MICROSOFT

Office 2000

Brief Concepts and Techniques

WORD 2000   EXCEL 2000   ACCESS 2000   POWERPOINT 2000

Gary B. Shelly
Thomas J. Cashman
Misty E. Vermaat

Contributing Authors
Steven G. Forsythe
Mary Z. Last
Philip J. Pratt
James S. Quasney
Susan L. Sebok
Denise M. Woods

COURSE
TECHNOLOGY

COURSE TECHNOLOGY
ONE MAIN STREET
CAMBRIDGE MA 02142

an International Thomson Publishing company I(T)P

SHELLY
CASHMAN
SERIES®

CAMBRIDGE • ALBANY • BONN • CINCINNATI • LONDON • MADRID • MELBOURNE

MEXICO CITY • NEW YORK • PARIS • SAN FRANCISCO • TOKYO • TORONTO • WASHINGTON

COURSE
TECHNOLOGY

Course Technology
One Main Street
Cambridge, Massachusetts 02142, USA

ITP GmbH
Konigswinterer Strasse 418
53227 Bonn, Germany

ITP Europe
Berkshire House
168-173 High Holborn
London, WC1V 7AA, United Kingdom

International Thomson Editores
Saneca, 53
Colonia Polanco
11560 Mexico D.F. Mexico

ITP Asia
60 Albert Street, #15-01
Albert Complex
Singapore 189969

ITP Australia
102 Dodds Street
South Melbourne
Victoria 3205 Australia

ITP Nelson Canada
1120 Birchmount Road
Scarborough, Ontario
Canada M1K 5G4

ITP Japan
Hirakawa-cho Kyowa Building, 3F
2-2-1 Hirakawa-cho, Chiyoda-ku
Tokyo 102, Japan

ISBN 0-7895-4651-5 (Perfect bound)
ISBN 0-7895-4657-4 (Spiral bound)

8 9 10   BC   04 03 02 01

MICROSOFT

Office 2000

Brief Concepts and Techniques

WORD 2000   EXCEL 2000   ACCESS 2000   POWERPOINT 2000

C O N T E N T S

Microsoft Word 2000

Microsoft Excel 2000

PROJECT 1

CREATING A WORKSHEET AND EMBEDDED CHART

PROJECT 2

FORMULAS, FUNCTIONS, FORMATTING, AND WEB QUERIES

● PROJECT 2

USING OUTLINE VIEW AND CLIP ART
TO CREATE A SLIDE SHOW

● WEB FEATURE

CREATING A PRESENTATION ON THE WEB USING POWERPOINT

● APPENDIX A

MICROSOFT OFFICE 2000 HELP SYSTEM   MO A.1

● APPENDIX B

PUBLISHING OFFICE WEB PAGES TO A WEB SERVER   MO B.1

● APPENDIX C

RESETTING THE MENUS AND TOOLBARS   MO C.1

● APPENDIX D

MICROSOFT OFFICE USER SPECIALIST CERTIFICATION PROGRAM   MO D.1

Preface

The Shelly Cashman Series® offers the finest textbooks in computer education. We are proud of the fact that our Microsoft Office 4.3, Microsoft Office 95, and Microsoft Office 97 textbooks have been the most widely used books in computer education. Each edition of our Office textbooks has included innovations, many based on comments made by the instructors and students who use our books. The Microsoft Office 2000 books continue with the innovation, quality, and reliability that you have come to expect from the Shelly Cashman Series.

Office 2000 is the most significant upgrade ever to the Office suite. Microsoft has enhanced Office 2000 in the following areas: (1) interface changes; (2) application-specific features; (3) multi-language pack; (4) round tripping HTML files back to an Office 2000 application; (5) collaboration; and (6) new applications. Each one of these enhancements is discussed in detail.

In our Office 2000 books, you will find an educationally sound and easy-to-follow pedagogy that combines a step-by-step approach with corresponding screens. All projects and exercises in this book are designed to take full advantage of the Office 2000 enhancements. The popular Other Ways and More About features offer in-depth knowledge of Office 2000. The project openers provide a fascinating perspective of the subject covered in the project. The project material is developed carefully to ensure that students will see the importance of learning Office 2000 applications for future course work.

Objectives of This Textbook

Microsoft Office 2000: Brief Concepts and Techniques is intended for a course that covers Microsoft Word 2000, Microsoft Excel 2000, Microsoft Access 2000, and Microsoft PowerPoint 2000, with an overview of Windows. No experience with a computer is assumed, and no mathematics beyond the high school freshman level is required. The objectives of this book are:

- To teach the fundamentals of Microsoft Office 2000
- To expose students to practical examples of the computer as a useful tool
- To acquaint students with the proper and correct way to create documents, workbooks, databases, and presentations suitable for course work, professional purposes, and personal use
- To develop an exercise-oriented approach that allows students to learn by example
- To encourage independent study, and help those who are working alone in a distance education environment

The Shelly Cashman Approach

Features of the Shelly Cashman Series Office 2000 books include:

- **Project Orientation:** Each project in the book presents a practical problem and complete solution in an easy-to-understand approach.
- **Screen-by-Screen, Step-by-Step Instructions:** Each of the tasks required to complete a project is identified throughout the development of the project. The steps are accompanied by full-color screens.

Other Ways

1. Type title text, press ENTER, click Demote button on Formatting toolbar, type subtitle text, press ENTER
2. Type title text, press ENTER, press TAB, type subtitle text, press ENTER

More About 2000

Joining Tables

One of the key features that distinguishes database management systems from file systems is the ability to join tables, that is, to create queries that draw data from two or more tables. Several types of joins are available. For more information, visit the Access 2000 More About Web page (www.scsite.com/ac2000/more.htm) and click Join Types.

- **Thoroughly Tested Projects:** Every screen in the book is correct because it is produced by the author only after performing a step, resulting in unprecedented quality.

- **Other Ways Boxes and Quick Reference Summary:** Office 2000 provides a variety of ways to carry out a given task. The Other Ways boxes displayed at the end of most of the step-by-step sequences specify the other ways to do the task completed in the steps. Thus, the steps and the Other Ways box make a comprehensive reference unit. In addition, a Quick Reference Summary, available on the Web, summarizes the way application-specific tasks can be completed.

- **More About Feature:** These marginal annotations provide background information that complements the topics covered, adding depth and perspective to the learning process.

- **Integration of the World Wide Web:** We have integrated the World Wide Web into the students' Office 2000 learning experience in different ways. For example, we have added (1) More Abouts that send students to Web sites for up-to-date information and alternative approaches to tasks; (2) a MOUS information Web page and a MOUS map Web page so students can better prepare for the Microsoft Office Use Specialist (MOUS) Certification examinations; (3) an Office 2000 Quick Reference Summary Web page that summarizes the ways to complete tasks (mouse, menu, shortcut menu, and keyboard); and (4) project reinforcement Web pages in the form of true/false, multiple choice, and short answer questions, and other types of student activities.

Organization of This Textbook

Microsoft Office 2000: Brief Concepts and Techniques is divided into nine projects, a Web Feature, and four appendices as follows:

An Introduction to Windows 98 and Microsoft Office 2000

Students learn about user interfaces, Windows 98, Windows Explorer, and each Office 2000 application. Topics include using the mouse; minimizing, maximizing, and restoring windows; sizing and scrolling windows; launching and quitting an application; displaying the contents of a folder; creating a folder; selecting and copying a group of files; renaming and deleting a file and a folder; using Windows 98 Help; and shutting down Windows 98. Topics pertaining to Office 2000 include a brief explanation of Word 2000, Excel 2000, Access, 2000, PowerPoint 2000, Publisher 2000, FrontPage 2000, PhotoDraw 2000, and Outlook 2000 and examples of how these applications take advantage of the Internet and World Wide Web.

Microsoft Word 2000

Project 1 - Creating and Editing a Word Document In Project 1, students are introduced to Word terminology and the Word window by preparing an announcement. Topics include starting and quitting Word; entering text; checking spelling while typing; saving a document; selecting characters, words, lines, and paragraphs; changing the font and font size of text; centering, right-aligning, and formatting text in bold and italic; undoing commands and actions; inserting clip art into a document; resizing a graphic; printing a document; opening a document; correcting errors; and using the Word Help system.

Project 2 – Creating a Research Paper In Project 2, students use the MLA style of documentation to create a research paper. Topics include changing margins; adjusting line spacing; using a header to number pages; entering text using Click and Type; first-line indenting paragraphs; using Word's AutoCorrect feature; adding a footnote; modifying a style; inserting a symbol; inserting a manual page break; creating a hanging indent; creating a text hyperlink; sorting paragraphs; moving text; finding a synonym; counting words in a document; and checking spelling and grammar at once.

Microsoft Excel 2000

Project 1 - Creating a Worksheet and Embedded Chart In Project 1, students are introduced to Excel terminology, the Excel window, and the basic characteristics of a worksheet and workbook. Topics include starting and quitting Excel; entering text and numbers; selecting a range; using the AutoSum button; copying using the fill handle; changing font size; formatting in bold; centering across columns; using the Auto-Format command; charting using the ChartWizard; saving and opening a workbook; editing a worksheet; using the AutoCalculate area; and using the Excel Help system.

Project 2 – Formulas, Functions, Formatting, and Web Queries In Project 2, students use formulas and functions to build a worksheet and learn more about formatting and printing a worksheet. Topics include entering formulas; using functions; verifying formulas; formatting text; formatting numbers; conditional formatting; drawing borders and adding colors; changing the widths of columns and rows; spell checking; previewing a worksheet; printing a section of a worksheet; and displaying and printing the formulas in a worksheet. This project also introduces students to accessing real-time data using Web Queries and sending the open workbook as an e-mail attachment directly from Excel.

Microsoft Access 2000

Project 1 - Creating a Database Using Design and Datasheet Views In Project 1, students are introduced to the concept of a database and shown how to use Access to create a database. Topics include creating a database; creating a table; defining the fields in a table; opening a table; adding records to a table; closing a table; and previewing and printing the contents of a table. Additional topics include using a form to view data; using the Report Wizard to create a report; and using the Access Help system. Students also learn how to design a database to eliminate redundancy.

Project 2 - Querying a Database Using the Select Query Window In Project 2, students learn to use queries to obtain information from the data in their databases. Topics include creating queries; running queries; and printing the results. Specific query topics include displaying only selected fields; using character data in criteria; using wildcards; using numeric data in criteria; using various comparison operators; and creating compound criteria. Other related topics include sorting; joining tables; and restricting records in a join. Students also use computed fields, statistics, and grouping.

Microsoft PowerPoint 2000

Project 1 - Using a Design Template and AutoLayouts to Create a Presentation In Project 1, students are introduced to PowerPoint terminology, the PowerPoint window, and the basics of creating a multi-level bulleted list presentation. Topics include selecting a design template; increasing font size; changing font style; ending a slide show with a black slide; saving a presentation; viewing the slides in a presentation; checking a presentation for spelling and style errors; changing line spacing on the Slide Master; printing copies of the slides; and using the PowerPoint Help system.

Project 2 – Using Outline View and Clip Art to Create a Slide Show In Project 2, students create a presentation in outline view, insert clip art, and add animation effects. Topics include creating a slide presentation by promoting and demoting text in outline view; changing slide layouts; inserting clip art; changing clip art size; adding slide transition effects; adding text animation effects; animating clip art; running an animated slide show; printing audience handouts from an outline; and e-mailing a slide show from within PowerPoint.

PowerPoint Web Feature – Creating a Presentation on the Web Using PowerPoint In the Web Feature, students are introduced to saving a presentation as a Web page. Topics include saving an existing PowerPoint presentation as an HTML file; viewing the presentation as a Web page; editing a Web page through a browser; and viewing the editing change.

Appendices

The book concludes with four appendices. Appendix A presents a detailed step-by-step introduction to the Microsoft Office Help system. Students learn how to use the Office Assistant, as well as the Contents, Answer Wizard, and Index sheets in the Help window. Appendix B describes how to publish Office Web pages to a Web server. Appendix C shows students how to reset the menus and toolbars in any Office application. Appendix D introduces students to the Microsoft Office User Specialist (MOUS) Certification program.

End-of-Project Student Activities

A notable strength of the Shelly Cashman Series Office 2000 books is the extensive student activities at the end of each project. Well-structured student activities can make the difference between students merely participating in a class and students retaining the information they learn. The activities in the Shelly Cashman Series Office 2000 books include the following.

- **What You Should Know** A listing of the tasks completed within a project together with the pages where the step-by-step, screen-by-screen explanations appear. This section provides a perfect study review for students.

- **Project Reinforcement on the Web** Every project has a Web page accessible from www.scsite.com/off2000/reinforce.htm. The Web page includes true/false, multiple choice, and short answer questions, and additional project-related reinforcement activities that will help students gain confidence in their Office 2000 abilities.

- **Apply Your Knowledge** This exercise requires students to open and manipulate a file on the Data Disk for the Office 2000 books. To obtain a copy of the Data Disk, follow the instructions on the inside back cover of this textbook.

- **In the Lab** Three in-depth assignments per project require students to apply the knowledge gained in the project to solve problems on a computer.

- **Cases and Places** Up to seven unique case studies that require students to apply their knowledge to real-world situations.

Shelly Cashman Series Teaching Tools

A comprehensive set of Teaching Tools accompanies this textbook in the form of a CD-ROM. The CD-ROM includes an Instructor's Manual and teaching and testing aids. The CD-ROM (ISBN 0-7895-4636-1) is available through your Course Technology representative or by calling one of the following telephone numbers: Colleges and Universities, 1-800-648-7450; High Schools, 1-800-824-5179; and Career Colleges, 1-800-477-3692. The contents of the CD-ROM are listed below.

- **Instructor's Manual** The Instructor's Manual is made up of Microsoft Word files. The files include lecture notes, solutions to laboratory assignments, and a large test bank. The files allow you to modify the lecture notes or generate quizzes and exams from the test bank using your own word processing software. Where appropriate, solutions to laboratory assignments are embedded as icons in the files. When an icon appears, double-click it and the application will start and the solution will display on the screen. The Instructor's Manual includes the following for each project: project objectives; project overview; detailed lesson plans with page number references; teacher notes and activities; answers to the end-of-project exercises; test bank of 110 questions for every project (25 multiple-choice, 50 true/false, and 35 fill-in-the-blank) with page number references; and transparency references. The transparencies are available through the Figures in the Book. The test bank questions are numbered the same as in Course Test Manager. Thus, you can print a copy of the project test bank and use the printout to select your questions in Course Test Manager.

- **Figures in the Book** Illustrations of the figures and tables in the textbook are available in Figures in the Book. Use this ancillary to create a slide show from the illustrations for lecture or to print transparencies for use in lecture with an overhead projector.

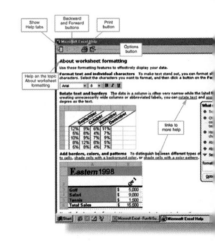

- **Course Test Manager** Course Test Manager is a powerful testing and assessment package that enables instructors to create and print tests from the large test bank. Instructors with access to a networked computer lab (LAN) can administer, grade, and track tests online. Students also can take online practice tests, which generate customized study guides that indicate where in the textbook students can find more information for each question.

- **Course Syllabus** Any instructor who has been assigned a course at the last minute knows how difficult it is to come up with a course syllabus. For this reason, sample syllabi are included for each of the Office 2000 products that can be customized easily to a course.

- **Lecture Success System** Lecture Success System files are for use with the application software, a personal computer, and projection device to explain and illustrate the step-by-step, screen-by-screen development of a project in the textbook without entering large amounts of data.

- **Instructor's Lab Solutions** Solutions and required files for all the In the Lab assignments at the end of each project are available.

- **Lab Tests/Test Outs** Tests that parallel the In the Lab assignments are supplied for the purpose of testing students in the laboratory on the material covered in the project or testing students out of the course.

- **Project Reinforcement** True/false, multiple choice, and short answer questions, and additional project-related reinforcement activities for each project help students gain confidence in their Office 2000 abilities.

- **Student Files** All the files that are required by students to complete the Apply Your Knowledge exercises are included.

- **Interactive Labs** Eighteen hands-on interactive labs that take students from ten to fifteen minutes each to step through help solidify and reinforce mouse and keyboard usage and computer concepts. Student assessment is available in each interactive lab by means of a Print button. The assessment requires students to answer questions.

Microsoft Office 2000 Supplements

Three supplements can be used in combination with the Shelly Cashman Series Microsoft Office 2000 books. These supplements reinforce the concepts and techniques presented in the books.

Microsoft Office 2000 Workbook

This highly popular supplement (ISBN 0-7895-4690-6) includes a variety of activities that help students recall, review, and master Office 2000 concepts and techniques. The workbook complements the end-of-project material with a guided project outline, a self-test consisting of true/false, multiple choice, short answer, fill-in, and matching questions, an entertaining puzzle, and other challenging exercises.

Course Assessment Live

Course Assessment Live (ISBN 0-619-00147-X) is a performance-based testing program that measures students' proficiency in Microsoft Office 2000. Previously known as SAM, Course Assessment Live is available for Office 2000 in both live and simulated environments. You can use Course Assessment Live to place students into or out of courses, monitor their performance throughout a course, and help prepare them for the MOUS certification exams.

Course CBT

Enhance your students' Office 2000 classroom learning experience with self-paced computer-based training on CD-ROM (ISBN 0-619-00151-8). Course CBT engages students with interactive multimedia and hands-on simulations that reinforce and complement the concepts and skills covered in the textbook. All the content is aligned with the Microsoft Office User Specialist (MOUS) program, making it a great preparation tool for the certification exams. Course CBT also includes extensive pre- and post-assessments that test students' mastery of skills. These pre- and post-assessments automatically generate a custom learning path through the course that highlights only the topics with which students need help.

Shelly Cashman Series MOUS Web Page

The Shelly Cashman Series MOUS Web page has more than fifteen Web pages you can visit to obtain additional information on the MOUS Certification Program. The Web page (www.scsite.com/off2000/cert.htm) includes links to general information on certification, choosing an application for certification, preparing for the certification exam, and taking and passing the certification exam.

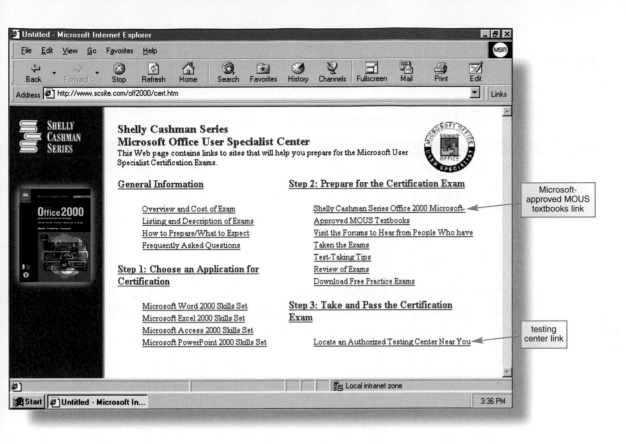

Acknowledgments

The Shelly Cashman Series would not be the leading computer education series without the contributions of outstanding publishing professionals. First, and foremost, among them is Becky Herrington, director of production and designer. She is the heart and soul of the Shelly Cashman Series, and it is only through her leadership, dedication, and tireless efforts that superior products are made possible. Becky created and produced the award-winning Windows series of books.

Under Becky's direction, the following individuals made significant contributions to these books: Doug Cowley, production manager; Ginny Harvey, series specialist and developmental editor; Ken Russo, senior Web designer; Mike Bodnar, associate production manager; Mark Norton, Web designer; Stephanie Nance, Ellana Russo, Marlo Mitchem, Chris Schneider, Hector Arvizu, graphic artists; Jeanne Black and Betty Hopkins, Quark experts; Nancy Lamm and Lyn Markowicz, copy editors; Marilyn Martin, Mary Steinman, and Kim Kosmatka, proofreaders; Cristina Haley, indexer; Sarah Evertson of Image Quest, photo researcher; and Susan Sebok and Ginny Harvey, contributing writers.

Special thanks go to Richard Keaveny, managing editor; Jim Quasney, series consultant; Lora Wade, product manager; Meagan Walsh, associate product manager; Francis Schurgot, Web product manager; Tonia Grafakos, associate Web product manager; Scott Wiseman, online developer; Rajika Gupta, marketing manager; and Erin Bennett, editorial assistant. Special mention must go to Suzanne Biron, Becky Herrington, and Michael Gregson for the outstanding book design; Becky Herrington for the cover design; and Stephanie Nance for the cover illustrations.

Gary B. Shelly
Thomas J. Cashman
Misty E. Vermaat

Shelly Cashman Series – Traditionally Bound Textbooks

The Shelly Cashman Series presents the following computer subjects in a variety of traditionally bound textbooks. For more information, see your Course Technology representative or call 1-800-648-7450. For Shelly Cashman Series information, visit Shelly Cashman Online at **www.scseries.com**

	COMPUTERS
Computers	Discovering Computers 2000: Concepts for a Connected World, Web and CNN Enhanced
	Discovering Computers 2000: Concepts for a Connected World, Web and CNN Enhanced Brief Edition
	Teachers Discovering Computers: A Link to the Future, Web and CNN Enhanced
	Discovering Computers 98: A Link to the Future, World Wide Web Enhanced
	Discovering Computers 98: A Link to the Future, World Wide Web Enhanced Brief Edition
	Exploring Computers: A Record of Discovery 2e with CD-ROM
	Study Guide for Discovering Computers 2000: Concepts for a Connected World, Web and CNN Enhanced
	Essential Introduction to Computers 3e (32-page)

	WINDOWS APPLICATIONS
Microsoft Office	Microsoft Office 2000: Essential Concepts and Techniques (5 projects)
	Microsoft Office 2000: Brief Concepts and Techniques (9 projects)
	Microsoft Office 2000: Introductory Concepts and Techniques (15 projects)
	Microsoft Office 2000: Advanced Concepts and Techniques (11 projects)
	Microsoft Office 2000: Post Advanced Concepts and Techniques (11 projects)
	Microsoft Office 97: Introductory Concepts and Techniques, Brief Edition (6 projects)
	Microsoft Office 97: Introductory Concepts and Techniques, Essentials Edition (10 projects)
	Microsoft Office 97: Introductory Concepts and Techniques, Enhanced Edition (15 projects)
	Microsoft Office 97: Advanced Concepts and Techniques
Microsoft Works	Microsoft Works 4.5[1] • Microsoft Works 3.0[1]
Windows	Microsoft Windows 98: Essential Concepts and Techniques (2 projects)
	Microsoft Windows 98: Introductory Concepts and Techniques (3 projects)
	Microsoft Windows 98: Introductory Concepts and Techniques Web Style Edition (3 projects)
	Microsoft Windows 98: Complete Concepts and Techniques (6 projects)
	Microsoft Windows 98: Comprehensive Concepts and Techniques (9 projects)
	Introduction to Microsoft Windows NT Workstation 4
	Microsoft Windows 95: Introductory Concepts and Techniques (2 projects)
	Introduction to Microsoft Windows 95 (3 projects)
	Microsoft Windows 95: Complete Concepts and Techniques
Word Processing	Microsoft Word 2000[2] • Microsoft Word 97[1] • Microsoft Word 7[1]
	Corel WordPerfect 8 • Corel WordPerfect 7 • WordPerfect 6.1[1]
Spreadsheets	Microsoft Excel 2000[2] • Microsoft Excel 97[1] • Microsoft Excel 7[1] • Microsoft Excel 5[1] • Lotus 1-2-3 97[1]
Database	Microsoft Access 2000[2] • Microsoft Access 97[1] • Microsoft Access 7[1]
Presentation Graphics	Microsoft PowerPoint 2000[2] • Microsoft PowerPoint 97[1] • Microsoft PowerPoint 7[1]
Desktop Publishing	Microsoft Publisher 2000[1]

	PROGRAMMING
Programming	Microsoft Visual Basic 6: Complete Concepts and Techniques[1]
	Microsoft Visual Basic 5: Complete Concepts and Techniques[1]
	QBasic • QBasic: An Introduction to Programming • Microsoft BASIC
	Structured COBOL Programming

	INTERNET
Browser	Microsoft Internet Explorer 5: An Introduction • Microsoft Internet Explorer 4: An Introduction Netscape Navigator 4: An Introduction
Web Page Creation	HTML: Complete Concepts and Techniques[1] • Microsoft FrontPage 98: Complete Concepts and Techniques[1] • Netscape Composer • JavaScript: Complete Concepts and Techniques[1]

	SYSTEMS ANALYSIS
Systems Analysis	Systems Analysis and Design, Third Edition

	DATA COMMUNICATIONS
Data Communications	Business Data Communications: Introductory Concepts and Techniques, Second Edition

[1] Also available as an Introductory Edition, which is a shortened version of the complete book

[2] Also available as an Introductory Edition, which is a shortened version of the complete book and also as a Comprehensive Edition, which is an extended version of the complete book

Windows 98/Office 2000

PROJECT

1

Microsoft Windows 98
and Office 2000

An Introduction to Windows 98 and Office 2000

You will have mastered the material in this project
when you can:

O
B
J
E
C
T
I
V
E
S

- Describe the Microsoft Windows 98 user interface
- Identify the objects on the Microsoft Windows 98 desktop
- Perform the basic mouse operations: point, click, right-click, double-click, drag, and right-drag
- Open, minimize, maximize, restore, scroll, and close a window
- Move and resize a window on the desktop
- Understand keyboard shortcut notation
- Identify the three desktop views: Classic style, Web style, and Custom style
- Launch and quit an application program
- Identify the elements of the Exploring – My Computer window
- Create. expand, and collapse a folder
- Select and copy one file or a group of files
- Rename and delete a folder or file
- Use Windows 98 Help
- Quit Windows Explorer and shut down Windows 98
- Identify each application in Microsoft Office 2000
- Define World Wide Web, intranet, and Internet
- Explain how each Microsoft Office 2000 application uses the Internet
- Understand the Microsoft Office 2000 Help system

Doing Windows
Graphical Computing
Clicks with Users

Doing Windows" has an entirely new meaning since Bill Gates announced plans to add graphical capabilities to the IBM personal computer in 1983. The Microsoft CEO decided to take this step to help current personal computer users work more effectively and entice others to buy systems.

Up until this time, users were typing cumbersome disk operating system (DOS) commands to run their computers. When IBM decided to design a personal computer in 1980, corporate executives approached Gates to develop its new operating system. Gates declined the offer and suggested that IBM contact Gary Kildall at Digital Research, a leading microcomputer software developer. Kildall had developed a widely used operating system called CP/M.

Kildall, however, decided not to attend the meeting at IBM headquarters. The frustrated IBM executives contacted Gates once again, and this time he reconsidered, even though he knew very little about operating systems. By chance, a neighboring company in Washington named Seattle Computer Products was developing an operating system it called QDOS (QDOS was an acronym for Quick and Dirty Operating System). Bill Gates made a proposal to the company, and in December 1980, Microsoft obtained nonexclusive rights to QDOS. Later, Microsoft acquired all rights for a total purchase price of $1 million, and renamed the system MS-DOS (an

MS–DOS

acronym for Microsoft Disk Operating System).

Microsoft modified the program, and then shipped it in the first IBM personal computer, the IBM PC, unveiled in August 1981. The sale of millions of IBM PCs and consequently millions of copies of the operating system, propelled Microsoft to the world's largest software company.

Gates's graphical intentions were fueled by work being done at Xerox's Palo Alto Research Center in California. He saw researchers there using an invention they called a mouse to move a pointer instead of using arrow keys on the keyboard to move a cursor.

Then, working with Apple, Microsoft developed software for the Macintosh computer. Combining its original innovations with those of Xerox, Microsoft created the graphical user interface and experimented with the use of various icons and fonts to make the screen user-friendly. In addition, Microsoft introduced Word and Excel for the Macintosh platform. When the Mac was released in 1984, it became a success among users, particularly students.

Microsoft's next step was to develop these applications for the IBM PC and IBM-compatible computers. The company's innovations resulted in the release of Windows 3.1 and Windows 95 prior to Windows 98. Currently more than 100 million computers worldwide use the Windows operating system.

Programmers at Microsoft use a process the corporation calls continuous reinvention to constantly add new features to enhance Windows performance. Microsoft also allows anyone to write programs for the Windows platform without requiring prior permission. Indeed, today many of the thousands of Windows-based programs compete with Microsoft's own programs.

Gates predicts his company will continue to release new Windows versions every two or three years. He is convinced that individuals will want to take advantage of user interface enhancements and innovations that make computing easier, more reliable, faster, and integrated with the Internet.

Using Windows 98 in this project, you will launch an application, create folders and documents, and access Windows Help. The latest enhancements to the applications in the Office 2000 suite are introduced including new programs, integration with the World Wide Web, and the extensive Office Help system.

Windows 98/Office 2000

Microsoft Windows 98
and Office 2000

An Introduction to Windows 98 and Office 2000

PROJECT
1

C A S E   P E R S P E C T I V E

After weeks of planning, your organization finally switched from Microsoft Windows 95 to Microsoft Windows 98 and installed Microsoft Office 2000 on all computers. As the computer trainer for the upcoming in-house seminar, you realize you should know more about Windows 98 and Office 2000. Since installing Windows 98 and Office 2000, many employees have come to you with questions. You have taken the time to answer their questions by sitting down with them at their computers and searching for the answers using the Microsoft Help system.

From their questions, you determine the seminar should cover the basics of Windows 98, including basic mouse operations, working within a window, launching an application, performing file maintenance using Windows Explorer, and searching for answers to employees' questions using Windows 98 Help. In addition, the seminar should familiarize the participants with each of the Office 2000 applications. Your goal in this project is to become familiar with Windows 98 and the Office 2000 applications in order to teach the seminar.

Introduction

Microsoft Windows 98 is a widely used version of the Microsoft Windows operating system. Microsoft Windows 98 is an easy-to-use program that allows you to communicate with and control your computer readily and customize it to fit your individual needs.

In this project, you will learn about Microsoft Windows 98 and how to use the Windows 98 graphical user interface to simplify the process of working with documents and applications, transfer data between documents, organize the manner in which you interact with your computer, and use your computer to access information on the Internet and/or intranet.

In the first part of this project, you will work with the desktop and the windows available on the desktop, learn the basic mouse operations, launch an application program, and create and modify documents using Microsoft Word 2000. Using Windows Explorer, you will learn to view the contents of files and folders, create and delete folders, select and copy files and folders, rename and delete files, and use Microsoft Windows 98 Help.

Microsoft Office 2000, the latest edition of the world's best-selling office suite, is a collection of the more popular Microsoft application software products that work similarly and together if they were a single program. Microsoft Office 2000 integrates these applications and combines them with the power of the Internet so you can move quickly among applications, transfer text and graphics easily among them, and interact seamlessly with the World Wide Web. An explanation of each of the application software programs in Microsoft Office 2000 is given at the end of this project.

What Is Microsoft Windows 98?

An **operating system** is the set of computer instructions, called a computer program, that controls the allocation of computer hardware, such as memory, disk devices, printers, and CD-ROM and DVD drives, and provides you with the capability of communicating with your computer. The most popular and widely used operating system for personal computers is **Microsoft Windows 98** (called **Windows 98** for the rest of this book).

Windows 98 is an operating system that performs every function necessary to enable you to communicate with and use your computer. Windows 98 is called a **32-bit operating system** because it uses 32 bits for addressing and other purposes, which means the operating system can address more than four gigabytes of RAM (random-access memory) and perform tasks faster than older operating systems. Windows 98 includes **Microsoft Internet Explorer (IE),** a browser software program developed by Microsoft Corporation, that integrates the Windows 98 desktop and the Internet. Internet Explorer allows you to work with programs and files in a similar fashion, whether they are located on your computer, a local network, or the Internet.

Windows 98 is designed to be compatible with all existing **application programs,** which are programs that perform an application-related function such as word processing. To use the application programs that can be executed under Windows 98, you must know about the Windows 98 user interface.

What Is a User Interface?

A **user interface** is the combination of hardware and software that you use to communicate with and control your computer. Through the user interface, you are able to make selections on your computer, request information from your computer, and respond to messages displayed by your computer. Thus, a user interface provides the means for dialogue between you and your computer.

Hardware and software together form the user interface. Among the hardware devices associated with a user interface are the monitor, keyboard, and mouse (Figure 1-1). The **monitor** displays messages and provides information. You respond by entering data in the form of a command or other response using the **keyboard** or **mouse.** Among the responses available to you are responses that specify what application program to run, what document to open, when to print, and where to store data for future use.

More About

Windows

For information about the Windows operating system, visit the Office 2000 More About Web page (www.scsite.com/off2000/more.htm) and then click Windows.

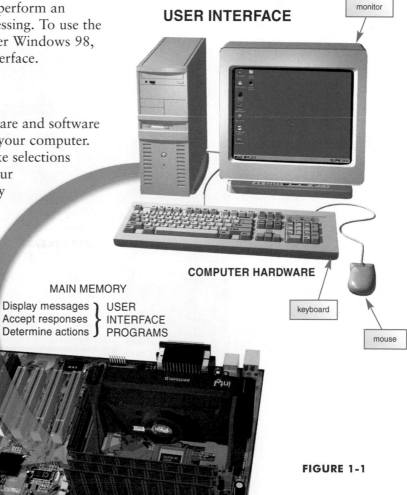

USER INTERFACE

monitor

COMPUTER HARDWARE

keyboard

mouse

MAIN MEMORY

Display messages ⎫ USER
Accept responses ⎬ INTERFACE
Determine actions ⎭ PROGRAMS

COMPUTER SOFTWARE

FIGURE 1-1

The Windows 98 Interface

The Windows 98 graphical user interface, although similar to the Windows 95 graphical user interface, has been improved greatly. Thousands of hours were spent accomplishing this. Of tremendous importance to the development of this version were the usability labs where all levels of users interacted with the various versions of the interface. One of the most significant improvements that emerged from the labs was the Quick Launch toolbar.

The computer software associated with the user interface consists of the programs that engage you in dialogue (Figure 1-1 on the previous page). The computer software determines the messages you receive, the manner in which you should respond, and the actions that occur based on your responses.

The goal of an effective user interface is to be **user friendly**, meaning that the software can be used easily by individuals with limited training. Research studies have indicated that the use of graphics can play an important role in aiding users to interact effectively with a computer. A **graphical user interface**, or **GUI** (pronounced gooey), is a user interface that displays graphics in addition to text when it communicates with the user.

The Windows 98 graphical user interface was designed carefully to be easier to set up, simpler to learn, faster and more powerful, and better integrated with the Internet than previous versions of Microsoft Windows.

Launching Microsoft Windows 98

When you turn on your computer, an introductory screen consisting of the Windows logo and Windows 98 name displays on a blue sky and clouds background in the middle of the screen. The screen clears and several items display on a background called the **desktop.** The default color of the desktop background is green, but your computer may display a different color. Your screen will display as shown in Figure 1-2. It may also display without the Welcome screen shown in Figure 1-2.

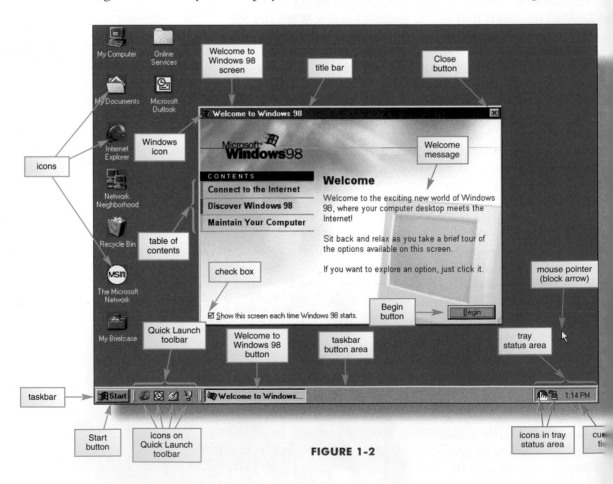

FIGURE 1-2

The items on the desktop shown in Figure 1-2 include nine icons and their titles on the left side of the desktop and the taskbar at the bottom of the desktop. Using the nine **icons**, you can view the contents of your computer (**My Computer**), store documents in one location (**My Documents**), connect to and browse the Internet (**Internet Explorer**), work with other computers connected to your computer (**Network Neighborhood**), discard unneeded objects (**Recycle Bin**), connect to The Microsoft Network online service (**The Microsoft Network**), transfer documents or folders to and from a portable computer (**My Briefcase**), investigate other online services (**Online Services**), and receive and send e-mail (**Microsoft Outlook**). Your computer's desktop may contain more, fewer, or some different icons because the desktop of the computer can be customized.

The **taskbar** at the bottom of the screen shown in Figure 1-2 contains the Start button, Quick Launch toolbar, taskbar button area, and the tray status area. The **Start button** allows you to launch a program quickly, find or open a document, change your computer's settings, shut down the computer, and perform many more tasks. The **Quick Launch toolbar** contains four icons that allow you to launch Internet Explorer (**Launch Internet Explorer Browser**), launch Microsoft Outlook (**Launch Microsoft Outlook**), view an uncluttered desktop at any time (**Show Desktop**), and view a list of channels (**View Channels**).

The **taskbar button area** contains buttons to indicate which windows are open on the desktop. In Figure 1-2, the Welcome to Windows 98 screen displays on the desktop and the Welcome to Windows 98 button displays in the taskbar button area. The **tray status area** contains **The Microsoft Network icon** to connect to The Microsoft Network online service, the **Internet connection icon** to indicate a modem is being used to connect to the Internet, and the current time (1:14 PM). The tray status area on your desktop may contain more, fewer, or some different icons because the contents of the tray status area change.

The Welcome to Windows 98 screen that may display on your desktop when you launch Windows 98 is shown in Figure 1-2. The **title bar** at the top of the screen, which is dark blue in color, contains the Windows icon, identifies the name of the screen (Welcome to Windows 98), and contains the Close button to close the Welcome to Windows 98 screen.

On the Welcome to Windows 98 screen, a table of contents contains three options (Connect to the Internet, Discover Windows 98, and Maintain Your Computer). The options in the table of contents allow you to perform different tasks such as connecting to the Internet, learning Windows 98 using the Discover Windows 98 tutorial, and improving the performance of your computer. A welcome message (Welcome) to the right of the table of contents welcomes you to the world of Windows 98. Pointing to an option in the table of contents replaces the Welcome message with an explanation of the option. The **Begin button** in the lower-right corner begins the process of connecting to the Internet, and a check mark in the **check box** in the left corner of the screen indicates the Welcome to Windows 98 screen will display each time you start Windows 98.

In the lower-right corner of the desktop is the mouse pointer. On the desktop, the **mouse pointer** is the shape of a block arrow. The mouse pointer allows you to point to objects on the desktop and may change shape as it points to different objects.

Nearly every item on the Windows 98 desktop is considered an object. Even the desktop itself is an object. Every **object** has properties. The **properties** of an object are unique to that specific object and may affect what can be done to the object or what the object does. For example, the properties of an object may be the color of the object, such as the color of the desktop.

The Windows 98 Desktop

Because Windows 98 is customized easily, the desktop on your computer may not resemble the desktop in Figure 1-2. For example, the icon titles on the desktop may be underlined or objects not shown in Figure 1-2 may display on your desktop. If this is the case, contact your instructor for instructions for selecting the default desktop view settings to change the desktop view.

Windows Tips and Tricks

For undocumented Windows tips and tricks, visit the Office 2000 More About Web page (www.scsite.com/off2000/more.htm) and then click Tips and Tricks.

Windows Performance

To improve Windows performance and view information about Windows Second Edition, visit the Office 2000 More About Web page (www.scsite.com/off2000/more.htm) and then click Windows Performance.

Closing the Welcome Screen

As noted, the Welcome screen may display when you launch Windows 98. If the Welcome screen does display on the desktop, you should close it prior to beginning any other operations using Windows 98. To close the Welcome screen, complete the following step.

TO CLOSE THE WELCOME SCREEN

1 Press and hold the ALT key on the keyboard and then press the F4 key on the keyboard. Release the ALT key.

The Welcome to Windows 98 screen closes.

The Desktop as a Work Area

The Windows 98 desktop and the objects on the desktop were designed to emulate a work area in an office or at home. You may think of the Windows desktop as an electronic version of the top of your desk. You can move objects around on the desktop, look at them and then put them aside, and so on. In Project 1, you will learn how to interact with the Windows 98 desktop.

More About

The Mouse

The mouse, though invented in the 1960s, was not used widely until the Apple Macintosh computer became available in 1984. Even then, some highbrows called mouse users "wimps." Today, the mouse is an indispensable tool for every computer user.

Communicating with Microsoft Windows 98

The Windows 98 interface provides the means for dialogue between you and your computer. Part of this dialogue involves your requesting information from your computer and responding to messages displayed by your computer. You can request information and respond to messages using either a mouse or a keyboard.

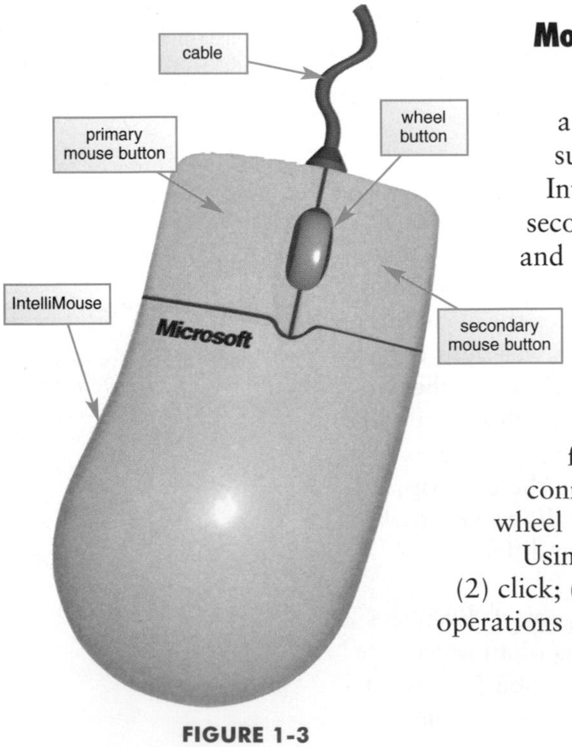

Mouse Operations

A **mouse** is a pointing device that is attached to the computer by a cable. Although not required when using Windows 98, Windows supports the use of the **Microsoft IntelliMouse** (Figure 1-3). The IntelliMouse contains three buttons; the primary mouse button, the secondary mouse button, and the wheel button between the primary and secondary mouse buttons. Typically, the **primary mouse button** is the left mouse button and the **secondary mouse button** is the right mouse button although Windows 98 allows you to switch them. In this book, the left mouse button is the primary mouse button and the right mouse button is the secondary mouse button. The functions the **wheel button** and wheel perform depends on the software application being used. If the mouse connected to your computer is not an IntelliMouse, it will not have a wheel button between the primary and secondary mouse buttons.

Using the mouse, you can perform the following operations: (1) point; (2) click; (3) right-click; (4) double-click; (5) drag; and (6) right-drag. These operations are demonstrated on the following pages.

cable

primary mouse button

wheel button

IntelliMouse

Microsoft

secondary mouse button

FIGURE 1-3

Point and Click

Point means you move the mouse across a flat surface until the mouse pointer rests on the item of choice on the desktop. As you move the mouse across a flat surface, the movement of a ball on the underside of the mouse (Figure 1-4) is sensed electronically, and the mouse pointer moves across the desktop in the same direction.

Click means you press and release the primary mouse button, which in this book is the left mouse button. In most cases, you must point to an item before you click. To become acquainted with the use of the mouse, perform the following steps to point to and click various objects on the desktop.

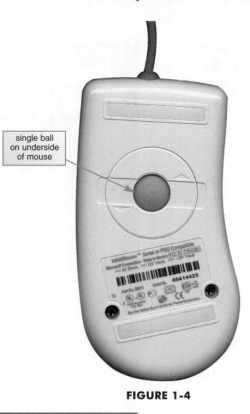

single ball
on underside
of mouse

FIGURE 1-4

teps **To Point and Click**

1 **Point to the Start button on the taskbar by moving the mouse across a flat surface until the mouse pointer rests on the Start button.**

The mouse pointer on the Start button displays a ScreenTip (Click here to begin.) (Figure 1-5). The ScreenTip, which provides instructions, displays on the desktop for approximately five seconds. Other ScreenTips display on the screen until you move the mouse pointer off the object.

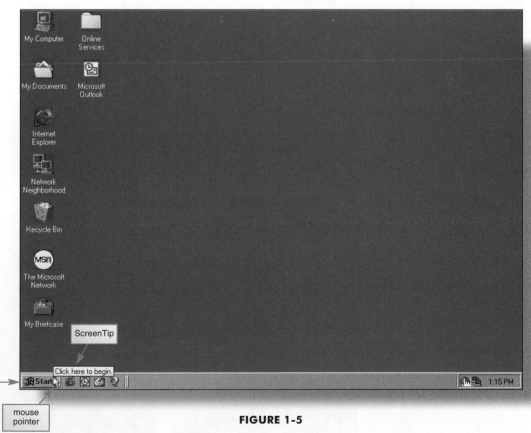

FIGURE 1-5

2 **Click the Start button on the taskbar by pressing and releasing the left mouse button.**

The *Start menu* displays and the Start button is recessed on the taskbar (Figure 1-6). A *menu* is a list of related commands. A *command* directs Windows 98 to perform a specific action such as shutting down the operating system. Each command on the Start menu consists of an icon and a command name. A *right arrow* follows some commands to indicate pointing to the command will open a submenu. Three commands (Run, Log Off Steven Forsythe, and Shut Down) are followed by an *ellipsis* (...) to indicate more information is required to execute these commands.

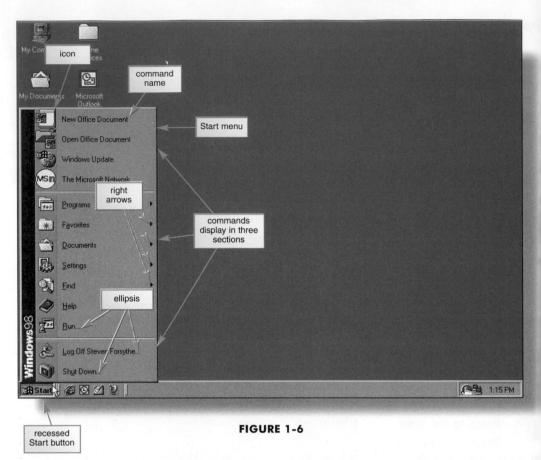

FIGURE 1-6

3 **Point to Programs on the Start menu.**

When you point to Programs, Windows 98 highlights the Programs command on the Start menu and the *Programs submenu* displays (Figure 1-7). A *submenu, or cascading menu,* is a menu that displays when you point to a command that is followed by a right arrow. Whenever you point to a command on a menu, the command is highlighted.

FIGURE 1-7

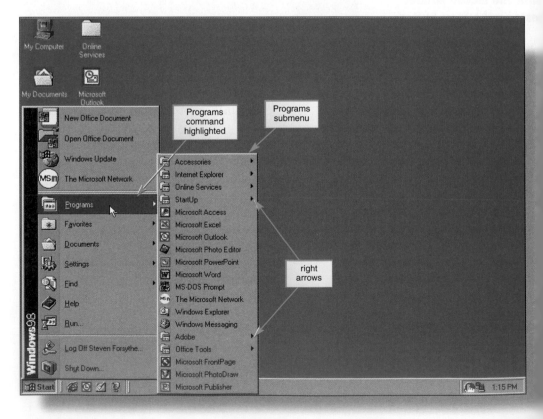

④ Point to an open area of the desktop and then click the open area of the desktop.

The Start menu and Programs submenu close (Figure 1-8). The mouse pointer points to the desktop. To close a menu anytime, click any open area of the desktop except on the menu itself. The Start button is no longer recessed.

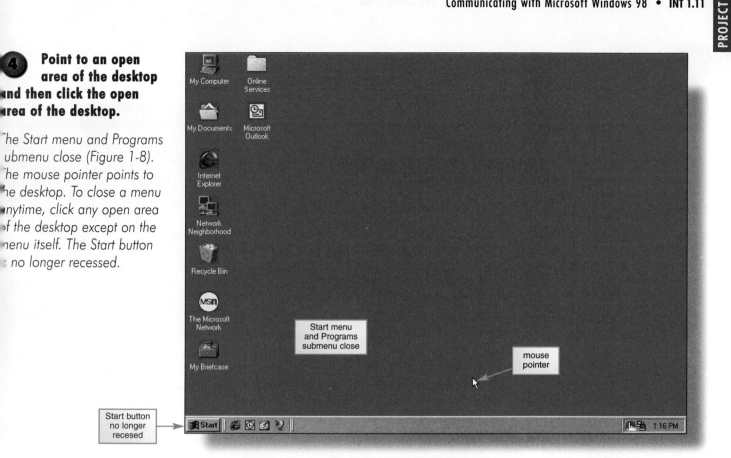

FIGURE 1-8

The Start menu shown in Figure 1-6 is divided into three sections. The top section contains commands to create or open a Microsoft Office document (New Office Document and Open Office Document), launch the Windows Update application (Windows Update), and connect to The Microsoft Network (The Microsoft Network), the middle section contains commands to launch an application, work with documents or Web sites, customize options, and search for files or Help (Programs, Favorites, Documents, Settings, Find, Help, and Run); and the bottom section contains basic operating tasks (Log Off Steven Forsythe and Shut Down).

When you click an object such as the Start button in Figure 1-6, you must point to the object before you click. In the steps that follow, the instruction that directs you to point to a particular item and then click is, Click the particular item. For example, Click the Start button means point to the Start button and then click.

Right-Click

Right-click means you press and release the secondary mouse button, which in this book is the right mouse button. As directed when using the primary mouse button for clicking an object, normally you will point to an object before you right-click it. Perform the steps on the next page to right-click the desktop.

Buttons

Buttons on the desktop and in programs are an integral part of Windows 98. When you point to them, their function displays in a ScreenTip. When you click them, they appear to recess on the screen to mimic what would happen if you pushed an actual button. All buttons in Windows 98 behave in the same manner.

The Right Mouse Button

The earliest versions of Microsoft Windows made little use of the right mouse button. In Windows 98, you will find using the right mouse button essential.

Steps **To Right-Click**

1 **Point to an open area of the desktop and then press and release the right mouse button.**

A shortcut menu displays (Figure 1-9). The shortcut menu consists of eight commands. Right-clicking an object, such as the desktop, opens a **shortcut menu** *that contains a set of commands specifically for use with that object. When a command on a menu appears dimmed, such as the Paste command and the Paste Shortcut command, that command is unavailable.*

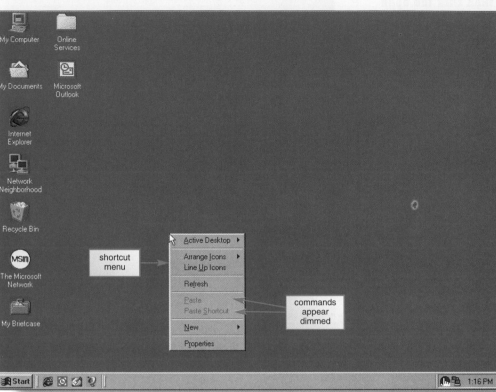

FIGURE 1-9

2 **Point to New on the shortcut menu.**

When you move the mouse pointer to the New command, Windows 98 highlights the New command and opens the New submenu (Figure 1-10). The New submenu contains a variety of commands. The number of commands and the actual commands that display on your computer may be different.

3 **Point to an open area of the desktop and click the open area to close the shortcut menu and the New submenu.**

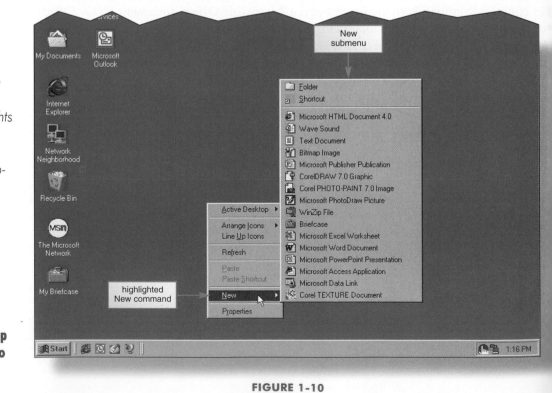

FIGURE 1-10

Whenever you right-click an object, a shortcut menu (also referred to as an object menu) will display. As you will see, the use of shortcut menus speeds up your work and adds flexibility to your interface with the computer.

Double-Click

To **double-click**, you quickly press and release the left mouse button twice without moving the mouse. In most cases, you must point to an item before you double-click. Perform the following step to open the My Computer window on the desktop by double-clicking the My Computer icon.

More About

Right-Clicking

Right-clicking an object other than the desktop will display a different shortcut menu with commands useful to that object. Right-clicking an object is thought to be the fastest method of performing an operation on an object.

Steps To Open a Window by Double-Clicking

1 **Point to the My Computer icon on the desktop and then double-click by quickly pressing and releasing the left mouse button twice without moving the mouse.**

The My Computer window opens (Figure 1-11). The recessed My Computer button is added to the taskbar button area.

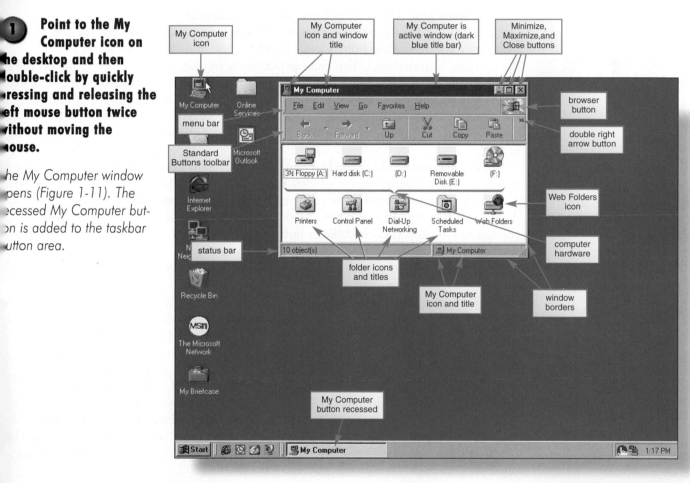

FIGURE 1-11

The My Computer window, the only open window, is the active window. The **active window** is the window currently being used. Whenever you click an object that can be opened, such as the My Computer icon, Windows 98 will open the object; and the open object will be identified by a recessed button in the taskbar button area. The recessed button identifies the active window.

The contents of the My Computer window on your computer may be different from the contents of the My Computer window in Figure 1-11.

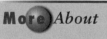

More About

Double-Clicking

When double-clicking, many people have a tendency to move the mouse before they click a second time. You should find, however, that with a little practice, double-clicking becomes quite natural.

More About

My Computer

The trade press and media have poked fun at the icon name, My Computer. One wag said no one should use Windows 98 for more than five minutes without changing the name (which is easily done). Microsoft responds that in their usability labs, beginning computer users found the name, My Computer, easier to understand.

More About

The My Computer Window

Because Windows 98 is customized easily, the My Computer window on your computer may not resemble the window in Figure 1-11 on the previous page. If this is the case, check the commands on the View menu by clicking View on the menu bar. If a check mark precedes the as Web Page command, click the as Web Page command. If a large dot does not precede the Large Icons command, click the Large Icons command.

More About

Minimizing Windows

Windows management on the Windows 98 desktop is important in order to keep the desktop uncluttered. You will find yourself frequently minimizing windows and then later reopening them with a click of a button in the taskbar button area.

My Computer Window

The thin line, or **window border**, surrounding the My Computer window shown in Figure 1-11 on the previous page determines its shape and size. The **title bar** at the top of the window contains a small icon that is the same as the icon on the desktop and the **window title** (My Computer) that identifies the window. The color of the title bar (dark blue) and the recessed My Computer button in the taskbar button area indicate the My Computer window is the active window. The color of the active window on your computer may be different from the dark blue color shown in Figure 1-11.

Clicking the icon at the left on the title bar will open the **System menu**, which contains commands to carry out the actions associated with the My Computer window. At the right on the title bar are three buttons, the Minimize button, the Maximize button, and the Close button, that can be used to specify the size of the window and close the window.

The **menu bar**, which is the horizontal bar below the title bar of a window (see Figure 1-11 on the previous page), contains a list of menu names for the My Computer window: File, Edit, View, Go, Favorites, and Help. One letter in each menu name is underlined. You can open a menu by clicking the menu name on the menu bar or by typing the corresponding underlined letter on the keyboard in combination with the ALT key. At the right end of the menu bar is a button containing the Windows logo. Clicking this button starts the Microsoft Internet Explorer Web browser and displays one of the Web pages in the Microsoft Web site in the browser window.

Below the menu bar is the **Standard Buttons toolbar** containing buttons that allow you to navigate through open windows on the desktop (Back, Forward, and Up) and copy and move text within a window or between windows (Cut, Copy, and Paste). Additional buttons display when the size of the window is increased or the double right arrow button is clicked. Each button contains a **text label** and an icon describing its function.

The area below the Standard Buttons toolbar contains 10 icons. A title below each icon identifies the icon. The five icons in the top row, called **drive icons**, represent a 3½ Floppy (A:) drive, a Hard disk (C:) drive, a different area on the same hard disk (D:), a Removable Disk (E:) drive, and a CD-ROM drive (F:).

The first four icons in the second row are folders on your computer. A **folder** is an object created to contain related documents, applications, and other folders. A folder in Windows 98 contains items in much the same way a folder on your desk contains items. The Web folders icon, which is associated with Microsoft Office, allows you to publish documents for viewing in a Web browser.

A message at the left on the **status bar** located at the bottom of the window indicates the right panel contains ten objects (see Figure 1-11 on the previous page). The My Computer icon and My Computer icon title display to the right of the message on the status bar.

Minimize Button

Two buttons on the title bar of a window, the Minimize button and the Maximize button, allow you to control the way a window displays or does not display on the desktop. When you click the **Minimize button** (see Figure 1-11 on the previous page), the My Computer window no longer displays on the desktop and the recessed My Computer button in the taskbar button area changes to a non-recessed button. A minimized window still is open but it does not display on the screen. To minimize and then redisplay the My Computer window, complete these steps.

Steps **To Minimize and Redisplay a Window**

1 **Point to the Minimize button on the title bar of the My Computer window.**

The mouse pointer points to the Minimize button on the My Computer window title bar (Figure 1-12). A ScreenTip displays below the Minimize button and the My Computer button in the taskbar button area is recessed.

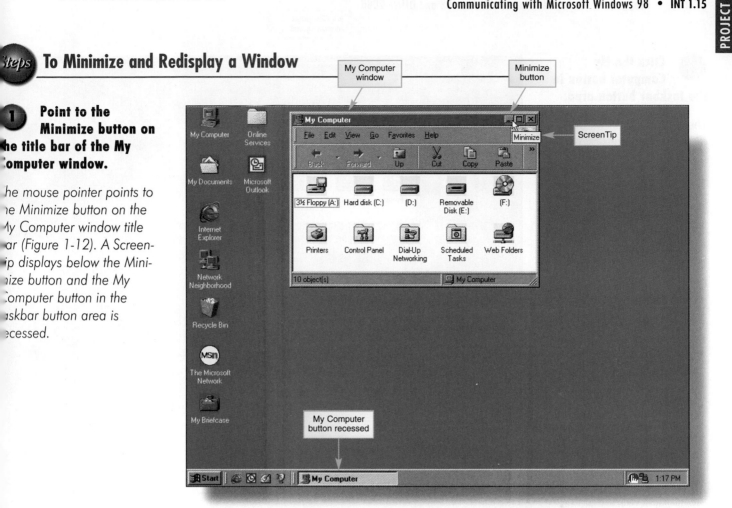

FIGURE 1-12

2 **Click the Minimize button.**

When you minimize the My Computer window, Windows 98 removes the My Computer window from the desktop and the My Computer button changes to a non-recessed button (Figure 1-13).

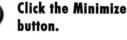

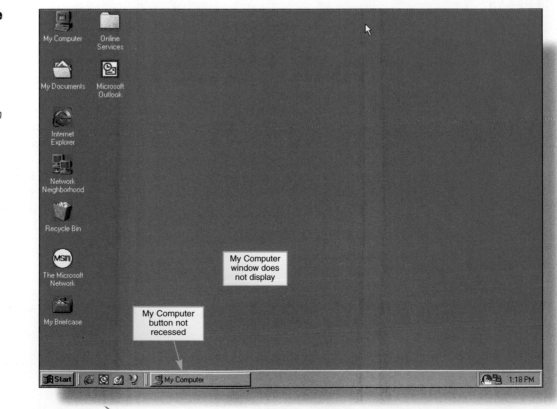

FIGURE 1-13

 **Click the My Computer button in the taskbar button area.**

The My Computer window displays on the desktop in the same place and size as it was before being minimized (Figure 1-14). In addition, the My Computer window is the active window because it contains the dark blue title bar, and the My Computer button in the taskbar button area is recessed.

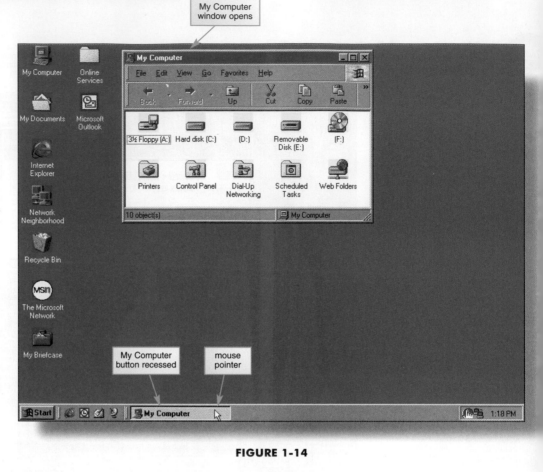

FIGURE 1-14

Whenever a window is minimized, it does not display on the desktop but a non-recessed button for the window does display in the taskbar button area. Whenever you want a minimized window to display and be the active window, click its button in the taskbar button area.

Maximize and Restore Buttons

Sometimes when information is displayed in a window, the information is not completely visible. One method to display the entire contents of a window is to enlarge the window using the **Maximize button**. The Maximize button maximizes a window so the window fills the entire screen, making it easier to see the contents of the window. When a window is maximized, the **Restore button** replaces the Maximize button on the title bar. Clicking the Restore button will return the window to its size before maximizing. To maximize and restore the My Computer window, complete the following steps.

Steps To Maximize and Restore a Window

1 **Point to the Maximize button on the title bar of the My Computer window (Figure 1-15).**

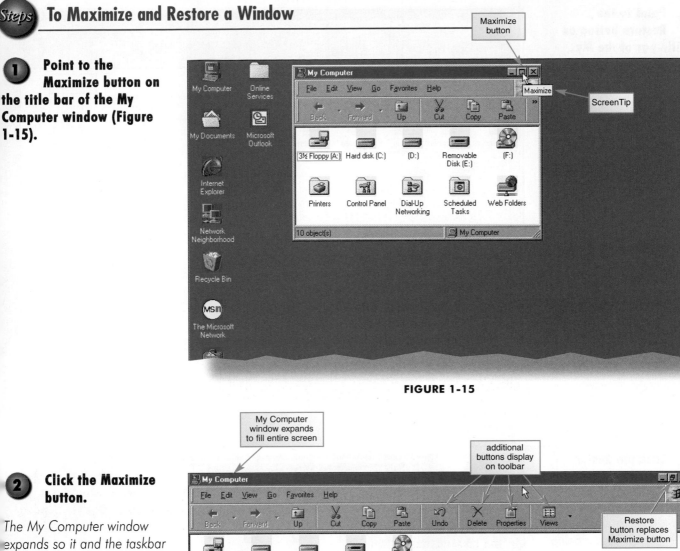

FIGURE 1-15

2 **Click the Maximize button.**

The My Computer window expands so it and the taskbar fill the entire screen (Figure 1-16). The Restore button replaces the Maximize button and the My Computer button on the taskbar button area remains recessed. The My Computer window still is the active window and additional buttons display on the Standard Buttons toolbar that allow you to undo a previous action (Undo), delete text (Delete), display the properties of an object (Properties), and change the desktop view (Views).

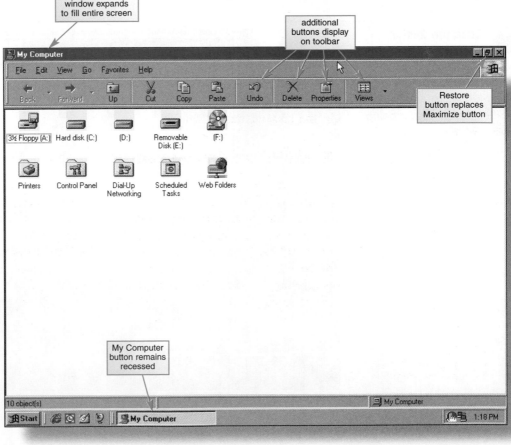

FIGURE 1-16

3 Point to the Restore button on the title bar of the My Computer window (Figure 1-17).

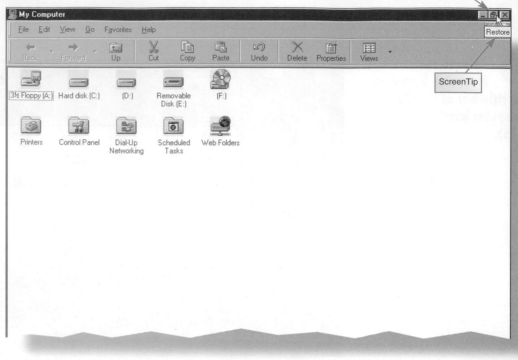

FIGURE 1-17

4 Click the Restore button.

The My Computer window returns to the size and position it occupied before being maximized (Figure 1-18). The My Computer button does not change. The Maximize button replaces the Restore button.

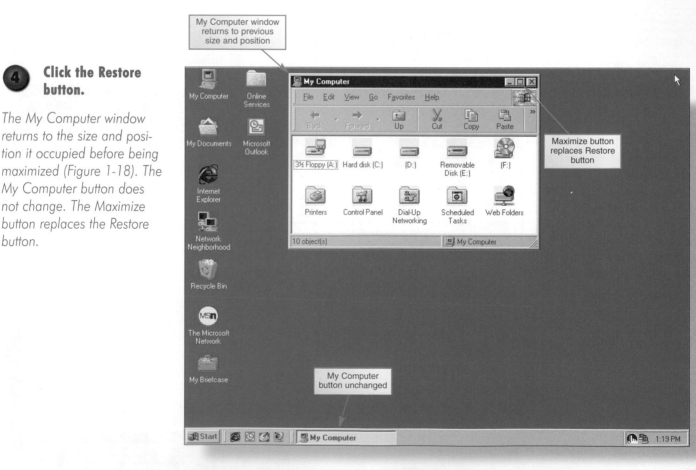

FIGURE 1-18

When a window is maximized, such as shown in Figure 1-16 on page INT 1.17, you also can minimize the window by clicking the Minimize button. If, after minimizing the window, you click its button in the taskbar button area, the window will return to its maximized size.

Close Button

The **Close button** on the title bar of a window closes the window and removes the window button from the taskbar. To close and then reopen the My Computer window, complete the following steps.

More About

The Close Button

The Close button was new in Windows 95. Before Windows 95, the user had to double-click a button or click a command on a menu to close the window. The choice of how to perform an operation such as closing a window is a matter of personal preference. In most cases, you will want to choose the easiest method.

Steps **To Close a Window and Reopen a Window**

1 Point to the Close button on the title bar of the My Computer window (Figure 1-19).

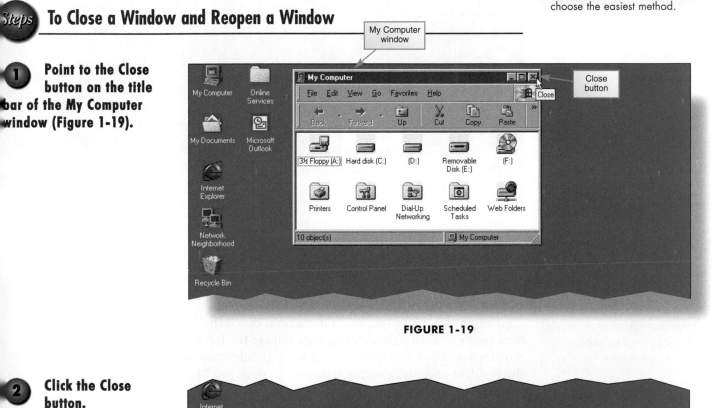

FIGURE 1-19

2 Click the Close button.

The My Computer window closes and the My Computer button no longer displays in the taskbar button area (Figure 1-20).

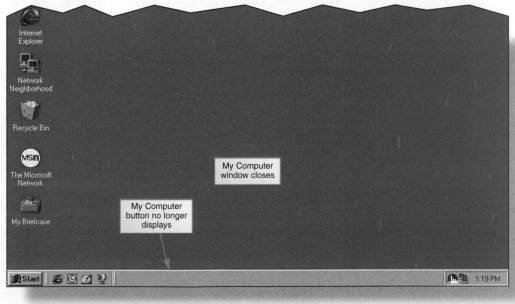

FIGURE 1-20

3 **Double-click the My Computer icon on the desktop.**

The My Computer window opens and displays on the screen (Figure 1-21). The My Computer button displays in the taskbar button area.

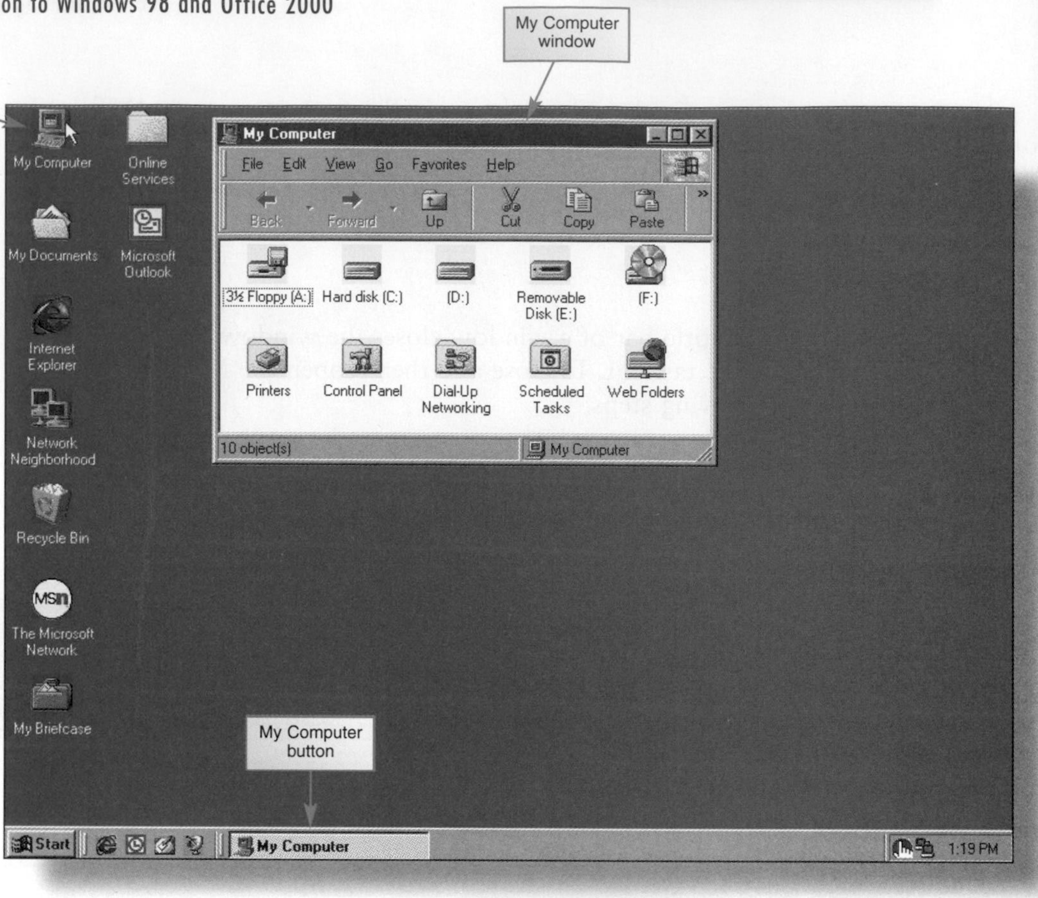

My Computer window

My Computer icon

My Computer button

FIGURE 1-21

More About

Dragging

Dragging is the second-most difficult skill to learn with a mouse. You may want to practice dragging a few times so you are comfortable with it.

Drag

Drag means you point to an item, hold down the left mouse button, move the item to the desired location, and then release the left mouse button. You can move any open window to another location on the desktop by pointing to the title bar of the window and dragging the window. To drag the My Computer window to another location on the desktop, perform the following steps.

Steps To Move an Object by Dragging

1 **Point to the My Computer window title bar (Figure 1-22).**

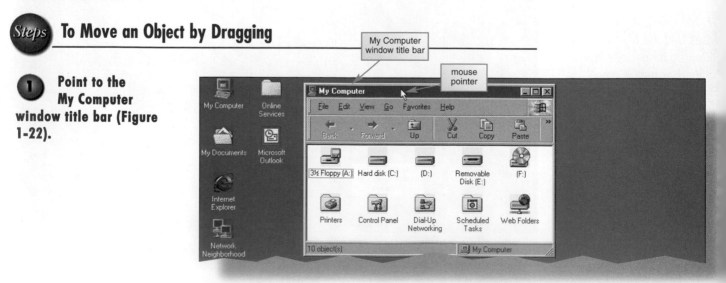

My Computer window title bar

mouse pointer

FIGURE 1-22

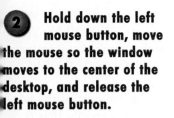

2 Hold down the left mouse button, move the mouse so the window moves to the center of the desktop, and release the left mouse button.

As you drag the mouse, the My Computer window moves across the desktop. When you release the left mouse button, the window displays in its new location (Figure 1-23).

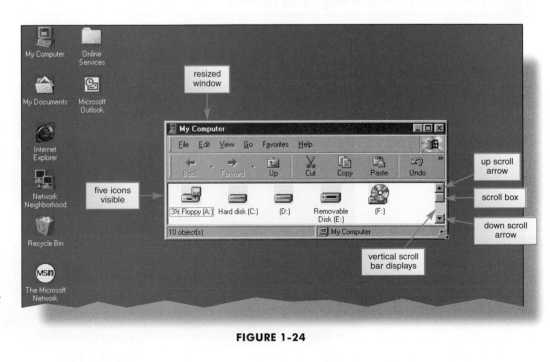

FIGURE 1-23

Sizing a Window by Dragging

You can use dragging for more than just moving an object. For example, you can drag the border of a window to change the size of the window. To change the size of the My Computer window, perform the following step.

 ## To Size a Window by Dragging

1 Position the mouse pointer over the lower-right corner of the My Computer window until the mouse pointer changes to a two-headed arrow. Drag the lower-right corner upward and to the right until the window on your desktop resembles the window shown in Figure 1-24.

As you drag the lower-right corner, the window changes size and a vertical scroll bar displays (Figure 1-24). Five of the ten icons in the window are visible in the resized window in Figure 1-24.

FIGURE 1-24

Window Sizing

Windows 98 remembers the size of the window when you close the window. When you reopen the window, it will display in the same size as when you closed it.

Scrolling

Most people either will maximize a window or size it so all the objects in the window are visible to avoid scrolling because scrolling takes time. It is more efficient not to have to scroll in a window.

A scroll bar is a bar that displays at the right edge and/or bottom edge of a window when the window contents are not completely visible. A vertical scroll bar contains an **up scroll arrow**, a **down scroll arrow**, and a **scroll box** that enable you to view areas of the window not currently visible. A vertical scroll bar displays in the My Computer window shown in Figure 1-24 on the previous page.

The size of the scroll box in any window is dependent on the amount of the window that is not visible. The smaller the scroll box, the more of the window that is not visible. In Figure 1-24, the scroll box occupies approximately half of the scroll bar. This indicates that approximately half of the contents of the window are not visible. If the scroll box were a tiny rectangle, a large portion of the window would not be visible.

In addition to dragging a corner of a window, you also can drag any of the borders of a window. If you drag a vertical border, such as the right border, you can move the border left or right. If you drag a horizontal border, such as the bottom border, you can move the border of the window up or down.

As mentioned earlier, maximizing a window is one method to enlarge a window and display more information in the window. Dragging a window to enlarge the window is a second method to display information in a window that is not visible.

Scrolling in a Window

Previously, two methods were shown to display information that was not completely visible in the My Computer window. These methods were maximizing the My Computer window and changing the size of the My Computer window. A third method uses the scroll bar in the window.

Scrolling can be accomplished in three ways: (1) click the scroll arrows; (2) click the scroll bar; and (3) drag the scroll box. On the following pages, you will use the scroll bar to scroll the contents of the My Computer window. Perform the following steps to scroll the My Computer window using the scroll arrows.

Steps **To Scroll a Window Using Scroll Arrows**

1 **Point to the down scroll arrow on the vertical scroll bar (Figure 1-25).**

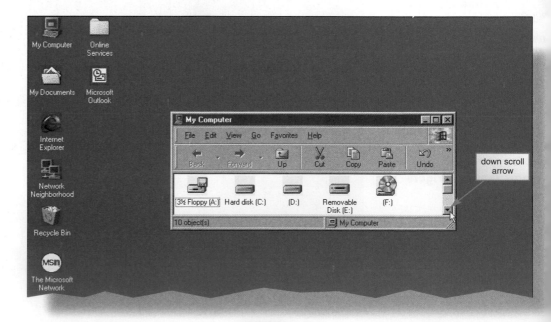

FIGURE 1-25

Click the down
scroll arrow one
time.

The window scrolls down (the icons move up in the window) and displays the tops of the icons previously not visible (Figure 1-26). Because the window size does not change when you scroll, the contents of the window will change, as seen in the difference between Figure 1-25 and Figure 1-26.

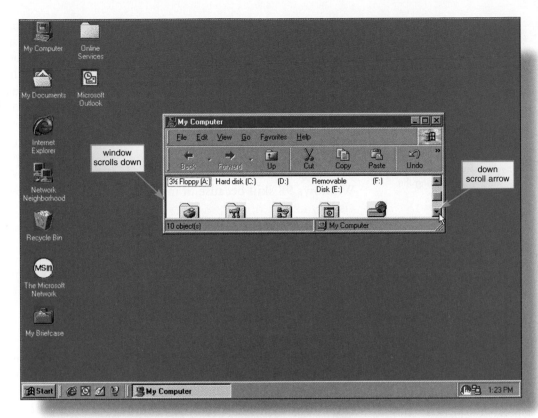

FIGURE 1-26

Click the down
scroll arrow two
more times.

The scroll box moves to the bottom of the scroll bar and the remaining icons in the window display (Figure 1-27).

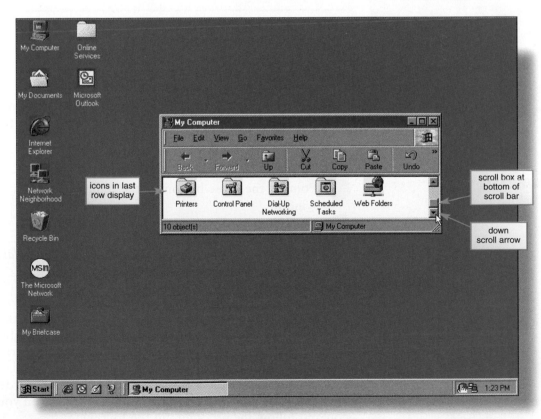

FIGURE 1-27

The Scroll Bar

In many application programs, clicking the scroll bar will move the window a full screen's worth of information up or down. You can step through a word processing document screen by screen, for example, by clicking the scroll bar.

The Scroll Box

Dragging the scroll box is the most efficient technique to scroll long distances. In many application programs, such as Microsoft Word, as you scroll using the scroll box, the page number of the document displays next to the scroll box.

Scrolling Guidelines

General scrolling guidelines: (1) To scroll short distances (line by line), click the scroll arrows; (2) To scroll one screen at a time, click the scroll bar; and (3) To scroll long distances, drag the scroll box.

Right-Dragging

Right-dragging was not available on some earlier versions of Windows, so you might find people familiar with Windows who do not even consider right-dragging. Because it always produces a shortcut menu, however, right-dragging is the safest way to drag.

You can scroll continuously through a window using scroll arrows by pointing to the up or down scroll arrow and holding down the left mouse button. The window continues to scroll until you release the left mouse button or you reach the top or bottom of the window. You also can scroll by clicking the scroll bar itself. When you click the scroll bar, the window moves up or down a greater distance than when you click the scroll arrows.

The third way in which you can scroll through a window to view its contents is by dragging the scroll box. When you drag the scroll box, the window moves up or down as you drag.

Being able to view the contents of a window by scrolling is an important Windows 98 skill because in many cases the entire contents of a window are not visible.

Resizing a Window

After moving and resizing a window, you may wish to return the window to approximately its original size. To return the My Computer window to about its original size, complete the following steps.

TO RESIZE A WINDOW

1. Position the mouse pointer over the lower-right corner of the My Computer window border until the mouse pointer changes to a two-headed arrow.
2. Drag the lower-right corner of the My Computer window until the window is the same size as shown in Figure 1-23 on page INT 1.21, and then release the mouse button.

The My Computer window is approximately the same size as before you made it smaller.

Closing a Window

After you have completed your work in a window, normally you will close the window. To close the My Computer window, complete the following steps.

TO CLOSE A WINDOW

1. Point to the Close button on the right of the title bar in the My Computer window.
2. Click the Close button.

The My Computer window closes and the desktop contains no open windows.

Right-Drag

Right-drag means you point to an item, hold down the right mouse button, move the item to the desired location, and then release the right mouse button. When you right-drag an object, a shortcut menu displays. The shortcut menu contains commands specifically for use with the object being dragged. To right-drag the My Briefcase icon to the right of its current position on the desktop, perform the following steps. If the My Briefcase icon does not display on your desktop, choose another icon and follow the procedure in the following steps.

To Right-Drag

1 Point to the My Briefcase icon on the desktop, hold down the right mouse button, drag the icon to the right toward the middle of the desktop, and then release the right mouse button.

The dimmed My Briefcase icon and a shortcut menu display in the middle of the desktop (Figure 1-28). The My Briefcase icon remains at its original location. The shortcut menu contains four commands: Move Here, Copy Here, Create Shortcut(s) Here, and Cancel. The Move Here command in bold (dark) type identifies what would happen if you were to drag the My Briefcase icon with the left mouse button.

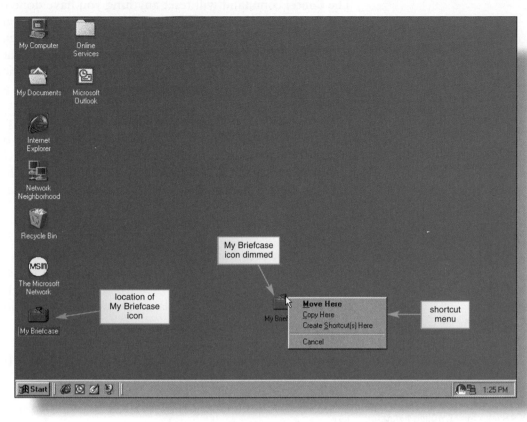

FIGURE 1-28

2 Point to Cancel on the shortcut menu.

The Cancel command is highlighted (Figure 1-29).

3 Click Cancel on the shortcut menu.

The shortcut menu and the dragged My Briefcase icon disappear from the screen.

FIGURE 1-29

Whenever you begin an operation but do not want to complete the operation, you can click Cancel on a shortcut menu or click the Cancel button in a dialog box. The **Cancel** command will reset anything you have done in the operation.

If you click **Move Here** on the shortcut menu shown in Figure 1-28 on the previous page, Windows 98 will move the icon from its current location to the new location. If you click **Copy Here**, the icon will be copied to the new location and two icons will display on the desktop. Windows 98 automatically will give the second icon a different title. If you click **Create Shortcut(s) Here**, a special object called a shortcut will be created.

Although you can move icons by dragging with the primary (left) mouse button and by right-dragging with the secondary (right) mouse button, it is strongly suggested you right-drag because a menu displays and you can specify the exact operation you want to occur. When you drag using the left mouse button, a default operation takes place and the operation may not do what you want.

Summary of Mouse and Windows Operations

You have seen how to use the mouse to point, click, right-click, double-click, drag, and right-drag in order to accomplish certain tasks on the desktop. The use of a mouse is an important skill when using Windows 98. In addition, you have learned how to move around and display windows on the Windows 98 desktop.

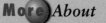

The Keyboard and Keyboard Shortcuts

The **keyboard** is an input device on which you manually key, or type, data. Figure 1-30a shows the enhanced IBM 101-key keyboard, and Figure 1-30b shows a Microsoft Natural keyboard designed specifically for use with Windows. Many tasks you accomplish with a mouse also can be accomplished using a keyboard.

To perform tasks using the keyboard, you must understand the notation used to identify which keys to press. This notation is used throughout Windows 98 to identify **keyboard shortcuts**.

The Microsoft Keyboard

The Microsoft keyboard in Figure 1-30(b) not only has special keys for Windows 98, but also is designed ergonomically so you type with your hands apart. It takes a little time to get used to, but several authors on the Shelly Cashman Series writing team report they type faster with more accuracy and less fatigue when using this keyboard.

FIGURE 1-30a

FIGURE 1-30b

Keyboard shortcuts consist of: (1) pressing a single key (example: press the ENTER key); or (2) pressing and holding down one key and then pressing a second key, as shown by two key names separated by a plus sign (CTRL+ESC). For example, to obtain Help about Windows 98, you can press the F1 key; to open the Start menu, hold down the CTRL key and then press the ESC key (press CTRL+ESC).

Often, computer users will use keyboard shortcuts for operations they perform frequently. For example, many users find pressing the F1 key to launch Windows 98 Help easier than using the Start menu as shown later in this project. As a user, you probably will find the combination of keyboard and mouse operations that particularly suit you, but it is strongly recommended that generally you use the mouse.

The Windows 98 Desktop Views

Windows 98 provides several ways to view your desktop and the windows that open on the desktop. The three desktop views are the Web style, Classic style, and Custom style. The desktop view you choose will affect the appearance of your desktop, how you open and work with windows on the desktop, and how you work with the files and folders on your computer.

The **Classic style** causes the desktop and the objects on the desktop to display and function as they did in Windows 95, the previous version of Windows. The icon titles are not underlined and you double-click an icon to open the window associated with the icon. In **Web style**, the icon titles on the desktop are underlined and you click, instead of double-click, an icon to open its window. Additional desktop items that are designed to allow you to access information on the Internet easily also may display on the desktop.

The **Custom style** is a combination of Classic style and Web style settings. The icon titles on the desktop may display with or without an underline, and you either click or double-click an icon to open its window. Unless you change the settings after installing Windows 98, the desktop will display in the Custom style as shown in the figures illustrated previously in this project.

For more information about desktop views and how to change the desktop view, read the instructions in the Using Windows Help section later in this project and then use Windows Help to search for information about desktop views.

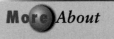

More About

Desktop Views

The Classic style was included in the Windows 98 operating system to allow Windows 95 users to upgrade easily to the newer Windows 98 operating system. Responses from people in the Beta Test program, which is a program designed to test software prior to the public sale of the software, indicated that most Windows 95 users had little difficulty switching to Windows 98, and experienced users liked the Web style.

Launching an Application Program

One of the basic tasks you can perform using Windows 98 is to launch an application program. A **program** is a set of computer instructions that carries out a task on your computer. An **application program** is a program that allows you to accomplish a specific task for which that program is designed. For example, a **word processing program** is an application program that allows you to create written documents; a **presentation graphics program** is an application program that allows you to create graphic presentations for display on a computer; and a **Web browser program** is an application program that allows you to search for and display Web pages.

The most popular activity using a computer is launching an application program to accomplish tasks. Windows allows you to launch an application in a variety of ways. When several methods are available, you have the opportunity to select the method that best fits your needs.

More About

Application Programs

Some application programs, such as Internet Explorer, are part of Windows 98. Most application programs, however, such as Microsoft Office, Lotus SmartSuite, and others must be purchased separately from Windows 98.

Launching an Application Using the Start Button

One method to launch an application program is to use the Start menu. Perform the steps on the next page to launch Internet Explorer using the Start menu and Internet Explorer command.

Steps **To Launch a Program Using the Start Menu**

1 **Click the Start button on the taskbar. Point to Programs on the Start menu. Point to Internet Explorer on the Programs submenu. Point to Internet Explorer on the Internet Explorer submenu.**

*The Start menu, Programs submenu, and Internet Explorer submenu display (Figure 1-31). The Internet Explorer submenu contains the **Internet Explorer command** to launch the Internet Explorer program. You may find a different set of commands on the submenus on your computer.*

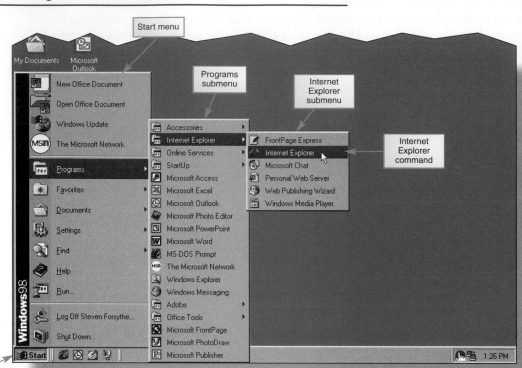

FIGURE 1-31

2 **Click Internet Explorer.**

Windows 98 launches the Internet Explorer program by opening the MSN.COM window on the desktop, displaying the MSN Web page in the window, and adding a recessed button to the taskbar button area (Figure 1-32). The URL for the Web page displays on the Address bar. Because Web pages are modified frequently, the Web page that displays on your desktop may be different from the Web page in Figure 1-32.

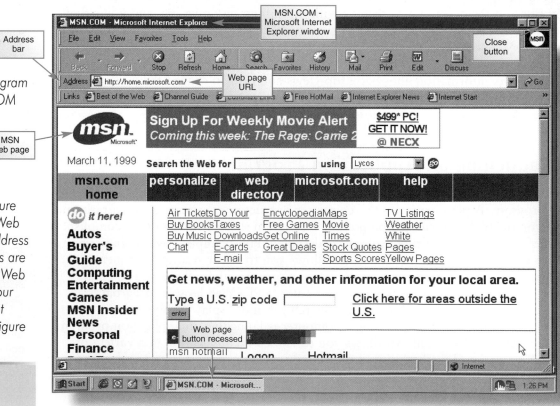

FIGURE 1-32

Other Ways

1. Click Launch Internet Explorer icon on Quick Launch toolbar
2. Double-click Internet Explorer icon on desktop

After you have launched Internet Explorer, you can use the program to search for and display different Web pages.

Windows 98 provides a number of ways to accomplish a particular task. In the previous section, one method to launch the Internet Explorer program was illustrated, and then alternate methods were listed in the Other Ways box. The remainder of this book will use the same format: a single set of steps will illustrate how to accomplish a task; and if you can perform the same task using other methods, the Other Ways box will specify the other methods. In each case, the method shown in the steps is the preferred method, but it is important for you to be aware of all the techniques you can use.

Quitting a Program

When you have completed your work using a program, you should quit the program. Perform the following steps to quit the Internet Explorer program.

Steps To Quit a Program

1 **Point to the Close button in the Internet Explorer window (Figure 1-33).**

2 **Click the Close button.**

Windows 98 quits Internet Explorer, closes the Internet Explorer window, and removes the Internet Explorer button from the taskbar.

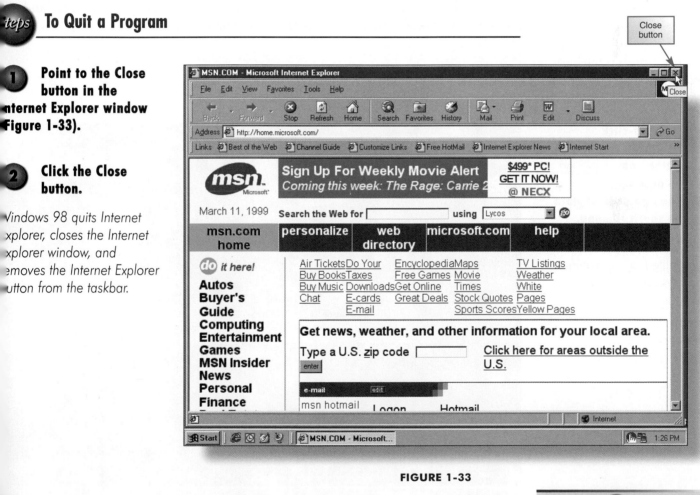

FIGURE 1-33

Other Ways

1. Double-click Internet Explorer logo on title bar
2. On File menu click Close
3. Press ALT+F4

In the preceding sections, you launched Internet Explorer and then quit the Internet Explorer program. In the next section, you will launch the Windows Explorer application program. Windows Explorer is another application program included with Windows 98. This program allows you to view the contents of the computer, the hierarchy of folders on the computer, and the files and folders in each folder.

Windows Explorer

Windows Explorer is an application program included with Windows 98 that allows you to view the contents of the computer, the hierarchy of folders on the computer, and the files and folders in each folder.

Windows Explorer also allows you to organize the files and folders on the computer by copying and moving the files and folders. In this project, you will use Windows Explorer to (1) work with the files and folders on your computer; (2) select and copy a group of files between the hard drive and a floppy disk; (3) create, rename, and delete a folder on a floppy disk; and (4) rename and delete a file on a floppy disk. These are common operations that you should understand how to perform.

Starting Windows Explorer and Maximizing Its Window

To explore the files and folders on the computer, start Windows Explorer and maximize its window by performing the following steps.

Steps **To Start Windows Explorer and Maximize Its Window**

1 **Right-click the My Computer icon on the desktop and then point to Explore on the shortcut menu.**

The My Computer icon is highlighted, a shortcut menu displays, and the Explore command is highlighted (Figure 1-34).

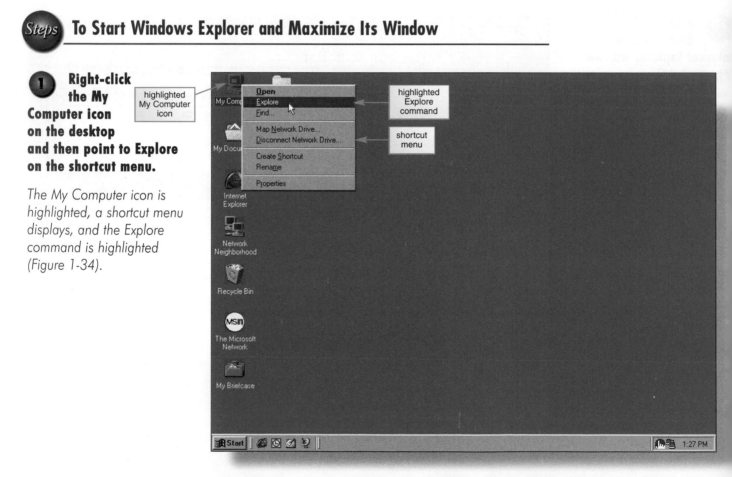

FIGURE 1-34

② **Click Explore and then click the Maximize button on the Exploring - My Computer title bar.**

The Exploring - My Computer window opens and is maximized. The recessed Exploring - My Computer button is added to the taskbar button area (Figure 1-35).

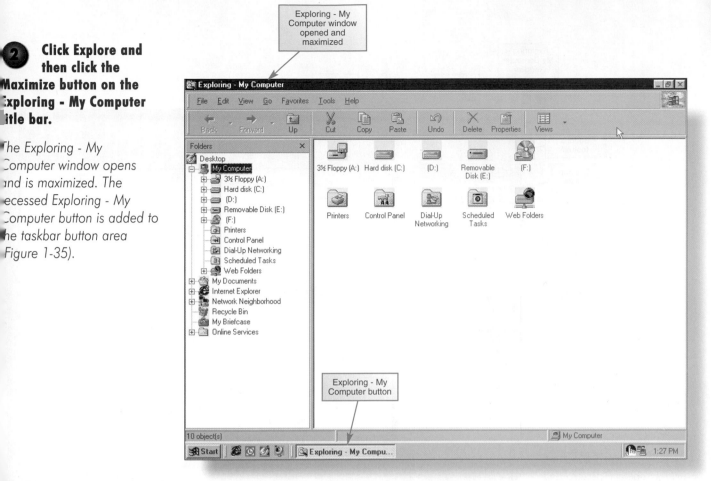

Exploring - My Computer window opened and maximized

Exploring - My Computer button

FIGURE 1-35

The Exploring – My Computer Window

When you start Windows Explorer by right-clicking the My Computer icon and then clicking the Explore command on the shortcut menu, Windows 98 opens the Exploring - My Computer window (Figure 1-36 on the next page). The menu bar contains the File, Edit, View, Go, Favorites, Tools, and Help menu names. These menus contain commands to organize and work with the drives on the computer and the files and folders on those drives. Below the menu bar is the Standard Buttons toolbar.

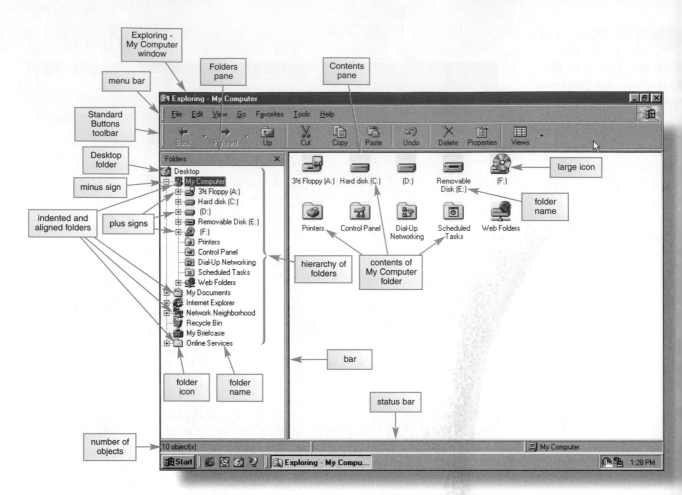

FIGURE 1-36

The main window is divided into two panes separated by a bar. The left pane of the window, identified by the Folders title, contains a **hierarchy** of folders on the computer. The right pane of the window displays the contents of the My Computer folder. In Figure 1-36, the Contents pane contains the icons and folder names of ten folders (3½ Floppy (A:), Hard disk (C:), (D:), Removable Disk (E:), (F:), Printers, Control Panel, Dial-Up Networking, Scheduled Tasks, and Web Folders) in the My Computer folder. These folders may be different on your computer. You can change the size of the Folders and Contents panes by dragging the bar that separates the two panes.

Each folder in the Folders pane is represented by an icon and folder name. The first folder, consisting of an icon and the Desktop folder name, represents the desktop of the computer. The seven folders indented and aligned below the Desktop folder name (My Computer, My Documents, Internet Explorer, Network Neighborhood, Recycle Bin, My Briefcase, and Online Services) are connected to the vertical line below the Desktop icon. These folders correspond to seven of the nine icons displayed on the left edge of the desktop (see Figure 1-2 on page INT 1.6). These folders may be different on your computer.

Windows 98 displays a minus sign (–) in a box to the left of an icon in the Folders pane to indicate the corresponding folder contains one or more folders that are visible in the Folders pane. These folders, called **subfolders**, are indented and aligned below the folder name.

In Figure 1-36, a minus sign precedes the My Computer icon, and 10 subfolders are indented and display below the My Computer folder name. The 10 subfolders (3½ Floppy (A:), Hard disk (C:), (D:), Removable Disk (E:), (F:), Printers, Control Panel, Dial-Up Networking, Scheduled Tasks, and Web Folders) correspond to the 10 folders in the Contents pane. Clicking the minus sign, referred to as **collapsing the folder**, removes the indented subfolders from the hierarchy of folders in the Folders pane and changes the minus sign to a plus sign.

Windows 98 displays a plus sign (+) in a box to the left of an icon to indicate the corresponding folder consists of one or more subfolders that are not visible in the Folders pane. In Figure 1-36, a plus sign precedes the first five icons indented and aligned below the My Computer name (3½ Floppy (A:), Hard disk (C:), (D:), Removable Disk (E:), and (F:) icons). Clicking the plus sign, referred to as **expanding the folder**, displays a list of indented subfolders and changes the plus sign to a minus sign.

If neither a plus sign nor a minus sign displays to the left of an icon, the folder does not contain subfolders. In Figure 1-36, the Printers, Control Panel, Dial-Up Networking, Scheduled Tasks, Recycle Bin, and My Briefcase icons are not preceded by a plus or minus sign and do not contain subfolders.

The status bar at the bottom of the Exploring - My Computer window indicates the number of folders, or objects, displayed in the Contents pane of the window (10 object(s)). Depending on the objects displayed in the Contents pane, the amount of disk space the objects occupy and the amount of unused disk space also may display on the status bar. If the status bar does not display in the Exploring - My Computer window on your computer, click View on the menu bar and then click Status Bar.

In addition to using Windows Explorer to explore your computer by right-clicking the My Computer icon, you also can use Windows Explorer to explore different aspects of your computer by right-clicking the Start button on the taskbar and the My Documents, Internet Explorer, Network Neighborhood, Recycle Bin, My Briefcase, and Online Services icons on the desktop.

Displaying the Contents of a Folder

In Figure 1-36, the Contents pane contains the subfolders in the My Computer folder. In addition to displaying the contents of the My Computer folder, the contents of any folder in the Folders pane can be displayed in the Contents pane. Perform the steps on the next page to display the contents of the Hard disk (C:) folder.

To Display the Contents of a Folder

1 **Point to the Hard disk (C:) folder name in the Folders pane of the Exploring - My Computer window (Figure 1-37).**

2 **Click the Hard disk (C:) folder name.**

The highlighted Hard disk (C:) folder name displays in the Folders pane, the contents of the Hard disk (C:) folder display in the Contents pane, the window title and button in the taskbar button area change to reflect the folder name, and the messages on the status bar change (Figure 1-38).

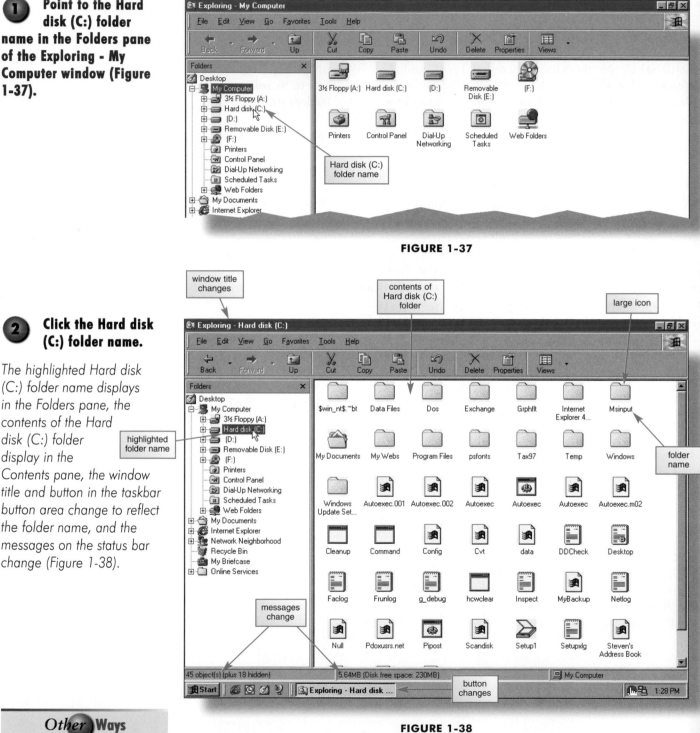

FIGURE 1-37

FIGURE 1-38

Other Ways

1. Double-click Hard disk (C:) icon in Contents pane
2. Press TAB to select any icon in Folders pane, press DOWN ARROW or UP ARROW to select Hard disk (C:) icon in Contents pane

The status bar messages shown in Figure 1-38 indicate 45 objects, the objects occupy 5.64MB of disk space, and the amount of unused (free) disk space is 230MB. The contents of the Hard disk (C:) folder may be different on your computer.

In addition to displaying the contents of the Hard disk (C:) folder, you can display the contents of the other folders by clicking the corresponding icon or folder name in the Folders pane. The contents of the folder you click then will display in the Contents pane of the window.

Expanding a Folder

Currently, the Hard disk (C:) folder is highlighted in the Folders pane of the Exploring - Hard disk (C:) window, and the contents of the Hard disk (C:) folder display in the Contents pane. Windows 98 displays a plus sign (+) to the left of the Hard disk (C:) icon to indicate the folder contains subfolders that are not visible in the hierarchy of folders in the Folders pane. To expand the Hard disk (C:) folder and display its subfolders, perform the following steps.

Steps To Expand a Folder

1 Point to the plus sign to the left of the Hard disk (C:) icon in the Folders pane (Figure 1-39).

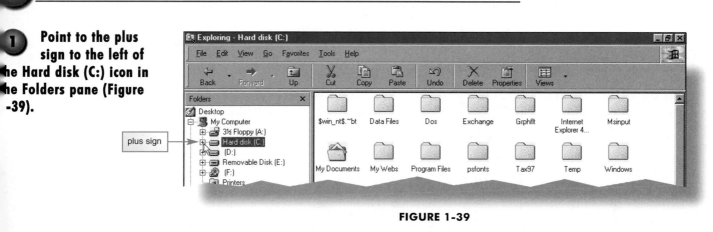

plus sign

FIGURE 1-39

2 Click the plus sign to display the subfolders in the Hard disk (C:) folder.

A minus sign replaces the plus sign preceding the Hard disk (C:) icon, a vertical scroll bar displays, and the Hard disk (C:) folder expands (Figure 1-40). The window title and the files and folders in the Contents pane remain unchanged.

minus sign replaces plus sign

subfolders

closed folder icon

scroll bar

folder name

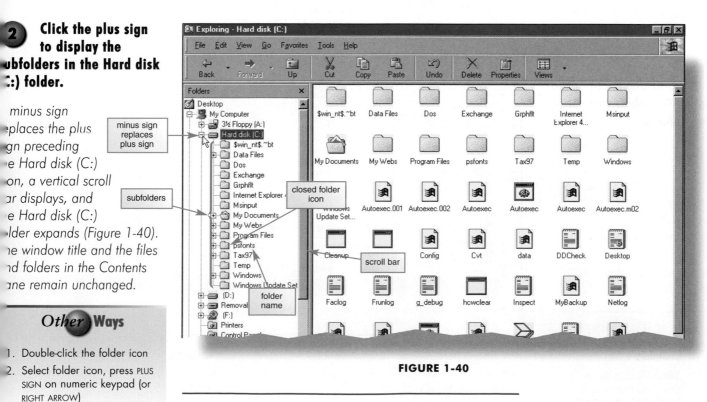

FIGURE 1-40

Other Ways

1. Double-click the folder icon
2. Select folder icon, press PLUS SIGN on numeric keypad (or RIGHT ARROW)

The subfolders in the expanded Hard disk (C:) folder shown in Figure 1-40 on the previous page are indented and aligned below the Hard disk (C:) folder name. A closed folder icon and folder name identify each subfolder in the Hard disk (C:) folder.

Collapsing a Folder

Currently, the subfolders in the Hard disk (C:) folder display indented and aligned below the Hard disk (C:) folder name (see Figure 1-40 on the previous page). Windows 98 displays a minus sign (–) to the left of the Hard disk (C:) icon to indicate the folder is expanded. To collapse the Hard disk (C:) folder and then remove its subfolders from the hierarchy of folders in the Folders pane, perform the following steps.

Steps **To Collapse a Folder**

1 **Point to the minus sign preceding the Hard disk (C:) icon in the Folders pane (Figure 1-41).**

minus sign

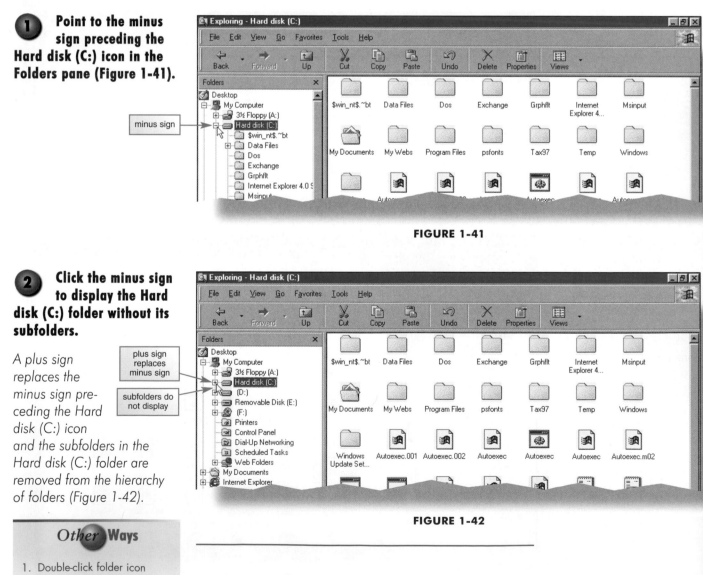

FIGURE 1-41

2 **Click the minus sign to display the Hard disk (C:) folder without its subfolders.**

A plus sign replaces the minus sign preceding the Hard disk (C:) icon and the subfolders in the Hard disk (C:) folder are removed from the hierarchy of folders (Figure 1-42).

plus sign replaces minus sign

subfolders do not display

FIGURE 1-42

Other Ways

1. Double-click folder icon
2. Select folder icon, press MINUS SIGN on numeric keypad (or LEFT ARROW)

Copying Files to a Folder on a Floppy Disk

One common operation that every student should understand how to perform is copying a file or group of files from one disk to another disk or from one folder to another folder. On the following pages, you will create a new folder, named My Files, on the floppy disk in drive A, select a group of files in the Windows folder on drive C, and copy the files from the Windows folder on drive C to the My Files folder on drive A.

When copying files, the drive and folder containing the files to be copied are called the **source drive** and **source folder**, respectively. The drive and folder to which the files are copied are called the **destination drive** and **destination folder,** respectively. Thus, the Windows folder is the source folder, drive C is the source drive, the My Files folder is the destination folder, and drive A is the destination drive.

Creating a New Folder

In preparation for selecting and copying files from a folder on the hard drive to a folder on the floppy disk in drive A, a new folder with the name of My Files will be created on the floppy disk. Perform the following steps to create the new folder.

Steps To Create a New Folder

1 Insert a formatted floppy disk into drive A on your computer.

2 Click the 3½ Floppy (A:) folder name in the Folders pane and then point to an open area of the Contents pane.

The 3½ Floppy (A:) folder name is highlighted, the contents of the 3½ Floppy (A:) folder display in the Contents pane, and the messages on the status bar change (Figure 1-43). The 3½ Floppy (A:) folder name displays in the window title and on the button in the taskbar button area. Currently, no files or folders display in the Contents pane. The files and folders may be different on your computer.

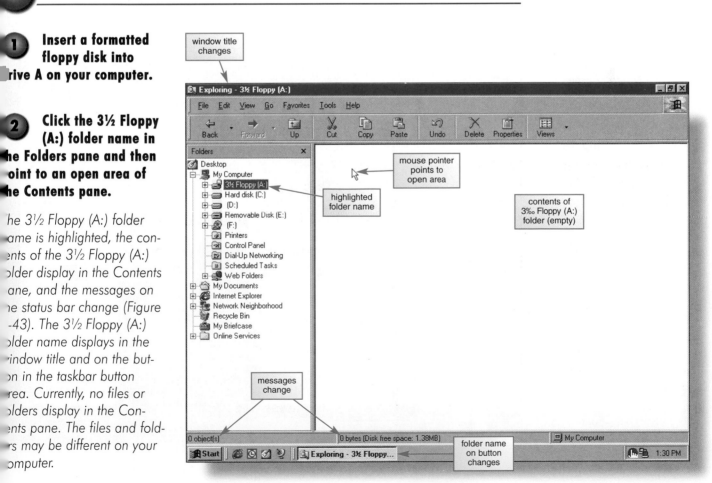

FIGURE 1-43

3 Right-click the open area of the Contents pane and then point to New on the shortcut menu.

A shortcut menu and the New submenu display and the New command is highlighted on the shortcut menu (Figure 1-44). Although no subfolders display in the Contents pane and no plus sign should precede the 3½ Floppy (A:) icon in the Folders pane, a plus sign precedes the icon.

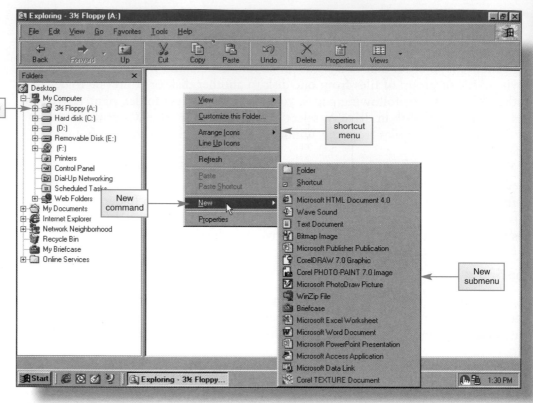

FIGURE 1-44

4 Point to Folder on the New submenu.

The Folder command is highlighted on the New submenu (Figure 1-45). Clicking the Folder command will create a folder in the Contents pane using the default folder name, New Folder.

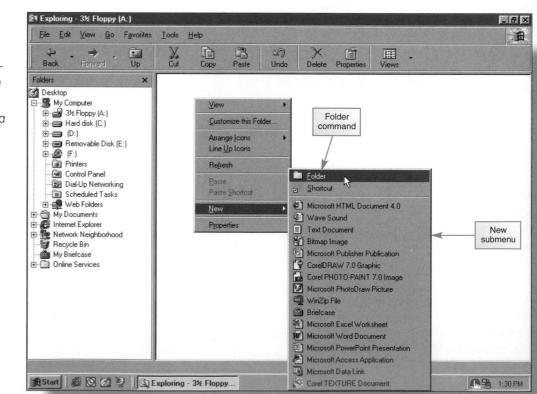

FIGURE 1-45

⑤ Click Folder on the New submenu.

The New Folder icon displays in the Contents pane (Figure 1-46). The text box below the icon contains the highlighted default folder name, New Folder, and an insertion point. A plus sign continues to display to the left of the 3½ Floppy (A:) icon to indicate the 3½ Floppy (A:) folder contains the New Folder subfolder. The message on the status bar indicates one object is selected in the Contents pane.

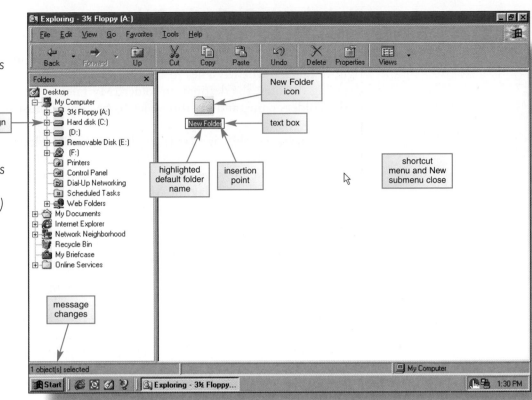

FIGURE 1-46

⑥ Type My Files **In the text box and then press the ENTER key.**

The new folder name, My Files, is entered and the text box is removed (Figure 1-47).

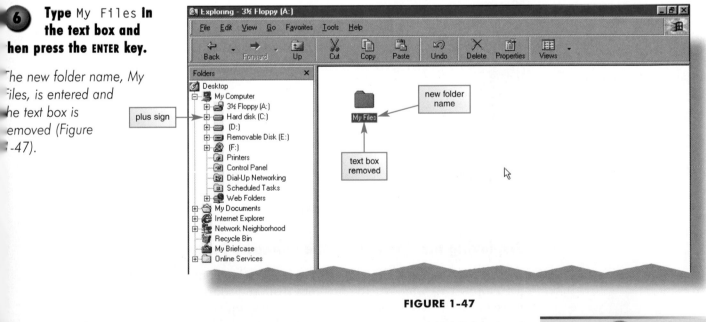

FIGURE 1-47

After creating the My Files folder on the floppy disk in drive A, you can save files in the folder or copy files from other folders to the folder. On the following pages, you will copy a group of files consisting of the Black Thatch, Bubbles, and Circles files from the Windows folder on drive C to the My Files folder on drive A.

> **Other Ways**
>
> 1. Select drive in Folders pane, on File menu point to New, click Folder on New submenu

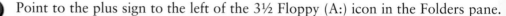
Displaying the Destination Folder

To copy the three files from the Windows folder on drive C to the My Files folder on drive A, the files to be copied will be selected in the Contents pane and right-dragged to the My Files folder in the Folders pane. Prior to selecting and right-dragging the files, the destination folder (My Files folder on drive A) must be visible in the Folders pane, and the three files to be copied must be visible in the Contents pane.

Currently, the plus sign (+) to the left of the 3½ Floppy (A:) icon indicates the folder contains one or more subfolders that are not visible in the Folders pane (see Figure 1-47 on the previous page). Perform the following steps to expand the 3½ Floppy (A:) folder to display the My Files subfolder.

TO EXPAND A FOLDER

1 Point to the plus sign to the left of the 3½ Floppy (A:) icon in the Folders pane.

2 Click the plus sign to display the subfolders in the 3½ Floppy (A:) folder.

A minus sign replaces the plus sign preceding the 3½ Floppy (A:) folder, the folder name is highlighted, and the My Files subfolder displays in the 3½ Floppy (A:) folder, indented and aligned below the 3½ Floppy (A:) folder name (Figure 1-48).

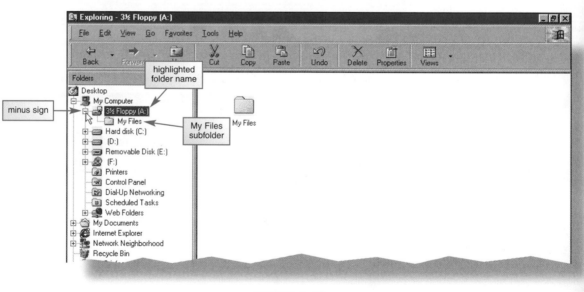

FIGURE 1-48

Displaying the Contents of the Windows Folder

Currently, the My Files folder displays in the Contents pane of the Exploring - 3½ Floppy (A:) window. To copy files from the source folder (Windows folder on drive C) to the My Files folder, the Windows folder must be visible in the Folders pane. To make the Windows folder visible, you must expand the Hard disk (C:) folder and then click the Windows folder name to display the contents of the Windows folder in the Contents pane. Perform the following steps to display the contents of the Windows folder.

To Display the Contents of a Folder

1 Click the plus sign to the left of the Hard disk (C:) icon in the Folders pane and then point to the Windows folder name.

A minus sign replaces the plus sign to the left of the Hard disk (C:) icon and the subfolders in the Hard disk (C:) folder display (Figure 1-49). In addition to folders and other files, the Windows folder contains a series of predefined graphics, called **clip art files**, that can be used with application programs.

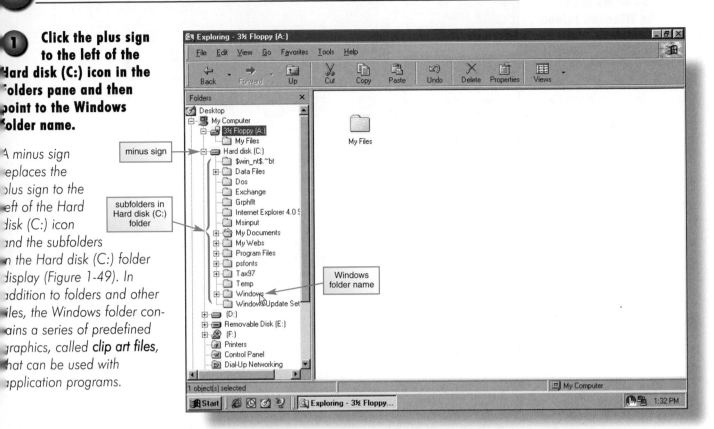

FIGURE 1-49

2 Click the Windows folder name.

The Windows folder name is highlighted in the Folders pane, the closed folder icon to the left of the Windows folder name changes to an open folder icon, and the contents of the Windows folder display in the Contents pane (Figure 1-50).

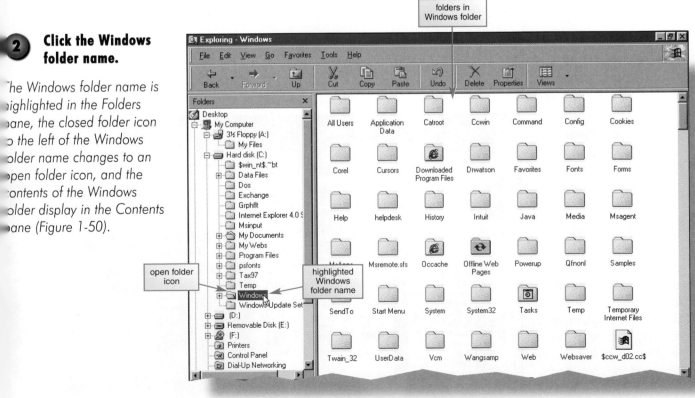

FIGURE 1-50

3 **Scroll the Contents pane to make the files in the Windows folder visible.**

The files in the Windows folder display in the Contents pane (Figure 1-51). Each file is identified by a large icon and a file name. The files in the Windows folder may be different and file extensions may display as part of the file names on your computer.

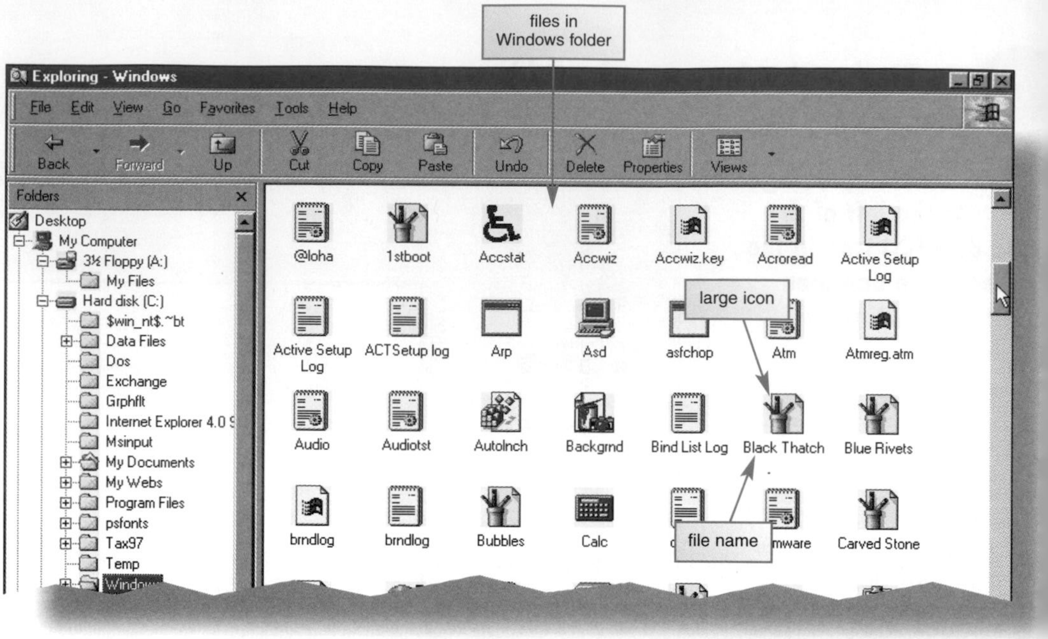

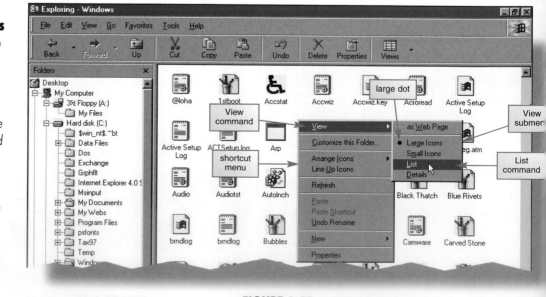

FIGURE 1-51

Changing the View

In Figure 1-51, the files in the Contents pane of the Exploring - Windows window display in Large Icons view. In **Large Icons view**, each file is represented by a large icon and a file name. Other views include Small Icons, List, and Details. List view often is useful when copying or moving files from one location to another location. In **List view**, each file is represented by a smaller icon and name, and the files are arranged in columns. Perform the following steps to change from Large Icons view to List view.

Steps **To Change to List View**

1 **Right-click an open area in the Contents pane, point to View on the shortcut menu, and then point to List on the View submenu.**

A shortcut menu displays, the View command is highlighted on the shortcut menu, the View submenu displays, and the List command is highlighted on the View submenu (Figure 1-52). A large dot to the left of the Large Icons command indicates files and folders in the Contents pane display in Large Icons view.

FIGURE 1-52

② Click List.

The files and folders in the Contents pane display in List view (Figure 1-53).

files and folders display in List view

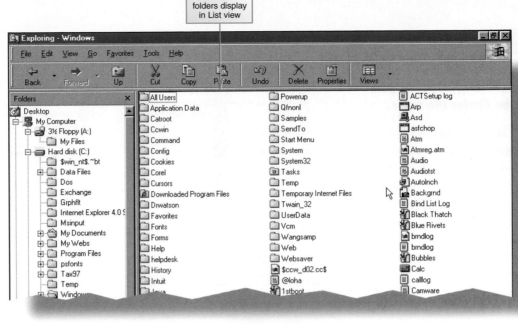

FIGURE 1-53

Other Ways

1. Click Views button on Standard Buttons toolbar repeatedly until files and folder display in List view
2. Click Views button arrow on Standard Buttons toolbar, click List
3. On View menu click List
4. Press ALT+V, press L

Selecting a Group of Files

You easily can copy a single file or group of files from one folder to another folder using Windows Explorer. To copy a single file, select the file in the Contents pane and right-drag the highlighted file to the folder in the Folders pane where the file is to be copied. Group files are copied in a similar fashion by clicking the icon or file name of the first file in a group of files to select it. You select the remaining files in the group by pointing to each file icon or file name, holding down the CTRL key, and clicking the file icon or file name. Perform the following steps to select the group of files consisting of the Black Thatch, Bubbles, and Circles files.

Steps To Select a Group of Files

① Select the Black Thatch file by clicking the Black Thatch file name, and then point to the Bubbles file name.

The Black Thatch file is highlighted in the Contents pane and two messages display on the status bar (Figure 1-54). The messages indicate that one file is selected (1 object(s) selected) and the size of the file is 182 bytes.

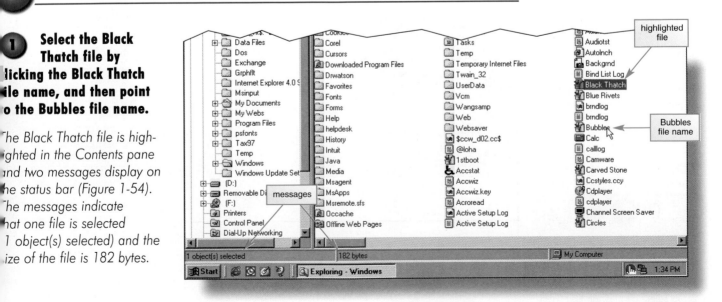

FIGURE 1-54

2 Hold down the CTRL key, click the **Bubbles** file name, release the CTRL key, and then point to the **Circles** file name.

The Black Thatch and Bubbles files are highlighted and the two messages on the status bar change to reflect the additional file selected (Figure 1-55). The messages indicate two files are selected (2 object(s) selected) and the size of the two files (2.24KB).

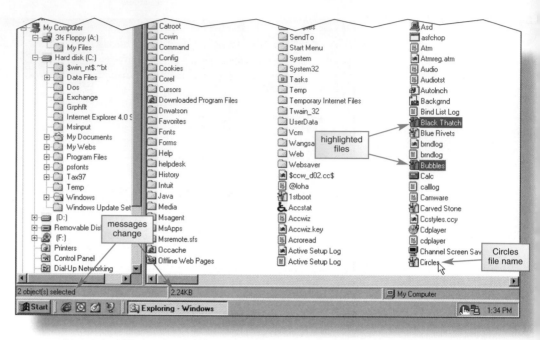

FIGURE 1-55

3 Hold down the CTRL key, click the **Circles** file name, and then release the CTRL key.

The group of files consisting of the Black Thatch, Bubbles, and Circles files is highlighted and the messages on the status bar change to reflect the selection of a third file (Figure 1-56). The messages indicate three files are selected (3 object(s) selected) and the size of the three files (2.43KB).

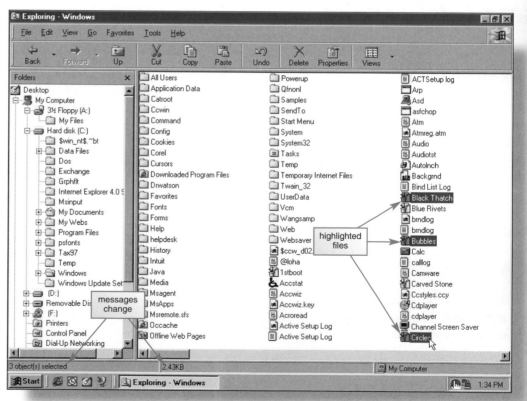

FIGURE 1-56

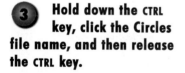

1. To select contiguous files, select first file name, hold down SHIFT key, click last file name
2. To select all files, on Edit menu click Select All

Copying a Group of Files

After selecting a group of files, copy the files to the My Files folder on drive A by pointing to any highlighted file name in the Contents pane and right-dragging the file name to the My Files folder in the Folders pane. Perform the following steps to copy a group of files.

Steps To Copy a Group of Files

1 If necessary, scroll the Folders pane to make the My Files folder visible. Point to the highlighted Black Thatch file name in the Contents pane.

The pointer points to the highlighted Black Thatch file name in the Contents pane and the My Files folder is visible in the Folders pane (Figure 1-57).

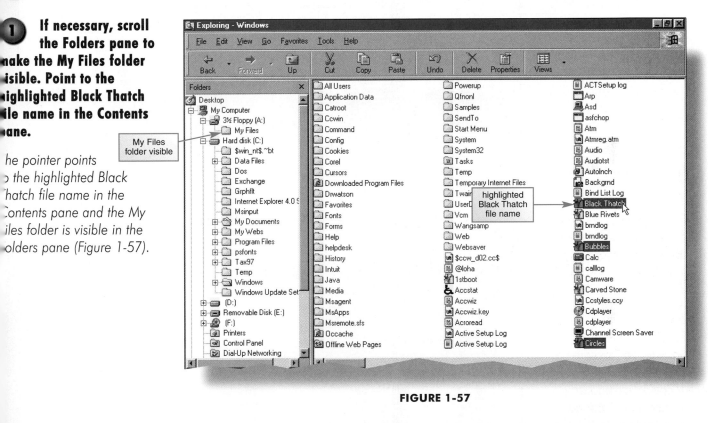

FIGURE 1-57

2 Right-drag the Black Thatch file over the My Files folder name in the Folders pane.

As you drag the file, an outline of three icons and three horizontal lines displays and the My Files folder name is highlighted (Figure 1-58). The mouse pointer contains a plus sign to indicate the group of files is being copied, not moved.

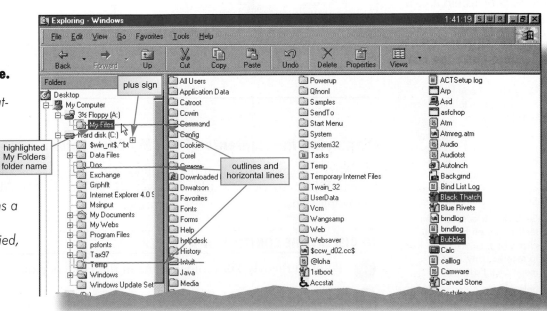

FIGURE 1-58

Release the right mouse button and then point to Copy Here on the shortcut menu.

A shortcut menu displays and the Copy Here command is highlighted (Figure 1-59).

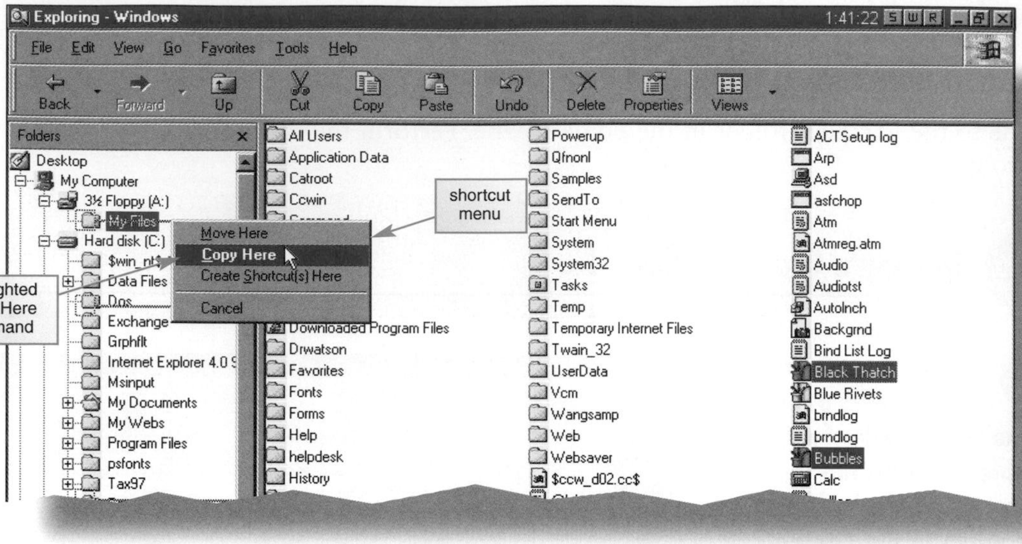

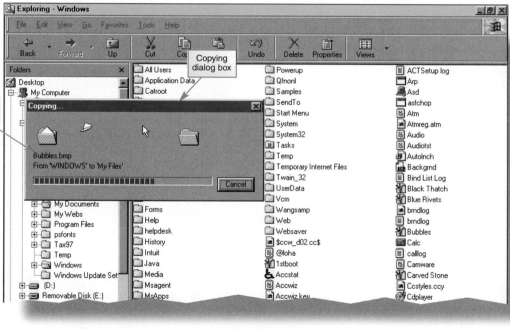

FIGURE 1-59

 Click Copy Here.

The Copying dialog box displays and remains on the screen while each file is copied to the My Files folder (Figure 1-60). A dialog box displays whenever Windows 98 needs to supply information to you or requires you to enter information or select among several options. The Copying dialog box shown in Figure 1-60 indicates the Bubbles.bmp file is being copied.

FIGURE 1-60

Other Ways

1. Drag file to copy from Contents pane to folder icon in Folders pane
2. Select file to copy in Contents pane, click Copy button on Standard Buttons toolbar, select folder icon to receive copy, click Paste button on Standard Buttons toolbar
3. Select file to copy in Contents pane, on Edit menu click Copy, select folder icon to receive copy, on Edit menu click Paste
4. Select file to copy, press CTRL+C, select folder icon to receive copy, press CTRL+V

Displaying the Contents of the My Files Folder

After copying a group of files, you should verify the files were copied into the correct folder. To view the files that were copied to the My Files folder, perform the following steps.

TO DISPLAY THE CONTENTS OF A FOLDER

1 Point to the My Files folder name in the Folders pane.

2 Click the My Files folder name.

The highlighted My Files folder name displays in the Folders pane, the open folder icon replaces the closed folder icon to the left of the My Files folder name, the contents of the My Files folder display in the Contents pane, and the message on the status bar changes (Figure 1-61). The status bar message indicates 1.38MB of free disk space on the disk in drive A.

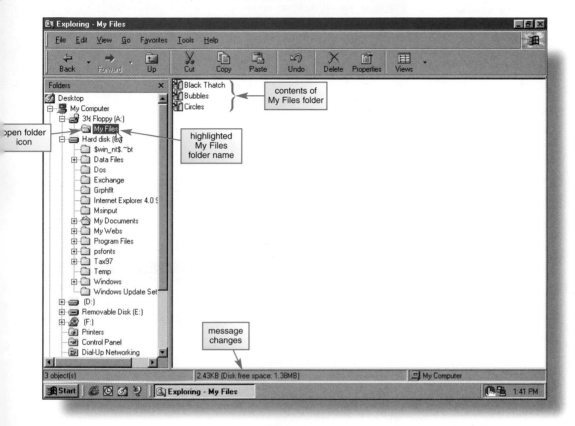

FIGURE 1-61

Renaming a File or Folder

For various reasons, you may wish to change the name of a file or folder on disk. Perform the following steps to change the name of the Circles file on drive A to Blue Circles.

To Rename a File

1 **Point to the Circles file name in the Contents pane (Figure 1-62).**

The mouse pointer points to the Circles file name.

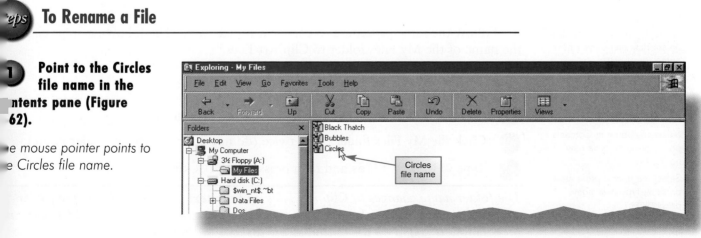

FIGURE 1-62

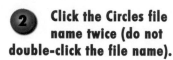

Click the Circles file name twice (do not double-click the file name).

A text box containing the highlighted Circles file name and insertion point displays (Figure 1-63).

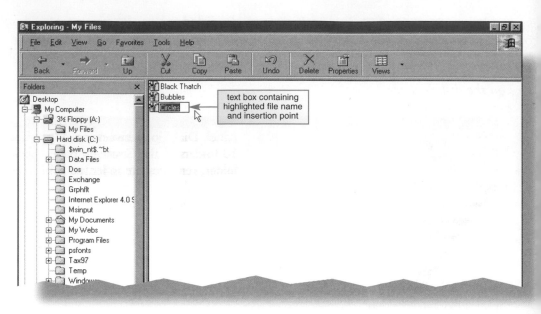

text box containing highlighted file name and insertion point

FIGURE 1-63

Type Blue Circles **and then press the ENTER key.**

The file name changes to Blue Circles and the text box surrounding the file name is removed (Figure 1-64).

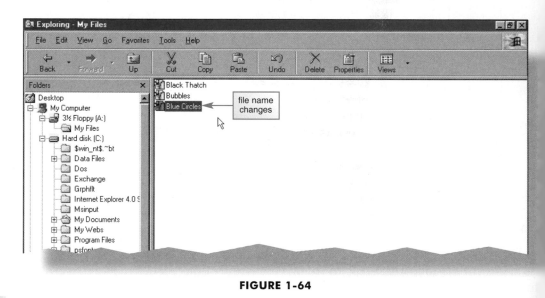

file name changes

FIGURE 1-64

Other Ways

1. Right-click file name in Contents pane, click Rename on shortcut menu, type new name, press ENTER

2. Select file name in Contents pane, on File menu click Rename, type new name, press ENTER

3. Select file name in Contents pane, press F2, type new name, press ENTER

4. Select file name, press ALT+F, press M, type new name, press ENTER

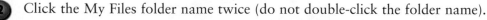

Follow the same procedure to change a folder name. The following steps change the name of the My Files folder to Clip Art Files.

TO RENAME A FOLDER

1 Point to the My Files folder name in the Folders pane.

2 Click the My Files folder name twice (do not double-click the folder name).

3 Type Clip Art Files and then press the ENTER key.

The folder name changes to Clip Art Files and the text box surrounding the folder name is removed (Figure 1-65). The new folder name replaces the old folder name in the window title and on the button in the taskbar button area.

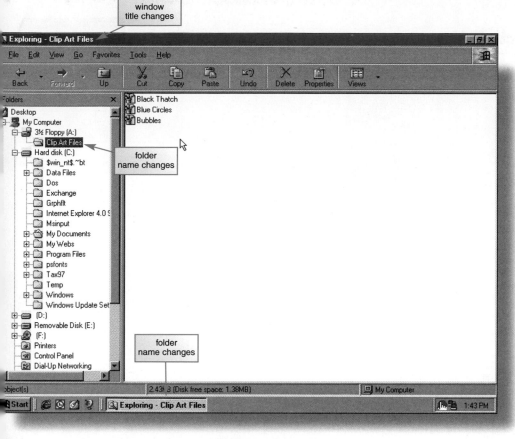

FIGURE 1-65

Deleting a File or Folder

When you no longer need a file or folder, you can delete it. When you delete a file or folder on the hard drive using the Recycle Bin, Windows 98 temporarily stores the deleted file or folder in the Recycle Bin until you permanently discard the contents of the Recycle Bin by emptying the Recycle Bin. Until the Recycle Bin is emptied, you can retrieve the files and folders you have deleted previously by mistake or other reasons. Unlike deleting files or folders on the hard drive, when you delete a file or folder located on a floppy disk, the file or folder is deleted immediately and not stored in the Recycle Bin.

Deleting a File by Right-Clicking Its File Name

Right-clicking a file name produces a shortcut menu that contains the Delete command. To illustrate how to delete a file by right-clicking, perform the steps on the next two pages to delete the Bubbles file.

Steps **To Delete a File by Right-Clicking**

1 **Right-click the Bubbles file name in the Contents pane and then point to the Delete command on the shortcut menu.**

The Bubbles file name is highlighted and a shortcut menu displays (Figure 1-66).

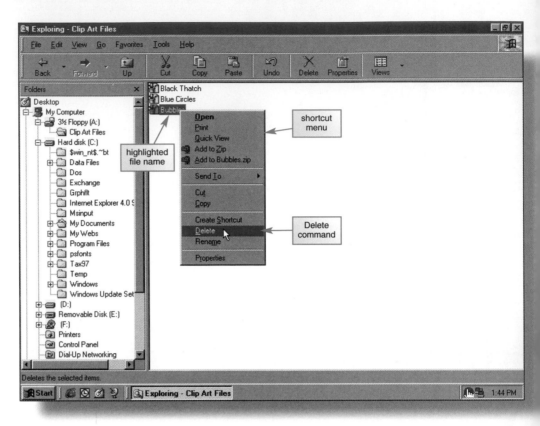

FIGURE 1-66

2 **Click Delete. When the Confirm File Delete dialog box displays, point to the Yes button.**

The Confirm File Delete dialog box displays (Figure 1-67). The dialog box contains the message, Are you sure you want to delete 'Bubbles'?, and the Yes and No command buttons.

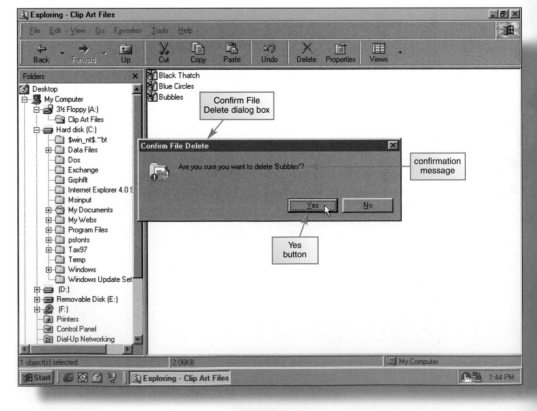

FIGURE 1-67

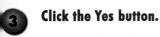

3 Click the Yes button.

\ Deleting dialog box dis- ›lays while the file is being ‑leleted, and then the ʒubbles file is removed from ʰe Contents pane (Figure -68).

FIGURE 1-68

Other Ways

1. Click file name, click Delete button on Standard Buttons toolbar, click Yes button
2. Right-drag file name over Recycle Bin icon, click Move Here, click Yes button
3. Drag file name over Recycle Bin icon, click Yes button

You can use the file selection techniques illustrated earlier in this project to delete group of files. When deleting a group of files, click the Yes button in the Confirm Aultiple File Delete dialog box to confirm the deletion of the group of files.

eleting a Folder

Follow the same procedure to delete a folder. When you delete a folder, Windows 8 deletes any files or subfolders in the folder. Perform the following steps to delete ie Clip Art Files folder on drive A.

O DELETE A FOLDER

1. Right-click the Clip Art Files folder name in the Folders pane.
2. Click Delete on the shortcut menu.
3. Click the Yes button in the Confirm Folder Delete dialog box.
4. Remove the floppy disk from drive A.

Deleting dialog box displays while the folder is being deleted, the Clip Art Files ›lder is removed from the Folders pane, and a plus sign replaces the minus sign pre- ›ding the 3½ Floppy (A:) icon (Figure 1-69).

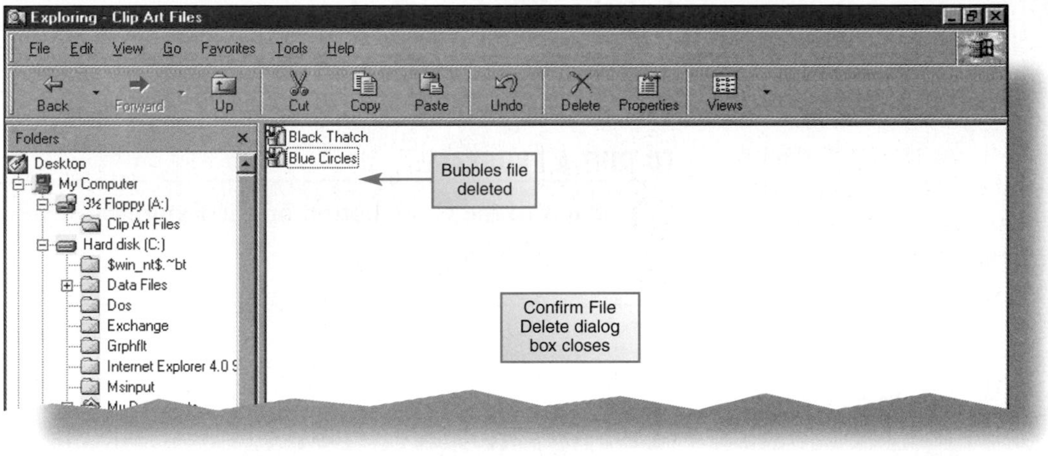

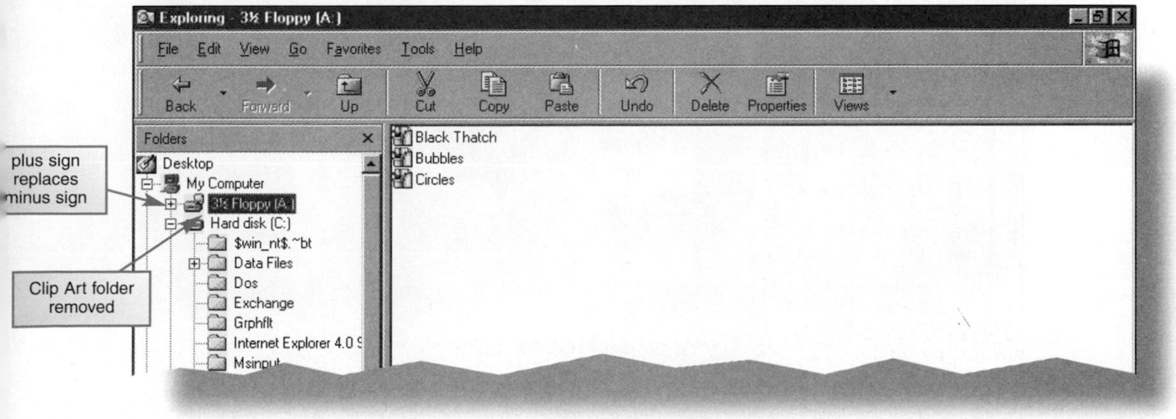

FIGURE 1-69

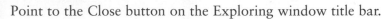

Quitting Windows Explorer

After completing your work with Windows Explorer, you should quit Windows Explorer. Perform the following steps to quit Windows Explorer.

TO QUIT A PROGRAM

(1) Point to the Close button on the Exploring window title bar.

(2) Click the Close button.

Windows 98 closes the Windows Explorer window and quits Windows Explorer.

More About

Windows 98 Help

If you purchased an operating system or application program five years ago, you received thick, heavy technical manuals that explained the software. With Windows 98, you receive a skinny manual less than 100 pages in length. The online Help feature of Windows 98 replaces reams and reams of printed pages in hard-to-understand technical manuals.

Using Windows Help

One of the more powerful application programs for use in Windows 98 is Windows Help. Windows Help is available when using Windows 98, or when using any application program running under Windows 98, to assist you in using Windows 98 and the various application programs. It contains answers to many questions you can ask with respect to Windows 98.

Contents Sheet

Windows Help provides a variety of ways in which to obtain information. One method to find a Help topic involves using the **Contents sheet** to browse through Help topics by category. To illustrate this method, you will use Windows Help to determine how to find a topic in Help. To launch Help, complete the following steps.

 To Launch Windows Help

(1) **Click the Start button on the taskbar. Point to Help on the Start menu (Figure 1-70).**

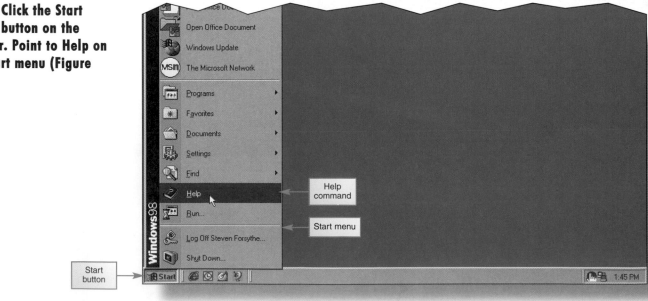

FIGURE 1-70

2 **Click Help.
Click the
Maximize button on the
Windows Help title bar. If
the Contents sheet does not
display, click the Contents
tab.**

*The Windows Help window
opens and maximizes (Figure
1-71). The window contains
the Help toolbar and two
frames. The left frame contains three **tabs** (Contents,
Index, and Search). The
Contents sheet is visible in
the left frame. The right
frame contains information
about the Welcome to Help
topic.*

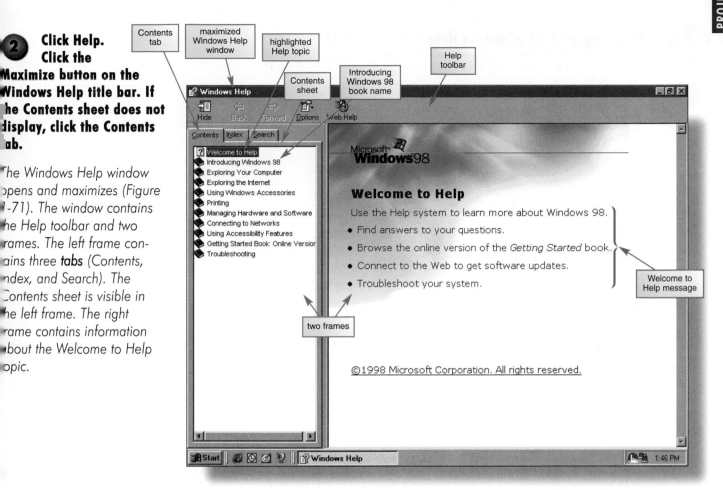

FIGURE 1-71

The Contents sheet contains a **Help topic** preceded by a question mark icon and
followed by 10 books. Each book consists of a closed book icon followed by a book
name. The Help topic, Welcome to Help, is highlighted. In the left frame, a closed
book icon indicates that Help topics or more books are contained in the book. The
question mark icon indicates a Help topic without any further subdivisions. Clicking
either the Index tab or the Search tab in the left frame opens the Index or Search
sheet, respectively.

In addition to launching Help by using the Start button, you also can launch
Help by pressing the F1 key.

After launching Help, the next step is to find the topic in which you are interested. To find the topic that describes how to find a topic in Help, complete the
steps on the next two pages.

Other **Ways**

1. Press F1
2. Press WINDOWS+H (WINDOWS
   key on Microsoft Natural
   keyboard)

Steps **To Use Help to Find a Topic in Help**

1 **Point to the Introducing Windows 98 closed book icon.**

The mouse pointer changes to a hand when positioned on the icon and the Introducing Windows 98 book name displays in blue font and underlined (Figure 1-72).

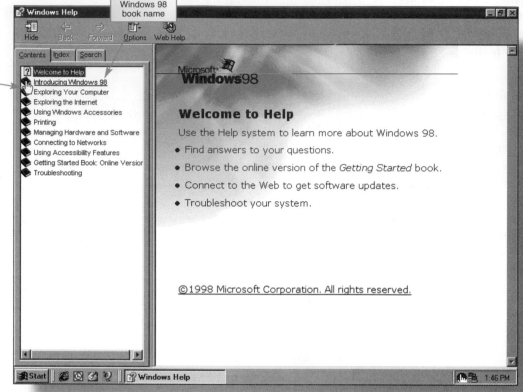

FIGURE 1-72

2 **Click the Introducing Windows 98 closed book icon and then point to the How to Use Help closed book icon.**

Windows 98 opens the Introducing Windows 98 book, changes the closed book icon to an open book icon, highlights the Introducing Windows 98 book name, underlines the How to Use Help book name, and displays the name and underline in blue font (Figure 1-73).

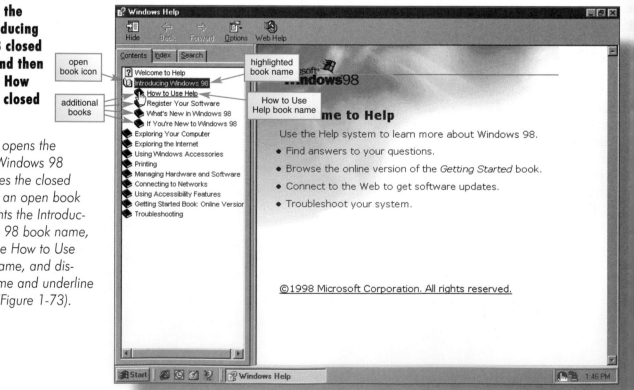

FIGURE 1-73

3 Click the How to Use Help closed book icon and then point to Find a topic in the opened How to Use Help book.

Windows 98 opens the How to Use Help book and displays several Help topics in the book, changes the closed book icon to an open book icon, highlights the How to Use Help book name, underlines the Find a topic Help topic name, and displays the topic name and underline in blue font (Figure 1-74).

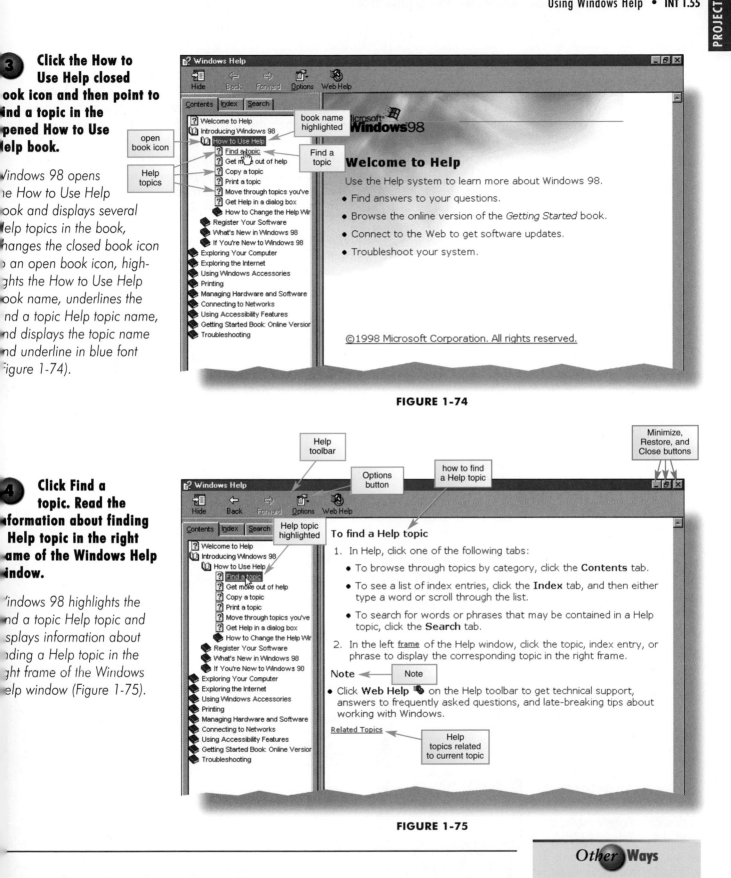

FIGURE 1-74

4 Click Find a topic. Read the information about finding a Help topic in the right frame of the Windows Help window.

Windows 98 highlights the Find a topic Help topic and displays information about finding a Help topic in the right frame of the Windows Help window (Figure 1-75).

FIGURE 1-75

Other **Ways**

1. Press DOWN ARROW key until book or topic is highlighted, press ENTER, continue until Help topic displays, read Help topic

In Figure 1-75 on the previous page, if you click the **Hide button** on the Help toolbar, Windows 98 hides the tabs in the left frame and displays only the right frame in the Windows Help window. Clicking the **Back button** or **Forward button** displays a previously displayed Help topic in the right frame. Clicking the **Options button** allows you to hide or display the tabs in the left frame, display previously displayed Help topics in the right frame, return to the Help home page, stop the display of a Help topic, refresh the currently displayed Help topic, access Web Help, and print a Help topic. The **Web Help command** on the Options menu and the **Web Help button** on the Help toolbar allow you to use the Internet to obtain technical support, answers to frequently asked questions, and tips about working with Windows 98.

Notice also in Figure 1-75 that the Windows Help title bar contains a Minimize button, Restore button, and Close button. You can minimize or restore the Windows Help window as needed and also close the Windows Help window.

Index Sheet

A second method of finding answers to your questions about Windows 98 or application programs running under Windows 98 is the Index sheet. The **Index sheet** lists a large number of index entries, each of which references one or more Help screens. To learn more about the Classic style and Web style, complete the following steps.

More About

The Index Sheet

The Index sheet probably is the best source of information in Windows Help because you can enter the subject you are interested in. Sometimes, however, you will have to be creative to discover the index entry that answers your question because the most obvious entry will not always lead to your answer.

Steps **To Use the Help Index Sheet**

1 Click the Index tab. Type classic style **(the flashing insertion point is positioned in the text box) in the text box. Point to the Display button at the bottom of the left frame.**

The Index sheet displays in the left frame and includes a list of entries that can be referenced (Figure 1-76). When you type an entry, the list automatically scrolls and the entry you type, such as classic style, is highlighted. To see additional entries, use the scroll bar at the right of the list. To highlight an entry in the list, click the entry.

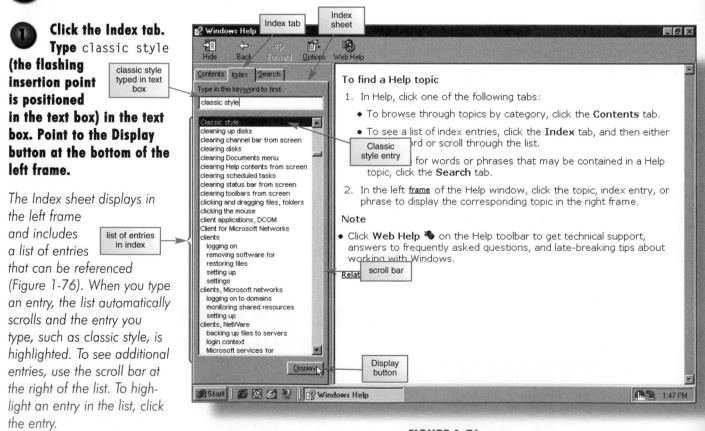

FIGURE 1-76

Click the Display button in the Windows Help window. Point to the Display button in the Topics Found dialog box.

The Topics Found dialog box displays on top of the Windows Help window and two Help topics display in the dialog box (Figure 1-77). The first topic, Choosing Web or Classic style for folders, is highlighted. This topic contains information about the Web and Classic styles.

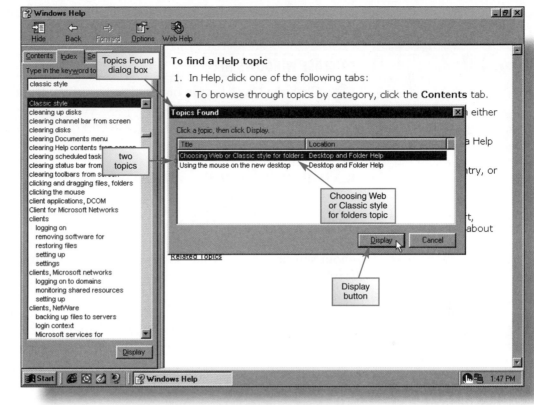

FIGURE 1-77

Click the Display button.

Information about the Web and Classic style and several hyperlinks display in the right frame of the Windows Help window (Figure 1-78).

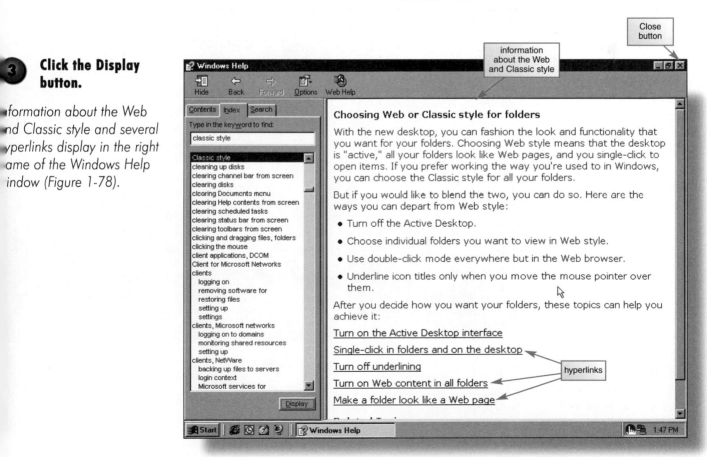

FIGURE 1-78

After viewing the index entries, normally you will close Windows Help. To close Windows Help, complete the following step.

 *About*

Shut Down Procedures

Some users of Windows 98 have turned off their computers without following the shut down procedure only to find data they thought they had stored on disk was lost. Because of the way Windows 98 writes data on the disk, it is important you shut down Windows properly so you do not lose your work.

TO CLOSE WINDOWS HELP

1 Click the Close button on the title bar of the Windows Help window.

Windows 98 closes the Windows Help window.

Shutting Down Windows 98

After completing your work with Windows 98, you may want to shut down Windows 98 using the **Shut Down command** on the Start menu. If you are sure you want to shut down Windows 98, perform the following steps. If you are not sure about shutting down Windows 98, read the following steps without actually performing them.

 To Shut Down Windows 98

1 **Click the Start button on the taskbar and then point to Shut Down on the Start menu (Figure 1-79).**

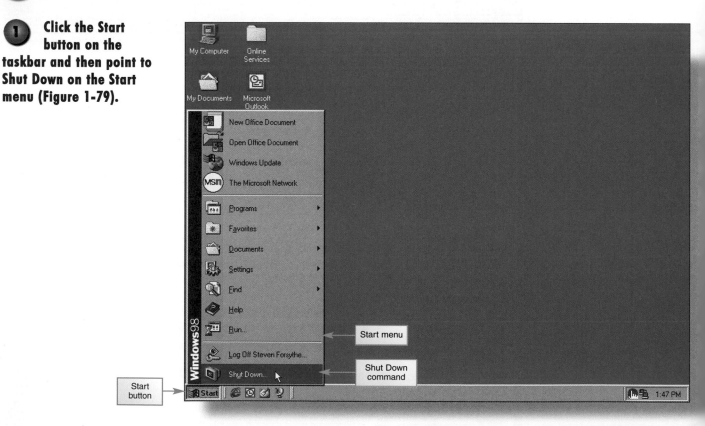

FIGURE 1-79

2 Click Shut Down. Point to the OK button in the Shut Down Windows dialog box.

The desktop darkens and the Shut Down Windows dialog box displays (Figure 1-80). The dialog box contains three option buttons. The selected option button, Shut down, indicates that clicking the OK button will shut down Windows 98.

3 Click the OK button.

Windows 98 is shut down.

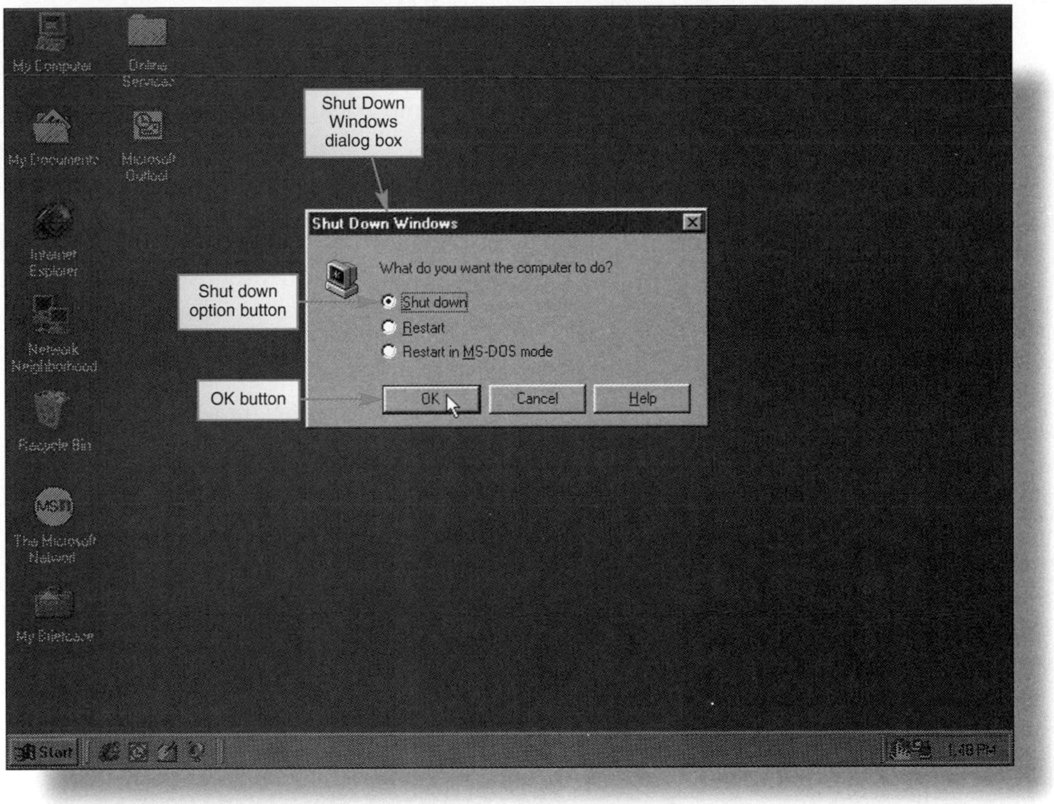

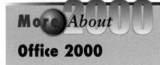

FIGURE 1-80

Two screens display while Windows 98 is shutting down. The first screen containing the Windows logo, Windows 98 name, and the text, Windows is shutting down, displays momentarily while Windows 98 is being shut down. Then, a second screen containing the text, It's now safe to turn off your computer, displays. At this point you can turn off your computer. Some computers are programmed to turn off automatically at this point. When shutting down Windows 98, you should never turn off your computer before these two screens display.

If you accidentally click Shut Down on the Start menu and you do not want to shut down Windows 98, click the Cancel button in the Shut Down Windows dialog box to return to normal Windows 98 operation.

Other Ways

1. Press CTRL+ESC, press U, Press UP ARROW or DOWN ARROW key to select Shut down option button, press ENTER
2. Press ALT+F4, press UP ARROW or DOWN ARROW key to select Shut down option button, press ENTER

What Is Microsoft Office 2000?

Microsoft Office 2000, the latest edition of the world's best-selling office suite, is a collection of the more popular Microsoft application software products. Microsoft Office 2000 is available in Standard, Small Business, Professional, Premium, and Developer editions. The **Microsoft Office 2000 Premium Edition** includes Microsoft Word 2000, Microsoft Excel 2000, Microsoft Access 2000, Microsoft PowerPoint 2000, Microsoft Publisher 2000, Microsoft FrontPage 2000, Microsoft PhotoDraw 2000, Microsoft Outlook 2000, and Internet Explorer. Microsoft Office 2000 allows you to work more efficiently, communicate better, and improve the appearance of the documents you create.

More About 2000

Office 2000

For more information about any Microsoft Office 2000 application, click Help on the menu bar of any Office 2000 application window, and click Office on the Web. Explore a Web page by clicking a hyperlink. After clicking a hyperlink, click the Back button to display the last Web page.

One of the CD-ROMs that accompanies Microsoft Office 2000 contains a clip art gallery that you can use in any of the applications to enhance the appearance of a document. The gallery contains over 16,000 clip art images, sounds, photographs, animations, themes, and backgrounds. In addition, thousands of additional images are available from the Microsoft Clipart Gallery Live found on the Microsoft Web site. Hundreds of new images are added each month to this collection.

Menus and toolbars adjust to the way in which you work. As Microsoft Office detects which commands you use more frequently, these commands display at the top of the menu, and the infrequently used commands are placed in reserve. A button at the bottom of the menu allows you to expand the menu in order to view all its commands. More frequently used buttons on a toolbar display on the toolbar, while less frequently used buttons are not displayed.

Microsoft Office applications are self-repairing. If you accidentally delete a file that is needed to run an Office application, the Self-Repairing Application feature automatically finds the deleted file and reinstalls the file. This feature reduces the number of calls to technical support and increases user productivity.

In addition, Microsoft Office 2000 integrates its applications with the power of the Internet so you can share information, collaborate on projects, and conduct online meetings.

The Internet, World Wide Web, and Intranets

Microsoft Office 2000 allows you to take advantage of the Internet, the World Wide Web, and intranets. The **Internet** is a worldwide network of thousands of computer networks and millions of commercial, educational, government, and personal computers. The **World Wide Web** is an easy-to-use graphical interface for exploring the Internet. The World Wide Web consists of many individual Web sites. A **Web site** can consist of a single **Web page** or multiple Web pages linked together. The first Web page in the Web site is called the **home page** and a unique address, called a **Uniform Resource Locator (URL)**, identifies each Web page. Web sites are located on computers called **Web servers**.

A software tool, called a **browser**, allows you to locate and view a Web page. One method of viewing a Web page is to use the browser to enter the URL for the Web page. A widely used browser, called **Microsoft Internet Explorer**, is included with Microsoft Office CD 2000. Another method of viewing Web pages allows you to click a hyperlink. A **hyperlink** is colored or underlined text or a graphic that, when clicked, connects to another Web page.

An **intranet** is a special type of Web that is available only to the users of a particular type of computer network, such as a network used within a company or organization for internal communication. Like the Internet, hyperlinks are used within an intranet to access documents, pages, and other destinations on the intranet.

Microsoft Office 2000 and the Internet

Microsoft Office 2000 was designed in response to customer requests to streamline the process of information sharing and collaboration within their organizations. Organizations that, in the past, made important information available only to a select few, now want their information accessible to a wider range of individuals who are using tools such as Microsoft Office and Microsoft Internet Explorer. Microsoft Office 2000 allows users to utilize the Internet or an intranet as a central location to view documents, manage files, and work together.

Each of the Microsoft Office 2000 applications makes publishing documents on a Web server as simple as saving a file on a hard disk. Once the file is placed on the Web server, users can view and edit the documents, and conduct Web discussions and live online meetings.

More *About*

Microsoft Office 2000

To subscribe to a free Office 2000 weekly newsletter delivered via e-mail, visit the Office 2000 More About Web page (www.scsite.com/off2000/more.htm) and then click Office 2000 Newsletter.

An explanation of each Microsoft Office 2000 application software program in the Premium Edition along with how it is used to access an intranet or the Internet is given on the following pages.

Microsoft Word 2000

Microsoft Word 2000 is a full-featured word processing program that allows you to create many types of personal and business communications, including announcements, letters, memos, business documents, and academic reports, as well as other forms of written documents. Figure 1-81 illustrates the top portion of the announcement that students create in one of the exercises in Project 1 of the Microsoft Word section of this book. The steps to create an announcement are shown in Project 1 of Microsoft Word 2000.

More About

Microsoft Word 2000

For more information about Microsoft Word 2000, click Help on the menu bar of the Microsoft Word window, and click Office on the Web. Explore a Web page by clicking a hyperlink. After clicking a hyperlink, click the Back button to display the last Web page.

FIGURE 1-81

The Microsoft Word AutoCorrect, Spelling, and Grammar features allow you to proofread documents for errors in spelling and grammar by identifying the errors and offering corrections as you type. As you create a specific document, such as a business letter or resume, Word provides wizards, which ask questions and then use your answers to format the document before you type the text of the document.

The Collect and Paste feature allows you to cut or copy as many as 12 objects (text, pictures, e-mail messages, and so on) and collect them on the Office Clipboard. Then you can paste them into the same document or different documents. Collect and Paste can be used within a single Office 2000 application or among multiple Office 2000 applications.

Microsoft Word automates many often-used tasks and provides you with powerful desktop publishing tools to use as you create professional-looking brochures, advertisements, and newsletters. The drawing tools allow you to design impressive 3-D effects by including shadows, textures, and curves. Floating tables permit you to position a table in an exact location on a page and then wrap text around the table.

Microsoft Word 2000 and the Internet

Microsoft Word makes it possible to access Web pages and search for information, design and publish Web pages on an intranet or the Internet, insert a hyperlink to a Web page in a word processing document, and retrieve pictures from other Web pages. Figure 1-82 illustrates the top portion of a cover letter that contains a hyperlink (e-mail address) that allows you to send an e-mail message to the sender.

Clicking the hyperlink starts the Microsoft Outlook mail program and allows you to send an e-mail message to the author of the cover letter. In Figure 1-83, the Resume and Cover Letter - Message [Rich Text] window that allows you to compose a new e-mail message contains the recipient's e-mail address (brandon@lenox.com), subject of the e-mail message (Resume and Cover Letter), and a brief message.

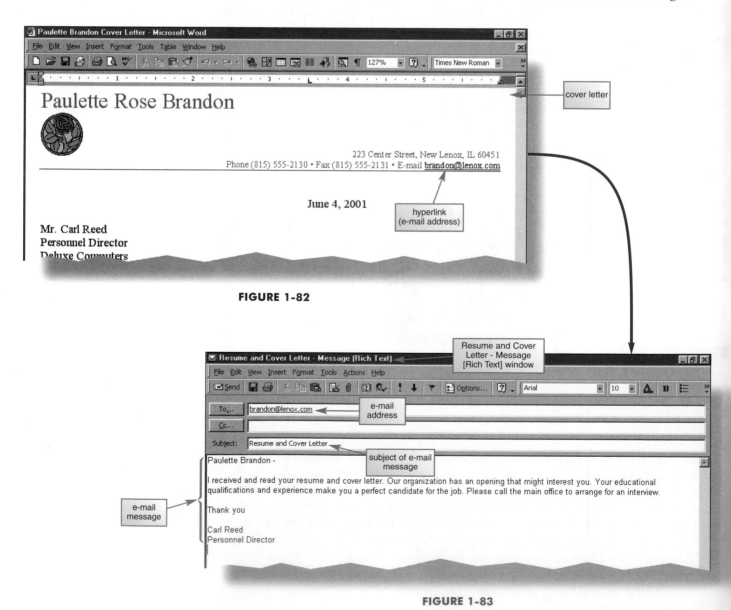

FIGURE 1-82

FIGURE 1-83

Microsoft Excel 2000

Microsoft Excel 2000 is a spreadsheet program that allows you to organize data, complete calculations, make decisions, graph data, develop professional looking reports, publish organized data on the Web, and access real-time data from Web sites. Figure 1-84 illustrates the Microsoft Excel window that contains the worksheet and 3-D column chart created in Project 1 of the Microsoft Excel section of this book.

More About

Microsoft Excel 2000

For more information about Microsoft Excel 2000, click Help on the menu bar of the Microsoft Excel window, and click Office on the Web. Explore a Web page by clicking a hyperlink. After clicking a hyperlink, click the Back button to display the last Web page.

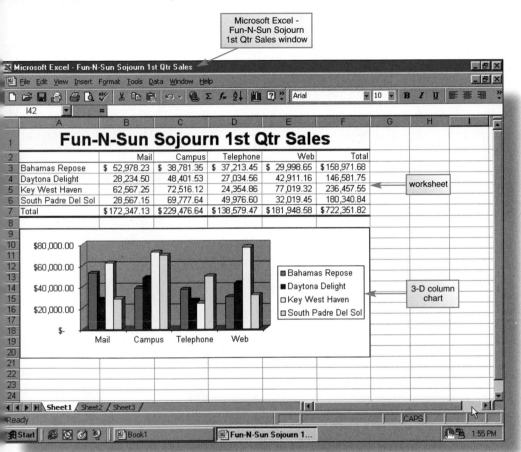

FIGURE 1-84

Microsoft Excel 2000 and the Internet

Using Microsoft Excel, you can create hyperlinks within a worksheet to access other Office 2000 documents on the network, an organization's intranet, or the Internet. You also can save worksheets as static and dynamic Web pages that can be viewed using your browser. Static Web pages cannot be changed by the person viewing them. Dynamic Web pages give the person viewing them many Excel capabilities in their browser. In addition, you can create and run queries to retrieve information from a Web page directly into a worksheet.

Figure 1-85 illustrates a worksheet created by running a Web query to retrieve stock market information for two stocks (CMGI, Inc. and America Online, Inc.). The two hyperlinks were created using the Insert HyperLink button on the Standard toolbar, and the information in the worksheet was obtained from the Microsoft Investor Web site. The Refresh All button on the External Data toolbar allows you to update the last price of the stocks (Last).

Clicking the Refresh All button locates the Microsoft Investor Web site, retrieves current information for the stocks in the worksheet, and displays the updated information in the worksheet (Figure 1-86). Notice that the stock prices and information in this worksheet differ from what was displayed in the worksheet in Figure 1-85.

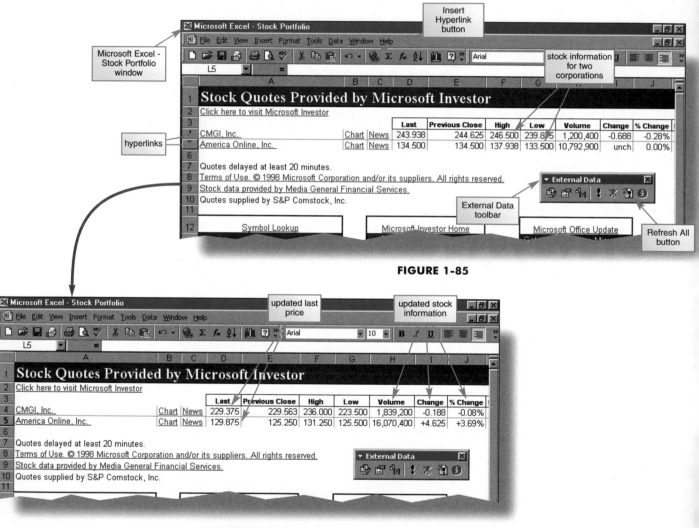

FIGURE 1-85

FIGURE 1-86

Microsoft Access 2000

Microsoft Access 2000 is a comprehensive **database management system (DBMS)**. A **database** is a collection of data organized in a manner that allows access, retrieval, and use of that data. Microsoft Access allows you to create a database; add, change, and delete data in the database; sort data in the database; retrieve data from the database; and create forms and reports using the data in the database.

The database created in Project 1 of the Microsoft Access section of this book displays in the Microsoft Access - [Marina : Table] window illustrated in Figure 1-87. The steps to create this database are shown in Project 1 of Access.

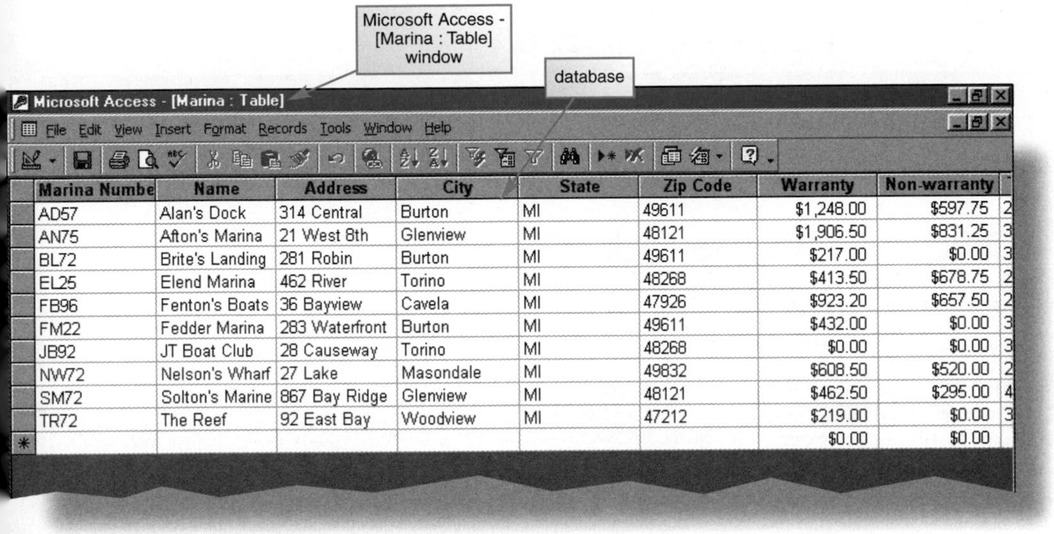

Microsoft Access - [Marina : Table] window

database

Marina Number	Name	Address	City	State	Zip Code	Warranty	Non-warranty	
AD57	Alan's Dock	314 Central	Burton	MI	49611	$1,248.00	$597.75	2
AN75	Afton's Marina	21 West 8th	Glenview	MI	48121	$1,906.50	$831.25	3
BL72	Brite's Landing	281 Robin	Burton	MI	49611	$217.00	$0.00	3
EL25	Elend Marina	462 River	Torino	MI	48268	$413.50	$678.75	2
FB96	Fenton's Boats	36 Bayview	Cavela	MI	47926	$923.20	$657.50	2
FM22	Fedder Marina	283 Waterfront	Burton	MI	49611	$432.00	$0.00	3
JB92	JT Boat Club	28 Causeway	Torino	MI	48268	$0.00	$0.00	3
NW72	Nelson's Wharf	27 Lake	Masondale	MI	49832	$608.50	$520.00	2
SM72	Solton's Marine	867 Bay Ridge	Glenview	MI	48121	$462.50	$295.00	4
TR72	The Reef	92 East Bay	Woodview	MI	47212	$219.00	$0.00	3
*						$0.00	$0.00	

FIGURE 1-87

Microsoft Access 2000 and the Internet

Databases provide a central location to store related pieces of information. Microsoft Access simplifies the creation of databases with a wizard that can build one of more than a dozen types of databases quickly. You also can transform lists or worksheets into databases using Access wizards. Data access pages allow you to share a database with other computer users on a network, intranet, or over the Internet, as well as allowing the users to view and edit the database. The database shown in Figure 1-88 contains information (order number, customer number, order date, product number, and quantity) about three orders entered over the Internet using the Microsoft Internet Explorer browser.

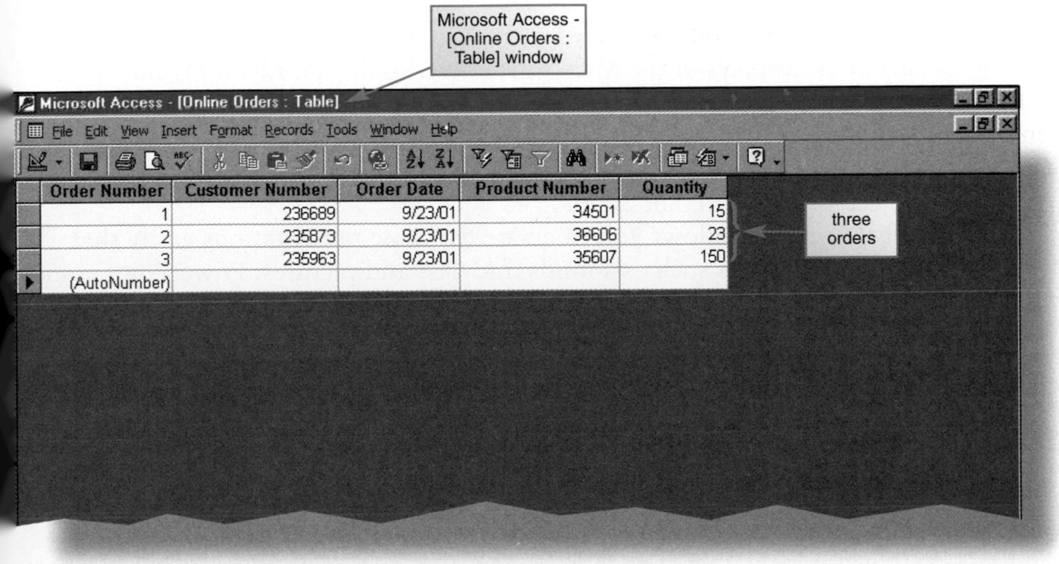

Microsoft Access - [Online Orders : Table] window

Order Number	Customer Number	Order Date	Product Number	Quantity	
1	236689	9/23/01	34501	15	
2	235873	9/23/01	36606	23	three orders
3	235963	9/23/01	35607	150	
(AutoNumber)					

FIGURE 1-88

Figure 1-89 illustrates a simple online order form created to enter order information into the database shown in Figure 1-88 on the previous page. The order form, containing information about order number 4, displays in the Online Orders - Microsoft Internet Explorer window.

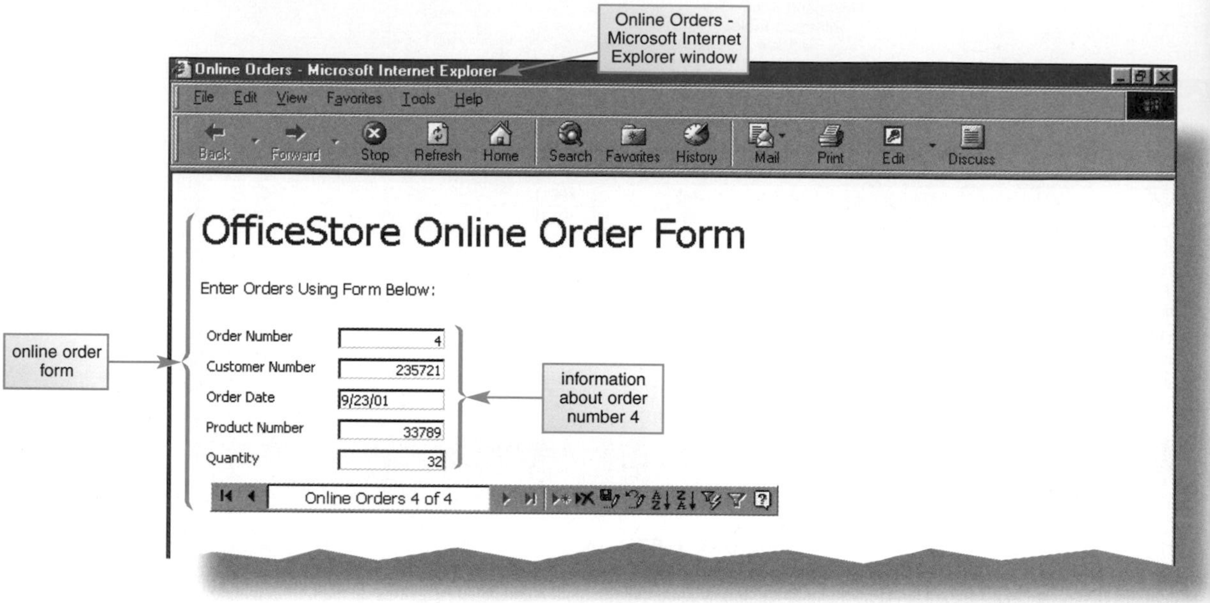

FIGURE 1-89

More About

Microsoft PowerPoint 2000

For more information about Microsoft PowerPoint 2000, click Help on the menu bar of the Microsoft PowerPoint window, and click Office on the Web. Explore a Web page by clicking a hyperlink. After clicking a hyperlink, click the Back button to display the last Web page.

Microsoft PowerPoint 2000

Microsoft PowerPoint 2000 is a complete **presentation graphics program** that allows you to produce professional-looking presentations. PowerPoint gives you the flexibility to make informal presentations using overhead transparencies, make electronic presentations using a projection device attached to a personal computer, make formal presentations using 35mm slides, or run virtual presentations on the Internet.

In PowerPoint 2000, you create a presentation in Normal view. Normal view allows you to view the outline pane, slide pane, and notes pane at the same time. The first slide in the presentation created in Project 1 of the Microsoft PowerPoint section of this book displays in the Microsoft PowerPoint - [Studying] window illustrated in Figure 1-90. The window contains the outline pane with the presentation outline, the slide pane displaying the first slide in the presentation, and the note pane showing a note about the presentation. The steps to create this presentation are shown in Project 1 of PowerPoint 2000.

Microsoft PowerPoint allows you to create dynamic presentations easily that include multimedia features such as sounds, movies, and pictures. PowerPoint comes with templates that assist you in designing a presentation that can be used to create a slide show. PowerPoint also contains formatting for tables, so that you do not have to create the tables using Excel or Word. The Table Draw tool used in Word to draw tables also is available in PowerPoint.

Microsoft PowerPoint 2000 and the Internet

PowerPoint allows you to publish presentations on the Internet or an intranet. Figure 1-91 illustrates the first slide in a presentation to be published on the Internet. The slide displays in Slide view and contains a title (Microsoft Office 2000), subtitle (Guide to Office Applications), and creation date (Created: October 2001). The additional slides in this presentation do not display in Figure 1-91.

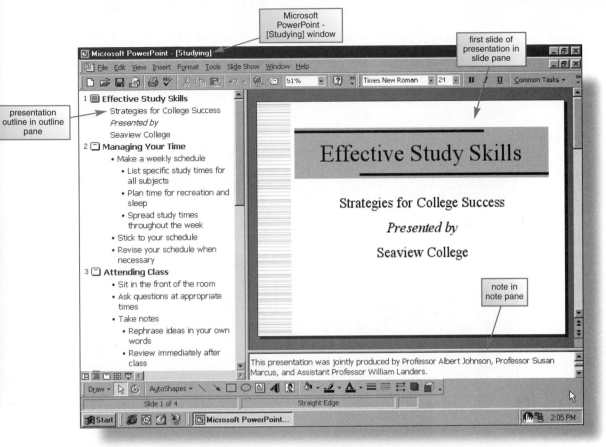

FIGURE 1-90

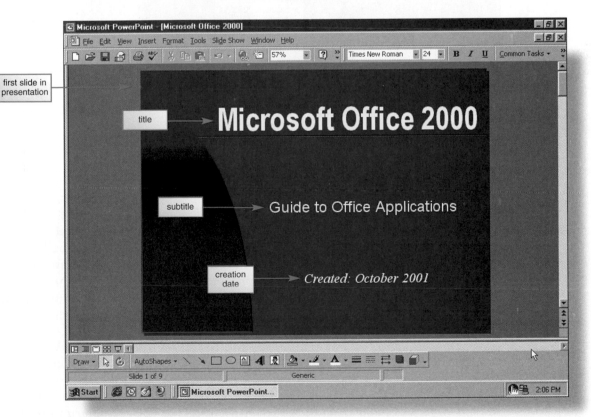

FIGURE 1-91

Figure 1-92 shows the first Web page in a series of Web pages created from the presentation illustrated in Figure 1-91 on the previous page. The Web page displays in the Microsoft Office 2000 - Microsoft Internet Explorer window. Navigation buttons below the Web page allow you to view additional Web pages in the presentation.

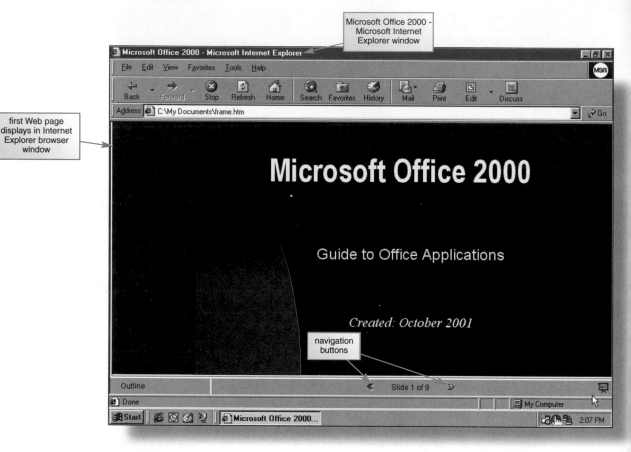

FIGURE 1-92

The Web Toolbar

The easiest method of navigating an intranet or the Internet is to use the Web toolbar. The Web toolbar allows you to search for and open Microsoft Office 2000 documents that have been placed on an intranet or the Internet. The Web toolbar in the Paulette Brandon Cover Letter - Microsoft Word window shown in Figure 1-93 is available in all Microsoft Office 2000 applications except Microsoft Publisher, Microsoft PhotoDraw, and Microsoft FrontPage. Currently, a Word document (cover letter) displays in the window, and the path and file name of the document display in the text box on the Web toolbar.

The buttons and text box on the Web toolbar allow you to jump to Web pages you have viewed previously, cancel a jump to a Web page, update the contents of the current Web page, or replace all other toolbars with the Web toolbar. In addition, you can view the first Web page displayed, search the Web for new Web sites, and add any Web pages you select to the Favorites folder, so you can return to them quickly in the future.

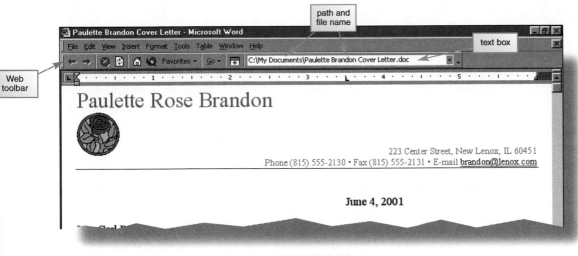

FIGURE 1-93

Microsoft Publisher 2000

Microsoft Publisher 2000 is a **desktop publishing (DTP) program** that allows you to design and produce professional-quality documents (newsletters, flyers, brochures, business cards, Web sites, and so on) that combine text, graphics, and photographs. Desktop publishing software provides a variety of tools, including design templates, graphic manipulation tools, color schemes or libraries, and various page wizards and templates. For large jobs, businesses use desktop publishing software to design publications that are **camera ready**, which means the files are suitable for production by outside commercial printers.

Publisher allows you to design a unique image, or logo, using one of more than 1,600 professional-looking design sets. This, in turn, permits you to use the same design for all your printed documents (letter, business cards, brochures, and advertisements) and Web pages. Microsoft Publisher includes 60 coordinated color schemes, more than 10,000 high-quality clip art images, 1,500 photographs, 1,000 Web-art graphics, 175 fonts, 340 animated graphics, and hundreds of unique Design Gallery elements (quotations, sidebars, and so on). In addition, you can download an additional 100 images from Microsoft Clipart Gallery Live on the Microsoft Web site each month.

In the Business Card - Hank Landers - Microsoft Publisher window shown in Figure 1-94, a business card that was created using the Business Card wizard and the Arcs design set displays.

More About

Microsoft Publisher 2000

For more information about Microsoft Publisher 2000, click Help on the menu bar of the Microsoft Publisher window, and click Office on the Web. Explore a Web page by clicking a hyperlink. After clicking a hyperlink, click the Back button to display the last Web page.

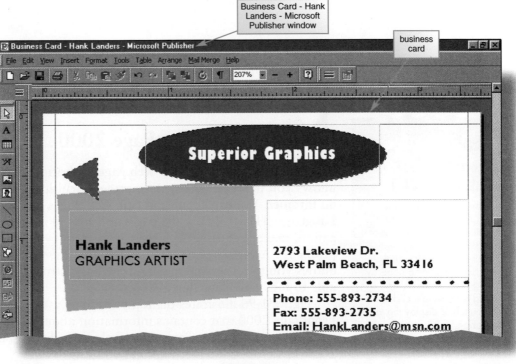

FIGURE 1-94

Microsoft Publisher and the Internet

Microsoft Publisher allows you to create a multi-page Web site with custom color schemes, photo images, animated images, and sounds easily. Figure 1-95 illustrates the Superior Graphics - Microsoft Internet Explorer window displaying the top portion of the home page in a Web site created using the Web page wizard and Arcs design set.

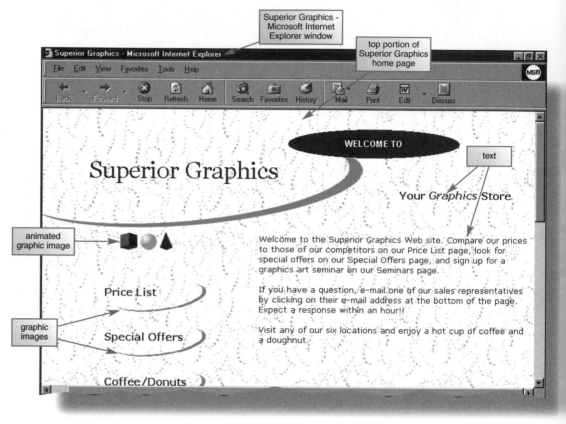

FIGURE 1-95

The home page in the Superior Graphics Web site contains text, graphic images, animated graphic images, and displays using the same design set (Arcs) as the business card illustrated in Figure 1-94 on the previous page.

More About

Microsoft FrontPage 2000

For more information about Microsoft FrontPage 2000, click Help on the menu bar of the Microsoft FrontPage window, and click Office on the Web. Explore a Web page by clicking a hyperlink. After clicking a hyperlink, click the Back button to display the last Web page.

Microsoft FrontPage 2000

Microsoft FrontPage 2000 is a Web page authoring and site management program that allows you to create and manage professional-looking Web sites on the Internet or an intranet. You can create and edit Web pages without knowing HyperText Markup Language (HTML), view the pages and files in the Web site and control their organization, manage existing Web sites, import and export files, and diagnose and fix problems. A variety of templates, including the new Workgroup Web template that allows you to set up and maintain the basic structure of a workgroup Web, are available to facilitate managing a Web site.

Figure 1-96 illustrates the top portion of a Web page created using Microsoft FrontPage 2000 that contains information about the Discovering Computers 2000 textbook published by Course Technology. It displays in the Discovering Computers 2000 - Microsoft Internet Explorer window.

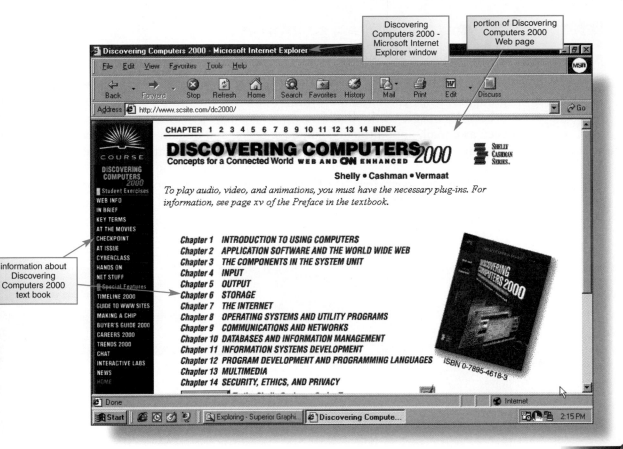

FIGURE 1-96

Microsoft PhotoDraw 2000

Microsoft PhotoDraw 2000 is a business graphics software program that allows you to create eye-catching business graphics to be used in documents and presentations on the Web. Microsoft PhotoDraw contains over 20,000 professional images (photos, logos, three-dimensional text, and Web banners), a complete set of graphics tools, 200 built-in special effects, and 300 professionally designed templates. Figure 1-97 illustrates the Microsoft PhotoDraw - [Mystery Falls] window displaying an enhanced, or retouched, photograph that has been outlined using the Soft Edges tool.

More About

Microsoft PhotoDraw 2000

For more information about Microsoft PhotoDraw 2000, click Office on the Web on the PhotoDraw Help menu. Explore a Web page by clicking a hyperlink; click the Back button to display the last Web page.

FIGURE 1-97

Microsoft Outlook 2000

For more information about Microsoft Outlook 2000, click Help on the menu bar of the Microsoft Outlook window, and click Office on the Web. Explore a Web page by clicking a hyperlink. After clicking a hyperlink, click the Back button to display the last Web page.

Microsoft Outlook 2000

Microsoft Outlook 2000 is an integrated **desktop information management (DIM)** program that helps you organize information on the desktop and share information with others. Microsoft Outlook allows you to manage personal and business information such as e-mail, appointments, contacts, tasks, and documents, and keep a journal of your activities. Outlook organizes and stores this information in folders on your desktop.

When you start Microsoft Outlook, the Inbox - Microsoft Outlook window displays and the contents of the Inbox folder (your e-mail messages) display in the window (Figure 1-98).

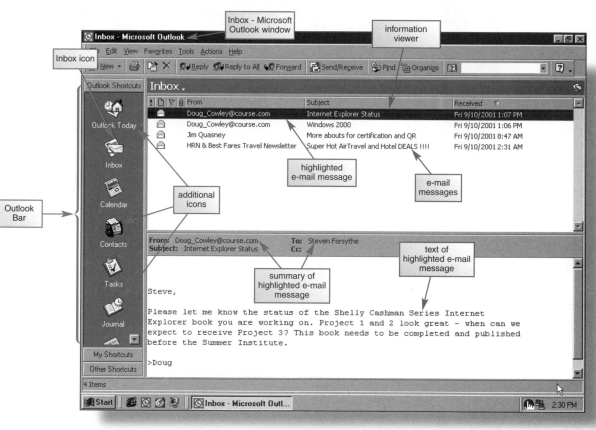

FIGURE 1-98

The Inbox icon, representing the Inbox folder, displays on the Outlook Bar on the left side of the window and the information viewer displays on the right side of the window. The contents of the Inbox folder (one highlighted e-mail message and three e-mail messages) display at the top of the information viewer. Summary information (From:, To:, Subject:, and Cc:) and the text of the highlighted e-mail message displays at the bottom of the information viewer. Also visible on the Outlook Bar are the Outlook Today, Calendar, Contacts, Tasks, and Journal icons. Clicking an icon in the Outlook Bar displays the contents of the associated folder in the information viewer.

When you click the Outlook Today button on the Outlook Bar, the Personal Folders - Microsoft Outlook window displays (Figure 1-99). The window contains the current date (Monday, September 10, 2001); a list of scheduled events, appointments, and meetings for the week; a list of tasks to perform; and a summary of the e-mail messages.

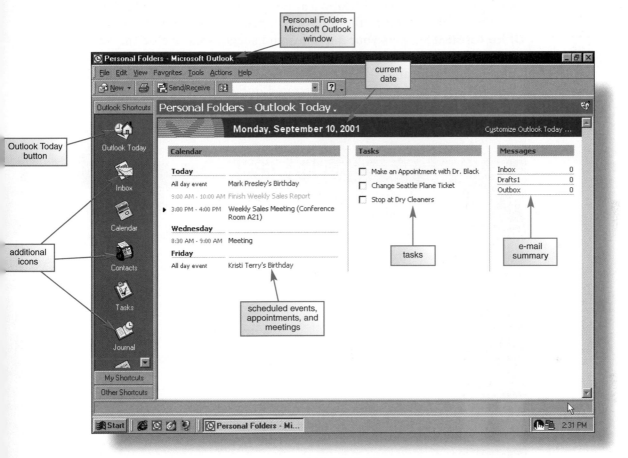

FIGURE 1-99

Microsoft Outlook also allows you to click the Calendar icon to schedule activities (events, appointments, and meetings), click the Contacts icon to maintain a list of contacts and e-mail addresses, and click the Tasks button to view a detailed list of tasks. In addition, you can click the Journal button to view a log of your Outlook activities and store and click the Notes button to make and review electronic reminders, or notes.

More About

Assistant

To change the Office Assistant, right-click the Office Assistant window, click Options on the shortcut menu, if necessary click Gallery tab, click Next button to select Office Assistant, and click the OK button.

The Microsoft Office 2000 Help System

At any time while you are using one of the Microsoft Office 2000 applications, you can interact with the Help system for that application and display information on any topic associated with the application. Several categories of help are available to you. One of the easiest methods to obtain help is to use the Office Assistant. The **Office Assistant** answers your questions and suggests more efficient ways to complete a task. The Office Assistant and balloon display whenever you start any Microsoft Office 2000 application. The Office Assistant and balloon that display in the Notes - Microsoft Outlook window are illustrated in Figure 1-100.

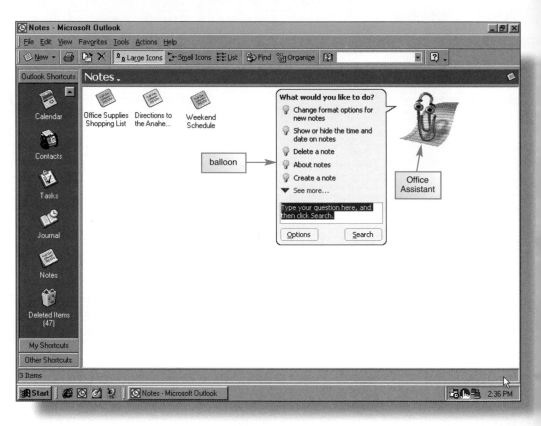

FIGURE 1-100

The Office Assistant (an animated two-dimensional paper clip) is completely customizable so you can select one of nine Office Assistants and the options that best suit the way you work. Detailed instructions for using the Office Assistant and the other categories of Help are explained in Appendix A of this book.

CASE PERSPECTIVE SUMMARY

While continuing to answer questions about Windows 98 and Office 2000 in the workplace, you spent nearly every free moment in the next two weeks learning about the newly installed operating system and application software. Then, the daily training sessions kept you busy for the following three months. You taught 37 workshops and trained all of the 473 employees in the company. Your supervisor, who attended the Windows 98 and Excel 2000 seminars, complimented your success by giving you a sizeable pay raise and time off to attend the Shelly Cashman Institute at Purdue University.

Project Summary

Project 1 illustrated the Microsoft Windows 98 graphical user interface and the Microsoft Office 2000 applications. You started Windows 98, learned the components of the desktop and the six mouse operations. You opened, closed, moved, resized, minimized, maximized, and scrolled a window. You used Windows Explorer to select and copy a group of files, display the contents of a folder, create a folder, expand and collapse a folder, and rename and delete a file and a folder. You obtained help about using Microsoft Windows 98 and shut down Windows 98.

Brief explanations of the Microsoft Word, Microsoft Excel, Microsoft Access, Microsoft PowerPoint, Microsoft Publisher, Microsoft FrontPage, Microsoft PhotoDraw, and Microsoft Outlook applications and examples of how these applications interact with the Internet, World Wide Web, and intranets were given. With this introduction, you are ready to begin a more in-depth study of each of the Microsoft Office 2000 applications explained in this book.

What You Should Know

Having completed this project, you now should be able to perform the following tasks:

Change to List View *(INT 1.42)*

Close a Window *(INT 1.24)*

Close a Window and Reopen a Window *(INT 1.19)*

Close the Welcome Screen *(INT 1.8)*

Close Windows Help *(INT 1.58)*

Collapse a Folder *(INT 1.36)*

Copy a Group of Files *(INT 1.45)*

Create a New Folder *(INT 1.37)*

Delete a File by Right-Clicking *(INT 1.50)*

Delete a Folder *(INT 1.51)*

Display the Contents of a Folder *(INT 1.34, INT 1.41, INT 1.46)*

Expand a Folder *(INT 1.35, INT 1.40)*

Launch a Program Using the Start Menu *(INT 1.28)*

Launch Windows Help *(INT 1.52)*

Maximize and Restore a Window *(INT 1.17)*

Minimize and Redisplay a Window *(INT 1.15)*

▶ Move an Object by Dragging *(INT 1.20)*

▶ Open a Window by Double-Clicking *(INT 1.13)*

▶ Point and Click *(INT 1.9)*

▶ Quit a Program *(INT 1.29, INT 1.52)*

▶ Rename a File *(INT 1.47)*

▶ Rename a Folder *(INT 1.48)*

▶ Resize a Window *(INT 1.24)*

▶ Right-Click *(INT 1.12)*

▶ Right-Drag *(INT 1.25)*

▶ Scroll a Window Using Scroll Arrows *(INT 1.22)*

▶ Select a Group of Files *(INT 1.43)*

▶ Shut Down Windows 98 *(INT 1.58)*

▶ Size a Window by Dragging *(INT 1.21)*

▶ Start Windows Explorer and Maximize Its Window *(INT 1.30)*

▶ Use Help to Find a Topic in Help *(INT 1.54)*

▶ Use the Help Index Sheet *(INT 1.56)*

In the Lab

1 Improving Your Mouse Skills

Instructions: Use a computer to perform the following tasks.

1. If necessary, start Microsoft Windows 98.
2. Click the Start button on the taskbar, point to Programs on the Start menu, point to Accessories on the Programs submenu, point to Games on the Accessories submenu, and then click Solitaire on the Games submenu. If you cannot find the Games command on the Accessories submenu, ask your instructor if the game have been removed from your computer.
3. Click the Maximize button in the Solitaire window.
4. Click Help on the Solitaire menu bar and then click Help Topics.
5. If the Contents sheet does not display, click the Contents tab.
6. Review the Playing Solitaire and Choosing a scoring system topics on the Contents sheet.
7. After reviewing the Help topics, close the Solitaire Help window.
8. Play the game of Solitaire.
9. Click the Close button on the Solitaire title bar to close the game.

2 Using the Discover Windows 98 Tutorial

Instructions: To use the Discover Windows 98 tutorial, you will need a copy of the Windows 98 CD-ROM. If this CD-ROM is not available, skip this lab assignment. Otherwise, use a computer and the CD-ROM to perform the following tasks.

1. If necessary, start Microsoft Windows 98.
2. Insert the Windows 98 CD-ROM in your CD-ROM drive. If the Windows 98 CD-ROM window displays, click the Close button on the title bar to close the window.
3. Click the Start button on the taskbar, point to Programs on the Start menu, point to Accessories on the Programs submenu, point to System Tools on the Accessories submenu, and then click Welcome to Windows on the System Tools submenu.
4. Click Discover Windows 98 in the Welcome to Windows 98 window to display the Discover Windows 98 Contents.
5. Click the Computer Essentials title (hyperlink) in the Discover Windows 98 Contents screen (Figure 1-101) The Computer Essentials tutorial starts and fills the desktop. The left panel contains a list of lessons. A left-pointing arrow to the right of a lesson indicates the current lesson. Pressing the RIGHT ARROW key on the keyboard displays the next screen in the lesson. Pressing the UP ARROW key quits the Computer Essentials tutorial. Clicking the Contents button displays the Table of Contents in the Discover Windows 98 Contents screen.
6. Press the RIGHT ARROW key to begin the Introduction.
7. When appropriate, press the number 1 key to begin the Meeting Your Computer section. Complete this lesson. The lesson takes approximately 10 minutes.

In the Lab

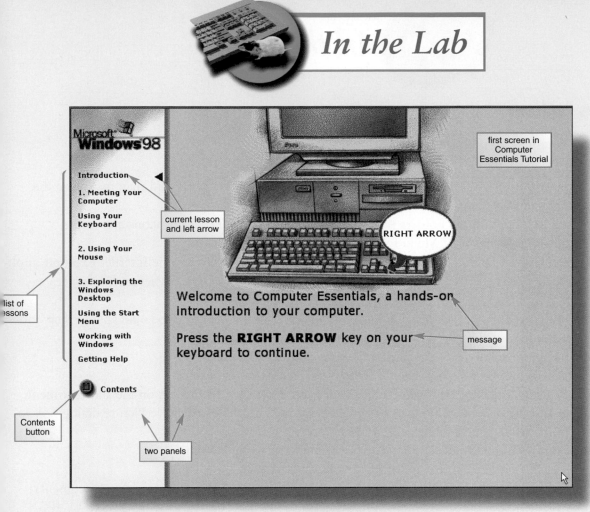

FIGURE 1-101

8. Click the Contents button to display the Discover Windows 98 Contents screen.
9. If you have experience using Windows 3.0 or Windows 3.1 and are learning to use Windows 98, click the Windows 98 Overview title. Otherwise, go to Step 10. This lesson takes approximately 10 minutes.
10. If you have experience using Windows 95 and are learning to use Windows 98, click the What's New title. Otherwise, go to Step 11. Press any key on the keyboard to begin the lesson. Features are organized into five groups. Click each feature (hyperlink) in each group to view a demonstration. When you have finished, click the Exit button. This lesson takes approximately 20 minutes.
11. If time permits, click the More Windows 98 Resources title. Click the Microsoft Windows 98 Starts Here title (1) and then click the Microsoft Press title (2) to view additional information about Windows 98. Click each of the three hyperlinks below the Resources title to explore three Windows-related Web sites. When you have finished, click the Close button in the Microsoft Internet Explorer window and click the Contents button.
12. Click the Close button in the Discover Windows 98 Contents screen.
13. Click the Yes button in the Discover Windows 98 dialog box.
14. Click the Close button in the Welcome to Windows 98 window.
15. Remove the Windows 98 CD-ROM from your CD-ROM drive.

In the Lab

3 Windows Explorer

Instructions: Use a computer to perform the following tasks.

1. Start Microsoft Windows 98 and connect to the Internet.
2. Right-click the Start button on the taskbar, click Explore on the shortcut menu, and then maximize the Exploring - Start Menu window.
3. If necessary, scroll to the left in the Folders pane so the Start Menu and Programs icons are visible.
4. Click the Programs icon in the Start Menu folder.
5. Double-click the Internet Explorer shortcut icon in the Contents pane to launch the Internet Explorer application. What is the URL of the Web page that displays in the Address bar in the Microsoft Internet Explorer window? _____
6. Click the URL in the Address bar in the Internet Explorer window to select it. Type www.scsite.com and then press the ENTER key.
7. Scroll the Web page to display the Shelly Cashman Series textbook titles.
8. Click the Microsoft Windows 98 Complete Concepts and Techniques hyperlink.
9. Right-click the Space Needle clip art image on the Web page, click Save Picture As on the shortcut menu, type Space Needle in the File name box, and then click the Save button in the Save Picture dialog box to save the image in the My Documents folder.
10. Click the Close button in the Windows 98 - Microsoft Internet Explorer window.
11. Scroll to the top of the Folders pane to make the drive C icon visible.
12. Click the minus sign in the box to the left of the drive C icon. The 3½ Floppy (A:) and My Documents icons should be visible.
13. Click the My Documents icon.
14. Right-click the Space Needle icon and then click Properties on the shortcut menu.
    a. What type of file is the Space Needle file? _____
    b. When was the file last modified? _____
    c. What is the size of the file in bytes? _____
15. Click the Cancel button in the Properties dialog box.
16. Insert a formatted floppy disk in drive A of your computer.
17. Right-drag the Space Needle icon over the 3½ Floppy (A:) icon in the Folders pane. Click Move Here on the shortcut menu. Click the 3½ Floppy (A:) icon in the Folders pane. Is the Space Needle file stored on drive A? _____
18. Click the Close button in the Exploring - 3½ Floppy (A:) window.

4 Using Windows Help

Instructions: Use Windows Help and a computer to perform the following tasks.

Part 1: *Using the Question Mark Button*

1. If necessary, start Microsoft Windows 98.
2. Click the Start button on the taskbar.
3. Point to Settings on the Start menu.

In the Lab

4. Click Folder Options on the Settings submenu.
5. Click the General tab in the Folder Options dialog box.
6. Click the Question Mark button on the title bar. The mouse pointer changes to a block arrow with a question mark (Figure 1-102).
7. Click the preview monitor in the General sheet. A pop-up window displays explaining the contents of the preview monitor. Read the information in the pop-up window.

FIGURE 1-102

8. Click an open area of the General sheet to remove the pop-up window.
9. Click the Question Mark button on the title bar and then click the Web style option button. A pop-up window displays explaining what happens when you select this option. Read the information in the pop-up window. Click an open area on the General sheet to remove the pop-up window.
0. Click the Question Mark button on the title bar and then click the Classic style option button. A pop-up window displays explaining what happens when you select this option. Read the information in the pop-up window. Click an open area on the General sheet to remove the pop-up window.
1. Click the Question Mark button on the title bar and then click the Custom style option button. A pop-up window displays explaining what happens when you select this option. Read the information in the pop-up window. Click an open area on the General sheet to remove the pop-up window.
2. Click the Question Mark button on the title bar and then click the Settings button. A pop-up window displays explaining the function of the button. Read the information in the pop-up window. Click an open area on the General sheet to remove the pop-up window.
3. Summarize the function of the Question Mark button. _____
4. Click the Close button in the Folder Options dialog box.

art 2: *Finding What's New in Windows 98*

1. Click the Start button and then click Help on the Start menu.
2. Click the Maximize button on the Windows Help title bar.
3. If the Contents sheet does not display, click the Contents tab. Click the Introducing Windows 98 closed book icon.
4. Click the What's New in Windows 98 closed book icon.

(continued)

In the Lab

Using Windows Help *(continued)*

5. Click the True Web integration Help topic. Seven hyperlinks display in the right frame (Figure 1-103).

6. Click the Active Desktop hyperlink in the right frame and read the information about the Active Desktop.

7. Click the Channels hyperlink and read the information about channels.

8. Click the Options button on the Help toolbar to display the Options menu and then click Print.

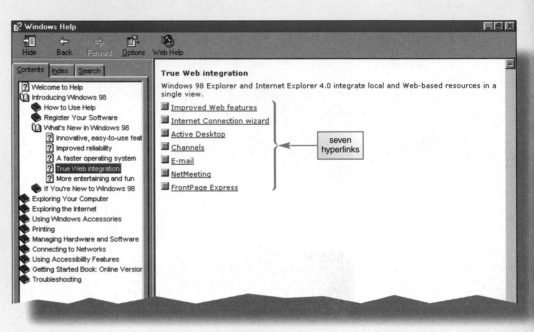

FIGURE 1-103

9. Click the OK button in the Print Topics dialog box to print the True Web integration screen.

Part 3: *Reading About the Online Getting Started Manual*

1. Click the Getting Started Book: Online Version closed book icon in the left frame.
2. Click the Microsoft Windows 98 Getting Started Book Help topic. Read the information Windows 98 displays about the Getting Started Book in the right frame. The Getting Started Book is the online version of the printed manual for Windows 98.
3. Click the Click here hyperlink in the right frame to open the Getting Started window.
4. If the Contents sheet does not display, click the Contents tab. Click the Introducing Getting Started closed book icon. Click and read each of the four Help topics that display.
5. Click the Welcome closed book icon. Three Help topics and two closed book icons display in the open book. Click and read the Overview, Windows 98 at a Glance, and If You're New to Windows topics.
6. Click the Where to Find Information closed book icon.
7. Click the Resources Included with Windows 98 closed book icon. Click and read the Overview topic.
8. Click the Online Tutorial: Discover Windows 98 topic. Read the information about the topic.
9. Click the Troubleshooters topic. Read the information about the topic.
10. Click the Back button on the Help toolbar to display the previous screen (Online Tutorial: Discover Windows 98) in the right frame.
11. Click the Options button on the Help toolbar, click Print, and then click the OK button to print the Help topic.
12. Click the Close button in the Getting Started window.
13. Click the Close button in the Windows Help window.

MICROSOFT

Word 2000

Microsoft **Word 2000**

Microsoft Word 2000

PROJECT 1

Creating and Editing a Word Document

OBJECTIVES

You will have mastered the material in this project when you can:

- Start Word
- Describe the Word window
- Zoom page width
- Change the default font size of all text
- Enter text into a document
- Check spelling as you type
- Scroll through a document
- Save a document
- Select text
- Change the font of selected text
- Change the font size of selected text
- Bold selected text
- Right-align a paragraph
- Center a paragraph
- Undo commands or actions
- Italicize selected text
- Underline selected text
- Insert clip art into a document
- Resize a graphic
- Print a document
- Open a document
- Correct errors in a document
- Use Microsoft Word Help
- Quit Word

Wobbling Words

Help for the Spelling Challenged

" *My spelling is Wobbly.*
It's good spelling, but it Wobbles,
and the letters get in the wrong places. "

Winnie-the-Pooh

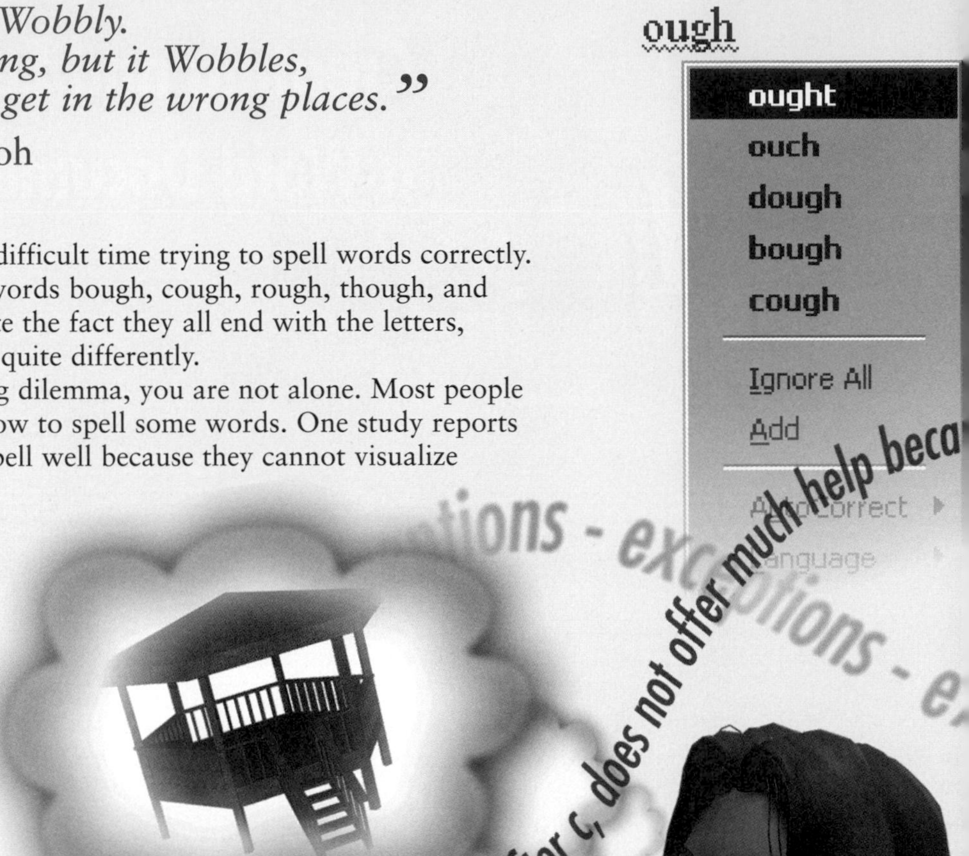

ough

ought
ouch
dough
bough
cough

Ignore All

Add

AutoCorrect ▶

Language

N o wonder Pooh has a difficult time trying to spell words correctly. If he pronounces the words bough, cough, rough, though, and through, he realizes that despite the fact they all end with the letters, ough, they all are pronounced quite differently.

If you share Pooh's spelling dilemma, you are not alone. Most people have difficulty remembering how to spell some words. One study reports 20 percent of writers do not spell well because they cannot visualize words. Even remembering the simple rules such as, i before e except after c, does not offer much assistance because of the slew of exceptions such as the words, weird science.

A spelling error in a flyer distributed on campus, a resume sent to a potential employer, or an e-mail message forwarded to an associate

gazebo

...ould lessen your credibility, cause a reader to doubt ...e accuracy of your statements, and leave a negative ...mpression. In this project, Microsoft Word will ...heck your typing for possible spelling errors as you ...reate an announcement for the Student Government ...ssociation's upcoming winter break ski trip at ...ummit Peak Resort.

If you type a word that does not appear in ...Vord's dictionary, Word will flag the possible error ...ith a wavy red underline. If the spelling is correct, ...ou can instruct Word to ignore the flagged word. ...f it is misspelled, the spelling feature will offer a list ...f suggested corrections. Despite this assistance from ...he spelling checker, one study indicates college ...udents repeatedly ignore or override the flagged ...ords.

Word's spelling checker is a useful alternative to ...dictionary, but you must not rely on it 100 percent. ...will not flag commonly misused homophones, ...hich are words that are pronounced alike but are ...pelled differently. For example, it is easy to confuse ...he homophones in the sentence, The Web site con-...ins an incorrect cite to the reference materials dis-...ussing regaining sight after experiencing blindness.

Then what is a spelling-challenged writer to do? English teachers emphasize that you can learn to spell better, but not by strictly memorizing long lists or having someone mark all the errors in a paper. Instead, you need to try the following strategies to improve awareness of spelling difficulties.

First, identify error patterns. For example, do you misspell the same words repeatedly? If so, write them in a list and have a friend dictate them to you. Then write the words again. If you involve your senses, hear the words spelled correctly, and then visualize the words, you increase your awareness of the problem.

Next, always consult a dictionary when you are uncertain of a word's spelling. Note the word's etymology — its origin and history. For example, the word, science, originated from the Latin word, scientia, a form of the verb to know.

As you proofread, read from right to left. Use a pencil to point at each word as you say it aloud.

Using Microsoft Word's spelling checker and a good dictionary should enhance your spelling skills, and stop your words from *Wobbling*.

Microsoft Word 2000

Creating and Editing a Word Document

P R O J E C T

1

What Is Microsoft Word 2000?

Microsoft Word is a full-featured word processing program that allows you to create professional looking documents such as announcements, letters, resumes, and reports, and revise them easily. You can use Word's desktop publishing features to create high-quality brochures, advertisements, and newsletters. Word also provides many tools that enable you to create Web pages with ease. From within Word, you even can place these Web pages directly on a Web server.

Word has many features designed to simplify the production of documents. With Word, you easily can include borders, shad-ing, tables, graphics, pictures, and Web addresses in your docu-ments. You can instruct Word to create a template, which is a form you can use and customize to meet your needs. While you are typing, Word can perform tasks automatically. For example, Word can detect and correct spelling and grammar errors in a variety of languages. Word also can format text such as headings, lists, fractions, borders, and Web addresses as you type them. Word's thesaurus allows you to add variety and precision to your writing. Within Word, you can e-mail a copy of your Word docu-ment to an e-mail address.

Project One — Summit Peak Announcement

To illustrate the features of Word, this book presents a series of projects that use Word to create documents similar to those you will encounter in academic and business environments. Project 1 uses Word to produce the announcement shown in Figure 1-1.

Feel the Thrill...

...Seize the Slopes! ◄— headline

graphic of skier

body title —►

SUMMIT PEAK RESORT

Summit Peak is the *largest* ski resort in the country. Breathtaking mountains provide more than 5,200 acres of groomed slopes and pristine lakes for skiing, sledding, snowboarding, ice skating, and ice fishing.

Summit Peak offers a range of vacation packages for every taste and budget, from traditional ski lodges to luxurious condominiums. Add transportation, meals, lift tickets, gear, and lessons for an exceptional value. ◄— body copy

Call <u>(970) 555-SNOW</u> for reservations.

FIGURE 1-1

More About

Word 2000

For more information on the features of Microsoft Word 2000, visit the Word 2000 More About Web page (www.scsite.com/wd2000/more.htm) and then click Microsoft Word 2000 Features.

The announcement informs students about exciting vacation packages offered by Summit Peak Resort during winter break. The announcement begins with a headline that is followed by a graphic of a skier. Below the graphic of the skier is the body title, SUMMIT PEAK RESORT, followed by the body copy that consists of a brief paragraph about the resort and another paragraph about the vacation packages. Finally, the last line of the announcement lists the resort's telephone number. The appearance of the text and graphic in the announcement is designed to catch the attention of the reader.

Starting Word

Follow these steps to start Word, or ask your instructor how to start Word for your system.

To Start Word

1 **Click the Start button on the taskbar and then point to New Office Document.**

*The programs on the Start menu display above the Start button (Figure 1-2). The New Office Document command is highlighted on the Start menu. A **highlighted command** displays as light text on a dark background.*

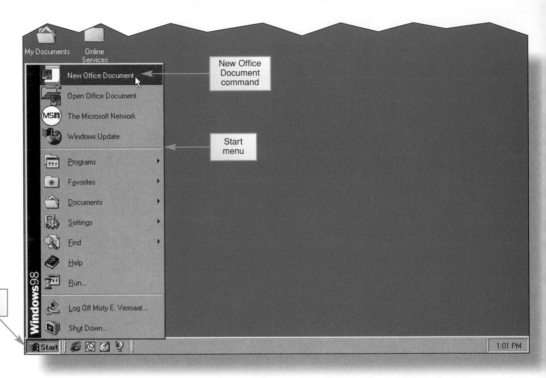

FIGURE 1-2

2 **Click New Office Document. If necessary, click the General tab when the New Office Document dialog box first displays. Point to the Blank Document icon.**

Office displays several icons in the General sheet in the New Office Document dialog box (Figure 1-3). The icons are large because the Large Icons button is selected. Each icon represents a different type of document you can create in Microsoft Office.

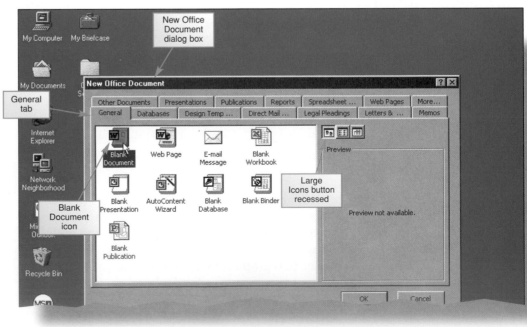

FIGURE 1-3

3 **Double-click the Blank Document Icon.**

Office starts Word. While Word is starting, the mouse pointer changes to the shape of an hourglass. After a few moments, an empty document titled Document1 displays in the Word window (Figure 1-4).

4 **If the Word window is not maximized, double-click its title bar to maximize it. If the Office Assistant displays, right-click it and then click Hide on the shortcut menu. If your screen differs from Figure 1-4, click View on the menu bar and then click Normal.**

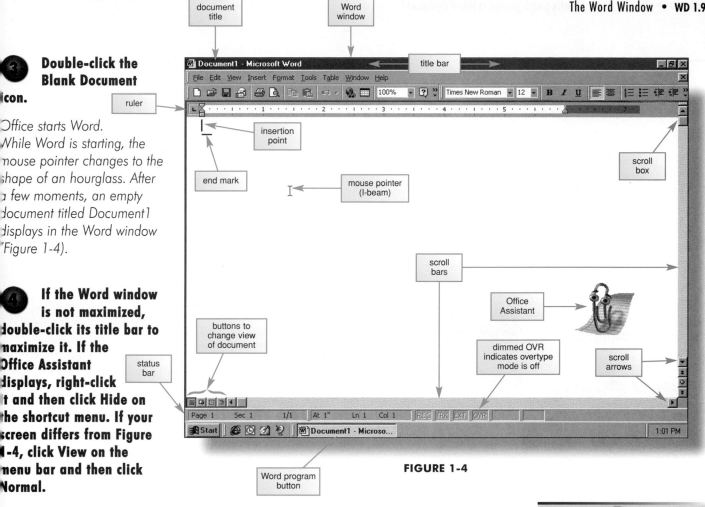

FIGURE 1-4

The Windows taskbar at the bottom of the screen displays the Word program button, indicating the Word program is open.

The Word Window

The **Word window** (Figure 1-4) consists of a variety of components to make your work more efficient and documents more professional. The following sections discuss these components.

Document Window

The document window displays text, tables, graphics, and other items as you type or insert them into a document. Only a portion of your document, however, displays on the screen at one time. You view the portion of the document displayed on the screen through the **document window** (Figure 1-5 on the next page).

Other Ways

1. Right-click Start button, click Open, double-click New Office Document, click General tab, double-click Blank Document icon

2. Click New Office Document button on Microsoft Office Shortcut Bar, click General tab, double-click Blank Document icon

3. On Start menu point to Programs, click Microsoft Word

FIGURE 1-5

The document window contains several elements commonly found in other applications, as well as some elements unique to Word. The main elements of the Word document window are the insertion point, end mark, mouse pointer, rulers, scroll bars, and status bar (see Figure 1-4 on the previous page).

INSERTION POINT The **insertion point** is a blinking vertical bar that indicates where text will be inserted as you type. As you type, the insertion point moves to the right and, when you reach the end of a line, it moves downward to the next line. You also can insert graphics, tables, and other items at the location of the insertion point.

END MARK The **end mark** is a short horizontal line that indicates the end of your document. Each time you begin a new line, the end mark moves downward.

MOUSE POINTER   The **mouse pointer** becomes different shapes depending on the task you are performing in Word and the pointer's location on the screen. The mouse pointer in Figure 1-4 has the shape of an I-beam. Other mouse pointer shapes are described as they appear on the screen during this and subsequent projects.

RULERS   At the top edge of the document window is the **horizontal ruler**. You use the horizontal ruler, sometimes simply called the **ruler**, to set tab stops, indent paragraphs, adjust column widths, and change page margins.

An additional ruler, called the **vertical ruler**, sometimes displays at the left edge of the window when you perform certain tasks. The purpose of the vertical ruler is discussed as it displays on the screen in a later project. If your screen displays a vertical ruler, click View on the menu bar and then click Normal.

SCROLL BARS   You use the **scroll bars** to display different portions of your document in the document window. At the right edge of the document window is a vertical scroll bar, and at the bottom of the document window is a horizontal scroll bar. On both the vertical and horizontal scroll bars, the position of the **scroll box** reflects the location of the portion of the document displaying in the document window.

On the left edge of the horizontal scroll bar are four buttons you use to change the view of your document, and on the bottom of the vertical scroll bar are three buttons you can use to scroll through a document. These buttons are discussed as they are used in later projects.

STATUS BAR   The status bar displays at the bottom of the document window, above the Windows taskbar. The **status bar** presents information about the location of the insertion point, the progress of current tasks, as well as the status of certain commands, keys, and buttons.

From left to right, the following information displays on the status bar in Figure 1-5: the page number, the section number, the page containing the insertion point followed by the total number of pages in the document, the position of the insertion point in inches from the top of the page, the line number and column number of the insertion point, followed by several status indicators. If you perform a task that requires several seconds (such as saving a document), the status bar displays a message informing you of the progress of the task.

You use the **status indicators** to turn certain keys or modes on or off. Four of these status indicators (REC, TRK, EXT, and OVR) display darkened when on and dimmed when off. For example, the dimmed OVR indicates overtype mode is off. To turn these four status indicators on or off, double-click the status indicator. These status indicators are discussed as they are used in the projects.

The next status indicators display icons as you perform certain tasks. When you begin typing in the document window, a Spelling and Grammar Status icon displays. When Word is saving your document, a Background Save Status icon displays. When you print a document, a Background Print Status icon displays.

When you point to various areas on the status bar, Word displays a ScreenTip to help you identify it. A **ScreenTip** is a short descriptive name of a button, icon, or command associated with the item to which you are pointing.

Menu Bar and Toolbars

The menu bar displays at the top of the screen just below the title bar (Figure 1-6a on the next page). The Standard toolbar and Formatting toolbar are preset to share a single row that displays immediately below the menu bar.

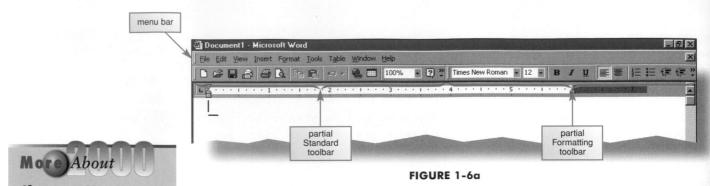

FIGURE 1-6a

More About 2000

Shortcut Menus

Right-clicking an object displays a shortcut menu (also called a context-sensitive or object menu). Depending on the object, the commands in the shortcut menu vary.

MENU BAR The **menu bar** displays the Word menu names. Each menu contains a list of commands you can use to perform tasks such as retrieving, storing, printing, and formatting data in your document. When you click a menu name on the menu bar, a **short menu** displays that lists your most recently used commands (Figure 1-6b). To display a menu, such as the View menu, click the menu name on the menu bar. If you point to a command on a menu with an arrow to its right, a submenu displays from which you choose a command.

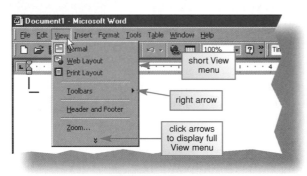

FIGURE 1-6b

If you wait a few seconds or click the arrows at the bottom of the short menu, it expands into a full menu. A **full menu** lists all the commands associated with a menu (Figure 1-6c). You also can display a full menu immediately by double-clicking the menu name on the menu bar. In this book, when you display a menu, always display the full menu using one of these techniques:

1. Click the menu name on the menu bar and then wait a few seconds.
2. Click the menu name and then click the arrows at the bottom of the short menu.
3. Click the menu name and then point to the arrows at the bottom of the short menu.
4. Double-click the menu name.

When a full menu displays, some of the commands are recessed into lighter gray background and some also are unavailable. A recessed command is called a **hidden command** because it does not display on a short menu. As you use Word, it automatically personalizes the short menus for you based on how often you use commands. That is, as you use hidden commands, Word *unhides* them and places them on the short menu. An **unavailable command** displays dimmed, which indicates it is not available for the current selection.

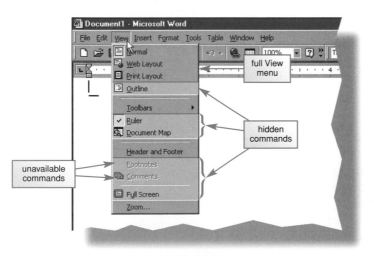

FIGURE 1-6c

TOOLBARS Word has many pre-defined, or built-in, toolbars. A **toolbar** contains buttons, boxes, and menus that allow you to perform tasks more quickly than using the menu bar and related menus. For example, to print a document, you click the Print button on the toolbar. Each button on a toolbar displays an image to help you remember its function. Also, when you point to a button or box on a toolbar, a ScreenTip (the item's name) displays below the mouse pointer (see Figure 1-10 on page WD 1.15).

Two built-in toolbars are the Standard toolbar and the Formatting toolbar. Figure 1-7a illustrates the Standard toolbar and identifies its buttons and boxes. Figure 1-7b illustrates the Formatting toolbar. Each button and box is explained in detail as it is used in the projects throughout the book.

The Standard toolbar and Formatting toolbar are preset to display docked on the same row immediately below the menu bar. A **docked toolbar** is one that is attached to the edge of the Word window. Because both of these toolbars cannot fit entirely on a single row, a portion or all of the Standard toolbar displays on the left of the row and a portion or all of the Formatting toolbar displays on the right (Figure 1-8a). The buttons that display on the toolbar are the more frequently used buttons.

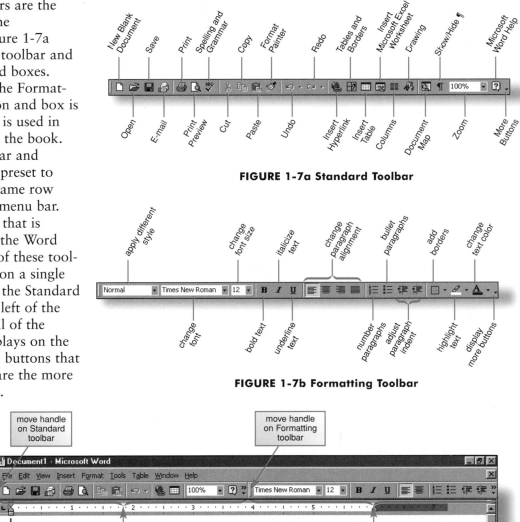

FIGURE 1-7a Standard Toolbar

FIGURE 1-7b Formatting Toolbar

FIGURE 1-8a

To display the entire Standard toolbar, double-click its **move handle**, which is the vertical bar at the left edge of a toolbar. When you display the complete Standard toolbar, only a portion of the Formatting toolbar displays (Figure 1-8b). To display the entire Formatting toolbar, double-click its move handle. When you display the complete Formatting toolbar, only a portion of the Standard toolbar displays (Figure 1-8c on the next page).

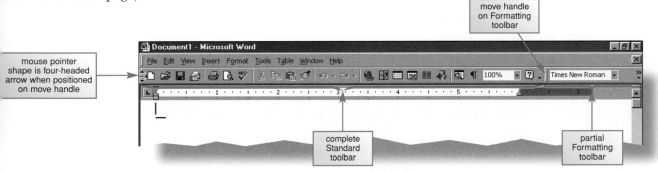

FIGURE 1-8b

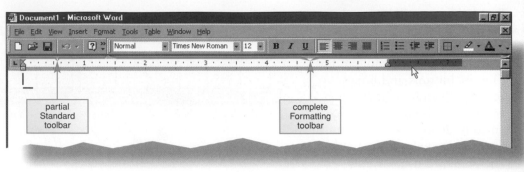

FIGURE 1-8c

An alternative to double-clicking the move handle to display an entire toolbar is to click the More Buttons button at the right edge of the toolbar. When you click a toolbar's **More Buttons** button, Word displays a **More Buttons list** that contains the toolbar's hidden buttons (Figure 1-8d).

FIGURE 1-8d

As with menus, Word personalizes toolbars. That is, once you click a hidden button in the More Buttons list, Word removes the button from the More Buttons list and places it on the toolbar. For example, if you click the Drawing button in Figure 1-8d, Word displays this button on the Standard toolbar and removes a less frequently used button to make room for the Drawing button. By adapting to the way you work, this intelligent personalization feature of Word is designed to increase your productivity.

Additional toolbars may display on the Word screen, depending on the task you are performing. These additional toolbars display either stacked below the row containing the Standard and Formatting toolbars or floating in the Word window. A **floating toolbar** is not attached to an edge of the Word window. You can rearrange the order of docked toolbars and can move floating toolbars anywhere in the Word window. Later in this book, steps are presented that show you how to float a docked toolbar or dock a floating toolbar.

Resetting Menus and Toolbars

Each project in this book begins with the menu bars and toolbars appearing as they did at the initial installation of the software. To reset your menus and toolbars so they appear exactly as shown in this book, follow the steps in Appendix C.

Displaying the Entire Standard Toolbar

Perform the following step to display the entire Standard toolbar.

Steps To Display the Entire Standard Toolbar

1 **Double-click the move handle on the Standard toolbar.**

Word displays the entire Standard toolbar (Figure 1-9).

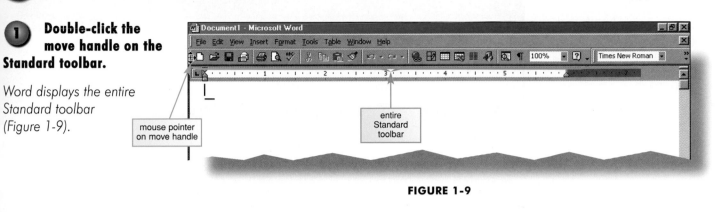

FIGURE 1-9

Zooming Page Width

Depending on your Windows and Word settings, the horizontal ruler at the top of the document window may show more inches or fewer inches than the ruler shown in Figure 1-9. The more inches of ruler that display, the smaller the text will be on the screen. The fewer inches of ruler that display, the larger the text will be on the screen. To minimize eyestrain, the projects in this book display the text as large as possible without extending the right margin beyond the right edge of the document window.

Two factors that affect how much of the ruler displays in the document window are the Windows screen resolution and the Word zoom percentage. The screens in this book use a resolution of 800 x 600. With this resolution, you can increase the preset zoom percentage beyond 100% so that the right margin extends to the edge of the document window. To increase or decrease the size of the displayed characters to a point where both the left and right margins are at the edges of the document window, use the **zoom page width** command as shown in the following steps.

Steps To Zoom Page Width

1 **Point to the Zoom box arrow on the Standard toolbar.**

The mouse pointer shape is a left-pointing block arrow when positioned on a toolbar button or box (Figure 1-10). When you point to a toolbar button or box, Word displays a ScreenTip.

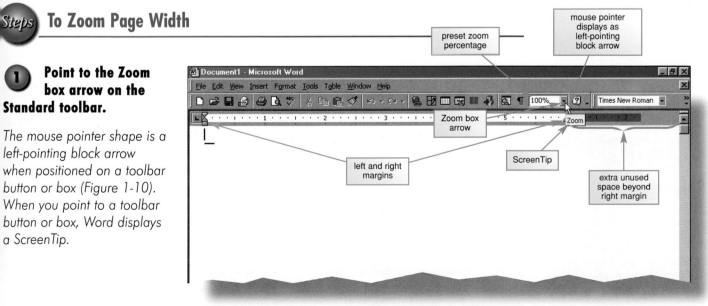

FIGURE 1-10

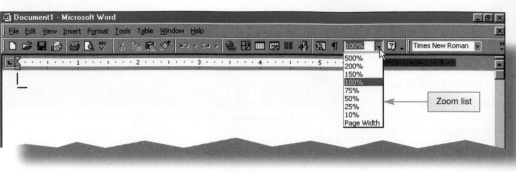

Click the Zoom box arrow.

Word displays a list of available zoom percentages and the Page Width option in the Zoom list (Figure 1-11).

FIGURE 1-11

Point to Page Width in the Zoom list.

Word highlights Page Width in the Zoom list (Figure 1-12).

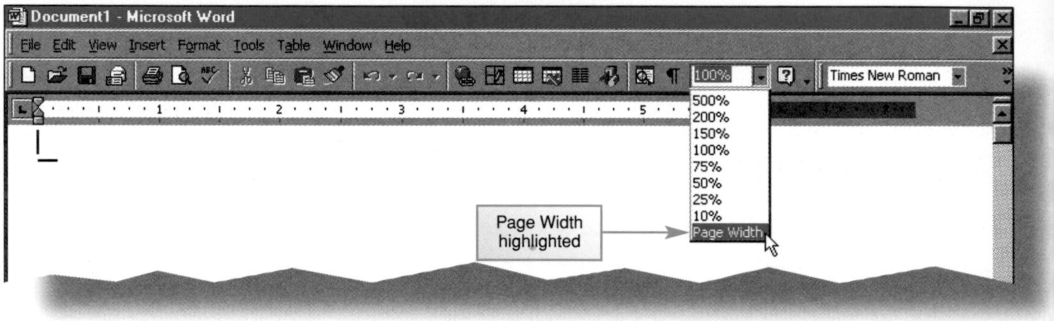

FIGURE 1-12

Click Page Width.

Word extends the right margin to the right edge of the document window (Figure 1-13).

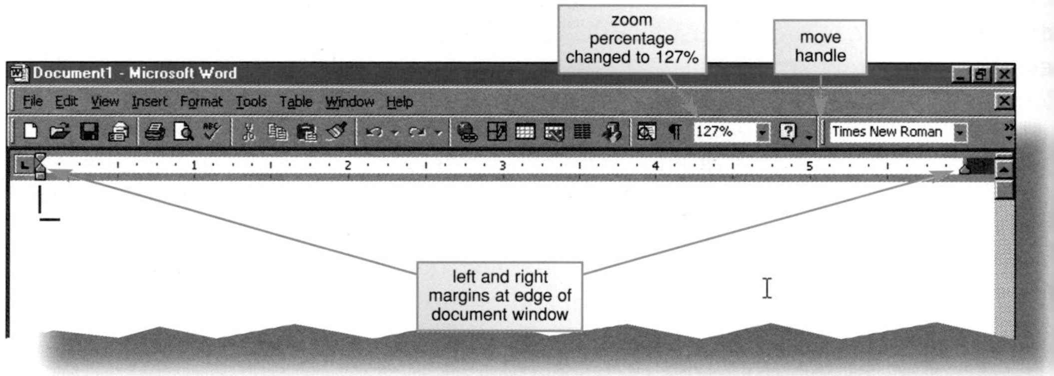

FIGURE 1-13

Other Ways

1. On View menu click Zoom, select Page Width, click OK button

Zooming

If you want to zoom to a percentage not displayed in the Zoom list, you can click the Zoom box on the Standard toolbar, type the desired percentage, and then press the ENTER key; or click view on the menu bar, click Zoom, and then enter the desired zoom percentage.

If your Zoom list (Figure 1-12) displayed additional options, click View on the menu bar and then click Normal.

The Zoom box in Figure 1-13 displays 127%, which Word computes based on a variety of settings. Your percentage may be different depending on your system configuration.

Changing the Default Font Size

Characters that display on the screen are a specific shape, size, and style. The **font**, or typeface, defines the appearance and shape of the letters, numbers, and special characters. The preset, or **default**, font is Times New Roman (Figure 1-14). **Font size** specifies the size of the characters. Font size is determined by a measurement system called points. A single **point** is about 1/72 of one inch in height. Thus, a character with a font size of ten is about 10/72 of one inch in height.

If Word 2000 is installed on a new computer, then the default font size most likely is 12. If, however, you upgrade from a previous version of Word when installing Word 2000, your default font most likely is 10.

If more of the characters in your document require a larger font size than the default, you easily can change the default font size before you type. In Project 1, many of the characters in the announcement are a font size of 16. Follow these steps to increase the font size before you begin entering text.

To Increase the Default Font Size Before Typing

1 **Double-click the move handle on the Formatting toolbar to display the entire toolbar. Click the Font Size box arrow on the Formatting toolbar and then point to 16.**

A list of available font sizes displays in the Font Size list (Figure 1-14). The available font sizes depend on the current font, which is Times New Roman.

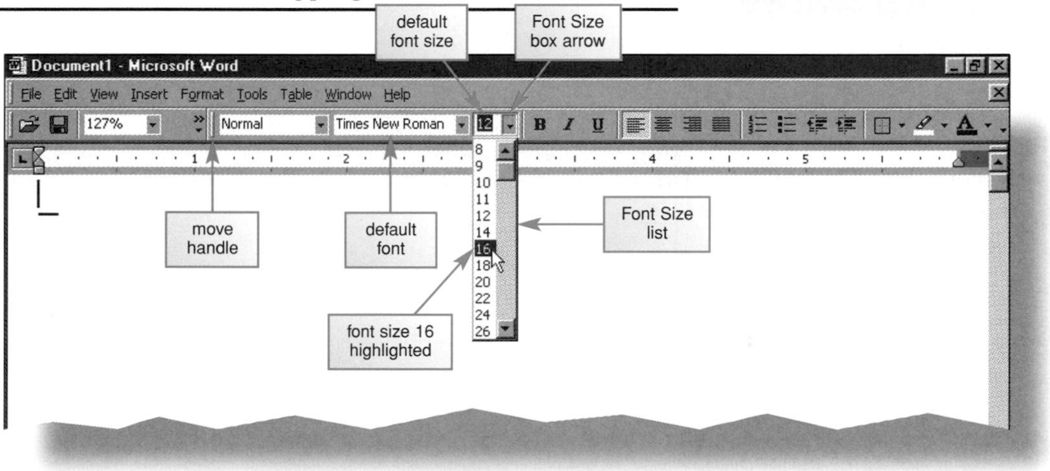

FIGURE 1-14

2 **Click 16.**

The font size for characters in this document changes to 16 (Figure 1-15). The size of the insertion point increases to reflect the new font size.

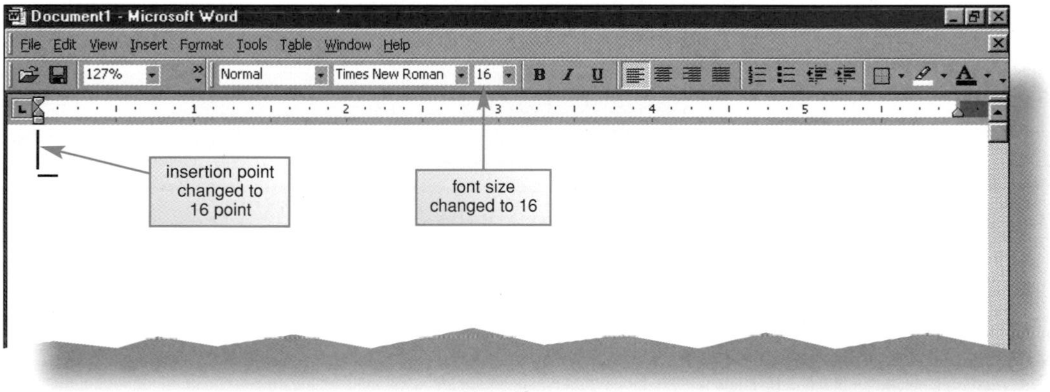

FIGURE 1-15

The new font size takes effect immediately in your document. Word uses this font size for characters you type into this announcement.

Entering Text

To create a document that contains text, you enter the text by typing on the keyboard. The example on the next page explains the steps to enter both lines of the headline of the announcement. These lines will be positioned at the left margin. Later in this project, you will format the headline so that both lines are bold and enlarged and the second line is positioned at the right margin.

Steps **To Enter Text**

1 **Type** Feel the Thrill **and then press the** PERIOD **key (.) three times. If you make an error while typing, press the** BACKSPACE **key until you have deleted the text in error and then retype the text correctly.**

As you type, the insertion point moves to the right (Figure 1-16).

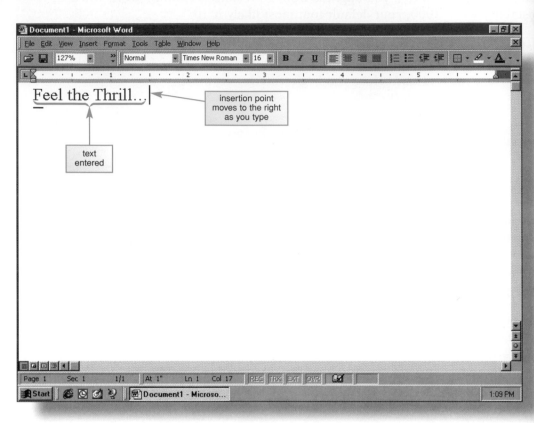

FIGURE 1-16

2 **Press the** ENTER **key.**

Word moves the insertion point to the beginning of the next line (Figure 1-17). Notice the status bar indicates the current position of the insertion point. That is, the insertion point currently is on line 2 column 1.

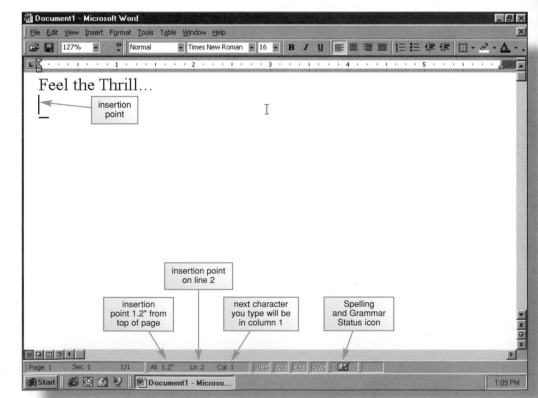

FIGURE 1-17

3 **Press the PERIOD key three times and then type** Seize the Slopes! **Press the ENTER key.**

The headline is complete (Figure 1-18). The insertion point is on line 3.

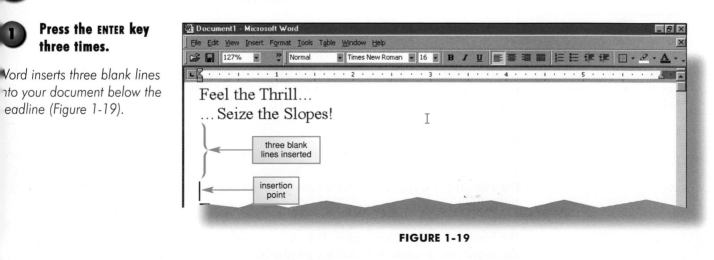

Feel the Thrill...
...Seize the Slopes! — headline entered

— insertion point

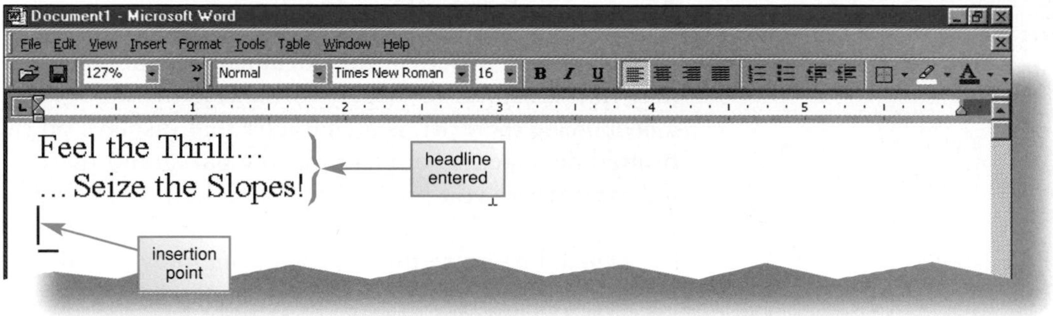

FIGURE 1-18

When you begin entering text into a document, the **Spelling and Grammar Status icon** displays at the right of the status bar (Figure 1-17). As you type, the Spelling and Grammar Status icon shows an animated pencil writing on paper, which indicates Word is checking for possible errors. When you stop typing, the pencil changes to either a red check mark or a red X. In Figure 1-17, the Spelling and Grammar Status icon displays a red check mark.

In general, if all of the words you have typed are in Word's dictionary and your grammar is correct, a red check mark displays on the Spelling and Grammar Status icon. If you type a word not in the dictionary (because it is a proper name or misspelled), a red wavy underline displays below the word. If you type text that may be grammatically incorrect, a green wavy underline displays below the text. When Word flags a possible spelling or grammar error, it also changes the red check mark on the Spelling and Grammar Status icon to a red X. As you enter text into the announcement, your Spelling and Grammar Status icon may show a red X instead of a red check mark. Later in this project, you will check the spelling of these words. At that time, the red X will return to a red check mark.

Entering Blank Lines into a Document

To enter a blank line into a document, press the ENTER key without typing any text on the line. The following example explains how to enter three blank lines below the headline.

To Enter Blank Lines into a Document

1 **Press the ENTER key three times.**

Word inserts three blank lines into your document below the headline (Figure 1-19).

Feel the Thrill...
...Seize the Slopes!

— three blank lines inserted

— insertion point

FIGURE 1-19

Displaying Formatting Marks

To indicate where in the document you press the ENTER key or SPACEBAR, you may find it helpful to display formatting marks. A **formatting mark**, sometimes called a **nonprinting character**, is a character that displays on the screen but is not visible on a printed document. For example, the paragraph mark (¶) is a formatting mark that indicates where you pressed the ENTER key. A raised dot (•) shows where you pressed the SPACEBAR. Other formatting marks are discussed as they display on the screen.

Depending on settings made during previous Word sessions, your screen may already display formatting marks (see Figure 1-21). If the formatting marks are not already displaying on your screen, perform the following steps to display them.

Steps **To Display Formatting Marks**

1 **Double-click the move handle on the Standard toolbar to display the entire toolbar. Point to the Show/Hide ¶ button on the Standard toolbar (Figure 1-20).**

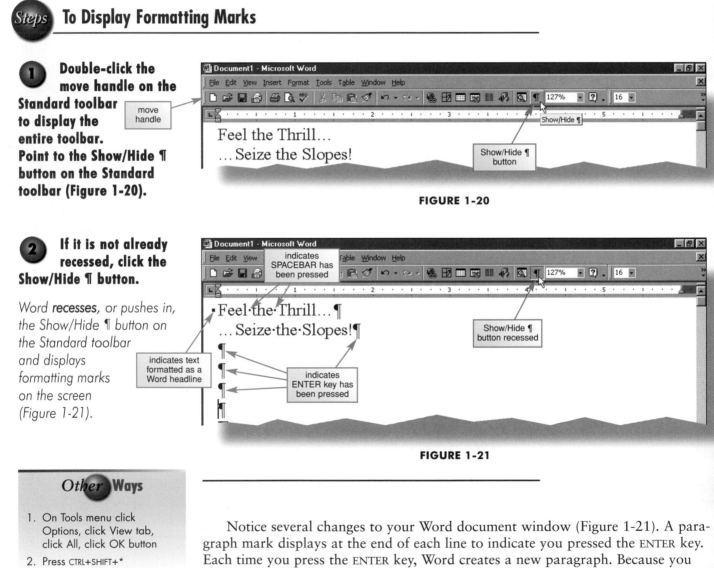

FIGURE 1-20

2 **If it is not already recessed, click the Show/Hide ¶ button.**

*Word **recesses**, or pushes in, the Show/Hide ¶ button on the Standard toolbar and displays formatting marks on the screen (Figure 1-21).*

FIGURE 1-21

Other **Ways**

1. On Tools menu click Options, click View tab, click All, click OK button
2. Press CTRL+SHIFT+*

Notice several changes to your Word document window (Figure 1-21). A paragraph mark displays at the end of each line to indicate you pressed the ENTER key. Each time you press the ENTER key, Word creates a new paragraph. Because you changed the font size, the paragraph marks are 16 point. Notice Word places a paragraph mark above the end mark – you cannot delete this paragraph mark. Between each word, a raised dot appears, indicating you pressed the SPACEBAR. A small square at the beginning of the first line in the announcement indicates it is formatted using the Heading 1 style. Styles are discussed in a later project. Finally, the Show/Hide ¶ button is recessed to indicate it is selected.

If you feel the formatting marks clutter your screen, you can hide them by clicking the Show/Hide ¶ button again. It is recommended that you display formatting marks; therefore, the document windows presented in this book show the formatting marks.

Entering More Text

The body title (SUMMIT PEAK RESORT) in the announcement is capitalized. The next step is to enter this body title in all capital letters into the document window as explained below.

TO ENTER MORE TEXT

1 Press the CAPS LOCK key on the keyboard to turn on capital letters. Verify the CAPS LOCK indicator is lit on your keyboard.

2 Type SUMMIT PEAK RESORT and then press the CAPS LOCK key to turn off capital letters.

3 Press the ENTER key twice.

The body title displays on line 6 as shown in Figure 1-22 below.

Using Wordwrap

Wordwrap allows you to type words in a paragraph continually without pressing the ENTER key at the end of each line. When the insertion point reaches the right margin, Word positions it automatically at the beginning of the next line. As you type, if a word extends beyond the right margin, Word also positions that word automatically on the next line with the insertion point.

Thus, as you enter text using Word, do not press the ENTER key when the insertion point reaches the right margin. Because Word creates a new paragraph each time you press the ENTER key, press the ENTER key only in these circumstances:

1. To insert blank lines into a document
2. To begin a new paragraph
3. To terminate a short line of text and advance to the next line
4. In response to certain Word commands

Perform the following step to become familiar with wordwrap.

More About

Wordwrap

Your printer controls where wordwrap occurs for each line in your document. For this reason, it is possible that the same document could word-wrap on different words if printed on different printers.

Steps To Wordwrap Text as You Type

1 **Type** Summit Peak is the largest ski resort in the country. Breathtaking mountains provide **as the beginning of the body copy.**

Word wraps the word, mountains, to the beginning of line 9 because it is too long to fit on line 8 (Figure 1-22). Your document may wordwrap differently depending on the type of printer you are using.

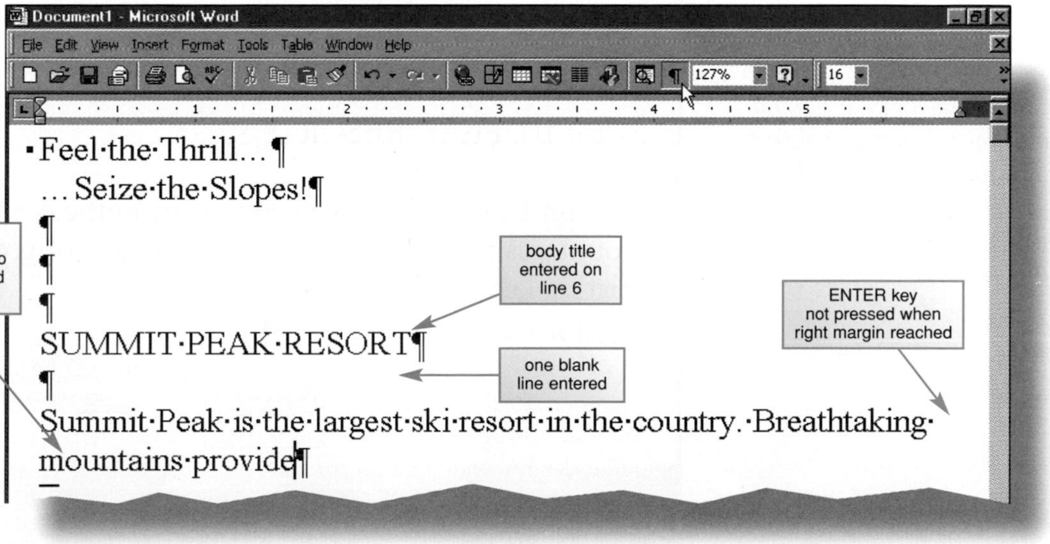

Document1 - Microsoft Word

File Edit View Insert Format Tools Table Window Help

127% 16

·Feel·the·Thrill...¶

...Seize·the·Slopes!¶

¶

¶ *the word, mountains, could not fit on line 8, so Word wrapped it around to beginning of line 9*

¶ *body title entered on line 6*

SUMMIT·PEAK·RESORT¶ *ENTER key not pressed when right margin reached*

¶ *one blank line entered*

Summit·Peak·is·the·largest·ski·resort·in·the·country.·Breathtaking· mountains·provide¶

FIGURE 1-22

Checking Spelling Automatically as You Type

As you type text into the document window, Word checks your typing for possible spelling and grammar errors. If a word you type is not in the dictionary, a red wavy underline displays below it. Likewise, if text you type contains possible grammar errors, a green wavy underline displays below the text. In both cases, the Spelling and Grammar Status icon on the status bar displays a red X, instead of a check mark. Although you can check the entire document for spelling and grammar errors at once, you also can check these errors immediately.

To verify that the check spelling as you type feature is enabled, right-click the Spelling and Grammar Status icon on the status bar and then click Options on the shortcut menu. When the Spelling & Grammar dialog box displays, be sure Check spelling as you type has a check mark and Hide spelling errors in this document does not have a check mark.

When a word is flagged with a red wavy underline, it is not in Word's dictionary. A flagged word, however, is not necessarily misspelled. For example, many names, abbreviations, and specialized terms are not in Word's main dictionary. In these cases, you tell Word to ignore the flagged word. As you type, Word also detects duplicate words. For example, if your document contains the phrase, to the the store, Word places a red wavy underline below the second occurrence of the word, the. To display a list of suggested corrections for a flagged word, you right-click it.

In the following example, the word, sledding, has been misspelled intentionally as sleding to illustrate Word's check spelling as you type feature. If you are doing this project on a personal computer, your announcement may contain different misspelled words, depending on the accuracy of your typing.

More *About*

Entering Sentences

Word processing documents use variable character fonts; for example, the letter w takes up more space than the letter i. With these fonts, it often is difficult to determine how many times the SPACEBAR has been pressed between sentences. Thus, the rule is to press the SPACEBAR only once after periods, colons, and other punctuation marks.

To Check Spelling as You Type

1 **Press the SPACEBAR once. Type** more than 5,200 acres of groomed slopes and pristine lakes for skiing, sleding, **and then press the SPACEBAR.**

Word flags the misspelled word, sledding, by placing a red wavy underline below it (Figure 1-23). Notice the Spelling and Grammar Status icon on the status bar now displays a red X, indicating Word has detected a possible spelling or grammar error.

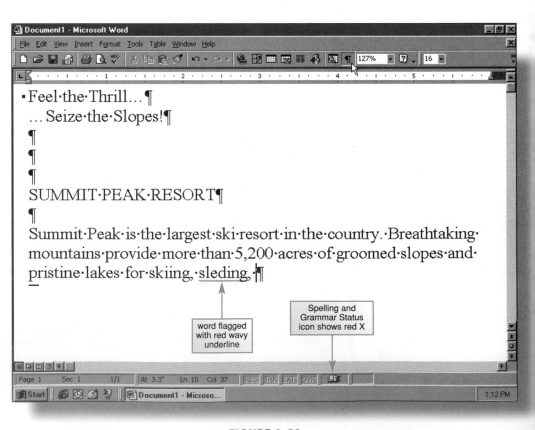

FIGURE 1-23

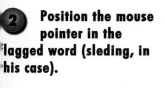

2 **Position the mouse pointer in the flagged word (sleding, in this case).**

The mouse pointer's shape is an I-beam when positioned in a word (Figure 1-24).

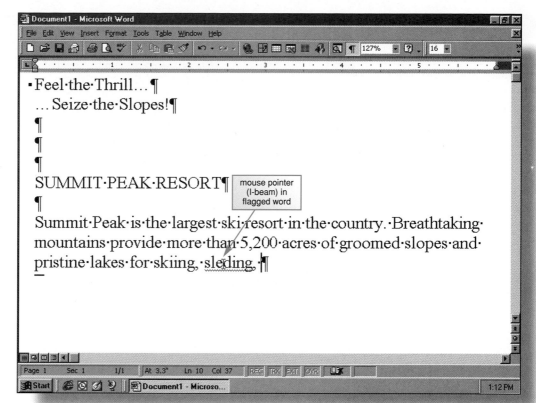

FIGURE 1-24

3 **Right-click the flagged word, sleding. When the shortcut menu displays, point to sledding.**

Word displays a shortcut menu that lists suggested spelling corrections for the flagged word (Figure 1-25).

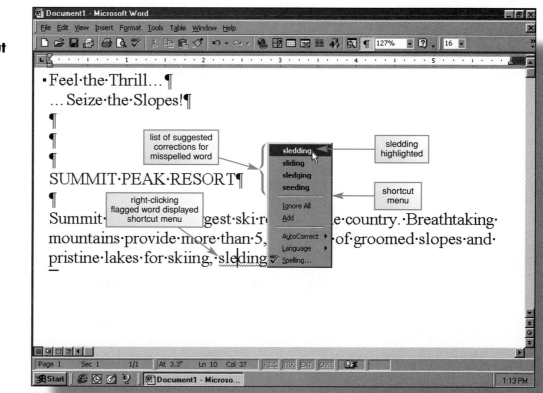

FIGURE 1-25

4 **Click sledding. Press the END key and then type the remainder of the sentence:** snowboarding, ice skating, and ice fishing.

Word replaces the misspelled word with the selected word on the shortcut menu (Figure 1-26). Word replaces the red X with a check mark on the Spelling and Grammar Status icon.

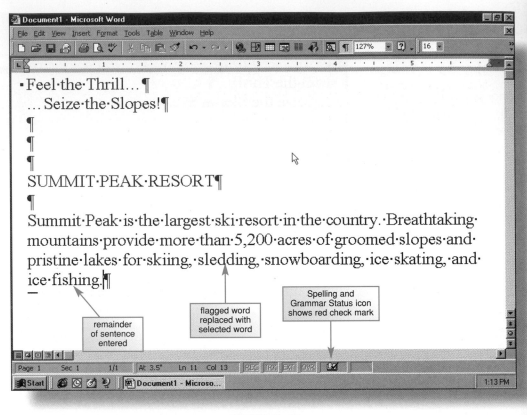

FIGURE 1-26

Other Ways

1. Click flagged word, double-click Spelling and Grammar Status icon on status bar, click correct word on short-cut menu

Scrolling

Computer users frequently switch between the keyboard and the mouse during a word processing session, which places strain on the wrist. To help prevent wrist injury, mini-mize switching. If your fingers are already on the keyboard, use keyboard keys to scroll; if your hand is already on the mouse, use the mouse to scroll.

If the word actually is spelled correctly and, for example, is a proper name, you can right-click it and then click Ignore All on the shortcut menu (Figure 1-25 on the previous page). If, when you right-click the misspelled word, your desired correction is not in the list on the shortcut menu, you can click outside the shortcut menu to make the menu disappear and then retype the correct word, or you can click Spelling on the shortcut menu to display the Spelling dialog box. The Spelling dialog box is discussed in Project 2.

If you feel the wavy underlines clutter your document window, you can hide them temporarily until you are ready to check for spelling errors. To hide spelling errors, right-click the Spelling and Grammar Status icon on the status bar and then click Hide Spelling Errors on the shortcut menu. To hide grammar errors, right-click the Spelling and Grammar Status icon on the status bar and then click Hide Grammatical Errors on the shortcut menu.

Entering Text that Scrolls the Document Window

As you type more lines of text than Word can display in the document window, Word **scrolls** the top portion of the document upward off the screen. Although you cannot see the text once it scrolls off the screen, it remains in the document. You have learned that the document window allows you to view only a portion of your document at one time (Figure 1-5 on page WD 1.10).

Perform the following step to enter text that scrolls the document window.

teps **To Enter Text that Scrolls the Document Window**

1 **Press the ENTER key twice. Type** Summit Peak offers a range of vacation packages for every taste and budget, from traditional ski lodges to luxurious condominiums. Add transportation, meals, lift tickets, gear, and lessons for an exceptional value. **Press the ENTER key twice. Type** Call (970) 555-SNOW for reservations.

Word scrolls the headline off the top of the screen (Figure 1-27). Your screen may scroll differently depending on the type of monitor you are using.

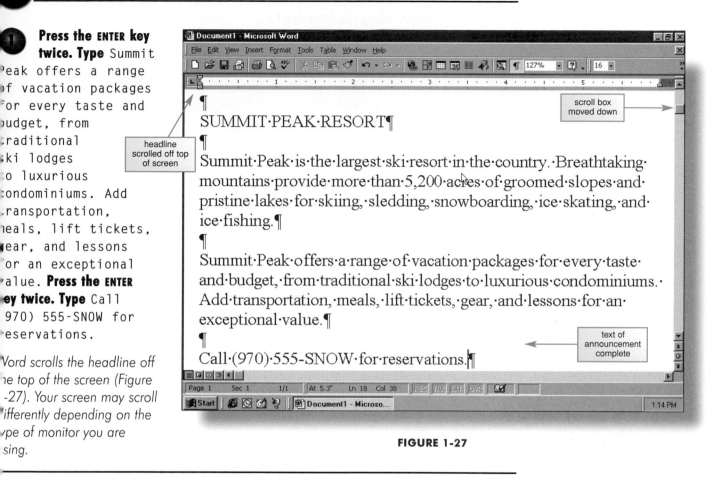

FIGURE 1-27

When Word scrolls text off the top of the screen, the scroll box on the scroll bar at the right edge of the document window moves downward (Figure 1-27). The **scroll box** indicates the current relative location of the insertion point in the document. You may use either the mouse or the keyboard to move the insertion point to a different location in a document.

With the mouse, you use the scroll arrows or the scroll box to display a different portion of the document in the document window, and then click the mouse to move the insertion point to that location. Table 1-1 explains various techniques for vertically scrolling with the mouse.

More About

Microsoft IntelliMouse®

For more information on the scrolling with the Microsoft IntelliMouse, visit the Word 2000 More About Web page (www.scsite.com/wd2000/more.htm) and then click Microsoft IntelliMouse.

Table 1-1	Techniques for Scrolling with the Mouse
SCROLL DIRECTION	**MOUSE ACTION**
Up	Drag the scroll box upward.
Down	Drag the scroll box downward.
Up one screen	Click anywhere above the scroll box on the vertical scroll bar.
Down one screen	Click anywhere below the scroll box on the vertical scroll bar.
Up one line	Click the scroll arrow at the top of the vertical scroll bar.
Down one line	Click the scroll arrow at the bottom of the vertical scroll bar.

When you use the keyboard to scroll, the insertion point moves automatically when you press the appropriate keys. Table 1-2 outlines various techniques to scroll through a document using the keyboard.

Table 1-2   Techniques for Scrolling with the Keyboard

SCROLL DIRECTION	KEY(S) TO PRESS	SCROLL DIRECTION	KEY(S) TO PRESS
Left one character	LEFT ARROW	Down one paragraph	CTRL+DOWN ARROW
Right one character	RIGHT ARROW	Up one screen	PAGE UP
Left one word	CTRL+LEFT ARROW	Down one screen	PAGE DOWN
Right one word	CTRL+RIGHT ARROW	To top of document window	ALT+CTRL+PAGE UP
Up one line	UP ARROW	To bottom of document window	ALT+CTRL+PAGE DOWN
Down one line	DOWN ARROW	Previous page	CTRL+PAGE UP
To end of a line	END	Next page	CTRL+PAGE DOWN
To beginning of a line	HOME	To the beginning of a document	CTRL+HOME
Up one paragraph	CTRL+UP ARROW	To the end of a document	CTRL+END

More About 2000

Saving

When you save a document, you use meaningful file names. A file name can be up to 255 characters, including spaces. The only invalid characters are backslash (\), slash (/), colon (:), asterisk (*), question mark (?), quotation mark ("), less than symbol (<), greater than symbol (>), and vertical bar (|).

Saving a Document

As you create a document in Word, the computer stores it in memory. If you turn off the computer or if you lose electrical power, the document in memory is lost. Hence, it is mandatory to save on disk any document that you will use later. The following steps illustrate how to save a document on a floppy disk inserted in drive A using the Save button on the Standard toolbar.

 To Save a New Document

1 **Insert a formatted floppy disk into drive A. Click the Save button on the Standard toolbar.**

Word displays the Save As dialog box (Figure 1-28). The first line from the document displays highlighted in File name text box as the default file name. With this file name selected, you can change it by immediately typing the new name.

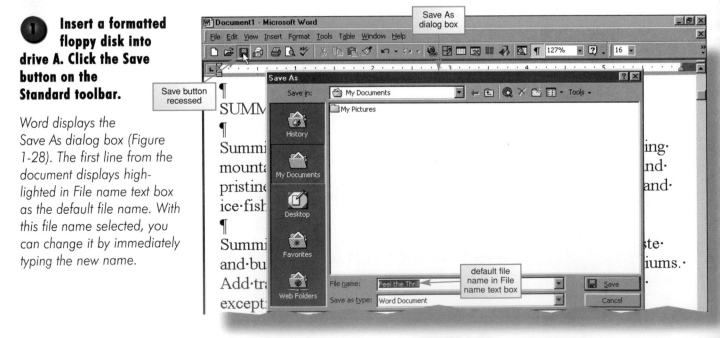

FIGURE 1-28

Type Summit Peak
Announcement **in
the File name text box. Do
not press the ENTER key
after typing the file name.**

*The file name, Summit Peak
Announcement, displays in
the File name text box (Figure
1-29). Notice that the current
save location is the My
Documents folder. A **folder**
is a specific location on a
disk. To change to a different
save location, you use the
Save in box.*

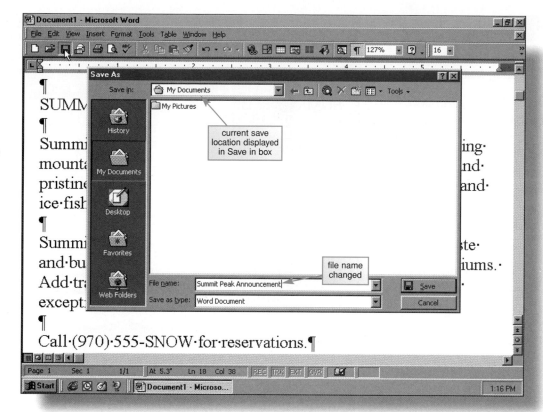

FIGURE 1-29

**Click the Save in
box arrow and then
point to 3½ Floppy (A:).**

*A list of the available save
locations displays (Figure
1-30). Your list may differ
depending on your system
configuration.*

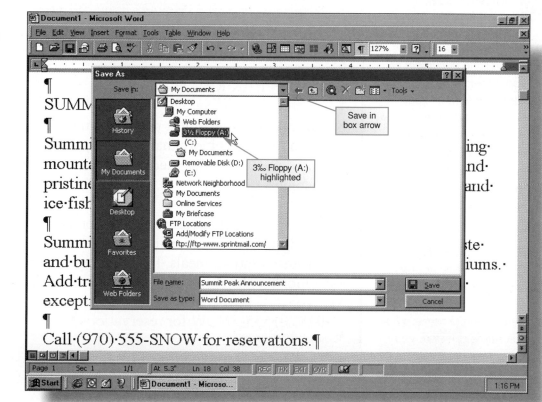

FIGURE 1-30

4 **Click 3½ Floppy (A:)
and then point to
the Save button in the Save
As dialog box.**

*The 3½ Floppy (A:) drive
becomes the save location
(Figure 1-31). The names of
existing files stored on the
floppy disk in drive A display.
In Figure 1-31, no Word files
currently are stored on the
floppy disk in drive A.*

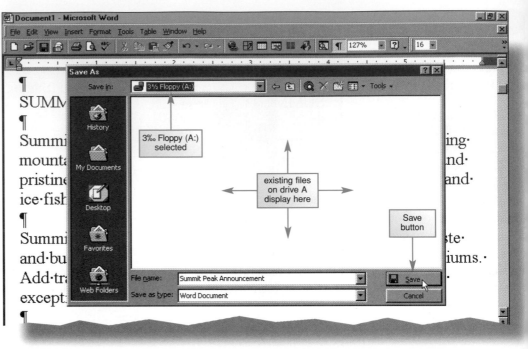

FIGURE 1-31

 5 **Click the Save
button in the Save
As dialog box.**

*Word saves the document on
the floppy disk in drive A with
the file name Summit Peak
Announcement (Figure 1-32).
Although the announcement
is saved on a floppy disk, it
also remains in main memory
and displays on the screen.*

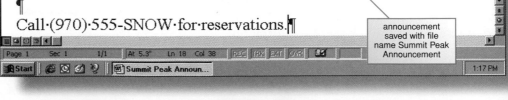

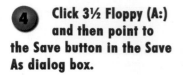 **Ways**

1. On File menu click Save,
   type file name, select location in Save in box, click
   Save button in dialog box

2. Press CTRL+S, type file name,
   select location in Save in
   box, click Save button in
   dialog box

FIGURE 1-32

Formatting Paragraphs and Characters in a Document

The text for Project 1 now is complete. The next step is to format the characters and paragraphs in the announcement. Paragraphs encompass the text up to and including a paragraph mark (¶). **Paragraph formatting** is the process of changing the appearance of a paragraph. For example, you can center or indent a paragraph.

Characters include letters, numbers, punctuation marks, and symbols. **Character formatting** is the process of changing the way characters appear on the screen and in print. You use character formatting to emphasize certain words and improve readability of a document.

With Word, you can format before you type or apply new formats after you type. Earlier, you changed the font size before you typed any text, and then you entered the text. In this section, you format existing text.

Figure 1-33a shows the announcement before formatting the paragraphs and characters. Figure 1-33b shows the announcement after formatting. As you can see from the two figures, a document that is formatted not only is easier to read, but it looks more professional.

More About

Formatting

Character formatting includes changing the font, font style, font size; adding an underline, color, strikethrough, shadow, outline; embossing; engraving; making a superscript or subscript; and changing the case of the letters. Paragraph formatting includes alignment; indentation; and spacing above, below, and in between lines.

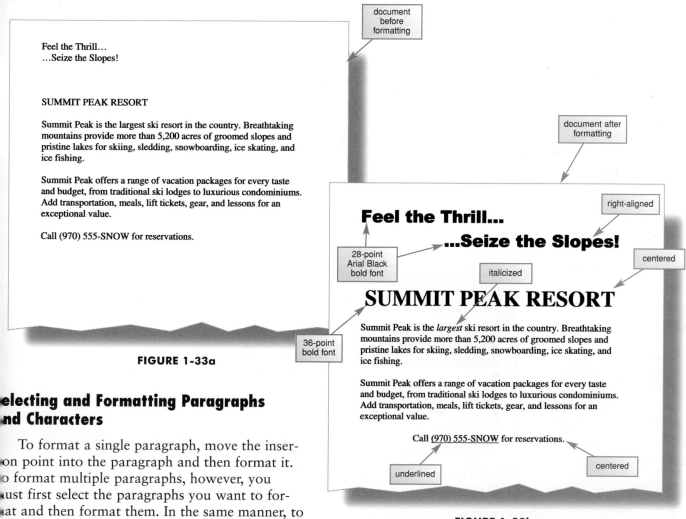

FIGURE 1-33a

FIGURE 1-33b

Selecting and Formatting Paragraphs and Characters

To format a single paragraph, move the insertion point into the paragraph and then format it. To format multiple paragraphs, however, you must first select the paragraphs you want to format and then format them. In the same manner, to format characters, a word, or words, you first must select the characters, word, or words to be formatted and then format your selection.

Selected text is highlighted. That is, if your screen normally displays dark letters on a light background, then selected text displays light letters on a dark background.

Selecting Multiple Paragraphs

The first formatting step in this project is to change the font of the characters in the headline. The headline consists of two separate lines, each ending with a paragraph mark. You have learned that each time you press the ENTER key, Word creates a new paragraph. Thus, the headline actually is two separate paragraphs.

To change the font of the characters in the headline, you must first **select**, or highlight, both paragraphs in the headline as shown in the following steps.

To Select Multiple Paragraphs

1 Press CTRL+HOME; that is, press and hold the CTRL key, then press the HOME key, and then release both keys. Move the mouse pointer to the left of the first paragraph to be selected until the mouse pointer changes to a right-pointing block arrow.

The mouse pointer changes to a right-pointing block arrow when positioned to the left of a paragraph (Figure 1-34). CTRL + HOME positions the insertion point at the top of the document.

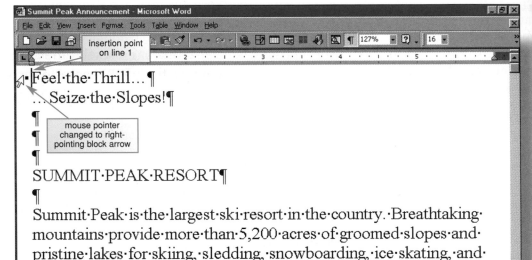

FIGURE 1-34

2 Drag downward until both paragraphs are highlighted.

Word selects both of the paragraphs (Figure 1-35). Recall that dragging is the process of holding down the mouse button while moving the mouse and finally releasing the mouse button.

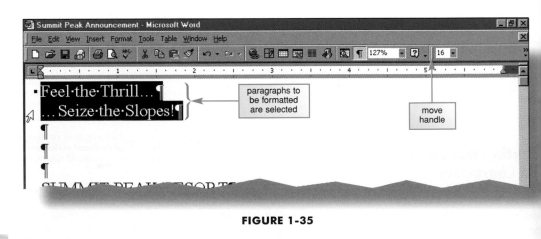

FIGURE 1-35

Other Ways

1. With insertion point at beginning of first paragraph, press CTRL+SHIFT+DOWN ARROW repeatedly

Changing the Font of Selected Text

You have learned that the default font is Times New Roman. Word, however, provides many other fonts to add variety to your documents. Thus, change the font of the headline in the announcement to Arial Black as shown in these steps.

To Change the Font of Selected Text

1 Double-click the move handle on the Formatting toolbar to display the entire toolbar. While the text is selected, click the Font box arrow on the Formatting toolbar, scroll through the list until Arial Black displays, and then point to Arial Black.

Word displays a list of available fonts (Figure 1-36). Your list of available fonts may differ, depending on the type of printer you are using.

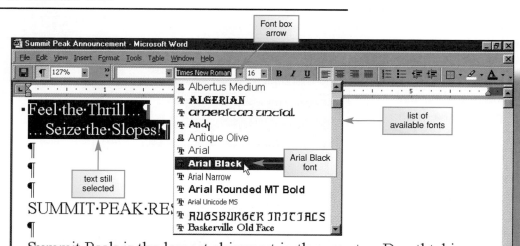

FIGURE 1-36

2 Click Arial Black.

Word changes the font of the selected text to Arial Black (Figure 1-37).

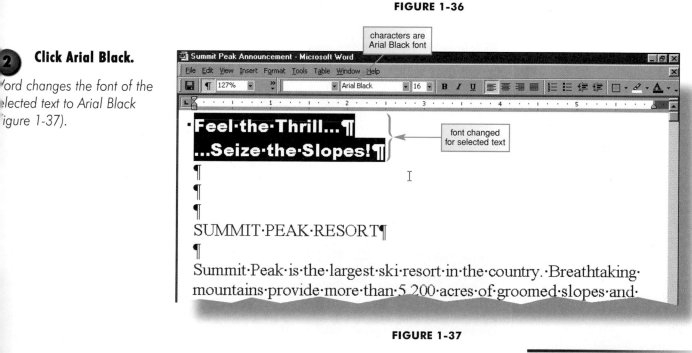

FIGURE 1-37

Changing the Font Size of Selected Text

The next step is to increase the font size of the characters in the selected headline. Recall that the font size specifies the size of the characters. Earlier in this project, you changed the font size for characters in the entire announcement to 16. To give the headline more impact, it has a font size larger than the body copy. Follow the steps on the next page to increase the font size of the headline from 16 to 28 points.

Other Ways

1. Right-click selected text, click Font on shortcut menu, click Font tab, select desired font in Font list, click OK button

2. On Format menu click Font, click Font tab, select desired font in Font list, click OK button

3. Press CTRL+SHIFT+F, press DOWN ARROW key until desired font displays, press ENTER

To Change the Font Size of Selected Text

1 **While the text is selected, click the Font Size box arrow on the Formatting toolbar and then point to the down scroll arrow on the Font Size scroll bar.**

Word displays a list of the available font sizes (Figure 1-38). Available font sizes vary depending on the font and printer driver.

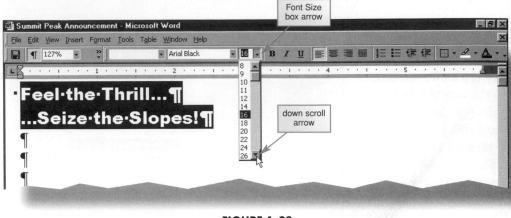

FIGURE 1-38

2 **Click the down scroll arrow on the scroll bar until 28 displays in the list and then point to 28.**

Word highlights 28 in the list (Figure 1-39).

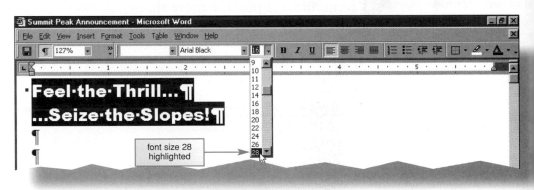

FIGURE 1-39

3 **Click 28.**

Word increases the font size of the headline from 16 to 28 (Figure 1-40). The Font Size box on the Formatting toolbar displays 28, indicating the selected text has a font size of 28.

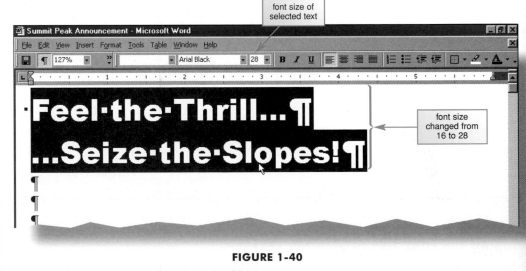

FIGURE 1-40

 Other Ways

1. Right-click selected text, click Font on shortcut menu, click Font tab, select desired point size in Size list, click OK button
2. On Format menu click Font, click Font tab, select desired point size in Size list, click OK button
3. Press CTRL+SHIFT+P, type desired point size, press ENTER

Bold Selected Text

Bold characters display somewhat thicker than those that are not bold. To further emphasize the headline of the announcement, perform the following step to bold its characters.

To Bold Selected Text

1 **While the text is selected, click the Bold button on the Formatting toolbar.**

Word formats the headline in bold (Figure 1-41). The Bold button is recessed.

FIGURE 1-41

When the selected text is bold, the Bold button on the Formatting toolbar is recessed. If, for some reason, you wanted to remove the bold format of the selected text, you would click the Bold button a second time.

Right-Align a Paragraph

The default alignment for paragraphs is **left-aligned**; that is, flush at the left edge of the document with uneven right edges. In Figure 1-42, the Align Left button is recessed to indicate the current paragraph is left-aligned.

The second line of the headline, however, is to be **right-aligned**; that is, flush at the right edge of the document with uneven left edges. Recall that the second line of the headline is a paragraph and that paragraph formatting does not require you to select the paragraph prior to formatting. Just position the insertion point in the paragraph to be formatted and then format it accordingly.

Perform the following steps to right-align the second line of the headline.

To Right-Align a Paragraph

1 **Click somewhere in the paragraph to be right-aligned. Point to the Align Right button on the Formatting toolbar.**

Word positions the insertion point at the location you clicked (Figure 1-42).

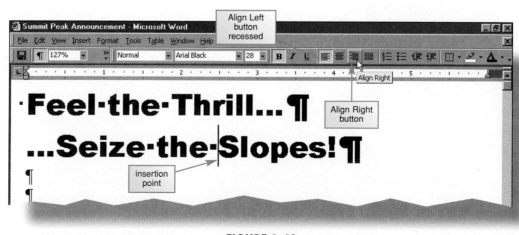

FIGURE 1-42

Other Ways

1. Right-click selected text, click Font on shortcut menu, click Font tab, click Bold in Font style list, click OK button
2. On Format menu click Font, click Font tab, click Bold in Font style list, click OK button
3. Press CTRL+B

2 **Click the Align Right button.**

The second line of the headline is right-aligned (Figure 1-43). Notice that you did not have to select the paragraph before right-aligning it; paragraph formatting only requires the insertion point be positioned somewhere in the paragraph.

FIGURE 1-43

1. Right-click paragraph, click Paragraph on shortcut menu, click Indents and Spacing tab, click Alignment box arrow, click Right, click OK button

2. With insertion point in desired paragraph, on Format menu click Paragraph, click Indents and Spacing tab, click Alignment box arrow, click Right, click OK button

3. Press CTRL+R

When a paragraph is right-aligned, the Align Right button on the Formatting toolbar is recessed. If, for some reason, you wanted to return the selected paragraph to left-aligned, you would click the Align Left button on the Formatting toolbar.

Center a Paragraph

The body title currently is left-aligned. Perform the following step to **center** it, that is, position the body title horizontally between the left and right margins on the page.

More About Centering

The Center button on the Formatting toolbar centers text horizontally. You also can center text vertically between the top and bottom margins. To do this, click File on the menu bar, click Page Setup, click the Layout tab, click the Vertical alignment box arrow, click Center in the list, and then click the OK button.

To Center a Paragraph

1 **Click somewhere in the paragraph to be centered. Click the Center button on the Formatting toolbar.**

Word centers the body title between the left and right margins (Figure 1-44). The Center button on the Formatting toolbar is recessed, which indicates the paragraph containing the insertion point is centered.

FIGURE 1-44

When a paragraph is centered, the Center button on the Formatting toolbar is recessed. If, for some reason, you wanted to return the selected paragraphs to left-aligned, you would click the Align Left button on the Formatting toolbar.

Undoing Commands or Actions

Word provides an **Undo button** on the Standard toolbar that you can use to cancel your recent command(s) or action(s). For example, if you format text incorrectly, you can *undo* the format and try it again. If, after you undo an action, you decide you did not want to perform the undo, you can use the **Redo button** to undo the undo. Some actions, such as saving or printing a document, cannot be undone or redone.

Perform the steps on the next page to *uncenter* the body title and then re-center

Other Ways

1. Right-click paragraph, click Paragraph on shortcut menu, click Indents and Spacing tab, click Alignment box arrow, click Centered, click OK button

2. On Format menu click Paragraph, click Indents and Spacing tab, click Alignment box arrow, click Centered, click OK button

3. Press CTRL+E

Steps **To Undo an Action**

1 **Double-click the move handle on the Standard toolbar to display the entire toolbar. Click the Undo button on the Standard toolbar.**

Word left-aligns the body title (Figure 1-45). Word returns the body title to its formatting prior to you issuing the command to center it.

2 **Click the Redo button on the Standard toolbar.**

Word re-applies the center format to the body title (see Figure 1-46).

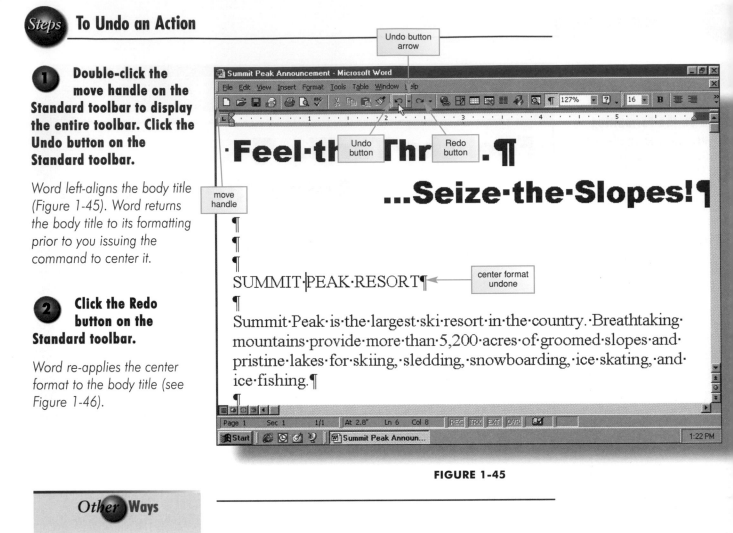

FIGURE 1-45

Other **Ways**

1. On Edit menu click Undo
2. Press CTRL+Z

You also can cancel a series of prior actions by clicking the Undo button arrow (Figure 1-45) to display the undo actions list and then dragging through the actions you wish to be undone.

Whereas undo cancels an action you did not want to perform, Word also provides a **Repeat command**, which duplicates an action you wish to perform again. For example, if you format a paragraph and wish to format another paragraph the exact same way, you could click in the second paragraph to format and then click Repeat on the Edit menu.

Selecting a Line and Formatting It

The next series of steps selects the body title, SUMMIT PEAK RESORT, and formats the characters in it. First, you select the body title. To select the body title, perform the following step.

Steps **To Select a Line**

1 Move the mouse pointer to the left of the line to be selected (SUMMIT PEAK RESORT) until it changes to a right-pointing block arrow and then click.

The entire line to the right of the mouse pointer is highlighted (Figure 1-46).

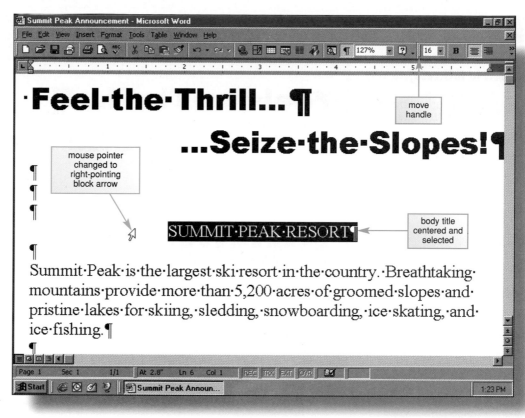

FIGURE 1-46

The next step is to increase the font size of the selected characters to 36 point and bold the selected characters, as explained in the following steps.

TO FORMAT A LINE OF TEXT

1 Double-click the move handle on the Formatting toolbar to display the entire toolbar. While the text is selected, click the Font Size box arrow on the Formatting toolbar and then scroll to 36 in the list. Click 36.

2 Click the Bold button on the Formatting toolbar.

The characters in the body title are enlarged and bold (Figure 1-47 on the next page).

Selecting a Word

To format characters in a word, you must select the entire word first. Follow the steps on the next page to select the word, largest, so you can italicize it.

Other Ways

1. Drag through the line
2. With insertion point at beginning of desired line, press SHIFT+DOWN ARROW

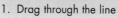

More About 2000

The Formatting Toolbar

Many of the buttons on the Formatting toolbar are toggles; that is, click them once to format the selected text; and click them again to remove the format from the selected text. For example, clicking the Bold button bolds selected text; clicking the Bold button again removes the bold.

To Select a Word

1 **Position the mouse pointer somewhere in the word to be formatted (largest, in this case).**

The mouse pointer's shape is an I-beam when you position it in unselected text in the document window (Figure 1-47).

FIGURE 1-47

2 **Double-click the word to be selected.**

The word, largest, is high-lighted (Figure 1-48). Notice that when the mouse pointer is positioned in a selected word, its shape is a left-pointing block arrow.

FIGURE 1-48

Other Ways

1. Drag through the word
2. With insertion point at beginning of desired word, press CTRL+SHIFT+RIGHT ARROW

Italicize Selected Text

To italicize the word, largest, perform the following step.

Steps: To Italicize Selected Text

1 **With the text still selected, click the Italic button on the Formatting toolbar.**

Word italicizes the text (Figure 1-49). The Italic button on the Formatting toolbar is recessed.

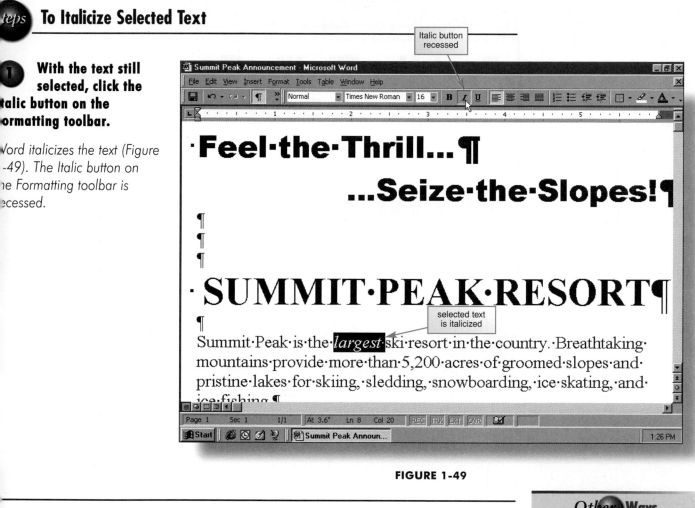

Italic button recessed

selected text is italicized

FIGURE 1-49

When the selected text is italicized, the Italic button on the Formatting toolbar is recessed. If, for some reason, you wanted to remove the italics from the selected text, you would click the Italic button a second time, or you immediately could click the Undo button on the Standard toolbar.

Scrolling

Continue formatting the document by scrolling down one screen so the bottom portion of the announcement displays in the document window. Perform the steps on the next page to display the lower portion of the document.

Other Ways

1. Right-click selected text, click Font on shortcut menu, click Font tab, click Italic in Font style list, click OK button

2. On Format menu click Font, click Font tab, click Italic in Font style list, click OK button

3. Press CTRL+I

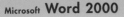
 To Scroll Through the Document

1 **Position the mouse pointer below the scroll box on the vertical scroll bar (Figure 1-50).**

2 **Click below the scroll box on the vertical scroll bar.**

Word scrolls down one screenful in the document (see Figure 1-51). Depending on your monitor type, your screen may scroll differently.

FIGURE 1-50

Other Ways

1. Drag scroll box on vertical scroll bar
2. Click scroll arrows on vertical scroll bar
3. Press PAGE DOWN or PAGE UP
4. See Tables 1-1 and 1-2 on pages WD 1.25 and WD 1.26

The next step is to center the last line of the announcement as described in the following steps.

TO CENTER A PARAGRAPH

1 Click somewhere in the paragraph to be centered.

2 Click the Center button on the Formatting toolbar.

Word centers the last line of the announcement (see Figure 1-51).

Selecting a Group of Words

The next step is to underline the telephone number in the last line of the announcement. Because the telephone number contains spaces and other punctuation, Word considers it a group of words. Thus, the telephone number is a group of words. Select the telephone number by performing the following steps.

To Select a Group of Words

1 Position the mouse pointer immediately to the left of the first character of the text to be selected.

The mouse pointer, an I-beam, is to the left of the parenthesis in the telephone number (Figure 1-51).

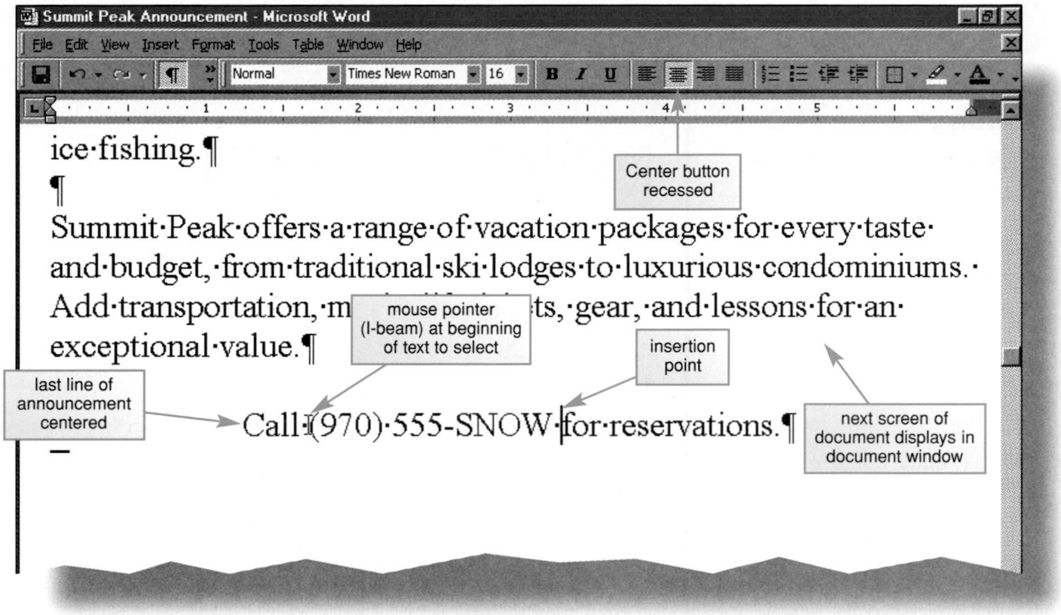

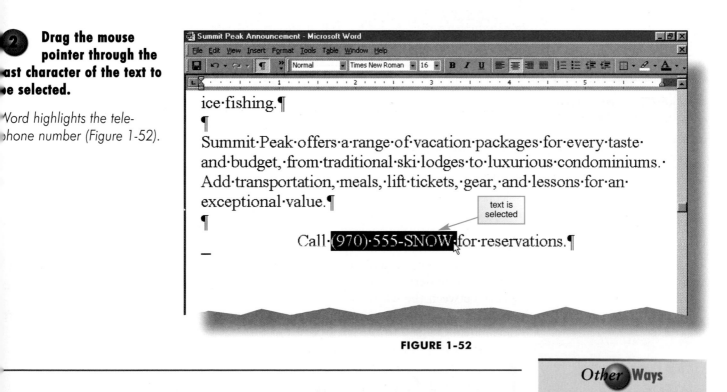

FIGURE 1-51

2 Drag the mouse pointer through the last character of the text to be selected.

Word highlights the telephone number (Figure 1-52).

FIGURE 1-52

Underlining Selected Text

Underlined text prints with an underscore (_) below each character. Like bold, it is used to emphasize or draw attention to specific text. Follow the step on the next page to underline the selected telephone number.

Other Ways

1. With insertion point at beginning of first word in the group, press CTRL+SHIFT+RIGHT ARROW until words are selected

To Underline Selected Text

1 **With the text still selected, click the Underline button on the Formatting toolbar. Click inside the selected text to remove the highlight.**

Word underlines the text and positions the insertion point inside the underlined text (Figure 1-53). When the insertion point is inside the underlined text, the Underline button is recessed.

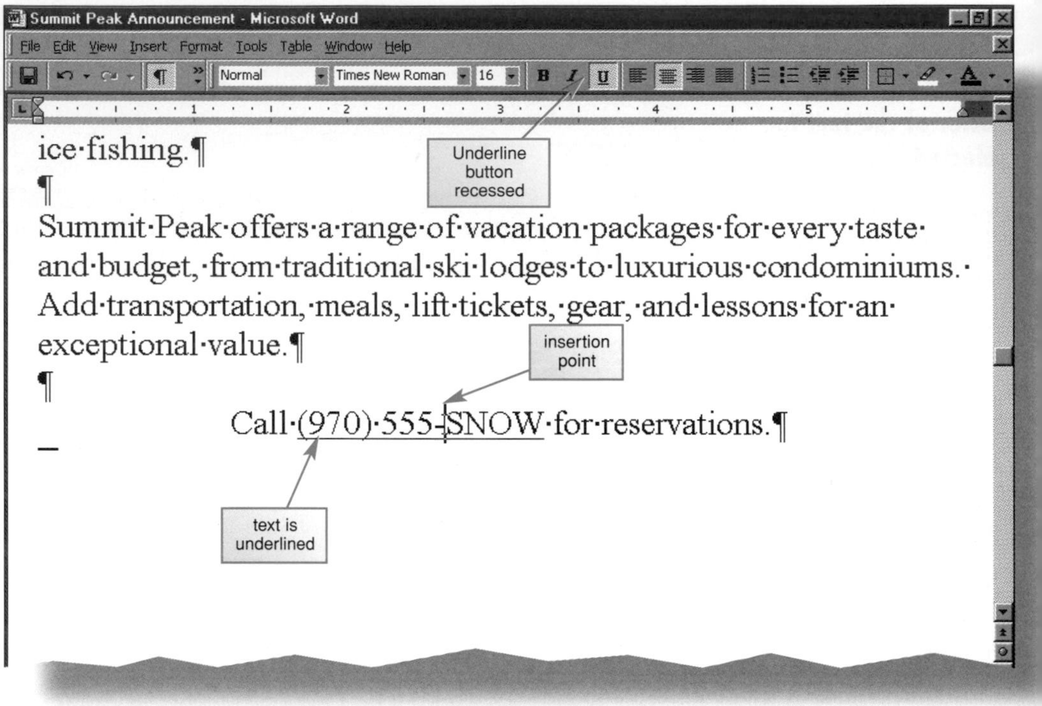

FIGURE 1-53

Other Ways

1. Right-click selected text, click Font on shortcut menu, click Font tab, click Underline style box arrow, click desired underline style, click OK button
2. On Format menu click Font, click Font tab, click Underline style box arrow, click desired underline style, click OK button
3. Press CTRL+U

More About

The Font Dialog Box

If a character formatting operation is not available on the Formatting toolbar, use the Font dialog box to perform the operation. To display the Font dialog box, click Format on the menu bar and then click Font.

To remove a highlight, click the mouse. If you click inside the highlight, the Formatting toolbar displays the formatting characteristics of the characters and paragraphs containing the insertion point.

When the selected text is underlined, the Underline button on the Formatting toolbar is recessed. If, for some reason, you wanted to remove the underline from the selected text, you would click the Underline button a second time, or you immediately could click the Undo button on the Standard toolbar.

In addition to the basic underline shown in Figure 1-53, Word has many decorative underlines that are available in the Font dialog box. For example, you can use double underlines, dotted underlines, and wavy underlines. You also can change the color of an underline and instruct Word to underline only the words and not the spaces between the words.

The formatting for the announcement is now complete. The next step is to insert a graphical image into the document and then resize the image.

Inserting Clip Art into a Word Document

Files containing graphical images, also called **graphics**, are available from a variety of sources. Word 2000 includes a series of predefined graphics called **clip art** that you can insert into a Word document. Clip art is located in the **Clip Gallery**, which contains a collection of **clips**, including clip art, as well as photographs, sounds, and video clips. The Clip Gallery contains its own Help system to assist you in locating clips suited to your application.

Inserting Clip Art

The next step in the project is to insert a graphic of a skier into the announcement. Perform the following steps to insert a graphic into the document.

Steps **To Insert Clip Art into a Document**

1 To position the insertion point where you want the clip art to be located, press CTRL+HOME and then press the DOWN ARROW key three times. Click Insert on the menu bar.

The insertion point is positioned on the second paragraph mark below the headline, and the Insert menu displays (Figure 1-54). Remember that a short menu initially displays, which expands into a full menu after a few seconds.

FIGURE 1-54

2 Point to Picture and then point to Clip Art.

The Picture submenu displays (Figure 1-55). You have learned that when you point to a command that has a small arrow to its right, Word displays a submenu associated with that command.

FIGURE 1-55

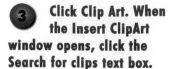

3 **Click Clip Art. When the Insert ClipArt window opens, click the Search for clips text box.**

Word opens the Insert ClipArt window (Figure 1-56). The text in the Search for clips text box is highlighted. When you enter a description of the desired graphic in this text box, Word searches the Clip Gallery for clips that match the description.

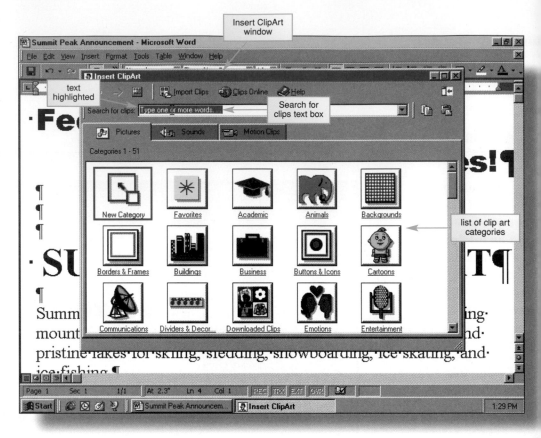

FIGURE 1-56

4 **Type** ski **and then press the ENTER key.**

A list of clips that match the description, ski, displays (Figure 1-57).

FIGURE 1-57

5 Click the desired image and then point to the Insert clip button on the Pop-up menu.

Word displays a Pop-up menu (Figure 1-58). The Pop-up menu contains four buttons: (1) Insert clip, (2) Preview clip, (3) Add clip to Favorites or other category, and (4) Find similar clips.

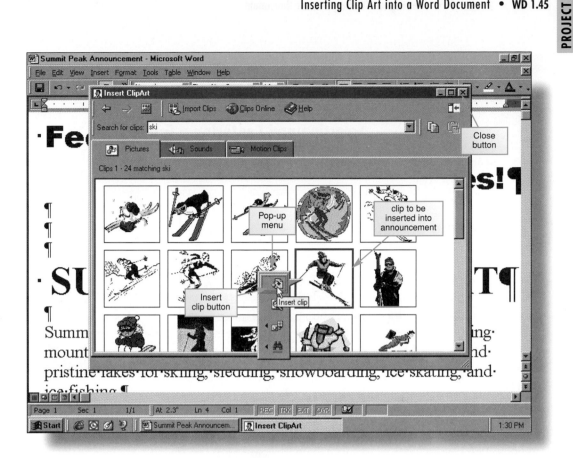

FIGURE 1-58

6 Click the Insert clip button. Click the Close button at the right edge of the Insert ClipArt window's title bar. Press the UP ARROW key twice to display part of the headline.

Word inserts the clip into the document at the location of the insertion point (Figure 1-59). The graphic of the skier displays below the headline in the announcement.

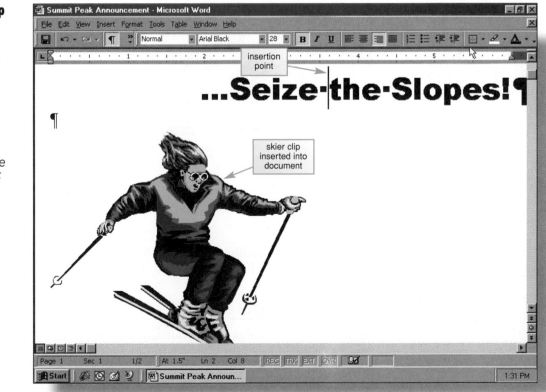

FIGURE 1-59

Obtaining Graphics

If you have a scanner or digital camera attached to your computer, Word can insert a graphic directly from these devices.

The clip art in the document is part of a paragraph. Because that paragraph is left-aligned, the clip art also is left-aligned. You can, however, use any of the paragraph alignment buttons on the Formatting toolbar to reposition the clip art.

Selecting and Centering a Graphic

To center a graphic, you first must select it. Perform the following steps to select and then center the graphic.

Steps | To Select a Graphic

1 **Click anywhere in the graphic. If your screen does not display the Picture toolbar, click View on the menu bar, point to Toolbars, and then click Picture.**

*Word selects the graphic (Figure 1-60). A selected graphic displays surrounded by a **selection rectangle** that has small squares, called **sizing handles**, at each corner and middle location. You use the sizing handles to change the size of the graphic. When a graphic is selected, the Picture toolbar automatically displays on the screen.*

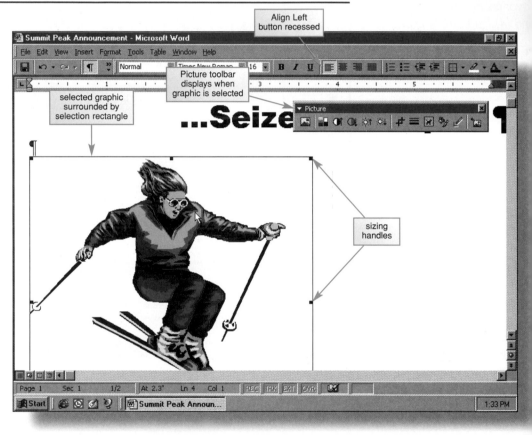

FIGURE 1-60

Graphics

Emphasize a graphic by placing it at the optical center of the page. To determine optical center, divide the page in half horizontally and vertically. The optical center is located one third of the way up the vertical line from the point of intersection of the two lines.

If the Picture toolbar covers the Standard and Formatting toolbars you can drag the title bar of the Picture toolbar to move the toolbar to a different location.

TO CENTER A SELECTED GRAPHIC

1 With the graphic still selected, click the Center button on the Formatting toolbar.

Word centers the selected graphic between the left and right margins of the document (see Figure 1-61). The Center button is recessed.

When you center the graphic, Word may scroll down so the graphic is positioned at the top of the document window. The graphic is a little too large for this announcement. The next step is to resize the graphic.

esizing a Graphic

Once you have inserted a graphic into a document, you easily can change its size. **esizing** includes both enlarging and reducing the size of a graphic. To resize a graphic, you first must select it. The following steps show how to resize the graphic you just inserted and selected.

More About

Resizing Graphics

When you drag the sizing handles to resize a graphic, you might distort its proportions. To maintain the proportions of the graphic, press the SHIFT key while you drag a corner sizing handle.

teps To Resize a Graphic

1 With the graphic still selected, point o the upper-left corner izing handle.

The mouse pointer changes o a two-headed arrow when t is on a sizing handle Figure 1-61). To resize a graphic, you drag the sizing handles until the graphic is he desired size.

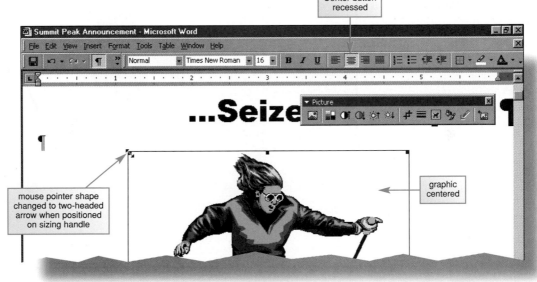

FIGURE 1-61

2 Drag the sizing handle diagonally oward the center of the graphic until the dotted election rectangle is ositioned approximately s shown in Figure 1-62.

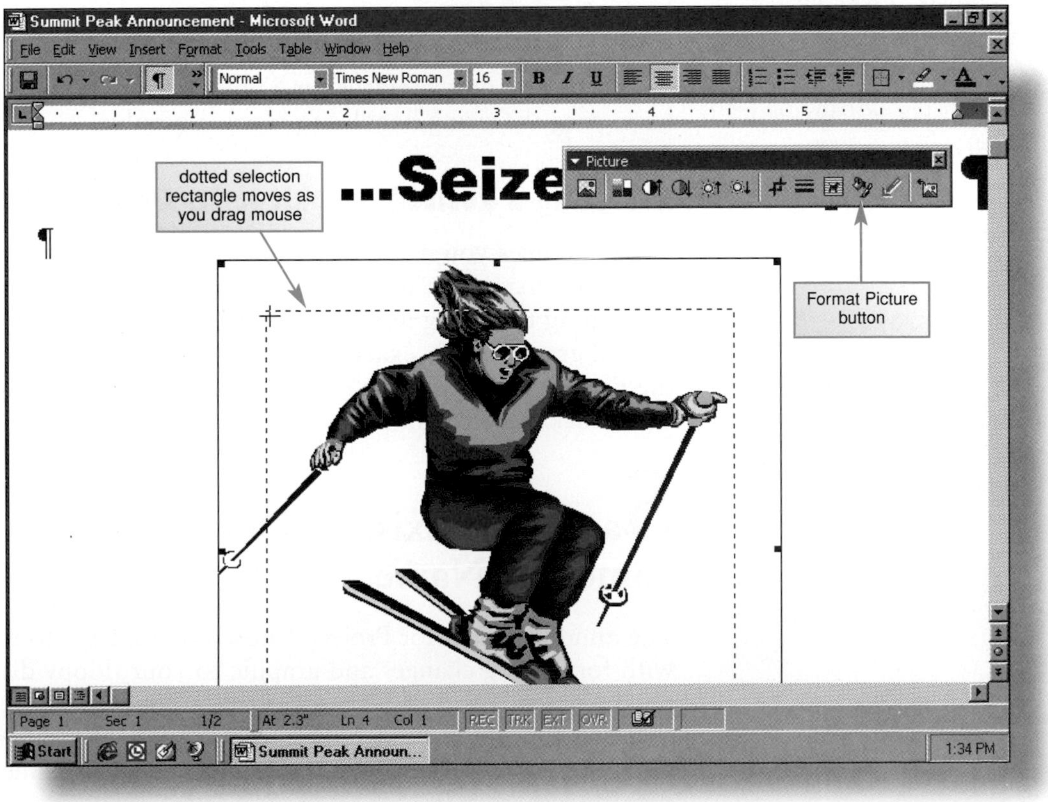

FIGURE 1-62

3 **Release the mouse button. Press**

CTRL + HOME.

Word resizes the graphic (Figure 1-63). When you click outside of a graphic or press a key to scroll through a document, Word deselects the graphic. The Picture toolbar disappears from the screen when you deselect the graphic.

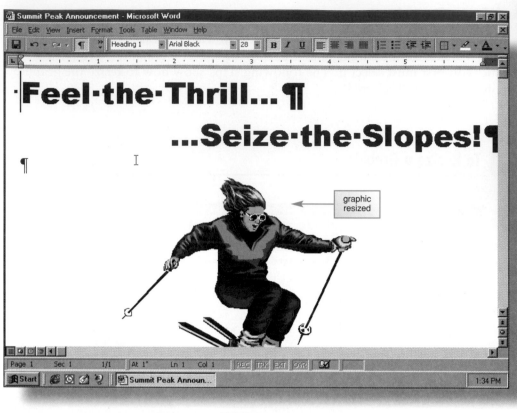

FIGURE 1-63

Instead of resizing a selected graphic with the mouse, you also can use the Format Picture dialog box to resize a graphic by clicking the Format Picture button (Figure 1-62 on the previous page) on the Picture toolbar and then clicking the Size tab. Using the Size sheet, you enter exact height and width measurements. If you have a precise measurement for a graphic, use the Format Picture dialog box; otherwise, drag the sizing handles to resize a graphic.

Restoring a Resized Graphic to Its Original Size

Sometimes you might resize a graphic and realize it is the wrong size. In these cases, you may want to return the graphic to its original size and start again. You could drag the sizing handle until the graphic resembles its original size. To restore a resized graphic to its exact original size, click the graphic to select it and then click the Format Picture button on the Picture toolbar to display the Format Picture dialog box. Click the Size tab and then click the Reset button. Finally, click the OK button.

Saving an Existing Document with the Same File Name

The announcement for Project 1 now is complete. To transfer the modified document with formatting changes and graphic to your floppy disk in drive A, you must save the document again. When you saved the document the first time, you assigned a file name to it (Summit Peak Announcement). If you use the following procedure, Word automatically assigns the same file name to the document each time you subsequently save it.

Steps **To Save an Existing Document with the Same File Name**

1 **Double-click the move handle on the Standard toolbar to display the entire toolbar. Click the Save button on the Standard toolbar.**

Word saves the document on a floppy disk inserted in drive A using the currently assigned file name, Summit Peak Announcement (Figure 1-64).

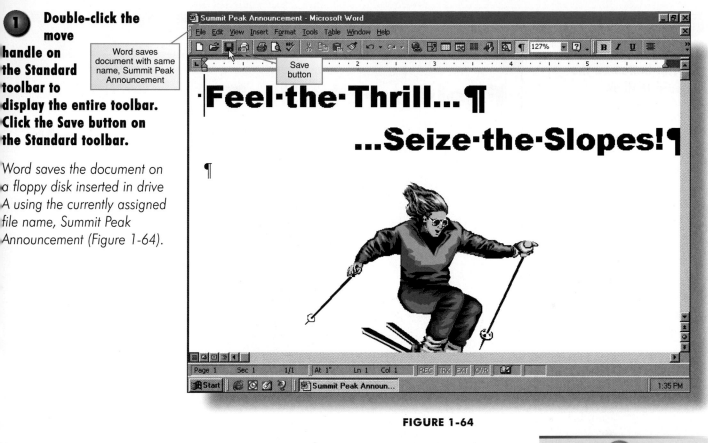

Word saves document with same name, Summit Peak Announcement

Save button

FIGURE 1-64

While Word is saving the document, the Background Save Status icon displays at the right edge of the status bar. When the save is complete, the document remains in memory and on the screen.

If, for some reason, you want to save an existing document with a different file name, click Save As on the File menu to display the Save As dialog box. Then, fill in the Save As dialog box as discussed in Steps 2 through 5 on pages WD 1.27 and WD 1.28.

Printing a Document

The next step is to print the document you created. A printed version of the document is called a **hard copy** or **printout**. Perform the steps on the next page to print the announcement created in Project 1.

More *About*

Save As

In the Save As dialog box, you can create a new Windows folder by clicking the Create New Folder button. You also can delete or rename files by selecting the file and then clicking the Tools button arrow in the Save As dialog box. To display the Save As dialog box, click File on the menu bar and then click Save As.

Steps **To Print a Document**

1 **Ready the printer according to the printer instructions. Click the Print button on the Standard toolbar.**

The mouse pointer briefly changes to an hourglass shape as Word prepares to print the document. While the document is printing, a printer icon displays in the tray status area on the taskbar (Figure 1-65).

2 **When the printer stops, retrieve the printout (see Figure 1-1 on page WD1.7).**

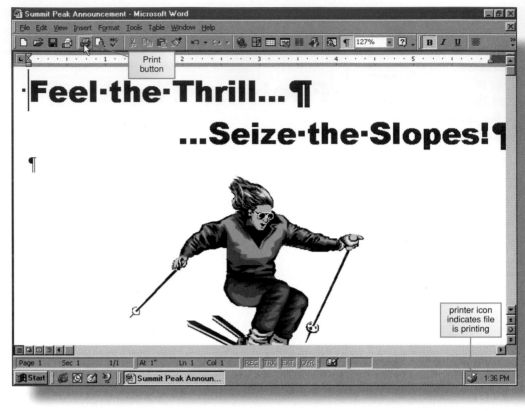

FIGURE 1-65

More About

Print Preview

To view a document before you print it, click the Print Preview button on the Standard toolbar. To return to the document window, click the Close Preview button on the Print Preview toolbar.

When you use the Print button to print a document, Word prints the entire document automatically. You then may distribute the hard copy or keep it as a permanent record of the document.

If you wanted to print multiple copies of the document, click File on the menu bar and then click Print to display the Print dialog box. This dialog box has several printing options, including specifying the number of copies to print.

If you wanted to cancel your job that is printing or one you have waiting to be printed, double-click the printer icon on the taskbar (Figure 1-65). In the printer window, click the job to be canceled and then click Cancel Printing on the Document menu.

Quitting Word

After you create, save, and print the announcement, Project 1 is complete. To quit Word and return control to Windows, perform the following steps.

Steps To Quit Word

1 Point to the Close button in the upper-right corner of the title bar (Figure 1-66).

2 Click the Close button.

The Word window closes.

FIGURE 1-66

If you made changes to the document since the last save, Word displays dialog box asking if you want to save the changes. Clicking the Yes button saves the changes; clicking the No button ignores the changes; and clicking the Cancel button returns to the document. If you did not make any changes since you saved the document, this dialog box does not display.

You created and formatted the announcement, inserted clip art into it, printed it, and saved it. You might decide, however, to change the announcement at a later date. To do this, you must start Word and then retrieve your document from the floppy disk in drive A.

Opening a Document

Earlier, you saved the Word document created in Project 1 on a floppy disk using the file name Summit Peak Announcement. Once you have created and saved a document, you often will have reason to retrieve it from the disk. For example, you might want to revise the document or print it. The steps on the next page illustrate how to open the file Summit Peak Announcement.

More About 2000

Opening Files

In Word, you can open a recently used file by clicking File on the menu bar and then clicking the file name on the File menu. To instruct Word to show the recently used documents on the File menu, click Tools on the menu bar, click Options, click the General tab, click Recently used file list, and then click the OK button.

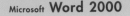
Steps **To Open a Document**

1 **Click the Start button on the taskbar and then point to Open Office Document (Figure 1-67).**

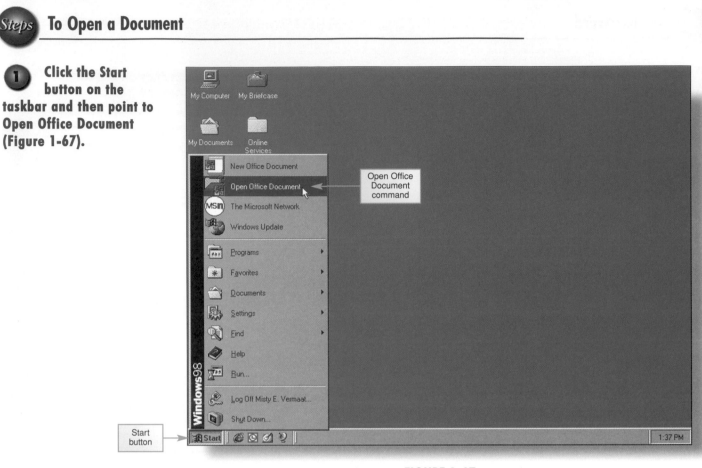

FIGURE 1-67

2 **Click Open Office Document. If necessary, click the Look in box arrow and then click 3½ Floppy (A:). If it is not selected already, click the file name Summit Peak Announcement. Point to the Open button.**

Office displays the Open Office Document dialog box (Figure 1-68). Office displays the files on the floppy disk in drive A.

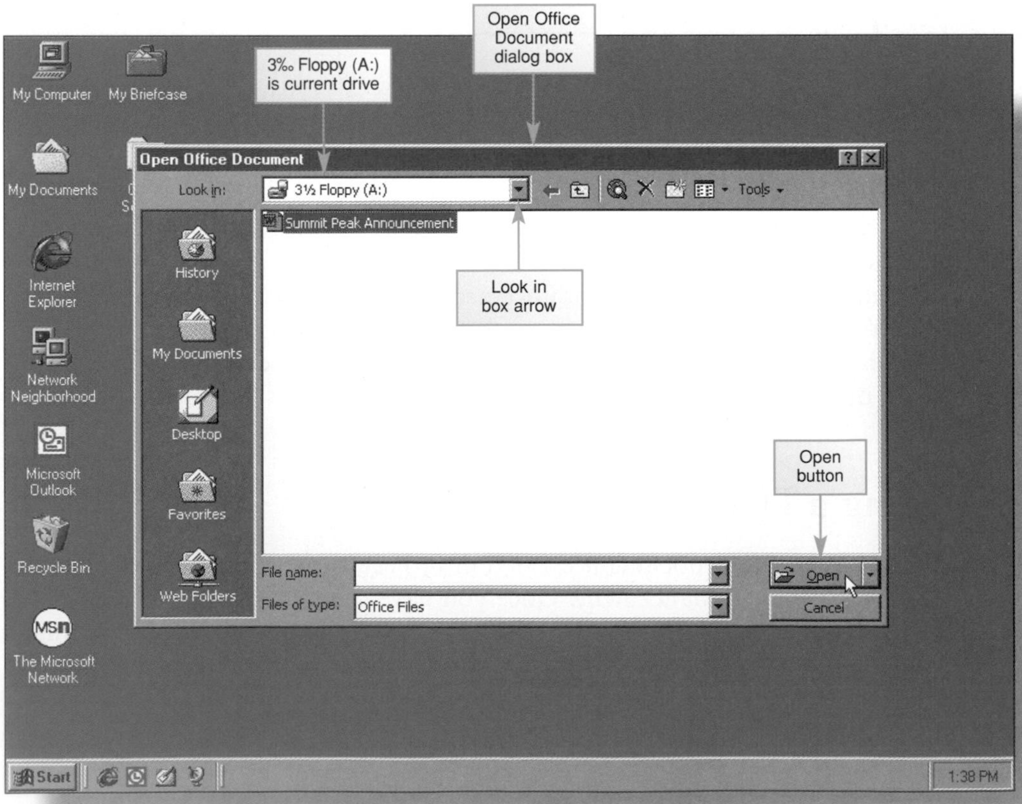

FIGURE 1-68

③ Click the Open button.

Office starts Word, and then Word opens the document, Summit Peak Announcement, from the floppy disk in drive A and displays the document on the screen (Figure 1-69).

FIGURE 1-69

Correcting Errors

After creating a document, you often will find you must make changes to it. Changes can be required because the document contains an error or because of new circumstances.

Types of Changes Made to Documents

The types of changes made to documents normally fall into one of the three following categories: additions, deletions, or modifications.

ADDITIONS Additional words, sentences, or paragraphs may be required in a document. Additions occur when you omit text from a document and want to insert it later. For example, you may want to insert the word, winter, in front of vacation packages to differentiate winter packages from summer packages.

DELETIONS Sometimes, text in a document is incorrect or is no longer needed. For example, the resort might remove transportation from their package deals. In this case, you would delete the word, transportation, from the list.

MODIFICATIONS If an error is made in a document or changes take place that affect the document, you might have to revise the word(s) in the text. For example, the resort might purchase more land and have 6,500 acres of slopes and lakes; thus, you would change the number from 5,200 to 6,500.

Word provides several methods for correcting errors in a document. For each of the error correction techniques, you first must move the insertion point to the error.

Other Ways

1. In Microsoft Word, click Open button on Standard toolbar, select file name, click Open button in dialog box
2. In Microsoft Word, on File menu click Open, select file name, click Open button in dialog box
3. In Microsoft Word, press CTRL+O, select file name, press ENTER

Inserting Text into an Existing Document

If you leave a word or phrase out of a sentence, you can include it in the sentence by positioning the insertion point where you intend to insert the text. Word is preset to insert the text to the left of the insertion point. The text to the right of the insertion point moves to the right and downward to accommodate the new text.

TO INSERT TEXT INTO AN EXISTING DOCUMENT

 1 Click to left of location to insert new text.

2 Type new text.

In Word, the default typing mode is insert mode. In **insert mode**, as you type a character, Word inserts the character and moves all the characters to the right of the typed character one position to the right. You can change to overtype mode by double-clicking the **OVR status indicator** on the status bar (see Figure 1-4 on page WD 1.9). In **overtype mode**, Word replaces characters to the right of the insertion point. Double-clicking the OVR status indicator a second time returns you to insert mode.

Deleting Text from an Existing Document

It is not unusual to type incorrect characters or words in a document. You have learned that you can click the Undo button on the Standard toolbar to undo a command or action – this includes typing. Word also provides other methods of correcting typing errors. For example, you may want to delete certain letters or words.

TO DELETE AN INCORRECT CHARACTER IN A DOCUMENT

1 Click next to the incorrect character.

2 Press the BACKSPACE key to erase to the left of the insertion point; or press the DELETE key to erase to the right of the insertion point.

TO DELETE AN INCORRECT WORD OR PHRASE IN A DOCUMENT

1 Select the word or phrase you want to erase.

2 Right-click the selected word or phrase, and then click Cut on the shortcut menu; or click the Cut button on the Standard toolbar (Figure 1-7a on page WD 1.13); or press the DELETE key.

Closing the Entire Document

Sometimes, everything goes wrong. If this happens, you may want to close the document entirely and start over. You also may want to close a document when you are finished with it so you can begin your next document.

TO CLOSE THE ENTIRE DOCUMENT AND START OVER

1 Click File on the menu bar and then click Close.

2 If Word displays a dialog box, click the No button to ignore the changes since the last time you saved the document.

 3 Click the New Blank Document button (see Figure 1-7a on page WD 1.13) on the Standard toolbar.

You also can close the document by clicking the Close button at the right edge of the menu bar.

Word Help System

At any time while you are using Word, you can get answers to questions by using the **Word Help system**. Used properly, this form of online assistance can increase your productivity and reduce your frustrations by minimizing the time you spend learning how to use Word.

The following section shows how to obtain answers to your questions using the Office Assistant. For additional information on using help, see Appendix A.

Using the Office Assistant

The **Office Assistant** answers your questions and suggests more efficient ways to complete a task. With the Office Assistant active, for example, you can type a question, word, or phrase in a text box and the Office Assistant provides immediate help on the subject. Also, as you create a document, the Office Assistant accumulates tips that suggest more efficient ways to do the tasks you completed while creating a document, such as formatting, printing, and saving. This tip feature is part of the **IntelliSense technology** that is built into Word, which understands what you are trying to do and suggests better ways to do it. When the light bulb displays above the Office Assistant, click it to see a tip.

The following steps show how to use the Office Assistant to obtain information on changing the size of a toolbar.

More About 2000

Help

If you purchased an application program five years ago, you probably received one or more thick technical manuals explaining the software. With Microsoft Word 2000, you receive a small manual. The online Help feature of Microsoft Word 2000 replaces the reams and reams of printed pages in complicated technical manuals.

Steps **To Obtain Help Using the Office Assistant**

1 If the Office Assistant is not on the screen, click Help on the menu bar and then click Show the Office Assistant. With the Office Assistant on the screen, click it. Type change toolbar size in the What would you like to do? text box. Point to the Search button (Figure 1-70).

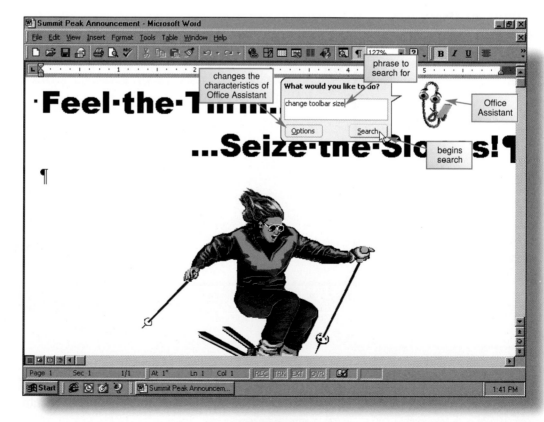

FIGURE 1-70

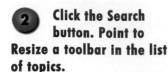**2** **Click the Search button. Point to Resize a toolbar in the list of topics.**

The Office Assistant displays a list of topics relating to the typed question, change toolbar size (Figure 1-71). The mouse pointer changes to a pointing hand.

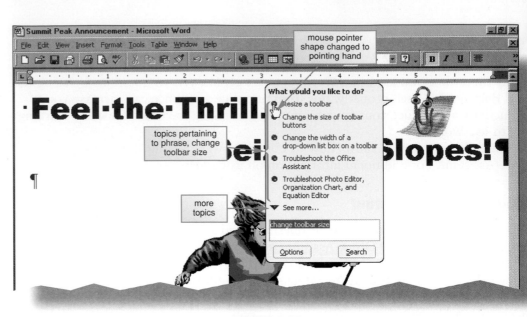

FIGURE 1-71

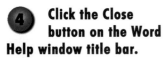**3** **Click Resize a toolbar. When Word opens the Word Help window, click its Maximize button. If necessary, drag the Office Assistant out of the way of the Help text.**

The Office Assistant opens a Word Help window that provides Help information on resizing toolbars (Figure 1-72).

4 **Click the Close button on the Word Help window title bar.**

The Word Help window closes and the Word document window again is active.

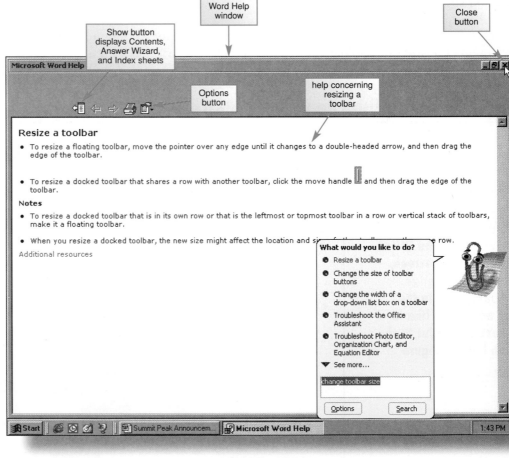

FIGURE 1-72

Other Ways

1. If the Office Assistant is on, click Microsoft Word Help button or click Microsoft Word Help on the Help menu

You can use the Office Assistant to search for Help on any topic concerning Word.

Table 1-3 summarizes the nine categories of help available to you. Because of the way the Word Help system works, please review the right-most column of Table 1-3 if you have difficulties activating the desired category of help.

Table 1-3	Word Help System		
TYPE	DESCRIPTION	HOW TO ACTIVATE	TURNING THE OFFICE ASSISTANT ON AND OFF
Answer Wizard	Similar to the Office Assistant in that it answers questions that you type in your own words.	Click the Microsoft Word Help button on the Standard toolbar. If necessary, maximize the Help window by double-clicking its title bar. Click the Answer Wizard tab.	If the Office Assistant displays, right-click it, click Options, click Use the Office Assistant to remove the check mark, click the OK button.
Contents sheet	Groups Help topics by general categories. Use when you know only the general category of the topic in question. Similar to a table of contents in a book.	Click the Microsoft Word Help button on the Standard toolbar. If necessary, maximize the Help window by double-clicking its title bar. Click the Contents tab.	If the Office Assistant displays, right-click it, click Options, click Use the Office Assistant to remove the check mark, click the OK button.
Detect and Repair	Automatically finds and fixes errors in the application.	Click Detect and Repair on the Help menu.	
Hardware and Software Information	Shows Product ID and allows access to system information and technical support information.	Click About Microsoft Word on the Help menu and then click the appropriate button.	
Index sheet	Similar to an index in a book; use when you know exactly what you want.	Click the Microsoft Word Help button on the Standard toolbar. If necessary, maximize the Help window by double-clicking its title bar. Click the Index tab.	If the Office Assistant displays, right-click it, click Options, click Use the Office Assistant to remove the check mark, click the OK button.
Office Assistant	Answers questions that you type in your own words, offers tips, and provides Help for a variety of Word features.	Click the Microsoft Word Help button on the Standard toolbar or double-click the Office Assistant icon. Some dialog boxes also include the Microsoft Word Help button.	If the Office Assistant does not display, click Show the Office Assistant on the Help menu.
Office on the Web	Used to access technical resources and download free product enhancements on the Web.	Click Office on the Web on the Help menu.	
Question Mark button and What's This? command	Used to identify unfamiliar items on the screen.	In a dialog box, click the Question Mark button and then click an item in the dialog box. Click What's This? on the Help menu, and then click an item on the screen.	
WordPerfect Help	Used to assist WordPerfect users who are learning Microsoft Word.	Click WordPerfect Help on the Help menu.	

The final step in this project is to quit Word.

O QUIT WORD

1 Click the Close button in the Word window.

he Word window closes.

Quick Reference

For a table that lists how to complete the tasks covered in this book using the mouse, menu, shortcut menu, and keyboard, visit the Shelly Cashman Series Office Web page (www.scsite.com/off2000/qr.htm) and then click Microsoft Word 2000.

CASE PERSPECTIVE SUMMARY

Jackie is thrilled with the completed announcement. The characters in the headline and body title are large enough so students can read them from a distance and the graphic is quite eye-catching. She takes the announcement to the school's Promotions Department and receives approval to post it in several locations around campus, have it printed in the school newspaper, and mailed to each student's home. Members of the SGA assist Jackie with these activities.

Project Summary

Project 1 introduced you to starting Word and creating a document. Before entering any text in the document, you learned how to change the font size. You also learned how to save and print a document. You used Word's check spelling as you type feature. Once you saved the document, you learned how to format its paragraphs and characters. Then, you inserted and resized clip art. You learned how to move the insertion point so you could insert, delete, and modify text. Finally, you learned one way to use Word Help.

What You Should Know

Having completed this project, you now should be able to perform the following tasks:

- Bold Selected Text *(WD 1.33)*
- Center a Paragraph *(WD 1.35 and WD 1.40)*
- Center a Selected Graphic *(WD 1.46)*
- Change the Font of Selected Text *(WD 1.31)*
- Change the Font Size of Selected Text *(WD 1.32)*
- Check Spelling as You Type *(WD 1.22)*
- Close the Entire Document and Start Over *(WD 1.54)*
- Delete an Incorrect Character in a Document *(WD 1.54)*
- Delete an Incorrect Word or Phrase in a Document *(WD 1.54)*
- Display Formatting Marks *(WD 1.20)*
- Displays the Entire Standard Toolbar *(WD 1.15)*
- Enter Blank Lines into a Document *(WD 1.19)*

- Enter More Text *(WD 1.21)*
- Enter Text *(WD 1.18)*
- Enter Text that Scrolls the Document Window *(WD 1.25)*
- Format a Line of Text *(WD 1.37)*
- Increase the Default Font Size Before Typing *(WD 1.17)*
- Insert Clip Art into a Document *(WD 1.43)*
- Insert Text into an Existing Document *(WD 1.54)*
- Italicize Selected Text *(WD 1.39)*
- Obtain Help Using the Office Assistant *(WD 1.55)*
- Open a Document *(WD 1.52)*
- Print a Document *(WD 1.50)*
- Quit Word *(WD 1.51)*
- Resize a Graphic *(WD 1.47)*
- Right-Align a Paragraph *(WD 1.33)*
- Save a New Document *(WD 1.26)*
- Save an Existing Document with the Same File Name *(WD 1.49)*
- Scroll Through the Document *(WD 1.40)*
- Select a Graphic *(WD 1.46)*
- Select a Group of Words *(WD 1.41)*
- Select a Line *(WD 1.37)*
- Select a Word *(WD 1.38)*
- Select Multiple Paragraphs *(WD 1.30)*
- Start Word *(WD 1.8)*
- Underline Selected Text *(WD 1.42)*
- Undo an Action *(WD 1.36)*
- Wordwrap Text as You Type *(WD 1.21)*
- Zoom Page Width *(WD 1.15)*

More About 2000

Microsoft Certification

The Microsoft Office User Specialist (MOUS) Certification program provides an opportunity for you to obtain a valuable industry credential — proof that you have the Word 2000 skills required by employers. For more information, see Appendix D or visit the Shelly Cashman Series MOUS Web page at www.scsite.com/off2000/cert.htm.

Apply Your Knowledge

➕ Project Reinforcement at www.scsite.com/off2000/reinforce.htm

1 Checking Spelling of a Document

Instructions: Start Word. Open the document, Meeting Announcement, on the Data Disk. If you did not download the Data Disk, see the inside back cover for instructions for downloading the Data Disk or see your instructor.

As shown in Figure 1-73, the document is a meeting announcement that contains many spelling and grammar errors. You are to right-click each of the errors and then click the appropriate correction on the shortcut menu.

You have learned that Word flags spelling errors with a red wavy underline. A green wavy underline indicates that Word has detected a possible grammar error. *Hint:* If your screen does not display the grammar errors, use the Word Help system to determine how to enable the check grammar feature. Perform the following tasks:

1. Position the insertion point at the beginning of the document. Right-click the flagged word, Notise. Change the incorrect word, Notise, to Notice by clicking Notice on the shortcut menu.

2. Right-click the flagged word, Januery. Change the incorrect word, Januery, to January by clicking January on the shortcut menu.

3. Right-click the flagged word, be. Click Delete Repeated Word on the shortcut menu to remove the duplicate occurrence of the word, be.

spelling and grammar errors are flagged on printout to help you identify them

Meeting Notise
All Employees

NEW HEALTH INSURANCE PLAN

Effective Januery 1, Kramer Enterprises will be be switching to a new insurance providor for major medical coverage. At that time, all employees must begin submitting claims and directing all claim-related questions to ofr new provider, Health America.

Representative's from Health America will be visiting our office on Friday, December 1, to discuss our nesw insurance plan. Please plan to attend either the morning session at 9:00 a.m. or the afternoon session at 2:00 p.m. Both session will be in the lunchroom.

insurance cards will be distributed at these meetings!

FIGURE 1-73

4. Right-click the flagged word, providor. Change the incorrect word, providor, to provider by clicking provider on the shortcut menu.

5. Right-click the flagged word, ofr. Because the shortcut menu does not display the correct word, click outside the shortcut menu to remove it from the screen. Correct the misspelled word, ofr, to the correct word, our, by removing the letter f and replacing it with the letter u.

6. Right-click the flagged word, Representative's. Change the word, Representative's, to its correct plural by clicking the word, Representatives, on the shortcut menu.

7. Right-click the incorrect word, nesw. Change the incorrect word, nesw, to new by clicking new on the shortcut menu.

8. Right-click the flagged word, session. Change the incorrect word, session, to its plural by clicking sessions on the shortcut menu.

9. Right-click the flagged word, insurance. Capitalize the word, insurance, by clicking Insurance on the shortcut menu.

10. Click File menu on the menu bar and then click Save As. Save the document using Corrected Meeting Announcement as the file name.

11. Print the revised document.

In the Lab

1 Creating an Announcement with Clip Art

Problem: The Director of the Harbor Theatre Company at your school has requested that each student in your Marketing 102 class prepare an announcement for auditions of its upcoming play. The student that creates the winning announcement will receive five complimentary tickets to the play. You prepare the announcement shown in Figure 1-74. *Hint:* Remember, if you make a mistake while formatting the announcement, you can click the Undo button on the Standard toolbar to undo your mistake.

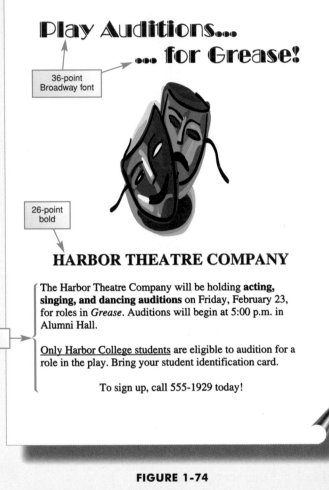

FIGURE 1-74

Instructions:

1. Change the font size from 10 to 18 by clicking the Font Size box arrow on the formatting toolbar and then clicking 18.
2. If necessary, click the Show/Hide ¶ button on Standard toolbar to display formatting marks.
3. Create the announcement shown in Figure 1-74. Enter the document first without clip art and unformatted; that is without any bold, underlined, italicized, right-aligned, or centered text. If Word flags any misspelled words as you type, check the spelling of these words and correct them.
4. Save the document on a floppy disk with Grease Announcement as the file name.
5. Select the two lines of the headline. Change their font to Broadway, or a similar font. Change their font size from 18 to 36.
6. Click somewhere in the second line of the headline. Right-align it.
7. Click somewhere in the body title line. Center it.
8. Select the body title line. Increase its font size from 18 to 26. Bold it.
9. In the first paragraph of the body copy, select the following phrase: acting, singing, and dancing auditions. Bold the phrase.
10. In the same paragraph, select the word, Grease. Italicize it.
11. In the second paragraph of the body copy, select the following phrase: Only Harbor College students. Underline the phrase.
12. Click somewhere in the last line of the announcement. Center it.
13. Insert the graphic of the drama masks between the headline and the body title line. Search for the text, drama, in the Clip Gallery to locate the graphic.
14. Click the graphic to select it. Center the selected graphic.
15. Save the announcement again with the same file name.
16. Print the announcement.

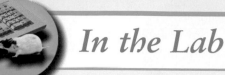

In the Lab

2 Creating an Announcement with Resized Clip Art

Problem: You are an assistant for the Marketing Manager at Taylor Business School. She has asked you to prepare an announcement for Fall Registration. The announcement must include clip art. You prepare the announcement shown in Figure 1-75. *Hint:* Remember, if you make a mistake while formatting the announcement, you can click the Undo button on the Standard toolbar to undo your mistake.

Instructions:

1. Change the font size from 10 to 18 by clicking the Font Size box arrow on the Formatting toolbar and then clicking 18.
2. If it is not already selected, click the Show/Hide ¶ button on the Standard toolbar to display formatting marks.
3. Create the announcement shown in Figure 1-75. Enter the document first without the clip art and unformatted; that is without any bold, underlined, italicized, right-aligned, or centered text. If Word flags any misspelled words as you type, check the spelling of these words and correct them.
4. Save the document on a floppy disk with Registration Announcement as the file name.
5. Select the two lines of the headline. Change their font to Arial, or a similar font. Change their font size from 20 to 36. Bold both lines.
6. Click somewhere in the second line of the headline. Right-align it.
7. Click somewhere in the body title line. Center it.
8. Select the body title line. Increase its font size from 18 to 28. Bold it.
9. Select the words, and much more, in the first paragraph of the body copy. Italicize the words.
10. Select the word, variety, in the second paragraph of the body copy. Underline it.
11. Click somewhere in the last line of the announcement. Center it.
12. Insert the graphic of the classroom between the headline and the body title line. Search for the text, classroom, in the Clip Gallery to locate the graphic.
13. Enlarge the graphic of the classroom. If you make the graphic too large, the announcement may flow onto two pages. If this occurs, reduce the size of the graphic so the announcement fits on a single page. *Hint:* Use Help to learn about **print preview**, which is a way to see the page before you print it. To exit print preview and return to the document window, click the Close button on the Print Preview toolbar.
14. Click the graphic to select it. Center the selected graphic.
15. Save the announcement again with the same file name.
16. Print the announcement.

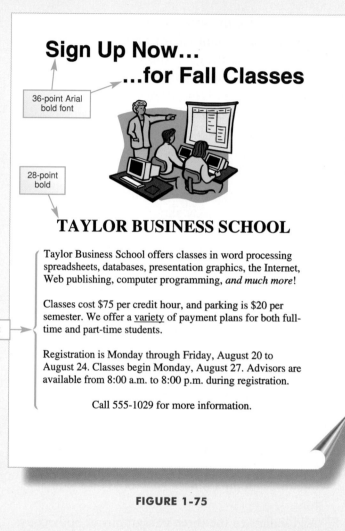

FIGURE 1-75

In the Lab

3 Creating an Announcement with Resized Clip Art and a Bulleted List

Problem: You are the secretary of The Computer Club at your school. One of your responsibilities is to announce the monthly meetings. For the February meeting, you prepare the announcement shown in Figure 1-76. *Hint:* Remember, if you make a mistake while formatting the announcement, you can click the Undo button on the Standard toolbar to undo your mistake.

Instructions:

1. Change the font size from 10 to 18.
2. If they are not already showing, display formatting marks.
3. Create the announcement shown in Figure 1-76. Enter the document first without the clip art and unformatted; that is without any bulleted, bold, underlined, italicized, right-aligned, or centered text. Check spelling as you type.
4. Save the document on a floppy disk with February Announcement as the file name.
5. Format the two lines of the headline to 28-point Arial Rounded MT Bold or a similar font.
6. Right-align the second line of the headline.
7. Center the body title line. Format the body title line to 22-point Courier New bold or a similar font.
8. Add bullets to the three paragraphs of body copy. A **bullet** is a symbol positioned at the beginning of a paragraph. In Word, the default bullet symbol is a small darkened circle. A list of paragraphs with bullets is called a **bulleted list**. *Hint*: Use Help to learn how to add bullets to a list of paragraphs.
9. Bold the date, Monday, February 19, in the first paragraph of the body copy.
10. Italicize the phrase, Word 2000, in the third paragraph of the body copy.
11. Center the last line of the announcement.
12. Insert the graphic of the computer between the headline and the body title line. Search for the text, academic computer, in the Clip Gallery to locate the graphic.
13. Enlarge the graphic of the computer. If you make the graphic too large, the announcement may flow onto two pages. If this occurs, reduce the size of the graphic so the announcement fits on a single page. *Hint*: Use Help to learn about **print preview**, which is a way to see the page before you print it. To exit print preview and return to the document window, click the Close button on the Print Preview toolbar.
14. Center the graphic.
15. Save the announcement again with the same file name.
16. Print the announcement.

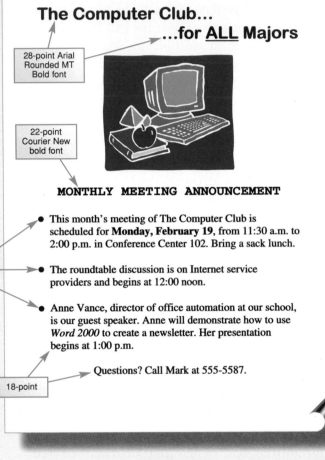

FIGURE 1-76

Cases and Places

The difficulty of these case studies varies:
▶ are the least difficult; ▶▶ are more difficult; and ▶▶▶ are the most difficult.

1 ▶ You have been assigned the task of preparing an announcement for Starport Airlines. The announcement is to contain a graphic of an airplane from the Clip Gallery. Use the following text: first line of headline – Fly With Us…; second line of headline – … We Have Your Ticket; body title – Starport Airlines; first paragraph of body copy – For the month of October, we are offering flights to 25 cities nationwide for the unbelievable rate of $100 per person round trip.; second paragraph of body copy – Take advantage of these low, low rates and make your travel arrangements now for a vacation, a business trip, or a family reunion.; last line – For reservations, call 555-9898. Use the concepts and techniques presented in this project to create and format this announcement. Ask your instructor if you should bullet the list of paragraphs of the body copy.

2 ▶ You have been assigned the task of preparing an announcement for the Lake Shore Carnival. The announcement contains a graphic of a carnival from the Clip Gallery. Use the following text: first line of headline – It's Time…; second line of headline – …for Our Carnival; body title – Lake Shore Carnival; first paragraph of body copy – Join us for fun, food, entertainment, crafts, contests, and rides at the Lake Shore Carnival on the weekend of July 21 and 22.; second paragraph of body copy – Admission is $10 per adult and $5 for children under 10 years old. Gates open at 8:00 a.m. each day and close at midnight.; last line – For information, call 555-9383. Use the concepts and techniques presented in this project to create and format this announcement. Ask your instructor if you should bullet the list of paragraphs of the body copy.

3 ▶▶ Your Uncle John, a graduate of Eagle High School, will be celebrating his twenty-fifth high school reunion this year. He has asked you to prepare an announcement that can be sent to each member of the graduating class. He asks that you include a graphic of the school's mascot, an eagle. The reunion will be held at Fisher Country Club and will feature live entertainment by The Jazzicians, a local band. The reunion will be held on Saturday, October 27. The doors open at 6:00 p.m. with dinner at 7:00 p.m., followed by entertainment from 8:00 p.m. until 11:00 p.m. Cost is $50 per person. Guests will have the opportunity to reminisce about old times, catch up on current projects, and share future plans. More information can be obtained by calling Sue Nordic at 555-9808. Use the concepts and techniques presented in this project to create the announcement. Ask your instructor if you should bullet the list of paragraphs of the body copy.

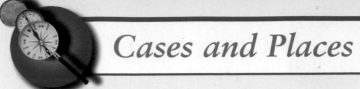

Cases and Places

4 ▶▶ Your parents own a campground called Quiet Oaks. With the new season just around the corner, they have asked you to prepare an announcement for their campground. Located at the intersection of I-293 and SR-35 in southern Louisiana, Quiet Oaks is a secluded campground situated in wooded, rolling hills. It has 75 paved pull-through sites and 46 gravel sites. All have city water and electric hook-ups. Facilities include restrooms, showers, dump, security, laundry, public telephone, and a data port. Recreation includes lake fishing, swimming pool, playground, horseshoes, and a game room. The campground is open from April 1 through October 31. Rates begin at $15 per night. Call 555-9393 for more information. Use the concepts and techniques presented in this project to create the announcement. Be sure to include an appropriate graphic from the Clip Gallery. Ask your instructor if you should bullet the list of paragraphs of the body copy.

5 ▶▶ You have a part-time job as the assistant to the Marketing Director at a new office supply store called Office World. The Director has asked you to prepare an announcement for the store's grand opening. Office World stocks thousands of office products including supplies, furniture, electronics, and computer software. Office World's low price guarantee states it will refund double a customer's money if the customer finds a comparable product for a lower price within ten days of purchase. Customers can purchase at the store, via fax or telephone, or on the Web at www.officeworld.com. Fax number is 555-2982 and telephone number is 555-2983. For purchases over $45.00, delivery is free. For a catalog, customers or potential customers can call 555-2900. Use the concepts and techniques presented in this project to create the announcement. Be sure to include an appropriate graphic from the Clip Gallery. Ask your instructor if you should bullet the list of paragraphs of the body copy.

6 ▶▶▶ Schools, churches, libraries, grocery stores, and other public places have bulletin boards for announcements and other postings. Often, these bulletin boards have so many announcements that some go unnoticed. At one of the above-mentioned organizations, find a posted announcement that you think might be overlooked. Copy the text from the announcement. Using this text, together with the techniques presented in this project, create an announcement that would be more likely to catch a reader's eye. Format the announcement effectively and include a bulleted list and suitable graphic from the Clip Gallery.

7 ▶▶▶ Advertisements are a company's way of announcing products or services to the public. You can find advertisements in printed media such as newspapers and magazines. Many companies also advertise on the World Wide Web. Find a printed advertisement or one on the Web that you feel lacks luster. Copy the text from the announcement. Using this text, together with the techniques presented in this project, create an announcement that would be more likely to catch a reader's eye. Format the announcement effectively and include a bulleted list and suitable graphic from the Clip Gallery.

Microsoft **Word 2000**

Microsoft Word 2000

P R O J E C T

2

Creating a
Research Paper

O B J E C T I V E S

You will have mastered the material in this project
when you can:

● Describe the MLA documentation style for
  research papers
● Change the margin settings in a document
● Adjust line spacing in a document
● Use a header to number pages of a document
● Enter text using Click and Type
● Apply formatting using shortcut keys
● Indent paragraphs
● Use Word's AutoCorrect feature
● Add a footnote to a research paper
● Modify a style
● Insert a symbol automatically
● Insert a manual page break
● Create a hanging indent
● Create a hyperlink
● Sort selected paragraphs
● Go to a specific location in a document
● Find and replace text
● Move text
● Find a synonym for a word
● Count the words in a document
● Check spelling and grammar at once
● Display the Web site associated with a hyperlink
● E-mail a copy of a document

Elvis and Aliens Abound

Research Net Sources Carefu

The checkout line at your local grocery store is longer than the conga line at your best friend's wedding. You grab a cola and a bag of pretzels off the strategically placed displays. Then, as you shuffle to the registers, you decide to peruse the headlines of the magazines on display. You learn that two-headed aliens have abducted Elvis, that researchers are coming closer to finding a cure for the common cold, and that the Chicago Cubs are in contention for the National League pennant. Which stories do you believe? And what criteria do you use to make these decisions?

These questions are relevant not only at the grocery store but also in the computer lab. When you sit down and surf the Internet for the latest news, celebrity sightings, sports scores, and reference sources, you make decisions on which sites to visit and which sites to avoid.

Not so long ago, students relied on books and magazines in the library for the bulk of their research material. These permanent sources were professionally evaluated and edited. Not so with the Internet. The Net is chock full of everything from reliable research to fictitious opinions. No one performs quality control checks to verify accuracy and reliability. Anyone can build a Web site and fill it with any content imaginable. And this content can be updated before your eyes.

In this project, you will create a research paper on the topic of Web publishing, which is the method of developing, maintaining, and posting Web pages. You will include a hyperlink that will permit you to navigate to a specific Internet site. Your Works Cited page will list the three sources used to obtain information for the paper. Two of these sources are books; one is an article available on the Shelly Cashman Series Web site

(www.scsite.com). How can you judge the reliability of these materials, particularly the article posted on the Web? Just remember the three S's: structure, source, and style.

Structure – Does the information seem objective or biased? Are authorities used as sources? When was the site created or updated? Is a contact person listed so you can verify information? Are working hyperlinks provided that refer you to additional sources?

Source – Examine the Web address to find out the site's sponsor. Is it a nonprofit organization (.org), a school (.edu), the government (.gov), or a commercial business (.com)? Is the purpose of the site to provide information or to make a profit?

Style – Does the site look organized and professional? Can you navigate easily with a minimum of mouse clicks? Does it contain an index and the capability of searching for specific information?

William Miller, a former president of the Association of College and Research Libraries, says that on the Web, "Much of what purports to be serious information is simply junk – not current, objective, or trustworthy." And by following the three S's, you will be able to decide that neither Elvis's abduction nor the Cubs's pennant seems likely.

Microsoft Word 2000

Creating a Research Paper

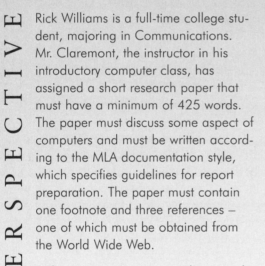

PROJECT

2

CASE PERSPECTIVE

Rick Williams is a full-time college student, majoring in Communications. Mr. Claremont, the instructor in his introductory computer class, has assigned a short research paper that must have a minimum of 425 words. The paper must discuss some aspect of computers and must be written according to the MLA documentation style, which specifies guidelines for report preparation. The paper must contain one footnote and three references – one of which must be obtained from the World Wide Web.

Rick's Internet service provider recently announced that all subscribers are entitled to 6 MB of free Web space for a personal Web page. Rick plans to publish his own Web page, so he decides to write the research paper on Web publishing. Rick intends to review computer magazines at the school's library, surf the Internet, contact his Internet service provider, and interview the Webmaster at his school for information on Web publishing. He also plans to use the Internet to obtain the guidelines for the MLA style of documentation. Because you are familiar with the Internet, Rick has asked you to assist him with the Web searches.

Introduction

In both academic and business environments, you will be asked to write reports. Business reports range from proposals to cost justifications to five-year plans to research findings. Academic reports focus mostly on research findings. Whether you are writing a business report or an academic report, you should follow a standard style when preparing it.

Many different styles of documentation exist for report preparation, depending on the nature of the report. Each style requires the same basic information; the differences among styles appear in the manner of presenting the information. For example, one documentation style may use the term *bibliography*, whereas another uses *references*, and yet a third prefers *works cited*. Two popular documentation styles for research papers are the **MLA** (**Modern Language Association of America**) and **APA** (**American Psychological Association**) styles. This project uses the MLA documentation style.

Project Two – Web Publishing Research Paper

Project 2 illustrates the creation of a short research paper describing Web publishing. As shown in Figure 2-1, the paper follows the MLA documentation style. The first two pages present the research paper and the third page lists the works cited alphabetically.

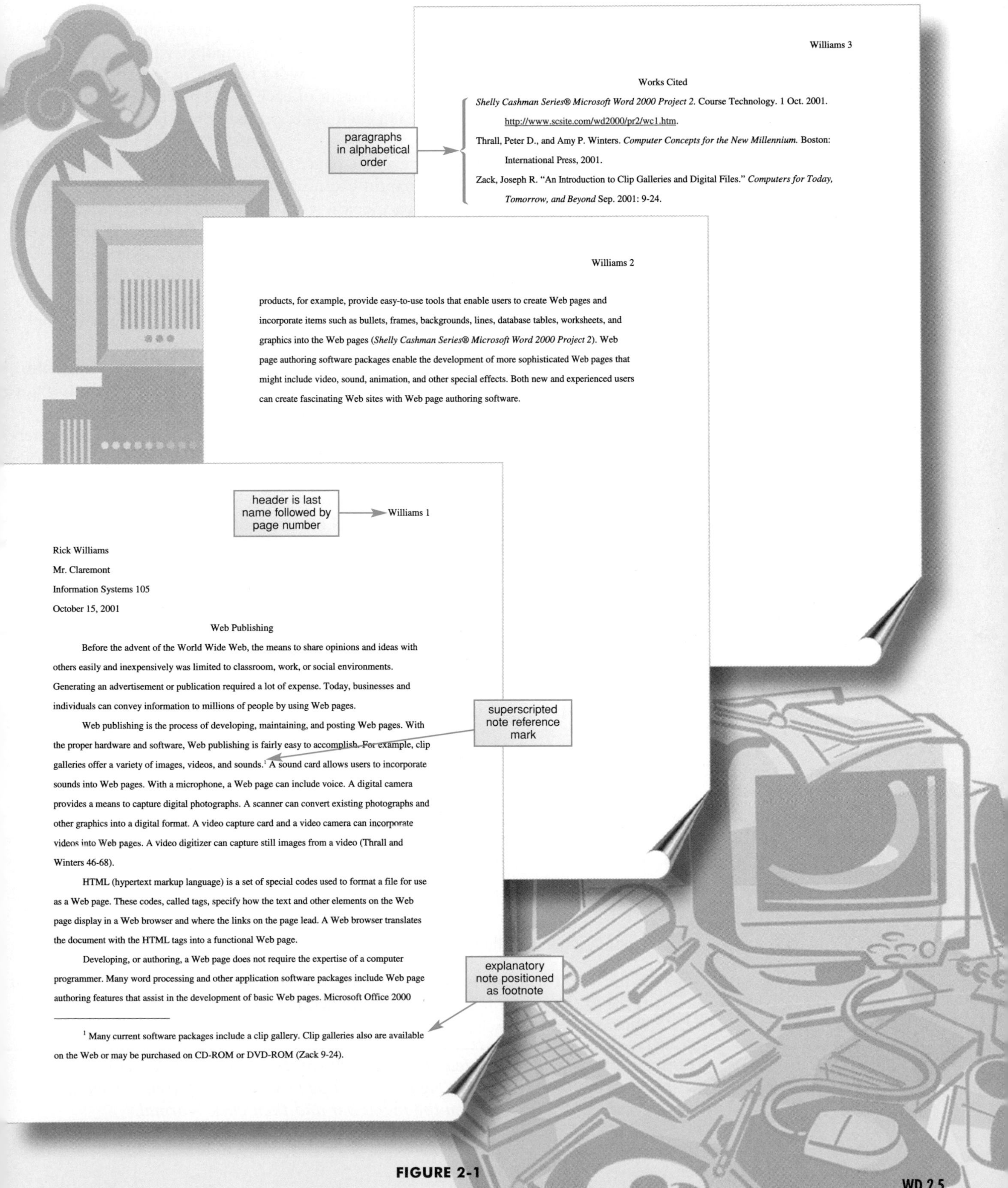

Williams 3

Works Cited

Shelly Cashman Series® Microsoft Word 2000 Project 2. Course Technology. 1 Oct. 2001.

http://www.scsite.com/wd2000/pr2/wc1.htm.

paragraphs in alphabetical order →

Thrall, Peter D., and Amy P. Winters. *Computer Concepts for the New Millennium.* Boston:

International Press, 2001.

Zack, Joseph R. "An Introduction to Clip Galleries and Digital Files." *Computers for Today,*

Tomorrow, and Beyond Sep. 2001: 9-24.

Williams 2

products, for example, provide easy-to-use tools that enable users to create Web pages and

incorporate items such as bullets, frames, backgrounds, lines, database tables, worksheets, and

graphics into the Web pages (*Shelly Cashman Series® Microsoft Word 2000 Project 2*). Web

page authoring software packages enable the development of more sophisticated Web pages that

might include video, sound, animation, and other special effects. Both new and experienced users

can create fascinating Web sites with Web page authoring software.

header is last name followed by page number → Williams 1

Rick Williams

Mr. Claremont

Information Systems 105

October 15, 2001

Web Publishing

Before the advent of the World Wide Web, the means to share opinions and ideas with

others easily and inexpensively was limited to classroom, work, or social environments.

Generating an advertisement or publication required a lot of expense. Today, businesses and

individuals can convey information to millions of people by using Web pages.

Web publishing is the process of developing, maintaining, and posting Web pages. With

the proper hardware and software, Web publishing is fairly easy to accomplish. For example, clip

superscripted note reference mark

galleries offer a variety of images, videos, and sounds.[1] A sound card allows users to incorporate

sounds into Web pages. With a microphone, a Web page can include voice. A digital camera

provides a means to capture digital photographs. A scanner can convert existing photographs and

other graphics into a digital format. A video capture card and a video camera can incorporate

videos into Web pages. A video digitizer can capture still images from a video (Thrall and

Winters 46-68).

HTML (hypertext markup language) is a set of special codes used to format a file for use

as a Web page. These codes, called tags, specify how the text and other elements on the Web

page display in a Web browser and where the links on the page lead. A Web browser translates

the document with the HTML tags into a functional Web page.

Developing, or authoring, a Web page does not require the expertise of a computer

programmer. Many word processing and other application software packages include Web page

explanatory note positioned as footnote

authoring features that assist in the development of basic Web pages. Microsoft Office 2000

---

[1] Many current software packages include a clip gallery. Clip galleries also are available

on the Web or may be purchased on CD-ROM or DVD-ROM (Zack 9-24).

FIGURE 2-1

MLA and APA

The MLA documentation style is the standard in the humanities, and the APA style is preferred in the social sciences. For more information from the MLA about its guidelines, visit the Word 2000 More About Web page (www.scsite.com/wd2000/more.htm) and then click MLA. For more information from the APA about its guidelines, visit the Word 2000 More About Web page (www.scsite.com/wd2000/more.htm) and then click APA.

APA Style

In the APA style, double-space all pages of the paper with 1.5" top, bottom, left, and right margins. Indent the first word of each paragraph .5" from the left margin. In the upper-right margin of each page, place a running head that consists of the page number double-spaced below a summary of the paper title.

MLA Documentation Style

When writing papers, you should adhere to some style of documentation. The research paper in this project follows the guidelines presented by the MLA. To follow the MLA style, double-space text on all pages of the paper with one-inch top, bottom, left, and right margins. Indent the first word of each paragraph one-half inch from the left margin. At the right margin of each page, place a page number one-half inch from the top margin. On each page, precede the page number by your last name.

The MLA style does not require a title page; instead, place your name and course information in a block at the left margin beginning one inch from the top of the page. Center the title one double-space below your name and course information.

In the body of the paper, place author references in parentheses with the page number(s) where the referenced information is located. The MLA style uses these in-text **parenthetical citations** instead of footnoting each source at the bottom of the page or at the end of the paper. In the MLA style, footnotes are used only for explanatory notes. In the body of the paper, use **superscripts** (raised numbers) for **note reference marks**, which signal that an explanatory note exists.

According to the MLA style, explanatory notes are optional. **Explanatory notes** are used to elaborate on points discussed in the body of the paper. Explanatory notes may be placed either at the bottom of the page as footnotes or at the end of the paper as endnotes. Double-space the explanatory notes. Superscript each note reference mark, and indent it one-half inch from the left margin. Place one space following the note reference mark before beginning the note text. At the end of the note text, you may list bibliographic information for further reference.

The MLA style uses the term **works cited** for the bibliographical references. The works cited page alphabetically lists works that are referenced directly in the paper by each author's last name, or, if the author's name is not available, by the title of the work. Place the works cited on a separate numbered page. Center the title, Works Cited, one inch from the top margin. Double-space all lines. Begin the first line of each entry at the left margin; indent subsequent lines of the same entry one-half inch from the left margin.

Starting Word

Follow these steps to start Word or ask your instructor how to start Word for your system.

TO START WORD

 Click the Start button on the taskbar.

2 Click New Office Document on the Start menu. If necessary, click the General tab when the New Office Document dialog box first displays.

3 Double-click the Blank Document icon in the General sheet.

4 If the Word window is not maximized, double-click its title bar to maximize it. If the Office Assistant displays, right-click it and then click Hide on the shortcut menu.

Office starts Word. After a few moments, an empty document titled Document1 displays in the Word window (Figure 2-2 on page WD 2.8). If your screen differs from Figure 2-2, click View on the menu bar and then click Normal.

Resetting Menus and Toolbars

To set the menus and toolbars so they appear exactly as shown in this book, you should reset your menus and toolbars as outlined in Appendix C or follow these steps.

TO RESET MENUS AND TOOLBARS

1 Click View on the menu bar and then point to Toolbars. Click Customize on the Toolbars submenu.

2 When the Customize dialog box displays, click the Options tab, make sure the top three check boxes have check marks and then click the Reset my usage data button. When the Microsoft Word dialog box displays, click the Yes button.

3 Click the Toolbars tab. Click Standard in the Toolbars list and then click the Reset button. When the Reset Toolbar dialog box displays, click the OK button.

4 Click Formatting in the Toolbars list and then click the Reset button. When the Reset Toolbar dialog box displays, click the OK button. Click the Close button.

Word resets the menus and toolbars.

Displaying Formatting Marks

As discussed Project 1, it is helpful to display **formatting marks** that indicate where in the document you pressed the ENTER key, SPACEBAR, and other keys. Follow this step to display formatting marks.

TO DISPLAY FORMATTING MARKS

1 Double-click the move handle on the Standard toolbar to display the entire toolbar. If the Show/Hide ¶ button on the Standard toolbar is not already recessed, click it.

Word displays formatting marks in the document window, and the Show/Hide ¶ button on the Standard toolbar is recessed (Figure 2-2 on the next page).

Changing the Margins

Word is preset to use standard 8.5-by-11-inch paper, with 1.25-inch left and right margins and 1-inch top and bottom margins. These margin settings affect every page in the document. Often, you may want to change these default margin settings. You have learned that the MLA documentation style requires one-inch top, bottom, left, and right margins throughout the paper.

The steps on the next page illustrate how to change the margin settings for a document when your screen is in normal view. To verify your screen is in normal view, click View on the menu bar and then click Normal.

Writing Papers

The World Wide Web contains a host of information, tips, and suggestions on writing research papers. College professors and fellow students develop many of these Web pages. For a list of Web links to sites on writing research papers, visit the Word 2000 More About Web page (www.scsite.com/wd2000/more.htm) and then click Links to Sites on Writing Research Papers.

Changing Margins

In print layout view, you can change margins using the horizontal and vertical rulers. Current margin settings are shaded in gray. The margin boundary is located where the gray meets the white. To change a margin, drag the margin boundary. Hold down the ALT key while dragging the margin boundary to display the margin settings.

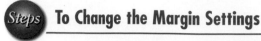

To Change the Margin Settings

1 **Click File on the menu bar and then point to Page Setup (Figure 2-2).**

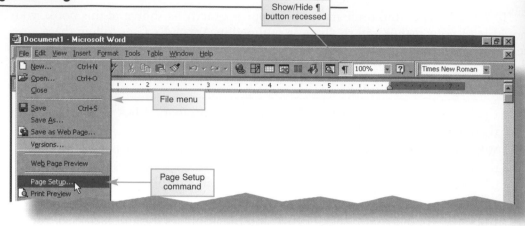

FIGURE 2-2

2 **Click Page Setup. If necessary, click the Margins tab when the Page Setup dialog box first displays.**

Word displays the Page Setup dialog box (Figure 2-3). Word lists the current margin settings in the text boxes.

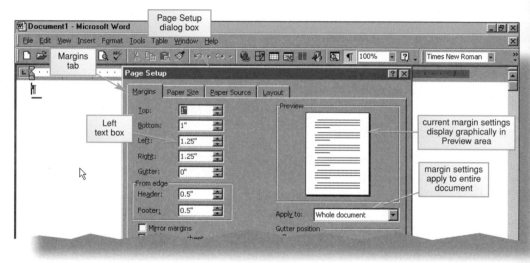

FIGURE 2-3

3 **Drag through the text in the Left text box to highlight 1.25". Type 1 and then press the TAB key. Type 1 and then point to the OK button.**

The new left and right margin settings are 1 inch (Figure 2-4).

4 **Click the OK button.**

Word changes the left and right margins.

Other **Ways**

1. In print layout view, drag margin boundary(s) on ruler

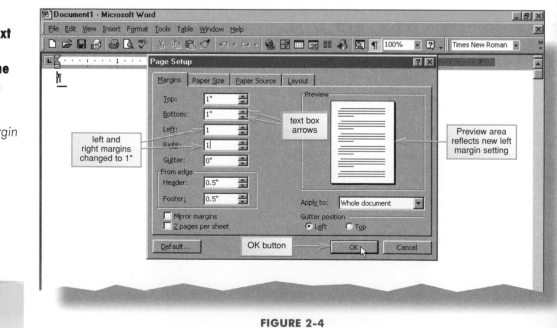

FIGURE 2-4

The new margin settings take effect in the document immediately, and Word uses these margins for the entire document.

When you change the margin settings in the text boxes in the Page Setup dialog box, the Preview area (Figure 2-4) does not adjust to reflect a changed margin setting until the insertion point leaves the respective text box. That is, you must press the TAB or ENTER key or click in another text box if you want to view the changes in the Preview area.

Zooming Page Width

As you learned in Project 1, when you **zoom page width**, Word displays text on the screen as large as possible without extending the right margin beyond the right edge of the document window. Perform the following steps to zoom page width.

TO ZOOM PAGE WIDTH

1. Click the Zoom box arrow on the Standard toolbar.

2. Click Page Width in the Zoom list.

Word extends the right margin to the right edge of the document window (Figure 2-5). Word computes the zoom percentage based on a variety of settings. Your percentage may be different depending on your system configuration.

Adjusting Line Spacing

Line spacing is the amount of vertical space between lines of text in a document. Word, by default, single-spaces between lines of text and automatically adjusts line height to accommodate various font sizes and graphics. The MLA documentation style requires that you **double-space** the entire paper; that is, one blank line should display between each line of text. Thus, you must adjust the line spacing from single to double as described in the following steps.

More About

Line Spacing

Sometimes, the top of characters or a graphic is chopped off. This occurs when the line spacing is set to Exactly. To remedy the problem, change the line spacing to Single, 1.5 lines, Double, or At least in the Paragraph dialog box, all of which accommodate the largest font or graphic.

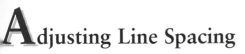 **To Double-Space a Document**

1. **Right-click the paragraph mark above the end mark in the document window. Point to Paragraph on the shortcut menu (Figure 2-5).**

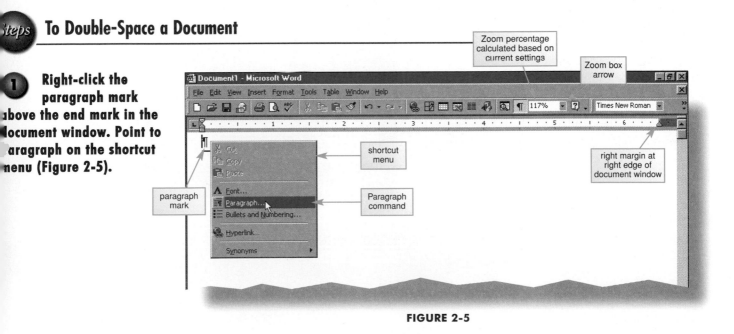

FIGURE 2-5

2 **Click Paragraph. If necessary, click the Indents and Spacing tab when the Paragraph dialog box first displays. Click the Line spacing box arrow and then point to Double.**

Word displays the Paragraph dialog box, which lists the current settings in the text boxes and displays them graphically in the Preview area (Figure 2-6). A list of available line spacing options displays.

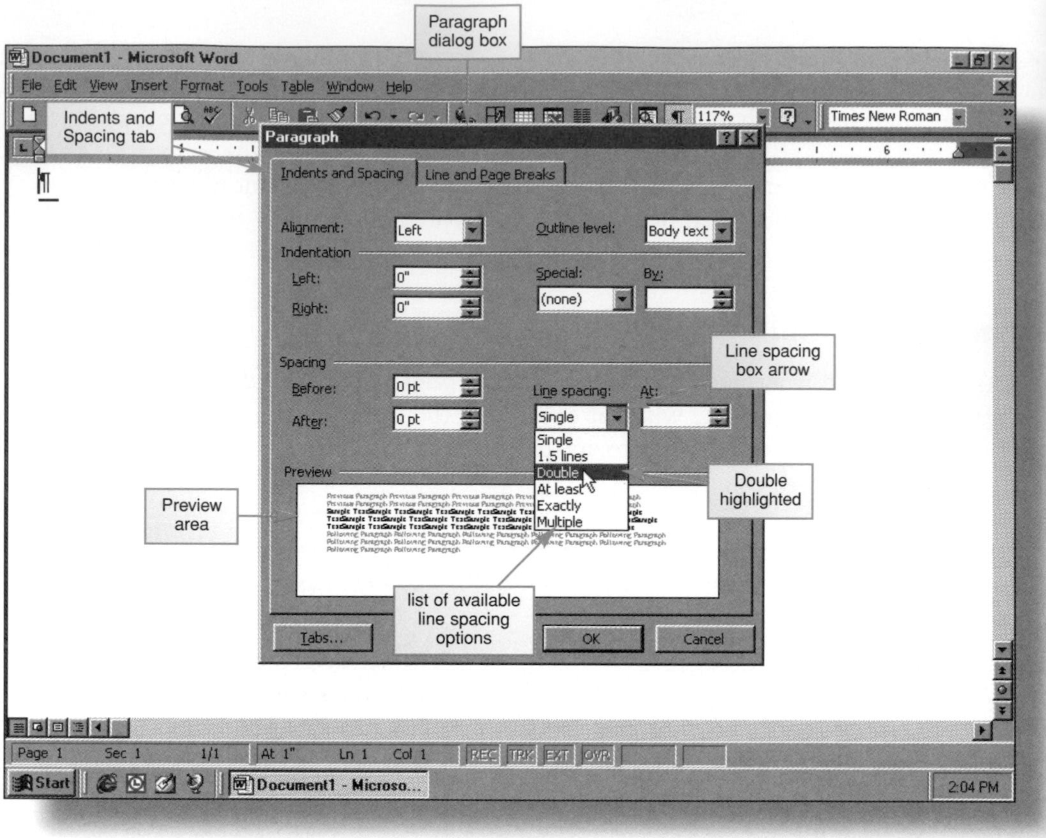

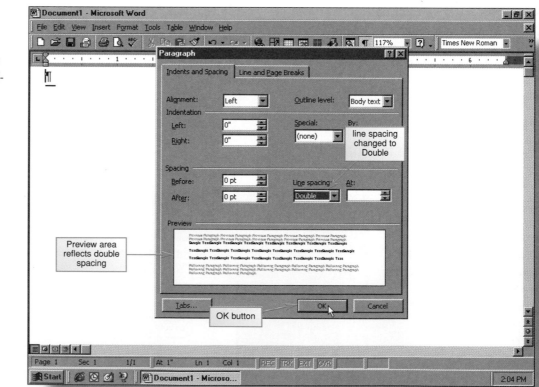

FIGURE 2-6

3 **Click Double. Point to the OK button.**

Word displays Double in the Line spacing box and graphically portrays the new line spacing in the Preview area (Figure 2-7).

FIGURE 2-7

④ Click the OK button.

Word changes the line spacing to double in the current document (Figure 2-8).

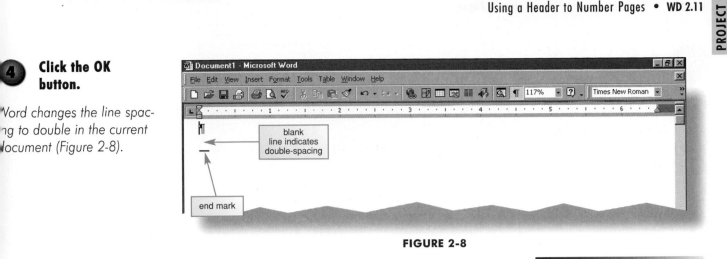

FIGURE 2-8

Notice that when line spacing is double (Figure 2-8), the end mark is positioned one blank line below the insertion point.

The Line spacing list (Figure 2-6) contains a variety of settings for the line spacing. The default, Single, and the options 1.5 lines and Double instruct Word to adjust line spacing automatically to accommodate the largest font or graphic on a line. The next two options, At least and Exactly, enable you to specify a line spacing not provided in the first three options. The difference is that the At least option instructs Word to increase the designation if necessary, whereas the Exactly option does not allow Word to increase the specification to accommodate larger fonts or graphics. With the last option, Multiple, you enter a value, which represents a percentage by which Word should increase or decrease the line spacing. For example, with the number 1 representing single-spacing, a multiple of 1.3 increases the line spacing by 30 percent and a multiple of .8 decreases the line spacing by 20 percent.

Using a Header to Number Pages

In Word, you can number pages easily by clicking Insert on the menu bar and then clicking Page Numbers. Using the Page Numbers command, you can specify the location (top or bottom of page) and alignment (right, left, or centered) of the page numbers. You cannot, however, place your name as required by the MLA style in front of the page number with the Page Numbers command. To place your name in front of the page number, you must create a header that contains the page number.

Headers and Footers

A **header** is text you want printed at the top of each page in the document. A **footer** is text you want printed at the bottom of every page. In Word, headers are printed in the top margin one-half inch from the top of every page, and footers are printed in the bottom margin one-half inch from the bottom of each page, which meets the MLA style. Headers and footers can include text and graphics, as well as the page number, total number of pages, current date, and current time.

In this project, you are to precede the page number with your last name placed one-half inch from the top of each page. Your name and the page number should print right-aligned; that is, at the right margin.

To create the header, first you display the header area in the document window and then you can enter the header text into the header area. Use the procedures on the following pages to create the header with page numbers according to the MLA documentation style.

Other Ways

1. On Format menu click Paragraph, click Indents and Spacing tab, click Line spacing box arrow, click Double, click OK button
2. Press CTRL+2

More About

Data and Statistics

When researching for a paper, you may need to access data, graphs of data, or perform statistical computations on data. For more information on statistical formulas and available data and graphs, visit the Word 2000 More About Web page (www.scsite.com/wd2000/more.htm) and then click Data and Statistics.

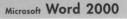
 Steps **To Display the Header Area**

① **Click View on the menu bar and then point to Header and Footer (Figure 2-9).**

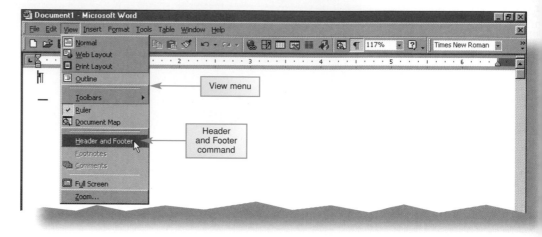

FIGURE 2-9

② **Click Header and Footer.**

*Word switches from normal view to print layout view and displays the **Header and Footer toolbar** (Figure 2-10). You type header text in the **header area**.*

FIGURE 2-10

Print Layout View

You also can switch to print layout view by clicking the Print Layout View button on the horizontal scroll bar. Print layout view shows the positioning of headers, footers, and footnotes. To move forward or backward an entire page, click the double arrows on the bottom of the vertical scroll bar.

The Header and Footer toolbar initially floats in the document window. To move a floating toolbar, drag its title bar. You can **dock**, or attach, a floating toolbar below the Standard and Formatting toolbars by double-clicking the floating toolbar's title bar. To move a docked toolbar, drag its move handle. Recall that the move handle is the vertical bar to the left of the first button on a toolbar. If you drag a floating toolbar to an edge of the window, the toolbar snaps to the edge of the window. If you drag a docked toolbar to the middle of the window, the toolbar floats in the Word window. If you double-click between two buttons or boxes on a docked toolbar, it floats in its original floating position.

The header area does not display on the screen when the document window is in normal view because it tends to clutter the screen. To display the header in the document window with the rest of the text, you must display the document in print preview, which is discussed in a later project, or switch to print layout view. When you click the Header and Footer command on the View menu, Word automatically switches to **print layout view**, which displays the document exactly as it will print.

Entering Text using Click and Type

When in print layout view, you can use **Click and Type** to format and enter text, graphics, and other items. To use Click and Type, you double-click a blank area of the document window. Word automatically formats the item you enter according to the location where you double-click. Perform the following steps to use Click and Type to right-align and then enter the last name into the header area.

Steps To Click and Type

1. **Point to right edge of the header area so a right-align icon displays next to the I-beam.**

   As you move the *Click and Type pointer* around the window, the icon changes to represent formatting that will be applied if you double-click at that location (Figure 2-11).

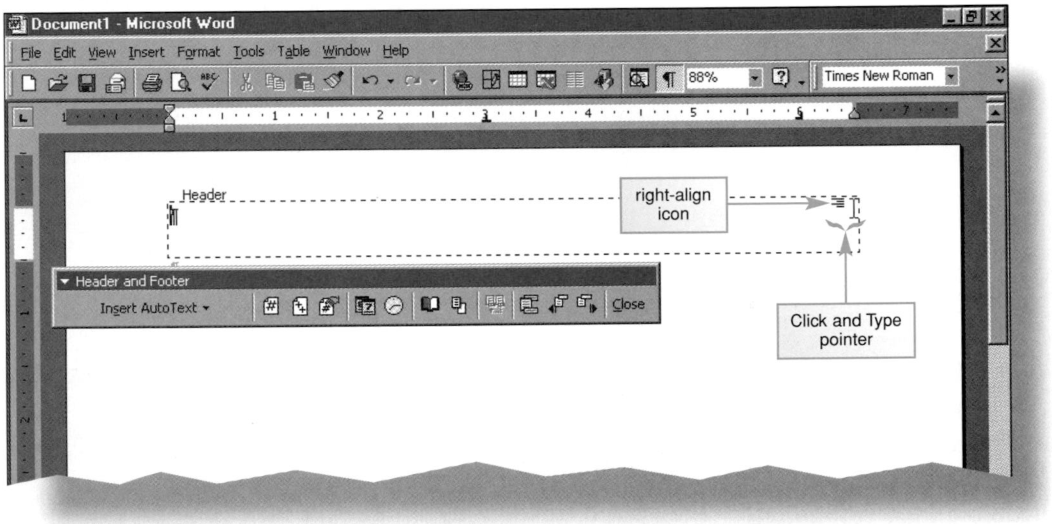

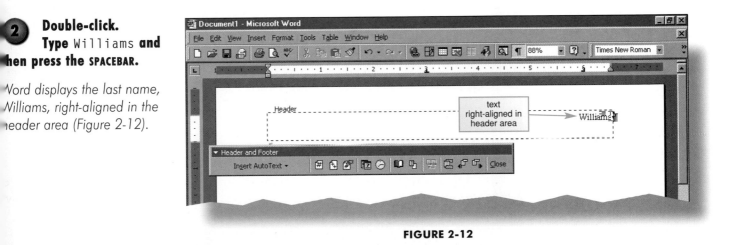

right-align icon

Click and Type pointer

FIGURE 2-11

2. **Double-click. Type** Williams **and then press the SPACEBAR.**

   Word displays the last name, Williams, right-aligned in the header area (Figure 2-12).

Header

text right-aligned in header area

Williams

FIGURE 2-12

The next step is to enter the page number into the header area and then format it.

Entering a Page Number into the Header

Word formats the text in the header area using the current font size. Perform the steps on the next page to enter a page number into the header area and then, if necessary, format the entire line of text to 12 point.

To Enter and Format a Page Number

1 **Click the Insert Page Number button on the Header and Footer toolbar.**

Word displays the page number 1 in the header area (Figure 2-13).

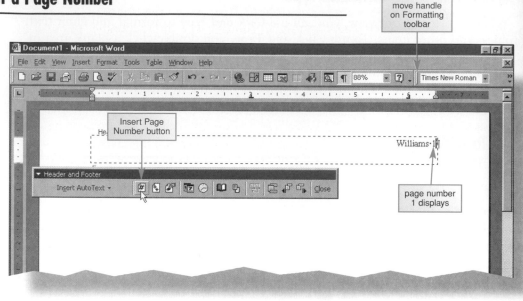

FIGURE 2-13

2 **Select the text, Williams 1, by dragging through it. Double-click the move handle on the Formatting toolbar to display the entire toolbar. If necessary, click the Font Size box arrow on the Formatting toolbar and then click 12 (Figure 2-14).**

3 **Click the Close Header and Footer button on the Header and Footer toolbar.**

Word closes the Header and Footer toolbar and returns the screen to normal view (see Figure 2-15 on page WD 2.16).

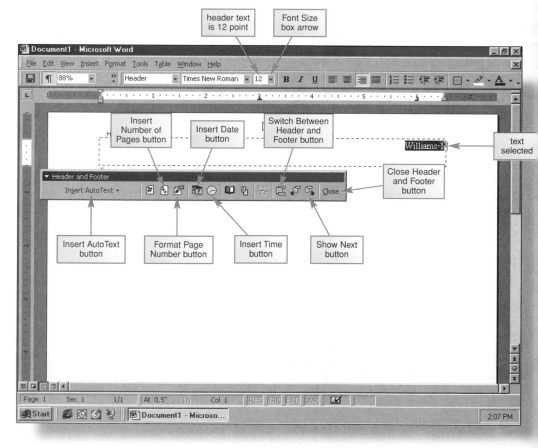

FIGURE 2-14

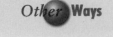 **Ways**

1. On Insert menu click Page Numbers, click OK button

Just as the Insert Page Number button on the Header and Footer toolbar inserts the page number into the document, three other buttons on the Header and Footer toolbar (Figure 2-14) insert items into the document. The Insert Number of Pages button inserts the total number of pages in the document; the Insert Date button inserts the current date into the document; and the Insert Time button inserts the current time.

To edit an existing header, you can follow the same procedure that you use to create a new header. That is, click View on the menu bar and then click Header and Footer to display the header area; or switch to print layout view by clicking the Print Layout View button on the horizontal scroll bar and then double-click the dimmed header. If you have multiple headers, click the Show Next button on the Header and Footer toolbar (Figure 2-14) until the appropriate header displays in the header area. Edit the header as you would any Word text and then click the Close Header and Footer button on the Header and Footer toolbar.

To create a footer, click View on the menu bar, click Header and Footer, click the Switch Between Header and Footer button on the Header and Footer toolbar, and then follow the same procedure as you would to create a header.

Typing the Body of the Research Paper

The body of the research paper encompasses the first two pages in Figure 2-1 on page WD 2.5. The steps on the following pages illustrate how to enter the body of the research paper.

Changing the Default Font Size

You learned in Project 1 that depending on how Word 2000 was installed on your computer, your default font size might be either 10 or 12. A font size of 10 point is difficult for some people to read. In this project, all characters in all paragraphs should be a font size of 12. If your default font size is 10, perform the following steps to change it to 12.

TO CHANGE THE DEFAULT FONT SIZE

1 If necessary, click the Font Size box arrow on the Formatting toolbar.

2 Click 12.

Word changes the font size to 12 (Figure 2-15 on the next page).

Entering Name and Course Information

You have learned that the MLA style does not require a separate title page for research papers. Instead, place your name and course information in a block at the top of the page at the left margin. Thus, follow the step on the next page to begin entering the body of the research paper.

More About

Writing Papers

When preparing to write a paper, many students take notes to keep track of information. One method is to summarize, or condense, the information. Another is to paraphrase, or rewrite the information in your own words. A third method is to quote, or record, the exact words of the original. Be sure to use quotation marks when directly quoting a source.

More About

APA Guidelines

APA guidelines require a title page as a separate page of a research paper, instead of placing name and course information on the paper's first page. The running head (a brief summary of the title and the page number) also is on the title page, along with the page number 1.

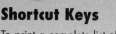 **To Enter Name and Course Information**

1 **Type** Rick Williams **and then press the ENTER key. Type** Mr. Claremont **and then press the ENTER key. Type** Information Systems 105 **and then press the ENTER key. Type** October 15, 2001 **and then press the ENTER key.**

The student name displays on line 1, the professor name on line 2, the course name on line 3, and the paper due date on line 4 (Figure 2-15).

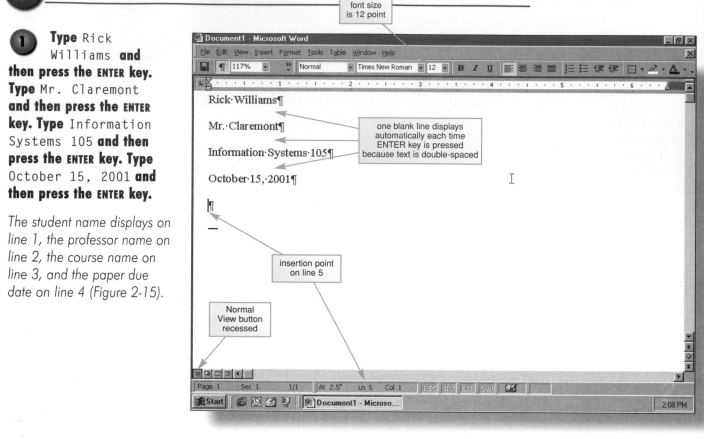

FIGURE 2-15

Notice in Figure 2-15 that the insertion point currently is on line 5. Each time you press the ENTER key, Word advances two lines on the screen, but increments the line counter on the status bar by only one because earlier you set line spacing to double.

If you watch the screen as you type, you may have noticed that as you typed the first few characters in the month, Octo, Word displayed the **AutoComplete tip**, October, above the characters. To save typing, you could press the ENTER key while the AutoComplete tip displays, which instructs Word to place the text of the AutoComplete tip at the location of your typing.

Applying Formatting Using Shortcut Keys

The next step is to enter the title of the research paper centered between the page margins. As you type text, you may want to format paragraphs and characters as you type them, instead of entering them and then formatting them later. In Project 1, you typed the characters in the document and then selected the ones to be formatted and applied the desired formatting using toolbar buttons. When your fingers are already on the keyboard, it sometimes is more efficient to use **shortcut keys**, or key z board key combinations, to format text as you type it. Perform the following steps to center a paragraph with the CTRL+E keys and then left-align a paragraph with the CTRL+L keys. (Recall from Project 1 that a notation such as CTRL+E means to press the letter E while holding the CTRL key.)

To Use Shortcut Keys to Format Text

1 Press the **CTRL + E** keys. Type Web Publishing and then press the ENTER key.

Word centers the title between the left and right margins (Figure 2-16). The paragraph mark and insertion point are centered because the formatting specified in the previous paragraph is carried forward to the next paragraph.

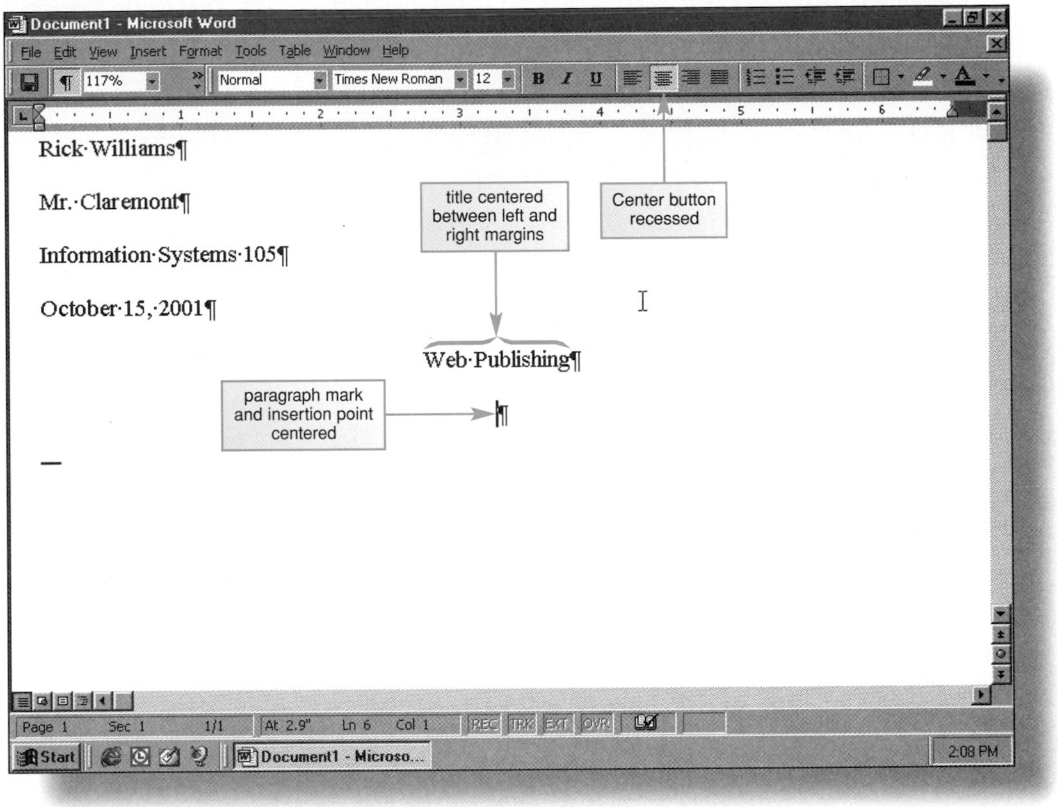

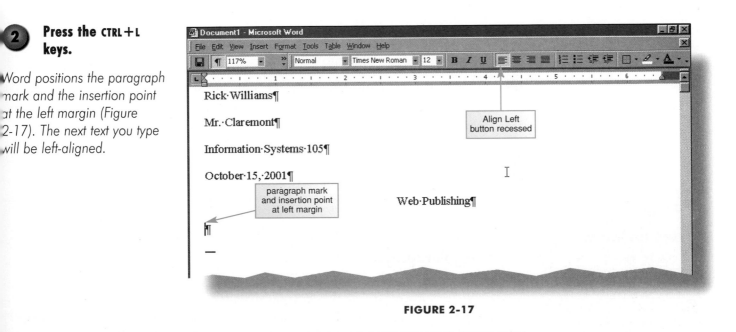

FIGURE 2-16

2 Press the **CTRL + L** keys.

Word positions the paragraph mark and the insertion point at the left margin (Figure 2-17). The next text you type will be left-aligned.

FIGURE 2-17

Word has many shortcut keys for your convenience while typing. Table 2-1 on the next page lists the common shortcut keys for formatting characters, and Table 2-2 on the next page lists common shortcut keys for formatting paragraphs.

Table 2-1 Shortcut Keys for Formatting Characters	
CHARACTER FORMATTING TASK	SHORTCUT KEYS
All capital letters	CTRL+SHIFT+A
Bold	CTRL+B
Case of letters	SHIFT+F3
Decrease font size	CTRL+SHIFT+<
Decrease font size 1 point	CTRL+[
Double-underline	CTRL+SHIFT+D
Increase font size	CTRL+SHIFT+>
Increase font size 1 point	CTRL+]
Italic	CTRL+I
Remove character formatting (plain text)	CTRL+SPACEBAR
Small uppercase letters	CTRL+SHIFT+K
Subscript	CTRL+=
Superscript	CTRL+SHIFT+PLUS SIGN
Underline	CTRL+U
Underline words, not spaces	CTRL+SHIFT+W

Table 2-2 Shortcut Keys for Formatting Paragraphs	
PARAGRAPH FORMATTING TASK	SHORTCUT KEYS
1.5 line spacing	CTRL+5
Add/remove one line above	CTRL+0
Center paragraph	CTRL+E
Decrease paragraph indent	CTRL+SHIFT+M
Double-space lines	CTRL+2
Hanging indent	CTRL+T
Increase paragraph indent	CTRL+M
Justify paragraph	CTRL+J
Left-align paragraph	CTRL+L
Remove hanging indent	CTRL+SHIFT+T
Remove paragraph formatting	CTRL+Q
Right-align paragraph	CTRL+R
Single-space lines	CTRL+1

Saving the Research Paper

You should save your research paper. For a detailed example of the procedure summarized below, refer to pages WD 1.26 through WD 1.28 in Project 1.

TO SAVE A DOCUMENT

1 Insert your floppy disk into drive A.

2 Double-click the move handle on the Standard toolbar to display the entire toolbar. Click the Save button on the Standard toolbar.

3 Type the file name Web Publishing Paper in the File name text box.

4 Click the Save in box arrow and then click 3½ Floppy (A:).

5 Click the Save button in the Save As dialog box.

Word saves your document with the name Web Publishing Paper (Figure 2-18).

First-Line Indent

You may be tempted to use the TAB key to indent the first line of each paragraph in your research paper. Using the TAB key for this task is inefficient because you must press it each time you begin a new paragraph. First-line indent is a paragraph format; thus, it is carried forward automatically each time you press the ENTER key.

Indenting Paragraphs

According to the MLA style, the first line of each paragraph in the research paper is to be indented one-half inch from the left margin. This procedure, called **first-line indent**, can be accomplished using the horizontal ruler. The **First Line Indent marker** is the top triangle at the 0" mark on the ruler (Figure 2-18). The small square at the 0" mark is the **Left Indent marker**. The Left Indent marker is used to change the entire left margin, whereas the First Line Indent marker affects only the first line of the paragraph. Perform the following steps to first-line indent Word paragraphs in the research paper.

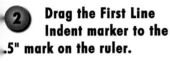

Steps **To First-Line Indent Paragraphs**

1 With the insertion point on the paragraph mark in line 6, point to the First Line Indent marker on the ruler (Figure 2-18).

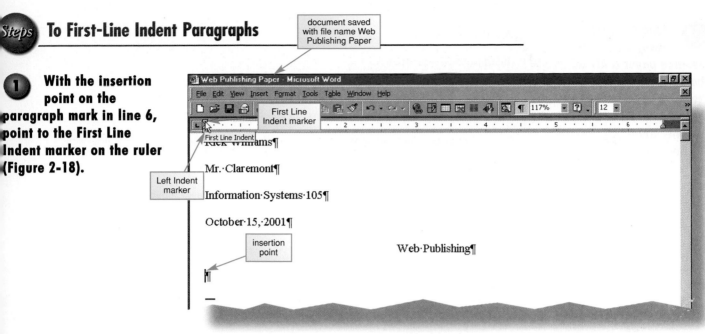

FIGURE 2-18

2 Drag the First Line Indent marker to the .5" mark on the ruler.

As you drag the mouse, a vertical dotted line displays in the document window, indicating the proposed location of the first line of the paragraph (Figure 2-19).

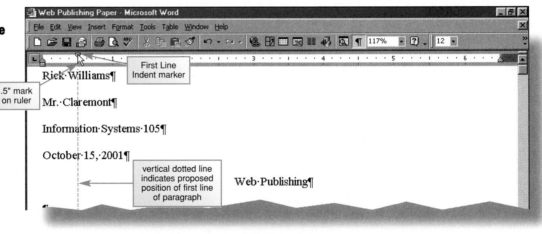

FIGURE 2-19

3 Release the mouse button.

The First Line Indent marker displays at the .5" mark on the ruler, or one-half inch from the left margin (Figure 2-20). The paragraph mark containing the insertion point in the document window also moves one-half inch to the right.

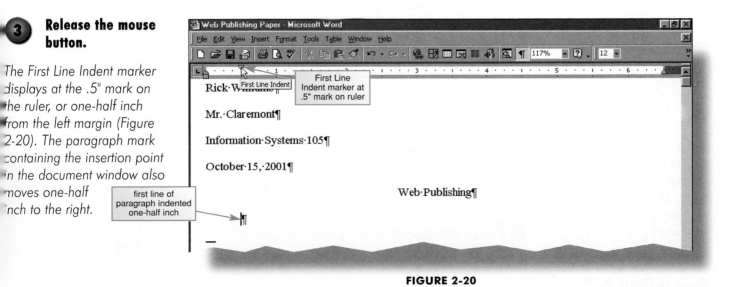

FIGURE 2-20

4 **Type the first paragraph of the research paper body as shown in Figure 2-21. Press the ENTER key. Type** Web publishing is the process of developing, maintaining, and posting Web pages.

Word automatically indents the first line of the second paragraph by one-half inch (Figure 2-21).

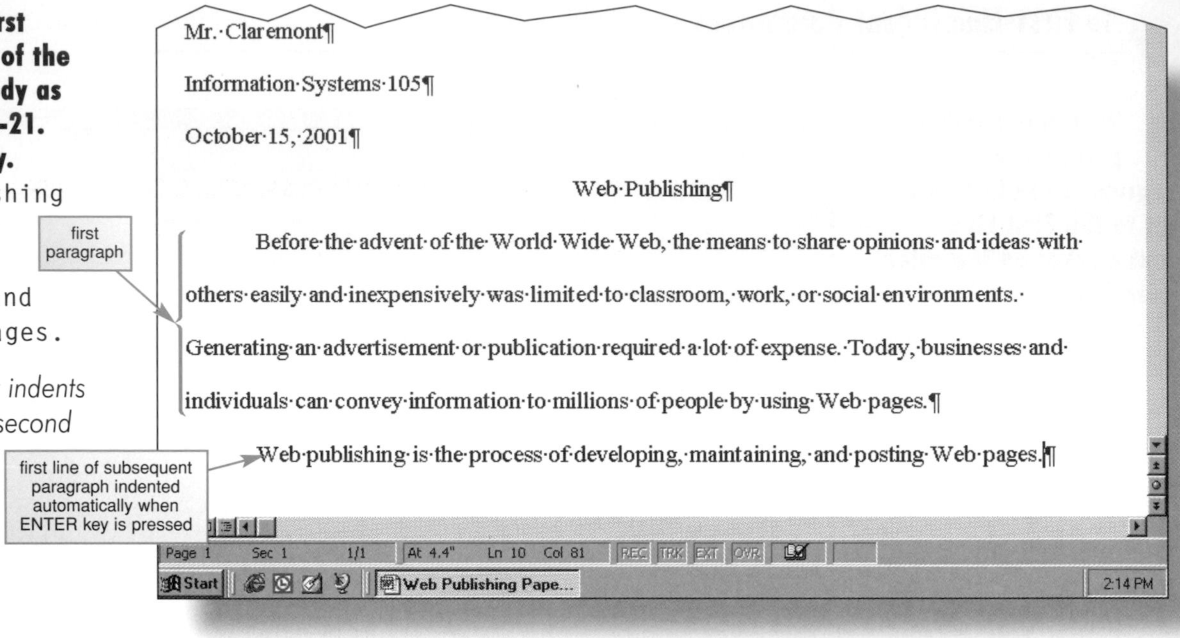

Mr.·Claremont¶

Information·Systems·105¶

October·15,·2001¶

Web·Publishing¶

Before·the·advent·of·the·World·Wide·Web,·the·means·to·share·opinions·and·ideas·with·others·easily·and·inexpensively·was·limited·to·classroom,·work,·or·social·environments.·Generating·an·advertisement·or·publication·required·a·lot·of·expense.·Today,·businesses·and·individuals·can·convey·information·to·millions·of·people·by·using·Web·pages.¶

Web·publishing·is·the·process·of·developing,·maintaining,·and·posting·Web·pages.¶

first paragraph

first line of subsequent paragraph indented automatically when ENTER key is pressed

Page 1   Sec 1   1/1   At 4.4"   Ln 10   Col 81   REC   TRK   EXT   OVR

Start   Web Publishing Pape...   2:14 PM

FIGURE 2-21

Recall that each time you press the ENTER key, the paragraph formatting in the previous paragraph is carried forward to the next paragraph. Thus, once you set the first-line indent, its format is carried automatically to each subsequent paragraph you type.

Using Word's AutoCorrect Feature

Because you may make typing, spelling, capitalization, or grammar errors as you type, Word provides an **AutoCorrect** feature that automatically corrects these errors as you type them into the document. For example, if you type the text, ahve, Word automatically changes it to the word, have, for you when you press the SPACEBAR or a punctuation mark key. Word has predefined many commonly misspelled words, which it automatically corrects for you. Perform the following steps to use the AutoCorrect as you type feature.

 To AutoCorrect As You Type

1 **Press the SPACEBAR. Type the beginning of the next sentence and misspell the word, accomplish, as follows:** With the proper hardware and software, Web publishing is fairly easy to acomplish **as shown in Figure 2-22.**

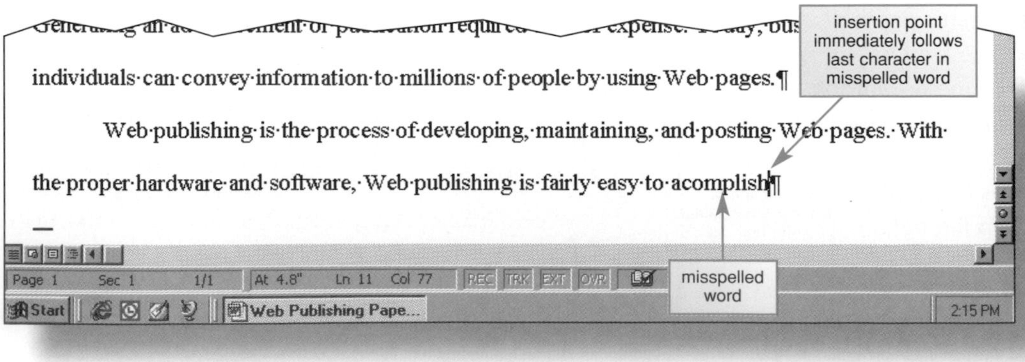

insertion point immediately follows last character in misspelled word

Generating·an·advertisement·or·publication·required·a·lot·of·expense.·Today,·businesses·and·individuals·can·convey·information·to·millions·of·people·by·using·Web·pages.¶

Web·publishing·is·the·process·of·developing,·maintaining,·and·posting·Web·pages.·With·the·proper·hardware·and·software,·Web·publishing·is·fairly·easy·to·acomplish¶

misspelled word

Page 1   Sec 1   1/1   At 4.8"   Ln 11   Col 77   REC   TRK   EXT   OVR

Start   Web Publishing Pape...   2:15 PM

FIGURE 2-22

② Press the PERIOD key.

As soon as you press the PERIOD key, Word's AutoCorrect feature detects the misspelling and corrects the misspelled word (Figure 2-23).

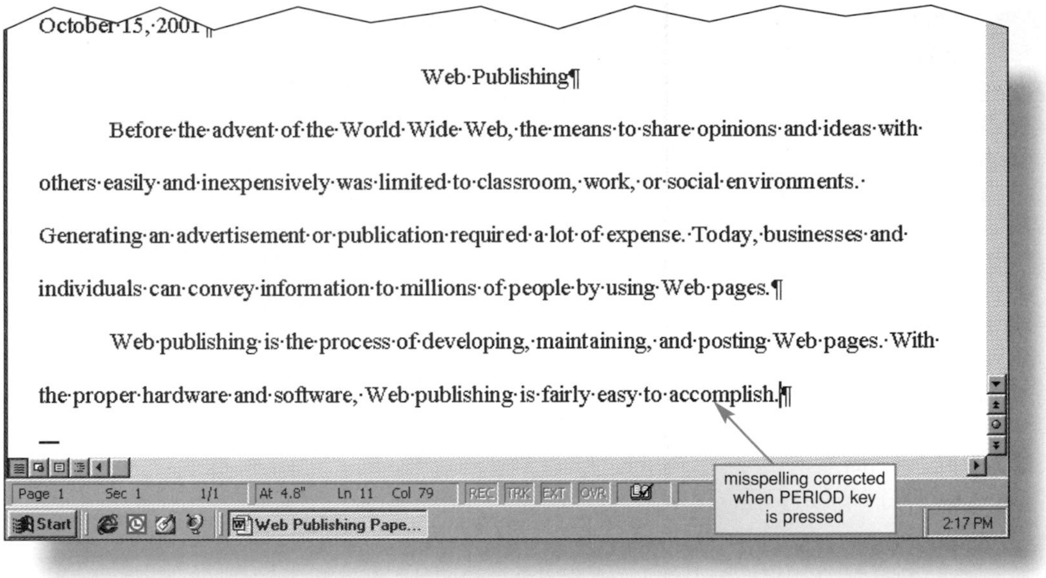

October 15, 2001

Web·Publishing¶

Before·the·advent·of·the·World·Wide·Web,·the·means·to·share·opinions·and·ideas·with·others·easily·and·inexpensively·was·limited·to·classroom,·work,·or·social·environments.·Generating·an·advertisement·or·publication·required·a·lot·of·expense.·Today,·businesses·and·individuals·can·convey·information·to·millions·of·people·by·using·Web·pages.¶

Web·publishing·is·the·process·of·developing,·maintaining,·and·posting·Web·pages.·With·the·proper·hardware·and·software,·Web·publishing·is·fairly·easy·to·accomplish.¶

Page 1   Sec 1   1/1   At 4.8"   Ln 11   Col 79   REC TRK EXT OVR

Start   Web Publishing Pape...   2:17 PM

misspelling corrected when PERIOD key is pressed

FIGURE 2-23

Word has a list of predefined typing, spelling, capitalization, and grammar errors that AutoCorrect can detect and correct. In addition to the predefined list, you can create your own AutoCorrect entries to add to the list. For example, if you often misspell the word, camera, as canera, you should create an AutoCorrect entry for it as shown in these steps.

To Create an AutoCorrect Entry

① Click Tools on the menu bar and then point to AutoCorrect (Figure 2-24).

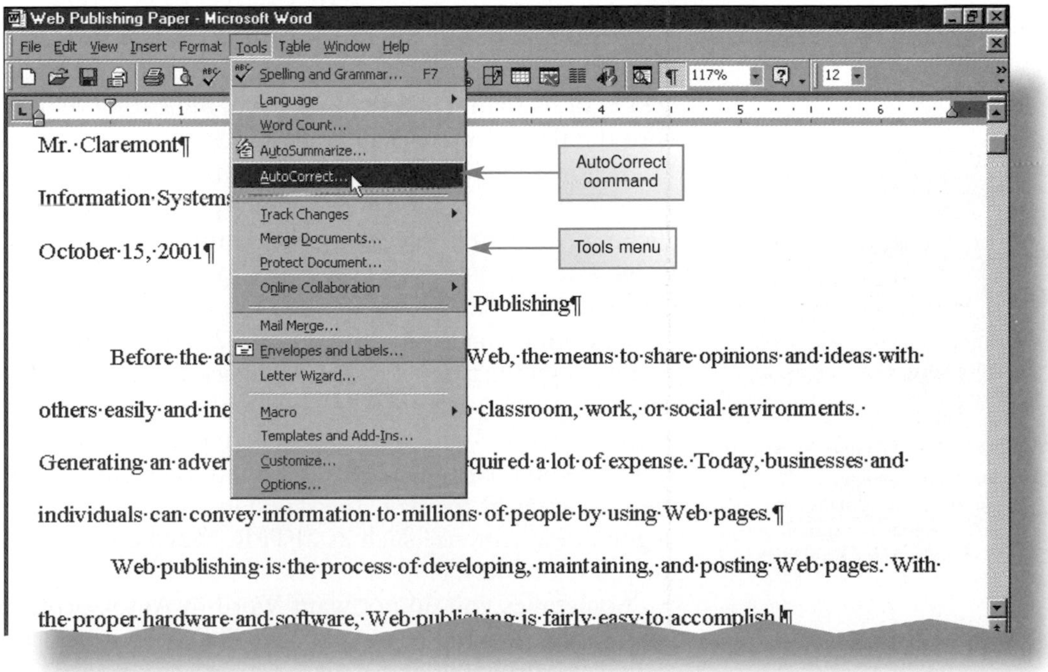

Web Publishing Paper - Microsoft Word

File Edit View Insert Format Tools Table Window Help

Spelling and Grammar...   F7
Language
Word Count...
AutoSummarize...
AutoCorrect...
Track Changes
Merge Documents...
Protect Document...
Online Collaboration
Mail Merge...
Envelopes and Labels...
Letter Wizard...
Macro
Templates and Add-Ins...
Customize...
Options...

AutoCorrect command

Tools menu

Mr.·Claremont¶

Information·Systems

October·15,·2001¶

·Publishing¶

Before·the·ad   Web,·the·means·to·share·opinions·and·ideas·with·others·easily·and·ine   ·classroom,·work,·or·social·environments.·Generating·an·adver   quired·a·lot·of·expense.·Today,·businesses·and·individuals·can·convey·information·to·millions·of·people·by·using·Web·pages.¶

Web·publishing·is·the·process·of·developing,·maintaining,·and·posting·Web·pages.·With·the·proper·hardware·and·software,·Web·publishing·is·fairly·easy·to·accomplish.¶

FIGURE 2-24

2 **Click AutoCorrect. When the AutoCorrect dialog box displays, type** canera **in the Replace text box. Press the TAB key and then type** camera **in the With text box.**

Word displays the AutoCorrect dialog box. The Replace text box contains the misspelled word, and the With text box contains its correct spelling (Figure 2-25).

3 **Click the Add button. (If your dialog box displays a Replace button instead, click it and then click the Yes button in the Microsoft Word dialog box.) Click the OK button.**

Word adds the entry alphabetically to the list of words to correct automatically as you type.

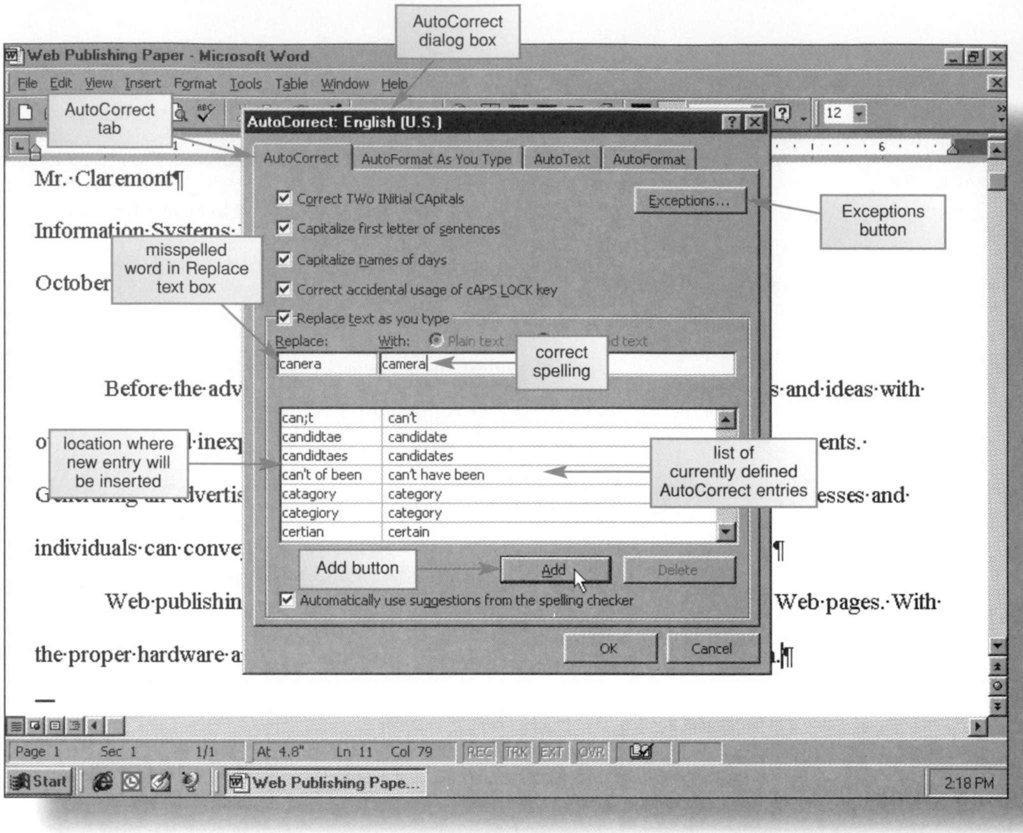

FIGURE 2-25

AutoCorrect

If you have installed the Microsoft Office 2000 Proofing Tools and have enabled editing for another language, Word automatically can detect the language you are using to create the document - as you type. These Proofing Tools provide fonts and templates, check spelling and grammar, and include AutoCorrect lists.

In addition to creating AutoCorrect entries for words you commonly misspell, you can create entries for abbreviations, codes, and so on. For example, you could create an AutoCorrect entry for asap, indicating that Word should replace this text with the phrase, as soon as possible.

If, for some reason, you do not want Word to correct automatically as you type, you can turn off the replace as you type feature by clicking Tools on the menu bar, clicking AutoCorrect, clicking the AutoCorrect tab (Figure 2-25), clicking the Replace text as you type check box to remove the check mark, and then clicking the OK button.

The AutoCorrect sheet (Figure 2-25) also contains four other check boxes that correct capitalization errors if the check boxes are selected. If you type two capital letters in a row such as TH, Word makes the second letter lowercase, Th. If you begin a sentence with a lowercase letter, Word capitalizes the first letter of the sentence. If you type the name of a day in lowercase such as tuesday, Word capitalizes the first letter of the day, Tuesday. Finally, if you leave the CAPS LOCK key on and begin a new sentence such as aFTER, Word corrects the typing, After, and turns off the CAPS LOCK key.

Sometimes you do not want Word to AutoCorrect a particular word or phrase. For example, you may use the code WD. in your documents. Because Word automatically capitalizes the first letter of a sentence, the character you enter following the period will be capitalized (in the previous sentence, it would capitalize the letter i in

he word, in). To allow the code WD. to be entered into a document and still leave
he AutoCorrect feature turned on, you need to set an exception. To set an exception
o an AutoCorrect rule, click Tools on the menu bar, click AutoCorrect, click the
AutoCorrect tab, click the Exceptions button in the AutoCorrect sheet (Figure 2-25),
click the appropriate tab in the AutoCorrect Exceptions dialog box, type the excep-
ion entry in the text box, click the Add button, click the Close button in the
AutoCorrect Exceptions dialog box, and then click the Close button in the
AutoCorrect dialog box.

Adding Footnotes

You have learned that explanatory notes are optional in the MLA documentation
style. They are used primarily to elaborate on points discussed in the body of the
paper. The style specifies that a superscript (raised number) be used for a note reference mark to signal that an explanatory note exists either at the bottom of the page
as a **footnote** or at the end of the document as an **endnote**.

Word, by default, places notes at the bottom of each page. In Word, **note text** can
be any length and format. Word automatically numbers notes sequentially for you by
placing a **note reference mark** in the body of the document and also in front of the
note text. If you insert, rearrange, or remove notes, any subsequent note text and
reference marks are renumbered according to their new sequence in the document.
Perform the following steps to add a footnote to the research paper.

More About

MLA and APA

Both the MLA and APA guidelines suggest the use of in-text
parenthetical citations, as
opposed to footnoting each
source of material in a paper.
These parenthetical acknowl-
edgments guide the reader to
the end of the paper for complete information on the
source.

Steps ## To Add a Footnote

1 **Press the SPACEBAR
and then type** For
example, clip
galleries offer a
variety of images,
videos, and sounds.
**Click Insert on the menu
bar and then point to
Footnote.**

*The insertion point is posi-
tioned immediately after the
period following the end of
the sentence (Figure 2-26).*

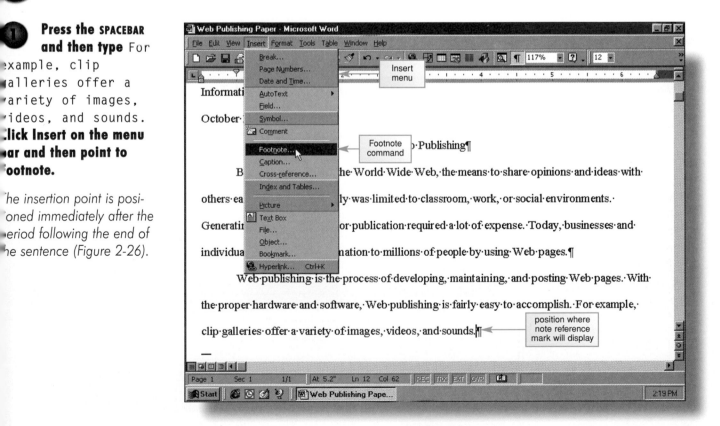

FIGURE 2-26

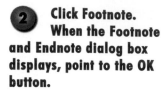

**Click Footnote.
When the Footnote
and Endnote dialog box
displays, point to the OK
button.**

*Word displays the Footnote
and Endnote dialog box
(Figure 2-27).*

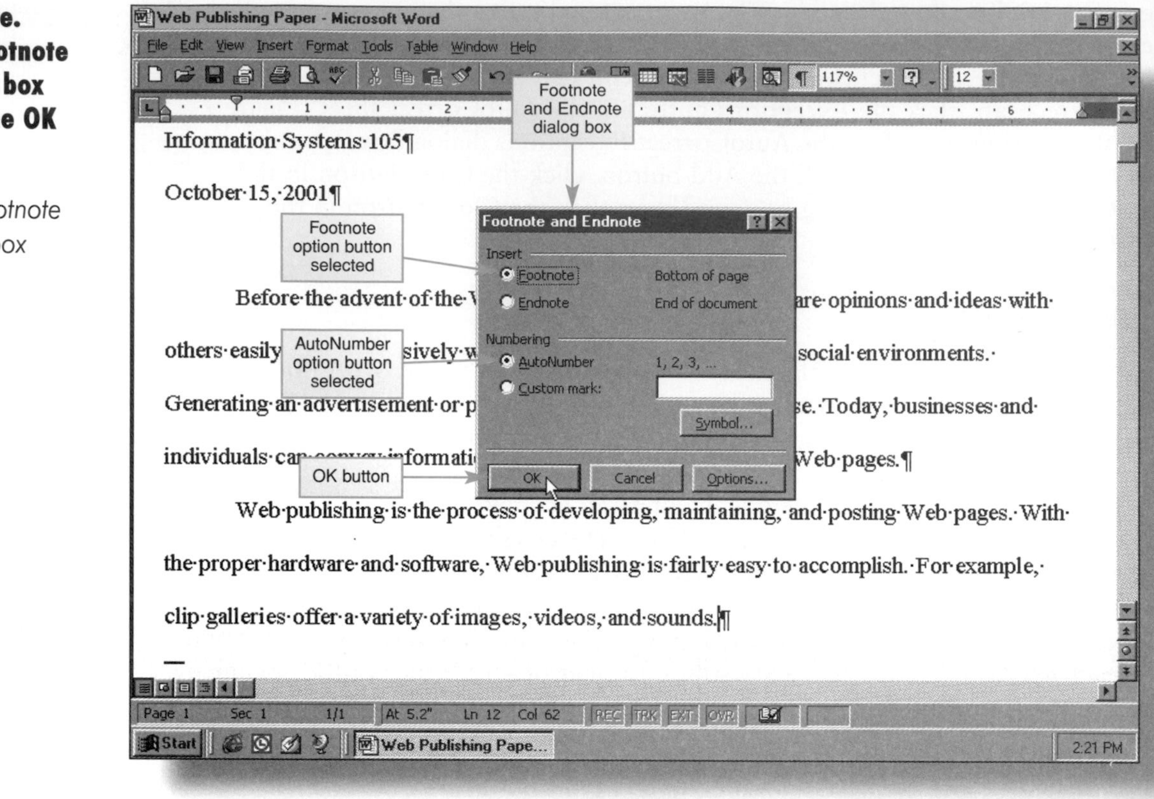

FIGURE 2-27

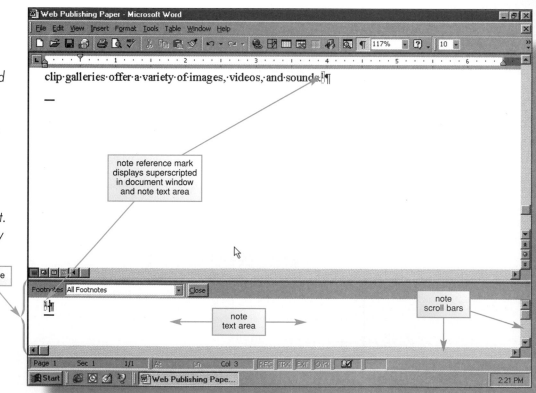

**Click the OK
button.**

*Word opens a **note pane** in
the lower portion of the Word
window with the note reference mark (a superscripted
1) positioned at the left margin of the note pane (Figure
2-28). The note reference
mark also displays in the
document window at the
location of the insertion point.
Note reference marks are, by
default, superscripted;
that is, raised
above other letters.*

FIGURE 2-28

④ **Type** Many
current software
packages include a
clip gallery. Clip
galleries also are
available on the Web
or may be purchased
on CD-ROM or DVD-ROM
(Zack 9-24).

*Word enters the note text in
the note pane (Figure 2-29).*

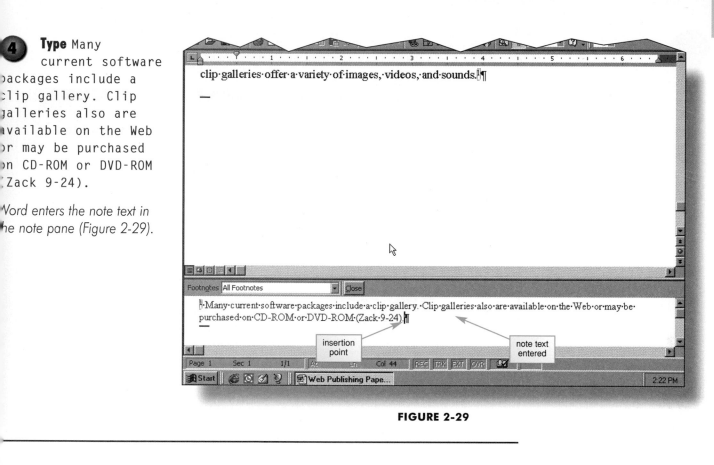

FIGURE 2-29

The footnote is not formatted according to the MLA style. Thus, the next step is to modify the style of the footnote.

Modifying a Style

A **style** is a customized format that you can apply to text. The formats defined by a style include character formatting such as the font and font size, and paragraph formatting such as line spacing and text alignment. Word has many built-in, or predefined, styles that you may use to format text. You can modify the formatting associated with these styles, or you can define new styles.

The base style for new Word documents is called the **Normal style**, which for a new installation of Word 2000 more than likely uses 12-point Times New Roman font for characters and single-spaced, left-aligned paragraphs. Recall from Project 1 that when you upgrade to Word 2000 from a previous version of Word, the default point size more than likely is 10 instead of 12.

In Figure 2-29, the insertion point is in the note text area, which is formatted using the Footnote Text style. The Footnote Text style is based on the Normal style. Thus, the text of the footnote you entered is single-spaced and left-aligned.

You could change the paragraph formatting of the footnote text to first-line indent and double-spacing as you did for the text in the document window. If you use this technique, however, you will have to change the format of the footnote text for each footnote you enter into the document. A more efficient technique is to modify the format of the Footnote Text style so paragraphs based on this style are double-spaced with a first-line indent format. Thus, by changing the formatting associated with the Footnote Text style, every footnote you enter will use the formats defined in this style. Perform the steps on the next page to modify the Footnote Text style.

To Modify a Style

1 Click Format on the menu bar and then point to Style (Figure 2-30).

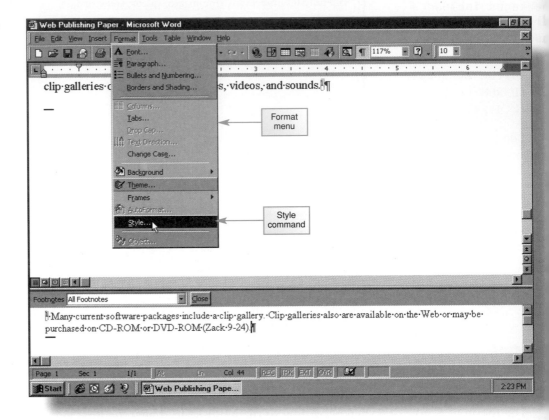

FIGURE 2-30

2 Click Style. When the Style dialog box displays, click Footnote Text in the Styles list, if necessary, and then point to the Modify button.

Word displays the Style dialog box (Figure 2-31). Footnote Text is highlighted in the Styles list. The Description area shows the formatting associated with the selected style.

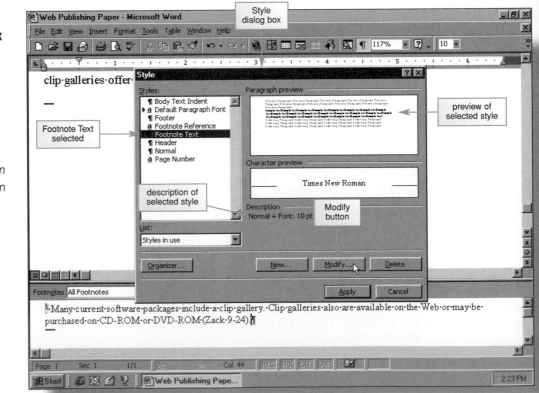

FIGURE 2-31

3 **Click the Modify button. When the Modify Style dialog box displays, click the Format button and then point to Paragraph.**

Word displays the Modify Style dialog box (Figure 2-32). A list of formatting commands displays above or below the Format button.

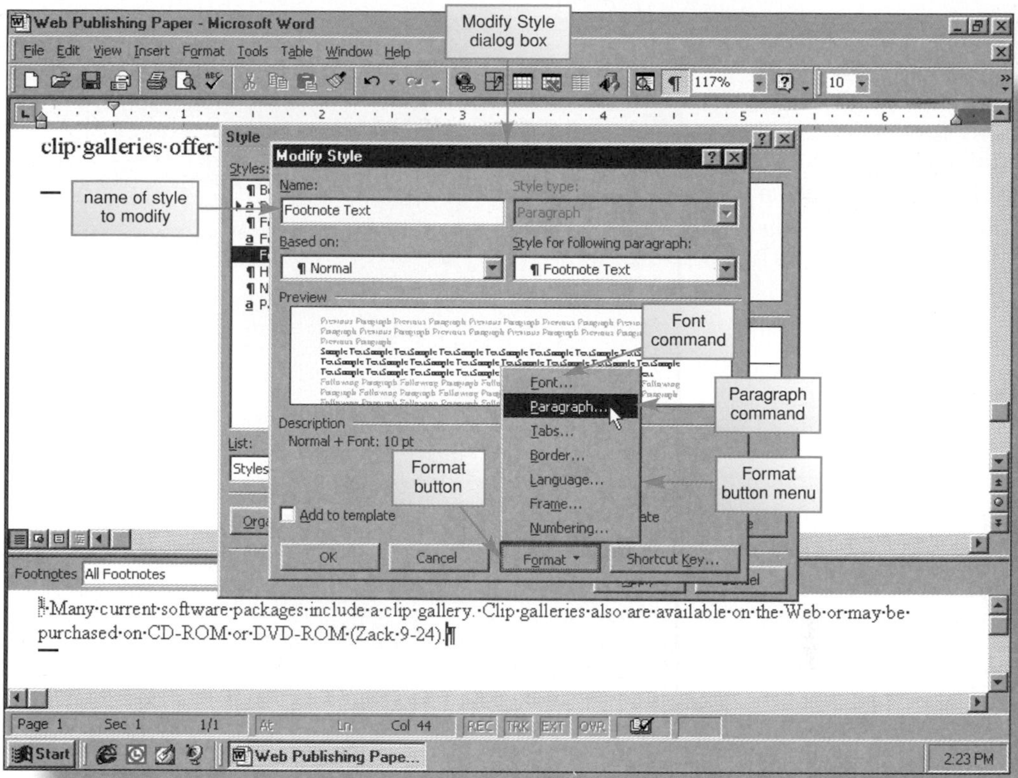

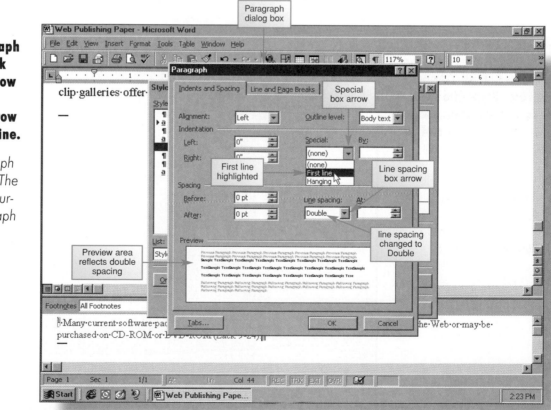

FIGURE 2-32

4 **Click Paragraph. When the Paragraph dialog box displays, click the Line spacing box arrow and then click Double. Click the Special box arrow and then point to First line.**

Word displays the Paragraph dialog box (Figure 2-33). The Preview area reflects the current settings in the Paragraph dialog box.

FIGURE 2-33

Click First line. Point to the OK button.

Word displays First line in the Special box and Double in the Line spacing box (Figure 2-34). Notice the default first-line indent is .5".

 Click the OK button.

Word removes the Paragraph dialog box, and the Modify Style dialog box (see Figure 2-32 on the previous page) is visible again.

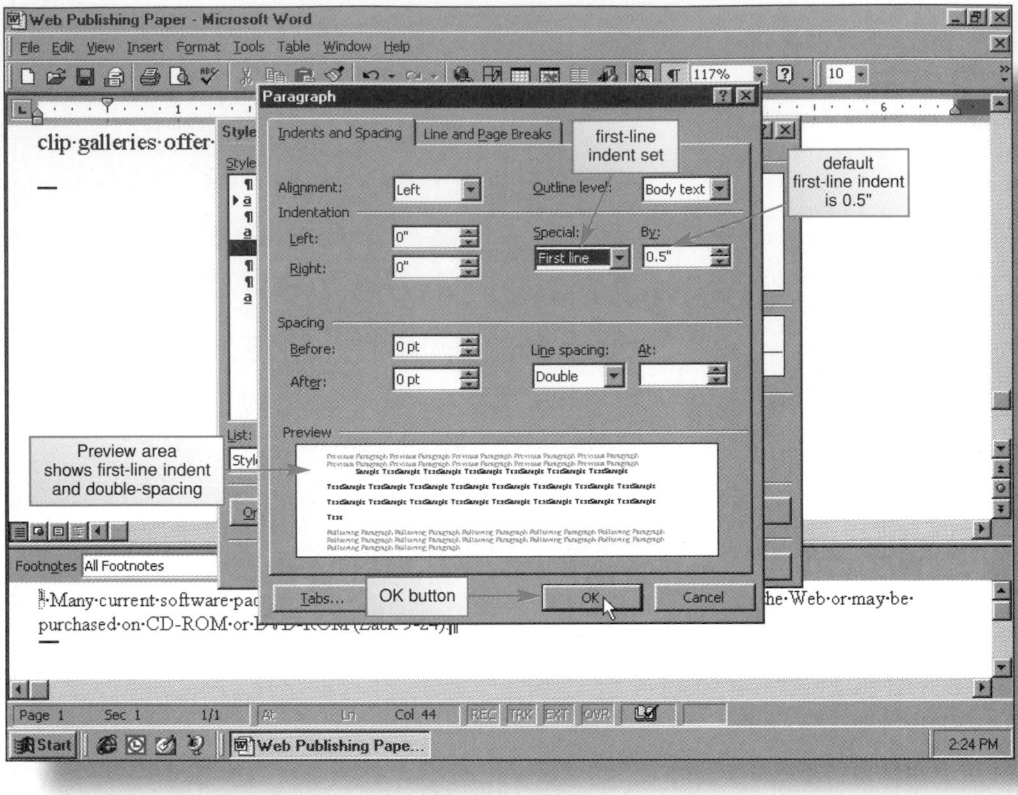

FIGURE 2-34

7 **In the Modify Style dialog box, click the Format button and then click Font. When the Font dialog box displays, click 12 in the Size list. Point to the OK button.**

Word displays the Font dialog box (Figure 2-35). Depending on your installation of Word 2000, the Size box already may display 12.

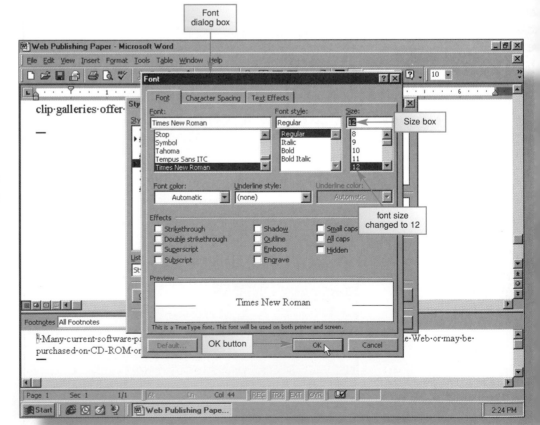

FIGURE 2-35

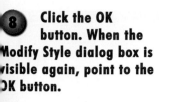

8 **Click the OK button. When the Modify Style dialog box is visible again, point to the OK button.**

Word removes the Font dialog box, and the Modify Style dialog box is visible again (Figure 2-36). Word modifies the Footnote Text style to a 12-point font with double-spaced and first-line indented paragraphs.

9 **Click the OK button. When the Style dialog box is visible again, click the Apply button. Click the note pane up scroll arrow to display the entire footnote.**

Word indents the first line of the note by one-half inch and sets the line spacing for the note to double (Figure 2-37 below).

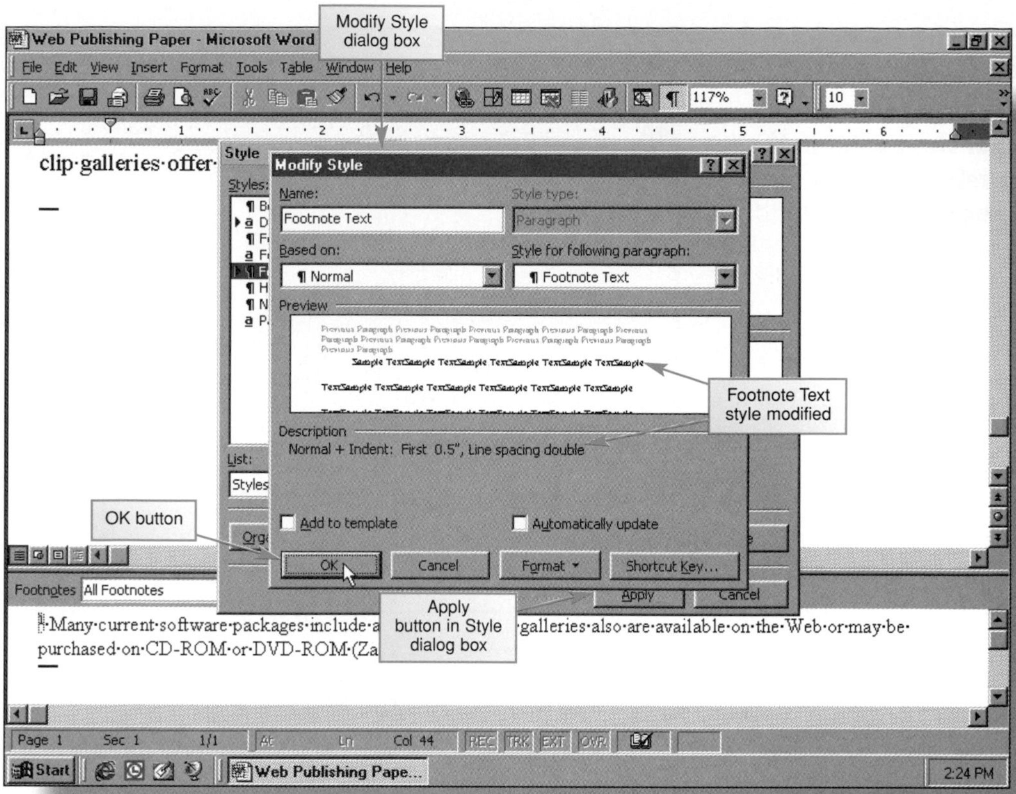

FIGURE 2-36

Any future footnotes entered into the document will use a 12-point font with first-line indented and double-spaced paragraphs. The footnote is complete. The next step is to close the note pane.

To Close the Note Pane

1 **Point to the Close button in the note pane (Figure 2-37).**

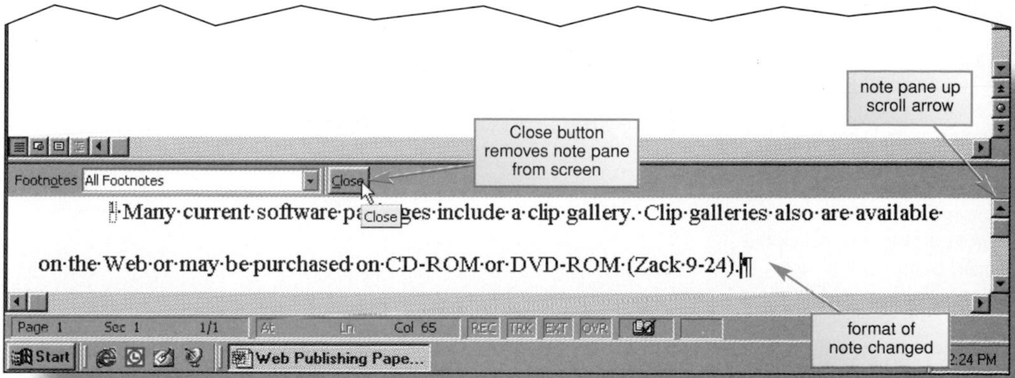

FIGURE 2-37

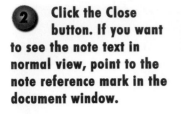

Click the Close button. If you want to see the note text in normal view, point to the note reference mark in the document window.

Word closes the note pane (Figure 2-38).

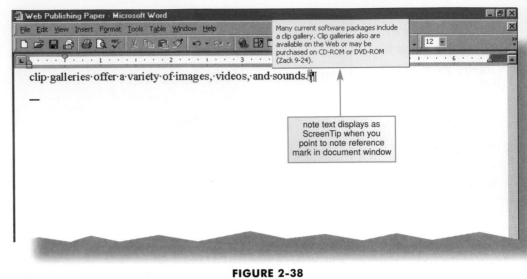

clip·galleries·offer·a·variety·of·images,·videos,·and·sounds.

note text displays as ScreenTip when you point to note reference mark in document window

Many current software packages include a clip gallery. Clip galleries also are available on the Web or may be purchased on CD-ROM or DVD-ROM (Zack 9-24).

FIGURE 2-38

When Word closes the note pane and returns to the document window, the note text disappears from the screen. Although the note text still exists, it usually is not visible as a footnote in normal view. If, however, you point to the note reference mark, the note text displays above the note reference mark as a **ScreenTip** (Figure 2-38).

To delete a note, you select the note reference mark in the document window (not in the note pane) by dragging through the note reference mark and then clicking the Cut button on the Standard toolbar. Another way to delete a note is to click to the right of the note reference mark in the document window and then press BACKSPACE key twice, or click to the left of the note reference mark in the document window and then press the DELETE key twice. To move a note to a different location in a document, you select the note reference mark in the document window (not in the note pane), click the Cut button on the Standard toolbar, click the location where you want to move the note, and then click the Paste button on the Standard toolbar. When you move or delete notes, Word automatically renumbers any remaining notes in the correct sequence.

You edit note text using the note pane at the bottom of the Word window. To display the note text in a note pane, double-click the note reference mark in the document window or click View on the menu bar and then click Footnotes. Edit the note as you would any Word text and then click the Close button in the note pane. If you want to verify that the note text is positioned correctly on the page, you must switch to print layout view or display the document in print preview. These views are discussed later.

The next step is to enter more text into the body of the research paper. Follow these steps to enter more text.

Notes

To convert current footnotes to endnotes, click Insert on the menu bar and then click Footnote. Click the Options button in the Footnote and Endnote dialog box. Click the Convert button in the Note Options dialog box. Click Convert all footnotes to endnotes and then click the OK button in each of the dialog boxes.

'O ENTER MORE TEXT

1 Press the SPACEBAR. Type the remainder of the second paragraph of the paper as shown in Figure 2-39.

2 Press the ENTER key. Type the third paragraph of the paper as shown in Figure 2-39.

The second and third paragraphs are entered (Figure 2-39).

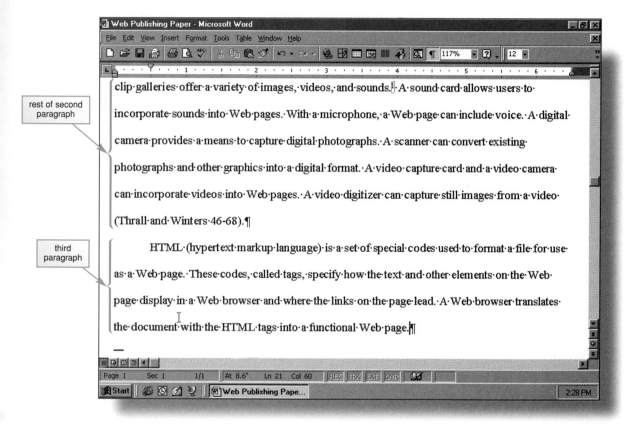

rest of second paragraph

third paragraph

FIGURE 2-39

utomatic Page Breaks

As you type documents that exceed one page, Word automatically inserts page reaks, called **automatic page breaks** or **soft page breaks**, when it determines the text as filled one page according to paper size, margin settings, line spacing, and other ettings. If you add text, delete text, or modify text on a page, Word recomputes ie position of automatic page breaks and adjusts them accordingly. Word performs age recomputation between the keystrokes; that is, in between the pauses in our typing. Thus, Word refers to the automatic page break task as **background pagination**. In normal view, automatic page breaks display on the Word screen as single dotted horizontal line. Word's automatic page break feature is illustrated in ie step on the next page.

More About

APA and MLA Documentation Styles

The World Wide Web contains a host of information on the APA and MLA documentation styles. College professors and fellow students develop many of these Web pages. For a list of Web links to sites on the APA and MLA styles, visit the Word 2000 More About Web page (www.scsite.com/wd2000/more.htm) and then click Links to Sites on the APA and MLA Styles.

Steps To Page Break Automatically

1 Press the ENTER key and then type the first two sentences of the fourth paragraph of the paper, as shown in Figure 2-40.

As you begin typing the paragraph, Word places an automatic page break between the third and fourth paragraphs in the paper (Figure 2-40). The status bar now displays Page 2 as the current page.

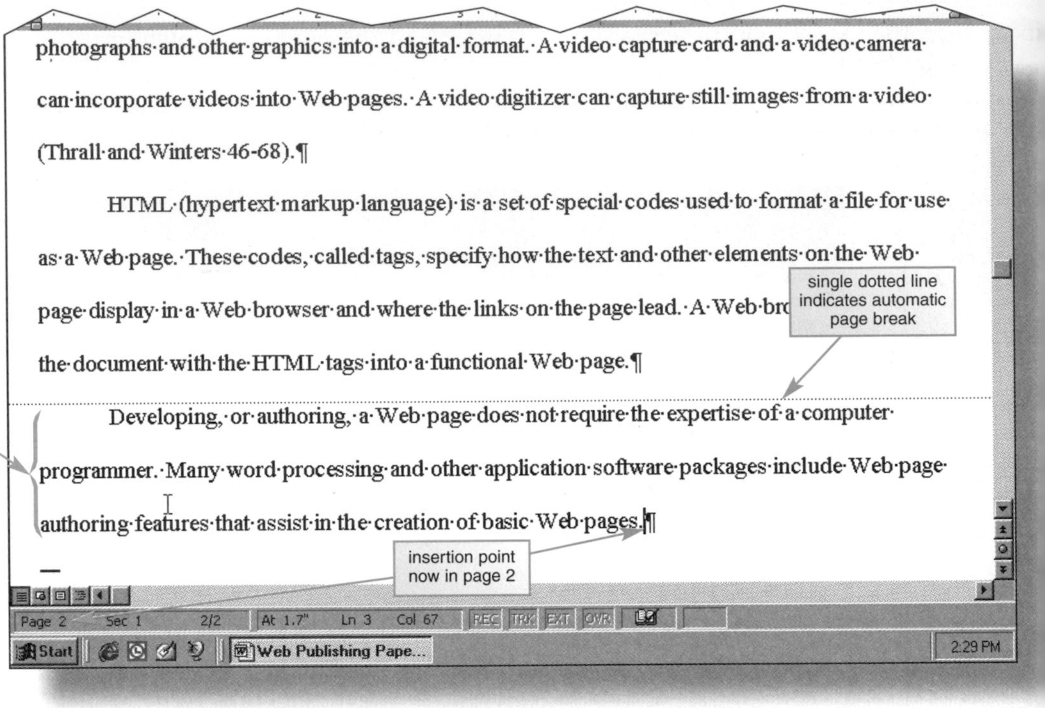

photographs·and·other·graphics·into·a·digital·format.·A·video·capture·card·and·a·video·camera·can·incorporate·videos·into·Web·pages.·A·video·digitizer·can·capture·still·images·from·a·video·(Thrall·and·Winters·46-68).¶

HTML·(hypertext·markup·language)·is·a·set·of·special·codes·used·to·format·a·file·for·use·as·a·Web·page.·These·codes,·called·tags,·specify·how·the·text·and·other·elements·on·the·Web·page·display·in·a·Web·browser·and·where·the·links·on·the·page·lead.·A·Web·bro the·document·with·the·HTML·tags·into·a·functional·Web·page.¶

two sentences entered

single dotted line indicates automatic page break

Developing,·or·authoring,·a·Web·page·does·not·require·the·expertise·of·a·computer·programmer.·Many·word·processing·and·other·application·software·packages·include·Web·page·authoring·features·that·assist·in·the·creation·of·basic·Web·pages.¶

insertion point now in page 2

Page 2   Sec 1   2/2   At 1.7"   Ln 3   Col 67   REC TRK EXT OVR

Start   Web Publishing Pape...   2:29 PM

FIGURE 2-40

Your page break may occur at a different location, depending on your printer type.

The header, although not shown in normal view, contains the name Williams and the page number 2. If you wanted to view the header, click View on the menu bar and then click Header and Footer. Then, click the Close button on the Header and Footer toolbar to return to normal view.

Word, by default, prevents widows and orphans from occurring in a document. A **widow** is created when the last line of a paragraph displays by itself at the top of a page, and an **orphan** occurs when the first line of a paragraph displays by itself at the bottom of a page. You turn this setting on and off through the Paragraph dialog box. If, for some reason, you wanted to allow a widow or an orphan in a document, you would right-click the paragraph in question, click Paragraph on the shortcut menu, click the Line and Page Breaks tab in the Paragraph dialog box, click Widow/Orphan control to select or deselect the check box, and then click the OK button.

The Line and Page Breaks sheet in the Paragraph dialog box also contains two other check boxes that control how Word places automatic page breaks. If you did not want a page break to occur within a particular paragraph, you would right-click the paragraph you wanted to keep together, click Paragraph on the shortcut menu, click the Line and Page Breaks tab in the Paragraph dialog box, click Keep lines together to select the check box, and then click the OK button. If you did not want a page break to occur between two paragraphs, you would select the two paragraphs, right-click the selection, click Paragraph on the shortcut menu, click the Line and Page Breaks tab in the Paragraph dialog box, click Keep with next to select the check box, and then click the OK button.

Inserting Arrows, Faces, and Other Symbols Automatically

Earlier in this project, you learned that Word has predefined many commonly misspelled words, which it automatically corrects for you as you type. In addition to words, this built-in list of **AutoCorrect entries** also contains many commonly used symbols. For example, to insert a smiling face into a document, you type :) and Word automatically changes it to ☺. Table 2-3 lists the characters you type to insert arrows, faces, and other symbols into a Word document.

You also can enter the first four symbols in Table 2-3 by clicking Insert on the menu bar, clicking Symbol, clicking the Special Characters tab, clicking the desired symbol in the Character list, clicking the Insert button, and then clicking the Close button in the Symbol dialog box.

If you do not like a change that Word automatically makes in a document, undo the change by clicking the Undo button on the Standard toolbar; clicking Edit on the menu bar and then clicking Undo; or pressing CTRL+Z.

The next step in the research paper is to enter a sentence that uses the registered trademark symbol. Perform the following steps to insert automatically the registered trademark symbol into the research paper.

Table 2-3 Word's Automatic Symbols		
TO DISPLAY	DESCRIPTION	TYPE
©	copyright symbol	(c)
®	registered trademark symbol	(r)
™	trademark symbol	(tm)
…	ellipsis	...
☺	smiley face	:) or :-)
☹	indifferent face	:| or :-|
☹	frowning face	:(or :-(
→	thin right arrow	-->
←	thin left arrow	<--
→	thick right arrow	==>
←	thick left arrow	<==
⇔	double arrow	<=>

To Insert a Symbol Automatically

With the insertion point positioned as shown in Figure 2-40, press the SPACEBAR. Type Microsoft Office 2000 products, for example, provide easy-to-use tools that enable users to create Web pages and include items such as bullets, frames, backgrounds, lines, database tables, worksheets, and graphics into the Web pages (**as the beginning of the sentence. Press CTRL+I to turn on italics. Type** Shelly Cashman Series(r **as shown in Figure 2-41.**

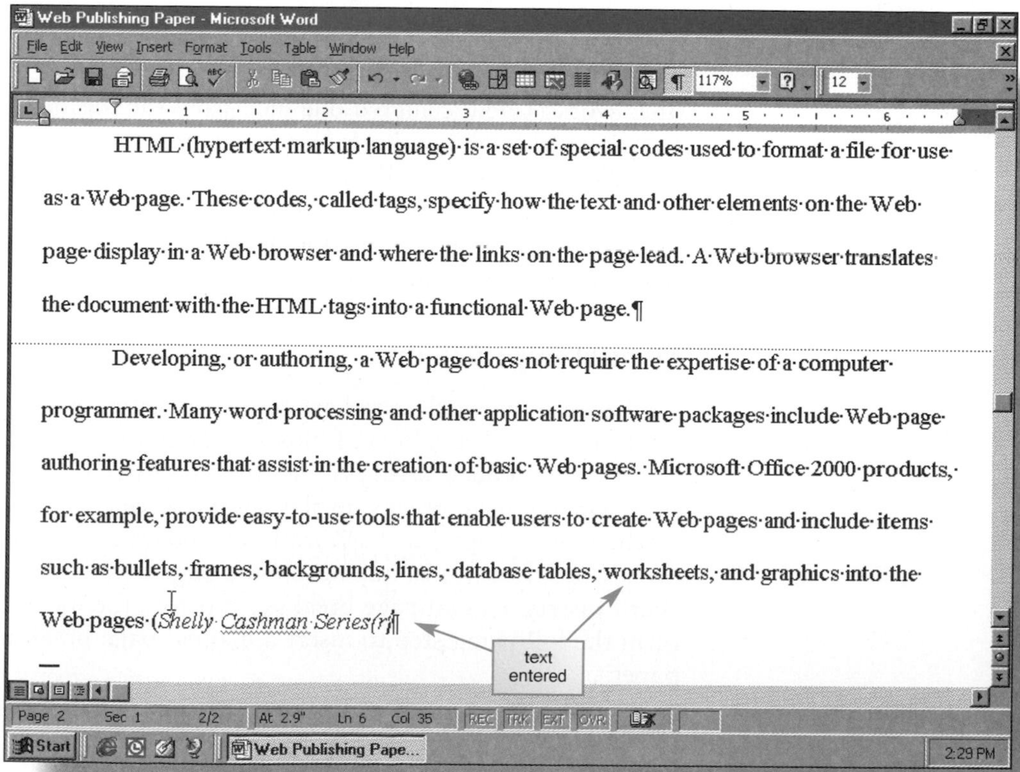

FIGURE 2-41

2 **Press the RIGHT PARENTHESIS key.**

Word automatically converts the (r) to ®, the registered trademark symbol.

3 **Press the SPACEBAR. Type** `Microsoft Word 2000 Project 2` **and then press CTRL+I to turn off italics. Press the RIGHT PARENTHESIS key and then press the PERIOD key. Press the SPACEBAR. Enter the last two sentences of the research paper as shown in Figure 2-42.**

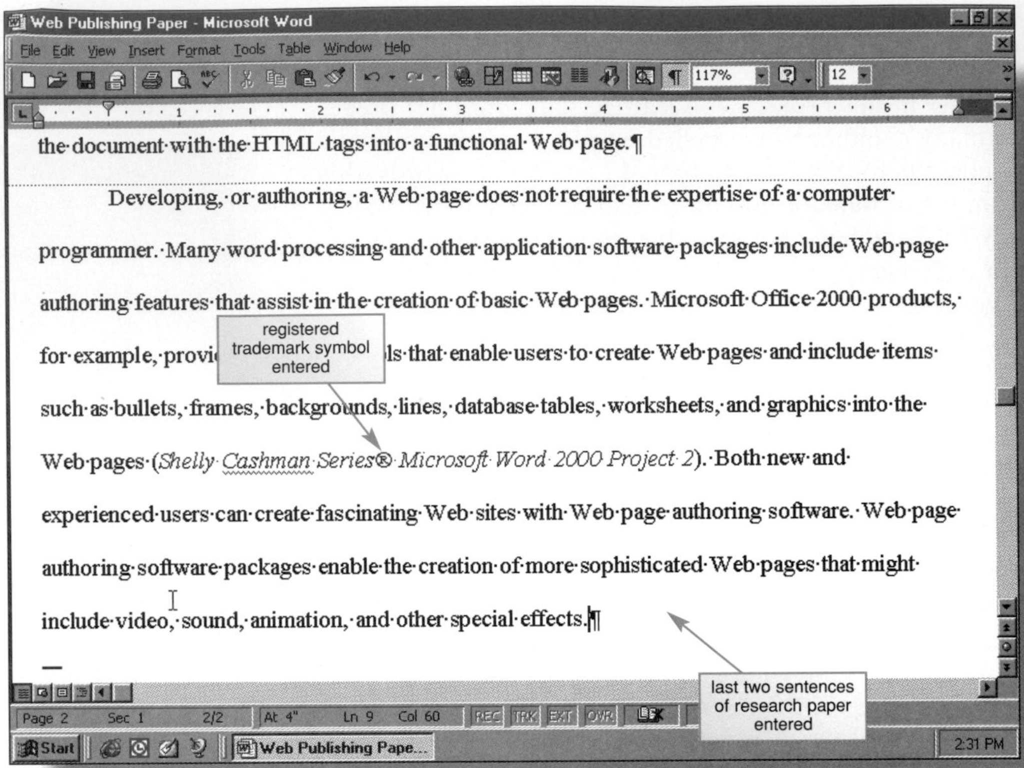
Web Publishing Paper - Microsoft Word
File Edit View Insert Format Tools Table Window Help
117%
12
the·document·with·the·HTML·tags·into·a·functional·Web·page.¶
Developing,·or·authoring,·a·Web·page·does·not·require·the·expertise·of·a·computer·
programmer.·Many·word·processing·and·other·application·software·packages·include·Web·page·
authoring·features·that·assist·in·the·creation·of·basic·Web·pages.·Microsoft·Office·2000·products,·
for·example,·provi
ls·that·enable·users·to·create·Web·pages·and·include·items·
such·as·bullets,·frames,·backgrounds,·lines,·database·tables,·worksheets,·and·graphics·into·the·
Web·pages·(Shelly·Cashman·Series®·Microsoft·Word·2000·Project·2).·Both·new·and·
experienced·users·can·create·fascinating·Web·sites·with·Web·page·authoring·software.·Web·page·
authoring·software·packages·enable·the·creation·of·more·sophisticated·Web·pages·that·might·
include·video,·sound,·animation,·and·other·special·effects.¶
registered trademark symbol entered
last two sentences of research paper entered
Page 2
Sec 1
2/2
At 4"
Ln 9
Col 60
REC
TRK
EXT
OVR
Start
Web Publishing Pape...
2:31 PM

FIGURE 2-42

Creating an Alphabetical Works Cited Page

According to the MLA style, the **works cited page** is a bibliographical list of works you reference directly in your paper. The list is placed on a separate page with the title, Works Cited, centered one inch from the top margin. The works are to be alphabetized by the author's last name or, if the work has no author, by the work's title. The first line of each entry begins at the left margin; subsequent lines of the same entry are indented one-half inch from the left margin.

The first step in creating the works cited page is to force a page break so the works cited display on a separate page.

Manual Page Breaks

Because the works cited are to display on a separate numbered page, you must insert a manual page break following the body of the research paper. A **manual page break,** or **hard page break,** is one that you force into the document at a specific location. Manual page breaks display on the screen as a horizontal dotted line, separated by the words, Page Break. Word never moves or adjusts manual page breaks; however, Word does adjust any automatic page breaks that follow a manual page break. Word inserts manual page breaks just before the location of the insertion point. Perform the following step to insert a manual page break after the body of the research paper.

steps To Page Break Manually

1 With the insertion point at the end of the research paper, press the ENTER key. Then, press the CTRL+ENTER keys.

The shortcut keys, CTRL+ENTER, instruct Word to insert a manual page break immediately above the insertion point and position the insertion point immediately below the manual page break (Figure 2-43). The status bar indicates the insertion point is located on page 3.

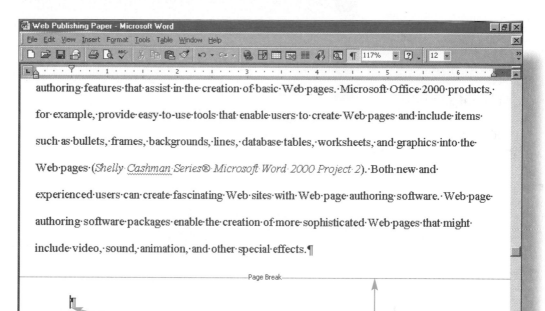

FIGURE 2-43

The manual page break displays as a horizontal dotted line with the words, Page Break, in the middle of the line. The header, although not shown in normal view, contains the name Williams and the page number 3. If you wanted to view the header, click View on the menu bar and then click Header and Footer. Then, click the Close button on the Header and Footer toolbar to return to normal view.

If, for some reason, you wanted to remove a manual page break from your document, you must first select it by double-clicking it. Then, press the DELETE key; or click the Cut button on the Standard toolbar; or right-click the selection and then click Cut on the shortcut menu.

Entering the Title of the Works Cited Page

The works cited title is to be centered between the margins. If you simply click the Center button on the Formatting toolbar, the title will not be centered properly; instead, it will be one-half inch to the right of the center point because earlier you set first-line indent at one-half inch. Thus, the first line of every paragraph is indented one-half inch. To properly center the title of the works cited page, you must move the First Line Indent marker back to the left margin before clicking the Center button as described in the steps on the next page.

Other Ways

1. On Format menu click Insert, click Break, click OK button

More *About*

Documentation Styles

The MLA documentation style uses the title *Works Cited* for the page containing bibliographical references, whereas the APA style uses the title *References*. APA guidelines for preparing the reference list entries differ significantly from the MLA style. Refer to an APA handbook for specifics.

TO CENTER THE TITLE OF THE WORKS CITED PAGE

 1 Drag the First Line Indent marker to the 0" mark on the ruler.

2 Double-click the move handle on the Formatting toolbar to display the entire toolbar. Click the Center button on the Formatting toolbar.

3 Type Works Cited as the title.

4 Press the ENTER key.

5 Because your fingers are on the keyboard, press the CTRL+L keys to left-align the paragraph mark.

The title displays centered properly and the insertion point is left-aligned (Figure 2-44).

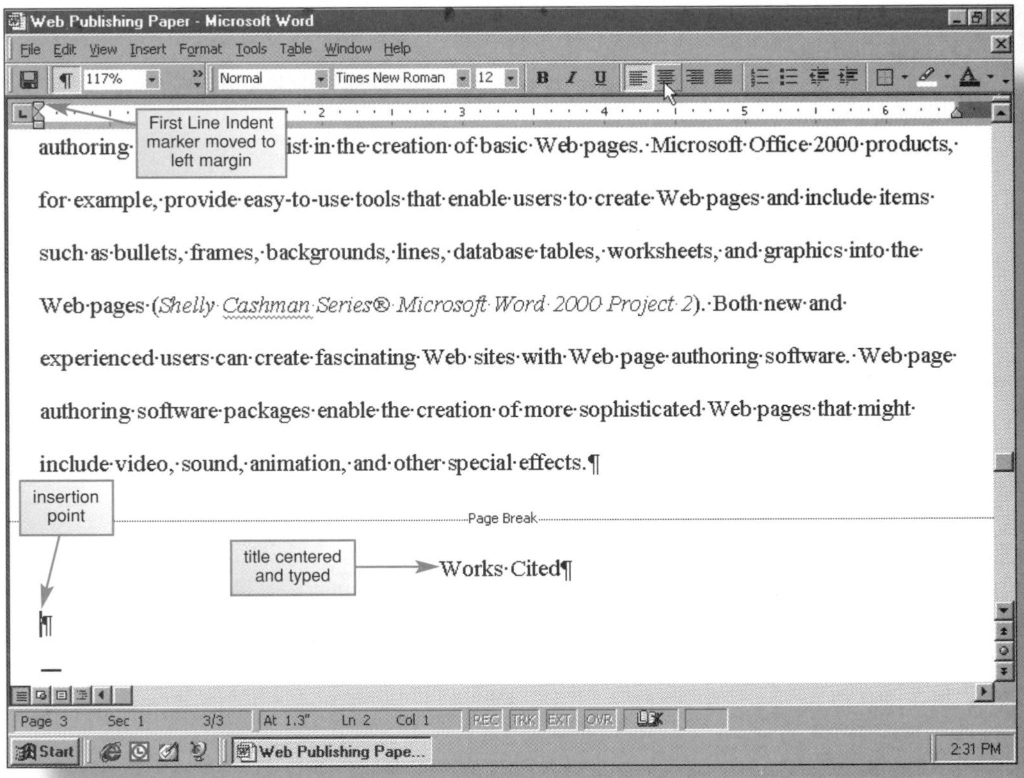

More *About*

Formatting

Minimize strain on your wrist by switching between the mouse and keyboard as little as possible. If your fingers are already on the keyboard, use shortcut keys to format text; if your fingers are already on the mouse, use the mouse to format text.

FIGURE 2-44

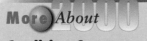

More *About*

Crediting Sources

When writing a research paper, you must acknowledge sources of information. Citing sources is a matter of ethics and honesty. Use caution when summarizing or paraphrasing a source. Be sure to avoid plagiarism, which includes using someone else's words or ideas and claiming them as your own.

Creating a Hanging Indent

On the works cited page, the first line of each entry begins at the left margin. Subsequent lines in the same paragraph are indented one-half inch from the left margin. In essence, the first line *hangs* to the left of the rest of the paragraph; thus, this type of paragraph formatting is called a **hanging indent**.

One method of creating a hanging indent is to use the horizontal ruler. The **Hanging Indent marker** is the bottom triangle at the 0" mark on the ruler (Figure 2-45). You have learned that the small square at the 0" mark is called the Left Indent marker. Perform the following steps to create a hanging indent.

teps ## To Create a Hanging Indent

1 With the insertion point in the paragraph to format (see Figure 2-44), point to the Hanging Indent marker on the ruler (Figure 2-45).

[Web Publishing Paper - Microsoft Word screen. Rulers and toolbars shown. Callout labels: "Hanging Indent marker", "Left Indent marker", "Hanging Indent".]

Text in document: ...features·that·assist·in·the·creation·of·basic·Web·pages.·Microsoft·Office·2000·products,· for·example,·provide·easy-to-use·tools·that·enable·users·to·create·Web·pages·and·include·items· such·as·bullets,·frames,·backgrounds,·lines,·database·tables,·worksheets,·and·graphics·into·the· Web·pages·(*Shelly·Cashman·Series®·Microsoft·Word·2000·Project·2*).·Both·new·and· experienced·users·can·create·fascinating·Web·sites·with·Web·page·authoring·software.·Web·page·

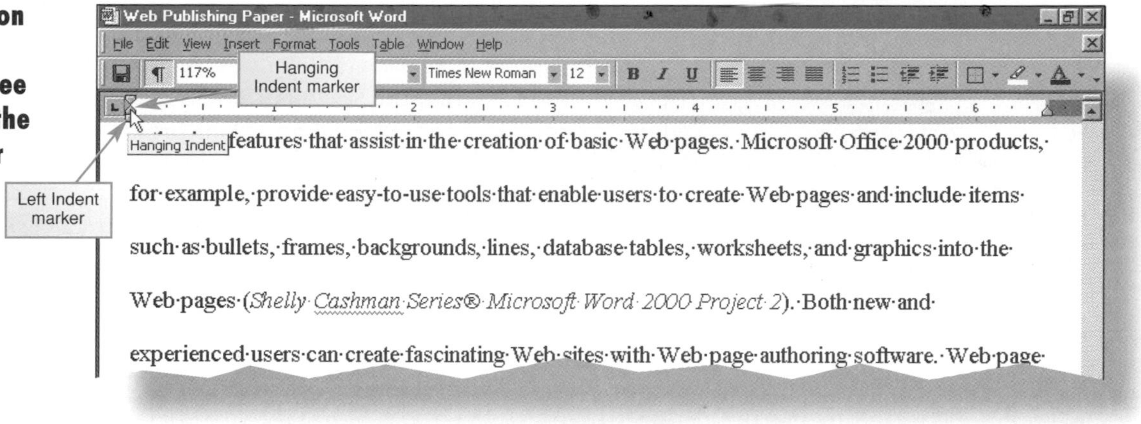

FIGURE 2-45

2 Drag the Hanging Indent marker to the ½" mark on the ruler.

The Hanging Indent marker and Left Indent marker display one-half inch from the left margin (Figure 2-46). When you drag the Hanging Indent marker, the Left Indent marker moves with it. The insertion point in the document window remains at the left margin because only subsequent lines in the paragraph are to be indented.

[Web Publishing Paper - Microsoft Word screen. Callout labels: "Hanging Indent marker positioned .5" from left margin", "paragraph mark remains at left margin".]

Text in document: authoring·features·that·assist·in·the·creation·of·basic·Web·pages.·Microsoft·Office·2000·products,· for·example,·provide·easy-to-use·tools·that·enable·users·to·create·Web·pages·and·include·items· such·as·bullets,·frames,·backgrounds,·lines,·database·tables,·worksheets,·and·graphics·into·the· Web·pages·(*Shelly·Cashman·Series®·Microsoft·Word·2000·Project·2*).·Both·new·and· experienced·users·can·create·fascinating·Web·sites·with·Web·page·authoring·software.·Web·page· authoring·software·packages·enable·the·creation·of·more·sophisticated·Web·pages·that·might· include·video,·sound,·animation,·and·other·special·effects.¶

————Page Break————

Works·Cited¶

¶

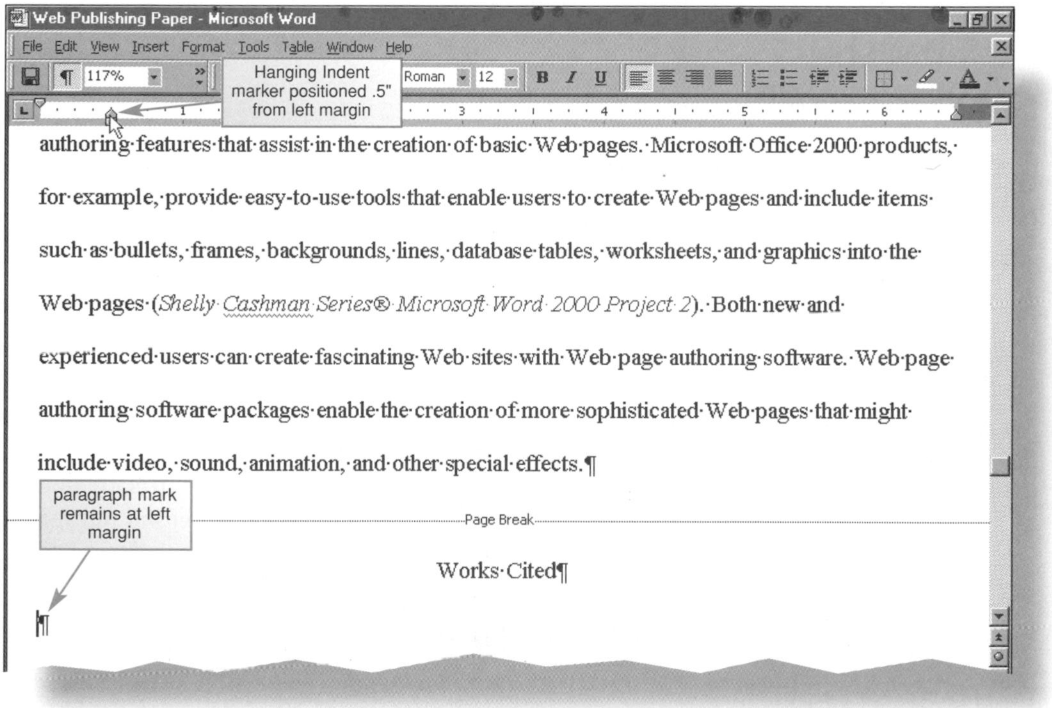

FIGURE 2-46

To drag both the First Line Indent and Hanging Indent markers at the same time, you drag the Left Indent marker on the ruler.

Enter the first two works in the works cited as explained in the steps on the next page.

Other Ways

1. Right-click paragraph, click Paragraph on shortcut menu, click Indents and Spacing tab, click Special box arrow, click Hanging, click OK button
2. On Format menu click Paragraph, click Indents and Spacing tab, click Special box arrow, click Hanging, click OK button
3. Press CTRL+T

Citing Sources
Information that commonly is known or accessible to the audience constitutes common knowledge and does not need to be listed as a parenthetical citation or in the bibliography. If you question whether certain information is common knowledge, you should cite it – just to be safe.

TO ENTER WORK CITED PARAGRAPHS

1 Type Thrall, Peter D., and Amy P. Winters. Press the SPACEBAR. Press CTRL+I. Type Computer Concepts for the New Millennium. Press CTRL+I. Press the SPACEBAR. Type Boston: International Press, 2001. Press the ENTER key.

2 Type Zack, Joseph R. "An Introduction to Clip Galleries and Digital Files." Press the SPACEBAR. Press CTRL+I. Type Computers for Today, Tomorrow, and Beyond and then press CTRL+I. Press the SPACEBAR. Type Sep. 2001: 9-24. Press the ENTER key.

The first two works cited paragraphs are entered (Figure 2-47).

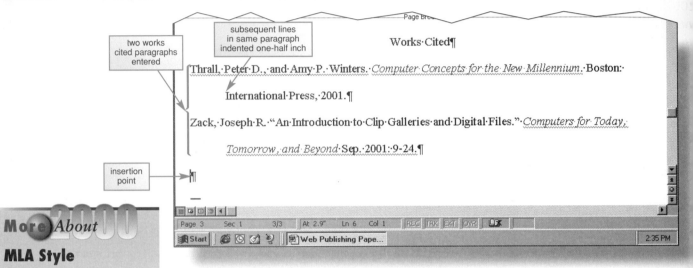

FIGURE 2-47

MLA Style
Titles of books, periodicals, and Web sites typically are underlined when a research paper is submitted in printed form. Some instructors require that Web addresses be hyperlinks for online access. Word formats hyperlinks with an underline. To distinguish hyperlinks from titles, the MLA allows titles to be italicized, if approved by the instructor.

When Word wraps the text in each works cited paragraph, it automatically indents the second line of the paragraph by one-half inch. When you press the ENTER key at the end of the first paragraph of text, the insertion point returns automatically to the left margin for the next paragraph. Recall that each time you press the ENTER key, the paragraph formatting in the previous paragraph is carried forward to the next paragraph.

Creating a Hyperlink

In Word, you can create a hyperlink simply by typing the address of the file or Web page to which you want to jump and then pressing the SPACEBAR or the ENTER key. A **hyperlink** is a shortcut that allows a user to jump easily and quickly to another location in the same document or to other documents or Web pages. **Jumping** is the process of following a hyperlink to its destination. For example, by clicking a hyperlink in the document window, you jump to another document on your computer, on your network, or on the World Wide Web. When you close the hyperlink destination page or document, you return to the original location in your Word document.

Hyperlinks
To verify that Word will automatically convert your Web addresses to hyperlinks, click Tools on the menu bar, click AutoCorrect, click the AutoFormat As You Type tab, verify that the Internet and network paths with hyperlinks check box contains a check mark, and then click the OK button.

In this project, one of the works cited is from a Web page on the Internet. When someone displays your research paper on the screen, you want him or her to be able to click the Web address in the work and jump to the associated Web site for more information. If you wish to create a hyperlink to a Web page from a Word document, you do not have to be connected to the Internet. Perform the following steps to create a hyperlink as you type.

teps **To Create a Hyperlink as You Type**

1 **Press CTRL+I. Type**
Shelly Cashman
Series(r) Microsoft
Word 2000 Project 2.
Press CTRL+I. Press the
SPACEBAR. Type Course
Technology. 1 Oct.
2001. http://
www.scsite.com/
wd2000/pr2/wc1.htm.

The insertion point immedi-
tely follows the Web address
(Figure 2-48).

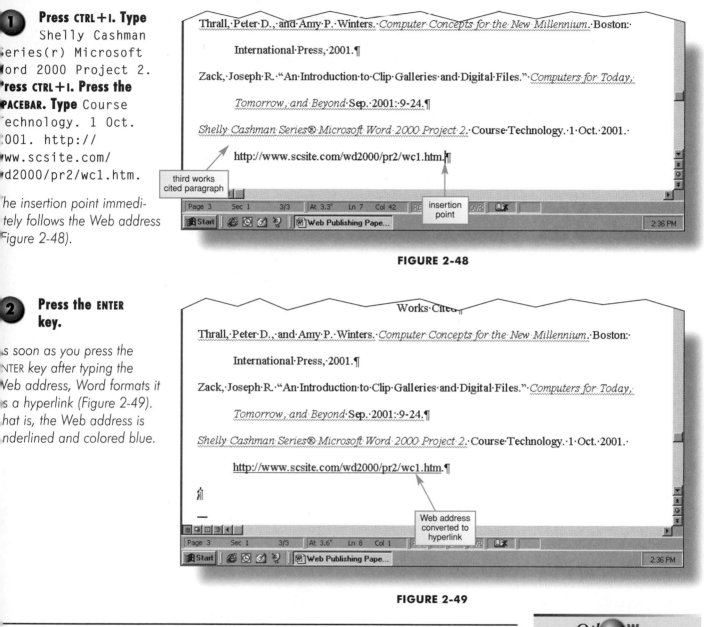

FIGURE 2-48

2 **Press the ENTER**
key.

As soon as you press the
ENTER key after typing the
Web address, Word formats it
as a hyperlink (Figure 2-49).
That is, the Web address is
underlined and colored blue.

FIGURE 2-49

Later in this project, you will jump to the hyperlink destination.

orting Paragraphs

The MLA style requires that the works cited be listed in alphabetical order by
author's last name. With Word, you can arrange paragraphs in alphabetic, numeric,
or date order based on the first character in each paragraph. Ordering characters in
his manner is called **sorting**. Arrange the works cited paragraphs in alphabetic order
as illustrated in the steps on the next page.

Other Ways

1. Right-click text, click
Hyperlink on shortcut menu,
click Existing File or Web
Page in the Link to list, type
Web address in Type the file
or Web page name text
box, click OK button

2. Click text, click Insert
Hyperlink button on
Standard toolbar, click
Existing File or Web Page
in the Link to list, type Web
address in Type the file or
Web page name text box,
click OK button

Steps **To Sort Paragraphs**

1 **Select all the works cited paragraphs by pointing to the left of the first paragraph and dragging down. Click Table on the menu bar and then point to Sort.**

Word displays the Table menu (Figure 2-50). All of the paragraphs to be sorted are selected.

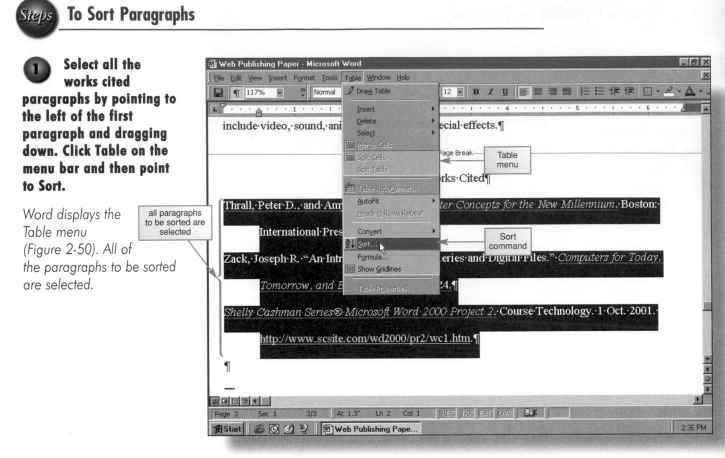

FIGURE 2-50

2 **Click Sort. Point to the OK button.**

Word displays the Sort Text dialog box (Figure 2-51). In the Sort by area, Ascending is selected. Ascending sorts in alphabetic, numeric, or earliest to latest date order.

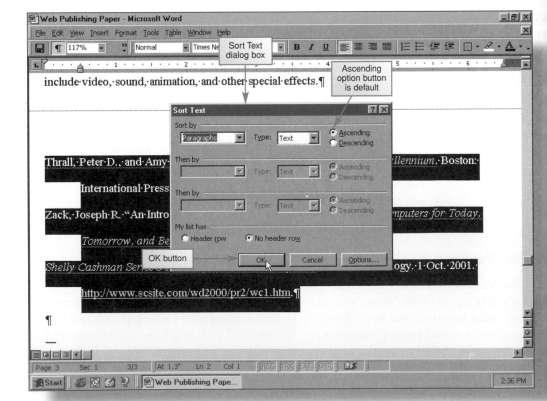

FIGURE 2-51

③ **Click the OK button. Click outside of the selection to remove the highlight.**

Word sorts the works cited paragraphs alphabetically (Figure 2-52).

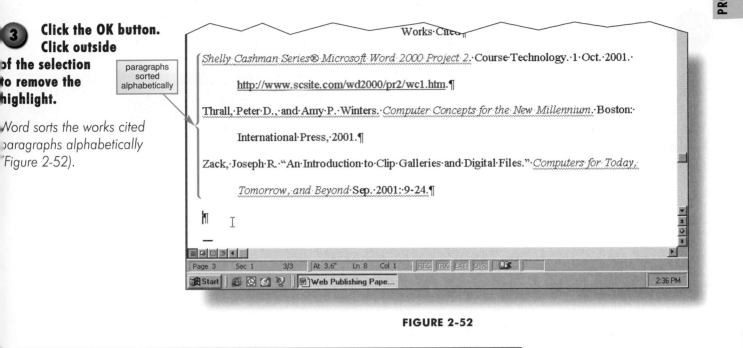

paragraphs sorted alphabetically

Works·Cited¶

Shelly·Cashman·Series®·Microsoft·Word·2000·Project·2.·Course·Technology.·1·Oct.·2001.·

http://www.scsite.com/wd2000/pr2/wc1.htm.¶

Thrall,·Peter·D.,·and·Amy·P.·Winters.·*Computer·Concepts·for·the·New·Millennium.*·Boston:·

International·Press,·2001.¶

Zack,·Joseph·R.·"An·Introduction·to·Clip·Galleries·and·Digital·Files."·*Computers·for·Today,·

Tomorrow,·and·Beyond.*·Sep.·2001:·9-24.¶

Page 3   Sec 1   3/3   At 3.6"   Ln 8   Col 1   REC TRK EXT OVR

Start   Web Publishing Pape...   2:36 PM

FIGURE 2-52

If you accidentally sort the wrong paragraphs, you can undo a sort by clicking the Undo button on the Standard toolbar.

In the Sort Text dialog box (Figure 2-51), the default sort order is Ascending. By default, Word orders in **ascending sort order**, which means from the beginning of the alphabet to the end of the alphabet, smallest number to the largest number, or earliest date to the most recent date. For example, if the first character of each paragraph to be sorted is a letter, Word sorts the selected paragraphs alphabetically.

You also can sort in descending order by clicking Descending in the Sort Text dialog box. **Descending sort order** means sorting from the end of the alphabet to the beginning of the alphabet, the largest number to the smallest number, or the most recent date to the earliest date.

Proofing and Revising the Research Paper

As discussed in Project 1, once you complete a document, you might find it necessary to make changes to it. Before submitting a paper to be graded, you should proofread it. While **proofreading**, you look for grammatical errors and spelling errors. You want to be sure the transitions between sentences flow smoothly and sentences themselves make sense. Very often, you may count the words in a paper to meet minimum word guidelines specified by an instructor. To assist you in this proofreading effort, Word provides several tools. These tools are discussed in the following pages.

Going to a Specific Location in a Document

Often, you would like to bring a certain page, footnote, or other object into view in the document window. To accomplish this, you could scroll through the document to find the desired page, footnote, or item. Instead of scrolling through the document, Word provides an easier method of going to a specific location via the **Select Browse Object menu**. Perform the steps on the next page to go to the top of page two in the research paper.

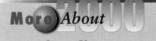

More About

Proofreading

When proofreading a paper, ask yourself these questions: Is the purpose clear? Does the title suggest the topic? Does the paper have an introduction, body, and conclusion? Is the thesis clear? Does each paragraph in the body relate to the thesis? Is the conclusion effective? Are all sources acknowledged?

To Browse by Page

1 **Click the Select Browse Object button on the vertical scroll bar. When the Select Browse Object menu displays, point to Browse by Page.**

Word displays the Select Browse Object menu (Figure 2-53). As you point to various commands on the Select Browse Object menu, Word displays the command name at the bottom of the menu.

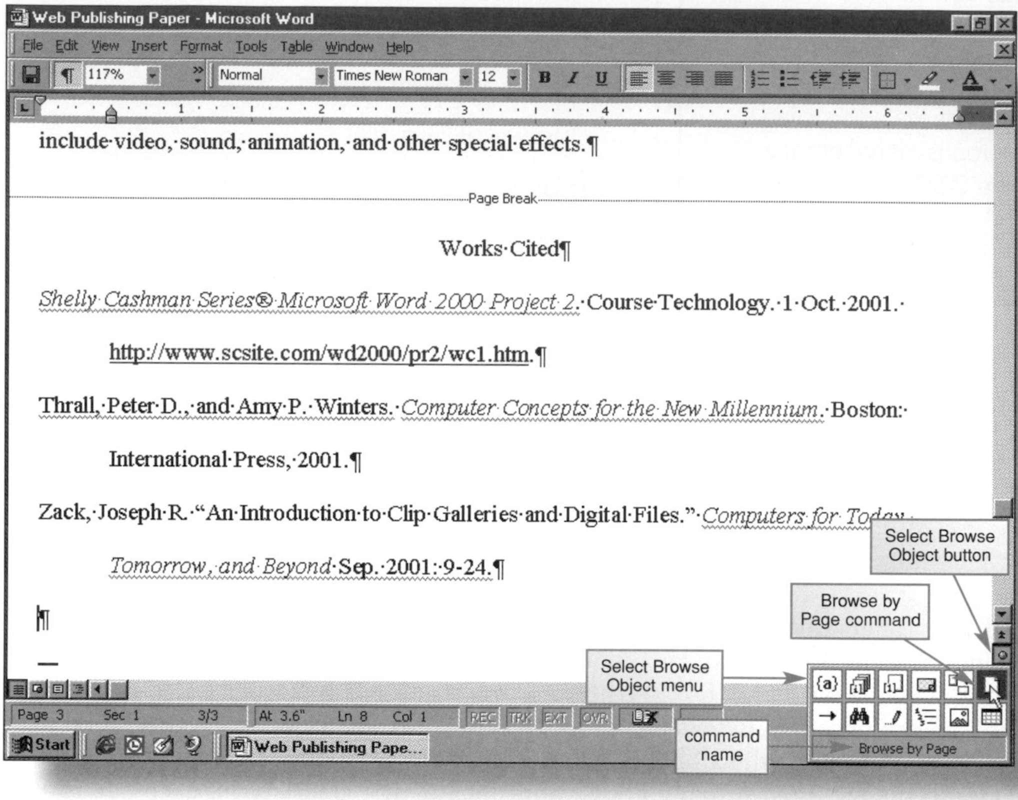

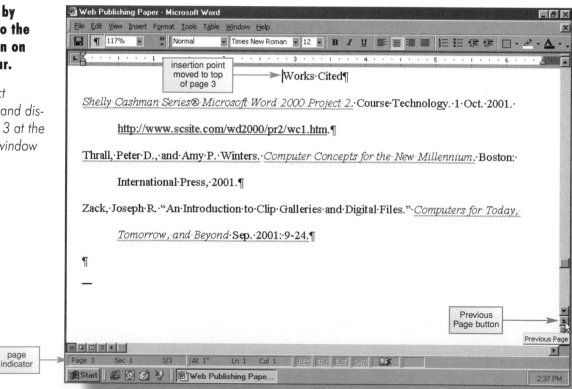

FIGURE 2-53

2 **Click Browse by Page. Point to the Previous Page button on the vertical scroll bar.**

Word closes the Select Browse Object menu and displays the top of page 3 at the top of the document window (Figure 2-54).

FIGURE 2-54

3 Click the Previous Page button.

Word places the top of page 2 (the previous page) at the top of the document window (Figure 2-55).

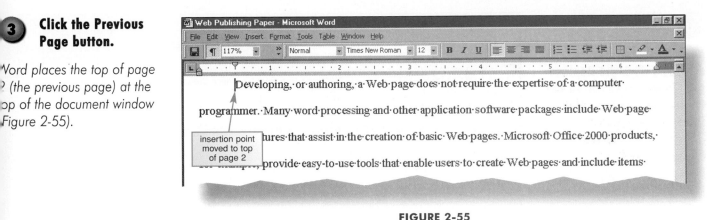

FIGURE 2-55

Depending on the command you click in the Select Browse Object menu, the function of the buttons above and below the Select Browse Object button on the vertical scroll bar changes. When you select Browse by Page, the buttons become Previous Page and Next Page buttons; when you select Browse by Footnote, the buttons become Previous Footnote and Next Footnote buttons, and so on.

Finding and Replacing Text

While proofreading the paper, you notice that it contains the word, creation, more than once in the document (see Figure 2-56 below); and you would rather use the word, development. Therefore, you wish to change all occurrences of the word, creation, to the word, development. To do this, you can use Word's find and replace feature, which automatically locates each occurrence of a specified word or phrase and then replaces it with specified text as shown in these steps.

Other Ways

1. Double-click page indicator on status bar (Figure 2-54), click Page in Go to what list, type page number in Enter page number text box, click Go To button, click Close button
2. On Edit menu click Go To, and then proceed as described in 1 above starting with click Page in Go to what list
3. Press CTRL+G, and then proceed as described in 1 above starting with click Page in Go to what list

Steps: To Find and Replace Text

1 Click the Select Browse Object button on the vertical scroll bar. Point to Find on the Select Browse Object menu (Figure 2-56).

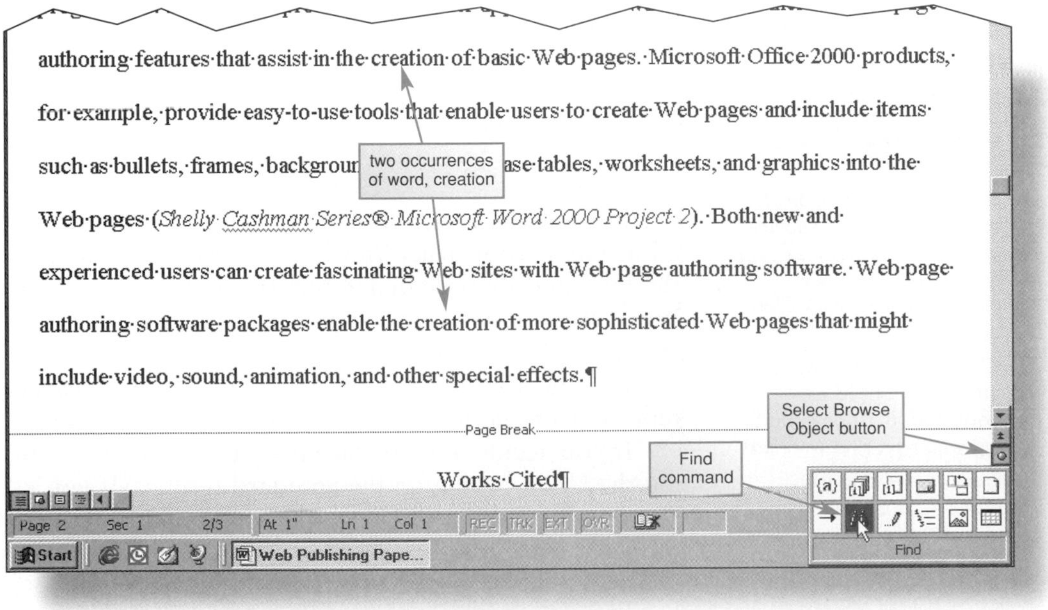

authoring·features·that·assist·in·the·creation·of·basic·Web·pages.·Microsoft·Office·2000·products,·

for·example,·provide·easy-to-use·tools·that·enable·users·to·create·Web·pages·and·include·items·

such·as·bullets,·frames,·background   two occurrences of word, creation   ·se·tables,·worksheets,·and·graphics·into·the·

Web·pages·(*Shelly·Cashman·Series® Microsoft·Word·2000·Project·2*).·Both·new·and·

experienced·users·can·create·fascinating·Web·sites·with·Web·page·authoring·software.·Web·page·

authoring·software·packages·enable·the·creation·of·more·sophisticated·Web·pages·that·might·

include·video,·sound,·animation,·and·other·special·effects.¶

----------Page Break----------

Works·Cited¶

Find command

Select Browse Object button

Page 2   Sec 1   2/3   At 1"   Ln 1   Col 1   REC TRK EXT OVR   Find

Start   Web Publishing Pape...

FIGURE 2-56

2 Click Find. When the Find and Replace dialog box displays, click the Replace tab. Type creation in the Find what text box. Press the TAB key. Type development in the Replace with text box. Point to the Replace All button.

Word displays the Find and Replace dialog box (Figure 2-57). The Replace All button replaces all occurrences of the Find what text with the Replace with text.

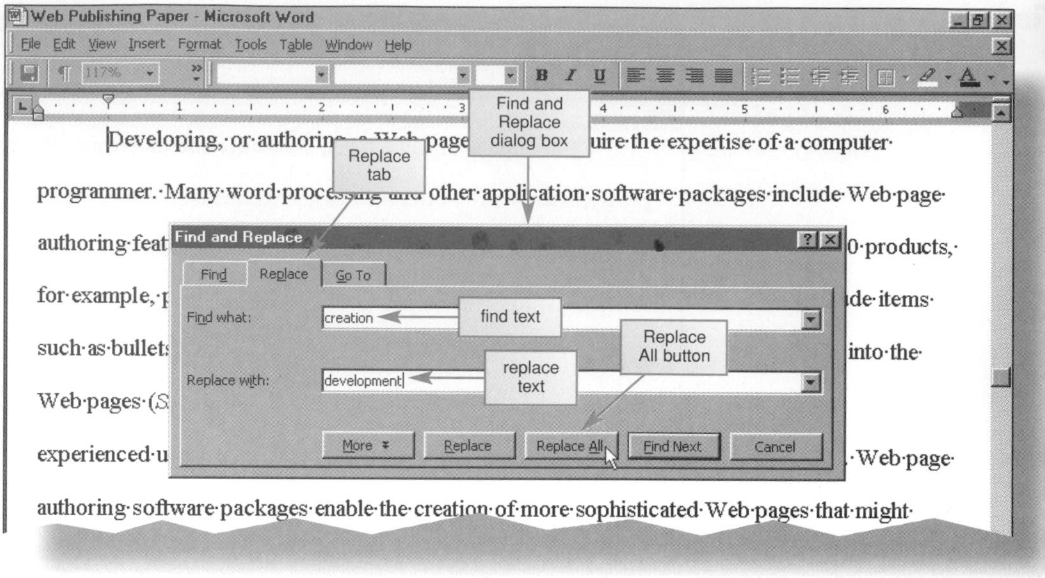

FIGURE 2-57

3 Click the Replace All button.

A Microsoft Word dialog box displays indicating the total number of replacements made (Figure 2-58).

4 Click the OK button. Click the Close button in the Find and Replace dialog box.

The word, development, displays in the document instead of the word, creation (see Figure 2-59).

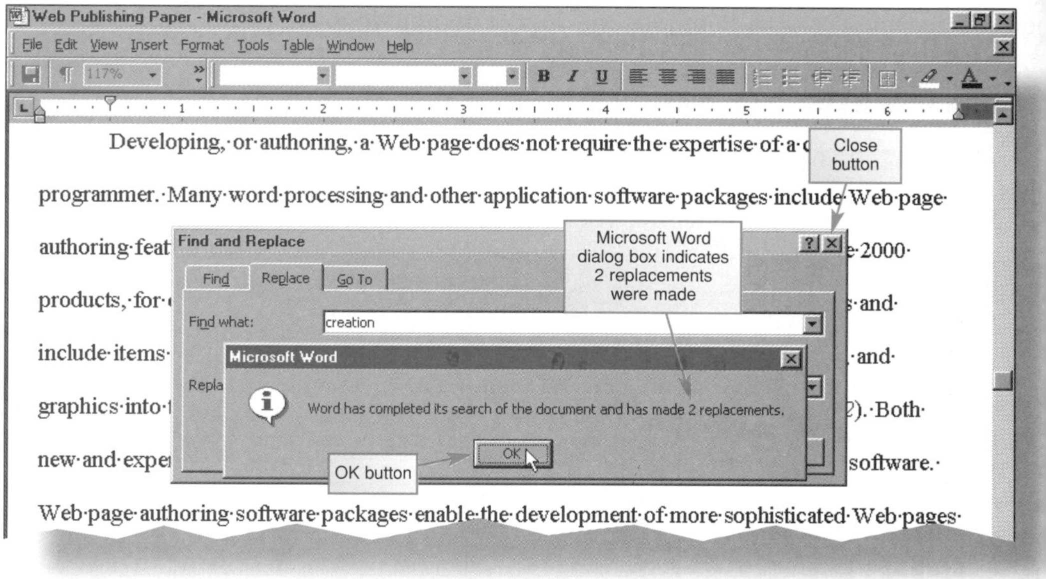

FIGURE 2-58

Other **Ways**

1. Double-click page indicator on status bar, click Replace tab, type Find what text, type Replace with text, click OK button, click Close button

2. On Edit menu click Replace, and then proceed as described in 1 above starting with type Find what text

3. Press CTRL+H, and then proceed as described in 1 above starting with type Find what text

In some cases, you may want to replace only certain occurrences of the text, not all of them. To instruct Word to confirm each change, click the Find Next button in the Find and Replace dialog box (Figure 2-57), instead of the Replace All button. When Word locates an occurrence of the text, it pauses and waits for you to click either the Replace button or the Find Next button. Clicking the Replace button changes the text; clicking the Find Next button instructs Word to disregard the replacement and look for the next occurrence of the Find what text.

If you accidentally replace the wrong text, you can undo a replacement by clicking the Undo button on the Standard toolbar. If you used the Replace All button, Word undoes all replacements. If you used the Replace button, Word undoes only the most recent replacement.

Finding Text

Sometimes, you may want to find only text, instead of find *and* replace text. To search for just a single occurrence of text, you would follow these steps.

TO FIND TEXT

1 Click the Select Browse Object button on the vertical scroll bar and then click Find on the Select Browse Object menu.

2 Type the text to locate in the Find what text box and then click the Find Next button. To edit the text, click the Close button in the Find and Replace dialog box; to find the next occurrence of the text, click the Find Next button.

Moving Text

While proofreading the research paper, you might realize that text in the last paragraph would flow better if the last two sentences were reversed. That is, you want to move the fourth sentence in the last paragraph to the end of the paragraph.

To move text, such as words, characters, sentences, or paragraphs, you first select the text to be moved and then use drag-and-drop editing or the cut-and-paste technique to move the selected text. With **drag-and-drop editing**, you drag the selected item to the new location and then insert, or drop, it there. **Cutting** involves removing the selected item from the document and then placing it on the **Office Clipboard**, which is a temporary storage area. **Pasting** is the process of copying an item from the Clipboard into the document at the location of the insertion point.

Use drag-and-drop editing to move an item a short distance. To drag-and-drop a sentence in the research paper, first select a sentence as shown below.

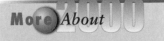

More About

Finding

To search for formatting or special characters, click the More button in the Find dialog box. To find formatting, click the Format button, select the formats you want to search for, then click the Find button. To find a special character, click the Special button, click the special character you desire, and then click the Find button.

More About

Cutting and Pasting

To move text a long distance (from one page to another page), the cut-and-paste technique is more efficient. When you paste text into a document, the contents of the Office Clipboard are not erased.

Steps To Select a Sentence

1 Position the mouse pointer (an I-beam) in the sentence to be moved. Press and hold the CTRL key. While holding the CTRL key, click the sentence. Release the CTRL key.

Word selects the entire sentence (Figure 2-59). Notice the space after the period is included in the selection.

authoring·features·that·assist·in·the·development·of·basic·Web·pages.·Microsoft·Office·2000·

products,·for·example,·provide·easy-to-use·tools·that·enable·users·to·create·Web·pages·and·

include·items·such·as·bullets,·frames,·backg [creation changed to development] ·database·tables,·worksheets,·and·

graphics·into·the·Web·pages·(*Shelly·Cashman·Series® Microsoft·Word·2000·Project·2*).·Both·

new·and·experienced·users·can·create·fascinating·Web·sites·with·Web·page·authoring·software.·

Web·page·authoring·software·packages·enable·the·development·of·more·sophisticated·Web·pages·

that·might·include·video,·sound,·animation,·and·other·special·effects.¶

Page Break

Works·Cited¶

sentence selected

Page 2   Sec 1   2/3   At 2.9"   Ln 6   Col 85   REC TRK EXT OVR

Start   Web Publishing Pape...   2:39 PM

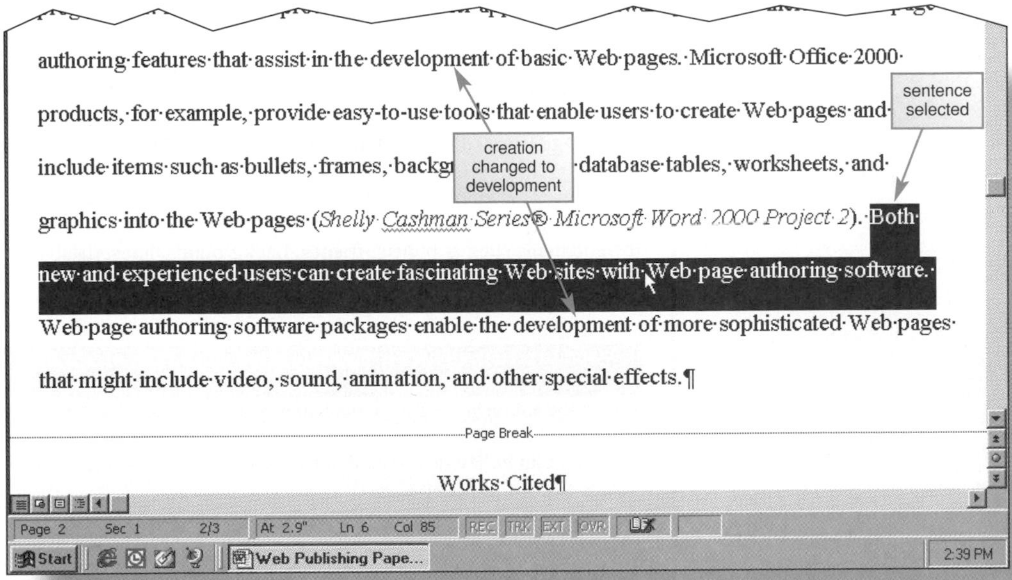

FIGURE 2-59

Other Ways

1. Drag through the sentence

Table 2-4 Techniques for Selecting Items with the Mouse

ITEM TO SELECT	MOUSE ACTION
Block of text	Click at beginning of selection, scroll to end of selection, position mouse pointer at end of selection, hold down SHIFT key and then click
Character(s)	Drag through character(s)
Document	Move mouse to left of text until mouse pointer changes to a right-pointing block arrow, then triple-click
Graphic	Click the graphic
Line	Move mouse to left of line until mouse pointer changes to a right-pointing block arrow, then click
Lines	Move mouse to left of first line until mouse pointer changes to a right-pointing block arrow, then drag up or down
Paragraph	Triple-click paragraph; or move mouse to left of paragraph until mouse pointer changes to a right-pointing block arrow, then double-click
Paragraphs	Move mouse to left of paragraph until mouse pointer changes to a right-pointing block arrow, double-click, then drag up or down
Sentence	Press and hold CTRL key, then click sentence
Word	Double-click the word
Words	Drag through words

Throughout Projects 1 and 2, you have selected text and then formatted it. Because selecting text is such a crucial function of Word, Table 2-4 summarizes the techniques used to select various items with the mouse.

With the sentence to be moved selected, you can use drag-and-drop editing to move it. You should be sure that drag-and-drop editing is enabled by clicking Tools on the menu bar, clicking Options, clicking the Edit tab, verifying a check mark is next to Drag and drop text editing, and then clicking the OK button. Follow these steps to move the selected sentence to the end of the paragraph.

Steps To Move Text

1 **With the mouse pointer in the selected text, press and hold the mouse button.**

*When you begin to drag the selected text, the insertion point changes to a **dotted insertion point** (Figure 2-60).*

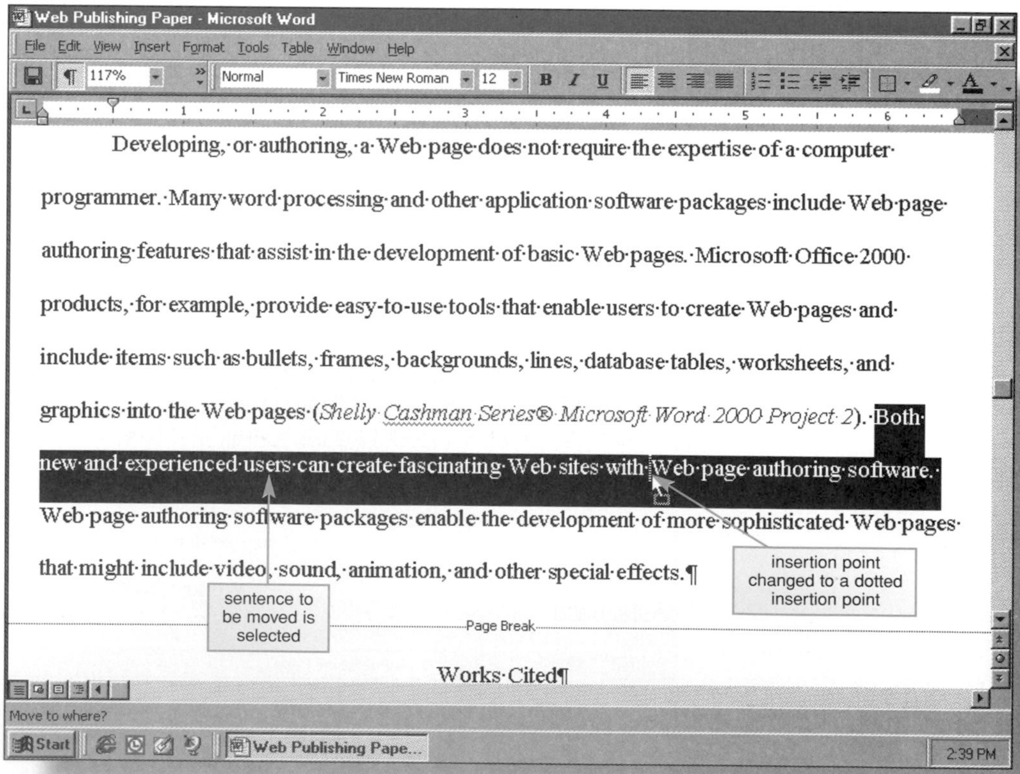

FIGURE 2-60

2 Drag the dotted insertion point to the location where the selected text is to be moved.

The dotted insertion point is at the end of the paragraph (Figure 2-61).

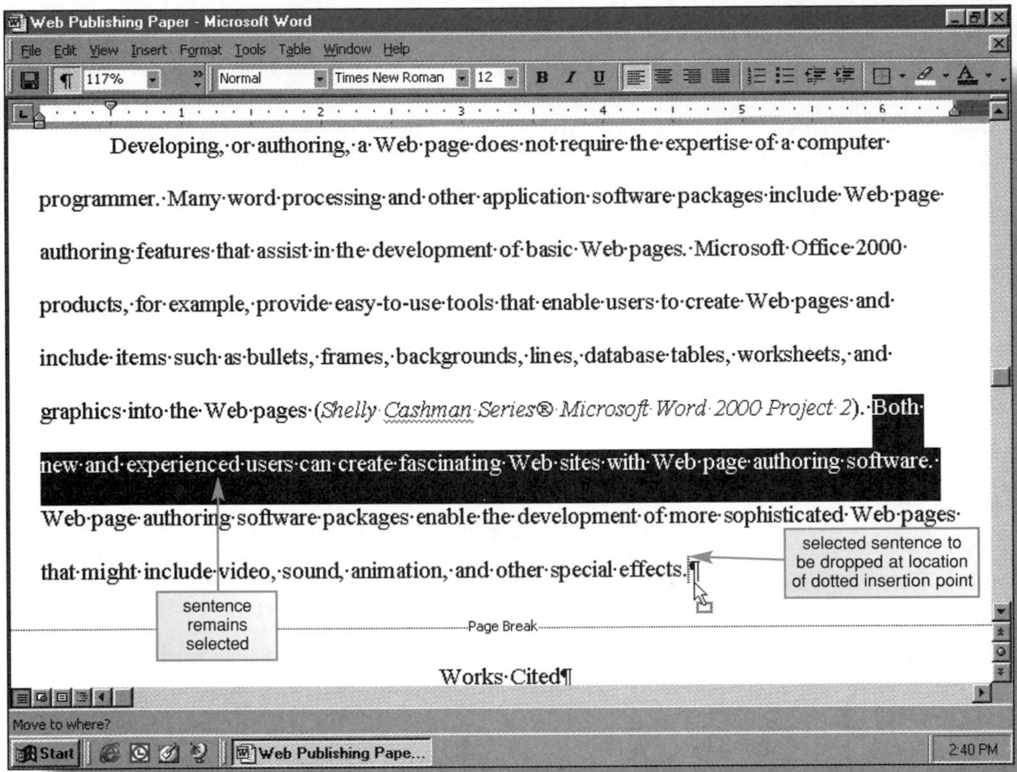

FIGURE 2-61

Web Publishing Paper - Microsoft Word

File Edit View Insert Format Tools Table Window Help

117%   Normal   Times New Roman   12   **B** *I* U

Developing, or authoring, a Web page does not require the expertise of a computer programmer. Many word processing and other application software packages include Web page authoring features that assist in the development of basic Web pages. Microsoft Office 2000 products, for example, provide easy-to-use tools that enable users to create Web pages and include items such as bullets, frames, backgrounds, lines, database tables, worksheets, and graphics into the Web pages (*Shelly Cashman Series® Microsoft Word 2000 Project 2*). Both new and experienced users can create fascinating Web sites with Web page authoring software. Web page authoring software packages enable the development of more sophisticated Web pages that might include video, sound, animation, and other special effects.

selected sentence to be dropped at location of dotted insertion point

sentence remains selected

Page Break

Works Cited¶

Move to where?

Start | Web Publishing Pape... | 2:40 PM

3 Release the mouse button. Click outside selection to remove the highlight.

Word moves the selected text to the location of the dotted insertion point (Figure 2-62).

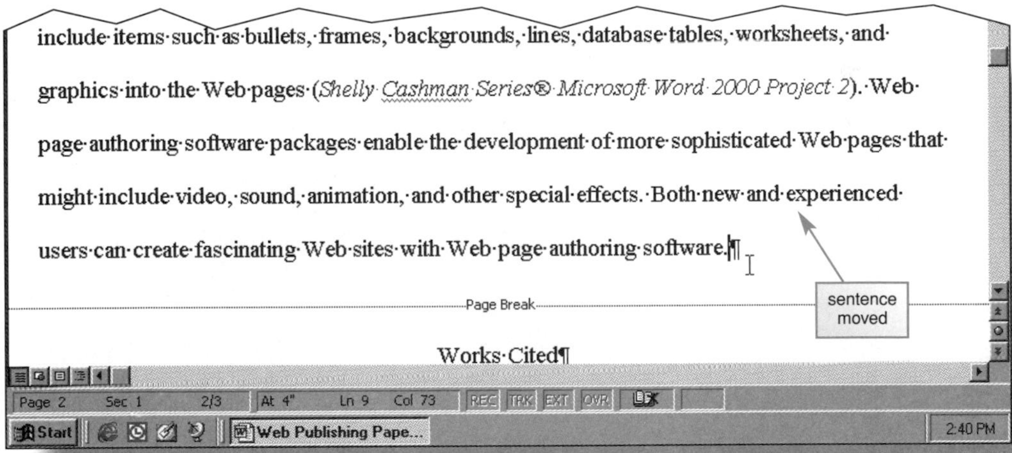

FIGURE 2-62

include items such as bullets, frames, backgrounds, lines, database tables, worksheets, and graphics into the Web pages (*Shelly Cashman Series® Microsoft Word 2000 Project 2*). Web page authoring software packages enable the development of more sophisticated Web pages that might include video, sound, animation, and other special effects. Both new and experienced users can create fascinating Web sites with Web page authoring software.¶

Page Break

Works Cited¶

sentence moved

Page 2   Sec 1   2/3   At 4"   Ln 9   Col 73   REC TRK EXT OVR

Start | Web Publishing Pape... | 2:40 PM

You can click the Undo button on the Standard toolbar if you accidentally drag text to the wrong location.

You can use drag-and-drop editing to move any selected item. That is, you can select words, sentences, phrases, and graphics and then use drag-and-drop editing to move them.

If you hold the CTRL key while dragging the selected item, Word copies the item instead of moving it.

Other Ways

1. Click Cut button on Standard toolbar, click where text is to be pasted, click Paste button on Standard toolbar

2. On Edit menu click Cut, click where text is to be pasted, on Edit menu click Paste

3. Press CTRL+X, position insertion point where text is to be pasted, press CTRL+V

More About

Synonyms

For access to an online thesaurus, visit the Word 2000 More About Web page (www.scsite.com/wd2000/more.htm) and then click Online Thesaurus.

Finding a Synonym

When writing, you may find that you used the same word in multiple locations or that a word you used was not quite appropriate. In these instances, you will want to look up a word similar in meaning to the duplicate or inappropriate word. These similar words are called **synonyms**. A book of synonyms is referred to as a **thesaurus**. Word provides synonyms and a thesaurus for your convenience. In this project, you would like a synonym for the word, include, in the middle of the last paragraph of the research paper. Perform the following steps to find an appropriate synonym.

Steps To Find a Synonym

1 Right-click the word for which you want to look up a synonym (include). Point to Synonyms on the shortcut menu and then point to the appropriate synonym (incorporate) on the Synonyms submenu.

Word displays a list of synonyms for the word containing the insertion point (Figure 2-63).

2 Click the synonym you want (incorporate).

Word replaces the word, include, in the document with the selected word, incorporate (Figure 2-64).

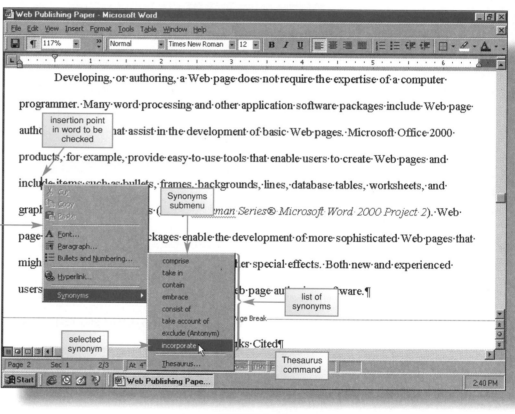

FIGURE 2-63

Other Ways

1. Click word, on Tools menu point to Language, on Language menu click Thesaurus, click appropriate meaning in Meanings list, click desired synonym in Replace with Synonym list, click Replace button
2. Click word, press SHIFT+F7, click appropriate meaning in Meanings list, click desired synonym in Replace with Synonym list, click Replace button

If the synonyms list does not display an appropriate word, you can display the Thesaurus dialog box by clicking Thesaurus on the Synonyms submenu (Figure 2-63). In the Thesaurus dialog box, you can look up synonyms for a different meaning of the word. You also can look up **antonyms**, or words with an opposite meaning.

Using Word Count

Often when you write papers, you are required to compose a paper with a minimum number of words. The requirement for the research paper in this project was a minimum of 425 words. Word provides a command that displays the number of words, as well as the number of pages, characters, paragraphs, and lines in your document. Perform the following steps to use word count.

steps To Count Words

1 Click Tools on the menu bar and then point to Word Count (Figure 2-64).

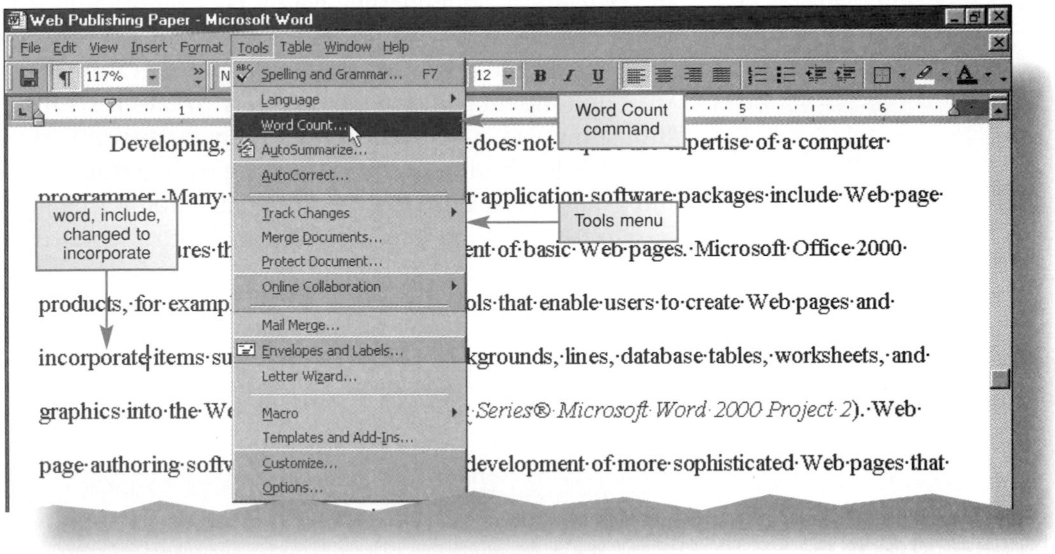

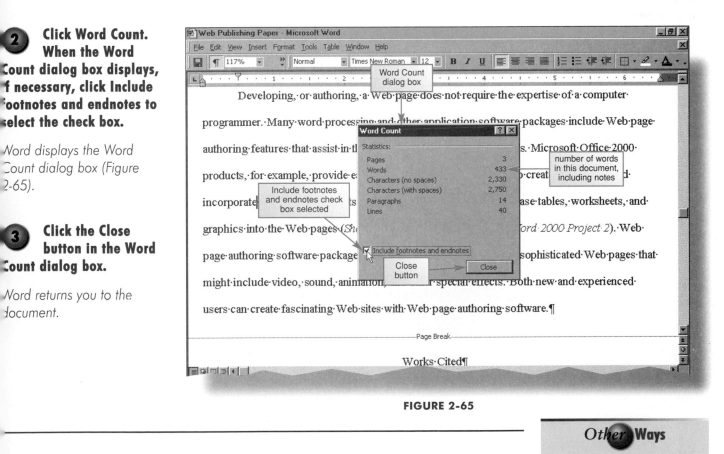

FIGURE 2-64

2 Click Word Count. When the Word Count dialog box displays, if necessary, click Include footnotes and endnotes to select the check box.

Word displays the Word Count dialog box (Figure 2-65).

3 Click the Close button in the Word Count dialog box.

Word returns you to the document.

FIGURE 2-65

Other Ways

1. On File menu click Properties, click Statistics tab, click OK button

The Word Count dialog box presents a variety of statistics about the current document, including number of pages, words, characters, paragraphs, and lines (Figure 2-65). You can choose to have note text included or not included in these statistics. If you want statistics on only a section of your document, select the section and then invoke the Word Count command.

Flagged Words

If you right-click a word, a shortcut menu displays. Recall that commands in a shortcut menu differ depending on the object that you right-click. If you right-click a word flagged with a red or green wavy underline, the shortcut menu displays spelling or grammar corrections for the flagged word.

Checking Spelling and Grammar at Once

As discussed in Project 1, Word checks your spelling and grammar as you type and places a wavy underline below possible spelling or grammar errors. You learned in Project 1 how to check these flagged words immediately. You also can wait and check the entire document for spelling and grammar errors at once.

The following steps illustrate how to check spelling and grammar in the Web Publishing Paper at once. In the following example the word, maintaining, has been misspelled intentionally as maintining to illustrate the use of Word's check spelling and grammar at once feature. If you are doing this project on a personal computer, your research paper may contain different misspelled words, depending on the accuracy of your typing.

Steps To Check Spelling and Grammar At Once

1 Press the CTRL+HOME keys to move the insertion point to the beginning of the document. Double-click the move handle on the Standard toolbar to display the entire toolbar. Point to the Spelling and Grammar button on the Standard toolbar.

Word will begin the spelling and grammar check at the location of the insertion point, which is at the beginning of the document (Figure 2-66).

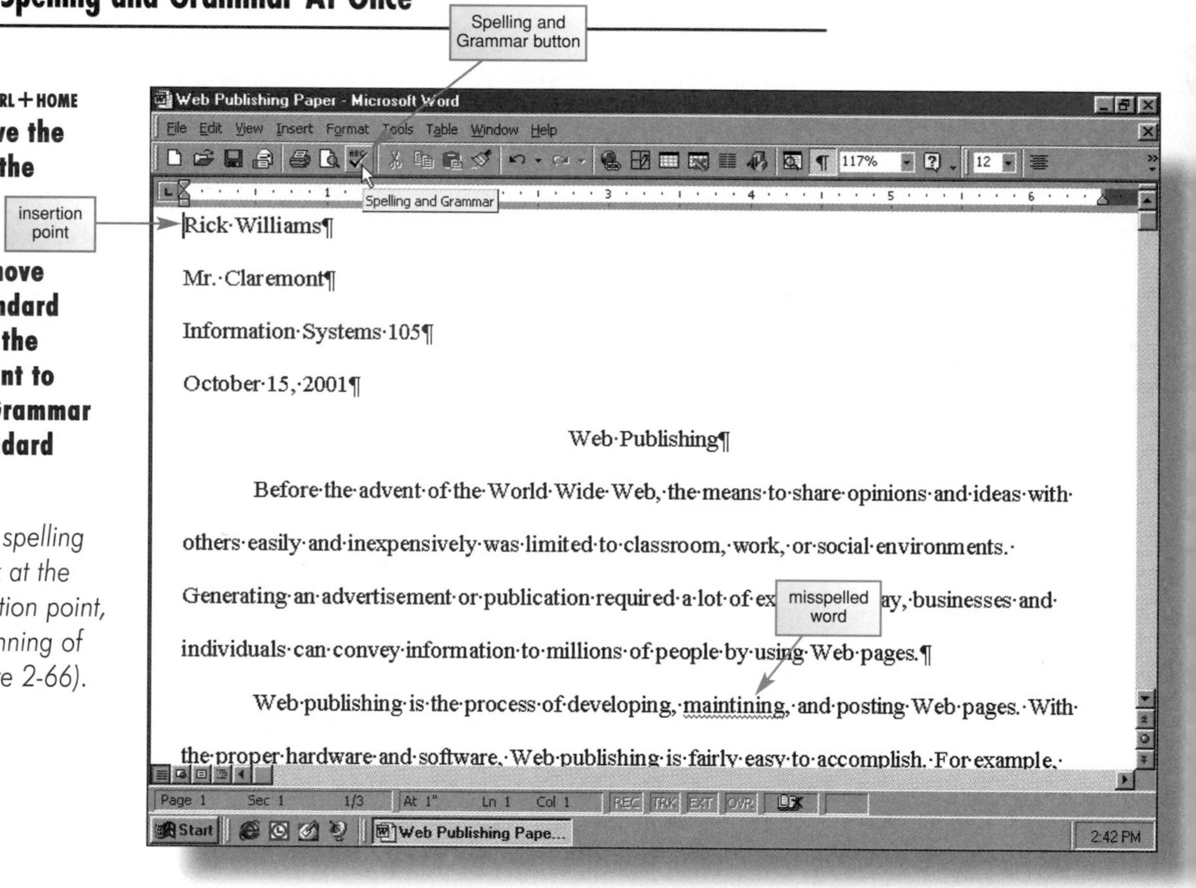

FIGURE 2-66

2 Click the Spelling and Grammar button. When the Spelling and Grammar dialog box displays, click maintaining in the Suggestions list and then point to the Change button.

Word displays the Spelling and Grammar dialog box (Figure 2-67). Word did not find the misspelled word, maintining, in its dictionary. The Suggestions list displays suggested corrections for the flagged word.

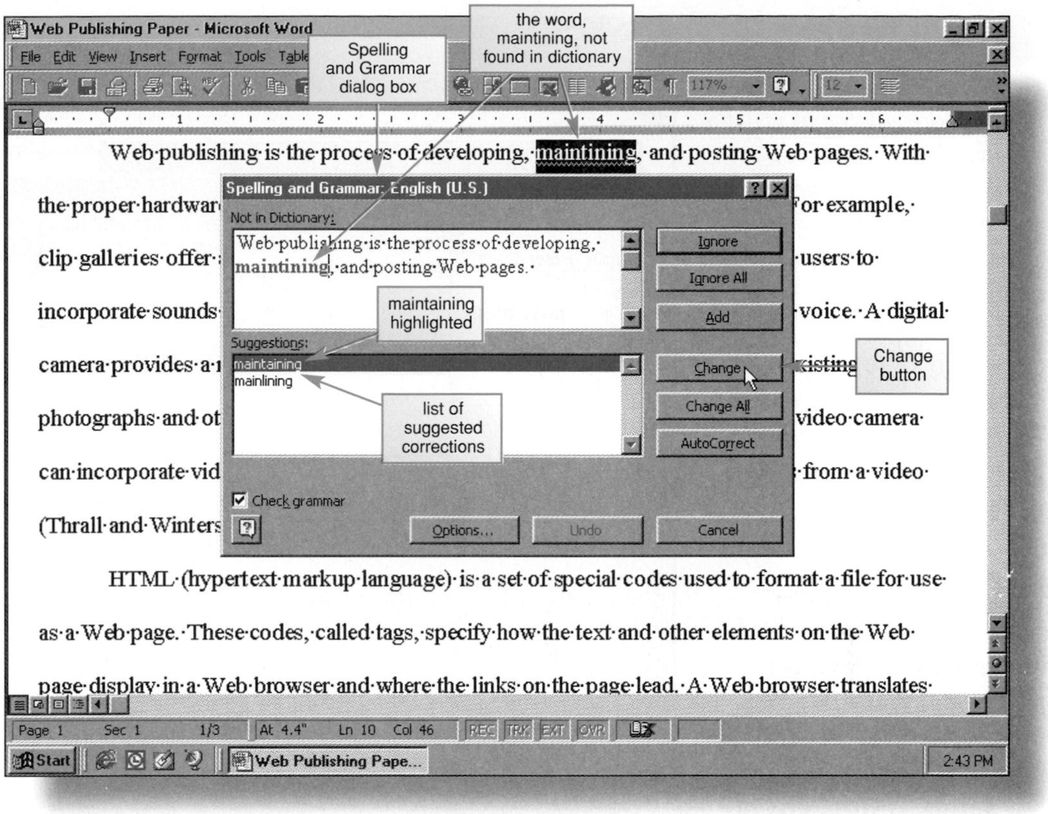

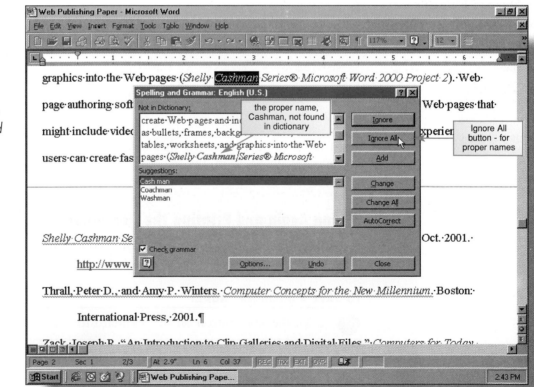

FIGURE 2-67

3 Click the Change button.

Word continues the spelling and grammar check until it finds the next error or reaches the end of the document (Figure 2-68). Word did not find Cashman in its dictionary because Cashman is a proper name. Cashman is spelled correctly.

FIGURE 2-68

4 Click the Ignore All button.

Word ignores all future occurrences of the word, Cashman. Word continues the spelling and grammar check until it finds the next error or reaches the end of the document. Word flags a grammar error on the Works Cited page (Figure 2-69). The works cited is written correctly.

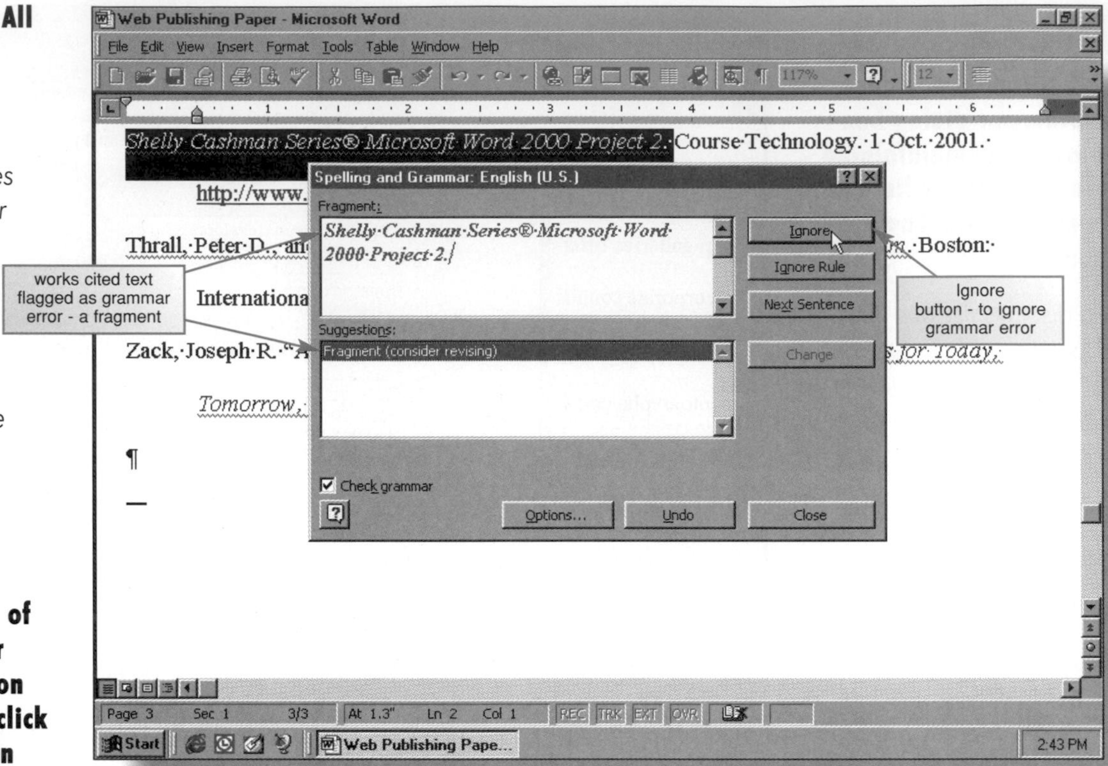

5 Click the Ignore button. For each of the remaining grammar errors that Word flags on the Works Cited page, click the Ignore button. When the Microsoft Word dialog box displays indicating Word has completed the spelling and grammar check, click the OK button.

Word returns to the document window.

FIGURE 2-69

Other Ways

1. Right-click flagged word, click Spelling on shortcut menu
2. On Tools menu click Spelling and Grammar
3. Press F7

Your document no longer displays red and green wavy underlines below words and phrases. In addition, the red X on the Spelling and Grammar Status icon has returned to a red check mark.

Saving Again and Printing the Document

The document now is complete. You should save the research paper again and print it, as described in the following steps.

TO SAVE A DOCUMENT AGAIN

1 Click the Save button on the Standard toolbar.

Word saves the research paper with the same file name, Web Publishing Paper.

TO PRINT A DOCUMENT

1 Click the Print button on the Standard toolbar.

The completed research paper prints as shown in Figure 2-1 on page WD 2.5.

Navigating to a Hyperlink

Recall that one requirement of this research paper is that one of the works be a Web site and be formatted as a hyperlink. Perform the following steps to check your hyperlink.

 To Navigate to a Hyperlink

1 **Display the third page of the research paper in the document window and then point to the hyperlink.**

When you point to a hyperlink in a Word document, the mouse pointer shape changes to a pointing hand (Figure 2-70).

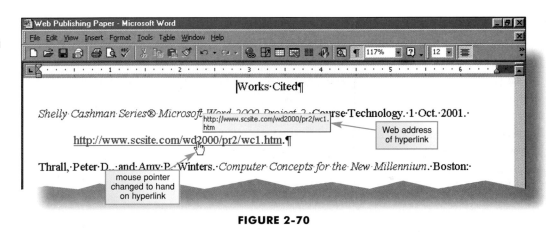

FIGURE 2-70

2 **Click the hyperlink.**

If you currently are not connected to the Web, Word connects you using your default browser. The www.scsite.com/wd2000/pr2/wc1.htm Web page displays (Figure 2-71).

3 **Close the browser window. If necessary, click the Microsoft Word program button on the taskbar to redisplay the Word window. Press CTRL+HOME.**

The first page of the research paper displays in the Word window.

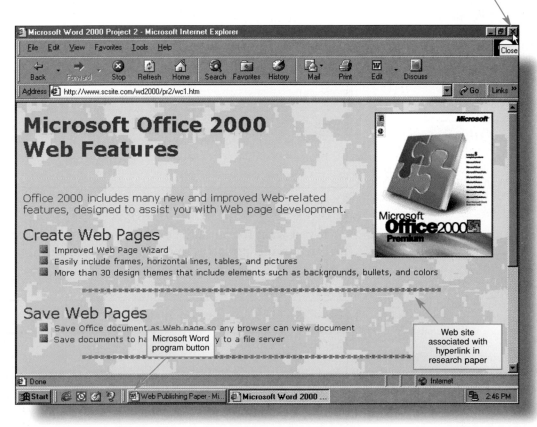

FIGURE 2-71

E-mailing

To e-mail a document as an attachment, click File on the menu bar, point to Send To, and then click Mail Recipient (as Attachment).

E-mailing a Copy of the Research Paper

Your instructor, Mr. Claremont, has requested you e-mail him a copy of your research paper so he can verify your hyperlink. Perform the following step to e-mail the document from within Word.

Steps **To E-mail a Document**

1 **Click the E-mail button on the Standard toolbar. Fill in the To text box with Mr. Claremont's e-mail address and the Subject text box (Figure 2-72) and then click the Send a Copy button.**

Word displays certain buttons and boxes from your e-mail editor inside the Word window. The document is e-mailed to the recipient named in the To text box.

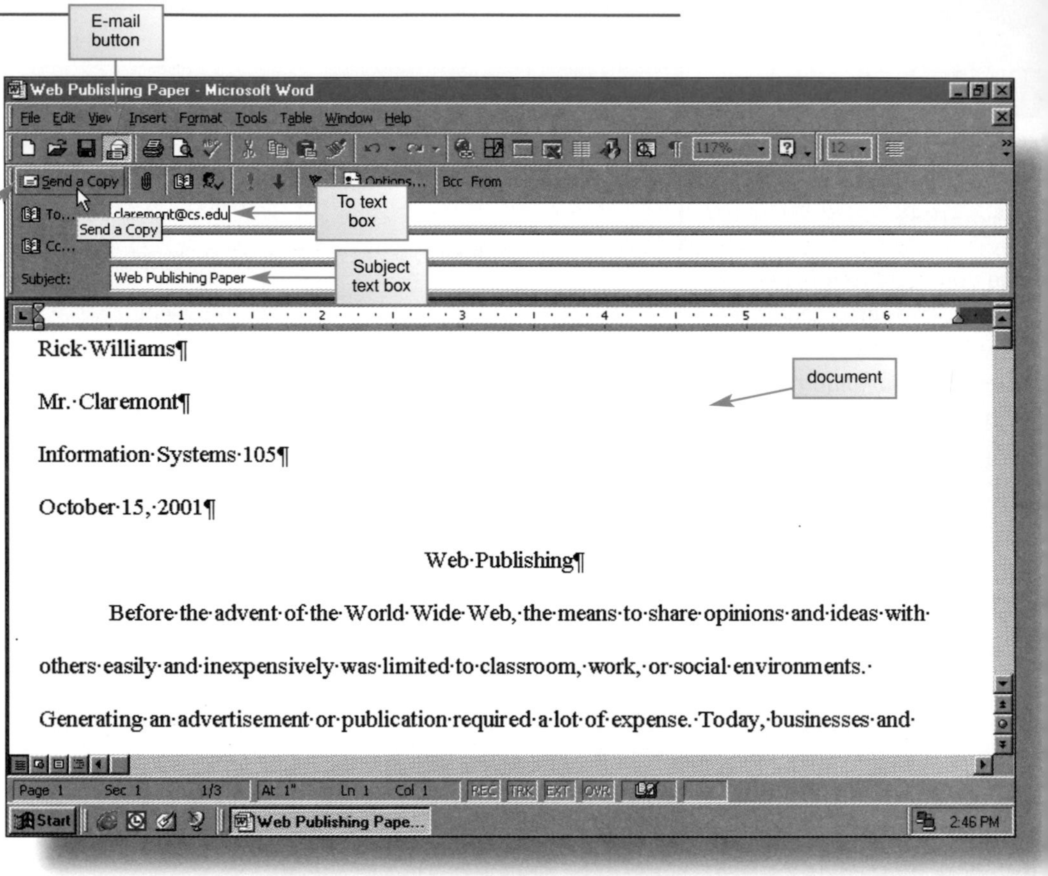

FIGURE 2-72

Other Ways

1. On File menu point to Send To, on Send To menu click Mail Recipient

Quick Reference

For a table that lists how to complete the tasks covered in this book using the mouse, menu, shortcut menu, and keyboard, visit the Office 2000 Web page (www.scsite.com/off2000/qr.htm) and then click Microsoft Word 2000.

If you want to cancel the e-mail operation, click the E-mail button again. The final step in this project is to quit Word, as described in the following step.

TO QUIT WORD

1 Click the Close button in the Word window.

The Word window closes.

CASE PERSPECTIVE SUMMARY

Rick accomplished his goal — learning about the basics of Web publishing while completing Mr. Claremont's research paper assignment. Now he is ready to create a personal Web page and publish it to a Web server. Rick decides to use Word's Web Page Wizard to create his Web page. He also contacts his Internet service provider to set up his free 6 MB of Web space. After receiving his personal Web site address from his Internet service provider, Rick publishes his Web page for the world to see. (For more information on publishing Web pages to a Web server, see Appendix B.) He shows Mr. Claremont the Web page, who in turn shows Rick's classmates.

Project Summary

Project 2 introduced you to creating a research paper using the MLA documentation style. You learned how to change margin settings, adjust line spacing, create headers with page numbers, and indent paragraphs. You learned how to use Word's AutoCorrect feature. Then, you added a footnote in the research paper. You alphabetized the works cited page by sorting its paragraphs and included a hyperlink to a Web page in one of the works. You learned how to browse through a Word document, find and replace text, and move text. You looked up a synonym and saw how to display statistics about your document. Finally, you navigated to a hyperlink and e-mailed a copy of a document.

What You Should Know

Having completed this project, you now should be able to perform the following tasks:

Add a Footnote *(WD 2.23)*

AutoCorrect As You Type *(WD 2.20)*

Browse by Page *(WD 2.42)*

Center the Title of the Works Cited Page *(WD 2.36)*

Change the Default Font Size *(WD 2.15)*

Change the Margin Settings *(WD 2.8)*

Check Spelling and Grammar at Once *(WD 2.50)*

Click and Type *(WD 2.13)*

Close the Note Pane *(WD 2.29)*

Count Words *(WD 2.49)*

Create a Hanging Indent *(WD 2.37)*

Create a Hyperlink as You Type *(WD 2.39)*

Create an AutoCorrect Entry *(WD 2.21)*

Display Formatting Marks *(WD 2.7)*

Display the Header Area *(WD 2.12)*

Double-Space a Document *(WD 2.9)*

E-mail a Document *(WD 2.54)*

Enter and Format a Page Number *(WD 2.14)*

Enter More Text *(WD 2.30)*

Enter Name and Course Information *(WD 2.16)*

Enter Works Cited Paragraphs *(WD 2.38)*

Find a Synonym *(WD 2.48)*

Find and Replace Text *(WD 2.43)*

Find Text *(WD 2.45)*

▶ First-Line Indent Paragraphs *(WD 2.19)*

▶ Insert a Symbol Automatically *(WD 2.33)*

▶ Modify a Style *(WD 2.26)*

▶ Move Text *(WD 2.46)*

▶ Navigate to a Hyperlink *(WD 2.53)*

▶ Page Break Automatically *(WD 2.32)*

▶ Page Break Manually *(WD 2.35)*

▶ Print a Document *(WD 2.52)*

▶ Quit Word *(WD 2.54)*

▶ Reset Menus and Toolbars *(WD 2.7)*

▶ Save a Document *(WD 2.18)*

▶ Save a Document Again *(WD 2.52)*

▶ Select a Sentence *(WD 2.45)*

▶ Sort Paragraphs *(WD 2.40)*

▶ Start Word *(WD 2.6)*

▶ Use Shortcut Keys to Format Text *(WD 2.17)*

▶ Zoom Page Width *(WD 2.9)*

More *About*

Microsoft Certification

The Microsoft Office User Specialist (MOUS) Certification program provides an opportunity for you to obtain a valuable industry credential — proof that you have the Word 2000 skills required by employers. For more information, see Appendix D or visit the Shelly Cashman Series MOUS Web page at www.scsite.com/off2000/cert.htm.

Apply Your Knowledge

Project Reinforcement at www.scsite.com/off2000/reinforce.htm

1 Revising a Document

Instructions: Start Word. Open the document, Internet Paragraph, on the Data Disk. If you did not download the Data Disk, see the inside back cover for instructions for downloading the Data Disk or see your instructor.

The document is a paragraph of text. You are to move two sentences in the paragraph and change all occurrences of the word, Web, to the phrase, World Wide Web. The revised paragraph is shown in Figure 2-73.

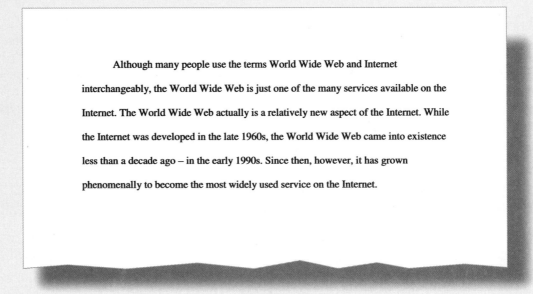

> Although many people use the terms World Wide Web and Internet interchangeably, the World Wide Web is just one of the many services available on the Internet. The World Wide Web actually is a relatively new aspect of the Internet. While the Internet was developed in the late 1960s, the World Wide Web came into existence less than a decade ago – in the early 1990s. Since then, however, it has grown phenomenally to become the most widely used service on the Internet.

FIGURE 2-73

Perform the following tasks:

1. Press and hold the CTRL key. While holding the CTRL key, click in the third sentence, which begins, The Web actually is..., to select the sentence. Release the CTRL key.
2. Press and hold down the left mouse button. Drag the dotted insertion point to the left of the letter W in the second sentence beginning, While the Internet was..., and then release the mouse button to move the sentence. Click outside the selection to remove the highlight.
3. Click the Select Browse Object button on the vertical scroll bar and then click Find on the Select Browse Object menu.
4. When the Find and Replace dialog box displays, click the Replace tab. Type Web in the Find what text box, press the TAB key, and then type World Wide Web in the Replace with text box. Click the Replace All button.
5. Click the OK button in the Microsoft Word dialog box. Click the Close button in the Find and Replace dialog box.
6. Click File on the menu bar and then click Save As. Use the file name, Revised Internet Paragraph, and then save the document on your floppy disk.
7. Print the revised paragraph.

In the Lab

1 Preparing a Research Paper

Problem: You are a college student currently enrolled in an English composition class. Your assignment is to prepare a short research paper (400-425 words) about digital cameras. The requirements are that the paper be presented according to the MLA documentation style and have three references (Figures 2-74a through 2-74c shown below and on the next page). One of the three references must be from the Internet and formatted as a hyperlink on the Works Cited page.

Thornton 1

Anne Thornton

Ms. Baxter

English 105

March 12, 2001

Digital Cameras

Digital cameras allow computer users to take pictures and store the photographed images

digitally instead of on traditional film. With some digital cameras, a user downloads the stored

pictures from the digital camera to a computer using special software included with the camera.

With others, the camera stores the pictures directly on a floppy disk or on a PC Card. A user then

copies the pictures to a computer by inserting the floppy disk into a disk drive or the PC Card

into a PC Card slot (Chambers and Norton 134). Once stored on a computer, the pictures can be

edited with photo-editing software, printed, faxed, sent via electronic mail, included in another

document, or posted to a Web site for everyone to see.

Three basic types of digital cameras are studio cameras, field cameras, and point-and-

shoot cameras (*Shelly Cashman Series® Microsoft Word 2000 Project 2*). The most expensive

and highest quality of the three, a studio camera, is a stationary camera used for professional

studio work. Photojournalists frequently use field cameras because they are portable and have a

variety of lenses and other attachments. As with the studio camera, a field camera can be quite

expensive.

Reliable and lightweight, the point-and-shoot camera provides acceptable quality

photographic images for the home or small business user. A point-and-shoot camera enables

these users to add pictures to personalized greeting cards, a computerized photo album, a family

FIGURE 2-74a

(continued)

In the Lab

Preparing a Research Paper *(continued)*

Thornton 2

newsletter, certificates, awards, or a personal Web site. Because of its functionality, it is an ideal

camera for mobile users such as real estate agents, insurance agents, and general contractors.

    The image quality produced by a digital camera is measured by the number of bits it

stores in a dot and the resolution, or number of dots per inch. The higher each number, the better

the quality, but the more expensive the camera. Most of today's point-and-shoot digital cameras

are at least 24-bit with a resolution ranging from 640 x 480 to 1024 x 960 (Walker 57-89). Home

and small business users can find an affordable camera with a resolution in this range that

delivers excellent detail for less than $400.

FIGURE 2-74b

Thornton 3

Works Cited

Chambers, John Q., and Theresa R. Norton. *Understanding Computers in the New Century*.

    Chicago: Midwest Press, 2001.

Shelly Cashman Series® Word 2000 Project 2. Course Technology. 5 Mar. 2001.

     http://www.scsite.com/wd2000/pr2/wc2.htm.

Walker, Marianne L. "Understanding the Resolutions of Digital Cameras and Imaging Devices."

    Computing for the Home Feb. 2001: 57-89.

FIGURE 2-74c

Instructions:

1. If necessary, click the Show/Hide ¶ button on the Standard toolbar. Change all margins to one inch. Adjust line spacing to double. Create a header to number pages. If necessary, change the font size of all characters to 12 point. Type the name and course information at the left margin. Center and type the title. First-line indent all paragraphs in the paper.
2. Type the body of the paper as shown in Figure 2-74a on the previous page and Figure 2-74b. At the end of the body of the research paper, press the ENTER key and insert a manual page break.
3. Create the works cited page (Figure 2-74c).
4. Check the spelling of the paper at once.
5. Save the document on a floppy disk with Digital Camera Paper as the file name.
6. If you have access to the Web, test your hyperlink by clicking it.
7. Print the research paper. Above the title of your printed research paper, handwrite the number of words in the research paper.

In the Lab

2 Preparing a Research Report with Footnotes

Problem: You are a college student currently enrolled in an English composition class. Your assignment is to prepare a short research paper in any area of interest to you. The requirements are that the paper be presented according to the MLA documentation style and have three references. One of the three references must be from the Internet and formatted as a hyperlink on the works cited page. You decide to prepare a paper on virtual reality (Figures 2-75 below and on the next page).

Jameson 1

Casey Jameson

Mr. Brookfield

English 105

September 14, 2001

Virtual Reality

Virtual reality (VR) is the use of a computer to create an artificial environment that appears and feels like a real environment and allows users to explore a space and manipulate the environment. In its simplest form, a VR application displays what appears to be a three-dimensional view of a place or object, such as a landscape, building, molecule, or red blood cell, which users can explore. For example, architects can use VR software to show clients how a building will look after a construction or remodeling project.

In more advanced forms, VR software requires that users wear specialized headgear, body suits, and gloves to enhance the experience of the artificial environment (Vance and Reed 34-58). The headgear displays the artificial environment in front of a user's eyes.[1] The body suit and the gloves sense motion and direction, allowing a user to move through, pick up, or hold items displayed in the virtual environment. Experts predict that eventually the body suits will provide tactile feedback so users can experience the touch and feel of the virtual world.

Many games, such as flight simulators, use virtual reality. In these games, special visors allow users to see the computer-generated environment. As the user walks around the game's electronic landscape, sensors in the surrounding game machine record movements and change the view of the landscape accordingly.

---

[1] According to Vance and Reed, patients in one dental office wear VR headsets to relax them during their visit with the dentist.

FIGURE 2-75a

(continued)

In the Lab

Preparing a Research Report with Footnotes *(continued)*

Jameson 2

Companies increasingly are using VR for more practical commercial applications, as well. Automobile dealers, for example, use virtual showrooms in which customers can view the exterior and interior of available vehicles. Airplane manufacturers use virtual prototypes to test new models and shorten product design time. Many firms use personal computer-based VR applications for employee training (*Shelly Cashman Series® Microsoft Word 2000 Project 2*). As computing power and the use of the Web increase, practical applications of VR continue to emerge in education, business, and entertainment.[2]

---

[2] Henry Davidson, a developer of VR applications, predicts that in the future, moviegoers will be able to pretend they are one of a movie's characters. In this environment, the VR technology will link the moviegoer's sensory system (sight, smell, hearing, taste, and touch) to the character's sensory system (Holloway 46-52).

FIGURE 2-75b

In the Lab

Part 1 Instructions: Perform the following tasks to create the research paper:

1. If necessary, click the Show/Hide ¶ button on the Standard toolbar. Change all margin settings to one inch. Adjust line spacing to double. Create a header to number pages. If necessary, change the font size of all characters to 12 point. Type the name and course information at the left margin. Center and type the title. First-line indent all paragraphs in the paper.

2. Type the body of the paper as shown in Figure 2-75a on page WD 2.59 and Figure 2-75b. At the end of the body of the research paper, press the ENTER key once and insert a manual page break.

3. Create the works cited page. Enter the works cited shown below as separate paragraphs and then sort the paragraphs.

   (a) *Shelly Cashman Series® Microsoft Word 2000 Project 2*. Course Technology. 3 Sep. 2001. http://www.scsite.com/wd2000/pr2/wc3.htm.

   (b) Holloway, April I. "The Future of Virtual Reality Applications." *Computers for Today, Tomorrow, and Beyond* Sep. 2001: 46-52.

   (c) Vance, Dale W., and Karen P. Reed. *The Complete Book of Virtual Reality*. Dallas: Worldwide Press, 2001.

4. Check the spelling of the paper.

5. Save the document on a floppy disk with Virtual Reality Paper as the file name.

6. If you have access to the Web, test your hyperlink by clicking it.

7. Print the research paper. Above the title of your printed research paper, handwrite the number of words, including the footnotes, in the research paper.

Part 2 Instructions: Perform the following tasks to modify the research paper:

1. Use Word to find a synonym of your choice for the word, eventually, in the second paragraph.

2. Change all occurrences of the word, artificial, to the word, simulated.

3. In the second footnote, change the word, link, to the word, connect.

4. Convert the footnotes to endnotes. You have learned that endnotes appear at the end of a document. *Hint:* Use Help to learn about converting footnotes to endnotes.

5. Modify the Endnote text style to 12-point font, double-spaced text with a first-line indent. Insert a page break so the endnotes are placed on a separate numbered page. Center the title, Endnotes, double-spaced above the notes.

6. Change the format of the note reference marks from Arabic numbers (1., 2., etc.) to capital letters (A., B., etc.). *Hint*: Use Help to learn about changing the number format of note reference marks.

7. Save the document on a floppy disk with Revised Virtual Reality Paper as the file name.

8. Print the revised research paper.

In the Lab

3 Composing a Research Paper from Notes

Problem: You have drafted the notes shown in Figure 2-76. Your assignment is to prepare a short research paper from these notes. Review the notes and then rearrange and reword them. Embellish the paper as you deem necessary. Add a footnote elaborating on a personal experience you have had. Present the paper according to the MLA documentation style.

Instructions: Perform the following tasks:

1. Change all margin settings to one inch. Adjust line spacing to double. Create a header to number pages. If necessary, change the font size of all characters to 12 point. Type the name and course information at the left margin. Center and type the title. First-line indent all paragraphs in the paper.

Productivity software makes people more efficient and effective in their daily activities. Three popular applications are (1) word processing, (2) spreadsheet, and (3) database.

Word Processing: Widely used application for creating, editing, and formatting text-based documents such as letters, memos, reports, fax cover sheet, mailing labels, and newsletters. Formatting features include changing font and font size, changing color of characters, organizing text into newspaper-style columns. Other features include adding clip art, changing margins, finding and replacing text, checking spelling and grammar, inserting headers and footers, providing a thesaurus, developing Web pages, and inserting tables. Source: "Evaluating Word Processing and Spreadsheet Software," an article in Computers Weekly, January 12, 2001 issue, pages 45-78, author Kimberly G. Rothman.

Spreadsheet: Used to organize data in rows and columns in a worksheet. Data is stored in cells, the intersection of rows and columns. Worksheets have more than 16 millions cells that can hold data. Cells can hold numbers, formulas, or functions. Formulas and functions perform calculations. When data in cells changes, the formulas and functions automatically recalculate formulas and display new values. Many spreadsheet packages allow you to create macros, which hold a series of keystrokes and instructions – a real timesaver. Most also include the ability to create charts, e.g. line charts, column charts, and pie charts, from the data. Source: same as for word processing software.

Database: Used to collect data and allow access, retrieval, and use of that data. Data stored in tables, which consists of rows (records) and columns (fields). Data can contain text, numbers, dates, or hyperlinks. When data is entered, it can be validated (compared to a set of stored rules or values to determine if the entered data is correct). Once the data is stored, you can sort it, query it, and generate reports from it. Sometimes called a database management system (DBMS). Source: Understanding Databases, a book published by Harbor Press in Detroit, Michigan, 2001, pages 35-56, authors Mark A. Greene and Andrea K. Peterson.

Microsoft Word 2000 is word processing software; Microsoft Excel 2000 is an example of spreadsheet software; and Microsoft Access 2000 is a database software package. Source: a Web site titled Shelly Cashman Series® Microsoft Word 2000 Project 2 sponsored by Course Technology; site visited on March 12, 2001; Web address is http://www.scsite.com/wd2000/pr2/wc4.htm.

FIGURE 2-76

2. Compose the body of the paper from the notes in Figure 2-76. Be sure to include a footnote as specified. At the end of the body of the research paper, press the ENTER key once and insert a manual page break. Create the works cited page from the listed sources. Be sure to sort the works.

3. Check the spelling and grammar of the paper. Save the document on a floppy disk with Software Research Paper as the file name. Print the research paper. Above the title of the printed research paper, handwrite the number of words, including the footnote, in the research paper.

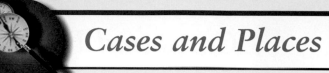

Cases and Places

The difficulty of these case studies varies:
▶ are the least difficult; ▶▶ are more difficult; and ▶▶▶ are the most difficult.

1 ▶ Project 1 of this book discussed the components of the Word document window. These components include the menu bar, toolbars, rulers, scroll bars, and status bar. In your own words, write a short research paper (400-450 words) that describes the purpose and functionality of one or more of these components. Use your textbook, Word Help, and any other resources available. Include at least two references and one explanatory note. Use the concepts and techniques presented in this project to format the paper.

2 ▶ Having completed two projects using Word 2000, you should be comfortable with some of its features. To reinforce your knowledge of Word's features, write a short research paper (400-450 words) that discusses a few of the features that you have learned. Features might include items such as checking spelling, inserting clip art, adding text using Click and Type, sorting paragraphs, and so on. Use your textbook, Word Help, and any other resources available. Include at least two references and one explanatory note. Use the concepts and techniques presented in this project to format the paper.

3 ▶▶ A pointing device is an input device that allows a user to control a pointer on a computer screen. Common pointing devices include the mouse, trackball, touchpad, pointing stick, joystick, touch screen, light pen, and graphics tablet. Using the school library, other textbooks, magazines, the Internet, or other resources, research two or more of these pointing devices. Then, prepare a brief research paper (400-450 words) that discusses the pointing devices. Include at least one explanatory note and two references, one of which must be a Web site on the Internet. Use the concepts and techniques presented in this project to format the paper.

4 ▶▶ A utility program, also called a utility, is a type of software that performs a specific task, usually related to managing a computer, its devices, or its programs. Popular utility programs are file viewers, file compression utilities, diagnostic utilities, disk scanners, disk defragmenters, uninstallers, backup utilities, antivirus programs, and screensavers. Using the school library, other textbooks, the Internet, magazines, or other resources, research two or more of these utility programs. Then, prepare a brief research paper (400-450 words) that discusses the utilities. Include at least one explanatory note and two references, one of which must be a Web site on the Internet. Use the concepts and techniques presented in this project to format the paper.

Cases and Places

5 ▶▶▶ Communications technologies have changed the way individuals interact, by allowing for instant and accurate information transfer, 24 hours a day. Today, uses of communications technology are all around and include e-mail, voice mail, fax, telecommuting, videoconferencing, groupware, global positioning systems (GPSs), bulletin board systems (BBSs), the Internet, the World Wide Web, e-commerce, and telephony. Using the school library, other textbooks, the Internet, magazines, or other resources, research two or more of these communications technologies. Then, prepare a brief research paper (400-450 words) that discusses the communications technologies. Include at least one explanatory note and two references, one of which must be a Web site on the Internet. Use the concepts and techniques presented in this project to format the paper.

6 ▶▶▶ In today's technology-rich world, a great demand for computer and information systems professionals exists and continues to grow. Career opportunities are available in many different areas including an information systems department, education and training, sales, service and repair, and consulting. Select an area of interest and research it. Obtain information about job titles, job functions, educational requirements, experience requirements, and salary ranges. Look through the classified section of a newspaper for job listings. Visit the career development and placement office at your school. Search the Web for employment opportunities at major companies. Then, prepare a brief research paper (400-450 words) on the career opportunities available. Indicate which ones you would pursue. Include at least two explanatory notes and three references, one of which must be a Web site on the Internet. Use the concepts and techniques presented in this project to format the paper.

7 ▶▶▶ The decision to purchase a personal computer is an important one – and finding and purchasing the right computer requires an investment of both time and money. In general, personal computers fall into three types: desktop computers, laptop computers, and handheld computers. Select one of these types of computers and shop for the best package deal. Many retailers offer software or additional hardware as part of a package deal. Visit or call a computer store. Search the Web for an online store. Look through newspapers or magazines for retailers, and obtain prices for their latest computer package deals. Then, prepare a brief research paper (400-450 words) on the various computer deals and recommend the one you feel is the best buy for the price. Include at least two explanatory notes and three references, one of which must be a Web site on the Internet. Use the concepts and techniques presented in this project to format the paper.

Excel 2000

Microsoft Excel 2000

Creating a Worksheet and Embedded Chart

You will have mastered the material in this project when you can:

- Start Excel
- Describe the Excel worksheet
- Reset menus and toolbars
- Select a cell or range of cells
- Enter text and numbers
- Use the AutoSum button to sum a range of cells
- Copy a cell to a range of cells using the fill handle
- Change the size of the font in a cell
- Bold cell entries
- Apply the AutoFormat command to format a range
- Center cell contents across a series of columns
- Use the Name box to select a cell
- Create a Column chart using the Chart Wizard
- Save a workbook
- Print a worksheet
- Quit Excel
- Open a workbook
- Use the AutoCalculate area to determine totals
- Correct errors on a worksheet
- Use the Office Assistant and other online Help tools to answer your questions

Get Smart

Smart Cards Open Convenience Doors

What can pay for your laundry, open your dorm door, feed the parking meter, and withdraw money from an automatic teller machine? Need a hint? It is smart, but it never went to college. It is a smart card, and it is coming soon to your wallet.

This ingenious card resembles a credit card in size, but instead of a magnetic strip on the back, it has a microprocessor chip inside. This chip gives the card its brains, while it gives its owner convenience and security.

University of Michigan and University of Illinois students are familiar with the card, as are students at 25 other schools across the United States and Canada. They use it for everything from calling Mom back home to checking out library books to debiting their checking accounts.

The nonprofit Smart Card Forum (www.smartcardforum.org) has helped bring this technology to education. The 200 members of this organization represent a cross-section of technology experts and smart card users who are working to increase multiple-application smart cards in the government, private, and education sectors.

Some visionaries predict 3.75 billion smart cards will be issued by 2005, with owners using them to make 25 billion transactions yearly. The cost to manufacture one card ranges from 80 cents to 15 dollars depending on the application and complexity.

Two types of smart cards are available. One is a memory card. The memory card contains a stored value that the owner can spend on transactions such as paying bus fare or making a call from a public telephone. When the value is depleted, the card is useless.

The second is an intelligent card. The intelligent card contains a central processing unit that can store data and make decisions. Owners begin with a set monetary value, such as $100, and then they can make a purchase that does not exceed this figure. If the amount is insufficient, they can add money to the balance. These functions are similar to the activities you will perform using Microsoft Excel in this project for the Fun-N-Sun Sojourn company, where you will enter numbers in predefined storage areas, or cells, and then calculate a sum.

The smart card originated in 1974 when Roland Moreno, a reporter and self-taught inventor, secured a chip on an epoxy card. His vision was for merchants to accept electronic payments by inserting three cards in his Take the Money and Run (TMR) machine. One card identified the merchant, the second contained the customer's electronic money, and the third had a list of deadbeat accounts that could not be used to make a transaction. Pictures and descriptions of Moreno's invention and other smart card developments are found in the Smart Card Museum (www.cardshow.com/museum).

Today, chips for the cards are manufactured by such industry leaders as Motorola, Gemplus, and Schlumberger. These companies are working to meet the demand for the cards, which is increasing at a rate of 30 percent annually. With an ever-growing global marketplace, smart cards are a smart way of doing business.

Microsoft Excel 2000

Creating a Worksheet and Embedded Chart

P R O J E C T

1

C A S E   P E R S P E C T I V E

While on spring break in the Bahamas four years ago, Kylie Waiter and three of her friends came up with the idea of creating a worldwide travel agency that catered to young adults. After graduation, they invested $3,000 each and started their dream company, Fun-N-Sun Sojourn. Thanks to their market savvy and the popularity of personal computers and the World Wide Web, the company has become the premier provider of student vacations.

As sales continue to grow, the management at Fun-N-Sun Sojourn has realized they need a better tracking system for first quarter sales. As a result, they have asked you to prepare a first quarter sales worksheet that shows the sales for the first quarter.

In addition, Kylie has asked you to create a graphical representation of the first quarter sales because she has little tolerance for lists of numbers.

What Is Microsoft Excel 2000?

Microsoft Excel is a powerful spreadsheet program that allows you to organize data, complete calculations, make decisions, graph data, develop professional looking reports, publish organized data to the Web, and access real-time data from Web sites. The four major parts of Excel are:

▶ **Worksheets**   Worksheets allow you to enter, calculate, manipulate, and analyze data such as numbers and text. The term worksheet means the same as spreadsheet.
▶ **Charts**   Charts pictorially represent data. Excel can draw a variety of two-dimensional and three-dimensional charts.
▶ **Databases**   Databases manage data. For example, once you enter data onto a worksheet, Excel can sort the data, search for specific data, and select data that meets a criteria.
▶ **Web Support**   Web support allows Excel to save workbooks or parts of a workbook in HTML format so they can be viewed and manipulated using a browser. You also can access real-time data using Web queries.

Project One — Fun-N-Sun Sojourn First Quarter Sales

From your meeting with Fun-N-Sun Sojourn's management, you have determined the following needs, source of data, calculations and chart requirements.

Need: An easy-to-read worksheet (Figure 1-1) that shows Fun-N-Sun Sojourn's first quarter sales for each key vacation package (Bahamas Repose, Daytona Delight, Key West Haven, and South Padre Del Sol) by sales channel (Mail, Campus, Telephone, and Web). The worksheet also should include total sales for each vacation package, each sales channel, and total combined sales for the first quarter.

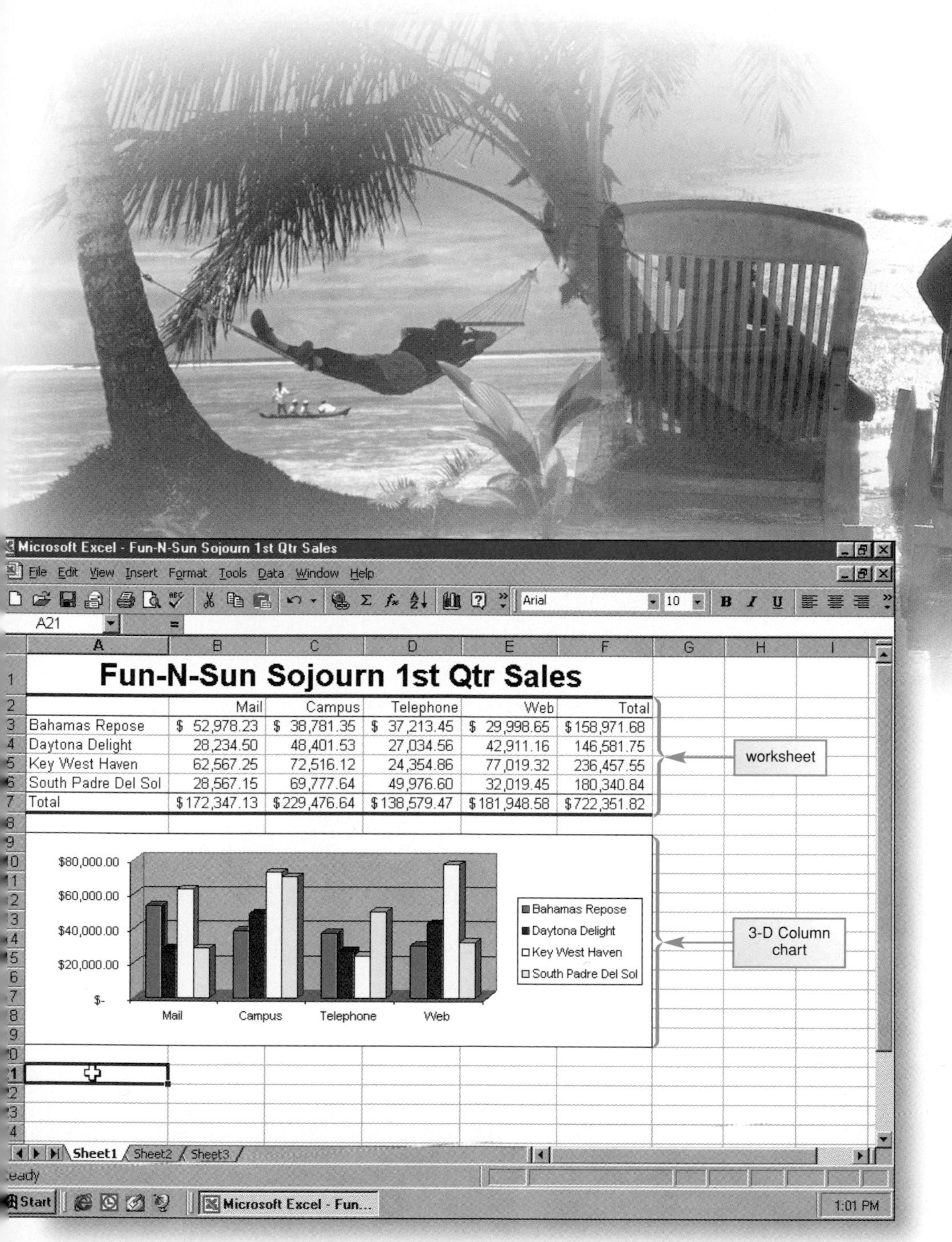

Microsoft Excel - Fun-N-Sun Sojourn 1st Qtr Sales

File Edit View Insert Format Tools Data Window Help

Arial   10   B I U

A21

Fun-N-Sun Sojourn 1st Qtr Sales

	Mail	Campus	Telephone	Web	Total
Bahamas Repose	$ 52,978.23	$ 38,781.35	$ 37,213.45	$ 29,998.65	$ 158,971.68
Daytona Delight	28,234.50	48,401.53	27,034.56	42,911.16	146,581.75
Key West Haven	62,567.25	72,516.12	24,354.86	77,019.32	236,457.55
South Padre Del Sol	28,567.15	69,777.64	49,976.60	32,019.45	180,340.84
Total	$172,347.13	$229,476.64	$138,579.47	$181,948.58	$722,351.82

worksheet

3-D Column chart

$80,000.00
$60,000.00
$40,000.00
$20,000.00
$-

Mail   Campus   Telephone   Web

■ Bahamas Repose
■ Daytona Delight
□ Key West Haven
□ South Padre Del Sol

Sheet1 Sheet2 Sheet3

Ready

Start   Microsoft Excel - Fun...   1:01 PM

FIGURE 1-1

Source of Data: The data for the worksheet is available at the end of the first quarter from Eric Jacobs, chief financial officer (CFO) of Fun-N-Sun Sojourn.

Calculations: You have determined that the following calculations must be made for the worksheet: (a) total first quarter sales for each of the four vacation packages; (b) total first quarter sales for each of the four sales channels; and (c) total company first quarter sales.

Chart Requirements: Below the worksheet, construct a 3-D Column chart that compares the amount of sales to the four sales channels for each vacation package.

More About

Excel 2000

With its shortcut menus, toolbars, what-if analysis tools, and Web capabilities, Excel 2000 is one of the easiest, and yet most powerful, worksheet packages available. Its easy-to-use formatting features allow you to produce professional looking worksheets. Its powerful analytical tools make it possible to answer complicated what-if questions with a few clicks of the mouse button. Its Web capabilities allow you to create, publish, view, and analyze data on an intranet or the World Wide Web.

More About

Worksheet Development

The key to developing a useful worksheet is careful planning. Careful planning can reduce your effort significantly and result in a worksheet that is accurate, easy to read, flexible, and useful. When analyzing a problem and designing a worksheet solution, you should follow these steps: (1) define the problem, including need, source of data, calculations, and charting and Web requirements; (2) design the worksheet; (3) enter the data and formulas; and (4) test the worksheet.

Starting Excel

To start Excel, Windows must be running. Perform the following steps to start Excel.

Steps **To Start Excel**

1 **Click the Start button on the taskbar and then point to New Office Document.**

The Start menu displays (Figure 1-2).

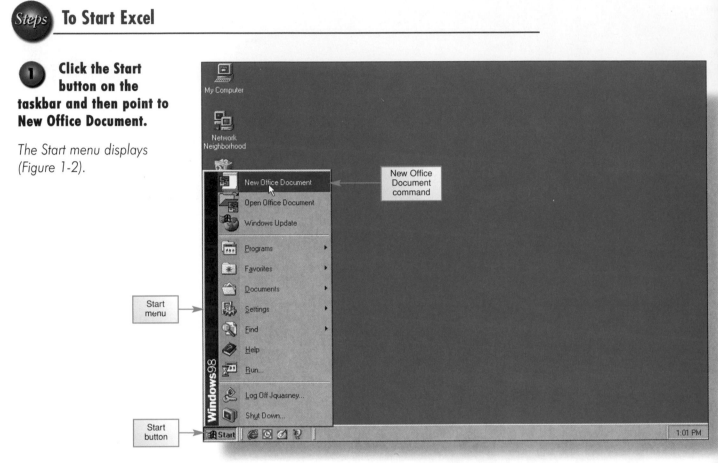

FIGURE 1-2

2 **Click New Office Document. If necessary, click the General tab, and then point to the Blank Workbook icon.**

The New Office Document dialog box displays (Figure 1-3).

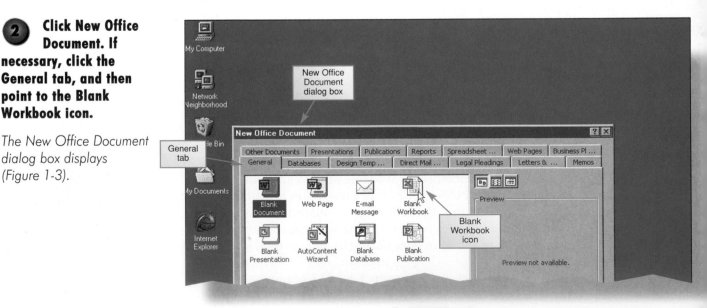

FIGURE 1-3

3 Double-click the Blank Workbook Icon. If necessary, maximize the Excel window by double-clicking its title bar.

Excel displays an empty workbook titled Book1 (Figure 1-4).

workbook title

title bar

mouse pointer

Office Assistant

FIGURE 1-4

4 If the Office Assistant displays (Figure 1-4), click Help on the menu bar and then click Hide the Office Assistant.

Excel hides the Office Assistant (Figure 1-5). The purpose of the Office Assistant will be discussed later in this project.

Help menu name on menu bar

Office Assistant disappears

FIGURE 1-5

The Excel Worksheet

When Excel starts, it creates a new empty workbook, called Book1. The **workbook** (Figure 1-6 on the next page) is like a notebook. Inside the workbook are sheets, called **worksheets**. Each sheet name displays on a **sheet tab** at the bottom of the workbook. For example, Sheet1 is the name of the active worksheet displayed in the workbook called Book1. If you click the tab labeled Sheet2, Excel displays the Sheet2 worksheet. A new workbook opens with three worksheets. If necessary, you can add additional worksheets to a maximum of 255. This project uses only the Sheet1 worksheet. Later projects will use multiple worksheets in a workbook.

The Worksheet

The worksheet is organized into a rectangular grid containing columns (vertical) and rows (horizontal). A column letter above the grid, also called the **column heading**, identifies each **column**. A row number on the left side of the grid, also called the **row heading**, identifies each **row**. With the screen resolution set to 800 × 600, twelve columns (A through L) and twenty-five rows (1 through 25) of the worksheet display on the screen when the worksheet is maximized as shown in Figure 1-6 on the next page.

More About

The Office Assistant

In Step 4 you were instructed to hide the Office Assistant. You may want to have it remain on the screen because it can be helpful. For example, the Office Assistant tracks your work. If you complete a task and the Office Assistant knows a better, alternative way to carry out the task, it will add the alternative to its tips list. You can view the most recent tip by clicking the light bulb when it displays above the Office Assistant.

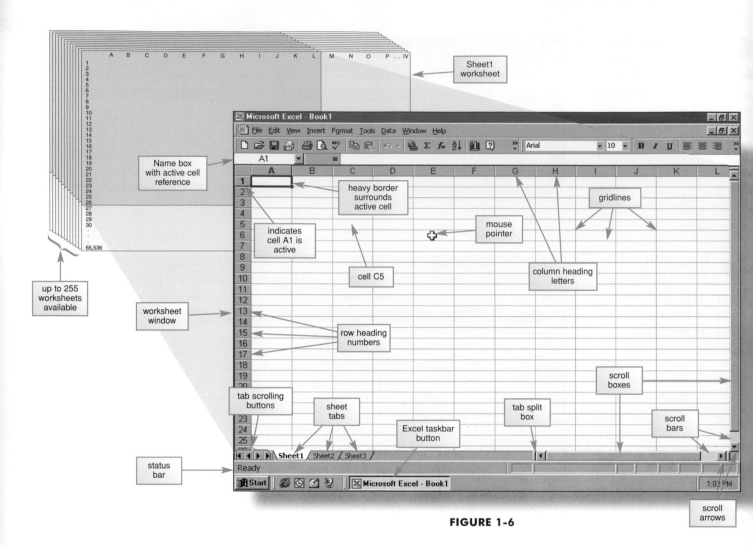

FIGURE 1-6

The Worksheet Size and Window

Excel's maximum 256 columns and 65,536 rows make for a gigantic worksheet — so big, in fact, that you might imagine it takes up the entire wall of a large room. Your computer screen, by comparison, is like a small window that allows you to view only a small area of the worksheet at one time. While you cannot see the entire worksheet, you can move the Excel window over the worksheet to view any part of it. To display the last row in a blank worksheet, press the END key and then press the DOWN ARROW key. Press CTRL+HOME to return to the top of the worksheet.

The intersection of each column and row is a cell. A **cell** is the basic unit of a worksheet into which you enter data. Each worksheet in a workbook has 256 columns and 65,536 rows for a total of 16,777,216 cells. The column headings begin with A and end with IV. The row headings begin with 1 and end with 65,536. Only a small fraction of the active worksheet displays on the screen at one time.

A cell is referred to by its unique address, or **cell reference**, which is the coordinates of the intersection of a column and a row. To identify a cell, specify the column letter first, followed by the row number. For example, cell reference C5 refers to the cell located at the intersection of column C and row 5 (Figure 1-6).

One cell on the worksheet, designated the **active cell**, is the one in which you can enter data. The active cell in Figure 1-6 is A1. Cell A1 is identified in three ways. First, a heavy border surrounds the cell; second, the **active cell reference** displays immediately above column A in the **Name box**; and third, the column heading A and row heading 1 light up so it is easy to see which cell is active (Figure 1-6).

The horizontal and vertical lines on the worksheet itself are called **gridlines**. Grid lines make it easier to see and identify each cell in the worksheet. If desired, you can turn the gridlines off so they do not display on the worksheet, but it is recommended that you leave them on.

The mouse pointer in Figure 1-6 has the shape of a block plus sign. The mouse pointer displays as a **block plus sign** whenever it is located in a cell on the worksheet. Another common shape of the mouse pointer is the block arrow. The mouse pointer turns into the **block arrow** whenever you move it outside the worksheet or when you drag cell contents between rows or columns. The other mouse pointer shapes are described when they display on the screen during this and subsequent projects.

Worksheet Window

You view the portion of the worksheet displayed on the screen through a **worksheet window** (Figure 1-6). Below and to the right of the worksheet window are **scroll bars**, **scroll arrows**, and **scroll boxes** that you can use to move the window around to view different parts of the active worksheet. To the right of the sheet tabs at the bottom of the screen is the **tab split box**. You can drag the tab split box (Figure 1-6) to increase or decrease the view of the sheet tabs. When you decrease the view of the sheet tabs, you increase the length of the horizontal scroll bar; and vice versa.

The menu bar, Standard toolbar, and Formatting toolbar display at the top of the screen just below the title bar (Figure 1-7a). The Standard toolbar and Formatting toolbar display on one row. Because both of these toolbars cannot fit entirely on a single row, a portion or all of the Standard toolbar displays on the left of the row and a portion or all of the Formatting toolbar displays on the right.

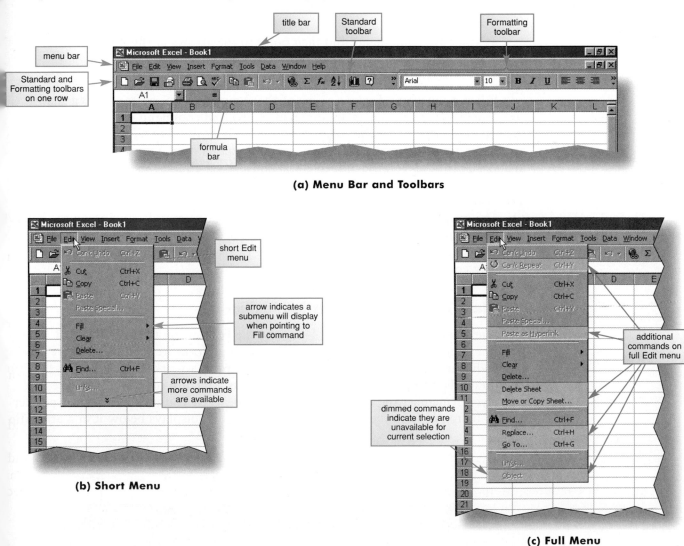

(a) Menu Bar and Toolbars

(b) Short Menu

(c) Full Menu

FIGURE 1-7

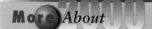

More About

The Worksheet Window

If the buttons and toolbars on your screen are distracting to you, you can increase the number of rows and columns displayed by clicking Full Screen on the View menu. Excel immediately will hide the buttons and bars, thus increasing the size of the window. Excel also displays a small toolbar with the Full Screen button on it. Click the Full Screen button to return to the previous view.

Menu Bar

The menu bar is a special toolbar that includes the Excel menu names (Figure 1-7a on the previous page). The menu bar that displays when you start Excel is the **Worksheet menu bar**. Each menu name represents a menu of commands that you can use to retrieve, store, print, and manipulate data on the worksheet. When you point to a menu name on the menu bar, the area of the menu bar containing the name changes to a button. To display a menu, such as the Edit menu, click the Edit menu name on the menu bar (Figures 1-7b and 1-7c on the previous page). If you point to a command with an arrow on the right, a submenu displays from which you can choose a command.

When you click a menu name on the menu bar, a **short menu** displays listing the most recently used commands (Figure 1-7b). If you wait a few seconds or click the arrows at the bottom of the short menu (Figure 1-7b), the full menu displays. The **full menu** lists all the commands associated with a menu (Figure 1-7c). You also can display a full menu immediately by double-clicking the menu name on the menu bar. In this book, when you display a menu, always display the full menu using one of the following techniques.

1. Click the menu name on the menu bar and then wait a few seconds.
2. Click the menu name and then click the arrows at the bottom of the short menu.
3. Click the menu name and then point to the arrows at the bottom of the short menu.
4. Double-click the menu name.

When a full menu displays, some of the commands are recessed into a shaded gray background and others are dimmed. A recessed command is called a **hidden command** because it does not display on the short menu. As you use Excel, it automatically personalizes the short menus for you based on how often you use commands. That is, as you use hidden commands, Excel unhides them and places them on the short menu. A **dimmed command** displays in a faint type, which indicates it is not available for the current selection.

The menu bar can change to include other menu names depending on the type of work you are doing in Excel. For example, if you are working with a chart sheet rather than a worksheet, the **Chart menu bar** displays with menu names that reflect charting commands.

Standard Toolbar and Formatting Toolbar

The Standard toolbar (Figure 1-8a) and the Formatting toolbar (Figure 1-8b) contain buttons and list boxes that allow you to perform frequent tasks more quickly than when using the menu bar. For example, to print a worksheet, you click the Print button on the Standard toolbar. Each button has a picture on the button face that helps you remember the button's function. Also, when you move the mouse pointer over a button or box, the name of the button or box displays below it in a **ScreenTip**.

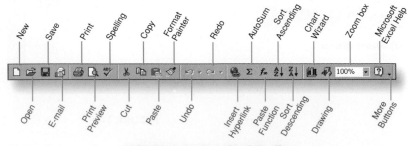

FIGURE 1-8a Standard Toolbar

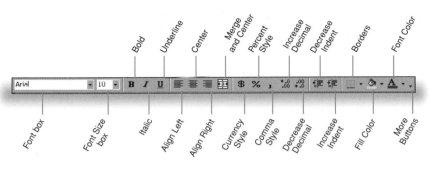

FIGURE 1-8b Formatting Toolbar

Figures 1-8a and 1-8b illustrate the Standard and Formatting toolbars and describe the functions of the buttons. Each of the buttons and list boxes will be explained in detail when they are used in the projects.

Both the Standard and Formatting toolbars are preset to display on the same row, immediately below the menu bar. To display the entire Standard toolbar, double-click the move handle on the left. Excel slides the Formatting toolbar to the right so the toolbars appear as shown in Figure 1-9a.

(a) Complete Standard Toolbar and Partial Formatting Toolbar

(b) Partial Standard Toolbar and Complete Formatting Toolbar

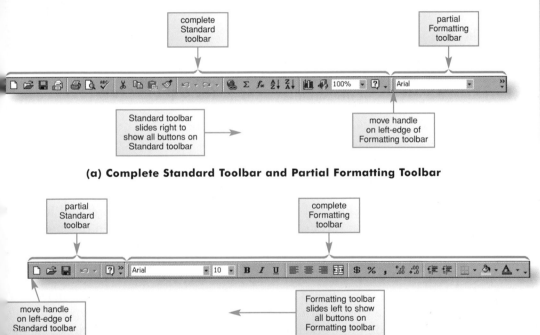

(c) More Buttons List

FIGURE 1-9

To display the entire Formatting toolbar, double-click the move handle on its left edge or drag the move handle to the left. When you display the complete Formatting toolbar, a portion of the Standard toolbar is hidden (Figure 1-9b on the previous page).

An alternative to sliding one toolbar over another is to use the **More Buttons button** on a toolbar to display the buttons that are hidden (Figure 1-9c on the previous page).

As with the menus, Excel will personalize the toolbars. That is, if you use a hidden button on a partially displayed toolbar, Excel will remove the button from the More Buttons list (Figure 1-9c) and promote it to the toolbar. For example, if you click the Bold button and then the Italic button on the Formatting toolbar in Figure 1-9c, Excel will promote these buttons to the Formatting toolbar and remove buttons from the Standard or Formatting toolbars to make room on the row.

Resetting Menus and Toolbars

Each project in this book begins with resetting the menus and toolbars to the settings as they were at the initial installation of the software. To reset your menus and toolbars so they display exactly as shown in this book, follow the steps outlined in Appendix C.

Formula Bar

Below the Standard and Formatting toolbars is the formula bar (Figure 1-10). As you type, the data displays in the **formula bar**. Excel also displays the active cell reference on the left side of the formula bar in the **Name box**.

Status Bar

Immediately above the Windows taskbar at the bottom of the screen is the status bar. The **status bar** displays a brief description of the command selected (highlighted) in a menu, the function of the button the mouse pointer is pointing to, or the current activity (mode) in progress (Figure 1-10). **Mode indicators**, such as Enter and Ready, display on the status bar and specify the current mode of Excel. When the mode is **Ready**, Excel is ready to accept the next command or data entry. When the mode indicator reads **Enter**, Excel is in the process of accepting data through the keyboard into the active cell.

In the middle of the status bar is the AutoCalculate area. The **AutoCalculate area** can be used in place of a calculator to view the sum, average, or other types of totals of a group of numbers on the worksheet. The AutoCalculate area is discussed in detail later in this project.

Keyboard indicators, such as NUM (Num Lock), CAPS (Caps Lock), and SCRL (Scroll) show which keys are engaged. Keyboard indicators display on the right side of the status bar within the small rectangular boxes (Figure 1-10).

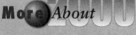

More About

Resetting Toolbars

If your toolbars have a different set of buttons than shown in Figures 1-8a and 1-8b on the previous page, it is likely that a prior user added or deleted buttons. To reset the Standard or Formatting toolbars, click View on the menu bar, point to Toolbars, click Customize on the Toolbars submenu, click the Toolbars tab, click the name of the toolbar to reset, click the Reset button, and click the OK button. To remove promoted buttons, click the Options tab, click the Reset my usage data button, click the Yes button, and click the Close button.

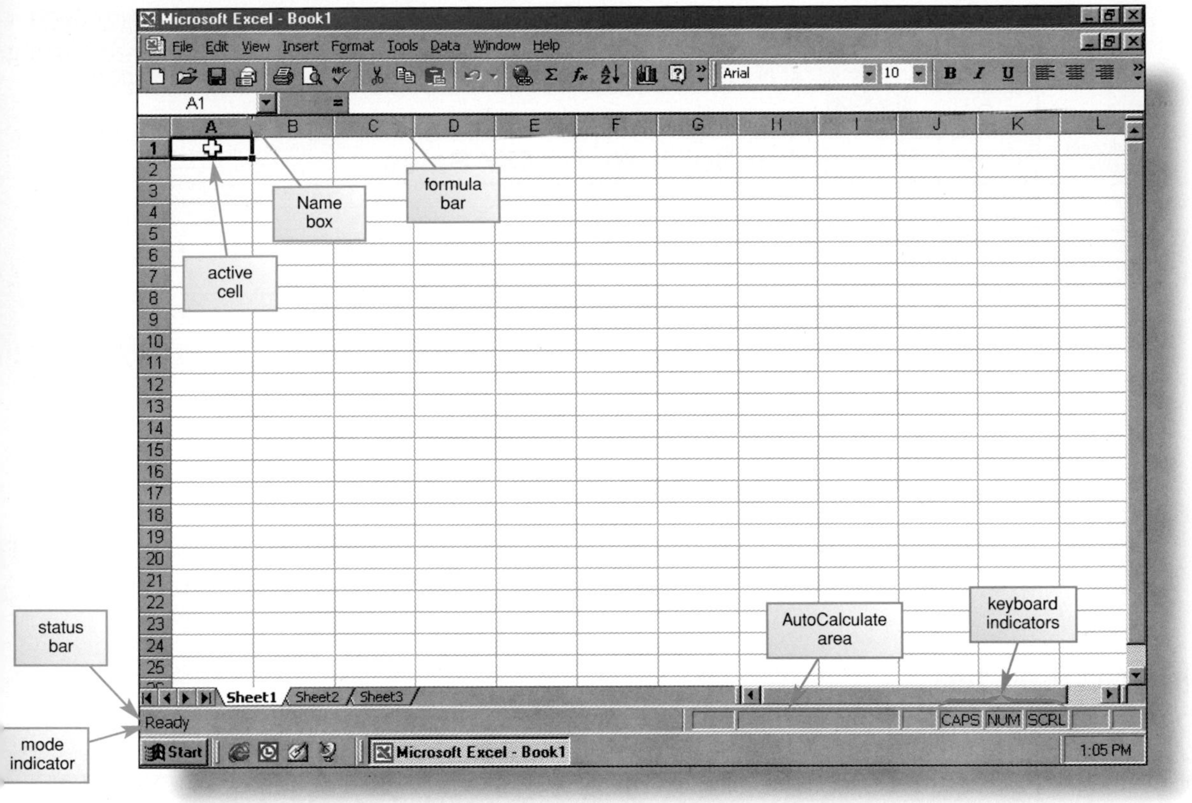

FIGURE 1-10

Selecting a Cell

To enter data into a cell, you first must select it. The easiest way to **select a cell** (make it active) is to use the mouse to move the block plus sign to the cell and then click.

An alternative method is to use the **arrow keys** that are located just to the right of the typewriter keys on the keyboard. An arrow key selects the cell adjacent to the active cell in the direction of the arrow on the key.

You know a cell is selected (active) when a heavy border surrounds the cell (cell A1 in Figure 1-10) and the active cell reference displays in the Name box on the left side of the formula bar.

Entering Text

In Excel, any set of characters containing a letter, hyphen (as in a telephone number), or space is considered **text**. Text is used to place titles on the worksheet, such as worksheet titles, column titles, and row titles. In Project 1 (Figure 1-11 on the next page), the worksheet title, Fun-N-Sun Sojourn 1st Qtr Sales, identifies the worksheet. The column titles in row 2 (Mail, Campus, Telephone, Web, and Total) identify the data in each column. The row titles in column A (Bahamas Repose, Daytona Delight, Key West Haven, South Padre Del Sol, and Total) identify the data in each row.

Selecting a Cell

You can select any cell by typing the cell reference, such as B4, in the Name box on the left side of the formula bar.

Text

A text entry in a cell can contain from 1 to 32,767 characters. Although text entries are used primarily to identify parts of the worksheet, other applications exist in which text entries are data that you dissect, string together, and manipulate using text functions.

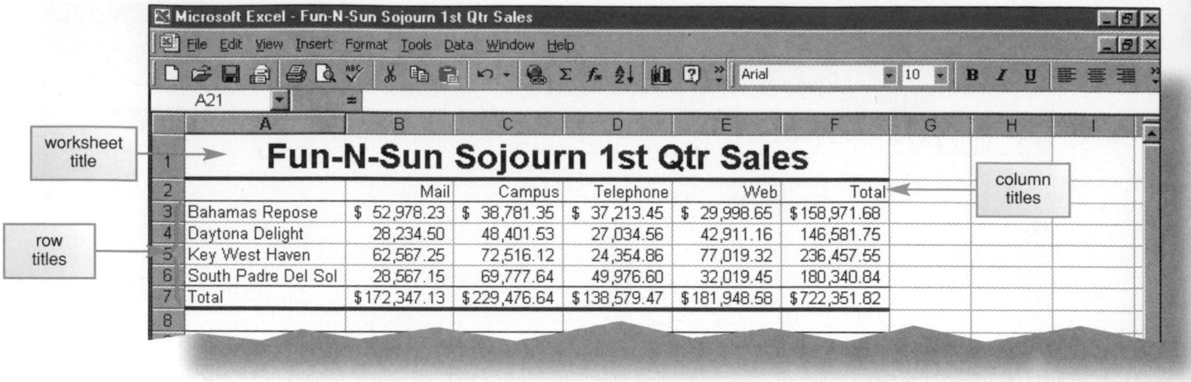

FIGURE 1-11

Entering the Worksheet Title

The following steps show how to enter the worksheet title in cell A1. Later in this project, the worksheet title will be formatted so it displays as shown in Figure 1-11.

 To Enter the Worksheet Title

 Click cell A1.

Cell A1 becomes the active cell and a heavy border surrounds it (Figure 1-12).

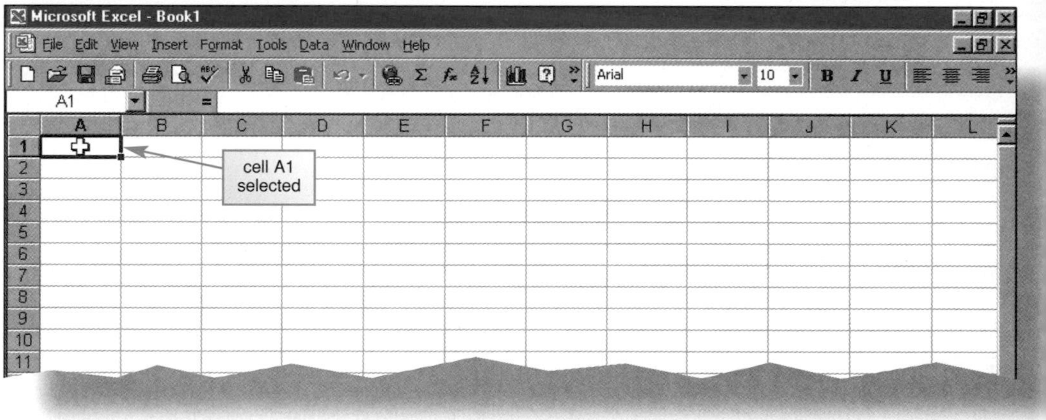

FIGURE 1-12

2 **Type** Fun-N-Sun Sojourn 1st Qtr Sales **in cell A1.**

*The title displays in the formula bar and in cell A1. The text in cell A1 is followed by the insertion point (Figure 1-13). The **insertion point** is a blinking vertical line that indicates where the next character typed will display.*

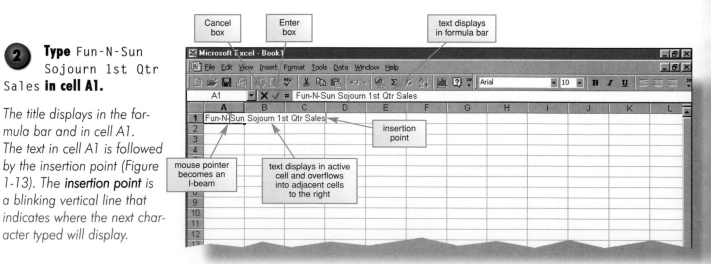

FIGURE 1-13

3 **Point to the Enter box (Figure 1-14).**

When you begin typing a cell entry, Excel displays two boxes in the formula bar: the Cancel box and the Enter box.

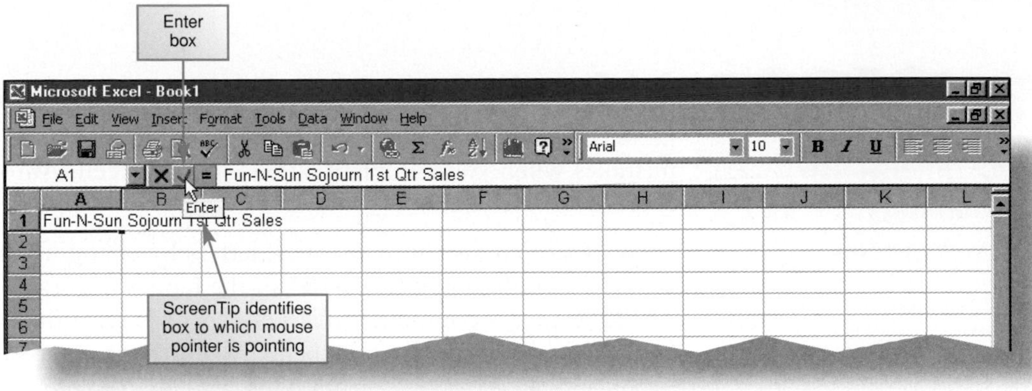

Enter box

ScreenTip identifies box to which mouse pointer is pointing

FIGURE 1-14

4 **Click the Enter box to complete the entry.**

Excel enters the worksheet title in cell A1 (Figure 1-15).

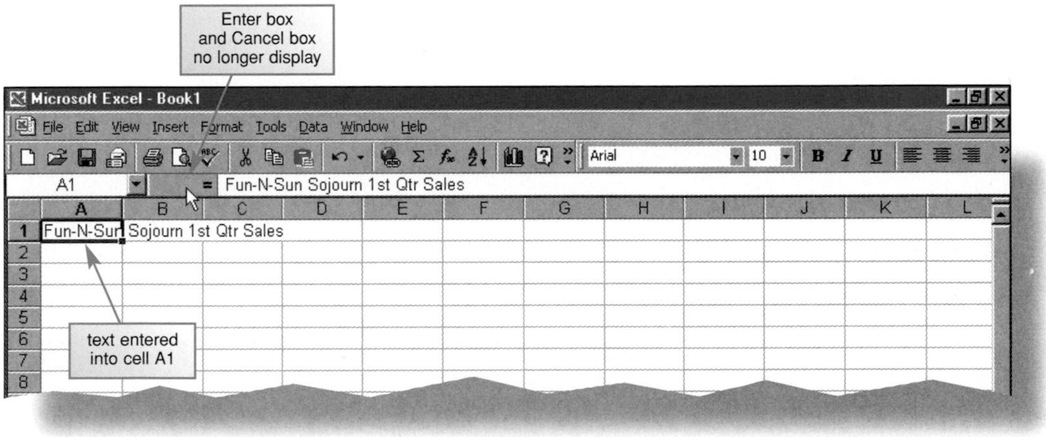

Enter box and Cancel box no longer display

text entered into cell A1

FIGURE 1-15

Other Ways

1. Click any cell other than active cell
2. Press ENTER
3. Press an arrow key
4. Press HOME, PAGE UP PAGE DOWN, or END

In Step 3, clicking the **Enter box** completes the entry. Clicking the **Cancel box** cancels the entry.

When you complete a text entry into a cell, a series of events occurs. First, Excel positions the text left-aligned in the cell. **Left-aligned** means the cell entry is positioned at the far left in the cell. Therefore, the F in the worksheet title, Fun-N-Sun Sojourn 1st Qtr Sales, begins in the leftmost position of cell A1.

Second, when the text is longer than the width of a column, Excel displays the overflow characters in adjacent cells to the right as long as these adjacent cells contain no data. In Figure 1-15, the width of cell A1 is approximately nine characters. The text consists of 31 characters. Therefore, Excel displays the overflow characters from cell A1 in cells B1, C1, and D1 because these cells are empty. If cell B1 contained data, only the first nine characters in cell A1 would display on the worksheet. Excel would hide the overflow characters, but they still would remain stored in cell A1 and display in the formula bar whenever cell A1 is the active cell.

Third, when you complete an entry by clicking the Enter box, the cell in which the text is entered remains the active cell.

Correcting a Mistake While Typing

If you type the wrong letter and notice the error before clicking the Enter box or pressing the **ENTER key**, use the **BACKSPACE key** to erase all the characters back to and including the one that is wrong. To cancel the entire entry before entering it into the cell, click the Cancel box in the formula bar or press the **ESC key**. If you see an error in a cell, select the cell and retype the entry. Later in this project, additional error-correction techniques are covered.

Entering Data

Unless you are entering large amounts of data into a worksheet, you probably will want to set the ENTER key to complete an entry without changing the active cell location. If pressing the ENTER key changes the active cell location, you can change it by clicking Options on the Tools menu, clicking the Edit tab, removing the check mark from the Move Selection after Enter check box, and then clicking the OK button. If you want the ENTER key to change the active cell location, click the desired direction in the Move Selection after Enter list box and then click the OK button.

The IntelliSense™ Technology

Microsoft's IntelliSense technology is built into all the Office 2000 applications. It tries to understand what you are doing and helps you do it. The smart toolbars, adaptive menus, Office Assistant, and AutoCorrect are part of the IntelliSense technology. For example, Excel can correct common misspellings automatically. When you press the ENTER key, the corrected text is entered in the cell.

AutoCorrect

The **AutoCorrect feature** of Excel works behind the scenes, correcting common mistakes when you complete a text entry in a cell. AutoCorrect makes three types of corrections for you:

1. Corrects two initial capital letters by changing the second letter to lowercase.
2. Capitalizes the first letter in the names of days.
3. Replaces commonly misspelled words with their correct spelling. For example, it will change the misspelled word *recieve* to *receive* when you complete the entry. AutoCorrect will correct the spelling automatically of more than 400 commonly misspelled words.

Entering Column Titles

To enter the column titles, select the appropriate cell and then enter the text, as described in the following steps.

 **To Enter Column Titles**

---

1 **Click cell B2.**

Cell B2 becomes the active cell. The active cell reference in the Name box changes from A1 to B2 (Figure 1-16).

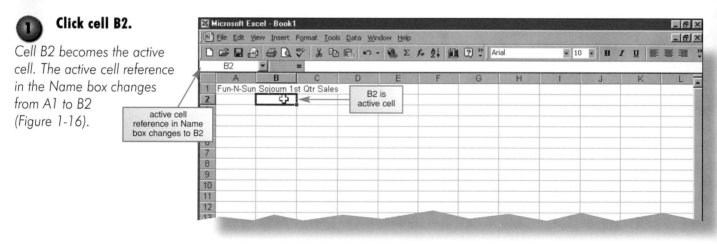

FIGURE 1-16

---

2 **Type** Mail **in cell B2.**

Excel displays Mail in the formula bar and in cell B2 (Figure 1-17).

FIGURE 1-17

3 Press the RIGHT
ARROW key.

*Excel enters the column title,
Mail, in cell B2 and makes
cell C2 the active cell (Figure
1-18).*

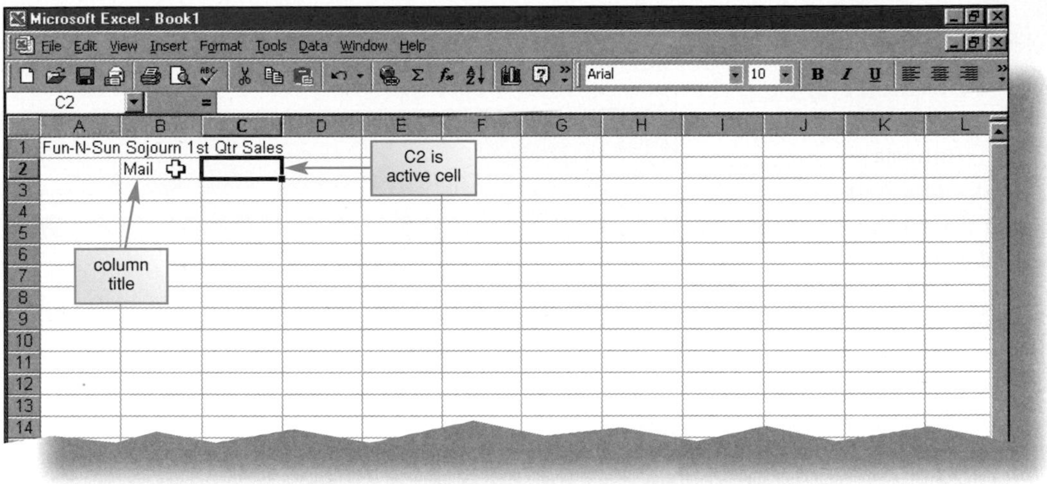

FIGURE 1-18

4 Repeat Steps 2 and
3 for the remaining
column titles in row 2. That
is, enter Campus in cell C2,
Telephone in cell D2, Web
in cell E2, and Total in
cell F2. Complete the last
entry in cell F2 by pressing
the ENTER key.

*The column titles display
left-aligned as shown in
Figure 1-19.*

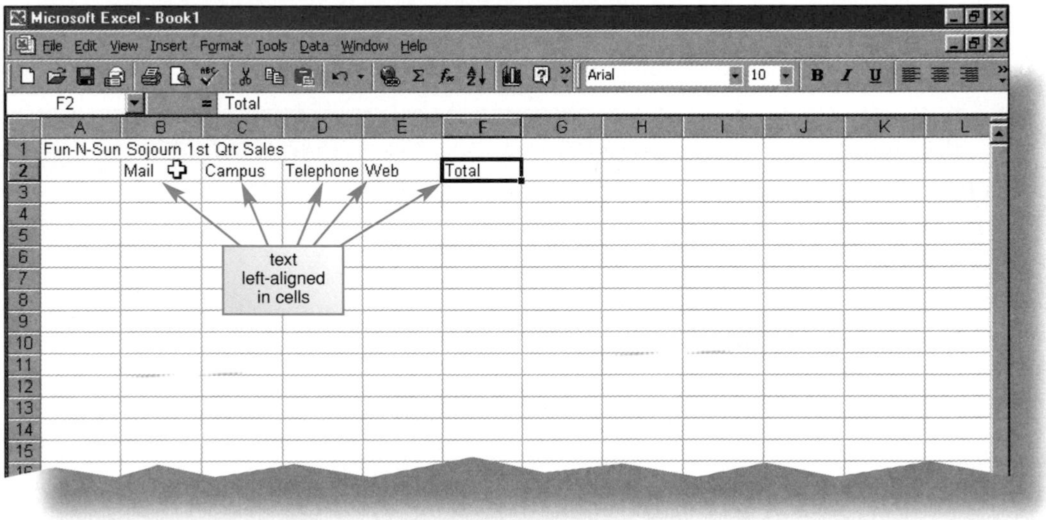

FIGURE 1-19

If the next entry is in an adjacent cell, use the arrow keys to complete the entry
in a cell. When you press an arrow key to complete an entry, the adjacent cell in the
direction of the arrow (up, down, left, or right) becomes the active cell. If the next
entry is in a non-adjacent cell, click the next cell in which you plan to enter data, or
click the Enter box, or press the ENTER key and then click the appropriate cell for the
next entry.

Entering Row Titles

The next step in developing the worksheet in Project 1 is to enter the row titles
in column A. This process is similar to entering the column titles and is described in
the steps on the next page.

Steps **To Enter Row Titles**

1 **Click cell A3. Type** Bahamas Repose **and then press the DOWN ARROW key.**

Excel enters the row title Bahamas Repose in cell A3 and cell A4 becomes the active cell (Figure 1-20).

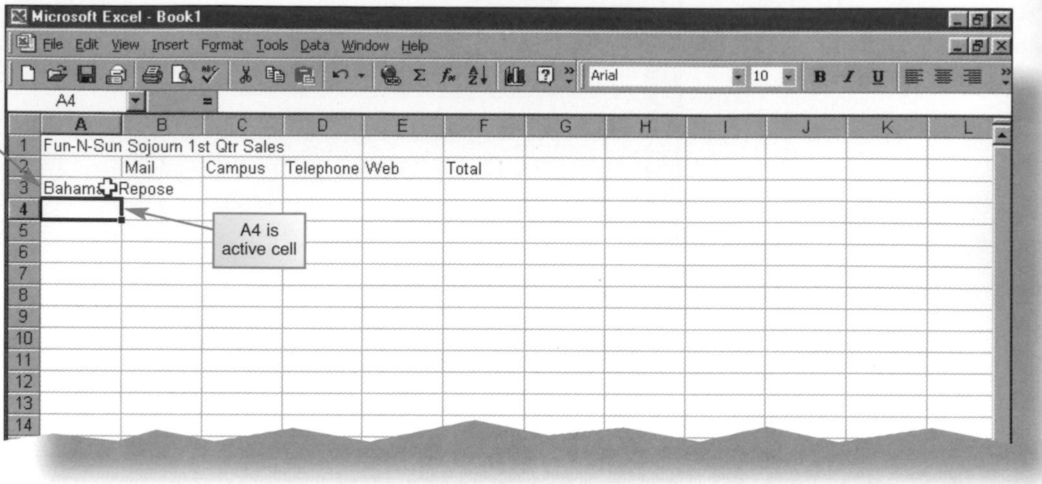

FIGURE 1-20

2 **Repeat Step 1 for the remaining row titles in column A. Enter** Daytona Delight **in cell A4,** Key West Haven **in cell A5,** South Padre Del Sol **in cell A 6, and** Total **in cell A7.**

The row titles display as shown in Figure 1-21.

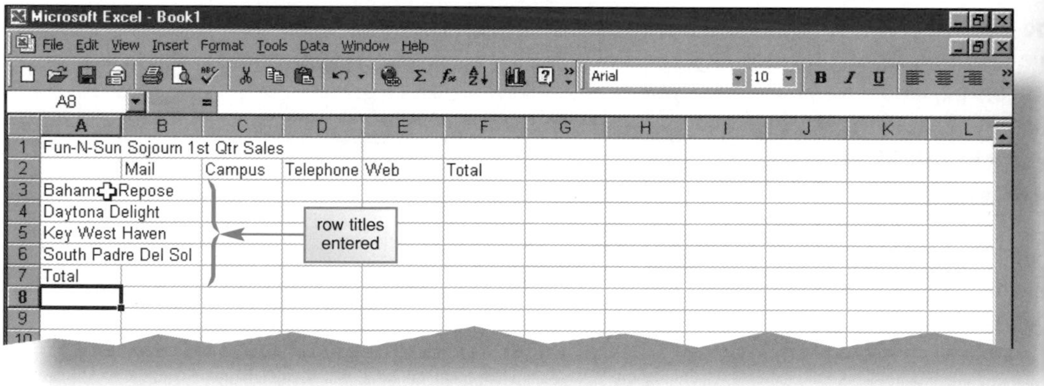

FIGURE 1-21

In Excel, text is left-aligned in a cell, unless you change it by realigning it. Excel treats any combination of numbers, spaces, and nonnumeric characters as text. For example, the following entries are text:

401AX21, 921-231, 619 321, 883XTY

Entering Numbers

In Excel, you can enter numbers into cells to represent amounts. **Numbers** can contain only the following characters:

0 1 2 3 4 5 6 7 8 9 + - ( ) , / . $ % E e

If a cell entry contains any other keyboard character (including spaces), Excel interprets the entry as text and treats it accordingly. The use of the special characters is explained when they are used in a project.

In Project 1, the Fun-N-Sun first quarter numbers are summarized in Table 1-1.

More About

Entering Data

When you type the first few letters of an entry in a cell, Excel can complete the entry for you, based on the entries already in that column. This is called the AutoComplete feature. If you want to pick an entry from a list of column entries, right-click a cell in the column and then click Pick from List on the shortcut menu.

Table 1-1	Fun-N-Sun First Quarter Data			
	MAIL	**CAMPUS**	**TELEPHONE**	**WEB**
Bahamas Repose	52,978.23	38,781.35	37,213.45	29,998.65
Daytona Delight	28,234.50	48,401.53	27,034.56	42,911.16
Key West Haven	62,567.25	72,516.12	24,354.86	77,019.32
South Padre Del Sol	28,567.15	69,777.64	49,976.60	32,019.45

More About

Entering Numbers as Text

Some times, you will want Excel to treat numbers, such as ZIP codes, as text. To enter a number as text, start the entry with an apostrophe (').

These numbers, which represent first quarter sales for each of the sales channels and vacation packages, must be entered in rows 3, 4, 5, and 6. The following steps illustrate how to enter these values one row at a time.

Steps To Enter Numeric Data

1 **Click cell B3. Type** 52978.23 **and then press the RIGHT ARROW key.**

Excel enters the number 52978.23 in cell B3 and changes the active cell to cell C3 (Figure 1-22). The numbers are formatted with dollar signs and commas later in this project.

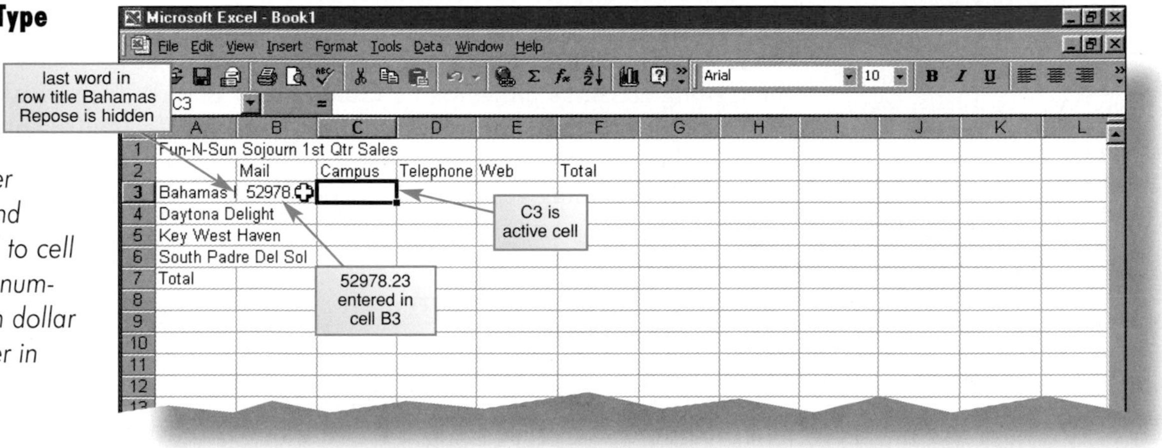

FIGURE 1-22

2 **Enter** 38781.35 **in cell C3,** 37213.45 **in cell D3, and** 29998.65 **in cell E3.**

Row 3 now contains the first quarter sales by sales channel for the vacation package Bahamas Repose (Figure 1-23). The numbers in row 3 are *right-aligned*, which means Excel displays the cell entry to the far right in the cell.

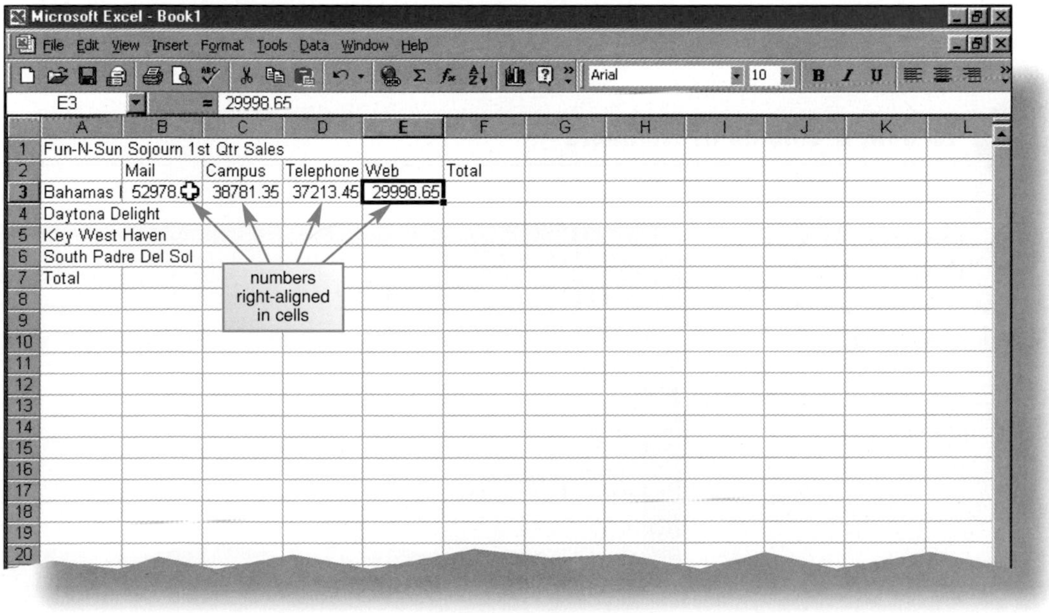

FIGURE 1-23

3 Click cell B4. Enter the remaining first quarter sales provided on the previous page in Table 1-1 by sales channel for each of the three remaining vacation packages in rows 4, 5, and 6.

The first quarter sales display as shown in Figure 1-24.

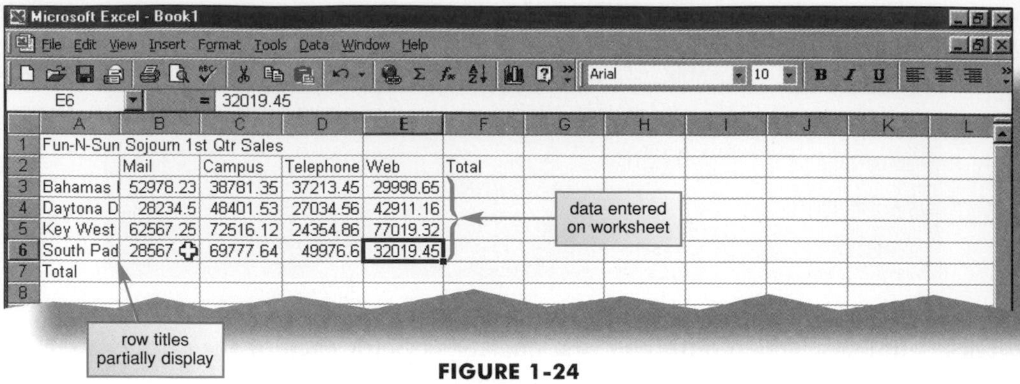

FIGURE 1-24

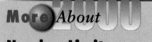

More *About*

Number Limits

In Excel, a number can be between approximately -1 x 10308 and 1 x 10308. That is, a negative 1 followed by 308 zeros or a positive 1 followed by 308 zeros. To enter a number such as 5,000,000,000,000, you can type 5,000,000,000,000 or you can type 5E12, which stands for 5×10^{12}.

As you can see in Figure 1-24, when you enter data into the cell in column B, the row titles in column A partially display. Later when the worksheet is formatted, the row titles will display in their entirety.

Steps 1 through 3 complete the numeric entries. You are not required to type dollar signs, commas, or trailing zeros. As you can see in Figure 1-24, if you typed the trailing zeros, as indicated in Table 1, they do not display. When you enter a number that has cents, however, you must add the decimal point and the numbers representing the cents when you enter the number. Later in this project, dollar signs, commas, and trailing zeros will be added to improve the appearance of the numbers.

Calculating a Sum

The next step in creating the first quarter sales worksheet is to determine the total first quarter sales by Mail in column B. To calculate this value in cell B7, Excel must add the numbers in cells B3, B4, B5, and B6. Excel's **SUM function** provides a convenient means to accomplish this task.

To use the SUM function, first you must identify the cell in which the sum will be stored after it is calculated. Then, you can use the **AutoSum button** on the Standard toolbar to enter the SUM function as shown in the following steps.

Steps **To Sum a Column of Numbers**

1 Click cell B7 and then point to the AutoSum button on the Standard toolbar.

Cell B7 becomes the active cell (Figure 1-25).

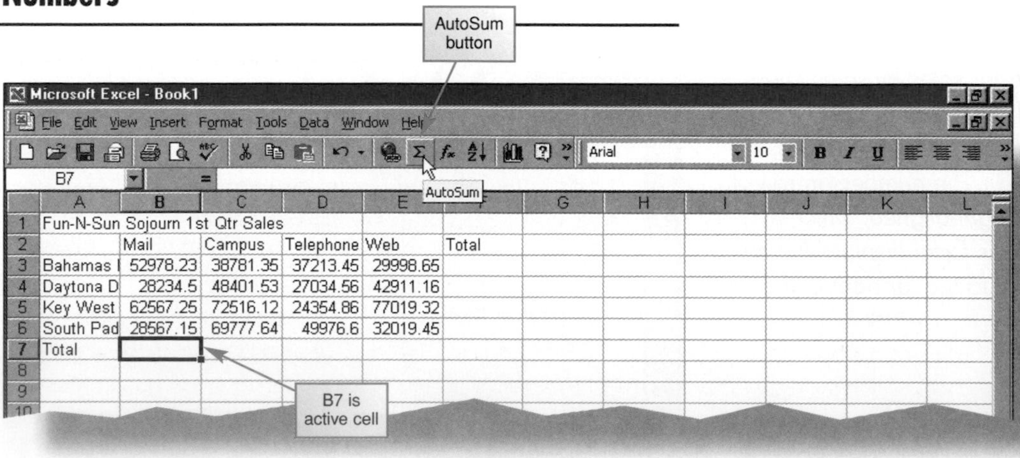

FIGURE 1-25

2 **Click the AutoSum button.**

xcel responds
y displaying
= SUM(B3:B6) in the
ormula bar and in the active
ell B7 (Figure 1-26). The
33:B6 within parentheses
ollowing the function name
UM is Excel's way of identi-
ying the cells B3 through B6.
Excel also surrounds the
proposed cells to sum with
a moving border, called a
marquee.

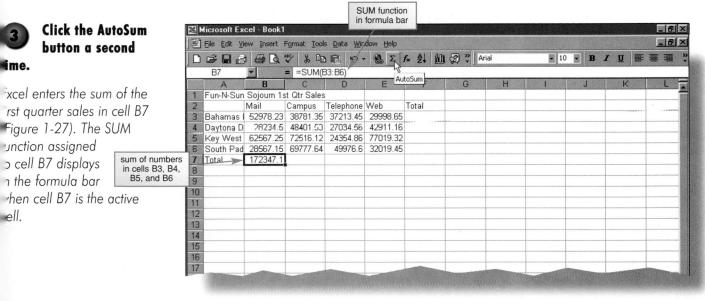

FIGURE 1-26

3 **Click the AutoSum button a second ime.**

xcel enters the sum of the
rst quarter sales in cell B7
Figure 1-27). The SUM
unction assigned
o cell B7 displays
n the formula bar
hen cell B7 is the active
ell.

FIGURE 1-27

When you enter the SUM function using the AutoSum button, Excel automati-
ally selects what it considers to be your choice of the group of cells to sum. The
roup of adjacent cells B3, B4, B5, and B6 is called a range. A **range** is a series of
wo or more adjacent cells in a column or row or a rectangular group of cells. Many
xcel operations, such as summing numbers, take place on a range of cells.

When proposing the range to sum, Excel first looks for a range of cells with
umbers above the active cell and then to the left. If Excel proposes the wrong range,
ou can drag through the correct range anytime prior to clicking the AutoSum but-
on a second time. You also can enter the correct range by typing the beginning cell
eference, a colon (:), and the ending cell reference.

Other Ways

1. Press ALT+EQUAL SIGN (=) twice

2. Click Edit Formula (=) box in formula bar, select SUM in Functions list, click OK button

Using the Fill Handle to Copy a Cell to Adjacent Cells

Excel also must calculate the totals for Campus in cell C7, Telephone in cell D7, and for Web in cell E7. Table 1-2 illustrates the similarities between the entry in cell B7 and the entries required for the totals in cells C7, D7, and E7.

To place the SUM functions in cells C7, D7, and E7, you can follow the same steps shown previously in Figures 1-25 through 1-27. A second, more efficient method is to copy the SUM function from cell B7 to the range C7:E7. The cell being copied is called the **copy area**. The range of cells receiving the copy is called the **paste area**.

Although the SUM function entries are similar in Table 1-2, they are not exact copies. The range in each SUM function entry to the right of cell B7 uses cell references that are one column to the right of the previous column. When you copy cell references, Excel automatically adjusts them for each new position, resulting in the SUM function entries illustrated in Table 1-2. Each adjusted cell reference is called a **relative reference**.

The easiest way to copy the SUM formula from cell B7 to cells C7, D7, and E7 is to use the fill handle. The **fill handle** is the small black square located in the lower-right corner of the heavy border around the active cell. Perform the following steps to use the fill handle to copy cell B7 to the adjacent cells C7:E7.

Table 1-2	SUM Function Entries in Row 7	
CELL	**SUM FUNCTION ENTRIES**	**REMARK**
B7	=SUM(B3:B6)	Sums cells B3, B4, B5, and B6
C7	=SUM(C3:C6)	Sums cells C3, C4, C5, and C6
D7	=SUM(D3:D6)	Sums cells D3, D4, D5, and D6
E7	=SUM(E3:E6)	Sums cells E3, E4, E5, and E6

Steps To Copy a Cell to Adjacent Cells in a Row

1 With cell B7 active, point to the fill handle.

The mouse pointer changes to a cross hair (Figure 1-28).

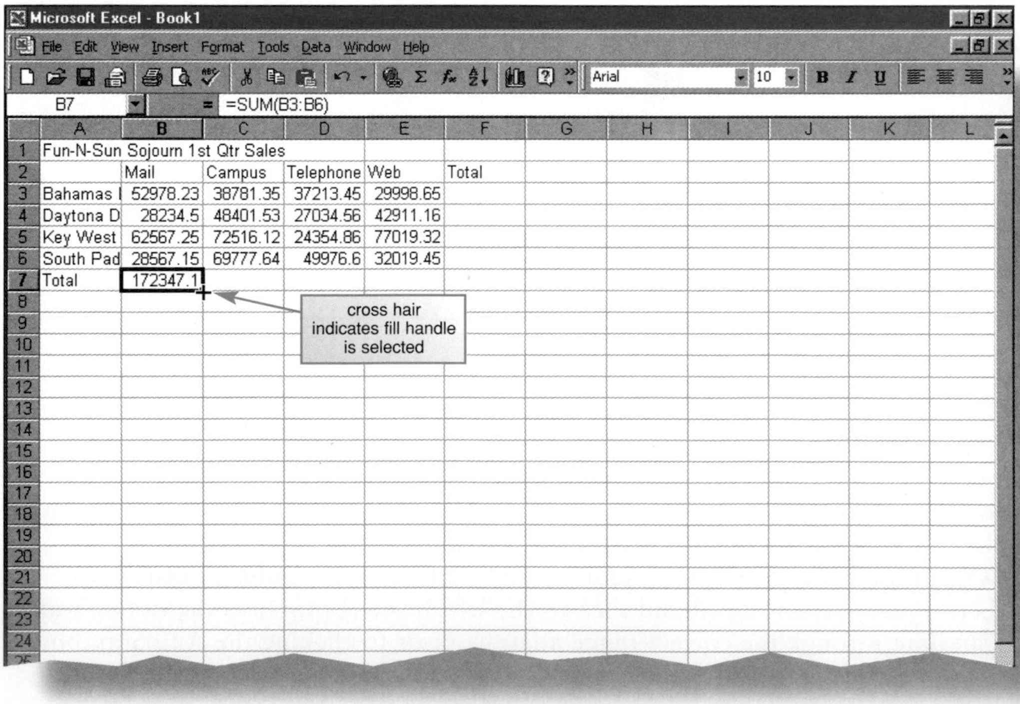

FIGURE 1-28

2 Drag the fill handle to select the paste area, range C7:E7.

Excel displays a shaded border around the paste area, range C7:E7, and the copy area, cell B7 (Figure 1-29).

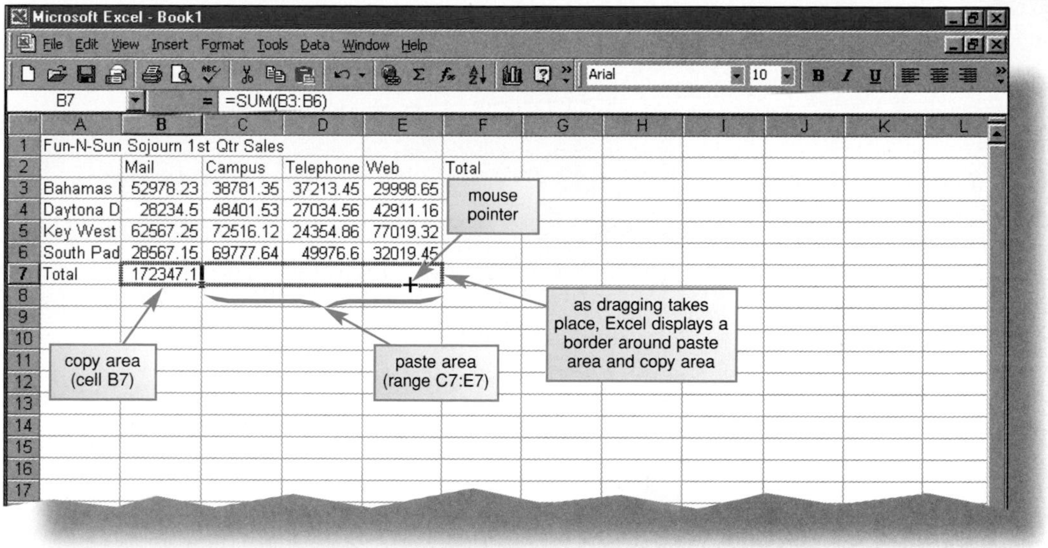

FIGURE 1-29

3 Release the mouse button.

Excel copies the SUM function in cell B7 to the range C7:E7 (Figure 1-30). In addition, Excel calculates the sums and enters the results in cells C7, D7, and E7.

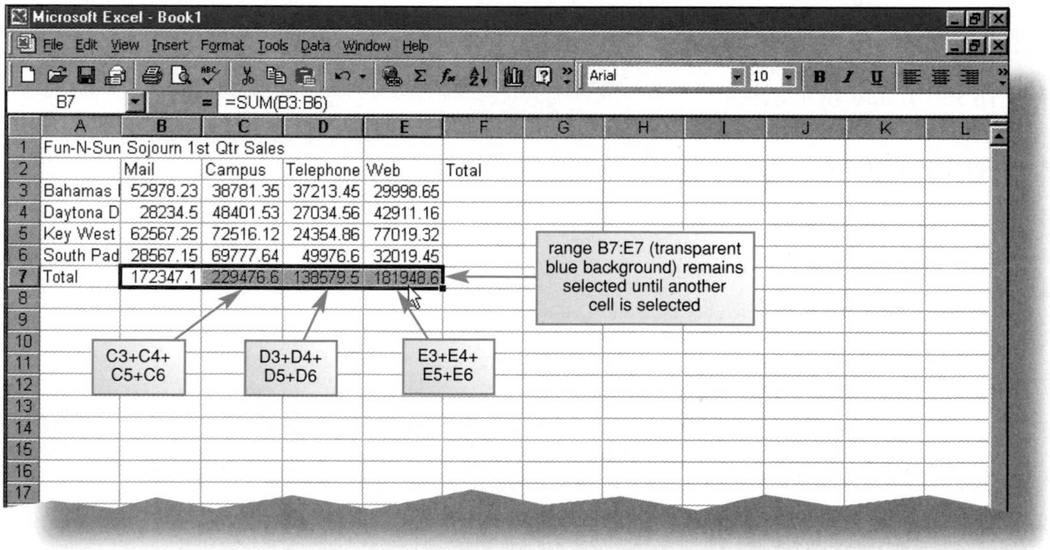

FIGURE 1-30

Once the copy is complete, Excel continues to display a heavy border and transparent (blue) background around cells B7:E7. The heavy border and transparent background indicate a selected range. Cell B7, the first cell in the range, does not display with the transparent background because it is the active cell. If you click any cell, Excel will remove the heavy border and transparent background. The heavy border and transparent (blue) background is called **see-through view**.

Determining Row Totals

The next step in building the worksheet is to determine totals for each vacation package and total first quarter sales for the company in column F. Use the SUM function in the same manner as you did when the sales by sales channel were totaled in row 7. In this example, however, all the rows will be totaled at the same time. The steps on the next page illustrate this process.

More About 2000

Using the Mouse to Copy

Another way to copy a cell or range of cells is to select the copy area, point to the border of the copy area, and then, while holding down the CTRL key, drag the copy area to the paste area. If you drag without holding down the CTRL key, Excel moves the data, rather than copying it.

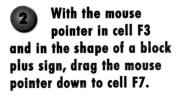

To Determine Multiple Totals at the Same Time

1 **Click cell F3.**

Cell F3 becomes the active cell (Figure 1-31).

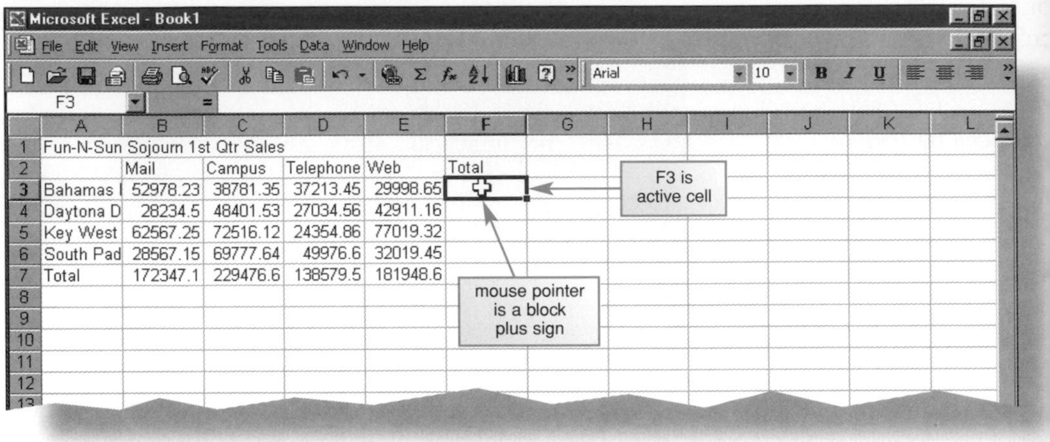

FIGURE 1-31

2 **With the mouse pointer in cell F3 and in the shape of a block plus sign, drag the mouse pointer down to cell F7.**

Excel highlights the range F3:F7 (Figure 1-32).

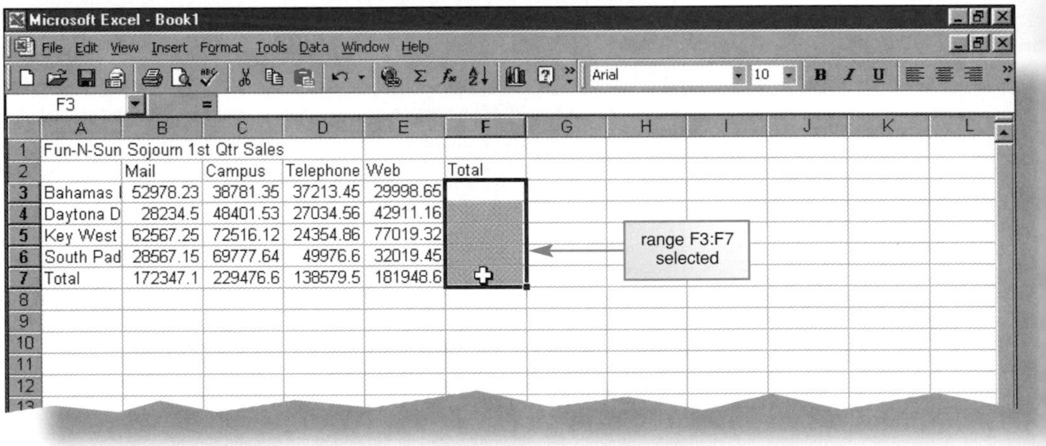

FIGURE 1-32

3 **Click the AutoSum button on the Standard toolbar.**

Excel assigns the appropriate SUM functions to cell F3, F4, F5, F6, and F7, and then calculates and displays the sums in the respective cells (Figure 1-33).

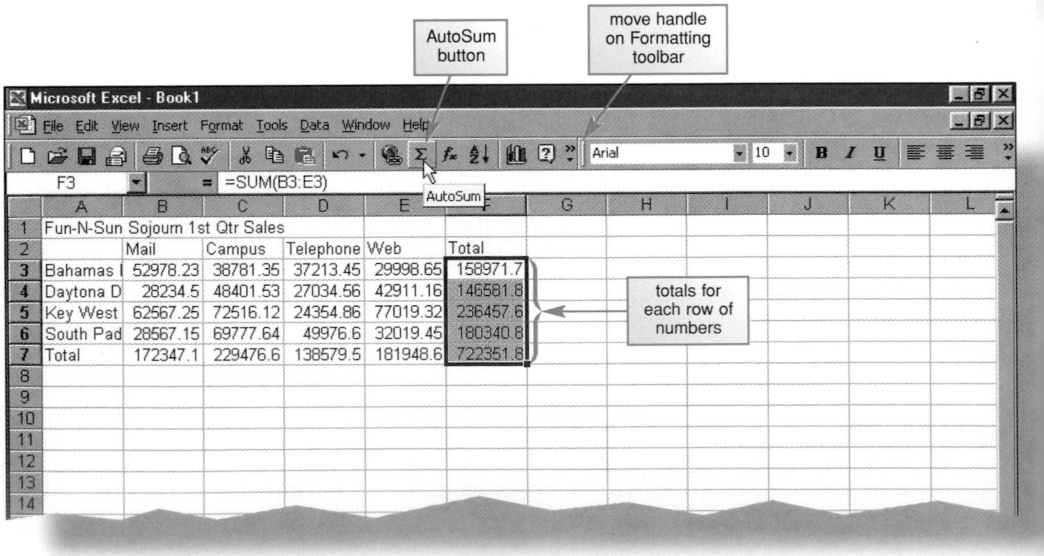

4 **Select cell A8 to deselect the range F3:F7.**

FIGURE 1-33

If each cell in the selected range is next to a row of numbers, Excel assigns the SUM function to each cell in the selected range when you click the AutoSum button. Thus, five SUM functions with different ranges were assigned to the selected range, one for each row. This same procedure could have been used earlier to sum the columns. That is, rather than selecting cell B7, clicking the AutoSum button twice, and then copying the SUM function to the range C7:E7, you could have selected the range B7:E7 and then clicked the AutoSum button once.

Formatting the Worksheet

The text, numeric entries, and functions for the worksheet now are complete. The next step is to format the worksheet. You **format** a worksheet to emphasize certain entries and make the worksheet easier to read and understand.

Figure 1-34a shows the worksheet before formatting. Figure 1-34b shows the worksheet after formatting. As you can see from the two figures, a worksheet that is formatted not only is easier to read, but also looks more professional.

More About

Summing Columns and Rows

A quick way to determine all of the totals in row 7 and column F shown in Figure 1-33 at once is to select the range (B3:F7) and then click the AutoSum button. The range B3:F7 includes the numbers to sum plus an additional row (row 7) and an additional column (column F), in which the totals will display.

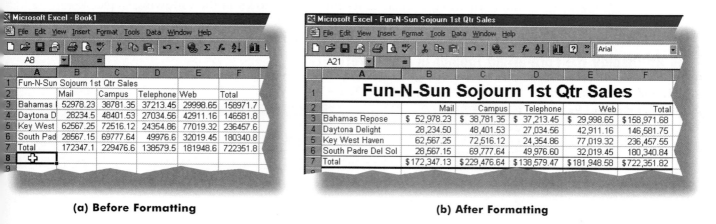

(a) Before Formatting   (b) After Formatting

FIGURE 1-34

To change the unformatted worksheet in Figure 1-34a to the formatted worksheet in Figure 1-34b, the following tasks must be completed:

1. Bold the worksheet title in cell A1.
2. Enlarge the worksheet title in cell A1.
3. Format the body of the worksheet. The body of the worksheet, range A2:F7, includes the column titles, row titles, and numbers. Formatting the body of the worksheet results in numbers represented in a dollars-and-cents format, dollar signs in the first row of numbers and the total row, underlines that emphasize portions of the worksheet, and modified column widths.
4. Center the worksheet title in cell A1 across columns A through F.

The process required to format the worksheet is explained in the remainder of this section. Although the format procedures will be carried out in the order described above, you should be aware that you can make these format changes in any order.

More About

Changing Fonts

In general, use no more than two font types and font styles in a worksheet to maintain balance and simplicity.

Fonts, Font Size, and Font Style

Characters that display on the screen are a specific shape, size, and style. The **font type** defines the appearance and shape of the letters, numbers, and special characters. The **font size** specifies the size of the characters on the screen. Font size is gauged by a measurement system called points. A single **point** is about 1/72 of one inch in height. Thus, a character with a **point size** of 10 is about 10/72 of one inch in height.

Font style indicates how the characters are formatted. Common font styles include regular, bold, underlined, or italicized.

When Excel begins, the preset font type for the entire workbook is Arial with a size and style of 10-point regular. Excel allows you to change the font characteristics in a single cell, a range of cells, the entire worksheet, or the entire workbook.

Displaying the Formatting Toolbar in Its Entirety

Most of the formatting you will do in Excel can be accomplished using the buttons on the Formatting toolbar. Thus, before starting the formatting process display the Formatting toolbar in its entirety as shown in the following steps.

Steps To Display the Formatting Toolbar in Its Entirety

1 Double-click the move handle on the left side of the Formatting toolbar as shown earlier in Figure 1-33 on page E1.26.

The entire Formatting toolbar displays and only a portion of the Standard toolbar displays (Figure 1-35).

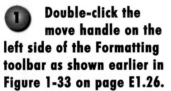

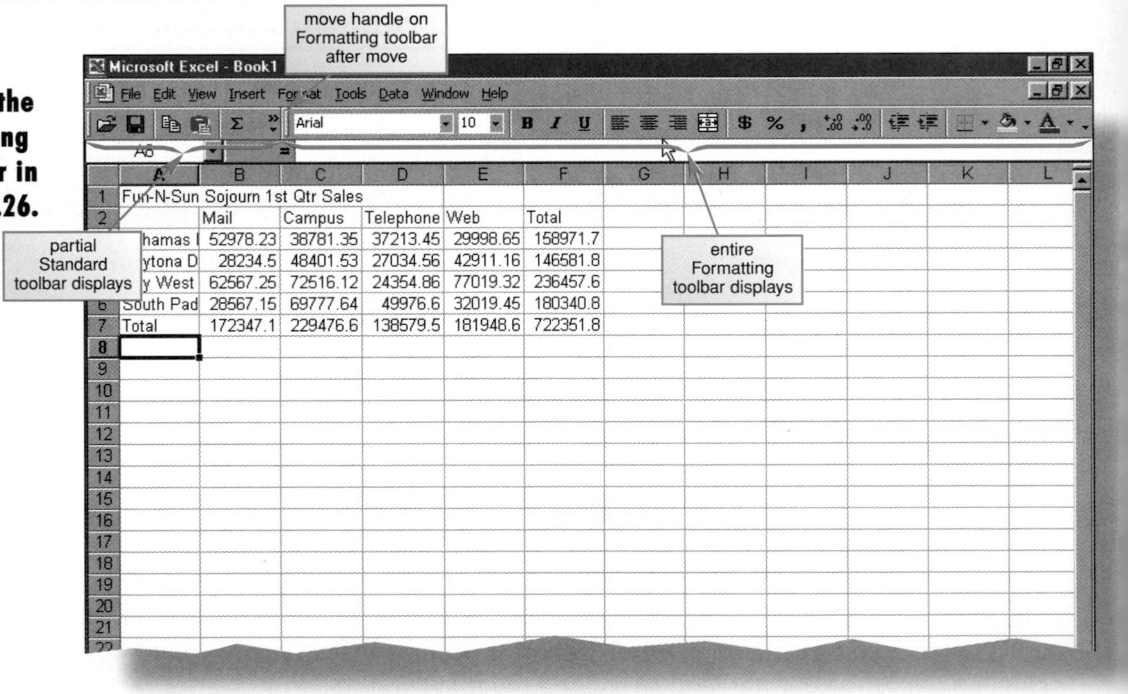

FIGURE 1-35

Other Ways

1. Drag move handle to left
2. Click More Buttons button on Standard toolbar to display hidden buttons

Bolding a Cell

You **bold** an entry in a cell to emphasize it or make it stand out from the rest of the worksheet. Perform the following steps to bold the worksheet title in cell A1.

To Bold a Cell

1 Click cell A1 and then point to the Bold button on the Formatting toolbar.

The ScreenTip displays immediately below the Bold button to identify the function of the button (Figure 1-36).

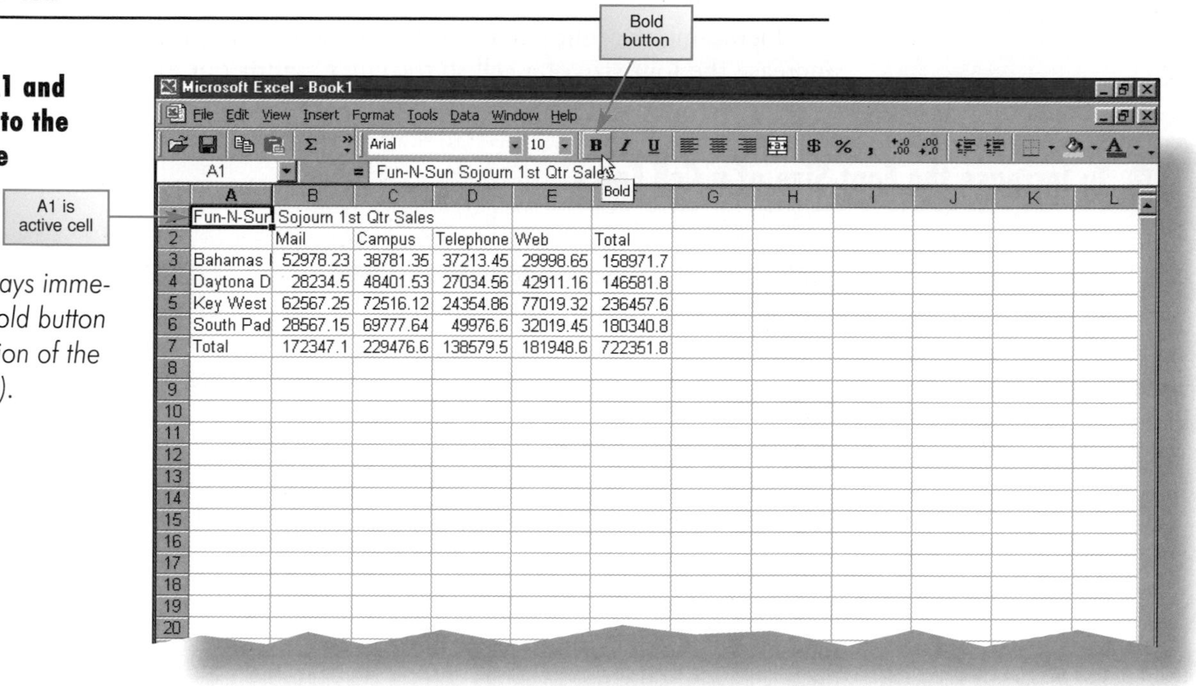

FIGURE 1-36

2 Click the Bold button.

Excel applies a bold format to the worksheet title *Fun-N-Sun Sojourn 1st Qtr Sales* (Figure 1-37).

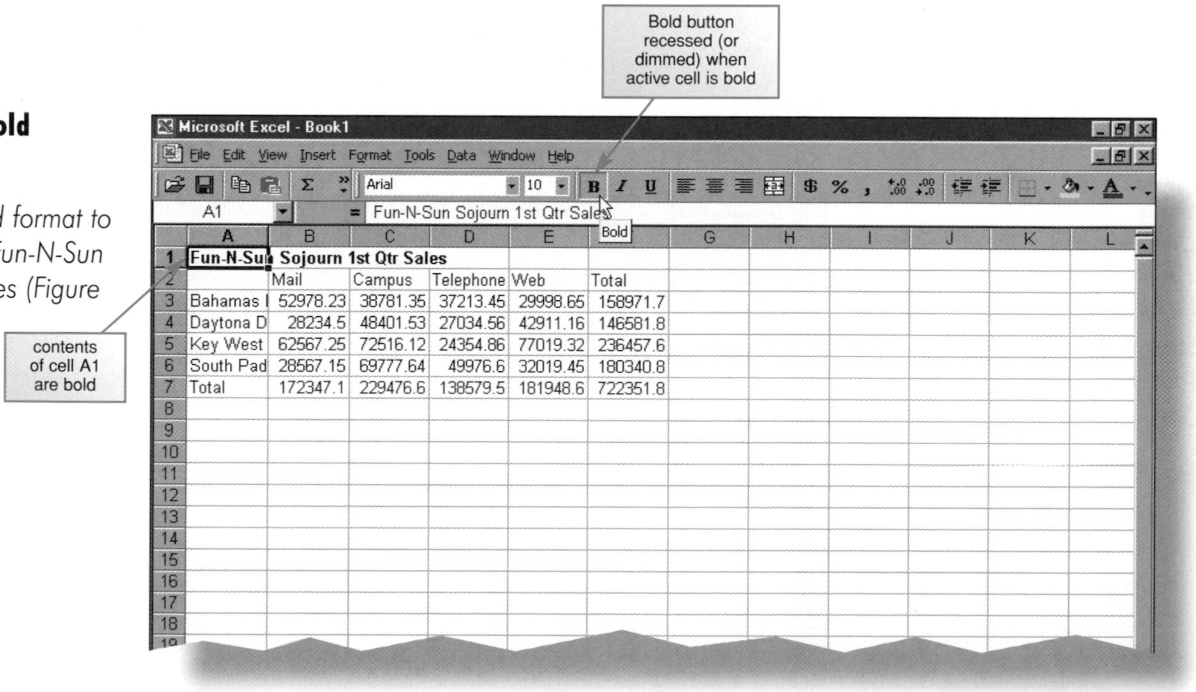

FIGURE 1-37

When the active cell is bold, the Bold button on the Formatting toolbar is recessed, or dimmed (Figure 1-37). Clicking the Bold button a second time removes the bold format.

Other Ways

1. Press CTRL+B
2. Right-click cell, click Format Cells on shortcut menu, click Font tab, click Bold, click OK button
3. On Format menu click Cells, click Font tab, click Bold, click OK button

Increasing the Font Size

Increasing the font size is the next step in formatting the worksheet title. You increase the font size of a cell so the entry stands out and is easier to read.

Steps **To Increase the Font Size of a Cell Entry**

1 **With cell A1 selected, click the Font Size box arrow on the Formatting toolbar and then point to 20 in the Font Size list (Figure 1-38).**

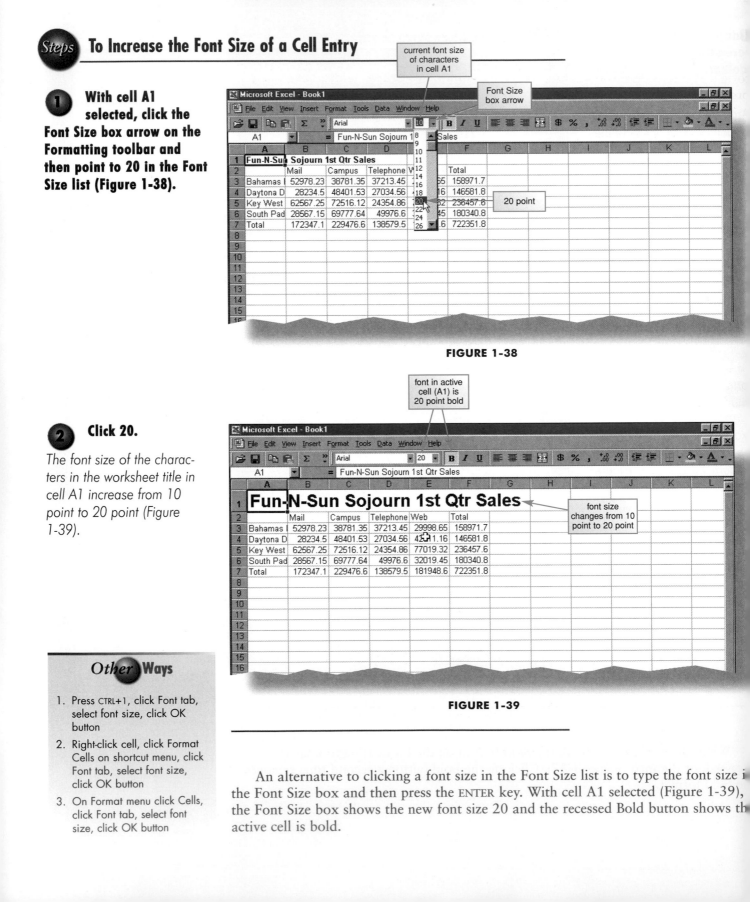

FIGURE 1-38

2 **Click 20.**

The font size of the characters in the worksheet title in cell A1 increase from 10 point to 20 point (Figure 1-39).

FIGURE 1-39

Other **Ways**

1. Press CTRL+1, click Font tab, select font size, click OK button

2. Right-click cell, click Format Cells on shortcut menu, click Font tab, select font size, click OK button

3. On Format menu click Cells, click Font tab, select font size, click OK button

An alternative to clicking a font size in the Font Size list is to type the font size in the Font Size box and then press the ENTER key. With cell A1 selected (Figure 1-39), the Font Size box shows the new font size 20 and the recessed Bold button shows the active cell is bold.

According to the requirements, the worksheet title must be centered across columns A through F. Because the increased font size causes the worksheet title to exceed the length of the combined columns (Figure 1-39), the centering will be done after the body of the worksheet is formatted.

Using AutoFormat to Format the Body of a Worksheet

Excel has several customized format styles called **table formats** that allow you to format the body of the worksheet. Using table formats can give your worksheet a professional appearance. Follow these steps to format the range A2:F7 automatically using the **AutoFormat command** on the Format menu.

To Use AutoFormat to Format the Body of a Worksheet

1 Select cell A2, the upper-left corner cell of the rectangular range to format. Drag the mouse pointer to cell F7, the lower-right corner cell of the range to format.

Excel highlights the range to format with a heavy border and blue background (Figure 1-40).

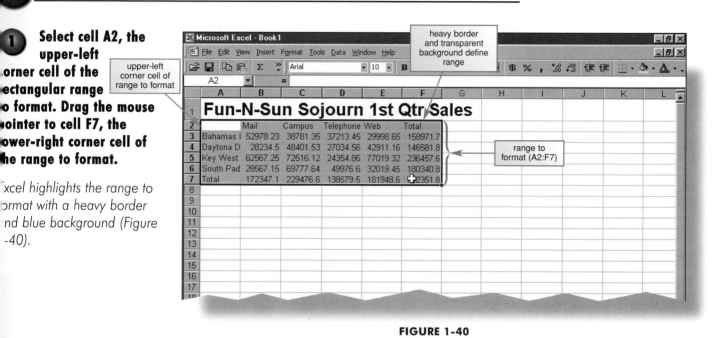

FIGURE 1-40

2 Click Format on the menu bar and then point to AutoFormat.

The Format menu displays (Figure 1-41).

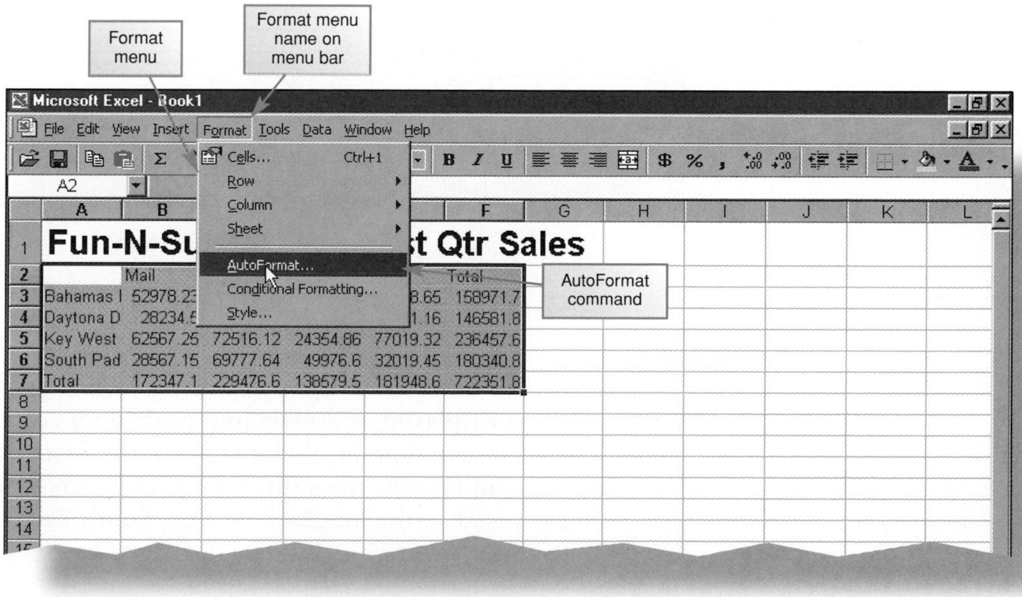

FIGURE 1-41

3 **Click AutoFormat. Click the Accounting 2 format (column 2, row 3) in the AutoFormat dialog box. Point to the OK button.**

The AutoFormat dialog box displays with a list of customized formats (Figure 1-42). Each format illustrates how the body of the worksheet will display if it is chosen.

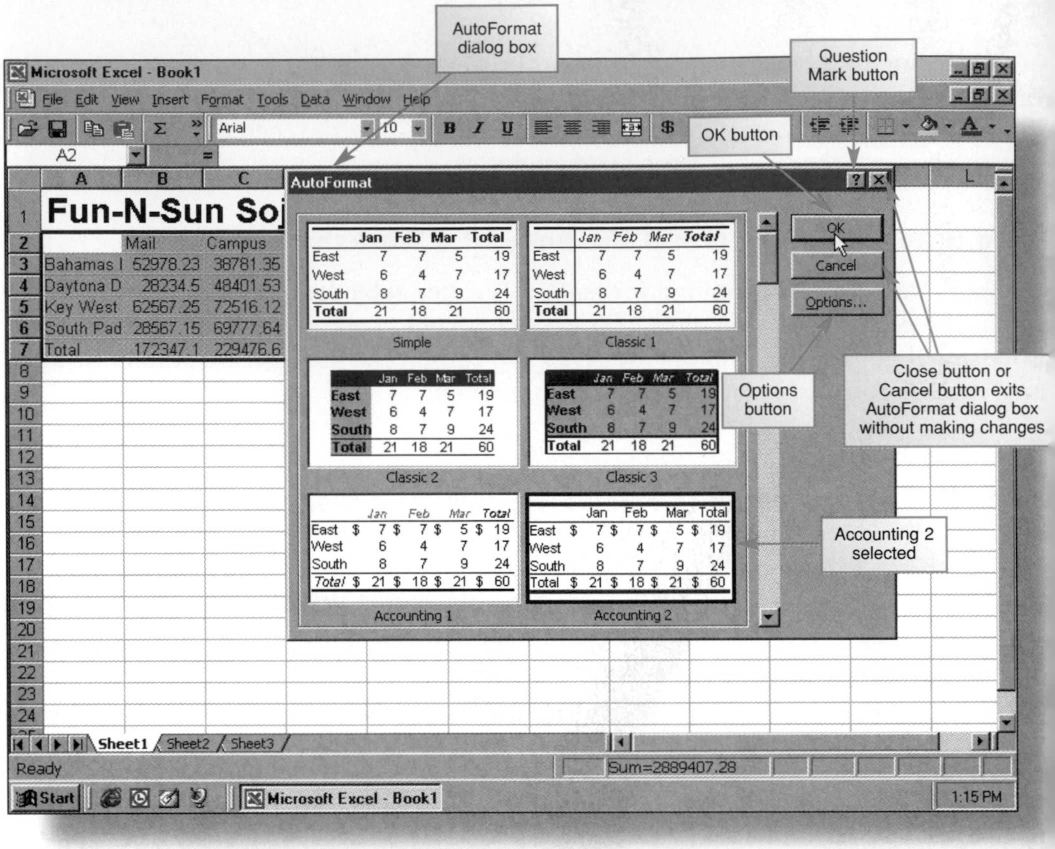

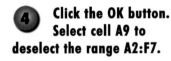

FIGURE 1-42

4 **Click the OK button. Select cell A9 to deselect the range A2:F7.**

Excel displays the worksheet with the range A2:F7 using the customized format, Accounting 2 (Figure 1-43).

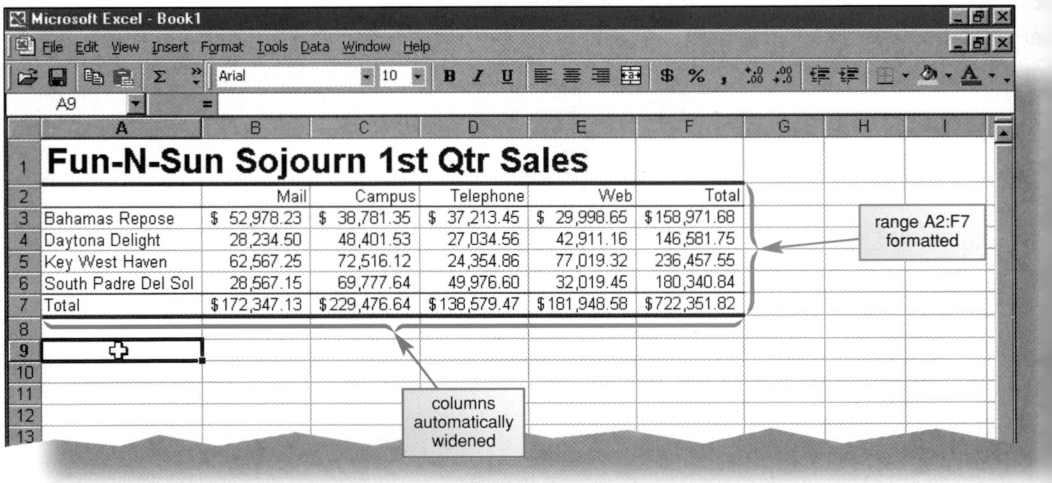

FIGURE 1-43

The formats associated with Accounting 2 include right-alignment of column titles, numbers displayed as dollars and cents with comma separators, numbers aligned on the decimal point, dollar signs in the first row of numbers and in the total row, and top and bottom rows display with borders. The width of column A also has been increased so the longest row title, South Padre Del Sol, just fits in the column. The widths of columns B through F have been increased so that the formatted numbers will fit in the cells.

The AutoFormat dialog box shown in Figure 1-42 includes 17 customized formats and five buttons. Use the scroll bar to view the 11 customized formats that do not display in the dialog box. Each one of these customized formats offers a different look. The one you choose depends on the worksheet you are creating.

The five buttons in the dialog box allow you to cancel, complete the entries, get Help, and adjust a customized format. The **Close button** terminates current activity without making changes. You also can use the **Cancel button**, immediately below the **OK button**, for this purpose. Use the **Question Mark button**, to obtain Help on any box or button located in the dialog box. The **Options button** allows you to select additional formats to assign as part of the selected customized format.

Centering the Worksheet Title Across Columns

With the column widths increased, the final step in formatting the worksheet title is to center it across columns A through F. Centering a worksheet title across the columns used in the body of the worksheet improves the worksheet's appearance.

More About

Customizing the AutoFormat

It is not uncommon to apply two or more of the customized formats shown in Figure 1-42 to the same range. If you assign two customized formats to a range, Excel does not remove the original format from the range; it simply adds the second customized format to the first. Thus, if you decide to change a customized format, first select the range, and then, in the AutoFormat dialog box, assign it the customized format titled None.

Steps To Center a Cell's Contents Across Columns

1 Click cell A1. Drag the block plus sign to the rightmost cell (F1) of the range to center (A1:F1). Point to the Merge and Center button on the Formatting toolbar.

When you drag through the range A1:F1, Excel highlights the cells (Figure 1-44).

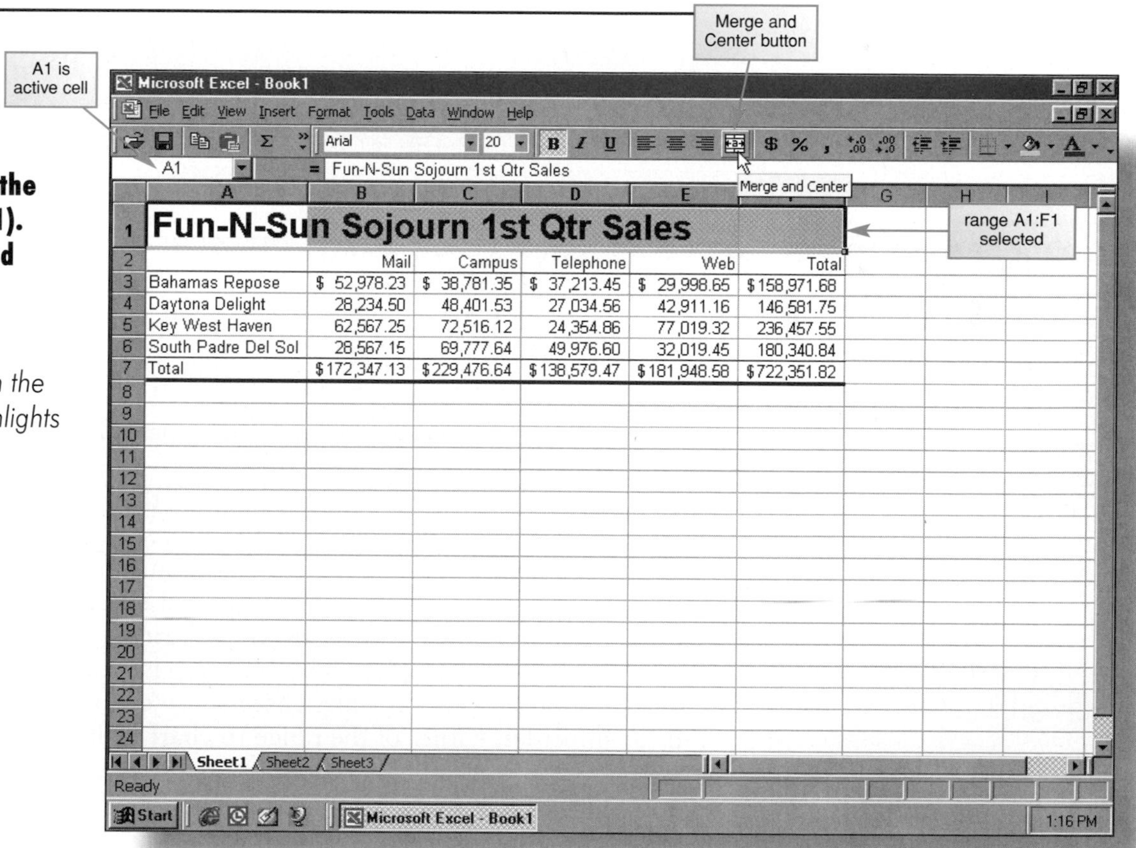

FIGURE 1-44

2 **Click the Merge and Center button.**

Excel merges the cells A1 through F1 to create a new cell A1 and centers the contents of cell A1 across columns A through F (Figure 1-45). After the merge, cells B1 through F1 no longer exist on the worksheet.

3 **Click cell A9 to deselect cell A1.**

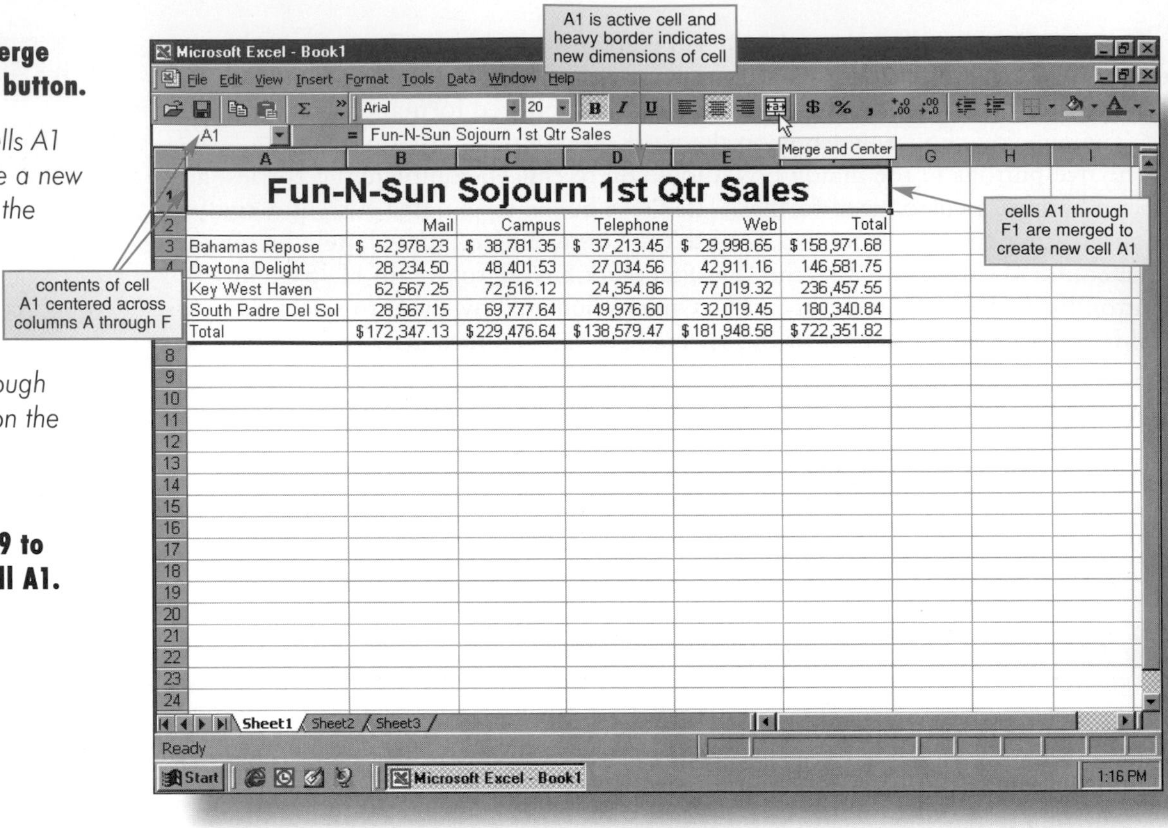

A1 is active cell and heavy border indicates new dimensions of cell

contents of cell A1 centered across columns A through F

cells A1 through F1 are merged to create new cell A1

	A	B	C	D	E	F
1	Fun-N-Sun Sojourn 1st Qtr Sales					
2		Mail	Campus	Telephone	Web	Total
3	Bahamas Repose	$ 52,978.23	$ 38,781.35	$ 37,213.45	$ 29,998.65	$158,971.68
4	Daytona Delight	28,234.50	48,401.53	27,034.56	42,911.16	146,581.75
5	Key West Haven	62,567.25	72,516.12	24,354.86	77,019.32	236,457.55
6	South Padre Del Sol	28,567.15	69,777.64	49,976.60	32,019.45	180,340.84
7	Total	$172,347.13	$229,476.64	$138,579.47	$181,948.58	$722,351.82

FIGURE 1-45

Excel not only centers the worksheet title, but also merges cells A1 through F1 into one cell, cell A1. Thus, the heavy border that defines the active cell in Figure 1-45 covers what originally was cells A1 through F1. For the Merge and Center button to work properly, all the cells except the leftmost cell in the range of cells must be empty.

Most formats assigned to a cell will display on the Formatting toolbar when the cell is selected. For example, the font type and font size display in their appropriate boxes. Recessed buttons indicate an assigned format. To determine if less frequently used formats are assigned to a cell, point to the cell and right-click. Next, click Format Cells, and then click each of the tabs in the Format Cells dialog box.

The worksheet now is complete. The next step is to chart the first quarter sales for the four vacation packages by sales channel. To create the chart, you must select the cell in the upper-left corner of the range to chart (cell A2). Rather than clicking cell A2 to select it, the next section describes how to use the Name box to select the cell.

Using the Name Box to Select a Cell

The **Name box** is located on the left side of the formula bar. To select any cell, click the Name box and enter the cell reference of the cell you want to select. Perform the following steps to select cell A2.

teps **To Use the Name Box to Select a Cell**

1 **Click the Name box in the formula bar. Type** a2 **in the Name box.**

Even though cell A9 is the active cell, the Name box displays the typed cell reference A2 (Figure 1-46).

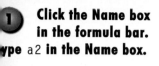
a2 typed in Name box

A9 is active cell

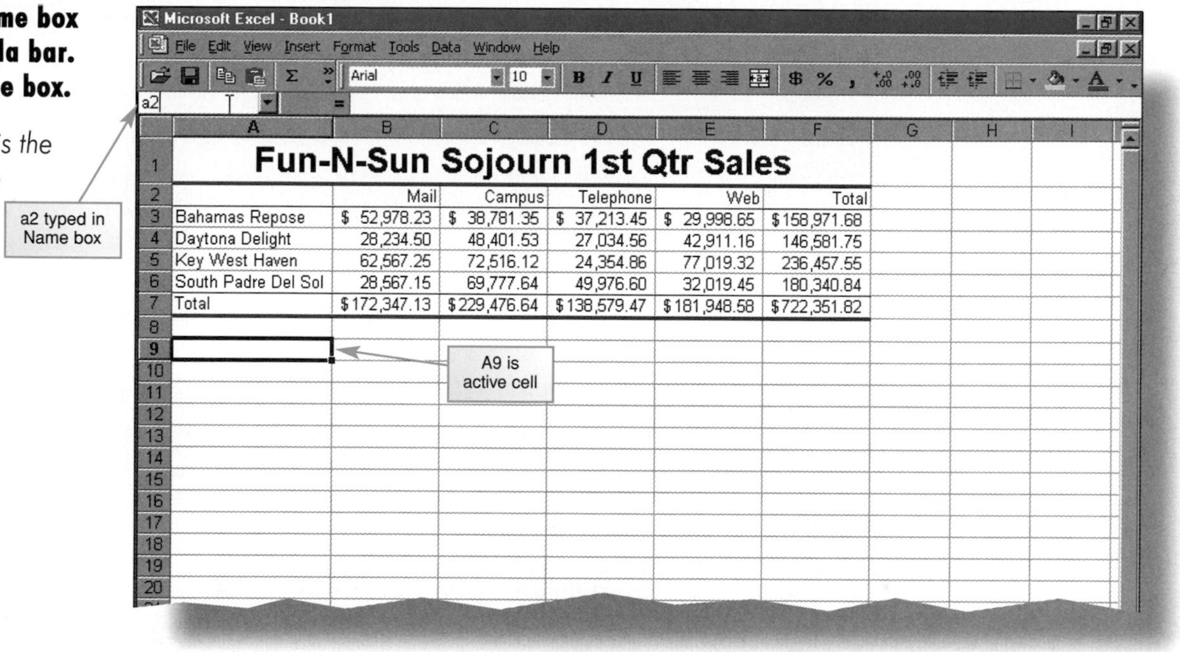

FIGURE 1-46

2 **Press the ENTER key.**

Excel changes the active cell from cell A9 to cell A2 (Figure 1-47).

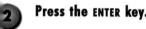
A2 is active cell

Name Box

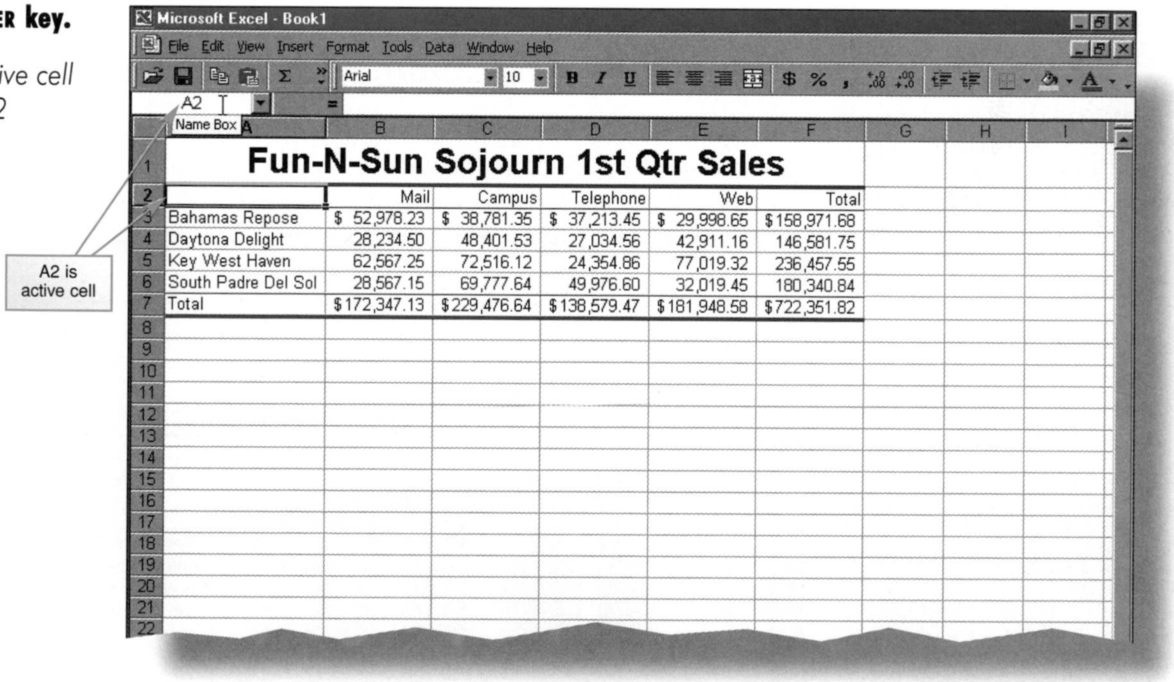

FIGURE 1-47

As you will see in later projects, besides using the Name box to select any cell in the worksheet, you also can use it to assign names to a cell or range of cells.

Excel supports several additional ways to select a cell, as summarized on the next page in Table 1-3.

Table 1-3   Selecting Cells in Excel

KEY, BOX, OR COMMAND	FUNCTION
ALT+PAGE DOWN	Selects the cell one window to the right and moves the window accordingly.
ALT+PAGE UP	Selects the cell one window to the left and moves the window accordingly.
ARROW	Selects the adjacent cell in the direction of the arrow on the key.
CTRL+ARROW	Selects the border cell of the worksheet in combination with the arrow keys and moves the window accordingly. For example, to select the rightmost cell in the row that contains the active cell, press CTRL+RIGHT arrow. You also can press the END key, release it, and then press the arrow key to accomplish the same task.
CTRL+HOME	Selects cell A1 or the cell one column and one row below and to the right of frozen titles and moves the the window accordingly.
Find command on Edit menu	Finds and selects a cell that contains specific contents that you enter in the Find dialog box. If necessary, Excel moves the window to display the cell. You can press SHIFT+F5 or CTRL+F to display the Find dialog box.
F5 or Go To command on Edit menu	Selects the cell that corresponds to the cell reference you enter in the Go To dialog box and moves the window accordingly. You can press CTRL+G to display the Find dialog box.
HOME	Selects the cell at the beginning of the row that contains the active cell and moves the window accordingly.
Name box	Selects the cell in the workbook that corresponds to the cell reference you enter in the Name box.
PAGE DOWN	Selects the cell down one window from the active cell and moves the window accordingly.
PAGE UP	Selects the cell up one window from the active cell and moves the window accordingly.

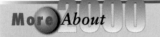

More About

Navigation

For more information on selecting cells that contain certain entries, such as constants or formulas, visit the Excel 2000 More About Web page (www.scsite.com/ex2000/more.htm) and click Using Go To Special.

Adding a 3-D Column Chart to the Worksheet

The 3-D Column chart (Figure 1-48) is called an **embedded chart** because it is drawn on the same worksheet as the data.

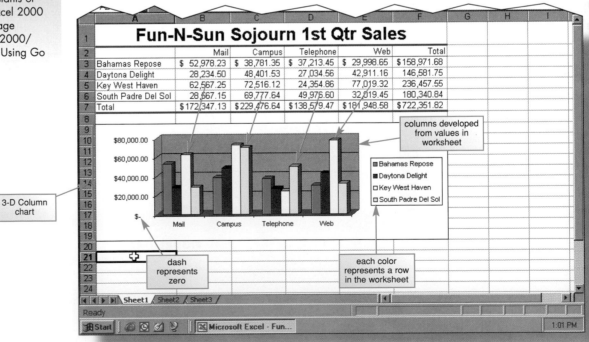

FIGURE 1-48

For the sales channel Mail, the light blue column represents the first quarter sales for the Bahamas Repose vacation package ($52,978.23); the purple column represents the first quarter sales for Daytona Delight ($28,234.50); the light yellow column represents the first quarter sales for Key West Haven ($62,567.25); and the turquoise column represents the first quarter sales for South Padre Del Sol ($28,567.15). For the sales channels Campus, Telephone, and Web, the columns follow the same color scheme to represent the comparable first quarter sales. The totals from the worksheet are not represented because the totals were not in the range specified for charting.

Excel derives the scale along the vertical axis (also called the **y-axis** or **value axis**) of the chart on the basis of the values in the worksheet. For example, no value in the range B3:E6 is less than zero or greater than $80,000.00. Excel also determines the $20,000.00 increments along the y-axis automatically. The format used by Excel for the numbers along the y-axis includes representing zero (0) with a dash (Figure 1-48).

With the range to chart selected, you click the **Chart Wizard button** on the Standard toolbar to initiate drawing the chart. The area on the worksheet where the chart displays is called the **chart location**. The chart location is the range A9:F20, immediately below the worksheet data.

Follow the steps below to draw a 3-D Column chart that compares the first quarter sales by vacation package for the four sales channels.

To Add a 3-D Column Chart to the Worksheet

1 Double-click the move handle on the left side of the Standard toolbar to display the entire toolbar. With cell A2 selected, position the block plus sign within the cell's border and drag the mouse pointer to the lower-right corner cell (cell E6) of the range to chart (A2:E6). Point to the Chart Wizard button on the Standard toolbar.

Excel highlights the range to chart (Figure 1-49).

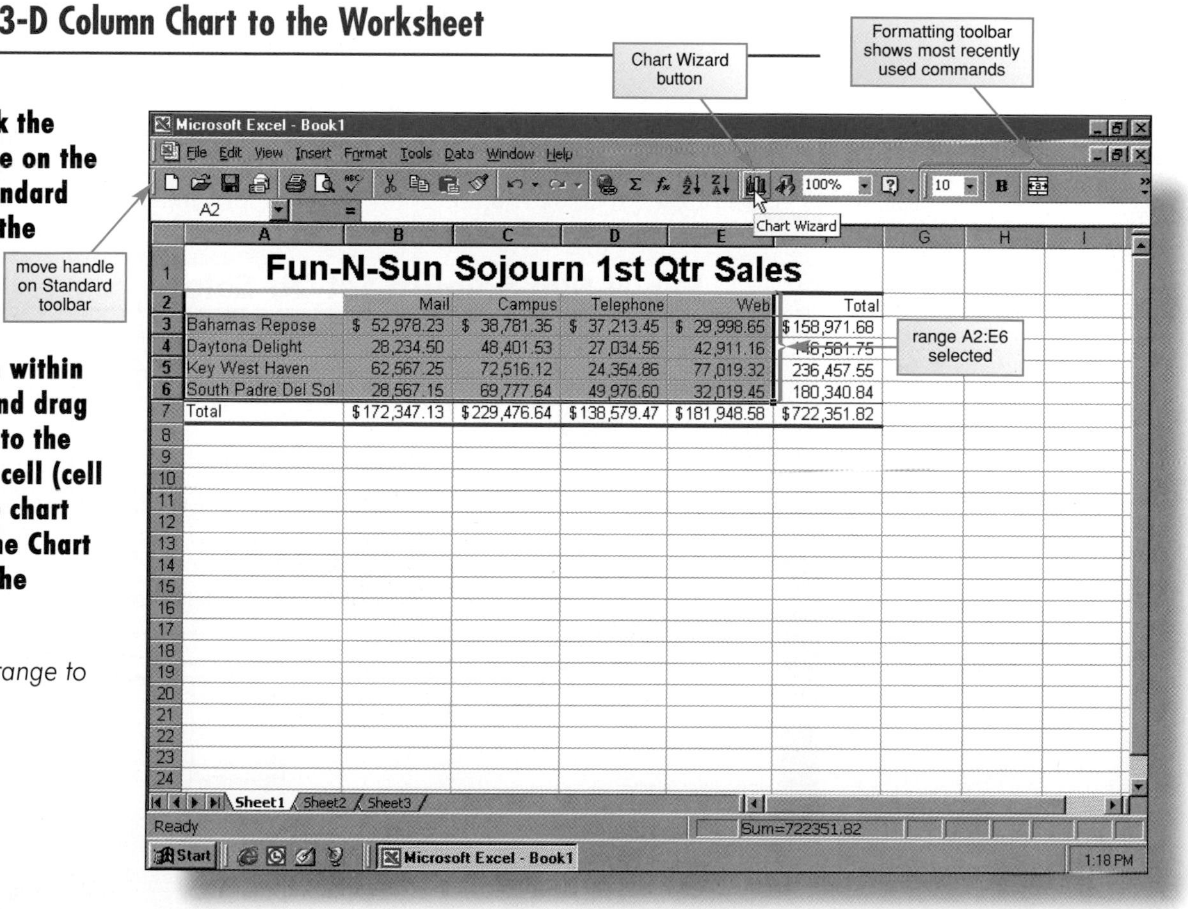

FIGURE 1-49

2 **Click the Chart Wizard button.**

The Chart Wizard – Step 1 of 4 – Chart Type dialog box displays.

3 **With Column selected in the Chart type list, click the 3-D Column chart sub-type (column 1, row 2) in the Chart sub-type area. Point to the Finish button.**

Column is highlighted in the Chart type list and Clustered column with a 3-D visual effect is highlighted in the Chart sub-type area (Figure 1-50).

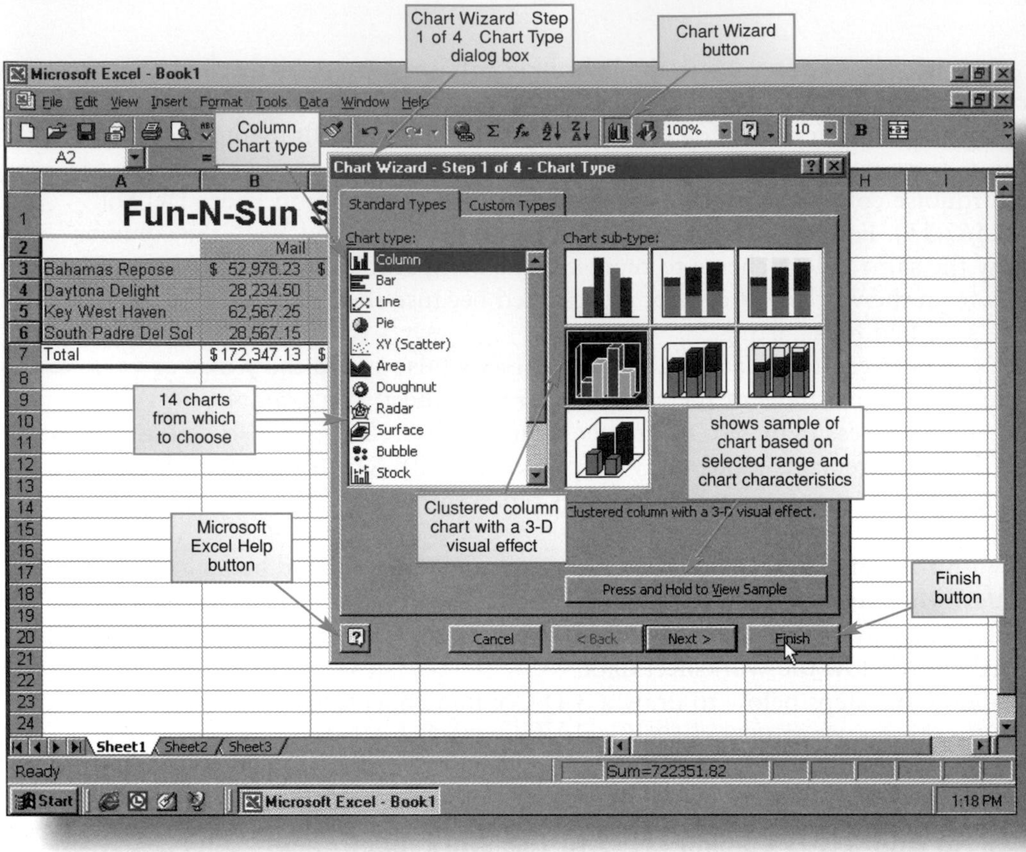

FIGURE 1-50

4 **Click the Finish button.**

Excel draws the 3-D Column chart (Figure 1-51). The chart displays in the middle of the window in a selection rectangle. The small sizing handles at the corners and along the sides of the selection rectangle indicate the chart is selected.

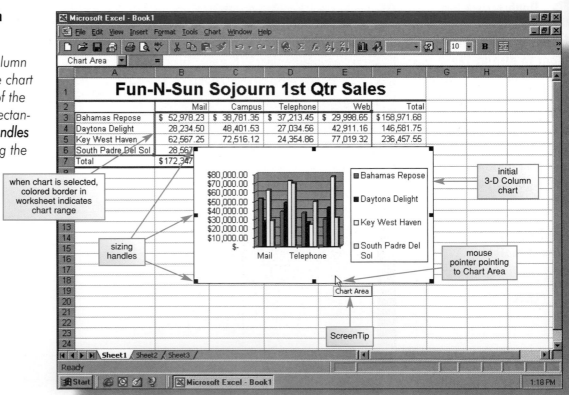

FIGURE 1-51

5 Point to an open area in the lower-right section of the Chart Area so the ScreenTip, Chart Area, displays (Figure 1-51). The ScreenTip defines the area of the chart that the mouse pointer is pointing to. Drag the chart down and to the left to position the upper-left corner of the dotted line rectangle over the upper-left corner of cell A9 (Figure 1-52).

Excel displays a dotted line rectangle showing the new chart location. As you drag the selected chart, the mouse pointer changes to a cross hair with four arrowheads.

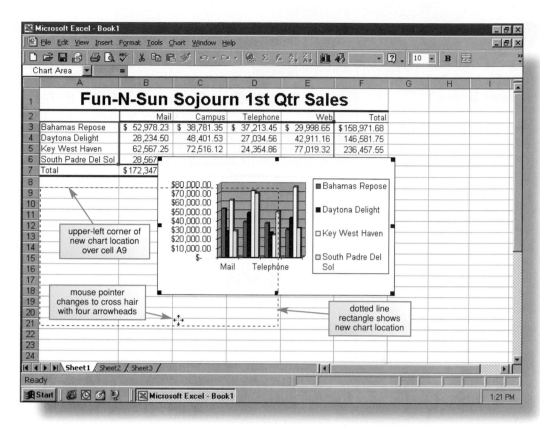

FIGURE 1-52

6 Release the mouse button. Point to the middle sizing handle on the right edge of the selection rectangle.

The chart displays in a new location (Figure 1-53). The mouse pointer changes to a horizontal line with two arrowheads when it points to a sizing handle.

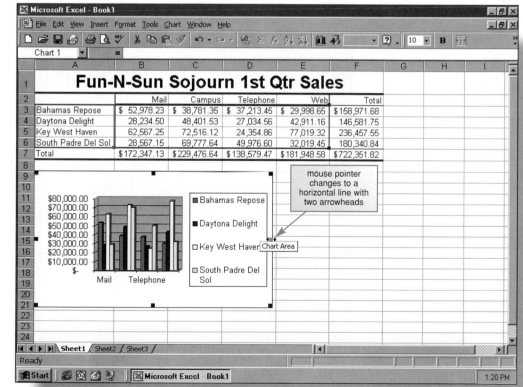

FIGURE 1-53

7 **While holding down the ALT key, drag the sizing handle to the right edge of column F. Release the mouse button.**

While you drag, the dotted line rectangle shows the new chart location (Figure 1-54). Holding down the ALT key while you drag a chart snaps (aligns) the new border to the worksheet gridlines.

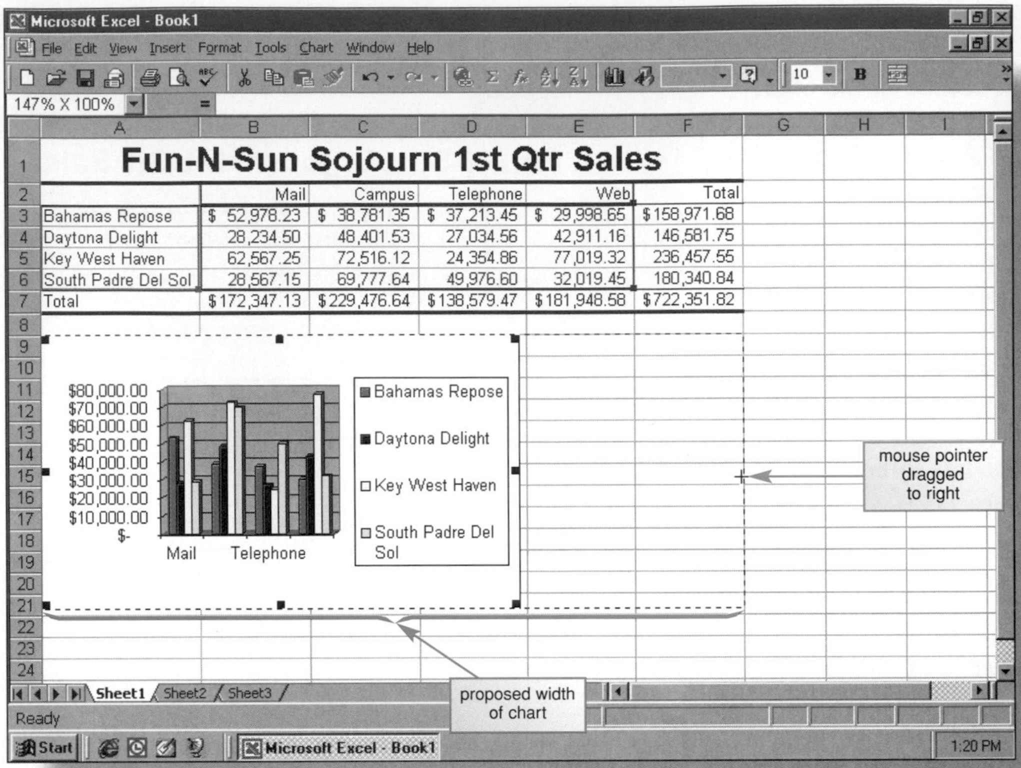

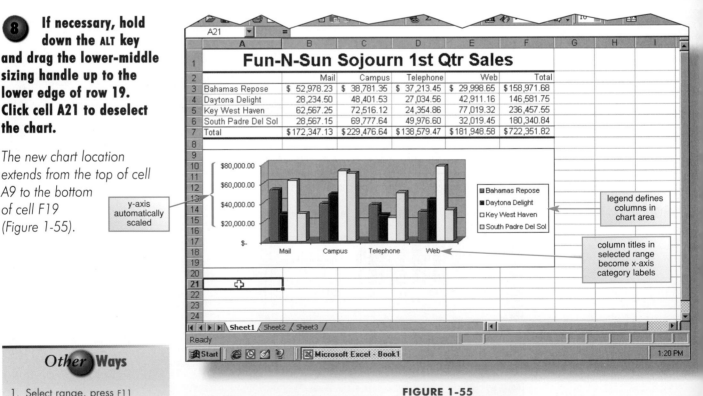

FIGURE 1-54

8 **If necessary, hold down the ALT key and drag the lower-middle sizing handle up to the lower edge of row 19. Click cell A21 to deselect the chart.**

The new chart location extends from the top of cell A9 to the bottom of cell F19 (Figure 1-55).

FIGURE 1-55

Other **Ways**

1. Select range, press F11
2. Select range, on Insert menu click Chart

The embedded 3-D Column chart in Figure 1-55 compares the first quarter sales for the four vacation packages within each sales channel. It also allows you to compare first quarter sales among the sales channels.

Excel automatically selects the entries in the topmost row of the range (row 2) as the titles for the horizontal axis (also called the **x-axis** or **category axis**) and draws a column for each of the 16 cells in the range containing numbers. The small box to the right of the column chart in Figure 1-55 contains the legend. The **legend** identifies each bar in the chart. Excel automatically selects the leftmost column of the range (column A) as titles within the legend. As indicated earlier, it also automatically scales the y-axis on the basis of the magnitude of the numbers in the chart range.

Excel offers 14 different chart types (Figure 1-50 on page E 1.38). The **default chart type** is the chart Excel draws if you click the Finish button in the first Chart Wizard dialog box. When you install Excel on a computer, the default chart type is the 2-D (two-dimensional) Column chart.

Saving a Workbook

While you are building a workbook, the computer stores it in memory. If the computer is turned off or if you lose electrical power, the workbook is lost. Hence, you must save on a floppy disk or hard disk any workbook that you will use later. A saved workbook is referred to as a **file** or **workbook**. The following steps illustrate how to save a workbook on a floppy disk in drive A using the Save button on the standard toolbar.

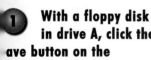

To Save a Workbook

1 **With a floppy disk in drive A, click the Save button on the standard toolbar.**

The Save As dialog box displays (Figure 1-56). The preset Save in folder is My Documents, the preset file name is Book1, and the file type is Microsoft Excel Workbook. The buttons on the top and on the side are used to select folders and change the display of file names and other information.

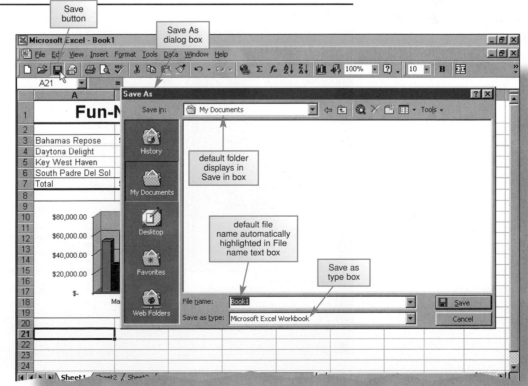

FIGURE 1-56

2 **Type** Fun-N-Sun Sojourn 1st Qtr Sales **in the File name text box.**

The new file name replaces Book1 in the File name text box (Figure 1-57). A file name can be up to 255 characters and can include spaces.

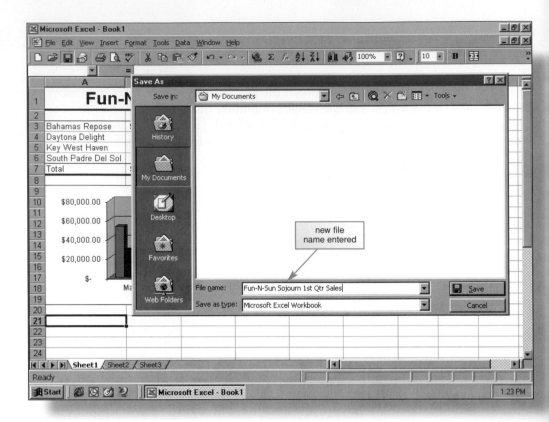

FIGURE 1-57

3 **Click the Save in box arrow and then point to 3½ Floppy (A:).**

A list of available drives and folders displays (Figure 1-58).

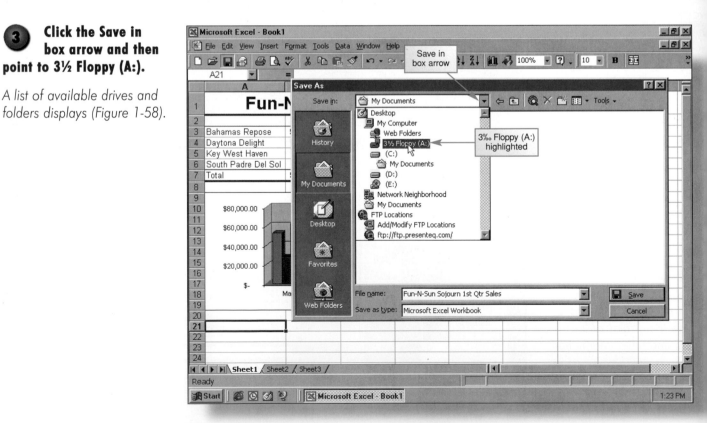

FIGURE 1-58

4 Click 3½ Floppy (A:) and then point to the Save button in the Save As dialog box.

Drive A becomes the selected drive (Figure 1-59).

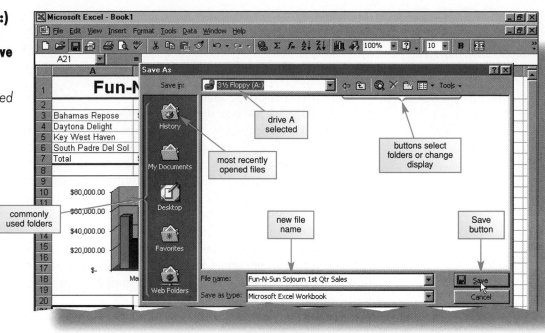

FIGURE 1-59

5 Click the Save button.

Excel saves the workbook on the floppy disk in drive A using the file name Fun-N-Sun Sojourn 1st Qtr Sales. Excel automatically appends the extension .xls to the file name you entered in Step 2, which stands for Excel workbook. Although the workbook is saved on a floppy disk, it also remains in memory and displays on the screen (Figure 1-60). Notice the file name in the title bar.

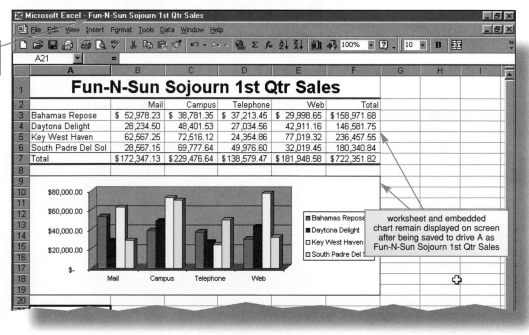

FIGURE 1-60

Other Ways

1. Press CTRL+S, type file name, select drive or folder, click OK button

2. Right-click workbook Control-menu icon on menu bar, click Save As on shortcut menu, type file name, select drive of folder, click OK button

3. On File menu click Save As, type file name, select drive of folder, click OK button

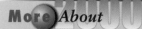

Saving a Worksheet as a Web Page

Excel allows you to save a worksheet in HTML format so you can publish it to the World Wide Web. Click Save as Web Page on the File menu. You have the option to save the worksheet as a static Web page or as a dynamic Web page. A static Web page means you can view the worksheet on the World Wide Web, but you cannot change cell contents. A dynamic Web page means you can modify the worksheet using a browser.

AutoSave

Are you worried about losing your work because your computer might crash? If so, you can use the AutoSave command on the Tools menu. The AutoSave command automatically saves your work every 10 minutes. If you prefer to change the time between saves, you can do so through the AutoSave dialog box that displays when you invoke the AutoSave command. AutoSave is an add-in program. If the AutoSave command does not display on your Tools menu, use the Add-Ins command on the Tools menu to add it.

While Excel is saving the workbook, it momentarily changes the word Ready on the status bar to Saving. It also displays a horizontal bar on the status bar indicating the amount of the workbook saved. After the save operation is complete, Excel changes the name of the workbook in the title bar from Book1 to Fun-N-Sun Sojourn 1st Qtr Sales (Figure 1-60 on the previous page).

When you click the **Tools button** in the Save As dialog box (Figure 1-59 on the previous page), a list box displays. The **General Options command** in the list allows you to save a backup copy of the workbook, create a password to limit access to the workbook, and carry out other functions that will be discussed later. Saving a **backup workbook** means that each time you save a workbook, Excel copies the current version of the workbook on disk to a file with the same name, but with the words, Backup of, appended to the front of the file name. In the case of a power failure or some other problem, use the backup version to restore your work.

You also can use the General Options command on the Tools list to assign a **password** to a workbook so others cannot open it. A password is case sensitive and can be up to 15 characters long. **Case sensitive** means Excel can differentiate between uppercase and lowercase letters. If you assign a password and forget the password, you cannot access the workbook.

The seven buttons at the top and to the right in the Save As dialog box (Figure 1-59) and their functions are summarized in Table 1-4.

Table 1-4	Save As Dialog Box Toolbar Buttons	
BUTTON	**BUTTON NAME**	**FUNCTION**
⇦	Default File Location	Displays contents of default file location
🗁	Up One Level	Displays contents of next level up folder
🔍	Search the Web	Starts browser and displays search engine
✕	Delete	Deletes selected file or folder
🗋	Create New Folder	Creates new folder
▦	Views	Changes view of files and folders
Tools ▾	Tools	Lists commands to print or modify file names and folders

The five buttons on the left of the Save As dialog box in Figure 1-59 allow you to select frequently used folders. The **History button** displays a list of shortcuts (pointers) to the most recently used files in a folder titled Recent. You can not save workbooks to the Recent folder.

Printing the Worksheet

Once you have created the worksheet and saved it on a floppy disk or hard disk, you might want to print it. A printed version of the worksheet is called a **hard copy** or **printout**.

You might want a printout for several reasons. First, to present the worksheet and chart to someone who does not have access to a computer, it must be in printed form. A printout, for example, can be handed out in a management meeting about first quarter sales. In addition, worksheets and charts often are kept for reference by people other than those who prepare them. In many cases, worksheets and charts are printed and kept in binders for use by others. This section describes how to print a worksheet and an embedded chart.

More About

Saving Paper

If you are an environmentalist interested in saving trees, you can preview the printout on your screen, make adjustments to the worksheet, and then print it only when it appears exactly as you desire. The Print Preview button is immediately to the right of the Print button on the Standard toolbar. Clicking it displays an onscreen image of how the printout will appear. Each time you preview rather than print, you save paper destined for the wastepaper basket, which, in turn, saves trees.

Steps — To Print a Worksheet

1 Ready the printer according to the printer instructions. Point to the Print button on the Standard toolbar (Figure 1-61).

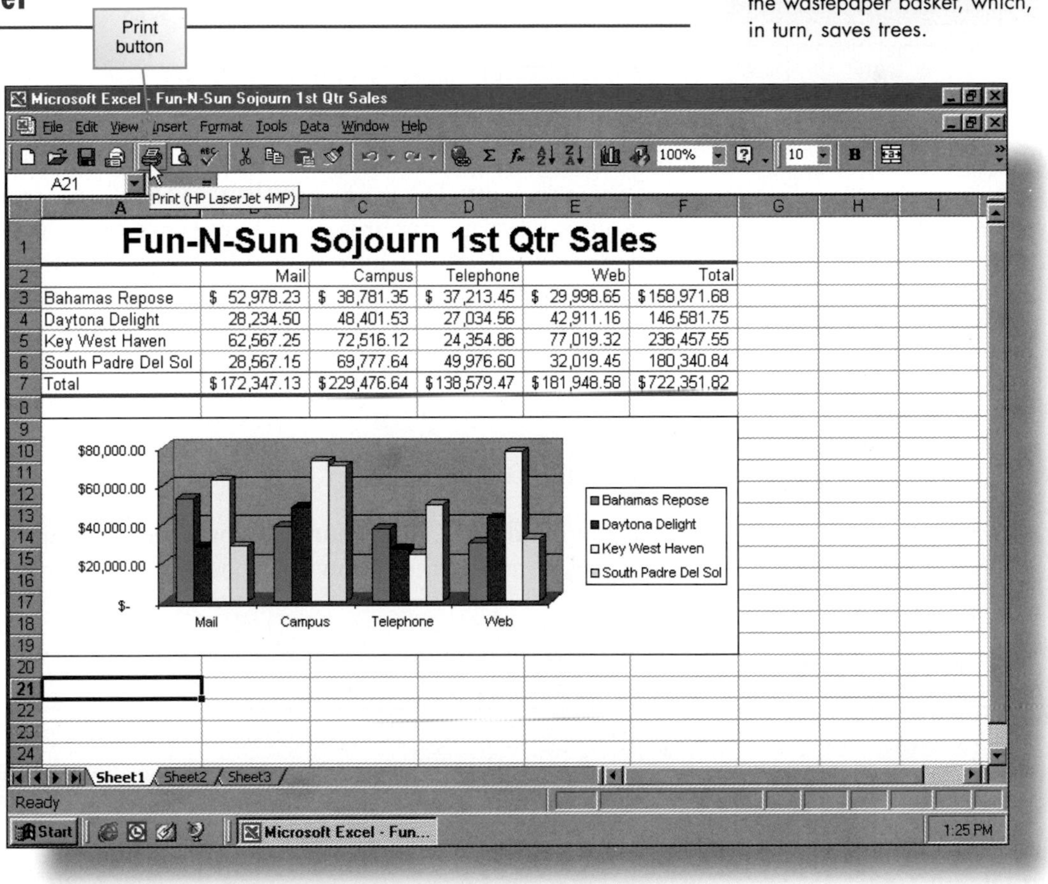

FIGURE 1-61

2 Click the Print button. When the printer stops printing the worksheet and the chart, retrieve the printout (Figure 1-62).

Excel displays the Printing dialog box that allows you to cancel the print job while the system is sending the worksheet and chart image to the printer.

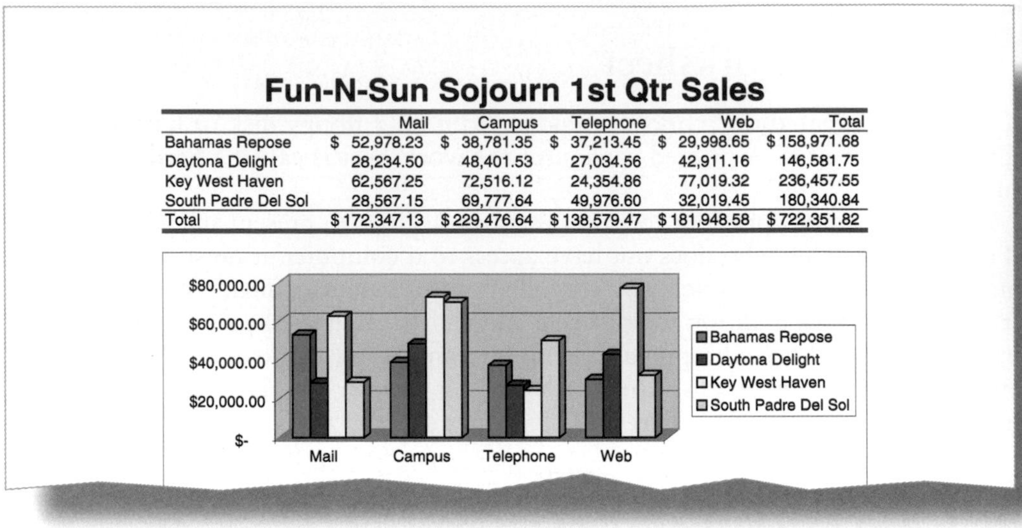

Fun-N-Sun Sojourn 1st Qtr Sales
Mail Campus Telephone Web Total
Bahamas Repose $ 52,978.23 $ 38,781.35 $ 37,213.45 $ 29,998.65 $ 158,971.68
Daytona Delight 28,234.50 48,401.53 27,034.56 42,911.16 146,581.75
Key West Haven 62,567.25 72,516.12 24,354.86 77,019.32 236,457.55
South Padre Del Sol 28,567.15 69,777.64 49,976.60 32,019.45 180,340.84
Total $ 172,347.13 $ 229,476.64 $ 138,579.47 $ 181,948.58 $ 722,351.82
$80,000.00
$60,000.00
$40,000.00
$20,000.00
$-
Mail
Campus
Telephone
Web
Bahamas Repose
Daytona Delight
Key West Haven
South Padre Del Sol

FIGURE 1-62

Other Ways

1. Press CTRL+P, click OK button
2. On File menu click Print, click OK button
3. Right-click workbook Control-menu icon on menu bar, click Print on shortcut menu, click OK button

Prior to clicking the Print button, you can select which columns and rows in the worksheet to print. The range of cells you choose to print is called the **print area**. If you do not select a print area, as was the case in the previous set of steps, Excel automatically selects a print area on the basis of used cells. As you will see in future projects, Excel has many different print options, such as allowing you to preview the printout on the screen to see if the printout is satisfactory prior to sending it to the printer. Several of these print options are discussed in Project 2.

Quitting Excel

After you build, save, and print the worksheet and chart, Project 1 is complete. To quit Excel, complete the following steps.

Steps To Quit Excel

1 Point to the Close button on the right side of the title bar (Figure 1-63).

Control-menu icon
Close button
workbook Close button
workbook Control-menu icon
Microsoft Excel - Fun-N-Sun Sojourn 1st Qtr Sales
File Edit View Insert Format Tools Data Window Help
Close
A21
Fun-N-Sun Sojourn 1st Qtr Sales
Mail Campus Telephone Web Total
Bahamas Repose $ 52,978.23 $ 38,781.35 $ 37,213.45 $ 29,998.65 $158,971.68
Daytona Delight 28,234.50 48,401.53 27,034.56 42,911.16 146,581.75
Key West Haven 62,567.25 72,516.12 24,354.86 77,019.32 236,457.55
South Padre Del Sol 28,567.15 69,777.64 49,976.60 32,019.45 180,340.84
Total $172,347.13 $229,476.64 $138,579.47 $181,948.58 $722,351.82
$80,000.00

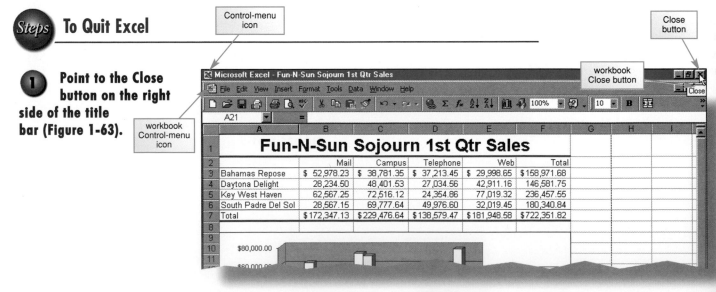

FIGURE 1-63

② Click the Close button.

If you made changes to the workbook, the Microsoft Excel dialog box displays the question, Do you want to save the changes you made to 'Fun-N-Sun Sojourn 1st Qtr Sales.xls'? (Figure 1-64). Clicking the Yes button saves the changes before quitting Excel. Clicking the No button quits Excel without saving the changes. Clicking the Cancel button stops the Exit command and returns to the worksheet.

③ Click the No button.

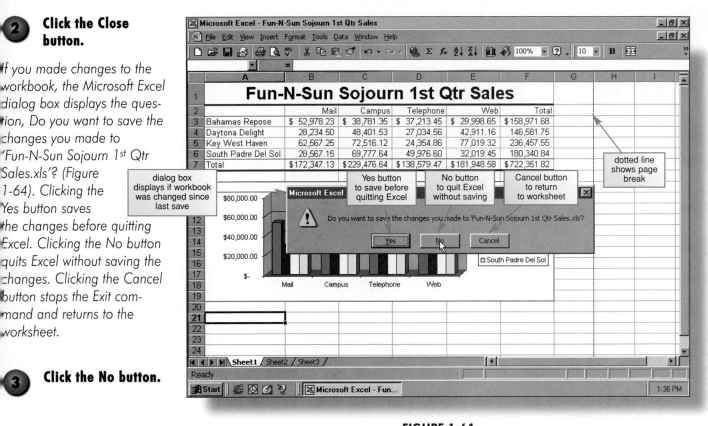

FIGURE 1-64

In Figure 1-63, you can see that two Close buttons and two Control-menu icons display. The Close button and Control-menu icon on the title bar close Excel. The Close button and Control-menu icon on the menu bar close the workbook.

Starting Excel and Opening a Workbook

Once you have created and saved a workbook, you often will have reason to retrieve it from a floppy disk. For example, you might want to review the calculations on the worksheet and enter additional or revised data on it. The steps on the next page assume Excel is not running.

Other Ways

1. Double-click Control-menu icon
2. Right-click Microsoft Excel button on taskbar, click Close on shortcut menu
3. On File menu click Exit

Steps **To Start Excel and Open a Workbook**

1 With your floppy disk in drive A, click the Start button on the taskbar and then point to Open Office Document (Figure 1-65).

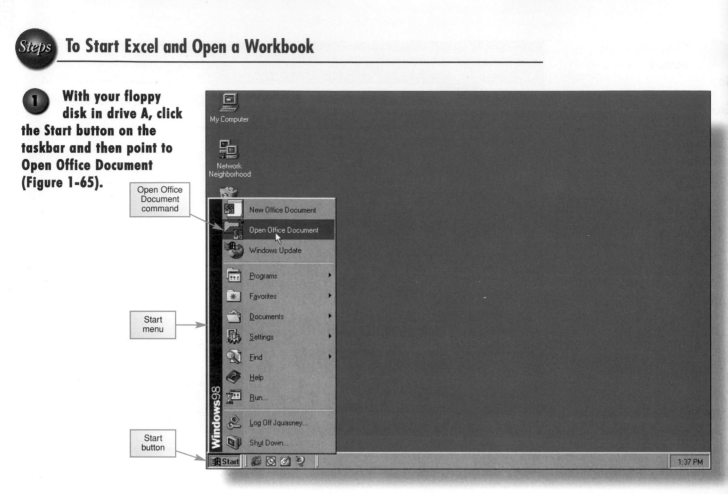

FIGURE 1-65

2 Click Open Office Document. If necessary, click the Look in box arrow and then click 3½ Floppy (A:).

The Open Office Document dialog box displays (Figure 1-66).

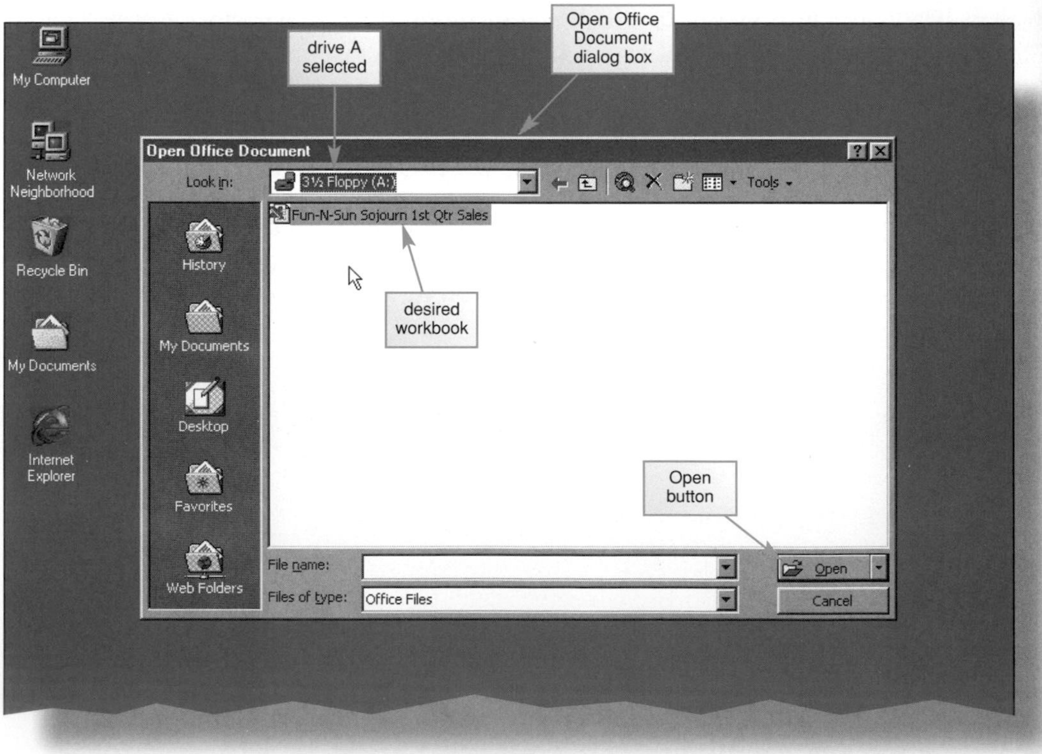

FIGURE 1-66

Double-click the file name Fun-N-Sun Sojourn 1ˢᵗ Qtr Sales.

Excel starts, opens the workbook Fun-N-Sun Sojourn 1st Qtr Sales.xls from drive A, and displays it on the screen (Figure 1-67). An alternative to double-clicking the file name is to click it and then click the Open button in the Open Office Document dialog box.

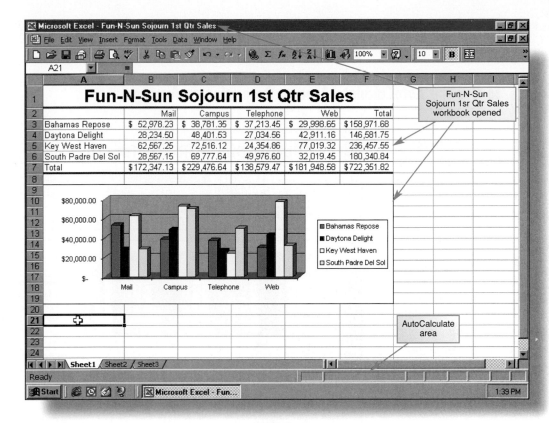

FIGURE 1-67

AutoCalculate

You easily can obtain a total, an average, or other information about the numbers in a range by using the **AutoCalculate area** on the status bar (bottom of Figure 1-67). All you need do is select the range of cells containing the numbers you want to check. Next, right-click the AutoCalculate area to display the shortcut menu (Figure 1-68 on the next page). The recessed check mark to the left of the active function (Sum) indicates that the sum of the selected range displays. The function commands on the AutoCalculate shortcut menu are described in Table 1-5.

Table 1-5 AutoCalculate Shortcut Menu Commands	
COMMAND	**FUNCTION**
Average	Displays the average of the numbers in the selected range
Count	Displays the number of nonblank cells in the selected range
Count Nums	Displays the number of cells containing numbers in the selected range
Max	Displays the highest value in the selected range
Min	Displays the lowest value in the selected range
Sum	Displays the sum of the numbers in the selected range

The following steps show how to display the average first quarter sales by sales channel for the Bahamas Repose vacation package.

Steps **To Use the AutoCalculate Area to Determine an Average**

1 **Select the range B3:E3. Right-click the AutoCalculate area on the status bar.**

The sum of the numbers in the range B3:E3 displays ($158,971.68) as shown in Figure 1-68 because Sum is active in the AutoCalculate area (you may see a total other than the Sum in your AutoCalculate area). The shortcut menu listing the various types of functions displays over the AutoCalculate area.

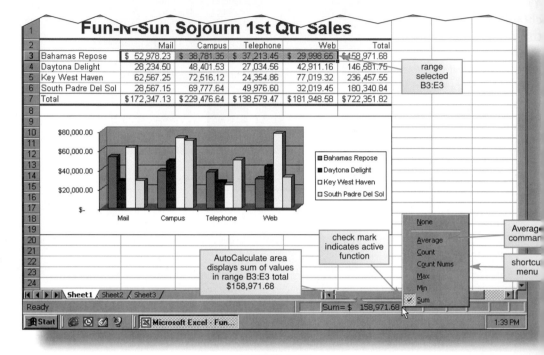

FIGURE 1-68

2 **Click Average on the shortcut menu.**

The average of the numbers in the range B3:E3 displays in the AutoCalculate area (Figure 1-69).

3 **Right-click the AutoCalculate area and then click Sum on the shortcut menu.**

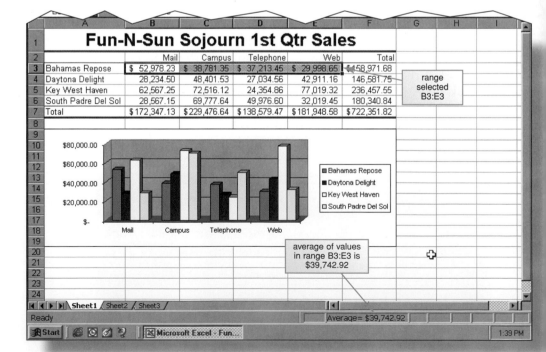

FIGURE 1-69

To change to any one of the other five functions for the range B3:E3, right-click the AutoCalculate area. Then click the desired function.

Correcting Errors

You can correct errors on a worksheet using one of several methods. The one you choose will depend on the extent of the error and whether you notice it while typing the data or after you have entered the incorrect data into the cell.

Correcting Errors While You Are Typing Data into a Cell

If you notice an error while you are typing data into a cell, press the BACKSPACE key to erase the portion in error and then type the correct characters. If the error is a major one, click the Cancel box in the formula bar or press the ESC key to erase the entire entry and then reenter the data from the beginning.

In-Cell Editing

If you find an error in the worksheet after entering the data, you can correct the error in one of two ways:

1. If the entry is short, select the cell, retype the entry correctly, and click the Enter box or press the ENTER key. The new entry will replace the old entry.
2. If the entry in the cell is long and the errors are minor, the **Edit mode** may be a better choice. Use the Edit mode as described below.
   a. Double-click the cell containing the error. Excel switches to Edit mode, the active cell contents display in the formula bar, and a flashing insertion point displays in the active cell (Figure 1-70). This editing procedure is called **in-cell editing** because you can edit the contents directly in the cell. The active cell contents also display in the formula bar.

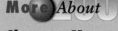

More About

Shortcut Menus

Shortcut menus display frequently used commands related to an object that the mouse pointer points to. To display a shortcut menu, right-click the object as shown in Step 1. In some cases, you also can display the shortcut menu by selecting the object, such as a cell or range of cells, and pressing SHIFT+F10. To hide a shortcut menu, click outside the shortcut menu or press the ESC key.

More About

Correcting Errors

Learning how to correct errors in a worksheet is critical to becoming proficient in Excel. Thus, carefully review this section on how to correct errors prior to entering data in a cell, how to perform in-cell editing, how to undo the last entry, and how to clear cells.

contents of cell E2 display in formula bar

insertion point displays in cell after double-clicking

	A	B	C	D	E	F	G	H	I
1	**Fun-N-Sun Sojourn 1st Qtr Sales**								
2		Mail	Campus	Telephone	Web	Total			
3	Bahamas Repose	$ 52,978.23	$ 38,781.35	$ 37,213.45	$ 29,998.65	$ 158,971.68			
4	Daytona Delight	28,234.50	48,401.53	27,034.56	42,911.16	146,581.75			
5	Key West Haven	62,567.25	72,516.12	24,354.86	77,019.32	236,457.55			
6	South Padre Del Sol	28,567.15	69,777.64	49,976.60	32,019.45	180,340.84			
7	Total	$ 172,347.13	$ 229,476.64	$ 47	$ 181,948.58	$ 722,351.82			

FIGURE 1-70

b. Make your changes, as specified below.
   (1) To insert between two characters, place the insertion point between the two characters and begin typing. Excel inserts the new characters at the location of the insertion point.
   (2) To delete a character in the cell, move the insertion point to the left of the character you want to delete and then press the DELETE key, or place the insertion point to the right of the character you want to delete and then press the BACKSPACE key. You also can use the mouse to drag through the character or adjacent characters you want to delete and then press the DELETE key or click the **Cut button** on the Standard toolbar.

More About

In-Cell Editing

An alternative to double-clicking the cell to edit is to select the cell and then press F2.

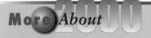

Editing the Contents of a Cell

Rather than using in-cell editing, you can select the cell and then click the formula bar to edit the contents.

(3) When you are finished editing an entry, click the Enter box or press the ENTER key.

When Excel enters the Edit mode, the keyboard usually is in Insert mode. In **Insert mode,** as you type a character, Excel inserts the character and moves all characters to the right of the typed character one position to the right. You can change to Overtype mode by pressing the INSERT key. In **Overtype mode,** Excel overtypes the character to the right of the insertion point. The INSERT key toggles the keyboard between Insert mode and Overtype mode.

While in Edit mode, you may have reason to move the insertion point to various points in the cell, select portions of the data in the cell, or switch from inserting characters to overtyping characters. Table 1-6 summarizes the most common tasks used during in-cell editing.

Table 1-6   Summary of In-Cell Editing Tasks

TASK	MOUSE	KEYBOARD
Move the insertion point to the beginning of data in a cell	Point to the left of the first character and click	Press HOME
Move the insertion point to the end of data in a cell	Point to the right of the last character and click	Press END
Move the insertion point anywhere in a cell	Point to the appropriate position and click the character	Press RIGHT ARROW or LEFT ARROW
Highlight one or more adjacent characters	Drag the mouse pointer through adjacent characters	Press SHIFT+RIGHT ARROW or SHIFT+LEFT ARROW
Select all data in a cell	Double-click the cell with the insertion point in the cell	
Delete selected characters	Click the Cut button on the Standard toolbar	Press DELETE
Toggle between Insert and Overtype modes		Press INSERT

Undoing the Last Entry

Excel provides the **Undo command** on the Edit menu and the **Undo button** on the Standard toolbar (Figure 1-71) that you can use to erase the most recent cell entry. Thus, if you enter incorrect data in a cell and notice it immediately, click the Undo command or Undo button and Excel changes the cell contents to what they were prior to entering the incorrect data.

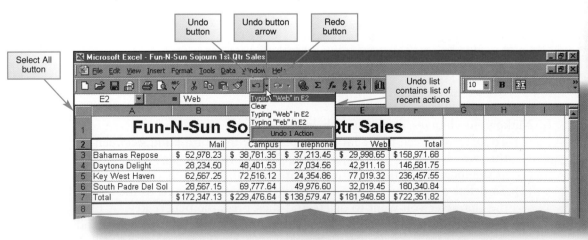

FIGURE 1-71

If Excel cannot undo an action, then the Undo button is inoperative. Excel remembers the last 16 actions you have completed. Thus, you can undo up to 16 previous actions by clicking the Undo box arrow to display the Undo list and clicking the action to be undone (Figure 1-71). You also can click Undo on the Edit menu rather than using the Undo button.

Next to the Undo button on the Standard toolbar is the Redo button. The **Redo button** allows you to repeat previous actions. You also can click Redo on the Edit menu rather than using the Redo button.

Clearing a Cell or Range of Cells

If you enter data into the wrong cell or range of cells, you can erase, or clear, the data using one of several methods. **Never press the SPACEBAR to clear a cell.** Pressing the SPACEBAR enters a blank character. A blank character is text and is different from an empty cell, even though the cell may appear empty.

Excel provides three methods to clear the contents of a cell or a range of cells.

TO CLEAR CELL CONTENTS USING THE FILL HANDLE

1. Select the cell or range of cells and point to the fill handle so the mouse pointer changes to a cross hair.
2. Drag the fill handle back into the selected cell or range until a shadow covers the cell or cells you want to erase. Release the mouse button.

TO CLEAR CELL CONTENTS USING THE SHORTCUT MENU

1. Select the cell or range of cells to be cleared.
2. Right-click the selection.
3. Click Clear Contents on the shortcut menu.

TO CLEAR CELL CONTENTS USING THE DELETE KEY

1. Select the cell or range of cells to be cleared.
2. Press the DELETE key.

TO CLEAR CELL CONTENTS USING THE CLEAR COMMAND

1. Select the cell or range of cells to be cleared.
2. Click Edit on the menu bar and then click Clear.
3. Click All on the submenu.

You also can select a range of cells and click the Cut button on the Standard toolbar or click Cut on the Edit menu. Be aware, however, that the **Cut button** or **Cut command** not only deletes the contents from the range, but also copies the contents of the range to the Office Clipboard.

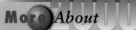
Clearing the Entire Worksheet

Sometimes, everything goes wrong. If this happens, you may want to clear the worksheet entirely and start over. To clear the worksheet, follow these steps.

TO CLEAR THE ENTIRE WORKSHEET

1 Click the Select All button on the worksheet (Figure 1-71 on page E 1.52).

2 Press the DELETE key or on the Edit menu click Clear and then click All on the submenu.

The **Select All button** selects the entire worksheet. Instead of clicking the Select All button, you also can press CTRL+A. You also can clear an unsaved workbook by clicking the workbook's Close button or by clicking **Close** on the File menu. If you close the workbook, click the **New button** on the Standard toolbar or click **New** on the File menu to begin working on the next workbook.

TO DELETE AN EMBEDDED CHART

1 Click the chart to select it.

2 Press the DELETE key.

Excel Help System

At any time while you are using Excel, you can get answers to questions by using the **Excel Help system**. Used properly, this form of online assistance can increase your productivity and reduce your frustrations by minimizing the time you spend learning how to use Excel.

The following section shows how to get answers to your questions using the Office Assistant. For additional information on using the Excel Help system, see Appendix A and Table 1-7 on page E1.57.

Using the Office Assistant

The **Office Assistant** answers your questions and suggests more efficient ways to complete a task. With the Office Assistant active, for example, you can type a question, word, or phrase in a text box and the Office Assistant provides immediate help on the subject. Also, as you create a worksheet, the Office Assistant accumulates tips that suggest more efficient ways to do the tasks you completed while building a worksheet, such as formatting, printing, and saving. This tip feature is part of the **IntelliSense™ technology** that is built into Excel, which understands what you are trying to do and suggests better ways to do it. When the light bulb displays above the Office Assistant, click it to see a tip.

The following steps show how to use the Office Assistant to obtain information on formatting a worksheet.

Steps To Obtain Help Using the Office Assistant

1 **If the Office Assistant is not on the screen, click Help on the menu bar and then click Show the Office Assistant. With the Office Assistant on the screen, click it. Type** formatting **in the What would you like to do? text box in the Office Assistant balloon. Point to the Search button (Figure 1-72).**

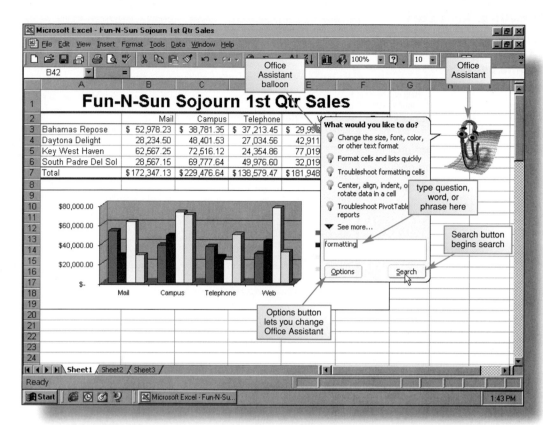

FIGURE 1-72

2 **Click the Search button. Point to the topic About worksheet formatting in the Office Assistant balloon.**

The Office Assistant displays a list of topics relating to the question, how do i format. The mouse pointer changes to a hand indicating it is pointing to a link (Figure 1-73).

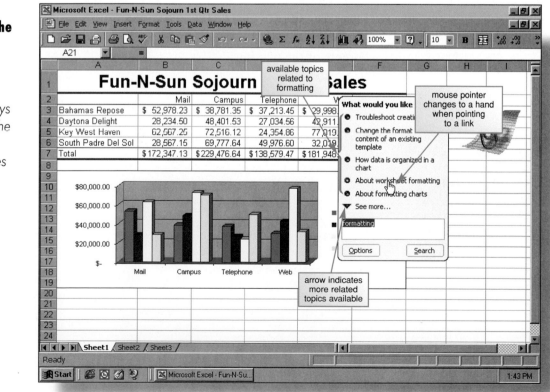

FIGURE 1-73

3 **Click About worksheet formatting. When Excel displays the Microsoft Excel Help window, double-click its title bar to maximize it.**

The Office Assistant displays a Microsoft Excel Help window that provides Help information about worksheet formatting (Figure 1-74).

4 **Click the Close button on the Microsoft Excel Help window title bar.**

The Microsoft Excel Help window closes and the worksheet is active.

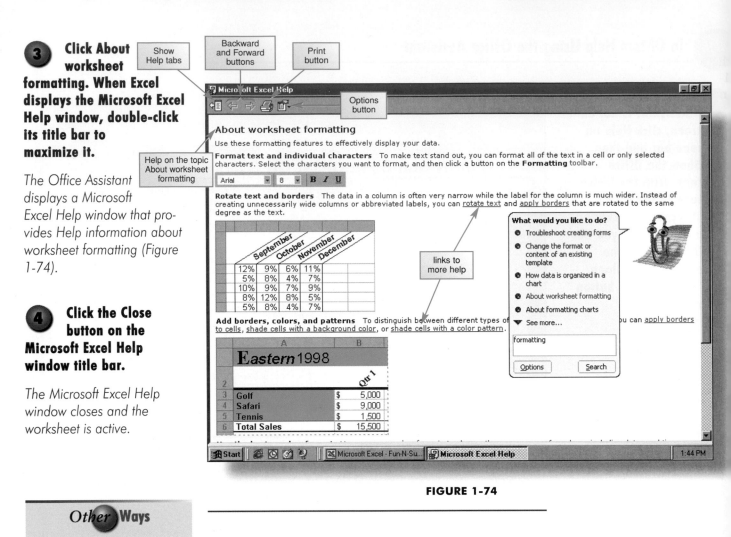

FIGURE 1-74

Use the buttons in the upper-left corner of the Microsoft Excel Help window (Figure 1-74) to navigate through the Help system, change the display, and print the contents of the window.

Table 1-7 summarizes the nine categories of Help available to you. Because of the way the Excel Help system works, please review the right most column of Table 1-7 if you have difficulties activating the desired category of Help. For additional information on using the Excel Help system, see Appendix A.

Table 1-7	Excel Help System		
TYPE	DESCRIPTION	HOW TO ACTIVATE	TURNING THE OFFICE ASSISTANT ON AND OFF
Answer Wizard	Similar to the Office Assistant in that it answers questions that you type in your own words.	Click the Microsoft Excel Help button on the Standard toolbar. If necessary, maximize the Help window by double-clicking its title bar. Click the Answer Wizard tab.	If the Office Assistant displays, right-click it, click Options on the shortcut menu, click Use the Office Assistant to remove the check mark, click the OK button.
Contents sheet	Groups Help topics by general categories. Use when you know only the general category of the topic in question.	Click the Microsoft Excel Help button on the Standard toolbar. If necessary, maximize the Help window by double-clicking its title bar. Click the Contents tab.	If the Office Assistant displays, right-click it, click Options, click Use the Office Assistant to remove the check mark, click the OK button.
Detect and Repair	Automatically finds and fixes errors in the application.	Click Detect and Repair on the Help menu.	
Hardware and Software Information	Shows Product ID and allows access to system information and technical support information.	Click About Microsoft Excel on the Help menu and then click the appropriate button.	
Help for Lotus 1-2-3 Users	Used to assist Lotus 1-2-3 users who are learning Microsoft Excel.	Click Lotus 1-2-3 Help on the Help menu.	
Index sheet	Similar to an index in a book. Use when you know exactly what you want.	Click the Microsoft Excel Help button on the Standard toolbar. If necessary, maximize the Help window by double-clicking its title bar. Click the Index tab.	If the Office Assistant displays, right-click it, click Options, click Use the Office Assistant to remove the check mark, click the OK button.
Office Assistant	Answers questions that you type in your own words, offers tips, and provides Help for a variety of Excel features.	Click the Microsoft Excel Help button on the Standard toolbar or double-click the Office Assistant icon. Some dialog boxes also include the Microsoft Excel Help button.	If the Office Assistant does not display, click Show the Office Assistant on the Help menu.
Office on the Web	Used to access technical resources and download free product enhancements on the Web.	Click Office on the Web on the Help menu.	
Question Mark button and What's This? command	Used to identify unfamiliar items on the screen.	In a dialog box, click the Question Mark button and then click an item in the dialog box. Click What's This? on the Help menu, and then click an item on the screen.	

Quitting Excel

To quit Excel, complete the following steps.

TO QUIT EXCEL

1. Click the Close button on the right side of the title bar (see Figure 1-63 on page E 1.46).

2. If the Microsoft Excel dialog box displays, click the No button.

More About 2000

Quitting Excel 2000

Do not forget to remove the floppy disk from drive A after quitting Excel, especially if you are working in a laboratory environment. Nothing can be more frustrating than leaving all of your hard work behind on a floppy disk for the next user.

CASE PERSPECTIVE SUMMARY

The worksheet created in this project (Figure 1-1 on page E 1.7) allows the management of the Fun-N-Sun Sojourn company to examine the first quarter sales for the four key vacation packages. Furthermore, the 3-D Column chart should meet the needs of Kylie Waiter, who as you recall, has little tolerance for lists of numbers.

Project Summary

In creating the Fun-N-Sun Sojourn 1st Quarter Sales worksheet and chart in this project, you gained a broad knowledge about Excel. First, you were introduced to starting Excel. You learned about the Excel window and how to enter text and numbers to create a worksheet. You learned how to select a range and how to use the AutoSum button to sum numbers in a column or row. Using the fill handle, you learned how to copy a cell to adjacent cells.

Once the worksheet was built, you learned how to change the font size of the title, bold the title, and center the title across a range using buttons on the Formatting toolbar. Using the steps and techniques presented in the project, you formatted the body of the worksheet using the AutoFormat command, and you used the Chart Wizard to add a 3-D Column chart. After completing the worksheet, you saved the workbook on disk and printed the worksheet and chart. You learned how to edit data in cells. Finally, you learned how to use the Excel Help system to answer your questions.

What You Should Know

Having completed this project, you now should be able to perform the following tasks:

- Add a 3-D Column Chart to the Worksheet *(E 1.37)*
- Bold a Cell *(E 1.29)*
- Center a Cell's Contents Across Columns *(E 1.33)*
- Clear Cell Contents Using the Clear Command *(E 1.53)*
- Clear Cell Contents Using the DELETE Key *(E 1.53)*
- Clear Cell Contents Using the Fill Handle *(E 1.53)*
- Clear Cell Contents Using the Shortcut Menu *(E 1.53)*
- Clear the Entire Worksheet *(E 1.54)*
- Copy a Cell to Adjacent Cells in a Row *(E 1.24)*
- Delete an Embedded Chart *(E 1.54)*
- Determine Multiple Totals at the Same Time *(E 1.26)*
- Display the Formatting Toolbar in Its Entirety *(E 1.28)*
- Enter Column Titles *(E 1.18)*
- Enter Numeric Data *(E 1.21)*
- Enter Row Titles *(E 1.20)*
- Enter the Worksheet Title *(E 1.16)*
- Increase the Font Size of a Cell Entry *(E 1.30)*
- Obtain Help Using the Office Assistant *(E 1.55)*
- Print a Worksheet *(E 1.45)*
- Quit Excel *(E 1.46, E 1.57)*
- Save a Workbook *(E 1.41)*
- Start Excel *(E 1.8)*
- Start Excel and Open a Workbook *(E 1.48)*
- Sum a Column of Numbers *(E 1.22)*
- Use AutoFormat to Format the Body of a Worksheet *(E 1.31)*
- Use the AutoCalculate Area to Determine an Average *(E 1.50)*
- Use the Name Box to Select a Cell *(E 1.35)*

Apply Your Knowledge

⊕ Project Reinforcement at www.scsite.com/off2000/reinforce.htm

1 Changing Data in a Worksheet

Instructions: Start Excel. Open the workbook Trevor's Shady Tree Service from the Data Disk. See the inside back cover of this book for instructions for downloading the Data Disk or see your instructor for information on accessing the files required in this book.

Make the changes to the worksheet described in Table 1-8 so it appears as shown in Figure 1-75. As you edit the values in the cells containing numeric data, watch the values in the total income (row 6), the total expenses (row 11), and the profit (row 12). The numbers in these three rows are based on formulas. When you enter a new value, Excel automatically recalculates the formulas. After you have successfully made the changes listed in the table, the profits in cells C12 through F12 should equal $18,580.17, $45,452.34, $44,101.35, and $26,996.44, respectively.

Save the workbook. Use the file name, Eric's Arborescent Service. Print the revised worksheet and hand in the printout to your instructor.

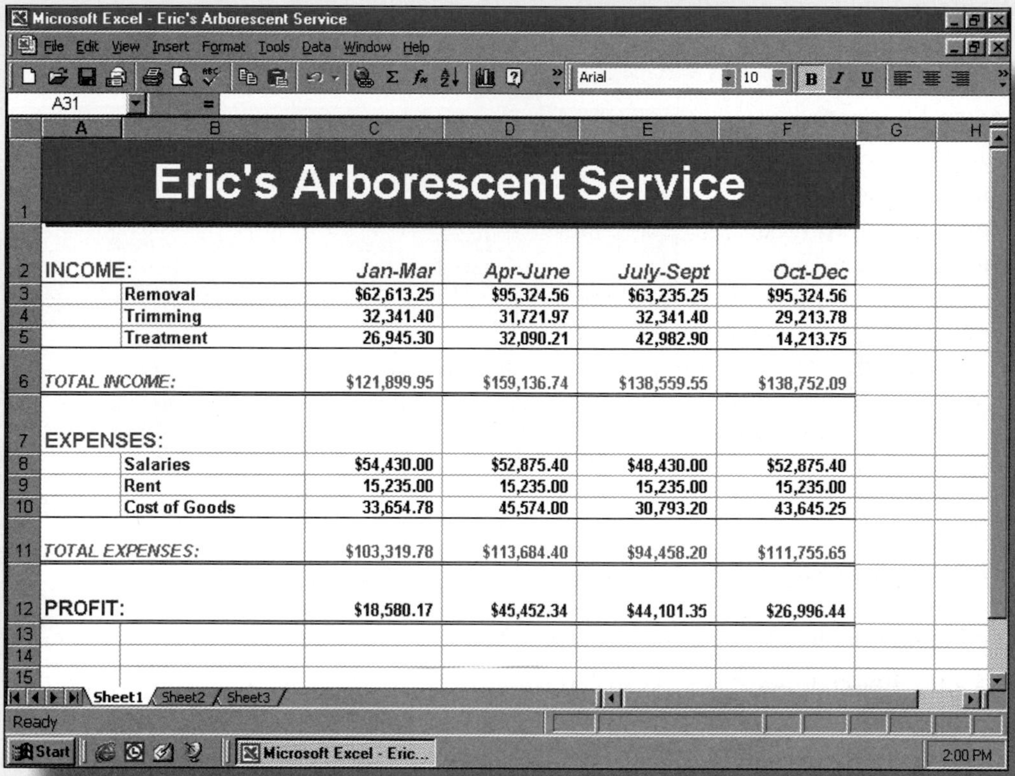

FIGURE 1-75

Table 1-8   New Worksheet Data

CELL	CHANGE CELL CONTENTS TO
A1	Eric's Arborescent Service
C3	62,613.25
D4	31,721.97
E5	42,982.90
F5	14,213.75
C8	54,430.00
E10	30,793.20
F10	43,645.25

Microsoft **Excel 2000**

In the Lab

1 Marvin's Music & Movie Mirage Sales Analysis Worksheet

Problem: The chief financial officer (CFO) of Marvin's Music & Movie Mirage needs a sales analysis worksheet similar to the one shown in Figure 1-76. Your task is to develop the worksheet. Table 1-9 provides the sales figures for the worksheet.

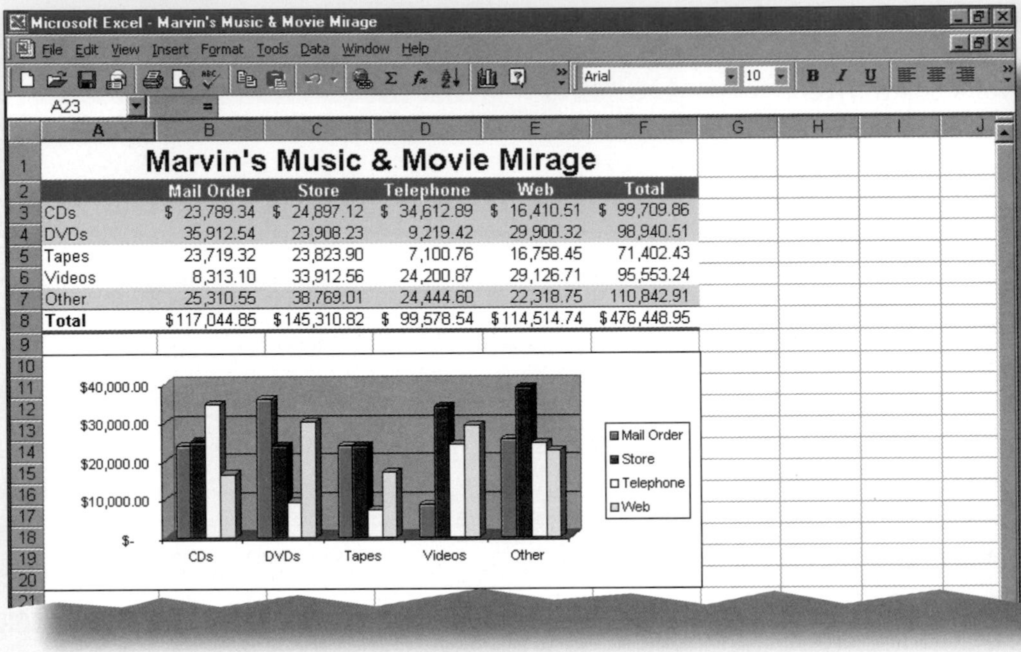

Instructions: Perform the following tasks.

1. Create the worksheet shown in Figure 1-76 using the title, sales amounts, and categories in Table 1-9.

2. Determine the totals for the types of products, sales channels, and company totals.

3. Format the worksheet title, Marvin's Music & Movie Mirage, in 18-point Arial, bold font, centered across columns A through F.

4. Format the range A2:F8 using the AutoFormat command on the Format menu as follows: (a) Select the range A2:F8 and then apply the table format Accounting 1; and (b) with the range A2:F8 still selected, apply the table format List 2. Excel 2000 appends the formats of List 2 to the formats of Accounting 1.

5. Select the range A2:E7 and then use the Chart Wizard button on the Standard toolbar to draw a Clustered column with a 3-D visual effect chart (column 1, row 2 in Chart sub-type list). Move the chart to the upper left corner of cell A10 and then drag the lower-right corner of the chart location to cell F20.

6. Enter your name, course, laboratory assignment number, date, and instructor name in cells A24 through A28.

7. Save the workbook using the file name Marvin's Music & Movie Mirage.

8. Print the worksheet.

9. Make the following two corrections to the sales amounts: $35,987.99 for DVDs sold in a store and $36,498.33 for Videos sold over the telephone. After you enter the corrections, the company totals should equal $157,390.58 in cell C8 and $111,876.00 in cell D8.

10. Print the revised worksheet. Close the workbook without saving the changes.

FIGURE 1-76

Table 1-9	Marvin's Music & Movie Mirage Data			
	MAIL ORDER	*STORE*	*TELEPHONE*	*WEB*
CDs	$23,789.34	$24,897.12	$34,612.89	$16,410.51
DVDs	35,912.54	23,908.23	9,219.42	29,900.32
Tapes	23,719.32	23,823.90	7,100.76	16,758.45
Videos	8,313.10	33,912.56	24,200.87	29,126.71
Other	25,310.55	38,769.01	24,444.60	22,318.75

In the Lab

2 Dollar Bill's Annual Software Sales Worksheet

Problem: As the assistant financial manager for Dollar Bill's Software, Inc., your supervisor has asked you to create a workbook to analyze the annual sales for the company by product group and store location. The software sales for the year are shown in Table 1-10.

Table 1-10 Dollar Bill's Data				
	SAN ANTONIO	SAN FRANCISCO	CLEVELAND	CHARLOTTE
Business	35,102.15	18,231.56	31,012.40	12,012.00
Database	42,970.50	57,210.00	29,089.12	29,765.23
Education	21,892.70	18,329.34	26,723.15	22,914.50
Graphics	9,312.45	12,923.21	9,012.56	8,910.32
Games	13,453.30	22,134.45	13,908.55	9,143.75

Instructions: Perform the following tasks.

1. Create the worksheet shown in Figure 1-77 using the sales amounts in Table 1-10.

2. Direct Excel to determine the totals for the four store locations, the product categories, and the company.

3. Format the worksheet title, Dollar Bill's Annual Software Sales, in 18-point Arial bold font, and centered across columns A through F.

4. Use the AutoFormat command on the Format menu to format the range A2:F8. Use the table format Accounting 2.

FIGURE 1-77

5. Use the ChartWizard button on the Standard toolbar to draw the 3-D Stacked Cylinder chart (column 3, row 1 in the Chart sub-type list), as shown in Figure 1-77. Chart the range A2:E7 and use the chart location A9:H22. Extend the chart location to the right, if necessary.

6. Enter your name in cell A25. Enter your course, computer laboratory assignment number, date, and instructor name in cells A26 through A29.

7. Save the workbook using the file name, Dollar Bill's Annual Software Sales. Print the worksheet.

8. Two corrections to the sales amounts were sent in from the accounting department. The correct sales amounts are $16,453.21 for Games in San Antonio and $42,781.50 for Database software in Charlotte. Enter the two corrections. After you enter the two corrections, the company total should equal $460,067.42 in cell F8. Print the revised worksheet.

9. Use the Undo button to change the worksheet back to the original numbers in Table 1-10.

10. Use the Redo button to change the worksheet back to the revised state.

11. Hand in all printouts to your instructor. Close the workbook without saving the changes.

In the Lab

3 Projected College Cash Flow Analysis

Problem: Attending college is an expensive proposition and your resources are limited. To plan for your four-year college career, you have decided to organize your anticipated expenses and resources in a worksheet. The data required to prepare your worksheet is shown in Table 1-11.

Part 1 Instructions: Using the numbers in Table 1-11, create the worksheet shown in Figure 1-78. Enter the worksheet title in cell A1 and the section titles, Expenses and Resources, in cells A2 and A10, respectively. Use the AutoSum button to calculate the totals in rows 9 and 16 and column F.

To format the worksheet, use the table format Accounting 1 for the range A3:F9 and again for the range A11:F16. Increase the font size of the worksheet title to 18 point and the section titles to 16 point. Bold the entire worksheet by first clicking the Select All button on the worksheet and then clicking the Bold button on the Formatting toolbar. Center the title across columns A through F. Enter your name in cell A19 and your course, laboratory assignment number, date, and instructor name in cells A20 through A23. Use Help to determine how to use the Font Color button on the Formatting toolbar to change the font color of the worksheet title and section titles as shown in Figure 1-78.

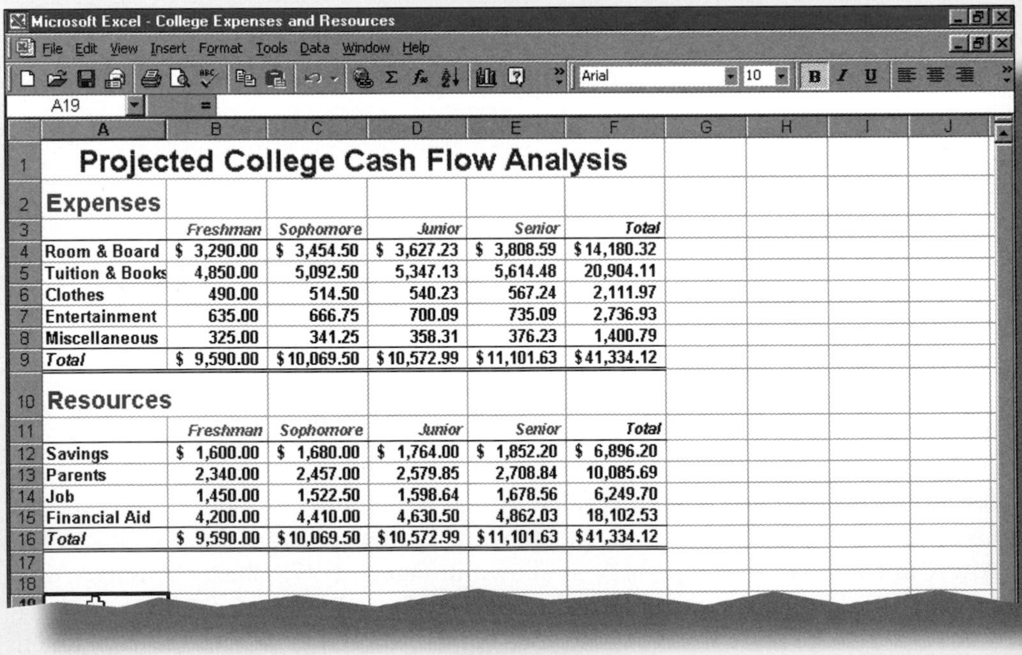

Save the workbook using the file name, College Expenses and Resources. Print the worksheet. Use the Office Assistant to learn how to print only a specific area of a worksheet and then print the selection A1:F9 of the worksheet.

Table 1-11	College Expenses and Resources			
EXPENSES	**FRESHMAN**	**SOPHOMORE**	**JUNIOR**	**SENIOR**
Room & Board	$3,290.00	$3,454.50	$3,627.23	$3,808.59
Tuition & Books	4,850.00	5,092.50	5,347.13	5,614.48
Clothes	490.00	514.50	540.23	567.24
Entertainment	635.00	666.75	700.09	735.09
Miscellaneous	325.00	341.25	358.31	376.23
RESOURCES	**FRESHMAN**	**SOPHOMORE**	**JUNIOR**	**SENIOR**
Savings	$1,600.00	$1,680.00	$1,764.00	$1,852.20
Parents	2,340.00	2,457.00	2,579.85	2,708.84
Job	1,450.00	1,522.50	1,598.64	1,678.56
Financial Aid	4,200.00	4,410.00	4,630.50	4,862.03

FIGURE 1-78

In the Lab

Increment all Junior-year expenses in column D by $500. Increment the financial aid for the Junior year by the amount required to cover the increase. The totals in cells F9 and F16 should equal $43,834.12. Print the worksheet. Close the workbook without saving changes. Hand in the three printouts to your instructor.

Part 2 Instructions: Open the workbook College Expenses and Resources created in Part 1. A close inspection of Table 1-11 shows a 5% increase each year over the previous year. Use the Office Assistant to determine how to enter the data for the last three years using a formula and the Copy command. For example, the formula to enter in cell C4 is =B4 * 1.5. Enter formulas to replace all the numbers in the range C4:E8 and C12:E15. If necessary, reformat the tables using Accounting 1 as you did in Part 1. The worksheet should appear as shown in Figure 1-78, except that some of the totals will be off by 0.01 due to round-off errors. Save the worksheet using the file name, College Expenses and Resources2. Print the worksheet. Press CTRL+` (left single quotation mark) to display the formulas. Print the formulas version. Hand in both printouts to your instructor.

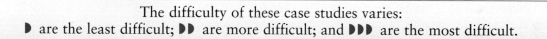

Cases and Places

The difficulty of these case studies varies:
▶ are the least difficult; ▶▶ are more difficult; and ▶▶▶ are the most difficult.

1 ▶ You just started as a summer intern at the Blue Suede Music Company. Your manager, Elma Presley, has asked you to prepare a worksheet and chart to help her analyze the yearly guitar sales by region and by guitar type (Table 1-12). Use the concepts and techniques presented in this project to create the worksheet and chart.

Table 1-12	Blue Suede Music Company Data			
	NORTH	EAST	WEST	SOUTH
Classical	6734	7821	4123	7989
Steel String	5423	2134	6574	3401
Electric	3495	6291	7345	7098
Bass	5462	2923	8034	5135

2 ▶ The number of new cars and trucks has increased each year from 1996 through 2000, as indicated in Table 1-13. Create a worksheet and 3-D Column chart that illustrates these increases. Show model year and type car and truck totals. Use the concepts and techniques presented in this project to create the worksheet and chart.

Table 1-13	1996 - 2000 New Cars and Trucks Data			
YEAR	DOMESTIC CARS*	IMPORT CARS*	DOMESTIC TRUCKS*	IMPORT TRUCKS*
1996	7,323	2,231	6,125	225
1997	7,498	2,356	6,315	257
1998	7,615	2,489	6,727	313
1999	7,734	2,501	6,501	407
2000	7,944	2,578	6,623	661
* in thousands				

Cases and Places

3 ▶ You are a teaching assistant for the Computer Information Systems department. The department head has asked you to take her grade ledger (Table 1-14), which shows her grade distributions for all her spring classes, and separate them into categories based on the class and the grade. She wants a worksheet and 3-D Column chart to make it easier to view the grades as well as the totals at a glance. Use the concepts and techniques presented in this project to create the worksheet and chart.

Table 1-14	Semester Grade Summary			
GRADE	CIS 104	CIS 205	CIS 299	CIS 331
A	2	1	4	2
B	22	7	2	3
C	15	10	11	9
D	20	5	15	6
F	11	8	19	3

4 ▶ The CheeseHeads restaurant in Green Bay, Wisconsin is trying to decide whether it is feasible to open another restaurant in the neighboring community of Oshkosh, Wisconsin. The owner, G. B. Pack, has asked you to develop a worksheet totaling all the revenue received last year. The revenue by quarter is: Quarter 1, $94,342.98; Quarter 2, $81,500.65; Quarter 3, $158,220.09; and Quarter 4, $225,435.50. Create a 3-D Pie chart to illustrate revenue contribution by quarter. Use the AutoCalculate area to find the average annual revenue.

5 ▶▶ The Palace Theater is a small movie house that shows almost-current releases at weekday evening, weekend matinee, and weekend evening screenings. Three types of tickets are sold at each presentation: general admission, senior citizen, and children. The theater management has asked you to prepare a worksheet, based on the revenue from a typical week, that can be used in reevaluating its ticket structure. During an average week, weekday evening shows generate $7,540 from general admission ticket sales, $3,575 from senior citizen ticket sales, and $1,375 from children ticket sales. Weekend matinee shows make $5,500 from general admission ticket sales, $1,950 from senior citizen ticket sales, and $2,500 from children ticket sales. Weekend evening shows earn $8,540 from general admission ticket sales, $7,350 from senior citizen ticket sales, and $1,100 from children ticket sales. Use the concepts and techniques presented in this project to prepare a worksheet that includes total revenues for each type of ticket and for each presentation time, and a Bar chart illustrating ticket revenues.

6 ▶▶▶ Some academic disciplines appear to attract more students of one gender than the other. Visit the Registrar's office at your school and find out how many males and how many females have declared majors in five disciplines. Using this information, create a worksheet showing the number of male, female, and total number of majors in each discipline. Include totals for each numeric column. Include a Column chart to illustrate your data.

Microsoft Excel 2000

Formulas, Functions, Formatting, and Web Queries

OBJECTIVES

You will have mastered the material in this project when you can:

- Enter multiple lines of text in the same cell
- Enter a formula using the keyboard
- Enter formulas using Point mode
- Identify the arithmetic operators +, −, *, /, %, and ^
- Apply the AVERAGE, MAX, and MIN functions
- Determine a percentage
- Verify a formula
- Change the font of a cell
- Color the characters and background of a cell
- Add borders to a range
- Format numbers using the Format Cells dialog box
- Add conditional formatting to a range of cells
- Align text in cells
- Change the width of a column and height of a row
- Check the spelling of a worksheet
- Preview how a printed copy of the worksheet will look
- Distinguish between portrait and landscape orientation
- Print a partial or complete worksheet
- Display and print the formulas version of a worksheet
- Print to fit
- Use a Web query to get real-time data from a Web site
- Rename sheets
- E-mail the active workbook from within Excel

Windy City Pedal Pushers

Riding L.A.T.E. into the Morning

Mountain bikes, helmets, and reflectors ready, very early morning cyclists do whatever it takes to prepare themselves to pedal their bikes 25 miles in Chicago during the annual Friends of the Parks' L.A.T.E. Ride. The event is aptly named. L.A.T.E. is an acronym for Long After Twilight Ends. The moonstruck ride occurs from 1:30 A.M. to sunrise and weaves through Chicago's downtown and north side neighborhoods and parks.

Friends of the Parks' mission is to preserve and improve Chicago's neighborhood, regional, and lakefront parks in addition to children's playlots. Every year, volunteers contribute time, funds, and effort to clean and maintain the park grounds. Friends of the Parks' has been representing Chicago citizens since 1975, and the L.A.T.E. Ride is one event, in addition to the annual Earth Day clean-up, that promotes its causes.

So how does the Friends of the Parks' organization attempt to manage and organize information about the more than 9,000 participants who take part in the L.A.T.E. Ride event each year? Staff, many of whom volunteer their time and expertise, use worksheets to organize, chart, and present all types of

NUMBER OF CYCLISTS

1989 350
1990 750
1991 1,800
1992 3,200
1993 4,500
1994 6,500
1995
1996
1997
1998

PEDAL PUSHERS: 1998 DEMOGRAPHICS

Residence

Chicago Suburbs (55%)

City of Chicago (34%)

Northwest Indiana (3%)
Other States (5%)
Other Areas in Illinois (3%)

Age

40-49yrs.
30-39yrs.

(5%)
60+ yrs.
10-14 yrs.
15-18 yrs. (4%)
19-22 yrs. (6%)

Chicago Suburbs (55% of total riders)

North and Northwest (42%)

Southwest (8%)
South (13%)

West and Far West (37%)

City of Chicago (34% of total riders)

WGN-TV Children's Charities Presents
Friends of the Parks'
L.A.T.E. Ride
July 11
1999

RIDER GUIDE

data with relative ease. They analyze and manipulate data; specifically, they input numbers and enter formulas to determine averages and percentages, as well as find the minimum and maximum numbers in a series. In addition, they create traditional Pie charts, Column charts, and other chart forms to represent the data visually.

If they want to determine, for example, the demographics of the L.A.T.E. bike riders, they can input participants' ages taken from a Friends of the Parks' survey and then allow the worksheet to generate Pie charts depicting the age breakdowns in a matter of seconds. Moreover, they can create a Column chart showing the number of participants from year to year. The Friends of the Parks' also can track how many participants live in Chicago, the suburbs, or other states and the number of male and female cyclists.

You will perform similar tasks in this project when you create a worksheet for the BetNet Stock Club. You will enter formulas, use the

AVERAGE, MAX, and MIN functions, and then verify the formulas for accuracy.

The L.A.T.E. Ride was established in 1989 with 350 cyclists; most recently nearly 10,000 bike riders have participated. It is not by sheer coincidence that the numbers have escalated dramatically. Once thc staff at the Friends of the Parks' collects survey data, they then input the numbers into worksheets using ranges of numbers, enter formulas, and apply formats for appropriate charts. Such data is important to determine marketing strategies or finalize the total number of glow-in-the-dark T-shirts and number tags needed for the participants to don for the ride.

So, if you are up for a challenge in the middle of the night in mid-July in the Windy City, grab your bike and head to the shores of Lake Michigan for the start of a L.A.T.E. night, pedal-pushing experience.

Microsoft Excel 2000

Formulas, Functions, Formatting, and Web Queries

P R O J E C T
2

CASE PERSPECTIVE

During their Freshman year in college, Michael Santos and six classmates began playing the Investment Challenge game on the Yahoo! Web site (quote.yahoo.com). In the game, each contestant is given $100,000 in fantasy money to make fantasy trades for a period of one month. Yahoo! awards the top finisher a $5,000 cash prize.

Recently, Michael and his classmates won the contest. With their newly gained confidence in investing, they used the prize money to start the BetNet Stock Club. They decided to invest in only the high-flying Internet stocks.

Each month, Michael summarizes the month-end financial status. As the club members approach graduation from college, the value of the club's portfolio has grown to nearly $900,000. As a result, the members voted to buy a new computer and Microsoft Office 2000 for Michael. With Office 2000, he plans to create a worksheet summarizing the club's stock activities that he can e-mail to the members. Michael has asked you to show him how to create the workbook and access real-time stock quotes over the Internet using Excel 2000.

Introduction

In Project 1, you learned how to enter data, sum values, make the worksheet easier to read, and draw a chart. You also learned about online Help and saving, printing, and loading a workbook from a floppy disk into memory. This project continues to emphasize these topics and presents some new ones.

The new topics include formulas, verifying formulas, changing fonts, adding borders, formatting numbers, conditional formatting, changing the widths of columns and heights of rows, spell checking, e-mailing from within an application, and alternative types of worksheet displays and printouts. One alternative display and printout shows the formulas rather than the values in the worksheet. When you display the formulas in the worksheet, you see exactly what text, data, formulas, and functions you have entered into it. Finally, this project covers Web queries to obtain real-time data from a Web site.

Project Two — BetNet Stock Club

The summary notes from your meeting with Michael include the following: need, source of data, calculations, and Web requirements.

Need: An easy-to-read worksheet that summarizes the club's investments (Figure 2-1a). For each stock, the worksheet is to include the name, symbol, date acquired, number of shares, initial price, initial cost, current price, current value, gain/loss, and percent gain/loss. Michael also has requested that the worksheet include totals and the average, highest value, and lowest value for each column of numbers. Finally, Michael wants to use Excel to access real-time stock quotes using Web queries (Figure 2-1b).

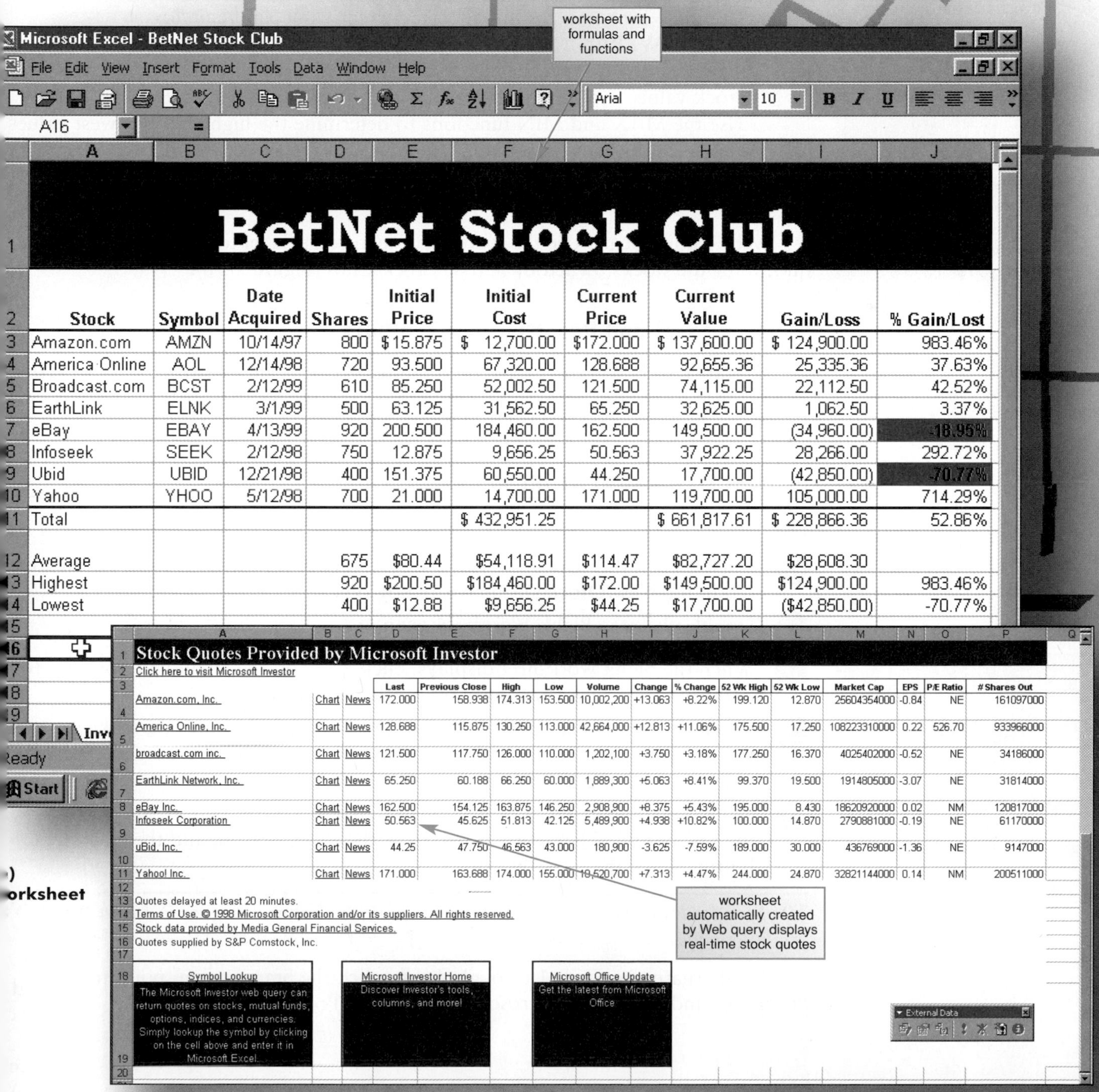

worksheet with formulas and functions

Microsoft Excel - BetNet Stock Club

File Edit View Insert Format Tools Data Window Help

Arial ▼ 10 ▼ **B** *I* U

A16 ▼ =

BetNet Stock Club

	Stock	Symbol	Date Acquired	Shares	Initial Price	Initial Cost	Current Price	Current Value	Gain/Loss	% Gain/Lost
3	Amazon.com	AMZN	10/14/97	800	$15.875	$ 12,700.00	$172.000	$ 137,600.00	$ 124,900.00	983.46%
4	America Online	AOL	12/14/98	720	93.500	67,320.00	128.688	92,655.36	25,335.36	37.63%
5	Broadcast.com	BCST	2/12/99	610	85.250	52,002.50	121.500	74,115.00	22,112.50	42.52%
6	EarthLink	ELNK	3/1/99	500	63.125	31,562.50	65.250	32,625.00	1,062.50	3.37%
7	eBay	EBAY	4/13/99	920	200.500	184,460.00	162.500	149,500.00	(34,960.00)	-18.95%
8	Infoseek	SEEK	2/12/98	750	12.875	9,656.25	50.563	37,922.25	28,266.00	292.72%
9	Ubid	UBID	12/21/98	400	151.375	60,550.00	44.250	17,700.00	(42,850.00)	-70.77%
10	Yahoo	YHOO	5/12/98	700	21.000	14,700.00	171.000	119,700.00	105,000.00	714.29%
11	Total					$ 432,951.25		$ 661,817.61	$ 228,866.36	52.86%
12	Average			675	$80.44	$54,118.91	$114.47	$82,727.20	$28,608.30	
13	Highest			920	$200.50	$184,460.00	$172.00	$149,500.00	$124,900.00	983.46%
14	Lowest			400	$12.88	$9,656.25	$44.25	$17,700.00	($42,850.00)	-70.77%

Inv...

Ready

Start

Stock Quotes Provided by Microsoft Investor

Click here to visit Microsoft Investor

				Last	Previous Close	High	Low	Volume	Change	% Change	52 Wk High	52 Wk Low	Market Cap	EPS	P/E Ratio	# Shares Out
	Amazon.com, Inc.	Chart	News	172.000	158.938	174.313	153.500	10,002,200	+13.063	+8.22%	199.120	12.870	25604354000	-0.84	NE	161097000
	America Online, Inc.	Chart	News	128.688	115.875	130.250	113.000	42,664,000	+12.813	+11.06%	175.500	17.250	108223310000	0.22	526.70	933966000
	broadcast.com inc.	Chart	News	121.500	117.750	126.000	110.000	1,202,100	+3.750	+3.18%	177.250	16.370	4025402000	-0.52	NE	34186000
	EarthLink Network, Inc.	Chart	News	65.250	60.188	66.250	60.000	1,889,300	+5.063	+8.41%	99.370	19.500	1914805000	-3.07	NE	31814000
	eBay Inc.	Chart	News	162.500	154.125	163.875	146.250	2,908,900	+8.375	+5.43%	195.000	8.430	18620920000	0.02	NM	120817000
	Infoseek Corporation	Chart	News	50.563	45.625	51.813	42.125	5,489,900	+4.938	+10.82%	100.000	14.870	2790881000	-0.19	NE	61170000
	uBid, Inc.	Chart	News	44.25	47.750	46.563	43.000	180,900	-3.625	-7.59%	189.000	30.000	436769000	-1.36	NE	9147000
	Yahoo! Inc.	Chart	News	171.000	163.688	174.000	155.000	18,520,700	+7.313	+4.47%	244.000	24.870	32821144000	0.14	NM	200511000

Quotes delayed at least 20 minutes.
Terms of Use. © 1998 Microsoft Corporation and/or its suppliers. All rights reserved.
Stock data provided by Media General Financial Services.
Quotes supplied by S&P Comstock, Inc.

worksheet automatically created by Web query displays real-time stock quotes

Symbol Lookup
The Microsoft Investor web query can return quotes on stocks, mutual funds, options, indices, and currencies. Simply lookup the symbol by clicking on the cell above and enter it in Microsoft Excel.

Microsoft Investor Home
Discover Investor's tools, columns, and more!

Microsoft Office Update
Get the latest from Microsoft Office

External Data

(b) Web Query

worksheet

FIGURE 2-1

Source of Data: The data supplied by Michael includes the stock names, symbols, dates acquired, number of shares, initial prices, and current prices. This data is shown in Table 2-1.

Calculations: The following calculations must be made for each of the stocks:

1. Initial Cost = Shares × Initial Price
2. Current Value = Shares × Current Price
3. Gain/Loss = Current Value – Initial Cost
4. Percentage Gain/Loss = $\dfrac{\text{Gain/Loss}}{\text{Initial Cost}}$
5. Compute the totals for initial cost, current value, and gain/loss.
6. Use the AVERAGE function to determine the average for the number of shares, initial price per share, initial stock cost, current stock price, current stock value, and gain/loss for each stock.
7. Use the MAX and MIN functions to determine the highest and lowest values for the number of shares, initial price per share, initial stock cost, current stock price, current stock value, gain/loss for each stock, and percent gain/loss.

Web Requirements: Use the Web query feature of Excel to get real-time stock quotes for the stocks owned by BetNet Stock Club (Figure 2-1b).

Starting Excel and Resetting the Toolbars

To start Excel, Windows must be running. Perform the following steps to start Excel. Once Excel displays, steps 4 through 6 reset the toolbars to their default. Step 6 is necessary only if you added or deleted new buttons on the toolbars.

TO START EXCEL AND RESET THE TOOLBARS

1 Click the Start button on the taskbar.

2 Click New Office Document on the Start menu. If necessary, click the General tab in the New Office Document dialog box.

3 Double-click the Blank Workbook icon.

4 When the blank worksheet displays, click View on the menu bar, point to Toolbars, and then click Customize on the Toolbars submenu.

5 When the Customize dialog box displays, click the Options tab, make sure the top three check boxes have check marks, click the Reset my usage data button, and then click the Yes button.

6 Click the Toolbars tab. Click Standard, click the Reset button, and then click the OK button. Click Formatting, click the Reset button, and the click the OK button. Click the Close button.

The Standard and Formatting toolbars display as shown in Figure 2-1a on the previous page.

An alternative to Steps 1 through 3 is to click the Start button, point to Programs, and then click Microsoft Excel on the Programs submenu.

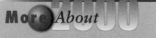

Web Queries

Thinking about being a day trader of stocks? If so, you will find Excel's Web Queries to be an invaluable tool. The Excel Web Query titled, Microsoft Investor Stock Quotes, can return near real-time stock quotes and links to breaking news for up to 20 stocks almost instantaneously. And you can refresh the results as often as you want.

Starting Excel

An alternative way to start Excel when you want to open a workbook is to start Explorer, display the contents of the folder containing the workbook, and then double-click the workbook name.

Entering the Titles and Numbers into the Worksheet

The worksheet title in Figure 2-1a is centered across columns A through J in row 1. Because the centered text first must be entered into the leftmost column of the area across which it is centered, it will be entered into cell A1.

TO ENTER THE WORKSHEET TITLE

1 Select cell A1. Type BetNet Stock Club in the cell.

2 Press the DOWN ARROW key.

The worksheet title displays in cell A1 as shown in Figure 2-2 on the next page.

The column titles in row 2 begin in cell A2 and extend through cell J2. As shown in Figure 2-1a, the column titles in row 2 include multiple lines of text. To start a new line in a cell, press ALT+ENTER after each line, except for the last line, which is completed by clicking the Enter box, pressing the ENTER key, or pressing one of the arrow keys. When you see ALT+ENTER in a step, while holding down the ALT key, press the ENTER key and then release both keys.

The stock names and the row titles Total, Average, Highest, and Lowest in column A begin in cell A3 and continue down to cell A14.

The stock club's investments are summarized in Table 2-1. These numbers are entered into rows 3 through 10. The steps required to enter the column titles, stock names and symbols, total row titles, and numbers as shown in Figure 2-2 are explained in the remainder of this section.

Table 2-1	BetNet Stock Club Portfolio				
STOCK	SYMBOL	DATE ACQUIRED	SHARES	INITIAL PRICE	CURRENT PRICE
Amazon.com	AMZN	10/14/97	800	15.875	172.00
America Online	AOL	12/14/98	720	93.50	126.688
Broadcast.com	BCST	2/2/99	610	85.25	121.5
EarthLink	ELNK	3/1/99	500	63.125	65.25
eBay	EBAY	4/13/99	920	200.50	162.50
Infoseek	SEEK	2/12/98	750	12.875	50.565
UBid	UBID	12/21/98	400	151.375	44.25
Yahoo	YHOO	5/12/98	700	21.00	171.00

TO ENTER THE COLUMN TITLES

1 With cell A2 active, type Stock and then press the RIGHT ARROW key.

2 Type Symbol and then press the RIGHT ARROW key.

3 Type Date and then press ALT+ENTER. Type Acquired and then press the RIGHT ARROW key.

4 Type Shares and then press the RIGHT ARROW key.

5 Type Initial and then press ALT+ENTER. Type Price and then press the RIGHT ARROW key.

6 Type Initial and then press ALT+ENTER. Type Cost and then press the RIGHT ARROW key.

7 Type Current and then press ALT+ENTER. Type Price and then press the RIGHT ARROW key.

More About 2000

Wrapping Text

If you have a long text entry, such as a paragraph, you can instruct Excel to wrap the text in a cell, rather than pressing ALT+ENTER to end a line. To wrap text, click Format Cells on the shortcut menu, click the Alignment tab, and click the Wrap Text check box. Excel will increase the height of the cell automatically so the additional lines will fit. If you want to control the contents of a line in a cell instead of letting Excel wrap based on the width of a cell, then you must end a line by pressing ALT+ENTER.

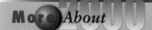
More About

Formatting a Worksheet

With early spreadsheet packages, users often skipped rows to improve the appearance of the worksheet. With Excel, it is not necessary to skip rows because you can increase the height of rows to add white space between information.

More About

Entering Two-Digit Years

When you enter a two-digit year value, Excel interprets the year as follows: (1) 00 through 29 as the years 2000 through 2029 and (2) 30 through 99 as the years 1930 through 1999. You may use four-digit years to ensure that Excel interprets year values the way you intend.

More About

Entering Numbers into a Range

An efficient way to enter data into a range of cells is first to select the range. Enter the number that you want to assign to the upper-left cell. Excel responds by entering the value and moving the active cell selection down one cell. When you enter the last value in the first column, Excel moves to the top of the next column.

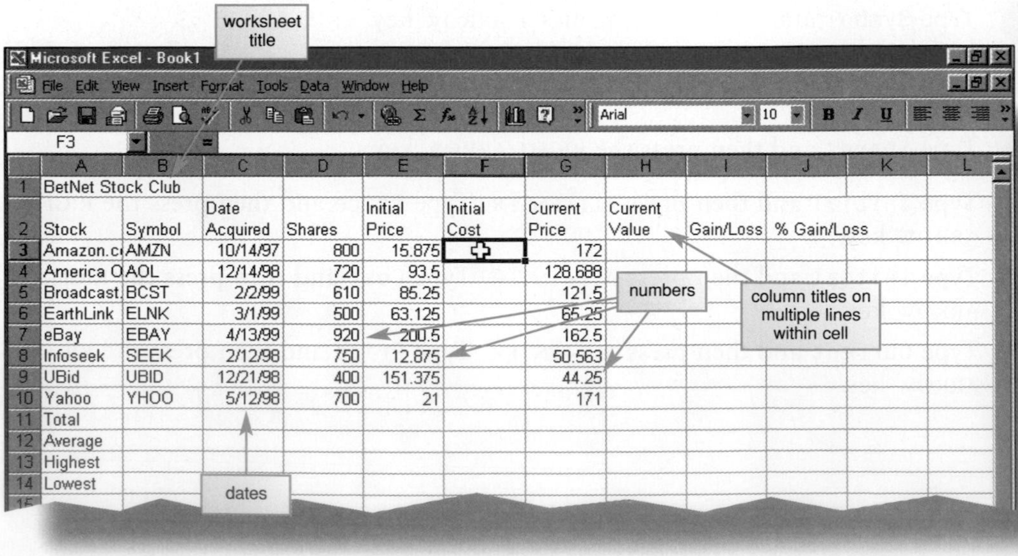

8 Type `Current` and then press ALT+ENTER. Type `Value` and then press the RIGHT ARROW key.

9 Type `Gain/Loss` and press the the RIGHT ARROW key.

10 Type `% Gain/Loss` and then click cell A3.

The column titles display as shown in row 2 of Figure 2-2 below. When you press ALT+ENTER to add more lines to a cell, Excel automatically increases the height of the entire row.

The stock data in Table 2-1 on the previous page includes a date on which each stock was acquired. Excel considers a date to be a number and, therefore, displays it right-aligned in the cell. When you enter a date, Excel automatically formats the date so it resembles the way you entered it. For example, if you enter May 20, 1999, Excel displays it as 20-May-99. If you enter the same date in the format 5/20/99, then Excel displays it as 5/20/99. The following steps describe how to enter the stock data shown in Table 2-1, which includes dates.

TO ENTER THE STOCK DATA

1 With cell A3 selected, type `Amazon.com` and then press the RIGHT ARROW key. Type `AMZN` and then press the RIGHT ARROW key.

2 With cell C3 selected, type `10/14/97` and then press the RIGHT ARROW key. Type `800` and then press the RIGHT ARROW key.

3 With cell E3 selected, type `15.875` and then press the RIGHT ARROW key twice. Type `331` and then press the ENTER key.

4 Click cell A4. Enter the data in Table 2-1 for the seven remaining stocks in rows 4 through 10.

The stock data displays in rows 3 through 10 as shown in Figure 2-2.

TO ENTER THE TOTAL ROW TITLES

1 Click cell A11. Type `Total` and then press the DOWN ARROW key. With cell A12 selected, type `Average` and then press the DOWN ARROW key.

2 With cell A13 selected, type `Highest` and then press the DOWN ARROW key. With cell A14 selected, type `Lowest` and then press the ENTER key. Click cell F3

The total row titles display as shown in Figure 2-2.

	A	B	C	D	E	F	G	H	I	J	K	L
1	BetNet Stock Club											
2	Stock	Symbol	Date Acquired	Shares	Initial Price	Initial Cost	Current Price	Current Value	Gain/Loss	% Gain/Loss		
3	Amazon.c	AMZN	10/14/97	800	15.875		172					
4	America O	AOL	12/14/98	720	93.5		128.688					
5	Broadcast	BCST	2/2/99	610	85.25		121.5					
6	EarthLink	ELNK	3/1/99	500	63.125		65.25					
7	eBay	EBAY	4/13/99	920	200.5		162.5					
8	Infoseek	SEEK	2/12/98	750	12.875		50.563					
9	UBid	UBID	12/21/98	400	151.375		44.25					
10	Yahoo	YHOO	5/12/98	700	21		171					
11	Total											
12	Average											
13	Highest											
14	Lowest											

FIGURE 2-2

Entering Formulas

The initial cost for each stock, which displays in column F, is equal to the number of shares in column D times the initial price in column E. Thus, the initial cost for Amazon.com in row 3 is obtained by multiplying 800 (cell D3) times 15.875 (cell E3).

One of the reasons Excel is such a valuable tool is that you can assign a **formula** to a cell and Excel will calculate the result. Consider, for example, what would happen if you had to multiply 800 × 15.875 and then manually enter the result, 12700, in cell F3. Every time the values in cells D3 and E3 changed, you would have to recalculate the product and enter the new value in cell F3. By contrast, if you enter a formula in cell F3 to multiply the values in cells D3 and E3, Excel recalculates the product whenever new values are entered into those cells and displays the result in cell F3. Complete the following steps to enter the formula using the keyboard.

More About

Recalculation of Formulas

Every time you enter a value into a cell in the worksheet, Excel recalculates all formulas. It makes no difference whether the worksheet contains one formula or hundreds of formulas. Excel recalculates the formulas instantaneously. This is one of the reasons why a spreadsheet package, such as Excel, is so powerful.

Steps To Enter a Formula Using the Keyboard

1 **With cell F3 selected, type** =d3*e3 **in the cell.**

The formula displays in the formula bar and in cell F3 (Figure 2-3).

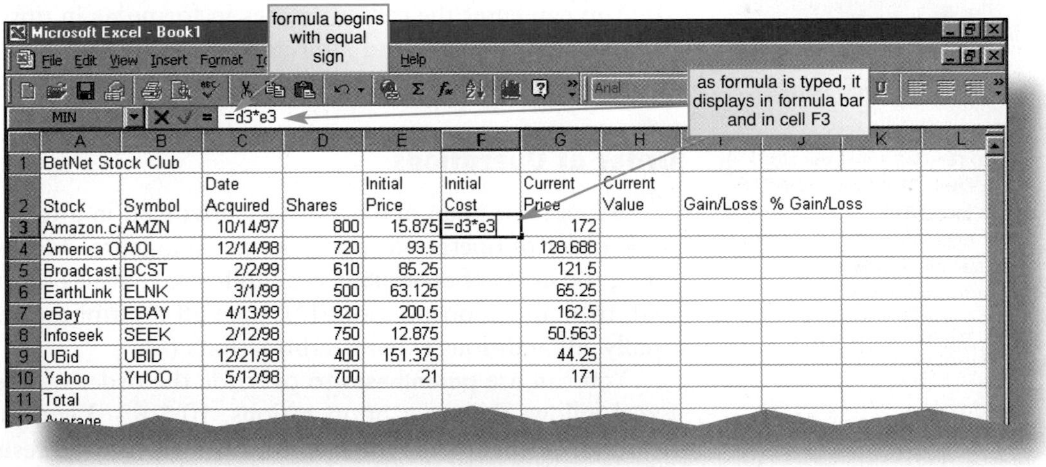

FIGURE 2-3

2 **Press the RIGHT ARROW key twice to select cell H3.**

Instead of displaying the formula in cell F3, Excel completes the arithmetic operation indicated by the formula and displays the result, 12700 (Figure 2-4).

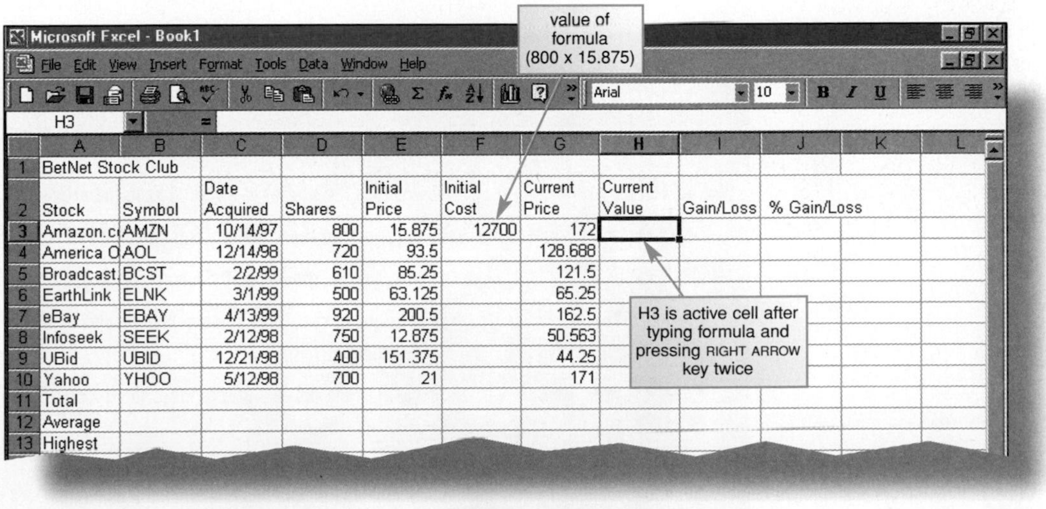

FIGURE 2-4

The equal sign (=) preceding d3*e3 is an important part of the formula, it alerts Excel that you are entering a formula or function and not text. The asterisk (*) following d3 is the arithmetic operator that directs Excel to perform the multiplication operation. The valid Excel arithmetic operators are described in Table 2-2.

More About

Entering Formulas

Besides the equal sign (=), you can start a formula with a plus sign (+) or a minus sign (-). If you do not begin with one of these characters, Excel interprets the formula as text.

Table 2-2   Summary of Arithmetic Operators

ARITHMETIC OPERATOR	MEANING	EXAMPLE OF USAGE	MEANING
−	Negation	−10	Negative 10
%	Percentage	=30%	Multiplies 30 by 0.01
^	Exponentiation	=2 ^ 3	Raises 2 to the third power, which in this example is equal to 8
*	Multiplication	=6.1 * A1	Multiplies the contents of cell A1 by 6.1
/	Division	=H3 / H5	Divides the contents of cell H3 by the contents of cell H5
+	Addition	=4 + 8	Adds 4 and 8
−	Subtraction	=D34 − 35	Subtracts 35 from the contents of cell D34

You can enter the cell references in formulas in uppercase or lowercase, and you can add spaces before and after arithmetic operators to make the formulas easier to read. That is, =d3*e3 is the same as =d3 * e3, =D3 * e3, or =D3 * E3.

Order of Operations

When more than one operator is involved in a formula, Excel follows the same basic order of operations that you use in algebra. Moving from left to right in a formula, the **order of operations** is as follows: first negation (−), then all percentages (%), then all exponentiations (^), then all multiplications (*) and divisions (/), and finally, all additions (+) and subtractions (−).

You can use **parentheses** to override the order of operations. For example, if Excel follows the order of operations, 10 * 6 − 3 equals 57. If you use parentheses, however, to change the formula to 10 * (6 − 3), the result is 30, because the parentheses instruct Excel to subtract 3 from 6 before multiplying by 10. Table 2-3 illustrates several examples of valid formulas and explains the order of operations.

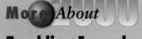

More About

Troubling Formulas

If Excel does not accept a formula, remove the equal sign from the left side and complete the entry as text. Later, after entering additional data or after you have determined the error, reinsert the equal sign.

Table 2-3   Examples of Excel Formulas

FORMULA	REMARK
=F6	Assigns the value in cell F6 to the active cell.
=6 + − 3^2	Assigns the sum of 6 + 9 (or 15) to the active cell.
=2 * K4 or =K4 * 2 or =(2 * K4)	Assigns two times the contents of cell K4 to the active cell.
=50% * 16	Assigns the product of 0.5 times 16 (or 8) to the active cell.
=− (J12 * S23)	Assigns the negative value of the product of the values contained in cells J12 and S23 to the active cell.
=5 * (L14 − H3)	Assigns the product of five times the difference between the values contained in cells H3 and L14 to the active cell.
=D1 / X6 − A3 * A4 + A5 ^ A6	From left to right: first exponentiation (A5 ^ A6), then division (D1 / X6), then multiplication (A3 * A4), then subtraction (D1 / X6) − (A3 * A4), and finally addition (D1 / X6 − A3 * A4) + (A5 ^ A6). If cells D1 = 10, A3 = 6, A4 = 2, A5 = 5, A6 = 2, and X6 = 2, then Excel assigns the active cell the value 18 (10 / 2 - 6 * 2 + 5 ^ 2 = 18).

The first formula (=d3*e3) in the worksheet was entered into cell F3 using the keyboard. The next section shows you how to enter the formulas in cells H3 and I3 using the mouse to select cell references in a formula.

Entering Formulas Using Point Mode

In the worksheet shown in Figure 2-1a on page E 2.5, the current value of each stock displays in column H. The current value for Amazon.com in cell H3 is equal to the number of shares in cell D3 times the current price in cell G3. The gain/loss for Amazon.com in cell I3 is equal to the current value in cell H3 minus the initial cost in cell F3. The percentage gain loss for Amazon.com in cell J3 is equal to the gain/loss in cell I3 divided by the initial cost in cell F3.

Instead of using the keyboard to enter the formulas =D3*G3 in cell H3, =H3 – F3 in cell I3, and =I3/F3 in cell J3, you can use the mouse and Point mode to enter these three formulas. **Point mode** allows you to select cells for use in a formula by using the mouse.

More About

Using Point Mode

Point mode allows you to create formulas using the mouse. Rather than typing a cell reference in a formula, simply click a cell and Excel appends the corresponding cell reference at the location of the insertion point. You also can use the Customize command on the shortcut menu that displays when you right-click a toolbar to create a Custom toolbar consisting of buttons that represent the operators. Thus, with Excel, you can enter entire formulas without ever touching the keyboard.

 To Enter Formulas Using Point Mode

 With cell H3 selected, type = (equal sign) to begin the formula and then click cell D3.

Excel surrounds cell D3 with a marquee and appends D3 to the equal sign (=) in cell H3 (Figure 2-5).

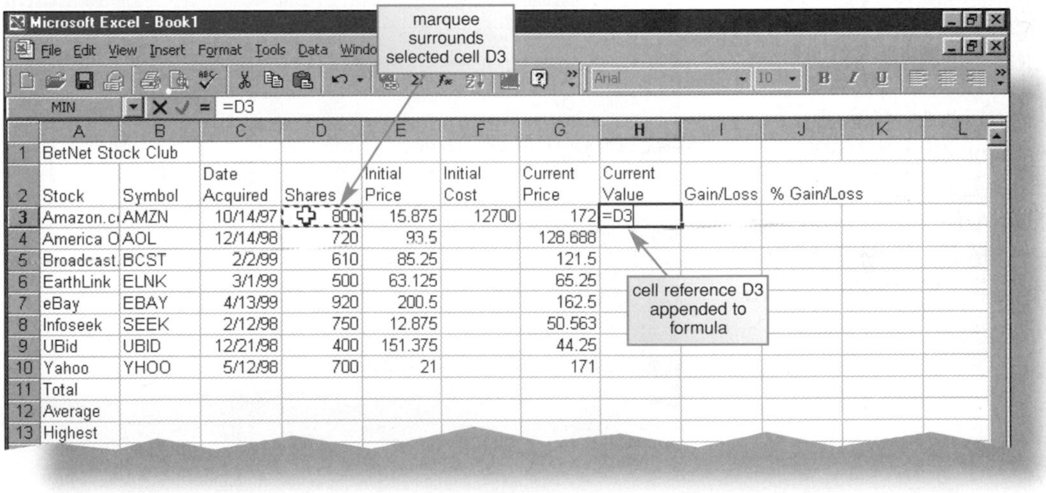

FIGURE 2-5

Type * (asterisk) and then click cell G3.

Excel surrounds cell G3 with a marquee and appends G3 to the asterisk (*) in cell H3 (Figure 2-6).

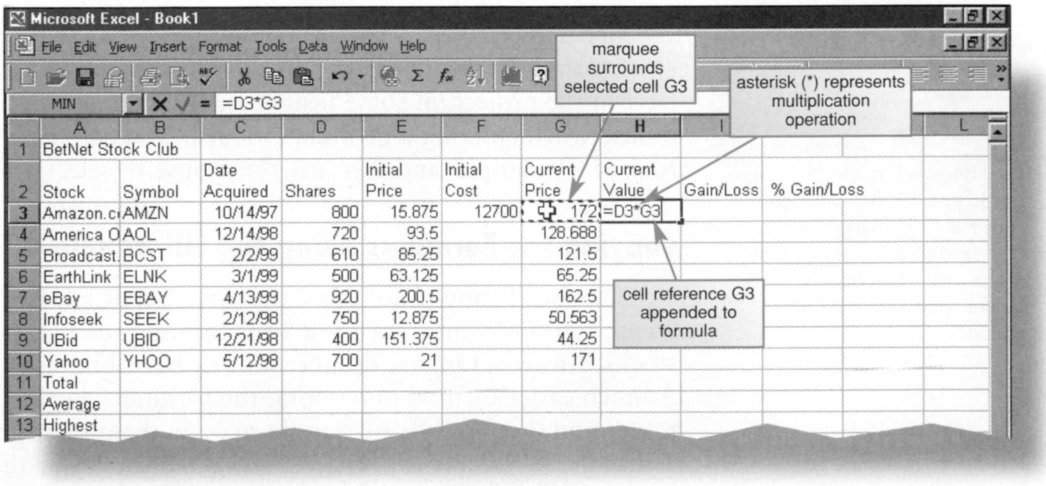

FIGURE 2-6

3   **Click the Enter box. Click cell I3. Type = (equal sign) and then click cell H3. Type − (minus sign) and then click cell F3.**

*Excel determines the product of =D3*G3 and displays the result, 137600, in cell H3. The formula =H3 − F3 displays in cell I3 and in the formula bar (Figure 2-7).*

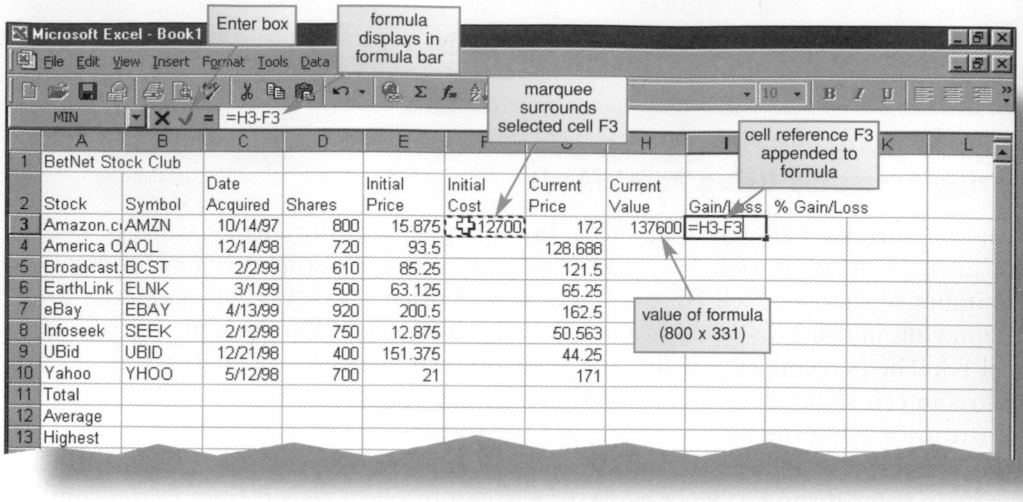

FIGURE 2-7

4   **Click the Enter box. Click cell J3. Type = (equal sign) and then click cell I3. Type / (division sign) and then click cell F3. Click the Enter box.**

The Gain/Loss for Amazon.com, 124900, displays in cell I3 and the % Gain/Loss for Amazon.com, 9.834646, displays in cell J3 (Figure 2-8). The 9.834646 represents 983.4646%.

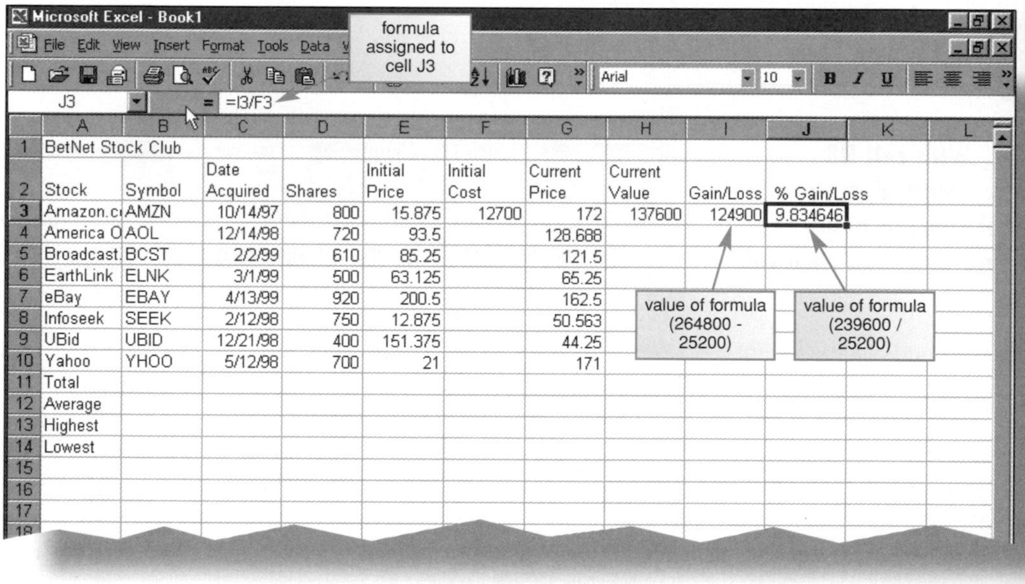

FIGURE 2-8

More About 2000

Formulas

To change a formula to a number (constant), select the cell, click the Copy button on the Standard toolbar, on the Edit menu click Paste Special, click Values, and click the OK button.

Depending on the length and complexity of the formula, using Point mode to enter formulas often is faster and more accurate than using the keyboard. As shown later in the project, in some instances, you may want to combine the keyboard and mouse when entering a formula in a cell. You can use the keyboard to begin the formula, for example, and then use the mouse to select a range of cells.

Copying the Formulas Using the Fill Handle

The four formulas for Amazon.com in cells F3, H3, I3, and J3 now are complete. You could enter the same four formulas one at a time for the seven remaining stocks, America Online, Broadcast.com, EarthLink, eBay, Infoseek, UBid, and Yahoo. A much easier method of entering the formulas, however, is to select the formulas in row 3 and then use the fill handle to copy them through row 10. Recall from Project 1 that the fill handle is a small rectangle in the lower-right corner of the active cell. Perform the following steps to copy the formulas.

To Copy Formulas Using the Fill Handle

1 Click cell F3 and then point to the fill handle. Drag the fill handle down through cell F10 and continue to hold down the mouse button.

A border surrounds the copy and paste areas (range F3:F10) and the mouse pointer changes to a cross hair (Figure 2-9).

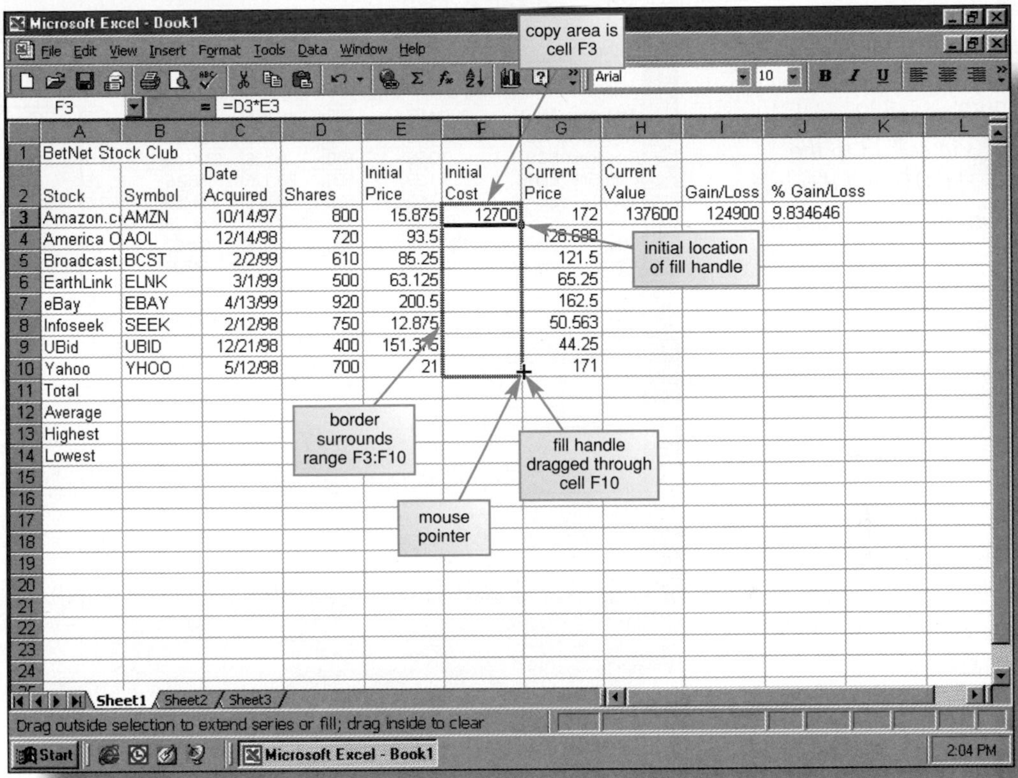

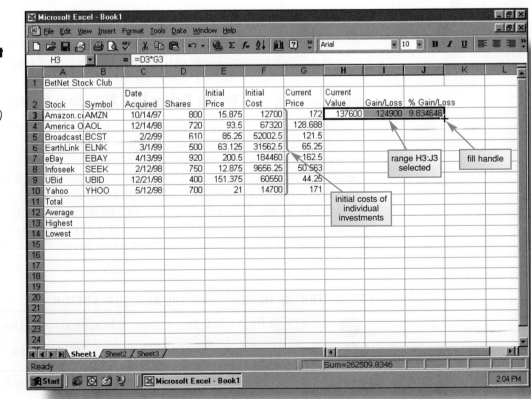

FIGURE 2-9

2 Release the mouse button. Select the range H3:J3 and then point to the fill handle.

*Excel copies the formula =D3*E3 to the range F4:F10 and displays the initial costs for the remaining seven stocks. The range H3:J3 is selected (Figure 2-10).*

FIGURE 2-10

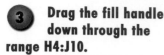

3 **Drag the fill handle down through the range H4:J10.**

Excel copies the three formulas =D3*G3 in cell H3, =H3-F3 in cell I3, and =I3/F3 in cell J3 to the range H4:J10 and displays the current value, gain/loss, and percentage gain/loss for the remaining seven stocks (Figure 2-11).

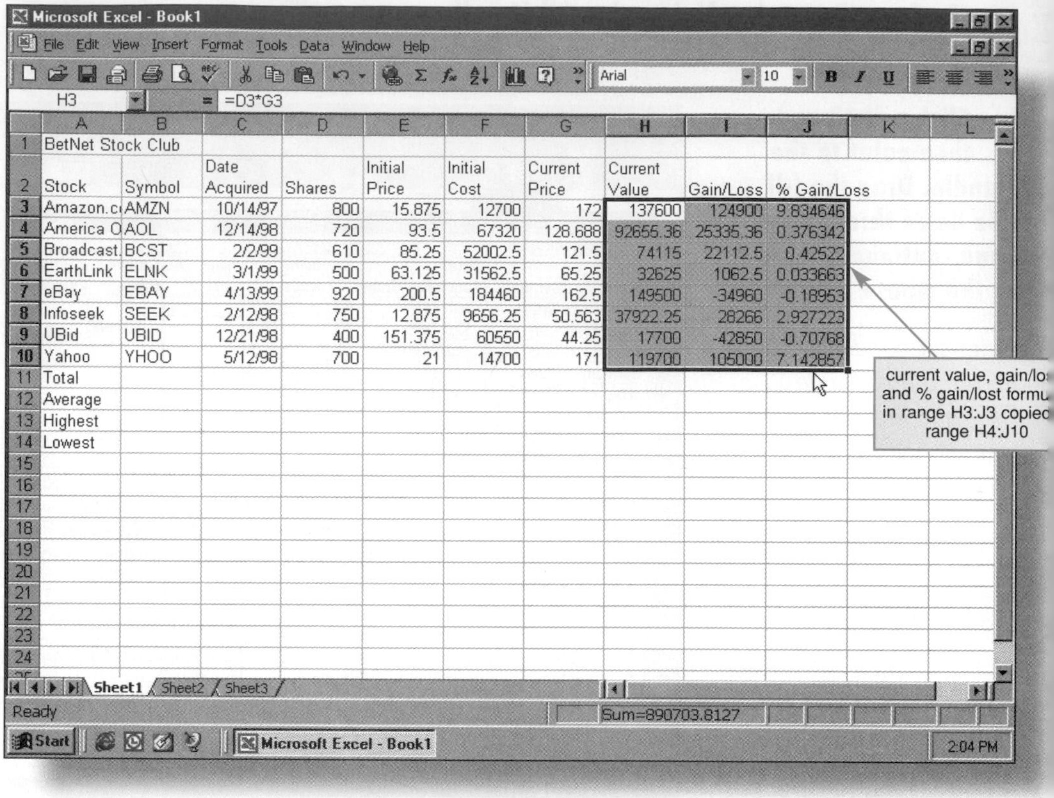

	A	B	C	D	E	F	G	H	I	J
1	BetNet Stock Club									
2	Stock	Symbol	Date Acquired	Shares	Initial Price	Initial Cost	Current Price	Current Value	Gain/Loss	% Gain/Loss
3	Amazon.c	AMZN	10/14/97	800	15.875	12700	172	137600	124900	9.834646
4	America O	AOL	12/14/98	720	93.5	67320	128.688	92655.36	25335.36	0.376342
5	Broadcast	BCST	2/2/99	610	85.25	52002.5	121.5	74115	22112.5	0.42522
6	EarthLink	ELNK	3/1/99	500	63.125	31562.5	65.25	32625	1062.5	0.033663
7	eBay	EBAY	4/13/99	920	200.5	184460	162.5	149500	-34960	-0.18953
8	Infoseek	SEEK	2/12/98	750	12.875	9656.25	50.563	37922.25	28266	2.927223
9	UBid	UBID	12/21/98	400	151.375	60550	44.25	17700	-42850	-0.70768
10	Yahoo	YHOO	5/12/98	700	21	14700	171	119700	105000	7.142857
11	Total									
12	Average									
13	Highest									
14	Lowest									

current value, gain/lo...
and % gain/lost formu...
in range H3:J3 copied...
range H4:J10

Sum=890703.8127

FIGURE 2-11

Other Ways

1. Select copy area, right-click copy area, click Copy on shortcut menu, select paste area, right-click paste area, click Paste on shortcut menu
2. Select copy area, click Copy button on Standard toolbar, select paste area, click Paste button on Standard toolbar
3. Select copy area, on Edit menu click Copy, select paste area, on Edit menu click Paste
4. Select copy area, press CTRL+C, select paste area, press CTRL+V

Recall that when you copy a formula, Excel adjusts the cell references so the new formulas contain references corresponding to the new location and performs calculations using the appropriate values. Thus, if you copy downward, Excel adjusts the row portion of cell references. If you copy across, then Excel adjusts the column portion of cell references. These cell references are called **relative references**.

Determining the Totals Using the AutoSum Button

The next step is to determine the totals in row 11 for the initial cost in column F, current value in column H, and gain/loss in column I. To determine the total initial cost in column F, you must sum cells F3 through F10. To do so, you can enter the function =sum(f3:f10) in cell F11, or you can select cell F11 and then click the Auto-Sum button on the Standard toolbar twice. Similar SUM functions or the AutoSum button can be used in cells H11 and I11 to determine total current value and total gain/loss, respectively. Recall from Project 1 that when you select one cell and use the AutoSum button, you must click the button twice. If you select a range, then you need only click the AutoSum button once.

TO DETERMINE TOTALS USING THE AUTOSUM BUTTON

1 Select cell F11. Click the AutoSum button twice. (Do not double-click.)

2 Select the range H11:I11. Click the AutoSum button.

The three totals display in row 11 as shown in Figure 2-12.

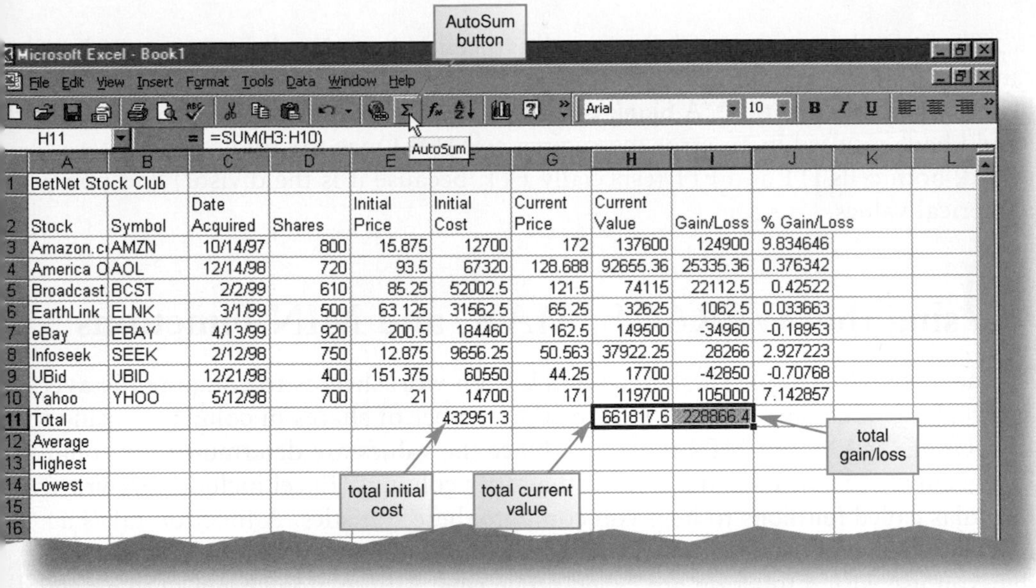

FIGURE 2-12

Rather than using the AutoSum function to calculate column totals individually, you can select all three cells before clicking the AutoSum button to calculate all three column totals at one time. To select the nonadjacent range F11, H11, and I11, select cell F11, and then, while holding down the CTRL key, drag through the range H11:I11. Next, click the AutoSum button.

Determining the Total Percentage Gain/Loss

With the totals in row 11 determined, you can copy the percentage gain/loss formula in cell J10 to cell J11 as shown in the following steps.

TO DETERMINE THE TOTAL PERCENTAGE GAIN/LOSS

1. Select cell J10 and then point to the fill handle.

2. Drag the fill handle down through cell J11.

The formula, =I10/F10, is copied to cell J11. The resultant formula in cell J11 is =I11/F11, which shows a total club gain on the club's holdings of 0.528619 or 52.8619% (Figure 2-13).

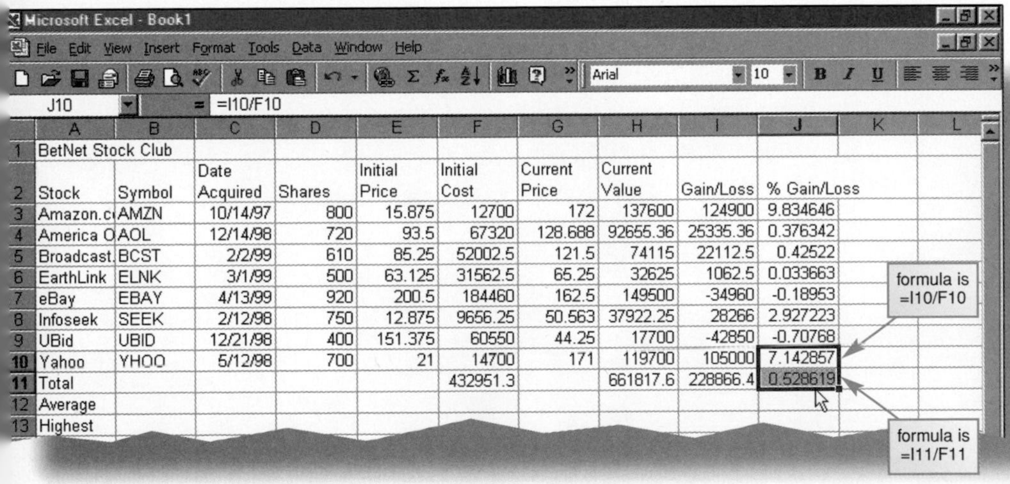

More About

Selecting a Range

If you dislike dragging to select a range, press F8 and use the arrow keys to select one corner of the range and then the cell diagonally opposite it in the proposed range. Make sure you press F8 to turn the selection off after you are finished with the range or you will continue to select ranges.

FIGURE 2-13

Formulas and Functions

For more information on entering formulas and functions, visit the Excel 2000 More About Web page (www.scsite.com/ex2000/more.htm) and click Using Formulas and Functions.

The formula was not copied originally to cell J11 when cell J3 was copied to the range J4:J10 because both cells involved in the computation (I11 and F11) were blank, or zero, at the time. A **blank cell** in Excel has a numerical value of zero, which would have resulted in an error message in cell J11. Once the totals were determined, both cells I11 and F11 (especially F11, because it is the divisor) had non-zero numerical values.

Using the AVERAGE, MAX, and MIN Functions

The next step in creating the BetNet Stock Club worksheet is to compute the average, highest value, and lowest value for the number of shares in column D using the AVERAGE, MAX, and MIN functions. Once the values are determined for column D, the entries can be copied across to the other columns. Excel includes prewritten formulas called **functions** to help you compute these statistics. A function takes a value or values, performs an operation, and returns a result to the cell. The values that you use with a function are called **arguments**. All functions begin with an equal sign and include
the arguments in parentheses after the function name. For example, in the function =AVERAGE(D3:D10), the function name is AVERAGE and the argument is the range D3:D10.

With Excel, you can enter functions using one of three methods: (1) the keyboard or mouse; (2) the Edit Formula box and Functions box; and (3) the Paste Function button on the Standard toolbar. The method you choose will depend on whether you can recall the function name and required arguments. In the following pages, each of the three methods will be used. The keyboard and mouse will be used to determine the average number of shares (cell D12). The Edit Formula box and Functions box will be used to determine the highest number of shares (cell D13). The Paste Function button will be used to determine the lowest number of shares (cell D14).

Determining the Average of a Range of Numbers

The **AVERAGE function** sums the numbers in the specified range and then divides the sum by the number of non-zero cells in the range. To determine the average of the numbers in the range D3:D10, use the AVERAGE function as shown in the following steps.

More About

The AVERAGE Function

A blank cell usually is considered to be equal to zero. The statistical functions, however, ignore blank cells. Thus, in Excel, the average of three cells with values of 2, blank, and 4 is 3 or (2 + 4) / 2, and not 2 or (2 + 0 + 4) / 3.

Steps **To Determine the Average of a Range of Numbers Using the Keyboard and Mouse**

1 **Select cell D12. Type** =average(**in the cell. Click cell D3, the first endpoint of the range to average. Drag through cell D10, the second endpoint of the range to average.**

A marquee surrounds the range D3:D10. When you click cell D3, Excel appends cell D3 to the left parenthesis in the formula bar and surrounds cell D3 with a marquee. When you begin dragging, Excel appends to the argument a colon (:) and the cell reference of the cell where the mouse pointer is located (Figure 2-14).

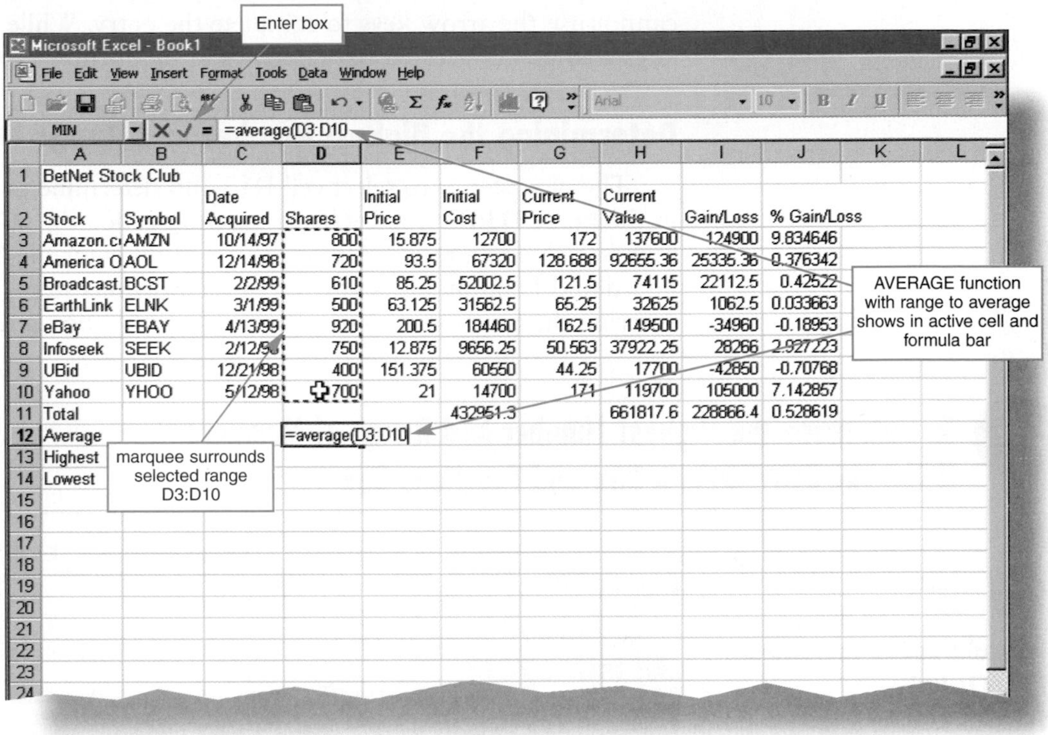

Enter box

AVERAGE function with range to average shows in active cell and formula bar

marquee surrounds selected range D3:D10

FIGURE 2-14

2 **Click the Enter box.**

Excel computes the average of the eight numbers in the range D3:D10 and displays the result, 633, in cell D12 (Figure 2-15). Thus, the average number of shares owned in the eight companies is 633.

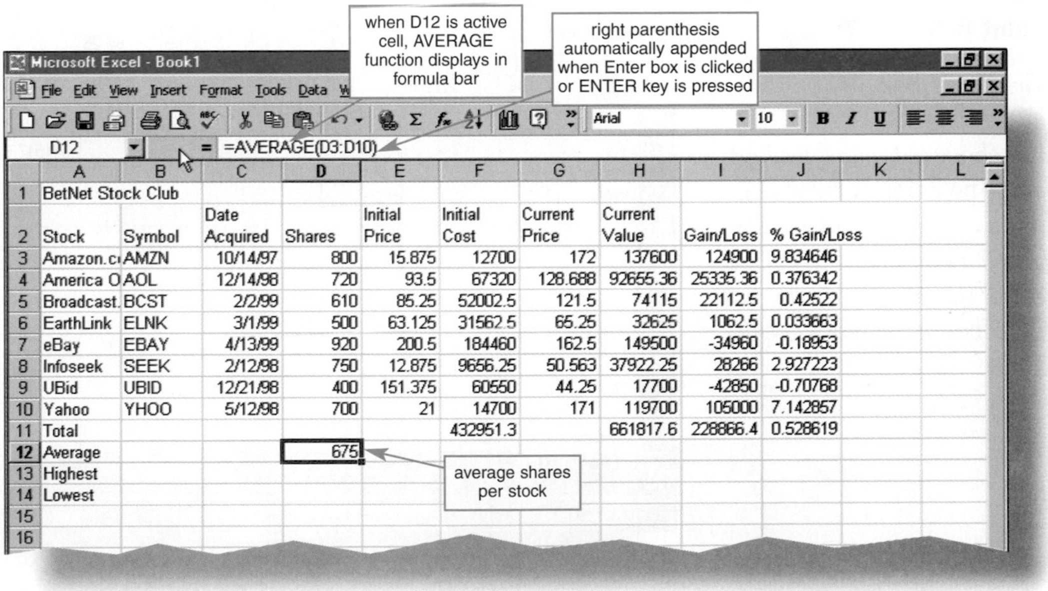

when D12 is active cell, AVERAGE function displays in formula bar

right parenthesis automatically appended when Enter box is clicked or ENTER key is pressed

average shares per stock

FIGURE 2-15

Other **Ways**

1. Click Edit Formula box in formula bar, click AVERAGE in Functions box
2. Click Paste Function button on Standard toolbar, click AVERAGE function

The AVERAGE function requires that the range (the argument) be included within parentheses following the function name. Excel thus automatically appends the right parenthesis to complete the AVERAGE function when you click the Enter box or press the ENTER key. When you use Point mode, as in the previous steps, you cannot use the arrow keys to complete the entry. While in Point mode, the arrow keys change the selected cell reference in the formula you are creating.

Determining the Highest Number in a Range of Numbers

The next step is to select cell D13 and determine the highest (maximum) number in the range D3:D10. Excel has a function called the **MAX function** that displays the highest value in a range. Although you could enter the MAX function using the keyboard and Point mode as you did in the previous steps, an alternative method to entering the function is to use the Edit Formula box and Functions box.

To Determine the Highest Number in a Range of Numbers Using the Edit Formula Box and Functions Box

1 **Select cell D13. Click the Edit Formula box in the formula bar. Click the Functions box arrow and then point to MAX.**

The Name box in the formula bar changes to the Functions box. The Formula Palette displays immediately below the formula bar (Figure 2-16). An equal sign displays in the formula bar and the active cell, D13.

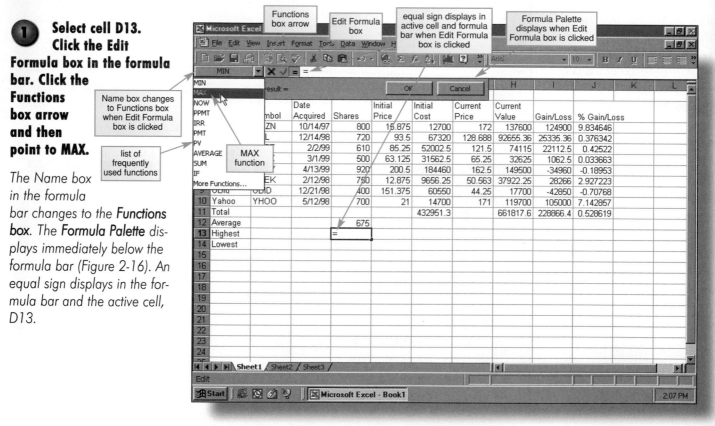

FIGURE 2-16

2 **Click MAX. When the MAX Formula Palette displays, type** d3:d10 **in the Number 1 edit box. Point to the OK button.**

The MAX Formula Palette displays with the range d3:d10 entered in the Number 1 edit box (Figure 2-17). The completed MAX function displays in the formula bar, and the end of the function displays in the active cell, D13.

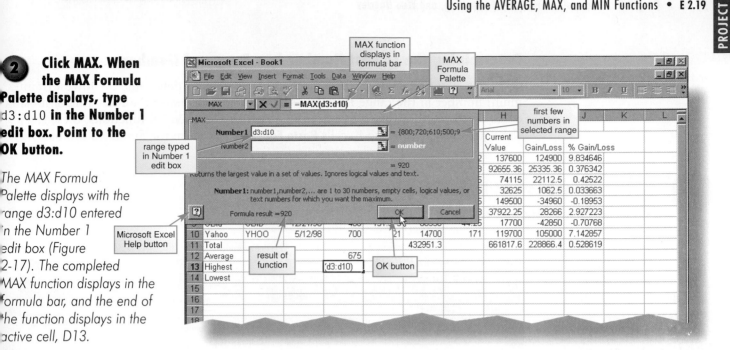

FIGURE 2-17

3 **Click the OK button.**

Excel determines that the highest value in the range D3:D10 is 934 (cell D7) and displays it in cell D13 (Figure 2-18).

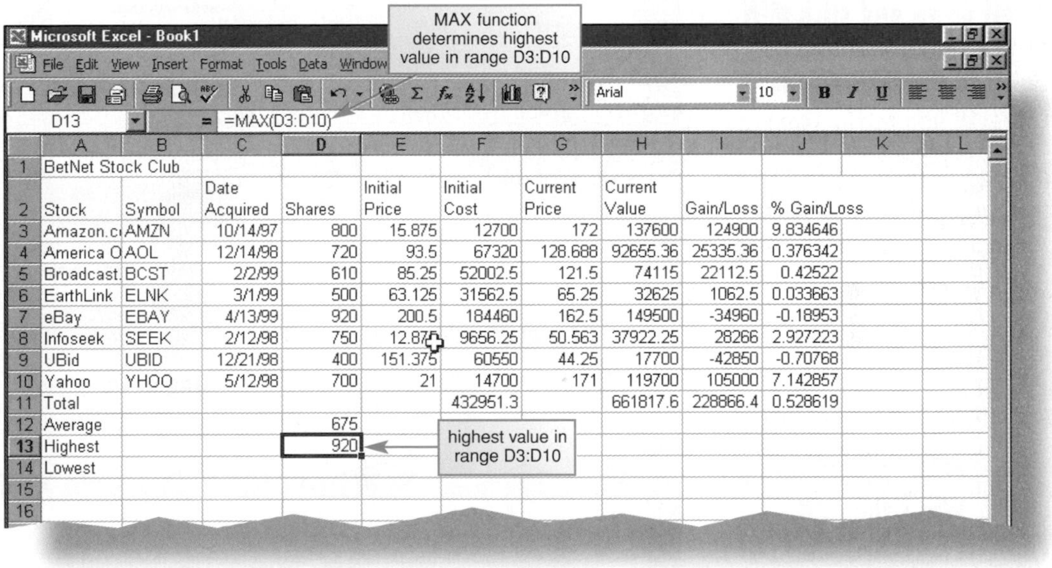

FIGURE 2-18

Other Ways

1. Click Paste Function button on Standard toolbar, click MAX function
2. Type MAX function in cell

As shown in Figure 2-17, the MAX Formula Palette displays the value the MAX function will return to cell D13. It also lists the first few numbers in the selected range, next to the Number 1 edit box.

In this example, rather than entering the MAX function, you easily could scan the range D3:D10, determine that the highest number of shares is 934, and enter the number as a constant in cell D13. The display would be the same as Figure 2-18. Because it contains a constant, cell D13 will continue to display 934, even if the values in the range D3:D10 change. If you use the MAX function, however, Excel will recalculate the highest value in the range D3:D10 each time a new value is entered into the worksheet. Manually determining the highest value in the range also would be more difficult if the club owned more stocks.

Determining the Lowest Number in a Range of Numbers

Next, you will enter the **MIN function** in cell D14 to determine the lowest (minimum) number in the range D3:D10. Although you can enter the MIN function using either of the methods used to enter the AVERAGE and MAX functions, these steps show an alternative using Excel's **Paste Function button** on the Standard toolbar.

To Determine the Lowest Number in a Range of Numbers Using the Paste Function Button

  Select cell D14. Click the Paste Function button on the Standard toolbar. When the Paste Function dialog box displays, click Statistical in the Function category list. Scroll down and click MIN in the Function name list. Point to the OK button.

The Paste Function dialog box displays (Figure 2-19). Statistical and MIN are selected. An equal sign displays in the formula bar and in the active cell, D14.

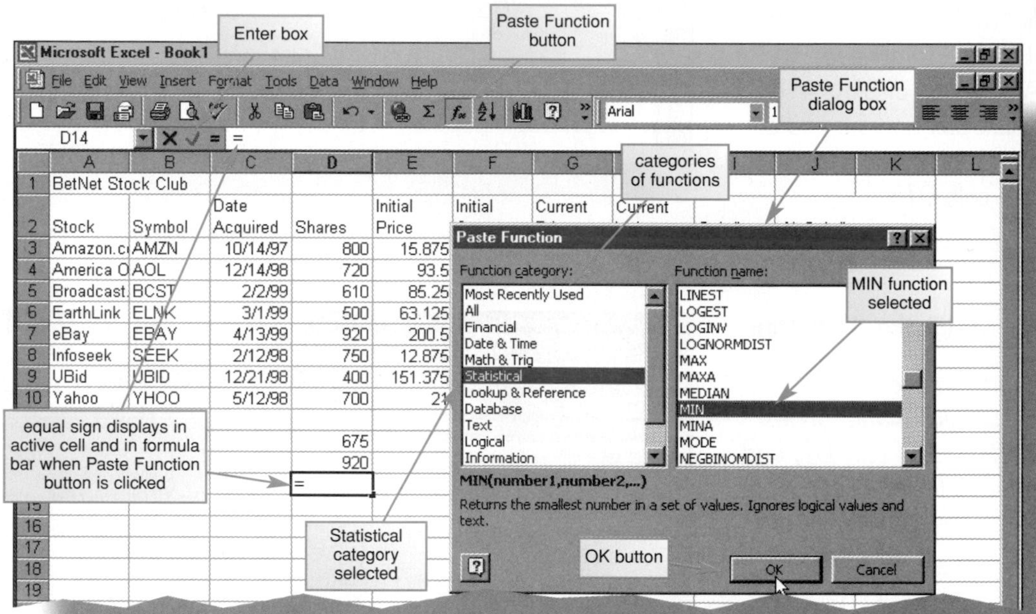

FIGURE 2-19

  Click the OK button. When the MIN Formula Palette displays, drag it to the bottom of the screen. Click cell D3 and then drag through cell D10.

The MIN Formula Palette displays at the bottom of the screen (Figure 2-20). The range D3:D10 displays in the Number 1 edit box. The MIN function displays in the formula bar and the end of the MIN function displays in the active cell, D14.

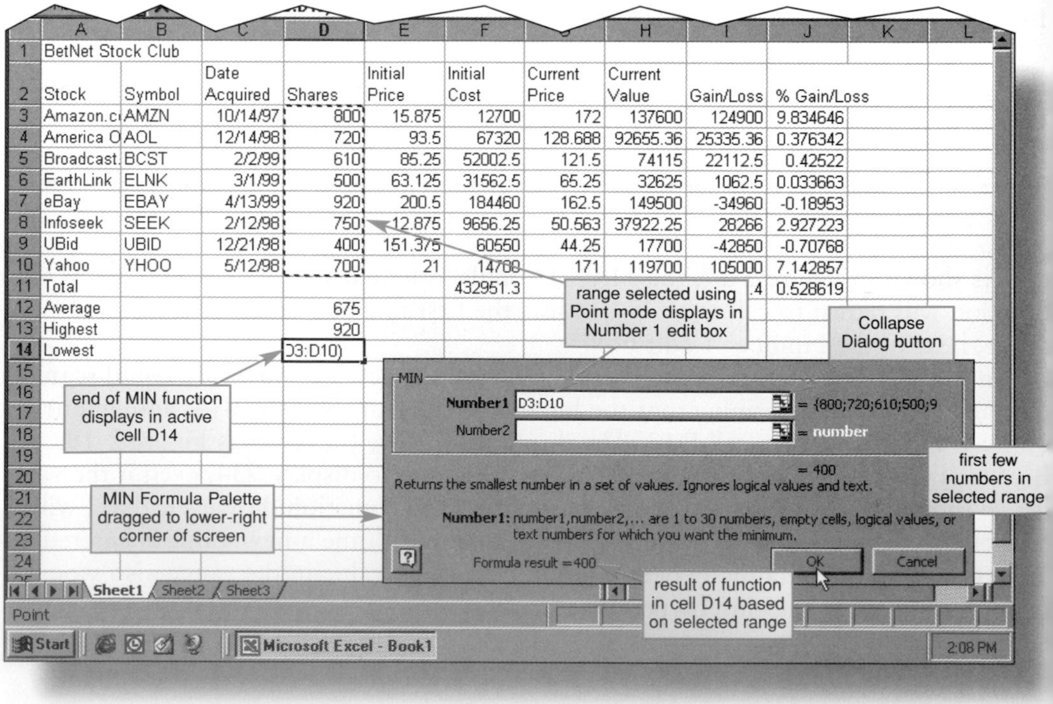

FIGURE 2-20

Click the Enter box.

Excel determines that the lowest value in the range D3:D10 is 350 and displays it in cell D14 (Figure 2-21).

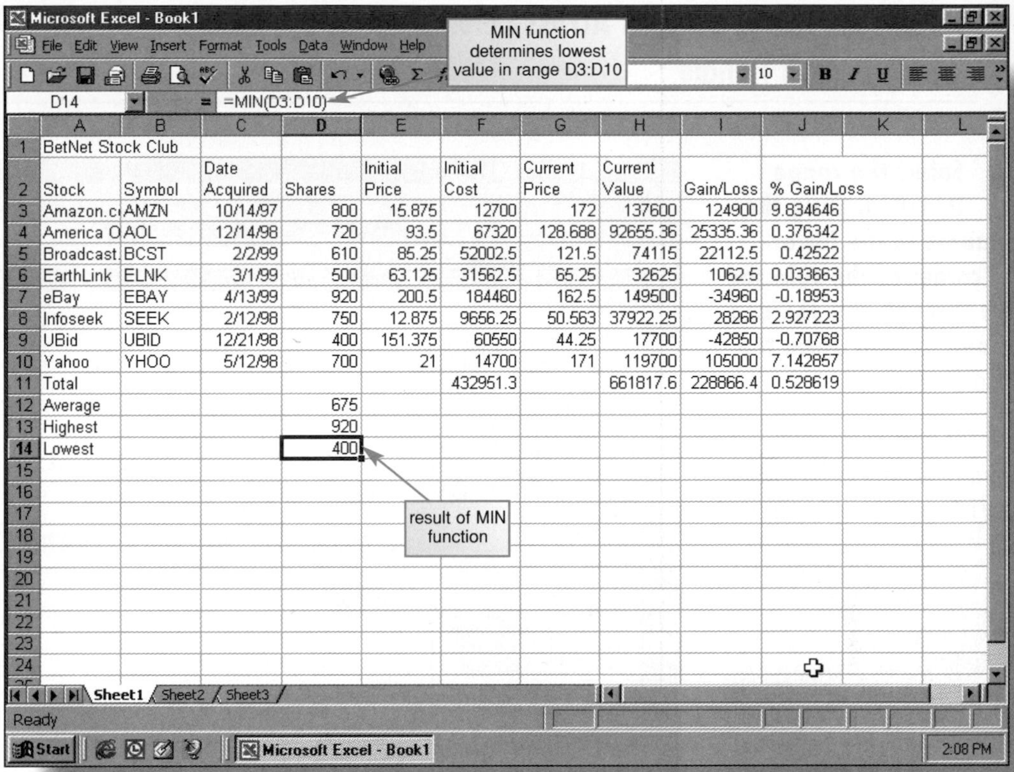

FIGURE 2-21

You can see from the previous example that using the Paste Function button on the Standard toolbar allows you to enter a function into a cell easily without requiring you to memorize its name or the required arguments. Anytime you desire to enter a function, but cannot remember the function name or the required arguments, simply click the Paste Function button on the Standard toolbar, select the desired function, and enter the arguments in the Formula Palette.

Thus far, you have learned to use the SUM, AVERAGE, MAX, and MIN functions. In addition to these four functions, Excel has more than 400 additional functions that perform just about every type of calculation you can imagine. These functions are categorized as shown in the Function category list box shown in Figure 2-19. To obtain a description of a selected function, select the Function name in the Paste Function dialog box. The description displays below the two list boxes in the dialog box.

Copying the AVERAGE, MAX, and MIN Functions

The next step is to copy the AVERAGE, MAX, and MIN functions in the range D12:D14 to the range E12:J14. The fill handle again will be used to complete the copy. The steps on the next page illustrate this procedure.

Other Ways

1. Click Edit Formula box in formula bar, click MIN function in Functions box
2. Type MIN function in cell

More About 2000

The Formula Palette

Rather than dragging the Formula Palette out of the way to use Point mode to select a range as was done in Step 2 on the previous page, you can click the Collapse Dialog button to the right of the Number 1 or Number 2 boxes to hide the Formula Palette. Once you select the range, click the button a second time to re-display the Formula Palette.

To Copy a Range of Cells Across Columns to an Adjacent Range Using the Fill Handle

1 **Select the range D12:D14. Drag the fill handle in the lower-right corner of the selected range through cell J14 and continue to hold down the mouse button.**

Excel displays an outline around the paste area (range D12:J14) as shown in Figure 2-22.

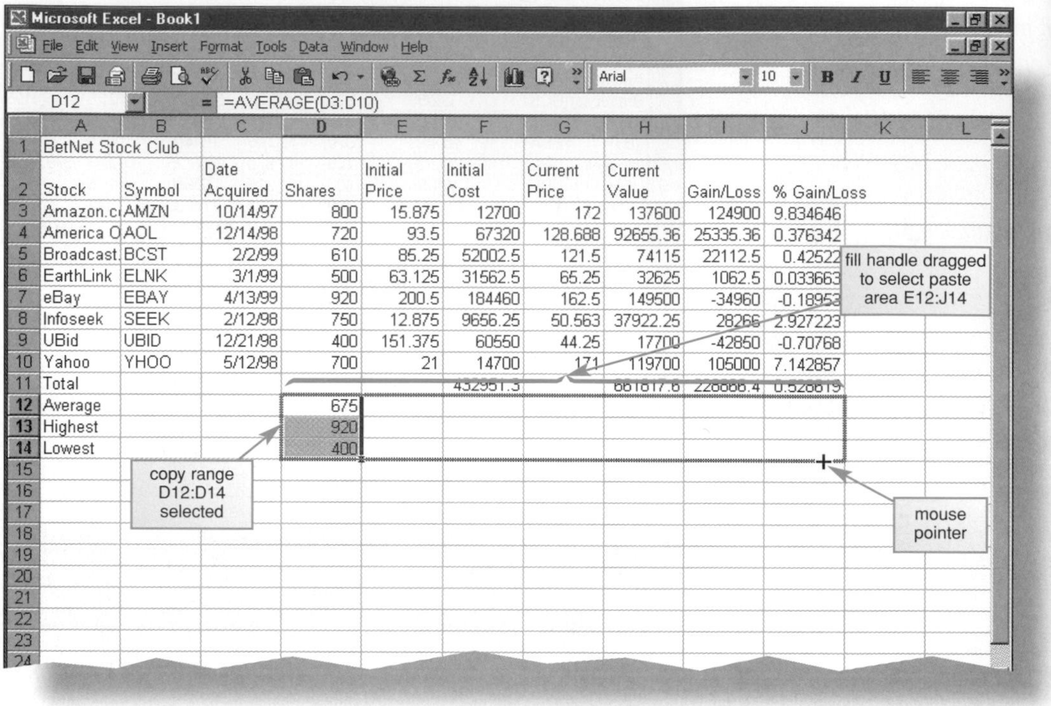

FIGURE 2-22

2 **Release the mouse button.**

Excel copies the three functions to the range E12:J14 (Figure 2-23).

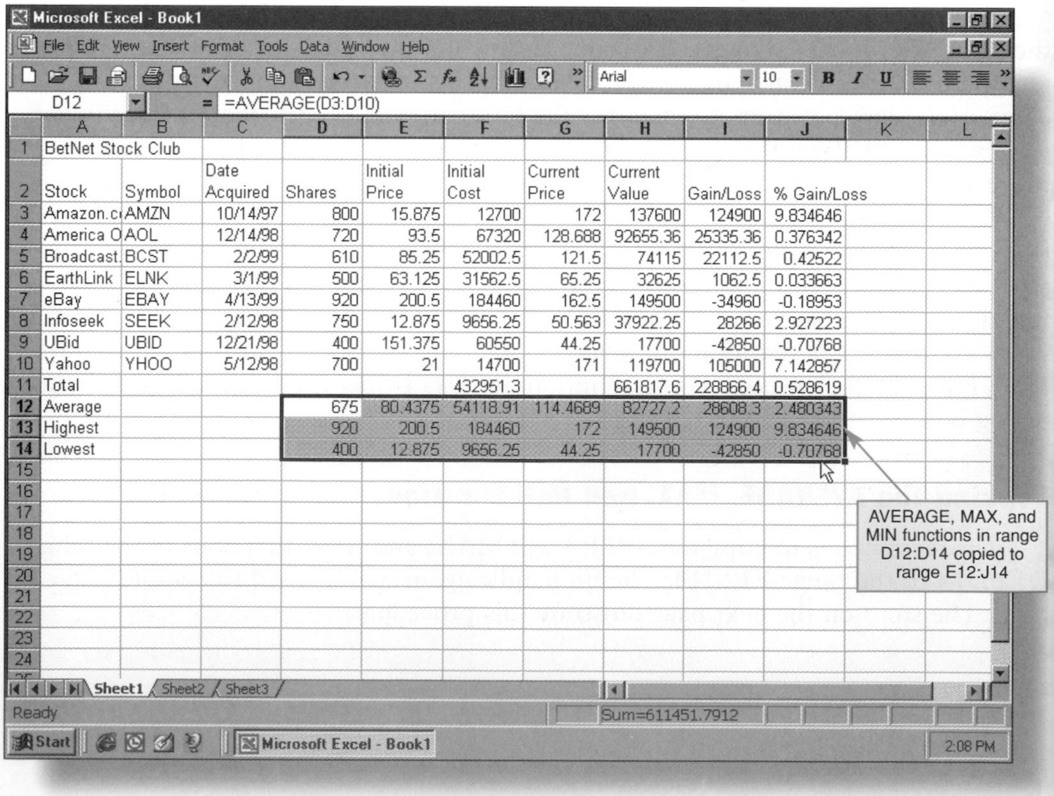

FIGURE 2-23

3 Select cell J12 and press the DELETE key to delete the average of the percentage gain/loss.

Cell J12 is blank (Figure 2-24).

4 Click the Save button on the standard toolbar. Type BetNet Stock Club in the File name text box. If necessary, click 3½ Floppy (A:) in the Save in box. Click the Save button in the Save As dialog box.

The file name in the title bar changes to BetNet Stock Club (Figure 2-24).

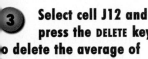

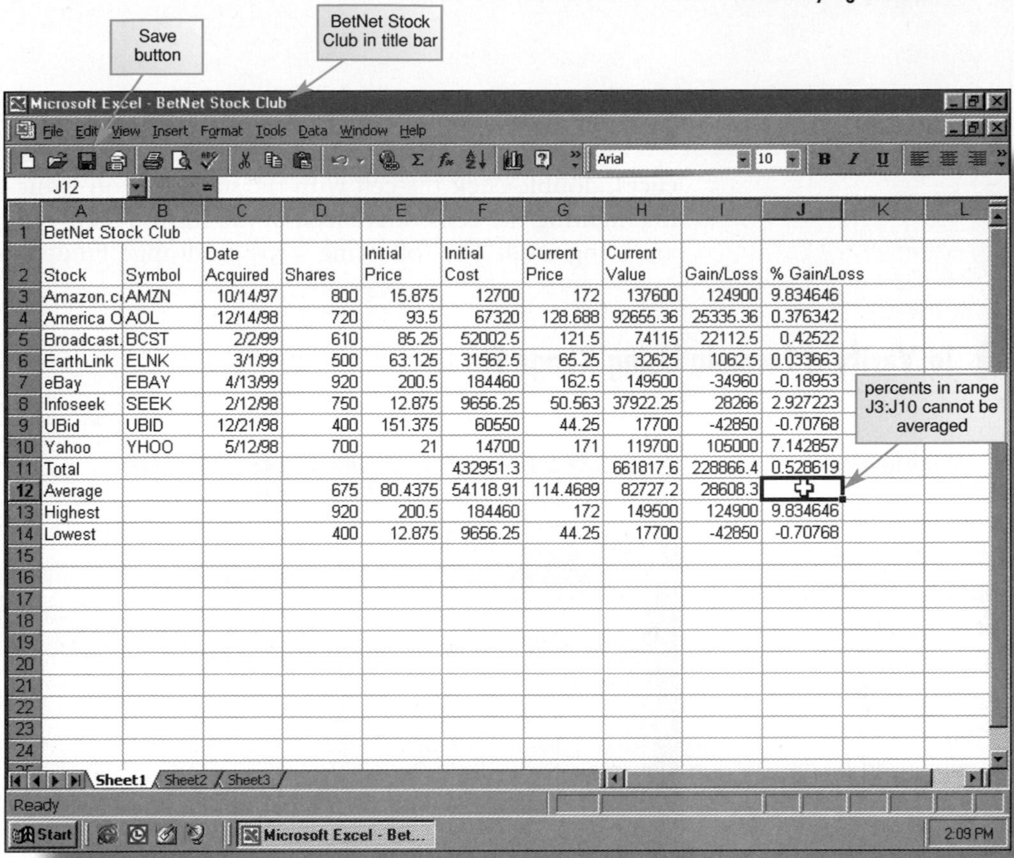

	A	B	C	D	E	F	G	H	I	J	K	L
1	BetNet Stock Club											
2	Stock	Symbol	Date Acquired	Shares	Initial Price	Initial Cost	Current Price	Current Value	Gain/Loss	% Gain/Loss		
3	Amazon.c	AMZN	10/14/97	800	15.875	12700	172	137600	124900	9.834646		
4	America O	AOL	12/14/98	720	93.5	67320	128.688	92655.36	25335.36	0.376342		
5	Broadcast	BCST	2/2/99	610	85.25	52002.5	121.5	74115	22112.5	0.42522		
6	EarthLink	ELNK	3/1/99	500	63.125	31562.5	65.25	32625	1062.5	0.033663		
7	eBay	EBAY	4/13/99	920	200.5	184460	162.5	149500	-34960	-0.18953		
8	Infoseek	SEEK	2/12/98	750	12.875	9656.25	50.563	37922.6	28266	2.927223		
9	UBid	UBID	12/21/98	400	151.375	60550	44.25	17700	-42850	-0.70768		
10	Yahoo	YHOO	5/12/98	700	21	14700	171	119700	105000	7.142857		
11	Total					432951.3		661817.6	228866.4	0.528619		
12	Average			675	80.4375	54118.91	114.4689	82727.2	28608.3			
13	Highest			920	200.5	184460	172	149500	124900	9.834646		
14	Lowest			400	12.875	9656.25	44.25	17700	-42850	-0.70768		

percents in range J3:J10 cannot be averaged

FIGURE 2-24

The average of the percentage gain/loss in cell J12 was deleted in Step 3 because an average of percents of this type is mathematically invalid.

Remember that Excel adjusts the ranges in the copied functions so each function refers to the column of numbers above it. Review the numbers in rows 12 through 14 in Figure 2-24. You should see that the functions in each column return the appropriate values, based on the numbers in rows 3 through 10 of that column.

This concludes entering the data and formulas into the worksheet. After saving the file, the worksheet remains on the screen with the file name, BetNet Stock Club, in the title bar. You immediately can continue with the next activity.

Verifying Formulas

One of the most common mistakes made with Excel is to include a wrong cell reference in a formula. Excel has two methods, the Auditing commands and Range Finder, to verify that a formula references the cells you want it to reference. The **Auditing commands** allow you to trace precedents and trace dependents. The **Trace Precedents command** highlights the cells in the worksheet that are referenced by the formula in the active cell. The **Trace Dependents command** highlights the cells with formulas in the worksheet that reference the active cell. The **Remove all Arrows command** removes the highlights.

As with the Trace Precedents command, **Range Finder** can be used to check which cells are being referenced in the formula assigned to the active cell. One of the advantages of Range Finder is that it allows you to make immediate changes to the cells referenced in a formula.

Verifying Formulas

If you lack confidence in your mathematical abilities, then you will find Range Finder and the Auditing commands to be useful to ensure the formulas you enter reference the correct cells.

Verifying a Formula Using Range Finder

To use Range Finder to verify that a formula contains the intended cell references, double-click the cell with the formula you want to check. Excel responds by highlighting the cells referenced in the formula so you can check that the correct cells are being used. The following steps use Range Finder to check the formula in cell J3.

Steps ## To Verify a Formula Using Range Finder

1 **Double-click cell J3.**

Excel responds by displaying the cells in the worksheet referenced by the formula in cell J3 using different color borders (Figure 2-25). The different colors allow you to see easily which cells are being referenced by the formula in cell J3.

2 **Click any cell or press the ESC key to quit Range Finder.**

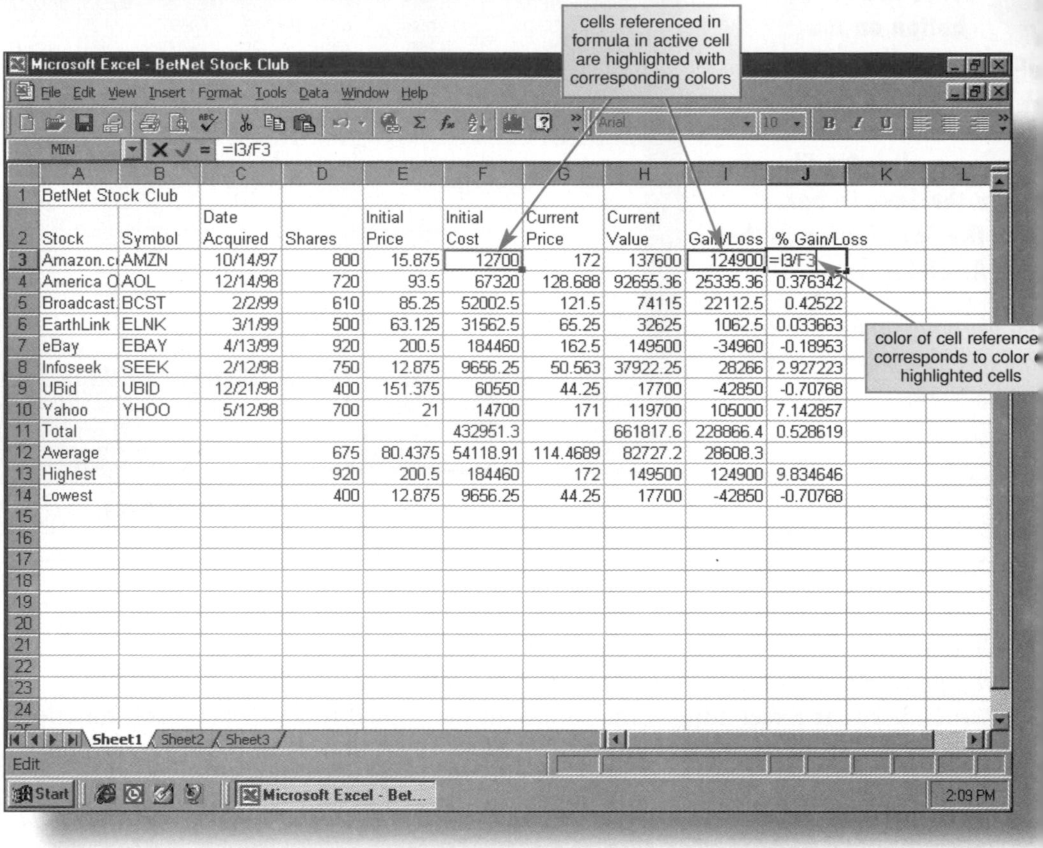

FIGURE 2-25

Not only does Range Finder show you the cells referenced in the formula in cell J3, but you can drag the colored borders to other cells and Excel will change the cell references in the formula to the newly selected cells. If you use Range Finder to change cells referenced in a formula, press the ENTER key to complete the edit.

Verifying a Formula Using the Auditing Commands

The following steps show how to use the Trace Precedent and Trace Dependent commands to verify a formula is referencing the correct cells and to determine the cells that reference the active cell.

To Verify a Formula Using the Auditing Commands

1 If necessary, click cell J3. Click Tools in the menu bar and then click the down arrows at the bottom of the Tools menu to display the full menu. Point to Auditing. When the Auditing submenu displays, point to Trace Precedents.

The Auditing submenu displays as shown in Figure 2-26.

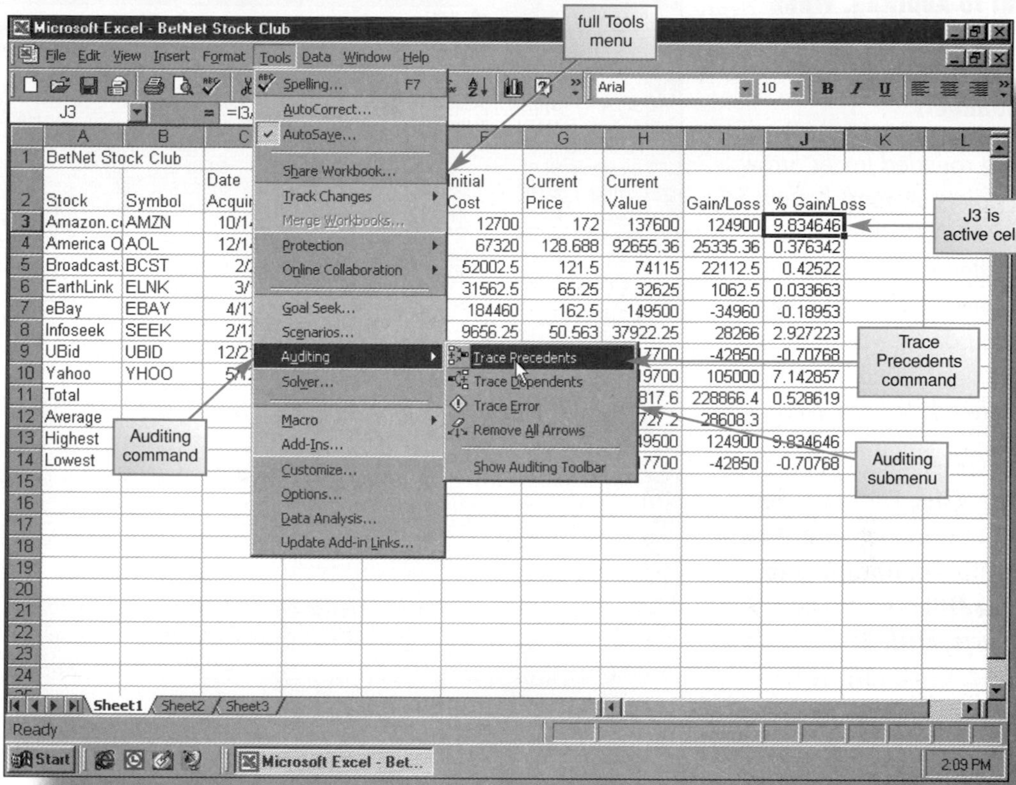

2 Click Trace Precedents.

Blue rounded tracer arrows that point upward display along a blue line in the cells (F3 and I3) that are used by the formula in the active cell, J3 (Figure 2-27). The horizontal arrow in cell J3 at the right end of the blue line indicates the active cell. You can use the blue line and arrows to verify that the correct cells are being used in the formula.

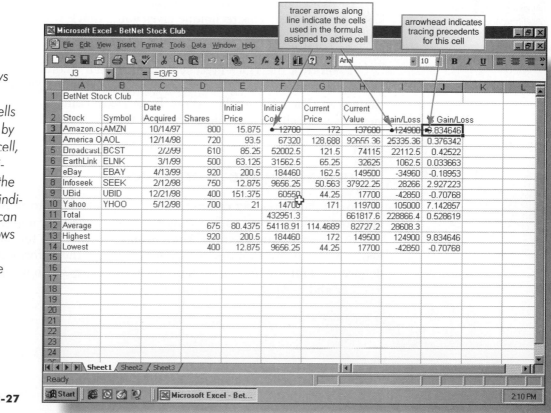

FIGURE 2-26

FIGURE 2-27

Click Tools on the menu bar and then point to Auditing. When the Auditing submenu displays, click Trace Dependents.

A blue rounded tracer arrow that points upward displays in the active cell, J3. A blue line extends downward to the two cells, J13 and J14 that depend on the value in cell J3. Cells J13 and J14 have arrowheads (Figure 2-28).

4 **Click Tools on the menu bar and then point to Auditing. When the Auditing submenu displays, click Remove All Arrows. Click cell A16.**

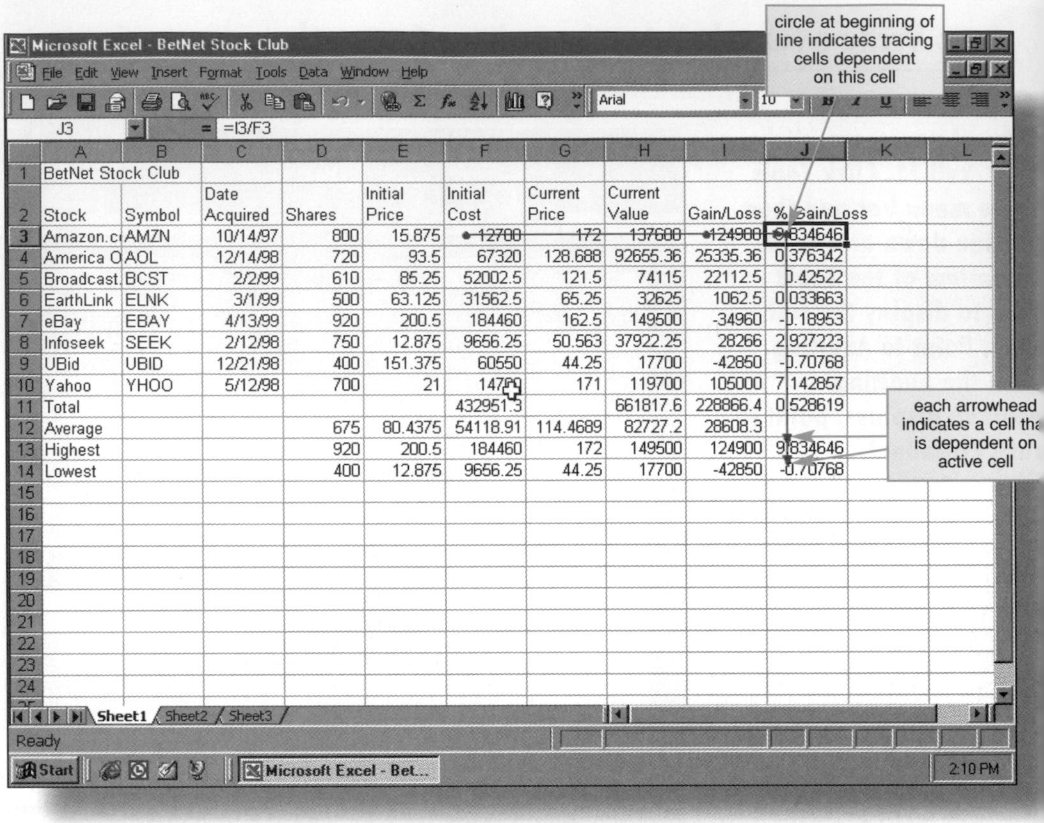

circle at beginning of line indicates tracing cells dependent on this cell

Microsoft Excel - BetNet Stock Club

File   Edit   View   Insert   Format   Tools   Data   Window   Help

J3   =   =I3/F3

	A	B	C	D	E	F	G	H	I	J	K	L
1	BetNet Stock Club											
2	Stock	Symbol	Date Acquired	Shares	Initial Price	Initial Cost	Current Price	Current Value	Gain/Loss	% Gain/Loss		
3	Amazon.c	AMZN	10/14/97	800	15.875	12700	172	137600	124900	834646		
4	America O	AOL	12/14/98	720	93.5	67320	128.688	92655.36	25335.36	0 376342		
5	Broadcast	BCST	2/2/99	610	85.25	52002.5	121.5	74115	22112.5	0.42522		
6	EarthLink	ELNK	3/1/99	500	63.125	31562.5	65.25	32625	1062.5	0 033663		
7	eBay	EBAY	4/13/99	920	200.5	184460	162.5	149500	-34960	-0.18953		
8	Infoseek	SEEK	2/12/98	750	12.875	9656.25	50.563	37922.25	28266	2 927223		
9	UBid	UBID	12/21/98	400	151.375	60550	44.25	17700	-42850	-0.70768		
10	Yahoo	YHOO	5/12/98	700	21	14700	171	119700	105000	7 142857		
11	Total					432951.3		661817.6	228866.4	0 528619		
12	Average			675	80.4375	54118.91	114.4689	82727.2	28608.3			
13	Highest			920	200.5	184460	172	149500	124900	9 834646		
14	Lowest			400	12.875	9656.25	44.25	17700	-42850	-0.70768		
15												

each arrowhead indicates a cell that is dependent on active cell

Sheet1 / Sheet2 / Sheet3

Ready

Start   Microsoft Excel - Bet...   2:10 PM

FIGURE 2-28

To change the active cell to the one at the other end of the blue line, double-click the blue line. This technique gives you a quick way to move from the active cell to one that provides data to the active cell. This is especially helpful in large worksheets.

If you click the Trace Precedents command a second time, Excel displays tracer arrows that show a second level of cells that are indirectly supplying data to the active cell. The same applies to the Trace Dependents command, only it shows the next level of cells that are dependent on the active cell.

Formatting the Worksheet

Although the worksheet contains the appropriate data, formulas, and functions, the text and numbers need to be formatted to improve their appearance and readability.

In Project 1, you used the AutoFormat command to format the majority of the worksheet. This section describes how to change the unformatted worksheet in Figure 2-29a to the formatted worksheet in Figure 2-29b using the Formatting toolbar and Format Cells command.

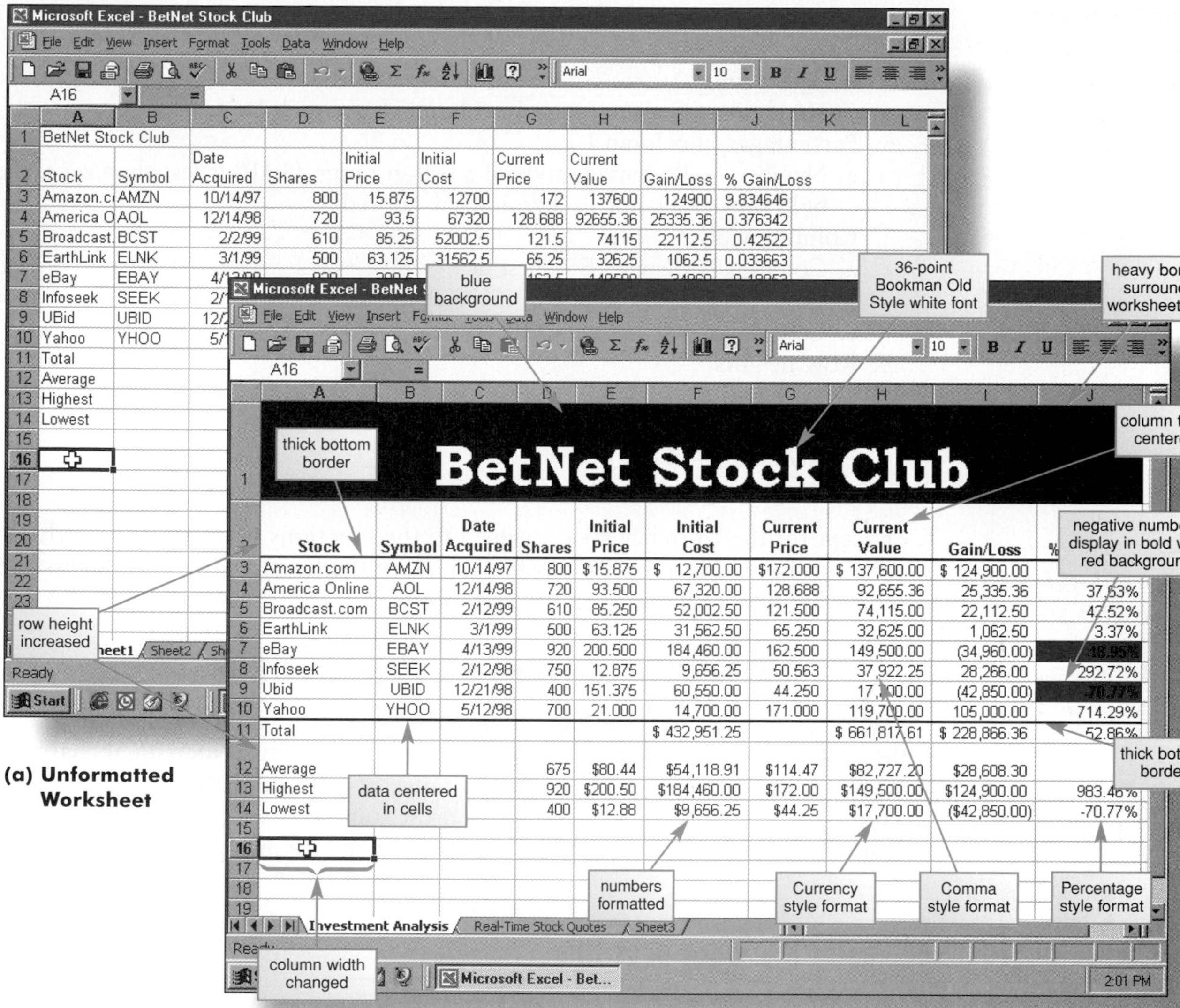

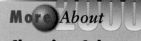

(a) Unformatted Worksheet

(b) Formatted Worksheet

FIGURE 2-29

The following outlines the type of formatting that is required in Project 2:

1. Worksheet title
   a. Font type — Bookman Old Style
   b. Font size — 36
   c. Alignment — center across columns A through J
   d. Background color (range A1:J1) — dark blue
   e. Font color — white
   f. Border — thick box border around range A1:J1
2. Column titles
   a. Font style — bold
   b. Alignment — center
   c. Border — thick bottom border on row 2
3. Data
   a. Alignment — center data in column B
   b. Numbers in top row (columns E through H in row 3) — Currency style
   c. Numbers below top row (rows 4 through 9) — Comma style
   d. Border — thick bottom border on row 10

More About 2000

Choosing Colors

Knowing how people perceive colors helps you emphasize parts of your worksheet. Warmer colors (red and orange) tend to reach toward the reader. Cooler colors (blue, green, and violet) tend to pull away from the reader. Bright colors jump out of a dark background and are easiest to see. White or yellow text on a dark blue, green, purple, or black background is ideal.

4. Total line
   a. Numbers — Currency style
5. Function lines
   a. Numbers — Currency style in columns E through I
6. Percentages in column J
   a. Numbers — Percentage style; if a cell in range J3:J10 is less than zero, then bold font and color background of cell red
7. Column widths
   a. Columns A through E — best fit
   b. Columns F, H through J — 12.00 characters
   c. Column G — 8.71 characters
8. Row heights
   a. Row 1 — 61.50 points
   b. Rows 2 — 36.00 points
   c. Row 12 —24.00 points
   d. Remaining rows — default

Except for the Currency style assigned to the functions in rows 12 through 14 and the conditional formatting in column J, all of the listed formats can be assigned to cells using the Formatting toolbar and mouse.

Changing the Font and Centering the Worksheet Title

When developing presentation-quality worksheets, different fonts often are used in the same worksheet. Excel allows you to change the font of individual characters in a cell or all the characters in a cell, in a range of cells, or in the entire worksheet. To emphasize the worksheet title in cell A1, the font type, size, and style are changed and the worksheet title is centered as described in the following steps.

Steps To Change the Font and Center the Worksheet Title

1 Click cell A1. Double-click the move handle on the left side of the Formatting toolbar to display it in its entirety. Click the Font box arrow on the Formatting toolbar and then point to Bookman Old Style (or Courier New if your system does not have Bookman Old Style).

The Font list displays with Bookman Old Style high-lighted (Figure 2-30).

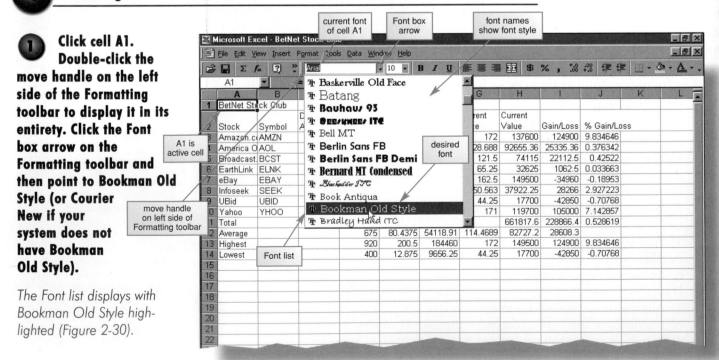

FIGURE 2-30

Step 2

Click Bookman Old Style (or Courier New). Click the Font Size box arrow on the Formatting toolbar and then point to 36.

The characters in cell A1 display using Bookman Old Style (or Courier New). The font size 36 is highlighted in the Font Size list (Figure 2-31).

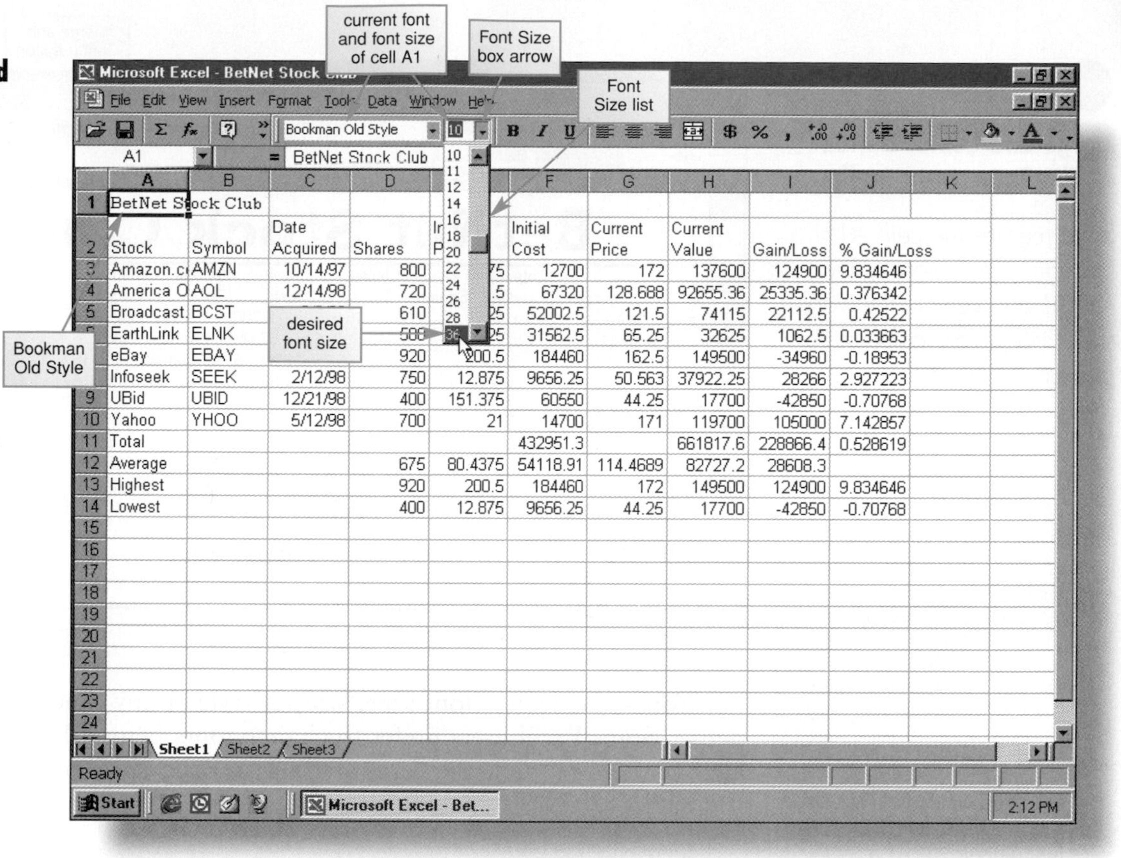

FIGURE 2-31

Step 3

Click 36. Click the Bold button on the Formatting toolbar.

The text in cell A1 displays in 36-point Bookman Old Style bold font. Excel automatically increases the height of row 1 so that the larger characters fit in the cells (Figure 2-32).

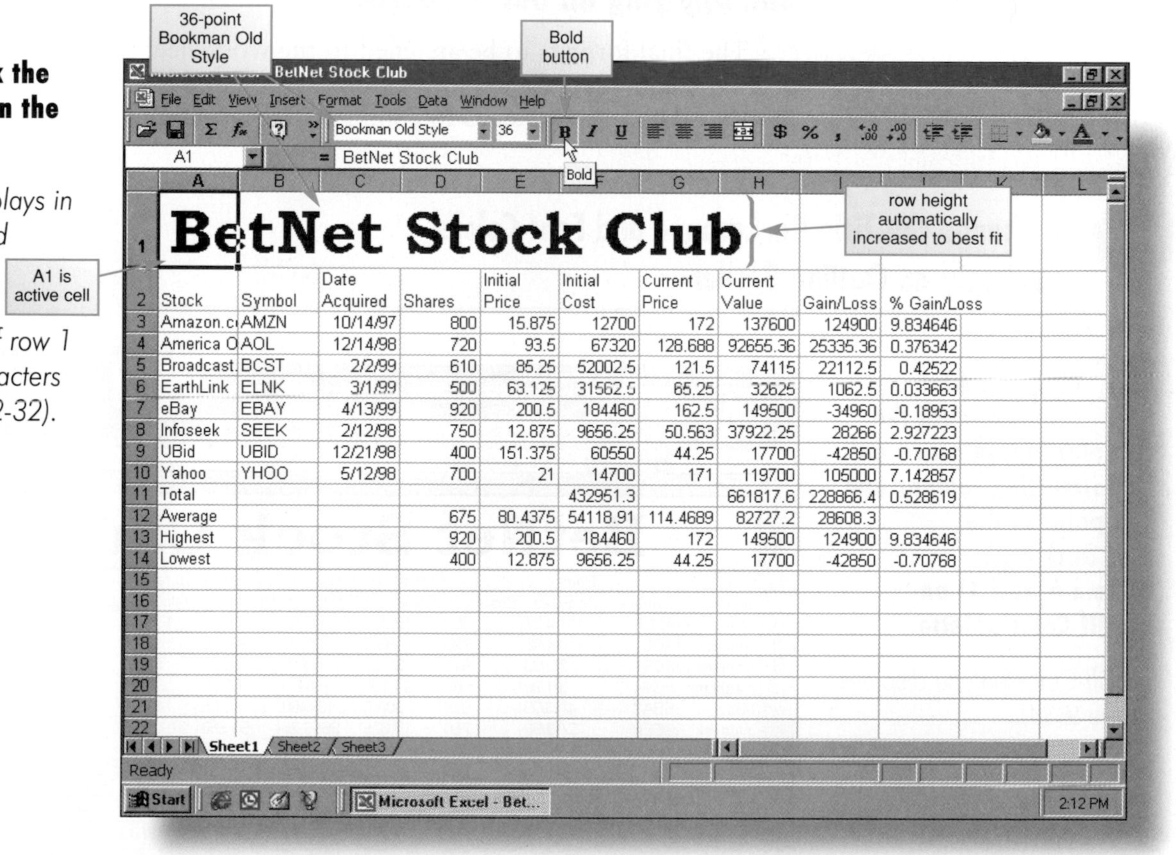

FIGURE 2-32

4 **Select the range A1:J1. Click the Merge and Center button on the Formatting toolbar.**

Excel merges the cells A1 through J1 to create a new cell A1 and centers the worksheet title across columns A through J (Figure 2-33).

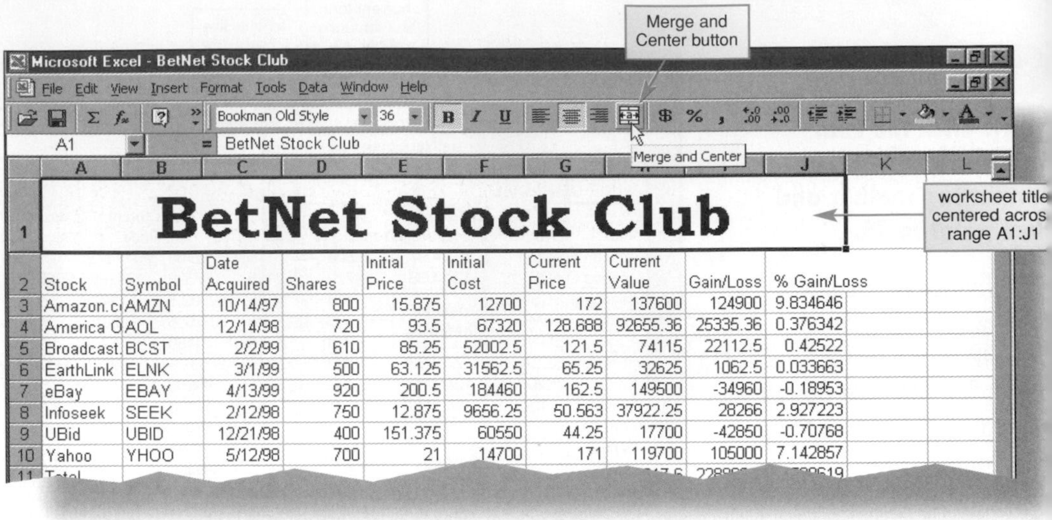

Merge and Center button

worksheet title centered across range A1:J1

FIGURE 2-33

You can change a font type, size, or style at any time while the worksheet is active. Some Excel users prefer to change fonts before they enter any data. Others change the font while they are building the worksheet or after they have entered all the data.

Changing the Worksheet Title Background and Font Colors and Applying an Outline Border

The final formats to be assigned to the worksheet title are the dark blue background color, white font color, and thick box border (Figure 2-29b on page E 2.27). Perform the following steps to complete the formatting of the worksheet title.

To Change the Title Background and Font Colors and Apply an Outline Border

1 **With cell A1 selected, click the Fill Color button arrow on the Formatting toolbar and then point to the color Dark Blue (column 6, row 1) on the Fill Color palette.**

The Fill Color palette displays (Figure 2-34).

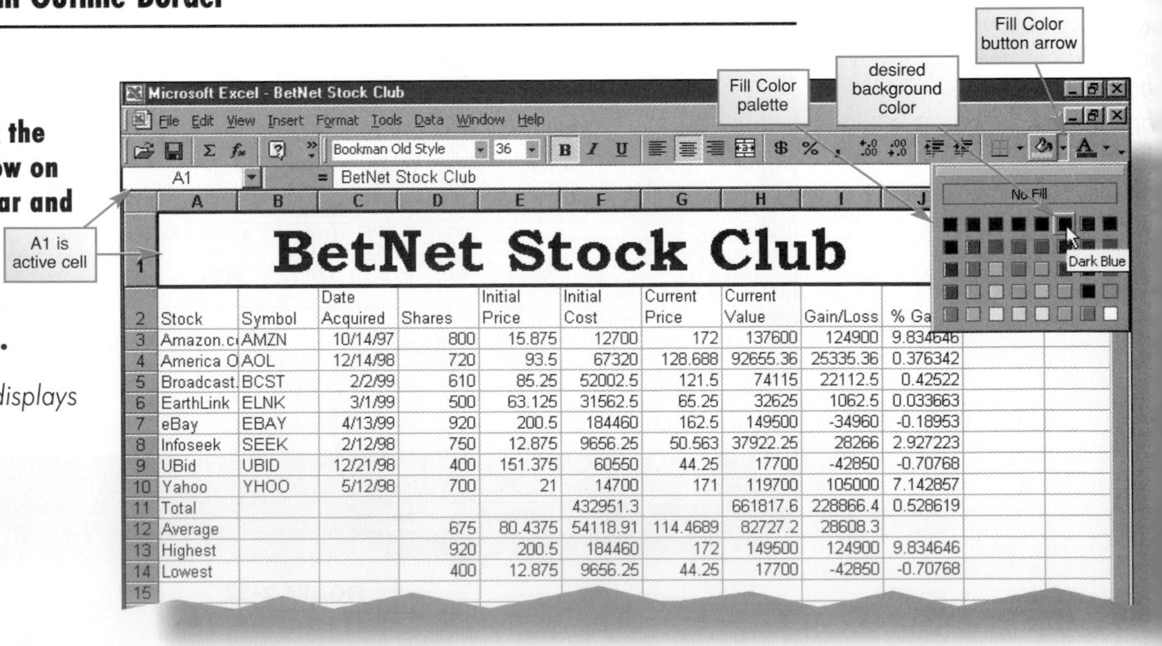

Fill Color button arrow

desired background color

Fill Color palette

A1 is active cell

No Fill

Dark Blue

FIGURE 2-34

2 Click the color Dark Blue. Click the Font Color button arrow on the Formatting toolbar. Point to the color White (column 8, row 5) on the Font Color palette.

The background color of cell A1 changes from white to dark blue. The Font Color palette displays (Figure 2-35).

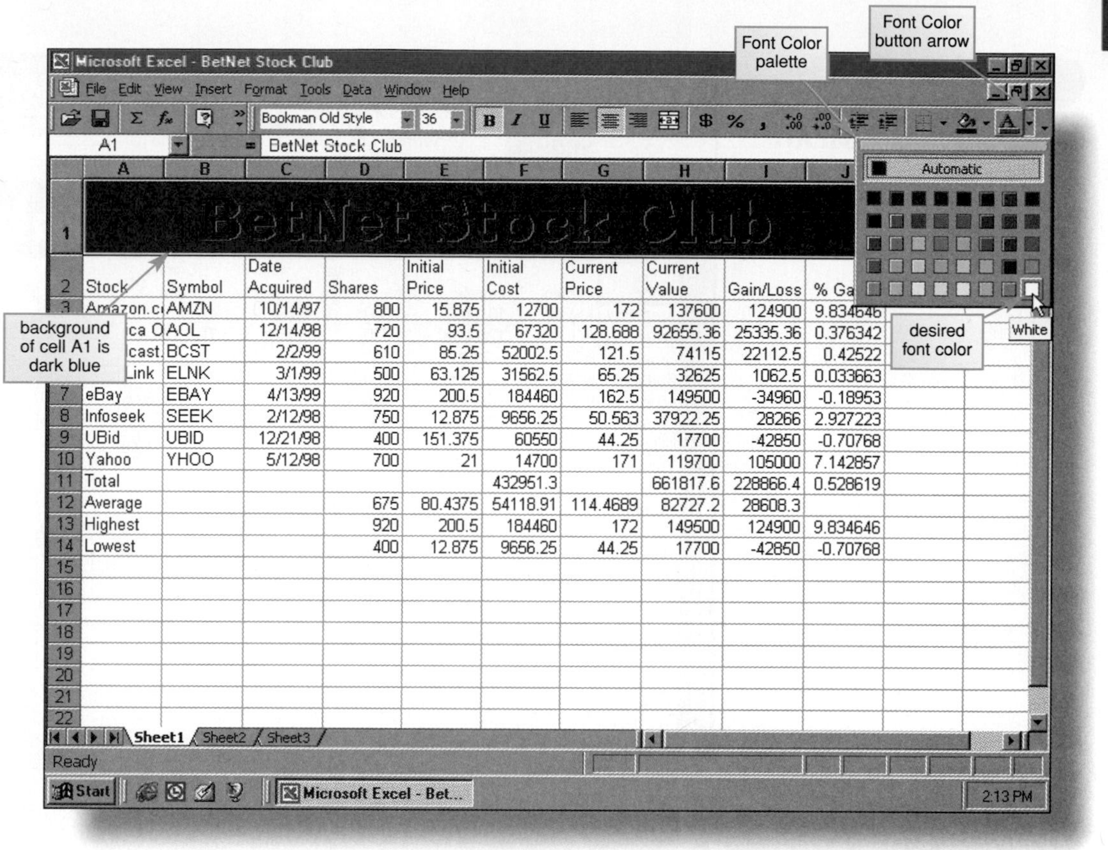

FIGURE 2-35

3 Click the color White. Click the Borders button arrow on the Formatting toolbar and then point to the Thick Box Border button (column 4, row 3) on the Borders palette.

The font in the worksheet title changes from black to white. The Borders palette displays (Figure 2-36).

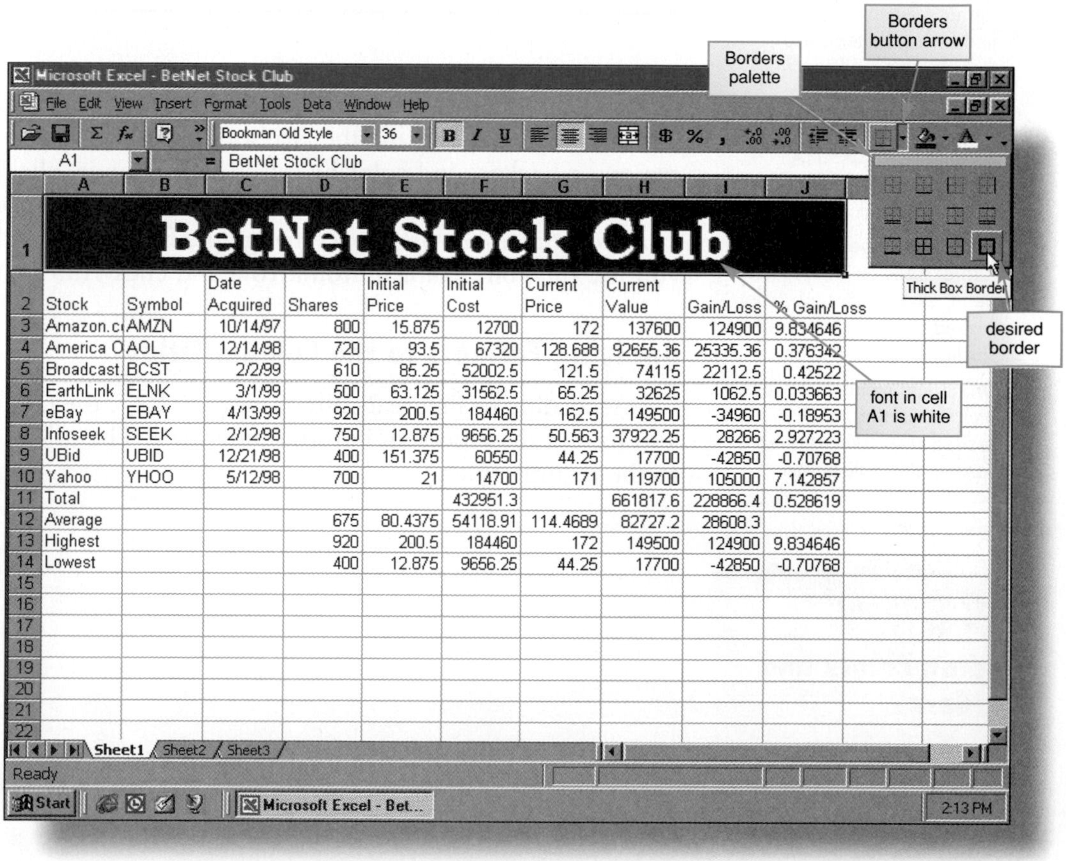

FIGURE 2-36

4 Click the Thick Box Border button. Click cell A2 to deselect cell A1.

Excel displays a thick box border around cell A1 (Figure 2-37).

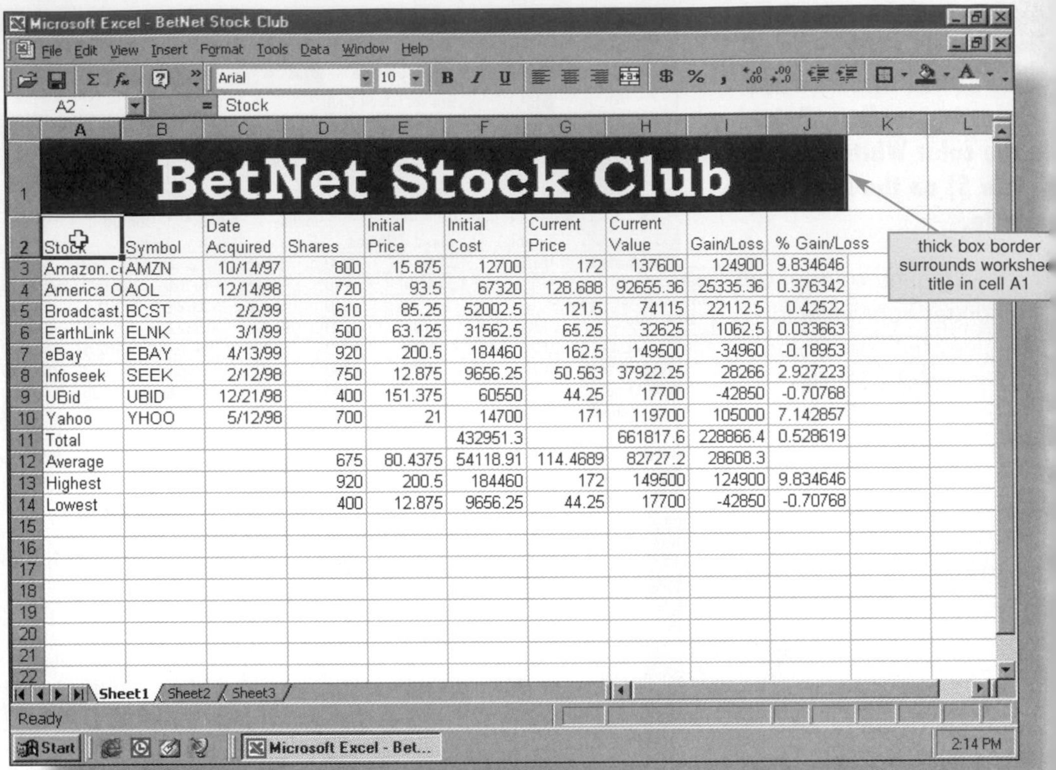

	A	B	C	D	E	F	G	H	I	J	K	L
1					BetNet Stock Club							
2	Stock	Symbol	Date Acquired	Shares	Initial Price	Initial Cost	Current Price	Current Value	Gain/Loss	% Gain/Loss		
3	Amazon.c	AMZN	10/14/97	800	15.875	12700	172	137600	124900	9.834646		
4	America O	AOL	12/14/98	720	93.5	67320	128.688	92655.36	25335.36	0.376342		
5	Broadcast.	BCST	2/2/99	610	85.25	52002.5	121.5	74115	22112.5	0.42522		
6	EarthLink	ELNK	3/1/99	500	63.125	31562.5	65.25	32625	1062.5	0.033663		
7	eBay	EBAY	4/13/99	920	200.5	184460	162.5	149500	-34960	-0.18953		
8	Infoseek	SEEK	2/12/98	750	12.875	9656.25	50.563	37922.25	28266	2.927223		
9	UBid	UBID	12/21/98	400	151.375	60550	44.25	17700	-42850	-0.70768		
10	Yahoo	YHOO	5/12/98	700	21	14700	171	119700	105000	7.142857		
11	Total					432951.3		661817.6	228866.4	0.528619		
12	Average			675	80.4375	54118.91	114.4689	82727.2	28608.3			
13	Highest			920	200.5	184460	172	149500	124900	9.834646		
14	Lowest			400	12.875	9656.25	44.25	17700	-42850	-0.70768		

thick box border surrounds workshee title in cell A1

FIGURE 2-37

You can remove borders, such as the thick box border around cell A1, by selecting the range and clicking the No Border button on the Borders palette. You can remove a background color by selecting the range, clicking the Fill Color button arrow on the Formatting toolbar, and clicking No Fill on the Fill Color palette. The same technique allows you to change the font color back to Excel's default, except you use the Font Color button arrow and click Automatic.

Applying Formats to the Column Titles

According to Figure 2-29b on page E 2.27, the column titles are bold, centered, and have a thick bottom border (underline). The following steps assign these formats to the column titles.

 **To Bold, Center, and Underline the Column Titles**

1 Select the range A2:J2. Click the Bold button on the Formatting toolbar. Click the Center button on the Formatting toolbar. Click the Borders button arrow on the Formatting toolbar and then point to the Thick Bottom Border button (column 2, row 2) on the Borders palette.

The column titles in row 2 are bold and centered. The Borders palette displays (Figure 2-38).

2 Click the Thick Bottom Border button.

Excel adds a thick bottom border to the range A2:J2.

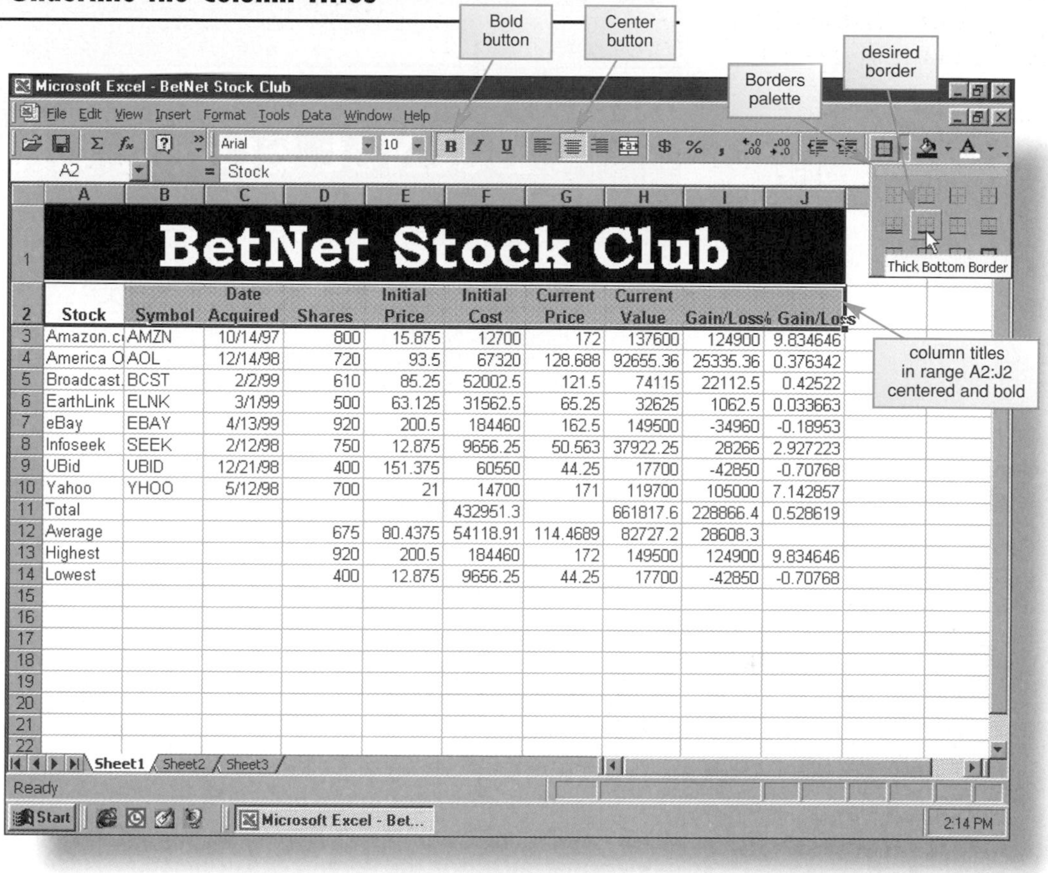

FIGURE 2-38

You can align the contents of cells in several different ways. Left alignment, center alignment, and right alignment are the more frequently used alignments. In fact, these three alignments are used so often that Excel has Left Align, Center, and Right Align buttons on the Formatting toolbar. In addition to aligning the contents of a cell horizontally, you also can align the contents of a cell vertically. You even can rotate the contents of a cell to various angles. For more information on alignment, on the Format menu click Cells and then click the Alignment tab.

Centering the Stock Symbols and Formatting the Numbers in the Worksheet

With the column titles formatted, the next step is to center the stock symbols in column B and format the numbers. If a cell entry is short, such as the stock symbols in column B, centering the entries within their respective columns improves the appearance of the worksheet. The following steps center the data in cells B3 to B10.

TO CENTER DATA IN CELLS

1 Select the range B3:B10. Click the Center button on the Formatting toolbar.

The stock symbols in column B are centered (Figure 2-39 on the next page).

Other Ways

1. Right-click cell, click Format Cells on shortcut menu, click Alignment tab, click Center in Horizontal list, click Font tab, click Bold in Font style list, click Border tab, click desired border, click OK button

2. On Format menu click Cells, click Alignment tab, click Center in Horizontal list, click Font tab, click Bold in Font style list, click Border tab, click desired border, click OK button

3. Press CTRL+1, click Alignment tab, click Center in Horizontal list, click Font tab, click Bold in Font style list, click Border tab, click desired border, click OK button

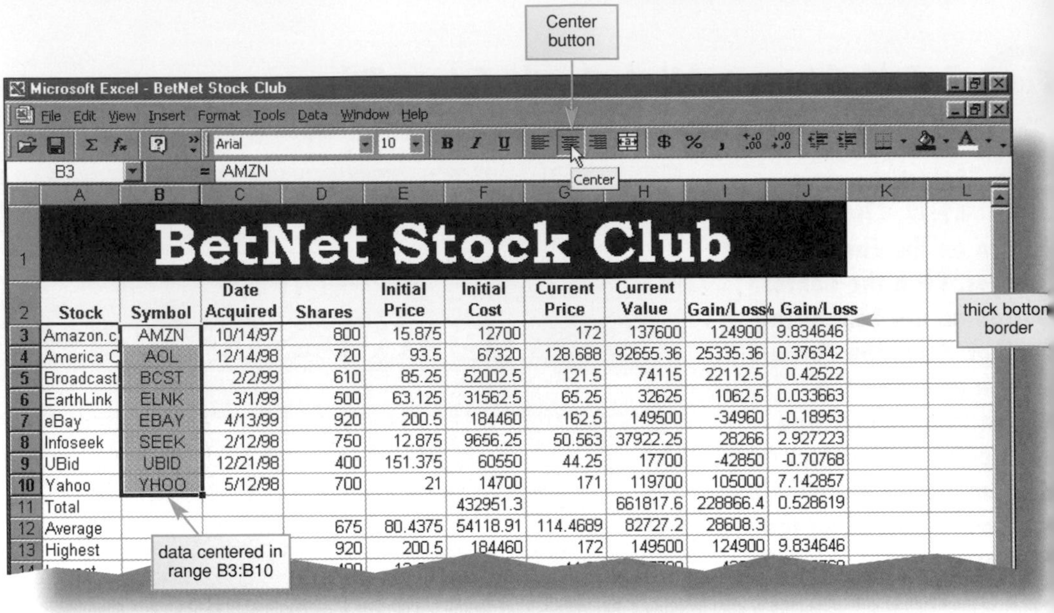

Center
button

Microsoft Excel - BetNet Stock Club

File Edit View Insert Format Tools Data Window Help

Arial   10   B I U   ≡ ≡ ≡ ⊞ $ % , ‰ ‰ ⊯ ⊯   ⊞ ・ ∂ ・ A ・

Center

B3   =   AMZN

BetNet Stock Club

	Stock	Symbol	Date Acquired	Shares	Initial Price	Initial Cost	Current Price	Current Value	Gain/Loss%	Gain/Loss
3	Amazon.c	AMZN	10/14/97	800	15.875	12700	172	137600	124900	9.834646
4	America C	AOL	12/14/98	720	93.5	67320	128.688	92655.36	25335.36	0.376342
5	Broadcast	BCST	2/2/99	610	85.25	52002.5	121.5	74115	22112.5	0.42522
6	EarthLink	ELNK	3/1/99	500	63.125	31562.5	65.25	32625	1062.5	0.033663
7	eBay	EBAY	4/13/99	920	200.5	184460	162.5	149500	-34960	-0.18953
8	Infoseek	SEEK	2/12/98	750	12.875	9656.25	50.563	37922.25	28266	2.927223
9	UBid	UBID	12/21/98	400	151.375	60550	44.25	17700	-42850	-0.70768
10	Yahoo	YHOO	5/12/98	700	21	14700	171	119700	105000	7.142857
11	Total					432951.3		661817.6	228866.4	0.528619
12	Average			675	80.4375	54118.91	114.4689	82727.2	28608.3	
13	Highest			920	200.5	184460	172	149500	124900	9.834646

thick bottom border

data centered in range B3:B10

FIGURE 2-39

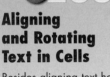

More About 2000

Aligning and Rotating Text in Cells

Besides aligning text horizontally in a cell, you can align text vertically (top, center, bottom, or justify). You can also rotate text. To align vertically or rotate the text, click Format Cells on the shortcut menu, click the Alignment tab, and then select the type of alignment you want.

Rather than selecting the range B3:B10 in the previous step, you could have clicked the column B heading immediately above cell B1, and then clicked the Center button on the Formatting toolbar. In this case, all cells in column B down to cell B65536 would have been assigned center alignment.

When using Excel, you can use the buttons on the Formatting toolbar to format numbers as dollar amounts, whole numbers with comma placement, and percentages. Customized numeric formats also can be assigned using the **Cells command** on the Format menu or the **Format Cells command** on the shortcut menu.

As shown in Figure 2-29b on page E 2.27, the worksheet is formatted to resemble an accounting report. For example, in columns E through I, the first row of numbers (row 3), the totals (row 11), and the rows below the totals (rows 13 and 14) display with dollar signs, while the remaining numbers (rows 4 through 10) in these columns do not. To display a dollar sign in a number, you should use the Currency style format.

The **Currency style format** displays a dollar sign to the left of the number, inserts a comma every three positions to the left of the decimal point, and displays numbers to the nearest cent (hundredths place). The **Currency Style button** on the Formatting toolbar will assign the desired Currency style format. When you use the Currency Style button, Excel displays a **fixed dollar sign** to the far left in the cell, often with spaces between it and the first digit. To assign a **floating dollar sign** that displays immediately to the left of the first digit with no spaces, you must use the Cells command on the Format menu or the Format Cells command on the shortcut menu. The project specifications call for a fixed dollar sign to be assigned to the numbers in columns E through I in rows 3 and 11, and a floating dollar sign to be assigned to the monetary amounts in columns E through I in rows 12 through 14.

To display monetary amounts with commas and no dollar signs, you will want to use the Comma style format. The **Comma style format** inserts a comma every three positions to the left of the decimal point and displays numbers to the nearest hundredths (cents).

The remainder of this section describes how to format the numbers as shown in Figure 2-29b on page E 2.27.

Formatting Numbers Using the Formatting Toolbar

The following steps show how to assign formats using the Currency Style button and the Comma Style button on the Formatting toolbar.

To Apply a Currency Style Format and Comma Style Format Using the Formatting Toolbar

1 Select the range E3:I3. While holding down the CTRL key, select the nonadjacent range F11:I11. Point to the Currency Style button on the Formatting toolbar.

The nonadjacent ranges display as shown in Figure 2-40.

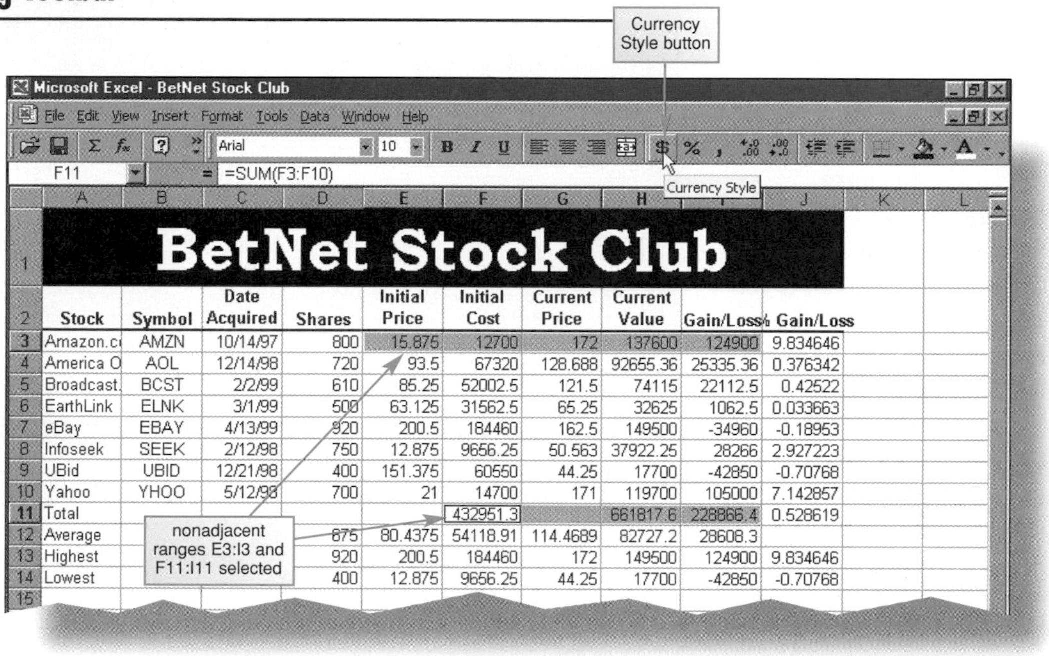

Currency Style button

	Stock	Symbol	Date Acquired	Shares	Initial Price	Initial Cost	Current Price	Current Value	Gain/Loss	% Gain/Loss
3	Amazon.c	AMZN	10/14/97	800	15.875	12700	172	137600	124900	9.834646
4	America O	AOL	12/14/98	720	93.5	67320	128.688	92655.36	25335.36	0.376342
5	Broadcast.	BCST	2/2/99	610	85.25	52002.5	121.5	74115	22112.5	0.42522
6	EarthLink	ELNK	3/1/99	500	63.125	31562.5	65.25	32625	1062.5	0.033663
7	eBay	EBAY	4/13/99	920	200.5	184460	162.5	149500	-34960	-0.18953
8	Infoseek	SEEK	2/12/98	750	12.875	9656.25	50.563	37922.25	28266	2.927223
9	UBid	UBID	12/21/98	400	151.375	60550	44.25	17700	-42850	-0.70768
10	Yahoo	YHOO	5/12/98	700	21	14700	171	119700	105000	7.142857
11	Total				432951.3			661817.6	228866.4	0.528619
12	Average			875	80.4375	54118.91	114.4689	82727.2	28608.3	
13	Highest			920	200.5	184460	172	149500	124900	9.834646
14	Lowest			400	12.875	9656.25	44.25	17700	-42850	-0.70768

nonadjacent ranges E3:I3 and F11:I11 selected

FIGURE 2-40

2 Click the Currency Style button. Select the range E4:I10 and then point to the Comma Style button on the Formatting toolbar.

Excel automatically increases the width of columns F, H, and I to best fit, so the numbers assigned the Currency Style format will fit in the cells (Figure 2-41). The range E4:I10 is selected.

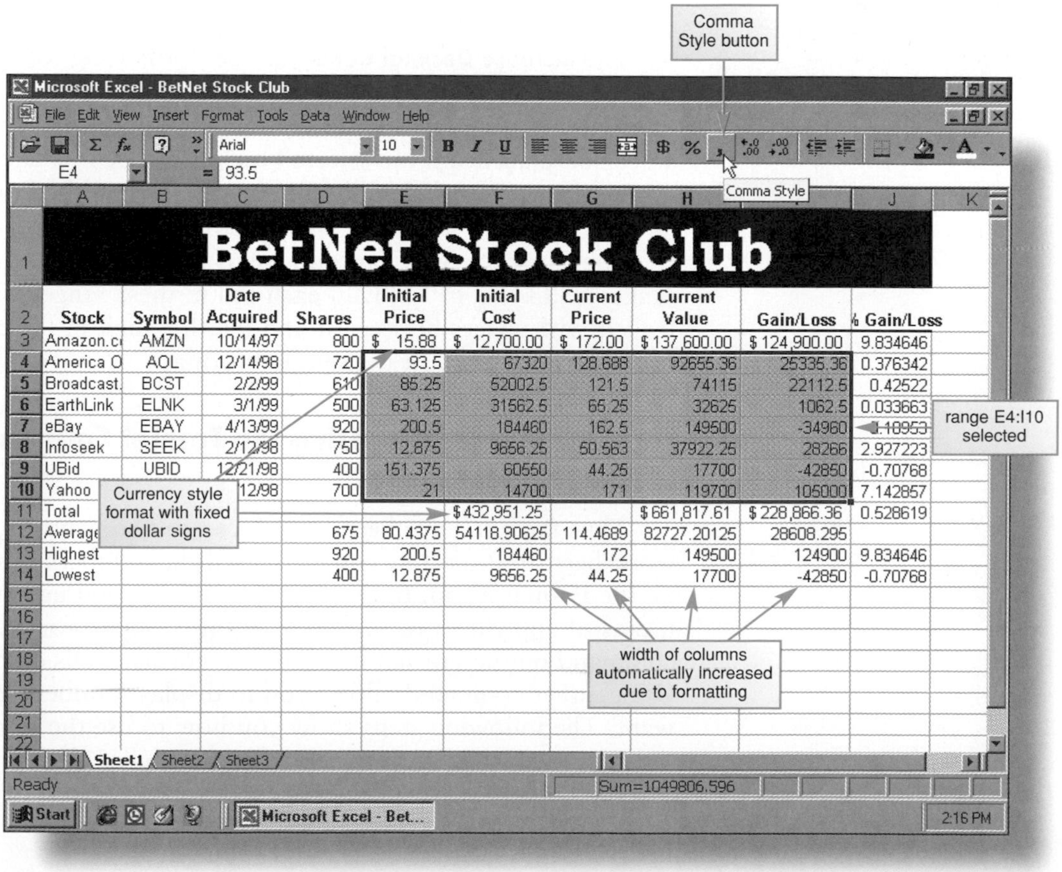

Comma Style button

	Stock	Symbol	Date Acquired	Shares	Initial Price	Initial Cost	Current Price	Current Value	Gain/Loss	% Gain/Loss
3	Amazon.c	AMZN	10/14/97	800	$ 15.88	$ 12,700.00	$ 172.00	$ 137,600.00	$ 124,900.00	9.834646
4	America O	AOL	12/14/98	720	93.5	67320	128.688	92655.36	25335.36	0.376342
5	Broadcast.	BCST	2/2/99	610	85.25	52002.5	121.5	74115	22112.5	0.42522
6	EarthLink	ELNK	3/1/99	500	63.125	31562.5	65.25	32625	1062.5	0.033663
7	eBay	EBAY	4/13/99	920	200.5	184460	162.5	149500	-34960	-0.18953
8	Infoseek	SEEK	2/12/98	750	12.875	9656.25	50.563	37922.25	28266	2.927223
9	UBid	UBID	12/21/98	400	151.375	60550	44.25	17700	-42850	-0.70768
10	Yahoo		12/98	700	21	14700	171	119700	105000	7.142857
11	Total				$ 432,951.25			$ 661,817.61	$ 228,866.36	0.528619
12	Average			675	80.4375	54118.90625	114.4689	82727.20125	28608.295	
13	Highest			920	200.5	184460	172	149500	124900	9.834646
14	Lowest			400	12.875	9656.25	44.25	17700	-42850	-0.70768

Currency style format with fixed dollar signs

range E4:I10 selected

width of columns automatically increased due to formatting

Sum=1049806.596

FIGURE 2-41

Click the Comma Style button. Select the range A10:J10 and then click the Borders button on the Formatting toolbar.

Excel assigns the Comma style format to the range E4:I10 and a thick bottom border to row 10.

 Click cell E3. Click the Increase Decimal button on the Formatting toolbar. Do the same to cell G3. Select the range E4:E10. Click the Increase Decimal button on the Formatting toolbar. Do the same to the range G4:G10. Click cell E12 to deselect the range G4:G10.

The initial prices and current prices display with three decimal positions (Figure 2-42).

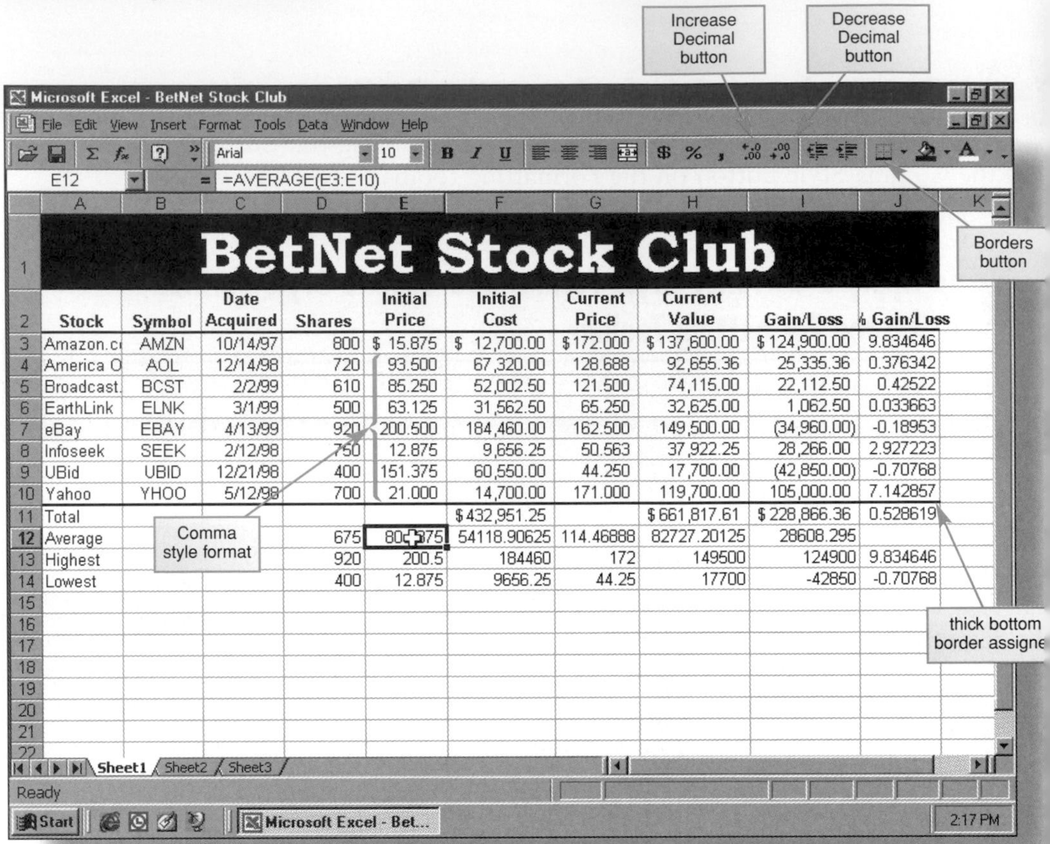

FIGURE 2-42

Other Ways

1. Right-click range, click Format Cells on shortcut menu, click Number tab, click Currency in Category list, click OK button
2. On Format menu click Cells, click Number tab, click Currency in Category list, click OK button

The **Increase Decimal button** on the Formatting toolbar is used to display additional decimal places in a cell. Each time you click the Increase Decimal button, Excel adds a decimal place to the selected cell. The **Decrease Decimal button** removes a decimal place from the selected cell each time it is clicked.

In Step 3, you clicked the Borders button on the Formatting toolbar because the Borders button is set to the thick bottom border that was assigned earlier to row 2.

The Currency Style button assigns a fixed dollar sign to the numbers in the ranges E3:I3 and F11:I11. In each cell in these ranges, the dollar sign displays to the far left with spaces between it and the first digit in the cell. Excel automatically rounds a number to fit the selected format.

Formatting Numbers Using the Format Cells Command on the Shortcut Menu

Thus far, you have been introduced to two ways of formatting numbers in a worksheet. In Project 1, you formatted the numbers using the AutoFormat command on the Format menu. In the previous section, you used the Formatting toolbar as a means of applying a format style. A third way to format numbers is to use the Cells command on the Format menu or the Format Cells command on the shortcut menu. Using either command allows you to display numbers in almost any format you want. The following steps show you how to use the Format Cells command to apply the Currency style format with a floating dollar sign to the totals in the range E12:I14.

To Apply a Currency Style Format with a Floating Dollar Sign Using the Format Cells Command

1 Select the range E12:I14. Right-click the selected range. Point to Format Cells on the shortcut menu.

The shortcut menu displays (Figure 2-43).

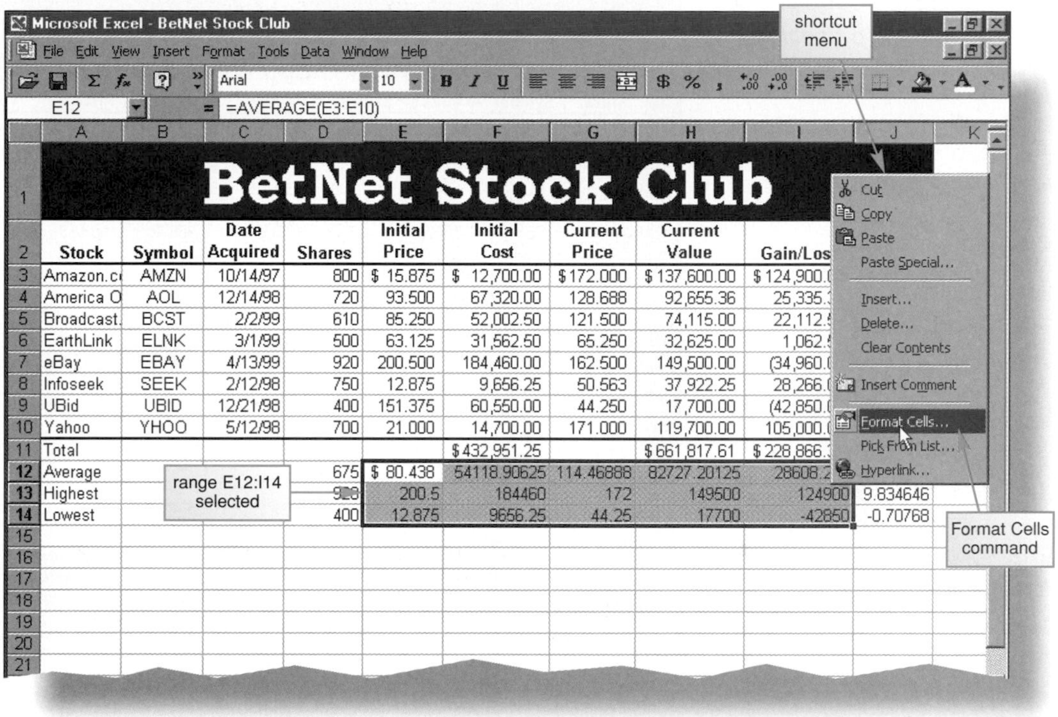

FIGURE 2-43

2 Click Format Cells. Click the Number tab in the Format Cells dialog box. Click Currency in the Category list, click the third style ($1,234.10) in the Negative numbers list, and then point to the OK button.

The Format Cells dialog box displays (Figure 2-44).

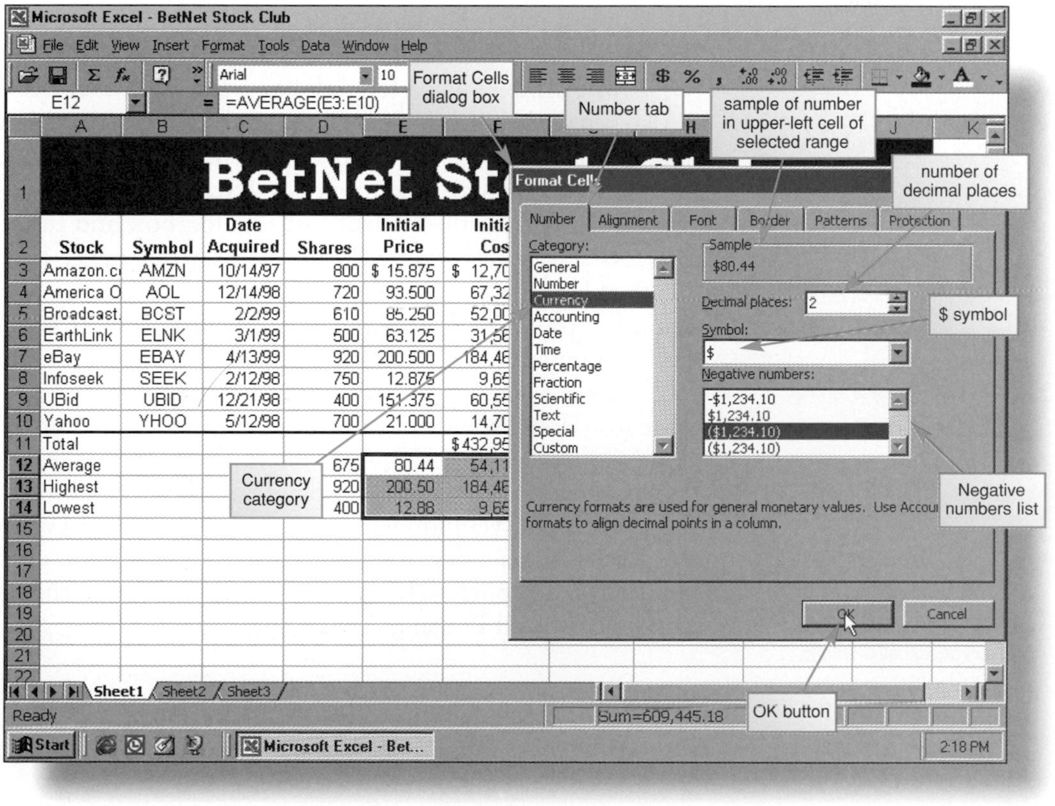

FIGURE 2-44

3 **Click the OK button.**

The worksheet displays with the totals in rows 12 through 14 assigned the Currency style format with a floating dollar sign (Figure 2-45).

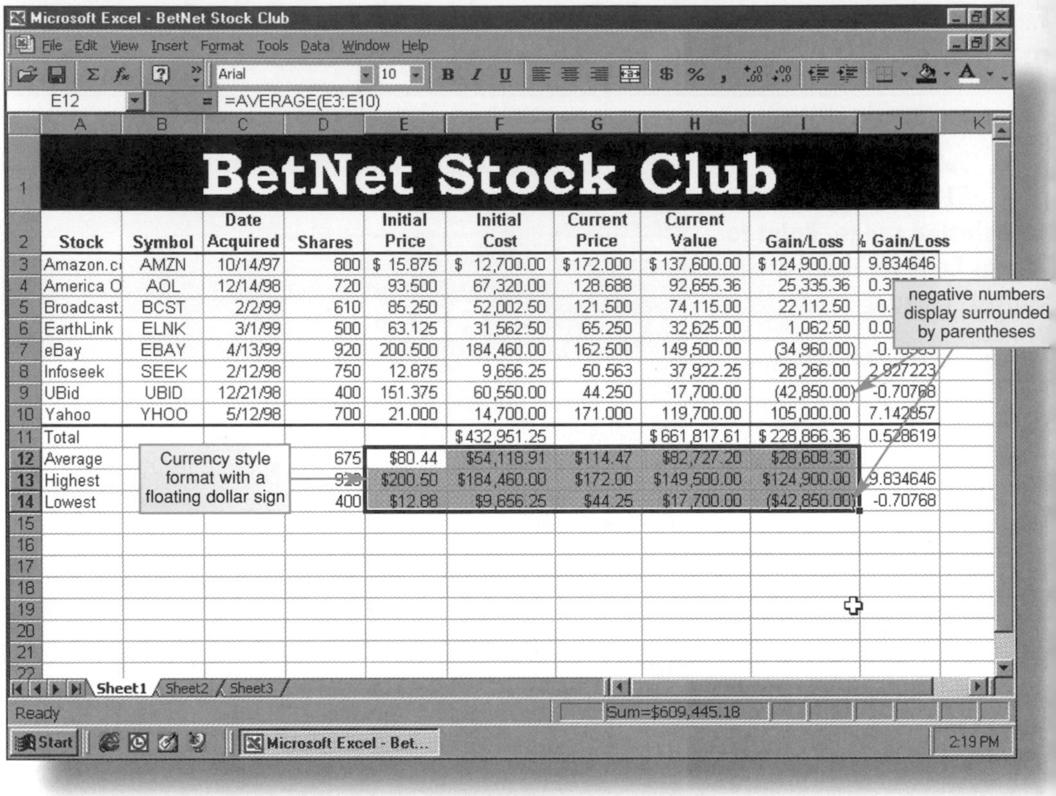

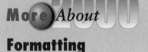

FIGURE 2-45

Other Ways

1. On Format menu click Cells, click Number tab, click Currency in Category list, select desired formats, click OK button
2. Press CTRL+SHIFT+DOLLAR SIGN

More About

Formatting Numbers as You Enter Them

You can format numbers when you enter them by entering a dollar sign ($), comma (,), or percent sign (%) as part of the number. For example, if you enter 1500, Excel displays 1500. If you enter $1500, however, Excel displays $1,500.

Recall that a floating dollar sign always displays immediately to the left of the first digit, and the fixed dollar sign always displays on the left side of the cell. Cell E3, for example, has a fixed dollar sign, while cell E12 has a floating dollar sign. Also recall that, while cells E3 and E12 both were assigned a Currency style format, the Currency style was assigned to cell E3 using the Currency Style button on the Formatting toolbar. The result is a fixed dollar sign. The Currency style was assigned to cell E12 using the Format Cells dialog box and the result is a floating dollar sign.

As shown in Figure 2-44 on the previous page, 12 categories of formats are available from which you can choose. Once you select a category, you can select the number of decimal places, whether or not a dollar sign should display, and how negative numbers should display.

Selecting the appropriate negative numbers format in Step 2 is important, because doing so adds a space to the right of the number (as do the Currency Style and Comma Style buttons). Some of the available negative number formats do not align the numbers in the worksheet on the decimal points.

The negative number format selected in the previous set of steps displays in cell I14, which has a negative entry. The third selection in the Negative numbers list box (Figure 2-44) purposely was chosen to agree with the negative number format assigned to cell I9 using the Comma Style button.

Formatting Numbers Using the Percent Style Button and Increase Decimal Button

The last entry in the worksheet that needs to be formatted is the percent gain/loss in column J. Currently, the numbers in column J display as a decimal fraction (9.834646 in cell J3). Follow these steps to change to the Percent style format with two decimal places.

Steps To Apply a Percent Style Format

1 Select the range J3:J14. Click the Percent Style button on the Formatting toolbar.

The numbers in column J display as a rounded whole percent.

2 Click the Increase Decimal button on the Formatting toolbar twice.

The numbers in column J display with two decimal places (Figure 2-46).

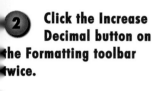

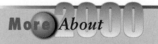

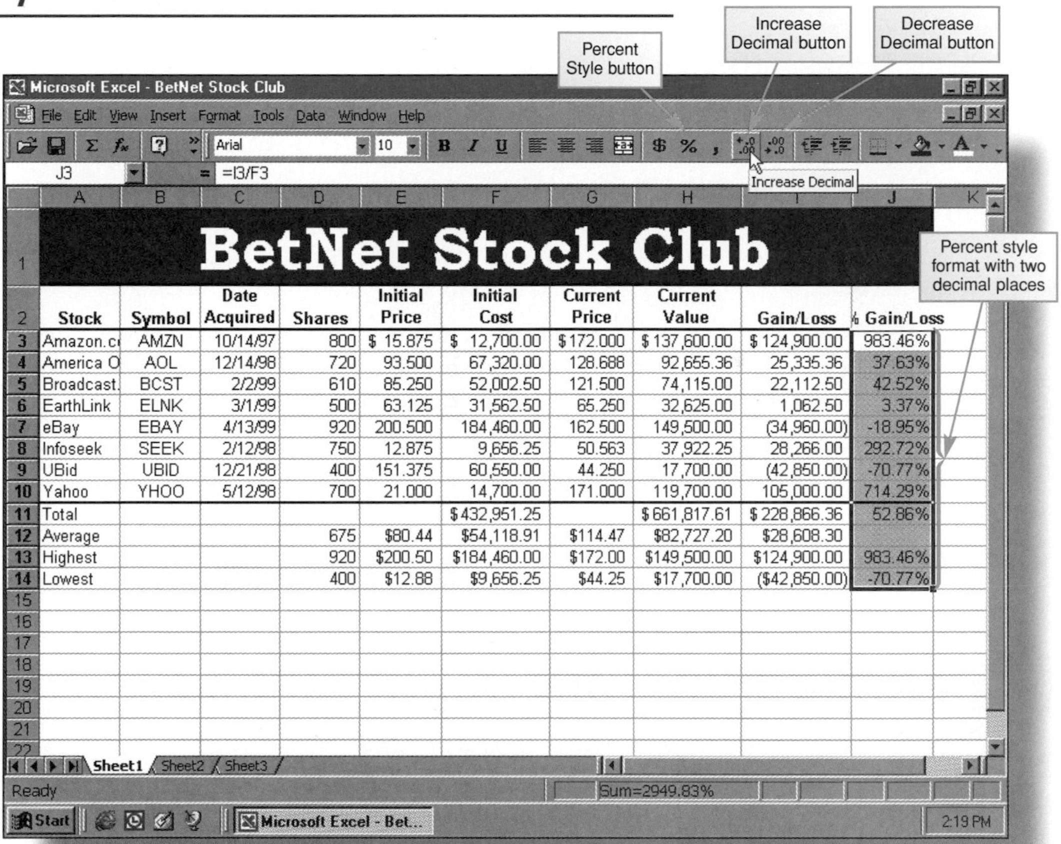

FIGURE 2-46

The **Percent Style button** on the Formatting toolbar is used to display a value determined by multiplying the cell entry by 100, rounding the result to the nearest percent, and adding a percent sign. For example, when cell J3 is formatted using the Increase Decimal button, the value 9.834646 displays as 983.46%. While they do not display, Excel does maintain all the decimal places for computational purposes. Thus, if cell J3 is used in a formula, the value used for computational purposes is 9.834646.

The last formatting requirement is to display the negative percents in column J in bold with a red background so they stand out. The **Conditional Formatting command** on the Format menu will be used to complete this task.

More About 2000

Rounding Numbers

When you instruct Excel to display a certain number of digits, it does maintain all the decimal places for computational purposes. For this reason, you may find a column sum to be off by a penny, because it is displaying data rounded to a specified number of digits, but it is using all the decimal places in the computation.

Conditional Formatting

Excel lets you apply formatting that appears only when the value in a cell meets conditions that you specify. This type of formatting is called **conditional formatting**. You can apply conditional formatting to a cell, a range of cells, the entire worksheet, or the entire workbook. Usually, you apply it to a range of cells that contains values you want to highlight if conditions warrant. For example, you can instruct Excel to bold and change the color of the background of a cell if the value in the cell meets a condition, such as being less than zero. For example, assume you assign the range J3:J10 the following condition:

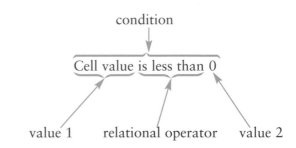

A **condition,** which is made up of two values and a relational operator, is true or false for each cell in the range. If the condition is true, then Excel applies the formatting. If the condition is false, then Excel suppresses the formatting. What makes conditional formatting so powerful is that the cell's appearance can change as you enter new values in the worksheet.

The following steps show how to assign conditional formatting to the range J3:J10. In this case, any cell value less than zero will cause the number in the cell to display in bold with a red background.

 To Apply Conditional Formatting

More About

Conditional Formatting

You can conditionally assign any format to a cell, a range of cells, the worksheet, or an entire workbook. If the value of the cell changes and no longer meets the specified condition, Excel temporarily suppresses the formats that highlight that condition.

1 **Select the range J3:J10. Click Format on the menu bar and then point to Conditional Formatting.**

The Format menu displays (Figure 2-47).

FIGURE 2-47

2 Click Conditional Formatting. If necessary, click the leftmost text box arrow and then click Cell Value Is. Click the middle text box arrow and then click less than. Type 0 in the rightmost text box. Point to the Format button.

The Conditional Formatting dialog box displays as shown in Figure 2-48.

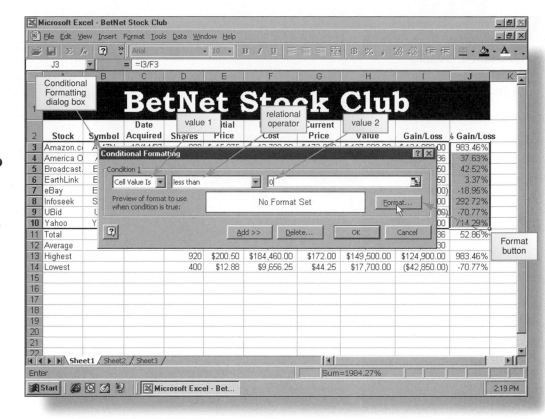

FIGURE 2-48

3 Click the Format button. When the Format Cells dialog box displays, click the Font tab and then click Bold in the font style list. Click the Patterns tab. Click the color red (column 1, row 3). Point to the OK button.

The Patterns sheet in the Format Cells dialog box displays as shown in Figure 2-49.

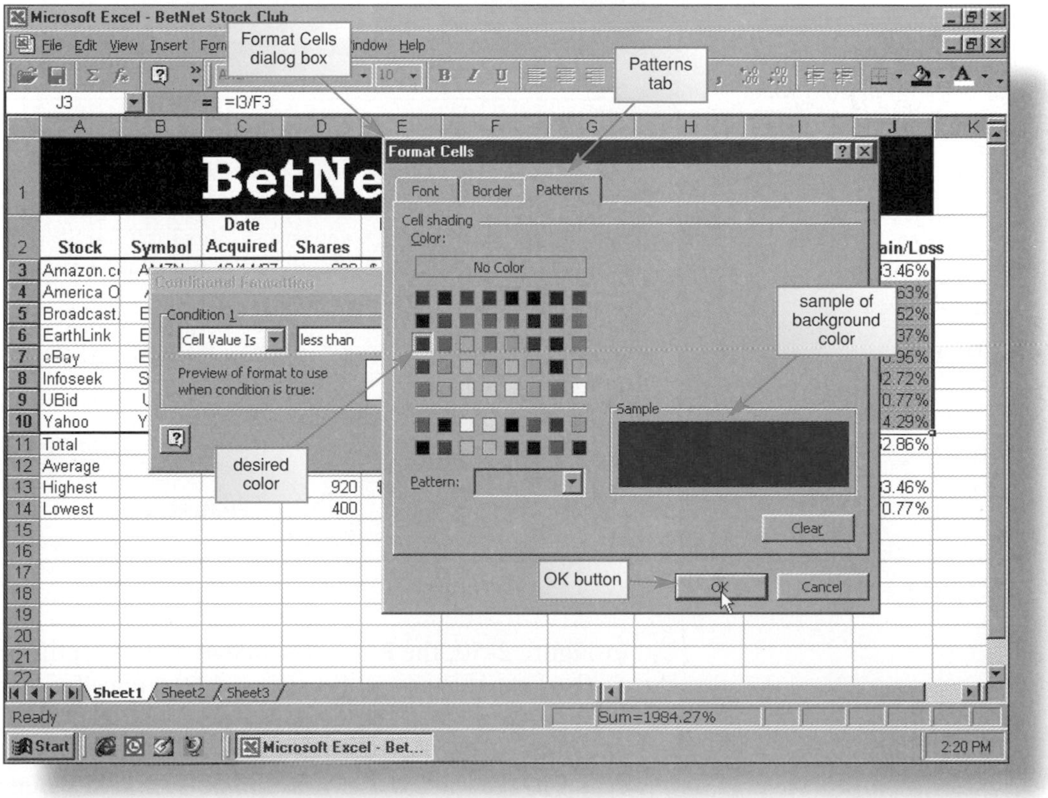

FIGURE 2-49

Click the OK button. When the Conditional Formatting dialog box displays, point to the OK button.

The Conditional Formatting dialog box displays as shown in Figure 2-50.

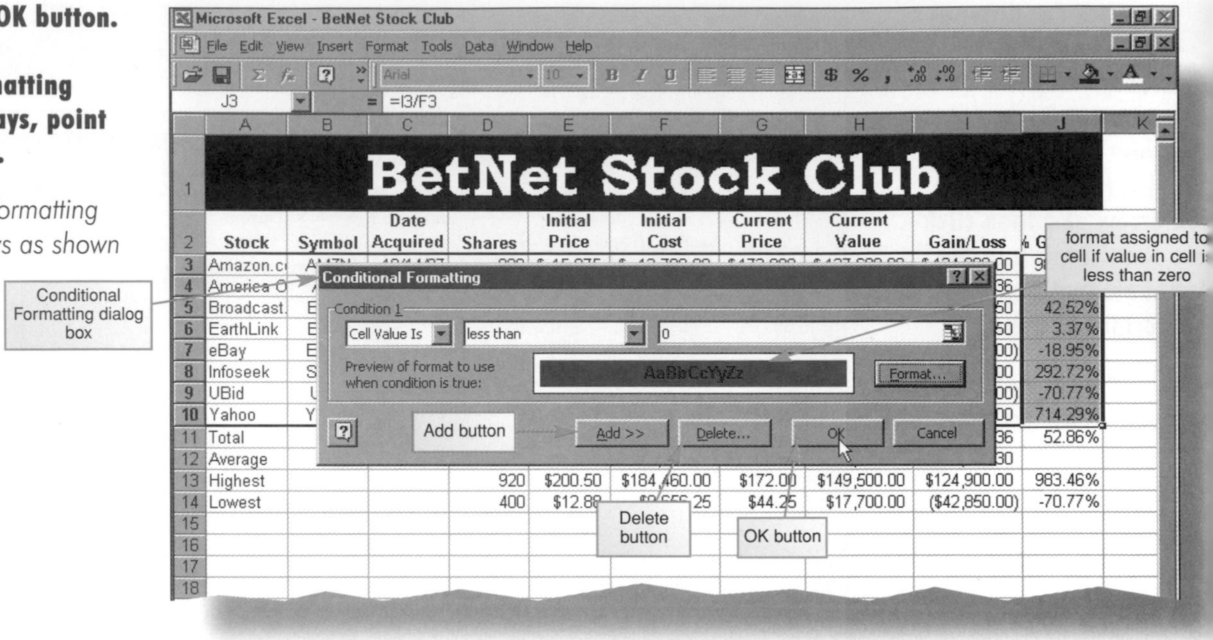

FIGURE 2-50

 Click the OK button. Click cell A16 to deselect the range J3:J10.

Excel assigns the conditional format to the range J3:J10. Any negative value in this range displays in bold with a red background (Figure 2-51).

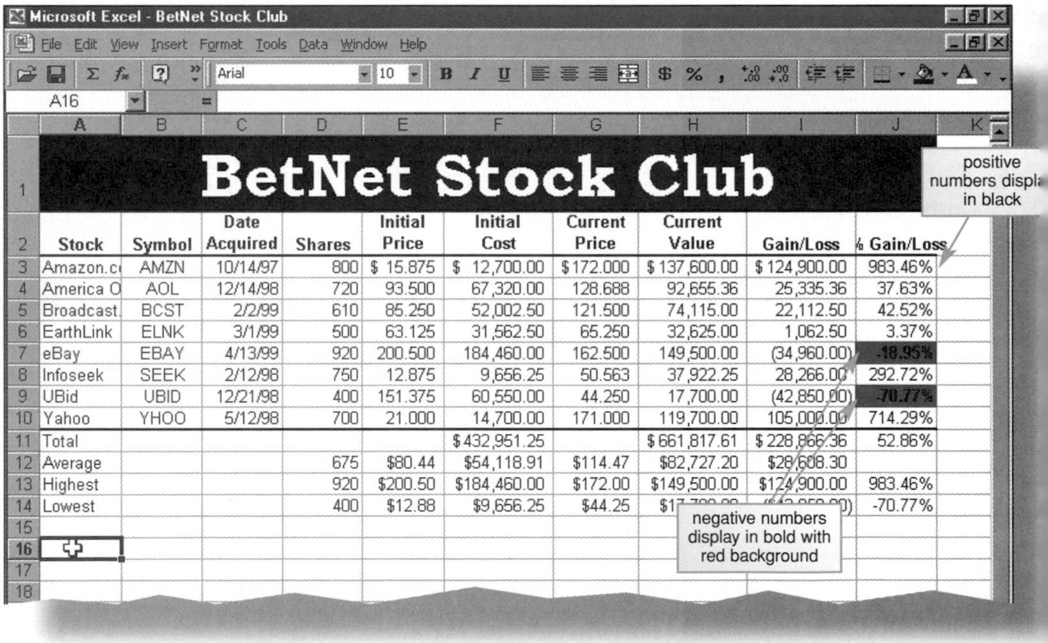

FIGURE 2-51

In Figure 2-50, the **Preview window** in the Conditional Formatting dialog box shows the format that will be assigned to any cells in the range J3:J10 that have a value less than zero. This preview allows you to modify the format before you click the OK button. The **Add button** in the Conditional Formatting dialog box allows you to add up to two additional conditions. The **Delete button** allows you to delete one or more active conditions.

The middle text box in the Conditional Formatting dialog box contains the relational operator. The eight different relational operators from which you can choose are summarized in Table 2-4

Table 2-4	Summary of Conditional Formatting Relational Operators
RELATIONAL OPERATOR	**DESCRIPTION**
Between	Cell value is between two numbers
Not between	Cell value is not between two numbers
Equal to	Cell value is equal to a number
Not equal to	Cell value is not equal to a number
Greater than	Cell value is greater than a number
Less than	Cell value is less than a number
Greater than or equal to	Cell value is greater than or equal to a number
Less than or equal to	Cell value is less than or equal to a number

Painting Formats

Painting is not an envious chore. In Excel, however, if you know how to paint, you can save yourself time and effort when formatting a worksheet. For example, if you see a cell that has the format you want to assign to another cell or range of cells, click the cell with the desired format, click the Format Painter button on the Standard toolbar, and then click the cell or drag through the cells you want to paint the format with.

With the number formatting complete, the next step is to change the column widths and row heights to make the worksheet easier to read.

Changing the Widths of Columns and Heights of Rows

When Excel starts and the blank worksheet displays on the screen, all of the columns have a default width of 8.43 characters, or 64 pixels. A **character** is defined as a letter, number, symbol, or punctuation mark in 10-point Arial font, the default font used by Excel. An average of 8.43 characters in this font will fit in a cell. Another measure is **pixels**, which is short for picture element. A pixel is a dot on the screen that contains a color. The size of the dot is based on your screen's resolution. At a common resolution of 800 × 600, 800 pixels display across the screen and 600 pixels display down the screen for a total of 480,000 pixels. It is these 480,000 pixels that form the font and other items you see on the screen.

The default row height in a blank worksheet is 12.75 points (or 17 pixels). Recall from Project 1 that a point is equal to 1/72 of an inch. Thus, 12.75 points is equal to about one-sixth of an inch. You can change the width of the columns or height of the rows at any time to make the worksheet easier to read or to ensure that an entry displays properly in a cell.

Changing the Widths of Columns

When changing the column width, you can set the width manually or you can instruct Excel to size the column to best fit. **Best fit** means that the width of the column will be increased or decreased so the widest entry will fit in the column. When the format you assign to a cell causes the entry to exceed the width of a column, Excel automatically changes the column width to best fit. This happened earlier when the Currency style format was used (Figure 2-41 on page E 2.35). If you do not assign a cell in a column a format, the width will remain 8.43 characters as is the case in columns A through D. To set a column width to best fit, double-click the right boundary of the column heading above row 1.

Sometimes, you may prefer more or less white space in a column than best fit provides. Excel thus allows you to change column widths manually. The following changes will be made to the column widths: columns A through E to best fit; column F to 12.00 characters, column G to 8.71 characters; and columns H through J to 2.00 characters.

Best Fit

Although Excel automatically increases the width of a column or the height of a row when you assign a format to a cell, it will not increase the column width or row height when a cell contains a formula and you change the value of a cell that is referenced in the formula. For example, if you change the number of shares in cell D3 from 800 to 10,0000, Excel will recalculate the formulas and display number signs (#) for the initial cost and gain/lost because the results of the formulas have more digits than can fit in the cell. You can fix the problem by double-clicking the right boundary of the column heading to change to best fit.

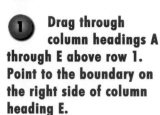

To Change the Widths of Columns

1 **Drag through column headings A through E above row 1. Point to the boundary on the right side of column heading E.**

The mouse pointer becomes a split double arrow (Figure 2-52).

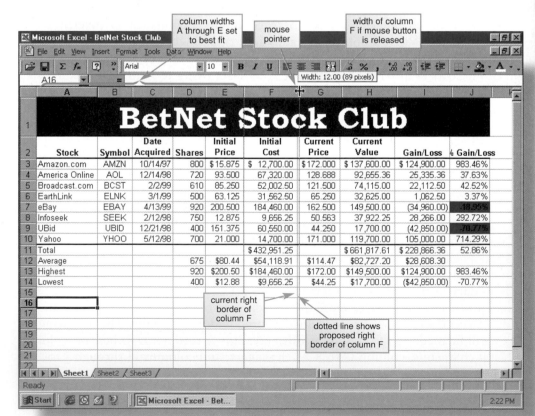

FIGURE 2-52

2 **Double-click the right boundary of column heading E. Click cell A16 to deselect columns A through E. Point to the boundary on the right side of the column F heading above row 1. Drag to the left until the ScreenTip, Width: 12.00 (89 pixels), displays.**

A dotted line shows the proposed right border of column F (Figure 2-53).

FIGURE 2-53

3 Release the mouse button. Point to the boundary on the right side of the column G heading above row 1. Drag to the right until the ScreenTip, Width: 8.71 (66 pixels), displays.

A dotted line shows the proposed right border of column G (Figure 2-54).

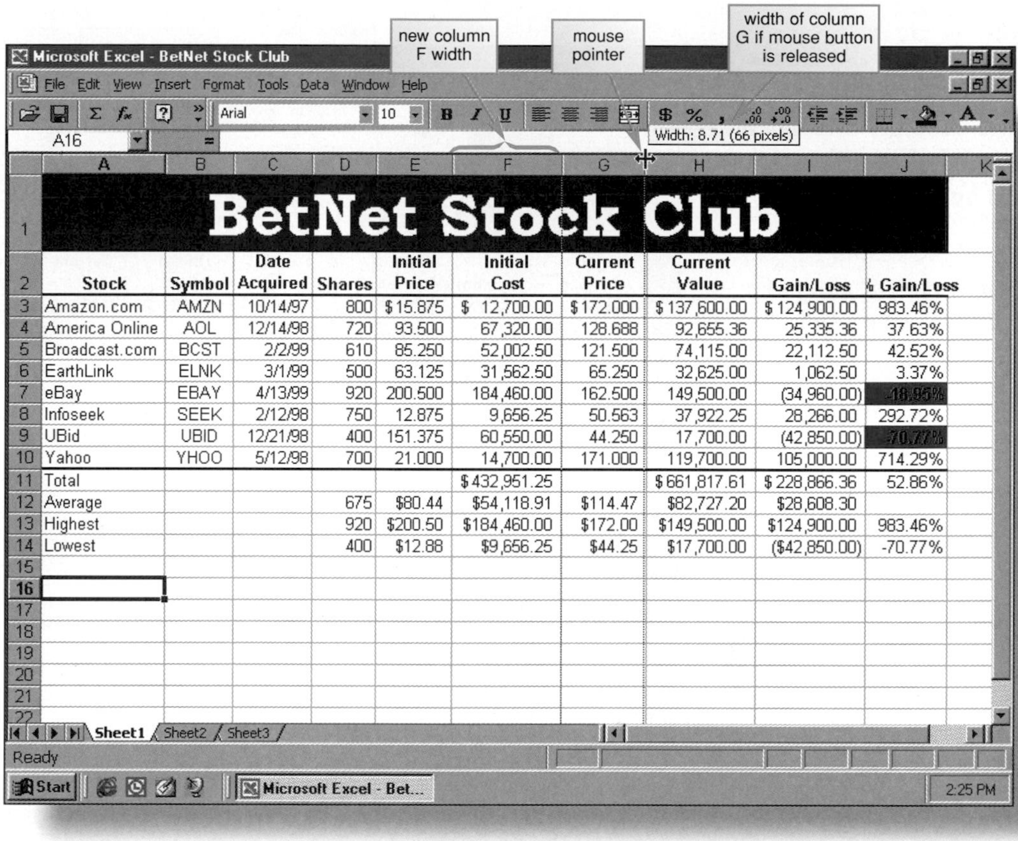

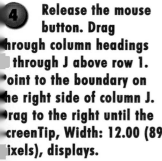

new column F width

mouse pointer

width of column G if mouse button is released

Width: 8.71 (66 pixels)

FIGURE 2-54

4 Release the mouse button. Drag through column headings H through J above row 1. Point to the boundary on the right side of column J. Drag to the right until the ScreenTip, Width: 12.00 (89 pixels), displays.

A dotted line shows the proposed right border of columns H through J (Figure 2-55).

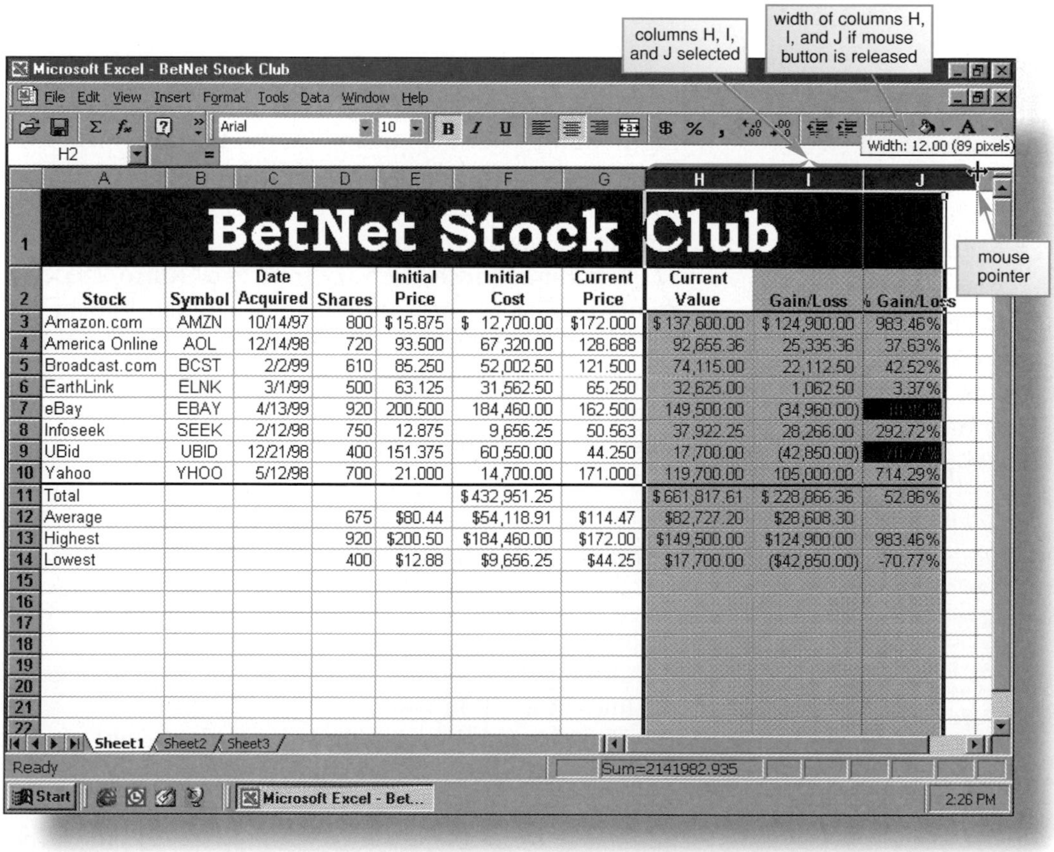

columns H, I, and J selected

width of columns H, I, and J if mouse button is released

Width: 12.00 (89 pixels)

mouse pointer

Sum=2141982.935

FIGURE 2-55

5 Release the mouse button. Click cell A16 to deselect columns H through J. Click File on the menu bar and then click Save.

The worksheet displays with the new columns widths (Figure 2-56).

width of columns A through E set to best fit

width of column F set to 12.00

width of column G set to 8.71

width of columns H through J set to 12.00

BetNet Stock Club

	Stock	Symbol	Date Acquired	Shares	Initial Price	Initial Cost	Current Price	Current Value	Gain/Loss	% Gain/Loss
3	Amazon.com	AMZN	10/14/97	800	$15.875	$ 12,700.00	$172.000	$ 137,600.00	$ 124,900.00	983.46%
4	America Online	AOL	12/14/98	720	93.500	67,320.00	128.688	92,655.36	25,335.36	37.63%
5	Broadcast.com	BCST	2/2/99	610	85.250	52,002.50	121.500	74,115.00	22,112.50	42.52%
6	EarthLink	ELNK	3/1/99	500	63.125	31,562.50	65.250	32,625.00	1,062.50	3.37%
7	eBay	EBAY	4/13/99	920	200.500	184,460.00	162.500	149,500.00	(34,960.00)	-18.95%
8	Infoseek	SEEK	2/12/98	750	12.875	9,656.25	50.563	37,922.25	28,266.00	292.72%
9	UBid	UBID	12/21/98	400	151.375	60,550.00	44.250	17,700.00	(42,850.00)	-70.77%
10	Yahoo	YHOO	5/12/98	700	21.000	14,700.00	171.000	119,700.00	105,000.00	714.29%
11	Total					$432,951.25		$ 661,817.61	$ 228,866.36	52.86%
12	Average			675	$80.44	$54,118.91	$114.47	$82,727.20	$28,608.30	
13	Highest			920	$200.50	$184,460.00	$172.00	$149,500.00	$124,900.00	983.46%
14	Lowest			400	$12.88	$9,656.25	$44.25	$17,700.00	($42,850.00)	-70.77%

FIGURE 2-56

Other Ways

1. Right-click column heading, click Column Width, enter desired column width, click OK button
2. Select cell or range of cells, on Format menu click Column, click Width, enter desired column width, click OK button

Hidden Columns

It often gets frustrating trying to use the mouse to unhide a range of columns. An alternative is to unhide columns using the keyboard. First select the columns to the right and left of the hidden ones and then press CTRL+SHIFT+RIGHT PARENTHE-SIS. To use the keyboard to hide a range of columns, press CTRL+0.

If you want to increase or decrease the column width significantly, you can use the Column Width command on the shortcut menu to change a column's width. To use this command, however, you must select one or more entire columns. As shown in the previous set of steps, you select entire columns by dragging through the column headings above row 1.

A column width can vary from zero (0) to 255 characters. If you decrease the column width to zero, the column is hidden. **Hiding** is a technique you can use to hide data that might not be relevant to a particular report or sensitive data that you do not want others to see. When you print a worksheet, hidden columns do not print. To display a hidden column, position the mouse pointer to the left of the column heading boundary where the hidden column is located and then drag to the right.

Changing the Heights of Rows

When you increase the font size of a cell entry, such as the title in cell A1, Excel automatically increases the row height to best fit so the characters display properly. Recall that Excel did this earlier (Figure 2-2 on page E 2.8) when you entered multiple lines in a cell in row 2.

You also can increase or decrease the height of a row manually to improve the appearance of the worksheet. The following steps show how to improve the appearance of the worksheet by increasing the height of row 1 to 61.50 points, row 2 to 36.00 points, and row 12 to 24.00 points. Perform the following steps to change the heights of these three rows.

To Change the Height of a Row by Dragging

1 Point to the boundary below row heading 1. Drag down until the ScreenTip, Height: 61.50 (82 pixels), displays.

The mouse pointer changes to a split double arrow (Figure 2-57). The distance between the dotted line and the top of row 1 indicates the proposed row height for row 1.

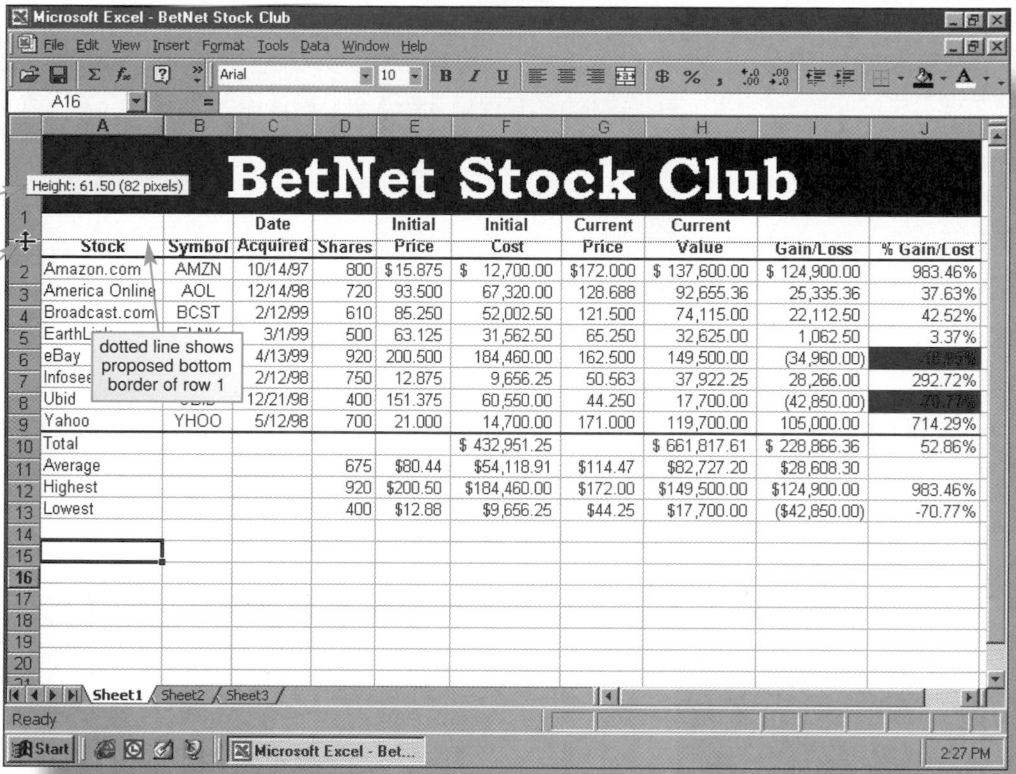

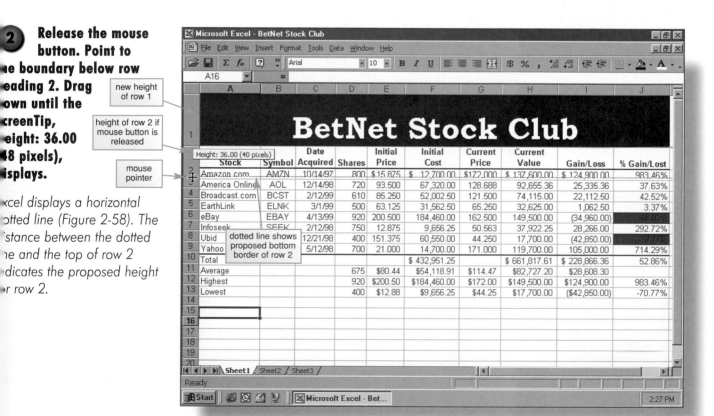

FIGURE 2-57

2 Release the mouse button. Point to the boundary below row heading 2. Drag down until the ScreenTip, Height: 36.00 (48 pixels), displays.

Excel displays a horizontal dotted line (Figure 2-58). The distance between the dotted line and the top of row 2 indicates the proposed height for row 2.

FIGURE 2-58

3 **Release the mouse button. Point to the boundary below row heading 12. Drag down until the ScreenTip, Height: 24.00 (32 pixels), displays. Release the mouse button.**

The Totals row and the Average row have additional white space between them, which improves the appearance of the worksheet. The formatting of the worksheet is complete (Figure 2-59).

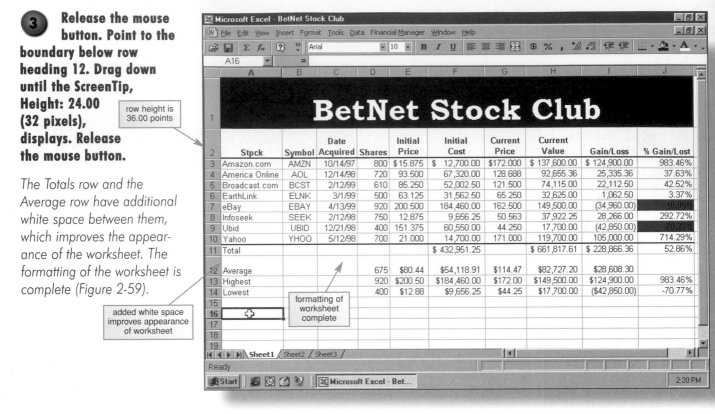

FIGURE 2-59

The row height can vary between zero (0) and 409 points. As with column widths, when you decrease the row height to zero, the row is hidden. To display a hidden row, position the mouse pointer just below the row heading boundary where the row is hidden and then drag down. To set a row height to best fit, double-click the bottom boundary of the row heading.

The task of formatting the worksheet is complete. The next step is to check the spelling of the worksheet.

Checking Spelling

Excel has a spell checker you can use to check the worksheet for spelling errors. The spell checker looks for spelling errors by comparing words on the worksheet against words contained in its standard dictionary. If you often use specialized terms that are not in the standard dictionary, you may want to add them to a custom dictionary using the Spelling dialog box.

When the spell checker finds a word that is not in either dictionary, it displays the word in the Spelling dialog box. You then can correct it if it is misspelled.

To illustrate how Excel responds to a misspelled word, the word, Stock, in cell A2 is misspelled purposely as the word, Stpck, as shown in Figure 2-60.

To Check Spelling on the Worksheet

Steps

1 **Double-click the move handle on the left side of the Standard toolbar to display the toolbar in its entirety. Select cell A2 and enter Stpck to misspell the word Stock. Select cell A1. Click the Spelling button on the Standard toolbar. When the spell checker stops on BetNet, click the Ignore button. When the spell checker stops on cell A2, click the word Stock in the Suggestions list.**

When the spell checker identifies the misspelled word, Stpck, the Spelling dialog box displays (Figure 2-60).

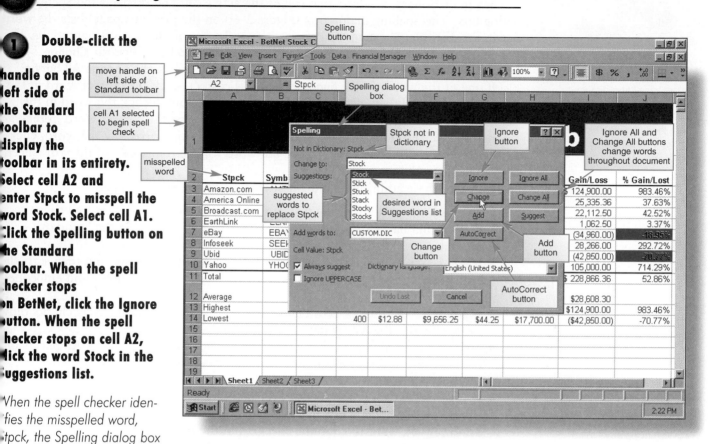

FIGURE 2-60

2 **Click the Change button. As the spell checker checks the remainder of the worksheet, click the Ignore and Change buttons as needed.**

The spell checker changes the misspelled word, Stpck, to the correct word, Stock, and continues spell checking the worksheet. When the spell checker is finished, it displays the Microsoft Excel dialog box with a message indicating that the spell check is complete for the entire sheet (Figure 2-61).

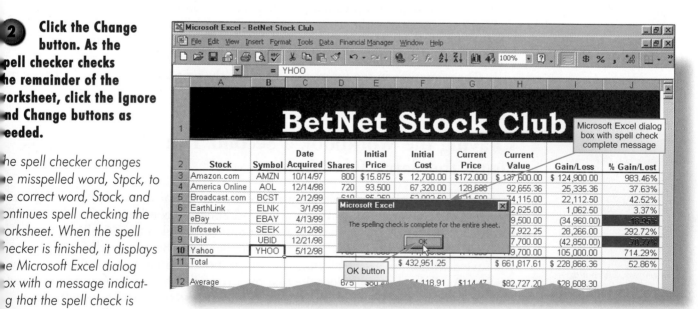

FIGURE 2-61

3 **Click the OK button.**

Other Ways

1. On the Tools menu click Spelling
2. Press F7

More About 2000

Checking Spelling

Always take the time to check the spelling of a worksheet before submitting it to your supervisor or instructor. Nothing deflates an impression more than a professional looking report with misspelled words.

When the spell checker identifies that a cell contains a word not in its standard or custom dictionary, it selects that cell as the active cell and displays the Spelling dialog box. The Spelling dialog box (Figure 2-60 on the previous page) lists the word not in the dictionary, a suggested correction, and a list of alternative suggestions. If you agree with the suggested correction in the **Change to box**, click the **Change button**. To change the word throughout the worksheet, click the **Change All button**.

If one of the words in the **Suggestions list** is correct, click the correct word in the Suggestions list and then click the Change button, or double-click the word in the Suggestions list. If none of the suggestions is correct, type the correct word in the Change to box and then click the Change button. To skip correcting the word, click the **Ignore button**. To have Excel ignore the word for the remainder of the worksheet, click the **Ignore All button**.

Consider these additional guidelines when using the spell checker:

▶ To check the spelling of the text in a single cell, double-click the cell to make the formula bar active and then click the Spelling button on the Standard toolbar.

▶ If you select a single cell so that the formula bar is not active and then start the spell checker, Excel checks the entire worksheet, including notes and embedded charts.

▶ If you select a range of cells before starting the spell checker, Excel checks only the spelling of the words in the selected range.

▶ To check the spelling of all the sheets in a workbook, click Select All Sheets on the sheet tab shortcut menu and then start the spell checker. To display the sheet tab shortcut menu, right-click the sheet tab.

▶ If you select a cell other than cell A1 before you start the spell checker, a dialog box will display when the spell checker reaches the end of the worksheet, asking if you want to continue checking at the beginning.

▶ To add words to the dictionary, click the **Add button** in the Spelling dialog box (Figure 2-60) when Excel identifies the word as not in the dictionary.

▶ Click the **AutoCorrect button** (Figure 2-60) to add the misspelled word and the correct version of the word to the AutoCorrect list. For example, suppose you misspell the word, do, as the word, dox. When the Spelling dialog box display the correct word, do, in the Change to box, click the AutoCorrect button. Then, anytime in the future that you type the word, dox, Excel will change it to the word, do.

Saving the Workbook a Second Time Using the Same File Name

Earlier in this project, you saved an intermediate version of the workbook using the file name, BetNet Stock Club. To save the workbook a second time using the same file name, click the Save button on the Standard toolbar. Excel automatically stores the latest version of the workbook using the same file name, BetNet Stock Club. When you save a workbook a second time using the same file name, Excel will not display the Save As dialog box as it does the first time you save the workbook. You also can click **Save** on the File menu or press SHIFT+F12 or CTRL+S to re-save a workbook.

If you want to save the workbook using a new name or on a different drive, click **Save As** on the File menu. Some Excel users, for example, use the Save button to save the latest version of the workbook on the default drive. Then, they use the Save As command to save a copy on another drive.

More About 2000

Saving

If you want to save the workbook under a new name, click the Save As command on the File menu. Some Excel users feel better if they save workbooks on two different drives. They use the Save button on the Standard toolbar to save the latest version of the workbook on the default drive. Then, they use the Save As command to save a second copy on another drive.

Previewing and Printing the Worksheet

In Project 1, you printed the worksheet without previewing it on the screen by clicking the Print button on the Standard toolbar. You can print the BetNet Stock Club worksheet the same way. By previewing the worksheet, however, you see exactly how it will look without generating a printout. Previewing allows you to see if the worksheet will print on one page in portrait orientation. **Portrait orientation** means the printout is printed across the width of the page. **Landscape orientation** means the printout is printed across the length of the page. Previewing a worksheet using the **Print Preview command** on the File menu or **Print Preview button** on the Standard toolbar can save time, paper, and the frustration of waiting for a printout only to discover it is not what you want.

More About

Print Preview

A popular button in the preview window (Figure 2-63) is the Margins button. The Margins button allows you to drag the top, bottom, left, and right margins to center a worksheet or add room to fit a wide or long worksheet on a page. You even can change the column widths.

To Preview and Print a Worksheet

1 Point to the Print Preview button on the Standard toolbar (Figure 2-62).

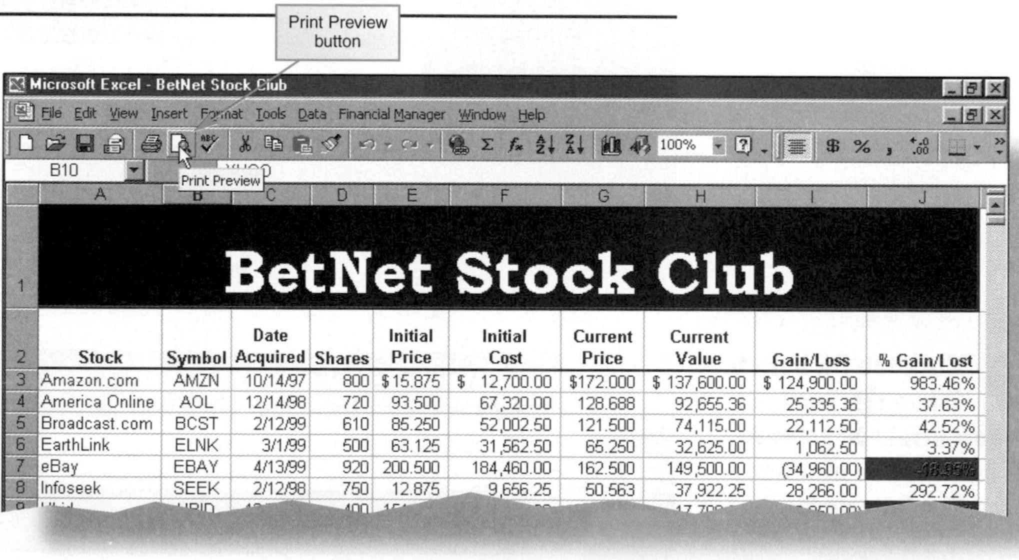

FIGURE 2-62

2 Click the Print Preview button. When the Preview window displays, point to the Setup button.

Excel displays a preview of the worksheet in portrait orientation. In portrait orientation, the worksheet does not fit on one page (Figure 2-63).

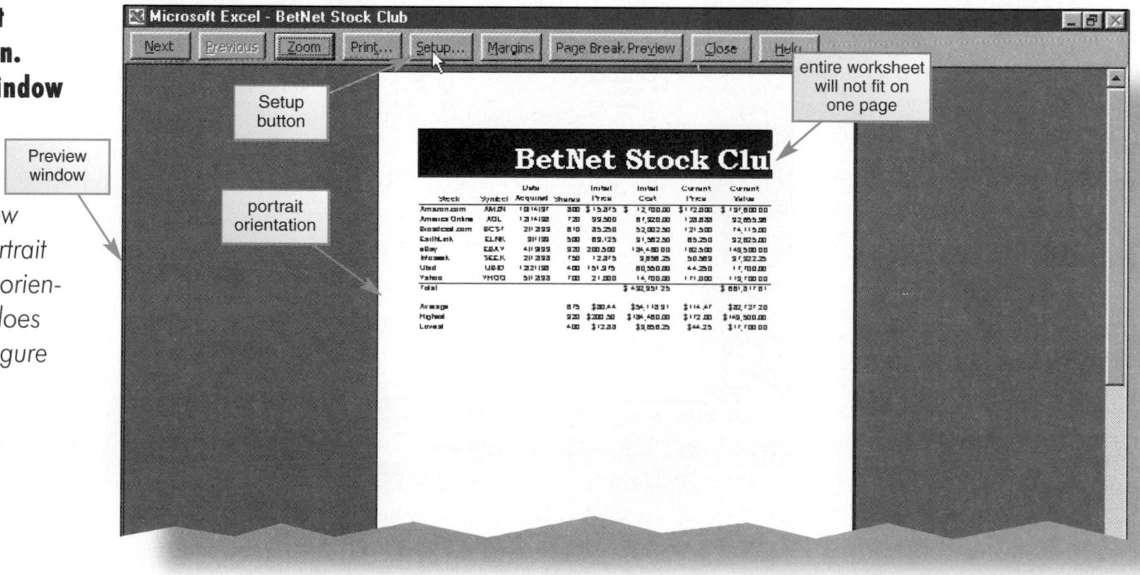

FIGURE 2-63

3 **Click the Setup button. When the Page Setup dialog box displays, click the Page tab and then click Landscape. Point to the OK button.**

The Page Setup dialog box displays. You have two choices in the Orientation area, Portrait or Landscape (Figure 2-64).

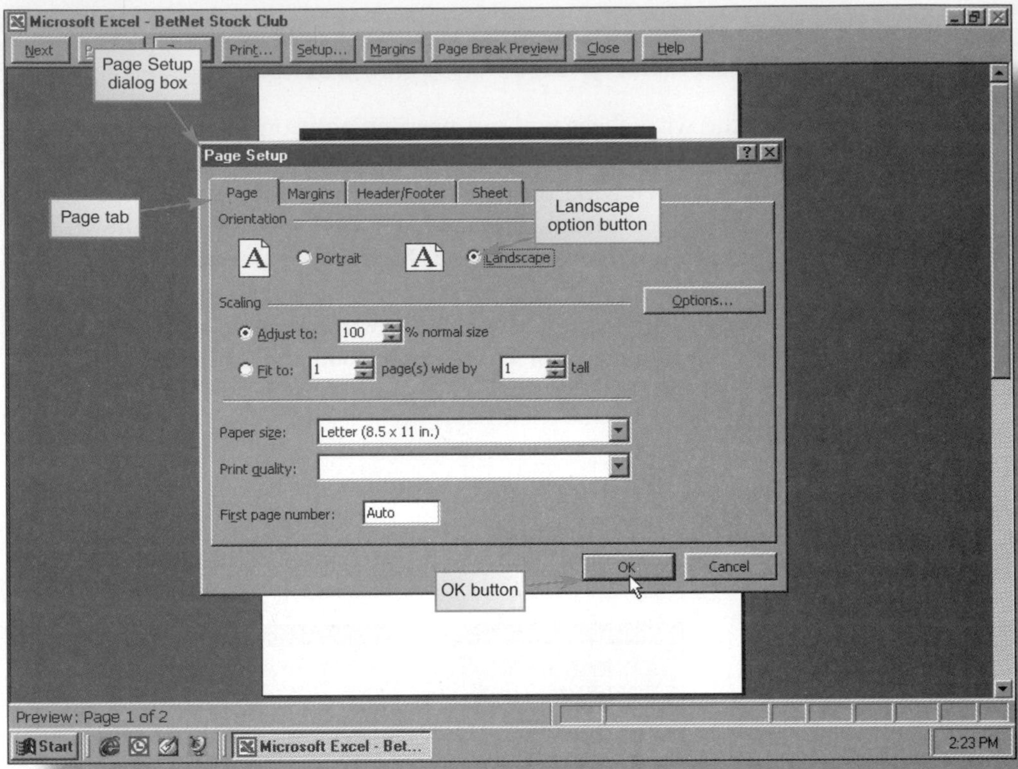

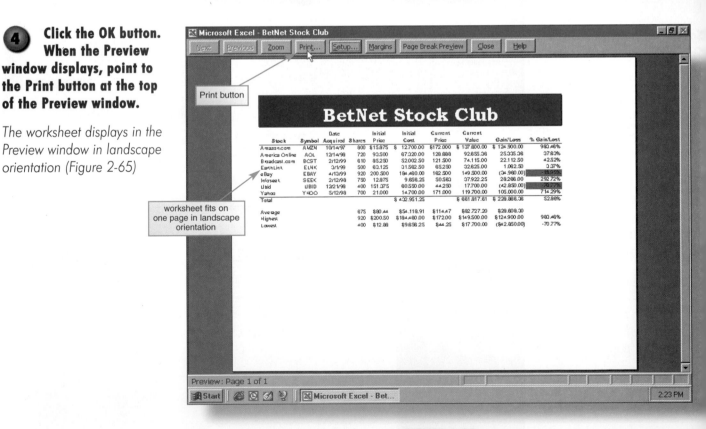

FIGURE 2-64

4 **Click the OK button. When the Preview window displays, point to the Print button at the top of the Preview window.**

The worksheet displays in the Preview window in landscape orientation (Figure 2-65)

FIGURE 2-65

5 **Click the Print button. When the Print dialog box displays, point to the OK button.**

The Print dialog box displays as shown in Figure 2-66.

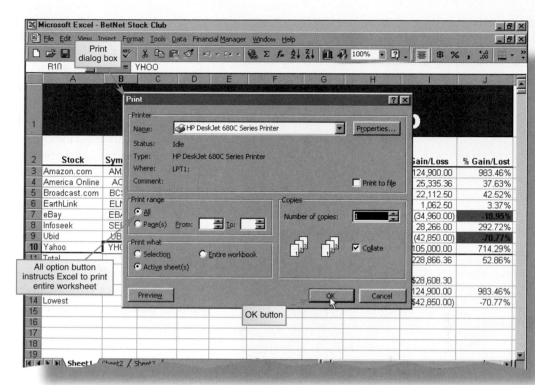

FIGURE 2-66

6 **Click the OK button. Click the Save button on the Standard toolbar.**

Excel prints the worksheet (Figure 2-67). The workbook is saved with the landscape orientation.

FIGURE 2-67

Once you change the orientation and save the workbook, it will remain until you change it. Excel sets the orientation for a new workbook to portrait.

There are several buttons at the top of the Preview window (Figure 2-65). The functions of these buttons are summarized in Table 2-5 on the next page.

Rather than click the Next and Previous buttons to move from page to page as described in Table 2-5, you can press the PAGE UP and PAGE DOWN keys. You also can click the previewed page in the Preview window when the mouse pointer shape is a magnifying glass to carry out the function of the Zoom button.

Other Ways

1. On the File menu click Print Preview

2. On the File menu click Page Setup, click Print Preview button

3. On File menu click Print, click Preview button

Table 2-5   Print Preview Buttons

BUTTON	FUNCTION
Next	Previews the next page
Previous	Previews the previous page
Zoom	Magnifies or reduces the print preview
Print...	Prints the worksheet
Setup...	Displays the Print Setup dialog box
Margins	Changes the print margins
Page Break Preview	Previews page breaks
Close	Closes the Preview window
Help	Displays Help about the Preview window

The Page Setup dialog box in Figure 2-64 on page E 2.52 allows you to make changes to the default settings for a printout. For example, on the Page tab, you can set the orientation as was done in the previous set of steps, scale the printout so it fits on one page, set the page size, and print quality. Scaling is an alternative to changing the orientation to fit a wide worksheet on one page. This technique will be discussed shortly. The Margins tab, Header/Footer tab, and Sheet tab in the Page Setup dialog box allow even more control of the way the printout will appear. These tabs will be discussed in later projects.

The Print dialog box shown in Figure 2-66 on the previous page displays when you use the Print command on the File menu or a Print button in a dialog box or Preview window. It does not display when you use the Print button on the Standard toolbar as was the case in Project 1. The Print dialog box allows you to select a printer, instruct Excel what to print, and indicate how many copies of the printout you want.

Printing a Section of the Worksheet

You might not always want to print the entire worksheet. You can print portions of the worksheet by selecting the range of cells to print and then clicking the Selection option button in the Print what area in the Print dialog box. The following steps show how to print the range A2:F11.

Steps **To Print a Section of the Worksheet**

1 **Select the range A2:F11. Click File on the menu bar and then click Print. Click Selection in the Print what area. Point to the OK button.**

The Print dialog box displays (Figure 2-68). Because the Selection option button is selected, Excel will print only the selected range.

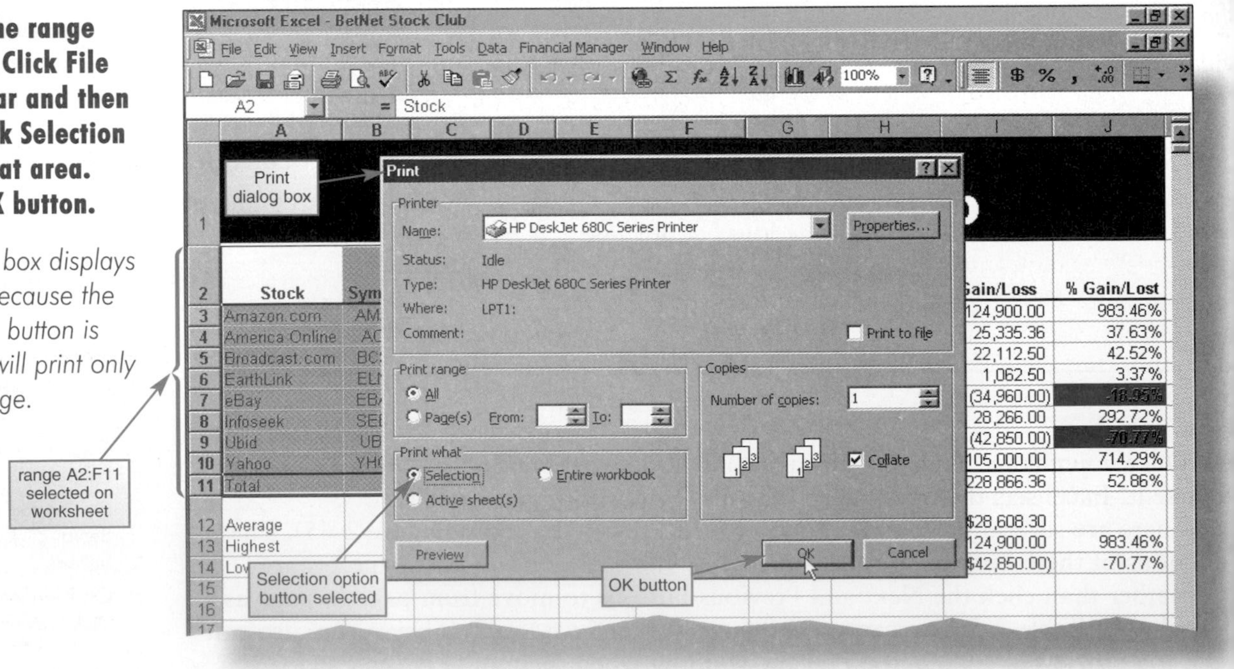

FIGURE 2-68

2 Click the OK button. Click cell A16 to deselect the range A2:F11.

Excel prints the selected range of the worksheet on the printer (Figure 2-69).

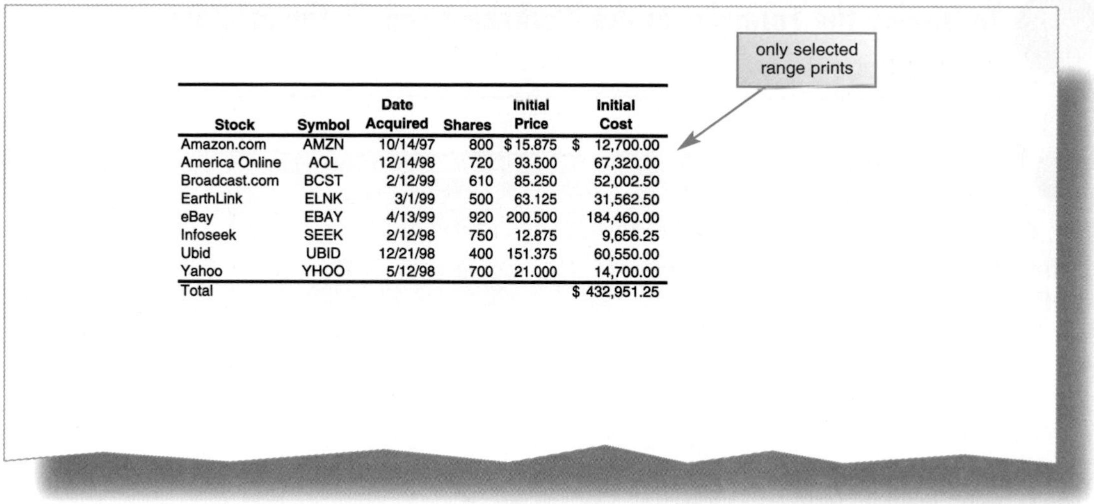

only selected range prints

Stock	Symbol	Date Acquired	Shares	Initial Price	Initial Cost
Amazon.com	AMZN	10/14/97	800	$15.875	$ 12,700.00
America Online	AOL	12/14/98	720	93.500	67,320.00
Broadcast.com	BCST	2/12/99	610	85.250	52,002.50
EarthLink	ELNK	3/1/99	500	63.125	31,562.50
eBay	EBAY	4/13/99	920	200.500	184,460.00
Infoseek	SEEK	2/12/98	750	12.875	9,656.25
Ubid	UBID	12/21/98	400	151.375	60,550.00
Yahoo	YHOO	5/12/98	700	21.000	14,700.00
Total					$ 432,951.25

FIGURE 2-69

Other Ways

1. Select range to print, on File menu click Print Area, click Set Print Area, click Print button on Standard toolbar; on File menu click Print Area, click Clear Print Area

Three option buttons display in the Print what area in the Print dialog box (Figure 2-68). As shown in the previous steps, the **Selection option button** instructs Excel to print the selected range. The **Active sheet(s) option button** instructs Excel to print the active sheet (the one displaying on the screen) or the selected sheets. Finally, the **Entire workbook option button** instructs Excel to print all the sheets with content in the workbook.

Displaying and Printing the Formulas Version of the Worksheet

Thus far, you have been working with the **values version** of the worksheet, which shows the results of the formulas you have entered, rather than the actual formulas. Excel also allows you to display and print the **formulas version** of the worksheet, which displays the actual formulas you have entered, rather than the resulting values. You can toggle between the values version and formulas version by pressing CTRL+LEFT SINGLE QUOTATION MARK (` to the left of the number 1 key).

The formulas version is useful for debugging a worksheet. **Debugging** is the process of finding and correcting errors in the worksheet. Because the formula version displays and prints formulas and functions, rather than the results, it makes it easier to see if any mistakes were made in the formulas.

When you change from the values version to the formulas version, Excel increases the width of the columns so the formulas and text do not overflow into adjacent cells on the right. The formulas version of the worksheet thus usually is significantly wider than the values version. To fit the wide printout on one page, you can use landscape orientation and the **Fit to option** on the Page tab in the Page Setup dialog box. To change from the values version to the formulas version of the worksheet and print the formulas on one page, perform the steps on the next page.

More About

Printing

A dark font on a dark background, such as a red font on a blue background, will not print properly on a black and white printer. For black and white printing, use a light colored font on a dark background and a dark font on a light colored background.

More About

Values versus Formulas

When completing class assignments, do not enter numbers in cells that require formulas. Most instructors require their students to hand in both the values version and formulas version of the worksheet. The formulas version verifies that you entered formulas, rather than numbers in formula-based cells.

Steps   To Display the Formulas in the Worksheet and Fit the Printout on One Page

1 **Press CTRL+LEFT SINGLE QUOTATION MARK (`). Click the right horizontal scroll arrow until column J displays.**

Excel changes the display of the worksheet from values to formulas (Figure 2-70). The formulas in the worksheet display showing unformatted numbers, formulas, and functions that were assigned to the cells. Excel automatically increases the column widths.

FIGURE 2-70

2 **Click File on the menu bar, and then click Page Setup. When the Page Setup dialog box displays, click the Page tab. If necessary, click Landscape, and then click Fit to. Point to the Print button in the Page Setup dialog box.**

Excel displays the Page Setup dialog box with the Landscape and Fit to option buttons selected (Figure 2-71).

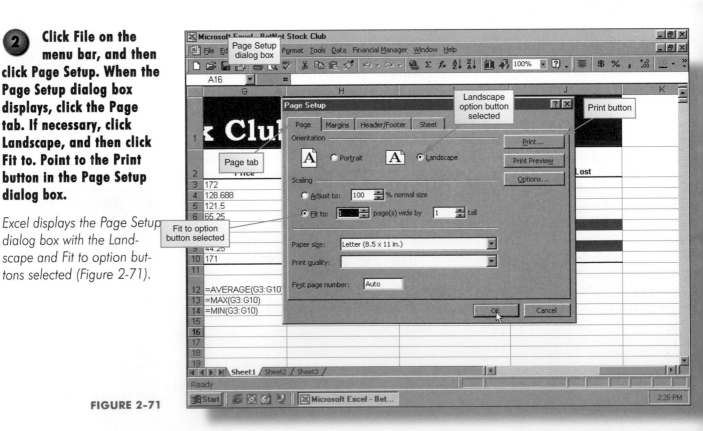

FIGURE 2-71

3 Click the Print button. When the Print dialog box displays, click the OK button. When you are done viewing and printing the formulas version, press CTRL + LEFT SINGLE QUOTATION MARK (`) to display the values version.

Excel prints the formulas in the worksheet on one page in landscape orientation (Figure 2-72).

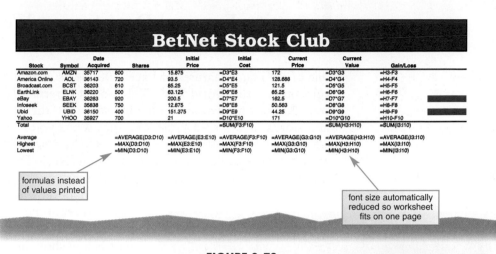

Stock	Symbol	Date Acquired	Shares	Initial Price	Initial Cost	Current Price	Current Value	Gain/Loss
Amazon.com	AMZN	35717	800	15.875	=D3*E3	172	=D3*G3	=H3-F3
America Online	AOL	36143	720	93.5	=D4*E4	128.688	=D4*G4	=H4-F4
Broadcast.com	BCST	36203	610	85.25	=D5*E5	121.5	=D5*G5	=H5-F5
EarthLink	ELNK	36220	500	63.125	=D6*E6	65.25	=D6*G6	=H6-F6
eBay	EBAY	36263	920	200.5	=D7*E7	162.5	=D7*G7	=H7-F7
Infoseek	SEEK	35838	750	12.875	=D8*E8	50.563	=D8*G8	=H8-F8
Ubid	UBID	36150	400	151.375	=D9*E9	44.25	=D9*G9	=H9-F9
Yahoo	YHOO	35927	700	21	=D10*E10	171	=D10*G10	=H10-F10
Total					=SUM(F3:F10)		=SUM(H3:H10)	=SUM(I3:I10)
Average			=AVERAGE(D3:D10)	=AVERAGE(E3:E10)	=AVERAGE(F3:F10)	=AVERAGE(G3:G10)	=AVERAGE(H3:H10)	=AVERAGE(I3:I10)
Highest			=MAX(D3:D10)	=MAX(E3:E10)	=MAX(F3:F10)	=MAX(G3:G10)	=MAX(H3:H10)	=MAX(I3:I10)
Lowest			=MIN(D3:D10)	=MIN(E3:E10)	=MIN(F3:F10)	=MIN(G3:G10)	=MIN(H3:H10)	=MIN(I3:I10)

BetNet Stock Club

formulas instead of values printed

font size automatically reduced so worksheet fits on one page

FIGURE 2-72

Other Ways

1. On Tools menu click Options, click View tab, click Formulas, click OK button

Although the formulas version of the worksheet was printed in the previous example, you can see from Figure 2-72 that the display on the screen also can be used for debugging the worksheet.

Changing the Print Scaling Option Back to 100%

Depending on your printer driver, you may have to change the Print Scaling option back to 100% after using the Fit to option. Complete the following steps to reset the Print Scaling option so future worksheets print at 100%, instead of being squeezed on one page.

TO CHANGE THE PRINT SCALING OPTION BACK TO 100%

1 Click File on the menu bar and then click Page Setup.

2 Click the Page tab in the Page Setup dialog box. Click Adjust to in the Scaling area.

3 If necessary, type 100 in the Adjust to box.

4 Click the OK button.

The print scaling is set to normal.

The **Adjust to box** allows you to specify the percentage of reduction or enlargement in the printout of a worksheet. The default percentage is 100%. When you click the Fit to option, this percentage automatically changes to the percentage required to fit the printout on one page.

More About

The Fit To Option

Do not take the Fit To option lightly. Most applications involve worksheets that extend well beyond the 8½-by-11-inch page. Most users, however, want the information on one page, at least with respect to the width of the worksheet. Thus, the Fit To option is a common choice among Excel users.

Getting External Data from a Web Source Using a Web Query

One of the major features of Excel 2000 is its capability of obtaining external data from sites on the World Wide Web. To get external data from a World Wide Web site, you must have access to the Internet. You then can run a **Web query** to retrieve data stored on a World Wide Web site. When you run a Web query, Excel returns the external data in the form of a worksheet. As described in Table 2-6, four Web queries are available when you first install Excel. Three of the four Web queries available relate to investment and stock market activities.

The data returned by the stock-related Web queries is real-time in the sense that it is no more than 20 minutes old during the business day. The steps below show how to get the most recent stock quotes for the eight stocks owned by the BetNet Stock Club — Amazon.com, America Online, eBay, UBid, Infoseek, Broadcast.com, EarthLink, and Yahoo. Although you can have a Web query return data to a blank workbook, the following steps have the data returned to a blank worksheet in the BetNet Stock Club workbook.

Table 2-6 Excel Web Queries	
QUERY	*EXTERNAL DATA RETURNED*
Get More Web	Download additional Web queries
Microsoft Investor Currency Rates	Currency rates
Microsoft Investor Major Indices	Major Indices
Microsoft Investor Stock Quotes	Up to 20 stocks of your choice

To Get External Data from a Web Source Using a Web Query

1 **With the BetNet Stock Club workbook open, click the Sheet2 tab at the bottom of the window. Click cell A1. Click Data on the menu bar, point to Get External Data and then point to Run Saved Query on the Get External Data submenu.**

The Get External Data sub-menu displays as shown in Figure 2-73.

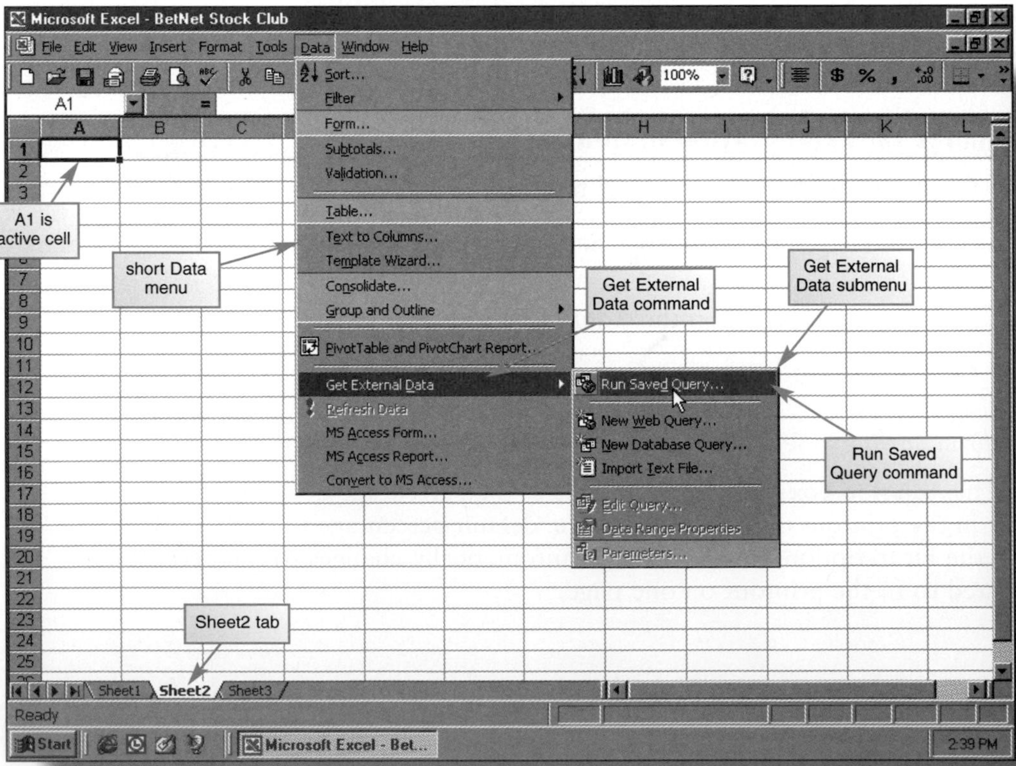

FIGURE 2-73

2 Click Run Saved Query. When the Run Query dialog box displays, click Microsoft Investor Stock Quotes. Point to the Get Data button.

The Run Query dialog box displays (Figure 2-74). If your display is different, ask your instructor for the folder location of the Web queries.

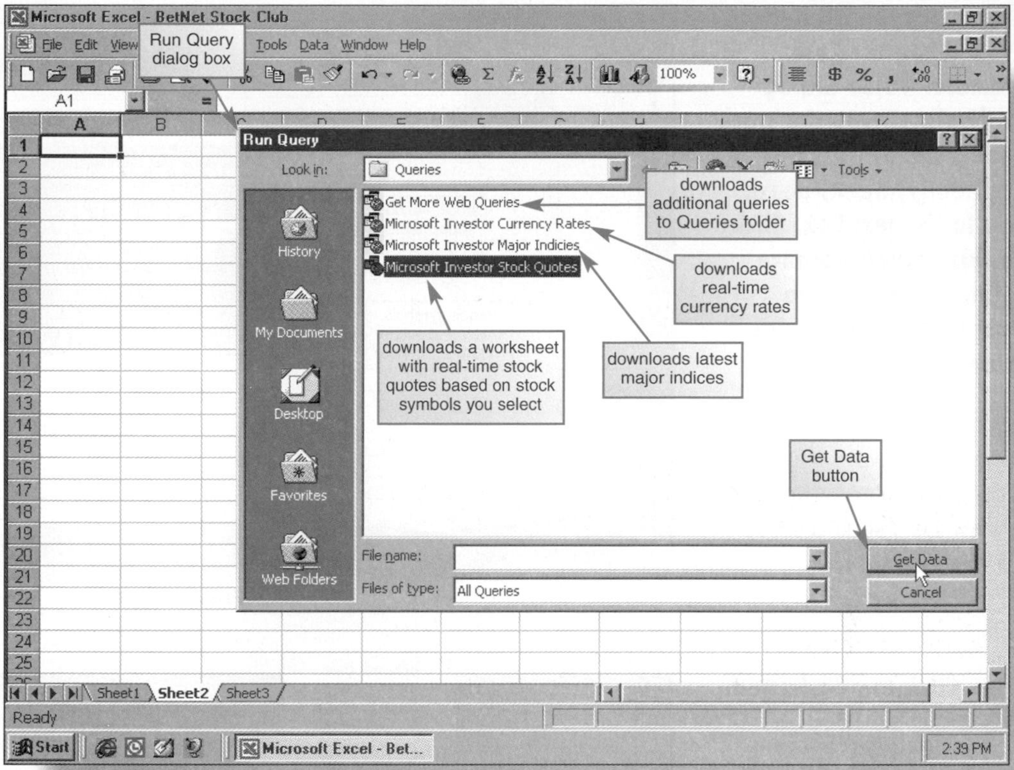

FIGURE 2-74

3 Click the Get Data button. When the Returning External Data to Microsoft Excel dialog box displays, click Existing worksheet, if necessary, to select it. Point to the OK button.

The Returning External Data to Microsoft Excel dialog box displays (Figure 2-75).

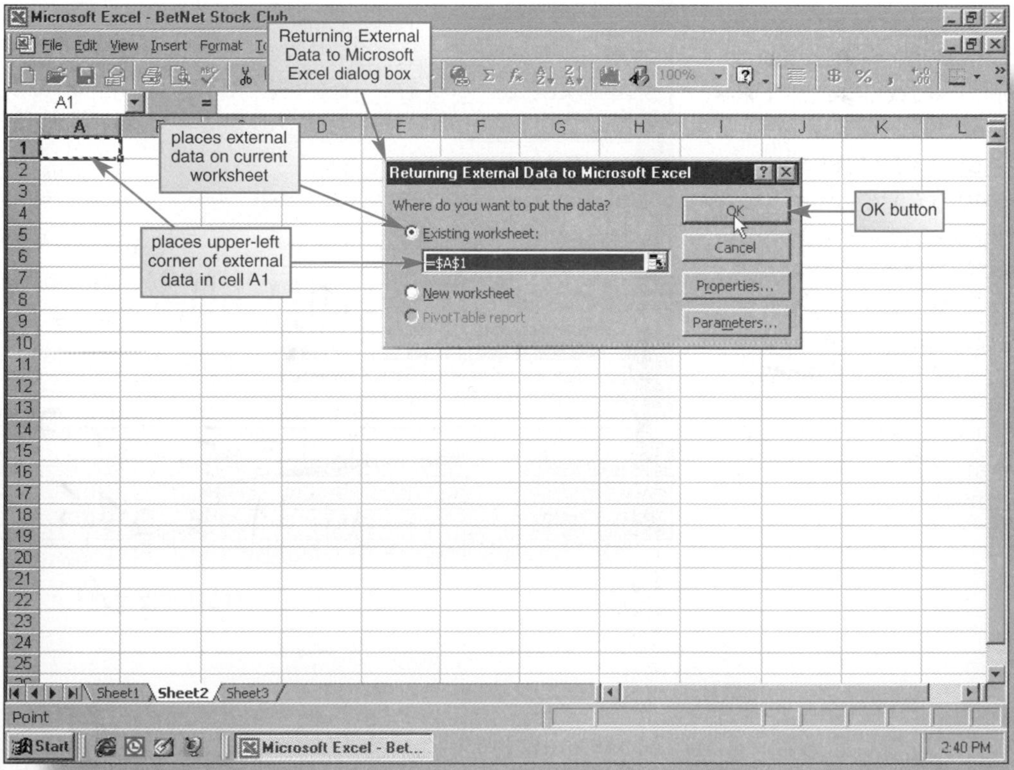

FIGURE 2-75

Click the OK button. When the Enter Parameter Value dialog box displays, type the stock symbols amzn, aol, bcst, elnk, ebay, seek, ubid, yhoo **in the text box. Click Use this value/reference for future refreshes to select it. Point to the OK button.**

The Enter Parameter Value dialog box displays (Figure 2-76). You can enter up to 20 stock symbols separated by commas (or spaces).

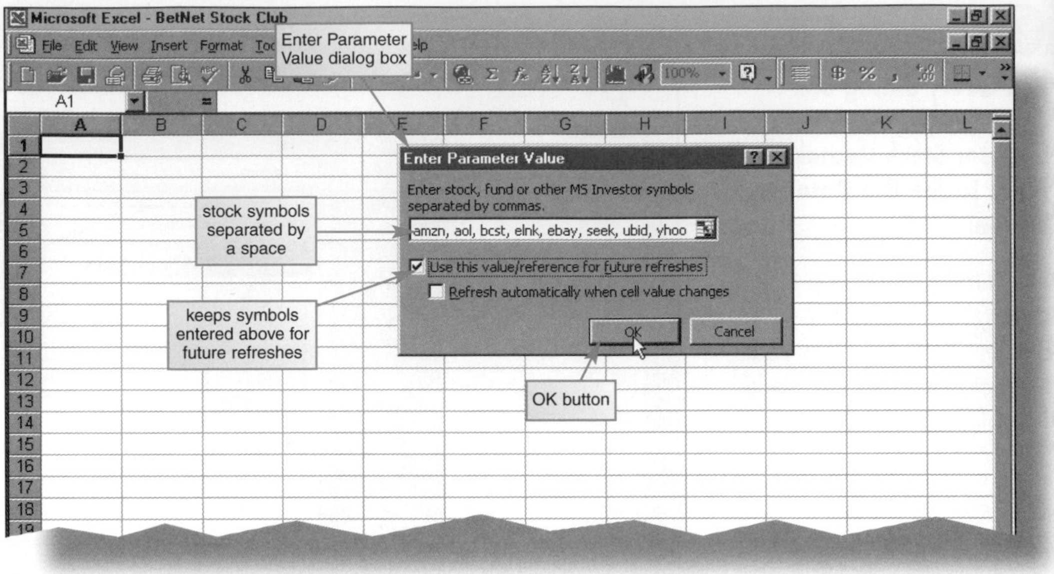

FIGURE 2-76

5 **Click the OK button.**

Once your computer connects to the Internet, a message displays to inform you that Excel is getting external data. After a short period, Excel displays a new worksheet with the desired data (Figure 2-77).

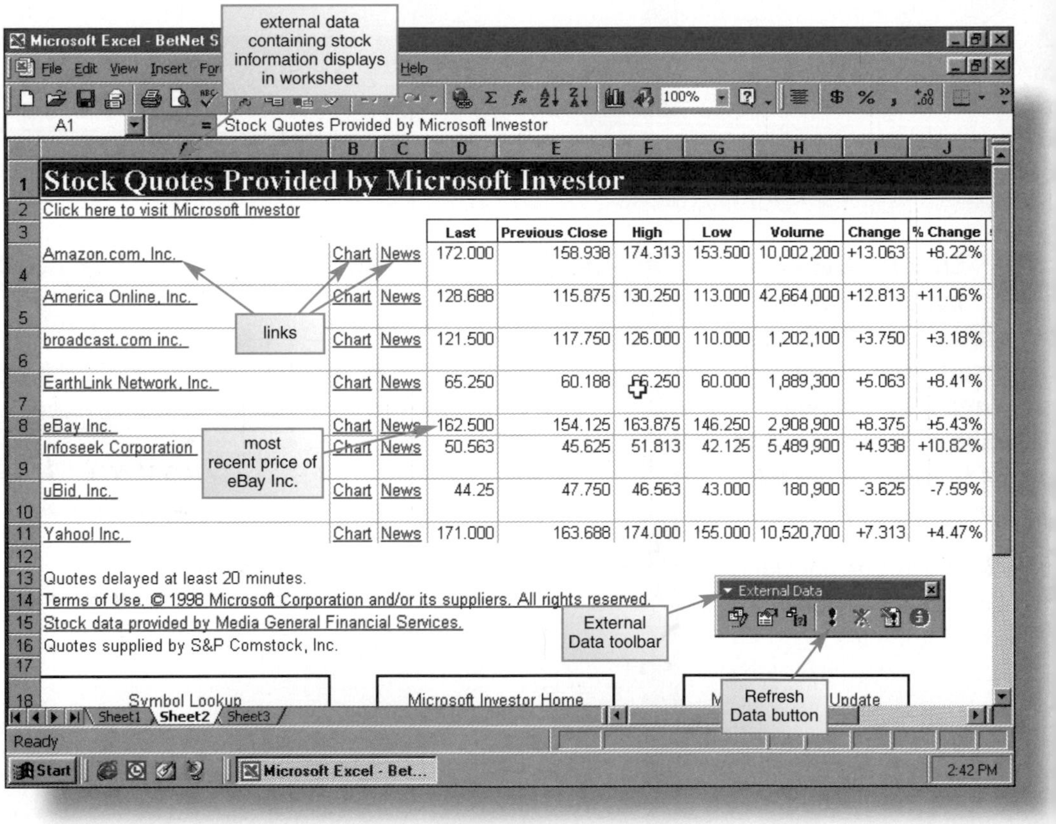

FIGURE 2-77

As shown in Figure 2-77, Excel displays the data returned from the Web query in an organized, formatted worksheet, which has a worksheet title, column titles, and a row of data for each stock symbol entered. Other than the first column, which contains the stock name and stock symbol, you have no control over the remaining columns of data returned. The latest price of each stock displays in column D.

Once the worksheet displays, you can refresh the data as often as you want. To refresh the data for all the stocks, click the **Refresh All button** on the **External Data toolbar** (Figure 2-78). Because the Use this value/reference for future refreshes check box was selected (Figure 2-76), Excel will continue to use the same stock symbols each time it refreshes. You can change the symbols by clicking the **Query Parameters button** on the External Data toolbar.

If the External Data toolbar does not display, right-click any toolbar and then click External Data. You also can invoke any Web query command by right-clicking the returned worksheet to display a shortcut menu.

This section gives you an idea of the potential of Web queries by having you use just one of Excel's many available Web queries. To reinforce the topics covered here, work through In the Lab 3 at the end of this project.

The workbook is nearly complete. The final step is to change the names of the sheets located on the sheet tabs at the bottom of the Excel window.

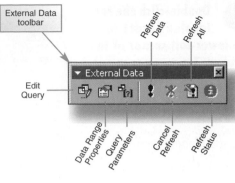

FIGURE 2-78

Changing the Sheet Names

At the bottom of the window (Figure 2-79) are the tabs that allow you to display any sheet in the workbook. You click the tab of the sheet you want to display. The names of the sheets are preset to Sheet1, Sheet2, and so on. These names become increasingly important as you move towards more sophisticated workbooks, especially those in which you reference cells between sheets. The following steps show how to rename sheets by double-clicking the sheet tabs.

More About

Web Queries

Most Excel specialists who perform Web queries use the worksheet returned from the Web query as an engine that supplies data to another worksheet in the workbook. With 3-D cell references, you can create a worksheet similar to the BetNet Stock Club, which feeds the Web query stock symbols and gets refreshed stock prices in return.

Steps **To Rename the Sheets**

1 Double-click the tab labeled Sheet2 in the lower-left corner of the window. Type Real-Time Stock Quotes as the sheet name and then click a cell on the worksheet.

The new sheet name displays on the tab (Figure 2-79).

FIGURE 2-79

2 Double-click the tab labeled Sheet1 in the lower-left corner of the window. Type Investment Analysis as the sheet name and then press the ENTER key.

The sheet name changes from Sheet1 to Investment Analysis (Figure 2-80).

3 Click the Save button on the Standard toolbar.

BetNet Stock Club

Stock	Symbol	Date Acquired	Shares	Initial Price	Initial Cost	Current Price	Current Value	Gain/Loss	% Gain/Lost
Amazon.com	AMZN	10/14/97	800	$15.875	$ 12,700.00	$172.000	$ 137,600.00	$ 124,900.00	983.46%
America Online	AOL	12/14/98	720	93.500	67,320.00	128.688	92,655.36	25,335.36	37.63%
Broadcast.com	BCST	2/12/99	610	85.250	52,002.50	121.500	74,115.00	22,112.50	42.52%
EarthLink	ELNK	3/1/99	500	63.125	31,562.50	65.250	32,625.00	1,062.50	3.37%
eBay	EBAY	4/13/99	920	200.500	184,460.00	162.500	149,500.00	(34,960.00)	-18.95%
Infoseek	SEEK	2/12/98	750	12.875	9,656.25	50.563	37,922.25	28,266.00	292.72%
Ubid	UBID	12/21/98	400	151.375	60,550.00	44.250	17,700.00	(42,850.00)	-70.77%
Yahoo	YHOO	5/12/98	700	21.000	14,700.00	171.000	119,700.00	105,000.00	714.29%
Total					$ 432,951.25		$ 661,817.61	$ 228,866.36	52.86%
Average			675	$80.44	$54,118.91	$114.47	$82,727.20	$28,608.30	
Highest			920	$200.50	$184,460.00	$172.00	$149,500.00	$124,900.00	983.46%
Lowest				$12.88	$9,656.25	$4...	...700.00	($42,850.00)	-70.77%

sheet name Sheet1 changed to Investment Analysis

tab split box

Investment Analysis / Real-Time Stock Quotes / Sheet3

Ready

Start — Microsoft Excel - Bet... — 2:43 PM

tab scrolling buttons

FIGURE 2-80

Sheet names can contain up to 31 characters (including spaces) in length. Longer sheet names, however, mean that fewer tabs will display. To display more sheet tabs, you can drag the **tab split box** (Figure 2-80) to the right. This will reduce the size of the scroll bar at the bottom of the screen. Double-click the tab split box to reset it to its normal position.

You also can use the **tab scrolling buttons** to the left of the sheet tabs (Figure 2-80) to move between sheets. The leftmost and rightmost scroll buttons move to the first or last sheet in the workbook. The two middle scroll buttons move one sheet to the left or right.

E-mailing a Workbook from within Excel

The most popular service on the Internet is electronic mail, or e-mail. Using **e-mail**, you can converse with friends across the room or on another continent. One of the features of e-mail is the ability to attach Office files, such as Word documents or Excel workbooks to an e-mail and send it to a co-worker. In the past, if you wanted to send a workbook you saved it, closed the file, launched your e-mail program, and then attached the workbook to the e-mail before sending it. A new feature of Office 2000 is the capability of e-mailing the worksheet or workbook directly from within Excel. For these steps to work properly, you must have an e-mail address and one of the following as your e-mail program: Outlook, Outlook Express, Microsoft Exchange Client, or another 32-bit e-mail program compatible with Messaging Application Programming Interface. The following steps show how to e-mail the workbook from within Excel to Michael Santos. Assume his e-mail address is michael_santo61@hotmail.com. If you do not have an E-mail button on the Standard toolbar, then this activity is not available to you.

To E-mail a Workbook from within Excel

 With the BetNet Stock Club workbook open, click the E-mail button on the Standard toolbar. If the E-mail dialog box displays, click Send the entire workbook as an attachment. Point to the OK button.

The E-mail dialog box displays as shown in Figure 2-81.

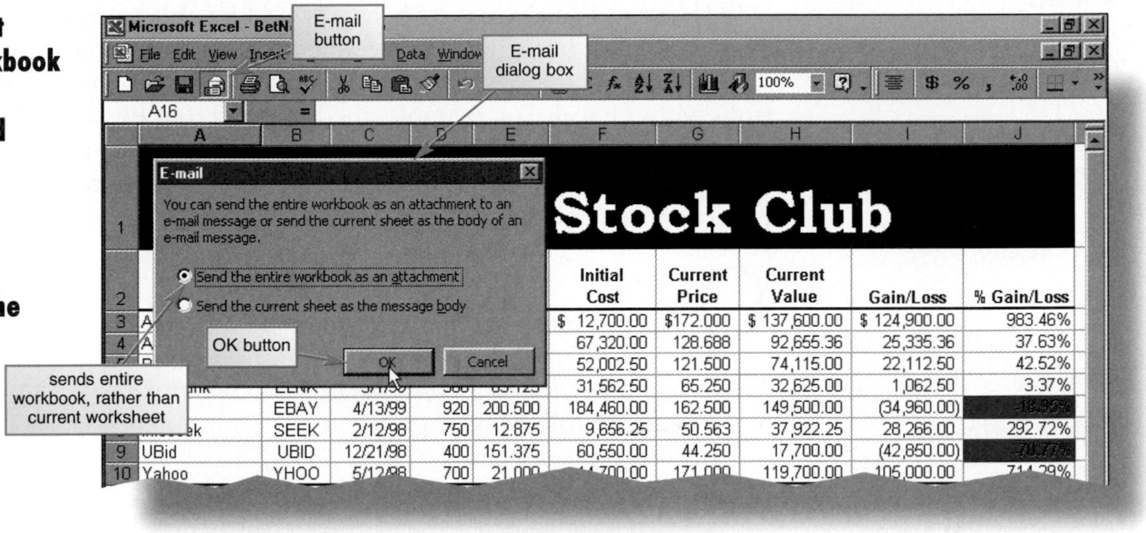

Microsoft Excel - BetN...

File Edit View Insert Data Window

E-mail button

E-mail dialog box

A16

E-mail

You can send the entire workbook as an attachment to an e-mail message or send the current sheet as the body of an e-mail message.

⦿ Send the entire workbook as an attachment

○ Send the current sheet as the message body

OK button

OK   Cancel

sends entire workbook, rather than current worksheet

			Initial Cost	Current Price	Current Value	Gain/Loss	% Gain/Loss
			$ 12,700.00	$172.000	$ 137,600.00	$ 124,900.00	983.46%
			67,320.00	128.688	92,655.36	25,335.36	37.63%
			52,002.50	121.500	74,115.00	22,112.50	42.52%
	ELNK	500	31,562.50	65.250	32,625.00	1,062.50	3.37%
EBAY	4/13/99	920	200.500	184,460.00	162.500	149,500.00	(34,960.00)	-18.95%
SEEK	2/12/98	750	12.875	9,656.25	50.563	37,922.25	28,266.00	292.72%
9 UBid UBID	12/21/98	400	151.375	60,550.00	44.250	17,700.00	(42,850.00)	-70.77%
10 Yahoo YHOO	5/12/98	700	21.000		171.000	119,700.00	105,000.00	714.29%

FIGURE 2-81

Click the OK button.

If the Choose Profile dialog box displays, click the OK button. When the e-mail Message window displays, type michael_santos @hotmail.com **in the To text box. Type** BetNet Stock Club workbook **in the Subject text box. Point to the Send button.**

Excel displays the e-mail Message window (Figure 2-82).

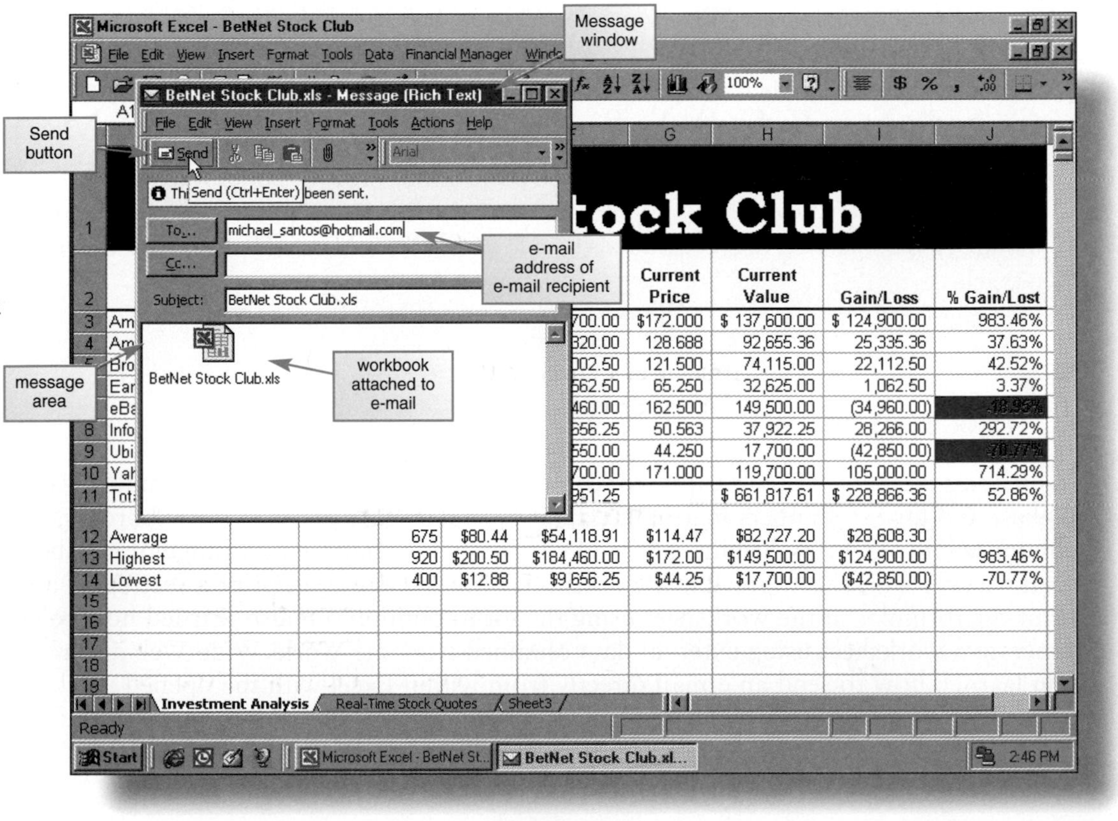

Microsoft Excel - BetNet Stock Club

File Edit View Insert Format Tools Data Financial Manager Window

Message window

BetNet Stock Club.xls - Message (Rich Text)

File Edit View Insert Format Tools Actions Help

Send button

Send (Ctrl+Enter)

Send   Arial

Thi   Send (Ctrl+Enter) been sent.

To...   michael_santos@hotmail.com

e-mail address of e-mail recipient

Cc...

Subject: BetNet Stock Club.xls

message area

BetNet Stock Club.xls

workbook attached to e-mail

tock Club

	Current Price	Current Value	Gain/Loss	% Gain/Lost
Am	700.00	$172.000	$ 137,600.00	$ 124,900.00	983.46%
Am	320.00	128.688	92,655.36	25,335.36	37.63%
Bro	002.50	121.500	74,115.00	22,112.50	42.52%
Ear	562.50	65.250	32,625.00	1,062.50	3.37%
eBa	460.00	162.500	149,500.00	(34,960.00)	-18.95%
Info	656.25	50.563	37,922.25	28,266.00	292.72%
Ubi	550.00	44.250	17,700.00	(42,850.00)	-70.77%
Yah	700.00	171.000	119,700.00	105,000.00	714.29%
Tot	951.25		$ 661,817.61	$ 228,866.36	52.86%

12 Average		675	$80.44	$54,118.91	$114.47	$82,727.20	$28,608.30	
13 Highest		920	$200.50	$184,460.00	$172.00	$149,500.00	$124,900.00	983.46%
14 Lowest		400	$12.88	$9,656.25	$44.25	$17,700.00	($42,850.00)	-70.77%

Investment Analysis / Real-Time Stock Quotes / Sheet3

Ready

Start   Microsoft Excel - BetNet St...   BetNet Stock Club.xl...   2:46 PM

Click the Send button.

The e-mail with the attached workbook is sent to michael_santos @hotmail.com.

FIGURE 2-82

More About

E-mail

Several Web sites are available that allow you to sign up for free e-mail. For more information on signing up for free e-mail, visit the Excel 2000 More About Web page (www.scsite.com/ex2000/more.htm) and click Signing Up for E-mail.

More About

Quick Reference

For a table that lists how to complete the tasks covered in this book using the mouse, menu, shortcut menu, and keyboard, visit the Office 2000 Web page (www.scsite.com/off2000/qr.htm), and then click Microsoft Excel 2000.

Because the workbook was sent as an attachment, Michael Santos can save the attachment and then open the workbook in Excel. The alternative in the E-mail dialog box in Figure 2-81 on the previous page is to send a copy of the worksheet in HTML format. In this case, Michael would be able to read the worksheet in the e-mail message, but would not be able to open it in Excel.

Many more options are available that you can choose when you send an e-mail from within Excel. For example, the Bcc and From buttons on the toolbar in the Message window give you the same capabilities as an e-mail program. The Options button on the toolbar allows you to send the e-mail to a group of people in a particular sequence and get responses along the route.

Quitting Excel

After completing the workbook and related activities, you can quit Excel by performing the following steps.

TO QUIT EXCEL

1 Click the Investment Analysis tab.

2 Click the Close button on the upper-right corner of the title bar.

3 When the Microsoft Excel dialog box displays, click the Yes button.

CASE PERSPECTIVE SUMMARY

The worksheet and Web query (Figure 2-1 on page E 2.5) you created for Michael Santos will serve his purpose well. The worksheet, which he plans to e-mail to the club members, contains valuable information in an easy-to-read format. Finally, the Web query allows Michael to obtain the latest stock prices to keep the workbook as up to date as possible.

Project Summary

In creating the BetNet Stock Club workbook, you learned how to enter formulas, calculate an average, find the highest and lowest numbers in a range, audit formulas, change fonts, draw borders, format numbers, change column widths and row heights, and add conditional formatting to a range of numbers. You learned how to spell check a worksheet, preview a worksheet, print a worksheet, print a section of a worksheet and display and print the formulas in the worksheet using the Fit to option. You also learned how to complete a Web query to generate a worksheet using external data obtained from the World Wide Web and rename sheet tabs. Finally, you learned how to send an e-mail directly from within Excel with the opened workbook attached.

What You Should Know

Having completed this project, you now should be able to perform the following tasks:

▶ Apply a Currency Style Format and Comma Style Format Using the Formatting Toolbar *(E 2.35)*

▶ Apply a Currency Style Format with a Floating Dollar Sign Using the Format Cells Command *(E 2.37*

▶ Apply a Percent Style Format *(E 2.39)*

▶ Apply Conditional Formatting *(E 2.40)*

▶ Bold, Center, and Underline the Column Titles *(E 2.33)*

▶ Center Data in Cells *(E 2.33)*

▶ Change the Title Background and Font Colors and Apply an Outline Border *(E 2.30)*

▶ Change the Font and Center the Worksheet Title *(E 2.28)*

▶ Change the Height of a Row by Dragging *(E 2.47)*

▶ Change the Print Scaling Option Back to 100% *(E 2.57)*

▶ Change the Widths of Columns *(E 2.44)*

▶ Check Spelling on the Worksheet *(E 2.49)*

▶ Copy a Range of Cells Across Columns to an Adjacent Range Using the Fill Handle *(E 2.22)*

▶ Copy Formulas Using the Fill Handle *(E 2.13)*

▶ Determine the Average of a Range of Numbers Using the Keyboard and Mouse *(E 2.17)*

▶ Determine the Highest Number in a Range of Numbers Using the Edit Formula Box and Function Box *(E 2.18)*

▶ Determine the Lowest Number in a Range of Numbers Using the Paste Function Button *(E 2.20)*

▶ Determine the Total Percentage Gain/Loss *(E 2.15)*

▶ Determine Totals Using the AutoSum Button *(E 2.14)*

▶ Display the Formulas in the Worksheet and Fit the Printout on One Page *(E 2.56)*

▶ Enter a Formula Using the Keyboard *(E 2.9)*

▶ Enter Formulas Using Point Mode *(E 2.11)*

▶ Enter the Column Titles *(E 2.7)*

▶ Enter the Stock Data *(E 2.8)*

▶ Enter the Total Row Titles *(E 2.8)*

▶ Enter the Worksheet Title *(E 2.7)*

▶ E-mail a Workbook from within Excel *(E 2.63)*

▶ Get External Data from a Web Source Using a Web Query *(E 2.58)*

▶ Preview and Print a Worksheet *(E 2.51)*

▶ Print a Section of the Worksheet *(E 2.54)*

▶ Quit Excel *(E 2.64)*

▶ Rename the Sheets *(E 2.61)*

▶ Start Excel and Reset the Toolbars *(E 2.6)*

▶ Verify a Formula Using the Auditing Commands *(E 2.25)*

▶ Verify a Formula Using Range Finder *(E 2.24)*

More About

Microsoft Certification

The Microsoft Office User Specialist (MOUS) Certification program provides an opportunity for you to obtain a valuable industry credential —- proof that you have the Excel 2000 skills required by employers. For more information, see Appendix D or visit the Shelly Cashman Series MOUS Web page at www.scsite.com/off2000/cert.htm.

Apply Your Knowledge

1 Sizes Galore and Much More Profit Analysis Worksheet

Instructions: Start Excel. Open the workbook Sizes Galore and Much More from the Data Disk. See the inside back cover of this book for instructions for downloading the Data Disk or see your instructor. The purpose of this exercise is to have you open a partially completed workbook, enter formulas and functions, copy the formulas and functions, and then format the numbers. As shown in Figure 2-83, the completed worksheet analyzes profits by product.

Microsoft Excel - Sizes Galore and Much More 2

File Edit View Insert Format Tools Data Window Help

A18

Sizes Galore and Much More
Profit Analysis

	Product	Description	Cost	Profit	Units Sold	Total Sales	Profit	% Profit
3	T211	Sweater	$ 92.95	$ 9.25	52,435	$ 5,358,857.00	$ 485,023.75	9.051%
4	C215	Dress	175.99	15.65	16,534	3,168,575.76	258,757.10	8.166%
5	D212	Jacket	110.60	11.58	32,102	3,922,222.36	371,741.16	9.478%
6	K214	Coat	160.50	26.82	43,910	8,225,221.20	1,177,666.20	14.318%
7	Q213	Suit	121.35	13.21	34,391	4,627,652.96	454,305.11	9.817%
8	X216	Custom	200.23	38.35	23,910	5,704,447.80	916,948.50	16.074%
9	D342	Sleepwear	50.65	8.45	45,219	2,672,442.90	382,100.55	14.298%
10	H567	Hat	34.20	5.83	63,213	2,530,416.39	368,531.79	14.564%
11	C289	Shirt	43.00	6.75	52,109	2,592,422.75	351,735.75	13.568%
12	K451	Slacks	38.25	7.25	76,145	3,464,597.50	552,051.25	15.934%
13	*Totals*				203,282	$ 42,266,856.62	$ 5,318,861.16	
14	Lowest		$34.20	$5.83	16,534	$2,530,416.39	$258,757.10	8.166%
15	Highest		$200.23	$38.35	76,145	$8,225,221.20	$1,177,666.20	16.074%
16	Average		$102.77	$14.31	43,997	$4,226,685.66	$531,886.12	

Report / Sheet2 / Sheet3

Ready

Start   Microsoft Excel - Size...   2:50 PM

FIGURE 2-83

Perform the following tasks.

1. Complete the following entries in row 3:
   a. Total Sales (cell F3) = Units Sold * (Cost + Profit) or =E3 * (C3+D3)
   b. Profit (cell G3) = Units Sold * Profit or = E3 * D3
      % Profit (cell H3) = Profit / Total Sales or = G3 / F3
2. Use the fill handle to copy the three formulas in the range F3:H3 to the range F4:H12.
3. Determine the Units Sold, Total Sales, and Profit column totals in row 13.
4. In the range C14:C16, determine the lowest value, highest value, and average value, respectively for the range C3:C12. Use the fill handle to copy the three functions to the range D14:H16. Delete the average from cell H16, because you can not average percents.
5. Use the Currency Style button on the Formatting toolbar to format the numbers in the ranges C3:D3, F3:G3, and F13:G13. Use the Comma Style button on the Formatting toolbar to format the numbers in cell E3 and the range C4:G12. Use the Decrease Decimal button on the Formatting toolbar to display the numbers in the range E3:E16 as whole numbers. Use the Percent Style and the Increase Decimal buttons on the Formatting toolbar to format the range H3:H15. Increase the decimal positions in this range to 3. Use the Format Cells command on the shortcut menu to format the numbers in the ranges C14:D16 and F14:G16 to a floating dollar sign.

Apply Your Knowledge

6. Use Range Finder and then the Auditing commands to verify the formula in cell G3. Check both precedents and dependents (Figure 2-83) using the Auditing commands. Use the Remove Arrows command on the Auditing submenu to remove the arrows.

7. Enter your name, course, laboratory assignment number (Apply 2-1), date, and instructor name in the range A20:A24.

8. Preview and print the worksheet in landscape orientation. Save the workbook. Use the file name, Sizes Galore and Much More 2.

9. Print the range A1:H13. Print the formulas version (press CTRL+LEFT QUOTATION MARK) of the worksheet in landscape orientation (Figure 2-84) using the Fit to option on the Page tab in the Page Setup dialog box.

10. In column D, use the keyboard to add manually $1.00 to the profit of each product whose profit is less than $10.00, or else add $2.00. You should end up with $5,909,676.16 in cell G13. Print the worksheet. Do not save the workbook. Hand in the printouts to your instructor.

Report

Sizes Galore and Much More
Profit Analysis

Product	Description	Cost	Profit	Units Sold	Total Sales	Profit	
T211	Sweater	92.95	9.25	52435	=E3*(C3+D3)	=E3*D3	
C215	Dress	175.99	15.65	16534	=E4*(C4+D4)	=E4*D4	
D212	Jacket	110.6	11.58	32102	=E5*(C5+D5)	=E5*D5	
K214	Coat	160.5	26.82	43910	=E6*(C6+D6)	=E6*D6	
Q213	Suit	121.35	13.21	34391	=E7*(C7+D7)	=E7*D7	
X216	Custom	200.23	38.35	23910	=E8*(C8+D8)	=E8*D8	
D342	Sleepwear	50.65	8.45	45219	=E9*(C9+D9)	=E9*D9	
H567	Hat	34.2	5.83	63213	=E10*(C10+D10)	=E10*D10	
C289	Shirt	43	6.75	52109	=E11*(C11+D11)	=E11*D11	
K451	Slacks	38.25	7.25	76145	=E12*(C12+D12)	=E12*D12	
Totals					=SUM(E3:E8)	=SUM(F3:F12)	=SUM(G3:G12)
Lowest		=MIN(C3:C12)	=MIN(D3:D12)	=MIN(E3:E12)	=MIN(F3:F12)	=MIN(G3:G12)	
Highest		=MAX(C3:C12)	=MAX(D3:D12)	=MAX(E3:E12)	=MAX(F3:F12)	=MAX(G3:G12)	
Average		=AVERAGE(C3:C12)	=AVERAGE(D3:D12)	=AVERAGE(E3:E12)	=AVERAGE(F3:F12)	=AVERAGE(G3:G12)	

Page 1

FIGURE 2-84

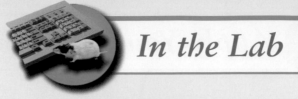

In the Lab

1 Stars and Stripes Automotive Weekly Payroll Worksheet

Problem: The Stars and Stripes Automotive Company has hired you as a summer intern in its software applications area. Because you took an Excel course last semester, the assistant manager has asked you to prepare a weekly payroll report for the six employees listed in Table 2-7.

Instructions: Perform the following tasks to create a worksheet similar to the one shown in Figure 2-85.

	A	B	C	D	E	F	G	H
1	Stars and Stripes Automotive Weekly Payroll							
2	Employee	Rate	Hours	Dep.	Gross Pay	Fed. Tax	State Tax	Net Pay
3	Breeze, Linus	27.50	40.25	4.00	1,106.88	190.61	35.42	880.85
4	Santiago, Juan	18.75	56.00	1.00	1,050.00	202.31	33.60	814.09
5	Webb, Trevor	28.35	38.00	3.00	1,077.30	192.38	34.47	850.44
6	Sabol, Kylie	21.50	46.50	6.00	999.75	153.80	31.99	813.96
7	Ali, Abdul	19.35	17.00	2.00	328.95	50.41	10.53	268.02
8	Goldstein, Kevin	17.05	28.00	5.00	477.40	57.02	15.28	405.10
9	Totals		225.75		5,040.28	846.52	161.29	4,032.46
10	Average	22.08	37.63	3.50	840.05	141.09	26.88	672.08
11	Highest	28.35	56.00	6.00	1,106.88	202.31	35.42	880.85
12	Lowest	17.05	17.00	1.00	328.95	50.41	10.53	268.02

FIGURE 2-85

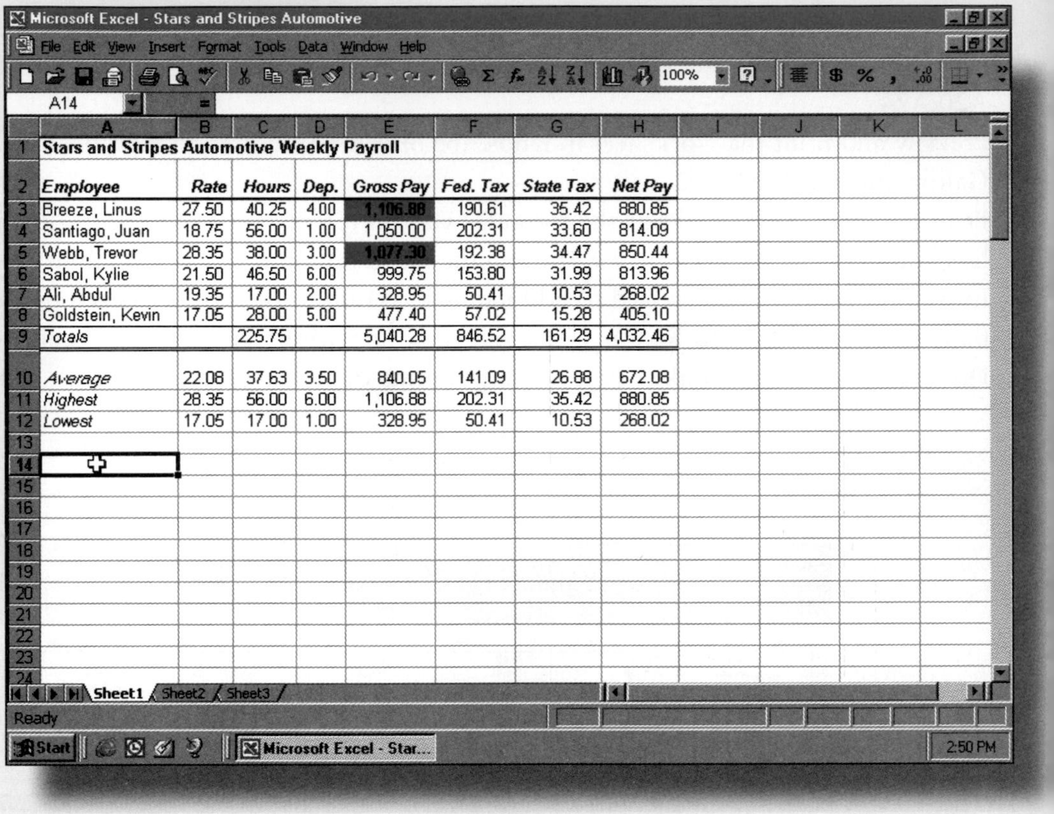

1. Enter the worksheet title `Stars and Stripes Automotive Weekly Payroll` in cell A1. Enter the column titles in row 2, the row titles in column A, and the data from Table 2-7 in columns B through D as shown in Figure 2-85.
2. Use the following formulas to determine the gross pay, federal tax, state tax, and net pay for the first employee
   a. Gross Pay (cell E3) = Rate*Hours or =B3*C3.
   b. Federal Tax (cell F3) = 20% * (Gross Pay – Dependents * 38.46) or =20% *(E3 – D3 * 38.46)
   c. State Tax (cell G3) = 3.2% * Gross Pay or =3.2% * E3
   d. Net Pay (cell H3) = Gross Pay – (Federal Tax + State Tax) or =E3 – (F3 + G3)

   Copy the formulas for the first employee to the remaining employees.
3. Calculate totals for hours, gross pay, federal tax, state tax, and net pay in row 9.
4. Use the appropriate functions to determine the average, highest, and lowest values of each column in rows 10 through 12.
5. Use Range Finder and then the Auditing commands to verify the formula entered in cell F3. Check both precedents and dependents with the Auditing commands. Remove all arrows.

Table 2-7 Payroll Data

EMPLOYEE	RATE	HOURS	DEPENDENTS
Breeze, Linus	27.50	40.25	4
Santiago, Juan	18.75	56.00	1
Webb, Trevor	28.35	38.00	3
Sabol, Kylie	21.50	46.50	6
Ali, Abdul	19.35	17.00	2
Goldstein, Kevin	17.05	28.00	5

In the Lab

6. Bold the worksheet title. Use buttons on the Formatting toolbar to assign the Comma style with two decimal places to the range B3:H12. Bold, italicize, and assign a thick bottom border (column 4, row 3 on the Borders palette) to the range A2:H2. Right-align the column titles in the range B2:H2. Italicize the range A9:A12. Assign a top border and double-line bottom border to the range A9:H9.

7. Change the width of column A to 15.00 characters. If necessary, change the widths of columns B through H to best fit. Change the height of rows 2 and 10 to 24.00 points.

8. Use the Conditional Formatting command on the Format menu to display bold font on a green background for any gross pay greater than $1,050.00 in the range E3:E8.

9. Enter your name, course, laboratory assignment number (Lab 2-1), date, and instructor name in the range A14:A18.

10. Save the workbook using the file name Stars and Stripes Automotive.

11. Preview and then print the worksheet.

12. Press CTRL+LEFT SINGLE QUOTATION MARK (`) to change the display from the values version to the formulas version. Print the formulas version of the worksheet in landscape orientation using the Fit to option on the Page tab in the Page Setup dialog box. After the printer is finished, press CTRL+LEFT SINGLE QUOTATION MARK (`) to reset the worksheet to display the values version. Reset the Scaling option to 100% by clicking the Adjust to option button in the Page sheet in the Page Setup dialog box and then setting the percent value to 100%.

13. Use the keyboard to increase manually the number of hours worked for each employee by 8 hours. The total net pay in cell H9 should equal $4,846.54. If necessary, increase the width of column F to best fit to view the new federal tax total. Preview and print the worksheet with the new values. Close the workbook without saving the changes. Hand in the printouts to your instructor.

2 Mortimer's Seaside Emporium Monthly Accounts Receivable Balance Sheet

Problem: You were recently hired as a part-time assistant in the Accounting department of Mortimer's Seaside Emporium, a popular Biloxi-based general merchandise company with several outlets along the Gulf coast. You have been asked to use Excel to generate a report (Figure 2-86 on the next page) that summarizes the monthly accounts receivable balance. A graphic breakdown of the data also is desired. The customer accounts receivable data in Table 2-8 is available for test purposes.

Table 2-8	Accounts Receivable Data				
CUSTOMER NUMBER	CUSTOMER NAME	BEGINNING BALANCE	PURCHASES	PAYMENTS	CREDITS
27839	Patel, Nipul	$2,356.15	$739.19	$175.00	$435.10
31982	Jaworski, Stanley	6,291.74	1,098.35	250.00	0.00
45012	Portugal, Juanita	4,103.75	620.75	4,000.00	25.00
56341	Country, James	5,691.45	4,352.12	250.00	35.25
76894	Santiago, Carlos	1,045.23	542.10	750.00	189.95

(continued)

In the Lab

Mortimer's Seaside Emporium Monthly Accounts Receivable Balance Sheet *(continued)*

![Microsoft Excel screenshot of Mortimer's Seaside Emporium worksheet]

	Customer Number	Customer Name	Beginning Balance	Purchases	Payments	Credits	Service Charge	New Balance
1	**Mortimer's Seaside Emporium**							
2	**Monthly Accounts Receivable Balance**							
4	27839	Patel, Nipul	$2,356.15	$739.19	$175.00	$435.10	$39.29	$2,524.53
5	31982	Jaworski, Stanley	6,291.74	1,098.35	250.00	0.00	135.94	7,276.03
6	45012	Portugal, Juanita	4,103.75	620.75	4,000.00	25.00	1.77	701.27
7	56341	Country, James	5,691.45	4,352.12	250.00	35.25	121.64	9,879.96
8	76894	Santiago, Carlos	1,045.23	542.10	750.00	189.95	2.37	649.75
9	Totals		$19,488.32	$7,352.51	$5,425.00	$685.30	$301.01	$21,031.54
10	Highest		$6,291.74	$4,352.12	$4,000.00	$435.10	$135.94	$9,879.96
11	Lowest		$1,045.23	$542.10	$175.00	$0.00	$1.77	$649.75

FIGURE 2-86

Instructions Part 1: Create a worksheet similar to the one shown in Figure 2-86. Include all six items in Table 2-8 on the previous page in the report, plus a service charge and a new balance for each customer. Assume no negative unpaid monthly balances. Perform the following tasks.

1. Click the Select All button (to the left of column heading A) and then click the Bold button on the Standard toolbar to bold the entire worksheet.

2. Assign the worksheet title, Mortimer's Seaside Emporium, to cell A1. Assign the worksheet subtitle, Monthly Accounts Receivable Balance, to cell A2.

3. Enter the column titles in the range A3:H3 as shown in Figure 2-86. Change the width of column A to 9.57. Change the widths of columns B through H to best fit.

4. Enter the customer numbers and row titles in column A. Enter the customer numbers as text, rather than numbers. To enter the customer numbers as text, begin each entry with an apostrophe ('). Enter the remaining data in Table 2-8.

5. Use the following formulas to determine the monthly service charge in column G and the new balance in column H for customer 27839. Copy the two formulas down through the remaining customers.
   a. Service Charge = 2.25% * (Beginning Balance – Payments – Credits)
   b. New Balance = Beginning Balance + Purchases – Payments – Credits + Service Charge

In the Lab

6. Calculate totals for beginning balance, purchases, payments, credits, service charge, and new balance in row 9.

7. Assign cell C10 the appropriate function to calculate the maximum value in the range C4:C8. Copy cell C10 to the range D10:H10.

8. Assign cell C11 the appropriate function to calculate the minimum value in the range C4:C8. Copy cell C11 to the range D11:H11.

9. Change the worksheet title in cell A1 to 28-point CG Times font. Format the worksheet subtitle in cell A2 to 20-point CG Times font. Center the worksheet titles in cells A1 and A2 across column A through H. Change the heights of rows 1 through 3 and row 10 to 27.75. Add a heavy outline to the range A1:H2 using the Borders button on the Formatting toolbar.

10. Select the range A1:H2 and then change the background color to Orange (column 2, row 2) on the Fill Color palette. Change the font color in the range A1:H2 to White (column 8, row 5) on the Font Color palette.

11. Italicize the column titles in row 3. Use the Borders button to add a thick bottom border to the column titles in row 3. Center the column titles in row 3. Italicize the titles in rows 9, 10, and 11. Use the Borders button to add a single top border and double-line bottom border to the range A9:H9 (column 4, row 2) on the Borders palette.

12. Use the Format Cells command on the shortcut menu to assign the Currency style with a floating dollar sign to the cells containing numeric data in row 4 and rows 9 through 11. Use the same command to assign the Comma style (currency with no dollar sign) to the range C5:H8. The Format Cells command is preferred over the Comma Style button because the worksheet specifications call for displaying zero as 0.00 rather than as a dash (-), as shown in Figure 2-86.

13. Use the Conditional Formatting command on the Format menu to bold the font and color the background orange of any cell in the range H4:H8 that contains a value greater than or equal to 3000.

14. Change the widths of columns B through H again to best fit, if necessary.

15. Rename the sheet Accounts Receivable.

16. Enter your name, course, laboratory assignment number (Lab 2-2), date, and instructor name in the range A13:A17.

17. Save the workbook using the file name Mortimer's Seaside Emporium. Preview and then print the worksheet. Print the range A3:C9.

18. Press CTRL+LEFT SINGLE QUOTATION MARK (`) to change the display from the values version to the formulas version and then print the worksheet to fit on one page in landscape orientation. After the printer is finished, press CTRL+LEFT SINGLE QUOTATION MARK (`) to reset the worksheet to display the values version. Reset the Scaling option to 100% by clicking the Adjust to option button on the Page tab in the Page Setup dialog box and then setting the percent value to 100%. Hand in the printouts to your instructor.

(continued)

In the Lab

Mortimer's Seaside Emporium Monthly Accounts Receivable Balance Sheet *(continued)*

Instructions Part 2: This part requires that you use the Chart Wizard button on the Standard toolbar to draw a Pie chart. If necessary, use the Office Assistant to obtain information on drawing a Pie chart.

Draw the 3-D Pie chart showing the contribution of each customer to the total new balance as shown in Figure 2-87. Select the nonadjacent chart ranges B4:B8 and H4:H8. That is, select the range B4:B8 and then hold down the CTRL key and select the range H4:H8. The category names in the range B4:B8 will identify the slices, while the data series in the range H4:H8 will determine the size of the slices. Click the Chart Wizard button on the Standard toolbar. Draw the 3-D Pie chart on a new chart sheet. Use the 3-D Pie chart sub-type (column 2, row 1). Add the chart title Contributions to Accounts Receivable.

Rename the Chart1 sheet 3-D Pie Chart. Drag the Accounts Receivable tab to the left of the 3-D Pie Chart tab. Save the workbook using the same file name as in Part 1. Preview and print the chart.

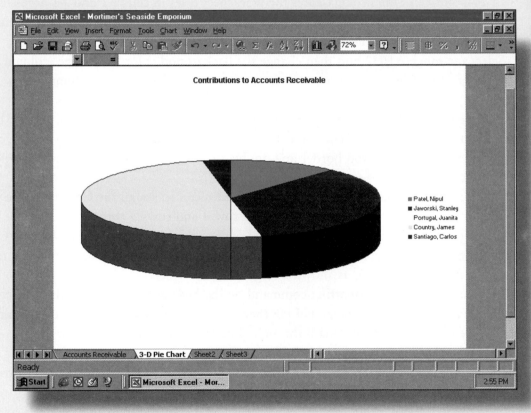

FIGURE 2-87

Instructions Part 3: Change the following purchases: account number 31982 to $3000.00; account number 76894 to $2500.00. The total new balance in cell H9 should equal $24,891.09. Select both sheets by holding down the SHIFT key and clicking the 3-D Pie Chart tab. Preview and print the selected sheets. Hand in the printouts to your instructor.

Instructions Part 4: With your instructor's permission, e-mail the workbook as an attachment to your instructor. Close the workbook without saving the changes.

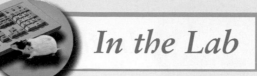

In the Lab

3 Equity Web Queries

Problem: The chief accountant at Rhine.com recently attended a Microsoft seminar and learned that Microsoft Excel 2000 can connect to the World Wide Web, download real-time stock data into a worksheet, and then refresh the data as often as needed. Because you have had courses in Excel and the Internet, she has hired you as a consultant to develop a stock analysis workbook. Her portfolio is listed in Table 2-9.

Table 2-9	Portfolio
COMPANY	STOCK SYMBOL
Dell	DELL
IBM	IBM
Caterpillar	CAT
Wal-Mart	WMT

Instructions Part 1: If necessary, connect to the Internet. Open a new Excel workbook and select cell A1. Perform the following steps to run a Web query to obtain multiple stock quotes, using the stock symbols in Table 2-9.

1. Point to Get External Data on the Data menu and then click Run Saved Query.
2. Double-click Microsoft Investor Stock Quotes in the Run Query dialog box. If the Queries folder does not display, see your instructor for its location.
3. Click the OK button in the Returning External Data to Microsoft Excel dialog box.
4. When the Enter Parameter Value dialog box displays, enter the stock symbols in Table 2-9 into the text box, being sure to separate them by a comma or space. Click the Use this value/reference for future refreshes check box, click the Refresh automatically when cell value changes, and then click the OK button. After several seconds, the stock data returned by the Web query displays in a worksheet as shown in Figure 2-88 on the next page. Because the stock data returned is real-time, the numbers on your worksheet may be different.
5. Enter your name, course, laboratory assignment number (Lab 2-3a), date, and instructor name in the range A20:A24.
6. Rename the sheet Multiple Quotes. Save the workbook using the file name Equities Online. Preview and then print the worksheet in landscape orientation using the Fit to option.
7. Click the following links and print each: Microsoft Investor, Dell Computer Corporation, Dell Chart, and Dell News. After printing each Web page, close the browser and click the Microsoft Excel button on the taskbar to activate Excel. Hand in the printouts to your instructor.

(continued)

In the Lab

Equity Web Queries *(continued)*

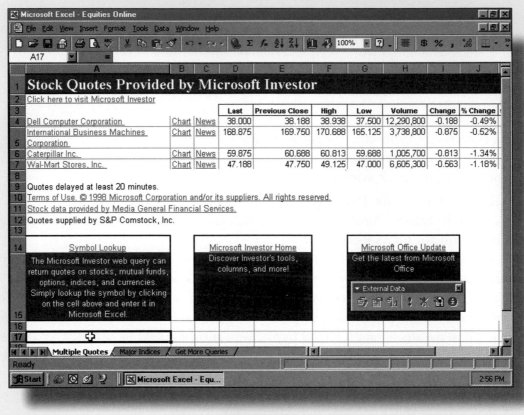

FIGURE 2-88

Instructions Part 2: Do the following to create a worksheet listing the major indices and their current values as shown in Figure 2-89.

1. With the workbook created in Part 1 open, click the Sheet2 tab. Point to Get External Data on the Data menu and then click Run Saved Query.
2. Double-click Microsoft Investor Major Indices in the Run Query dialog box.
3. Click the OK button in the Returning External Data to Microsoft Excel dialog box, starting the data in cell A1 of the existing worksheet.
4. The Web query returns the worksheet shown in Figure 2-89. Your results may differ.
5. Enter your name, course, laboratory assignment number (Lab 2-3b), date, and instructor name in the range A24:A28.
6. Rename the sheet Major Indices. Save the workbook using the same file as in Part 1. Preview and then print the worksheet in landscape orientation using the Fit to option. Hand in the printouts to your instructor.

In the Lab

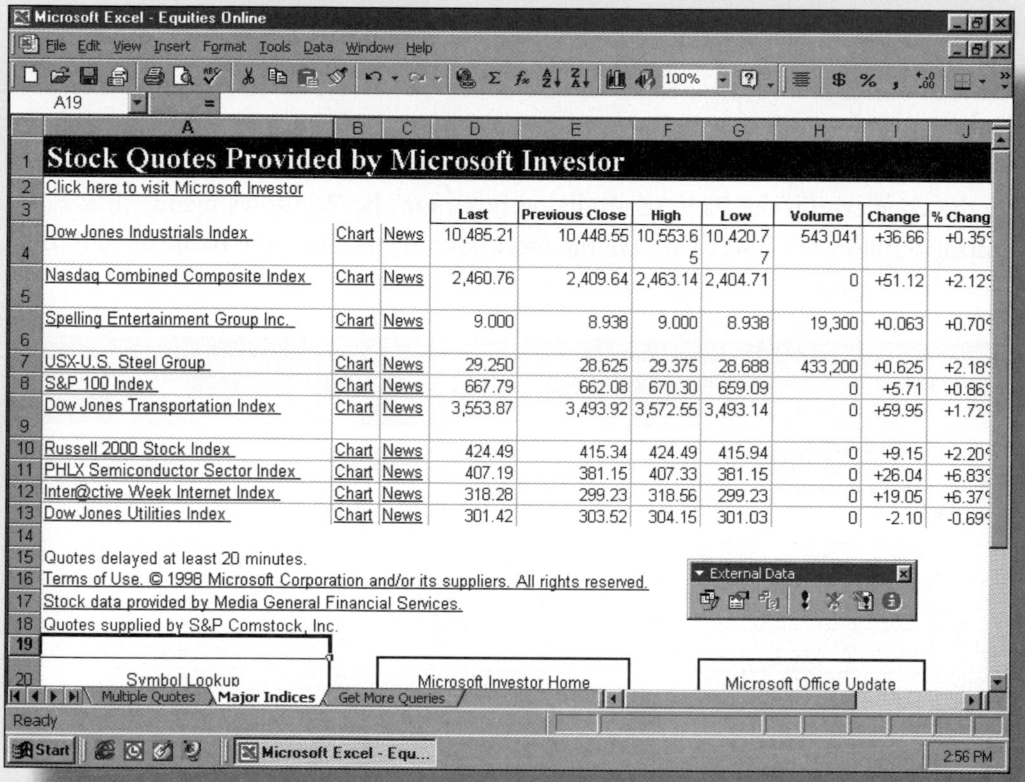

	A	B	C	D	E	F	G	H	I	J
1	Stock Quotes Provided by Microsoft Investor									
2	Click here to visit Microsoft Investor									
3				Last	Previous Close	High	Low	Volume	Change	% Chang
4	Dow Jones Industrials Index	Chart	News	10,485.21	10,448.55	10,553.6 5	10,420.7 7	543,041	+36.66	+0.35%
5	Nasdaq Combined Composite Index	Chart	News	2,460.76	2,409.64	2,463.14	2,404.71	0	+51.12	+2.12%
6	Spelling Entertainment Group Inc.	Chart	News	9.000	8.938	9.000	8.938	19,300	+0.063	+0.70%
7	USX-U.S. Steel Group	Chart	News	29.250	28.625	29.375	28.688	433,200	+0.625	+2.18%
8	S&P 100 Index	Chart	News	667.79	662.08	670.30	659.09	0	+5.71	+0.86%
9	Dow Jones Transportation Index	Chart	News	3,553.87	3,493.92	3,572.55	3,493.14	0	+59.95	+1.72%
10	Russell 2000 Stock Index	Chart	News	424.49	415.34	424.49	415.94	0	+9.15	+2.20%
11	PHLX Semiconductor Sector Index	Chart	News	407.19	381.15	407.33	381.15	0	+26.04	+6.83%
12	Inter@ctive Week Internet Index	Chart	News	318.28	299.23	318.56	299.23	0	+19.05	+6.37%
13	Dow Jones Utilities Index	Chart	News	301.42	303.52	304.15	301.03	0	-2.10	-0.69%
14										
15	Quotes delayed at least 20 minutes.									
16	Terms of Use. © 1998 Microsoft Corporation and/or its suppliers. All rights reserved.									
17	Stock data provided by Media General Financial Services.									
18	Quotes supplied by S&P Comstock, Inc.									
19										
20	Symbol Lookup			Microsoft Investor Home			Microsoft Office Update			

FIGURE 2-89

Instructions Part 3: Create a worksheet showing the latest commodity prices (Figure 2-90 on the next page). The Web query for commodity prices is not one of the queries available in the Queries folder by default. Thus, you must download it from the World Wide Web.

Perform the following tasks.

1. With the workbook Equities Online created in Parts 1 and 2 open, click Sheet3. Rename the Sheet3 tab Get More Queries.
2. Point to Get External Data on the Data menu, and then click Run Saved Query. Double-click Get More Web Queries in the Run Query dialog box.
3. Click the OK button in the Returning External Data to Microsoft Excel dialog box, starting the data in cell A1 of the existing worksheet.
4. When the worksheet titled Microsoft Excel Web Queries displays, scroll down and click the link CNN Commodities under Commodities.
5. If the File in Use dialog box displays, click the Notify button. When the File Now Available dialog box displays, click the Read-Write button. The query creates a Read-Only workbook (Book2) and a Read-Write workbook (Book3).
6. With Book3 active, scroll down so row 15 displays at the top of your screen (Figure 2-90).

(continued)

In the Lab

Equity Web Queries *(continued)*

7. Enter your name, course, laboratory assignment number (Lab 2-3c), date, and instructor name below the entries in column A, in separate but adjacent cells.

8. After viewing the Commodities worksheet, preview and print it in portrait orientation with scaling adjusted to 100% (see the Page tab on the Page Setup dialog box). On the Windows menu, click Equities Online. Click the Multiple Quotes tab and then save the workbook using the same name as in Part 1. Hand in the printout to your instructor.

FIGURE 2-90

Instructions Part 4: Click the Multiple Quotes tab. Right-click a toolbar and click External Data on the shortcut menu. Refresh the data by clicking the Refresh All button on the External Data toolbar. Click the Click here to visit Microsoft Investor link. When the MSN Money Central investor page displays, find the latest prices for the following symbols: MSFT, INTC, YHOO, and GE. Print the Web page for each. Hand in the printouts to your instructor.

Cases and Places

The difficulty of these case studies varies:
▶ are the least difficult; ▶▶ are more difficult; and ▶▶▶ are the most difficult.

1 ▶ The household electric bill has just arrived in the mail, and you have been accused of driving up the total by burning the midnight oil. You are convinced your late-night studying has little effect on the total amount due. You obtain a brochure from the electric company that lists the typical operating costs of appliances based on average sizes and local electricity rates (Figure 2-91).

With this data, you produce a worksheet to share with your family. Use the concepts and techniques presented in this project to create and format the worksheet.

APPLIANCE	COST PER HOUR	HOURS USED DAILY	TOTAL COST PER DAY	TOTAL COST PER MONTH (30 DAYS)
Clothes dryer	$0.5331	2		
Iron	$0.1173	0.5		
Light bulb (150 watt)	$0.0160	5		
Personal computer	$0.0213	3		
Radio	$0.0075	2		
Refrigerator	$0.0113	24		
Stereo	$0.0053	4		
Television	$0.0128	6		
VCR	$0.0032	2		

FIGURE 2-91

2 ▶ In order to determine the effectiveness of their endangered species recovery plan, the Fish and Wildlife Department traps and releases red wolves in selected areas and records how many are pregnant. To obtain a representative sample, the department tries to trap approximately 20% of the population. The sample for 5 sections is shown in Table 2-10.

Use the following formula to determine the total red wolf population for each section:

Wolves in a Section = 5 * (Total Catch + Pregnant Wolves) – 5 * Death Rate * (Total Catch + Pregnant Wolves)

Use the concepts and techniques presented in this project to create the worksheet. Determine appropriate totals. Finally, estimate the total state red wolf population if 898 sections are in the state.

Table 2-10	Red Wolf Catch Data		
SECTION	WOLVES CAUGHT	WOLVES PREGNANT	ANNUAL DEATH RATE
1	55	21	19%
2	32	7	22%
3	26	8	32%
4	29	17	8%
5	72	28	29%

Cases and Places

3 ▶ The Student Loan Office has a special assistance program that offers emergency short-term loans at simple interest. The five types of emergency loans, end-of-year principal, rate, and time are shown in Table 2-11.

Create a worksheet that includes the information in Table 2-11, the interest, and amount due. Use the following formulas:

Interest = Principal x Rate x Time
Amount Due = Principal + Interest

Also include a total, maximum value, and minimum value for Principal, Interest, and Amount Due. Format the worksheet using the techniques presented in this project.

Table 2-11	Emergency Loans		
LOAN TYPE	PRINCIPAL	RATE	TIME IN YEARS
Tuition Assistance	$96,000	9%	0.4
Academic Supplies	$32,000	11%	0.3
Room and Board	56,250	8%	0.2
Personal Emergency	$7,500	7%	0.17
Travel Expenses	$6,275	15%	0.33

4 ▶ Rich's Oil Production Company drills oil in six states. The management has asked you to develop a worksheet for the company's next meeting from the data in Table 2-12. The worksheet should determine the gross value of the oil, the taxes, and the net value for each state, as well as the net value for all the states. Use these formulas:

Gross Value = Barrels of Oil Produced × Price Per Barrel
Taxes = Gross Value * 7%
Net Value = Gross Value − Taxes

Include appropriate totals, averages, minimums, and maximums. Draw a pie chart on a separate sheet that shows the barrels of oil contribution of each state.

Table 2-12	Oil Production Data	
STATE	BARRELS OF OIL PRODUCED	PRICE PER BARREL
Alaska	12,890	$14.25
California	4,321	$13.50
Louisiana	8,500	$15.25
Montana	4,250	$13.50
Oklahoma	9,705	$11.75
Texas	7,543	$14.25

5 ▶▶ Use the concepts and techniques described in this project to run the Web queries titled Microsoft Investor Dow30 and Microsoft Investor Currency Rates on separate worksheets shortly after the stock market opens. Print each worksheet to fit on one page in landscape orientation. Refresh the worksheets later in the day near the stock market close. Print the worksheets and compare them.

Run Get More Web Queries through the Run Saved Query command. Print the list on queries available on the Web. Download three of the queries. Run each one and print the results. For more information, see In the Lab Part 3 on page E 2.75.

Cases and Places

6 ▶▶ The Woodbridge Furniture Company has decided to pay a 5% commission to its salespeople to stimulate sales. The company currently pays each employee a base salary. The management has projected each employee's sales for the next quarter. this information - employee name, employee base salary, and projected sales - follows: Baker, Tim, $6,000.00, $225,456.00; Learner, Joseph, $7,500.00, $264,888.00; Albright, Barbara, $8,500.00, $235,250.00; Mourissee, Lynn, $7,250.00, $258,450.00; Noble, Richard, $4,250.00, $325,456.00.

With this data, you have been asked to develop a worksheet calculating the amount of commission and the quarterly salary for each employee. the following formulas can be used to obtain this information:

Commission Amount = 5% x Projected Sales

Quarterly Salary = Employee Base Salary + Commission Amount

Include a total, Average Value, Highest Value, and Lowest Value for Employee Base Salary, Commission Amount, and Quarterly Salary. Create an appropriate chart illustrating the portion each employee's quarterly salary contributes to the total quarterly salary. Use the concepts and techniques presented in this project to create and format the worksheet and chart.

7 ▶▶▶ Regular, moderate exercise lowers cholesterol and blood pressure, reduces stress, controls weight, and increases bone strength. Fitness experts recommend individuals who need to lose weight do so at the rate of 1½ to 2 pounds per week. If an individual maintains a regular, sensible diet and burns 750 extra calories each day, he or she will lose about 1½ pounds of fatty tissue a week. Visit a fitness center at your school or in your community to discuss various exercise options. Find out the types of activities offered (for example, aerobics, swimming, jogging, tennis, racquetball, and basketball). Then, list how many calories are burned per hour when performing each of these activities. Using this information, create a worksheet showing the activities offered, the number of calories burned per hour performing these activities, the number of calories burned and pounds lost if you exercise two hours, four hours, and seven hours a week while performing each of these activities.

MICROSOFT

Access 2000

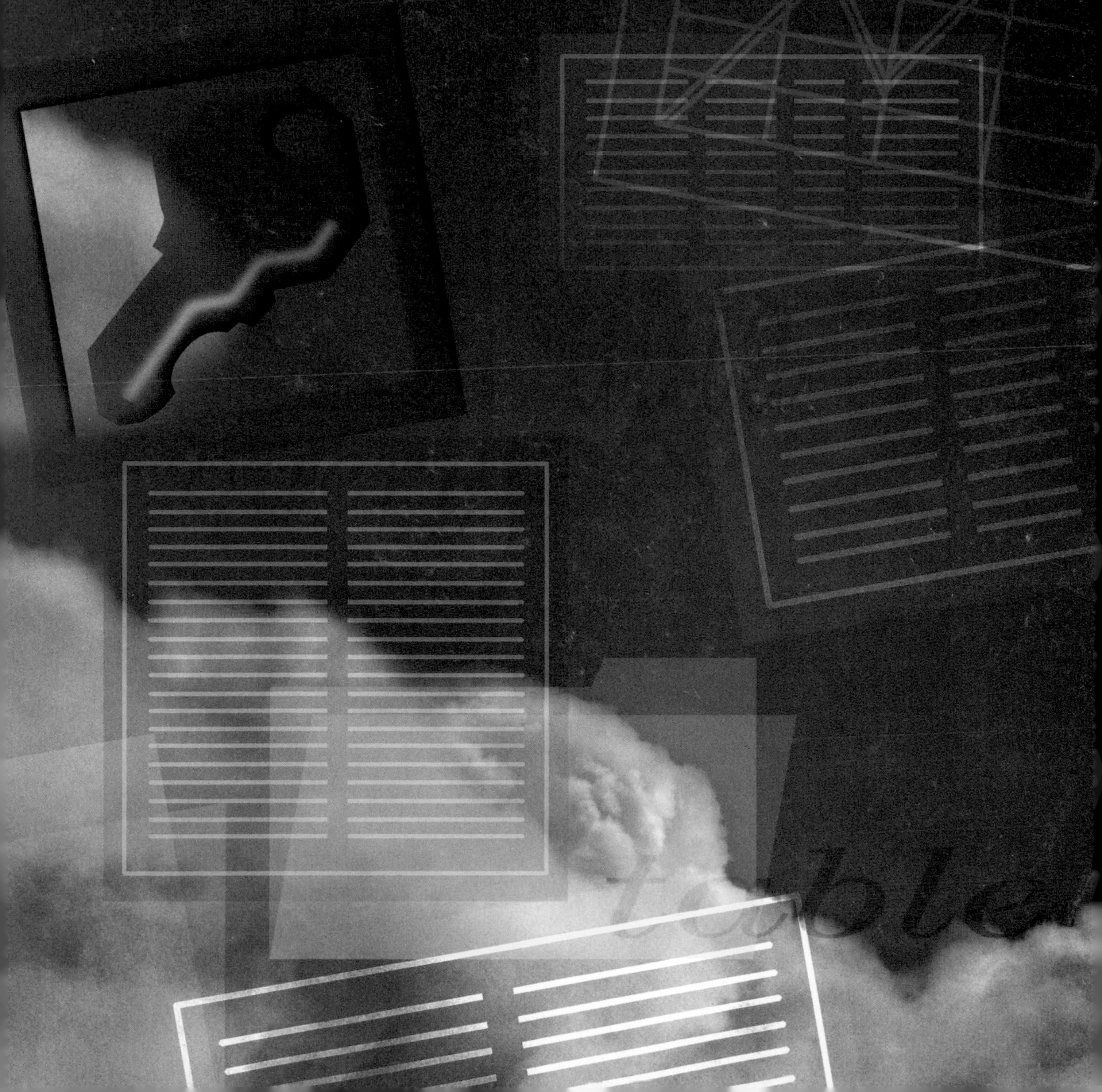

Microsoft Access 2000

P R O J E C T

1

Creating a Database Using Design and Datasheet Views

You will have mastered the material in this project when you can:

O B J E C T I V E S

- Describe databases and database management systems
- Start Access
- Describe the features of the Access screen
- Create a database
- Create a table
- Define the fields in a table
- Open a table
- Add records to an empty table
- Close a table
- Close a database and quit Access
- Open a database
- Add records to a nonempty table
- Print the contents of a table
- Use a form to view data
- Create a custom report
- Use Microsoft Access Help
- Design a database to eliminate redundancy

A Match Made in Computer Heaven

Mentoring Unites Experts and Schools

Educational issues dominate the airwaves and print media. From decorum in the classroom to equal access to the Internet, school-related topics are broadcast on the evening news and published in the morning newspapers. Then discussions take place around family dinner tables and at study sessions. Often these dialogues focus on improving the classroom experience by strengthening the relationship among educators, students, community members, and funding sources.

One effective way of enriching the learning process is to involve various groups in education. For example, college students are earning federal work-study funds by helping students in elementary grades learn to read and do math in the America Reads and the America Counts programs. More than 900 public schools have received grants in the 21st Century Community Learning Centers program to provide safe places for children to gather. Business leaders critique middle school students' writing samples as part of the National School Network Exchange, a

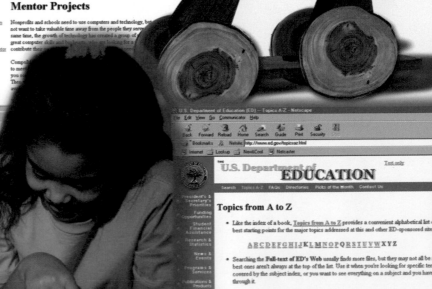

grant-funded program that links more than 500 schools, companies, museums, and governmental agencies via the Internet.

In mythology, Mentor advised Odysseus, who lead the Greeks in the Trojan War. In today's world, mentors advise people needing direction and coaching. These partnerships are common in the computer field. For example, network experts collaborate with a culturally diverse school district to network classrooms throughout the region. Technology buffs develop a distance education program for students living in remote areas. Software experts install donated copies of Microsoft Office in computer labs and then train teachers.

Building these partnerships requires superb technological and organizational skills, strong marketing, and dedicated staff members. Various local, regional, and national organizations have the right mix of technology expertise and qualified personnel to meet these requirements. The nation's largest nonprofit computerization assistance center, CompuMentor, is one of these successful partnering organizations. CompuMentor has linked its staff with more than 6,000 schools and other nonprofit organizations since 1987.

The heart of its success is matching computer experts with the appropriate school or organization. Some mentors volunteer long term, while others agree to work intensively for a few days, particularly in telecommunications areas. Potential mentors complete an application at CompuMentor's Web site (www.compumentor.org) by entering specific information in boxes, called fields, pertaining to their knowledge of operating systems, networking, and hardware repair. They give additional information about their available working hours, training experience, and special skills in office and accounting applications, databases, and desktop publishing.

This information structures records in the CompuMentor database. The staff then can search these records to find a volunteer whose skills match the school's or organization's needs. Similarly, in Project 1, you will use the Access database management system to enter records in the Bavant Marine Services database so the marina staff can match service technicians with boat owners whose vessels need repairs.

Uniting schools with appropriate experts increases awareness of educational issues and ultimately improves the learning process. For more information on building mentoring relationships, visit the U.S. Department of Education Web site (www.ed.gov) or call 1-800-USA-LEARN.

Microsoft Access 2000

Creating a Database Using Design and Datasheet Views

Microsoft Access 2000

P R O J E C T

1

With the popularity of water sports increasing, the number of recreational boaters has risen dramatically! Boats come in all shapes and sizes and are often stored at a marina.

Larger, full-service marinas typically have a service department. The department performs the requested work, such as engine repair, and bills the owner's account. Smaller marinas usually cannot provide on-site service departments, but can offer the same convenience to boat owners by contracting with Bavant Marine Services. A boat owner requiring service notifies the marina, which then contacts Bavant. Bavant sends a technician to perform the required labor and bills the marina.

To ensure operations run smoothly, Bavant Marine Services needs to maintain data on its technicians and their assigned marinas. Bavant wants to organize the data in a database, managed by a database management system such as Access. In this way, Bavant can keep its data current and accurate while management can analyze the data for trends and produce a variety of useful reports. Your task is to help Bavant Marine Services in creating and using their database.

What Is Microsoft Access 2000?

Microsoft Access 2000 is a powerful database management system (DBMS) that functions in the Windows environment and allows you to create and process data in a database. Some of the key features are:

▶ **Data entry and update** Access provides easy mechanisms for adding data, changing data, and deleting data, including the ability to make mass changes in a single operation.
▶ **Queries** (questions) Using Access, it is easy to ask complex questions concerning the data in the database and receive instant answers.
▶ **Forms** In Access, you can produce attractive and useful forms for viewing and updating data.
▶ **Reports** Access contains a feature to allow you to easily create sophisticated reports for presenting your data.
▶ **Web Support** Access allows you to save objects (reports, tables) in HTML format so they can be viewed using a browser. You also can create data access pages to allow real-time access to data in the database via the Internet.

Project One — Bavant Marine Services Database

Creating, storing, sorting, and retrieving data are important tasks. In their personal lives, many people keep a variety of records such as names, addresses, and telephone numbers of friends and business associates, records of investments, records of expenses for tax purposes, and so on. These records must be arranged for quick access. Businesses also must be able to store and access information quickly and easily. Personnel and inventory records, payroll information, client records, order data, and accounts receivable information all are crucial and must be available readily.

A 1.6

The term **database** describes a collection of data organized in a manner that allows access, retrieval, and use of that data. A database management system, such as Access, allows you to use a computer to create a database; add, change, and delete data in the database; sort the data in the database; retrieve data in the database; and create forms and reports using the data in the database.

In Access, a database consists of a collection of tables. Figure 1-1 shows a sample database for Bavant Marine Services. It consists of two tables. The Marina table contains information about the marinas that Bavant Marine Services provides service for. Each marina is assigned to a specific technician. The Technician table contains information about the technicians to whom these marinas are assigned.

fields

marinas of technician Trista Anderson

Marina table

MARINA NUMBER	NAME	ADDRESS	CITY	STATE	ZIP CODE	WARRANTY	NON-WARRANTY	TECH NUMBER
AD57	Alan's Docks	314 Central	Burton	MI	49611	$1,248.00	$597.75	23
AN75	Afton's Marina	21 West 8th	Glenview	MI	48121	$1,906.50	$831.25	36
BL72	Brite's Landing	281 Robin	Burton	MI	49611	$217.00	$0.00	36
EL25	Elend Marina	462 River	Torino	MI	48268	$413.50	$678.75	49
FB96	Fenton's Boats	36 Bayview	Cavela	MI	47926	$923.20	$657.50	23
FM22	Fedder Marina	283 Waterfront	Burton	MI	49611	$432.00	$0.00	36
JB92	JT Boat Club	28 Causeway	Torino	MI	48268	$0.00	$0.00	36
NW72	Nelson's Wharf	27 Lake	Masondale	MI	49832	$608.50	$520.00	23
SM72	Solton's Marine	867 Bay Ridge	Glenview	MI	48121	$462.50	$295.00	49
TR72	The Reef	92 East Bay	Woodview	MI	47212	$219.00	$0.00	36

records

Technician table

technician Trista Anderson

TECH NUMBER	LAST NAME	FIRST NAME	ADDRESS	CITY	STATE	ZIP CODE	HOURLY RATE	YTD EARNINGS
23	Anderson	Trista	283 Belton	Port Anton	MI	47989	$24.00	$17,862.00
36	Nichols	Ashton	978 Richmond	Hewitt	MI	47618	$21.00	$19,560.00
49	Gomez	Teresa	2855 Parry	Ashley	MI	47711	$22.00	$21,211.50

FIGURE 1-1

Databases in Access 2000

In some DBMS's, every table, query, form, or report is stored in a separate file. This is not the case in Access 2000, in which a database is stored in a single file on disk. The file contains all the tables, queries, forms, reports, and programs that you create for this database.

The rows in the tables are called **records**. A record contains information about a given person, product, or event. A row in the Marina table, for example, contains information about a specific marina.

The columns in the tables are called fields. A **field** contains a specific piece of information within a record. In the Marina table, for example, the fourth field, City, contains the city where the marina is located.

The first field in the Marina table is the Marina Number. This is a code assigned by Bavant Marine Services to each marina. Like many organizations, Bavant Marine Services calls it a *number* although it actually contains letters. The marina numbers have a special format. They consist of two uppercase letters followed by a two-digit number.

These numbers are unique; that is, no two marinas will be assigned the same number. Such a field can be used as a **unique identifier**. This simply means that a given marina number will appear only in a single record in the table. Only one record exists, for example, in which the marina number is BL72. A unique identifier also is called a **primary key**. Thus, the Marina Number field is the primary key for the Marina table.

The next eight fields in the Marina table are Name, Address, City, State, Zip Code, Warranty, Non-warranty, and Tech Number. The Warranty field contains the amount billed to the Marina that should be covered by the boat owner's warranty. The Non-warranty field contains the amount that is not covered by warranty.

For example, marina AD57 is Alan's Docks. It is located at 314 Central in Burton, Michigan. The zip code is 49611. The marina has been billed $1,248.00 that should be covered by warranty and $597.75 that will not be covered by warranty.

Each marina is assigned to a single technician. The last field in the Marina table, Tech Number, gives the number of the marina's technician.

The first field in the Technician table, Tech Number, is the number assigned by Bavant Marine Services to the technician. These numbers are unique, so Tech Number is the primary key of the Technician table.

The other fields in the Technician table are Last Name, First Name, Address, City, State, Zip Code, Hourly Rate, and YTD Earnings. The Hourly Rate field gives the technician's hourly billing rate, and the YTD Earnings field contains the total amount that has been paid to the technician for services so far this year.

For example, Technician 23 is Trista Anderson. She lives at 283 Belton in Port Anton, Michigan. Her zip code is 47989. Her hourly billing rate is $24.00 and her YTD earnings are $17,862.00.

The tech number displays in both the Marina table and the Technician table. It is used to relate marinas and technicians. For example, in the Marina table, you see that the tech number for marina AD57 is 23. To find the name of this technician, look for the row in the Technician table that contains 23 in the Tech Number field. Once you have found it, you know the marina is assigned to Trista Anderson. To find all the marinas assigned to Trista Anderson, on the other hand, look through the Marina table for all the marinas that contain 23 in the Tech Number field. Her marinas are AD57 (Alan's Docks), FB96 (Fenton's Boats), and NW72 (Nelson's Wharf).

Together with the management of Bavant Marine Services, you have determined the data that must be maintained in the database is that shown in Figure 1-1 on page A 1.7. You first must create the database and the tables it contains. In the process, you must define the fields included in the two tables, as well as the type of data each field will contain. You then must add the appropriate records to the tables. You also must print the contents of the tables. Finally, you must create a report with the Marina Number, Name, Warranty, and Non-warranty fields for each marina served by Bavant Marine Services. Other reports and requirements for the database at Bavant Marine Services will be addressed with the Bavant Marine Services management in the future.

Starting Access and Creating a New Database

In Access, all the tables, reports, forms, and queries that you create are stored in a single file called a database. Thus before creating any of these objects, you must first start Access and create the database that will hold them. To start Access, first make sure that Windows is running. Once you have done so, perform the following steps to start Access, create a new database, and save the database on a floppy disk.

 To Start Access

① **Place a formatted floppy disk in drive A, click the Start button, and then point to New Office Document on the Start menu.**

The Start menu displays (Figure 1-2).

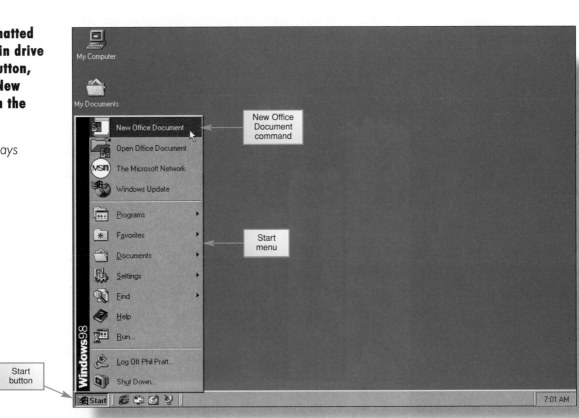

FIGURE 1-2

2 **Click New Office Document. If the General tab is not selected, that is, if it does not display in front of the other tabs, click the General tab. Click the Blank Database icon and then point to the OK button.**

The New Office Document dialog box displays (Figure 1-3). The Blank Database icon is selected.

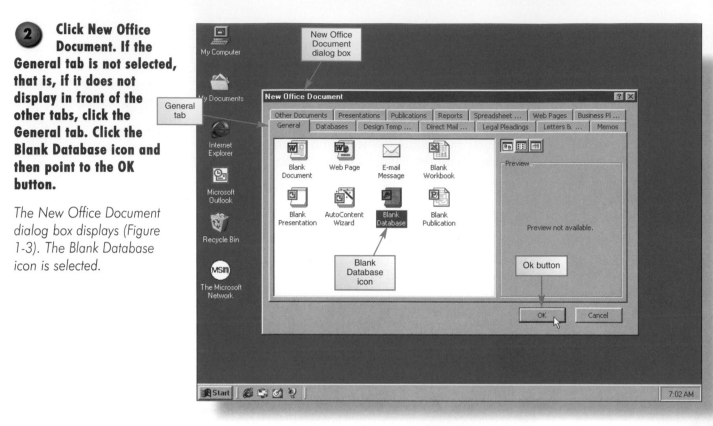

FIGURE 1-3

3 **Click the OK button and then point to the Save in box arrow.**

The File New Database dialog box displays (Figure 1-4).

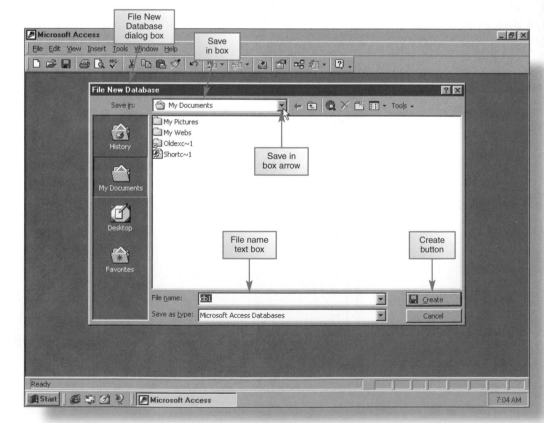

FIGURE 1-4

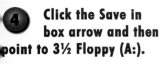 **Click the Save in box arrow and then point to 3½ Floppy (A:).**

The Save in list displays (Figure 1-5).

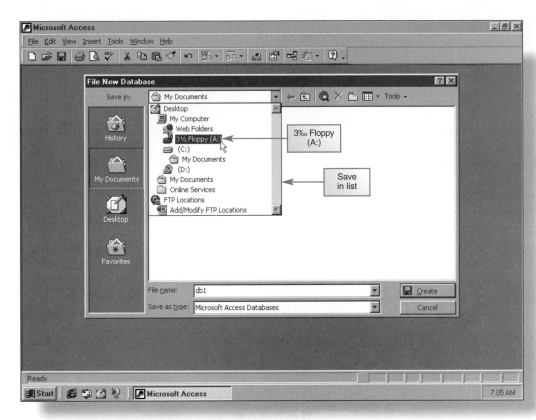

FIGURE 1-5

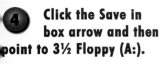 **Click 3½ Floppy (A:). Click the File name text box. Repeatedly press the BACKSPACE key to delete db1 (your number may be different) and then type** Bavant Marine Services **as the file name. Point to the Create button.**

The file name is changed to Bavant Marine Services (Figure 1-6).

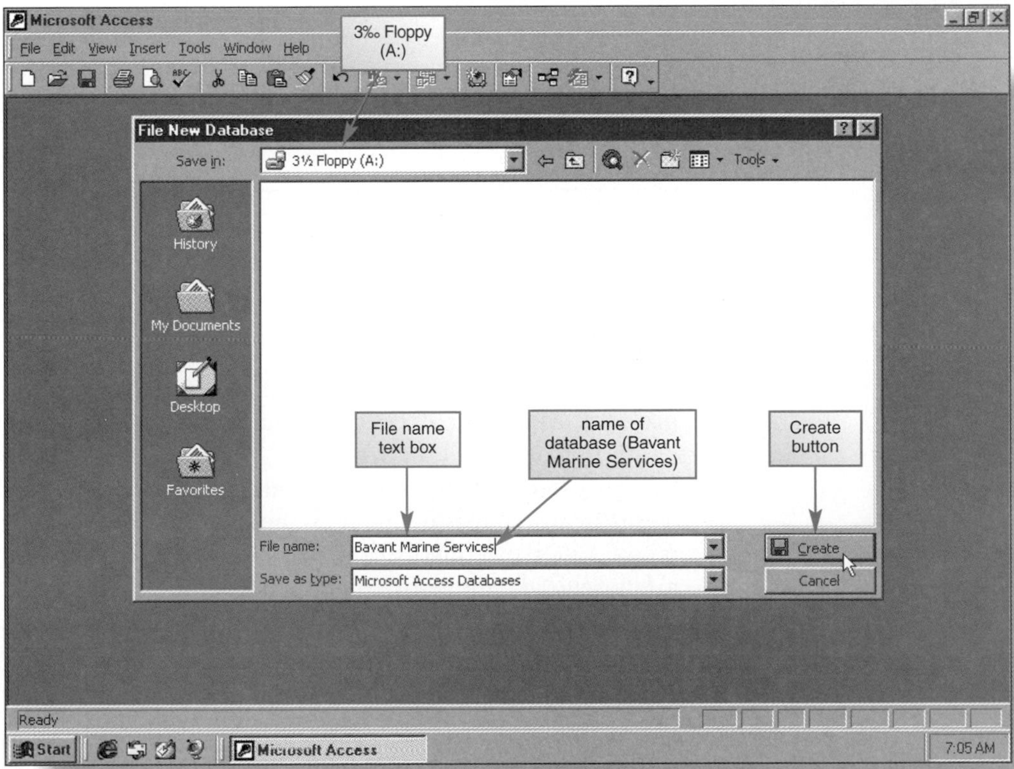

FIGURE 1-6

6 Click the Create button to create the database. If the Office Assistant displays, right-click the Office Assistant and then point to Hide on the shortcut menu.

The Bavant Marine Services database is created. The Bavant Marine Services : Database window displays on the desktop (Figure 1-7). The **Office Assistant**, a tool you can use to obtain help while working with Microsoft Access may display. (You will see how to use the Office Assistant later in this project.)

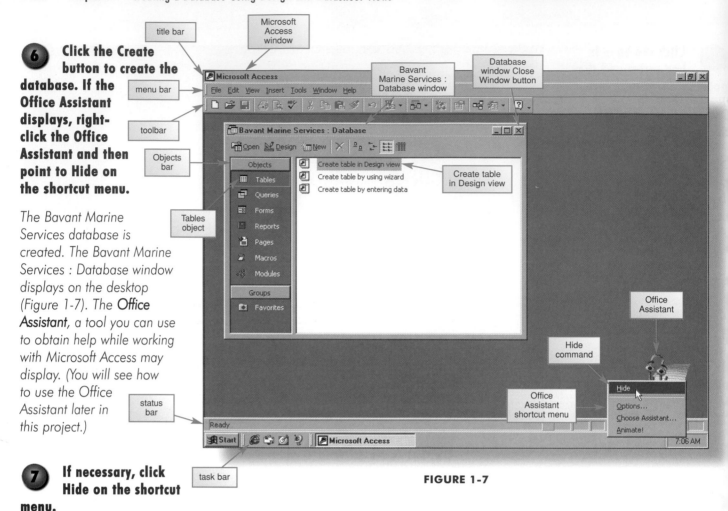

FIGURE 1-7

7 If necessary, click Hide on the shortcut menu.

The Office Assistant no longer displays.

Other Ways

1. Right-click Start button, click Open, double-click New Office Document
2. On Start menu click Programs, click Microsoft Access

Toolbars

Normally, the correct Access 2000 toolbar automatically will display. If it does not, click View on the menu bar, and then click Toolbars. Click the toolbar for the activity in which you are engaged. See Appendix C for additional details.

The Access Desktop and the Database Window

The first bar on the desktop (Figure 1-7) is the **title bar**. It displays the title of the product, Microsoft Access. The button on the right is the **Close button**. Clicking the Close button closes the window.

The second bar is the **menu bar**. It contains a list of menu names. To open a menu from the menu bar, click the menu name. Initially a personalized version of the menu, one that consists of commands you have selected most recently, displays. After a few seconds, the entire menu displays. If the command you wish to select is on the personalized menu, you can select it immediately. If not, wait a few seconds to view the entire menu. (The menus shown throughout this book are the full menus, the ones that display after a few seconds.)

The third bar is the **Database window toolbar**. The Database window toolbar contains buttons that allow you to perform certain tasks more quickly than using the menu bar. Each button contains a picture, or **icon**, depicting its function. The specific buttons on the Database window toolbar will vary, depending on the task on which you are working.

The **taskbar** at the bottom of the screen displays the Start button, any active windows, and the current time.

Immediately above the Windows taskbar is the **status bar** (Figure 1-7). It contains special information that is appropriate for the task on which you are working. Currently, it contains the word, Ready, which means Access is ready to accept commands.

The **Database window**, referred to in Figure 1-7 as the Bavant Marine Services : Database window, is a special window that allows you to access easily and rapidly a variety of objects such as tables, queries, forms, and reports. To do so, you will use the various components of the window.

More About

Creating a Table

Access 2000 includes Table Wizards that guide you by suggesting some commonly used tables and fields. If you already know the fields you need, however, it usually is easier to simply create the table yourself. For more information, visit the Access 2000 More About Web page (www.scsite.com/ac2000/more.htm) and then click Table Wizards.

Creating a Table

An Access database consists of a collection of tables. Once you have created the database, you must create each of the tables within it. In this project, for example, you must create both the Marina and Technician tables shown in Figure 1-1 on page A 1.7.

To create a table, you describe the **structure** of the table to Access by describing the fields within the table. For each field, you indicate the following:

1. **Field name** — Each field in the table must have a unique name. In the Marina table (Figure 1-8), for example, the field names are Marina Number, Name, Address, City, State, Zip Code, Warranty, Non-warranty, and Tech Number.

Structure of Marina table

FIELD NAME	DATA TYPE	FIELD SIZE	PRIMARY KEY?	DESCRIPTION
Marina Number	Text	4	Yes	Marina Number (Primary Key)
Name	Text	20		Marina Name
Address	Text	15		Street Address
City	Text	15		City
State	Text	2		State (Two-Character Abbreviation)
Zip Code	Text	5		Zip Code (Five-Character Version)
Warranty	Currency			Current Warranty Amount
Non-warranty	Currency			Current Non-warranty Amount
Tech Number	Text	2		Number of Marina's Technician

Data for Marina table

MARINA NUMBER	NAME	ADDRESS	CITY	STATE	ZIP CODE	WARRANTY	NON-WARRANTY	TECH NUMBER
AD57	Alan's Docks	314 Central	Burton	MI	49611	$1,248.00	$597.75	23
AN75	Afton's Marina	21 West 8th	Glenview	MI	48121	$1,906.50	$831.25	36
BL72	Brite's Landing	281 Robin	Burton	MI	49611	$217.00	$0.00	36
EL25	Elend Marina	462 River	Torino	MI	48268	$413.50	$678.75	49
FB96	Fenton's Boats	36 Bayview	Cavela	MI	47926	$923.20	$657.50	23
FM22	Fedder Marina	283 Waterfront	Burton	MI	49611	$432.00	$0.00	36
JB92	JT Boat Club	28 Causeway	Torino	MI	48268	$0.00	$0.00	36
NW72	Nelson's Wharf	27 Lake	Masondale	MI	49832	$608.50	$520.00	23
SM72	Solton's Marine	867 Bay Ridge	Glenview	MI	48121	$462.50	$295.00	49
TR72	The Reef	92 East Bay	Woodview	MI	47212	$219.00	$0.00	36

FIGURE 1-8

Data Types (General)

Different database management systems have different available data types. Even data types that are essentially the same can have different names. The Access 2000 Text data type, for example, is referred to as Character in some systems and Alpha in others.

Data Types (Access 2000)

Access 2000 offers a wide variety of data types, some of which have special options associated with them. For more information on data types, visit the Access 2000 More About Web page (www.scsite.com/ac2000/more.htm) and then click Data Types.

2. **Data type** — Data type indicates to Access the type of data the field will contain. Some fields can contain letters of the alphabet and numbers. Others contain only numbers. Others, such as Warranty and Non-warranty, can contain numbers and dollar signs.
3. **Description** — Access allows you to enter a detailed description of the field.

You also can assign field widths to text fields (fields whose data type is Text). This indicates the maximum number of characters that can be stored in the field. If you do not assign a width to such a field, Access assumes the width is 50.

You also must indicate which field or fields make up the **primary key**; that is, the unique identifier, for the table. In the sample database, the Marina Number field is the primary key of the Marina table and the Tech Number field is the primary key of the Technician table.

The rules for field names are:

1. Names can be up to 64 characters in length.
2. Names can contain letters, digits, and spaces, as well as most of the punctuation symbols.
3. Names cannot contain periods, exclamation points (!), or square brackets ([ ]).
4. The same name cannot be used for two different fields in the same table.

Each field has a **data type**. This indicates the type of data that can be stored in the field. The data types you will use in this project are:

1. **Text** — The field can contain any characters.
2. **Number** — The field can contain only numbers. The numbers either can be positive or negative. Fields are assigned this type so they can be used in arithmetic operations. Fields that contain numbers but will not be used for arithmetic operations usually are assigned a data type of Text. The Tech Number field, for example, is a text field because the tech numbers will not be involved in any arithmetic.
3. **Currency** — The field can contain only dollar amounts. The values will be displayed with dollar signs, commas, decimal points, and with two digits following the decimal point. Like numeric fields, you can use currency fields in arithmetic operations. Access assigns a size to currency fields automatically.

The field names, data types, field widths, primary key information, and descriptions for the Marina table are shown in Figure 1-8. With this information, you are ready to begin creating the table. To create the table, use the following steps.

Steps **To Create a Table**

① **Right-click Create table in Design view and then point to Open on the shortcut menu.**

The shortcut menu for creating a table in Design view displays (Figure 1-9).

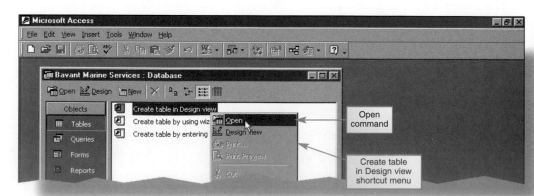

FIGURE 1-9

② Click Open.

The Table1 : Table window displays (Figure 1-10).

③ Click the Maximize button for the Table1 : Table window.

A maximized Table1 : Table window displays.

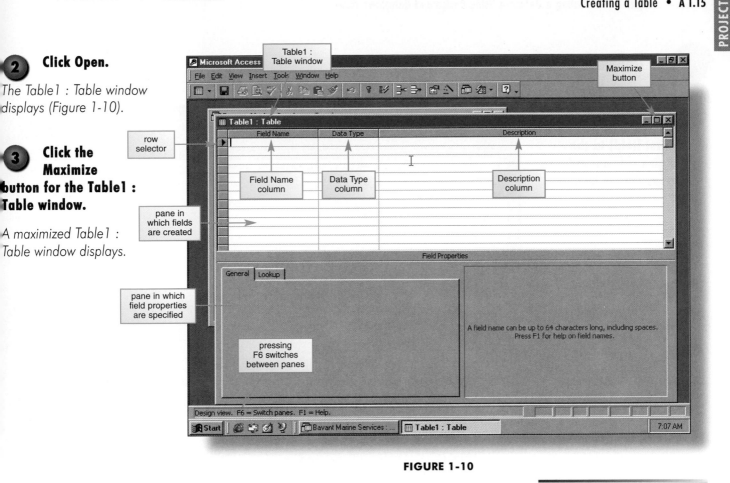

FIGURE 1-10

Defining the Fields

The next step in creating the table is to define the fields by specifying the required details in the Table window. Make entries in the Field Name, Data Type, and Description columns. Enter additional information in the Field Properties box in the lower portion of the Table window. Press the F6 key to move from the upper **pane** (portion of the screen), the one where you define the fields, to the lower pane, the one where you define field properties. Enter the appropriate field size and then press the F6 key to return to the upper pane. As you define the fields, the row selector (Figure 1-10) indicates the field you currently are describing. The **row selector** is a small box or bar that, when clicked, selects the entire row. It is positioned on the first field, indicating Access is ready for you to enter the name of the first field in the Field Name column.

Perform the steps on the next page to define the fields in the table.

Other Ways

1. Click New Object: AutoForm button arrow on Database window toolbar, click Table
2. On Insert menu click Table
3. Double-click Create table in Design view
4. Press ALT+N

Primary Keys

In some cases, the primary key consists of a combination of fields rather than a single field. For more information on determining primary keys in such situations, visit the Access 2000 More About Web page (www.scsite.com/ac2000/more.htm) and then click Primary Key.

Steps **To Define the Fields in a Table**

1 Type Marina Number (the name of the first field) in the Field Name column and then press the TAB key.

The words, Marina Number, display in the Field Name column and the insertion point advances to the Data Type column, indicating you can enter the data type (Figure 1-11). The word, Text, one of the possible data types, currently displays. The arrow in the Data Type column indicates a list of data types is available by clicking the arrow.

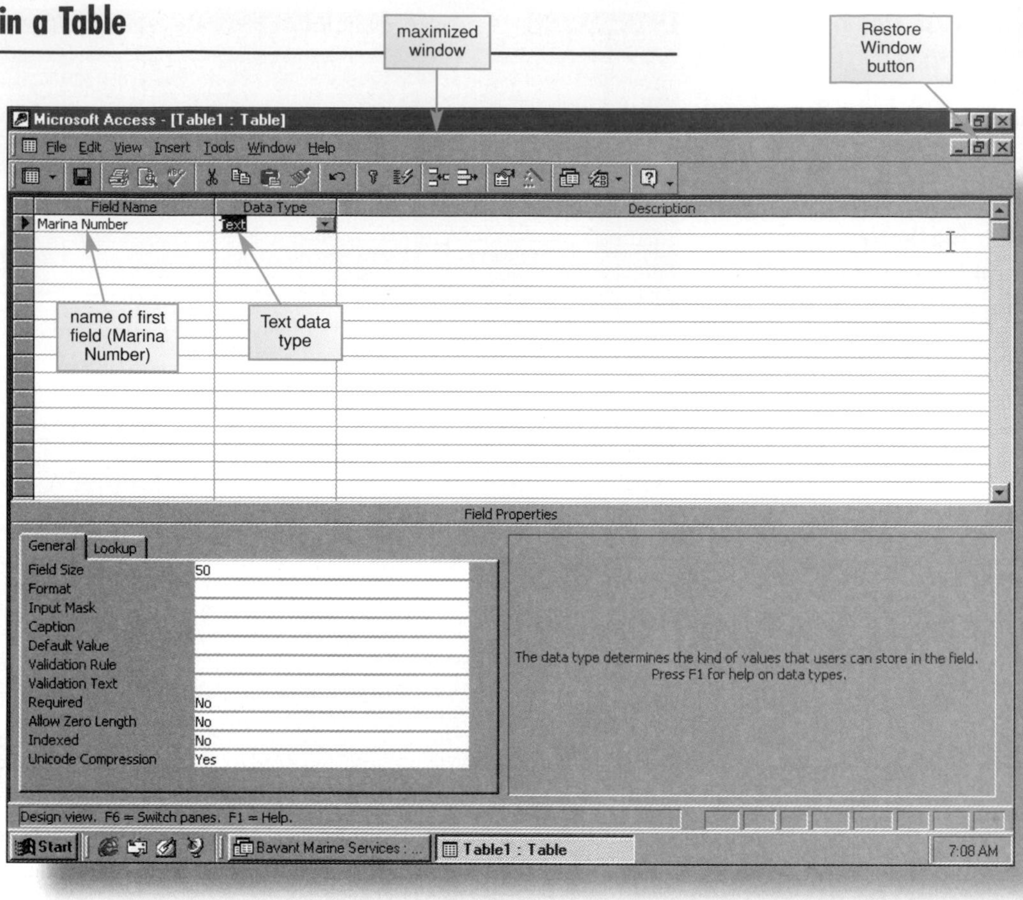

maximized window

Restore Window button

name of first field (Marina Number)

Text data type

The data type determines the kind of values that users can store in the field. Press F1 for help on data types.

FIGURE 1-11

2 Because Text is the correct data type, press the TAB key to move the insertion point to the Description column, type Marina Number (Primary Key) as the description and then point to the Primary Key button on the Database window toolbar.

A ScreenTip, which is a description of the button, displays partially obscuring the description of the first field (Figure 1-12).

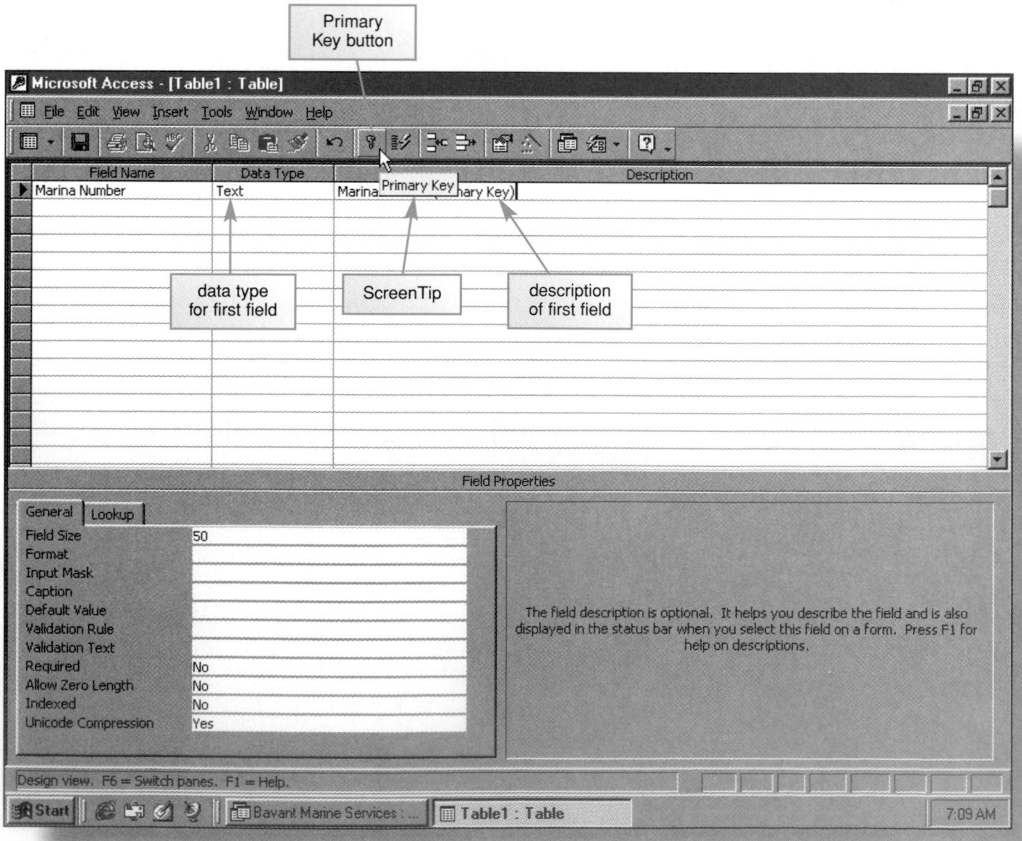

Primary Key button

data type for first field

ScreenTip

description of first field

The field description is optional. It helps you describe the field and is also displayed in the status bar when you select this field on a form. Press F1 for help on descriptions.

FIGURE 1-12

3 Click the Primary Key button to make Marina Number the primary key and then press the F6 key to move the insertion point to the Field Size text box.

The Marina Number field is the primary key as indicated by the key symbol that displays in the row selector (Figure 1-13). The current entry in the Field Size text box (50) is selected.

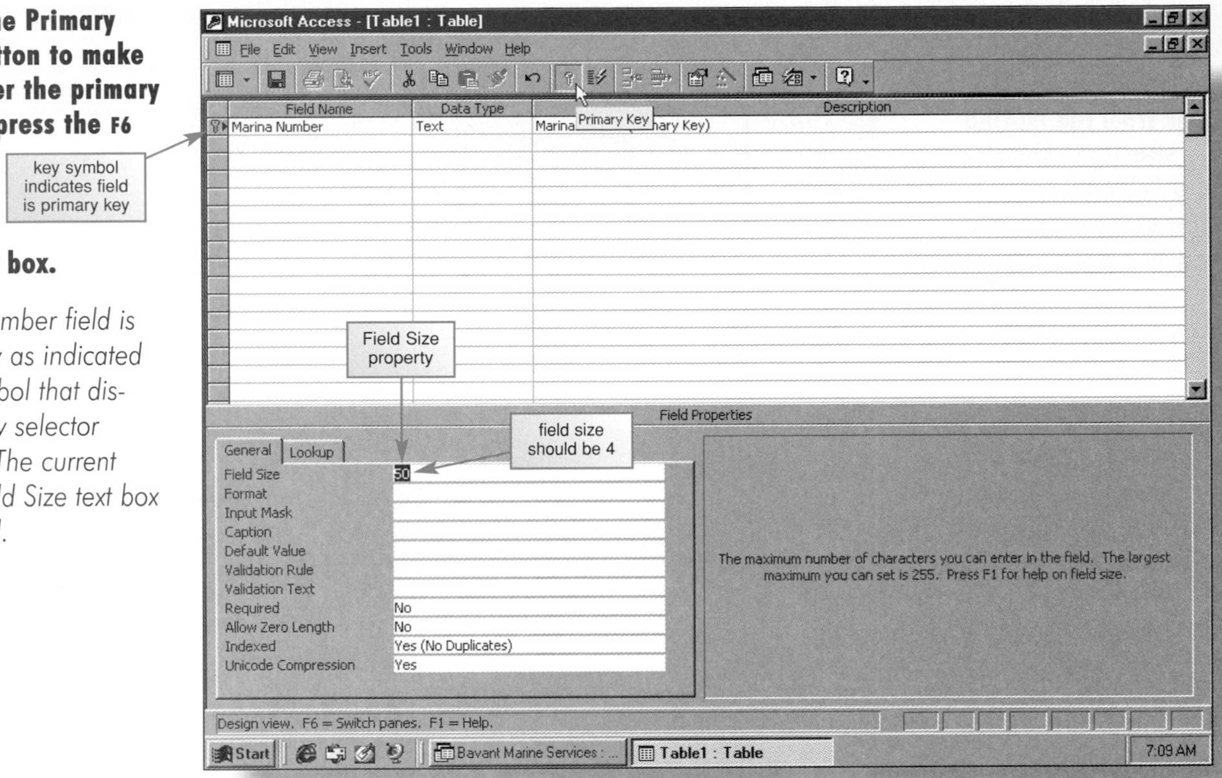

Microsoft Access - [Table1 : Table]

File Edit View Insert Tools Window Help

Field Name	Data Type	Description
Marina Number	Text	Marina Primary Key hary Key)

key symbol indicates field is primary key

Field Size property

field size should be 4

Field Properties

General | Lookup

Field Size: 50
Format:
Input Mask:
Caption:
Default Value:
Validation Rule:
Validation Text:
Required: No
Allow Zero Length: No
Indexed: Yes (No Duplicates)
Unicode Compression: Yes

The maximum number of characters you can enter in the field. The largest maximum you can set is 255. Press F1 for help on field size.

Design view. F6 = Switch panes. F1 = Help.

Start | Bavant Marine Services : ... | Table1 : Table | 7:09 AM

FIGURE 1-13

4 Type 4 as the size of the Marina Number field. Press the F6 key to return to the Description column for the Marina Number field and then press the TAB key to move to the Field Name column in the second row.

The row selector moves to the second row just below the field name Marina Number (Figure 1-14).

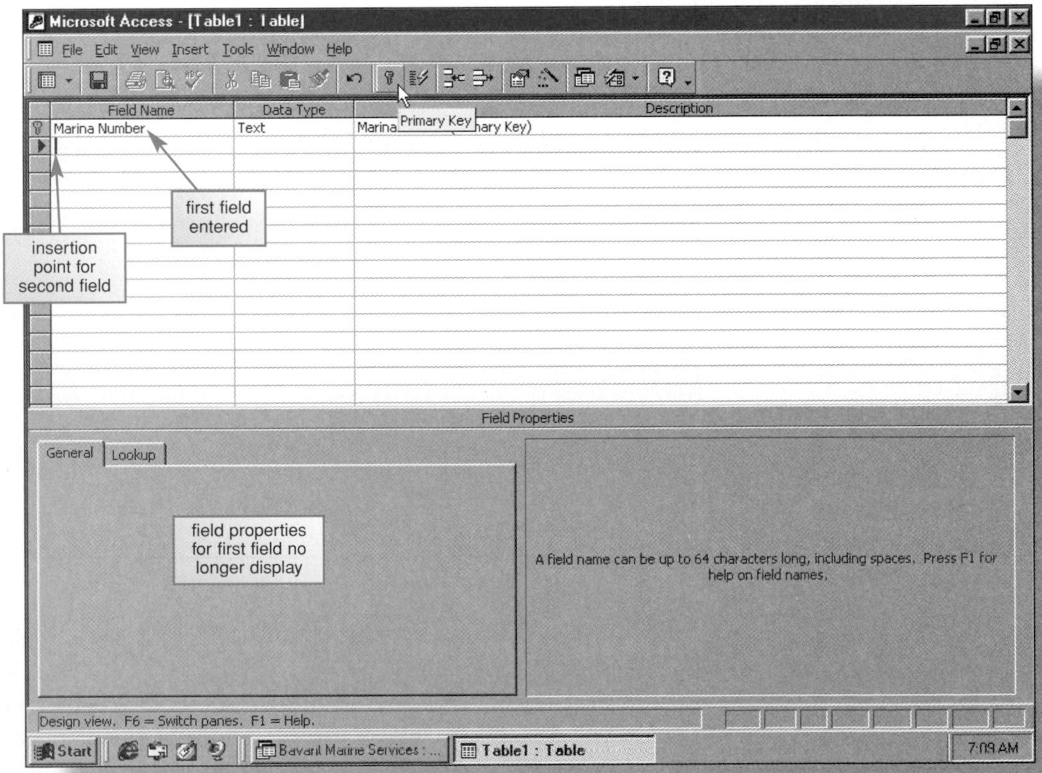

Microsoft Access - [Table1 : Table]

File Edit View Insert Tools Window Help

Field Name	Data Type	Description
Marina Number	Text	Marina Primary Key hary Key)

first field entered

insertion point for second field

Field Properties

General | Lookup

field properties for first field no longer display

A field name can be up to 64 characters long, including spaces. Press F1 for help on field names.

Design view. F6 = Switch panes. F1 = Help.

Start | Bavant Marine Services : ... | Table1 : Table | 7:09 AM

FIGURE 1-14

5 Use the techniques illustrated in Steps 1 through 4 to make the entries from the Marina table structure shown in Figure 1-8 on page A 1.13 up through and including the name of the Warranty field. Click the Data Type column arrow and then point to Currency.

The additional fields are entered (Figure 1-15). A list of available data types displays in the Data Type column for the Warranty field.

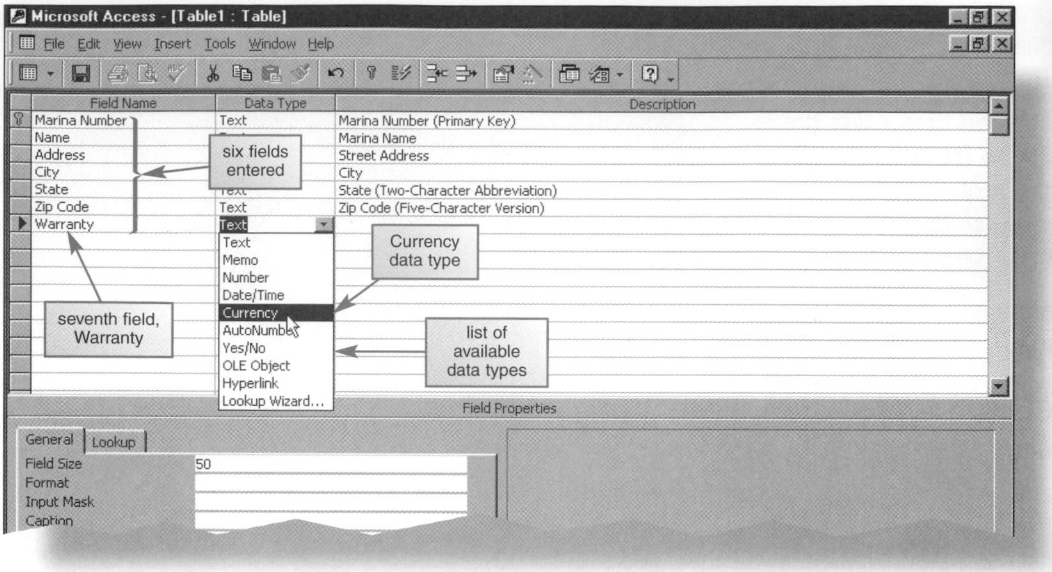

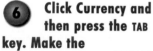

FIGURE 1-15

6 Click Currency and then press the TAB key. Make the remaining entries from the Marina table structure shown in Figure 1-8.

The fields are all entered (Figure 1-16).

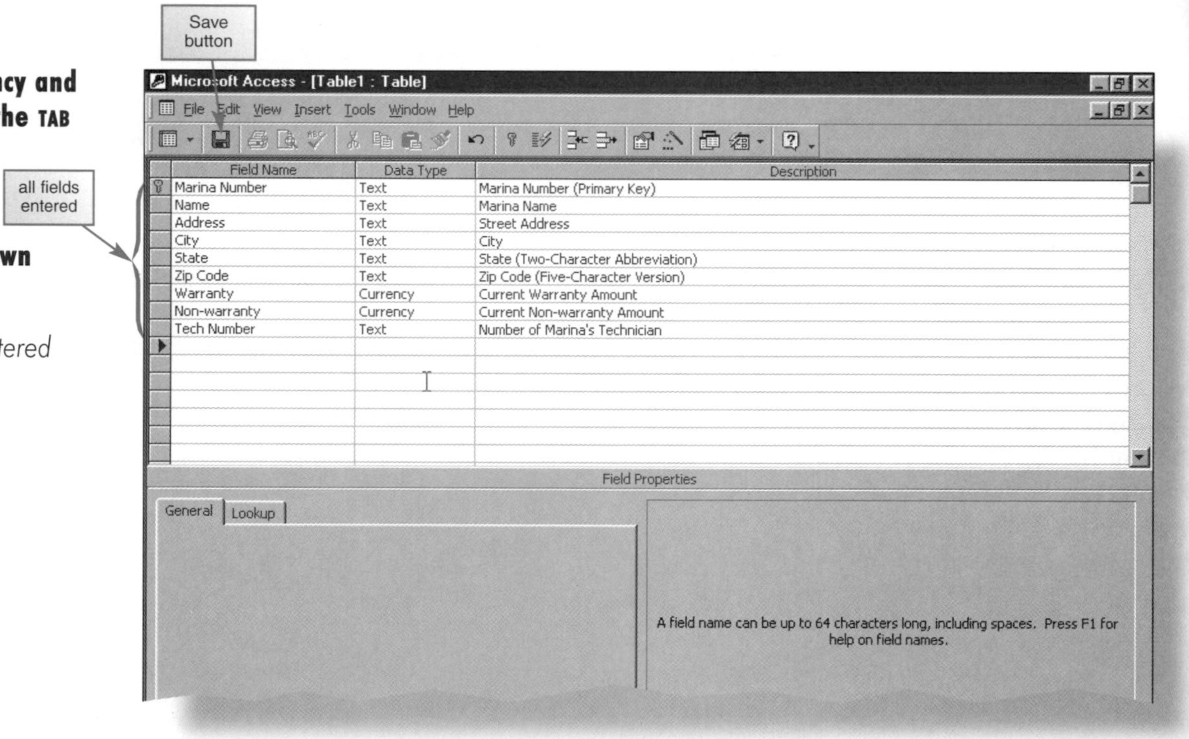

FIGURE 1-16

Correcting Errors in the Structure

When creating a table, check the entries carefully to ensure they are correct. If you make a mistake and discover it before you press the TAB key, you can correct the error by repeatedly pressing the BACKSPACE key until the incorrect characters are removed. Then, type the correct characters. If you do not discover a mistake until later, you can click the entry, type the correct value, and then press the ENTER key.

If you accidentally add an extra field to the structure, select the field by clicking the row selector (the leftmost column on the row that contains the field to be deleted). Once you have selected the field, press the DELETE key. This will remove the field from the structure.

If you forget a field, select the field that will follow the field you wish to add by clicking the row selector, and then press the INSERT key. The remaining fields move down one row, making room for the missing field. Make the entries for the new field in the usual manner.

If you made the wrong field a primary key field, click the correct primary key entry for the field and then click the Primary Key button on the Database window toolbar.

As an alternative to these steps, you may want to start over. To do so, click the Close button for the Table1 : Table window and then click No. The original desktop displays and you can repeat the process you used earlier.

More About 2000

Correcting Errors

Even after you have entered data, it still is possible to correct errors in the structure. Access 2000 will make all the necessary adjustments to the structure of the table as well as to the data within it. (It is simplest to make the correction, however, before any data is entered.)

Saving a Table

The Marina table structure now is complete. The final step is to save the table within the database. At this time, you should give the table a name.

Table names are from one to 64 characters in length and can contain letters, numbers, and spaces. The two table names in this project are Marina and Technician.

To save the table, complete the following steps.

Steps To Save a Table

1 Click the Save button on the Database window toolbar (see Figure 1-16 on page A 1.18). Type Marina **as the name of the table in the Table Name text box and then point to the OK button.**

The Save As dialog box displays (Figure 1-17). The name of the table displays in the Table Name text box.

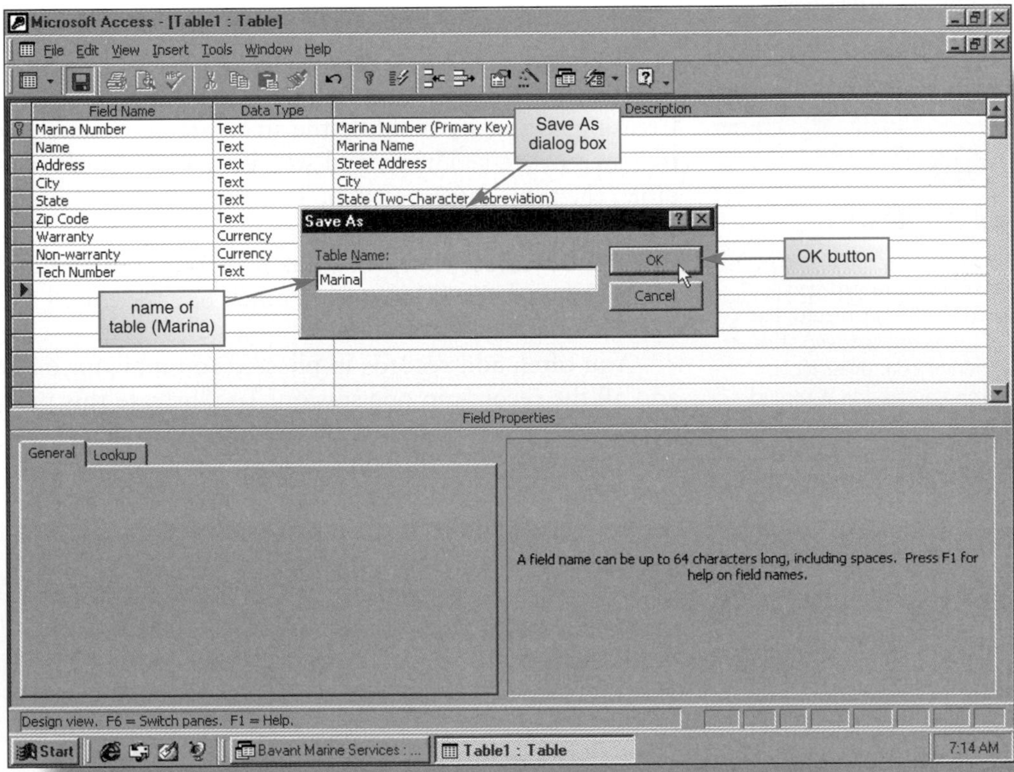

FIGURE 1-17

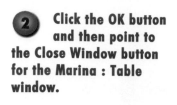
Microsoft Access 2000

2 **Click the OK button and then point to the Close Window button for the Marina : Table window.**

The table is saved on the floppy disk in drive A. The name of the table is now Marina as indicated on the title bar (Figure 1-18).

3 **Click the Close Window button for the Marina : Table window. (Be sure not to click the Close button on the Microsoft Access title bar, because this would close Microsoft Access.)**

The Marina : Table window no longer displays.

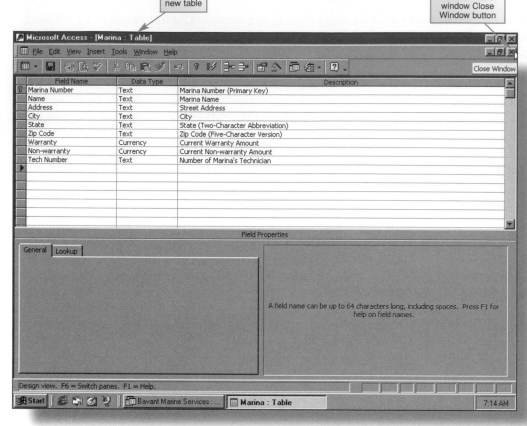

FIGURE 1-18

Other Ways

1. On File menu click Save
2. Press CTRL+S

More About

Adding Records

As soon as you have entered or modified a record and moved to another record, the original record is saved. This is different from other tools. The rows entered in a spreadsheet, for example, are not saved until the entire spreadsheet is saved.

Adding Records to a Table

Creating a table by building the structure and saving the table is the first step in a two-step process. The second step is to add records to the table. To add records to a table, the table must be open. To open a table, right-click the table in the Database window and then click Open on the shortcut menu. The table displays in Datasheet view. In **Datasheet view**, the table is represented as a collection of rows and columns called a **datasheet**. It looks very much like the tables shown in Figure 1-1 on page A 1.7.

You often add records in phases. You may, for example, not have enough time to add all the records in one session. To illustrate this process, this project begins by adding the first two records in the Marina table (Figure 1-19). The remaining records are added later.

Marina table (first 2 records)

MARINA NUMBER	NAME	ADDRESS	CITY	STATE	ZIP CODE	WARRANTY	NON-WARRANTY	TECH NUMBER
AD57	Alan's Docks	314 Central	Burton	MI	49611	$1,248.00	$597.75	23
AN75	Afton's Marina	21 West 8th	Glenview	MI	48121	$1,906.50	$831.25	36

FIGURE 1-19

To open the Marina table and then add records, use the following steps.

To Add Records to a Table

Steps

1 Right-click
Marina in the
Bavant Marine Services :
Database window and then
point to Open on the
shortcut menu.

*The shortcut menu
for the Marina table displays
(Figure 1-20). The Bavant
Marine Services : Database
window is maximized
because the previous window,
the Marina : Table window,
was maximized. (If you
wanted to restore the Database window to its original
size, you would click the
Restore Window button.)*

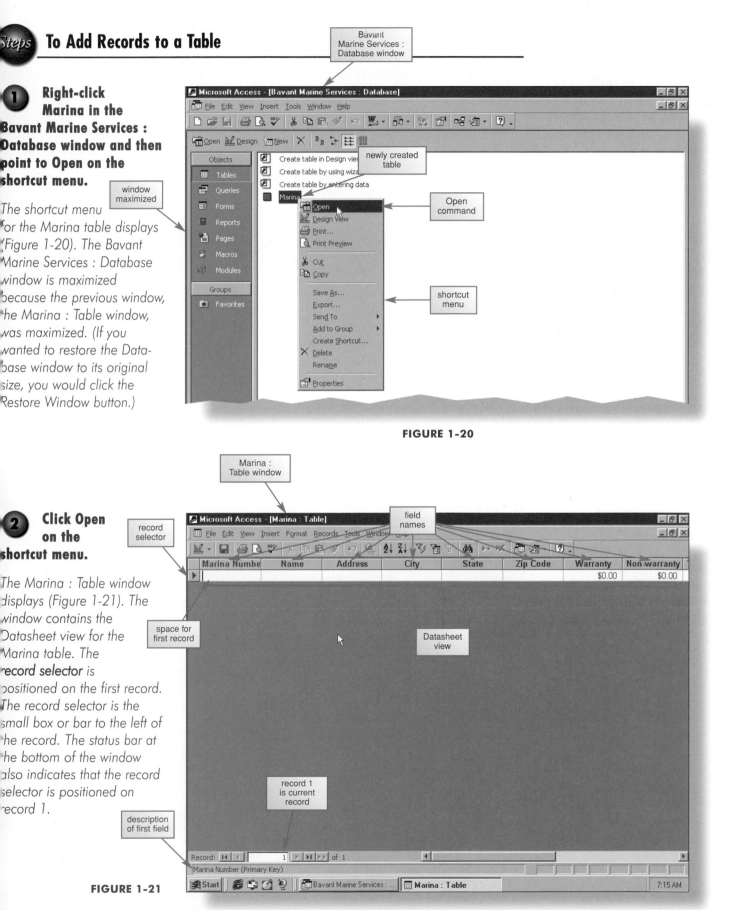

FIGURE 1-20

2 Click Open
on the
shortcut menu.

*The Marina : Table window
displays (Figure 1-21). The
window contains the
Datasheet view for the
Marina table. The
record selector is
positioned on the first record.
The record selector is the
small box or bar to the left of
the record. The status bar at
the bottom of the window
also indicates that the record
selector is positioned on
record 1.*

FIGURE 1-21

3 If your window is not already maximized, click the Maximize button to maximize the window containing the table. Type AD57 as the first marina number, as shown in Figure 1-19. Be sure you type the letters in uppercase, because that is the way they are to be entered in the database.

The marina number is entered, but the insertion point is still in the Marina Number field (Figure 1-22).

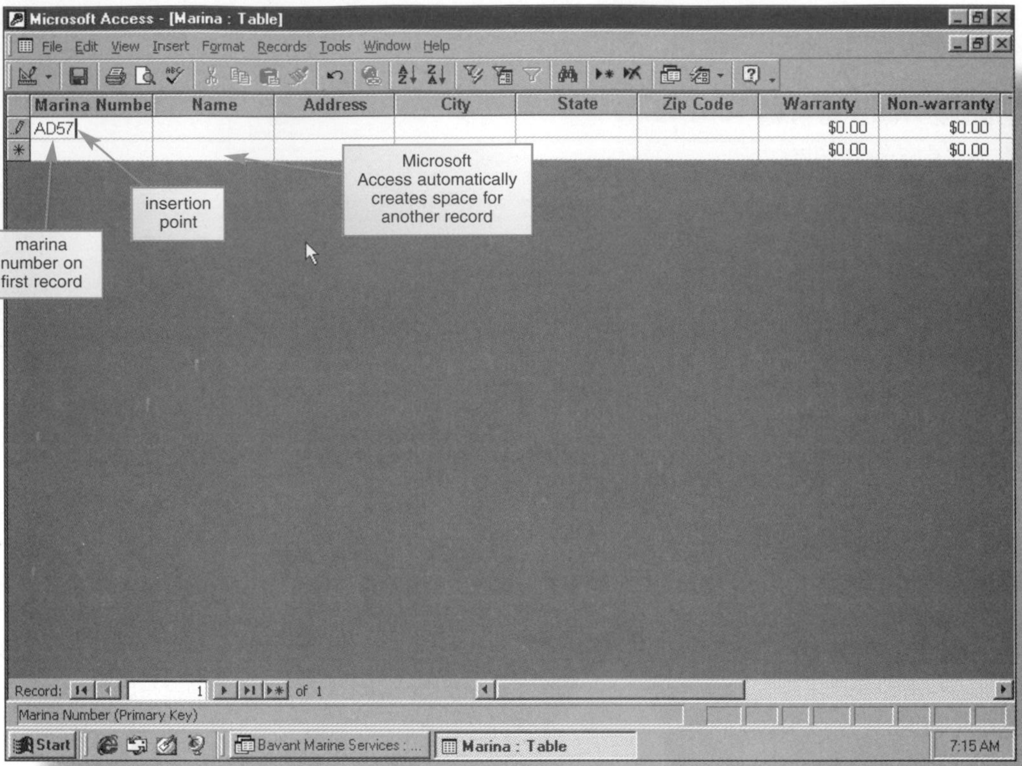

Microsoft Access - [Marina : Table]

File Edit View Insert Format Records Tools Window Help

Marina Numbe	Name	Address	City	State	Zip Code	Warranty	Non-warranty
AD57						$0.00	$0.00
						$0.00	$0.00

marina number on first record

insertion point

Microsoft Access automatically creates space for another record

Record: 1 of 1

Marina Number (Primary Key)

Start Bavant Marine Services : Marina : Table 7:15 AM

FIGURE 1-22

4 Press the TAB key to complete the entry for the Marina Number field. Type the following entries, pressing the TAB key after each one: Alan's Docks as the name, 314 Central as the address, Burton as the city, MI as the state, and 49611 as the zip code.

The Name, Address, City, State, and Zip Code fields are entered (Figure 1-23).

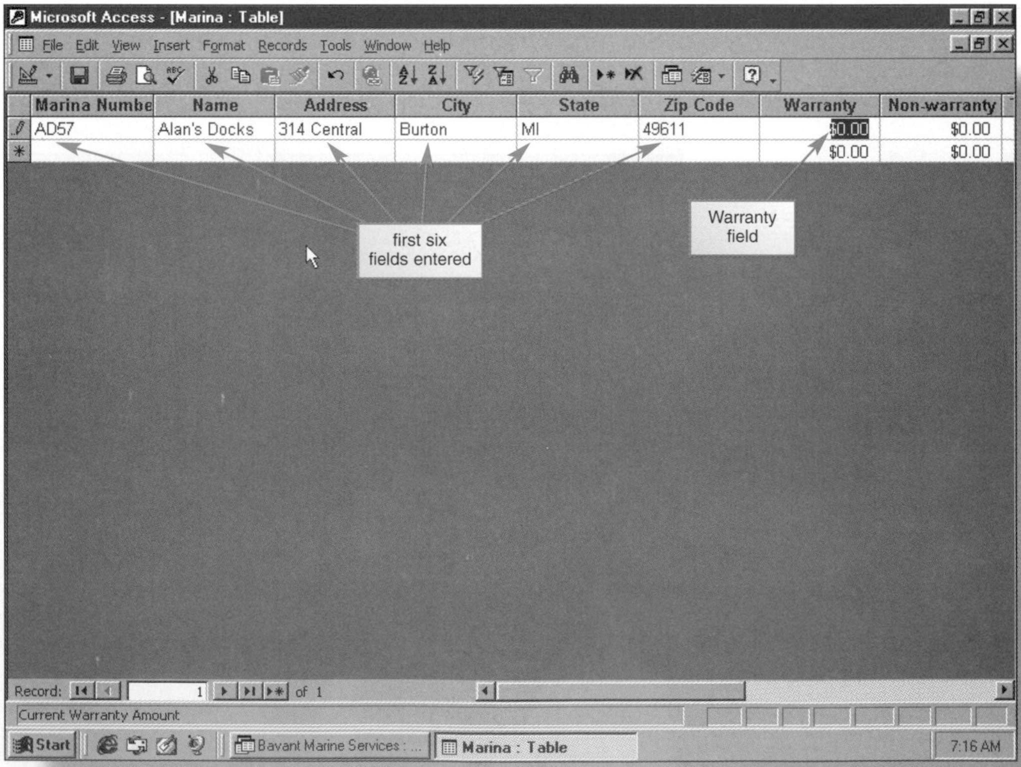

Microsoft Access - [Marina : Table]

File Edit View Insert Format Records Tools Window Help

Marina Numbe	Name	Address	City	State	Zip Code	Warranty	Non-warranty
AD57	Alan's Docks	314 Central	Burton	MI	49611	$0.00	$0.00
						$0.00	$0.00

first six fields entered

Warranty field

Record: 1 of 1

Current Warranty Amount

Start Bavant Marine Services : Marina : Table 7:16 AM

FIGURE 1-23

5 Type 1248 as the warranty amount and then press the TAB key. (You do not need to type dollar signs or commas. In addition, because the digits to the right of the decimal point were both zeros, you did not need to type the decimal point.) Type 597.75 as the non-warranty amount and then press the TAB key. Type 23 as the tech number to complete the record.

The fields have shifted to the left (Figure 1-24). The Warranty and Non-warranty values display with dollar signs and decimal points. The insertion point is positioned in the Tech Number field.

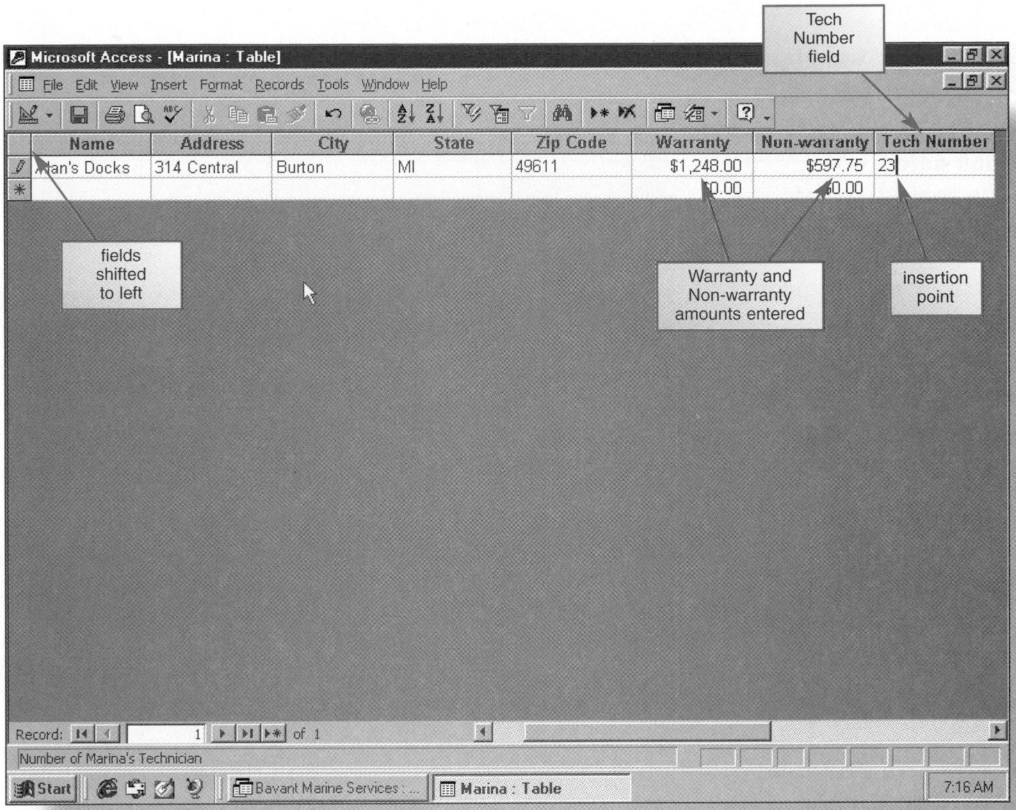

FIGURE 1-24

6 Press the TAB key.

The fields shift back to the right, the record is saved, and the insertion point moves to the marina number on the second row (Figure 1-25).

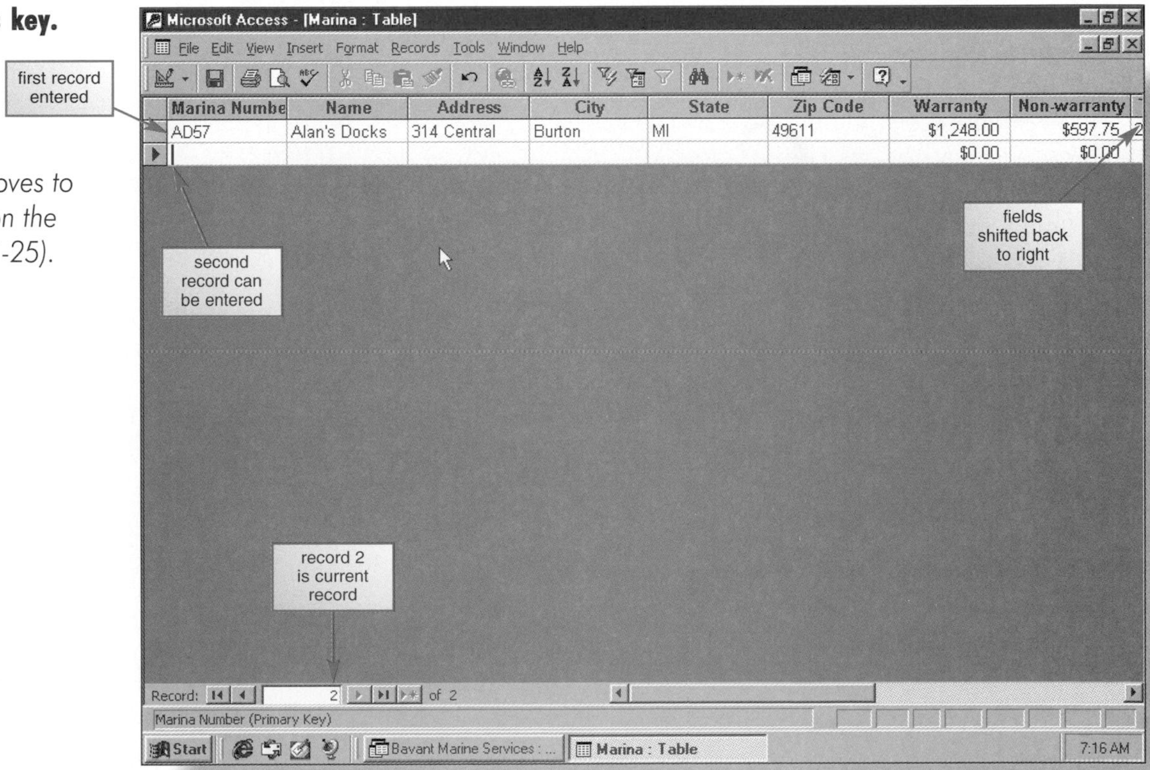

FIGURE 1-25

Use the techniques shown in Steps 3 through 6 to add the data for the second record in Figure 1-19.

The second record is added and the insertion point moves to the marina number on the third row (Figure 1-26).

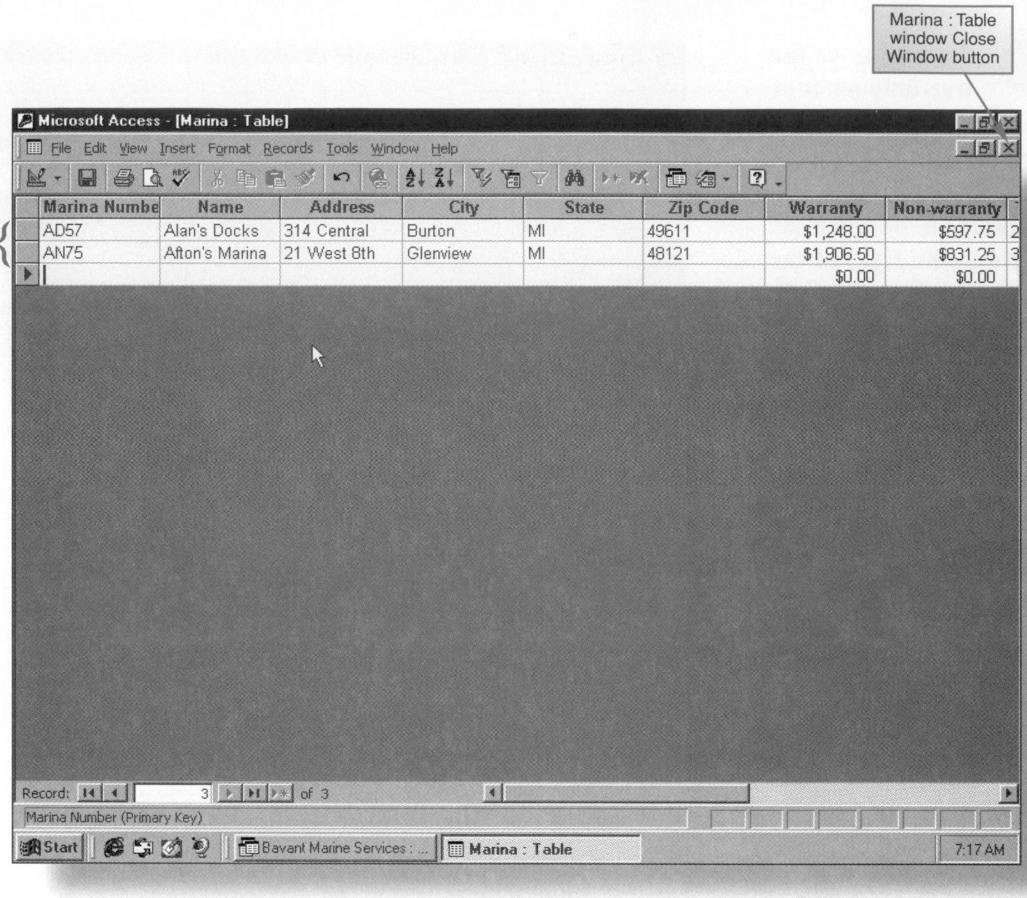

Marina : Table window Close Window button

two records currently in Marina table

Microsoft Access - [Marina : Table]

File   Edit   View   Insert   Format   Records   Tools   Window   Help

Marina Number	Name	Address	City	State	Zip Code	Warranty	Non-warranty
AD57	Alan's Docks	314 Central	Burton	MI	49611	$1,248.00	$597.75	2
AN75	Afton's Marina	21 West 8th	Glenview	MI	48121	$1,906.50	$831.25	3
						$0.00	$0.00	

Record: 14 ◀ 3 ▶ ▶l ▶* of 3

Marina Number (Primary Key)

Start   Bavant Marine Services : ...   Marina : Table   7:17 AM

FIGURE 1-26

Closing a Table and a Database and Quitting Access

It is a good idea to close a table as soon as you have finished working with it. It keeps the screen from getting cluttered and prevents you from making accidental changes to the data in the table. If you no longer will work with the database, you should close the database as well. With the creation of the Marina table complete, you can quit Access at this point.

Perform the following steps to close the table and the database and then quit Access.

To Close a Table and Database and Quit Access

Click the Close Window button for the Marina : Table window (see Figure 1-26 on page A 1.24).

The datasheet for the Marina table no longer displays (Figure 1-27).

Click the Close button for the Bavant Marine Services : Database window (see Figure 1-27).

The Bavant Marine Services : Database window no longer displays.

Click the Close button for the Microsoft Access window.

The Microsoft Access window no longer displays.

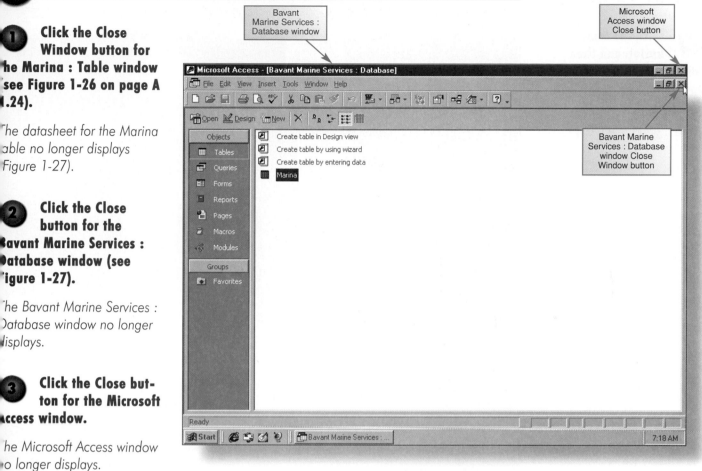

FIGURE 1-27

Opening a Database

To work with any of the tables, reports, or forms in a database, the database must be open. To open a database from the Windows desktop, click Open Office Document on the Start menu by performing the following steps. (The Other Ways box indicates ways to open a database from within Access.)

 To Open a Database

 Click the Start button and then point to Open Office Document (Figure 1-28).

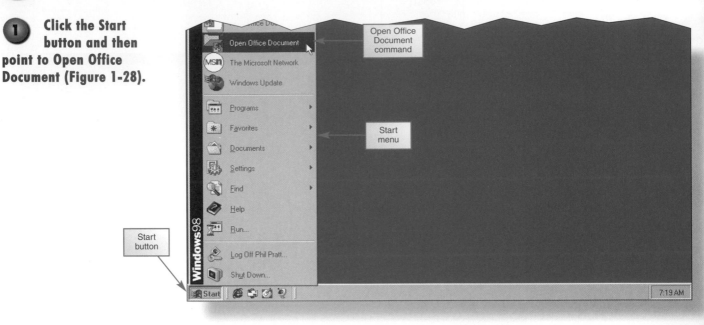

FIGURE 1-28

 Click Open Office Document. If necessary, click the Look in box arrow and then click 3½ Floppy (A:) in the Look in box. If it is not already selected, click the Bavant Marine Services database name. Point to the Open button.

The Open Office Document dialog box displays (Figure 1-29). The 3½ Floppy (A:) folder displays in the Look in box and the files on the floppy disk in drive A display. Your list may be different.

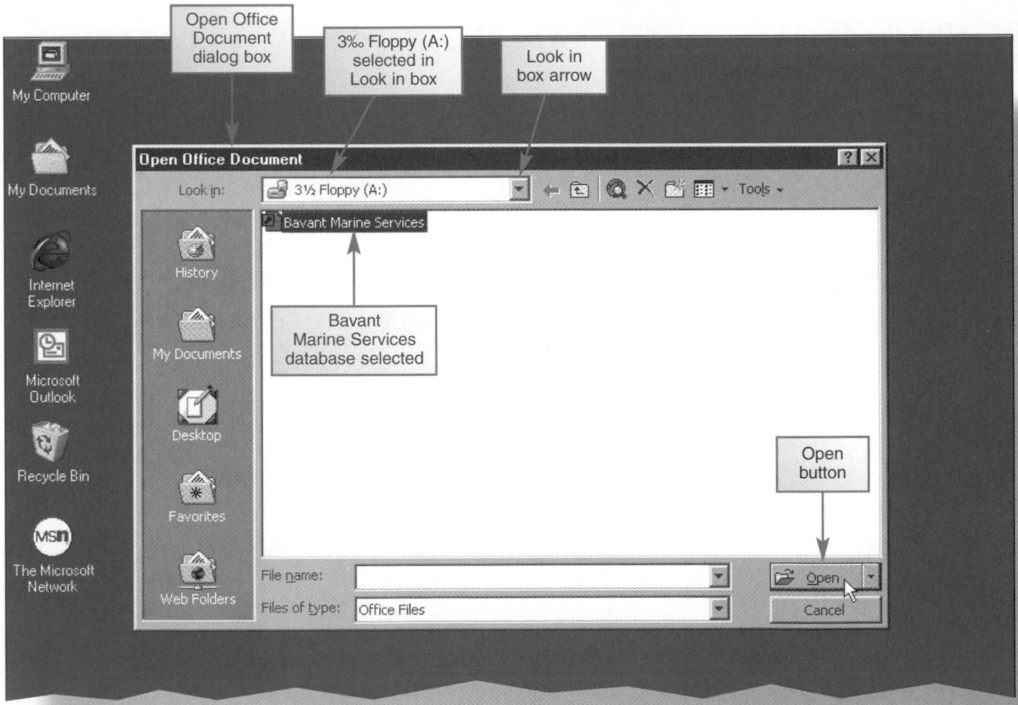

Click the Open button.

The database opens and the Bavant Marine Services : Database window displays.

FIGURE 1-29

Other Ways

1. Click Open button on Data-base window toolbar
2. On File menu click Open
3. Press CTRL+O

Adding Additional Records

You can add records to a table that already contains data using a process almost identical to that used to add records to an empty table. The only difference is that you place the insertion point after the last data record before you enter the additional data. To do so, use the **Navigation buttons** found near the lower-left corner of the screen. The purpose of each of the Navigation buttons is described in Table 1-1.

Table 1-1	Navigation Buttons in Datasheet View
BUTTON	PURPOSE
First Record	Moves to the first record in the table
Previous Record	Moves to the previous record
Next Record	Moves to the next record
Last Record	Moves to the last record in the table
New Record	Moves to the end of the table to a position for entering a new record

Complete the following steps to add the remaining records (Figure 1-30) to the Marina table.

Marina table (last 8 records)

MARINA NUMBER	NAME	ADDRESS	CITY	STATE	ZIP CODE	WARRANTY	NON-WARRANTY	TECH NUMBER
BL72	Brite's Landing	281 Robin	Burton	MI	49611	$217.00	$0.00	36
EL25	Elend Marina	462 River	Torino	MI	48268	$413.50	$678.75	49
FB96	Fenton's Boats	36 Bayview	Cavela	MI	47926	$923.20	$657.50	23
FM22	Fedder Marina	283 Waterfront	Burton	MI	49611	$432.00	$0.00	36
JB92	JT Boat Club	28 Causeway	Torino	MI	48268	$0.00	$0.00	36
NW72	Nelson's Wharf	27 Lake	Masondale	MI	49832	$608.50	$520.00	23
SM72	Solton's Marine	867 Bay Ridge	Glenview	MI	48121	$462.50	$295.00	49
TR72	The Reef	92 East Bay	Woodview	MI	47212	$219.00	$0.00	36

FIGURE 1-30

 **To Add Additional Records to a Table**

1 Right-click Marina in the Bavant Marine Services : Database window and then click Open on the shortcut menu.

2 When the Marina table displays, maximize the window by clicking the Maximize button. Point to the New Record button.

The datasheet displays (Figure 1-31).

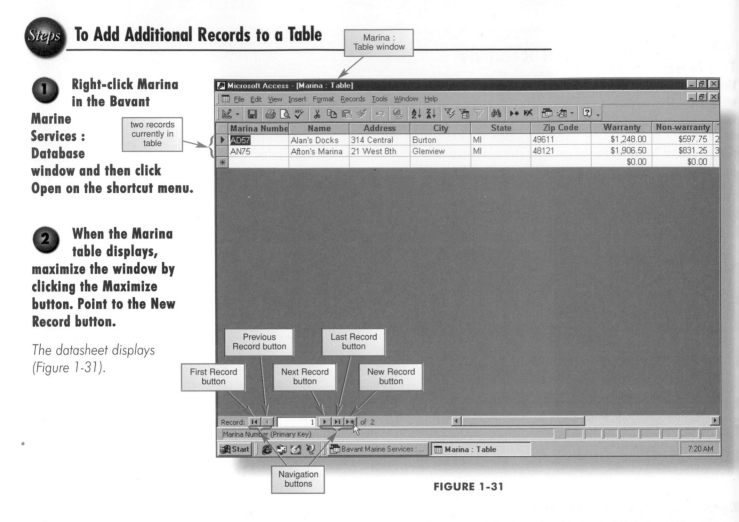

FIGURE 1-31

3 Click the New Record button.

Access places the insertion point in position to enter a new record (Figure 1-32).

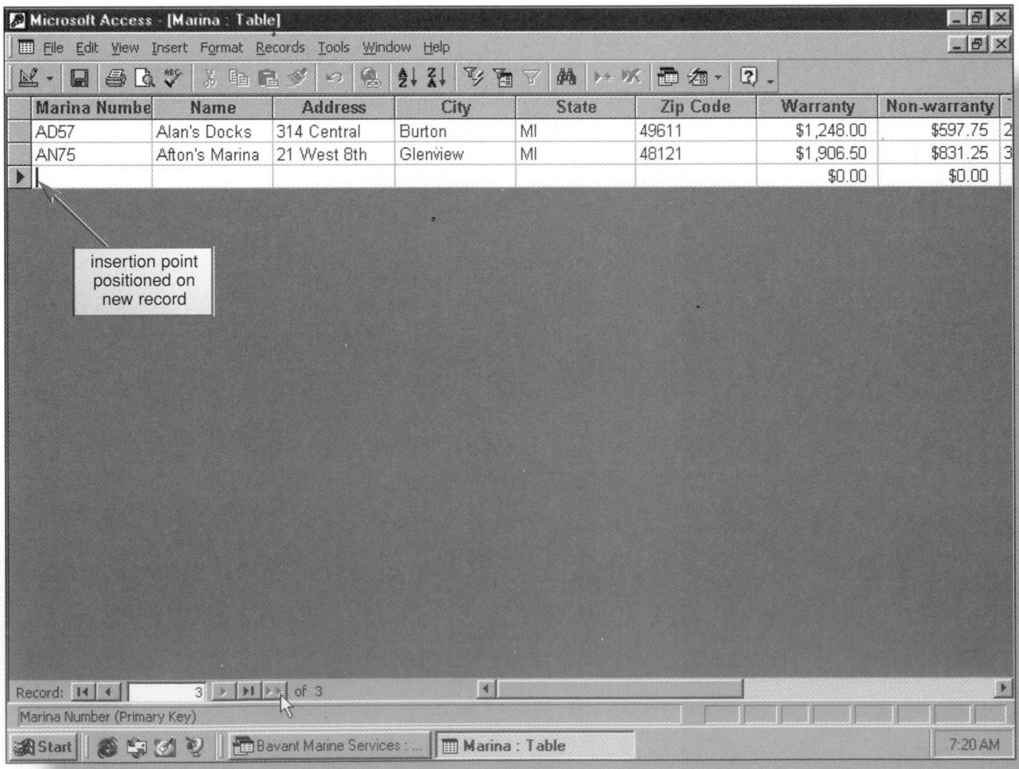

FIGURE 1-32

4 Add the remaining records from Figure 1-30 on page A 1.27 using the same techniques you used to add the first two records. Point to the Close Window button.

The additional records are added (Figure 1-33).

5 Click the Close Window button.

The window containing the table closes.

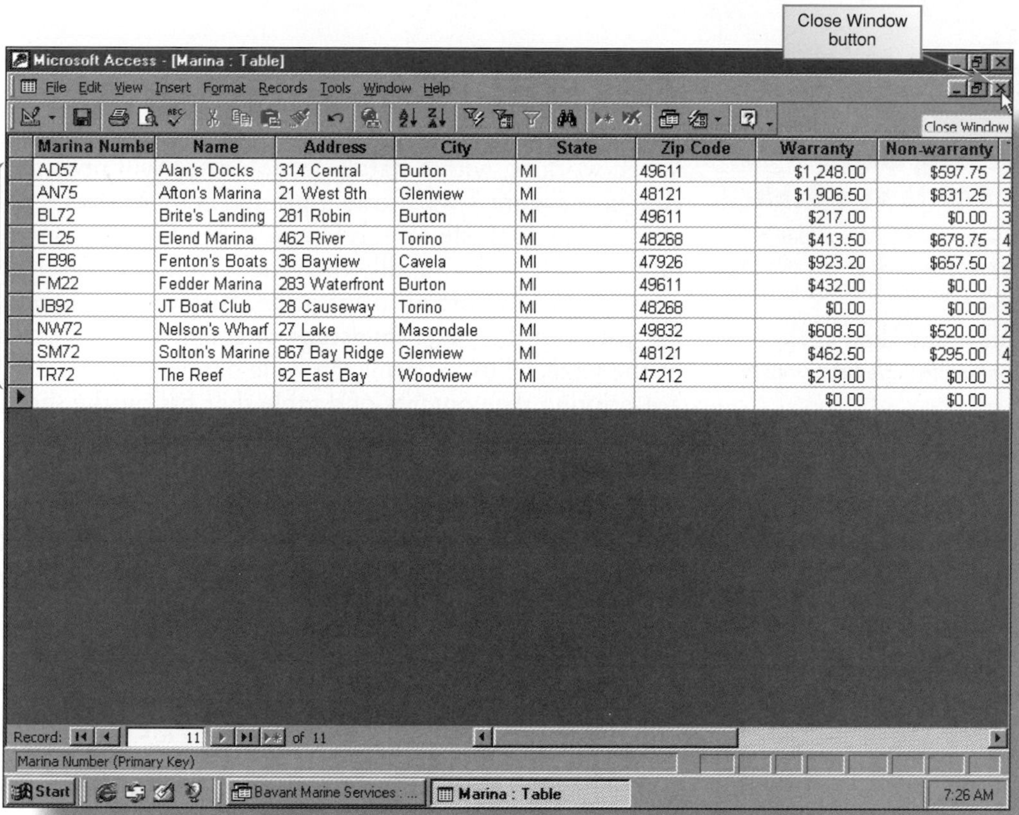

Close Window button

all ten records entered

Marina Numbe	Name	Address	City	State	Zip Code	Warranty	Non-warranty	
AD57	Alan's Docks	314 Central	Burton	MI	49611	$1,248.00	$597.75	2
AN75	Afton's Marina	21 West 8th	Glenview	MI	48121	$1,906.50	$831.25	3
BL72	Brite's Landing	281 Robin	Burton	MI	49611	$217.00	$0.00	3
EL25	Elend Marina	462 River	Torino	MI	48268	$413.50	$678.75	4
FB96	Fenton's Boats	36 Bayview	Cavela	MI	47926	$923.20	$657.50	2
FM22	Fedder Marina	283 Waterfront	Burton	MI	49611	$432.00	$0.00	3
JB92	JT Boat Club	28 Causeway	Torino	MI	48268	$0.00	$0.00	3
NW72	Nelson's Wharf	27 Lake	Masondale	MI	49832	$608.50	$520.00	2
SM72	Solton's Marine	867 Bay Ridge	Glenview	MI	48121	$462.50	$295.00	4
TR72	The Reef	92 East Bay	Woodview	MI	47212	$219.00	$0.00	3
						$0.00	$0.00	

Record: ⏮ ◀ | 11 | ▶ ⏭ ▶* | of 11

Marina Number (Primary Key)

FIGURE 1-33

Correcting Errors in the Data

Check your entries carefully to ensure they are correct. If you make a mistake and discover it before you press the TAB key, correct it by pressing the BACKSPACE key until the incorrect characters are removed and then typing the correct characters.

If you discover an incorrect entry later, correct the error by clicking the incorrect entry and then making the appropriate correction. If the record you must correct is not on the screen, use the Navigation buttons (Next Record, Previous Record, and so on) to move to it. If the field you want to correct is not visible on the screen, use the horizontal scroll bar along the bottom of the screen to shift all the fields until the one you want displays. Then make the correction.

If you add an extra record accidentally, select the record by clicking the record selector that immediately precedes the record. Then, press the DELETE key. This will remove the record from the table. If you forget a record, add it using the same procedure as for all the other records. Access will place it in the correct location in the table automatically.

If you cannot determine how to correct the data, you are, in effect, stuck on the record. Access neither allows you to move to any other record until you have made the correction, nor allows you to close the table. If you encounter this situation, simply press the ESC key. Pressing the ESC key will remove from the screen the record you are trying to add. You then can move to any other record, close the table, or take any other action you desire.

Other Ways

1. Click New Record button on Database window toolbar
2. On Insert menu click New Record

Printing the Contents of a Table

You can change the paper size, paper source, or the printer that will be used to print the report. To change any of these, select the Page sheet in the Page Setup dialog box.

Previewing and Printing the Contents of a Table

When working with a database, you often will need to print a copy of the table contents. Figure 1-34 shows a printed copy of the contents of the Marina table. (Yours may look slightly different, depending on your printer.) Because the Marina table is wider substantially than the screen, it also will be wider than the normal printed page in portrait orientation. **Portrait orientation** means the printout is across the width of the page. **Landscape orientation** means the printout is across the length of the page. Thus, to print the wide database table, use landscape orientation. If you are printing the contents of a table that fits on the screen, you will not need landscape orientation. A convenient way to change to landscape orientation is to **preview** what the printed copy will look like by using Print Preview. This allows you to determine whether landscape orientation is necessary and, if it is, to change easily the orientation to landscape. In addition, you also can use Print Preview to determine whether any adjustments are necessary to the page margins.

Marina   9/7/2001

Marina Number	Name	Address	City	State	Zip Code	Warranty	Non-warranty	Tech Number
AD57	Alan's Docks	314 Central	Burton	MI	49611	$1,248.00	$597.75	23
AN75	Afton's Marina	21 West 8th	Glenview	MI	48121	$1,906.50	$831.25	36
BL72	Brite's Landing	281 Robin	Burton	MI	49611	$217.00	$0.00	36
EL25	Elend Marina	462 River	Torino	MI	48268	$413.50	$678.75	49
FB96	Fenton's Boats	36 Bayview	Cavela	MI	47926	$923.20	$657.50	23
FM22	Fedder Marina	283 Waterfront	Burton	MI	49611	$432.00	$0.00	36
JB92	JT Boat Club	28 Causeway	Torino	MI	48268	$0.00	$0.00	36
NW72	Nelson's Wharf	27 Lake	Masondale	MI	49832	$608.50	$520.00	23
SM72	Solton's Marina	867 Bay Ridge	Glenview	MI	48121	$462.50	$295.00	49
TR72	The Reef	92 East Bay	Woodview	MI	47212	$219.00	$0.00	36

Page 1

FIGURE 1-34

Perform the following steps to use Print Preview to preview and then print the
Marina table.

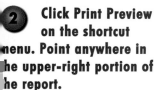

To Preview and Print the Contents of a Table

1 **Right-click Marina
and then point to
Print Preview on the
shortcut menu.**

*The shortcut menu for the
Marina table displays (Figure
1-35).*

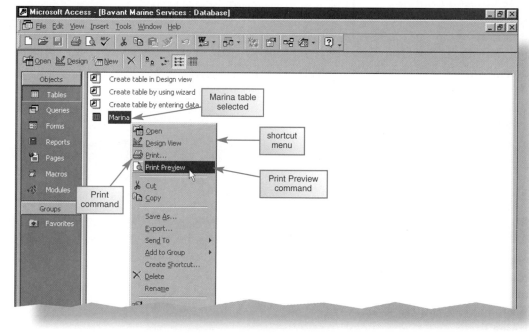

FIGURE 1-35

2 **Click Print Preview
on the shortcut
menu. Point anywhere in
the upper-right portion of
the report.**

*The preview of the report dis-
plays (Figure 1-36).*

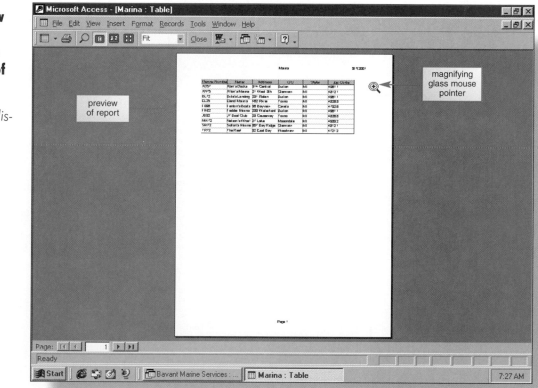

FIGURE 1-36

3 Click the magnifying glass mouse pointer in the approximate position shown in Figure 1-36.

The portion surrounding the mouse pointer is magnified (Figure 1-37). The last field that displays is the Zip Code field. The Warranty, Non-warranty, and Tech Number fields do not display. To display the additional fields, you will need to switch to landscape orientation.

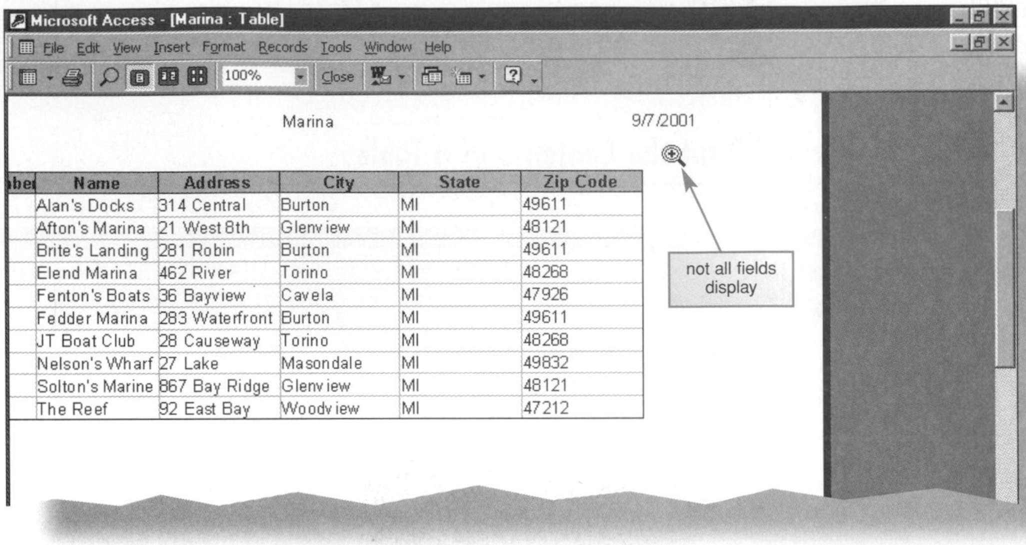

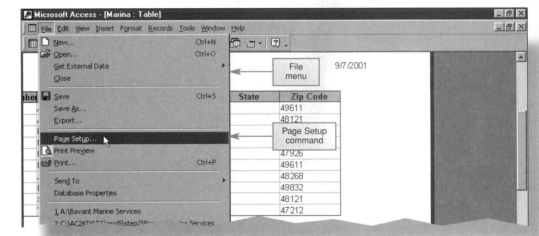

FIGURE 1-37

4 Click File on the menu bar and then point to Page Setup. (Remember that you might have to wait a few seconds for the entire menu to display.)

The File menu displays (Figure 1-38).

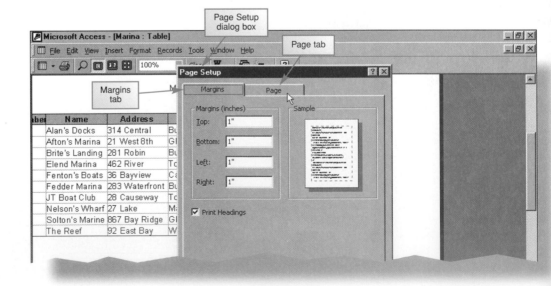

FIGURE 1-38

5 Click Page Setup and then point to the Page tab.

The Page Setup dialog box displays (Figure 1-39).

FIGURE 1-39

6 Click the Page tab and then point to the Landscape option button.

The Page sheet displays (Figure 1-40). The Portrait option button currently is selected. (*Option button* refers to the round button that indicates choices in a dialog box. When the corresponding option is selected, the button contains within it a solid circle. Clicking an option button selects it, and deselects all others.)

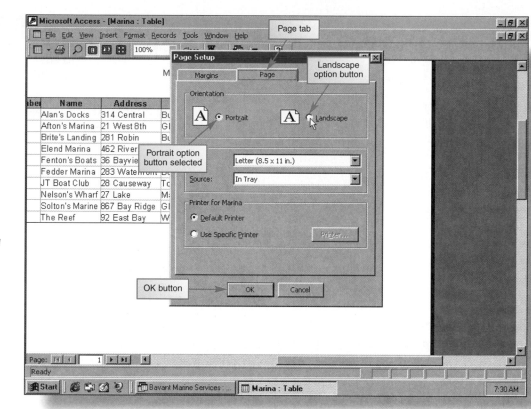

FIGURE 1-40

7 Click Landscape and then click the OK button. Click the mouse pointer anywhere within the report to view the entire report.

The orientation is changed to landscape as shown by the report that displays on the screen (Figure 1-41). The characters in the report are so small that it is difficult to determine whether all fields currently display. To zoom in on a portion of the report, click the desired portion of the report.

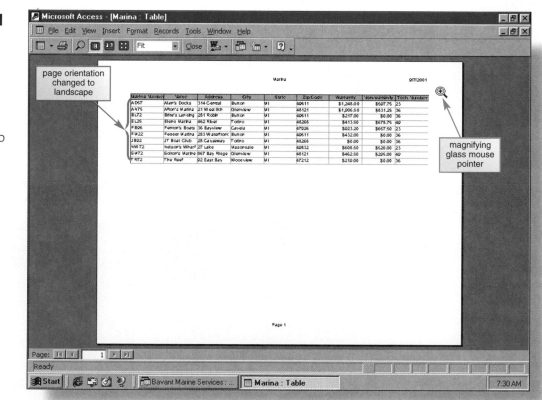

FIGURE 1-41

8 Click the magnifying glass mouse pointer in the approximate position shown in Figure 1-41.

The portion surrounding the mouse pointer is magnified (Figure 1-42). The last field that displays is the Tech Number field, so all fields currently display. If they did not, you could decrease the left and right margins; that is, the amount of space left by Access on the left and right edges of the report.

9 Click the Print button to print the report. Click the Close button when the report has been printed to close the Print Preview window.

The Print Preview window no longer displays.

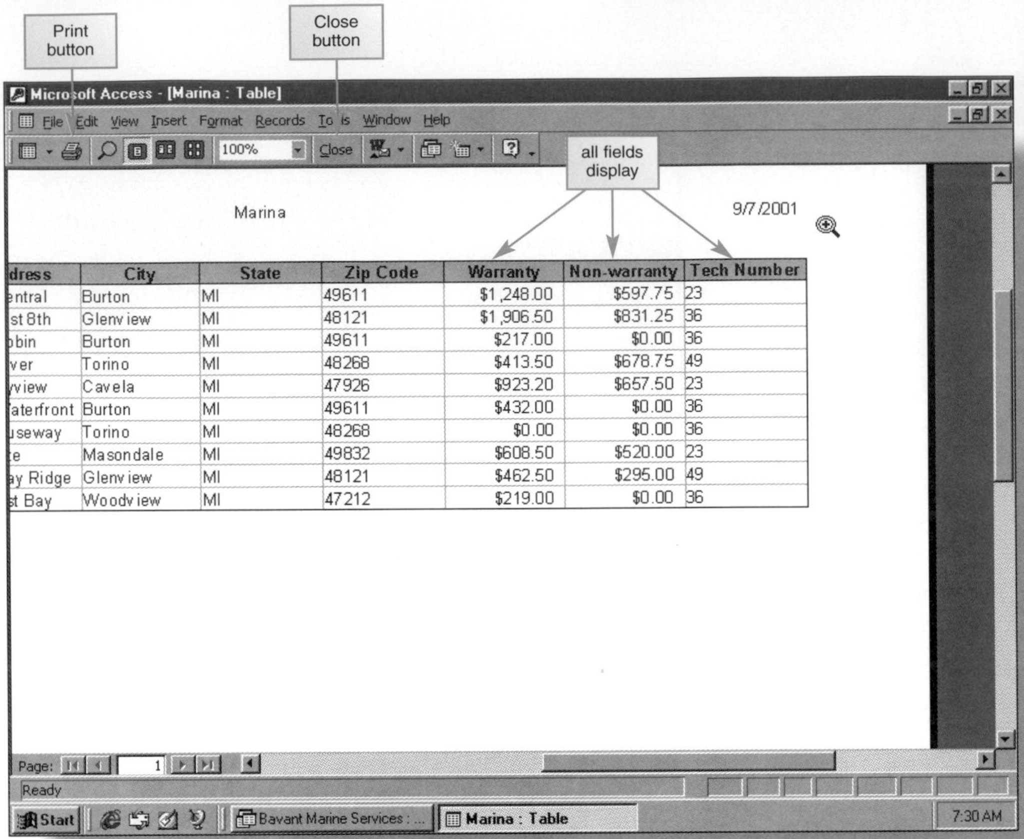

Other Ways

1. On File menu click Print Preview to preview
2. On File menu click Print to print
3. Press CTRL+P to print

Print button   Close button

Microsoft Access - [Marina : Table]

File   Edit   View   Insert   Format   Records   Tools   Window   Help

100%   Close

all fields display

Marina   9/7/2001

dress	City	State	Zip Code	Warranty	Non-warranty	Tech Number
entral	Burton	MI	49611	$1,248.00	$597.75	23
st 8th	Glenview	MI	48121	$1,906.50	$831.25	36
bbin	Burton	MI	49611	$217.00	$0.00	36
ver	Torino	MI	48268	$413.50	$678.75	49
view	Cavela	MI	47926	$923.20	$657.50	23
aterfront	Burton	MI	49611	$432.00	$0.00	36
seway	Torino	MI	48268	$0.00	$0.00	36
e	Masondale	MI	49832	$608.50	$520.00	23
y Ridge	Glenview	MI	48121	$462.50	$295.00	49
t Bay	Woodview	MI	47212	$219.00	$0.00	36

Page: 1

Ready

Start   Bavant Marine Services : ...   Marina : Table   7:30 AM

FIGURE 1-42

Creating Additional Tables

A database typically consists of more than one table. The sample database contains two, the Marina table and the Technician table. You need to repeat the process of creating a table and adding records for each table in the database. In the sample database, you need to create and add records to the Technician table. The structure and data for the table are given in Figure 1-43. The steps to create the table follow.

Structure of Technician table

FIELD NAME	DATA TYPE	FIELD SIZE	PRIMARY KEY?	DESCRIPTION
Tech Number	Text	2	Yes	Technician Number (Primary Key)
Last Name	Text	10		Last Name of Technician
First Name	Text	8		First Name of Technician
Address	Text	15		Street Address
City	Text	15		City
State	Text	2		State (Two-Character Abbreviation)
Zip Code	Text	5		Zip Code (Five-Character Version)
Hourly Rate	Currency			Hourly Rate of Technician
YTD Earnings	Currency			YTD Earnings of Technician

FIGURE 1-43

Data for Technician table

TECH NUMBER	LAST NAME	FIRST NAME	ADDRESS	CITY	STATE	ZIP CODE	HOURLY RATE	YTD EARNINGS
23	Anderson	Trista	283 Belton	Port Anton	MI	47989	$24.00	$17,862.00
36	Nichols	Ashton	978 Richmond	Hewitt	MI	47618	$21.00	$19,560.00
49	Gomez	Teresa	2855 Parry	Ashley	MI	47711	$22.00	$21,211.50

FIGURE 1-43 *(continued)*

To Create an Additional Table

1 Make sure the Bavant Marine Services database is open. Right-click Create table in Design view and then click Open on the shortcut menu. Enter the data for the fields for the Technician table from Figure 1-43. Be sure to click the Primary Key button when you enter the Tech Number field. Point to the Save button on the Database window toolbar after you have entered all the fields.

The entries display (Figure 1-44).

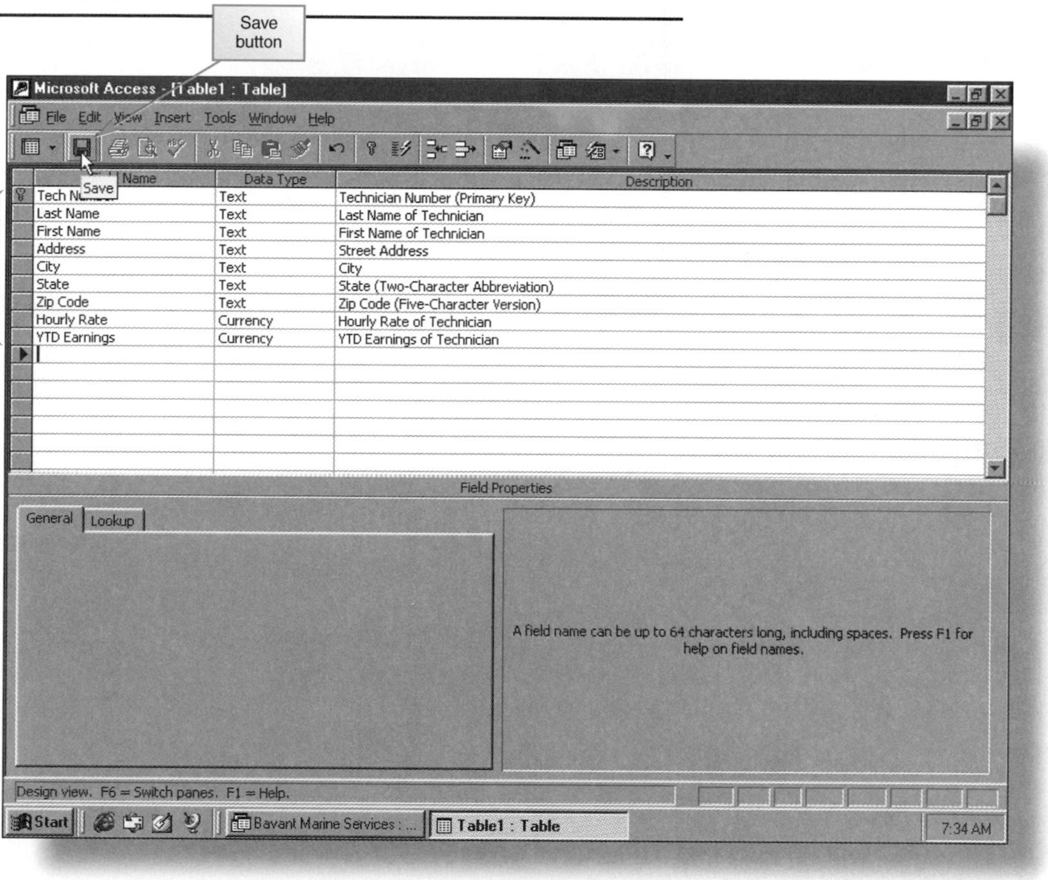

Save button

all fields entered for Technicial table

Field Name	Data Type	Description
Tech Number	Text	Technician Number (Primary Key)
Last Name	Text	Last Name of Technician
First Name	Text	First Name of Technician
Address	Text	Street Address
City	Text	City
State	Text	State (Two-Character Abbreviation)
Zip Code	Text	Zip Code (Five-Character Version)
Hourly Rate	Currency	Hourly Rate of Technician
YTD Earnings	Currency	YTD Earnings of Technician

A field name can be up to 64 characters long, including spaces. Press F1 for help on field names.

FIGURE 1-44

2 Click the Save button, type Technician as the name of the table, and then click the OK button. Click the Close Window button.

The table is saved in the Bavant Marine Services database. The Technician : Table window no longer displays.

Adding Records to the Additional Table

Now that you have created the Technician table, use the steps on the next page to add records to it.

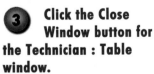

Steps **To Add Records to an Additional Table**

1 **Right-click Technician and point to Open on the shortcut menu.**

The shortcut menu for the Technician table displays (Figure 1-45).

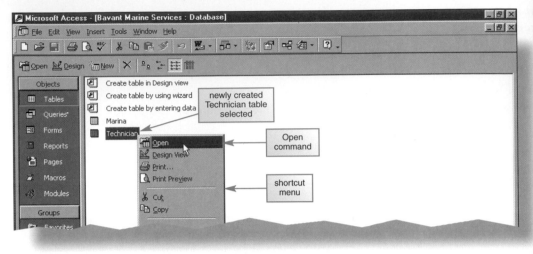

FIGURE 1-45

2 **Click Open on the shortcut menu and then enter the Technician data from Figure 1-43 on page A 1.34 into the Technician table.**

The datasheet displays with three records entered (Figure 1-46).

Tech Number	Last Name	First Name	Address	City	State	Zip Code	Hourly Rate
23	Anderson	Trista	283 Belton	Port Anton	MI	47989	$24.00
36	Nichols	Ashton	978 Richmond	Hewitt	MI	47618	$21.00
49	Gomez	Teresa	2855 Parry	Ashley	MI	47711	$22.00
							$0.00

all records entered

Close Window button

3 **Click the Close Window button for the Technician : Table window.**

Access closes the table and removes the datasheet from the screen.

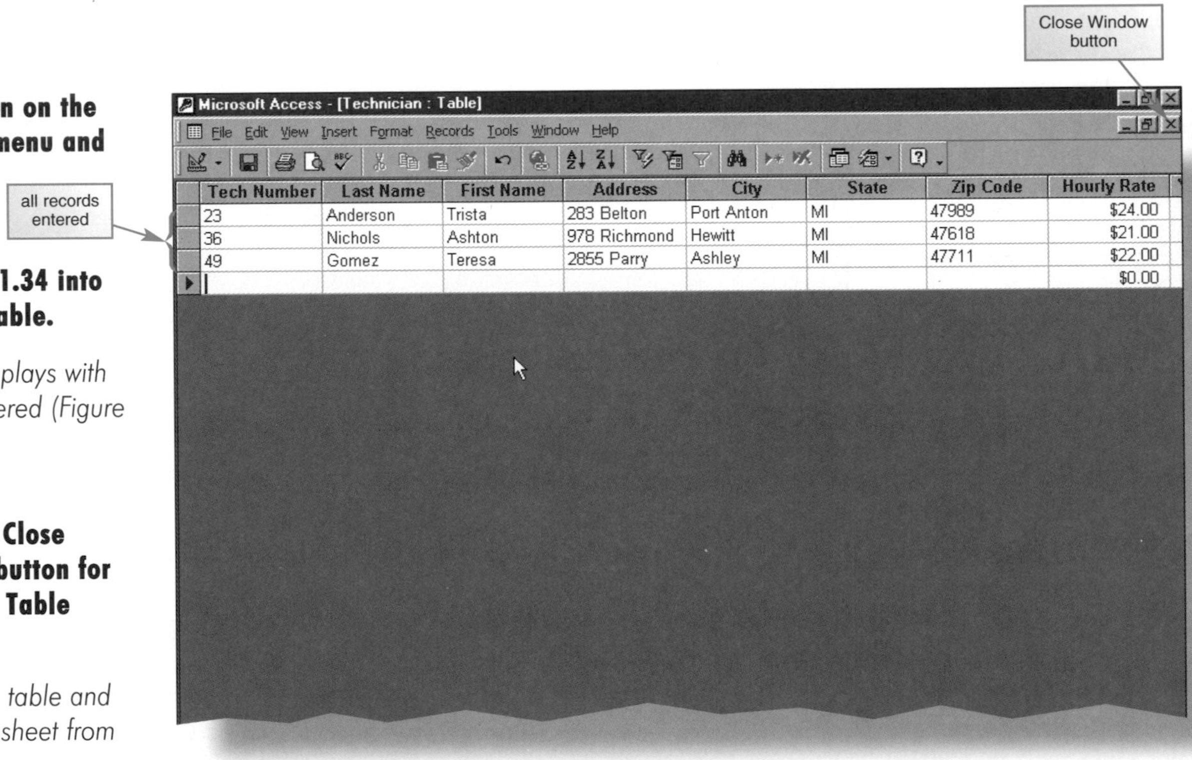

FIGURE 1-46

Using a Form to View Data

In creating tables, you have used Datasheet view; that is, the data on the screen displayed as a table. You also can use **Form view**, in which you see a single record at a time.

The advantage with Datasheet view is you can see multiple records at once. It has the disadvantage that, unless you have few fields in the table, you cannot see all the fields at the same time. With Form view, you see only a single record, but you can see all the fields in the record. The view you choose is a matter of personal preference.

Creating a Form

To use Form view, you first must create a form. The simplest way to create a form is to use the New Object: AutoForm button on the Database window toolbar. To do so, first select the table for which the form is to be created in the Database window and then click the New Object: AutoForm button. A list of available objects displays. Click AutoForm in the list to select it.

Perform the following steps using the New Object: AutoForm button to create a form for the Marina table.

More About

Forms

Attractive and functional forms can improve greatly the data entry process. Forms are not restricted to data from a single table, but can incorporate data from multiple tables as well as special types of data like pictures and sounds. A good DBMS like Access 2000 furnishes an easy way to create sophisticated forms.

Steps To Use the New Object: AutoForm Button to Create a Form

1 **Make sure the Bavant Marine Services database is open, the Database window displays, and the Marina table is selected. Point to the New Object: AutoForm button arrow on the Database window toolbar (Figure 1-47).**

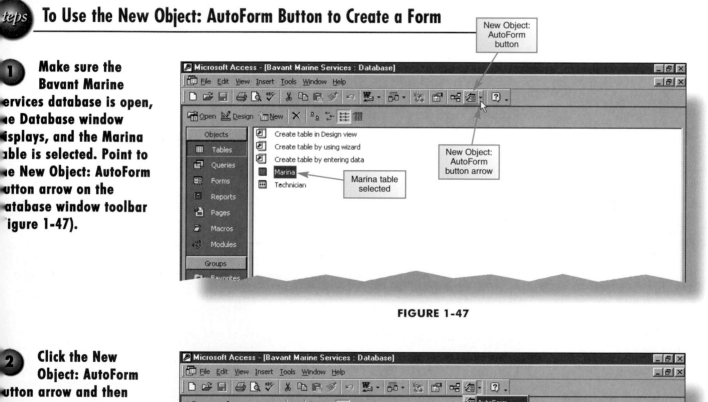

FIGURE 1-47

2 **Click the New Object: AutoForm button arrow and then point to AutoForm.**

A list of objects that can be created displays (Figure 1-48).

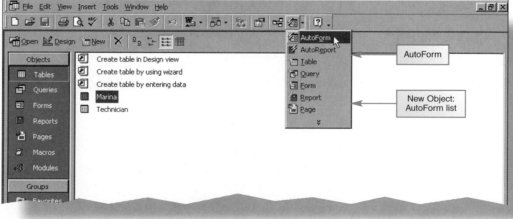

FIGURE 1-48

Close Window button

3 **Click AutoForm in the New Object: AutoForm list.**

Formatting toolbar

The form displays (Figure 1-49). An additional toolbar, the Formatting toolbar, also displays. (When you close the form, this toolbar no longer displays.)

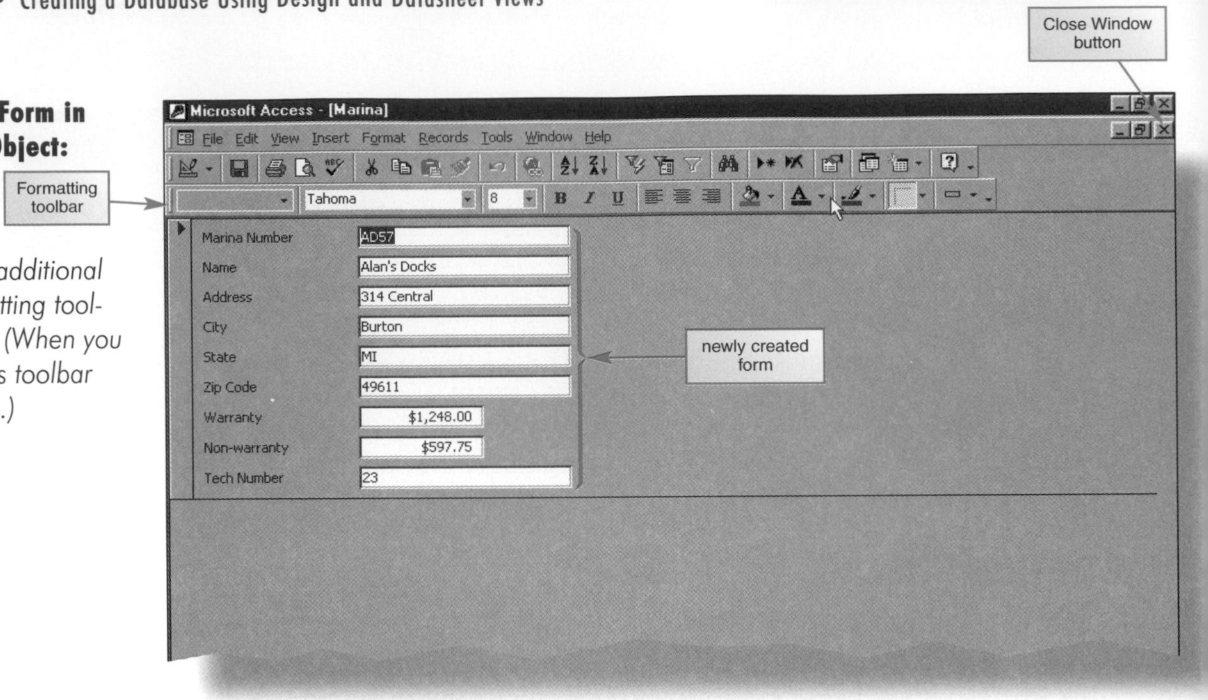

Microsoft Access - [Marina]

File Edit View Insert Format Records Tools Window Help

Tahoma   8   **B** *I* U

Marina Number	AD57
Name	Alan's Docks
Address	314 Central
City	Burton
State	MI
Zip Code	49611
Warranty	$1,248.00
Non-warranty	$597.75
Tech Number	23

newly created form

FIGURE 1-49

Closing and Saving the Form

Closing a form is similar to closing a table. The only difference is that you will be asked if you want to save the form unless you previously have saved it. Perform the following steps to close the form and save it as Marina.

Steps To Close and Save a Form

1 **Click the Close Window button for the Marina window (see Figure 1-49). Point to the Yes button.**

The Microsoft Access dialog box displays (Figure 1-50).

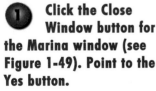

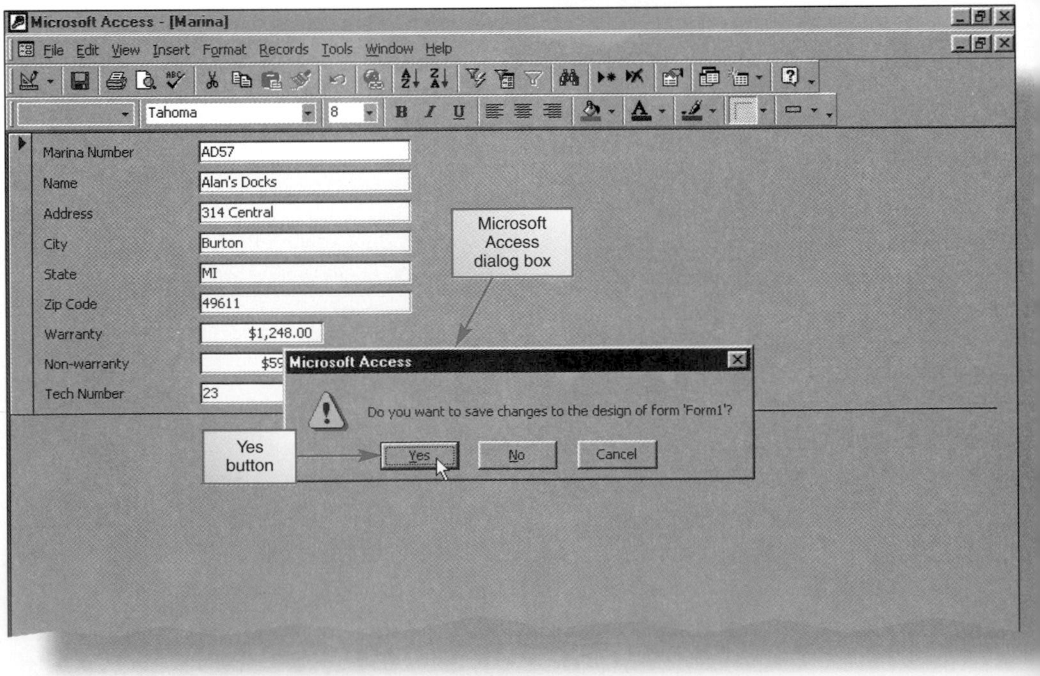

Microsoft Access - [Marina]

File Edit View Insert Format Records Tools Window Help

Tahoma   8   **B** *I* U

Marina Number	AD57
Name	Alan's Docks
Address	314 Central
City	Burton
State	MI
Zip Code	49611
Warranty	$1,248.00
Non-warranty	$59
Tech Number	23

Microsoft Access dialog box

Microsoft Access

Do you want to save changes to the design of form 'Form1'?

Yes button   Yes   No   Cancel

FIGURE 1-50

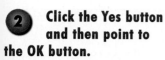

Click the Yes button and then point to the OK button.

The Save As dialog box displays (Figure 1-51). The name of the table (Marina) becomes the name of the form automatically. This name can be replaced with any name.

Click the OK button in the Save As dialog box.

The form is saved as part of the database and is removed from the screen. The Bavant Marine Services : Database window again displays.

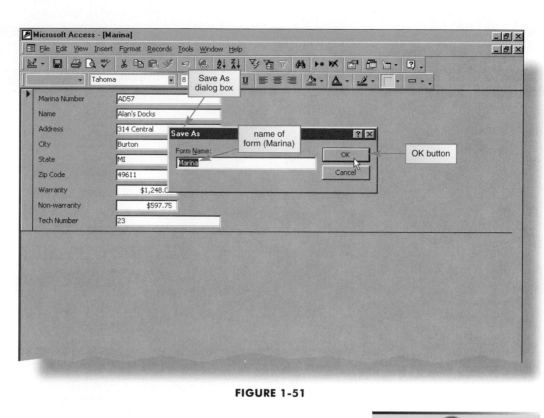

FIGURE 1-51

Other **Ways**

1. On File menu click Close

Opening the Saved Form

Once you have saved a form, you can use it at any time in the future by opening it. Opening a form is similar to opening a table; that is, make sure the form to be opened is selected, right-click, and then click Open on the shortcut menu. Before opening the form, however, the Forms object, rather than the Tables object, must be selected.

Perform the following steps to open the Marina form.

 To Open a Form

With the Bavant Marine Services database open and the Database window on the screen, point to Forms on the Objects bar (Figure 1-52).

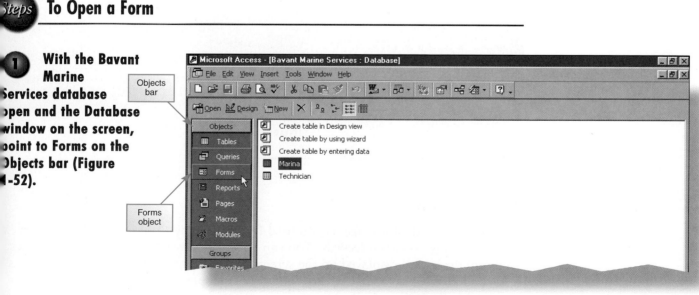

FIGURE 1-52

2 **Click Forms, right-click Marina, and then point to Open on the shortcut menu.**

The Forms object is selected and the list of available forms displays (Figure 1-53). Currently, the Marina form is the only form. The shortcut menu for the Marina form displays.

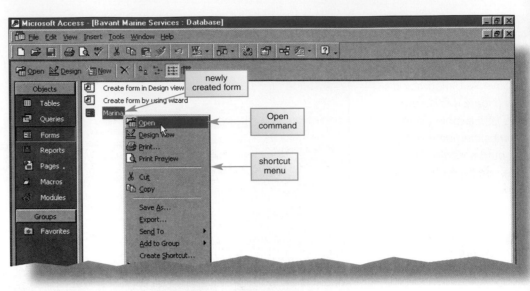

FIGURE 1-53

3 **Click Open on the shortcut menu.**

The Marina form displays (Figure 1-54).

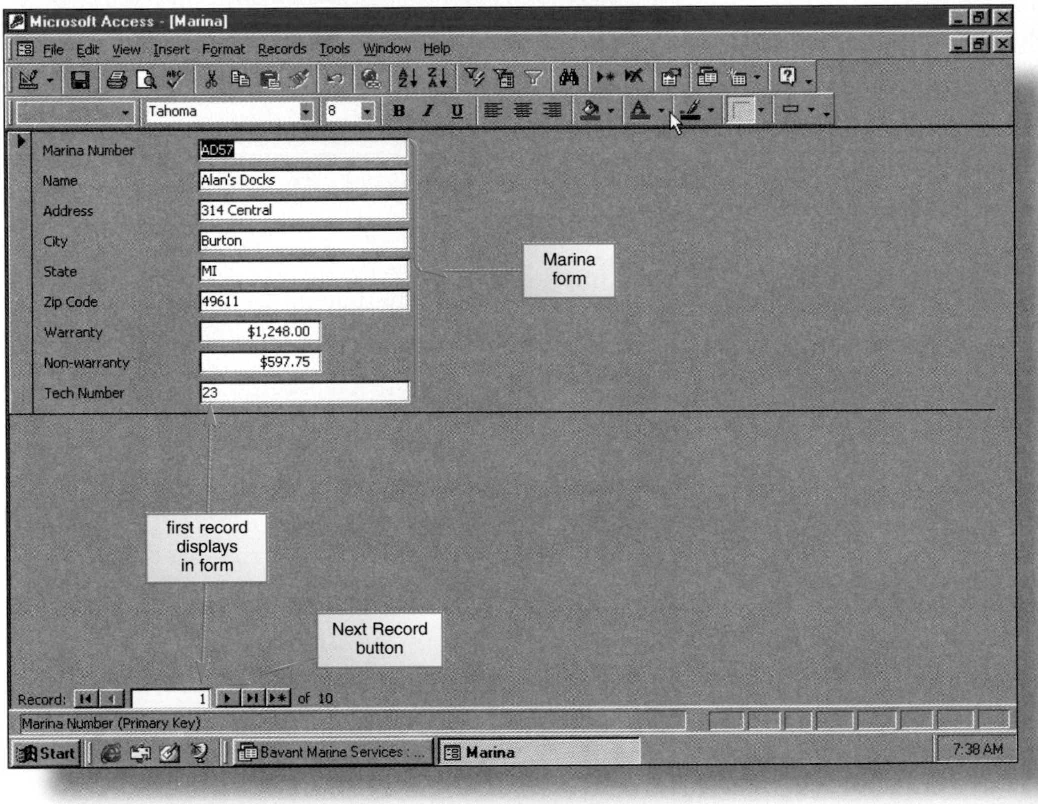

FIGURE 1-54

Using the Form

You can use the form just as you used Datasheet view. You use the Navigation buttons to move between records. You can add new records or change existing ones. To delete the record displayed on the screen, after selecting the record by clicking its record selector, press the DELETE key. Thus, you can perform database operations using either Form view or Datasheet view.

 Other Ways

1. Click Forms object, double-click desired form
2. Click desired form, click Open button
3. Click desired from, press ALT+O

Because you can see only one record at a time in Form view, to see a different record, such as the fifth record, use the Navigation buttons to move to it. To move from record to record in Form view, perform the following step.

Steps To Use a Form

1 Click the Next Record button four times.

The fifth record displays on the form (Figure 1-55).

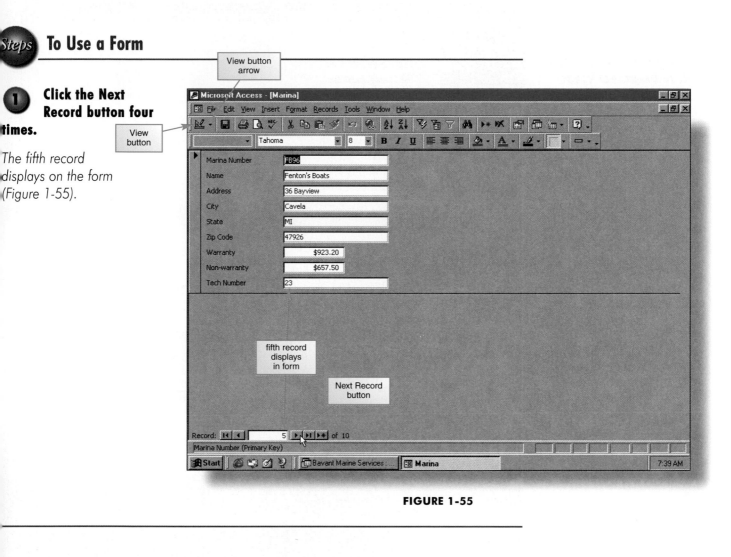

FIGURE 1-55

Switching Between Form View and Datasheet View

In some cases, once you have seen a record in Form view, you will want to move to Datasheet view to again see a collection of records. To do so, click the View button arrow on the Database window toolbar and then click Datasheet View in the list that displays.

Perform the steps on the next page to switch from Form view to Datasheet view.

To Switch from Form View to Datasheet View

1 **Click the View button arrow on the Database window toolbar (see Figure 1-55) and then point to Datasheet View.**

The list of available views displays (Figure 1-56).

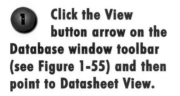

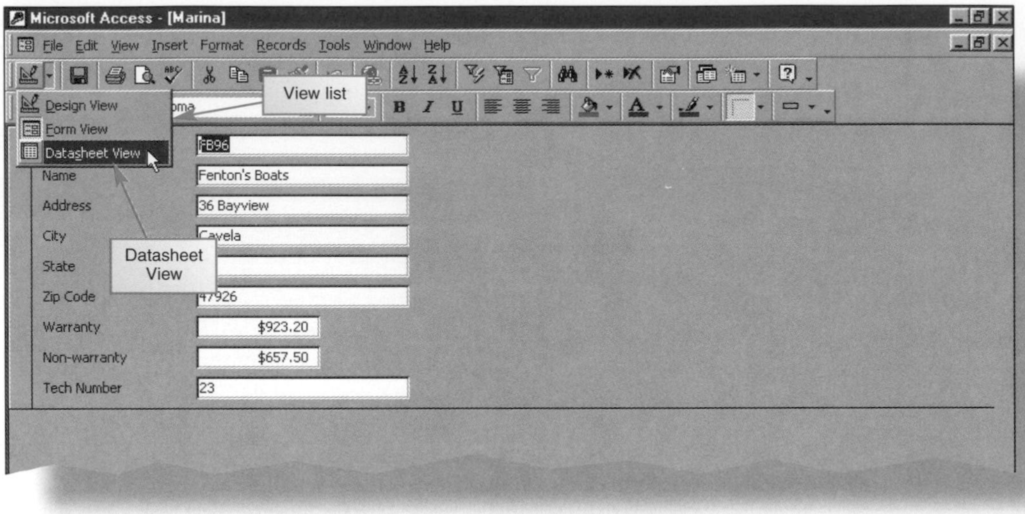

FIGURE 1-56

2 **Click Datasheet View.**

The table displays in Datasheet view (Figure 1-57). The record selector is positioned on the fifth record.

3 **Click the Close Window button.**

The Marina window closes and the datasheet no longer displays.

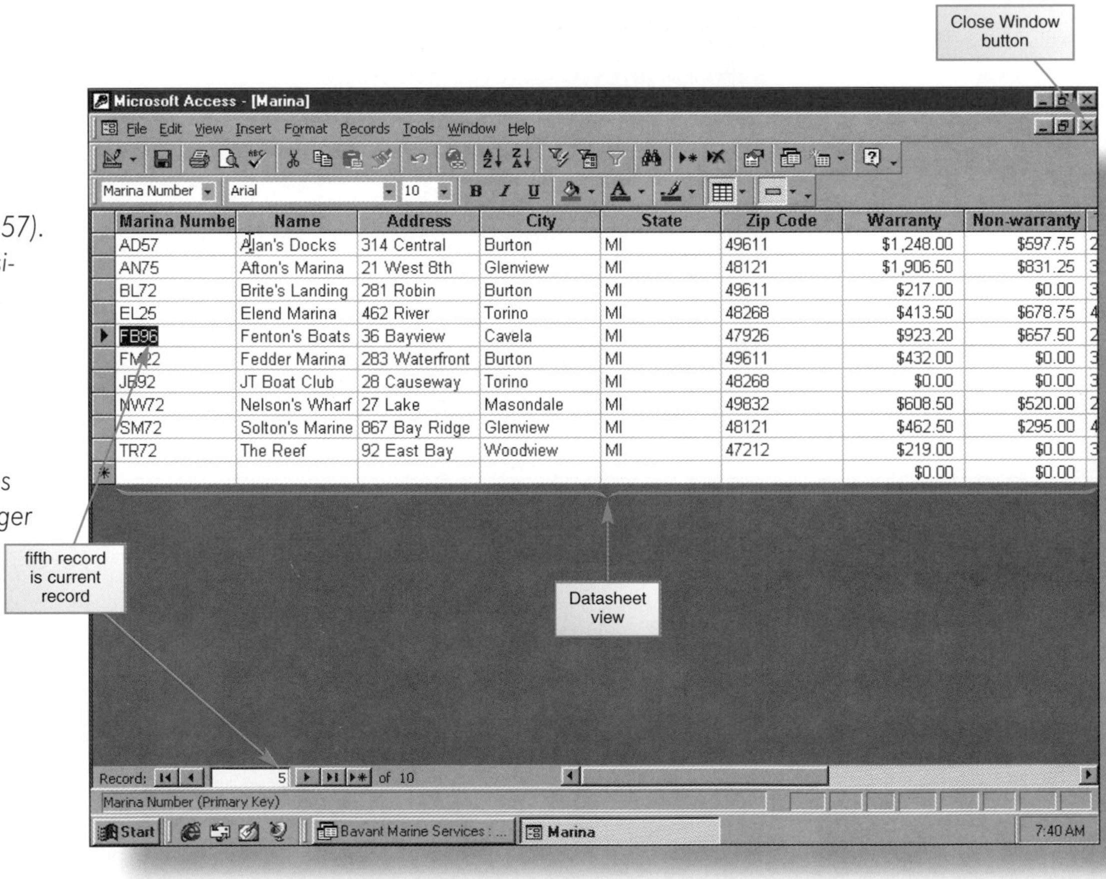

Marina Number	Name	Address	City	State	Zip Code	Warranty	Non-warranty
AD57	Alan's Docks	314 Central	Burton	MI	49611	$1,248.00	$597.75
AN75	Afton's Marina	21 West 8th	Glenview	MI	48121	$1,906.50	$831.25
BL72	Brite's Landing	281 Robin	Burton	MI	49611	$217.00	$0.00
EL25	Elend Marina	462 River	Torino	MI	48268	$413.50	$678.75
FB96	Fenton's Boats	36 Bayview	Cavela	MI	47926	$923.20	$657.50
FM22	Fedder Marina	283 Waterfront	Burton	MI	49611	$432.00	$0.00
JB92	JT Boat Club	28 Causeway	Torino	MI	48268	$0.00	$0.00
NW72	Nelson's Wharf	27 Lake	Masondale	MI	49832	$608.50	$520.00
SM72	Solton's Marine	867 Bay Ridge	Glenview	MI	48121	$462.50	$295.00
TR72	The Reef	92 East Bay	Woodview	MI	47212	$219.00	$0.00
						$0.00	$0.00

Record: 5 of 10
Marina Number (Primary Key)

FIGURE 1-57

1. On View menu click Datasheet View

Creating a Report

Earlier in this project, you printed a table using the Print button. The report you produced was shown in Figure 1-34 on page A 1.30. While this type of report presented the data in an organized manner, it was not very flexible. It included all the fields, but in precisely the same order in which they occurred in the table. A way to change the title was not presented; it remained Marina.

In this section, you will create the report shown in Figure 1-58. This report features significant differences from the one in Figure 1-34 on page A 1.30. The portion at the top of the report in Figure 1-58, called a **page header**, contains a custom title. The contents of this page header display at the top of each page. The **detail lines**, which are the lines that are printed for each record, contain only those fields you specify and in the order you specify.

Perform the following steps to create the report in Figure 1-58.

More About

Reports

Custom reports represent one of the more important ways of presenting the data in a database. Reports can incorporate data from multiple tables and can be formatted in a wide variety of ways. The ability to create sophisticated custom reports is one of the major benefits of a DBMS like Access 2000.

Billing Summary Report

Marina Number	Name	Warranty	Non-warranty
AD57	Alan's Docks	$1,248.00	$597.75
AN75	Afton's Marina	$1,906.50	$831.25
BL72	Brite's Landing	$217.00	$0.00
EL25	Elend Marina	$413.50	$678.75
FB96	Fenton's Boats	$923.20	$657.50
FM22	Fedder Marina	$432.00	$0.00
JB92	JT Boat Club	$0.00	$0.00
NW72	Nelson's Wharf	$608.50	$520.00
SM72	Solton's Marina	$462.50	$295.00
TR72	The Reef	$219.00	$0.00

FIGURE 1-58

Steps To Create a Report

1 Click Tables on the Objects bar. Make sure the Marina table is selected. Click the New Object: AutoForm button arrow on the Database window toolbar.

The list of available objects displays (Figure 1-59).

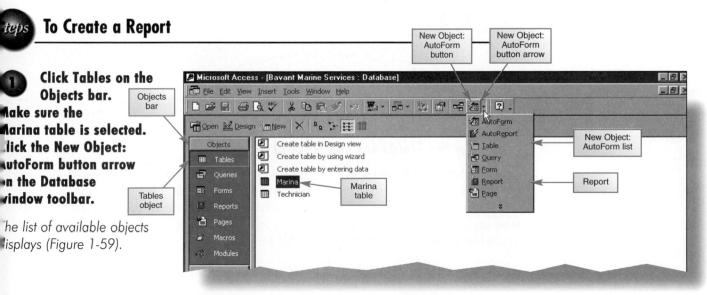

FIGURE 1-59

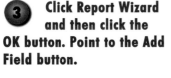

Click Report and then point to Report Wizard.

The New Report dialog box displays (Figure 1-60).

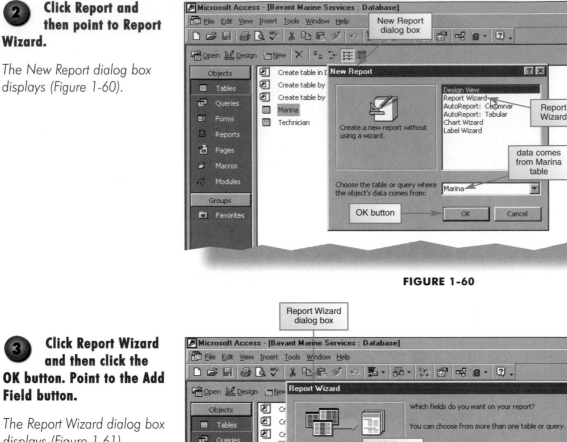

FIGURE 1-60

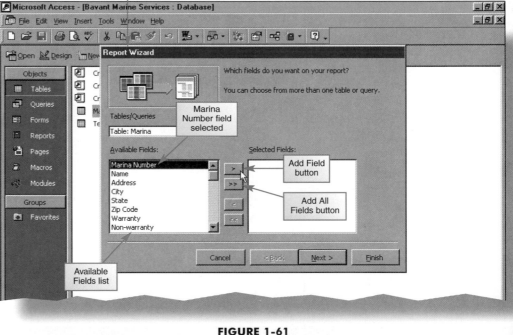

Click Report Wizard and then click the OK button. Point to the Add Field button.

The Report Wizard dialog box displays (Figure 1-61).

FIGURE 1-61

Other Ways

1. On Insert menu click Report
2. On Objects bar click Reports, click New

Selecting the Fields for the Report

To select a field for the report; that is, to indicate the field is to be included in the report, click the field in the Available Fields list. Next, click the Add Field button. This will move the field from the Available Fields box to the Selected Fields box thus including the field in the report. If you wanted to select all fields, a shortcut is available simply by clicking the Add All Fields button.

To select the Marina Number, Name, Warranty, and Non-warranty fields for the report, perform the following steps.

Steps **To Select the Fields for a Report**

① **Click the Add Field button to add the Marina Number field. Add the Name field by clicking it and then clicking the Add Field button. Add the Warranty and Non-warranty fields just as you added the Marina Number and Name fields.**

The fields for the report display in the Selected Fields box (Figure 1-62).

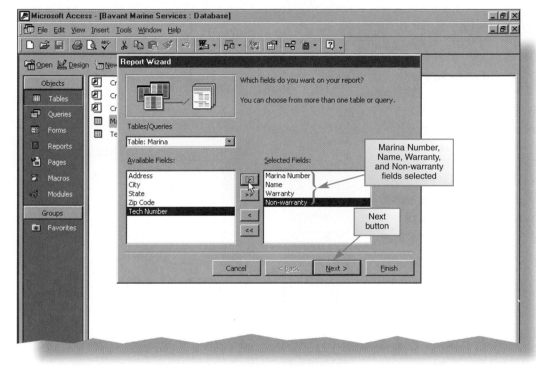

FIGURE 1-62

② **Click the Next button.**

The Report Wizard dialog box displays (Figure 1-63).

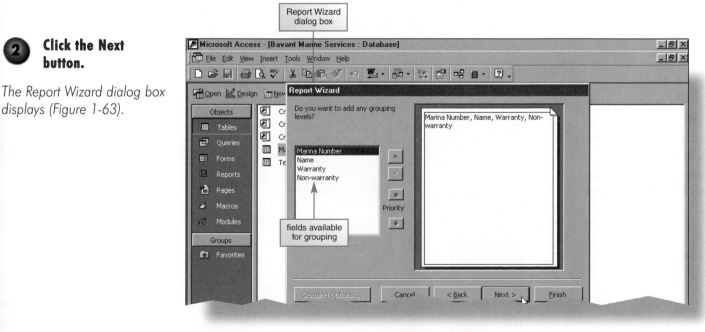

FIGURE 1-63

Other **Ways**

1. Double-click field

Completing the Report

Several additional steps are involved in completing the report. With the exception of changing the title, the Access selections are acceptable, so you simply will click the Next button.

Perform the following steps to complete the report.

 To Complete a Report

1 Because you will not specify any grouping, click the Next button in the Report Wizard dialog box (see Figure 1-63). Click the Next button a second time because you will not need to make changes on the screen that follows.

The Report Wizard dialog box displays (Figure 1-64). In this dialog box, you can change the layout or orientation of the report.

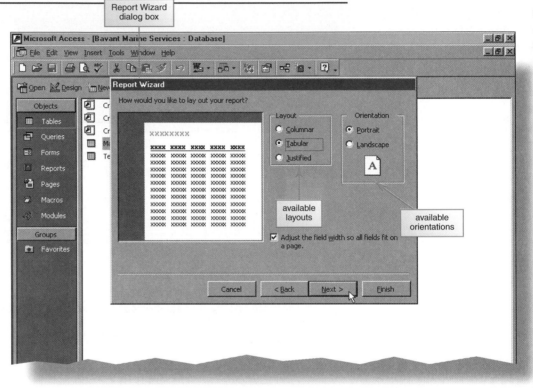

FIGURE 1-64

2 Make sure that Tabular is selected as the layout and Portrait is selected as the orientation and then click the Next button.

The Report Wizard dialog box displays (Figure 1-65). In this dialog box, you can select a style for the report.

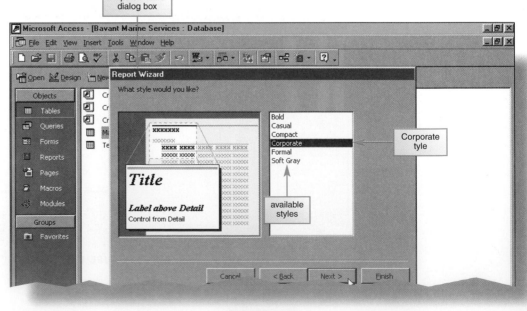

FIGURE 1-65

3 Be sure that the Corporate style is selected and then click the Next button.

The Report Wizard dialog box displays (Figure 1-66). In this dialog box, you can specify a title for the report.

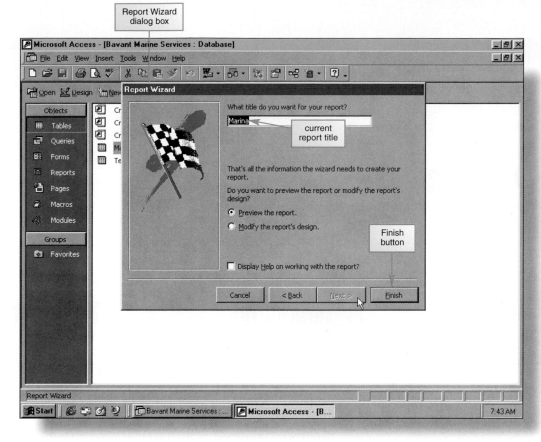

FIGURE 1-66

4 Type Billing Summary Report as the new title and then click the Finish button.

A preview of the report displays (Figure 1-67). Yours may look slightly different, depending on your printer.

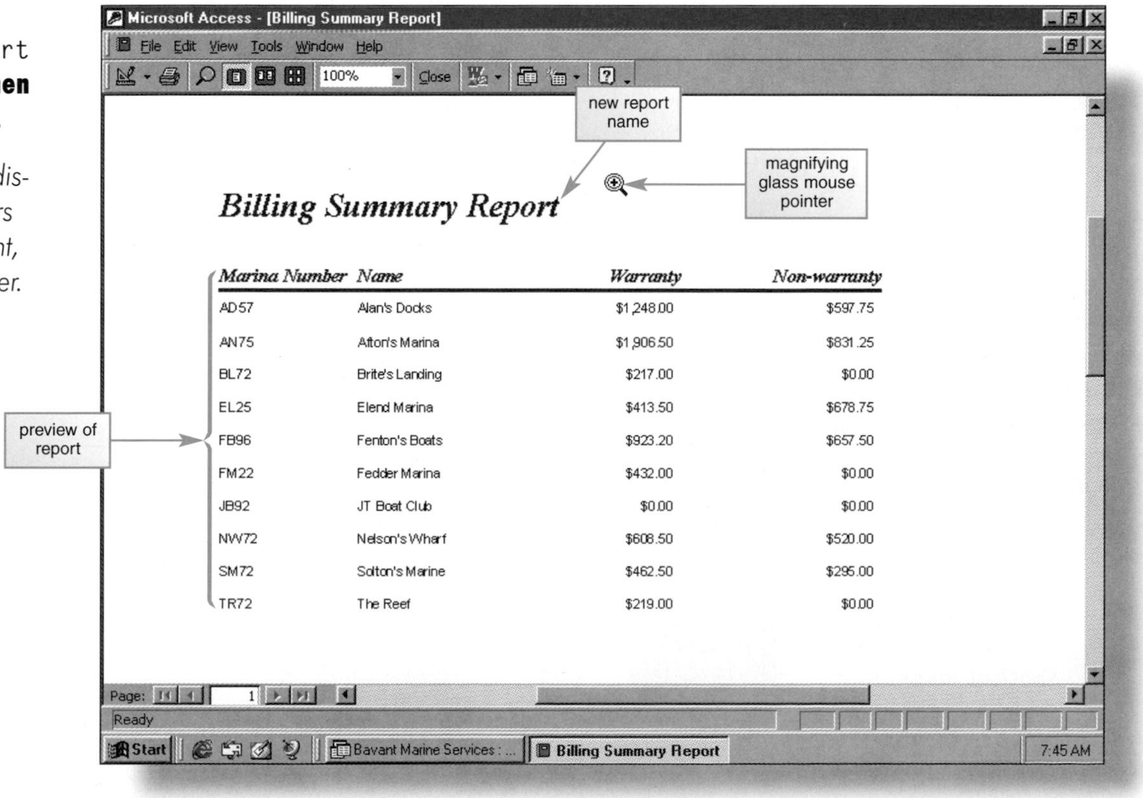

FIGURE 1-67

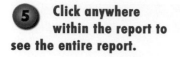

5 Click anywhere within the report to see the entire report.

The entire report displays (Figure 1-68).

6 Click the Close Window button in the Billing Summary Report window.

The report no longer displays. It has been saved automatically using the name Billing Summary Report.

FIGURE 1-68

Printing the Report

To print a report from the Database window, first right-click the report. Then click Print on the shortcut menu to print the report or click Print Preview on the shortcut menu to see a preview of the report on the screen.

Perform the following steps to print the report.

Steps **To Print a Report**

1 If necessary, click Reports on the Objects bar in the Database window, right-click Billing Summary Report, and then point to Print on the shortcut menu.

The shortcut menu for the Billing Summary Report displays (Figure 1-69).

2 Click Print on the shortcut menu.

The report prints. It should look similar to the one shown in Figure 1-58 on page A 1.43.

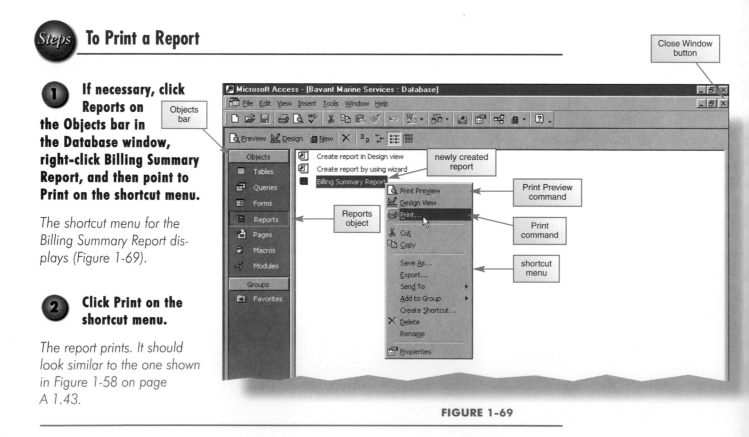

FIGURE 1-69

Closing the Database

Once you have finished working with a database, you should close it. The following step closes the database by closing its Database window.

TO CLOSE A DATABASE

1 Click the Close Window button for the Bavant Marine Services : Database window.

Access Help System

At any time while you are using Access, you can get answers to questions by using the **Access Help system**. Used properly, this form of online assistance can increase your productivity and reduce your frustrations by minimizing the time you spend learning how to use Access. Table 1-2 on page A 1.52, summarizes the eight categories of help available to you. Because of the way the Access Help system works, please review the rightmost column of Table 1-2 if you have difficulties activating the desired category of help.

The following section shows how to get answers to your questions using the Office Assistant. For additional information on using the Access Help system, see Appendix A.

Using the Office Assistant

The **Office Assistant** answers your questions and suggests more efficient ways to complete a task. With the Office Assistant active, for example, you can type a question, word, or phrase in a text box and the Office Assistant provides immediate help on the subject. Also, as you create a database, the Office Assistant accumulates tips that suggest more efficient ways to do the tasks you completed while creating a database, such as printing and saving. This tip feature is part of the **IntelliSense™ technology** built into Access, which understands what you are trying to do and suggests better ways to do it. When the light bulb displays above the Office Assistant, click it to see a tip.

The steps on the next page show how to use the Office Assistant to obtain information on setting and changing the primary key.

Quick Reference

For a table that lists how to complete the tasks covered in this book using the mouse, menu, shortcut menu, and keyboard, visit the Shelly Cashman Series Office Web page (www.scsite.com/off2000/qr.htm), and then click Microsoft Access 2000.

Steps ## To Obtain Help Using the Office Assistant

1 **If the Office Assistant does not display, click Show the Office Assistant on the Help menu. With the Office Assistant on the screen, click it. Type** how do i set the primary key **in the What would you like to do? text box in the Office Assistant balloon. Point to the Search button (Figure 1-70).**

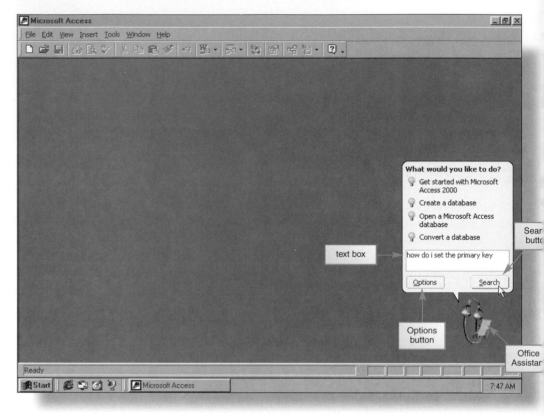

FIGURE 1-70

2 **Click the Search button. Point to the topic Set or change the primary key.**

The Office Assistant displays a list of topics relating to the question, "how do i set the primary key." (Your list may be different.) The mouse pointer changes to a hand (Figure 1-71).

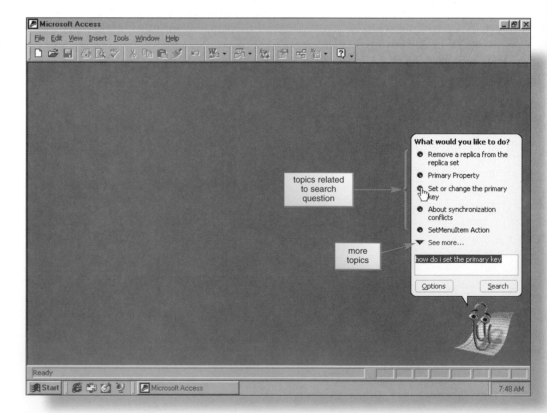

FIGURE 1-71

Click Set or change the primary key.

The Office Assistant displays a Microsoft Access Help window that provides Help information on setting or changing the primary key (Figure 1-72).

 Click the Close Window button on the Microsoft Access Help window title bar.

The Microsoft Access Help window closes.

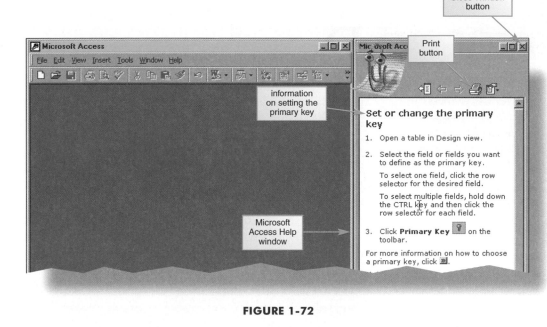

FIGURE 1-72

Table 1-2 summarizes the eight categories of Help available in Access 2000.

Table 1-2   Access Help System

TYPE	DESCRIPTION	HOW TO ACTIVATE	TURNING THE OFFICE ASSISTANT ON AND OFF
Answer Wizard	Similar to the Office Assistant in that it answers questions that you type in your own words.	Click the Microsoft Access Help button on the Database window toolbar. If necessary, maximize the Help window by double-clicking its title bar. Click the Answer Wizard tab.	If the Office Assistant displays, right-click it, click Options, click the Use the Office Assistant check box, and click the OK button.
Contents sheet	Groups Help topics by general categories. Use when you know only the general category of the topic in question.	Click the Microsoft Access Help button on the Database window toolbar. If necessary, maximize the Help window by double-clicking its title bar. Click the Contents tab.	If the Office Assistant displays, right-click it, click Options, click the Use the Office Assistant check box, and then click the OK button.
Detect and Repair	Automatically finds and fixes errors in the application.	Click Detect and Repair on the Help menu.	
Hardware and Software Information	Shows Product ID and allows access to system information and technical support information.	Click About Microsoft Access on the Help menu and then click the appropriate button.	
Index sheet	Similar to an index in a book; use when you know exactly what you want.	Click the Microsoft Access Help button on the Database window toolbar. If necessary, maximize the window by double-clicking its title bar. Click the Index tab.	If the Office Assistant displays, right-click it, click Options, click the Use the Office Assistant check box, and then click the OK button.
Office Assistant	Answers questions that you type in your own words, offers tips, and provides Help for a variety of Access features.	Click the Microsoft Access Help button on the Database window toolbar.	If the Office Assistant does not display, close the Microsoft Access Help window and then click Show the Office Assistant on the Help menu.
Office on the Web	Used to access technical resources and download free product enhancements on the Web.	Click Office on the Web on the Help menu.	
Question Mark button and What's This? command	Used to identify unfamiliar items on the screen.	Click the Question Mark button and click an item in the dialog box. Click What's This? on the Help menu, and then click an item on the screen.	

More About

Database Design (Normalization)

There is a special technique for identifying and eliminating redundancy, called **normalization**. For more information on normalization, visit the Access 2000 More About Web page (www.scsite.com/ac2000/more.htm) and then click Normalization.

Designing a Database

Database design refers to the arrangement of data into tables and fields. In the example in this project, the design is specified, but in many cases, you will have to determine the design based on what you want the system to accomplish.

With large, complex databases, the database design process can be extensive. Major sections of advanced database textbooks are devoted to this topic. Often, however, you should be able to design a database effectively by keeping one simple principle in mind: Design to remove redundancy. **Redundancy** means storing the same fact in more than one place.

To illustrate, you need to maintain the following information shown in Figure 1-73 on the next page. In the figure, all the data is contained in a single table. Notice that the data for a given technician (number, name, and so on) occurs on more than one record.

Marina table

MARINA NUMBER	NAME	ADDRESS	CITY	STATE	ZIP CODE	WARRANTY	NON WARRANTY	TECH NUMBER	LAST NAME	FIRST NAME
AD57	Alan's Docks	314 Central	Burton	MI	49611	$1,248.00	$597.75	23	Anderson	Trista
AN75	Afton's Marina	21 West 8th	Glenview	MI	48121	$1,906.50	$831.25	36	Nichols	Ashton
BL72	Brite's Landing	281 Robin	Burton	MI	49611	$217.00	$0.00	36	Nichols	Ashton
EL25	Elend Marina	462 River	Torino	MI	48268	$413.50	$678.75	49	Gomez	Teresa
FB96	Fenton's Boats	36 Bayview	Cavela	MI	47926	$923.20	$657.50	23	Anderson	Trista
FM22	Fedder Marina	283 Waterfront	Burton	MI	49611	$432.00	$0.00	36	Nichols	Ashton
JB92	JT Boat Club	28 Causeway	Torino	MI	48268	$0.00	$0.00	36	Nichols	Ashton
NW72	Nelson's Wharf	27 Lake	Masondale	MI	49832	$608.50	$520.00	23	Anderson	Trista
SM72	Solton's Marine	867 Bay Ridge	Glenview	MI	48121	$462.50	$295.00	49	Gomez	Teresa
TR72	The Reef	92 East Bay	Woodview	MI	47212	$219.00	$0.00	36	Nichols	Ashton

FIGURE 1-73

duplicate technician names

More About

Database Design (Design Method)

There are a variety of methods that have been developed for designing complex databases given a set of input and output requirements. For more information on database design methods, visit the Access 2000 More About Web page (www.scsite.com/ac2000/more.htm) and then click Database Design.

Storing this data on multiple records is an example of redundancy, which causes several problems, including:

1. Redundancy wastes space on the disk. The address of technician 23 (Trista Anderson), for example, should be stored only once. Storing this fact several times is wasteful.
2. Redundancy makes updating the database more difficult. If, for example, Trista Anderson moves, her address would need to be changed in several different places.
3. A possibility of inconsistent data exists. Suppose, for example, that you change the address of Trista Anderson on marina FB96's record to 146 Valley but do not change it on marina AD57's record. In both cases, the tech number is 23, but the addresses are different. In other words, the data is inconsistent.

The solution to the problem is to place the redundant data in a separate table, one in which the data will no longer be redundant. If, for example, you place the data for technicians in a separate table (Figure 1-74), the data for each technician will appear only once.

technician data is in separate table

Technician table

TECH NUMBER	LAST NAME	FIRST NAME	ADDRESS	CITY	STATE	ZIP CODE	HOURLY RATE	YTD EARNINGS
23	Anderson	Trista	283 Belton	Port Anton	MI	47989	$24.00	$17,862.00
36	Nichols	Ashton	978 Richmond	Hewitt	MI	47618	$21.00	$19,560.00
49	Gomez	Teresa	2855 Parry	Ashley	MI	47711	$22.00	$21,211.50

Marina table

MARINA NUMBER	NAME	ADDRESS	CITY	STATE	ZIP CODE	WARRANTY	NON-WARRANTY	TECH NUMBER
AD57	Alan's Docks	314 Central	Burton	MI	49611	$1,248.00	$597.75	23
AN75	Afton's Marina	21 West 8th	Glenview	MI	48121	$1,906.50	$831.25	36
BL72	Brite's Landing	281 Robin	Burton	MI	49611	$217.00	$0.00	36
EL25	Elend Marina	462 River	Torino	MI	48268	$413.50	$678.75	49
FB96	Fenton's Boats	36 Bayview	Cavela	MI	47926	$923.20	$657.50	23
FM22	Fedder Marina	283 Waterfront	Burton	MI	49611	$432.00	$0.00	36
JB92	JT Boat Club	28 Causeway	Torino	MI	48268	$0.00	$0.00	36
NW72	Nelson's Wharf	27 Lake	Masondale	MI	49832	$608.50	$520.00	23
SM72	Solton's Marine	867 Bay Ridge	Glenview	MI	48121	$462.50	$295.00	49
TR72	The Reef	92 East Bay	Woodview	MI	47212	$219.00	$0.00	36

FIGURE 1-74

Notice that you need to have the tech number in both tables. Without it, no way exists to tell which technician is associated with which marina. All the other technician data, however, was removed from the Marina table and placed in the Technician table. This new arrangement corrects the problems of redundancy in the following ways:

1. Because the data for each technician is stored only once, space is not wasted.
2. Changing the address of a technician is easy. You have only to change one row in the Technician table.
3. Because the data for a technician is stored only once, inconsistent data cannot occur.

Designing to omit redundancy will help you to produce good and valid database designs.

CASE PERSPECTIVE SUMMARY

In Project 1, you assisted Bavant Marine Service in their efforts to place their data in a database. You created the database that Bavant will use. Within this database, you created the Marina and Technician tables by defining the fields within them. You then added records to these tables. Once you created the tables, you printed the contents of the tables. You also used a form to view the data in the table. Finally, you used the Report Wizard to create a report containing the Marina Number, Name, Warranty, and Non-warranty fields for each marina served by Bavant Marine Services.

Project Summary

In Project 1, you learned about databases and database management systems. You learned how to create a database and how to create the tables within a database. You saw how to define the fields in a table by specifying the characteristics of the fields. You learned how to open a table, how to add records to it, and how to close it. You also printed the contents of a table. You created a form to view data on the screen and also created a custom report. You learned how to use Microsoft Access Help. Finally, you learned how to design a database to eliminate redundancy.

What You Should Know

Having completed this project, you now should be able to perform the following tasks:

▶ Add Additional Records to a Table *(A 1.27)*
▶ Add Records to a Table *(A 1.20)*
▶ Add Records to an Additional Table *(A 1.35)*
▶ Close a Database *(A 1.49)*
▶ Close a Table and Database and Quit Access *(A 1.24)*
▶ Close and Save a Form *(A 1.38)*
▶ Complete a Report *(A 1.46)*
▶ Create a Report *(A 1.43)*

▶ Create a Table *(A 1.13)*
▶ Create an Additional Table *(A 1.34)*
▶ Define the Fields in a Table *(A 1.15)*
▶ Obtain Help Using the Office Assistant *(A 1.50)*
▶ Open a Database *(A 1.25)*
▶ Open a Form *(A 1.39)*
▶ Preview and Print the Contents of a Table *(A 1.30)*
▶ Print a Report *(A 1.48)*
▶ Save a Table *(A 1.19)*
▶ Select the Fields for a Report *(A 1.45)*
▶ Start Access *(A 1.9)*
▶ Switch from Form View to Datasheet View *(A 1.41)*
▶ Use a Form *(A 1.36)*
▶ Use the New Object: AutoForm Button to Create a Form *(A 1.37)*

More About

Microsoft Certification

The Microsoft Office User Specialist (MOUS) Certification program provides an opportunity for you to obtain a valuable industry credential — proof that you have the Access 2000 skills required by employers. For more information, see Appendix D or visit the Shelly Cashman Series MOUS Web page at www.scsite.com/off2000/cert.htm.

Apply Your Knowledge

➕ Project Reinforcement at www.scsite.com/off2000/reinforce.htm

1 Changing Data and Creating Reports

Instructions: Start Access. Open the Sidewalk Scrapers document from the Access Data Disk. See the inside back cover for instructions for downloading the Access Data Disk or see your instructor for information on accessing the files required for this book. Sidewalk Scrapers is a snow removal service that was started by two high school juniors looking for ways to earn money for college. Sidewalk Scrapers provides snow removal to residences and businesses in a city that receives lots of snow during the winter months. The business has expanded rapidly and now employs high school and college students to shovel sidewalks, steps, and driveways. Sidewalk Scrapers has a database that keeps track of its workers and customers. The database has two tables. The Customer table contains data on the customers who use the services of Sidewalk Scrapers. The Worker table contains data on the students employed by Sidewalk Scrapers. The structure and data are shown for the Customer table in Figure 1-75 and for the Worker table in Figure 1-76.

Structure of Customer table

FIELD NAME	DATA TYPE	FIELD SIZE	PRIMARY KEY?	DESCRIPTION
Customer Number	Text	4	Yes	Customer Number (Primary Key)
Name	Text	20		Customer Name
Address	Text	15		Street Address
Telephone	Text	8		Telephone Number (999-9999 Version)
Balance	Currency			Amount Owed by Customer
Worker Id	Text	2		Id of Customer's Worker

Data for Customer table

CUSTOMER NUMBER	NAME	ADDRESS	TELEPHONE	BALANCE	WORKER ID
AL25	Arders, Lars	205 Norton	555-2050	$45.00	03
AT43	Atari Cleaners	147 Main	555-7410	$80.00	10
BH81	Bond, Laura	407 Scott	555-0704	$0.00	10
CH65	Chan's Bootery	154 Main	555-0504	$70.00	14
CI05	Cinco Gallery	304 Secord	555-1304	$29.00	03
JB51	Jordach, Ben	203 Norton	555-0213	$60.00	10
LK44	Lee, Kim	605 Thurston	555-5061	$0.00	10
MD60	Martinez, Dan	410 Orange	555-4110	$95.00	03
ME02	Meat Shoppe	75 Edgewater	555-7557	$0.00	14
ST21	Styling Salon	406 Secord	555-6454	$40.00	10

FIGURE 1-75

(continued)

Apply Your Knowledge

Project Reinforcement at www.scsite.com/off2000/reinforce.htm

Changing Data and Creating Reports (continued)

Structure of Worker table				
FIELD NAME	DATA TYPE	FIELD SIZE	PRIMARY KEY?	DESCRIPTION
Worker Id	Text	2	Yes	Worker Identification Number (Primary Key)
Last Name	Text	15		Last Name of Worker
First Name	Text	10		First Name of Worker
Address	Text	20		Street Address
Telephone	Text	8		Telephone Number (999-9999 Version)
Pay Rate	Currency			Hourly Pay Rate

Data for Worker table					
WORKER ID	LAST NAME	FIRST NAME	ADDRESS	TELEPHONE NUMBER	PAY RATE
03	Carter	Chris	467 Norton	555-7641	$4.50
10	Lau	John	56 Parker	555-5656	$4.25
14	Sanchez	Elena	211 Thurston	555-1122	$4.75

FIGURE 1-76

Perform the following tasks.

1. Open the Worker table in Datasheet view and add the following record to the table:

07	Ferrens	Louis	24 Scott	555-2442	4.25

Close the Worker table.

2. Open the Worker table again. Notice that the record you just added has been moved. It is no longer at the end of the table. The records are in order by the primary key, Worker Id.
3. Print the Worker table.
4. Open the Customer table.
5. Change the Worker Id for customer LK44 to 07.
6. Print the Customer table.
7. Create the report shown in Figure 1-77 for the Customer table.
8. Print the report.

Balance Due Report

Customer Number	Name	Balance
AL25	Arders, Lars	$45.00
AT43	Atari Cleaners	$80.00
BH81	Bond, Laura	$0.00
CH65	Chan's Bootery	$70.00
CI05	Cinco Gallery	$29.00
JB51	Jordach, Ben	$60.00
LK44	Lee, Kim	$0.00
MD60	Martinez, Dan	$95.00
ME02	Meat Shoppe	$0.00
ST21	Styling Salon	$40.00

FIGURE 1-77

In the Lab

1 Creating the School Connection Database

Problem: The Booster's Club at the local high school raises money by selling merchandise imprinted with the school logo to alumni. The Booster's Club purchases products from vendors that deal in school specialty items. The database consists of two tables. The Item table contains information on items available for sale. The Vendor table contains information on the vendors.

Instructions: Perform the following tasks.

1. Create a new database in which to store all the objects related to the merchandise data. Call the database School Connection.

2. Create the Item table using the structure shown in Figure 1-78. Use the name Item for the table.

3. Add the data shown in Figure 1-78 to the Item table.

4. Print the Item table.

5. Create the Vendor table using the structure shown in Figure 1-79. Use the name Vendor for the table.

6. Add the data shown in Figure 1-79 on the next page to the Vendor table.

7. Print the Vendor table.

8. Create a form for the Item table. Use the name Item for the form.

Structure of Item table

FIELD NAME	DATA TYPE	FIELD SIZE	PRIMARY KEY?	DESCRIPTION
Item Id	Text	4	Yes	Item Id Number (Primary Key)
Description	Text	25		Description of Item
On Hand	Number	Long Integer		Number of Units On Hand
Cost	Currency			Cost of Item
Selling Price	Currency			Selling Price of Item
Vendor Code	Text	2		Code of Item Vendor

Data for Item table

ITEM ID	DESCRIPTION	ON HAND	COST	SELLING PRICE	VENDOR CODE
BA02	Baseball Cap	15	$12.50	$15.00	AL
CM12	Coffee Mug	20	$3.75	$5.00	GG
DM05	Doormat	5	$14.25	$17.00	TM
OR01	Ornament	25	$2.75	$4.00	GG
PL05	Pillow	8	$13.50	$15.00	TM
PN21	Pennant	22	$5.65	$7.00	TM
PP20	Pen and Pencil Set	12	$16.00	$20.00	GG
SC11	Scarf	17	$8.40	$12.00	AL
TT12	Tie	10	$8.90	$12.00	AL
WA34	Wastebasket	3	$14.00	$15.00	GG

FIGURE 1-78

(continued)

In the Lab

Creating the School Connection Database *(continued)*

Structure of Vendor table

FIELD NAME	DATA TYPE	FIELD SIZE	PRIMARY KEY?	DESCRIPTION
Vendor Code	Text	2	Yes	Vendor Code (Primary Key)
Name	Text	30		Name of Vendor
Address	Text	20		Street Address
City	Text	20		City
State	Text	2		State (Two-Character Abbreviation)
Zip Code	Text	5		Zip Code (Five-Character Version)
Telephone Number	Text	12		Telephone Number (999-999-9999 Version)

Data for Vendor table

VENDOR CODE	NAME	ADDRESS	CITY	STATE	ZIP CODE	TELEPHONE NUMBER
AL	Alum Logo Inc.	1669 Queen	Aurora	WI	53595	608-555-9753
GG	GG Gifts	5261 Stream	Brisbane	NM	88061	505-555-8765
TM	Trinkets 'n More	541 Maple	Kentwood	VA	20147	804-555-1234

FIGURE 1-79

9. Create and print the report shown in Figure 1-80 for the Item table.

Inventory Report

Item Id	Description	On Hand	Cost
BA02	Baseball Cap	15	$12.50
CM12	Coffee Mug	20	$3.75
DM05	Doormat	5	$14.25
OR01	Ornament	25	$2.75
PP20	Pen and Pencil Set	12	$16.00
PN21	Pennant	22	$5.65
PL05	Pillow	8	$13.50
SC11	Scarf	17	$8.40
TT12	Tie	10	$8.90
WA34	Wastebasket	3	$14.00

FIGURE 1-80

In the Lab

2 Creating the City Area Bus Company Database

Problem: Like many urban transportation companies, the City Area Bus Company sells advertising. Local firms buy advertising from ad sales representatives who work for the bus company. Ad sales representatives receive a commission based on the advertising revenues they generate. The database consists of two tables. The Advertiser table contains information on the organizations that advertise on the buses. The Sales Rep table contains information on the representative assigned to the advertising account.

Instructions: Perform the following tasks.

1. Create a new database in which to store all the objects related to the advertising data. Call the database City Area Bus Company.
2. Create the Advertiser table using the structure shown in Figure 1-81. Use the name Advertiser for the table.
3. Add the data shown in Figure 1-81 to the Advertiser table.

Structure of Advertiser table

FIELD NAME	DATA TYPE	FIELD SIZE	PRIMARY KEY?	DESCRIPTION
Advertiser Id	Text	4	Yes	Advertiser Id (Primary Key)
Name	Text	20		Name of Advertiser
Address	Text	15		Street Address
City	Text	15		City
State	Text	2		State (Two-Character Abbreviation)
Zip Code	Text	5		Zip Code (Five-Character Version)
Balance	Currency			Amount Currently Owed
Amount Paid	Currency			Amount Paid Year-to-Date
Sales Rep Number	Text	2		Number of Advertising Sales Representative

Data for Advertiser table

ADVERTISER ID	NAME	ADDRESS	CITY	STATE	ZIP CODE	BALANCE	AMOUNT PAID	SALES REP NUMBER
AC25	Alia Cleaners	223 Michigan	Crescentville	MA	05431	$85.00	$585.00	24
BB99	Bob's Bakery	1939 Jackson	Richmond	MA	05433	$435.00	$1,150.00	29
CS46	Cara's Salon	787 Ottawa	Cheltenham	CT	06470	$35.00	$660.00	29
FS78	Franz and Sons	3294 Campeau	Richmond	MA	05434	$185.00	$975.00	31
GR75	G's Restaurant	1632 Shue	Manyunk	CT	06471	$0.00	$1,500.00	24
HC11	Hilde's Cards	3140 Main	Crescentville	MA	05431	$250.00	$500.00	29
MC34	Mom's Cookies	1805 Broadway	Crescentville	MA	05431	$95.00	$1,050.00	29
NO10	New Orient	2200 Lawrence	Manyunk	CT	06471	$150.00	$350.00	24
PJ24	Pajama Store	13 Monroe	Cheltenham	CT	06470	$0.00	$775.00	31
TM89	Tom's Market	39 Albert	Richmond	MA	05433	$50.00	$500.00	24

FIGURE 1-81

(continued)

In the Lab

Creating the City Area Bus Company Database (continued)

4. Print the Advertiser table.
5. Create the Sales Rep table using the structure shown in Figure 1-82. Use the name Sales Rep for the table. Be sure that the field size for the Comm Rate field is Double.
6. Add the data shown in Figure 1-82 to the Sales Rep table.
7. Print the Sales Rep table.
8. Create a form for the Advertiser table. Use the name Advertiser for the form.

Structure of Sales Rep table

FIELD NAME	DATA TYPE	FIELD SIZE	PRIMARY KEY?	DESCRIPTION
Sales Rep Number	Text	2	Yes	Advertising Sales Rep Number (Primary Key)
Last Name	Text	15		Last Name of Advertising Sales Rep
First Name	Text	10		First Name of Advertising Sales Rep
Address	Text	15		Street Address
City	Text	15		City
State	Text	2		State (Two-Character Abbreviation)
Zip Code	Text	5		Zip Code (Five-Character Version)
Comm Rate	Number	Double		Commission Rate
Commission	Currency			Year-to-Date Total Commissions

Data for Sales Rep table

SALES REP NUMBER	LAST NAME	FIRST NAME	ADDRESS	CITY	STATE	ZIP CODE	COMM RATE	COMMISSION
24	Chou	Peter	34 Second	Crescentville	MA	05431	0.09	$7,500.00
29	Ortiz	Elvia	45 Belmont	Cheltenham	CT	06470	0.09	$8,450.00
31	Reed	Pat	78 Farmwood	Richmond	MA	05433	0.08	$7,225.00

FIGURE 1-82

9. Open the form you created and change the address for Advertiser Number HC11 to 340 Mainline.
10. Change to Datasheet view and delete the record for Advertiser Number GR75.
11. Print the Advertiser table.
12. Create and print the report shown in Figure 1-83 for the Advertiser table.

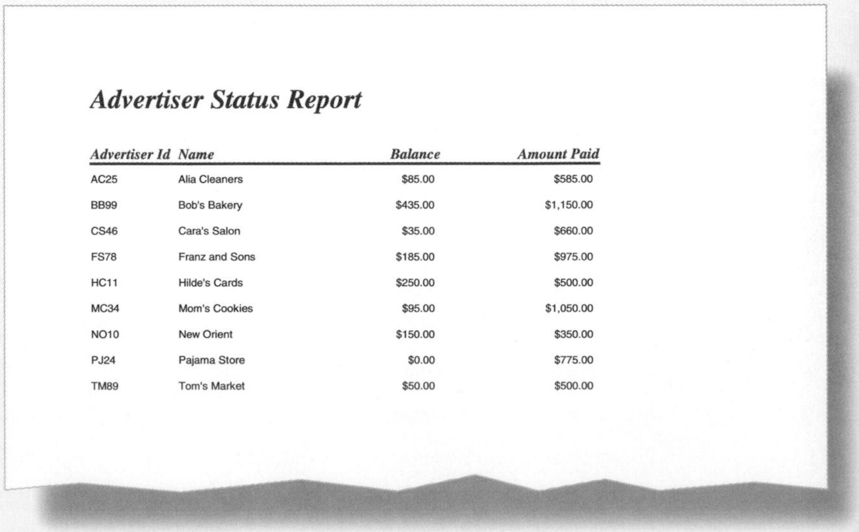

Advertiser Status Report

Advertiser Id	Name	Balance	Amount Paid
AC25	Alia Cleaners	$85.00	$585.00
BB99	Bob's Bakery	$435.00	$1,150.00
CS46	Cara's Salon	$35.00	$660.00
FS78	Franz and Sons	$185.00	$975.00
HC11	Hilde's Cards	$250.00	$500.00
MC34	Mom's Cookies	$95.00	$1,050.00
NO10	New Orient	$150.00	$350.00
PJ24	Pajama Store	$0.00	$775.00
TM89	Tom's Market	$50.00	$500.00

FIGURE 1-83

In the Lab

3 Creating the Resort Rental Database

Problem: A real estate company located in an ocean resort community provides a rental service for apartment/condo owners. The company rents units by the week to interested tourists and "snowbirds" (people who spend their winters in warmer climates). The database consists of two tables. The Rental Unit table contains information on the units available for rent. The Owner table contains information on the owners of the rental units.

Instructions: Perform the following tasks.

1. Create a new database in which to store all the objects related to the rental data. Call the database Resort Rentals.
2. Create the Rental Unit table using the structure shown in Figure 1-84. Use the name Rental Unit for the table. Note that the table uses a new data type, Yes/No for the Pool and Ocean View fields.
3. Add the data shown in Figure 1-84 to the Rental Unit table.

Structure of Rental Unit table

FIELD NAME	DATA TYPE	FIELD SIZE	PRIMARY KEY?	DESCRIPTION
Rental Id	Text	3	Yes	Rental Id (Primary Key)
Address	Text	20		Street Address of Rental Unit
City	Text	20		City
Bedrooms	Number			Number of Bedrooms
Bathrooms	Number			Number of Bathrooms
Sleeps	Number			Maximum Number that can sleep in rental unit
Pool	Yes/No			Does the rental unit have a pool?
Ocean View	Yes/No			Does the rental unit have an ocean view?
Weekly Rate	Currency			Weekly Rental Rate
Owner Id	Text	4		Id of Rental Unit's Owner

Data for Rental Unit table

RENTAL ID	ADDRESS	CITY	BED-ROOMS	BATH-ROOMS	SLEEPS	POOL	OCEAN VIEW	WEEKLY RATE	OWNER ID
101	521 Ocean	Hutchins	2	1	4	Y	Y	$750.00	ML10
103	783 First	Gulf Breeze	3	3	8	Y		$1,000.00	FH15
105	684 Beach	San Toma	1	1	3		Y	$700.00	PR23
108	96 Breeze	Gulf Breeze	1	1	2		Y	$650.00	PR23
110	523 Ocean	Hutchins	2	2	6	Y		$900.00	LD45
112	345 Coastal	Shady Beach	2	2	5		Y	$900.00	LD45
116	956 First	Gulf Breeze	2	2	6	Y	Y	$1,100.00	ML10
121	123 Gulf	San Toma	3	2	8	Y	Y	$1,300.00	FH15
134	278 Second	Shady Beach	2	1	4		Y	$1,000.00	FH15
144	24 Plantation	Hutchins	1	1	2	Y		$650.00	PR23

FIGURE 1-84

(continued)

In the Lab

Creating the Resort Rental Database *(continued)*

4. Use Microsoft Access Help to learn how to resize column widths in Datasheet view and then reduce the size of the Rental Id, Bedrooms, Bathrooms, Sleeps, Pool, Ocean View, Weekly Rate, and Owner Id columns.

5. Print the Rental Unit table.

6. Create the Owner table using the structure shown in Figure 1-85. Use the name Owner for the table.

7. Add the data shown in Figure 1-85 to the Owner table.

8. Print the Owner table.

Structure of Owner table

FIELD NAME	DATA TYPE	FIELD SIZE	PRIMARY KEY?	DESCRIPTION
Owner Id	Text	4	Yes	Owner Id (Primary Key)
Last Name	Text	15		Last Name of Owner
First Name	Text	10		First Name of Owner
Address	Text	15		Street Address
City	Text	15		City
State	Text	2		State (Two-Character Abbreviation)
Zip Code	Text	5		Zip Code (Five-Character Version)
Telephone	Text	12		Telephone Number (999-999-9999 Version)

Data for Owner table

OWNER ID	LAST NAME	FIRST NAME	ADDRESS	CITY	STATE	ZIP CODE	TELEPHONE NO
FH15	Franco	Hilda	1234 Oakley	Middleville	PA	19063	610-555-7658
LD45	Lakos	Daniel	45 Fanshawe	Grenard	MI	49441	616-555-9080
ML10	Manuel	Larry	78 Unruh	Dalute	CA	95518	916-555-8787
PR23	Peoples	Rita	5489 South	Johnson	LA	58345	504-555-9845

FIGURE 1-85

9. Create a form for the Rental Unit table. Use the name Rental Unit for the form.

10. Open the form you created and change the weekly rate for Rental Id 144 to $675.00.

11. Print the Rental Unit table.

12. Create and print the report shown in Figure 1-86 for the Rental Unit table.

Available Rental Units Report

Rental Id	Address	City	Weekly Rate
101	521 Ocean	Hutchins	$750.00
103	783 First	Gulf Breeze	$1,000.00
105	684 Beach	San Toma	$700.00
108	96 Breeze	Gulf Breeze	$650.00
110	523 Ocean	Hutchins	$900.00
112	345 Coastal	Shady Beach	$900.00
116	956 First	Gulf Breeze	$1,100.00
121	123 Gulf	San Toma	$1,300.00
134	278 Second	Shady Beach	$1,000.00
144	24 Plantation	Hutchins	$675.00

FIGURE 1-86

Cases and Places

The difficulty of these case studies varies:
▶ are the least difficult; ▶▶ are more difficult; and ▶▶▶ are the most difficult.

1 ▶ As a fund-raising project, the local college's Computer Science Club sells small computer accessories to students. Disks, disk cases, and mouse pads are some of the items that the club sells from a small kiosk in the student computer lab. The club has asked you to create a database that keeps track of their inventory and suppliers. The current inventory is shown in Figure 1-87.

Design and create a database to store the club's inventory. Then create the necessary tables, enter the data from Figure 1-87, and print the tables.

ITEM ID	DESCRIPTION	UNITS ON HAND	COST	SELLING PRICE	SUPPLIER CODE	SUPPLIER NAME	SUPPLIER TELEPHONE
1663	Antistatic Wipes	30	$0.15	$0.25	ER	Ergonomics Ltd.	517-555-3853
1683	CD Wallet	12	$3.45	$4.00	HI	Human Interface	317-555-4747
2563	Desktop Holder	4	$3.85	$4.75	ER	Ergonomics Ltd.	517-555-3853
2593	Disks	175	$0.20	$.75	HI	Human Interface	317-555-4747
3923	Disk Cases	12	$2.20	$2.75	HI	Human Interface	317-555-4747
3953	Mouse Holder	10	$0.80	$1.00	MT	Mouse Tracks	616-555-9228
4343	Mouse Pad	25	$2.25	$3.00	MT	Mouse Tracks	616-555-9228
5810	PC Tool Kit	9	$7.80	$9.00	ER	Ergonomics Ltd.	517-555-3853
5930	Wrist Rest	3	$2.90	$3.25	ER	Ergonomics Ltd.	517-555-3853

FIGURE 1-87

2 ▶ Sci-Fi Scene is a local bookstore that specializes in Science Fiction. The owner has asked you to create and update a database that she can use to keep track of the books she has in stock. You gather the information shown in Figure 1-88.

Design and create a database to store the book data. Then create the necessary tables, enter the data from Figure 1-88, and print the tables.

Cases and Places

BOOK CODE	TITLE	AUTHOR	UNITS ON HAND	PRICE	YEAR PUBLISHED	PUBLISHER CODE	PUBLISHER NAME
0488	Robot Wars	H Brawley	1	$5.95	1997	SI	Simpson-Ivan
0533	Albert's Way	H Brawley	2	$4.75	1999	SI	Simpson-Ivan
1019	Stargaze	G Chou	3	$5.50	1996	BB	Bertrand Books
128X	Comet Dust	R Eaton	2	$5.95	2000	PB	Peabody Books
1668	Android	E Dearling	3	$6.95	1999	VN	VanNester
3495	Dark Wind	G Chou	4	$4.95	1998	BB	Bertrand Books
3859	Infinity	R Torres	1	$4.75	1997	VN	VanNester
4889	The Galaxy	E Dearling	2	$6.75	2000	VN	VanNester
6517	Strange Alien	R Eaton	2	$9.95	1998	PB	Peabody Books
7104	Secret City	R Torres	1	$5.75	1997	VN	VanNester

FIGURE 1-88

3 ▶▶ The marching band director of your school has asked you to create a database of band members. He wants to keep track of the following data on each band member: name, address, telephone number, age, sex, emergency contact name, emergency telephone number, type of band instrument, band instrument number, whether the student owns or leases the instrument, and number of years in the band.

Design and create a database to meet the band director's needs. Create the necessary tables, enter some sample data, and print the tables to show the director.

4 ▶▶ You have been hired as an intern by the local humane society. The humane society would like you to computerize their adoption files. Currently, they keep all the information about animals that are placed for adoption on index cards. The cards include information on the family, for example, name, address, telephone number, number of children, any previous animal adoptions, and other family pets. Information on the animal also is kept, for example, type of animal, sex, age, name, and any medical problems.

Design and create a database to meet the humane society's needs. Create the necessary tables, enter some sample data, and print the tables to show the director of the humane society.

5 ▶▶▶ The Intramural Sports Club has decided that a good way to make money and help students would be to set up a used sports equipment co-operative similar to the secondhand sporting goods stores. As a member of the club, you are asked to create a database that can store data related to the sports equipment and the students who wish to sell their items.

Determine the type of data you will need, then design and create a database to meet the club's needs. Create the necessary tables, enter some sample data, and print the tables.

Microsoft Access 2000

PROJECT 2

Querying a Database Using the Select Query Window

OBJECTIVES

You will have mastered the material in this project when you can:

- State the purpose of queries
- Create a new query
- Use a query to display all records and all fields
- Run a query
- Print the answer to a query
- Close a query
- Clear a query
- Use a query to display selected fields
- Use text data in criteria in a query
- Use wildcards in criteria
- Use numeric data in criteria
- Use comparison operators
- Use compound criteria involving AND
- Use compound criteria involving OR
- Sort the answer to a query
- Join tables in a query
- Restrict the records in a join
- Use calculated fields in a query
- Calculate statistics in a query
- Use grouping with statistics
- Save a query
- Use a saved query

Where Have All the Children Gone?

National Database Helps Search for Missing Youngsters

All parents fear this situation: One minute their children are within eyesight; the next minute they have vanished, never to be seen again.

Nearly 4,600 children are abducted by non-family members each year, according to the U.S. Justice Department. Another 438,200 children are lost, injured, or otherwise missing. Yet, thousands of these children's records appear in a database maintained by the National Center for Missing and Exploited Children (NCMEC). Through this organization, the children, while they may be missing physically, appear in photo images.

NCMEC was created in 1984 as a public and private partnership to help the public search for missing children. Since the nonprofit Center opened, more than 1.3 million calls have been channeled through its national hotline (1-800-THE-LOST). In addition, NCMEC has partnered with the U.S. Department of

MILK

TO OPEN ▶

TO OPEN

HAVE YOU SEEN ME?

MILK

Name: Rain Ricardo

1-800-THE-LOST

Justice's Office of Juvenile Justice and Delinquency Prevention (www.ncjrs.org) to promote and raise public awareness of this crime.

Since its inception, NCMEC has evolved into a high-tech resource for family, friends, and loved ones of missing and abused children. With nearly 114,600 attempted abductions reported each year, such a resource desperately is needed. Because of these alarming rates, NCMEC has established sophisticated databases that contribute to recovery rates, which are termed child case completions. Currently, the completion rate is 90 percent, dramatically up from 66 percent, which was the norm in 1989. Through partnerships with Intel, IBM, and Tektronix, to name a few, NCMEC has grown into a solid force for solving child cases.

One example of the advanced technology utilized by NCMEC is a database that contains photographs of missing children. Investigators and Web users are able to open the database and create a precise query based on such fields as the child's name, age, eye color, and weight. Then they run the query, and within a matter of seconds they have answers to the requested information. You can create queries and view some of

these images at the NCMEC Web site (www.ncmec.org). Similarly, you will query the Bavant Marine Services Database in this project to obtain answers to questions regarding warranty amounts and marina names and locations.

Moreover, NCMEC's imaging specialists can alter a child's photograph to show how he might appear many years after he has disappeared. Subsequently, these images are stored in corresponding fields in the computerized imaging database. Many children who may not have been located otherwise have been found using this enhancement technology.

A recent technological development is the Multimedia Kiosk Program, which IBM donated to NCMEC. In this program, 50 kiosks have been placed in high pedestrian traffic areas such as LaGuardia Airport in New York and in large shopping malls throughout the country. They provide a functional database for the general public to learn about missing children and a means to transfer information quickly to affected friends and family.

Through the efforts of NCMEC, the nation now has a solid weapon and resource for the fight against child endangerment.

Microsoft Access 2000

Querying a Database Using the Select Query Window

C A S E   P E R S P E C T I V E

Now that Bavant Marine Services has created a database with marina and technician data, the management and staff of the organization hope to gain the benefits they expected when they set up the database. One of the more important benefits is the capability of easily asking questions concerning the data in the database and rapidly obtaining the answers. Among the questions they want answered are the following:

1. What are the warranty and non-warranty amounts for marina EL25?

2. Which marinas' names begin with Fe?

3. Which marinas are located in Burton?

4. What is the total amount (warranty amount plus non-warranty amount) for each marina?

5. Which marinas of technician 36 have warranty amounts of more than $1,000?

Your task is to assist Bavant Marine Services in obtaining answers to these questions as well as any other questions they deem important.

Introduction

A database management system such as Access offers many useful features, among them the capability of answering questions such as those posed by the management of Bavant Marine Services (Figure 2-1). The answers to these questions, and many more, are found in the database, and Access can find the answers quickly. When you pose a question to Access, or any other database management system, the question is called a query. A **query** is simply a question represented in a way that Access can understand.

Thus, to find the answer to a question, you first create a corresponding query using the techniques illustrated in this project. Once you have created the query, you instruct Access to run the query; that is, to perform the steps necessary to obtain the answer. When finished, Access will display the answer to your question in the format shown at the bottom of Figure 2-1.

Project Two — Querying the Bavant Marine Services Database

You must obtain answers to the questions posed by the management of Bavant Marine Services. These include the questions shown in Figure 2-1, as well as any other questions that the management deems important.

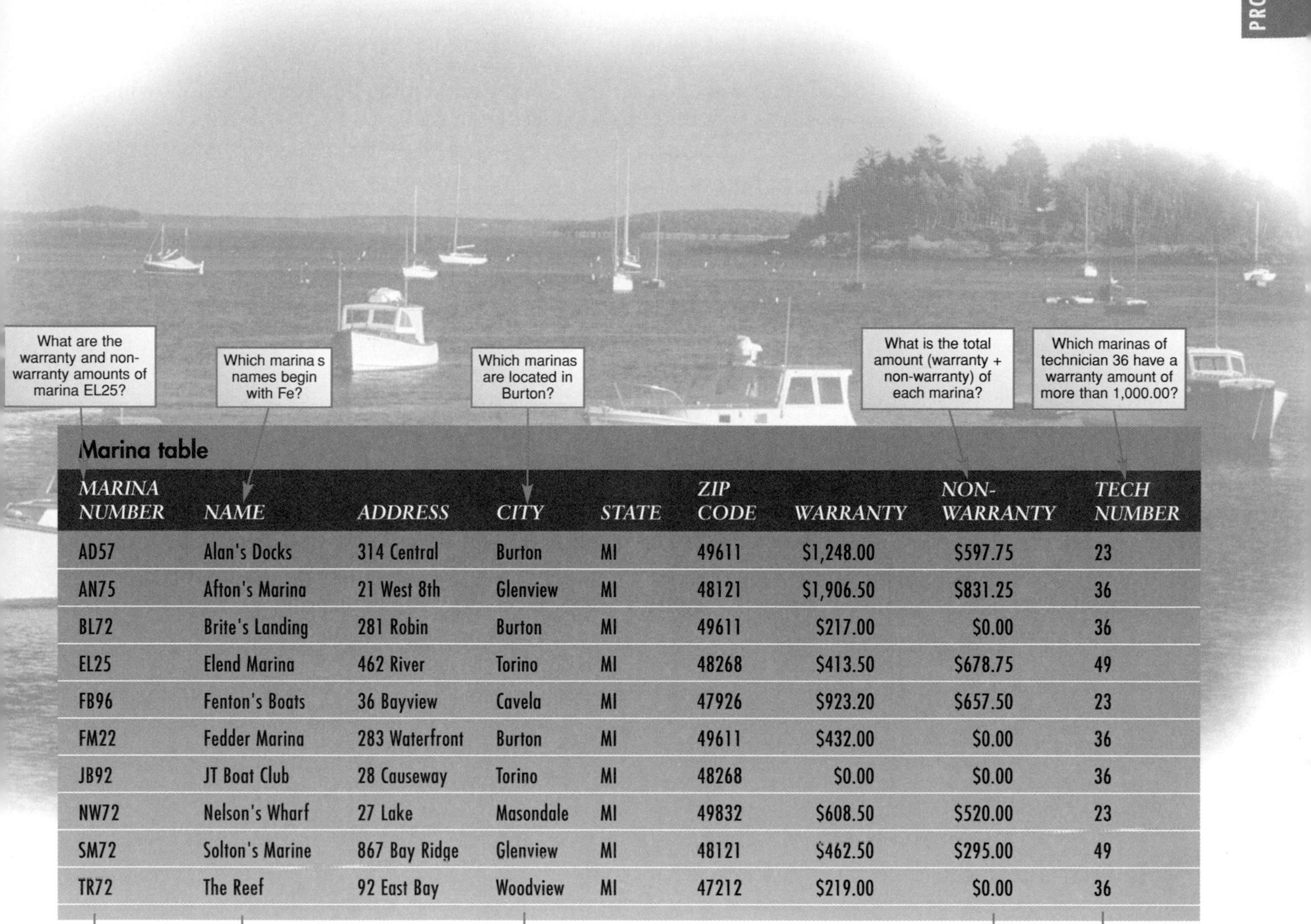

What are the warranty and non-warranty amounts of marina EL25?

Which marina s names begin with Fe?

Which marinas are located in Burton?

What is the total amount (warranty + non-warranty) of each marina?

Which marinas of technician 36 have a warranty amount of more than 1,000.00?

Marina table

MARINA NUMBER	NAME	ADDRESS	CITY	STATE	ZIP CODE	WARRANTY	NON-WARRANTY	TECH NUMBER
AD57	Alan's Docks	314 Central	Burton	MI	49611	$1,248.00	$597.75	23
AN75	Afton's Marina	21 West 8th	Glenview	MI	48121	$1,906.50	$831.25	36
BL72	Brite's Landing	281 Robin	Burton	MI	49611	$217.00	$0.00	36
EL25	Elend Marina	462 River	Torino	MI	48268	$413.50	$678.75	49
FB96	Fenton's Boats	36 Bayview	Cavela	MI	47926	$923.20	$657.50	23
FM22	Fedder Marina	283 Waterfront	Burton	MI	49611	$432.00	$0.00	36
JB92	JT Boat Club	28 Causeway	Torino	MI	48268	$0.00	$0.00	36
NW72	Nelson's Wharf	27 Lake	Masondale	MI	49832	$608.50	$520.00	23
SM72	Solton's Marine	867 Bay Ridge	Glenview	MI	48121	$462.50	$295.00	49
TR72	The Reef	92 East Bay	Woodview	MI	47212	$219.00	$0.00	36

MARINA NUMBER	NAME
FB96	Fenton's Boats
FM22	Fedder Marina

MARINA NUMBER	NAME
AN75	Afton's Marina

MARINA NUMBER	NAME	ADDRESS
AD57	Alan's Docks	314 Central
BL72	Brite's Landing	281 Robin
FM22	Fedder Marina	283 Waterfront

MARINA NUMBER	NAME	TOTAL AMOUNT
AD57	Alan's Docks	$1,845.75
AN75	Afton's Marina	$2,737.75
BL72	Brite's Landing	$217.00
EL25	Elend Marina	$1,092.25
FB96	Fenton's Boats	$1,580.70
FM22	Fedder Marina	$432.00
JB92	JT Boat Club	$0.00
NW72	Nelson's Wharf	$1,128.50
SM72	Solton's Marine	$757.50
TR72	The Reef	$219.00

MARINA NUMBER	NAME	WARRANTY	NON-WARRANTY
EL25	Elend Marina	$413.50	$678.75

FIGURE 2-1

Opening the Database

Before creating queries, first you must open the database. The following steps summarize the procedure to complete this task.

TO OPEN A DATABASE

1 Click the Start button on the taskbar.

2 Click Open Office Document and then click 3½ Floppy (A:) in the Look in box. Make sure the database called Bavant Marine Services is selected.

3 Click the Open button in the Open dialog box. If the Tables object is not already selected, click Tables on the Objects bar.

The database is open and the Bavant Marine Services : Database window displays.

Creating a New Query

You create a query by making entries in a special window called a **Select Query window**. Once the database is open, the first step in creating a query is to select the table for which you are creating a query in the Database window. Next, using the New Object: AutoForm button on the Database window toolbar, you will design the new query. The Select Query window will display. It typically is easier to work with the Select Query window if it is maximized. Thus, as a standard practice, maximize the Select Query window as soon as you have created it.

Perform the following steps to begin creating a query.

Steps **To Create a Query**

1 **Be sure the Bavant Marine Services database is open, the Tables object is selected, and the Marina table is selected. Click the New Object: AutoForm button arrow on the Database window toolbar. Point to Query on the New Object: AutoForm menu.**

The list of available objects displays (Figure 2-2).

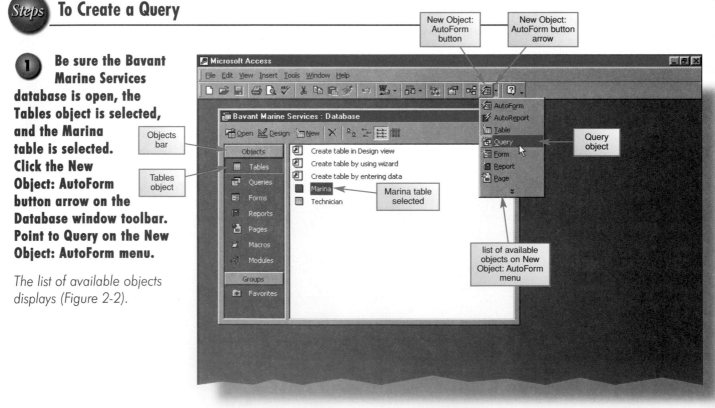

FIGURE 2-2

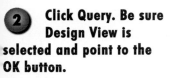 **Click Query. Be sure Design View is selected and point to the OK button.**

The New Query dialog box displays (Figure 2-3).

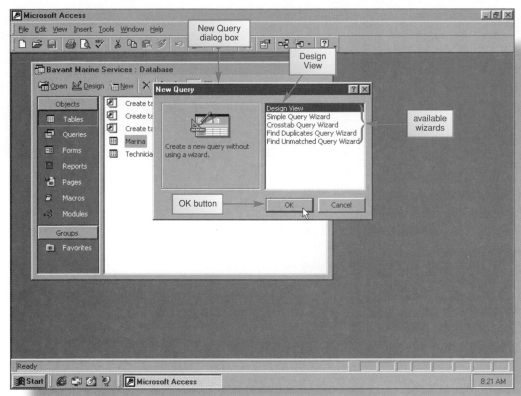

FIGURE 2-3

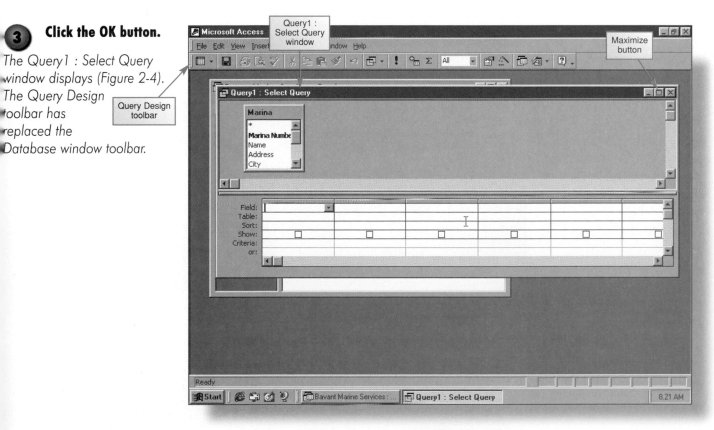 **Click the OK button.**

The Query1 : Select Query window displays (Figure 2-4). The Query Design toolbar has replaced the Database window toolbar.

FIGURE 2-4

**Maximize the
Query1 : Select
Query window by
clicking its
Maximize button,
and then point to
the dividing line
that separates the upper
and lower panes of the
window. The mouse pointer
will change shape to
a two-headed arrow
with a horizontal bar.**

The Query1 : Select Query
window is maximized (Figure
2-5). The upper pane con-
tains a field list for the
Marina table. The lower pane
contains the **design grid**,
which is the area where you
specify fields to be included,
sort order, and the criteria the
records you are looking for
must satisfy.

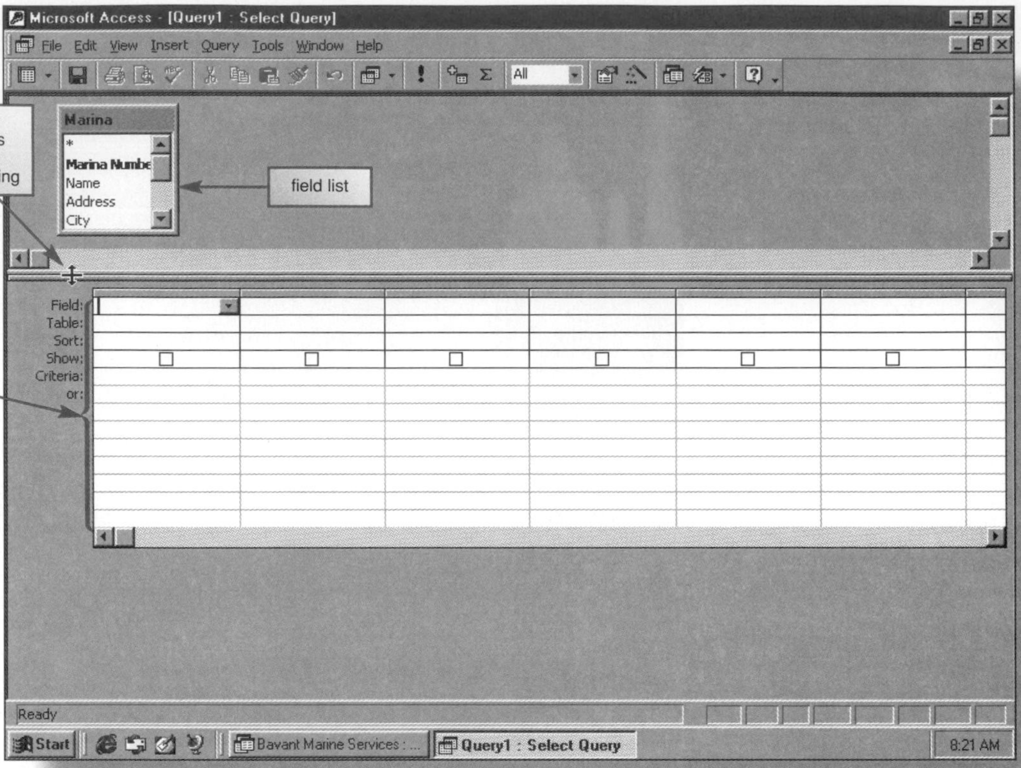

FIGURE 2-5

**Drag the line down
to the approximate
position shown in Figure
2-6 and then move the
mouse pointer to the lower
edge of the field box so it
changes shape to a two-
headed arrow.**

The two panes have been
resized.

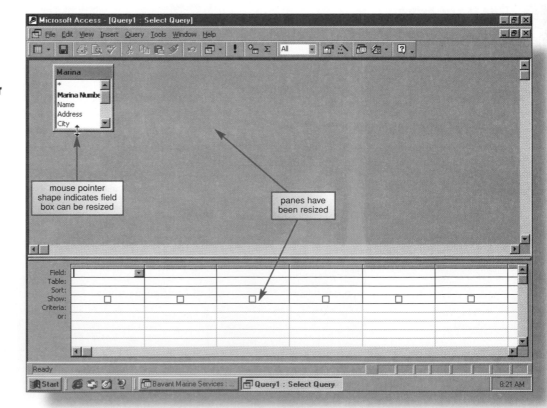

FIGURE 2-6

6 Drag the lower edge of the field box down far enough so all fields in the Marina table are visible.

All fields in the Marina table display (Figure 2-7).

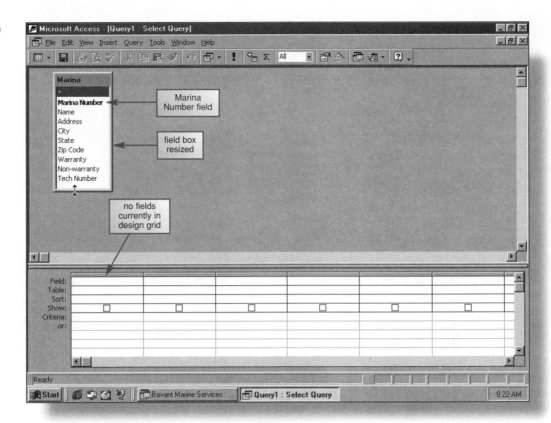

FIGURE 2-7

Using the Select Query Window

Once you have created a new Select Query window, you are ready to create the actual query by making entries in the design grid in the lower pane of the window. You enter the names of the fields you want included in the Field row in the grid. You also can enter criteria, such as the fact that the marina number must be EL25, in the Criteria row of the grid. When you do so, only the record or records that match the criterion will be included in the answer.

Displaying Selected Fields in a Query

Only the fields that appear in the design grid will be included in the results of the query. Thus, to display only certain fields, place only these fields in the grid, and no others. If you place the wrong field in the grid inadvertently, click Edit on the menu bar and then click Delete to remove it. Alternatively, you could click Clear Grid to clear the entire design grid and then start over.

The steps on the next page create a query to show the marina number, name, and technician number for all marinas by including only those fields in the design grid.

1. Click Queries object, double-click Create query in Design view
2. On Insert menu click Query

Queries: Query-by-Example

Query-by-Example, often referred to as QBE, was a query language first proposed in the mid 1970s. In this approach, users asked questions by filling in a table on the screen. The approach to queries taken by several DBMSs is based on Query-by-Example. For more information, visit the Access 2000 More About Web page (www.scsite.com/ ac2000/more.htm) and click QBE.

Steps To Include Fields in the Design Grid

1 **Make sure you have a maximized Query1 : Select Query window containing a field list for the Marina table in the upper pane of the window and an empty design grid in the lower pane (see Figure 2-7 on page A 2.9).**

2 **Double-click the Marina Number field to include the Marina Number field in the query.**

The Marina Number field is included as the first field in the design grid (Figure 2-8).

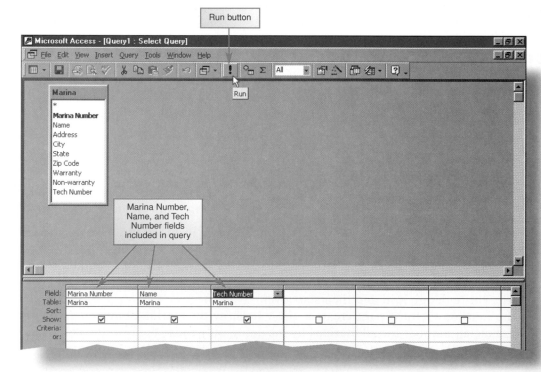

FIGURE 2-8

3 **Double-click the Name field to include it in the query. Include the Tech Number field using the same technique. Point to the Run button on the Query Design toolbar.**

The Marina Number, Name, and Tech Number fields are included in the query (Figure 2-9).

FIGURE 2-9

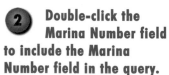

Running a Query

Once you have created the query, you need to run the query to produce the results. To do so, click the Run button. Access then will perform the steps necessary to obtain and display the answer. The set of records that makes up the answer will be displayed in Datasheet view. Although it looks like a table that is stored on your disk, it really is not. The records are constructed from data in the existing Marina table. If you were to change the data in the Marina table and then rerun this same query, the results would reflect the changes.

More About

Queries: SQL

The most widespread of all the query languages is a language called SQL. Many database management systems, including Access, offer SQL as one option for querying databases. For more information, visit the Access 2000 More About Web page (www.scsite.com/ac2000/more.htm) and click SQL.

Steps **To Run the Query**

1 **Click the Run button.**

The query is executed and the results display (Figure 2-10). The Query Datasheet toolbar replaces the Query Design toolbar. The Sort Ascending button on the Query Datasheet toolbar now occupies the position of the Run button. If you do not move the mouse pointer after clicking a button, the Screen-Tip for the button may obscure a portion of the first record, such as the ScreenTip for the Sort Ascending button. Moving the mouse pointer away from the toolbar after running the Query eliminates this problem.

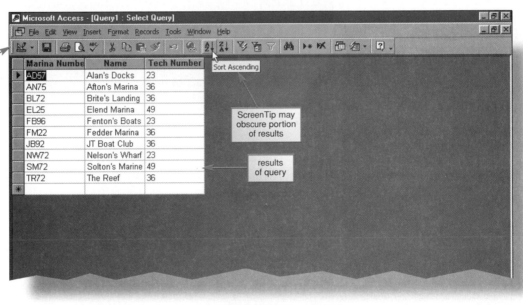

FIGURE 2-10

2 **Move the mouse pointer to a position that is outside of the data and is not on the Query Datasheet toolbar.**

The data displays without obstruction (Figure 2-11). Notice that an extra blank row, marking the end of the table, displays at the end of the results.

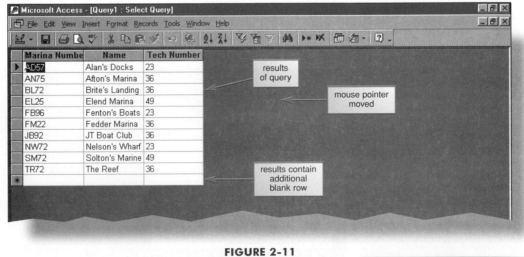

FIGURE 2-11

Other Ways

1. On Query menu click Run
2. On View menu click Datasheet View

In all future examples, after running a query, move the mouse pointer so the table displays without obstruction.

Printing the Results of a Query

To print the results of a query, click the Print button on the toolbar. Complete the following steps to print the query results that currently display on the screen.

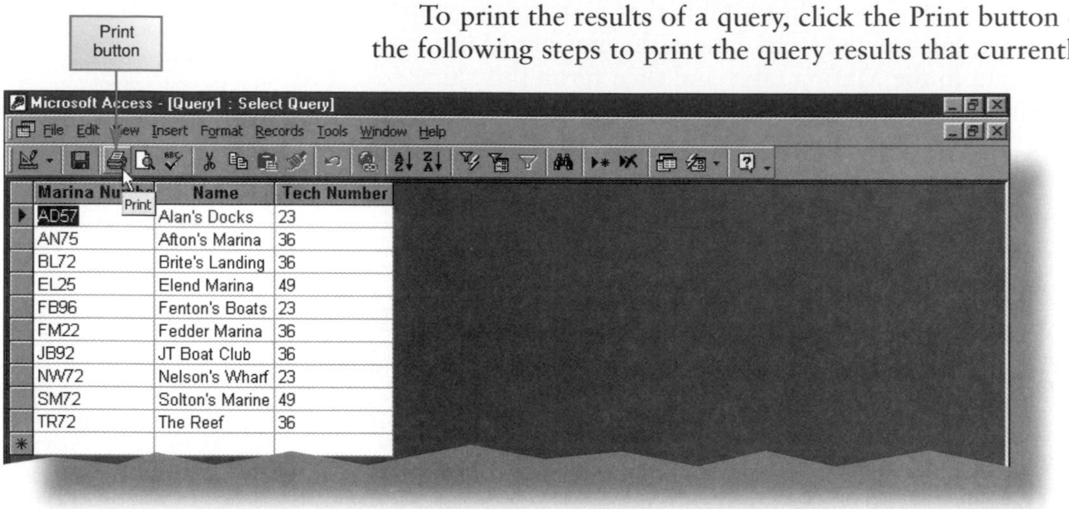

Print button

Print

FIGURE 2-12

TO PRINT THE RESULTS OF A QUERY

1   Ready the printer and then point to the Print button on the Query Datasheet toolbar (Figure 2-12).

2   Click the Print button.

The results print.

If the results of a query require landscape orientation, switch to landscape orientation before you click the Print button as indicated in Project 1 on page A 1.30.

Returning to Design View

You can examine the results of a query on your screen to see the answer to your question. You can scroll through the records, if necessary, just as you scroll through the records of any other table. You also can print a copy of the table. In any case, once you are finished working with the results, you can return to Design view to ask another question. To do so, use the View button arrow on the Query Datasheet toolbar as shown in the following steps.

Steps   **To Return to Design View**

1   **Point to the View button arrow on the Query Datasheet toolbar (Figure 2-13).**

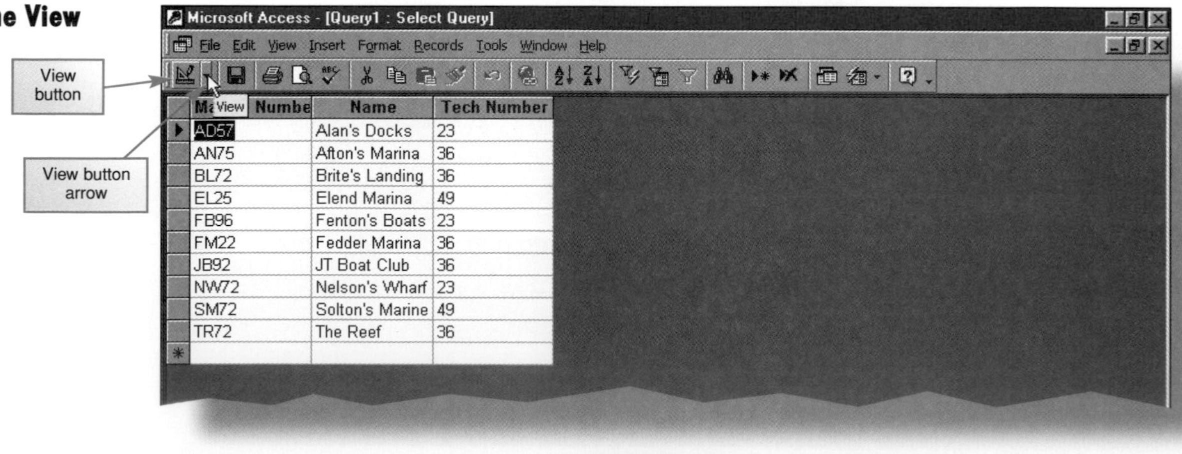

View button

View button arrow

FIGURE 2-13

Click the View button arrow and then point to Design View.

The View button menu displays (Figure 2-14).

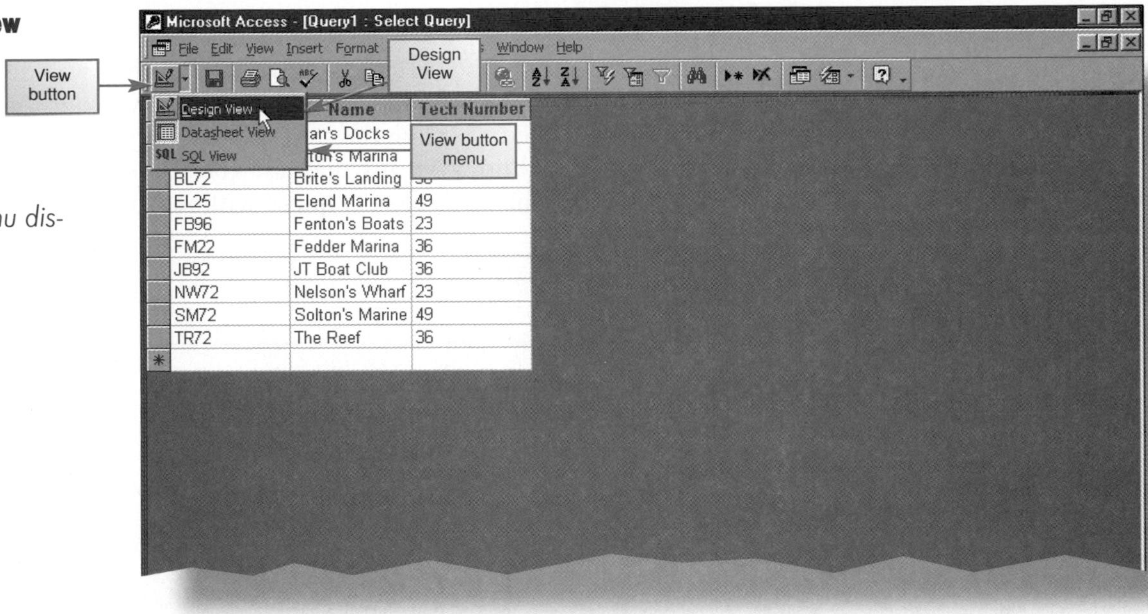

FIGURE 2-14

 Click Design View.

The Query1 : Select Query window displays (Figure 2-15).

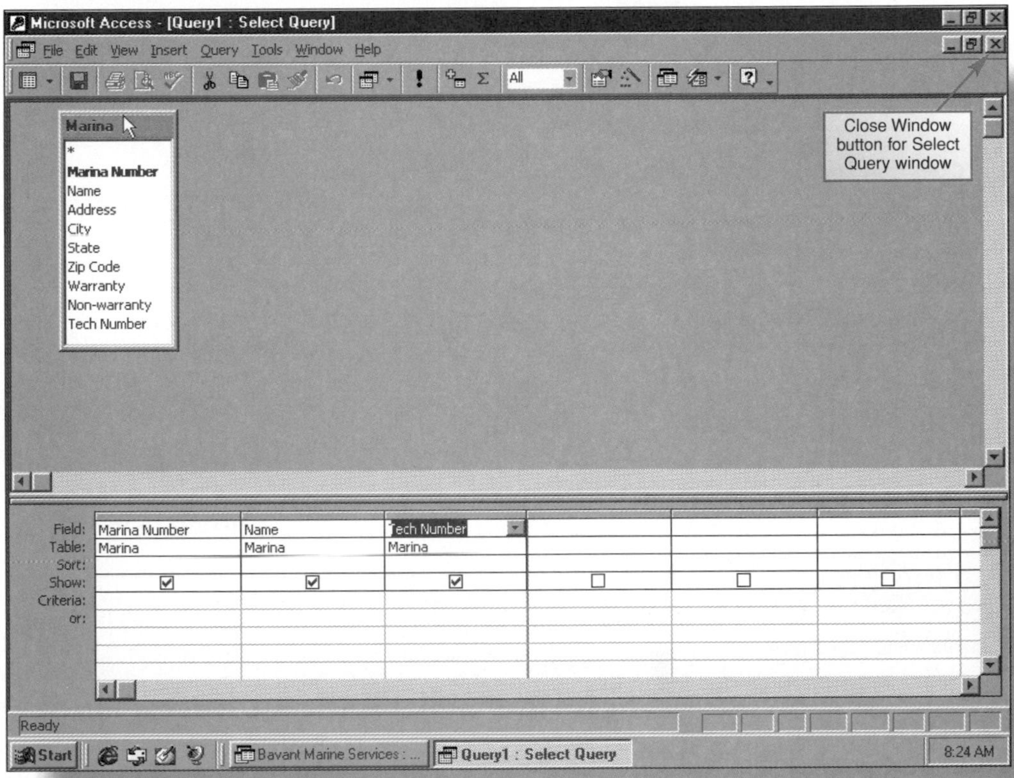

FIGURE 2-15

Other Ways

1. On View menu click Design View

Because Design View is the first command on the View button menu, you do not have to click the View button arrow and then click Design View. You simply can click the View button itself.

Closing a Query

To close a query, close the Select Query window. When you do so, Access displays the Microsoft dialog box asking if you want to save your query for future use. If you think you will need to create the same exact query often, you should save the query. For now, you will not save any queries. You will see how to save them later in the project. The following steps close a query without saving it.

 To Close the Query

1 Click the Close Window button for the Query1 : Select Query window. (See Figure 2-15 on page A 2.13.)

The Microsoft Access dialog box displays (Figure 2-16). Clicking the Yes button saves the query and clicking the No button closes the query without saving.

2 Click the No button in the Microsoft Access dialog box.

The Query1 : Select Query window closes and is removed from the desktop.

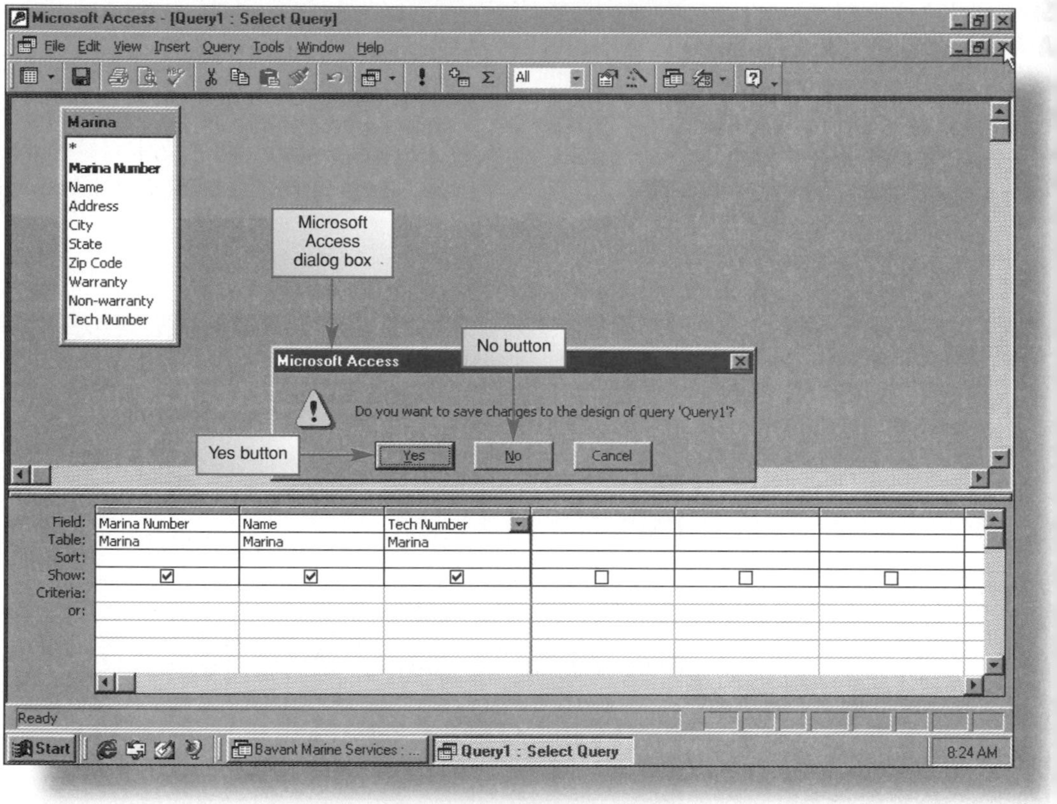

FIGURE 2-16

Other Ways

1. On File menu click Close

Including All Fields in a Query

If you want to include all fields in a query, you could select each field individually. A more simplified way exists to include all fields, however. By selecting the **asterisk (*)** in the field list, you are indicating that all fields are to be included. Complete the following steps to use the asterisk to include all fields.

To Include All Fields in a Query

1 Be sure you have a maximized Query1 : Select Query window containing a field list for the Marina table in the upper pane and an empty design grid in the lower pane. (See Steps 1 through 6 on pages A 2.6 through A 2.9 to create the query and resize the window.) Point to the asterisk at the top of the field list.

A maximized Query1 : Select Query window displays (Figure 2-17). The two panes have been resized.

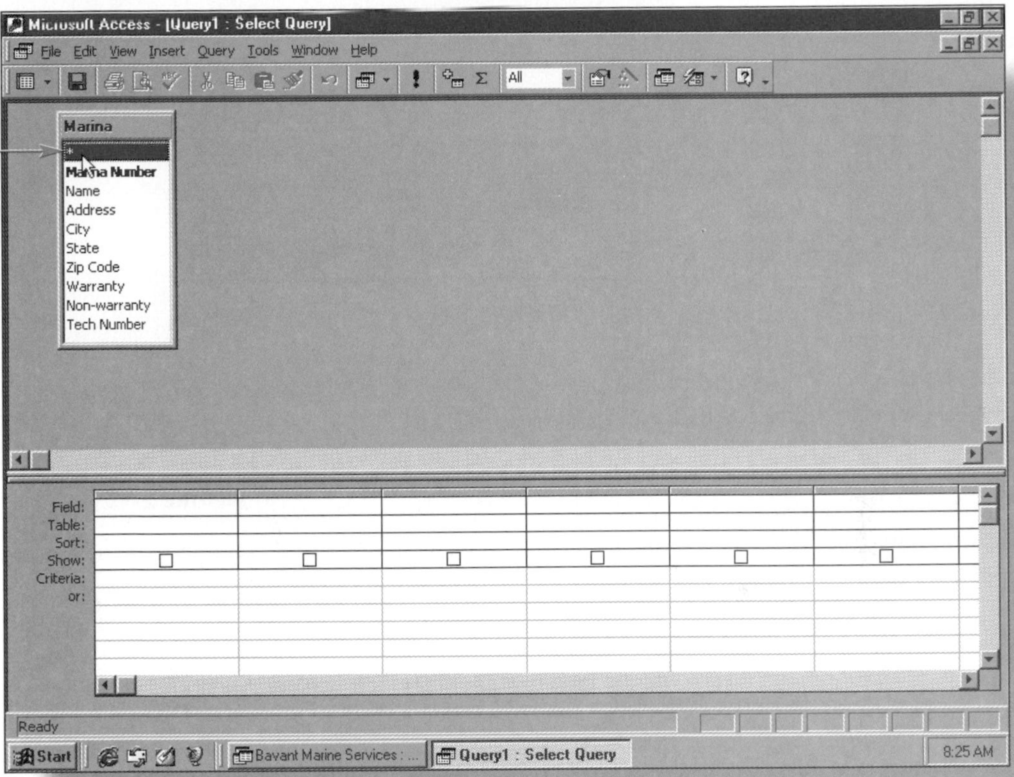

FIGURE 2-17

2 Double-click the asterisk in the field list and then point to the Run button on the Query Design toolbar.

The table name, Marina, followed by a period and an asterisk is added to the design grid (Figure 2-18), indicating all fields are included.

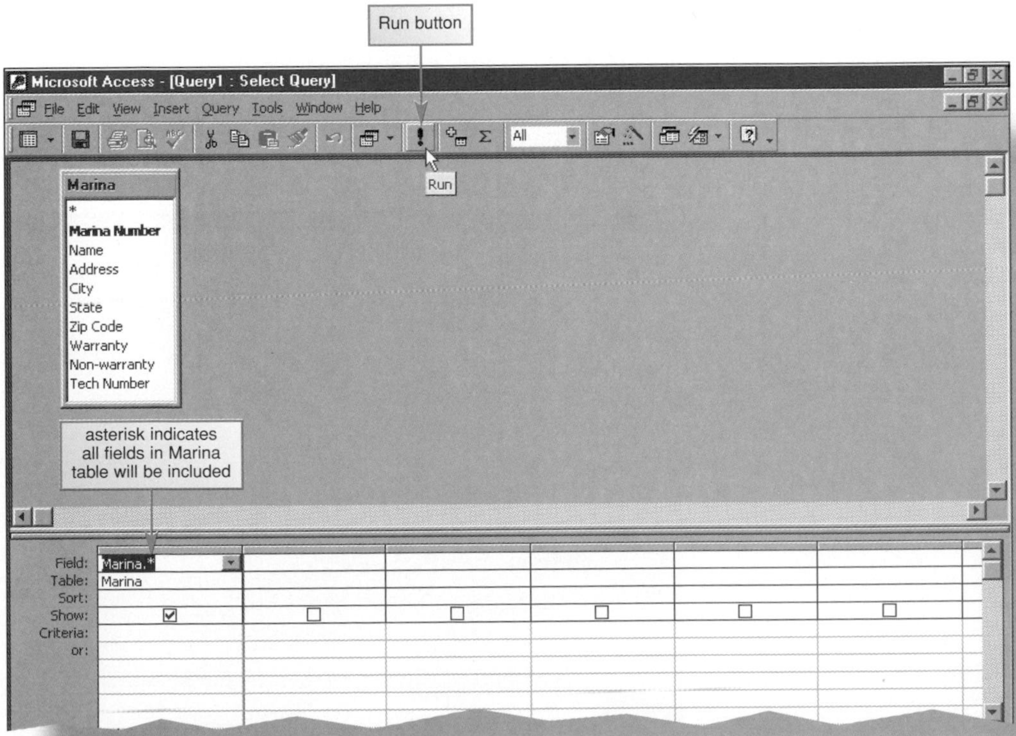

FIGURE 2-18

Click the Run button.

The results display and all fields in the Marina table are included (Figure 2-19). The Tech Number field does not display, because it does not fit on the screen.

Click the View button on the Query Datasheet toolbar to return to Design view.

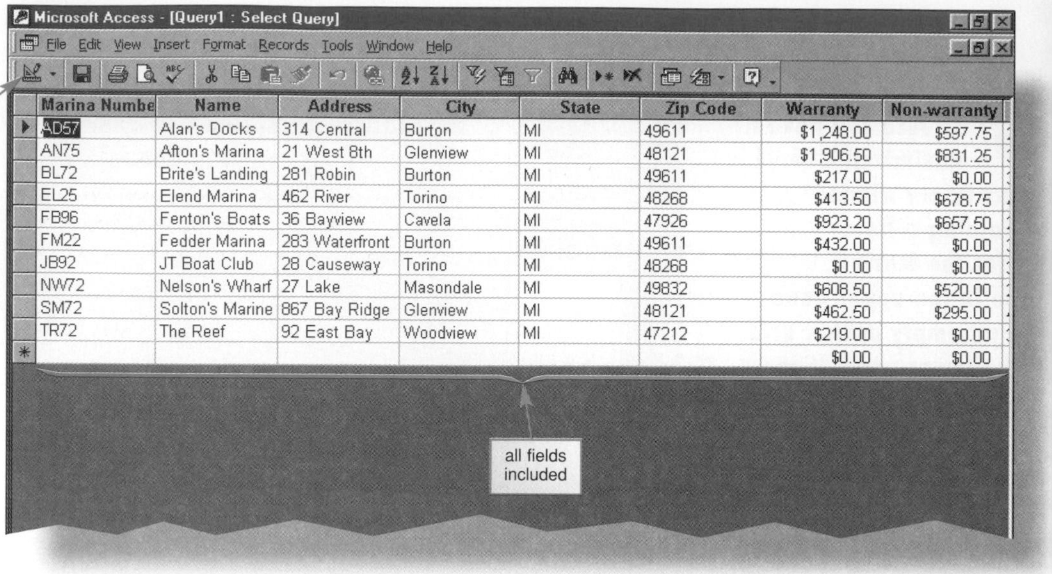

Microsoft Access - [Query1 : Select Query]

File Edit View Insert Format Records Tools Window Help

Marina Numbe	Name	Address	City	State	Zip Code	Warranty	Non-warranty
AD57	Alan's Docks	314 Central	Burton	MI	49611	$1,248.00	$597.75
AN75	Afton's Marina	21 West 8th	Glenview	MI	48121	$1,906.50	$831.25
BL72	Brite's Landing	281 Robin	Burton	MI	49611	$217.00	$0.00
EL25	Elend Marina	462 River	Torino	MI	48268	$413.50	$678.75
FB96	Fenton's Boats	36 Bayview	Cavela	MI	47926	$923.20	$657.50
FM22	Fedder Marina	283 Waterfront	Burton	MI	49611	$432.00	$0.00
JB92	JT Boat Club	28 Causeway	Torino	MI	48268	$0.00	$0.00
NW72	Nelson's Wharf	27 Lake	Masondale	MI	49832	$608.50	$520.00
SM72	Solton's Marine	867 Bay Ridge	Glenview	MI	48121	$462.50	$295.00
TR72	The Reef	92 East Bay	Woodview	MI	47212	$219.00	$0.00
*						$0.00	$0.00

View button

all fields included

FIGURE 2-19

Clearing the Design Grid

If you make mistakes as you are creating a query, you can fix each one individually. Alternatively, you simply may want to **clear the query**; that is, clear out the entries in the design grid and start over. One way to clear out the entries is to close the Select Query window and then start a new query just as you did earlier. A simpler approach, however, is to click Clear Grid on the Edit menu.

To Clear a Query

Click Edit on the menu bar.

The Edit menu displays (Figure 2-20).

Click Clear Grid.

Access clears the design grid so you can enter your next query.

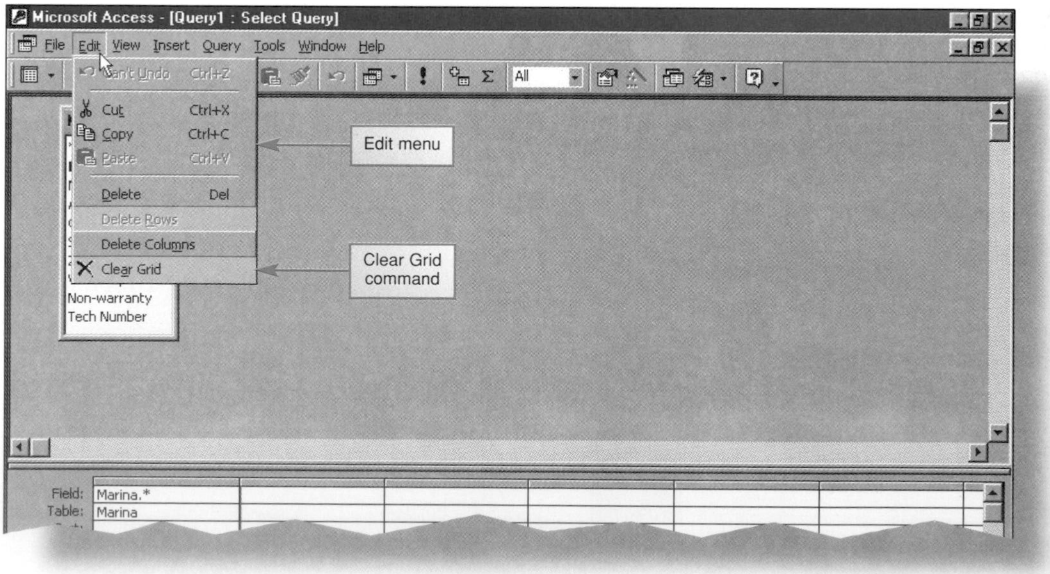

Microsoft Access - [Query1 : Select Query]

File Edit View Insert Query Tools Window Help

Can't Undo   Ctrl+Z
Cut   Ctrl+X
Copy   Ctrl+C
Paste   Ctrl+V

Delete   Del
Delete Rows
Delete Columns
Clear Grid

Non-warranty
Tech Number

Edit menu

Clear Grid command

Field: Marina.*
Table: Marina

FIGURE 2-20

Entering Criteria

When you use queries, usually you are looking for those records that satisfy some criterion. You might want the name, warranty, and non-warranty amounts of the marina whose number is EL25, for example, or of those marinas whose names start with the letters, Fe. To enter criteria, enter them on the Criteria row in the design grid below the field name to which the criterion applies. For example, to indicate that the marina number must be EL25, you would type EL25 in the Criteria row below the Marina Number field. You first must add the Marina Number field to the design grid before you can enter the criterion.

The next examples illustrate the types of criteria that are available.

Using Text Data in Criteria

To use **text data** (data in a field whose type is text) in criteria, simply type the text in the Criteria row below the corresponding field name. The following steps query the Marina table and display the marina number, name, warranty amount, and non-warranty amount of marina EL25.

More About

Using Text Data in Criteria

Some database systems require that text data must be enclosed in quotation marks. For example, to find customers in Michigan, "MI" would be entered as the criterion for the State field. In Access this is not necessary, because Access will insert the quotation marks automatically.

 To Use Text Data in a Criterion

1 **One by one, double-click the Marina Number, Name, Warranty, and Non-warranty fields to add them to the query. Point to the Criteria row for the first field in the design grid.**

The Marina Number, Name, Warranty, and Non-warranty fields are added to the design grid (Figure 2-21). The mouse pointer on the Criteria entry for the first field (Marina Number) has changed shape to an I-beam.

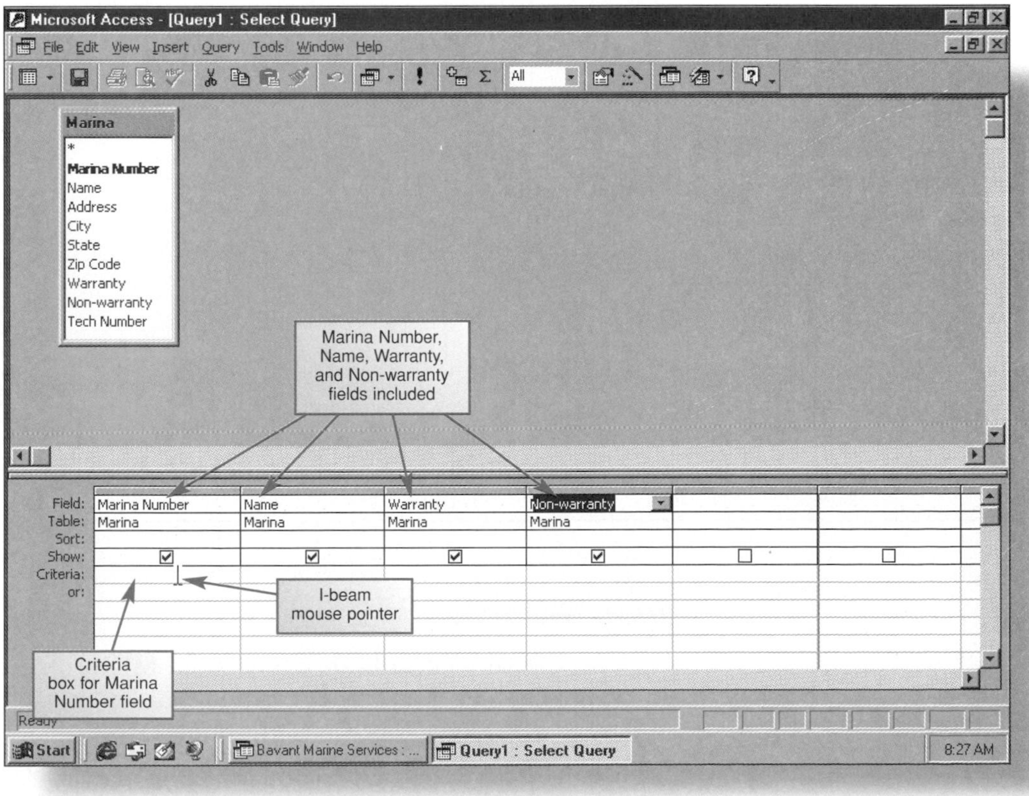

FIGURE 2-21

Microsoft Access 2000

 Click the Criteria row, type EL25 as the criterion for the Marina Number field.

The criterion is entered (Figure 2-22).

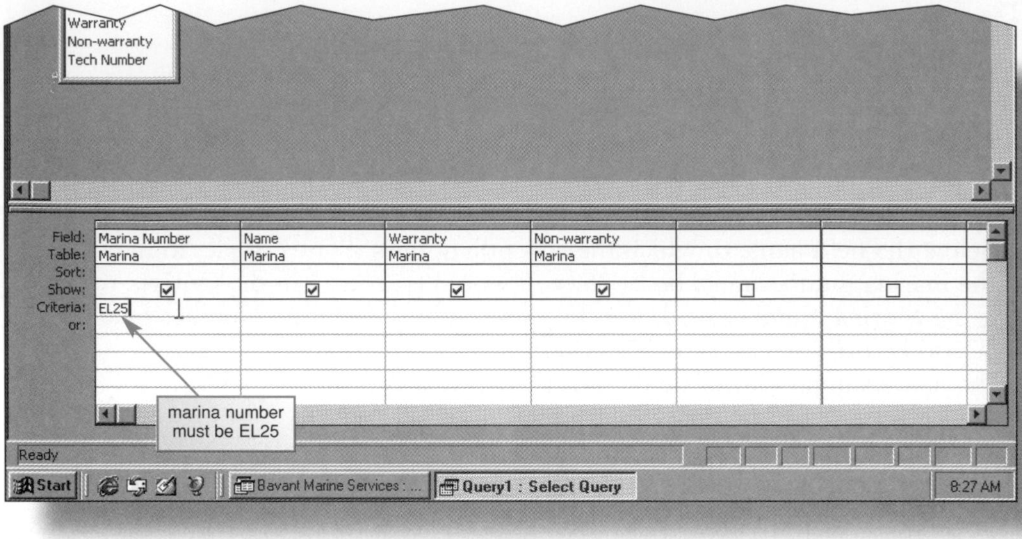

FIGURE 2-22

 Click the Run button to run the query.

The results display (Figure 2-23). Only marina EL25 is included. (The extra blank row contains $0.00 in the Warranty and Non-warranty fields. Unlike text fields, which are left blank, number and currency fields in the extra row contain 0. Because the Warranty and Non-warranty fields are currency fields, the values display as $0.00.)

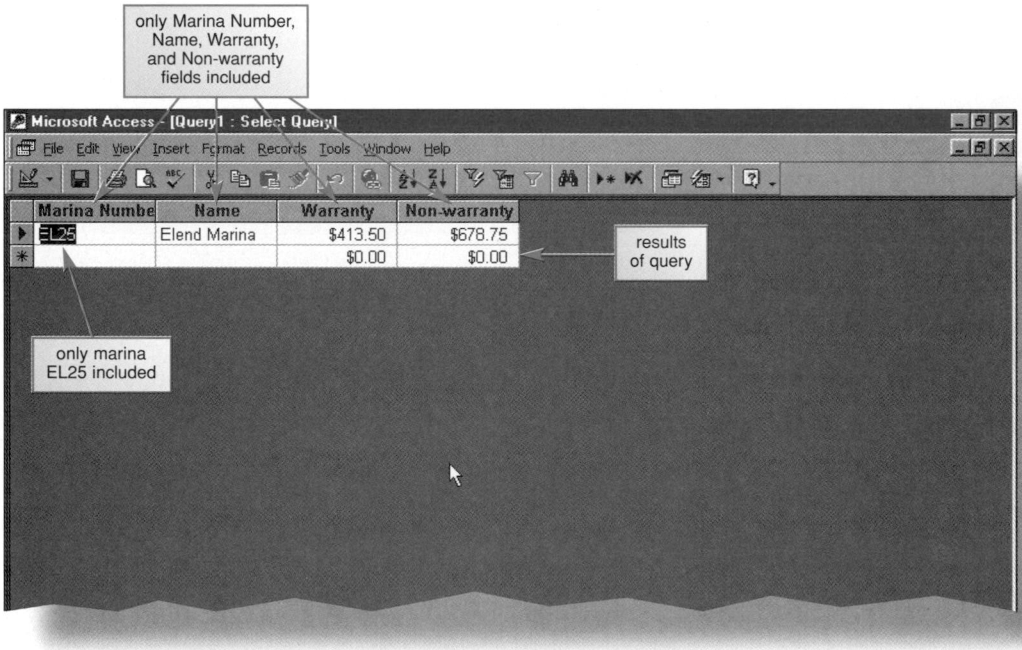

FIGURE 2-23

Using Wildcards

Two special wildcards are available in Microsoft Access. **Wildcards** are symbols that represent any character or combination of characters. The first of the two wildcards, the **asterisk (*)**, represents any collection of characters. Thus Gr* represents the letters, Gr, followed by any collection of characters. The other wildcard symbol is the **question mark (?)**, which represents any individual character. Thus t?m represents the letter, T, followed by any single character followed by the letter, m, such as Tim or Tom. To use a wildcard, begin the criterion with the special word LIKE.

The following steps use a wildcard to find the number, name, and address of those marinas whose names begin with Fe. Because you do not know how many characters will follow the Fe, the asterisk is appropriate.

Steps) **To Use a Wildcard**

① **Click the View button to return to Design view. Click the Criteria row under the Marina Number field and then use the DELETE or BACKSPACE key to delete the current entry (EL25). Click the Criteria row under the Name field. Type** LIKE Fe* **as the entry.**

The criterion is entered (Figure 2-24).

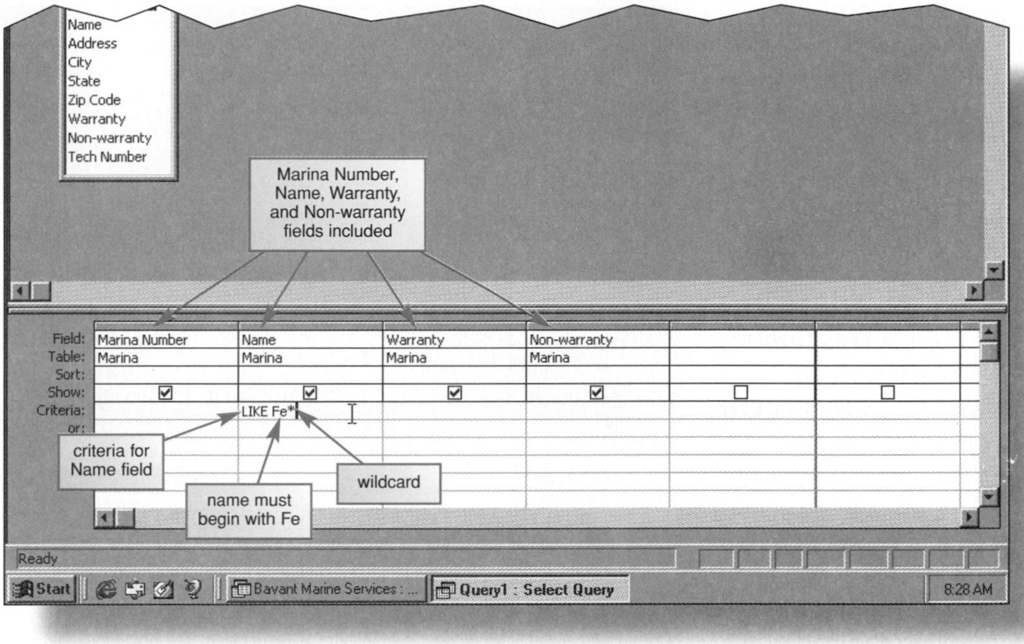

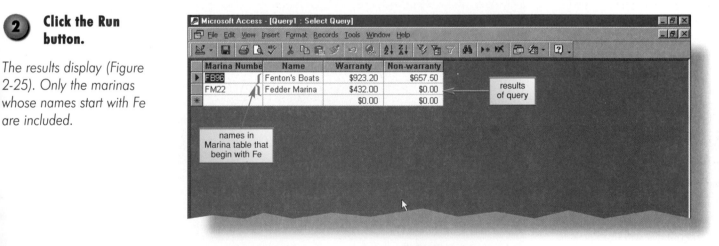

FIGURE 2-24

② **Click the Run button.**

The results display (Figure 2-25). Only the marinas whose names start with Fe are included.

FIGURE 2-25

Criteria for a Field Not in the Result

In some cases, you may have criteria for a particular field that should not appear in the results of the query. For example, you may wish to see the marina number, name, address, and warranty amounts for all marinas located in Burton. The criteria involve the City field, which is not one of the fields to be included in the results.

To enter a criterion for the City field, it must be included in the design grid. Normally, this also would mean it would appear in the results. To prevent this from happening, remove the check mark from its Show check box in the Show row of the grid. The following steps illustrate the process by displaying the marina number, name, and warranty amounts for marinas located in Burton.

Steps **To Use Criteria for a Field Not Included in the Results**

1 **Click the View button to return to Design view. On the Edit menu, click Clear Grid.**

Access clears the design grid so you can enter the next query.

2 **Include the Marina Number, Name, Address, Warranty, and City fields in the query. Type** Burton **as the criterion for the City field and then point to the City field's Show check box.**

The fields are included in the grid, and the criterion for the City field is entered (Figure 2-26).

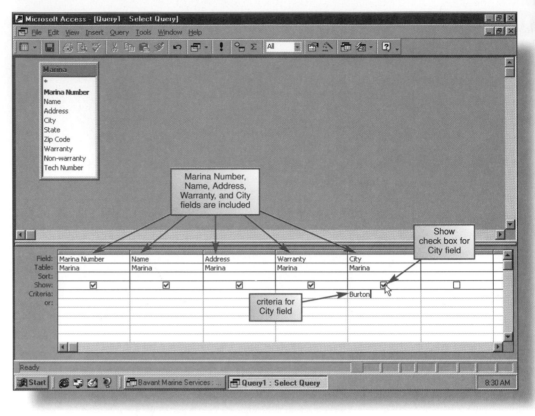

FIGURE 2-26

3 **Click the Show check box to remove the check mark.**

The check mark is removed from the Show check box for the City field (Figure 2-27), indicating it will not show in the result. Access has added quotation marks before and after Burton automatically.

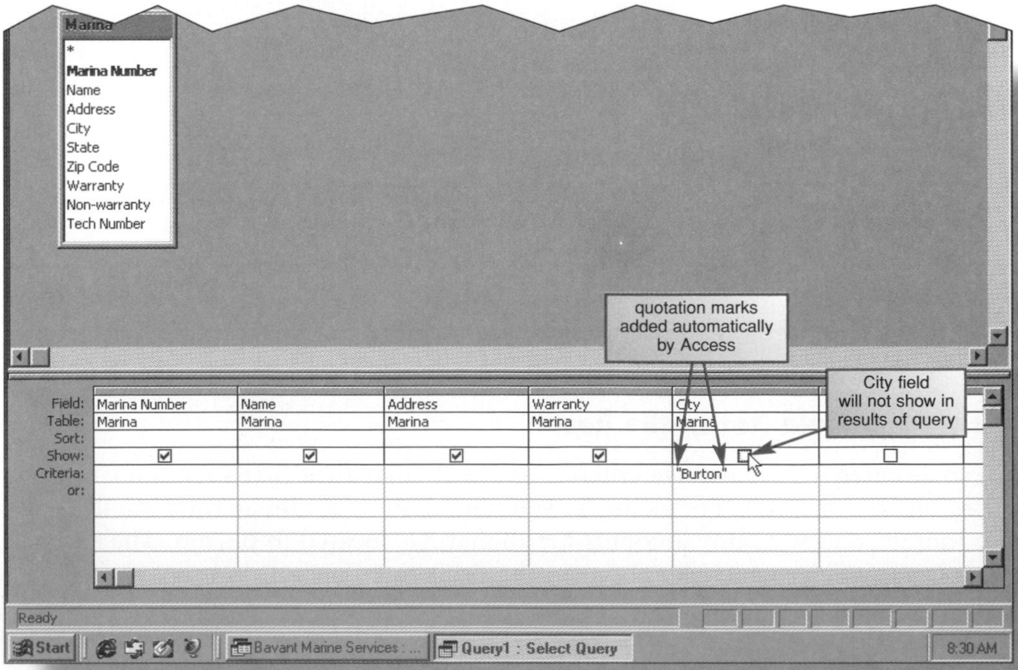

FIGURE 2-27

4 **Run the query by clicking the Run button.**

The results display (Figure 2-28). The City field does not display. The only marinas included are those located in Burton.

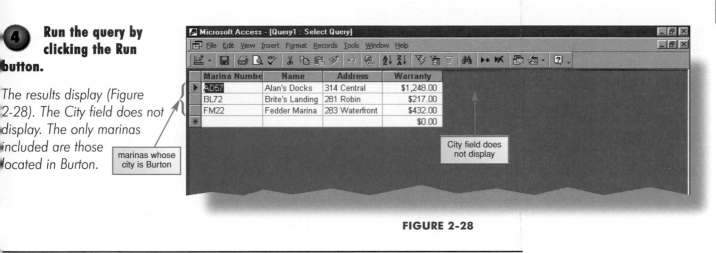

FIGURE 2-28

Using Numeric Data in Criteria

To enter a number in a criterion, type the number without any dollar signs or commas. Complete the following steps to display all marinas whose non-warranty amount is $0.00. To do so, you will need to type a 0 (zero) as the criterion for the Non-warranty field.

 To Use a Number in a Criterion

1 **Click the View button to return to Design view. On the Edit menu, click Clear Grid.**

Access clears the design grid so you can enter the next query.

2 **Include the Marina Number, Name, Warranty, and Non-warranty fields in the query. Type 0 as the criterion for the Non-warranty field. You need not enter a dollar sign or decimal point in the criterion.**

The fields are selected and the criterion is entered (Figure 2-29).

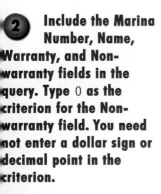

FIGURE 2-29

3 **Run the query by clicking the Run button.**

The results display (Figure 2-30). Only those marinas that have a non-warranty amount of $0.00 are included.

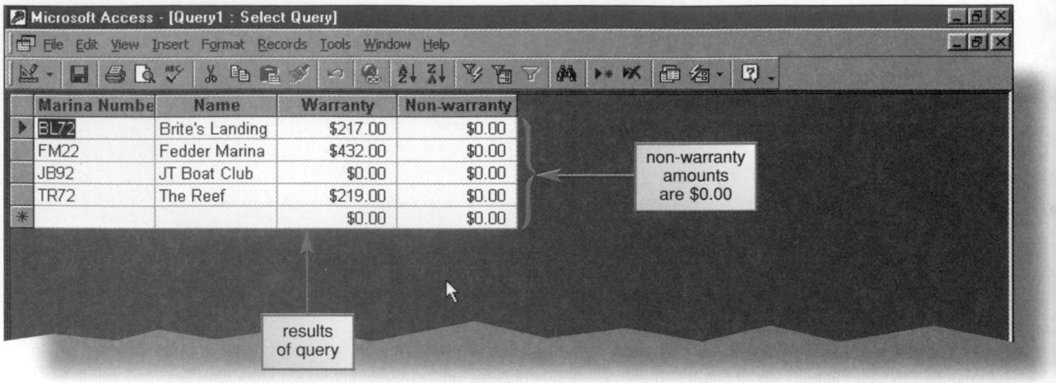

FIGURE 2-30

Using Comparison Operators

Unless you specify otherwise, Access assumes that the criteria you enter involve equality (exact matches). In the last query, for example, you were requesting those marinas whose non-warranty amount is equal to 0 (zero). If you want something other than an exact match, you must enter the appropriate **comparison operator**. The comparison operators are > (greater than), < (less than), >= (greater than or equal to), <= (less than or equal to), and NOT (not equal to).

Perform the following steps to use the > operator to find all marinas whose warranty amount is more than $1,000.

Steps **To Use a Comparison Operator in a Criterion**

1 **Click the View button to return to Design view. On the Edit menu, click Clear Grid.**

Access clears the design grid so you can enter the next query.

2 **Include the Marina Number, Name, Warranty, and Non-warranty fields in the query. Type >1000 as the criterion for the Warranty field.**

The fields are selected and the criterion is entered (Figure 2-31).

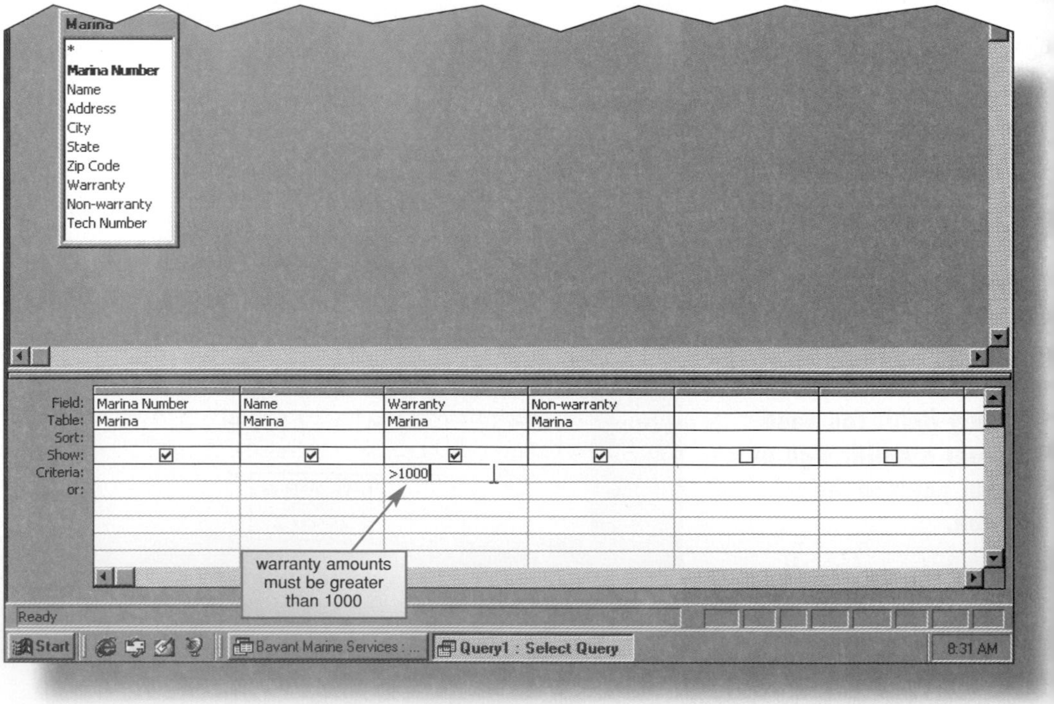

FIGURE 2-31

Run the query.

The results display (Figure 2-32). Only those marinas that have a warranty amount greater than $1,000 are included.

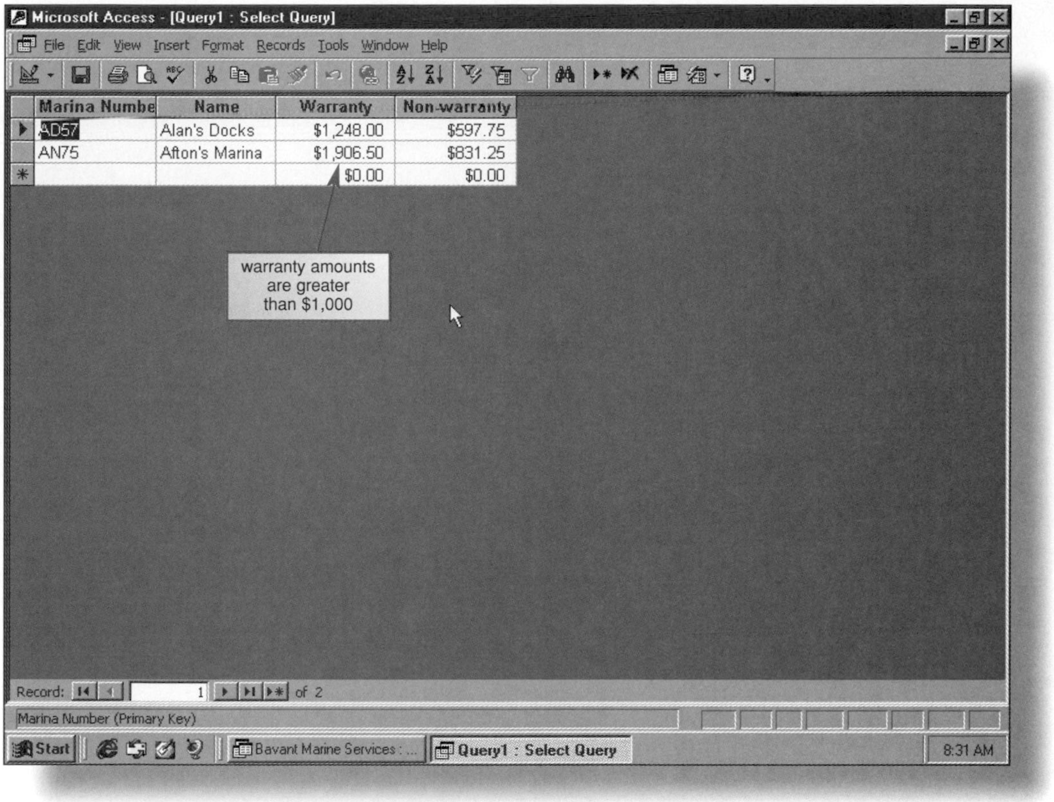

FIGURE 2-32

Using Compound Criteria

Often you will have more than one criterion that the data for which you are searching must satisfy. This type of criterion is called a **compound criterion**. Two types of compound criteria exist.

In **AND criterion**, each individual criterion must be true in order for the compound criterion to be true. For example, an AND criterion would allow you to find those marinas that have a warranty amount greater than $1,000 and whose technician is technician 36.

Conversely, an **OR criterion** is true provided either individual criterion is true. An OR criterion would allow you to find those marinas that have a warranty amount more than $1,000 or whose technician is technician 36. In this case, any marina whose warranty amount is greater than $1,000 would be included in the results whether or not the marina's technician is technician 36. Likewise, any marina whose technician is technician 36 would be included whether or not the marina had a warranty amount greater than $1,000.

Using AND Criteria

To combine criteria with AND, place the criteria on the same line. Perform the following steps to use an AND criterion to find those marinas whose warranty amount is greater than $1,000 and whose technician is technician 36.

Steps: To Use a Compound Criterion Involving AND

1 **Click the View button to return to Design view. Include the Tech Number field in the query. If necessary, click the Criteria entry for the Warranty field, and then type >1000 as the criterion for the Warranty field. Click the Criteria entry for the Tech Number field and then type 36 as the criterion for the Tech Number field.**

Criteria have been entered for the Warranty and Tech Number fields (Figure 2-33).

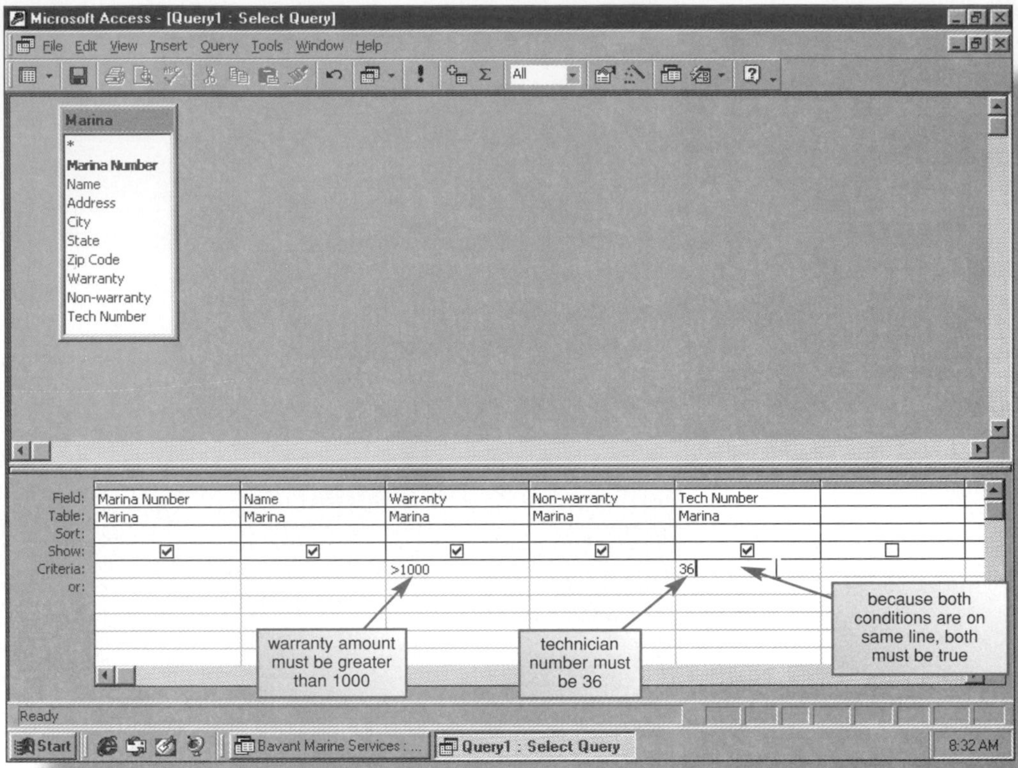

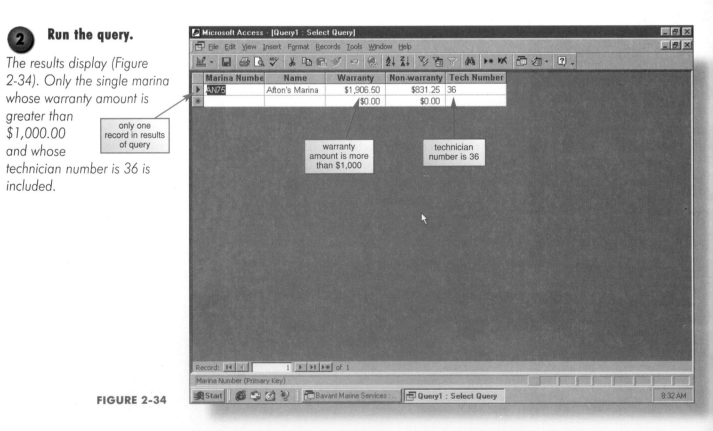

FIGURE 2-33

2 **Run the query.**

The results display (Figure 2-34). Only the single marina whose warranty amount is greater than $1,000.00 and whose technician number is 36 is included.

FIGURE 2-34

Using OR Criteria

To combine criteria with OR, the criteria must go on separate lines in the Criteria area of the grid. The following steps use an OR criterion to find those marinas whose warranty amount is greater than $1,000.00 or whose technician is technician 36 (or both).

To Use a Compound Criterion Involving OR

1 Click the View button to return to Design view.

2 Click the Criteria entry for the Tech Number field. Use the BACKSPACE key to delete the entry ("36"). Click the or row (below the Criteria row) for the Tech Number field and then type 36 as the entry.

The criteria are entered for the Warranty and Tech Number fields on different lines (Figure 2-35).

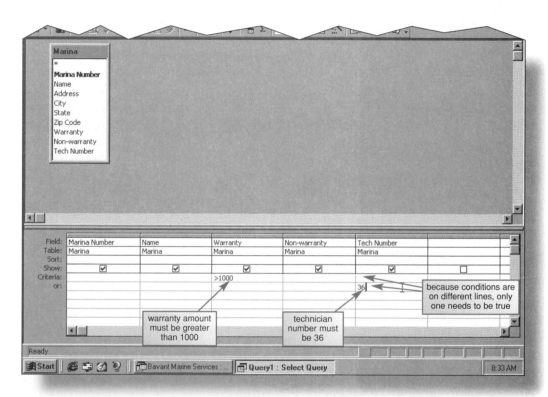

FIGURE 2-35

3 Run the query.

The results display (Figure 2-36). Only those marinas whose warranty amount is greater than $1,000.00 or whose technician number is 36 are included.

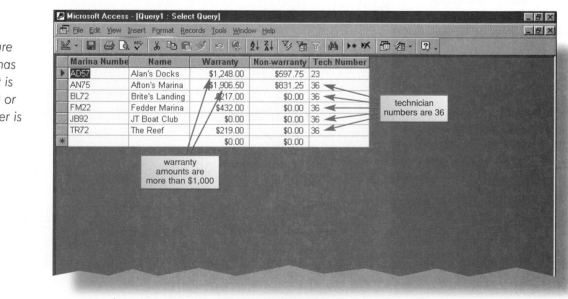

FIGURE 2-36

Sorting Data in a Query

In some queries, the order in which the records are displayed really does not matter. All you need be concerned about are the records that appear in the results. It does not matter which one is first or which one is last.

In other queries, however, the order can be very important. You may want to see the cities in which marinas are located and would like them arranged alphabetically. Perhaps you want to see the marinas listed by technician number. Further, within all the marinas of any given technician, you would like them to be listed by warranty amount.

To order the records in the answer to a query in a particular way, you **sort** the records. The field or fields on which the records are sorted is called the **sort key**. If you are sorting on more than one field (such as sorting by warranty amount within technician number), the more important field (Tech Number) is called the **major key** (also called the **primary sort key**) and the less important field (Warranty) is called the **minor key** (also called the **secondary sort key**).

To sort in Microsoft Access, specify the sort order in the Sort line of the design grid below the field that is the sort key. If you specify more than one sort key, the sort key on the left will be the major sort key and the one on the right will be the minor key.

The following steps sort the cities in the Marina table.

Compound Criteria

Access to compound criteria is precisely the approach that was proposed for Query-by-Example. (Placing criteria on the same line indicates they are connected by the word AND. Placing them on separate lines indicates they are connected by the word OR.)

Steps To Sort Data in a Query

1 **Click the View button to return to Design view. On the Edit menu, click Clear Grid.**

2 **Include the City field in the design grid. Click the Sort row below the City field, and then click the Sort row arrow that displays.**

The City field is included (Figure 2-37). A list of available sort orders displays.

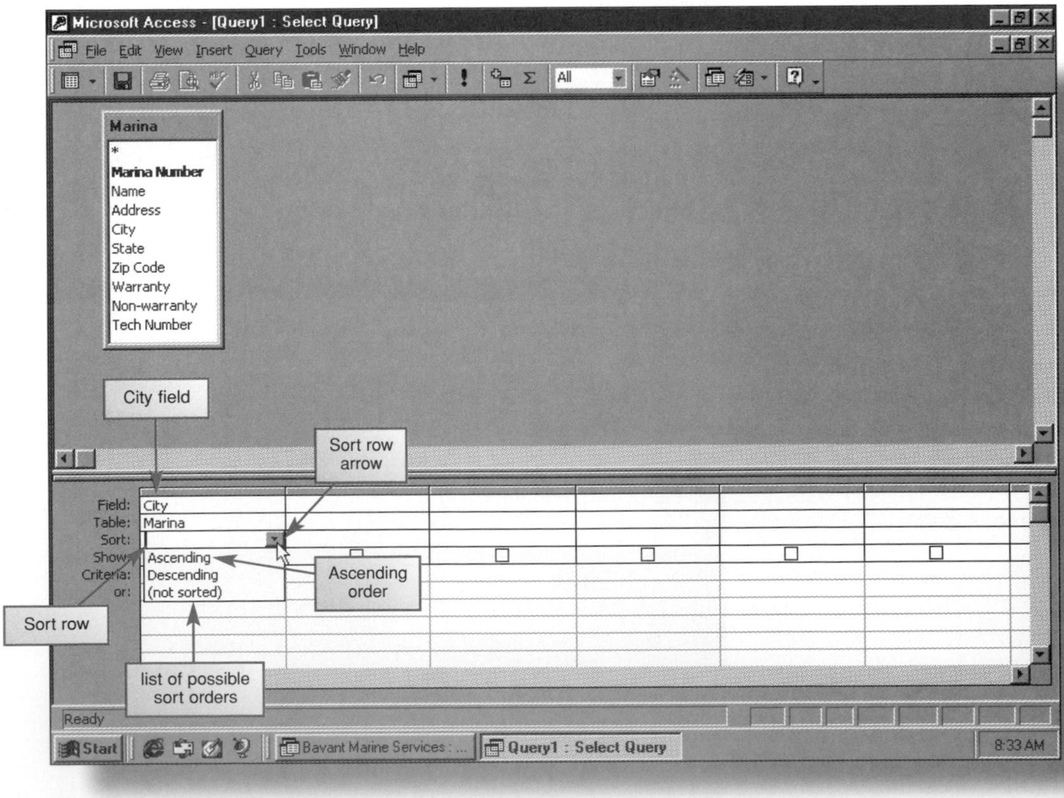

FIGURE 2-37

3 **Click Ascending.**

Ascending is selected as the order (Figure 2-38).

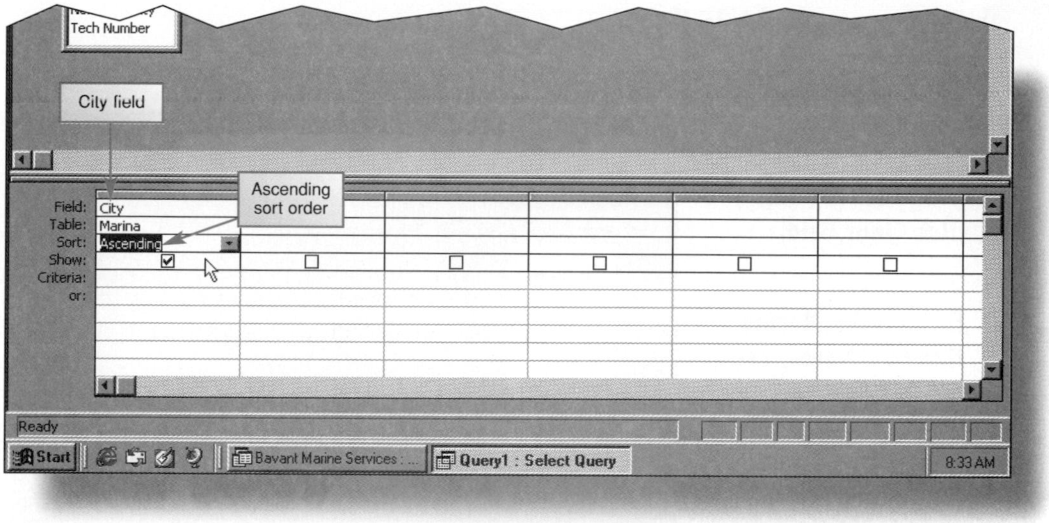

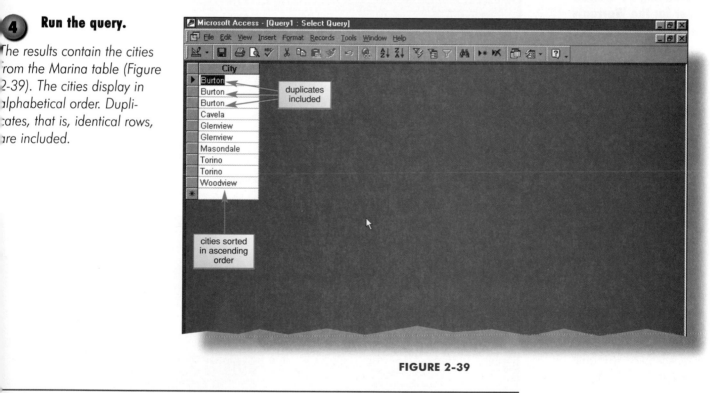

FIGURE 2-38

4 **Run the query.**

The results contain the cities from the Marina table (Figure 2-39). The cities display in alphabetical order. Duplicates, that is, identical rows, are included.

FIGURE 2-39

Sorting on Multiple Keys

The next example lists the number, name, technician number, and warranty amount for all marinas. The data is to be sorted by descending warranty amount (high to low) within technician number, which means that the Tech Number field is the major key and the Warranty field is the minor key. It also means that the Warranty field should be sorted in descending order.

The following steps accomplish this sorting by specifying the Tech Number and Warranty fields as sort keys and by selecting Descending as the sort order for the Warranty field.

Steps: To Sort on Multiple Keys

1 Click the View button to return to Design view. On the Edit menu, click Clear Grid.

2 Include the Marina Number, Name, Tech Number, and Warranty fields in the query in this order. Select Ascending as the sort order for the Tech Number field and Descending as the sort order for the Warranty field (Figure 2-40).

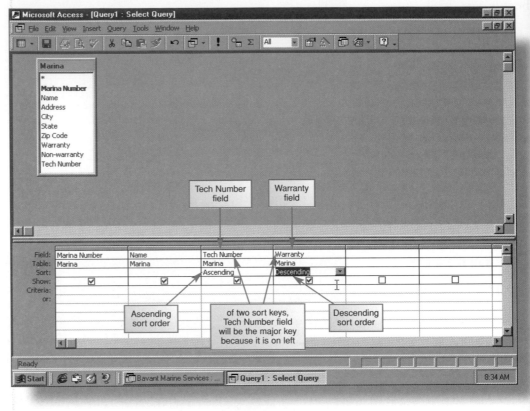

FIGURE 2-40

3 Run the query.

The results display (Figure 2-41). The marinas are sorted by technician number. Within the collection of marinas having the same technician, the marinas are sorted by descending warranty amount.

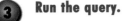

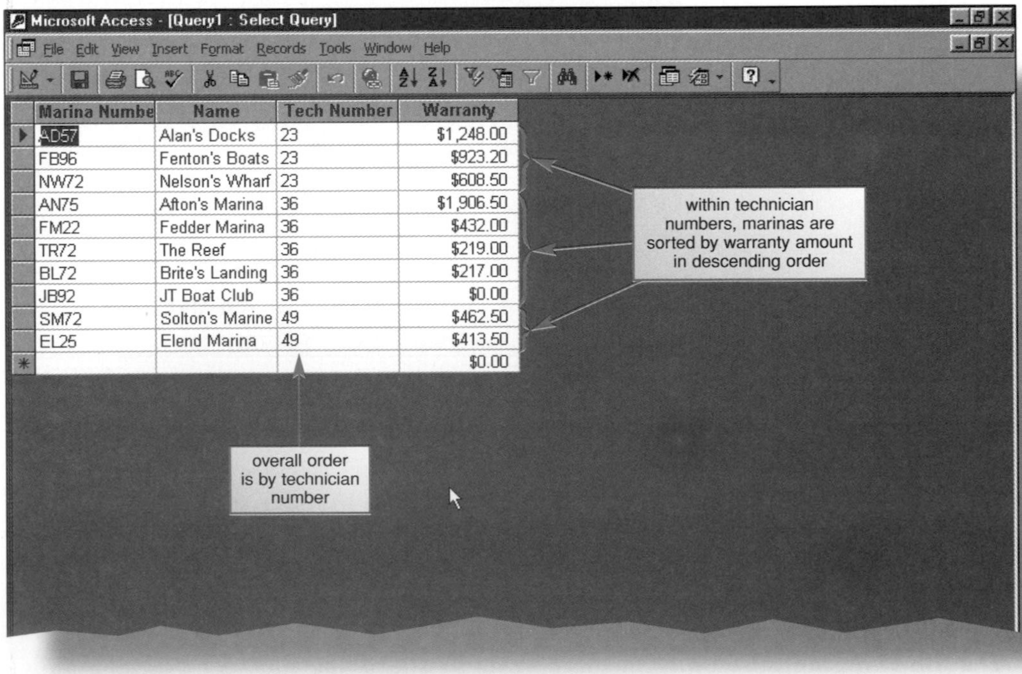

Marina Number	Name	Tech Number	Warranty
AD57	Alan's Docks	23	$1,248.00
FB96	Fenton's Boats	23	$923.20
NW72	Nelson's Wharf	23	$608.50
AN75	Afton's Marina	36	$1,906.50
FM22	Fedder Marina	36	$432.00
TR72	The Reef	36	$219.00
BL72	Brite's Landing	36	$217.00
JB92	JT Boat Club	36	$0.00
SM72	Solton's Marine	49	$462.50
EL25	Elend Marina	49	$413.50
*			$0.00

within technician numbers, marinas are sorted by warranty amount in descending order

overall order is by technician number

FIGURE 2-41

It is important to remember that the major sort key must appear to the left of the minor sort key in the design grid. If you attempted to sort by warranty amount within technician number, but placed the Warranty field to the left of the Tech Number field, your results would be incorrect.

Omitting Duplicates

As you saw earlier, when you sort data, duplicates are included. In Figure 2-39 on page A 2.27, for example, Glenview appeared twice, Burton appeared three times, and Torino appeared twice. If you do not want duplicates included, use the Properties command and change the Unique Values property to Yes. Perform the following steps to produce a sorted list of the cities in the Marina table in which each city is listed only once.

More About

Sorting Data in a Query

When sorting data in a query, the records in the underlying tables (the tables on which the query is based) are not actually rearranged. Instead, the DBMS will determine the most efficient method of simply displaying the records in the requested order. The records in the underlying tables remain in their original order.

Steps To Omit Duplicates

1 Click the View button to return to Design view. On the Edit menu, click Clear Grid.

2 Include the City field, click Ascending as the sort order, and right-click the second field in the design grid (the empty field following City). (You must right-click the second field or you will not get the correct results.)

The shortcut menu displays (Figure 2-42).

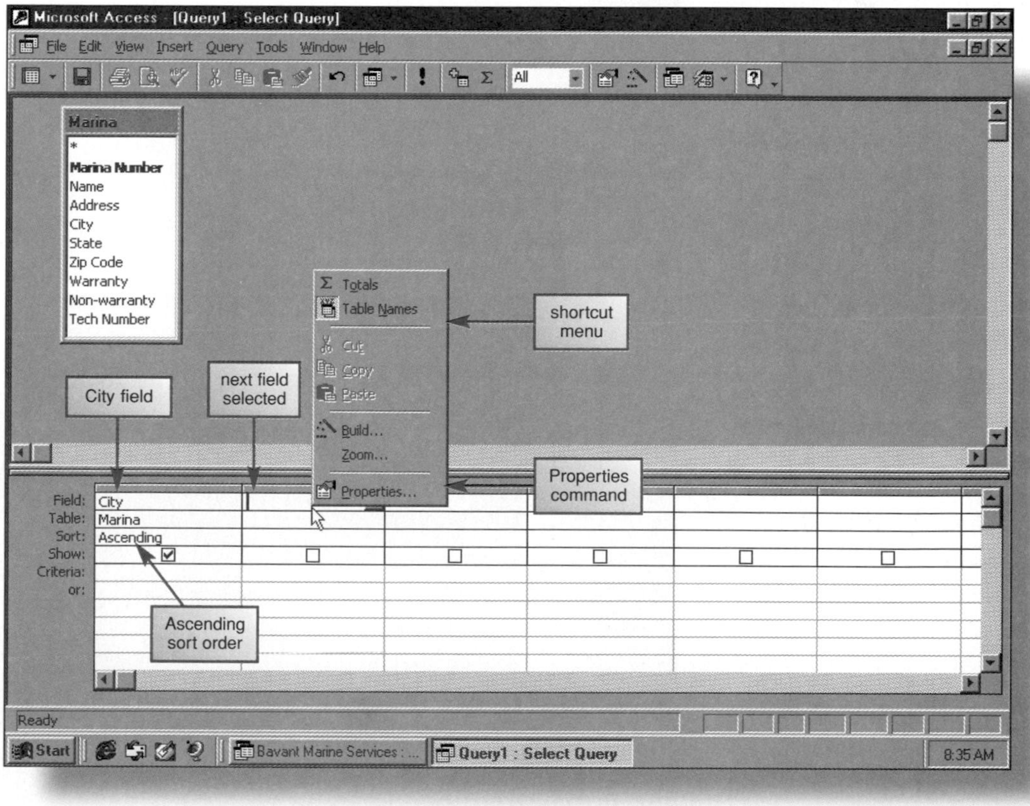

FIGURE 2-42

③ Click Properties on the shortcut menu.

The Query Properties sheet displays (Figure 2-43). (If your sheet looks different, you right-clicked the wrong place. Close the sheet that displays and right-click the second field in the grid.)

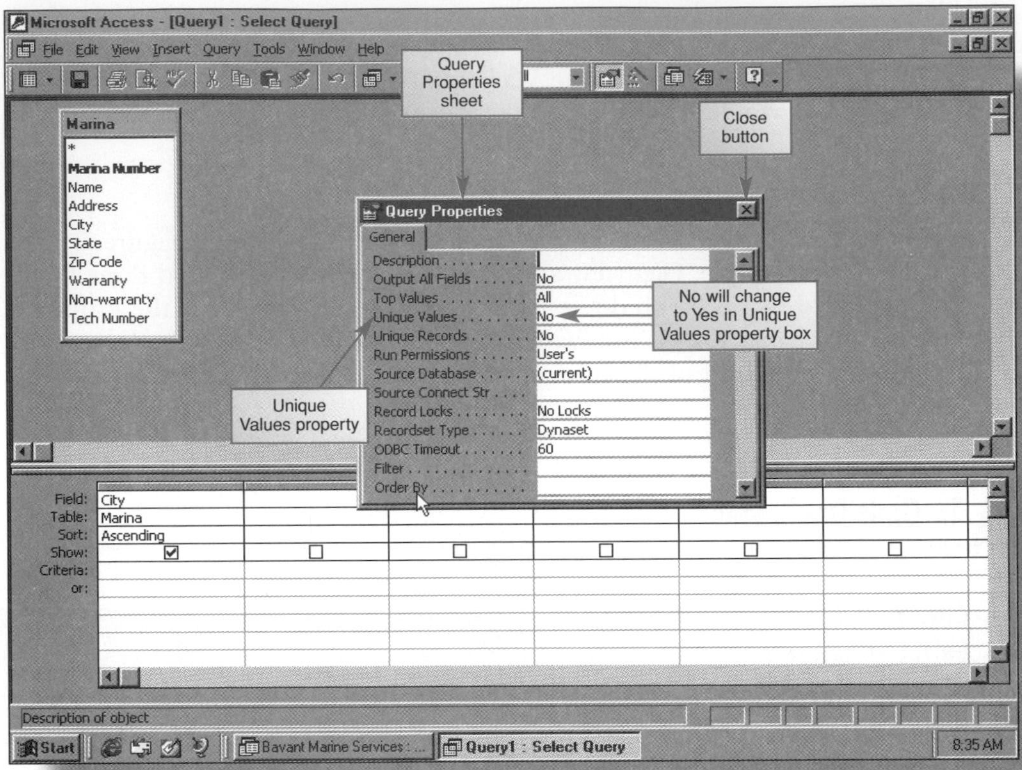

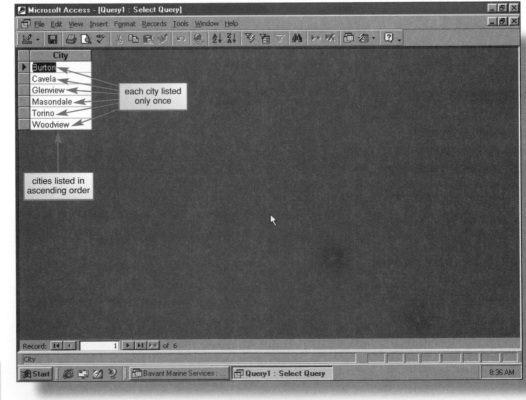

FIGURE 2-43

④ Click the Unique Values property box, and then click the arrow that displays to produce a list of available choices for Unique Values. Click Yes and then close the Query Properties sheet by clicking its Close button. Run the query.

The results display (Figure 2-44). The cities are sorted alphabetically. Each city is included only once.

Other Ways

1. Click Properties button on toolbar
2. On View menu click Properties

FIGURE 2-44

Joining Tables

Bavant Marine Services needs to list the number and name of each marina along with the number and name of the marina's technician. The marina's name is in the Marina table, whereas the technician's name is in the Technician table. Thus, this query cannot be satisfied using a single table. You need to **join** the tables; that is, to find records in the two tables that have identical values in matching fields (Figure 2-45). In this example, you need to find records in the Marina table and the Technician table that have the same value in the Tech Number fields.

More About

Joining Tables

One of the key features that distinguishes database management systems from file systems is the ability to join tables, that is, to create queries that draw data from two or more tables. Several types of joins are available. For more information, visit the Access 2000 More About Web page (www.scsite.com/ac2000/more.htm) and click Join Types.

give me the number and name of each Marina along with the number and name of the marina's technician

Marina table

MARINA NUMBER	NAME	. . .	TECH NUMBER
AD57	Alan's Docks	. . .	23
AN75	Afton's Marina	. . .	36
BL72	Brite's Landing	. . .	36
EL25	Elend Marina	. . .	49
FB96	Fenton's Boats	. . .	23
FM22	Fedder Marina	. . .	36
JB92	JT Boat Club	. . .	36
NW72	Nelson's Wharf	. . .	23
SM72	Solton's Marine	. . .	49
TR72	The Reef	. . .	36

Technician table

TECH NUMBER	LAST NAME	FIRST NAME	. . .
23	Anderson	Trista	. . .
36	Nichols	Ashton	. . .
49	Gomez	Teresa	. . .

MARINA NUMBER	NAME	. . .	TECH NUMBER	LAST NAME	FIRST NAME	. . .
AD57	Alan's Docks	. . .	23	Anderson	Trista	. . .
AN75	Afton's Marina	. . .	36	Nichols	Ashton	. . .
BL72	Brite's Landing	. . .	36	Nichols	Ashton	. . .
EL25	Elend Marina	. . .	49	Gomez	Teresa	. . .
FB96	Fenton's Boats	. . .	23	Anderson	Trista	. . .
FM22	Fedder Marina	. . .	36	Nichols	Ashton	. . .
JB92	JT Boat Club	. . .	36	Nichols	Ashton	. . .
NW72	Nelson's Wharf	. . .	23	Anderson	Trista	. . .
SM72	Solton's Marine	. . .	49	Gomez	Teresa	. . .
TR72	The Reef	. . .	36	Nichols	Ashton	. . .

FIGURE 2-45

Microsoft Access 2000

To join tables in Access, first you bring field lists for both tables to the upper pane of the Select Query window. Access will draw a line, called a **join line**, between matching fields in the two tables indicating that the tables are related. You then can select fields from either table. Access will join the tables automatically.

The first step is to add an additional table, the Technician table, to the query. A join line will display connecting the Tech Number fields in the two field lists. This join line indicates how the tables are related; that is, linked through these matching fields. (If you fail to give the matching fields the same name, Access will not insert the line. You can insert it manually, however, by clicking one of the two matching fields and dragging the mouse pointer to the other matching field.)

The following steps add the Technician table and then select the appropriate fields.

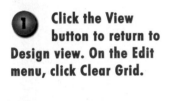

To Join Tables

1 Click the View button to return to Design view. On the Edit menu, click Clear Grid.

2 Right-click any open area in the upper pane of the Query1 : Select Query window.

The shortcut menu displays (Figure 2-46).

FIGURE 2-46

3 Click Show Table on the shortcut menu.

The Show Table dialog box displays (Figure 2-47).

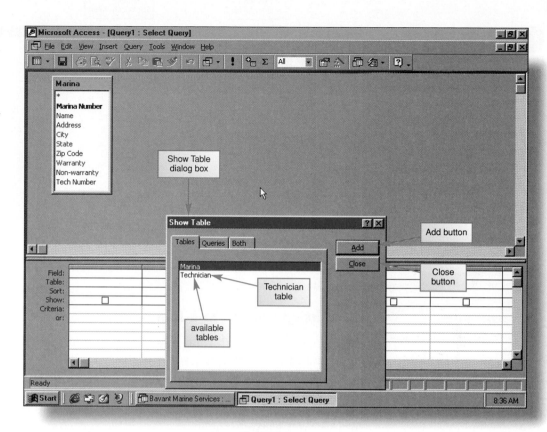

FIGURE 2-47

4 Click Technician to select the Technician table and then click the Add button. Close the Show Table dialog box by clicking the Close button. Expand the size of the field list so all the fields in the Technician table display. Include the Marina Number, Name, and Tech Number fields from the Marina table and the Last Name and First Name fields from the Technician table.

The fields from both tables are included (Figure 2-48).

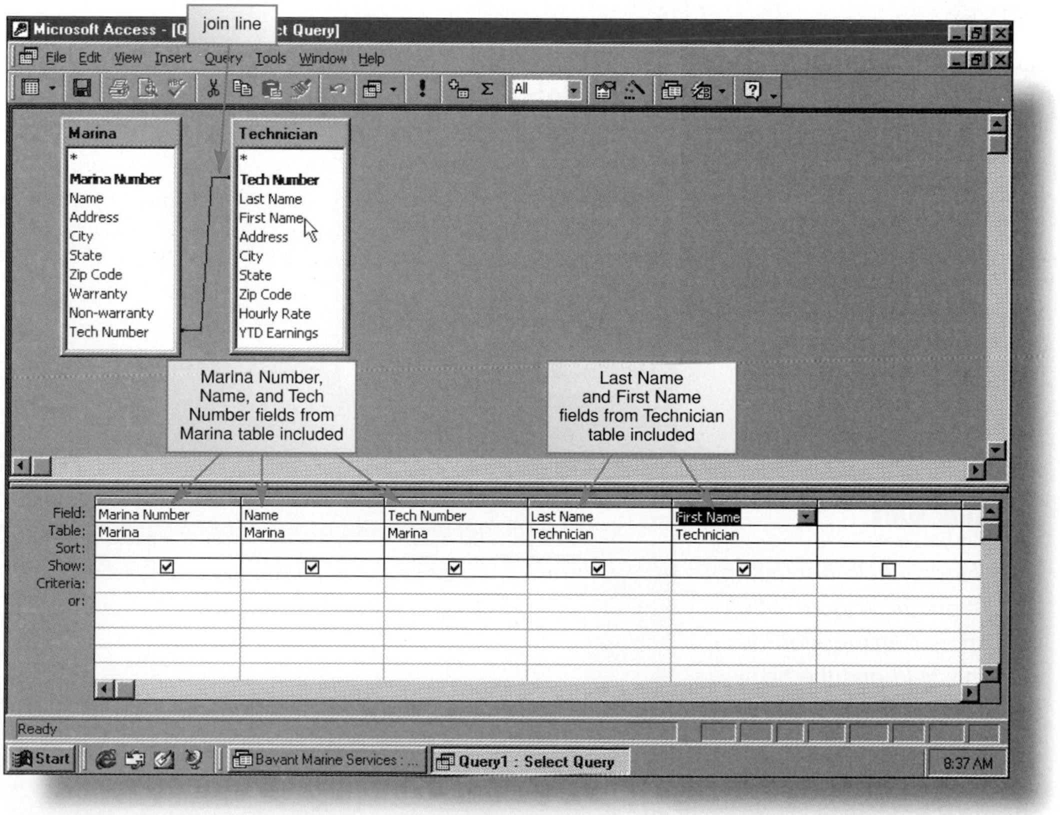

FIGURE 2-48

5 **Run the query.**

The results display (Figure 2-49) and contain data from both the Marina and the Technician tables.

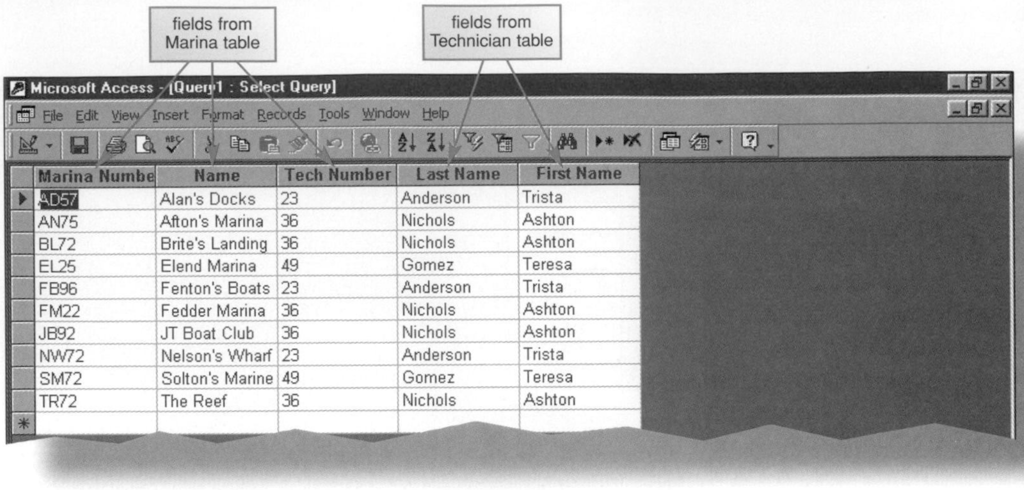

fields from
Marina table

fields from
Technician table

Microsoft Access - [Query1 : Select Query]

File Edit View Insert Format Records Tools Window Help

Marina Number	Name	Tech Number	Last Name	First Name
AD57	Alan's Docks	23	Anderson	Trista
AN75	Afton's Marina	36	Nichols	Ashton
BL72	Brite's Landing	36	Nichols	Ashton
EL25	Elend Marina	49	Gomez	Teresa
FB96	Fenton's Boats	23	Anderson	Trista
FM22	Fedder Marina	36	Nichols	Ashton
JB92	JT Boat Club	36	Nichols	Ashton
NW72	Nelson's Wharf	23	Anderson	Trista
SM72	Solton's Marine	49	Gomez	Teresa
TR72	The Reef	36	Nichols	Ashton
*				

FIGURE 2-49

Restricting Records in a Join

Sometimes you will want to join tables, but you will not want to include all possible records. In such cases, you will relate the tables and include fields just as you did before. You also will include criteria. For example, to include the same fields as in the previous query, but only those marinas whose warranty amount is more than $1,000, you will make the same entries as before and then also type >1000 as a criterion for the Warranty field.

The following steps modify the query from the previous example to restrict the records that will be included in the join.

 To Restrict the Records in a Join

1 **Click the View button to return to Design view. Add the Warranty field to the query. Type >1000 as the criterion for the Warranty field and then click the Show check box for the Warranty field to remove the check mark.**

The Warranty field displays in the design grid (Figure 2-50). A criterion is entered for the Warranty field and the Show check box is empty, indicating that the field will not display in the results of the query.

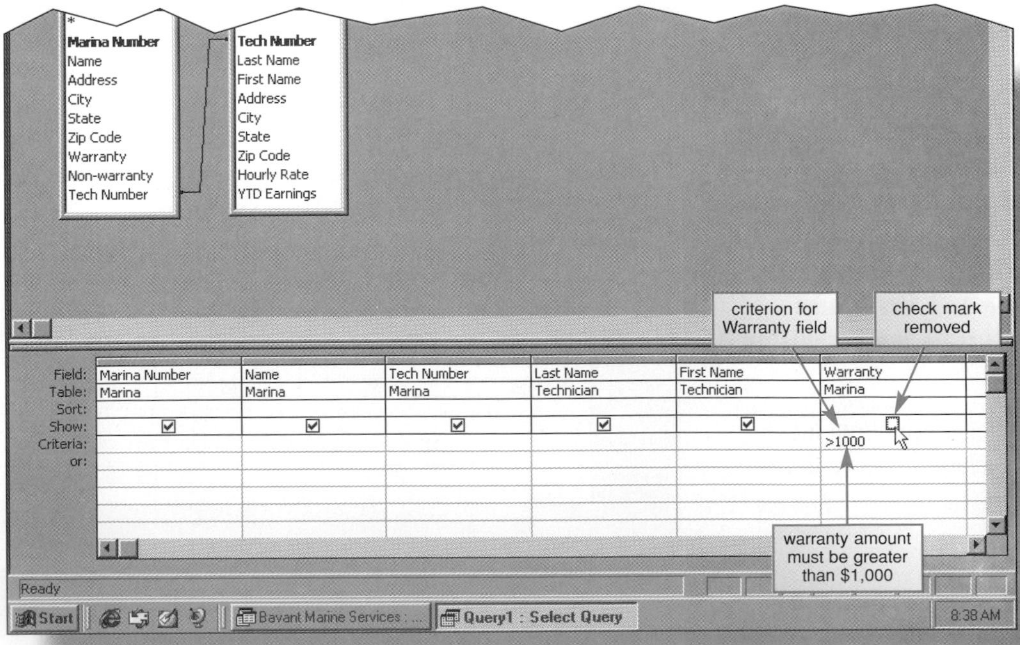

	Marina Number		Tech Number
	Name		Last Name
	Address		First Name
	City		Address
	State		City
	Zip Code		State
	Warranty		Zip Code
	Non-warranty		Hourly Rate
	Tech Number		YTD Earnings

criterion for
Warranty field

check mark
removed

Field:	Marina Number	Name	Tech Number	Last Name	First Name	Warranty
Table:	Marina	Marina	Marina	Technician	Technician	Marina
Sort:						
Show:	☑	☑	☑	☑	☑	☐
Criteria:						>1000
or:						

warranty amount
must be greater
than $1,000

Ready

Start | Bavant Marine Services : ... | Query1 : Select Query | 8:38 AM

FIGURE 2-50

Run the query.

The results display (Figure 2-51). Only those marinas with a warranty amount greater than $1,000 display in the result. The Warranty field does not display.

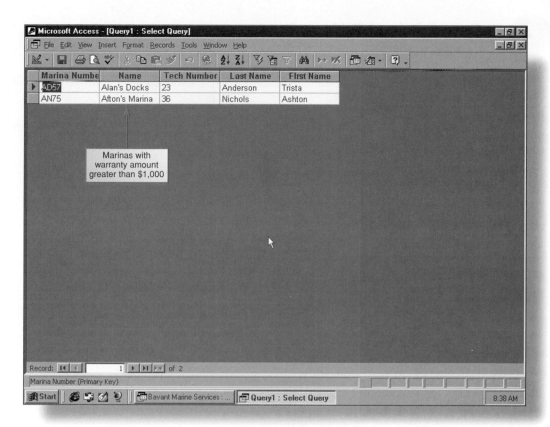

FIGURE 2-51

Using Calculated Fields in a Query

It is important to Bavant Marine Services to know the total amount for each marina; that is, the warranty amount plus the non-warranty amount. This poses a problem because the Marina table does not include a field for total amount. You can calculate it, however, because the total amount is equal to the warranty amount plus the non-warranty amount. Such a field is called a **calculated field**.

To include calculated fields in queries, you enter a name for the calculated field, a colon, and then the expression in one of the columns in the Field row. Any fields included in the expression must be enclosed in square brackets ([ ]). For the total amount, for example, you will type Total Amount:[Warranty]+[Non-warranty] as the expression.

You can type the expression directly into the Field row. You will not be able to see the entire entry, however, because the Field row is not large enough. The preferred way is to select the column in the Field row, right-click to display the shortcut menu, and then click Zoom. The Zoom dialog box displays where you can type the expression.

You are not restricted to addition in calculations. You can use subtraction (-), multiplication (*), or division (/). You also can include parentheses in your calculations to indicate which calculations should be done first.

Perform the following steps to remove the Technician table from the query (it is not needed), and then use a calculated field to display the number, name, and total amount of all marinas.

More About

Calculated Fields

Because it is easy to compute values in a query, there is no need to store calculated fields, also called computed fields, in a database. There is no need, for example, to store the total amount (the warranty amount plus the non-warranty amount), because it can be calculated whenever it is required.

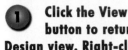

To Use a Calculated Field in a Query

1 **Click the View button to return to Design view. Right-click any field in the Technician table field list.**

The shortcut menu displays (Figure 2-52).

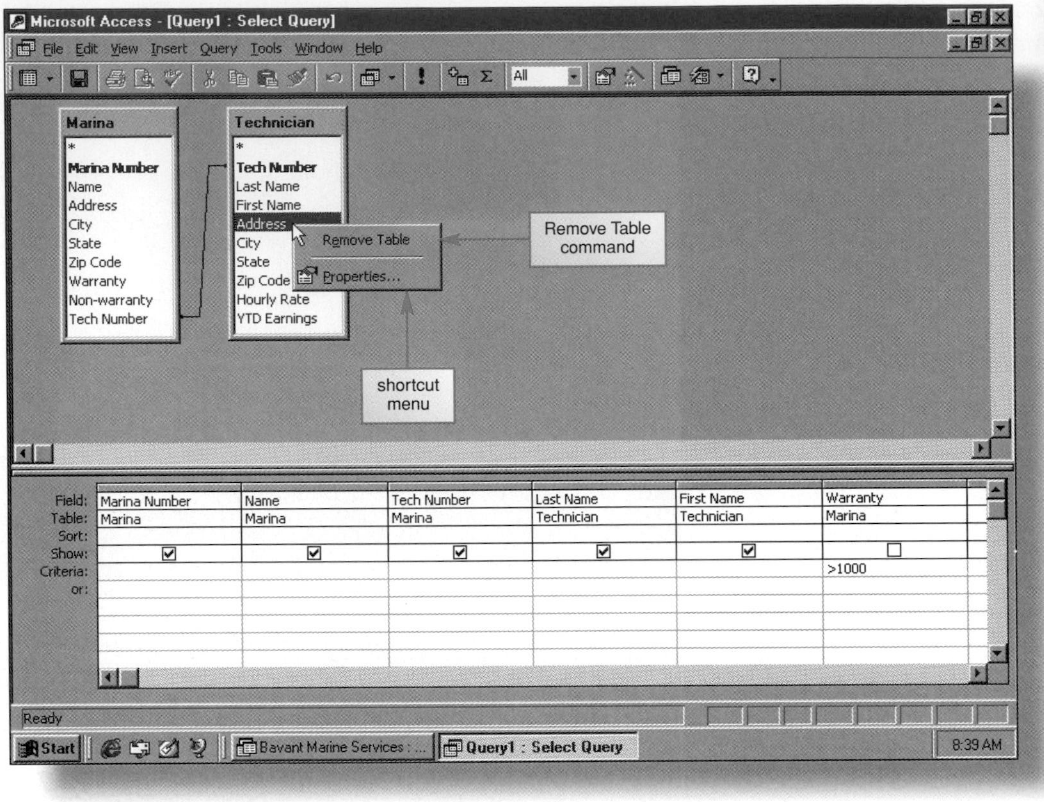

FIGURE 2-52

2 **Click Remove Table to remove the Technician table from the Query1 : Select Query window. On the Edit menu, click Clear Grid.**

3 **Include the Marina Number and Name fields. Right-click the Field row in the third column in the design grid and then click Zoom on the shortcut menu. Type** Total Amount:[Warranty]+ [Non-warranty] **in the Zoom dialog box that displays.**

The Zoom dialog box displays (Figure 2-53). The expression you typed displays within the dialog box.

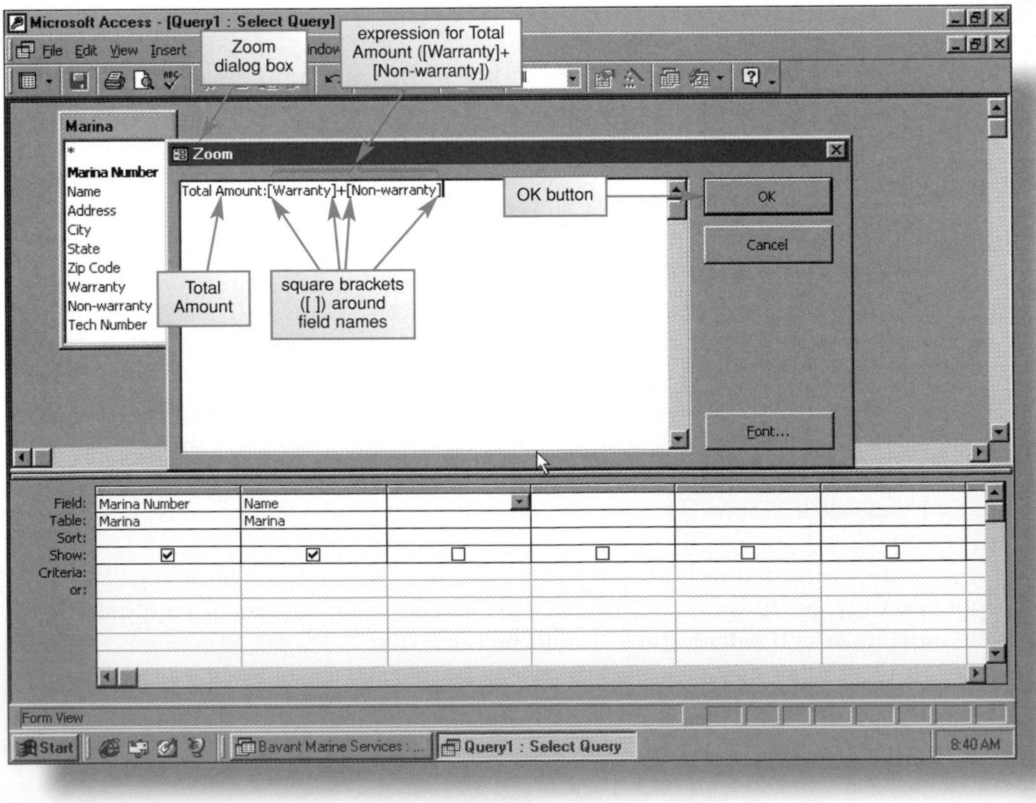

FIGURE 2-53

4 **Click the OK button.**

The Zoom dialog box no longer displays (Figure 2-54). A portion of the expression you entered displays in the third field in the design grid.

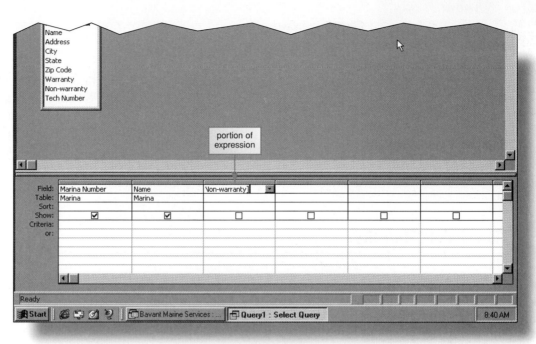

FIGURE 2-54

5 **Run the query.**

The results display (Figure 2-55). Microsoft Access has calculated and displayed the total amounts.

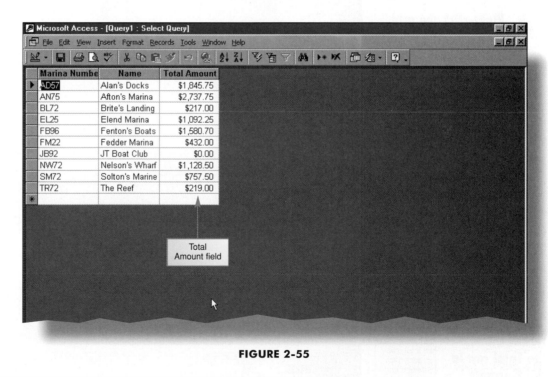

FIGURE 2-55

Rather than clicking Zoom on the shortcut menu, you can click Build. The Build dialog box then will display. This dialog box provides assistance in creating the expression. If you know the expression you will need, however, it usually is easier to enter it using Zoom.

Other Ways

1. Press SHIFT+F2

Calculating Statistics

Virtually all database management systems support the basic set of statistical calculations: sum, average, count, maximum, and minimum as part of their query feature. Some systems, including Access, add several more, such as standard deviation, variance, first, and last.

Calculating Statistics

Microsoft Access supports the built-in **statistics**: COUNT, SUM, AVG (average), MAX (largest value), MIN (smallest value), STDEV (standard deviation), VAR (variance), FIRST, and LAST. To use any of these in a query, you include it in the Total row in the design grid. The Total row routinely does not appear in the grid. To include it, right-click the grid, and then click Totals on the shortcut menu.

The following example illustrates how you use these functions by calculating the average warranty amount for all marinas.

Steps **To Calculate Statistics**

① Click the View button to return to Design view. On the Edit menu, click Clear Grid.

② Right-click the grid.

The shortcut menu displays (Figure 2-56).

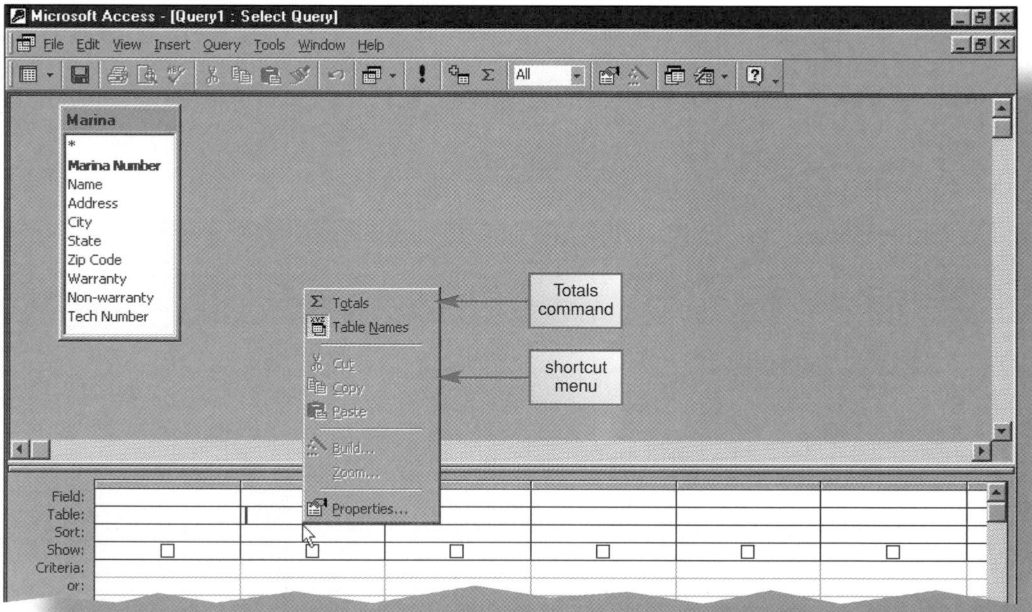

FIGURE 2-56

③ Click Totals on the shortcut menu and then include the Warranty field. Point to the Total row in the Warranty column.

The Total row now is included in the design grid (Figure 2-57). The Warranty field is included, and the entry in the Total row is Group By. The mouse pointer, which has changed shape to an I-beam, is positioned on the Total row under the Warranty field.

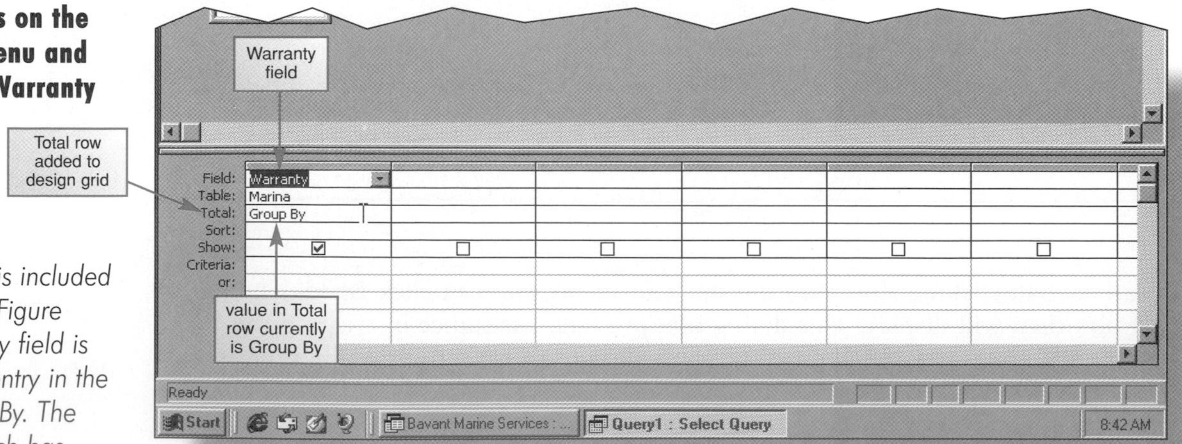

FIGURE 2-57

4 Click the Total row in the Warranty column, and then click the arrow that displays.

The list of available selections displays (Figure 2-58).

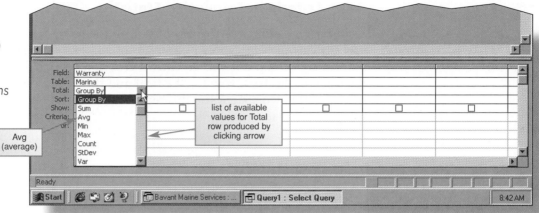

Avg (average)

list of available values for Total row produced by clicking arrow

FIGURE 2-58

5 Click Avg.

Avg is selected (Figure 2-59).

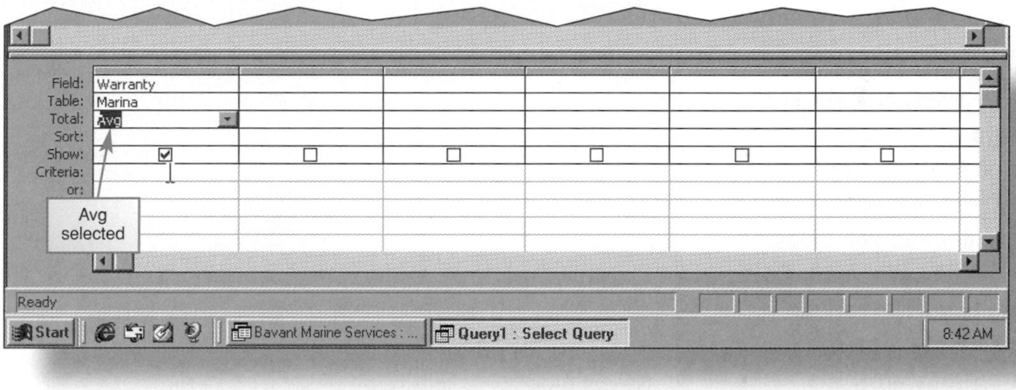

Avg selected

FIGURE 2-59

6 Run the query.

The result displays (Figure 2-60), showing the average warranty amount for all marinas.

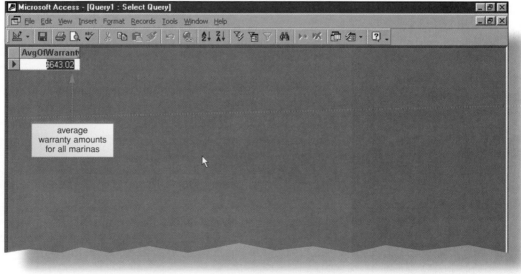

average warranty amounts for all marinas

FIGURE 2-60

Other **Ways**

1. Click Totals button on toolbar
2. On View menu click Totals

Using Criteria in Calculating Statistics

Sometimes calculating statistics for all the records in the table is appropriate. In other cases, however, you will need to calculate the statistics for only those records that satisfy certain criteria. To enter a criterion in a field, first you select Where as the entry in the Total row for the field and then enter the criterion in the Criteria row. The following steps use this technique to calculate the average warranty amount for marinas of technician 36.

Steps To Use Criteria in Calculating Statistics

1 Click the View button to return to Design view.

2 Include the Tech Number field in the design grid. Produce the list of available options for the Total row entry just as you did when you selected Avg for the Warranty field. Use the vertical scroll bar to move through the options until the word, Where, displays.

The list of available selections displays (Figure 2-61). The Group By entry in the Tech Number field may not be highlighted on your screen depending on where you clicked in the Total row.

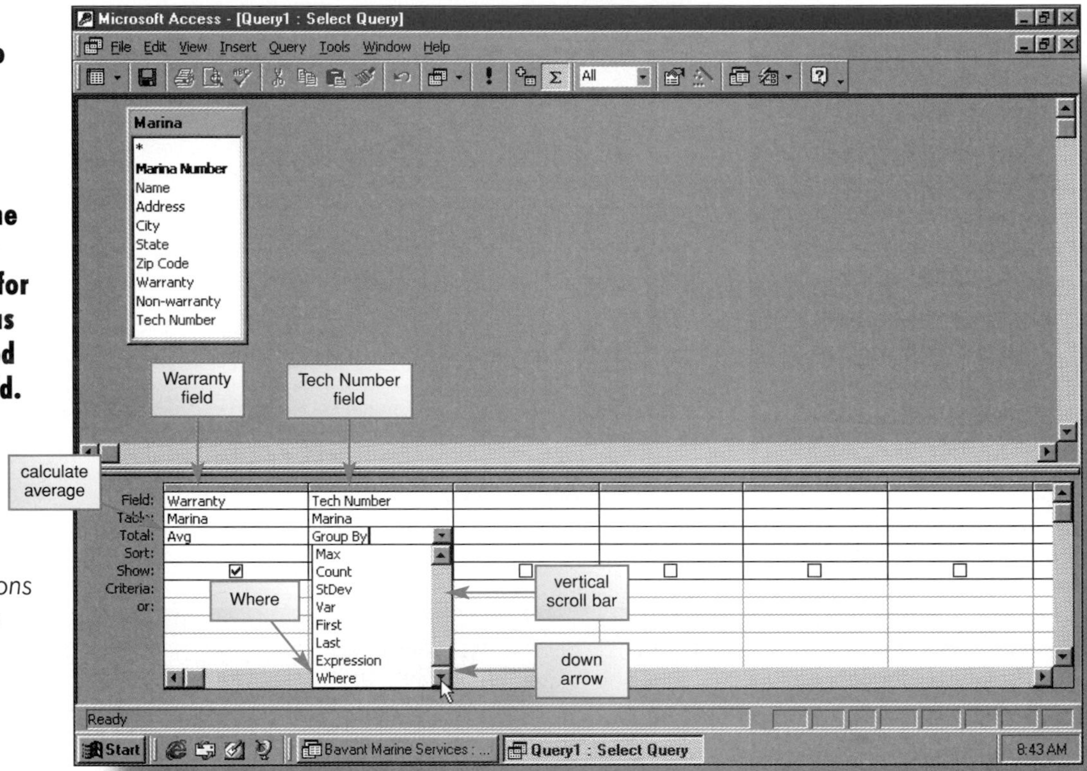

FIGURE 2-61

3 Click Where. Type 36 as the criterion for the Tech Number field.

Where is selected as the entry in the Total row for the Tech Number field (Figure 2-62) and 36 is entered as the Criterion.

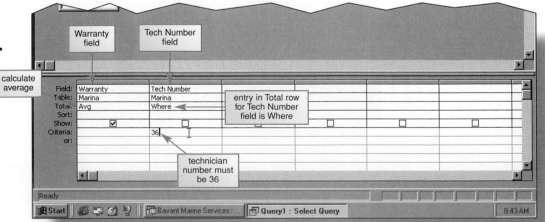

FIGURE 2-62

4 **Run the query.**

The result displays (Figure 2-63), giving the average warranty amount for marinas of technician 36.

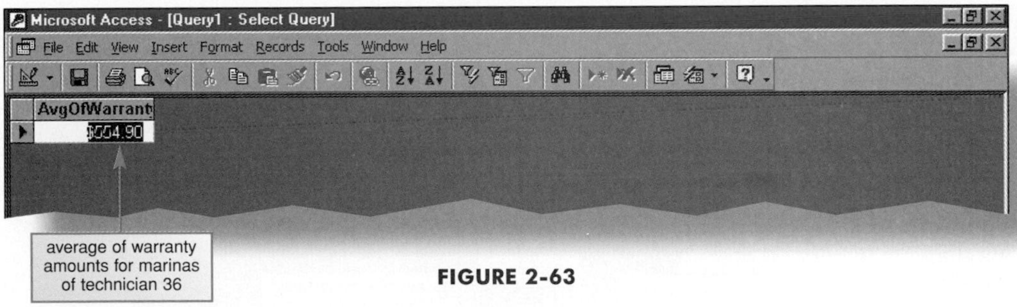

FIGURE 2-63

Grouping

Another way statistics often are used is in combination with grouping; that is, statistics are calculated for groups of records. You may, for example, need to calculate the average warranty amount for the marinas of each technician. You will want the average for the marinas of technician 23, the average for marinas of technician 36, and so on.

Grouping means creating groups of records that share some common characteristic. In grouping by Tech Number, for example, the marinas of technician 23 would form one group, the marinas of technician 36 would be a second, and the marinas of technician 49 form a third. The calculations then are made for each group. To indicate grouping in Access, select Group By as the entry in the Total row for the field to be used for grouping.

Perform the following steps to calculate the average warranty amount for marinas of each technician.

More *About*

Quick Reference

For a table that lists how to complete the tasks covered in this book using the mouse, menu, shortcut menu, and keyboard, visit the Office 2000 Web page (www.scsite.com/off2000/qr.htm), and then click Microsoft Access 2000.

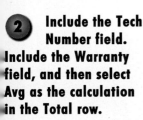 **To Use Grouping**

1 **Click the View button to return to Design view. On the Edit menu, click Clear Grid.**

2 **Include the Tech Number field. Include the Warranty field, and then select Avg as the calculation in the Total row.**

The Tech Number and Warranty fields are included (Figure 2-64). Group By currently is the entry in the Total row for the Tech Number field, which is correct; thus, it was not changed.

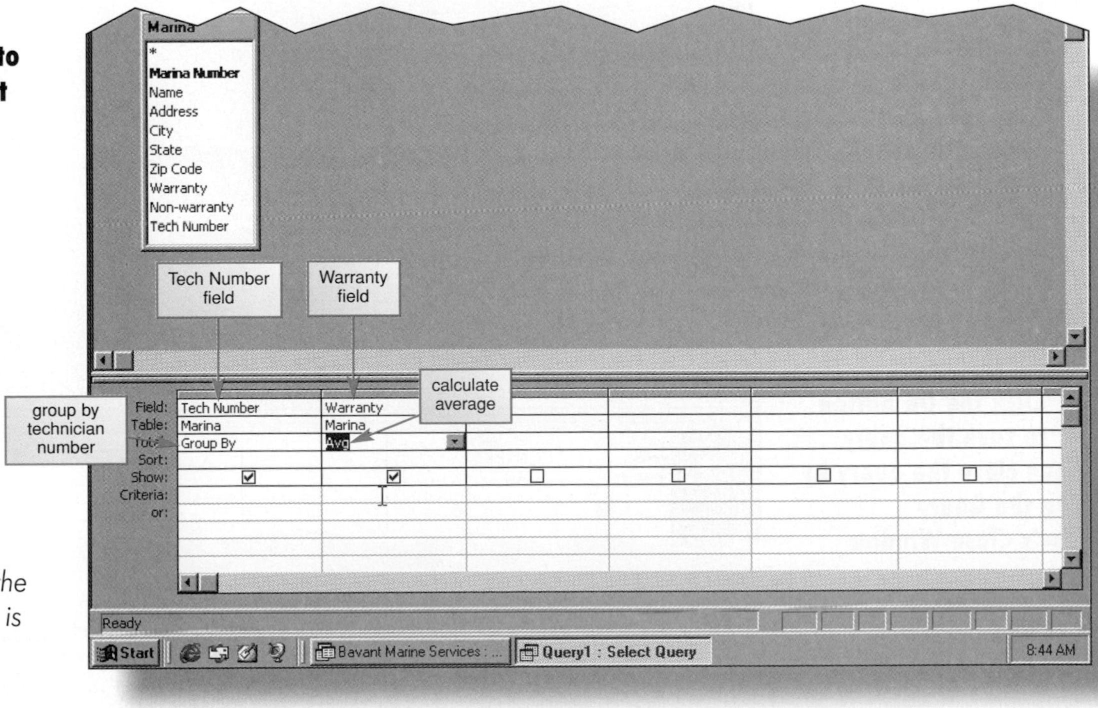

FIGURE 2-64

3 **Run the query.**

The result displays (Figure 2-65), showing each technician's number along with the average warranty amount for the marinas of that technician.

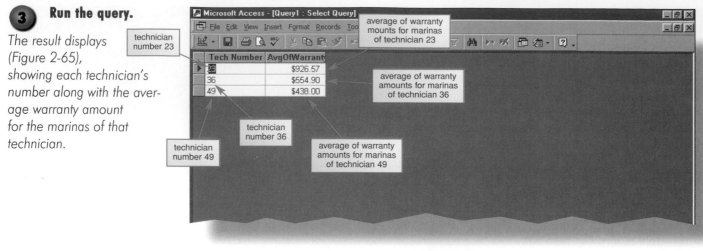

FIGURE 2-65

Saving a Query

In many cases, you will construct a query you will want to use again. By saving the query, you will eliminate the need to repeat all your entries. The following steps illustrate the process by saving the query you just have created and assigning it the name Average Warranty Amount by Technician.

Steps **To Save a Query**

1 **Click the View button and then click the Save button. Type** Average Warranty Amount by Technician **and then point to the OK button.**

The Save As dialog box displays with the query name you typed (Figure 2-66).

2 **Click the OK button to save the query, and then close the query by clicking the Query window's Close Window button.**

Access saves the query and closes the Query1 : Select Query window.

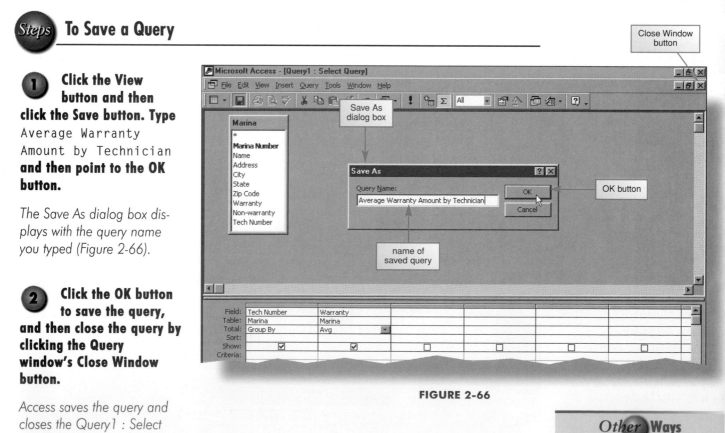

FIGURE 2-66

Other **Ways**

1. On File menu click Save
2. Press CTRL+S

Once you have saved a query, you can use it at any time in the future by opening t. Opening a query produces the same results as running the query from Design view. To open a saved query, click the Queries object in the Database window, right-click the query, and then click Open on the shortcut menu. You then could print the results by clicking the Print button. If you wish to change the design of the query, you would click Design View on the shortcut menu rather than Open. If you wanted to print it *without first opening it*, you would click Print on the shortcut menu.

The query is run against the current database. Thus, if changes have been made to the data since the last time you ran it, the results of the query may be different.

Closing a Database

The following step closes the database by closing its Database window.

TO CLOSE A DATABASE

1. Click the Close Window button for the Bavant Marine Services : Database window.

Microsoft Certification

The Microsoft Office User Specialist (MOUS) Certification program provides an opportunity for you to obtain a valuable industry credential — proof that you have the Access 2000 skills required by employers. For more information, see Appendix D or visit the Shelly Cashman Series MOUS Web page at www.scsite.com/off2000/cert.htm.

CASE PERSPECTIVE SUMMARY

You have been successful in assisting the management of Bavant Marine Services by creating and running queries to obtain answers to important questions. You used various types of criteria in these queries. You joined tables in some of the queries. Some Bavant Marine Services queries used calculated fields and statistics. Finally, you saved one of the queries for future use.

Project Summary

In Project 2, you created and ran a variety of queries. You learned how to select fields in a query. You used text data and wildcards in criteria. You also used comparison operators in criteria involving numeric data. You combined criteria with both AND and OR. You learned how to sort the results of a query, how to join tables, and how to restrict the records in a join. You created computed fields and calculated statistics. You learned how to use grouping as well as how to save a query for future use.

What You Should Know

Having completed this project, you now should be able to perform the following tasks:

- Calculate Statistics *(A 2.38)*
- Clear a Query *(A 2.16)*
- Close the Database *(A 2.43)*
- Close a Query *(A 2.14)*
- Create a Query *(A 2.6)*
- Include All Fields in a Query *(A 2.15)*
- Include Fields in the Design Grid *(A 2.10)*
- Join Tables *(A 2.32)*
- Omit Duplicates *(A 2.29)*
- Open a Database *(A 2.6)*
- Print the Results of a Query *(A 2.12)*
- Restrict the Records in a Join *(A 2.34)*
- Return to the Design View *(A 2.12)*
- Run the Query *(A 2.11)*
- Save a Query *(A 2.42)*
- Sort Data in a Query *(A 2.26)*
- Sort on Multiple Keys *(A 2.28)*
- Use a Comparison Operator in a Criterion *(A 2.22)*
- Use a Compound Criterion Involving AND *(A 2.24)*
- Use a Compound Criterion Involving OR *(A 2.25)*
- Use a Calculated Field in a Query *(A 2.36)*
- Use a Number in a Criterion *(A 2.21)*
- Use a Wildcard *(A 2.18)*
- Use Criteria for a Field Not Included in the Results *(A 2.20)*
- Use Criteria in Calculating Statistics *(A 2.40)*
- Use Grouping *(A 2.41)*
- Use Text Data in a Criterion *(A 2.17)*

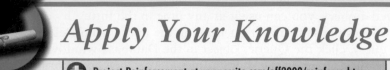

Microsoft **Access 2000**

Apply Your Knowledge

➕ Project Reinforcement at www.scsite.com/off2000/reinforce.htm

1 Querying the Sidewalk Scrapers Database

Instructions: Start Access. Open the Sidewalk Scrapers database from the Access Data Disk. See the inside back cover for instructions for downloading the Access Data Disk or see your instructor for information on accessing the files required for this book. Perform the following tasks.

1. Create a new query for the Customer table.
2. Add the Customer Number, Name, and Address fields to the design grid.
3. Restrict retrieval to only those records where the customer has an address on Secord.
4. Run the query and print the results.
5. Return to Design view and clear the grid.
6. Add the Customer Number, Name, Telephone, and Balance fields to the design grid.
7. Restrict retrieval to only those records where the balance is greater than $50.
8. Run the query and print the results.
9. Return to Design view and clear the grid.
10. Add the Customer Number, Name, Address, and Worker Id fields to the design grid.
11. Restrict retrieval to only those records where the Worker Id is either 03 or 07.
12. Run the query and print the results.
13. Return to Design view and clear the grid.
14. Join the Customer and Worker tables. Add the Customer Number, Name, and Worker Id fields from the Customer table and the First Name and Last Name fields from the Worker table.
15. Sort the records in ascending order by Worker Id.
16. Run the query and print the results.

In the Lab

1 Querying the School Connection Database

Problem: The Booster's Club has determined a number of questions they want the database management system to answer. You must obtain answers to the questions posed by the club.

Instructions: Use the database created in the In the Lab 1 of Project 1 for this assignment.
Perform the following tasks.

1. Open the School Connection database and create a new query for the Item table.
2. Display and print the Item Id, Description, and Selling Price fields for all records in the table as shown in Figure 2-67.
3. Display all fields and print all the records in the table.

In the Lab

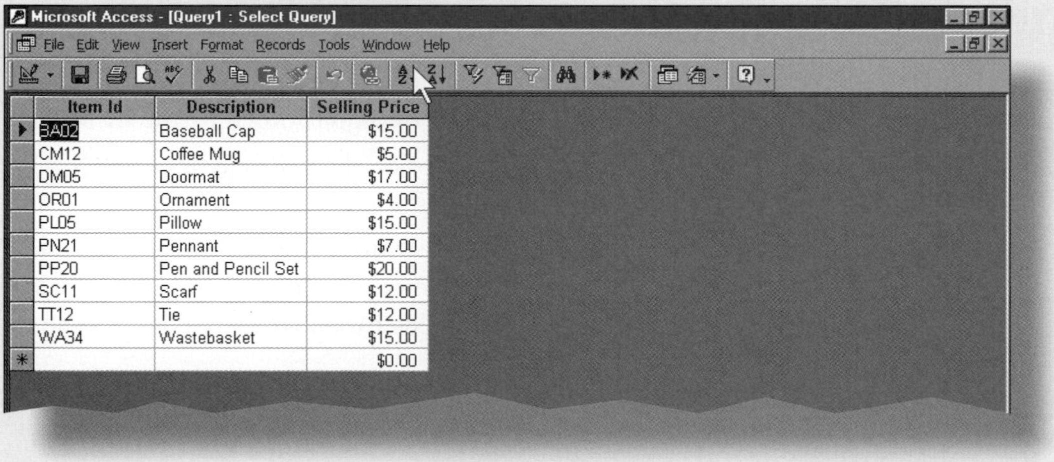

Item Id	Description	Selling Price
BA02	Baseball Cap	$15.00
CM12	Coffee Mug	$5.00
DM05	Doormat	$17.00
OR01	Ornament	$4.00
PL05	Pillow	$15.00
PN21	Pennant	$7.00
PP20	Pen and Pencil Set	$20.00
SC11	Scarf	$12.00
TT12	Tie	$12.00
WA34	Wastebasket	$15.00
*		$0.00

FIGURE 2-67

4. Display and print the Item Id, Description, Cost, and Vendor Code fields for all items where the Vendor Code is TM.
5. Display and print the Item Id and Description fields for all items where the Description begins with the letters, Pe.
6. Display and print the Item Id, Description, and Vendor Code fields for all items with a cost greater than $10.
7. Display and print the Item Id and Description for all items that have a selling price of $10 or less.
8. Display and print all fields for those items with a cost greater than $10 and where the number on hand is less than 5.
9. Display and print all fields for those items that have a vendor code of TM or have a selling price less than $10.
10. Join the Item table and the Vendor table. Display the Item Id, Description, Cost, Name, and Telephone Number fields. Run the query and print the results.
11. Restrict the records retrieved in task 10 above to only those items where the number on hand is less than 10. Display and print the results.
12. Remove the Vendor table and clear the design grid.
13. Include the Item Id and Description fields in the design grid. Calculate the on-hand value (on hand * cost) for all records in the table. Display and print the results.
14. Display and print the average selling price of all items.
15. Display and print the average selling price of items grouped by vendor code.
16. Join the Item and Vendor tables. Include the Vendor Code and Name fields from the Vendor table. Include the Item Id, Description, Cost, and On Hand fields from the Item table. Save the query as Vendors and Items. Run the query and print the results.

In the Lab

2 Querying the City Area Bus Company Database

Problem: The advertising sales manager has determined a number of questions that he wants the database management system to answer. You must obtain answers to the questions posed by the manager.

Instructions: Use the database created in the In the Lab 2 of Project 1 for this assignment. Perform the following tasks.

1. Open the City Area Bus Company database and create a new query for the Advertiser table.
2. Display and print the Advertiser Id, Name, Balance, and Amount Paid fields for all the records in the table.
3. Display and print the Advertiser Id, Name, and Balance fields for all advertisers where the sales rep number is 24.
4. Display and print the Advertiser Id, Name, and Balance fields for all advertisers where the balance is greater than $200.
5. Display and print the Advertiser Id, Name, and Amount Paid fields for all advertisers where the sales rep number is 29 and the amount paid is greater than $1,000.
6. Display and print the Advertiser Id, Name, and City fields of all advertisers where the city begins with C.
7. Display and print the Advertiser Id, Name, and Balance fields for all advertisers where the sales rep number is 29 or the balance is less than $50.
8. Include the Advertiser Id, Name, City, and State fields in the design grid. Sort the records in ascending order by city within state. Display and print the results. The City field should display in the result to the left of the State field. (*Hint:* Use Microsoft Access Help to solve this problem.) *Right*
9. Display and print the cities in ascending order. Each city should display only once.
10. Display and print the Advertiser Id, Name, Balance, and Amount Paid fields from the Advertiser table and the First Name, Last Name, and Comm Rate fields from the Sales Rep table.
11. Restrict the records retrieved in task 10 above to only those advertisers that are in MA. Display and print the results.
12. Clear the design grid and add the First Name, Last Name, and Comm Rate fields from the Sales Rep table to the grid. Add the Name and Balance fields from the Advertiser table. Calculate the pending commission (balance * comm rate) for the Sales Rep table. Sort the records in ascending order by last name and format pending commission as currency. (*Hint:* Use Microsoft Access Help to solve this problem.) Run the query and print the results.
13. Display and print the following statistics: the total balance and total amount paid for all advertisers; the total balance for advertisers of sales rep 29; and the total amount paid for each sales rep.
14. Display and print the Sales Rep Number, Last Name, First Name, Advertiser Id, Name, Balance, and Amount Paid fields. Save the query as Sales Reps and Advertisers.

3 Querying the Resort Rentals Database

Problem: The real estate company has determined a number of questions that they want the database management system to answer. You must obtain answers to the questions posed by the company.

Instructions: Use the database created in the In the Lab 3 of Project 1 for this assignment. Perform the following tasks.

1. Open the Resort Rentals database and create a new query for the Rental Unit table.

In the Lab

2. Display and print the Rental Id, Address, City, and Owner Id fields for all the records in the table as shown in Figure 2-68.

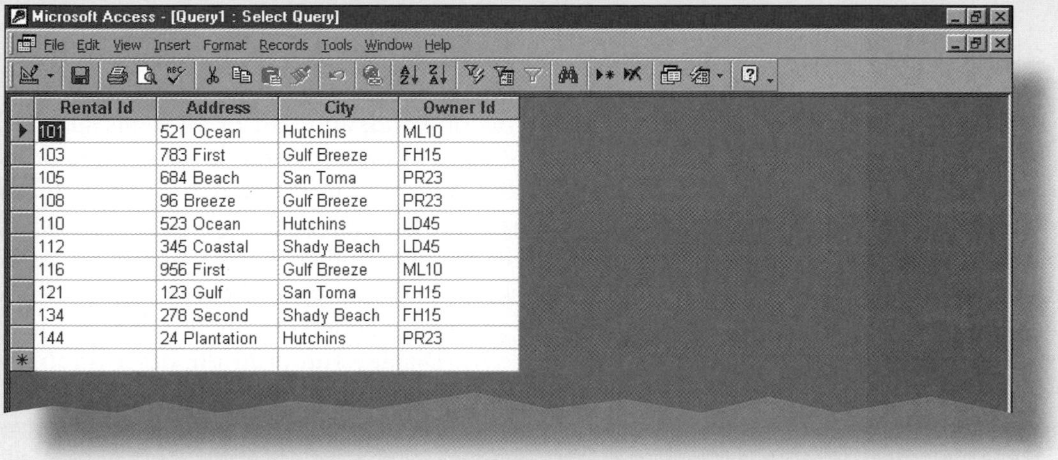

Rental Id	Address	City	Owner Id
101	521 Ocean	Hutchins	ML10
103	783 First	Gulf Breeze	FH15
105	684 Beach	San Toma	PR23
108	96 Breeze	Gulf Breeze	PR23
110	523 Ocean	Hutchins	LD45
112	345 Coastal	Shady Beach	LD45
116	956 First	Gulf Breeze	ML10
121	123 Gulf	San Toma	FH15
134	278 Second	Shady Beach	FH15
144	24 Plantation	Hutchins	PR23

FIGURE 2-68

3. Display and print the Rental Id, Address, City, and Weekly Rate fields for all units that rent for less than $1,000 per week.
4. Display and print the Rental Id, Address, and Weekly Rate fields for all units that sleep more than four people and have a pool.
5. Display and print the Rental Id, Address, City, and Weekly Rate fields for all units that are either in Hutchins or Gulf Breeze, have more than one bedroom and an ocean view. (*Hint:* Use Microsoft Access Help to solve this problem.)
6. Display and print the Rental Id, Address, and City fields of all units where the city begins with S.
7. Display and print the Rental Id, Address, and Weekly Rate fields for all units that have more than one bedroom and more than one bathroom.
8. Include the Rental Id, Address, City, Bedrooms, Sleeps, and Weekly Rate fields in the design grid. Sort the records in descending order by bedrooms within sleeps. The Bedrooms field should display in the result to the left of the Sleeps field. Display and print the results. (*Hint:* Use Microsoft Access Help to solve this problem.)
9. Display and print the weekly rates in descending order. Each rate should display only once.
10. Display and print the Rental Id, Address, City, and Weekly Rate fields from the Rental Unit table and the First Name, Last Name, and Phone Number fields from the Owner table.
11. Restrict the records retrieved in task 10 above to only those units that rent for more than $1,000 per week. Display and print the results.
12. Clear the design grid and remove the Owner table from the query. Owner ML10 offers a 15% discount on the weekly rate if renters rent for more than one week at a time. What is the discounted weekly rental rate for his units? Display the rental id, address, city, and discounted weekly rate in your result. Format the discounted weekly rate as currency. (*Hint:* Use Microsoft Access Help to solve this problem.) Run the query and print the results.
13. Display and print the average weekly rate for each owner.
14. Display and print the Owner Id, First Name, Last Name, Rental Id, Address, City, and Weekly Rate fields. Save the query as Owners and Rental Units.

Cases and Places

The difficulty of these case studies varies:
▌ are the least difficult; ▌▌ are more difficult; and ▌▌▌ are the most difficult.

1 ▌ Use the Computer Accessories database you created in Case Study 1 of Project 1 for this assignment. Perform the following: (a) The Computer Science Club has been unhappy with the supplier, Mouse Tracks. Display and print the description, units on hand, and cost of all items supplied by Mouse Tracks. (b) The club is considering raising the selling price of items costing less than one dollar. Find the current profit (selling price – cost) of these items and display and print the item id, description, cost, selling price, and current profit. (c) The faculty advisor for the club needs to know the on-hand value of the club's inventory. Display and print the item id, description, and on-hand value (units on hand * cost) for all items. (d) The club needs to replenish its stock. Display and print the item id, description, units on hand, supplier name, and supplier telephone for all items where there are less than 10 items on hand. (e) The club would like to display a list of items for sale. Display and print the description and selling price. Sort the list in ascending order by selling price.

2 ▌ Use the Bookstore database you created in Case Study 2 of Project 1 for this assignment. The owner of the bookstore has put together a list of the most common type of questions she would like to ask the database. She wants to know if the database you created can answer these questions. Perform the following: (a) Display and print the book code, title, price, and year published for all books written by H Brawley. (b) Display and print the authors in ascending order. List each author only once. (c) Display and print a count of the books grouped by author. (d) Display and print the book code, title, author, and price for all books published in the year 2000. (e) Display and print the book code, title, units on hand, price, and on-hand value (units on hand * price) for all books. (f) Display and print the book code, title, price, and publisher name for all books where the number of units on hand is less than two.

3 ▌▌ Use the Band database you created in Case Study 3 of Project 1 for this assignment. Perform the following: (a) The band director would like a telephone list of all band members. List the name and telephone number of all band members. (b) The band is going to a marching band competition this weekend and it is important that school officials be able to reach a parent/guardian in case of emergency. List the name and emergency contact information for all band members. (c) The local college is offering a special weekend camp for clarinet players. Identify all band members that play the clarinet. (d) Students who have been band members for two years or more are eligible for special recognition. List the name, age, sex, band instrument, and number of years in the band for these band members. (e) The school has just negotiated a new lease arrangement with a local music store. List the name, telephone number, and type of band instrument for those band members that lease their instrument. (f) The band needs an updated directory. List the band instrument type, member name, age, sex, and years in band for each member. The list should be in order by last name within band instrument type.

4 ▌▌ Use the Humane Society database you created in Case Study 4 of Project 1 for this assignment. Display and print the following: (a) The name, address, and telephone number of all families that have adopted pets. (b) A list of all animals that have been adopted. The list should include the animal's name, type, age, and sex. (c) A list of all adoptions. The list should include the name of the family, telephone number, the animal's name and type. (d) The average number of other pets owned by families that have adopted animals. (e) A list of the different types of animals that have been adopted. Each animal type should display only once.

PowerPoint 2000

1

2

3

4

5

6

Microsoft PowerPoint 2000

PROJECT 1

Using a Design Template and AutoLayouts to Create a Presentation

OBJECTIVES

You will have mastered the material in this project when you can:

- Start a presentation as a New Office document
- Describe the PowerPoint window
- Select a design template
- Create a title slide
- Describe and use text attributes such as font size and font style
- Save a presentation
- Add a new slide
- Create a multi-level bulleted list slide
- Move to another slide in normal view
- End a slide show with a black slide
- View a presentation in slide show view
- Quit PowerPoint
- Open a presentation
- Check the spelling and consistency of a presentation
- Edit a presentation
- Change line spacing on the slide master
- Display a presentation in black and white
- Print a presentation in black and white
- Use the PowerPoint Help system

Puttin' on the Glitz

Presentations Help COMDEX Shine

Microsoft's Bill Gates will be there. So will thousands of the world's computer industry executives. And they will be joined by hundreds of thousands of curious technology affectionados seeking the latest trends in hardware, software, and the Internet.

They will be attending COMDEX, North America's largest trade show. COMDEX/Fall is held in Las Vegas each November, and COMDEX/Spring is held in Chicago in April. Both shows feature speeches by industry leaders, tutorials on the latest technologies, and thousands of square feet of exhibits showcasing the latest in computer technology.

Information technology (IT) experts headline COMDEX as the premier IT event in the world. Indeed, more than 10,000 new products are unveiled at the Fall show. Since COMDEX's inception in 1979, some of the more notable product launches have been the IBM PC in 1981, COMPAQ's suitcase-sized portable computer, Microsoft's first version of Windows, Apple's original Macintosh computer, and CD-ROM drives.

Attendance and industry representation have grown steadily. The first show featured 150 exhibitions seen by 4,000 curious visitors. Six years later, more than 1,000 companies displayed their wares for more than 100,000 techies. Recent shows have produced as many as 2,400 booths visited by 250,000-plus attendees.

Computer companies realize their sales forces need to capture their audiences' attention, so they add sensory cues to their exhibits. They treat the trade show visitors to a multimedia blitz of sound, visuals, and action with the help of presentation software such as Microsoft PowerPoint 2000. This program enhances the presenters' speeches by highlighting keywords in the presentation, displaying graphs, pictures, and diagrams, and playing sound and video clips.

In this project, you will learn to use PowerPoint 2000 to create a presentation, which also is called a slide show, concerning effective study skills. You then will run the slide show and print handouts for the audience. In later projects you will add animation, pictures, and sound.

PowerPoint's roots stem from the innovative work performed by a small company called Forethought, Inc. Programmers at this pioneering business coined the phrase, desktop presentation graphics, for formal slide shows and created a complete software package that automated creating slides containing text, charts, and graphics. Microsoft liked the visual appeal of the software and acquired Forethought in 1987. Company executives decided to market the software to Apple Macintosh users because Mac computers were considered clearly superior to IBM-based personal computers for graphics applications.

Microsoft PowerPoint became a favorite among Mac users. Meanwhile, Lotus Freelance Graphics and Software Publishing Harvard Graphics were popular within the PC community. This division ceased, however, when Microsoft released Windows 3.0 in 1990 and subsequently developed a Windows version of PowerPoint to run on PCs.

Since that time, Macintosh and PC users alike have utilized the presentation power of PowerPoint. The package has grown to include animation, audio and video clips, and Internet integration. Certainly the technology gurus at COMDEX have realized PowerPoint's dazzling visual appeal. So will you as you complete the exercises in this textbook.

Microsoft PowerPoint 2000

Using a Design Template and AutoLayouts to Create a Presentation

P R O J E C T

1

Excellent study habits are the keys to college success. What matters is not how long people study — it is how well they use their time. Students who study well can maximize their hours, have time for other activities, make the highest grades, and have a better chance to get accepted to their desired school. Ultimately, they generally earn higher incomes because their good study habits carry over to the working environment.

Advisers in Seaview College's Counseling Department spend many hours each semester helping students organize their study times, maximize their classroom experiences, and read their textbooks for ultimate comprehension. Dr. Ramon Martinez, the dean of counseling, has asked you to develop a short presentation to run at next semester's Freshmen Orientation sessions. You agree to create the presentation using a computer and PowerPoint software with the theme of effective study habits. In addition, you will print handouts of the presentation for the incoming students and also print a copy of the presentation on transparency film to enable the advisers to project the slides using an overhead projector.

What Is Microsoft PowerPoint 2000?

Microsoft PowerPoint 2000 is a complete presentation graphics program that allows you to produce professional-looking presentations. A PowerPoint **presentation** also is called a **slide show**. PowerPoint gives you the flexibility to make presentations using a projection device attached to a personal computer (Figure 1-1a) and using overhead transparencies (Figure 1-1b). In addition, you can take advantage of the World Wide Web and run virtual presentations on the Internet (Figure 1-1c). PowerPoint also can create paper printouts of the individual slides, outlines, and speaker notes.

PowerPoint contains several features to simplify creating a slide show. For example, you can instruct PowerPoint to create a predesigned presentation, and then you can modify the presentation to fulfill your requirements. You quickly can format a slide show using one of the professionally designed presentation design templates. To make your presentation more impressive, you can add tables, charts, pictures, video, sound, and, animation effects. You also can check the spelling of your slide show as you type or after you have completed designing the presentation. For example, you can instruct PowerPoint to restrict the number of bulleted items on a slide or limit the number of words in each paragraph. Additional PowerPoint features include the following:

- **Word processing** —create bulleted lists, combine words and images, find and replace text, and use multiple fonts and type sizes.
- **Outlining** — develop your presentation using an outline format. You also can import outlines from Microsoft Word or other word processing programs.
- **Charting** —create and insert charts into your presentations. The two chart types are: standard, which includes bar, line, pie, and xy (scatter) charts; and custom, which displays floating bars, colored lines, and three-dimensional cones.

(a) Projection Device Connected to a Personal Computer

(b) Overhead Transparencies

FIGURE 1-1

(c) PowerPoint Presentation Over the World Wide Web

Projection Devices

Multimedia projectors have become the standard for today's presenters. The newest devices are about the size of a deli sandwich, weigh just five pounds, and fill the room with brilliant, clear images. For more information, visit the PowerPoint 2000 More About Web page (www.scsite.com/pp2000/more.htm) and click Projection.

▶ **Drawing** —form and modify diagrams using shapes such as arcs, arrows, cubes, rectangles, stars, and triangles.

▶ **Inserting multimedia** — insert artwork and multimedia effects into your slide show. Clip Gallery 5.0 contains hundreds of clip art images, pictures, photos, sounds, and video clips. You can search for clips by entering words or phrases that describe the subject you want, by looking for clips with similar artistic styles, colors, or shapes, or by connecting to a special Web site reserved for Clip Gallery users. You also can import art from other applications.

▶ **Web support** — save presentations or parts of a presentation in HTML format so they can be viewed and manipulated using a browser. You can publish your slide show to the Internet or to an intranet. You also can insert action buttons and hyperlinks to create a self-running or interactive Web presentation.

▶ **E-mailing** — send an individual slide as an e-mail message or your entire slide show as an attachment to an e-mail message.

▶ **Using Wizards** — quickly and efficiently create a presentation by answering prompts for specific content criteria. For example, the **AutoContent Wizard** gives prompts for the type of slide show you are planning, such as communicating bad news or motivating a team, and the type of output, such as an on-screen presentation or black and white overheads. If you are planning to run your presentation on another computer, the **Pack and Go Wizard** helps you bundle everything you need, including any objects associated with that presentation. If you cannot confirm that this other computer has PowerPoint installed, you also can include the **PowerPoint Viewer**, a program that allows you to run, but not edit, a PowerPoint slide show.

Project One — Effective Study Skills

This book presents a series of projects using PowerPoint to produce slides similar to those you would develop in an academic or business environment. Project 1 uses PowerPoint to create the presentation shown in Figures 1-2a through 1-2d. The objective is to produce a presentation, called Effective Study Skills, to be displayed using an overhead projector. As an introduction to PowerPoint, this project steps you through the most common type of presentation, which is a bulleted list. A **bulleted list** is a list of paragraphs, each preceded by a bullet. A **bullet** is a symbol such as a heavy dot (•) or other character that precedes text when the text warrants special emphasis.

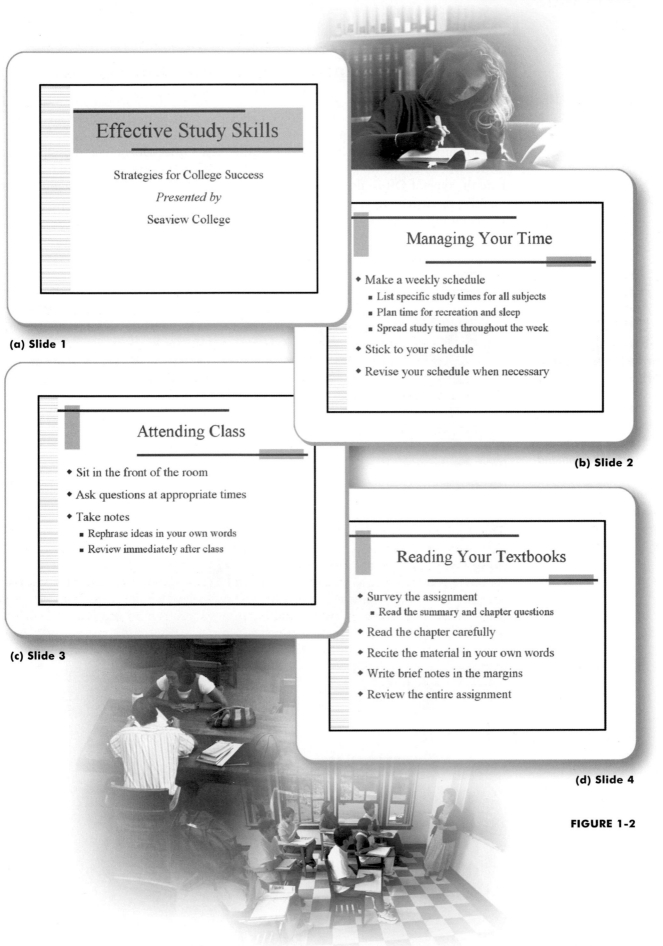

(a) Slide 1

Effective Study Skills

Strategies for College Success
Presented by
Seaview College

(b) Slide 2

Managing Your Time

- Make a weekly schedule
  - List specific study times for all subjects
  - Plan time for recreation and sleep
  - Spread study times throughout the week
- Stick to your schedule
- Revise your schedule when necessary

(c) Slide 3

Attending Class

- Sit in the front of the room
- Ask questions at appropriate times
- Take notes
  - Rephrase ideas in your own words
  - Review immediately after class

(d) Slide 4

Reading Your Textbooks

- Survey the assignment
  - Read the summary and chapter questions
- Read the chapter carefully
- Recite the material in your own words
- Write brief notes in the margins
- Review the entire assignment

FIGURE 1-2

Starting a Presentation as a New Office Document

The quickest way to begin a new presentation is to use the **Start button** on the **taskbar** at the bottom of your screen. When you click the Start button, the **Start menu** displays several commands for simplifying tasks in Windows. When Microsoft Office 2000 is installed, the Start menu displays the New Office Document and Open Office Document commands. You use the **New Office Document command** to designate the type of Office document you are creating. The Open Office Document command is discussed later in this project. Perform these steps to start a new presentation, or ask your instructor how to start PowerPoint on your system.

 To Start a New Presentation

1 Click the Start button on the taskbar and then point to New Office Document.

The programs on the Start menu display above the Start button (Figure 1-3). The New Office Document command is highlighted on the Start menu. Your computer system displays the time on the clock in the tray status area on the taskbar.

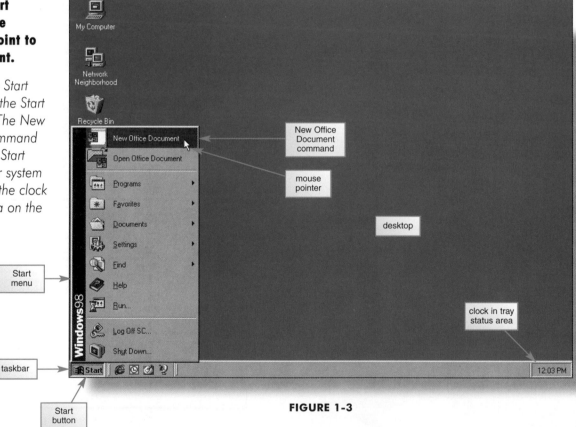

FIGURE 1-3

2 Click New Office Document. If necessary, click the General tab in the New Office Document dialog box, and then click the Blank Presentation icon.

Office displays several icons on the General sheet in the New Office Document dialog box (Figure 1-4). Each icon represents a different type of document you can create in Microsoft Office. In this project, you will create a new presentation using Microsoft PowerPoint, starting with a blank presentation.

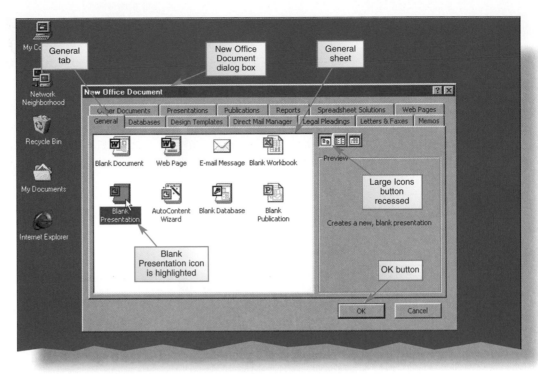

FIGURE 1-4

3 Click the OK button. If necessary, enlarge the PowerPoint window by double-clicking its title bar. If the Office Assistant displays, right-click the Office Assistant and then click Hide on the shortcut menu. Point to the OK button in the New Slide dialog box.

The New Slide dialog box displays (Figure 1-5). The Title Slide AutoLayout is selected, and its name displays in the lower-right corner of the New Slide dialog box. The Office Assistant will be discussed later in this project.

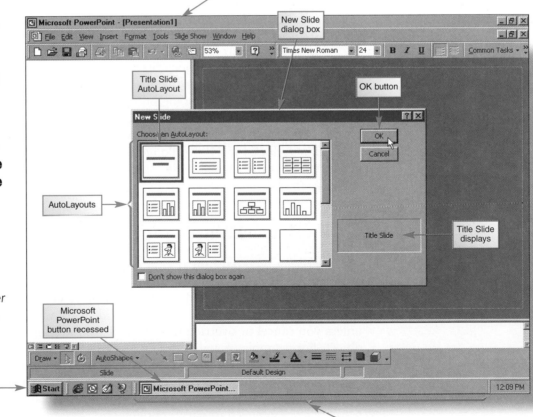

FIGURE 1-5

4 **Click the OK button.**

PowerPoint displays the Title Slide AutoLayout and the Default Design template on Slide 1 (Figure 1-6). The title bar identifies this window as a Microsoft PowerPoint presentation currently titled [Presentation1]. The status bar displays information about the current slide: the slide number and the name of the current design template.

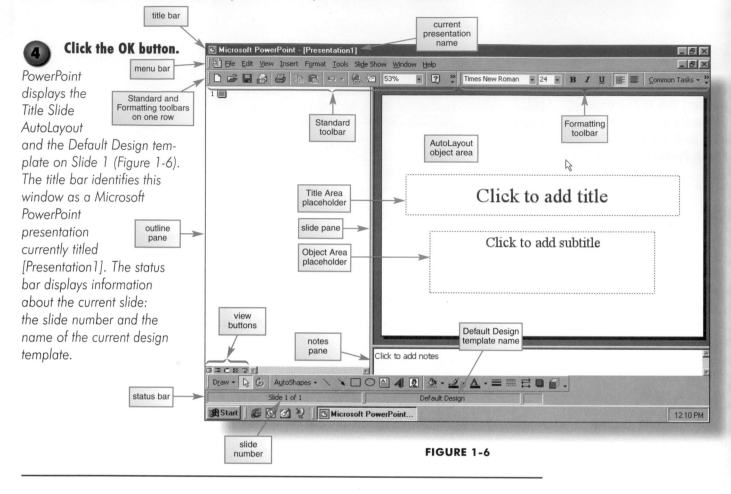

FIGURE 1-6

When an application is open, its name displays on a button in the **taskbar button area**. The **active application** is the one displaying on the foreground of the desktop. That application's corresponding button in the taskbar button area displays recessed.

The basic unit of a PowerPoint presentation is a **slide**. A slide contains one or many **objects**, such as a title, text, graphics, tables, charts, and drawings. An object is the building block for a PowerPoint slide. PowerPoint assumes the first slide in a new presentation is the **title slide**. The title slide's purpose is to introduce the presentation to the audience.

The PowerPoint Window

In PowerPoint, you have the option of using the PowerPoint default settings or establishing your own. A **default setting** is a particular value for a variable that PowerPoint assigns initially. It controls the placement of objects, the color scheme, the transition between slides, and other slide attributes, and it remains in effect unless you cancel or override it. **Attributes** are the properties or characteristics of an object. For example, if you underline the title of a slide, the title is the object, and the underline is the attribute. When you start PowerPoint, the default **slide layout** is **landscape orientation**, where the slide width is greater than its height. In landscape orientation, the slide size is preset to 10 inches wide and 7.5 inches high. The slide layout can be changed to **portrait orientation**, so that the slide height is greater than its width, by clicking Page Setup on the File menu. In portrait orientation, the slide width is 7.5 inches, and the height is 10 inches.

PowerPoint Views

PowerPoint has five views: normal view, outline view, slide view, slide sorter view, and slide show. A **view** is the mode in which the presentation displays on the screen. You may use any or all views when creating your presentation, but you can use only one at a time. Change views by clicking one of the view buttons found in the lower-left of the PowerPoint window above the status bar (Figure 1-6). The PowerPoint window display is dependent on the view. Some views are graphical while others are textual.

You generally will use normal view and slide sorter view when you are creating your presentation. Normal view is composed of three panes, which are the **outline pane**, **slide pane**, and **notes pane**. You can drag the pane borders to adjust the size of the panes. They allow you to work on various aspects of your presentation simultaneously (Figure 1-6). You can type the text of your presentation in the outline pane and easily rearrange bulleted lists, paragraphs, and individual slides. As you type in the outline pane, you can view this text in the slide pane. You also can enter text, graphics, animations, and hyperlinks directly in the slide pane. You can type notes and additional information in the notes pane. This text can consist of notes to yourself or remarks to share with your audience. After you have created at least two slides, **scroll bars**, **scroll arrows**, and **scroll boxes** will display below and to the right of the windows, and you can use them to view different parts of the panes.

Slide sorter view is helpful when you want to see all the slides in your presentation simultaneously. A miniature version of each slide displays, and you can rearrange their order, add transitions and timings to switch from one side to the next in your presentation, add and delete slides, and preview animations.

Table 1-1 identifies the view buttons and provides an explanation of each view.

More About

PowerPoint Views

The three panes in normal, outline, and slide views allow you to work on all aspects of your presentation simultaneously. You can drag the pane borders to make each area larger or smaller.

Table 1-1	View Buttons and Functions	
BUTTON	**NAME**	**FUNCTION**
⬜	Normal View	Displays three panes: the outline pane, the slide pane, and the notes pane.
⬜	Outline View	Displays a presentation in an outline format showing slide titles and text. It is best used for organizing and developing the content of your presentation. You can rearrange paragraphs and bullet points in this view.
⬜	Slide View	Displays a single slide as it appears in your presentation. Slide view is used to incorporate text, graphics, video, audio, hyperlinks, and animation and also to create line-by-line progressive disclosure, called build effects. Use slide view to create or edit a presentation.
⬜	Slide Sorter View	Displays miniature versions of all slides in your presentation. You then can copy, cut, paste, or otherwise change slide position to modify your presentation. Slide sorter view also is used to add timings, to select animated transitions, and to preview animations.
⬜	Slide Show View	Displays your slides as an electronic presentation on the full screen of your computer's monitor. Looking much like a slide projector display, you can see the effect of transitions, build effects, slide timings, and animations.

Placeholders, Title Area, Object Area, Mouse Pointer, and Scroll Bars

The PowerPoint window contains elements similar to the document windows in other Microsoft Office 2000 applications. Other features are unique to PowerPoint. The main elements are the Title Area and Object Area placeholders, the mouse pointer, and scroll bars.

PLACEHOLDERS **Placeholders** are boxes that display when you create a new slide. All AutoLayouts except the Blank AutoLayout contain placeholders. Depending on the particular slide layout selected, placeholders display for the slide title, text, charts, tables, organization charts, media clips, and clip art. You type titles, body text, and bulleted lists in **text placeholders**; you place graphic elements in chart placeholders, table placeholders, organizational chart placeholders, and clip art placeholders. A placeholder is considered an **object**, which is a single element of your slide. An empty placeholder is called an **unfilled object**; a placeholder containing text or graphics is called a **filled object**. When a filled object contains text, it is called a **text object**.

TITLE AREA Surrounded by a dotted outline, the **Title Area** is the location of the text placeholder where you will type the main heading of a new slide (Figure 1-6 on page PP 1.12).

OBJECT AREA Surrounded by a dotted outline, the **Object Area** is the empty area that displays below the Title Area on a slide. It can contain various placeholders for displaying subtitle or supporting information such as clip art and charts (Figure 1-6).

MOUSE POINTER The **mouse pointer** can have a different shape depending on the task you are performing in PowerPoint and the pointer's location on the screen. The different shapes are discussed when they display in subsequent projects.

SCROLL BARS When you add a second slide to your presentation, **vertical scroll bars** display on the right side of the outline and slide panes. PowerPoint allows you to use the scroll bars to move forward or backward through your presentation.

The **horizontal scroll bar** also displays when you add a second slide to your presentation. It is located on the bottom of the slide pane and allows you to display a portion of the slide when the entire slide does not fit on the screen.

Menu Bar, Standard Toolbar, Formatting Toolbar, Drawing Toolbar, and Status Bar

The menu bar, Standard toolbar, and Formatting toolbar display at the top of the screen just below the title bar (Figure 1-6). The Standard and Formatting toolbars are by default on one row. The Drawing toolbar and status bar display at the bottom of the screen above the Windows taskbar.

MENU BAR The menu bar displays the PowerPoint menu names (Figure 1-7a). Each menu name represents a menu of commands that you can use to retrieve, store, print, and manipulate objects in your presentation. When you point to a menu name on the menu bar, the area of the menu bar containing the name changes to a button. To display a menu, such as the Insert menu, click the Insert menu name on the menu bar (Figures 1-7b and 1-7c). If you point to a command with an arrow on the right, a submenu displays from which you can choose a command.

When you click a menu name on the menu bar, a **short menu** displays listing the most recently used commands (Figure 1-7b). If you wait a few seconds or click the arrows at the bottom of the short menu (Figure 1-7b), the full menu displays. The **full menu** shows all the commands associated with a menu (Figure 1-7c). As you use PowerPoint, it automatically personalizes the menus for you based on how often you use commands. In this book, when you display a menu, wait a few seconds or click the arrows at the bottom of the menu so the long menu displays. The **hidden commands** that display on the full menu are recessed. **Dimmed commands** (gray background) indicate they are not available for the current selection.

The menu bar can change to include other menu names depending on the type of work you are doing. For example, if you are adding a chart to a slide, Data and Chart menu names are added to the menu bar with commands that reflect charting options.

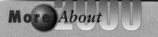

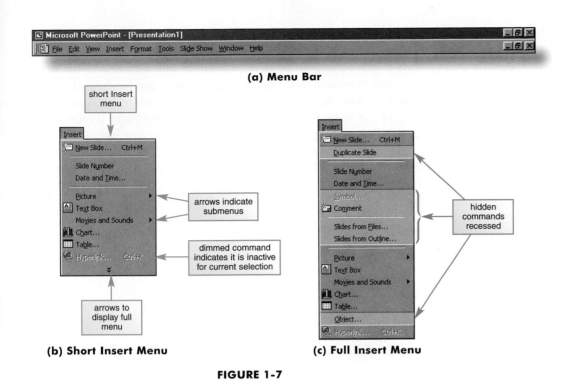

(a) Menu Bar

(b) Short Insert Menu

(c) Full Insert Menu

FIGURE 1-7

STANDARD, FORMATTING, AND DRAWING TOOLBARS The Standard toolbar (Figure 1-8a), Formatting toolbar (Figure 1-8b), and Drawing toolbar (Figure 1-8c) contain buttons and list boxes that allow you to perform frequent tasks more quickly than when using the menu bar. For example, to print a slide show, you click the Print button on the Standard toolbar. Each button has an image on the button that helps you remember the button's function. When you move the mouse pointer over a button or box, the name of the button or box also displays below it. This name is called a **ScreenTip**.

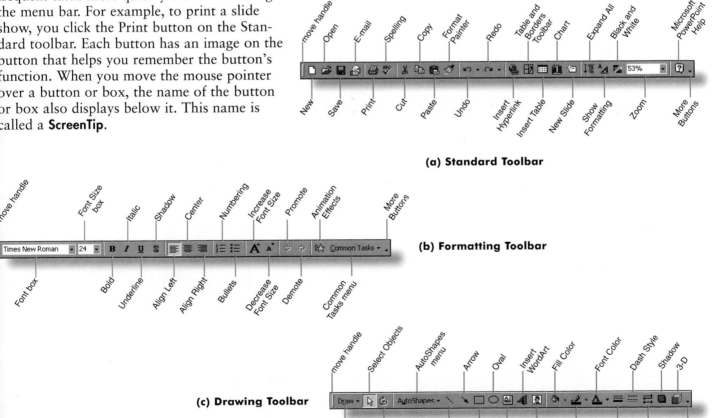

(a) Standard Toolbar

(b) Formatting Toolbar

(c) Drawing Toolbar

FIGURE 1-8

Toolbars

To display more of the PowerPoint window, you can hide a toolbar you no longer need. To hide a toolbar, right-click any toolbar and then click the check mark next to the toolbar you want to hide.

Figures 1-8a, 1-8b, and 1-8c on the previous page illustrate the Standard, Formatting, and Drawing toolbars and describe the functions of the buttons. Each of the buttons and list boxes will be explained in detail when they are used in the projects.

Remember, both the Standard and Formatting toolbars are by default on the same row immediately below the menu bar. Usually, the Standard toolbar displays on the left of the row and the Formatting toolbar displays on the right (Figure 1-9a).

To view the entire Formatting toolbar, double-click the move handle on its left edge or drag the move handle to the left. When you show the complete Formatting toolbar, a portion of the Standard toolbar is hidden (Figure 1-9b). To display the entire Standard toolbar, double-click its move handle. PowerPoint slides the Formatting toolbar to the right so the toolbars return to the way they look in Figure 1-9a.

An alternative to sliding one toolbar over another is to use the More Buttons button on a toolbar to display the buttons that are hidden (Figure 1-9c).

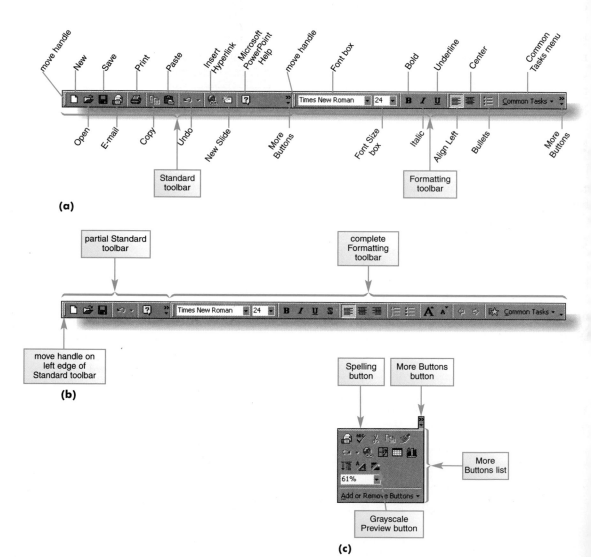

FIGURE 1-9

As with the menus, PowerPoint will personalize the toolbars. That is, if you use a hidden button on a partially displayed toolbar, PowerPoint will remove the button from the More Buttons list (Figure 1-9c) and place it on the toolbar. For example, if you click the Spelling button and then the Grayscale Preview button on the Standard toolbar (Figure 1-9c), PowerPoint will display these buttons on the Standard toolbar and remove buttons from the Standard or Formatting toolbars to make room on the row.

STATUS BAR Immediately above the Windows taskbar at the bottom of the screen is the status bar. The **status bar** consists of a message area and a presentation design template identifier (Figure 1-11 on page PP 1.18). Generally the message area displays the current slide number and the total number of slides in the slide show. For example, in Figure 1-11 the message area displays Slide 1 of 1. Slide 1 is the current slide, and of 1 indicates the slide show contains only 1 slide. The template identifier displays Default Design, which is the template PowerPoint uses initially.

PowerPoint has several additional toolbars you can display by pointing to Toolbars on the View menu and then clicking the respective name on the Toolbars submenu. You also can display a toolbar by pointing to a toolbar and right-clicking to display a shortcut menu, which lists the available toolbars. A **shortcut menu** contains a list of commands or items that relate to the item to which you are pointing when you right-click.

More About 2000

Personalizing

Have some fun building your presentation by adding sound cues. You can download files from the Microsoft Web site that play sounds when you scroll, open dialog boxes, and zoom in or out. For more information, visit the PowerPoint 2000 More About Web page (www.scsite.com/pp2000/more.htm) and click Personalizing.

Resetting Menus and Toolbars

Each project in this book begins with the menu bars and toolbars appearing as they did at initial installation of the software. To reset your toolbars and menus so they appear exactly as shown in this book, follow the steps outlined in Appendix C.

Displaying the Formatting Toolbar in Its Entirety

Perform the following steps to display the entire Formatting toolbar.

Steps To Display the Formatting Toolbar in Its Entirety

1 Point to the move handle on the Formatting toolbar (Figure 1-10).

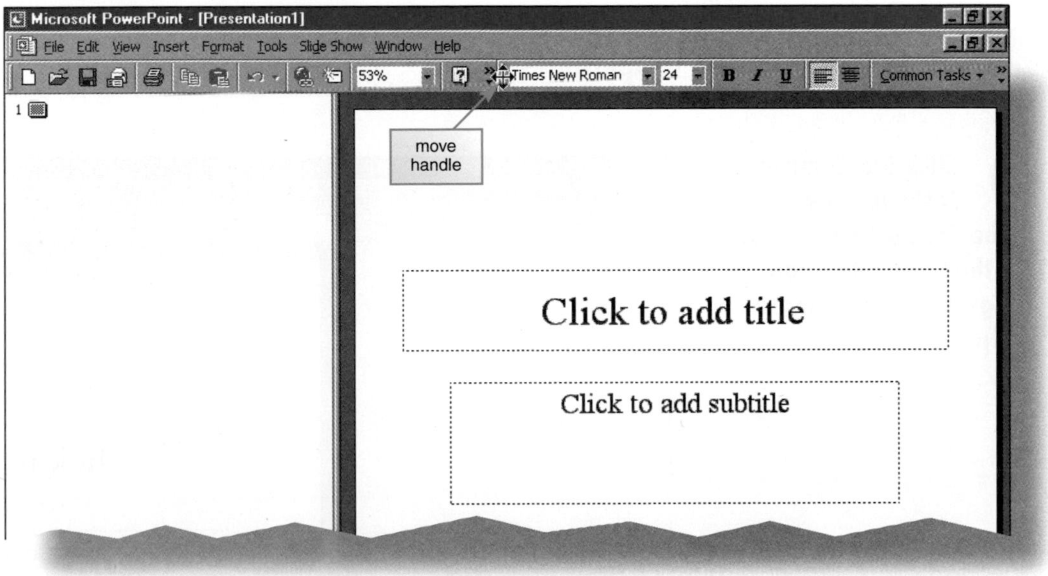

FIGURE 1-10

2 **Double-click the move handle on the Formatting toolbar.**

The entire Formatting toolbar displays (Figure 1-11).

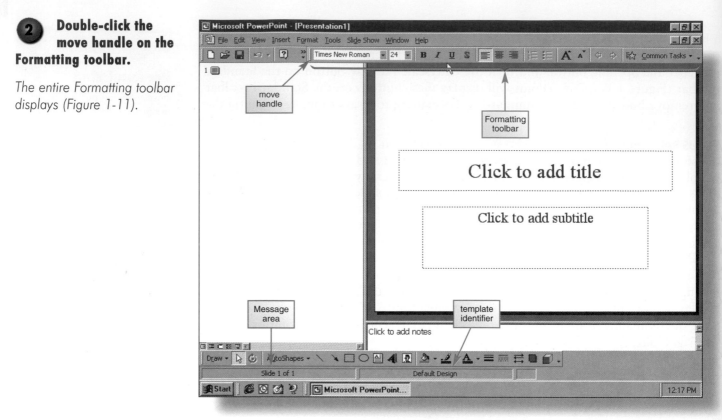

FIGURE 1-11

Choosing a Design Template

A **design template** provides consistency in design and color throughout the entire presentation. It determines the color scheme, font and font size, and layout of your presentation. Perform the following steps to choose a design template.

Steps **To Choose a Design Template**

1 **Click the Common Tasks menu button on the Formatting toolbar and then point to Apply Design Template (Figure 1-12).**

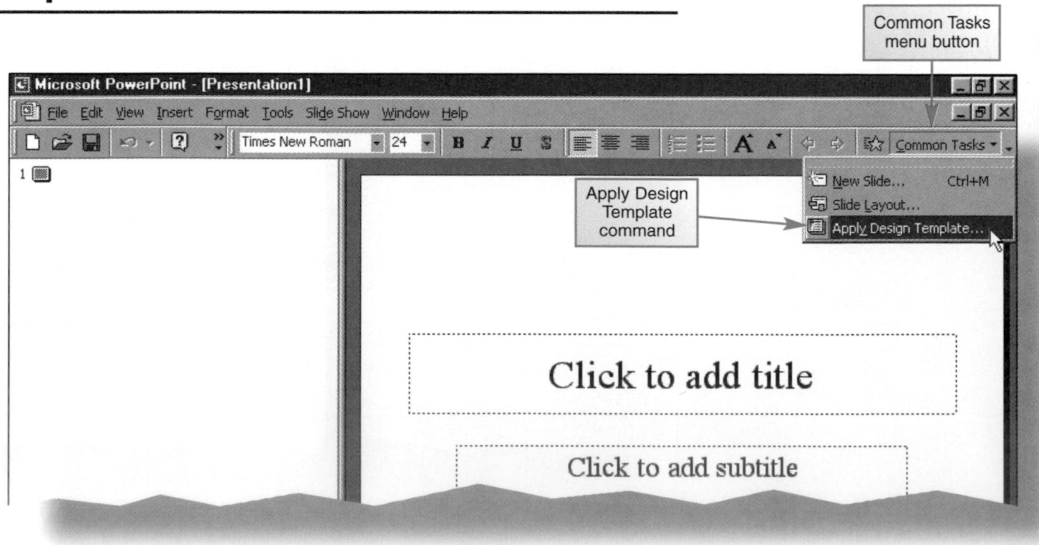

FIGURE 1-12

2 Click Apply Design Template.

The Apply Design Template dialog box displays (Figure 1-13). Numerous design template names display in the list box. Artsy is highlighted in the list, and a thumbnail view of the Artsy design template displays in the preview area. If the preview area does not display, click the Views button arrow and then click Preview. The Cancel button or the Close button can be used to close the Apply Design Template dialog box if you do not want to apply a new template.

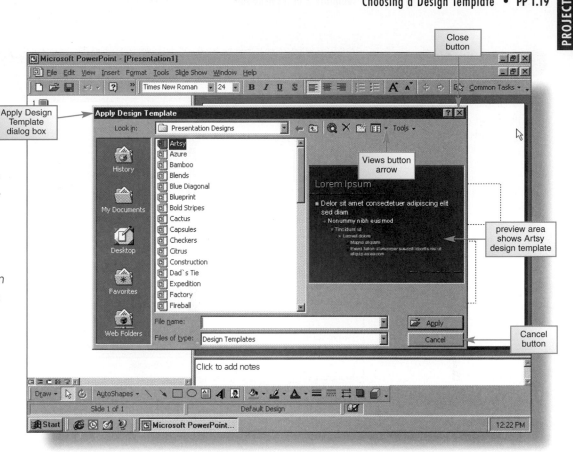

FIGURE 1-13

3 Click the down scroll arrow to scroll down the list of design templates until Straight Edge appears. Click Straight Edge. Point to the Apply button.

A preview of the Straight Edge design template displays in the preview area (Figure 1-14).

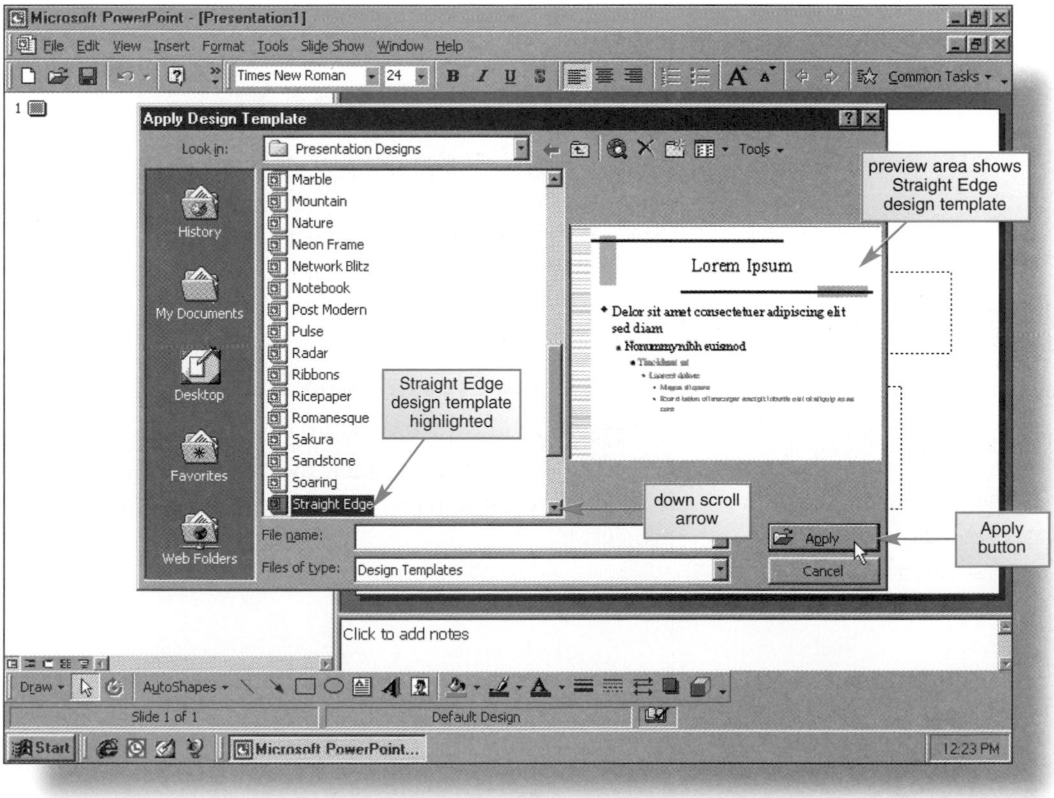

FIGURE 1-14

4 **Click the Apply button.**

Slide 1 displays with the Straight Edge design template (Figure 1-15).

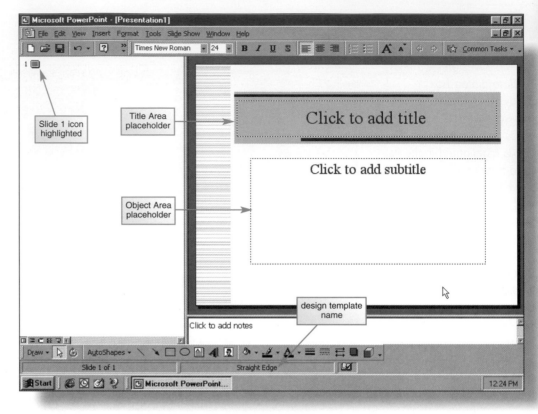

FIGURE 1-15

Creating a Title Slide

With the exception of a blank slide, PowerPoint also assumes every new slide has a title. To make creating your presentation easier, any text you type after a new slide displays becomes the title object. The AutoLayout for the title slide has a Title Area placeholder near the middle of the window and an Object Area placeholder directly below the Title Area placeholder (Figure 1-15).

Entering the Presentation Title

The presentation title for Project 1 is Effective Study Skills. As you begin typing in the Title Area placeholder, the title text displays immediately after the Slide 1 icon in the outline pane. Perform the following steps to create the title slide for this project.

To Enter the Presentation Title

1 **Click the label, Click to add title, located inside the Title Area placeholder.**

The insertion point is in the Title Area placeholder (Figure 1-16). The *insertion point* is a blinking vertical line (|), which indicates where the next character will display. The mouse pointer changes to an I-beam. A *selection rectangle* displays around the Title Area placeholder. The placeholder is selected as indicated by the border and sizing handles displaying on the edges.

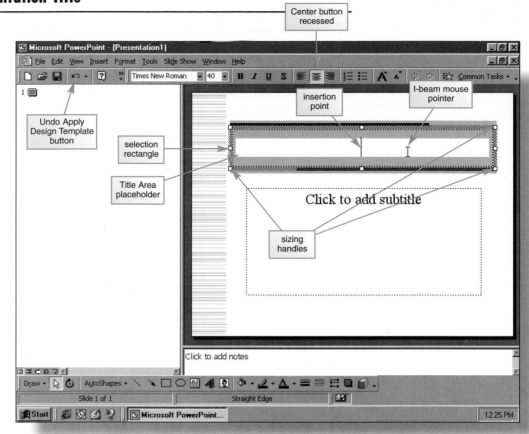

FIGURE 1-16

2 **Type** Effective Study Skills **in the Title Area placeholder. Do not press the ENTER key.**

The title text, Effective Study Skills, displays in the Title Area placeholder and in the outline pane (Figure 1-17). The current title text displays with the default font (Times New Roman) and default font size (40).

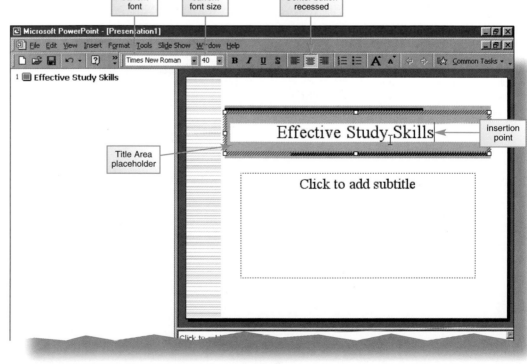

FIGURE 1-17

Enhancements

Microsoft touts the AutoFit text feature as an important PowerPoint 2000 upgrade. Other ease-of-use enhancements are the tri-pane view, the ability to create tables easily, and the self-paced introduction, which gives a useful overview of PowerPoint's key features. For more information, visit the PowerPoint 2000 More About Web page (www.scsite.com/pp2000/more.htm) and click Enhancements.

Notice that you do not press the ENTER key after the word Skills. If you press the ENTER key after typing the title, PowerPoint creates a new line, which would be a new second paragraph in the Title Area. You want only one paragraph in this text placeholder. A **paragraph** is a segment of text with the same format that begins when you press the ENTER key and ends when you press the ENTER key again. Therefore, do not press the ENTER key unless you want to create a two-paragraph title. Additionally, PowerPoint **line wraps** text that exceeds the width of the placeholder. For example, if the slide title was Effective College Study Skills, it would exceed the width of the Title Area placeholder and display on two lines.

One of PowerPoint's new features is **AutoFit text**. If you are creating your slide and need to squeeze an extra line in the text placeholder, PowerPoint will resize the existing text in the placeholder so that this extra line will fit on the screen.

Correcting a Mistake When Typing

If you type the wrong letter and notice the error before pressing the ENTER key, press the BACKSPACE key to erase all the characters back to and including the one that is incorrect. If you mistakenly press the ENTER key after entering the title and the insertion point is on the new line, simply press the BACKSPACE key to return the insertion point to the right of the letter s in the word Skills.

When you install PowerPoint, the default setting allows you to reverse up to the last 20 changes by clicking the **Undo button** on the Standard toolbar. The ScreenTip that displays when you point to the Undo button changes to indicate the type of change just made. For example, if you type text in the Title Area placeholder and then point to the Undo button, the ScreenTip that displays is Undo Typing. For clarity, when referencing the Undo button in this project, the name displaying in the ScreenTip is referenced. Another way to reverse changes is to click the Undo command on the Edit menu. Like the Undo button, the Undo command reflects the last type of change made to the presentation.

You can reapply a change that you reversed with the Undo button by clicking the Redo button on the Standard toolbar. Clicking the **Redo button** reverses the last undo action. The ScreenTip name reflects the type of reversal last performed.

Entering the Presentation Subtitle

The next step in creating the title slide is to enter the subtitle text into the Object Area placeholder. Perform the following steps to enter the presentation subtitle.

To Enter the Presentation Subtitle

1 **Click the label, Click to add subtitle, located inside the Object Area placeholder.**

The insertion point is in the Object Area placeholder (Figure 1-18). The mouse pointer changes to an I-beam indicating the mouse is in a text placeholder. The selection rectangle indicates the placeholder is selected. The default Object Area text font size is 32.

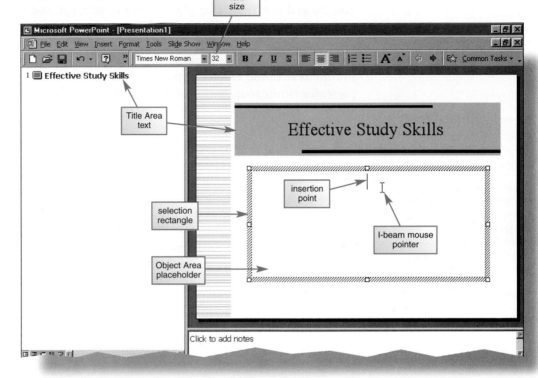

FIGURE 1-18

2 **Type** Strategies for College Success **and then press the ENTER key. Type** Presented by **and then press the ENTER key. Type** Seaview College **but do not press the ENTER key.**

The text displays in the Object Area placeholder and the outline pane (Figure 1-19). The insertion point displays after the letter e in College. A red wavy line displays under the word, Seaview, to indicate a possible spelling error. A light bulb may display in the top-left corner of the text place-holder, depending on your computer's settings. The Office Assistant generates this light bulb to give you design tips.

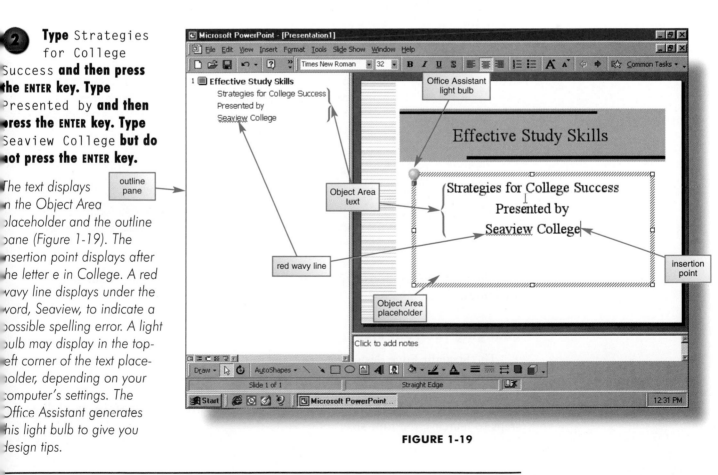

FIGURE 1-19

The previous section created a title slide using an AutoLayout for the title slide. PowerPoint displayed the title slide layout because you created a new presentation. You clicked the Title Area placeholder to select it and then typed your title. In general, to type text in any text placeholder, click the text placeholder and begin typing. You could, however, enter text in the Title Area placeholder without selecting this placeholder because PowerPoint assumes every slide has a title. You also added subtitle text in the Object Area placeholder. While this information identifying the presenter is not required, it often is useful for the audience.

Text Attributes

Text Attributes

An extensive glossary of typography terms is available at the Microsoft Web site. The information includes a diagram illustrating the text attributes. For more information, visit the PowerPoint 2000 More About Web page (www.scsite.com/pp2000/more.htm) and click Attributes.

This presentation is using the Straight Edge design template. Each design template has its own text attributes. A **text attribute** is a characteristic of the text, such as font, font size, font style, or text color. You can adjust text attributes any time before, during, or after you type the text. Recall that a design template determines the color scheme, font and font size, and layout of your presentation. Most of the time, you use the design template's text attributes and color scheme. Occasionally you may want to change the way your presentation looks, however, and still keep a particular design template. PowerPoint gives you that flexibility. You can use the design template and change the text's color, font size, font, and font style. Table 1-2 explains the different text attributes available in PowerPoint.

Table 1-2 Design Template Text Attributes	
ATTRIBUTE	DESCRIPTION
Color	Defines the color of text. Displaying text in color requires a color monitor. Printing text in color requires a color printer or plotter.
Font	Defines the appearance and shape of letters, numbers, and special characters.
Font size	Specifies the size of characters on the screen. Character size is gauged by a measurement system called points. A single point is about 1/72 of an inch in height. Thus, a character with a point size of eighteen is about 18/72 (or 1/4) of an inch in height.
Font style	Defines text characteristics. Font styles include plain, italic, bold, shadowed, and underlined. Text may have one or more font styles at a time.
Subscript	Defines the placement of a character in relationship to another. A subscript character displays or prints slightly below and immediately to one side of another character.
Superscript	Defines the placement of a character in relationship to another. A superscript character displays or prints above and immediately to one side of another character.

The next two sections explain how to change the font size and font style attributes.

Changing the Font Size

The Straight Edge design template default font size is 40 points for title text and 32 points for body text. A point is 1/72 of an inch in height. Thus, a character with a point size of 40 is about 40/72 (or 5/9) of an inch in height. Slide 1 requires you to increase the font size for the paragraph, Effective Study Skills. Perform the following steps to increase the font size.

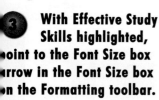

To Increase Font Size

1 **Position the mouse pointer in the Title Area placeholder and then triple-click.**

PowerPoint selects the entire line (Figure 1-20). You select an entire line quickly by triple-clicking any area within the Title Area placeholder.

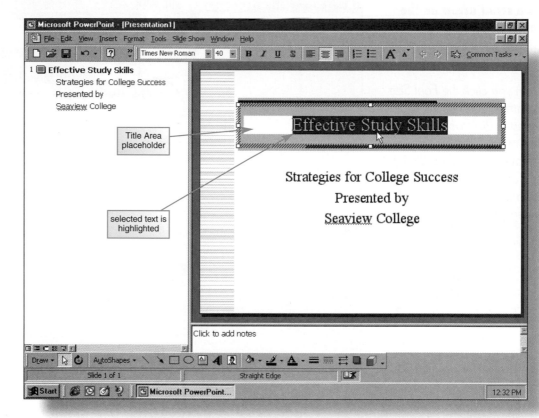

FIGURE 1-20

3 **With Effective Study Skills highlighted, point to the Font Size box arrow in the Font Size box on the Formatting toolbar.**

When you point to a button or other areas on a toolbar, PowerPoint displays a Screen-Tip. A ScreenTip contains the name of the tool to which you are pointing. When pointing to the Font Size box or the Font Size box arrow, the ScreenTip displays the words, Font Size (Figure 1-21). The Font Size box indicates that the title text is 40 points.

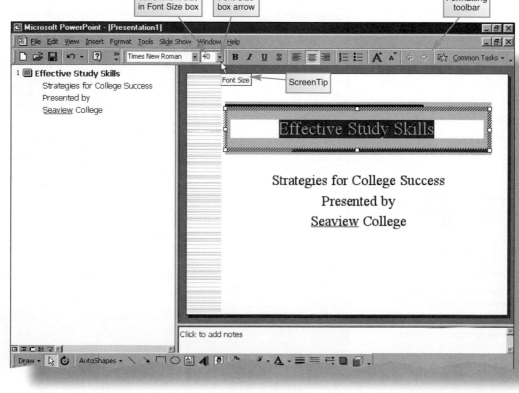

FIGURE 1-21

④ Click the Font Size box arrow, click the down scroll arrow on the Font Size scroll bar until 54 appears, and then point to 54.

*When you click the **Font Size box arrow**, a list of available font sizes displays in the Font Size list box. The font sizes displayed depend on the current font, which is Times New Roman. Font size 54 is highlighted (Figure 1-22).*

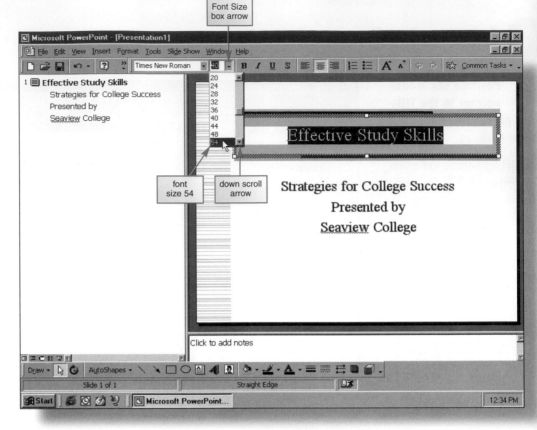

FIGURE 1-22

⑤ Click 54.

The title text, Effective Study Skills, increases in font size to 54 points (Figure 1-23). The Font Size box on the Formatting toolbar displays 54, indicating the selected text has a font size of 54.

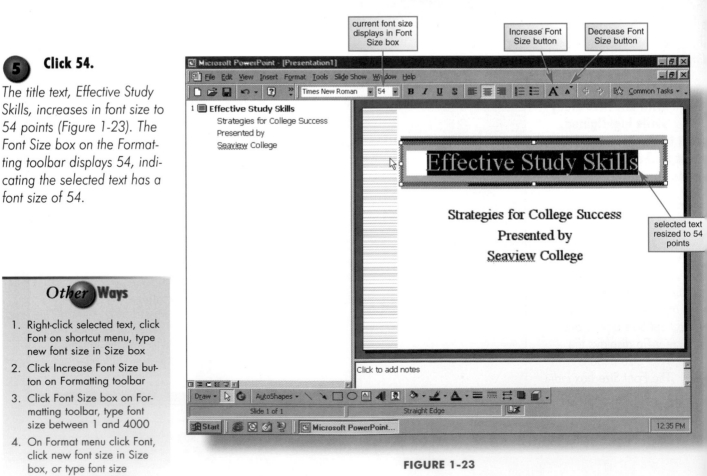

FIGURE 1-23

Other Ways

1. Right-click selected text, click Font on shortcut menu, type new font size in Size box

2. Click Increase Font Size button on Formatting toolbar

3. Click Font Size box on Formatting toolbar, type font size between 1 and 4000

4. On Format menu click Font, click new font size in Size box, or type font size between 1 and 4000

You also can use the **Increase Font Size button** on the Formatting toolbar to increase the font size. Each time you click the button, the font size becomes larger in preset increments. If you need to decrease the font size, click the Font Size box arrow and select a size smaller than 40. Another method is to click the **Decrease Font Size button** on the Formatting toolbar. The font size will become smaller in preset increments each time you click the button.

Changing the Style of Text to Italic

Text font styles include plain, italic, bold, shadowed, and underlined. PowerPoint allows you to use one or more text font styles in your presentation. Perform the following steps to add emphasis to the title slide by changing plain text to italic text.

Steps To Change the Text Font Style to Italic

1 **Triple-click the paragraph, Presented by, in the Object Area text placeholder, and then point to the Italic button on the Formatting toolbar.**

The paragraph, Presented by, is highlighted (Figure 1-24). The Italic button is three-dimensional.

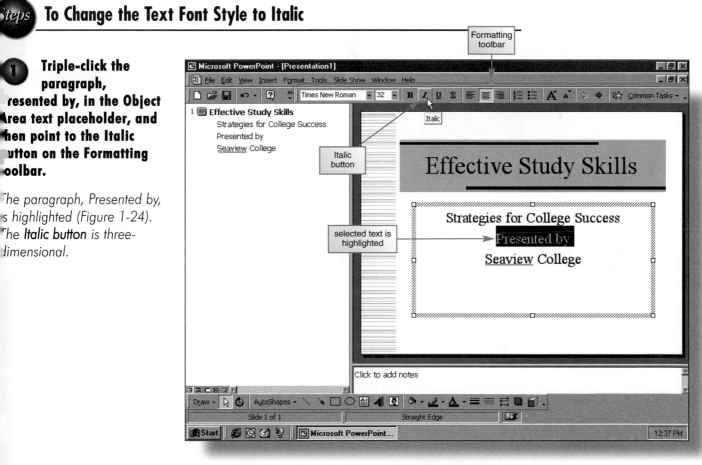

FIGURE 1-24

2 **Click the Italic button.**

The text is italicized in both the slide and outline panes, and the Italic button is recessed on the Formatting toolbar (Figure 1-25).

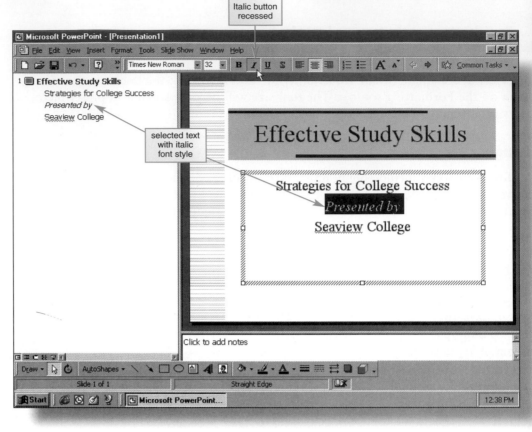

FIGURE 1-25

To remove italics from text, select the italicized text and then click the Italic button. As a result, the Italic button is not recessed, and the text does not have the italic font style.

Saving the Presentation on a Floppy Disk

While you are building your presentation, the computer stores it in main memory. It is important to save your presentation frequently because the presentation will be lost if the computer is turned off or you lose electrical power. Another reason to save your work is that if you run out of lab time before completing your project, you may finish the project later without starting over. You must, therefore, save any presentation you will use later. Before you continue with Project 1, save the work completed thus far. Perform the following steps to save a presentation on a floppy disk using the Save button on the Standard toolbar.

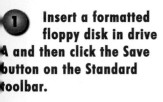

To Save a Presentation on a Floppy Disk

1 **Insert a formatted floppy disk in drive A and then click the Save button on the Standard toolbar.**

The Save As dialog box displays (Figure 1-26). The default folder, My Documents, displays in the Save in box. Effective Study Skills displays highlighted in the File name box because PowerPoint uses the words in the Title Area placeholder as the default file name. Presentation displays in the Save as type box. Clicking the Cancel button closes the Save As dialog box.

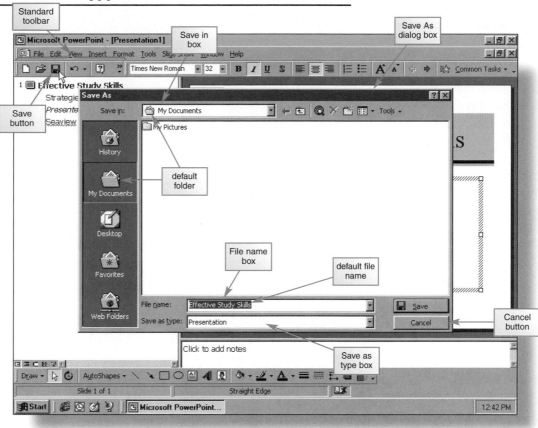

FIGURE 1-26

2 **Type** Studying **in the File name box. Do not press the ENTER key after typing the file name.**

The name, Studying, displays in the File name box (Figure 1-27).

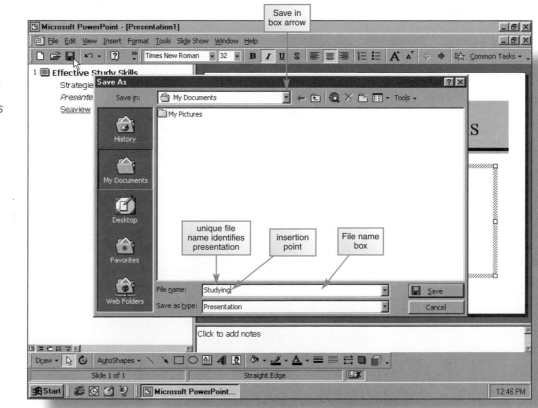

FIGURE 1-27

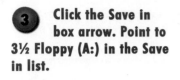

Click the Save in box arrow. Point to 3½ Floppy (A:) in the Save in list.

The Save in list displays a list of locations to which you can save your presentation (Figure 1-28). Your list may look different depending on the configuration of your system. 3½ Floppy (A:) is highlighted.

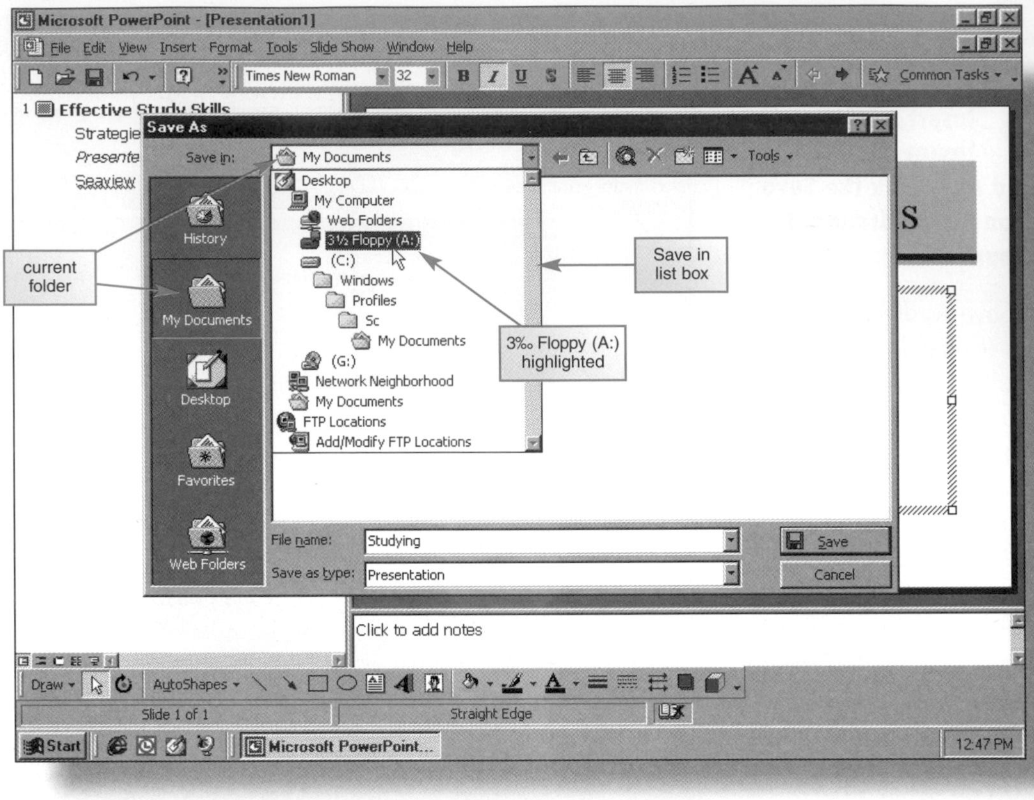

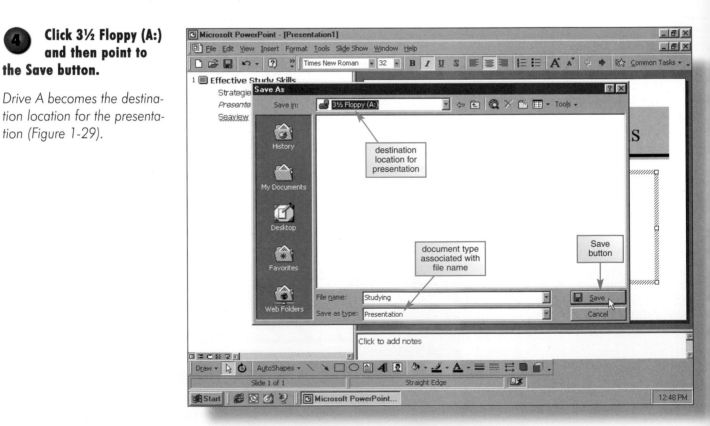

FIGURE 1-28

Click 3½ Floppy (A:) and then point to the Save button.

Drive A becomes the destination location for the presentation (Figure 1-29).

FIGURE 1-29

5 **Click the Save button.**

PowerPoint saves the presentation to your floppy disk in drive A. The title bar displays the file name, Studying, used to save the presentation (Figure 1-30).

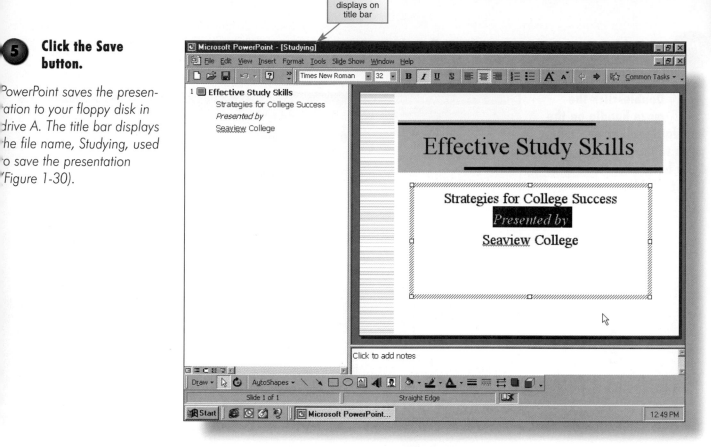

file name displays on title bar

FIGURE 1-30

PowerPoint automatically appends the extension .ppt to the file name, Studying. The **.ppt** extension stands for **PowerPoint**. Although the slide show, Studying, is saved on a floppy disk, it also remains in main memory and displays on the screen.

It is a good practice to save periodically while you are working on a project. By doing so, you protect yourself from losing all the work you have done since the last time you saved.

Other Ways

1. On File menu click Save As
2. Press CTRL+S or press SHIFT+F12

Adding a New Slide to a Presentation

The title slide for your presentation is created. The next step is to add the first bulleted list slide immediately after the current slide in Project 1. Usually when you create your presentation, you add slides with text, graphics, or charts. When you add a new slide, PowerPoint displays a dialog box for you to choose one of the 24 different AutoLayouts. These AutoLayouts have placeholders for various objects. Some placeholders allow you to double-click the placeholder and then access other PowerPoint objects. More information about using AutoLayout placeholders to add graphics follows in subsequent projects. Perform the steps on the next page to add a new slide using the Bulleted List AutoLayout.

Steps **To Add a New Slide Using the Bulleted List AutoLayout**

1 **Double-click the move handle on the Standard toolbar and then point to the New Slide button (Figure 1-31).**

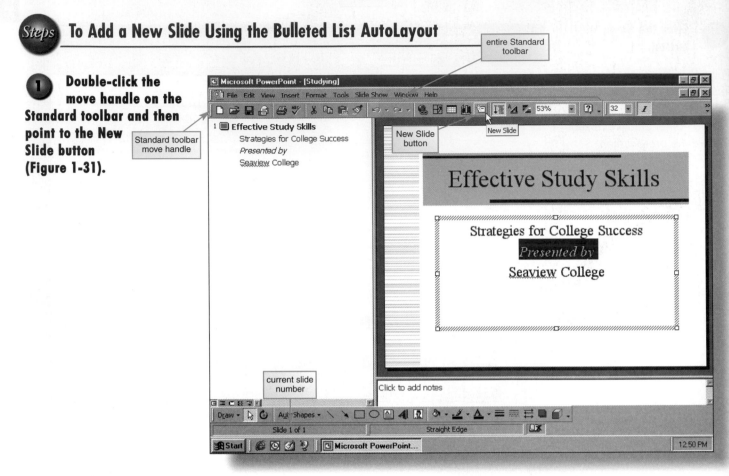

FIGURE 1-31

2 **Click the New Slide button. When the New Slide dialog box displays, point to the OK button.**

The New Slide dialog box displays (Figure 1-32). The Bulleted List AutoLayout is selected, and the AutoLayout title, Bulleted List, displays at the bottom-right corner of the New Slide dialog box.

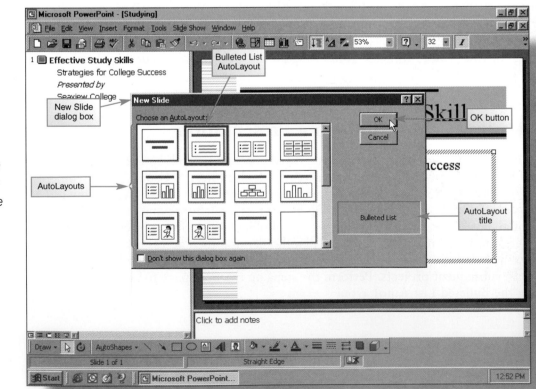

FIGURE 1-32

③ Click the OK button.

Slide 2 displays keeping the attributes of the Straight Edge design template using the Bulleted List AutoLayout (Figure 1-33). Slide 2 of 2 displays on the status bar. The vertical scroll bar displays in the slide pane. The bullet appears as a diamond.

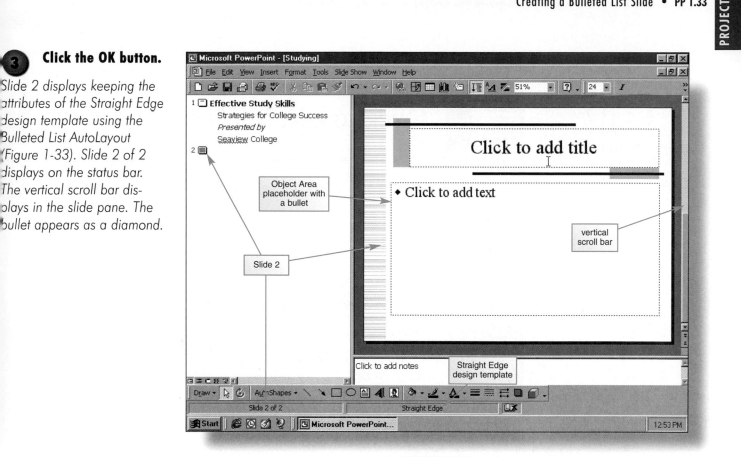

FIGURE 1-33

Because the Bulleted List AutoLayout was selected, PowerPoint displays Slide 2 with a Title Area placeholder and an Object Area placeholder with a bullet. You can change the layout for a slide at any time during the creation of your presentation by clicking the Common Tasks menu button on the Formatting toolbar and then clicking the Slide Layout button. You then can double-click the AutoLayout of your choice.

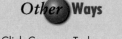

Other Ways

1. Click Common Tasks menu button on Formatting toolbar, click New Slide
2. On Insert menu click New Slide
3. Press CTRL+M

Creating a Bulleted List Slide

The bulleted list slides in Figure 1-2 on page PP 1.9 contain more than one level of bulleted text. A slide with more than one level of bulleted text is called a **multi-level bulleted list slide**. A **level** is a position within a structure, such as an outline, that indicates a magnitude of importance. PowerPoint allows for five paragraph levels. Each paragraph level has an associated bullet. The bullet font is dependent on the design template. Figure 1-34 on the next page identifies the five paragraph levels and the bullet fonts for the Straight Edge design template. Beginning with the Second level, each paragraph indents to the right of the preceding level.

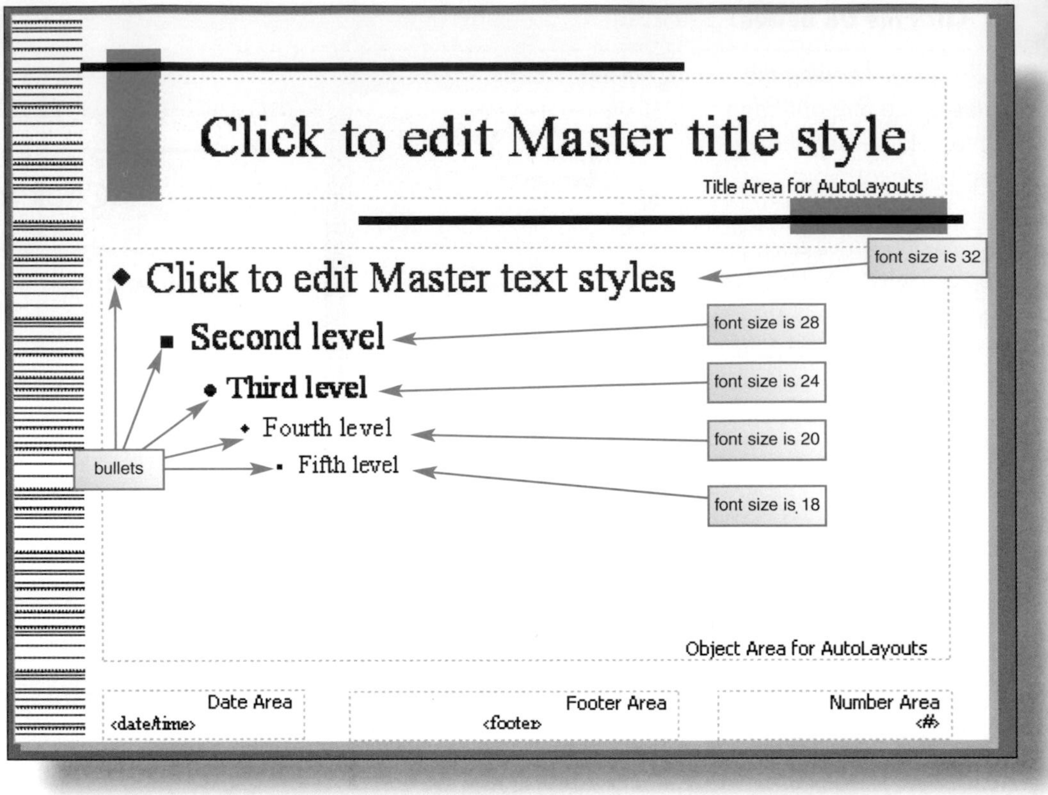

FIGURE 1-34

An indented paragraph is **demoted**, or pushed down to a lower level. For example, if you demote a First level paragraph, it becomes a Second level paragraph. This lower-level paragraph is a subset of the higher-level paragraph. It usually contains information that supports the topic in the paragraph immediately above it. You demote a paragraph by clicking the **Demote button** on the Formatting toolbar.

When you want to raise a paragraph from a lower level to a higher level, you **promote** the paragraph by clicking the **Promote button** on the Formatting toolbar.

Creating a multi-level bulleted list slide requires several steps. Initially, you enter a slide title in the Title Area placeholder. Next, you select the Object Area text placeholder. Then you type the text for the multi-level bulleted list, demoting and promoting paragraphs as needed. The next several sections explain how to add a multi-level bulleted list slide.

More About 2000

Slide Masters

Each design template has a corresponding slide master designed by Microsoft graphic artists. The text attributes and color schemes are developed to coordinate with each other and to evoke audience reactions, such as excitement or relaxation.

Entering a Slide Title

PowerPoint assumes every new slide has a title. The title for Slide 2 is Managing Your Time. Perform the following step to enter this title.

Steps ## To Enter a Slide Title

1 **If necessary, click the Title Area placeholder and then type** Managing your Time **as the title. Do not press the** ENTER **key.**

The title, Managing Your Time, displays in the Title Area placeholder and in the outline pane (Figure 1-35). The insertion point displays after the e in Time.

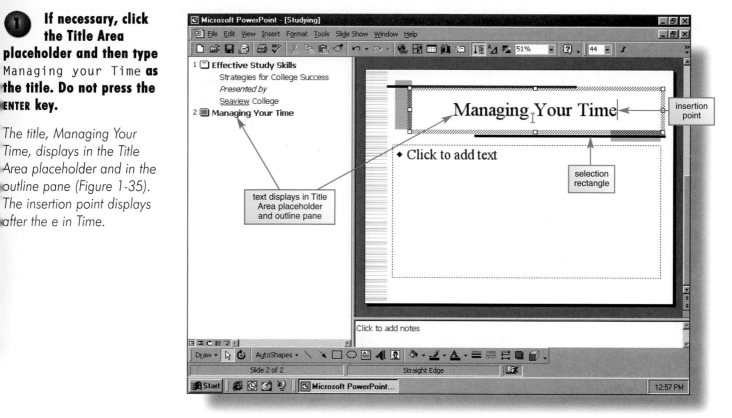

FIGURE 1-35

Selecting an Object Area Placeholder

Before you can type text in the Object Area placeholder, you first must select it. Perform the step on the next page to select the Object Area placeholder on Slide 2.

Steps **To Select an Object Area Placeholder**

① Click the bulleted paragraph labeled, Click to add text.

The insertion point displays immediately after the bullet on Slide 2 (Figure 1-36). The mouse pointer may change shape if you move it away from the bullet.

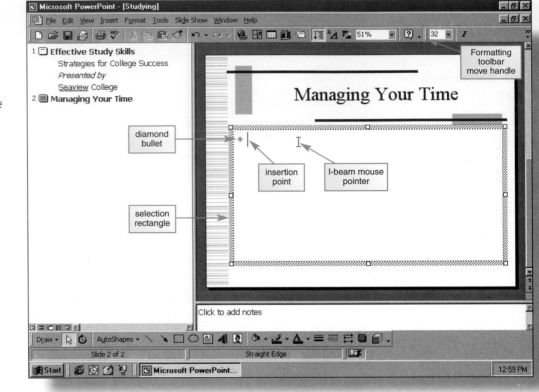

FIGURE 1-36

1. Press CTRL+ENTER

Typing a Multi-level Bulleted List

Recall that a bulleted list is a list of paragraphs, each of which is preceded by a bullet. Also recall that a paragraph is a segment of text ended by pressing the ENTER key. The next step is to type the multi-level bulleted list, which consists of the six entries (Figure 1-2 on page PP 1.9). Perform the following steps to type a multi-level bulleted list.

To Type a Multi-level Bulleted List

1 **Double-click the move handle on the Formatting toolbar. Type** Make a weekly schedule **and then press the ENTER key.**

The paragraph, Make a weekly schedule, displays (Figure 1-37). The font size is 32. The insertion point displays after the second bullet. When you press the ENTER key, PowerPoint ends one paragraph and begins a new paragraph. Because you are using the Bulleted List Auto-Layout, PowerPoint places a diamond bullet in front of the new paragraph.

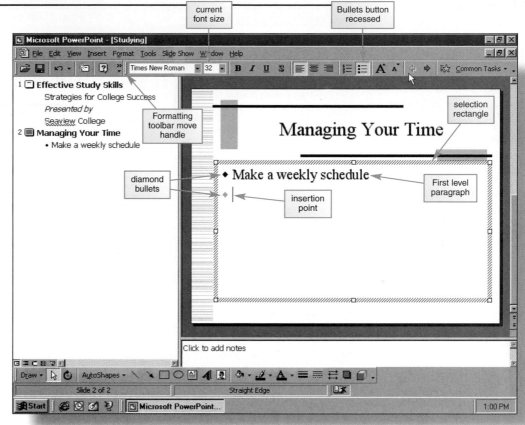

FIGURE 1-37

2 **Point to the Demote button (Figure 1-38).**

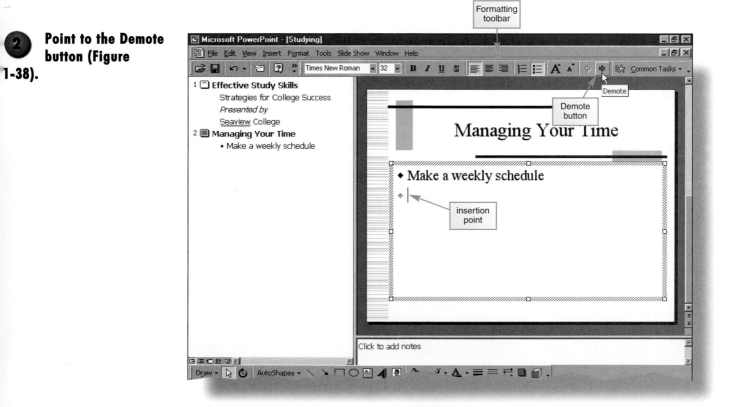

FIGURE 1-38

Microsoft **PowerPoint 2000**

③ Click the Demote button.

The second paragraph indents under the first and becomes a Second level paragraph (Figure 1-39). Notice the bullet in front of the second paragraph changes from a diamond to a box, and the font size for the demoted paragraph now is 28. The insertion point displays after the box.

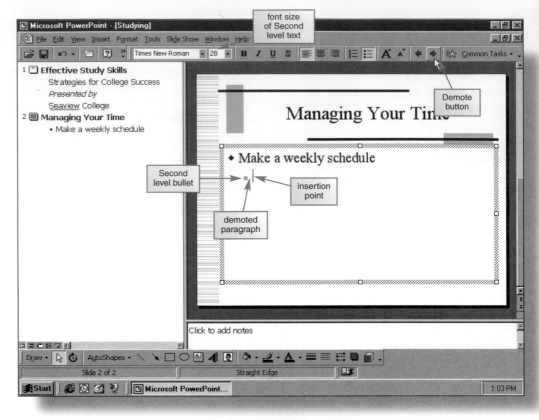

FIGURE 1-39

④ Type List specific study times for all subjects **and then press the ENTER key. Type** Plan time for recreation and sleep **and then press the ENTER key. Type** Spread study times throughout the week **and then press the ENTER key. Point to the Promote button.**

Three new Second level paragraphs display with boxes in both the slide and outline panes (Figure 1-40). When you press the ENTER key, PowerPoint adds a new paragraph at the same level as the previous paragraph.

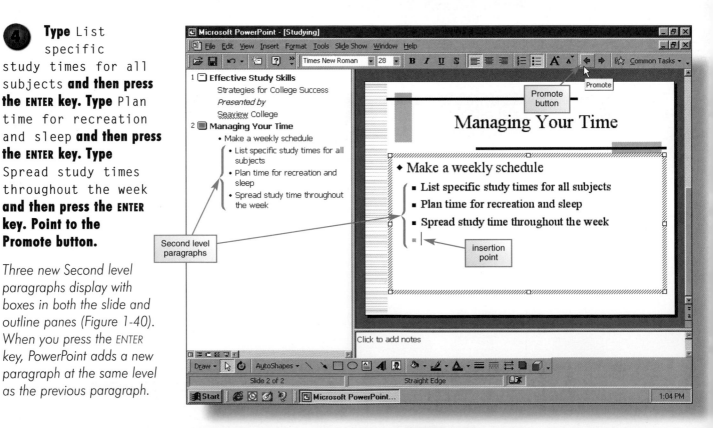

FIGURE 1-40

5 **Click the Promote button.**

The Second level paragraph becomes a First level paragraph (Figure 1-41). The bullet in front of the new paragraph changes from a box to a diamond, and the font size for the promoted paragraph is 32. The insertion point displays after the diamond bullet.

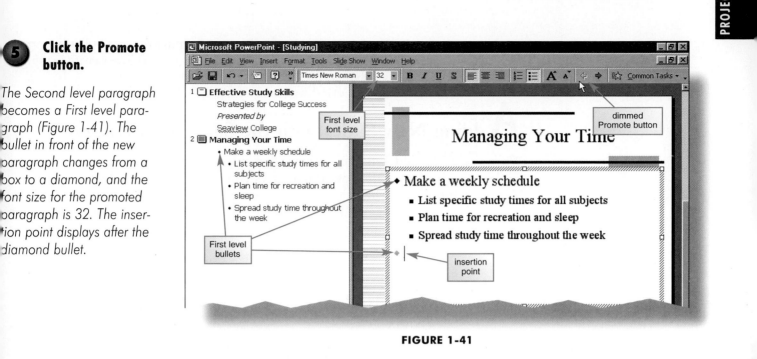

FIGURE 1-41

Perform the following steps to complete the text for Slide 2.

TO TYPE THE REMAINING TEXT FOR SLIDE 2

1 Type Stick to your schedule and then press the ENTER key.

2 Type Revise your schedule when necessary but do not press the ENTER key.

The insertion point displays after the y in necessary (Figure 1-42).

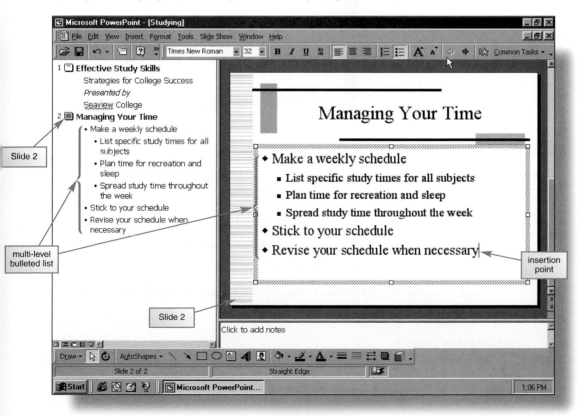

FIGURE 1-42

Notice that you did not press the ENTER key after typing the last bullet line in Step 2. If you press the ENTER key, a new bullet displays after the last entry on this slide. To remove an extra bullet, press the BACKSPACE key.

Adding New Slides with the Same AutoLayout

When you add a new slide to a presentation and want to keep the same AutoLayout used on the previous slide, PowerPoint gives you a shortcut. Instead of clicking the New Slide button and clicking an AutoLayout in the New Slide dialog box, you can press and hold down the SHIFT key and then click the New Slide button. Perform the following step to add a new slide (Slide 3) and keep the Bulleted List AutoLayout used on the previous slide.

Steps To Add a New Slide with the Same AutoLayout

1 **Press and hold down the SHIFT key, click the New Slide button on the Standard toolbar, and then release the SHIFT key.**

Slide 3 displays the Bulleted List AutoLayout (Figure 1-43). Slide 3 of 3 displays on the status bar.

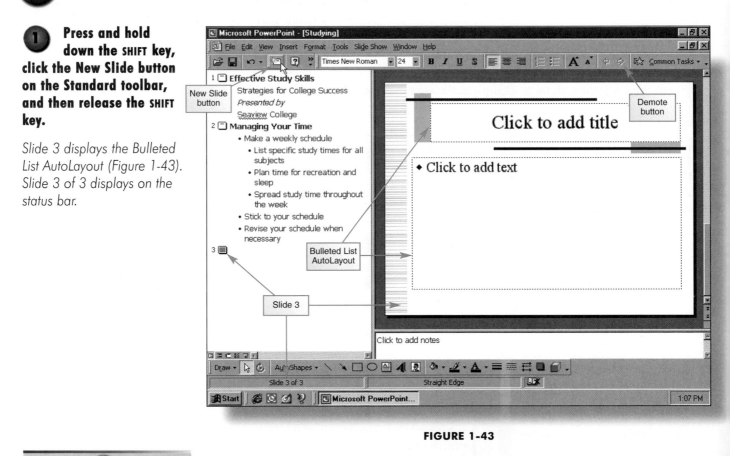

FIGURE 1-43

Other Ways

1. Press SHIFT+CTRL+M

Slide 3 is added to the presentation. Perform the following steps to add text to Slide 3 and to create a multi-level bulleted list.

TO COMPLETE SLIDE 3

1 Type Attending Class in the Title Area placeholder.

2 Press CTRL+ENTER to move the insertion point to the Object Area placeholder.

3 Type Sit in the front of the room and then press the ENTER key.

4 Type Ask questions at appropriate times and then press the ENTER key.

5 Type Take notes and then press the ENTER key.

6 Click the Demote button.

7 Type Rephrase ideas in your own words and then press the ENTER key.

8 Type Review immediately after class but do not press the ENTER key.

Slide 3 displays as shown in Figure 1-44. The Office Assistant light bulb may display to offer design help. If so, you may click the light bulb next to the Office Assistant to see a tip. For additional help on using the Office Assistant, refer to Appendix A.

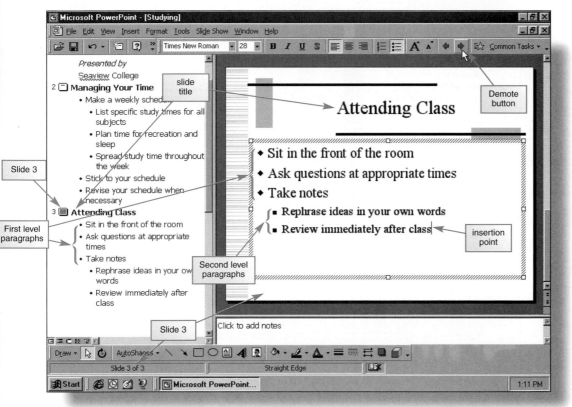

FIGURE 1-44

Slide 4, also a multi-level bulleted list, is the last slide in this presentation. Perform the following steps to create Slide 4.

TO CREATE SLIDE 4

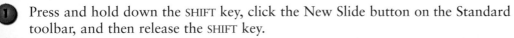

1 Press and hold down the SHIFT key, click the New Slide button on the Standard toolbar, and then release the SHIFT key.

2 Type Reading Your Textbooks in the Title Area placeholder.

3 Press CTRL+ENTER to move the insertion point to the Object Area placeholder.

4 Type Survey the assignment and then press the ENTER key.

5 Click the Demote button. Type Read the summary and chapter questions and then press the ENTER key.

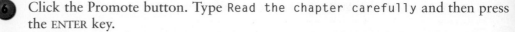

6 Click the Promote button. Type Read the chapter carefully and then press the ENTER key.

7 Type Recite the material in your own words and then press the ENTER key.

8 Type Write brief notes in the margins and then press the ENTER key.

9 Type Review the entire assignment but do not press the ENTER key.

The Title Area and Object Area text objects display in the slide and outline panes (Figure 1-45). The Office Assistant light bulb may display to offer design help.

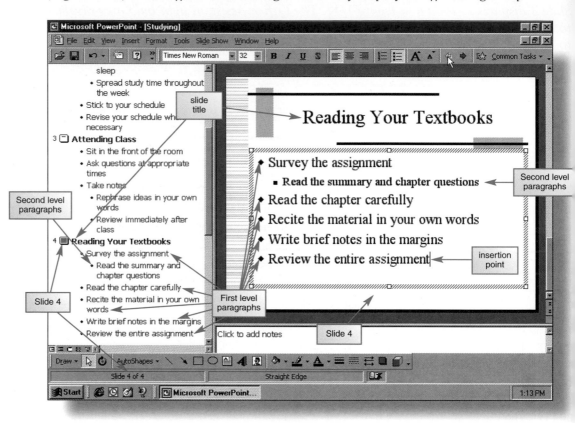

FIGURE 1-45

All slides for the Studying presentation are created. This presentation consists of a title slide and three multi-level bulleted list slides.

Ending a Slide Show with a Black Slide

After the last slide in the slide show displays, the default PowerPoint setting is to end your presentation with a black slide. This black slide displays only when the slide show is running and concludes your slide show gracefully so your audience never sees the PowerPoint window. A black slide ends all slide shows until the option setting is deactivated. Perform the following steps to verify the End with black slide option is activated.

More *About*

Black Slides

Insert a blank, black slide between sections of a large presentation or when you want to pause for discussion. The black slide focuses the audience's attention on you, the speaker, and away from the screen display.

To End a Slide Show with a Black Slide

1 **Click Tools on the menu bar and then point to Options (Figure 1-46).**

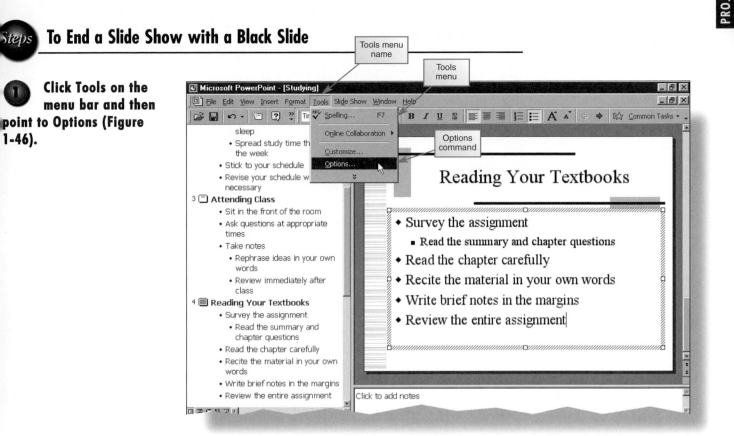

FIGURE 1-46

2 **Click Options. If necessary, click the View tab when the Options dialog box opens. Verify a check mark displays in the End with black slide check box. If a check mark does not display, click the End with black slide check box.**

The Options dialog box displays (Figure 1-47). The View sheet contains settings for the overall PowerPoint display and for a particular slide show.

3 **Click the OK button.**

The End with black slide option is activated.

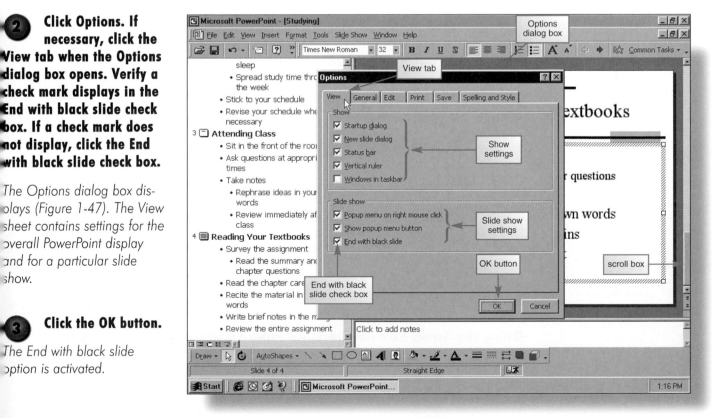

FIGURE 1-47

Now that all aspects of the presentation are complete, you need to save the additions and changes you have made to your Studying presentation.

Saving a Presentation with the Same File Name

Saving frequently cannot be overemphasized. When you first saved the presentation, you clicked the Save button on the Standard toolbar and the Save dialog box displayed. When you want to save the changes made to the presentation after your last save, you again click the Save button. This time, however, the Save dialog box does not display because PowerPoint updates the document called Studying.ppt on your floppy disk. Perform the following steps to save the presentation again.

TO SAVE A PRESENTATION WITH THE SAME FILE NAME

1 Be sure your floppy disk is in drive A.

2 Click the Save button on the Standard toolbar.

PowerPoint overwrites the old Studying.ppt document on the floppy disk in drive A with the revised presentation document. Slide 4 displays in the PowerPoint window.

Moving to Another Slide in Normal View

When creating or editing a presentation in normal view, you often want to display a slide other than the current one. You can move to another slide using several methods. In the outline pane, you can point to any of the text in a particular slide to display that slide in the slide pane, or you can drag the scroll box on the vertical scroll bar up or down to move through the text in your presentation. In the slide pane, you can click the **Previous Slide** or **Next Slide** buttons on the vertical scroll bar. Clicking the Next Slide button advances to the next slide in the presentation. Clicking the Previous Slide button backs up to the slide preceding the current slide. You also can drag the scroll box on the vertical scroll bar. When you drag the scroll box, the **slide indicator** displays the number and the title of the slide you are about to display. Releasing the mouse button displays the slide.

A slide's **Zoom setting** affects the portion of the slide displaying in the slide pane. PowerPoint defaults to a setting of approximately 50% so the entire slide displays. This percentage depends on the size and type of your monitor. If you want to display a small portion of the current slide, you would zoom in by clicking the Zoom box arrow and then clicking the desired magnification. You can display the entire slide in the slide pane by clicking Fit in the Zoom list. The Zoom setting affects the action of the vertical and horizontal scroll bars. If Zoom is set so that the entire slide is not visible in the slide pane, clicking the up scroll arrow on the vertical scroll bar displays the next portion of your slide, not the previous slide.

More About

Zoom

You can increase your Zoom setting to as large as 400% when you want to see details on small objects. Likewise, you can decrease your Zoom setting to as small as 10%.

Using the Scroll Box on the Slide Pane to Move to Another Slide

Before continuing with Project 1, you want to display the title slide. Perform the following steps to move from Slide 4 to the Slide 1 using the scroll box on the slide pane vertical scroll bar.

Steps **To Use the Scroll Box on the Slide Pane to Move to Another Slide**

1 Position the mouse pointer on the scroll box. Press and hold down the left mouse button.

Slide: 4 of 4 Reading Your Textbooks displays in the slide indicator (Figure 1-48). The Slide 4 icon is shaded in the outline pane.

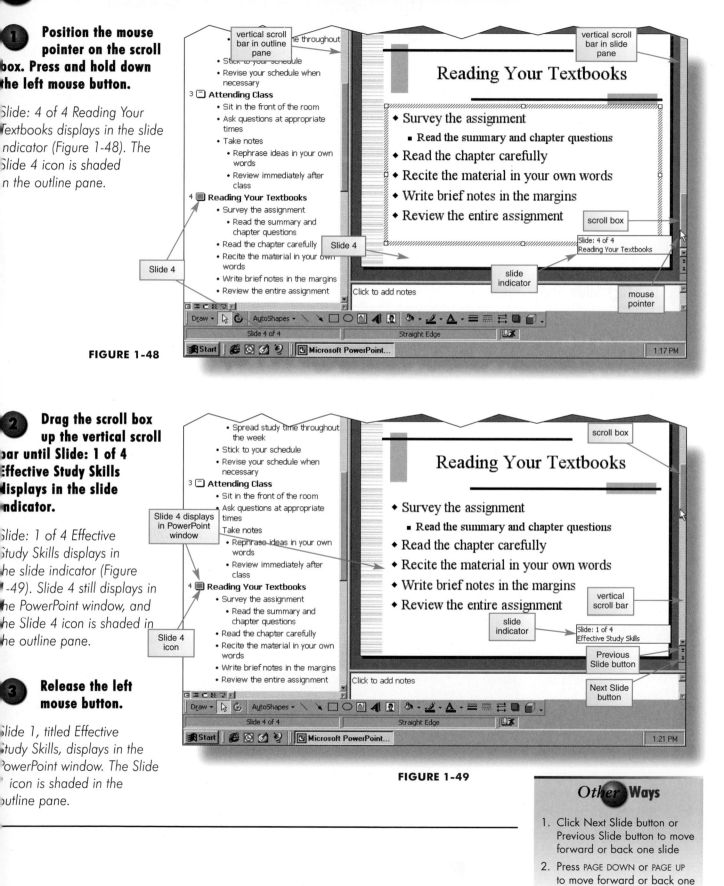

FIGURE 1-48

2 Drag the scroll box up the vertical scroll bar until Slide: 1 of 4 Effective Study Skills displays in the slide indicator.

Slide: 1 of 4 Effective Study Skills displays in the slide indicator (Figure 1-49). Slide 4 still displays in the PowerPoint window, and the Slide 4 icon is shaded in the outline pane.

3 Release the left mouse button.

Slide 1, titled Effective Study Skills, displays in the PowerPoint window. The Slide 1 icon is shaded in the outline pane.

FIGURE 1-49

Other Ways

1. Click Next Slide button or Previous Slide button to move forward or back one slide

2. Press PAGE DOWN or PAGE UP to move forward or back one slide

Viewing the Presentation Using Slide Show

The **Slide Show button**, located at the lower-left of the PowerPoint window above the status bar, allows you to display your presentation electronically using a computer. The computer acts like a slide projector, displaying each slide on a full screen. The full screen slide hides the toolbars, menus, and other PowerPoint window elements. Slide show view is used when making a presentation. You can start slide show view from any view: normal view, outline view, slide view, or slide sorter view.

Starting Slide Show View

Slide show view begins when you click the Slide Show button in the lower-left of the PowerPoint window above the status bar. PowerPoint then displays the current slide on the full screen without any of the PowerPoint window objects, such as the menu bar or toolbars. Perform the following steps to start slide show view.

Steps To Start Slide Show View

1 **Point to the Slide Show button in the lower-left of the PowerPoint window above the status bar.**

The Normal View button is recessed because you still are in normal view (Figure 1-50).

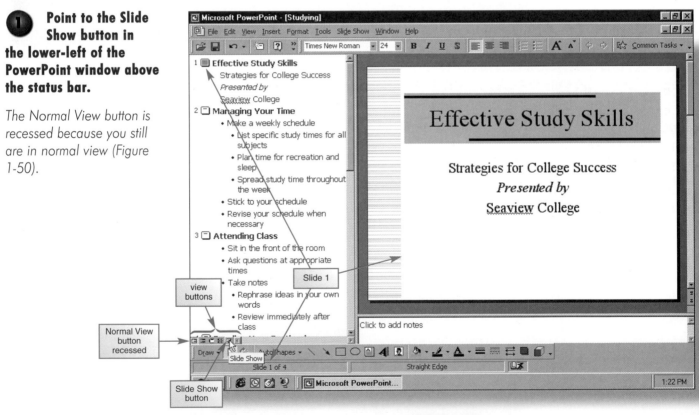

FIGURE 1-50

② Click the Slide Show button.

The title slide fills the screen (Figure 1-51). The PowerPoint window is hidden.

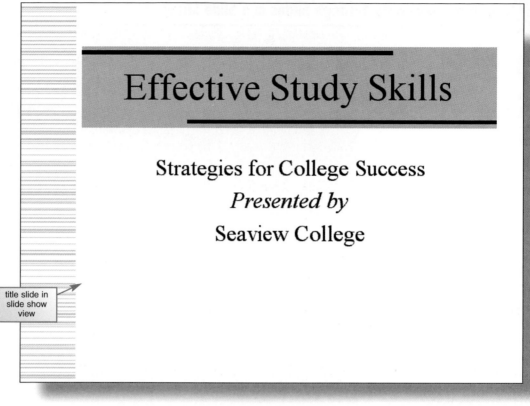

Effective Study Skills

Strategies for College Success
Presented by
Seaview College

title slide in slide show view

FIGURE 1-51

Other Ways

1. On View menu click Slide Show
2. Press F5

Advancing Through a Slide Show Manually

After you begin slide show view, you can move forward or backward through your slides. PowerPoint allows you to advance through your slides manually or automatically. Automatic advancing is discussed in a later project. Perform the steps on the next page to move manually through your slides.

Steps To Move Manually Through Slides in a Slide Show

1. **Click each slide until the Reading Your Textbooks slide (Slide 4) displays.**

Each slide in your presentation displays on the screen, one slide at a time. Each time you click the mouse button, the next slide displays.

2. **Click Slide 4.**

The black slide displays (Figure 1-52). The message at the top of the slide announces the end of the slide show. To return to normal view, click the black slide.

FIGURE 1-52

Other Ways

1. Press PAGE DOWN to advance one slide at a time, or press PAGE UP to go backward one slide at a time
2. Press RIGHT ARROW key to advance one slide at a time, or press LEFT ARROW key to go backward one slide at a time

Using the Popup Menu to Go to a Specific Slide

Slide show view has a shortcut menu, called **Popup menu**, that displays when you right-click a slide in slide show view. This menu contains commands to assist you during a slide show. For example, clicking the **Next command** moves you to the next slide. Clicking the **Previous command** moves you to the previous slide. You can go to any slide in your presentation by pointing to the **Go command** and then clicking Slide Navigator. The **Slide Navigator dialog box** contains a list of the slides in your presentation. Go to the requested slide by double-clicking the name of that slide.

Perform the following steps to go to the title slide (Slide 1) in your presentation.

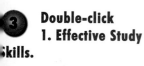

To Display the Popup Menu and Go to a Specific Slide

1 With the black slide displaying in slide show view, right-click the slide. Point to Go on the Popup menu, and then point to Slide Navigator on the Go submenu.

The Popup menu displays on the black slide, and the Go submenu displays (Figure 1-53). Your screen may look different because the Popup menu displays near the location of the mouse pointer at the time you right-click.

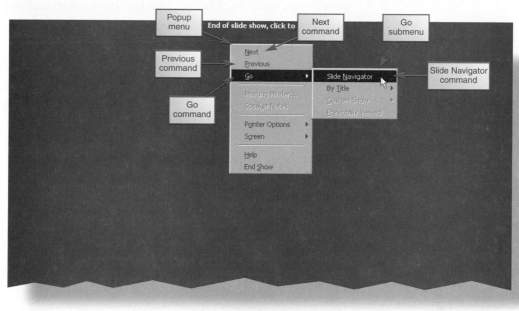

FIGURE 1-53

2 Click Slide Navigator. When the Slide Navigator dialog box displays, point to 1. Effective Study Skills in the Slide titles list.

The Slide titles list contains the title text of the slides in your presentation (Figure 1-54). You want to go to Slide 1 in your presentation. Slide 4 is the last slide viewed during your slide show.

3 Double-click 1. Effective Study Skills.

The title slide, Effective Study Skills, displays.

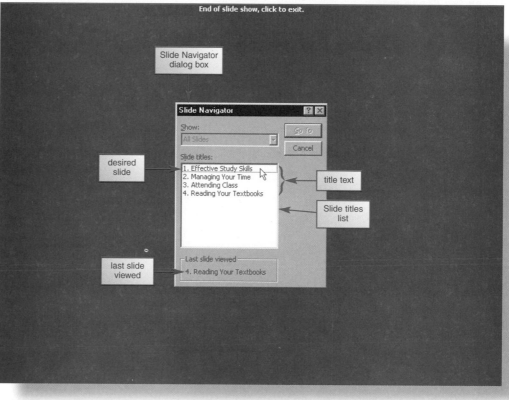

FIGURE 1-54

Other **Ways**

1. Right-click, point to Go, click Slide Navigator, type slide number, press ENTER

Additional Popup menu commands allow you to write meeting minutes or to create a list of action items during a slide show, change the mouse pointer to a pen that draws in various colors, blacken the screen, and end the slide show. Popup menu commands are discussed in subsequent projects.

Using the Popup Menu to End a Slide Show

The **End Show command** on the Popup menu exits slide show view and returns to the view you were in when you clicked the Slide Show button. Perform the following steps to end slide show view and return to normal view.

 To Use the Popup Menu to End a Slide Show

 Right-click the title slide.

The Popup menu displays on Slide 1.

2 **Point to End Show on the Popup menu.**

Your Popup menu may display in a different location (Figure 1-55).

3 **Click End Show.**

PowerPoint exits slide show view and returns to normal view. Slide 1 displays because it is the last slide displayed in slide show view.

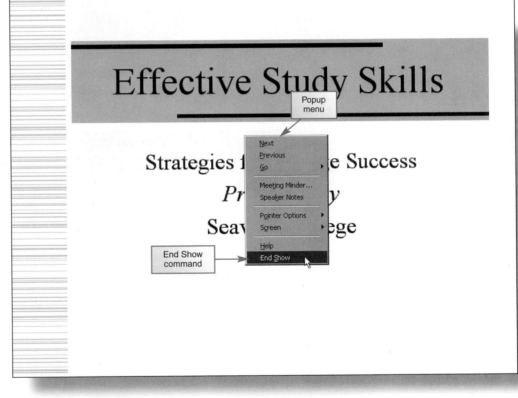

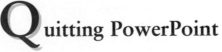

FIGURE 1-55

Other Ways

1. Click last slide in presentation to return to slide at which you began slide show view
2. Press ESC to display slide last viewed in slide show view

Quitting PowerPoint

The Studying presentation now is complete. When you quit PowerPoint, PowerPoint prompts you to save any changes made to the presentation since the last save, closes all PowerPoint windows, and then quits PowerPoint. Closing PowerPoint returns control to the desktop. Perform the following steps to quit PowerPoint.

To Quit PowerPoint

① **Point to the Close button on the title bar (Figure 1-56).**

② **Click the Close button.**

PowerPoint closes and the Windows desktop displays. If you made changes to the presentation since your last save, a Microsoft PowerPoint dialog box displays the question, Do you wish to save the changes you made to Studying?. Click the Yes button to save the changes to the presentation before closing PowerPoint. Click the No button to quit PowerPoint without saving the changes. Click the Cancel button to return to the presentation.

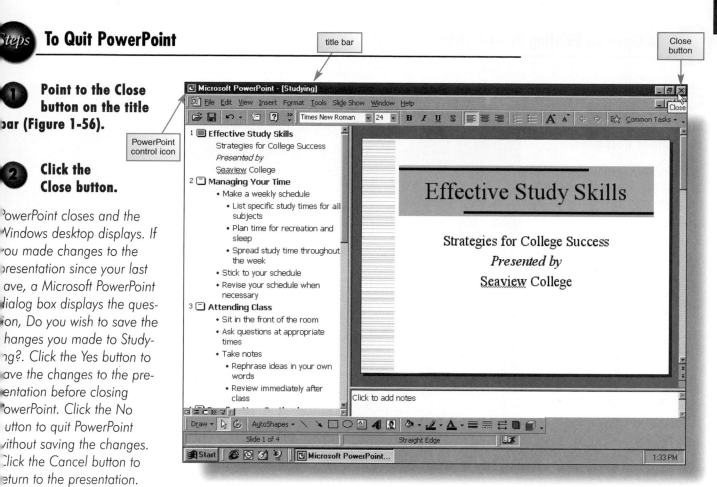

FIGURE 1-56

Other Ways

1. On title bar double-click PowerPoint control icon; or on title bar click PowerPoint control icon, click Close
2. On File menu click Exit
3. Press CTRL+Q or press ALT+F4

Opening a Presentation

Earlier, you saved the presentation on a floppy disk using the file name, Studying.ppt. Once you create and save a presentation, you may need to retrieve it from the floppy disk to make changes. For example, you may want to replace the design template or modify some text. Recall that a presentation is a PowerPoint document. Use the **Open Office Document command** to open an existing presentation.

Opening an Existing Presentation

Ensure that the floppy disk used to save Studying.ppt is in drive A. Then perform the steps on the next page to open the Studying presentation using the Open Office Document command on the Start menu.

Steps **To Open an Existing Presentation**

1 **Click the Start button on the taskbar and then point to Open Office Document.**

The Windows Start menu displays (Figure 1-57). Open Office Document is highlighted.

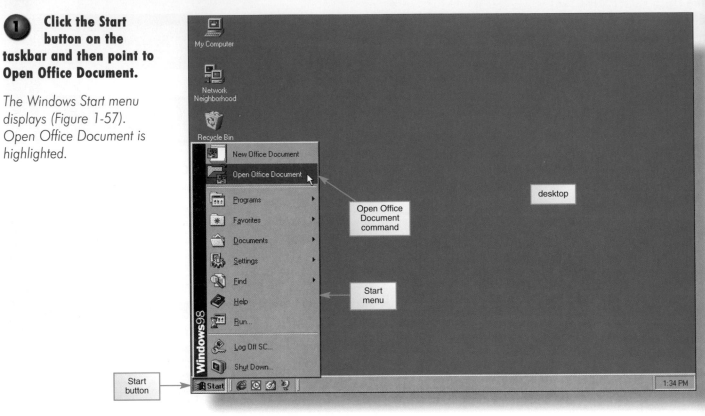

FIGURE 1-57

Click Open Office Document. When the Open Office Document dialog box displays, if necessary, click the Look in box arrow and then click 3½ Floppy (A:) (see Figures 1-28 and 1-29 on page 1.30 to review this process).

The Open Office Document dialog box displays (Figure 1-58). A list of existing files on drive A displays because your floppy disk is in drive A. Notice that Office Files displays in the Files of type box. The file, Studying, is highlighted. Your list of existing files may be different depending on the files saved on your floppy disk.

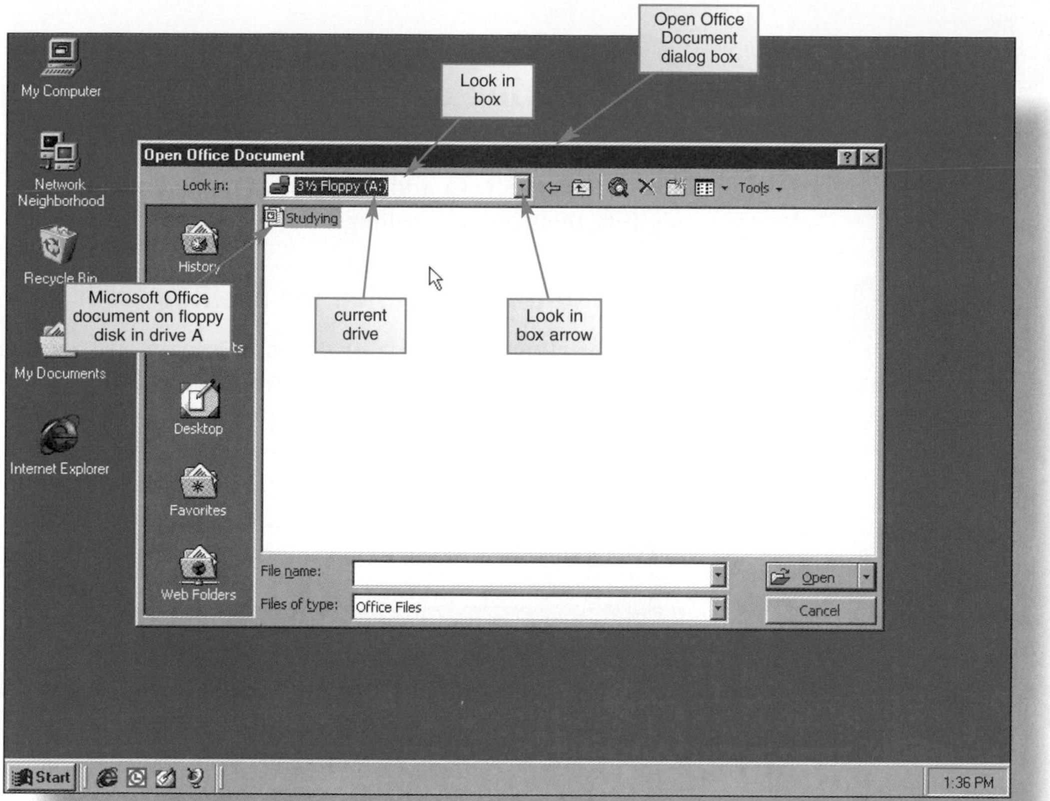

FIGURE 1-58

 Double-click Studying.

PowerPoint starts, opens Studying.ppt from drive A into main memory, and displays the first slide on the screen. The presentation displays in normal view because PowerPoint opens a presentation in the same view in which it was saved.

Other **Ways**

1. Click Open Office Document button on Microsoft Office Shortcut Bar, click folder or drive name in Look in list, double-click document name
2. On Start menu click Documents, click document name

When you start PowerPoint and open Studying.ppt, this application and the file name display on a recessed button in the taskbar button area. When more than one application is open, you can switch between applications by clicking the button labeled with the name of the application to which you want to switch.

Checking a Presentation for Spelling and Consistency

After you create a presentation, you should check it visually for spelling errors and style consistency. In addition, you can use PowerPoint's Spelling and Style tools to identify possible misspellings and inconsistencies.

Checking a Presentation for Spelling Errors

Dictionaries

Microsoft has partnered with publishing companies to produce the world's first global dictionary. More than 250 people worked to compile the three million English words contained in this work. The terms are used worldwide, for more than 80 percent of the world's computer-based communication uses the English language.

PowerPoint checks your entire presentation for spelling mistakes using a standard dictionary contained in the Microsoft Office group. This dictionary is shared with the other Microsoft Office applications such as Word and Excel. A **custom dictionary** is available if you want to add special words such as proper names, cities, and acronyms. When checking a presentation for spelling errors, PowerPoint opens the standard dictionary and the custom dictionary file, if one exists. When a word displays in the Spelling dialog box, you perform one of the actions listed in Table 1-3.

Table 1-3 Summary of Spelling Checker Actions	
FEATURE	**DESCRIPTION**
Ignore the word	Click Ignore when the word is spelled correctly but not found in the dictionaries. PowerPoint continues checking the rest of the presentation.
Ignore all occurrences of the word	Click Ignore All when the word is spelled correctly but not found in the dictionaries. PowerPoint ignores all occurrences of the word and continues checking the rest of the presentation.
Select a different spelling	Click the proper spelling of the word from the list in the Suggestions box. Click Change. PowerPoint corrects the word and continues checking the rest of the presentation.
Change all occurrences of the misspelling to a different spelling	Click the proper spelling of the word from the list in the Suggestions box. Click Change All. PowerPoint changes all occurrences of the misspelled word and continues checking the rest of the presentation.
Add a word to the custom dictionary	Click Add. PowerPoint opens the custom dictionary, adds the word, and continues checking the rest of the presentation.
View alternative spellings	Click Suggest. PowerPoint lists suggested spellings. Click the correct word from the Suggestions box or type the proper spelling. Then click Change. PowerPoint continues checking the rest of the presentation.
Add spelling error to AutoCorrect list	Click AutoCorrect. PowerPoint adds the spelling error and its correction to the AutoCorrect list. Any future misspelling of the word is corrected automatically as you type.
Close	Click Close to exit from the spelling checker and to return to the PowerPoint window.

The standard dictionary contains commonly used English words. It does not, however, contain proper names, abbreviations, technical terms, poetic contractions, or antiquated terms. PowerPoint treats words not found in the dictionaries as misspellings.

Starting the Spelling Checker

Start the Spelling checker by clicking the Spelling command on the Tools menu. Perform the following steps to start the Spelling checker and check your entire presentation.

To Start the Spelling Checker

1 Double-click the move handle on the Standard toolbar. Point to the Spelling button on the Standard toolbar (Figure 1-59).

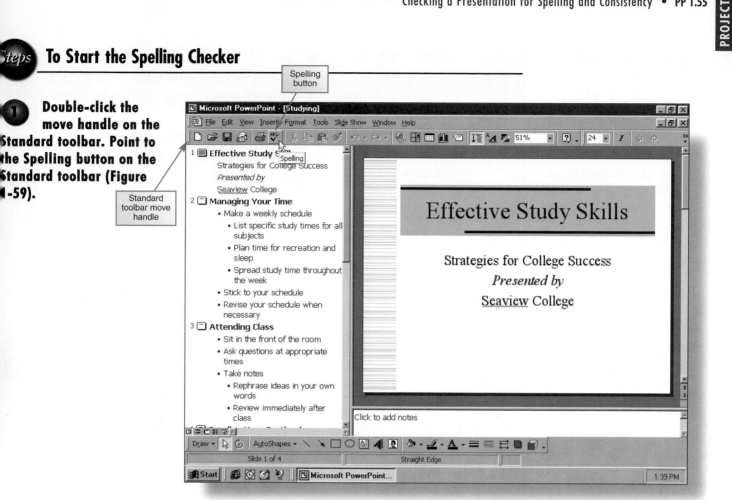

FIGURE 1-59

2 Click the Spelling button. When the Spelling dialog box displays, point to the Ignore button.

PowerPoint launches the spelling checker and displays the Spelling dialog box (Figure 1-60). The word, Seaview, displays in the Not in Dictionary box. Depending on your custom dictionary, Seaview may not be recognized as a misspelled word.

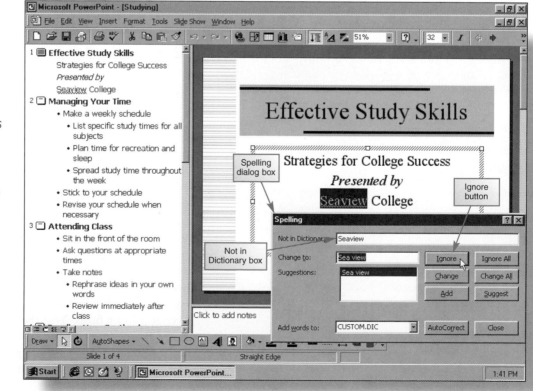

FIGURE 1-60

Click the Ignore button.

PowerPoint ignores the word, Seaview, and continues searching for additional misspelled words. PowerPoint may stop on additional words depending on your typing accuracy. When PowerPoint has checked all slides for misspellings, it displays the Microsoft PowerPoint dialog box informing you that the spelling check is complete (Figure 1-61).

 Click the OK button.

PowerPoint closes the Spelling checker and returns to the current slide, Slide 1, or to the slide where a possible misspelled word appeared.

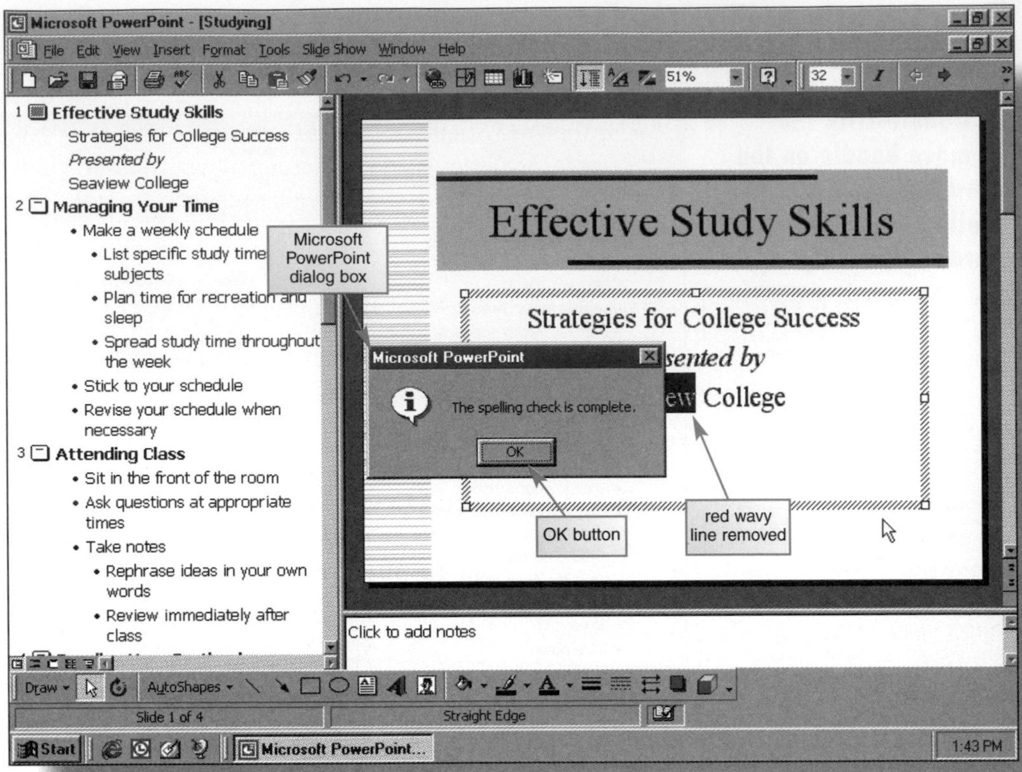

FIGURE 1-61

Other Ways

1. Press ALT+T, press S; when finished, press ENTER

The red wavy line under the word, Seaview, is gone because you instructed PowerPoint to ignore that word, which does not appear in the standard dictionary. You also could have added that word to the dictionary so it would not be flagged as a possible misspelled word in subsequent presentations you create using that word.

Checking a Presentation for Style Consistency

Recall that the Office Assistant may have generated a light bulb in the text placeholder when you were typing your title slide (see Figure 1-19 on page PP 1.23). The Office Assistant recognized you were starting to prepare a slide show and offered design tips. These tips can range from suggesting clip art to ensuring your presentation meets predefined criteria for style consistency. For example, in this Studying presentation the first word in each line of text begins with a capital letter, and each line does not end with a period. The Office Assistant automatically checks for case and end punctuation consistency and for visual clarity. It identifies problems on a screen by displaying a light bulb. You then can choose to correct or to ignore the elements PowerPoint flags. You can change the options to suit your design specifications. Table 1-4 identifies each option available in the Style checker and each default setting.

Table 1-4 Style Checker Options and Default Settings	
OPTION	SETTING
CASE	
Slide title style	Title Case
Body text style	Sentence case
END PUNCTUATION	
Slide title punctuation	Paragraphs have punctuation
Body punctuation	Paragraphs have consistent punctuation
VISUAL CLARITY	
Number of fonts should not exceed	3
Title text size should be at least	36
Body text size should be at least	20
Number of bullets should not exceed	6
Number of lines per title should not exceed	2
Number of lines per bullet should not exceed	2

Correcting Errors

After creating a presentation and running the Spelling checker, you may find that you must make changes. Changes may be required because a slide contains an error, the scope of the presentation shifts, or the style is inconsistent. This section explains the types of errors that commonly occur when creating a presentation.

Types of Corrections Made to Presentations

You generally make three types of corrections to text in a presentation: additions, deletions, and replacements.

- **Additions** —are necessary when you omit text from a slide and need to add it later. You may need to insert text in the form of a sentence, word, or single character. For example, you may want to add the rest of the presenter's first name on your title slide.
- **Deletions** —are required when text on a slide is incorrect or is no longer relevant to the presentation. For example, one of your slides may look cluttered. Therefore, you may want to remove one of the bulleted paragraphs to add more space.
- **Replacements** —are needed when you want to revise the text in your presentation. For example, you may want to substitute the word, their, for the word, there.

Editing text in PowerPoint is basically the same as editing text in a word processing package. The following sections illustrate the most common changes made to text in a presentation.

Deleting Text

You can delete text using one of three methods. One is to use the BACKSPACE key to remove text just typed. The second is to position the insertion point to the left of the text you wish to delete and then press the DELETE key. The third method is to drag through the text you wish to delete and then press the DELETE key. (Use the third method when deleting large sections of text.)

Replacing Text in an Existing Slide

When you need to correct a word or phrase, you can replace the text by selecting the text to be replaced and then typing the new text. As soon as you press any key on the keyboard, the highlighted text is deleted and the new text displays.

PowerPoint inserts text to the left of the insertion point. The text to the right of the insertion point moves to the right (and shifts downward if necessary) to accommodate the added text.

Changing Line Spacing

The bulleted lists on Slides 2, 3, and 4 look crowded; yet, there is ample blank space that could be used to separate the paragraphs. You can adjust the spacing on each slide, but when several slides need to be changed, you should change the slide master. Each PowerPoint component (slides, title slides, audience handouts, and speaker's notes) has a **master**, which controls its appearance. Slides have two masters, title master and slide master. The **title master** controls the appearance of the title slide. The **slide master** controls the appearance of the other slides in your presentation.

More About

Correcting Errors

While PowerPoint's Spelling checker and Style checker are valuable tools, they are not infallible. You should proofread your presentation carefully by saying each word aloud and pointing to each word as you say it. Be mindful of commonly misused words such as its and it's, their and they're, and you're and your

Table 1-5 Summary of Slide Master Components

ELEMENT	DESCRIPTION
Background items	Any object other than the title object or text object. Typical items include borders and graphics such as a company logo, page number, date, and time.
Color scheme	A coordinated set of eight colors designed to complement each other. Color schemes consist of background color, line and text color, shadow color, title text color, object fill color, and three different accent colors.
Date	Inserts the special symbol used to print the date the presentation was printed.
Font	Defines the appearance and shape of letters, numbers, and special characters.
Font size	Specifies the size of the characters on the screen. Character size is gauged by a measurement system called points. A single point is about 1/72 of an inch in height. Thus, a character with a point size of eighteen is about 18/72 of an inch in height.
Font style	Font styles include plain, italic, bold, shadowed, and underlined. Text may have more than one font style at a time.
Slide number	Inserts the special symbol used to print the slide number.
Text alignment	Position of text in a paragraph is left-aligned, right-aligned, centered, or justified. Justified text is proportionally spaced across the object.
Time	Inserts the special symbol used to print the time the presentation was printed.

Each design template has a specially designed slide master. If you select a design template but want to change one of its components, you can override that component by changing the slide master. Any change to the slide master results in changing every slide in the presentation, except the title slide. For example, if you change the line spacing to .5 inches before each paragraph on the slide master, each slide (except the title slide) changes line spacing after each paragraph to .5 inches. The slide master components more frequently changed are listed in Table 1-5.

Additionally, each view has its own master. You can access the master by holding down the SHIFT key while clicking the appropriate view button. For example, holding down the SHIFT key and clicking the Slide View button displays the slide master. To exit a master, click the view button to which you wish to return. To return to slide view, for example, click the Slide View button.

Displaying the Slide Master

Before you can change line spacing on the slide master, you first must display it. Perform the following steps to display the slide master.

Steps **To Display the Slide Master**

1 **Click the Next Slide button on the slide pane to display Slide 2. Press and hold down the SHIFT key and then point to the Slide View button.**

When you hold down the SHIFT key, the ScreenTip displays Slide Master View (Figure 1-62).

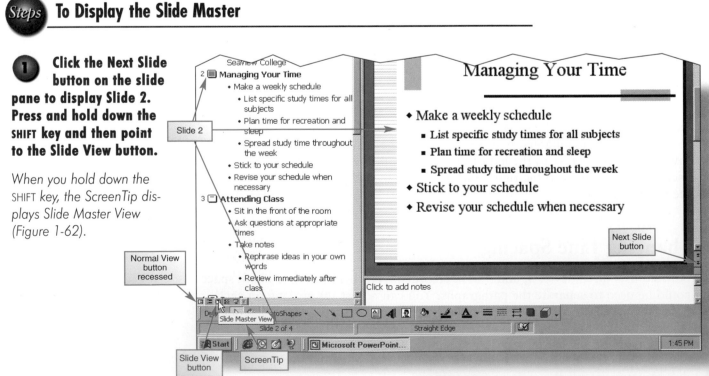

FIGURE 1-62

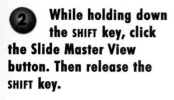

2 While holding down the SHIFT key, click the Slide Master View button. Then release the SHIFT key.

The slide master and Master toolbar display (Figure 1-63).

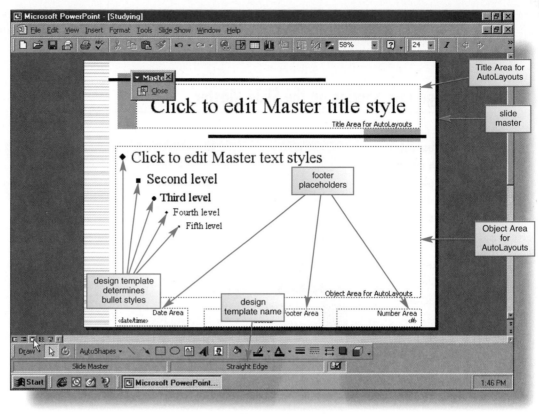

FIGURE 1-63

Changing Line Spacing on the Slide Master

Change line spacing by clicking the Line Spacing command on the Format menu. When you click the **Line Spacing command**, the Line Spacing dialog box displays. The Line Spacing dialog box contains three boxes, Line spacing, Before paragraph, and After paragraph, which allow you to adjust line spacing within a paragraph, before a paragraph, and after a paragraph, respectively.

Before paragraph line spacing is controlled by establishing the number of units before a paragraph. Units are either lines or points; lines are the default unit. Points may be selected by clicking the down arrow next to the Before paragraph box (see Figure 1-66 on page PP 1.61). Recall from page PP 1.24 that a single point is about 1/72 of an inch in height.

The Line spacing, Before paragraph, and After paragraph boxes each contain an amount of space box and a unit of measure box. To change the amount of space displaying between paragraphs, click the amount of space box up arrow or down arrow in the Line spacing box. To change the amount of space displaying before a paragraph, as you did in this project, click the amount of space box up arrow or down arrow in the Before paragraph box. To change the amount of space displaying after a paragraph, click the amount of space box up arrow or down arrow in the After paragraph box. To change the unit of measure from Lines to Points in the Line Spacing dialog box, click the arrow next to the appropriate unit of measure box and then click Points in the list.

In this project, you change the number in the amount of space box to increase the amount of space that displays before every paragraph, except the first paragraph, on every slide. For example, increasing the amount of space box to 0.5 lines increases the amount of space that displays before each paragraph.

Other **Ways**

1. On View menu point to Master, click Slide Master

Line Spacing

Blank space on a slide can be advantageous. The absence of text, called white space, helps the viewer focus attention on the presenter. Do not be afraid to increase line spacing to give your text some breathing room.

The first paragraph on every slide, however, does not change because of its position in the Object Area placeholder. Perform the following steps to change the line spacing.

 Steps **To Change Line Spacing on the Slide Master**

1 **Click the bulleted paragraph in the Object Area placeholder labeled, Click to edit Master text styles.**

The insertion point displays at the point you clicked (Figure 1-64). The Object Area placeholder is selected.

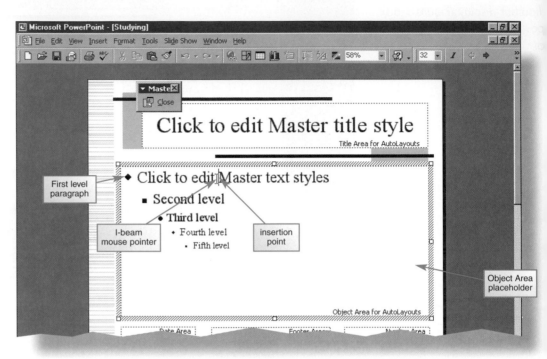

FIGURE 1-64

2 **Click Format on the menu bar and then point to Line Spacing. (Remember that you might have to wait a few seconds for the entire menu to display.)**

The Format menu displays (Figure 1-65).

FIGURE 1-65

3 **Click Line Spacing. Point to the Before Paragraph amount of space box up arrow.**

PowerPoint displays the Line Spacing dialog box (Figure 1-66). The default Before paragraph line spacing is set at 0.2 Lines.

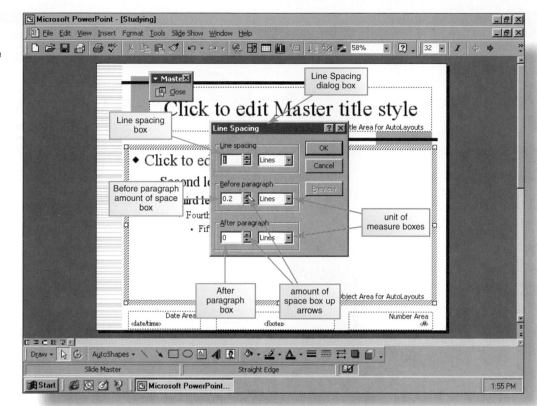

FIGURE 1-66

4 **Click the Before paragraph amount of space box up arrow six times.**

The Before paragraph amount of space box displays 0.5 (Figure 1-67). The Preview button is available after this change is made in the Line Spacing dialog box. If you click the Preview button, PowerPoint temporarily updates your presentation with the new amount of space setting. This new setting is not actually applied until you click the OK button.

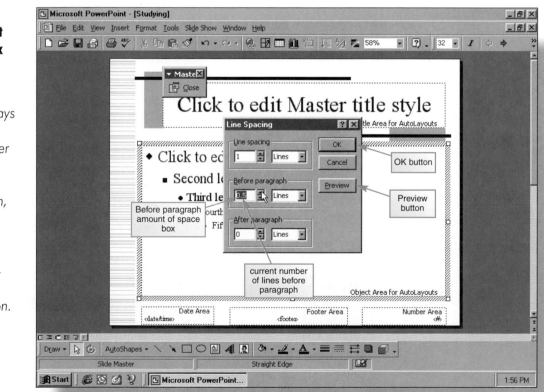

FIGURE 1-67

5 **Click the OK button.**

The slide master Object Area placeholder displays the new line spacing (Figure 1-68). Depending on the video drivers installed, the spacing on your screen may appear slightly different than this figure.

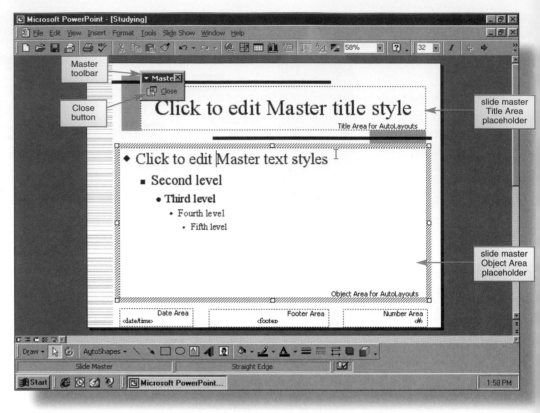

FIGURE 1-68

6 **Click the Close button on the Master toolbar to return to normal view.**

Slide 2 displays with the Before paragraph line spacing set to 0.5 Lines (Figure 1-69).

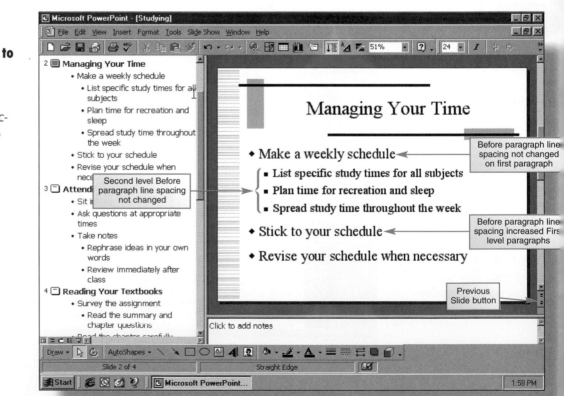

FIGURE 1-69

To display line spacing changes without making them permanent, click the Preview button in the Line Spacing dialog box. If you want to close the Line Spacing dialog box without applying the changes, click the Cancel button.

The placeholder at the top of the slide master (Figure 1-68) is used to edit the Master title style. The Object Area placeholder under the Master Title Area placeholder is used to edit the Master text styles. Here you make changes to the various bullet levels. Changes can be made to line spacing, bullet font, text and line color, alignment, and text shadow.

Displaying a Presentation in Black and White

You want to print handouts of your presentation and create overhead transparencies. The **Grayscale Preview button** allows you to display the presentation in black and white before you print. Table 1-6 identifies how PowerPoint objects display in black and white.

Perform the following steps to display the presentation in black and white.

Table 1-6 Appearance in Black and White View	
OBJECT	DISPLAY
Text	Black
Text shadows	Hidden
Embossing	Hidden
Fills	Grayscale
Frame	Black
Pattern fills	Grayscale
Lines	Black
Object shadows	Grayscale
Bitmaps	Grayscale
Slide backgrounds	White

Steps To Display a Presentation in Black and White

1 Click the Previous Slide button to display Slide 1. Point to the Grayscale Preview button on the Standard toolbar.

Slide 1 displays. The Grayscale Preview ScreenTip displays (Figure 1-70).

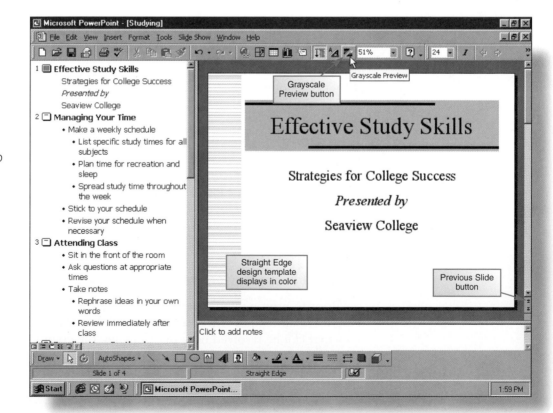

FIGURE 1-70

2 Click the Grayscale Preview button.

Slide 1 displays in black and white (Figure 1-71). The Grayscale Preview button is recessed on the Standard toolbar.

3 Click the Next Slide button three times to view all slides in the presentation in black and white.

4 Click the Grayscale Preview button.

Slide 4 displays with the default Straight Edge color scheme.

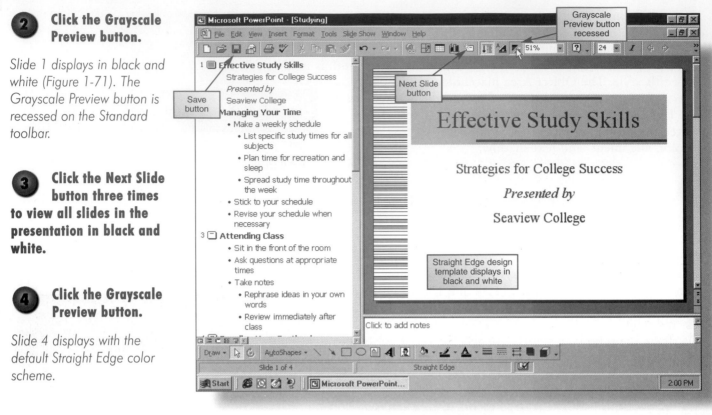

FIGURE 1-71

Other Ways

1. On View menu click Black and White

After you view the text objects in your presentation in black and white, you can make any changes that will enhance printouts produced from a black and white printer or photocopier.

Printing a Presentation

After you create a presentation, you often want to print it. A printed version of the presentation is called a **hard copy**, or **printout**. The first printing of the presentation is called a **rough draft**. The rough draft allows you to proofread the presentation to check for errors and readability. After correcting errors, you print the final copy of your presentation.

Saving a Presentation Before Printing

Prior to printing your presentation, you should save your work in the event you experience difficulties with the printer. You occasionally may encounter system problems that can be resolved only by restarting the computer. In such an instance, you will need to reopen your presentation. As a precaution, always save your presentation before you print. Perform the following steps to save the presentation before printing.

TO SAVE A PRESENTATION BEFORE PRINTING

1 Verify that your floppy disk is in drive A.

2 Click the Save button on the Standard toolbar.

All changes made after your last save now are saved on a floppy disk.

Printing the Presentation

After saving the presentation, you are ready to print. Clicking the **Print button** on the Standard toolbar causes PowerPoint to print all slides in the presentation. Perform the following steps to print the presentation slides.

Steps ## To Print a Presentation

1 Ready the printer according to the printer instructions. Then click the Print button on the Standard toolbar.

The printer icon in the tray status area on the taskbar indicates a print job is processing (Figure 1-72). After several moments, the slide show begins printing on the printer. When the presentation is finished printing, the printer icon in the tray status area on the taskbar no longer displays.

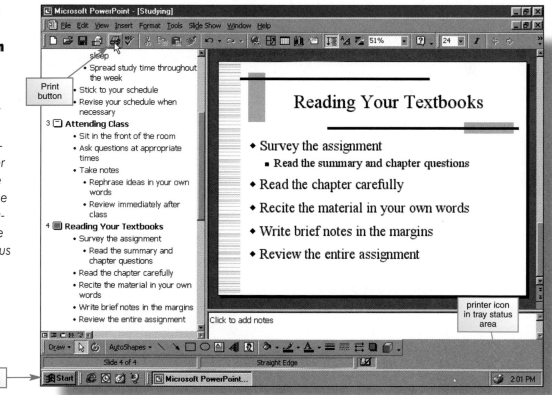

FIGURE 1-72

When the printer stops, retrieve the printouts of the slides.

The presentation, Studying, prints on four pages (Figures 1-73a through 1-73d).

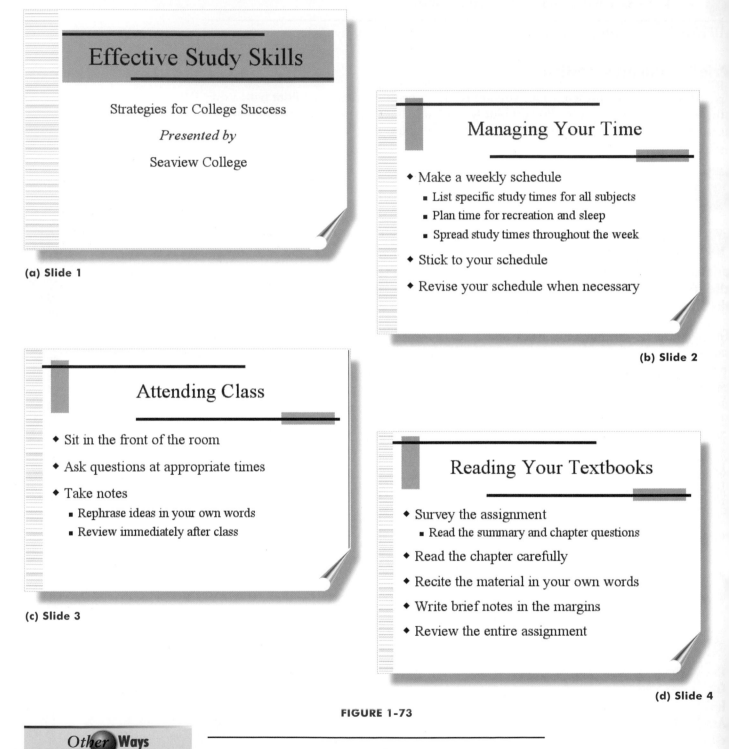

Effective Study Skills

Strategies for College Success

Presented by

Seaview College

(a) Slide 1

Managing Your Time

◆ Make a weekly schedule
- List specific study times for all subjects
- Plan time for recreation and sleep
- Spread study times throughout the week

◆ Stick to your schedule

◆ Revise your schedule when necessary

(b) Slide 2

Attending Class

◆ Sit in the front of the room

◆ Ask questions at appropriate times

◆ Take notes
- Rephrase ideas in your own words
- Review immediately after class

(c) Slide 3

Reading Your Textbooks

◆ Survey the assignment
- Read the summary and chapter questions

◆ Read the chapter carefully

◆ Recite the material in your own words

◆ Write brief notes in the margins

◆ Review the entire assignment

(d) Slide 4

FIGURE 1-73

Other **Ways**

1. On File menu click Print
2. Press CTRL+P or press CTRL+SHIFT+F12

You can click the printer icon next to the clock in the tray status area on the taskbar to obtain information about the presentations printing on your printer and to delete files in the print queue that are waiting to be printed.

Making a Transparency

Now that you have printed handouts, you want to make overhead transparencies. You can make transparencies using one of several devices. One device is a printer attached to your computer, such as an ink-jet printer or a laser printer. Transparencies produced on a printer may be in black and white or color, depending on the printer. Another device is a photocopier. Because each of these devices requires a special transparency film, check the user's manual for the film requirement of your specific device, or ask your instructor.

PowerPoint Help System

You can get answers to PowerPoint questions at any time by using the **PowerPoint Help system**. Used properly, this form of online assistance can increase your productivity and reduce your frustrations by minimizing the time you spend learning how to use PowerPoint. The following section shows how to get answers to your questions using the Office Assistant.

Using the Office Assistant

The **Office Assistant** answers your questions and suggests more efficient ways to complete a task. With the Office Assistant active, for example, you can type a question, word, or phrase in a text box and the Office Assistant provides immediate help on the subject. Also, as you create a worksheet, the Office Assistant accumulates tips that suggest more efficient ways to do the tasks you completed while building a presentation, such as formatting, printing, and saving. This tip feature is part of the **IntelliSense technology** that is built into PowerPoint, which understands what you are trying to do and suggests better ways to do it. When the light bulb displays above the Office Assistant, click it to see a tip.

The following steps show how to use the Office Assistant to obtain information on formatting a presentation.

Help

In previous versions of Microsoft PowerPoint and other software, users had to spend hours pouring through thick reference manuals to find relevant information. This task was particularly difficult for novice computer users. Today, the Office Assistant helps you search for relevant information instantly and easily.

Steps **To Obtain Help Using the Office Assistant**

1 **If the Office Assistant is not on the screen, click Show the Office Assistant on the Help menu. With the Office Assistant on the screen, click it. Type** how do i take meeting minutes **in the What would you like to do? text box in the Office Assistant balloon. Point to the Search button (Figure 1-74).**

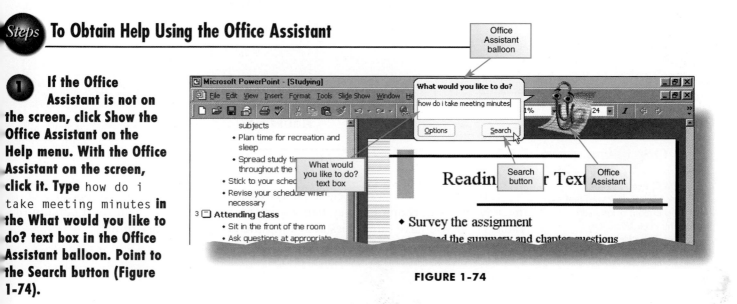

FIGURE 1-74

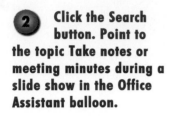

2 **Click the Search button. Point to the topic Take notes or meeting minutes during a slide show in the Office Assistant balloon.**

The Office Assistant displays a list of topics relating to the question how do i take meeting minutes (Figure 1-75). The mouse pointer changes to a hand.

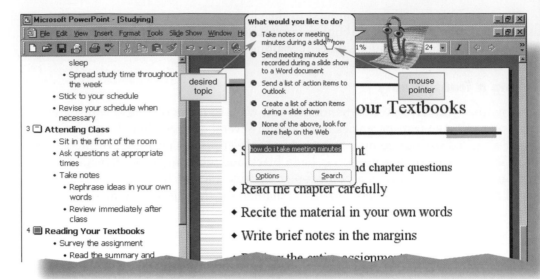

FIGURE 1-75

3 **Click Take notes or meeting minutes during a slide show.**

The Office Assistant displays a Microsoft PowerPoint Help window that provides Help information on taking notes or meeting minutes during a slide show (Figure 1-76).

4 **Click the Close button on the Microsoft PowerPoint Help window title bar.**

The Microsoft PowerPoint Help window closes, and the worksheet again is active.

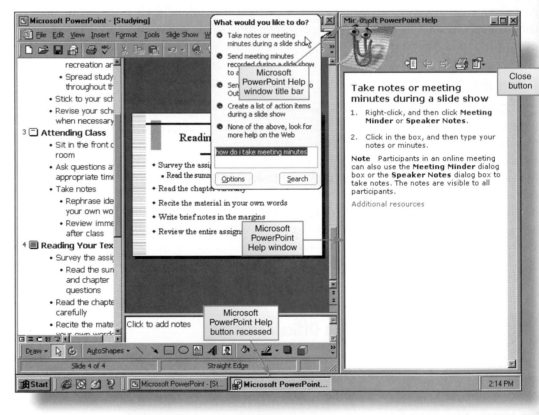

FIGURE 1-76

Other Ways

1. With Office Assistant on, click Microsoft PowerPoint Help button; or on Help menu click Microsoft PowerPoint Help

2. Press F1

Table 1-7 summarizes the eight categories of help available to you. Because of the way the PowerPoint Help system works, please review the right-most column of Table 1-7 if you have difficulties activating the desired category of help.

Table 1-7 PowerPoint Help System

TYPE	DESCRIPTION	HOW TO ACTIVATE	TURNING THE OFFICE ASSISTANT ON AND OFF
Answer Wizard	Similar to the Office Assistant in that it answers questions that you type in your own words.	Click the Microsoft PowerPoint Help button on the Standard toolbar. If necessary, maximize the Help window by double-clicking its title bar. Click the Answer Wizard tab.	If the Office Assistant displays, right-click it, click Options, click the Use the Office Assistant check box, and then click the OK button.
Contents sheet	Groups Help topics by general categories. Use when you know only the general category of the topic in question.	Click the Office Assistant button on the Standard toolbar. If necessary, maximize the Help window by double-clicking its title bar. Click the Contents tab.	If the Office Assistant displays, right-click it, click Options, click the Use the Office Assistant check box, and then click the OK button.
Detect and Repair	Automatically finds and fixes errors in the application.	Click Detect and Repair on the Help menu.	
Hardware and Software Information	Shows Product ID and allows access to system information and technical support information.	Click About Microsoft PowerPoint on the Help menu and then click the System Information or Technical Information button.	
Index sheet	Similar to an index in a book; use when you know exactly what you want.	Click the Microsoft PowerPoint Help button on the Standard toolbar. If necessary, maximize the Help window by double-clicking its title bar. Click the Index tab.	If the Office Assistant displays, right-click it, click Options, click Use the Office Assistant check box, and then click the OK button.
Office Assistant	Answers questions that you type in your own words, offers tips, and provides Help for a variety of PowerPoint features.	Click the Microsoft PowerPoint Help button on the Standard toolbar.	If the Office Assistant does not display, close the Microsoft PowerPoint Help window and then click Show the Office Assistant on the Help menu.
Office on the Web	Accesses technical resources and download free product enhancements on the Web.	Click Office on the Web on the Help menu.	
Question Mark button and What's This? command	Identifies unfamiliar items on the screen.	Click the Question Mark button and then click an item in the dialog box. Click What's This? on the Help menu, and then click an item on the screen.	

You can use the Office Assistant to search for Help on any topic concerning PowerPoint. For additional information on using the PowerPoint Help system, see Appendix A.

Quitting PowerPoint

Project 1 is complete. The final task is to close the presentation and quit PowerPoint. Perform the following steps to quit PowerPoint.

TO QUIT POWERPOINT

 1 Click the Close button on the title bar.

2 If prompted to save the presentation before quitting PowerPoint, click the Yes button in the Microsoft PowerPoint dialog box.

CASE PERSPECTIVE SUMMARY

Your Effective Study Skills PowerPoint slide show should help Dr. Martinez and the counseling staff present essential college survival skills to incoming freshmen attending orientation sessions at your school. The four slides display the key study habits all students need to succeed throughout college. The title slide identifies the topic of the presentation, and the next three slides give key pointers regarding time management, class attendance, and textbook usage. The counselors will use your overhead transparencies to organize their speeches, and the students will keep handouts of your slides for future reference.

Project Summary

Project 1 introduced you to starting PowerPoint and creating a multi-level bulleted list presentation. You learned about PowerPoint design templates, objects, and attributes. This project illustrated how to create an interesting introduction to a presentation by changing the text font style to italic and increasing font size on the title slide. Completing these tasks, you saved your presentation. Then, you created three multi-level bulleted list slides to explain how to study effectively in college. Next, you learned how to view the presentation in slide show view. Then you learned how to quit PowerPoint and how to open an existing presentation. You used the Spelling checker to search for spelling errors and learned how the Office Assistant Style checker identifies inconsistencies in design specifications. Using the slide master, you quickly adjusted the Before paragraph line spacing on every slide to make better use of white space. You learned how to display the presentation in black and white. Then, you learned how to print hard copies of your slides in order to make overhead transparencies. Finally, you learned how to use the PowerPoint Help system.

What You Should Know

Having completed this project, you now should be able to perform the following tasks:

- Add a New Slide Using the Bulleted List AutoLayout *(PP 1.32)*
- Add a New Slide with the Same AutoLayout *(PP 1.40)*
- Change Line Spacing on the Slide Master *(PP 1.60)*
- Change the Text Font Style to Italic *(PP 1.27)*

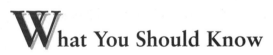

Microsoft Certification

You can prove to your employer that you have essential PowerPoint 2000 skills. The Microsoft Office User Specialist (MOUS) Certification program allows you to obtain this valuable credential known throughout the computer industry. For more information, see Appendix D or visit the Shelly Cashman Series MOUS Web page at www.scsite.com/off2000/cert.htm.

- Choose a Design Template *(PP 1.18)*
- Complete Slide 3 *(PP 1.40)*
- Create Slide 4 *(PP 1.41)*
- Display a Presentation in Black and White *(PP 1.63)*
- Display the Formatting Toolbar in its Entirety *(PP 1.17)*
- Display the Popup Menu and Go to a Specific Slide *(PP 1.49)*
- Display the Slide Master *(PP 1.58)*
- End a Slide Show with a Black Slide *(PP 1.43)*
- Enter a Slide Title *(PP 1.35)*
- Enter the Presentation Subtitle *(PP 1.23)*
- Enter the Presentation Title *(PP 1.21)*
- Increase Font Size *(PP 1.25)*
- Move Manually Through Slides in a Slide Show *(PP 1.48)*
- Obtain Help Using the Office Assistant *(PP 1.67)*
- Open an Existing Presentation *(PP 1.52)*

- Print a Presentation *(PP 1.65)*
- Quit PowerPoint *(PP 1.51, 1.69)*
- Save a Presentation Before Printing *(PP 1.65)*
- Save a Presentation on a Floppy Disk *(PP 1.29)*
- Save a Presentation with the Same File Name *(PP 1.44)*
- Select an Object Area Placeholder *(PP 1.36)*
- Start a New Presentation *(PP 1.10)*
- Start Slide Show View *(PP 1.46)*
- Start the Spelling Checker *(PP 1.55)*
- Type a Multi-level Bulleted List *(PP 1.37)*
- Type the Remaining Text for Slide 2 *(PP 1.39)*
- Use the Popup Menu to End a Slide Show *(PP 1.50)*
- Use the Scroll Box on the Slide Pane to Move to Another Slide *(PP 1.45)*

Apply Your Knowledge

Project Reinforcement at www.scsite.com/off2000/reinforce.htm

1 Computer Buying Basics

Instructions: Start PowerPoint. Open the presentation Apply-1 from the PowerPoint Data Disk. See the inside back cover for instructions for downloading the PowerPoint Data Disk or see your instructor for information on accessing the files required for this book. This slide lists questions to consider when buying a computer. Perform the following tasks to change the slide so it looks like the one in Figure 1-77.

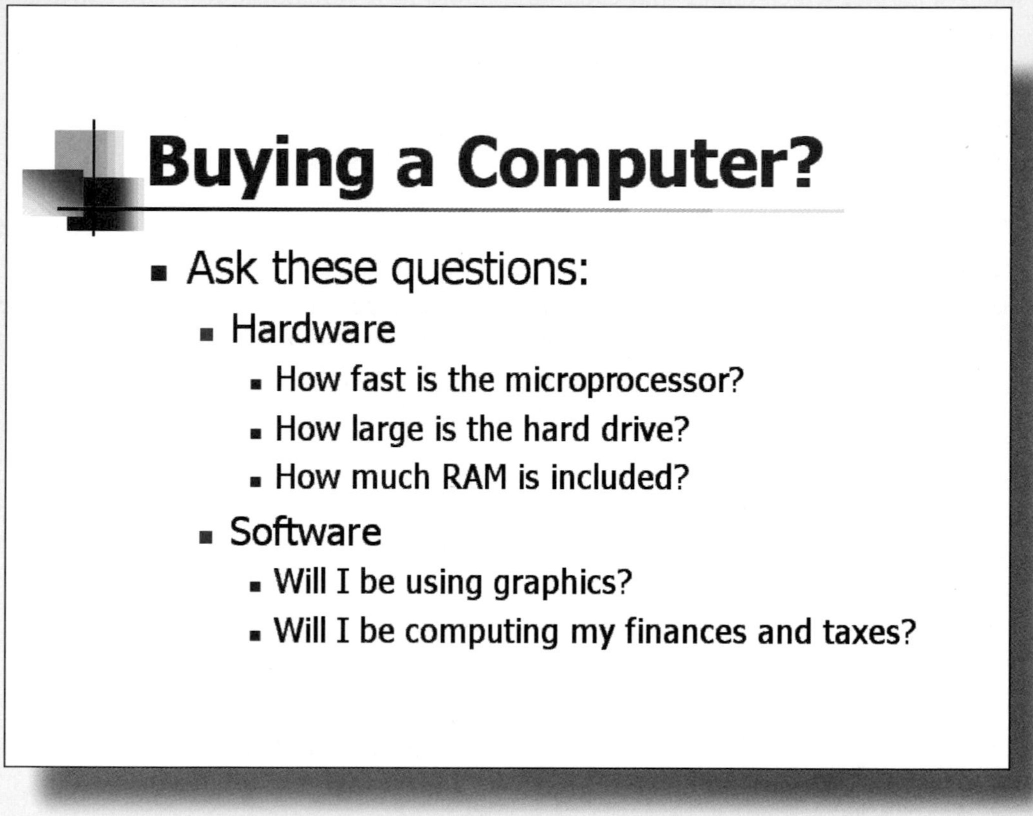

Buying a Computer?

- Ask these questions:
  - Hardware
    - How fast is the microprocessor?
    - How large is the hard drive?
    - How much RAM is included?
  - Software
    - Will I be using graphics?
    - Will I be computing my finances and taxes?

FIGURE 1-77

1. Click the Common Tasks menu button on the Formatting toolbar, and then click the Apply Design Template command. Choose the Blends design template.
2. Press and hold down the SHIFT key, and then click the Slide Master View button to display the slide master. Click the paragraph, Click to edit Master text styles. Click Format on the menu bar and then click Line Spacing. Increase the Before paragraph line spacing to 1 Lines. Click the OK button. Then click the Close button on the Master toolbar to return to normal view.
3. Select the text in the Title Area placeholder. Click the Bold button on the Formatting toolbar.
4. If necessary, select the text in the Title Area placeholder. Click the Font Size box arrow on the Font Size button on the Formatting toolbar. Click the down scroll arrow and then scroll down and click font size 48.
5. Click the paragraph in the Object Area placeholder, How fast is the microprocessor?. Click the Demote button on the Formatting toolbar.
6. Demote the four other paragraphs that end with a question mark.
7. Click File on the menu bar and then click Save As. Type Buying a Computer in the File name box. If drive A is not already displaying in the Save in box, click the Save in box arrow, and then click 3½ Floppy (A:). Click the Save button.
8. Click the Grayscale Preview button on the Standard toolbar to display the presentation in black and white.
9. Click the Print button on the Standard toolbar.
10. Click the Close button on the menu bar to quit PowerPoint.
11. Write your name on the printout, and hand it in to your instructor.

In the Lab

NOTE: These labs require you to create presentations based on notes. When you design these slide shows, use the 7 x 7 rule, which states that each line should have a maximum of seven words, and each slide should have a maximum of seven lines.

1 Financial Freedom at Community Savings & Loan

Problem: You work at the Community Savings & Loan. The institution's vice president wants you to help her prepare a presentation for an upcoming seminar for the community regarding achieving financial freedom. She hands you the notes in Figure 1-78, and you create the presentation shown in Figures 1-79a through 1-79d.

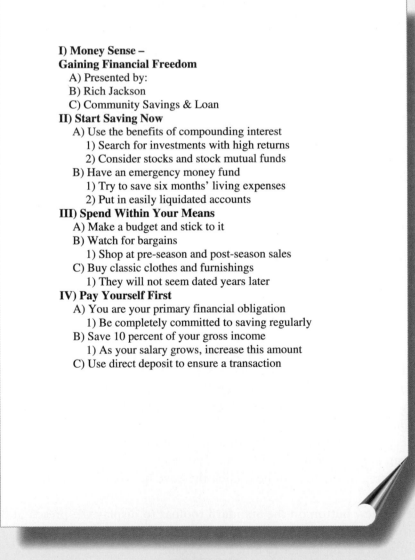

I) Money Sense –
Gaining Financial Freedom
  A) Presented by:
  B) Rich Jackson
  C) Community Savings & Loan
II) Start Saving Now
  A) Use the benefits of compounding interest
    1) Search for investments with high returns
    2) Consider stocks and stock mutual funds
  B) Have an emergency money fund
    1) Try to save six months' living expenses
    2) Put in easily liquidated accounts
III) Spend Within Your Means
  A) Make a budget and stick to it
  B) Watch for bargains
    1) Shop at pre-season and post-season sales
  C) Buy classic clothes and furnishings
    1) They will not seem dated years later
IV) Pay Yourself First
  A) You are your primary financial obligation
    1) Be completely committed to saving regularly
  B) Save 10 percent of your gross income
    1) As your salary grows, increase this amount
  C) Use direct deposit to ensure a transaction

FIGURE 1-78

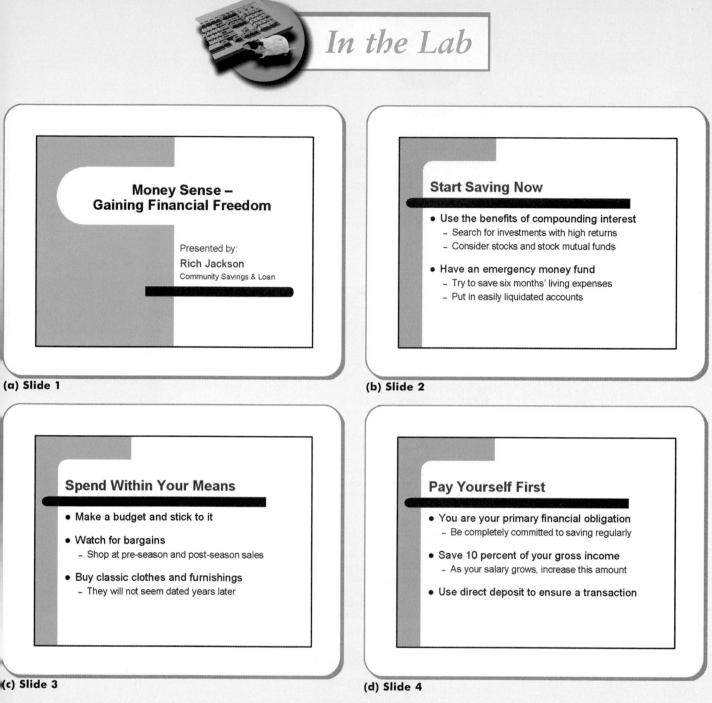

In the Lab

(a) Slide 1

Money Sense –
Gaining Financial Freedom

Presented by:

Rich Jackson
Community Savings & Loan

(b) Slide 2

Start Saving Now

- Use the benefits of compounding interest
  - Search for investments with high returns
  - Consider stocks and stock mutual funds
- Have an emergency money fund
  - Try to save six months' living expenses
  - Put in easily liquidated accounts

(c) Slide 3

Spend Within Your Means

- Make a budget and stick to it
- Watch for bargains
  - Shop at pre-season and post-season sales
- Buy classic clothes and furnishings
  - They will not seem dated years later

(d) Slide 4

Pay Yourself First

- You are your primary financial obligation
  - Be completely committed to saving regularly
- Save 10 percent of your gross income
  - As your salary grows, increase this amount
- Use direct deposit to ensure a transaction

FIGURE 1-79

Instructions: Perform the following tasks.

1. Create a new presentation using the Capsules design template.
2. Using the typed notes illustrated in Figure 1-78, create the title slide shown in Figure 1-79a using your name in place of Rich Jackson. Decrease the font size of the paragraph, Presented by:, to 24. Decrease the font size of the paragraph, Community Savings & Loan, to 20.
3. Using the typed notes in Figure 1-78, create the three bulleted list slides shown in Figures 1-79b through 1-79d. Increase the Before paragraph spacing to .8 Lines.
4. Click the Spelling button on the Standard toolbar. Correct any errors.
5. Save the presentation on a floppy disk using the file name, Money Freedom.
6. Display the presentation in black and white.
7. Print the black and white presentation. Quit PowerPoint.

In the Lab

2 Lake Shore Mall Fashion Show

Problem: You work in a clothing store at Lake Shore Mall, and your manager has asked you to participate in the annual fashion show. You decide to get involved with the segment promoting clothing to wear on job interviews. You determine that a PowerPoint presentation would help the commentator present key points as the models display accompanying clothing. You interview fashion coordinators at various stores in the mall and organize the list in Figure 1-80. Then you select a PowerPoint design template and decide to modify it. *Hint*: Use the PowerPoint Help system to solve this problem.

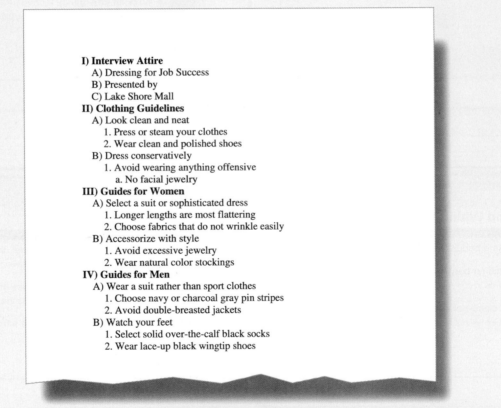

I) Interview Attire
 A) Dressing for Job Success
 B) Presented by
 C) Lake Shore Mall
II) Clothing Guidelines
 A) Look clean and neat
  1. Press or steam your clothes
  2. Wear clean and polished shoes
 B) Dress conservatively
  1. Avoid wearing anything offensive
   a. No facial jewelry
III) Guides for Women
 A) Select a suit or sophisticated dress
  1. Longer lengths are most flattering
  2. Choose fabrics that do not wrinkle easily
 B) Accessorize with style
  1. Avoid excessive jewelry
  2. Wear natural color stockings
IV) Guides for Men
 A) Wear a suit rather than sport clothes
  1. Choose navy or charcoal gray pin stripes
  2. Avoid double-breasted jackets
 B) Watch your feet
  1. Select solid over-the-calf black socks
  2. Wear lace-up black wingtip shoes

FIGURE 1-80

Instructions: Perform the following tasks.

1. Create a new presentation using the Post Modern design template.
2. Using the notes in Figure 1-80, create the title slide shown in Figure 1-81a. Increase the font size of the paragraph, Dressing for Job Success, to 36. Decrease the font size of the paragraph, Presented by, to 28.
3. Using the notes in Figure 1-80, create the three multi-level bulleted list slides shown in Figures 1-81b through 1-81d.
4. Display the slide master. Click the paragraph, Click to edit Master title style. Click the Bold button on the Formatting toolbar.
5. Click the paragraph, Click to edit Master text styles. On the Format menu, click Line Spacing, and then increase the Before paragraph line spacing to 0.75 Lines. Click the paragraph, Second level. On the Format menu, click Line Spacing, and then increase the After paragraph spacing to 0.25 Lines.

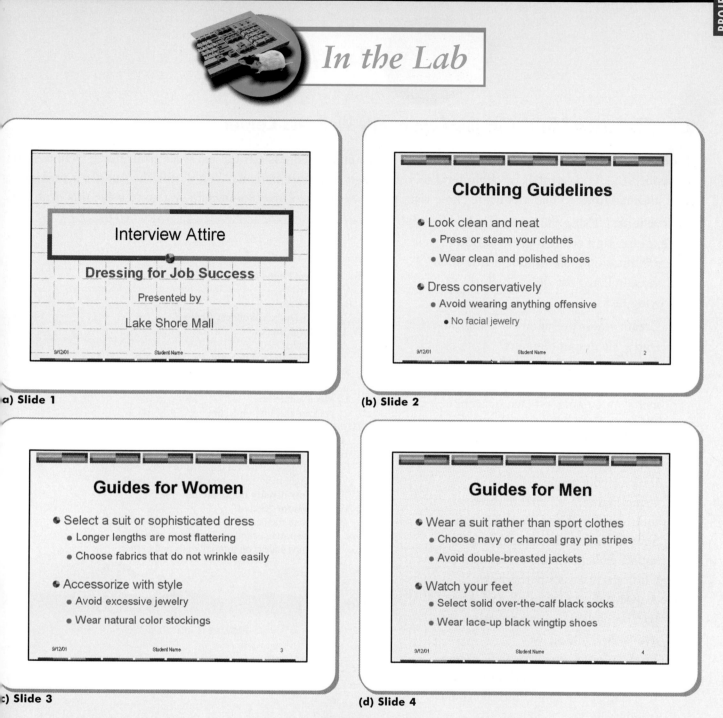

In the Lab

(a) Slide 1

Interview Attire

Dressing for Job Success

Presented by

Lake Shore Mall

(b) Slide 2

Clothing Guidelines

- Look clean and neat
  - Press or steam your clothes
  - Wear clean and polished shoes
- Dress conservatively
  - Avoid wearing anything offensive
    - No facial jewelry

(c) Slide 3

Guides for Women

- Select a suit or sophisticated dress
  - Longer lengths are most flattering
  - Choose fabrics that do not wrinkle easily
- Accessorize with style
  - Avoid excessive jewelry
  - Wear natural color stockings

(d) Slide 4

Guides for Men

- Wear a suit rather than sport clothes
  - Choose navy or charcoal gray pin stripes
  - Avoid double-breasted jackets
- Watch your feet
  - Select solid over-the-calf black socks
  - Wear lace-up black wingtip shoes

FIGURE 1-81

6. Drag the scroll box in the slide pane down to display the title master. Click the paragraph, Click to edit Master title style. Click the Bold button on the Formatting toolbar.

7. Return to normal view. On the View menu, click Header and Footer. If necessary, click the Slide tab. Add the date (so it updates automatically), a slide number, and your name to the footer. Display the footer on all slides.

8. Drag the scroll box to display Slide 1. Click the Slide Show button to start slide show view. Then click to display each slide.

9. Save the presentation on a floppy disk using the file name, Interview Attire. Display and print the presentation in black and white. Quit PowerPoint.

In the Lab

3 Cholesterol Basics at the Community Wellness Center

Problem: At your visit to the South Suburban Community Wellness Center last week, staff nurse Debbie Ortiz explained the fundamentals of cholesterol to you and several other patients. You decide she can use a presentation and handouts to better educate clinic visitors. *Hint*: Use the PowerPoint Help system to solve this problem.

Instructions: Using the list in Figure 1-82, design and create a presentation. The presentation must include a title slide and three bulleted list slides. Perform the following tasks.

1. Create a new presentation using the Dad's Tie design template.

2. Create a title slide titled, Cholesterol Highs and Lows. Include a subtitle, using your name in place of Debbie Ortiz. Decrease the font size for paragraphs Presented by: and South Suburban Wellness Center to 32. Italicize your name.

3. Using Figure 1-82, create three multi-level bulleted list slides. On Slide 2, use check marks instead of square bullets for the three main Cholesterol Basics paragraphs.

4. Adjust Before paragraph and After paragraph line spacing to utilize the available white space.

5. Insert a footer on every slide except the title slide that includes the current date, your name, and the slide number.

6. View the presentation in slide show view to look for errors. Correct any errors.

7. Check the presentation for spelling errors.

8. Save the presentation to a floppy disk with the file name, Cholesterol Basics. Print the presentation slides in black and white. Quit PowerPoint.

I) Cholesterol Highs and Lows
  A) Presented by:
  B) Debbie Ortiz
  C) South Suburban Wellness Center
II) Cholesterol Basics
  A) Needed by:
    1) Every cell in your body
  B) Builds:
    1) Brain and nerve tissues; bile
  C) Manufactured by:
    1) Liver and small intestine
III) HDL (high density lipids)
  A) H stands for "Healthy"
  B) Good for your heart
    1) Delivers cholesterol deposits in body to liver
      a) Liver disposes or recycles these deposits
IV) LDL (low density lipoproteins)
  A) L stands for "Lethal"
  B) Enemy of the heart
    1) Transports needed cholesterol to cells
    2) Dumps excess on arterial walls and tissues

FIGURE 1-82

Cases and Places

The difficulty of these case studies varies:
▶ are the least difficult; ▶▶ are more difficult; and ▶▶▶ are the most difficult.

1 ▶ Dr. Doug Gordon, chief ophthalmologist at the North Shore Eye Clinic, knows that many people take their eyesight for granted. They visit an eye doctor only when they are having difficulties, such as eye pain or extreme redness. He urges everyone, from newborns to senior citizens, to preserve their eyesight by scheduling regular eye exams. The times for these checkups varies by age. Dr. Gordon has contacted you to help him prepare a presentation that will be delivered at community fairs and at the local shopping mall. He has prepared the notes in Figure 1-83 and has asked you to use them to develop a title slide and additional slides that can be used on an overhead projector. Use the concepts and techniques introduced in this project to create the presentation.

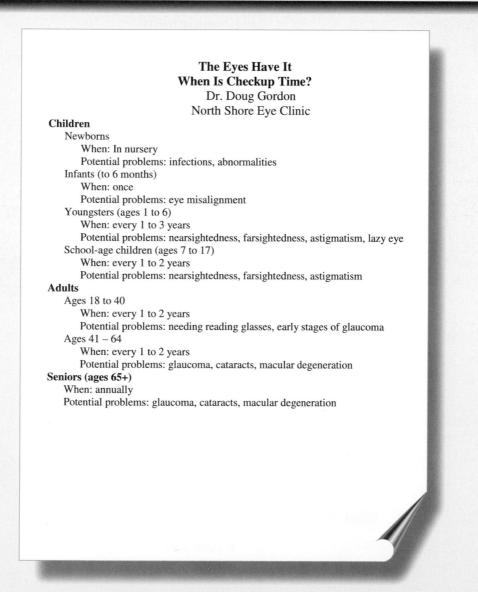

FIGURE 1-83

Cases and Places

2 ▶▶ This past holiday season, the Highland Shores police and fire departments experienced an unusually high number of calls for assistance. Many of these problems were the result of mishaps that easily could have been prevented. Police Chief Victor Halen and Fire Chief Norton Smits want to inform community residents at local block parties next summer about how they can follow a few safety precautions to reduce their chances of injuries. The chiefs want you to help them prepare a slide show and handouts for the community. They have typed safety tips for you (Figure 1-84), and they have asked you to prepare five slides that can be used on an overhead projector and as handouts. They want the title slide to introduce them and their topic. Use the concepts and techniques introduced in this project to create the presentation.

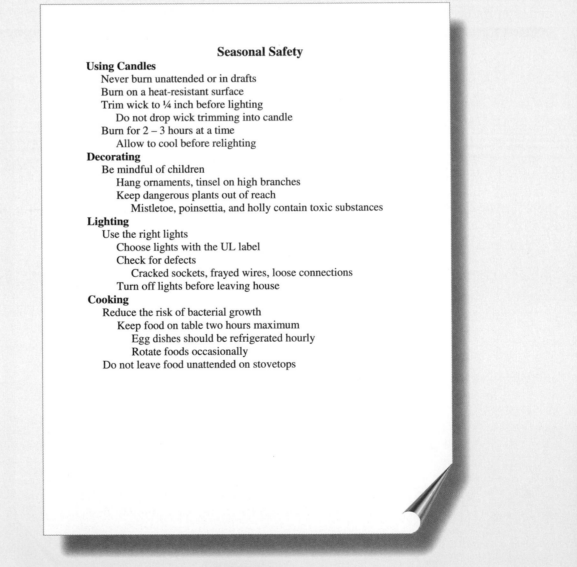

Seasonal Safety

Using Candles
   Never burn unattended or in drafts
   Burn on a heat-resistant surface
   Trim wick to ¼ inch before lighting
      Do not drop wick trimming into candle
   Burn for 2 – 3 hours at a time
      Allow to cool before relighting
Decorating
   Be mindful of children
      Hang ornaments, tinsel on high branches
      Keep dangerous plants out of reach
         Mistletoe, poinsettia, and holly contain toxic substances
Lighting
   Use the right lights
      Choose lights with the UL label
      Check for defects
         Cracked sockets, frayed wires, loose connections
      Turn off lights before leaving house
Cooking
   Reduce the risk of bacterial growth
      Keep food on table two hours maximum
         Egg dishes should be refrigerated hourly
         Rotate foods occasionally
   Do not leave food unattended on stovetops

FIGURE 1-84

Cases and Places

3 ▶▶ CPU-4-U is a computer repair store near campus that specializes in repairing computer systems and building custom computers. The co-owners, Warren Shilling and Mary Burg, want to attract new customers, and they have asked you to help them design a PowerPoint advertising campaign. Having graduated from your college, they are familiar with the hardware and software students need for their classes. Computer users can make appointments to bring their computers to the shop or to arrange for on-site service 24 hours a day. CPU-4-U also carries a complete line of supplies, including toner cartridges, paper, and labels. Many students consult with the technicians to plan for future computer purchases and to arrange financing for their new systems. The store is located in Tinley Mall, 6302 South State Street, Ypsilanti, Michigan. For more information call 555-2297. Using the techniques presented in this project, prepare a title slide and three bulleted list slides to be used for their presentation and for handouts.

4 ▶▶ The Poochy Humane Society in your town wants to increase community awareness of its services and facilities. The society's director, Jennifer Durkin, has decided that one way she can promote the shelter is by informing community residents on how they should react when a loose dog approaches them. She decides to address residents who regularly participate in activities at the local park district and who are walking, jogging, and biking in the community park. She wants to inform them that they can react in one of three ways when a stray dog approaches. They can be friendly by talking softly and by extending one of their hands palm down. Another behavior is to assert dominance. Using this approach, they should look at the dog sternly and yell, "Go away!" A third reaction is to act submissively by relaxing their muscles and glancing to the side. This technique is especially useful for an encounter with a big dog that thinks it is in control. The Poochy Humane Society is located at 10836 Windy Terrace; the telephone number is 555-DOGS. Using the concepts and techniques presented in this project, prepare a title slide and three bulleted list slides to be used on an overhead projector and as handouts for community residents.

5 ▶▶ Fat is one of the three essential components your body needs. The other two are protein and carbohydrates. Unfortunately, many people throughout the world consume too much fat in their diets. Although fat intake needs vary based on age and weight, following a low-fat diet can reduce the risk of heart disease. Some fats are healthy and actually help give energy, prevent blood clotting, and reduce cholesterol and triglyceride levels. These fats, commonly called essential fatty acids (EFAs) or Vitamin F, are found in cold-water fish and cold-temperature plant oils, such as flax seed and black currant. Monounsaturated fats also are healthy for the body. They are found in olive, almond, and canola oils, they all are liquid at room temperature, and they generally come from plant seeds. Although polyunsaturated fats can decrease cholesterol levels, they also can decrease the percentage of healthy HDL cholesterol (see In the Lab Project 3). Like monounsaturated fats, they come from plant seeds and are liquid at room temperature. They are found in safflower oil and corn oil. Saturated fats and hydrogenated fats are unhealthy because they can clog arteries and elevate cholesterol levels. They are found in animal foods, such as butter, margarine, and meat. Using the concepts and techniques presented in this project, prepare a presentation describing the various type of fats in our foods and their benefits or dangers to our health. Create a title slide and at least three additional slides that can be used with an overhead projector and as handouts.

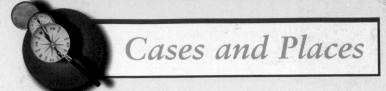

Cases and Places

6 ▶▶ Every day, two Americans are killed in collisions between trains and cars or between trains and pedestrians. Many more people suffer serious injuries from these accidents. Lighting is not a significant factor, for more than 50 percent of these accidents occur at crossings marked with gates and flashing lights, and more than 70 percent occur during the day. People involved in train accidents have one or more of these three personality traits: impatient, and not wanting to wait for a train; inattentive, and daydreaming or listening to loud music; or ignorant, and not aware of the impending danger. Drivers and pedestrians can reduce the risk of train accidents by looking both ways before crossing the tracks, never walking down a track, and assuming that a train can come at any time in either direction on any track. If your car stalls on a railroad track when a train is approaching, get out immediately and run away from the track in the same direction from which the train is coming. (If you run in the same direction the train is traveling, the train will hit your car, which can potentially hit you.) Using the concepts and techniques presented in this project, prepare a presentation to warn drivers and pedestrians of the dangers involved in crossing railroad tracks. Create a title slide and at least three additional slides that can be used with an overhead projector and as handouts.

7 ▶▶▶ In the Lab Project 1 discusses the need for developing techniques to achieve financial freedom. One of the suggestions is to invest in stocks or in stock mutual funds. These mutual funds pool shareholders' money and invest in a diversified portfolio of funds. Interview a financial planner or research the Internet for information on the various types of mutual funds and how they are managed. Determine the fees and expenses involved in this type of investment. Then, using the concepts and techniques presented in this project, prepare a presentation to report your findings. Create a title slide and at least three additional slides that can be used with an overhead projector and as handouts.

Microsoft PowerPoint 2000

P R O J E C T

2

Using Outline View and Clip Art to Create a Slide Show

You will have mastered the material in this project when you can:

- Create a presentation from an outline
- Start a presentation as a new PowerPoint document
- Use outline view
- Create a presentation in outline view
- Add a slide in outline view
- Create multi-level bulleted list slides in outline view
- Create a closing slide in outline view
- Save and review a presentation
- Change the slide layout
- Insert clip art from Microsoft Clip Gallery 5.0
- Move clip art
- Change clip art size
- Add a header and footer to outline pages
- Add animation and slide transition effects
- Apply animation effects to bulleted slides
- Animate clip art objects
- Format and animate a title slide
- Run an animated slide show
- Print a presentation outline
- E-mail a slide show from within PowerPoint

plan

prepare

practice

No Sweat

Deliver Your Presentation with Ease

What two words strike panic in the hearts of millions of people across the world? Public speaking.

Countless surveys throughout the decades have asked people to list their greatest fears. Going to the dentist always is near the top of the dreaded-events list. So are contracting a fatal disease and losing a job. The mere thought of standing in front of a group of people and trying to say something coherent, however, tops their lists every time. The memories of dry mouths, sweaty palms, queasy stomachs, and shaky

Sales

knees are enough to
guarantee a lifetime of
nightmares.

Fortunately, PowerPoint has
eased the pain of speechmaking
somewhat. As you learned in Project 1,
this software helps you organize your thoughts
and present your information in an orderly,
attractive manner. In Project 2, you will add to
your knowledge base by learning to change layouts and then insert drawings and photos in your
slides. Ultimately, your slide shows will have
visual appeal and ample content.

While the PowerPoint slide shows help you
plan your speeches, they also help your audience
absorb your message. People learn most effectively when their five senses are involved.
Researchers have determined that individuals
remember 10 percent of what they read, 20
percent of what they hear, 30 percent of what
they see, and an amazing 70 percent when they
both see and hear. That is why it is important to
attend class instead of copying your classmate's
notes. When you see and hear your instructor
deliver a lecture and write your own notes, you
are apt to interpret the concepts correctly and
recall this information at the ever-important final
exam.

The synergy of the speech-graphics combo
is recognized in a variety of venues. For example,
some college administrators and instructors are
requiring students to register for their

communications and
PowerPoint classes concurrently.
Bill Clinton's maps and Ross
Perot's charts are staples in their
speech repertoires.

The theories of structuring effective communication presentations are deep rooted. Dale
Carnegie wrote *How to Win Friends and Influ-
ence People* in 1936, and the millions of people
who have read that book have learned practical
advice on achieving success through communication. He formed the Dale Carnegie Institute,
which has taught 4.5 million graduates worldwide
the techniques of sharing ideas effectively and
persuading others. Microsoft has included
Carnegie's four-step process — plan, prepare,
practice, and present — in the PowerPoint Help
system.

In the days prior to PowerPoint, slides and
overhead transparencies were the domain of
artists in a corporation's graphic communications
department. With the influx of Microsoft Office
on desktops throughout a company, however,
employees from all departments now develop the
slide shows. According to Microsoft, the average
PowerPoint user now creates nine presentations
each month, which is double the number produced in 1995.

With all these presentations, that means a lot
of sweaty palms and shaky knees. But with planning and practice — and powerful PowerPoint presentations — these speakers can deliver their
messages confidently and successfully.

Microsoft PowerPoint 2000

Using Outline View and Clip Art to Create a Slide Show

P R O J E C T

2

CASE PERSPECTIVE

A college education no longer is considered an extravagance; instead, it is essential for landing and advancing in many jobs. The college experience has a price, however. Students often find their budgets maximized and their bank accounts drained. Financial aid in the form of scholarships, loans, and grants can help ease this burden. Each year millions of dollars of scholarship money go unclaimed because students do not know where or how to find these funds. Fortunately, a little effort can uncover an assortment of scholarship sources.

Many financially strapped students at your college visit the Office of Financial Aid in hopes of finding some relief. Dr. Mary Halen, the director of financial aid, has asked you to help prepare a student lecture on the topic of searching for scholarships. You suggest developing a short PowerPoint presentation to accompany her talk. The slide show will give an overview of researching scholarship sources, applying for the funds, considering merit scholarships and private sources, and surfing the Internet for additional information. You decide to add clip art and animation to increase visual interest. Then you e-mail the completed presentation to her.

Creating a Presentation from an Outline

At some time during either your academic or business life, you probably will make a presentation. The presentation may be informative by providing detailed information about a specific topic. Other presentations may be persuasive by selling a proposal or a product to a client, convincing management to approve a new project, or persuading the board of directors to accept the new fiscal budget. As an alternative to creating your presentation in the slide pane in normal view, as you did in Project 1, PowerPoint provides an outlining feature to help you organize your thoughts. When the outline is complete, it becomes the foundation for your presentation.

You can create your presentation outline using outline view. When you create an outline, you type all the text at one time, as if you were typing an outline on a sheet of paper. This technique differs from creating a presentation in the slide pane in normal view, where you type text as you create each individual slide and the text displays in both the slide and outline panes. PowerPoint creates the presentation as you type the outline by evaluating the outline structure and displaying a miniature view of the slide. Regardless of the view in which you build a presentation, PowerPoint automatically creates the five views discussed in Project 1: normal, outline, slide, slide sorter, and slide show.

The first step in creating a presentation in outline view is to type a title for the outline. The **outline title** is the subject of the presentation and later becomes the presentation title slide. Then you type the remainder of the outline, indenting appropriately to establish a structure or hierarchy. Once the outline is complete, you make your presentation more persuasive by adding graphics. This project uses outlining to create the presentation and clip art graphics to support the text visually.

Project Two — Searching for Scholarships

Project 2 uses PowerPoint to create the six-slide Searching for Scholarships presentation shown in Figures 2-1a through 2-1f. You create the presentation from the outline in Figure 2-2 on the next page.

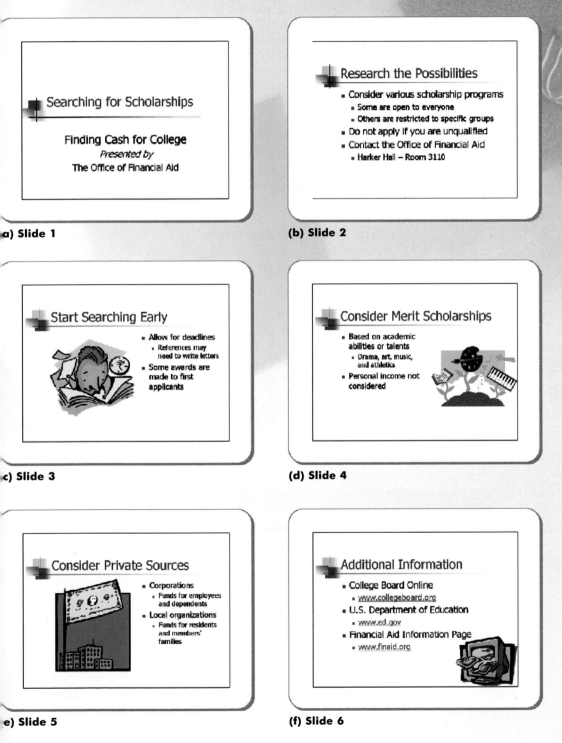

(a) Slide 1

(b) Slide 2

(c) Slide 3

(d) Slide 4

(e) Slide 5

(f) Slide 6

FIGURE 2-1

I. Searching for Scholarships
   A. Finding Cash for College
   B. Presented by
   C. The Office of Financial Aid
II. Research the Possibilities
   A. Consider various scholarship programs
      1. Some are open to everyone
      2. Others are restricted to specific groups
   B. Do not apply if you are unqualified
   C. Contact the Office of Financial Aid
      1. Harker Hall – Room 3110
III. Start Searching Early
   A. Allow for deadlines
      1. References may need to write letters
   B. Some awards are made to first applicants
IV. Consider Merit Scholarships
   A. Based on academic abilities or talents
      1. Drama, art, music, and athletics
   B. Personal income not considered
V. Consider Private Sources
   A. Corporations
      1. Funds for employees and dependents
   B. Local organizations
      1. Funds for residents and members' families
VI. Additional Information
   A. College Board Online
      1. www.collegeboard.org
   B. U.S. Department of Education
      1. www.ed.gov
   C. Financial Aid Information Page
      1. www.finaid.org

FIGURE 2-2

More About 2000

Using PowerPoint

The word "PowerPoint" traditionally is used as a noun to refer to the software you are using in these projects to create presentations. With our ever-changing language, however, the word has evolved into a synonym for the term presentation. You now can ask your instructor, Did you grade my PowerPoint?

Starting a New Presentation

Project 1 introduced you to starting a presentation document, choosing an AutoLayout, and applying a design template. The following steps summarize how to start a new presentation, choose an AutoLayout, apply a design template, and display the entire Formatting toolbar. For a more detailed explanation, see pages PP 1.10 through PP 1.20 in Project 1. To reset your toolbars and menus so they display exactly as shown in this book, follow the steps outlined in Appendix B. Perform the following steps to start a new presentation.

TO START A NEW PRESENTATION

1 Click the Start button on the taskbar.

2 Click New Office Document. If necessary, click the General tab in the New Office Document dialog box.

3 Double-click the Blank Presentation icon.

4 Click the OK button when the New Slide dialog box displays to select the Title Slide AutoLayout.

5 Double-click Default Design on the status bar. Double-click the Blends design template in the Presentation Designs list in the Apply Design template dialog box.

6 If the Office Assistant displays, right-click the Office Assistant and then click Hide on the shortcut menu.

7 Double-click the move handle on the Formatting toolbar in the Microsoft PowerPoint window to display it in its entirety.

PowerPoint displays the Title Slide AutoLayout and the Blends design template on Slide 1 in normal view (Figure 2-3).

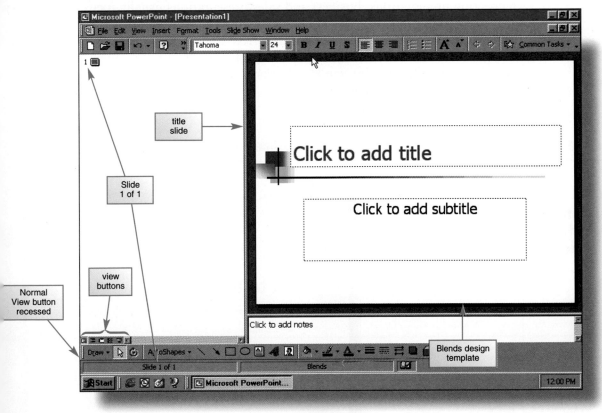

FIGURE 2-3

Using Outline View

Outline view provides a quick, easy way to create a presentation. Outlining allows you to organize your thoughts in a structured format. An outline uses indentation to establish a hierarchy, which denotes levels of importance to the main topic. An **outline** is a summary of thoughts, presented as headings and subheadings, often used as a preliminary draft when you create a presentation.

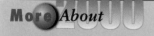
The three panes — outline, slide, and notes — shown in normal view also display in outline view. In outline view, however, the outline pane occupies the largest area on the left side of the window, and the slide pane shrinks to the upper-right corner to display how the current slide will look in normal view, slide view, slide sorter view, and slide show view. The notes pane displays under the slide pane. In the outline pane, the slide text displays along with a slide number and a slide icon. Body text is indented under the title text. Graphic objects, such as pictures, graphs, or tables, do not display in outline view. The slide icon is blank when a slide does not contain graphics. The attributes for text in outline view are the same as in normal view except for color and paragraph style.

PowerPoint limits the number of heading levels to six. The first heading level is the slide title and is not indented. The remaining five heading levels are the same as the five indent levels in slide view. Recall from Project 1 that PowerPoint allows for five indent levels and that each indent level has an associated bullet.

The outline begins with a title on **heading level 1**. The title is the main topic of the slide. Text supporting the main topic begins on **heading level 2** and indents under heading level 1. **Heading level 3** indents under heading level 2 and contains text to support heading level 2. **Heading level 4, heading level 5,** and **heading level 6** indent under heading level 3, heading level 4, and heading level 5, respectively. Use heading levels 4, 5, and 6 as required. They generally are used for very detailed scientific and engineering presentations. Business and sales presentations usually focus on summary information and use heading level 1, heading level 2, and heading level 3.

PowerPoint initially displays in normal view when you start a new presentation. Change from normal view to outline view by clicking the Outline View button at the lower left of the PowerPoint window. Perform the following steps to change the view from normal view to outline view.

Steps **To Change the View to Outline View and Display the Outline Toolbar**

1 Point to the Outline View button located at the lower left of the PowerPoint window (Figure 2-4).

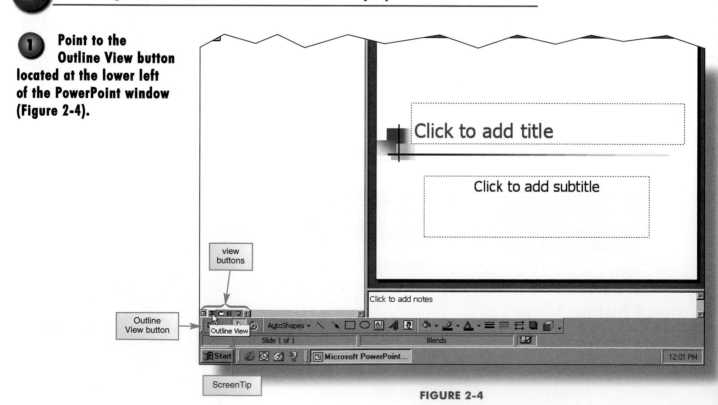

FIGURE 2-4

2 Click the Outline View button.

3 Click View on the menu bar and then point to Toolbars. Point to Outlining on the Toolbars submenu.

PowerPoint displays in outline view and the Toolbars submenu displays (Figure 2-5).

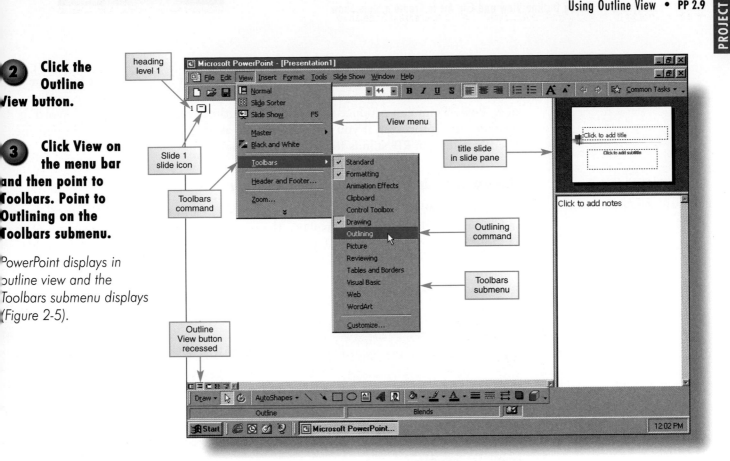

FIGURE 2-5

4 Click Outlining.

PowerPoint displays in outline view with the Outlining toolbar (Figure 2-6). PowerPoint displays the color view of Slide 1 in the slide pane.

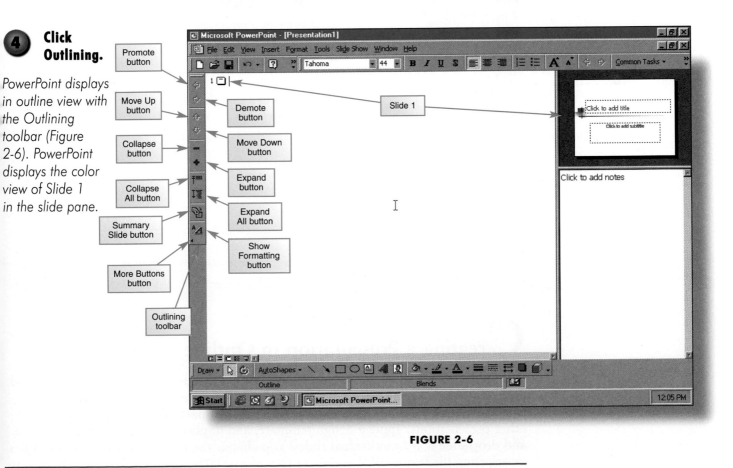

FIGURE 2-6

You can create and edit your presentation in outline view. Outline view also makes it easy to sequence slides and to relocate title text and body text from one slide to another. In addition to typing text to create a new presentation in outline view, PowerPoint can produce slides from an outline created in Microsoft Word or another word processor, if you save the outline as an RTF file or as a plain text file. The file extension **RTF** stands for **R**ich **T**ext **F**ormat.

The PowerPoint Window in Outline View

The PowerPoint window in outline view differs from the window in normal view because the Outlining toolbar displays, the outline pane occupies the majority of the window, and the slide pane displays a miniature version of the current slide. Table 2-1 describes the buttons on the Outlining toolbar.

Table 2-1	Buttons on the Outlining Toolbar	
BUTTON	**BUTTON NAME**	**DESCRIPTION**
	Promote	Moves the selected paragraph to the next-higher heading level (up one level, to the left).
	Demote	Moves the selected paragraph to the next-lower heading level (down one level, to the right).
	Move Up	Moves a selected paragraph and its collapsed (temporarily hidden) subordinate text above the preceding displayed paragraph.
	Move Down	Moves a selected paragraph and its collapsed (temporarily hidden) subordinate text down, below the following displayed paragraph.
	Collapse	Hides all but the title of selected slides. Collapsed text is represented by a gray line.
	Expand	Displays the titles and all collapsed text of selected slides.
	Collapse All	Displays only the title of each slide. Text other than the title is represented by a gray line below the title.
	Expand All	Displays the titles and all the body text for each slide.
	Summary Slide	Creates a new slide from the titles of the slides you select in slide sorter or normal view. The summary slide creates a bulleted list from the titles of the selected slides. PowerPoint inserts the summary slide in front of the first selected slide.
	Show Formatting	Shows or hides character formatting (such as bold and italic) in normal view. In slide sorter view, switches between showing all text and graphics on each slide and displaying titles only.
	More Buttons	Allows you to select the particular buttons you want to display on the toolbar.

Creating a Presentation in Outline View

Outline view enables you to view title and body text, add and delete slides, drag and drop slide text, drag and drop individual slides, promote and demote text, save a presentation, print an outline, print slides, copy and paste slides or text to and from other presentations, apply a design template, and import an outline. When you **drag and drop** slide text or individual slides, you change the order of the text or the slides by selecting the text or slide you want to move or copy and then dragging the text or slide to its new location.

Developing a presentation in outline view is quick because you type the text for .ll slides on one screen. Once you type the outline, the presentation fundamentally is omplete. If you choose, you then can go to normal view or slide view to enhance ·our presentation with graphics.

More About 2000

Design Templates

You can change design templates easily, even when you have completed creating each slide in your presentation. Each design template changes the color scheme, font attributes, and graphic objects throughout the entire file. For more information, visit the PowerPoint 2000 More About Web page (www.scsite.com/pp2000/more.htm) and click Design Templates.

:reating a Title Slide in Outline View

Recall from Project 1 that the title slide introduces the presentation to the ıudience. In addition to introducing the presentation, Project 2 uses the title slide o capture the attention of the students in your audience by using a design template vith colorful graphics. Perform the following steps to create a title slide in outline ·iew.

teps To Create a Title Slide in Outline View

1 Type `Searching for Scholarships` **ınd then press the ENTER ey.**

;earching for Scholarships s the title for ;lide 1 and is :alled heading level 1. A ;lide icon displays to the left ɔf each slide title. The font or heading level 1 is Tahoma ınd the font size is 44 points. ²ressing the ENTER key moves he insertion point to the next ine and maintains the same heading level. The insertion ɔoint is in position for typing he title for Slide 2 (Figure 2-7).

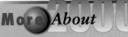

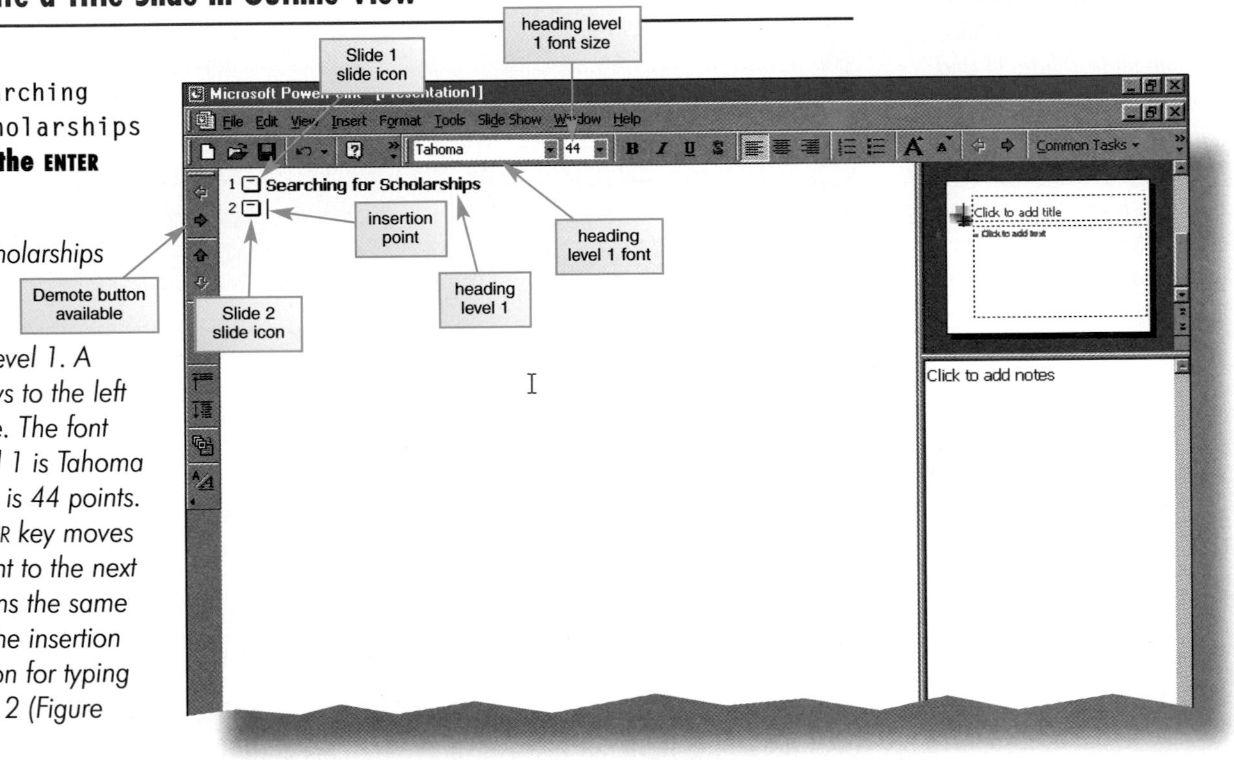

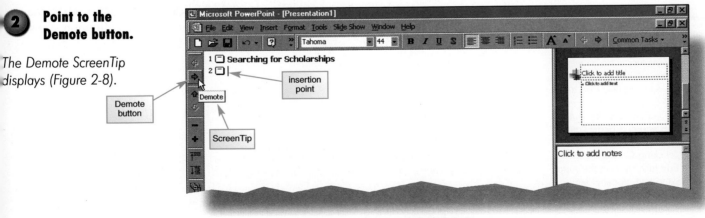

FIGURE 2-7

2 Point to the Demote button.

The Demote ScreenTip displays (Figure 2-8).

FIGURE 2-8

3 **Click the Demote button on the Outlining toolbar. Type** Finding Cash for College **and then press the ENTER key. Type** Presented by **and then press the ENTER key. Type** The Office of Financial Aid **and then press the ENTER key.**

The paragraphs, Finding Cash for College, Presented by, and The Office of Financial Aid, are subtitles on the title slide (Slide 1) and demote to heading level 2 (Figure 2-9). Heading level 2 is indented to the right under heading level 1. The heading level 2 font is Tahoma and the heading level 2 font size is 32 points. The Slide 2 slide icon does not display.

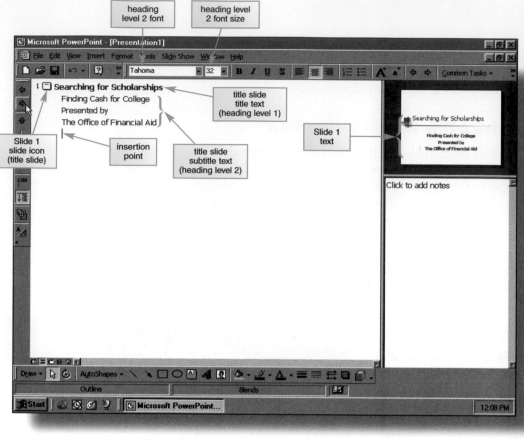

FIGURE 2-9

Auto-Fit Text

PowerPoint will reduce the point size of text automatically when you reach the bottom of the Object Area placeholder and need to squeeze an additional line on the slide. If you do not want to use this Auto-Fit feature, you can deactivate it by clicking Tools on the menu bar, clicking Options, clicking the Edit tab, clicking the Auto-fit text to text placeholder check box, and clicking OK.

The title slide text for the Searching for Scholarships presentation is complete. The next section explains how to add a slide in outline view.

Adding a Slide in Outline View

Recall from Project 1 that when you add a new slide in normal view, PowerPoint defaults to the Bulleted List AutoLayout. This action occurs in outline view as well. One way to add a new slide in outline view is to promote a paragraph to heading level 1 by clicking the Promote button on the outlining toolbar until the insertion point or the paragraph displays at heading level 1. A slide icon displays when the insertion point or paragraph reaches heading level 1. Perform the following steps to add a slide in outline view.

To Add a Slide in Outline View

1 Point to the Promote button on the Outlining toolbar.

The insertion point still is positioned at heading level 2 (Figure 2-10).

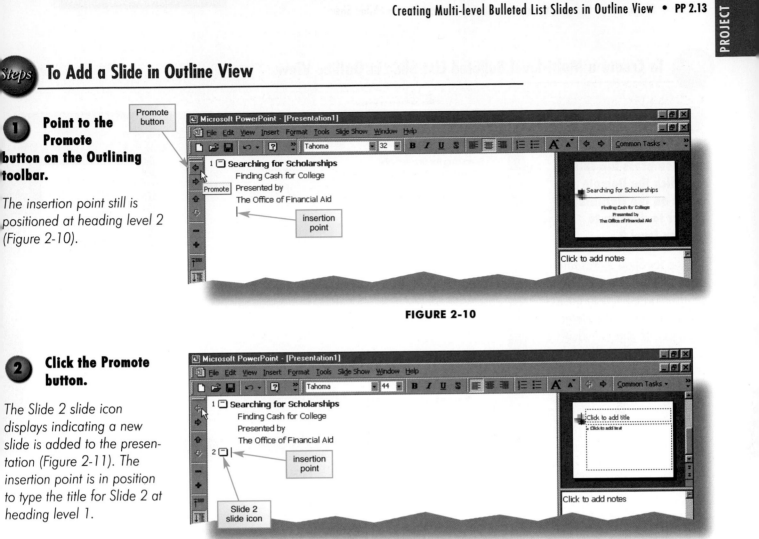

FIGURE 2-10

2 Click the Promote button.

The Slide 2 slide icon displays indicating a new slide is added to the presentation (Figure 2-11). The insertion point is in position to type the title for Slide 2 at heading level 1.

FIGURE 2-11

After you add a slide, you are ready to type the slide text. The next section explains how to create a multi-level bulleted list slide in outline view.

Creating Multi-level Bulleted List Slides in Outline View

To create a multi-level bulleted list slide, you demote or promote the insertion point to the appropriate heading level and then type the paragraph text. Recall from Project 1 that when you demote a paragraph, PowerPoint adds a bullet to the left of each heading level. Depending on the design template, each heading level has a different bullet font. Also recall that the design template determines font attributes, including the bullet font.

Slide 2 is the first **informational slide** for Project 2. Slide 2 introduces the main topic: students can conduct searches to find many scholarships available to them. Each of the three major points regarding finding scholarship information displays as heading level 2, and the first and third points have two supporting paragraphs, which display as heading level 3. The steps on the next page explain how to create a multi-level bulleted list slide in outline view.

1. Click New Slide button on Standard toolbar, click OK button
2. On Insert menu click New Slide, click OK button
3. Press ALT+I, press N, press ENTER
4. Press CTRL+M, press ENTER
5. Press and hold SHIFT, press TAB until paragraph or insertion point displays at heading level 1, release TAB

Steps   **To Create a Multi-level Bulleted List Slide in Outline View**

1 **Type**
Research
the Possibilities
**and then press the ENTER
key. Click the Demote
button on the Outlining
toolbar to demote to
heading level 2.**

*The title for Slide 2, Research
the Possibilities, displays and
the insertion point is in position to type the first bulleted
paragraph (Figure 2-12). A
bullet displays to the left of
the insertion point.*

FIGURE 2-12

2 **Type** Consider
various
scholarship programs
**and then press the ENTER
key. Click the Demote
button on the Outlining
toolbar to demote to
heading level 3. Type**
Some are open to
everyone **and then press
the ENTER key.**

*Slide 2 displays three head-
ing levels: the title, Research
the Possibilities, on heading
level 1, the first bulleted
paragraph on heading level
2, and the third bulleted
paragraph and insertion point
on heading level 3 (Figure
2-13). The heading level 3
font is Tahoma and the font
size is 28 points.*

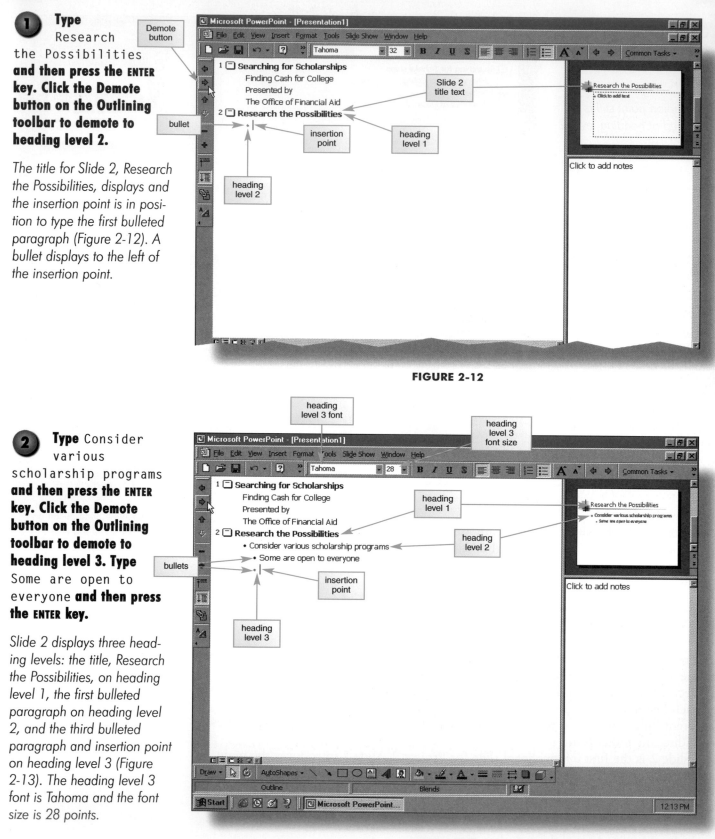

FIGURE 2-13

3 **Type** Others are restricted to specific groups **and then press the ENTER key. Click the Promote button on the Outlining toolbar to promote to heading level 2. Type** Do not apply if you are unqualified **and then press the ENTER key. Type** Contact the Office of Financial Aid **and then press the ENTER key. Click the Demote button on the Outlining toolbar to demote to heading level 3. Type** Harker Hall – Room 3110 **and then press the ENTER key.**

The text for Slide 2 is complete (Figure 2-14). Pressing the ENTER key begins a new paragraph at the same heading level as the previous paragraph. A red wavy line displays under the word Harker to indicate that particular word is not found in the Microsoft main dictionary or open custom dictionaries.

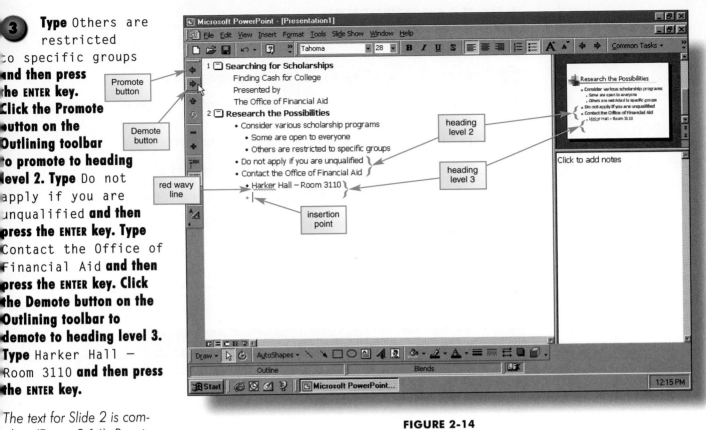

FIGURE 2-14

Creating Subordinate Slides

When developing your presentation, begin with a main topic and follow with **subordinate slides**, which are slides to support the main topic. Placing all your information on one slide may overwhelm your audience. In Project 1 you learned about the 7 × 7 rule, which recommends that each line should have a maximum of seven words, and each slide should have a maximum of seven lines. The steps on the next page use this 7 × 7 rule and explain how to create subordinate slides giving techniques for finding scholarships. The information on the next slide, Slide 3, provides information explaining the importance of looking for scholarships in a timely manner. Slides 4 and 5 list information on merit and private scholarships.

TO CREATE A SUBORDINATE SLIDE

1) Click the Promote button on the Outlining toolbar two times so that Slide 3 is added after Slide 2.

2) Type Start Searching Early and then press the ENTER key.

3) Click the Demote button on the Outlining toolbar to demote to heading level 2.

4) Type Allow for deadlines and then press the ENTER key.

5) Click the Demote button to demote to heading level 3.

6) Type References may need to write letters and then press the ENTER key.

7) Click the Promote button to promote to heading level 2.

8) Type Some awards are made to first applicants and then press the ENTER key.

The completed Slide 3 displays (Figure 2-15).

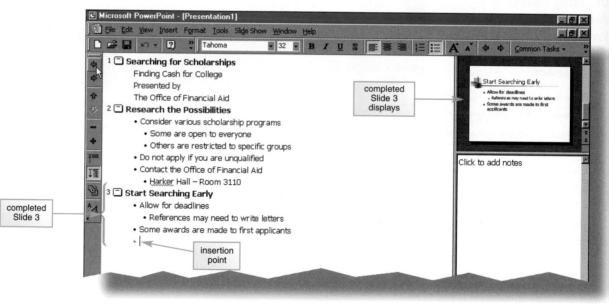

FIGURE 2-15

Creating a Second Subordinate Slide

The next step is to create Slide 4, which discusses merit scholarships. Perform the following steps to create this subordinate slide.

TO CREATE A SECOND SUBORDINATE SLIDE

1) Click the Promote button on the Outlining toolbar to add Slide 4 after Slide 3. Type Consider Merit Scholarships and then press the ENTER key.

2) Click the Demote button on the Outlining toolbar to demote to heading level 2. Type Based on academic abilities or talents and then press the ENTER key.

3) Click the Demote button to demote to heading level 3. Type Drama, art, music, and athletics and then press the ENTER key.

Click the Promote button to promote to heading level 2. Type `Personal income not considered` and then press the ENTER key.

The completed Slide 4 displays (Figure 2-16).

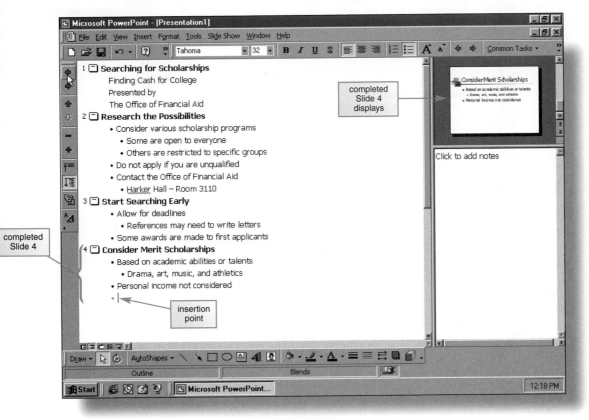

FIGURE 2-16

Creating a Third Subordinate Slide

The next step is to create Slide 5, which gives details on private sources of scholarship funds. Perform the following steps to create this subordinate slide.

TO CREATE A THIRD SUBORDINATE SLIDE

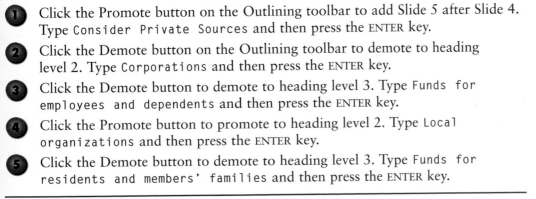

1. Click the Promote button on the Outlining toolbar to add Slide 5 after Slide 4. Type `Consider Private Sources` and then press the ENTER key.

2. Click the Demote button on the Outlining toolbar to demote to heading level 2. Type `Corporations` and then press the ENTER key.

3. Click the Demote button to demote to heading level 3. Type `Funds for employees and dependents` and then press the ENTER key.

4. Click the Promote button to promote to heading level 2. Type `Local organizations` and then press the ENTER key.

5. Click the Demote button to demote to heading level 3. Type `Funds for residents and members' families` and then press the ENTER key.

The completed Slide 5 displays (Figure 2-17 on the next page).

More About 2000

Smart Quotes

When you type an apostrophe and quotation marks, PowerPoint automatically converts these symbols to smart quotes, which also are called curly quotes. These symbols are in the shape of a dot and curved line (' " ' ") instead of a straight line (' "). If you want to use straight quotes instead, click Options on the Tools menu, click the Edit tab, and the click the Replace straight quotes with smart quotes check box.

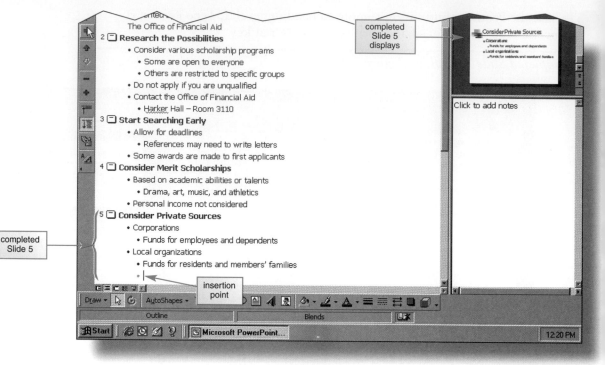

FIGURE 2-17

Creating a Closing Slide in Outline View

Starting Presentations

When faced with constructing a new PowerPoint presentation, you may find it helpful to start by designing your closing slide first. Knowing how you want the slide show to end helps you focus on reaching this conclusion. You can create each slide in the presentation with this goal in mind.

The last slide in your presentation is the closing slide. A **closing slide** gracefully ends a presentation. Often used during a question and answer session, the closing slide usually remains on the screen to reinforce the message delivered during the presentation. Professional speakers design the closing slide with one or more of these methods.

1. List important information. Tell the audience what to do next.
2. Provide a memorable illustration or example to make a point.
3. Appeal to emotions. Remind the audience to take action or accept responsibility.
4. Summarize the main points of the presentation.
5. Cite a quotation that directly relates to the main points of the presentation. This technique is most effective if the presentation started with a quotation.

The closing slide in this project lists three links to sites on the World Wide Web that have additional information on scholarships. Perform the following steps to create this closing slide.

TO CREATE A CLOSING SLIDE IN OUTLINE VIEW

 Click the Promote button on the Outlining toolbar two times so that Slide 6 is added to the end of the presentation. Type Additional Information as the slide title and then press the ENTER key.

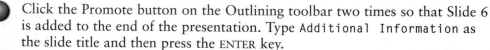 Click the Demote button on the Outlining toolbar to demote to heading level 2. Type College Board Online and then press the ENTER key.

 Click the Demote button to demote to heading level 3. Type www.collegeboard.org and then press the ENTER key.

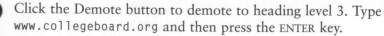 Click the Promote button to promote to heading level 2. Type U.S. Department of Education and then press the ENTER key.

5 Click the Demote button to demote to heading level 3. Type www.ed.gov and then press the ENTER key.

6 Click the Promote button to promote to heading level 2. Type Financial Aid Information Page and then press the ENTER key.

7 Click the Demote button to demote to heading level 3. Type www.finaid.org but do not press the ENTER key.

The completed Slide 6 displays (Figure 2-18). PowerPoint automatically displays the first two Internet addresses underlined and with a font color of red.

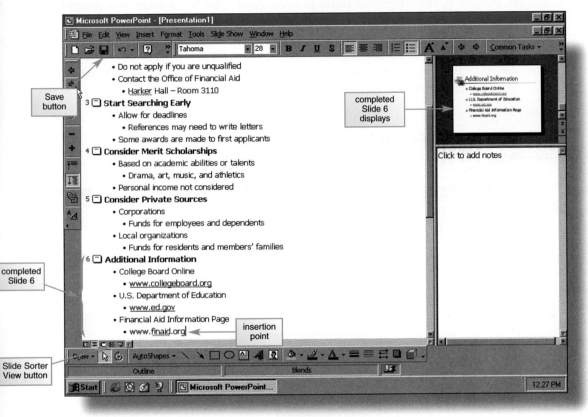

FIGURE 2-18

The outline now is complete and the presentation should be saved. The next section explains how to save the presentation.

Saving a Presentation

Recall from Project 1 that it is wise to save your presentation frequently. Now that you have created all the text for your presentation, you should save your presentation. For a detailed explanation of the following summarized steps, refer to pages PP 1.28 through PP 1.31 in Project 1.

TO SAVE A PRESENTATION

 Insert a formatted floppy disk in drive A and then click the Save button on the Standard toolbar.

2 Click the Save in box arrow. Click 3½ Floppy (A:) in the Save in list.

More About

Quick Reference

For a table that lists how to complete the tasks covered in this book using the mouse, menu, shortcut menu, and keyboard, visit the Office 2000 Web page (www.scsite.com/off2000/qr.htm) and then click Microsoft PowerPoint.

3 Click the Save button in the Save As dialog box.

The presentation is saved on the floppy disk in drive A under the file name Searching for Scholarships. PowerPoint uses the first text line in your presentation as the default file name. The file name displays on the title bar.

Reviewing a Presentation in Slide Sorter View

In Project 1, you displayed slides in slide show view to evaluate the presentation. Slide show view, however, restricts your evaluation to one slide at a time. Outline view is best for quickly reviewing all the text for a presentation. The slide sorter view allows you to look at several slides at one time, which is why it is the best view to use to evaluate a presentation for content, organization, and overall appearance. Perform the following step to change from outline view to slide sorter view.

Steps **To Change the View to Slide Sorter View**

1 **Click the Slide Sorter View button at the lower left of the PowerPoint window.**

PowerPoint displays the presentation in slide sorter view (Figure 2-19). Slide 6 is selected because it was the current slide in outline view.

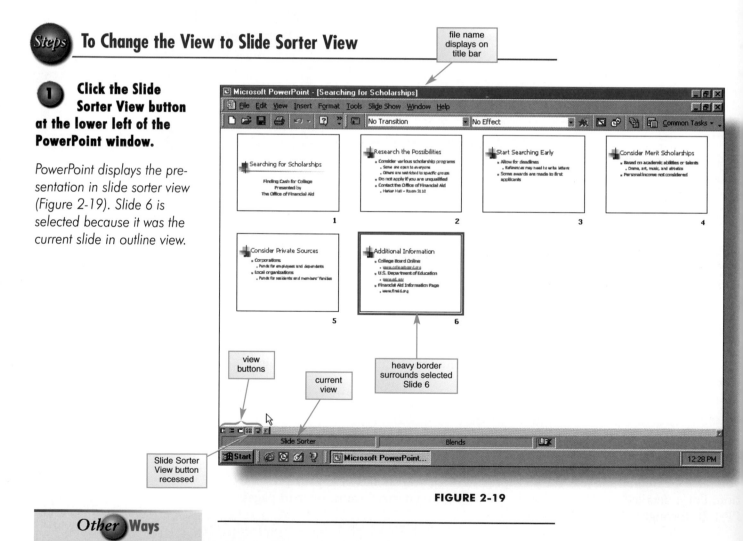

FIGURE 2-19

Other Ways

1. On View menu click Slide Sorter
2. Press ALT+V, press D

You can review the six slides in this presentation all in one window. Notice the slides have a significant amount of white space and look drab. These observations indicate a need to add visual interest to the slides by using graphics, such as clip art. The next several sections explain how to improve the presentation by changing slide layouts and adding clip art.

You can make changes to text in normal view, outline view, and slide view. It is best, however, to change the view to slide view when altering the slide layouts so you can see the result of your changes. Perform the following steps to change the view from slide sorter view to slide view.

Steps **To Change the View to Slide View**

1 **Point to the Slide 3 slide miniature (Figure 2-20).**

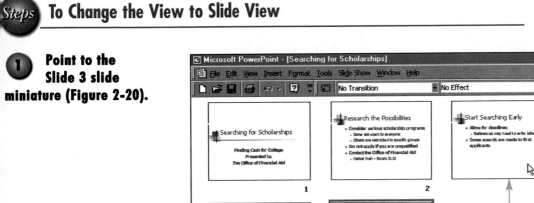

FIGURE 2-20

2 **Click the Slide 3 slide miniature. Click the Slide View button at the lower left of the PowerPoint window.**

Slide 3 displays in slide view (Figure 2-21). The Slide View button is recessed at the lower left of the PowerPoint window. The Slide 3 icon is highlighted in the outline pane.

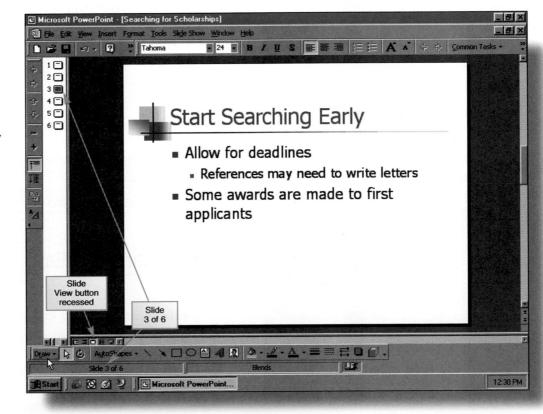

FIGURE 2-21

Changing Slide Layout

When you began developing this presentation, PowerPoint displayed the New Slide dialog box with the default Title Slide AutoLayout selected. When you added the five new slides to your presentation, PowerPoint used the default Bulleted List Auto-Layout. After creating a slide, you can change its layout by clicking the **Common Tasks button** on the Formatting toolbar and then clicking the Slide Layout command on the Common Tasks button menu. The Slide Layout dialog box then displays.

Like the AutoLayout dialog box, the **Slide Layout dialog box** allows you to choose one of the 24 different AutoLayouts that has placeholders arranged in various configurations for the title, text, clip art, graphs, tables, and media clips. The placement of the text, in relationship to nontext objects, depends on the slide layout. The nontext Object Area placeholder may be to the right or left of the text, above the text, or below the text. Additionally, some slide layouts are constructed with two nontext object placeholders.

When you change the layout of a slide, PowerPoint retains the text and graphics and repositions them into the appropriate placeholders. Using slide layouts eliminates the need to resize objects and the font size because PowerPoint automatically sizes the objects and text to fit the placeholders. If the objects are in landscape orientation, PowerPoint sizes them to the width of the placeholders. If the objects are in portrait orientation, PowerPoint sizes them to the height of the placeholder.

Before you insert clip art into an AutoLayout placeholder, you first must select one of the slide layouts that includes an Object Area placeholder with a clip art region. This Object Area placeholder contains instructions to open Microsoft Clip Gallery 5.0. Double-clicking the clip art region in the Object Area placeholder activates the instructions. The Object Area placeholders on Slides 3, 4, and 5 will hold clip art. Adding clip art to these slides requires two steps. First, change the slide layout to Clip Art & Text or Text & Clip Art. Then insert clip art into the Object Area placeholder. Perform the following steps to change the slide layout on Slide 3 from a bulleted list to Clip Art & Text.

Toolbar Buttons

You can customize your toolbars by using buttons that are larger than the ones normally displayed. To enlarge the buttons, click Customize on the Tools menu, click the Options tab, and then select the Large icons check box. This setting will affect all of your Microsoft Office programs.

 To Change Slide Layout to Clip Art & Text

1 **Click the Common Tasks button on the Formatting toolbar and then point to Slide Layout (Figure 2-22).**

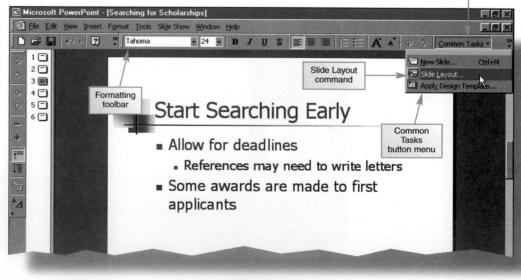

FIGURE 2-22

2 **Click Slide Layout on the Common Tasks button menu. Click the Clip Art & Text slide layout located in row three, column two when the Slide Layout dialog box displays. Point to the Apply button.**

The Slide Layout dialog box displays (Figure 2-23). The Clip Art & Text slide layout is selected. When you click a slide layout, its name displays in the box at the lower-right corner of the Slide Layout dialog box.

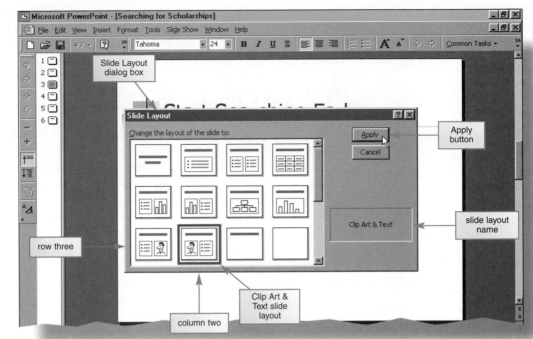

FIGURE 2-23

3 **Click the Apply button.**

Slide 3 displays the Clip Art & Text AutoLayout (Figure 2-24). PowerPoint moves the text object containing the bulleted list to the right side of the slide and automatically resizes the text to fit the object. The left side of the Object Area placeholder displays the message, Double click to add clip art.

Other Ways

1. Right-click slide anywhere except Title Area or Object Area placeholders, click Slide Layout, double-click desired slide layout

2. Click Common Tasks menu button, click Slide Layout, double-click desired slide layout

3. On Format menu click Slide Layout, double-click desired slide layout

4. Press ALT+O, press L, press arrow keys to select desired slide layout, press ENTER

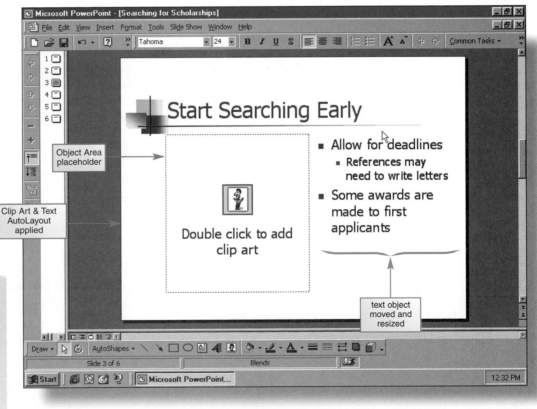

FIGURE 2-24

PowerPoint reduced the heading level 2 text in the Slide 3 placeholder from a font size of 32 points to 28 points and the heading level 3 text from 28 points to 24 points so all the words would fit into the text object.

Adding Clip Art to a Slide

Clip art offers a quick way to add professional-looking graphic images to your presentation without creating the images yourself. One clip art source is the Microsoft Clip Gallery 5.0. **Microsoft Clip Gallery 5.0** is a tool that accompanies Microsoft Office 2000 and allows you to insert pictures, photographs, audio clips, and video clips to a presentation. It contains a wide variety of clip art images and is shared with other Microsoft Office applications. Microsoft Clip Gallery 5.0 combines topic-related clip art images into categories, such as Academic, Business, Entertainment, and Healthcare & Medicine.

Table 2-2 shows four of the 57 categories from Microsoft Clip Gallery 5.0 and keywords of various clip art files in those categories. Clip art images have one or more keywords associated with various entities, activities, labels, and emotions. In most instances, the keywords give the name of the physical object and related categories. For example, an image of a horse in the Animals category has the keywords, animals, nature, creatures, mammals, domestic animals, and horses. You can enter these keywords in the Search for clips text box to find clip art when you know one of the words associated with the clip art image. Otherwise, you may find it necessary to scroll through several categories to find an appropriate picture.

More About

Legal Use of Clip Art

Be certain you have the legal right to use clip art, photographs, sounds, and movies in your slide show. Read the copyright notices that accompany clip art software and are posted on Web sites. The owners of these images and files often ask you to give them credit for using their work, which may be accomplished by stating where you obtained the images.

Table 2-2	Microsoft Clip Gallery 5.0 Category and Keyword Examples
CATEGORY	CLIP ART KEYWORDS
Academic	Books; activities; graduations; schools; academic, music, school bells; academic, books, education; academic, office, office
Business	Risks; decisions; light bulbs; goals; motivation; challenges; workers; teamwork; activities
Entertainment	Musicians; musical notes; majic; dance; motion pictures; juggling priorities
Healthcare & Medicine	Research; vaccinations; equipment; medical; surgery; nursing; chiropractors; veterinary medicine; dentistry

Depending on the installation of Microsoft Clip Gallery 5.0 on your computer, you may not have the clip art pictures used in this project. Contact your instructor if you are missing clip art when you perform the following steps.

Inserting Clip Art into an Object Area Placeholder

Now that the Clip Art & Text layout is applied to Slide 3, you insert clip art into the Object Area placeholder. Perform the following steps to insert clip art to the Object Area placeholder on Slide 3.

To Insert Clip Art into an Object Area Placeholder

1 **Position the mouse pointer anywhere within the clip art region of the Object Area placeholder.**

The mouse pointer is positioned inside the clip art region of the Object Area placeholder (Figure 2-25). The mouse pointer becomes a four-headed arrow. It is not necessary to point to the picture inside the placeholder.

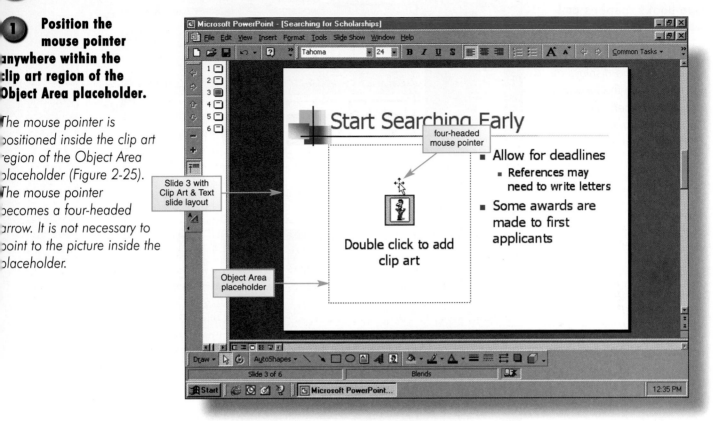

FIGURE 2-25

2 **Double-click the left side of the Object Area placeholder on Slide 3.**

PowerPoint displays the Microsoft Clip Gallery dialog box (Figure 2-26). The Pictures sheet displays clip art images by category, and New Category is the selected category. The Search for clips text box displays, Type one or more words. . . , as the entry.

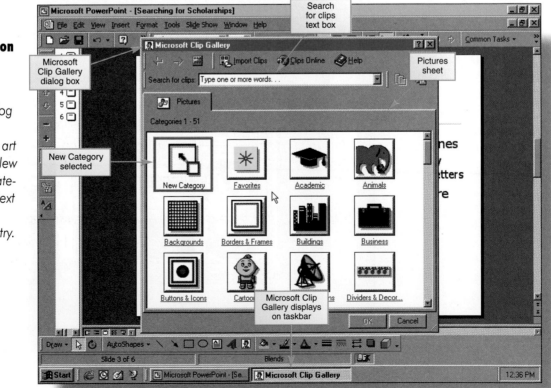

FIGURE 2-26

Click the Search for clips text box. Type books papers **and then press the ENTER key.**

The Microsoft Clip Gallery searches for and displays all pictures having the keywords, books and papers (Figure 2-27). The desired clip art image of a man looking in a book displays. Your images may be different depending on the clip art installed on your computer.

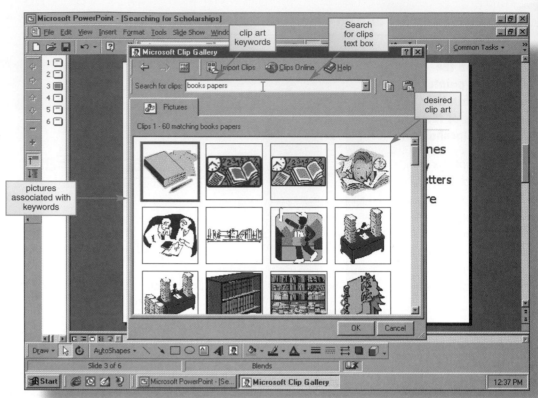

FIGURE 2-27

 Click the desired picture and then point to the Insert clip button.

When you click the desired picture, a Pop-up menu displays (Figure 2-28). If you want to see a larger image of the selected image, you would click Preview clip on the Pop-up menu.

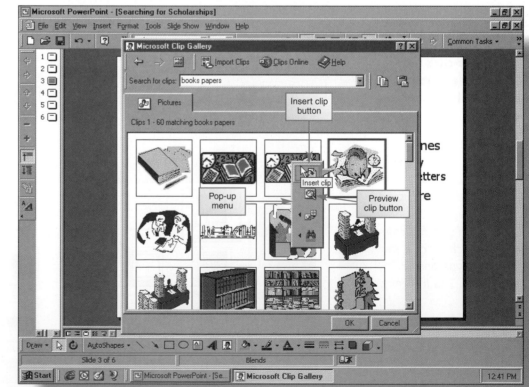

FIGURE 2-28

Step 5

Click the Insert clip button on the Pop-up menu.

The selected picture is inserted into the Object Area placeholder on Slide 3 (Figure 2-29). PowerPoint automatically sizes the picture to fit the placeholder.

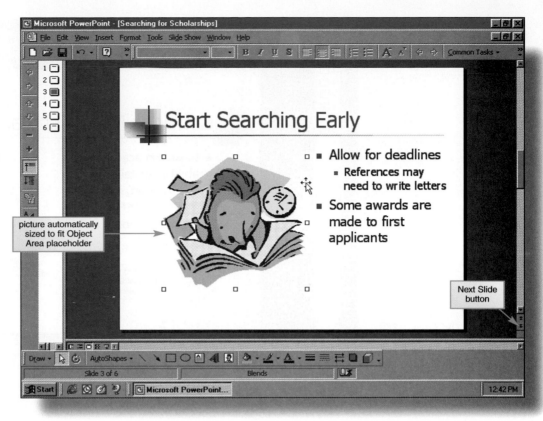

FIGURE 2-29

Inserting Clip Art on Other Slides

Slide 3 is complete, and you now want to add other clip art to Slides 4 and 5. Slide 5 also uses the Clip Art & Text slide layout, but Slide 4 uses the Text & Clip Art slide layout so the text displays on the left side of the slide and the clip art displays on the right side. Perform the following steps to change the slide layouts and then add clip art to Slide 4.

TO CHANGE THE SLIDE LAYOUT TO TEXT & CLIP ART AND INSERT CLIP ART

1 Click the Next Slide button on the vertical scroll bar to display Slide 4.

2 Click the Common Tasks menu button on the Formatting toolbar and then click Slide Layout.

3 Double-click the Text & Clip Art slide layout located in row three, column one.

4 Double-click the clip art region of the Object Area placeholder on the right side of Slide 4.

5 Type art music in the Search for clips text box and then press the ENTER key.

6 If necessary, scroll to display the desired clip art displaying a book, an artist's palette, and a keyboard. Click the desired clip art and then click Insert clip on the Pop-up menu.

The selected picture is inserted into the Object Area placeholder on Slide 4 (Figure 2-30 on the next page). PowerPoint automatically sizes the picture to fit the placeholder.

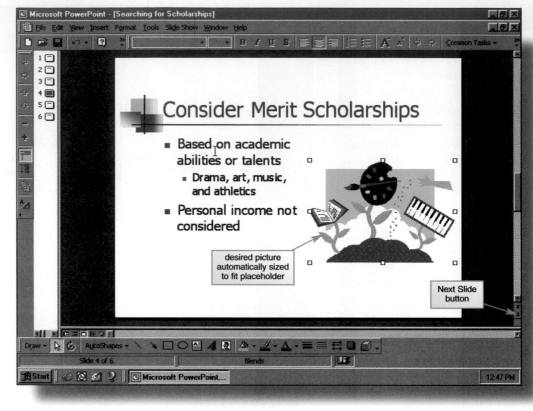

FIGURE 2-30

Slide 4 is complete. Your next step is to add other clip art to Slide 5, which also uses the Clip Art & Text slide layout you used in Slide 3. Perform the following steps to change the slide layouts and then add clip art to Slide 5.

TO CHANGE THE SLIDE LAYOUT TO CLIP ART & TEXT AND INSERT CLIP ART

1 Click the Next Slide button on the vertical scroll bar to display Slide 5.

2 Click the Common Tasks menu button on the Formatting toolbar and then click Slide Layout.

3 Double-click the Clip Art & Text slide layout located in row three, column two.

4 Double-click the clip art region of the Object Area placeholder on the left side of Slide 5.

5 Type buildings money in the Search for clips text box and then press the ENTER key.

6 If necessary, scroll to display the desired clip art displaying buildings with money on a flagpole. Click the desired clip art and then click Insert clip on the Pop-up menu.

The selected picture is inserted into the Object Area placeholder on Slide 5 (Figure 2-31). PowerPoint automatically sizes the picture to fit the placeholder.

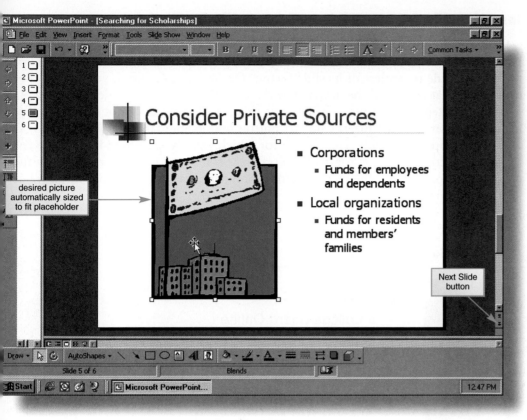

FIGURE 2-31

In addition to the clip art images in Microsoft Clip Gallery 5.0, other sources for clip art include retailers specializing in computer software, the Internet, bulletin board systems, and online information systems. Some popular online information systems are The Microsoft Network, America Online, CompuServe, and Prodigy. A **bulletin board system** is a computer system that allows users to communicate with each other and share files. Microsoft has created Clip Gallery Live, a special page on its World Wide Web site with new clips you can review and add to your Clip Gallery.

Besides clip art, you can insert pictures into your presentation. These may include scanned photographs, line art, and artwork from compact discs. To insert a picture into a presentation, the picture must be saved in a format that PowerPoint can recognize. Table 2-3 identifies some of the formats PowerPoint recognizes.

You can import files saved with the .emf, .gif, .jpg, .png, .bmp, .rle, .dib, and .wmf formats directly into your presentations. All other file formats require separate filters that are shipped with the PowerPoint installation software and must be installed. You can download additional graphics filters from the Microsoft Office Update Web site.

Table 2-3 Primary File Formats Recognized by PowerPoint	
FORMAT	*FILE EXTENSION*
Computer Graphics Metafile	*.cgm
CorelDRAW	*.cdr, .cdt, .cmx, and .pat
Encapsulated PostScript	*.eps
Enhanced Metafile	*.emf
FlashPix	*.fpx
Graphics Interchange Format	*.gif
Hanako	*.jsh, .jah, and .jbh
Joint Photographic Experts Group (JPEG)	*.jpg
Kodak Photo CD	*.pcd
Macintosh PICT	*.pct
PC Paintbrush	*.pcx
Portable Network Graphics	*.png
Tagged Image File Format	*.tif
Windows Bitmap	*.bmp, .rle, .dib
Microsoft Windows Metafile	*.wmf
WordPerfect Graphics	*.wpg

More About

Design

Graphic artists suggest designing a presentation in black and white and then adding color to emphasize particular areas on the slide. By starting with black letters on a white background, basic design principles, such as balance, contrast, rhythm, and harmony, are evident.

Inserting Clip Art on a Slide without a Clip Art Region

PowerPoint does not require you to use an AutoLayout containing a clip art region in the Object Area placeholder to add clip art to a slide. You can insert clip art on any slide regardless of its slide layout. On Slides 3, 4, and 5, you added clip art images that enhanced the message in the text. Recall that the slide layout on Slide 6 is the Bulleted List AutoLayout. Because this AutoLayout does not contain a clip art region, you click the Insert Clip Art button on the Standard toolbar to start Microsoft Clip Gallery 5.0. The picture for which you are searching has money coming out of a computer monitor. Its keywords are computer and dollars. Perform the following steps to insert the picture of this monitor on a slide that does not have a clip art region.

Steps To Insert Clip Art on a Slide without a Clip Art Region

1 Click the Next Slide button on the vertical scroll bar to display Slide 6.

2 Point to the Insert Clip Art button on the Drawing toolbar.

Clicking the Insert Clip Art button on the Drawing toolbar performs the same action as double-clicking an Object Area placeholder (Figure 2-32).

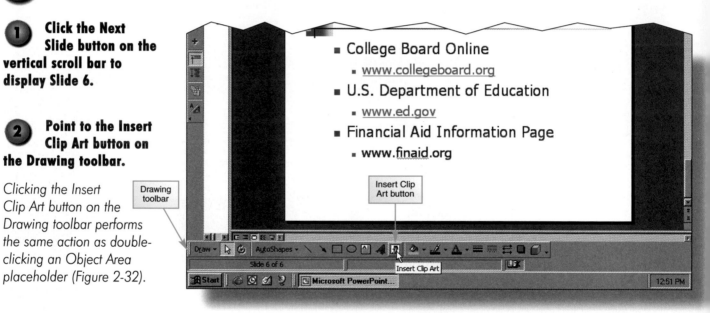

FIGURE 2-32

3 Click the Insert Clip Art button.

4 Type computer dollars in the Search for clips text box and then press the ENTER key. If necessary, scroll to display the desired clip art displaying a computer monitor with money.

The clip art image of money floating out of a computer monitor displays (Figure 2-33).

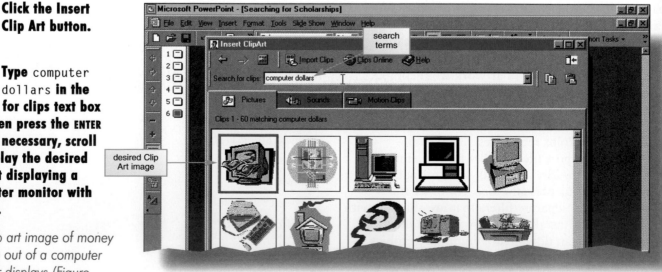

FIGURE 2-33

5 **Click the desired clip art and then click Insert clip on the shortcut menu. Point to the Close button on the Insert Clip Art title bar.**

PowerPoint inserts the desired clip art on Slide 6. Slide 6, however, is not visible until you close the Insert ClipArt dialog box (Figure 2-34).

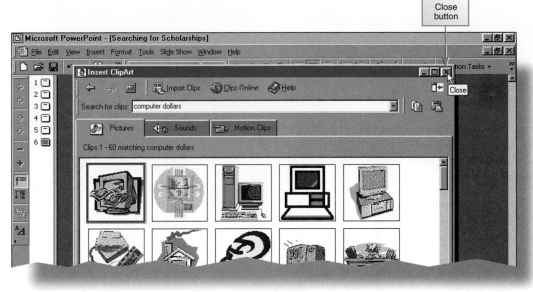

FIGURE 2-34

6 **Click the Close button on the Insert ClipArt title bar.**

The selected picture is inserted on Slide 6 (Figure 2-35). Sizing handles indicate the clip art is selected.

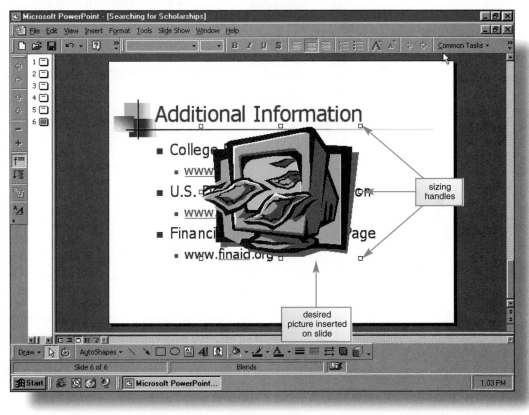

FIGURE 2-35

Moving Clip Art

After you insert clip art on a slide, you may want to reposition it. The picture of the monitor on Slide 6 overlays the bulleted list. You want to move the picture away from the text to the bottom-right corner of the slide. First move the picture and then change its size. Perform the steps on the next page to move the monitor to the bottom-right side of the slide.

Steps To Move Clip Art

1 **If the picture of the monitor is not already selected, use the mouse pointer to point to the monitor and then click.**

2 **Press and hold down the left mouse button. Drag the picture of the monitor to the bottom-right corner of the slide. Release the left mouse button.**

When you drag an object, a dotted box displays. The dotted box indicates the new position of the object. When you release the left mouse button, the picture of the monitor displays in the new location (Figure 2-36). Sizing handles display at the corners and along the edges of the monitor.

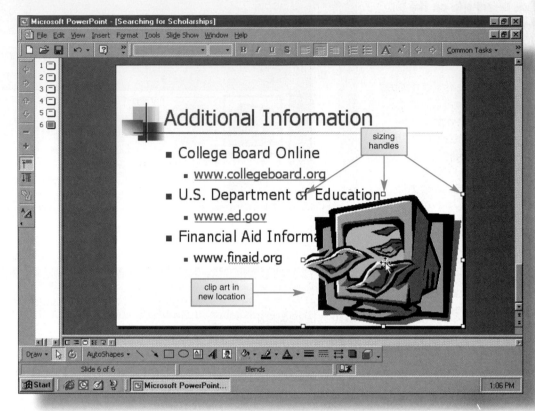

FIGURE 2-36

Other Ways

1. Select clip art, press arrow keys to move to new position

Changing Clip Art

If you alter a clip art image, be certain you have the legal right to make these modifications. For example, corporate logos are designed using specific colors and shapes and often cannot be changed. Photographs and illustrations cannot damage a person's reputation by casting them in a "false light," such as inserting a photograph of your teacher on the FBI's Top Ten Most Wanted list.

Changing the Size of Clip Art

Sometimes it is necessary to change the size of clip art. For example, on Slide 6, the monitor covers some of the bulleted text. To make the picture fit onto the slide, you reduce its size. To change the size of a clip art picture by an exact percentage, use the **Format Picture command.** The Format Picture dialog box contains six tabbed sheets with several options for formatting a picture. The **Size sheet** contains options for changing the size of a picture. You either enter the exact height and width in the Size and rotate area, or enter the height and width as a percentage of the original picture in the Scale area. When the **Lock aspect ratio check box** displays a check mark, the height and width settings change to maintain the aspect ratio of the original picture. **Aspect ratio** is the relationship between the height and width of an object. For example, a 3-by-5-inch picture scaled to 50 percent would become a 1½-by-2½-inch picture. Perform the following steps to reduce the size of the monitor.

Steps **To Change the Size of Clip Art**

1 **Right-click the monitor picture. Point to Format Picture (Figure 2-37).**

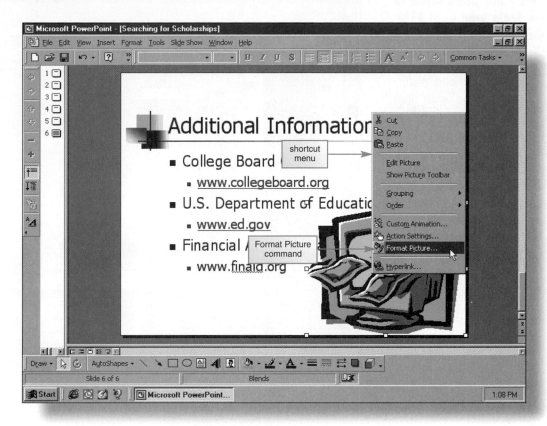

FIGURE 2-37

2 **Click Format Picture on the shortcut menu. Click the Size tab when the Format Picture dialog box displays.**

The Size sheet in the Format Picture dialog box displays (Figure 2-38). The Height and Width text boxes in the Scale area display the current percentage of the monitor picture, 100. Check marks display in the Lock aspect ratio and Relative to original picture size check boxes.

FIGURE 2-38

3 **Click the Height box down arrow in the Scale area until 65% displays and then point to the OK button.**

Both the Height and Width text boxes in the Scale area display 65% (Figure 2-39). PowerPoint automatically changes the Height and Width text boxes in the Size and rotate area to reflect changes made in the Scale area.

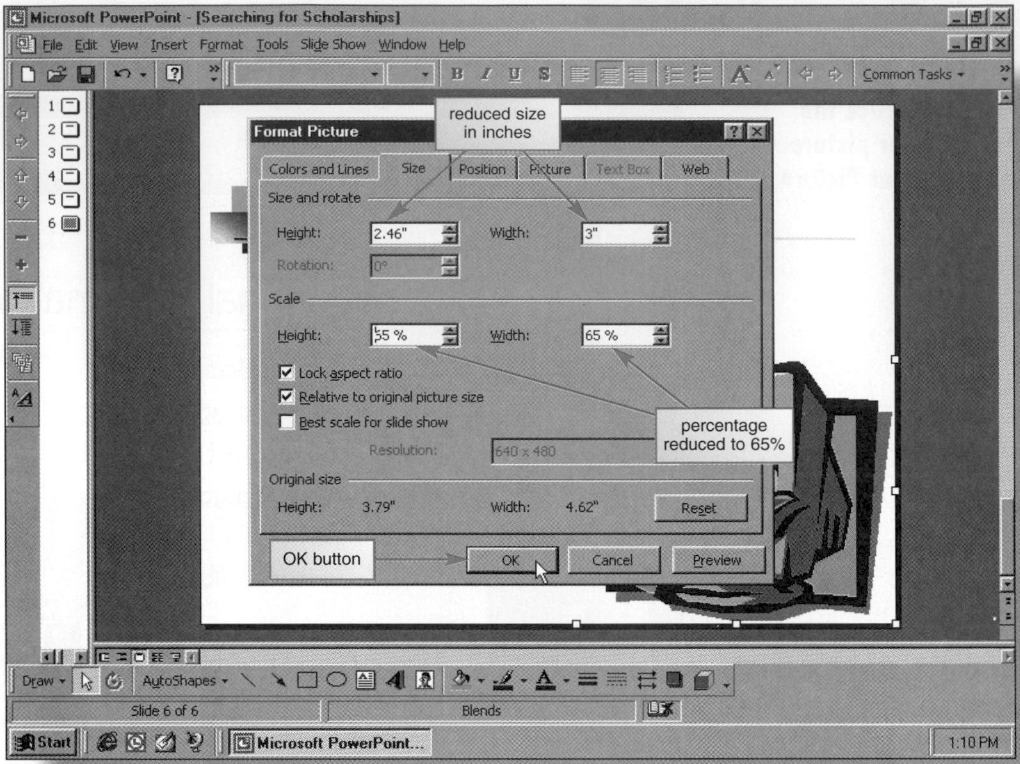

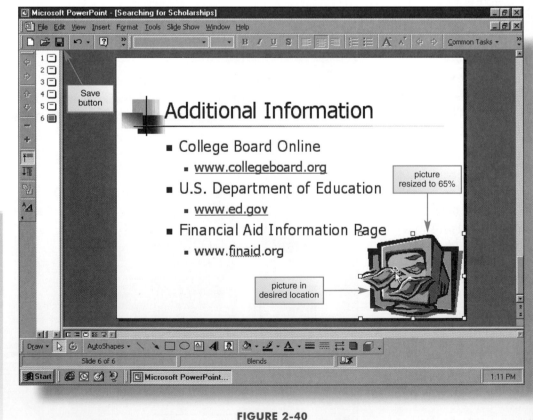

FIGURE 2-39

4 **Click the OK button. Drag the picture of the monitor to the bottom-right corner of the slide.**

PowerPoint closes the Format Picture dialog box and displays the reduced monitor picture in the desired location (Figure 2-40).

Other **Ways**

1. Click clip art object, on Format menu click Picture, click Size tab, click Height box up or down arrow in Scale area, click OK

2. Press ALT+O, press I, press CTRL+TAB three times to select Size tab, press TAB to select Height text box in Scale area, press up or down arrow keys to increase or decrease size, press ENTER

3. Click clip art object, drag a sizing handle until object is desired shape and size

FIGURE 2-40

Creating a Hyperlink

The Internet address in the last bulleted item on Slide 6 does not appear underlined and with a font color of red. When you were creating that slide, you typed the first two Web page addresses for the College Board Online and the U.S. Department of Education and then pressed the ENTER key after each address. When you performed this action, PowerPoint enabled the **AutoFormat as you type** option and changed the addresses' appearances to display as **hyperlinks**. A hyperlink is a shortcut that allows a user to jump from the presentation to another destination, such as a Web page on the Internet or another document on your computer. You did not press the ENTER key after you typed the address for the Financial Aid Information Web site, so the text did not change appearance and become a hyperlink. You can check to see if the AutoFormat as you type option is enabled by clicking Tools on the menu bar, clicking Options, and then verifying the AutoFormat as you type check box is selected.

To change the last bulleted line to a hyperlink, perform the following steps.

TO CREATE A HYPERLINK

1 Click the end of the last bulleted line, www.finaid.org.

2 Press the ENTER key.

3 Press the BACKSPACE key twice.

The last Internet address displays underlined and with a font color of red.

Saving the Presentation Again

To preserve the work completed, perform the following step to save the presentation again.

TO SAVE A PRESENTATION

1 Click the Save button on the Standard toolbar.

The changes made to the presentation after the previous save are saved on a floppy disk.

A default setting in PowerPoint allows for fast saves, which save only the changes made since the last time you saved. If you want to full save a copy of the complete presentation, click Tools on the menu bar, click Options on the Tools menu, and then click the Save tab. Remove the check mark in the Allow fast saves check box by clicking the check box and then click the OK button.

Adding a Header and Footer to Outline Pages

A printout of the presentation outline often is used as an audience handout. Distributing a copy of the outline provides the audience with paper on which to write notes or comments. Another benefit of distributing a copy of the outline is to help the audience see the text on the slides when lighting is poor or the room is too large. To help identify the source of the printed outline, add a descriptive header and footer. A **header** displays at the top of the sheet of paper or slide, and a **footer** displays at the bottom. Both contain specific information, such as the presenter's name or the company's telephone number. In addition, the current date and time and the slide or page number can display beside the header or footer information.

More *About*

Footers

If you are going to turn your PowerPoint slides into overhead transparencies, consider using page numbers and the presentation name in the footer. This information will help keep the transparencies organized.

Using the Notes and Handouts Sheet to Add Headers and Footers

You add headers and footers to outline pages by clicking the Notes and Handouts sheet in the Header and Footer dialog box and entering the information you wish to print. Perform the following steps to add the current date, header information, the page number, and footer information to the printed outline.

Steps To Use the Notes and Handouts Sheet to Add Headers and Footers

1 **Click View on the menu bar and then point to Header and Footer (Figure 2-41).**

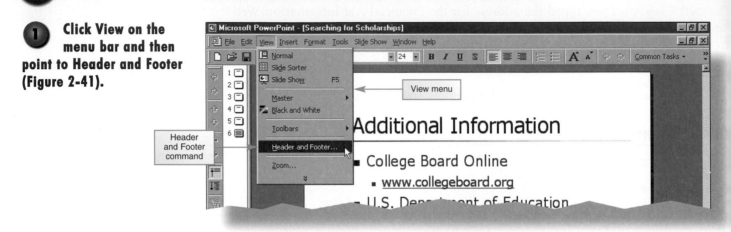

FIGURE 2-41

2 **Click Header and Footer on the View menu. Click the Notes and Handouts tab when the Header and Footer dialog box displays.**

The Notes and Handouts sheet in the Header and Footer dialog box displays (Figure 2-42). Check marks display in the Date and time, Header, Page number, and Footer check boxes. The Fixed option button is selected.

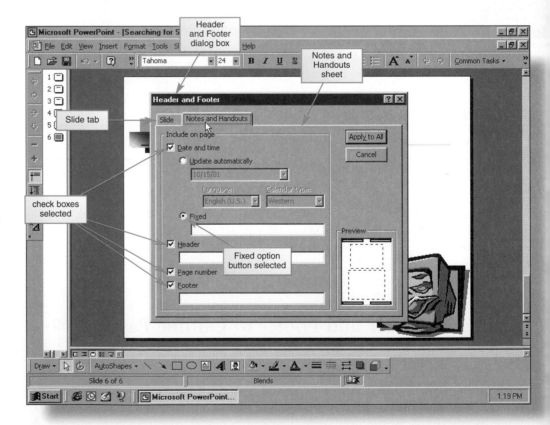

FIGURE 2-42

3 Click the Update automatically option button and then click the Header text box. Type Searching for Scholarships in the Header text box. Click the Footer text box. Type Office of Financial Aid in the Footer text box and then point to the Apply to All button (Figure 2-43).

4 Click the Apply to All button.

PowerPoint applies the header and footer text to the outline, closes the Header and Footer dialog box, and displays Slide 6. You cannot see header and footer text until you print the outline (see Figure 2-67 on page PP 2.53).

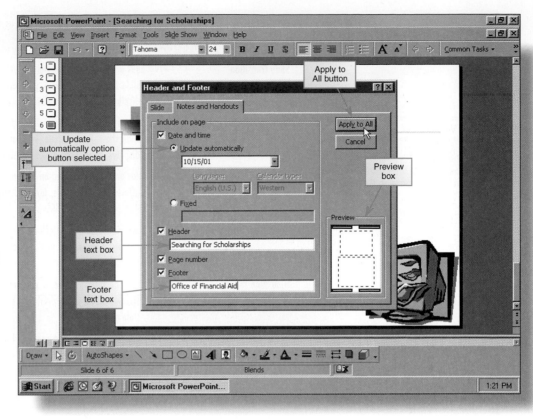

FIGURE 2-43

Adding Animation Effects

PowerPoint provides many animation effects to make your slide show presentation look professional. In this project you use slide transition and custom animation. A **slide transition** is a special effect used to progress from one slide to the next in a slide show. **Custom animation effects** define animation types and speeds and sound effects on a slide. The following pages discuss each of these animation effects in detail.

Slide Sorter Toolbar

PowerPoint provides you with multiple methods for accomplishing most tasks. Generally, the fastest method is to right-click to display a shortcut menu. Another frequently used method is to click a toolbar button. For example, you can apply slide transition effects by clicking the Slide Transition Effects list box on the Slide Sorter toolbar.

The Slide Sorter toolbar displays only when you are in slide sorter view. It displays to the right of the Standard toolbar, in place of the Formatting toolbar. The Slide Sorter toolbar contains tools to help you quickly add animation effects to your slide show. Table 2-4 on the next page explains the function of the buttons and boxes on the Slide Sorter toolbar.

Table 2-4	Buttons and Boxes on the Slide Sorter Toolbar	
BUTTON/BOX	*BUTTON/BOX NAME*	*FUNCTION*
	Slide Transition	Adds or changes the special effect that introduces a slide during a slide show. For example, you can play a sound when the slide displays, or you can make the slide fade from black.
Split Vertical Out ▼	Slide Transition Effects	Adds or changes the special effect that introduces a slide during a slide show. For example, you can play a sound when the slide displays, or you can make the slide fade from black.
Zoom In From Screen Center ▼	Animation Effects	Adds or changes animation effects on the current slide. Animation effects include sounds, text and object movements, and movies that occur during a slide show.
	Animation Preview	Runs all the animation effects for the current slide in a slide-miniature window so you can see how the animation will work during the slide show.
	Hide Slide	Hides the selected slide. If you are in slide view, hides the current slide so that it is not displayed automatically during an electronic slide show.
	Rehearse Timings	Runs your slide show in rehearsal mode, in which you can set or change the timing of your electronic slide show.
	Summary Slide	Creates a new slide from the titles of the slides you select in slide sorter view or normal view. The summary slide creates a bulleted list from the titles of the selected slides. PowerPoint inserts the summary slide in front of the first selected slide.
	Speaker Notes	Displays the speaker notes for the current slide. You can include speaker notes on your printed handouts, or you can print them to remember key points during a presentation.
Common Tasks ▼	Common Tasks	Contains the three more frequently used commands: New Slide, Slide Layout, and Apply Design Template.
▼	More Buttons	Allows you to select the particular buttons you want to display on the toolbar.

Adding Slide Transitions to a Slide Show

More *About* **2000**

Slide Transitions

Graphic designers suggest using a maximum of two different slide transition effects in one presentation. Any more than two can cause audience members to fixate on the visual effects and not on the slide content or the speaker.

PowerPoint allows you to control the way you advance from one slide to another by adding slide transitions to a slide show. PowerPoint has 42 different slide transitions, and you can vary the speed of each in your presentation. The name of the slide transition characterizes the visual effect that displays. For example, the slide transition effect, Split Vertical Out, displays the next slide by covering the previous slide with two vertical boxes moving from the center of the screen until the two boxes reach the left and right edges of the screen. The effect is similar to opening draw drapes over a window.

PowerPoint requires you to select at least one slide before applying slide transition effects. In this presentation, you apply slide transition effects to all slides except the title slide. Because Slide 6 already is selected, you must select Slides 2, 3, 4, and 5. The technique used to select more than one slide is the SHIFT+**click technique**. To perform the SHIFT+click technique in slide sorter view, press and hold down the SHIFT key as you click the starting and ending range of desired slides. After you click the slides to which you want to add animation effects, release the SHIFT key.

In the Searching for Scholarships presentation, you wish to display the Wipe Down slide transition effect between slides. That is, all slides begin stacked on top of one another, like a deck of cards. As you click the mouse to view the next slide, the new slide enters the screen by starting at the top of the slide and gliding down to the bottom of the slide. This effect resembles pulling down a window shade. Perform the following steps to apply the Wipe Down slide transition effect to the Searching for Scholarships presentation.

Steps To Add Slide Transitions to a Slide Show

1 **Click the Slide Sorter View button at the lower left of the PowerPoint window.**

PowerPoint displays the presentation in slide sorter view (Figure 2-44). Slide 6 is selected. Slide 6 currently does not have a slide transition effect, as noted in the Slide Transition Effects box on the Slide Sorter toolbar.

2 **Press and hold down the SHIFT key and then click Slide 2. Release the SHIFT key.**

Slides 2 through 6 are selected, as indicated by the heavy border around each slide (Figure 2-45).

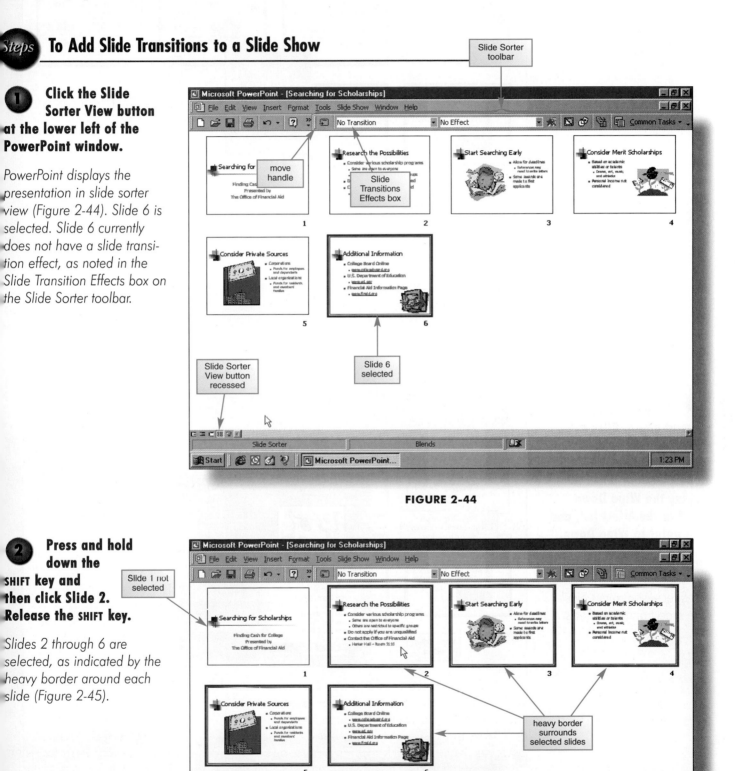

FIGURE 2-44

FIGURE 2-45

3 Point to Slide 2 and right-click. Point to Slide Transition (Figure 2-46).

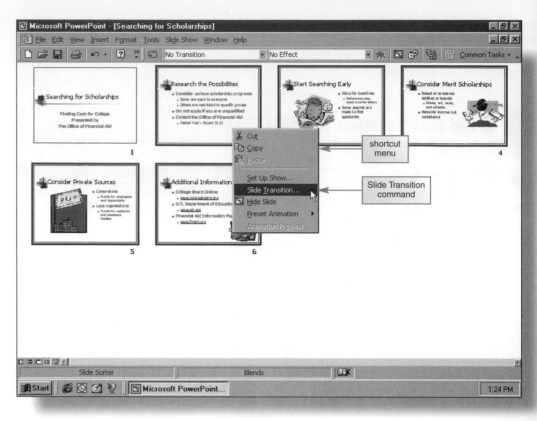

FIGURE 2-46

4 Click Slide Transition on the shortcut menu. Click the Effect box arrow when the Slide Transition dialog box displays. Scroll down to display the Wipe Down effect in the Effect list, and then point to Wipe Down.

The Slide Transition dialog box displays (Figure 2-47). The Effect list displays available slide transition effects.

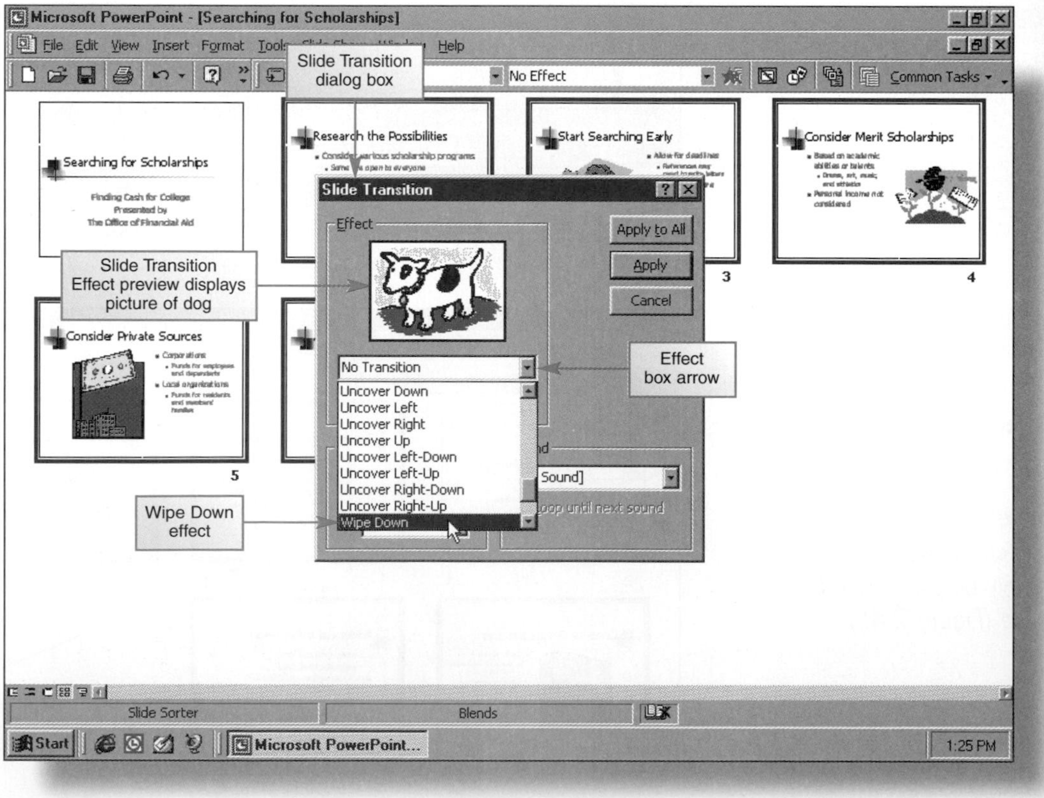

FIGURE 2-47

⑤ Click Wipe Down in the list. Point to the Apply button.

The Slide Transition Effect preview demonstrates the Wipe Down effect (Figure 2-48). To see the demonstration again, click the picture in the Slide Transition Effect preview.

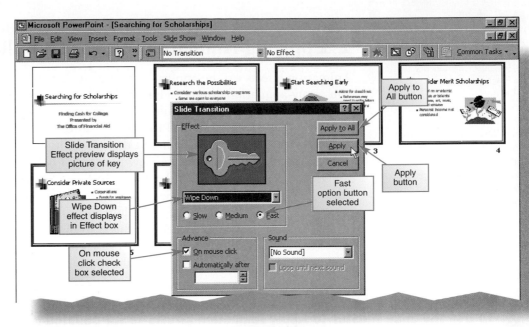

FIGURE 2-48

⑥ Click the Apply button.

PowerPoint displays the presentation in slide sorter view (Figure 2-49). A slide transition icon displays under each selected slide, which indicates that a slide transition effect has been added to those slides. The current slide transition effect, Wipe Down, displays in the Slide Transition Effects box.

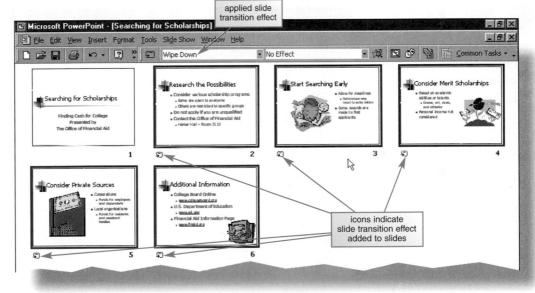

FIGURE 2-49

To adjust the speed at which the special effect runs during the slide show, click Slow, Medium, or Fast in the Effect area in the Slide Transition dialog box. When you click a particular speed option, PowerPoint runs that effect in the sample picture.

To apply slide transition effects to every slide in the presentation, right-click a slide, click Slide Transition on the shortcut menu, choose the desired slide transition effect, and then click the Apply to All button.

To remove slide transition effects when displaying the presentation in slide sorter view, select the slides to which slide transition effects are applied, click the Slide Transition Effects box arrow, and select No Transition.

The Wipe Down slide transition effect has been applied to the presentation. The next step in creating this slide show is to add animation effects to individual slides.

Other Ways

1. Select slide, right-click selected slide, click Slide Transition, click Effect box arrow, select desired effect, click Apply button

2. Select slide, on Slide Show menu click Slide Transition, click Effect box arrow, select desired effect, click Apply button

More About

Clip Gallery Live

Microsoft's Clip Gallery Live is an outstanding place to locate additional clip art. This Web site also contains movie clips, pictures, and sounds. To connect to the Clip Gallery Live site, click the Insert Clip Art button on the Drawing toolbar and then click the Clips Online button. Another method of connecting to this area is to visit the PowerPoint 2000 More About Web page (www.scsite.com/pp2000/more.htm) and click Clip Gallery Live.

Applying Animation Effects to Bulleted Slides

Animation effects can be applied to text as well as to objects, such as clip art. When you apply animation effects to bulleted text, you progressively disclose each bulleted paragraph. As a result, you build the slide paragraph by paragraph during the running of a slide show to control the flow of information. PowerPoint has a wide variety of custom animation effects and the capability to dim the paragraphs already displaying on the slide when the new paragraph is displayed.

The next step is to apply the Zoom In From Screen Center animation effect to Slides 2, 3, 4, 5, and 6 in the Searching for Scholarships presentation. All slides, except the title slide, will have the Zoom In From Screen Center animation effect. Recall from Project 1 that when you need to make a change that affects all slides, make the change to the slide master. Perform the following steps to apply animation effects to the bulleted paragraphs in this presentation.

Steps ▶ **To Use the Slide Master to Apply Animation Effects to All Bulleted Slides**

1 **Press and hold down the SHIFT key** and then click the Slide Master View button at the lower left of the PowerPoint window.

The slide master displays (Figure 2-50).

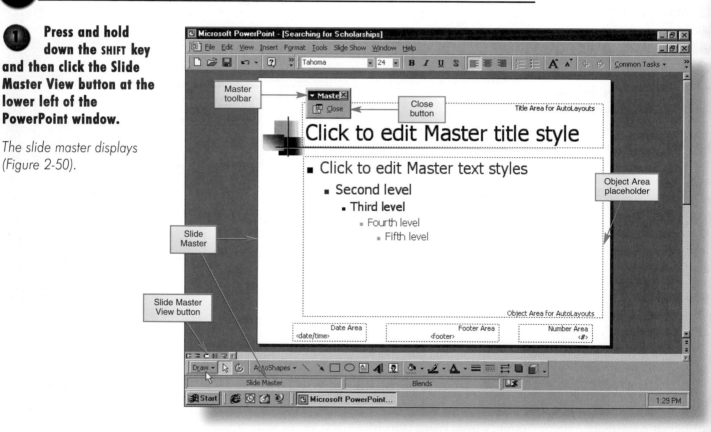

FIGURE 2-50

2 Right-click the Object Area placeholder in the slide master. Point to Custom Animation (Figure 2-51).

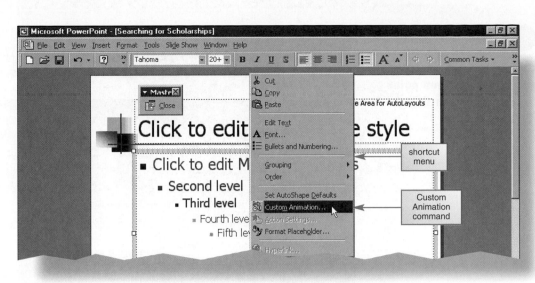

FIGURE 2-51

3 Click Custom Animation on the shortcut menu. If necessary, click the Effects tab when the Custom Animation dialog box displays.

The Custom Animation dialog box displays (Figure 2-52).

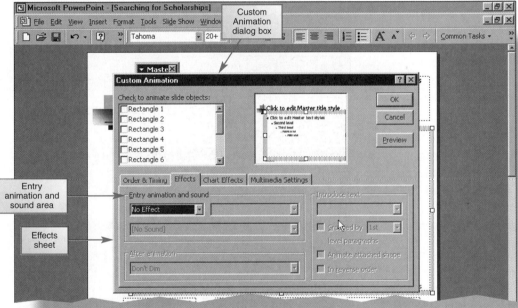

FIGURE 2-52

4 Click the left Entry animation and sound box arrow. Scroll down the list until Zoom displays and then point to Zoom (Figure 2-53).

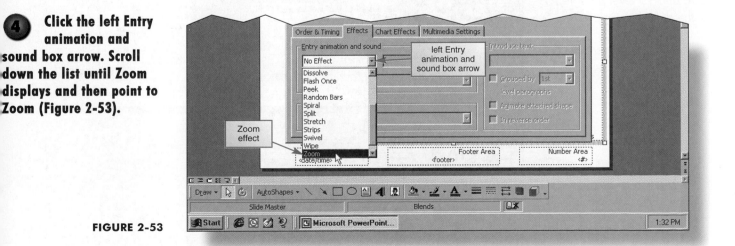

FIGURE 2-53

5 Click Zoom in the list. Click the right Entry animation and sound box arrow and then point to In From Screen Center (Figure 2-54).

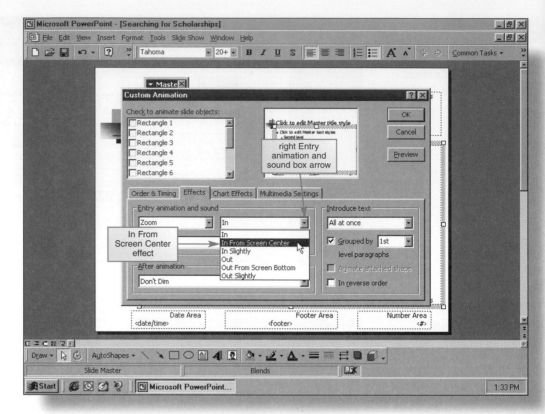

FIGURE 2-54

6 Click In From Screen Center in the list and then point to the Grouped by level paragraphs box arrow.

The Entry animation and sound boxes display Zoom and In From Screen Center, respectively (Figure 2-55). A check mark displays in the Grouped by level paragraphs box, and 1st level paragraphs is the default setting.

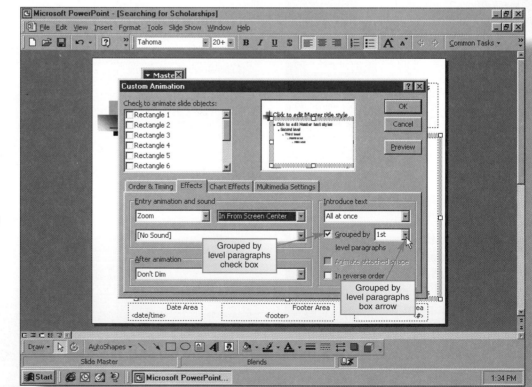

FIGURE 2-55

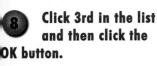

7 Click the Grouped by level paragraphs box arrow and then point to 3rd.

3rd is highlighted in the Grouped by level paragraphs list (Figure 2-56).

8 Click 3rd in the list and then click the OK button.

PowerPoint applies the animation effects to the slide master, closes the Custom Animation dialog box, and then displays the slide master.

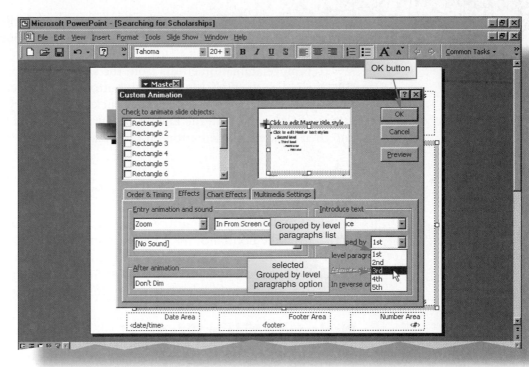

FIGURE 2-56

9 Click the Close button on the Master toolbar.

PowerPoint closes the slide master and returns to slide sorter view (Figure 2-57). The icons next to the slide transition effect icons indicate animation effects have been added to the slides.

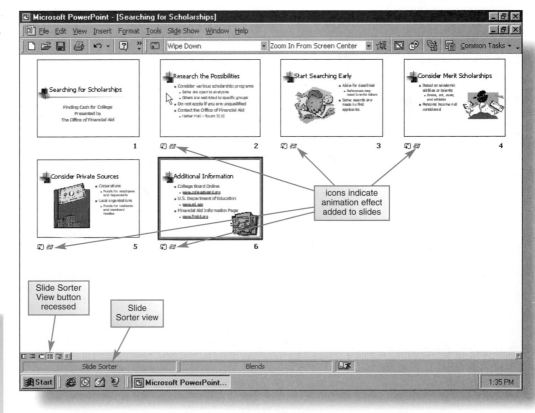

FIGURE 2-57

Other Ways

1. On View menu point to Master, click Slide Master, right-click Object Area placeholder, on Slide Show menu click Custom Animation, click Effects tab, click Entry animation and sound box arrow, click desired animation effect, click Grouped by level paragraphs box arrow, click appropriate paragraph level, click OK

The Zoom In From Screen Center animation effect displays for each bulleted paragraph on paragraph level 1, 2, or 3 on Slides 2 through 6 when the slide show is running.

To remove animation effects from the slide master, press and hold down the SHIFT key, click the Slide Master View button, release the SHIFT key, right-click the slide master, click Custom Animation, click the left Entry animation and sound box arrow, click No effect in the Entry animation and sound list, click the OK button, and then click the Close button on the Master toolbar.

Animating Clip Art Objects

To add visual interest to your presentation, you want the monitor clip art on Slide 6 to rise from the bottom of the screen. Animating a clip art object takes several steps. First, display the slide containing the clip art (Slide 6) in slide view. Then select the clip art object and display the Custom Animation dialog box. Next, select the animation effect. Finally, apply the animation effect as described in the following sections.

Displaying a Slide in Slide View

PowerPoint requires you to display a slide in slide view before adding animation effects to clip art. Before continuing with the animation of the monitor on Slide 6, display the slide in slide view as described in the following step.

TO DISPLAY A SLIDE IN SLIDE VIEW

1 Double-click Slide 6.

Slide 6 displays in slide view.

With Slide 6 displaying in slide view, you are ready to animate the monitor clip art as explained in the next section.

Animating Clip Art

PowerPoint allows you to animate clip art along with animating text. Because Slide 6 lists three sources on the Internet for current scholarship information, you want to emphasize these sites by having the monitor clip art pass from the left side of the screen to the right. One way of animating clip art is to select options in the Custom Animation dialog box, similarly to what you did to animate text. A quicker way is to choose an animation option from the Preset Animation list. Perform the following steps to add the Flying animation effect to the monitor on Slide 6.

More *About*

Finding Clip Art

Many Web sites offer thousands of clip art images that you can import directly into your presentations. Along with pictures sorted into easy-to-navigate categories, these sites contain bullets, lines, and buttons. Use a search engine to find public domain graphics for your presentations. Use the keywords clip art and clip+art.

Steps **To Animate Clip Art**

**1** **Click the monitor clip art object. Click Slide Show on the menu bar, point to Preset Animation, and then point to Flying.**

Animation options display in the Preset Animation submenu (Figure 2-58). The monitor clip art is selected.

2 **Click Flying on the Preset Animation submenu.**

PowerPoint applies the Flying animation effect to the clip art. You will see this effect when you run your slide show.

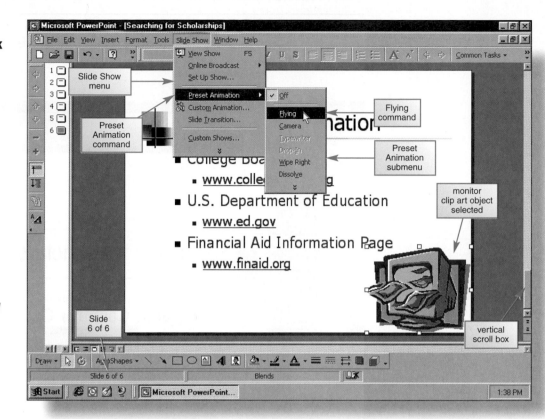

FIGURE 2-58

When you run the slide show, the names of each of the three Internet sites will display, and then the monitor clip art will begin moving from the left side of the slide and stop at the position where you inserted it onto Slide 6.

Formatting and Animating a Title Slide

The title slide of every presentation should seize the attention of the audience. In order to excite the audience with the Searching for Scholarships presentation, you want to intensify the subtitle object on the title slide. First, you italicize the words Presented by, and then you increase the size of the words, Finding Cash for College. Finally, you add animation effects to the subtitle.

The first step is to display Slide 1 and then format the title slide subtitle. Perform the following steps to format the subtitle object on Slide 1.

TO CHANGE TEXT FONT STYLE TO ITALIC AND INCREASE FONT SIZE

1 Drag the vertical scroll box to display Slide 1.

2 Triple-click the paragraph, Finding Cash for College.

3 Click the Font Size box arrow on the Formatting toolbar and then select the font size 40 in the list.

*Other* **Ways**

1. Click clip art, on Slide Show menu click Custom Animation, click Effects tab, click Entry animation and sound box arrows, click desired animation effects, click OK

2. Press TAB until clip art is selected, press ALT+D, press M, press DOWN ARROW key until desired animation effect selected, press ENTER

4 Triple-click the paragraph, Presented by, and then click the Italic button on the Formatting toolbar.

The formatted subtitle on Slide 1 displays (Figure 2-59). The paragraph, Finding Cash For College, displays in font size 40, and the words, Presented by, display the italic font style.

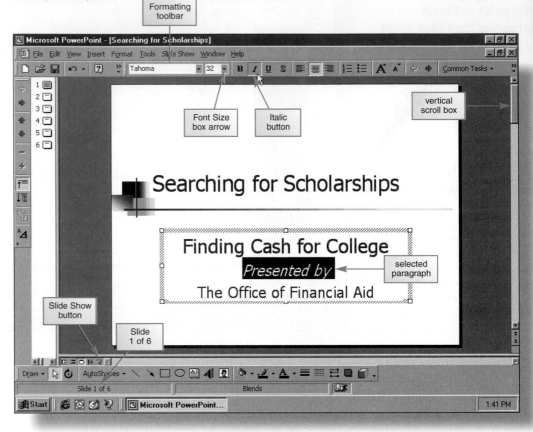

FIGURE 2-59

The next step is to apply the Dissolve animation effect to the subtitle text. Perform the following steps to animate the paragraphs in the subtitle object on Slide 1.

TO ANIMATE TEXT

1 Right-click the Object Area placeholder and then click Custom Animation on the shortcut menu.

2 If necessary, click the Effects tab in the Custom Animation dialog box.

3 Click the left Entry animation and sound box arrow.

4 Scroll down the list until Dissolve displays and then click Dissolve in the list.

5 Click the OK button.

The Object Area object, Text 2, is selected in the preview box and in the Check to animate slide objects box. Dissolve displays in the Entry animation and sound box. By default, the subtitle text is grouped by first level paragraphs. PowerPoint applies the animation effect, closes the Custom Animation dialog box, and then displays Slide 1.

Animation effects are complete for this presentation. You now are ready to review the presentation in slide show view.

Saving the Presentation Again

The presentation is complete. Perform the following step to save the finished presentation on a floppy disk before running the slide show.

TO SAVE A PRESENTATION ON A FLOPPY DISK

1 Click the Save button on the Standard toolbar.

PowerPoint saves the presentation on your floppy disk by saving the changes made to the presentation since the last save.

Running an Animated Slide Show

Project 1 introduced you to using slide show view to look at your presentation one slide at a time. This project introduces you to running a slide show with slide transition effects and text and object animation effects. When you run a slide show with slide transition effects, PowerPoint displays the slide transition effect when you click the mouse button to advance to the next slide. When a slide has text animation effects, each paragraph level displays as determined by the animation settings. Animated clip art objects display the selected animation effect in the sequence established in the Custom Animation dialog box. Perform the following steps to run the animated Searching for Scholarships slide show.

Steps To Run an Animated Slide Show

1 **With Slide 1 displaying, click the Slide Show button at the lower left of the PowerPoint window. When Slide 1 displays in slide show view, click the slide anywhere.**

PowerPoint first displays the title slide title object, Searching for Scholarships (Figure 2-60). When you click the slide, the first heading level 2 subtitle paragraph, Finding Cash for College, displays using the Dissolve animation effect.

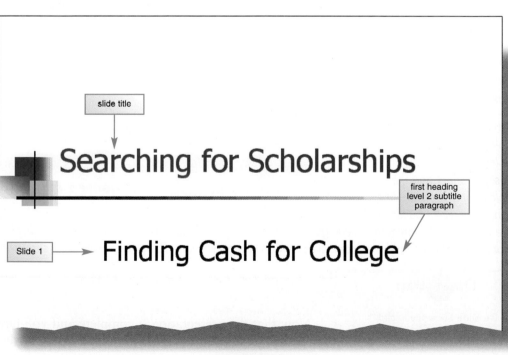

FIGURE 2-60

Click the slide again.

PowerPoint displays the second heading level 2 subtitle paragraph, Presented by, using the Dissolve animation effect (Figure 2-61). If the Popup Menu buttons display when you move the mouse pointer, do not click them.

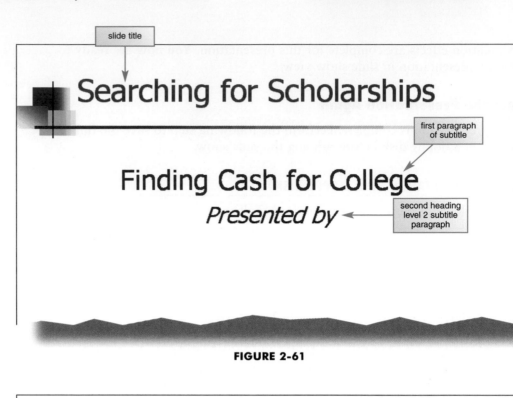

FIGURE 2-61

3 **Click the slide again.**

PowerPoint displays the third heading level 2 subtitle paragraph, The Office of Financial Aid, beneath the second heading level 2 subtitle paragraph. PowerPoint again uses the Dissolve animation effect (Figure 2-62).

4 **Continue clicking to finish running the slide show and return to normal view.**

Each time a new slide displays, PowerPoint first displays the Wipe Down slide transition effect and then displays only the slide title. Then, PowerPoint builds each slide based on the animation settings. When you click the slide after the last paragraph displays on the last slide of the presentation, PowerPoint displays a blank slide. When you click again, PowerPoint exits slide show view and returns to normal view.

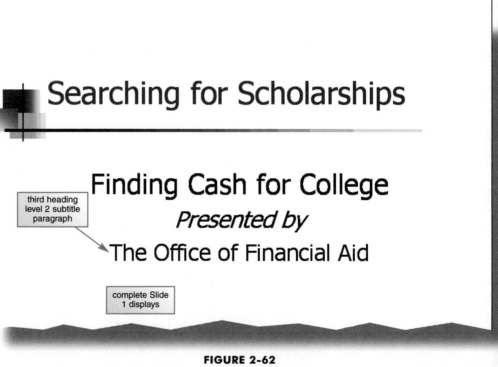

FIGURE 2-62

1. On Slide Show menu click View Show, click slide until slide show ends
2. Press ALT+D, press V, press ENTER until slide show ends

Now that the presentation is complete and you have tested the animation effects, the last step is to print the presentation outline and slides.

Printing in Outline View

When you click the Print button on the Standard toolbar, PowerPoint prints a hard copy of the presentation component last selected in the Print what box in the Print dialog box. To be certain to print the component you want, such as the presentation outline, use the Print command on the File menu. When the Print dialog box displays, you can select the appropriate presentation component in the Print what box. The next two sections explain how to use the Print command on the File menu to print the presentation outline and the presentation slides.

Printing an Outline

During the development of a lengthy presentation, it often is easier to review your outline in print rather than on the screen. Printing your outline also is useful for audience handouts or when your supervisor or instructor wants to review your subject matter before you develop your presentation fully.

Recall that the Print dialog box displays print options. When you wish to print your outline, select Outline View in the Print what list located in the Print dialog box. The outline, however, prints as last viewed in outline view. This means that you must select the Zoom setting to display the outline text as you wish it to print. If you are uncertain of the Zoom setting, you should return to outline view and review it prior to printing. Perform the following steps to print an outline from slide view.

More About

Outlines

You can send your PowerPoint outline to Microsoft Word and then create handouts and other documents using that text. To perform this action, click the Grayscale Preview button on the Standard toolbar, click File on the menu bar, point to Send To, click Microsoft Word, and then select the desired page layout.

Steps **To Print an Outline**

1 **Ready the printer according to the printer manufacturer's instructions. Click File on the menu bar and then point to Print.**

The File menu displays (Figure 2-63). The Collapse All button on the Outlining toolbar is recessed, so the entire outline will not print. If you want to print all the lines of text on the slides, you would click the Expand All button.

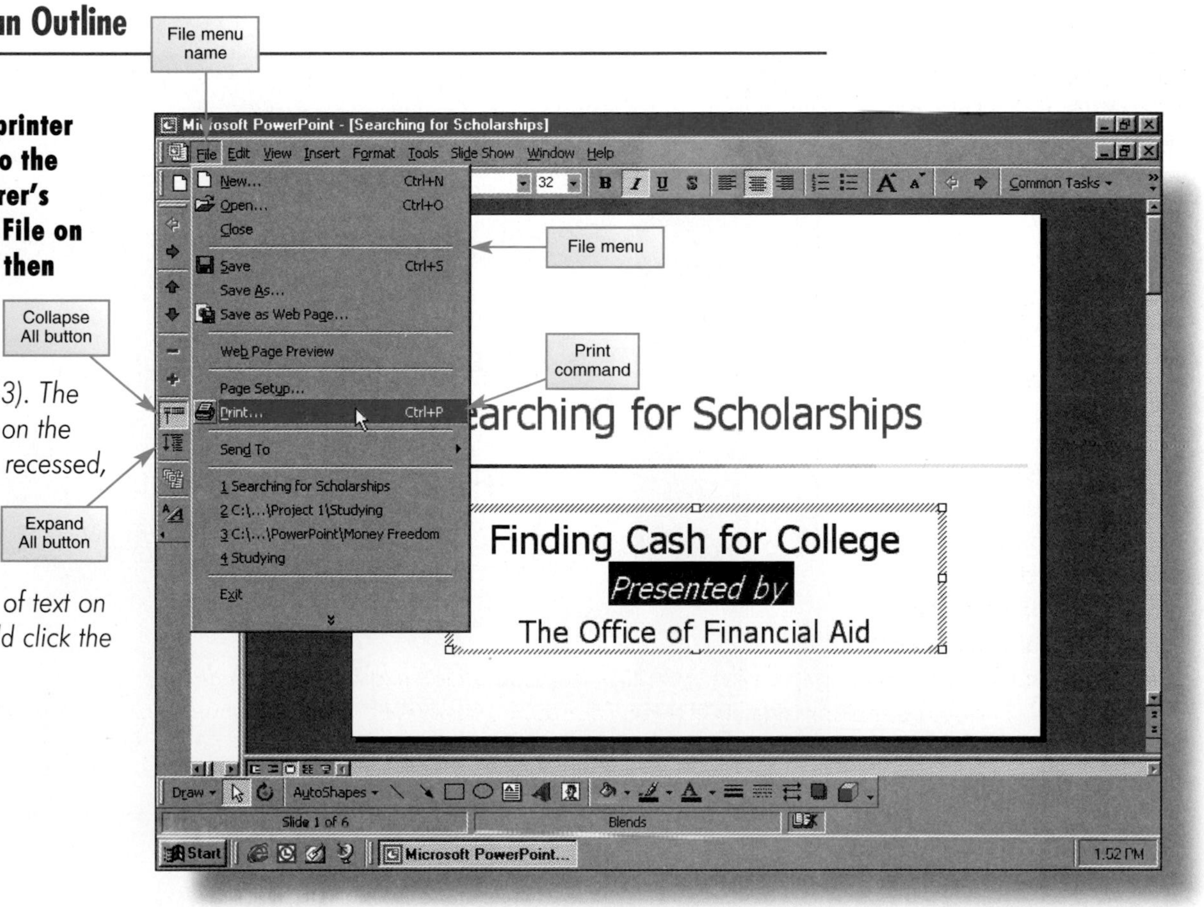

FIGURE 2-63

2 **Click Print on the File menu.**

The Print dialog box displays (Figure 2-64).

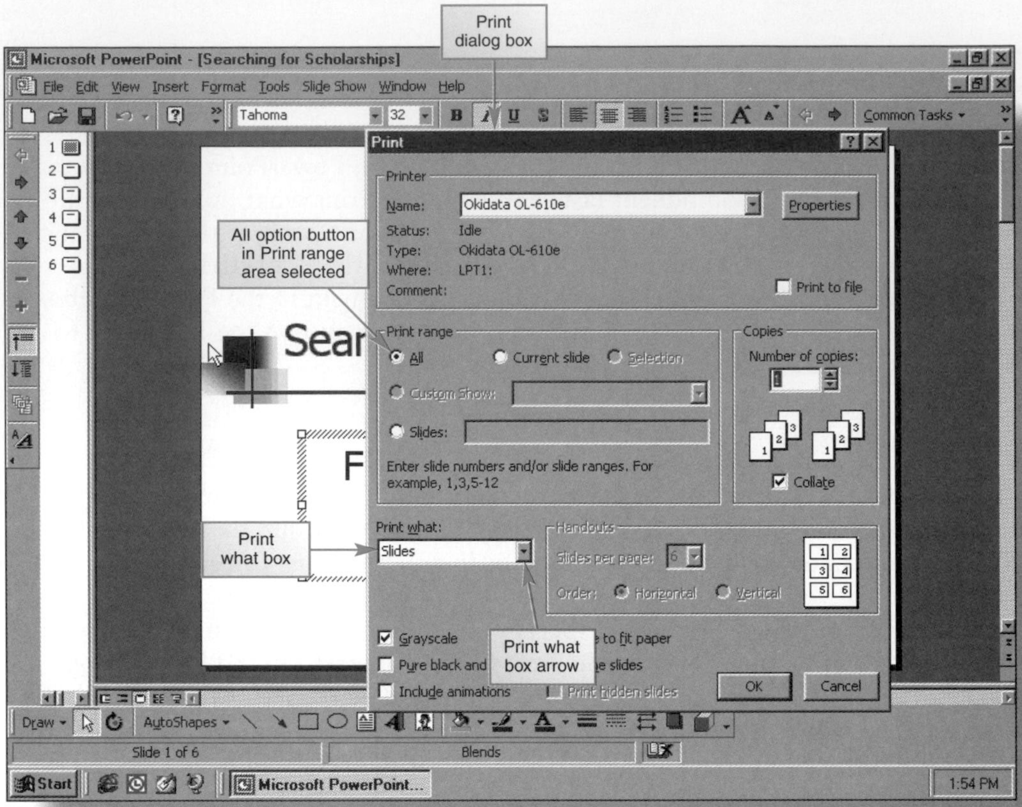

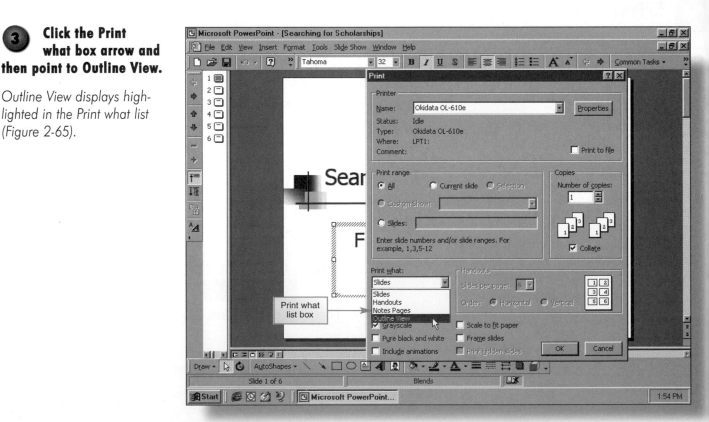

FIGURE 2-64

3 **Click the Print what box arrow and then point to Outline View.**

Outline View displays highlighted in the Print what list (Figure 2-65).

FIGURE 2-65

4 Click Outline View in the list and then point to the OK button (Figure 2-66).

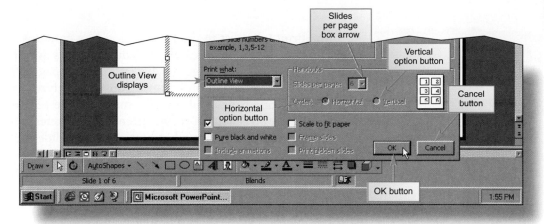

FIGURE 2-66

5 Click the OK button.

The outline prints. Clicking the Cancel button, cancels the printing request.

6 When the printer stops, retrieve the printout of the outline (Figure 2-67).

The six PowerPoint slides display in outline form. The words, Searching for Scholarships, and the current date display in the header, and the words, Office of Financial Aid, and the page number display in the footer.

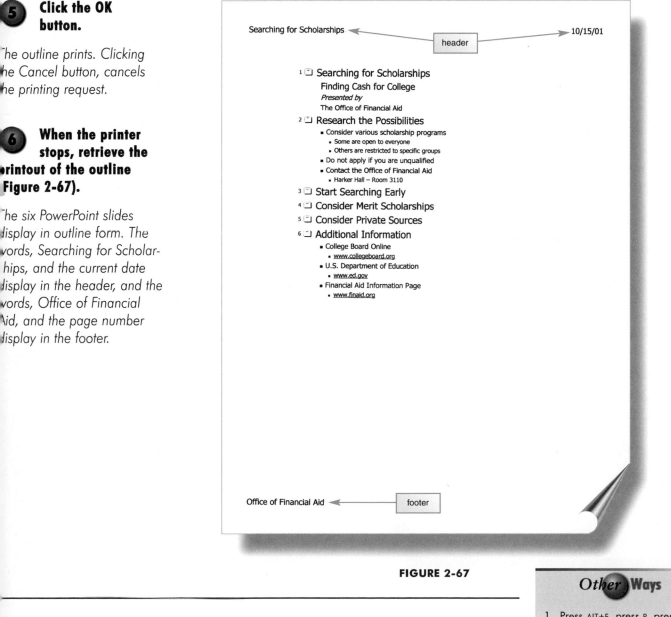

FIGURE 2-67

You may select the Print command from the File menu while in any view except slide show view.

Other Ways

1. Press ALT+F, press P, press TAB, press W, press down arrow until Outline View selected, press ENTER, press ENTER

More About

Printing

If your printer seems to print slowly, Microsoft suggests clearing at least two megabytes of space on your hard drive and also closing any unnecessary programs that are running simultaneously.

The Print what list in the Print dialog box contains options for printing handouts, and the Handouts area allows you to specify whether you want two, three, four, six, or nine slide images to display on each page. Printing handouts is useful for reviewing a presentation because you can analyze several slides displaying simultaneously on one page. Additionally, many businesses distribute handouts of the slide show before a presentation so the attendees can refer to a copy. To print handouts, click Handouts in the Print what box, click the Slides per page box arrow in the Handouts area, and then click 2, 3, 4, 6, or 9. You can change the order in which the Searching for Scholarships slides display on a page by clicking the Horizontal option button in the Order area, which displays Slides 1 and 2, 3 and 4, and 5 and 6 adjacent to each other, or the Vertical option button in the Order area, which displays Slides 1 and 4, 2 and 5, and 3 and 6 adjacent to each other.

Printing Presentation Slides

After correcting errors, you will want to print a final copy of your presentation. If you made any changes to your presentation since your last save, be certain to save your presentation before you print.

Perform the following steps to print the presentation.

TO PRINT PRESENTATION SLIDES

1 Ready the printer according to the printer manufacturer's instructions.

2 Click File on the menu bar and then click Print on the File menu.

3 When the Print dialog box displays, click the Print what box arrow.

4 Click Slides in the list.

5 Click the OK button. When the printer stops, retrieve the slide printouts.

The printouts should resemble the slides shown in Figures 2-68a through 2-68f.

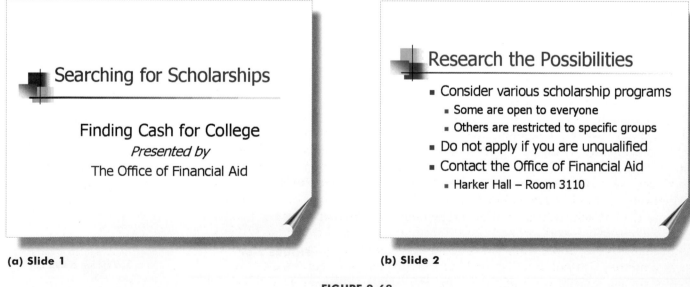

(a) Slide 1

(b) Slide 2

FIGURE 2-68

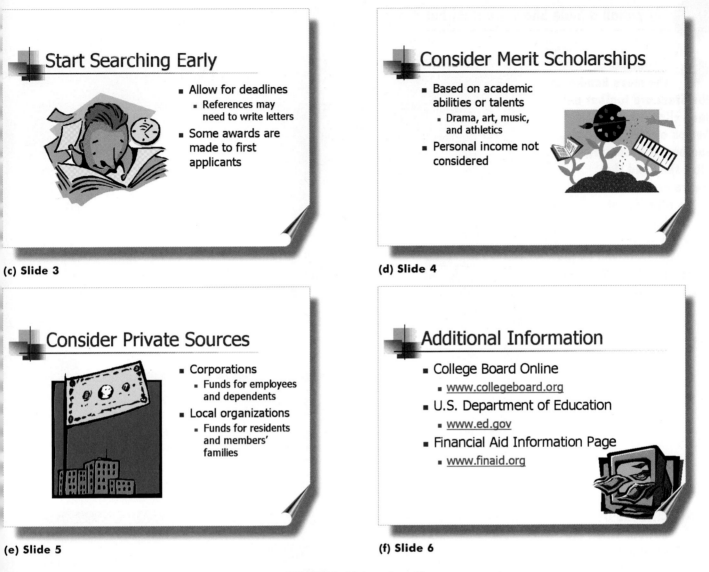

(c) Slide 3

(d) Slide 4

(e) Slide 5

(f) Slide 6

FIGURE 2-68 (continued)

E-mailing a Slide Show from within PowerPoint

Billions of e-mail messages are sent throughout the world each year. Computer users use this popular service on the Internet to send and receive plain text e-mail or to send and receive rich e-mail content that includes graphics, links to other Web pages, and file attachments. These attachments can include Office files, such as Word documents or PowerPoint slide shows. Using Office 2000, you can e-mail the presentation directly from within PowerPoint. In previous versions of Microsoft Office, to send a presentation you would have had to save it, close the file, launch your e-mail program, and then attach the presentation to the e-mail before sending it.

For these steps to work properly, users need an e-mail address and a 32-bit e-mail program compatible with a Messaging Application Programming Interface, such as Outlook, Outlook Express, or Microsoft Exchange Client. Free e-mail accounts are available at www.hotmail.com. The steps on the next page show how to e-mail the slide show from within PowerPoint to Dr. Mary Halen. Assume her e-mail address is mary_halen@hotmail.com. If you do not have an E-mail button on the Standard toolbar, then this activity is not available to you.

More About

E-mail

UCLA Professor Leonard Kleinrock sent the first e-mail message in 1969 to a colleague at Stanford University. Today, Americans send more than 2.2 billion e-mail messages daily, as compared to fewer than 300 million pieces of first-class mail.

Steps To E-mail a Slide Show from within PowerPoint

1 **Double-click the move handle on the Standard toolbar and then click the E-mail button on the Standard toolbar. If necessary, click the Send the entire presentation as an attachment option button or click the same message displayed by the Office Assistant. Point to the OK button.**

The E-mail dialog box displays (Figure 2-69).

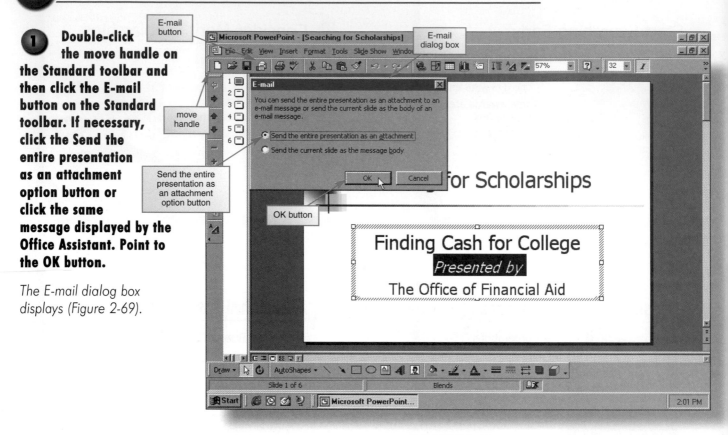

FIGURE 2-69

2 **Click the OK button. When the New Message window displays, type** mary_halen@ hotmail.com **in the To box. Type** Scholarships presentation **in the Subject box. Click the Message box.**

PowerPoint displays the E-mail area, which includes the title bar, menu bar, Standard Buttons toolbar, the To, Cc, Subject, and Attach boxes, and the Formatting Bar toolbar (Figure 2-70). The insertion point is in the Message box so you can type a message to Dr. Mary Halen.

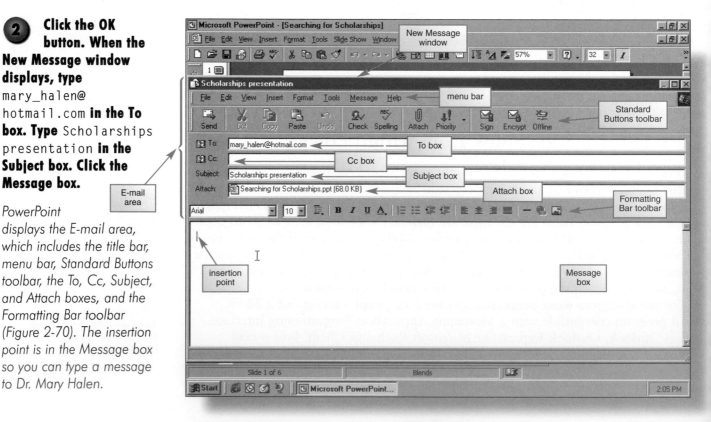

FIGURE 2-70

3 **Type** Attached is the PowerPoint presentation you can use to accompany your lecture on scholarships. **in the Message box. Point to the Send button.**

This message helps Dr. Halen understand the purpose of your e-mail when she opens her mail (Figure 2-71).

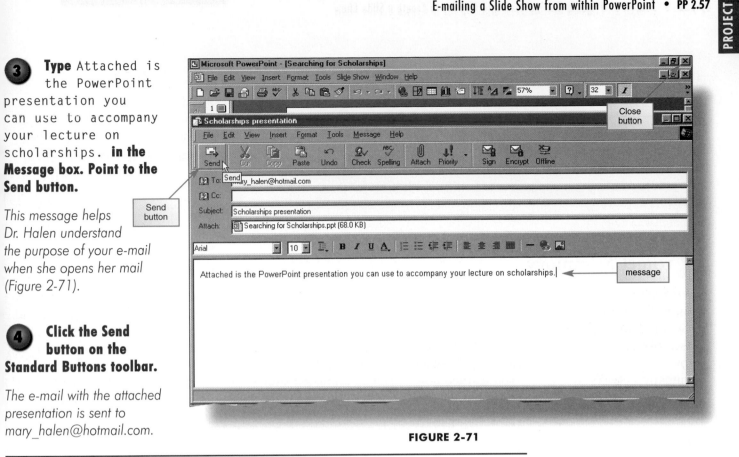

4 **Click the Send button on the Standard Buttons toolbar.**

The e-mail with the attached presentation is sent to mary_halen@hotmail.com.

FIGURE 2-71

Because the slide show was sent as an attachment, Dr. Halen can save the attachment and then open the presentation in PowerPoint. The alternative in the E-mail dialog box in Figure 2-69 on page PP 2.56 is to send a copy of the current slide as the e-mail message. In this case, Mary would be able to see the slide in her e-mail, but she would not be able to open it in PowerPoint.

You can choose many more options when you send e-mail from within PowerPoint. For example, the Apply Stationery command on the Format menu in the Outlook Express window adds graphics to your message, such as colorful candles for a birthday message or chicken soup for a get well note. In addition, the Encrypt message on the Standard Buttons toolbar allows you to send secure messages that only your intended recipient can read.

Saving and Quitting PowerPoint

If you made any changes to your presentation since your last save, you should save it again before quitting PowerPoint. For more details on quitting PowerPoint, refer to pages PP 1.50 through PP 1.51 in Project 1. Perform the following steps to save changes to the presentation and quit PowerPoint.

TO SAVE CHANGES AND QUIT POWERPOINT

1 Click the Close button on the Microsoft PowerPoint window title bar.

2 If prompted, click the Yes button.

PowerPoint saves any changes made to the presentation since the last save and then quits PowerPoint.

More *About*

Microsoft Certification

The Microsoft Office User Specialist (MOUS) Certification program allows you to prove your knowledge of essential PowerPoint 2000 skills. For more information, see Appendix D or visit the Shelly Cashman Series MOUS Web page at www.scsite.com/off2000/cert.htm.

CASE PERSPECTIVE SUMMARY

The Searching for Scholarships slide show should help some students at your school find sources of financial aid. These classmates viewing your presentation in the Office of Financial Aid will realize that many sources of scholarships are overlooked. When Dr. Halen runs your slide show, she will describe and expand upon the available scholarships you list in your slides. The audience members should have a better understanding of potential sources of scholarship money by knowing possible aid sources, the benefits of searching early, the difference between merit and private scholarships, and places to look on the Internet for more details.

Project Summary

Project 2 introduced you to outline view, clip art, and animation effects. You created a slide presentation in outline view where you entered all the text in the form of an outline. You arranged the text using the Promote and Demote buttons. Once your outline was complete, you changed slide layouts and added clip art to the Object Area placeholders. After adding clip art to another slide without a clip art region in the Object Area placeholder, you moved and sized the picture. You added slide transition effects and text animation effects. Then you applied animation effects to clip art. You learned how to run an animated slide show demonstrating slide transition and animation effects. Finally, you printed the presentation outline and slides using the Print command on the File menu and e-mailed the presentation.

What You Should Know

Having completed this project, you now should be able to perform the following tasks:

- Add a Slide in Outline View *(PP 2.13)*
- Add Slide Transitions to a Slide Show *(PP 2.39)*
- Animate Clip Art *(PP 2.47)*
- Animate Text *(PP 2.48)*
- Change the Size of Clip Art *(PP 2.33)*
- Change Slide Layout to Clip Art & Text *(PP 2.22)*
- Change the Slide Layout to Clip Art & Text and Insert Clip Art *(PP 2.28)*
- Change the Slide Layout to Text & Clip Art and Insert Clip Art *(PP 2.27)*
- Change the View to Outline View and Display the Outline Toolbar *(PP 2.8)*
- Change the View to Slide Sorter View *(PP 2.20)*
- Change the View to Slide View *(PP 2.21)*
- Change Text Font Style to Italic and Increase Font Size *(PP 2.47)*
- Create a Closing Slide in Outline View *(PP 2.18)*
- Create a Hyperlink *(PP 2.35)*
- Create a Multi-level Bulleted List Slide in Outline View *(PP 2.14)*
- Create a Second Subordinate Slide *(PP 2.16)*
- Create a Third Subordinate Slide *(PP 2.17)*
- Create a Subordinate Slide *(PP 2.16)*
- Create a Title Slide in Outline View *(PP 2.11)*
- Display a Slide in Slide View *(PP 2.46)*
- E-mail a Slide Show from within PowerPoint *(PP 2.56)*
- Insert Clip Art into an Object Area Placeholder *(PP 2.25)*
- Insert Clip Art on a Slide without a Clip Art Region *(PP 2.30)*
- Move Clip Art *(PP 2.32)*
- Print an Outline *(PP 2.51)*
- Print Presentation Slides *(PP 2.54)*
- Run an Animated Slide Show *(PP 2.49)*
- Save a Presentation *(PP 2.19, 2.35)*
- Save a Presentation on a Floppy Disk *(PP 2.49)*
- Save Changes and Quit PowerPoint *(PP 2.57)*
- Start a New Presentation *(PP 2.7)*
- Use the Notes and Handouts Sheet to Add Headers and Footers *(PP 2.36)*
- Use the Slide Master to Apply Animation Effects to All Bulleted Slides *(PP 2.42)*

Apply Your Knowledge

1 Intensifying a Presentation by Applying a Design Template, Changing Slide Layout, Inserting Clip Art, and Applying Animation Effects

Instructions: Start PowerPoint. Open the presentation Antique from the Data Disk. See the inside back cover of this book for instructions for downloading the Data Disk or see your instructor for information on accessing the files required in this book. Perform the following tasks to change the presentation to look like Figures 2-72a through 2-72e.

1. Apply the Dad's Tie design template. Add the current date, slide number, and your name to the notes and handouts footer.

2. On Slide 1, italicize the paragraph, Midwest College Art Department, and then decrease the font size to 28 points. Insert the gramophone clip art image shown in Figure 2-72a. Scale the clip art to 90% using the Format Picture command on the shortcut menu. Drag the gramophone clip art image to align the upper-left corner of the dotted box below the letter w in the word Show, as shown in Figure 2-72a. Apply the Spiral custom animation effect to the clip art.

(a) Slide 1

(b) Slide 2

(c) Slide 3

(d) Slide 4

(e) Slide 5

FIGURE 2-72

(continued)

Apply Your Knowledge

Intensifying a Presentation by Applying a Design Template, Changing Slide Layout, Inserting Clip Art, and Applying Animation Effect (continued)

3. Go to Slide 3. Change the slide layout to Clip Art & Text. Insert the vendor clip art image shown in Figure 2-72c. Change the size of the vendor clip art image to 275%. Move the vendor clip art image so the left edge of the selection rectangle aligns with the blue strip running down the slide.

4. Go to Slide 4. Change the slide layout to 2 Column Text. Select the bottom three categories (Furniture, Jewelry, Arts & Crafts), press and hold down the left mouse button, and drag the text to the right placeholder.

5. Go to Slide 5. Change the slide layout to Text & Clip Art. Insert the treasure chest clip art image shown in Figure 2-72e. Change the size of the treasure chest to 100%.

6. Add the Uncover Right slide transition effect to all slides except the title slide.

7. Save the presentation on a floppy disk using the file name, Antique Show.

8. Print the presentation in black and white. Print the presentation outline. Quit PowerPoint.

In the Lab

1 Adding Clip Art and Animation Effects to a Presentation Created in Outline View

Problem: Every fall and winter you experience the "winter blues." You feel depressed and lethargic, and you notice your friends are feeling the same symptoms. In the spring and summer months, however, these symptoms fade away. In your Health 101 class, you learn that these "winter blues" feelings are attributed to Seasonal Affective Disorder, commonly called SAD. They result from fewer hours of daylight, cold temperatures, and inclement weather. One of the assignments in this class is a research paper and accompanying five-minute presentation. You decide to conduct additional research on SAD and create the outline shown in Figure 2-73 to prepare your presentation. You use the outline to create the slide show shown in Figures 2-74a through 2-74d.

Instructions: Perform the following tasks.

1. Create a new presentation using the Sandstone design template.

2. Using the outline shown in Figure 2-73, create the title slide shown in Figure 2-74a.

I. Seasonal Affective Disorder
  A. Jacob Heilman
  B. Health 101
II. Symptoms of SAD
  A. Frequent depression
  B. Increasing appetite
    1. Craving carbohydrates
  C. Oversleeping
  D. Being irritable
III. Causes of SAD
  A. Increased melatonin
    1. A natural tranquilizer
    2. Secreted in greater amounts in darkness
  B. Internal clock desynchronized
IV. Relief for SAD
  A. Use light therapy
    1. Use bright lights in the morning
    2. Take a walk outside
  B. Avoid overeating
  C. Think spring!

FIGURE 2-73

Use your name instead of the name Jacob Heilman. Decrease the font size of the class name to 28 points. Insert the clip art that has the keywords, emotions, hearts, sadness, broken. Center the clip art under the class name.

3. Using the outline in Figure 2-73, create the three bulleted list slides shown in Figures 2-74b through 2-74d.

4. Change the slide layout on Slide 2 to Text & Clip Art. Using the Object Area placeholder, insert the clip art shown in Figure 2-74b that has the keywords, sorrow, grief, sadness, tears. Scale the clip art to 200%.

5. Change the slide layout on Slide 3 to Clip Art & Text. Using the Object Area placeholder, insert the clip art shown in Figure 2-74c that has the keywords, medicine, body parts, healthcare.

6. On Slide 4, change the slide layout to Text & Clip Art. Insert the clip art shown in Figure 2-74d that has the keywords, emotions, nature, seasons. Animate the sun clip art using the Spiral custom animation effect.

7. Add the slide number and your name to the slide footer. Display the footer on all slides except the title slide. Add your name to the outline header and your school's name to the outline footer.

8. Apply the Fade Through Black slide transition effect to Slides 2, 3, and 4.

9. Save the presentation on a floppy disk using the file name, SAD.

10. Print the presentation outline. Print the presentation. Quit PowerPoint.

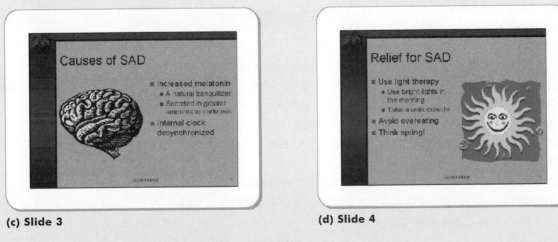

(a) Slide 1

(b) Slide 2

(c) Slide 3

(d) Slide 4

FIGURE 2-74

In the Lab

2 Animating a Slide Show

Problem: The park district in your community wants to develop a PowerPoint presentation that encourages residents to consider Nordic skiing at South Shore Park for fun and recreation. You have been active in many park district activities, so the marketing director asks you for assistance. She approves the outline you developed in Figure 2-75. When you practice your presentation, you decide to add animation effects to the slide show. The completed slide show is shown in Figures 2-76a through 2-76d. *Hint*: Use Help to solve this problem.

Instructions: Perform the following tasks.

1. Create a new presentation using the Nature design template and the outline shown in Figure 2-75.

2. On the title slide, increase the font size of Fun and Fitness to 36 points. Decrease the font size of the word, at, to 28 points. Using Figure 2-76a as a reference, insert the clip art that has the keywords, people, person, sports. Scale the clip art to 95% and drag it to the upper-right corner of the slide.

3. On Slide 2, change the slide layout to 2 Column Text. Drag the text into the right column placeholder so your slide looks like Slide 2 in Figure 2-76b.

4. On Slide 3, change the slide layout to Text & Clip Art. Insert the clip art shown in Figure 2-76c that has the keywords, animals, cartoons, nature, birds. Scale the clip art to 115%.

5. On Slide 4, change the slide layout to Clip Art & Text. Insert the clip art shown in Figure 2-76d that has the keywords, household, hats, clothes. Scale the clip art to 200%.

6. Add the current date, slide number, and your name to the slide footer. Display the footer on all slides except the title slide. Include the current date and your name on the outline header. Include South Shore Park and the page number on the outline footer.

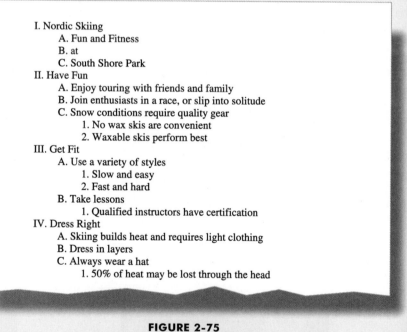

I. Nordic Skiing
  A. Fun and Fitness
  B. at
  C. South Shore Park
II. Have Fun
  A. Enjoy touring with friends and family
  B. Join enthusiasts in a race, or slip into solitude
  C. Snow conditions require quality gear
    1. No wax skis are convenient
    2. Waxable skis perform best
III. Get Fit
  A. Use a variety of styles
    1. Slow and easy
    2. Fast and hard
  B. Take lessons
    1. Qualified instructors have certification
IV. Dress Right
  A. Skiing builds heat and requires light clothing
  B. Dress in layers
  C. Always wear a hat
    1. 50% of heat may be lost through the head

FIGURE 2-75

7. Apply the Box Out slide transition effect to Slide 2 through 4. Apply the Peek From Top custom animation effect to the subtitle text on Slides 1 through 4. On Slide 1, introduce text grouped by 3rd level paragraphs.

8. Animate the clip art on Slide 1 using the Fly From Right custom animation effect so it displays immediately after the slide title when you run the slide show. Animate clip art on Slide 3 using the Fly From Top custom animation effect.

9. Save the presentation on a floppy disk using the file name, Nordic Skiing.

10. Print the presentation outline. Print the presentation slides. Print a handout with all four slides arranged vertically on one page. Quit PowerPoint.

In the Lab

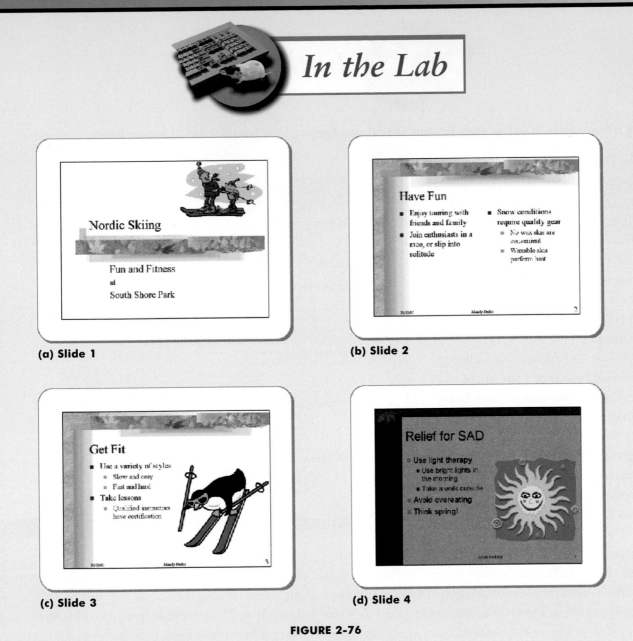

(a) Slide 1

(b) Slide 2

(c) Slide 3

(d) Slide 4

FIGURE 2-76

3 Creating a Presentation in Outline View, Inserting Clip Art, and Applying Slide Transition and Animation Effects

Problem: Bernice Simpson, the director of student life at your school, has asked you to help her prepare a lecture for students on the topic of stress management. You suggest developing a short PowerPoint presentation to accompany her talk. The slide show will describe how stress develops, how it affects studying and sleeping patterns, and what techniques can combat stress. It will conclude with describing how combating stress will improve the students' overall health and outlook toward life. You create the presentation using the outline shown in Figure 2-77 on the next page. You then refine the presentation using clip art, slide transitions, and animation effects to create the slide show shown in Figures 2-78a through 2-78f on page PP 2.65. *Hint:* Use Help to solve this problem.

Instructions: Perform the following tasks.

1. Create a new presentation using the Notebook design template and the outline in Figure 2-77.
2. On the title slide, animate the three subtitles with the Dissolve custom animation effect.

(continued)

In the Lab

Creating a Presentation in Outline View, Inserting Clip Art, and Applying Slide Transition and Animation Effects *(continued)*

3. Use Figure 2-78c as a reference. Change the slide layout on Slide 3 to Clip Art & Text. Then insert clip art that has the keywords, office, people, people at work.

4. Change the slide layout on Slide 4 (Figure 2-78d) to Text & Clip Art. Insert clip art that has the key-words household, people, signs, symbols.

5. On Slide 5 (Figure 2-78e), change the slide layout to Clip Art & Text. Insert the clip art that has the keyword, graduations.

6. On Slide 6 (Figure 2-78f), change the slide layout to Text & Clip Art. Insert the clip art that has the keywords, academic, people, schools. Scale the clip art to 100%.

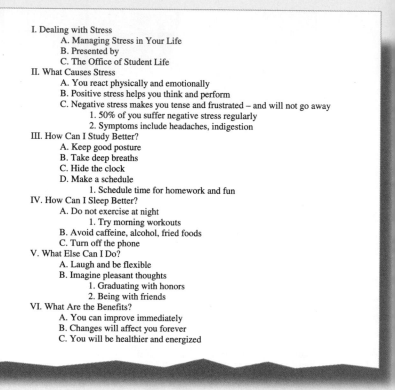

I. Dealing with Stress
    A. Managing Stress in Your Life
    B. Presented by
    C. The Office of Student Life
II. What Causes Stress
    A. You react physically and emotionally
    B. Positive stress helps you think and perform
    C. Negative stress makes you tense and frustrated – and will not go away
        1. 50% of you suffer negative stress regularly
        2. Symptoms include headaches, indigestion
III. How Can I Study Better?
    A. Keep good posture
    B. Take deep breaths
    C. Hide the clock
    D. Make a schedule
        1. Schedule time for homework and fun
IV. How Can I Sleep Better?
    A. Do not exercise at night
        1. Try morning workouts
    B. Avoid caffeine, alcohol, fried foods
    C. Turn off the phone
V. What Else Can I Do?
    A. Laugh and be flexible
    B. Imagine pleasant thoughts
        1. Graduating with honors
        2. Being with friends
VI. What Are the Benefits?
    A. You can improve immediately
    B. Changes will affect you forever
    C. You will be healthier and energized

FIGURE 2-77

7. Add the current date, your name, and slide number to the slide footer. Display the footer on all slides. Display your name and the current date on the outline header, and display the page number and the name of your school on the outline footer.

8. Apply the Wipe Down slide transition effect to Slides 2 through 6. Change the animation order so the clip art displays before the bulleted text. Apply the Split Horizontal In custom animation effect to all heading level 2 and 3 paragraphs on Slides 2 through 6. Apply the Fly From Right custom animation effect to the clip art on Slide 6.

9. Save the presentation on a floppy disk using the file name, Dealing With Stress.

10. Run the slide show.

11. Print the presentation outline. Print the presentation slides. Print a handout with all six slides arranged hori-zontally on one page. E-mail the presentation to Bernice using the address Bernice_Simpson@hotmail.com. Quit PowerPoint.

In the Lab

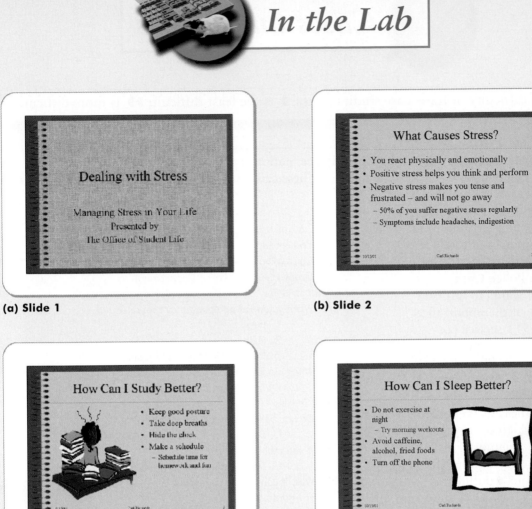

(a) Slide 1

(b) Slide 2

(c) Slide 3

(d) Slide 4

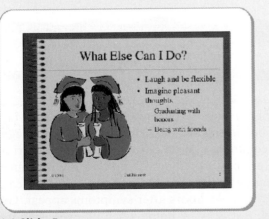

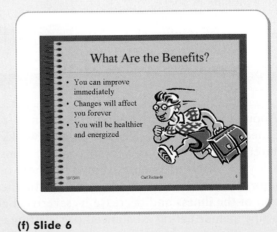

(e) Slide 5

(f) Slide 6

FIGURE 2-78

Cases and Places

The difficulty of these case studies varies: ❱ is the least difficult; ❱❱ is more difficult.

1 ❱ The dispatcher at the Brook Highlands Police Station is noticing an increase in the number of calls made to the emergency 911 telephone number. These calls, unfortunately, are not always emergencies. Community residents have been calling the number to obtain information on everything from the times of movies at the local theatre to the names of the local city trustees. Police Chief Wilbur Thiel wants to inform homeowners of the importance of using the 911 service correctly. He created the following outline (Figure 2-79) and asks you to help him prepare an accompanying PowerPoint presentation to show at the local mall and food stores. Using the concepts and techniques introduced in this project, together with Chief Thiel's outline, develop slides for a slide show. Include clip art and animation effects to add interest. Print the outline and slides as a one-page handout so they can be distributed to residents at the conclusion of the presentation.

I. 911 A Call for Help
A. Presented by
B. Chief Wilbur Thiel
C. Brook Highlands Police Department
II. What It Is For
A. When you need an emergency response
1. Fire
2. Police
3. Emergency Medical Personnel
B. When disaster occurs
1. Tornadoes, earthquakes, floods
III. How To Help
A. Do not call for general information
1. Consult local telephone directories
B. If you call by mistake
1. Tell the dispatcher you have misdialed
C. Wait if you hear a recording
IV. Other Information
A. Tell the telephone company if you change your name or address
1. This info displays on the dispatcher's screen
2. The dispatcher relies on this information
B. Be certain your house number can be seen from the street

FIGURE 2-79

2 ❱❱ About 25 percent of the population suffers from the flu each year from October through May. Flu-related symptoms generally last for two weeks and include sudden headaches, chills, dry coughs, high fevers, and body aches. Serious complications are common, and an estimated 20,000 Americans die each year from the disease. Annual flu shots can help prevent the illness, and they are recommended for high-risk individuals such as the elderly and healthcare workers. Some drugs will help shorten the duration of the illness and decrease its severity if given within 48 hours after symptoms appear. General health tips include eating a balanced diet, getting enough rest, staying home when ill, exercising frequently, and washing hands frequently with warm, soapy water. Your campus' health services department wants to develop a presentation for students informing them about the flu and giving advice to stay healthy. Using the techniques introduced in the project, create a presentation about the flu. Include appropriate clip art and animation effects.

Microsoft PowerPoint 2000

Creating a Presentation on the Web Using PowerPoint

C A S E   P E R S P E C T I V E

The advisers at Lake View College's Counseling Department are pleased with the Effective Study Skills presentation you developed in Project 1. The results indicate that students who view the slide show and read the handouts gain helpful information about time management, class attendance, and textbook usage. The counselors realize, however, that students who often have difficulty in class are those who have poor listening skills. The counselors refer these students to the Tutoring Center for help.

Now the Tutoring Center wants you to develop a similar presentation describing how students can improve their listening skills. Dr. Rachel Sims, the Tutoring Center director, knows that students can improve their listening capability by practicing some techniques. Dr. Sims decides the most effective way to disseminate this information is to have you prepare a PowerPoint slide show highlighting these skills and then make the presentation available on the World Wide Web to all students. The slide show, called Listen Up, will contain this information along with clip art and animation effects for visual interest. Dr. Sims then wants you to publish the presentation on the World Wide Web.

Introduction

The graphic design power of PowerPoint allows you to create vibrant presentations that convey information in a clear, interesting manner. Some of these presentations are created for small, specific audiences, such as a subcommittee planning a department golf outing. In this case, the presentation may be shown in an office conference room. On the other hand, other presentations are designed for large, general audiences, such as workers at a corporation's various offices across the country learning about a new computer system being installed. These employees can view the presentation on their company's **intranet**, which is an internal network that uses Internet technologies. On a grand scale, you can inform the entire world about the contents of your presentation by posting your slide show to the World Wide Web. To publish to the World Wide Web, you need an **FTP (File Transfer Protocol)** program to copy your presentation and related files to an **Internet service provider (ISP)** computer.

PowerPoint allows you to create Web pages in three ways. First, you can start a new presentation, as you did in Projects 1 and 2 when you produced the Effective Study Skills and Searching for Scholarships presentations. PowerPoint provides a Web Presentation template in the **AutoContent Wizard** option when you start PowerPoint. The wizard provides design and content ideas to help you develop an effective slide show for an intranet or for the Internet by opening a sample presentation that you can alter by adding your own text and graphics.

Second, by using the **Save as Web Page** command, you can convert an existing presentation to a format compatible with popular Web browsers, such as Microsoft Internet Explorer. This command allows you to create a Web page from a single slide or from a multiple-slide presentation. This Web feature illustrates opening the Listen Up presentation on the Data Disk and then saving the presentation as a Web page. PowerPoint will start your default browser and open your HTML file so you can view the presentation (Figures 1a through 1e). Finally, you will edit the presentation, save it again, and view it in your default browser.

FIGURE 1

Third, in PowerPoint you can preview your presentation as a Web page. This action opens your presentation in your default Web browser without saving HTML files. You could use this feature to review and modify your work in progress until you develop a satisfactory presentation.

Because you are converting the Listen Up presentation on the Data Disk to a Web page, the first step in this project is to open the Listen Up file. Then you will save the file as a Web page and view the presentation in your default browser. For instructional purposes in this Web feature, you create and save your Web page on a floppy disk. At times, this saving process may be slow, so you must be patient.

Saving a PowerPoint Presentation as a Web Page

Once a PowerPoint slide show is complete, you want to save it as a Web page so you can publish and then view it in a Web browser. PowerPoint allows you to **publish** the presentation by saving the pages to a Web folder or to an FTP location. The procedures for publishing Web pages to the World Wide Web in Microsoft Office are discussed in Appendix B. When you publish your presentation to the Web, it is available for other computer users to view on the Internet or through other means.

You can save and then view the presentation in two ways. First, you can save the entire presentation as a Web page, quit PowerPoint, open your browser, and open the Web page in your browser. Second, in this Web feature you will combine these steps by saving the presentation to drive A and then viewing the presentation. In this case, PowerPoint automatically will start the browser and display your presentation. Perform the steps on the next page to save and publish the Listen Up presentation as a Web page.

More *About*

The World Wide Web

More than three-fourths of college graduates use the World Wide Web for their job hunting efforts. They search for specific information on their careers, and then they turn to corporate Web sites for information on job vacancies and the annual report. They also e-mail their resumes to potential employers and post their resumes on online job services. For more information, visit the PowerPoint 2000 More About Web page (www.scsite.com/pp2000/more.htm) and click Jobs.

Steps **To Save a PowerPoint Presentation as a Web Page**

1 **Start PowerPoint and then open the Listen Up file on the Data Disk. Reset your toolbars as described in Appendix C. Click the notes pane and then type** We receive most of our information by listening to others, yet few people have had listening training. **Click File on the menu bar and then point to Save as Web Page.**

PowerPoint opens and displays the presentation in normal view (Figure 2). The notes pane lets you type speaker notes to remind you of information you want to share with your audience. The File menu displays.

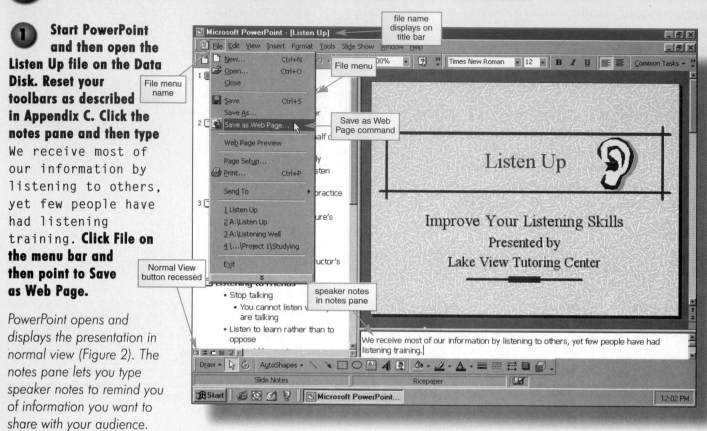

FIGURE 2

2 **Click Save as Web Page. When the Save As dialog box displays, type** Listening Well **in the File name text box.**

PowerPoint displays the Save As dialog box (Figure 3). Web Page displays in the Save as type box.

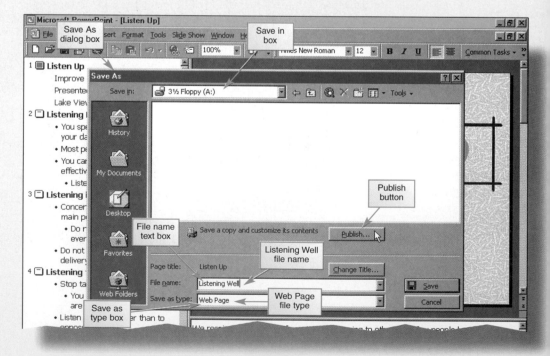

FIGURE 3

3 **Click the Publish button. If the Office Assistant displays, click No, don't provide help now. When the Publish as Web Page dialog box displays, triple-click the Publish a copy as File name text box and then type** A:\Listening Well **in the text box. Be certain the Open published Web page in browser check box is selected. Point to the Publish button.**

The Publish as Web Page dialog box displays (Figure 4). PowerPoint defaults to publishing the complete presentation, although you can choose to publish one or a range of slides. The Open published Web page in browser check box is selected, which means the Listening Well presentation will open in your default browser when you click the Publish button.

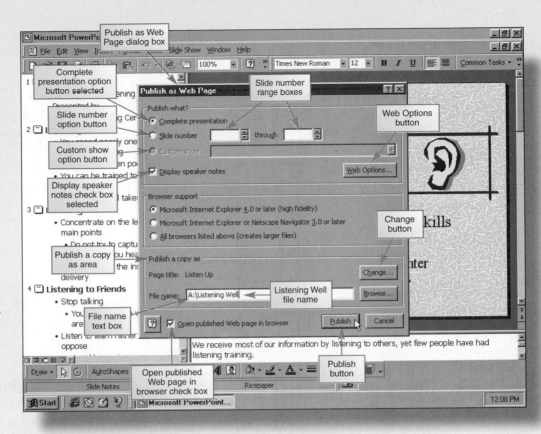

FIGURE 4

4 **Click the Publish button.**

PowerPoint saves the presentation as Listening Well.htm on your Data Disk in drive A. After a few seconds, PowerPoint opens your default Web browser in a separate window (Figure 5).

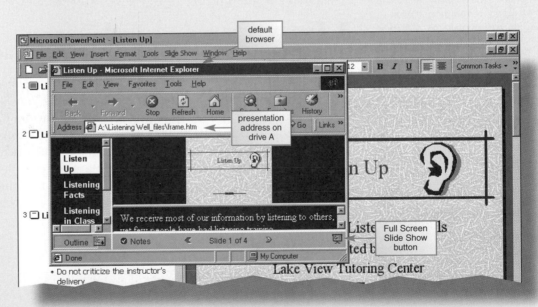

FIGURE 5

Other Ways

1. Press ALT+F, press G, type new file name, press SHIFT+TAB two times, press P, change file name in Publish copy as box, press ENTER

Publishing provides customizing options that are not available when you merely save the entire publication and then start your browser. The Publish as Web Page dialog box provides several options to customize your Web page. For example, you can change the page title that displays in the browser's title bar and history list. People visiting your Web site can store a link to your Web page, which will display in their favorites list. To change the page title, you click the Change button in the Publish a copy as area (see Figure 4 on the previous page) and then type a new title.

The Publish what? area of the Publish as Web Page dialog box allows you to publish parts of your presentation. PowerPoint defaults to publishing the complete presentation, but you can select specific slides by clicking the Slide number option button and then entering the range of desired slide numbers. In addition, you can publish a custom show you have created previously. A **custom show** is a subset of your presentation that contains slides tailored for a specific audience. For example, you may want to show Slides 1, 2, and 4 to one group and Slides 1, 3, and 4 to another group.

You can choose to publish only the publication slides, and not the accompanying speaker notes. By default, the **Display speaker notes check box** is selected in the Publish what? area. You typed speaker notes for Slide 1 of this presentation, so they will display in the browser window. If you do not want to make your notes available to users, click the Display speaker notes check box to remove the check mark.

The Web Options button in the Publish what? area allows you to select options to determine how your presentation will look when viewed in a Web browser. You can choose options such as allowing slide animation to show, selecting the screen size, and having the notes and outline panes display when viewing the presentation in a Web browser.

Now that you have opened the Listen Up file and saved the presentation as a Web page, you want to view the slide show using your default browser.

Viewing a Presentation as a Web Page

PowerPoint makes it easy to create a presentation and then view how it will display on an intranet or the World Wide Web. By viewing your slide show, you can decide which features look good and which need modification. The left side of the window contains the outline pane showing a table of contents consisting of each slide's title text. You can click the **Expand/Collapse Outline button** below the outline pane to view the complete slide text. The right side displays the complete slide in the slide pane. The speaker notes display in the notes pane under the slide pane. Perform the following steps to view your Listening Well presentation as a Web page.

More *About* 2000

Speaker Notes

When you prepare speaker notes for your presentation, remember that audiences want to hear you explain the concepts on the slides. Each slide should list the key points, and your notes should guide you with the supplemental information you will deliver. Your listeners can retain a maximum of six major points you make, so these facts and your explanation should comprise the majority of your presentation. For more information, visit the PowerPoint 2000 More About Web page (www.scsite.com/pp2000/more.htm) and click Speaker Notes.

More *About* 2000

Viewing Presentations

The PowerPoint Viewer allows users to see your Web presentation without installing PowerPoint. This application is handy when you are going to deliver your slide show at a remote site on a computer other than your own. Microsoft distributes this software free of charge. For more information, visit the PowerPoint 2000 More About Web page (www.scsite.com/pp2000/more.htm) and click Viewer.

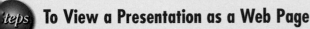

To View a Presentation as a Web Page

1 If necessary, double-click the Microsoft Internet Explorer title bar to maximize the browser window. Point to the Full Screen Slide Show button.

The title text and ear clip art of the first slide of the Listening Well presentation display in the slide pane in the browser window (Figure 6). The outline pane contains the table of contents, which consists of the title text of each slide. The notes pane displays the speaker notes.

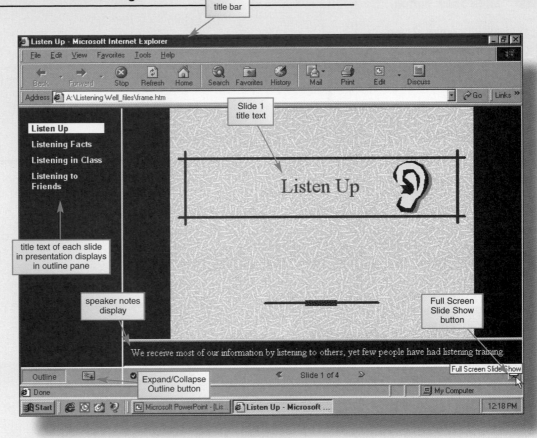

FIGURE 6

Click the Full Screen Slide Show button.

Slide 1 fills the entire screen (Figure 7). The Slide 1 title text and ear clip art display.

 Click to display the first line of the Object Area placeholder text.

The first line of the Slide 1 Object Area placeholder text displays.

4 **Continue clicking each slide in the presentation. When the black slide displays, click it. Point to the Expand/ Collapse Outline button below the outline pane.**

Each of the four slides in the Listening Well presentation displays. The message on the black slide, End of slide show, click to exit., indicates the conclusion of the slide show.

5 **Click the Expand/ Collapse Outline button.**

The text of each slide displays in the outline pane (Figure 8). Lines display to the left and under the text of the current slide in this pane. To display only the title of each slide, you would click the Expand/ Collapse Outline button again.

FIGURE 7

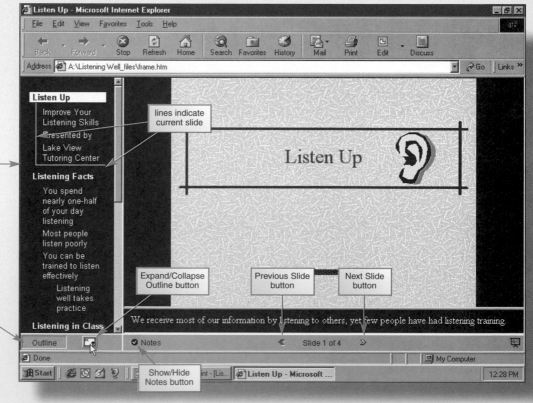

FIGURE 8

You can alter the browser window by choosing to display or hide the outline and notes panes. To eliminate the outline pane, click the **Show/Hide Outline button** below the outline pane. If you later want to display the outline pane, you would click the **Show/Hide Outline button** again. Similarly, the **Show/Hide Notes button** below the slide pane allows you to display or conceal the speaker notes on a particular slide.

To advance through the Web pages, click the **Next Slide button** below the slide pane. Likewise, to display a slide appearing earlier in the slide show, click the **Previous Slide button**.

Editing a Web Page through a Browser

Dr. Rachel Sims, the Tutoring Center director, informs you that she wants her name to display on the title slide so that students can contact her for further information. She suggests you change the last line of the Slide 1, Lake View Tutoring Center, to her name. Perform the following steps to modify Slide 1.

More About

Persuading Audiences

As you choose to show or hide your outline and notes, consider the needs of your audience. Some researchers believe listeners are more attentive on Sundays, Mondays, and Tuesdays because they are more relaxed than at the middle and end of a week. Thus, you may need to provide more information via the outline and notes when your audience is less focused.

Steps) To Edit a Web Page through a Browser

1 **Point to the Edit button** on the **Standard Buttons toolbar.**

Slide 1 displays in the browser (Figure 9). The ScreenTip, Edit with Microsoft PowerPoint for Windows, indicates you can modify the presentation using PowerPoint directly from the browser window. Your computer may indicate other editing options, such as using Windows Notepad.

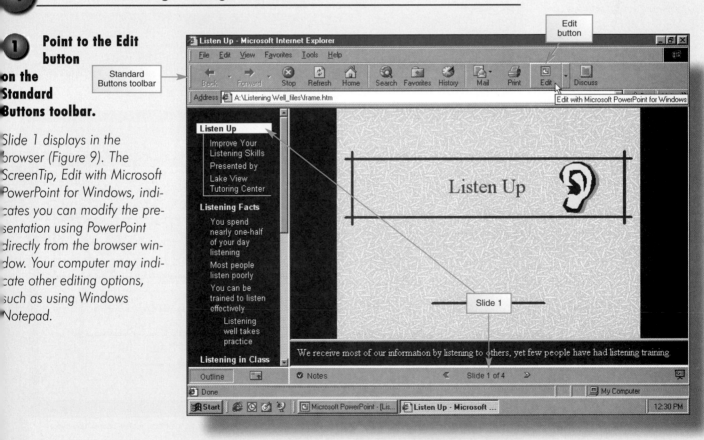

FIGURE 9

2 **Click the Edit button. Triple-click the last second level line, Lake View Tutoring Center.**

When you click the Edit button, PowerPoint returns control to the PowerPoint window, as indicated by the title bar and the recessed Microsoft PowerPoint – [Listening Well] button (Figure 10). A selection rectangle displays around the Object Area placeholder text. The last line is highlighted.

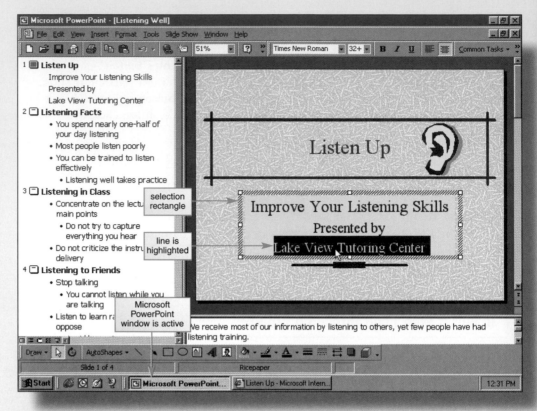

FIGURE 10

3 **Type** Dr. Rachel Sims **and then point to the Save button on the Standard toolbar.**

The last line is modified (Figure 11).

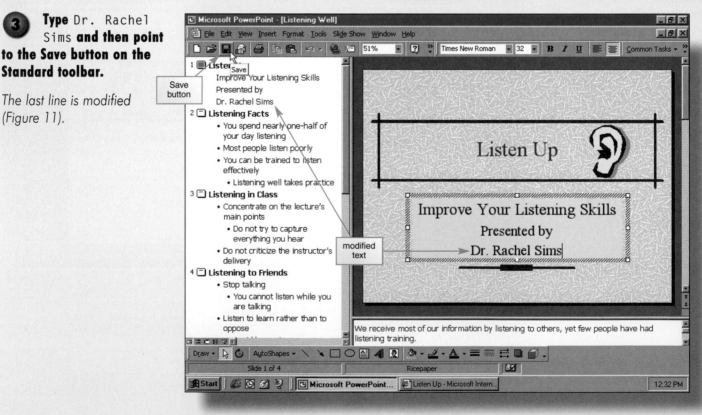

FIGURE 11

4 Click the Save
button. Point to the
Listen Up – Microsoft
Internet Explorer button on
the taskbar.

*PowerPoint saves the changes
to the Listening Well.htm file
on the Data Disk. The buttons
on the taskbar indicate that
both PowerPoint and the
browser are open
(Figure 12).*

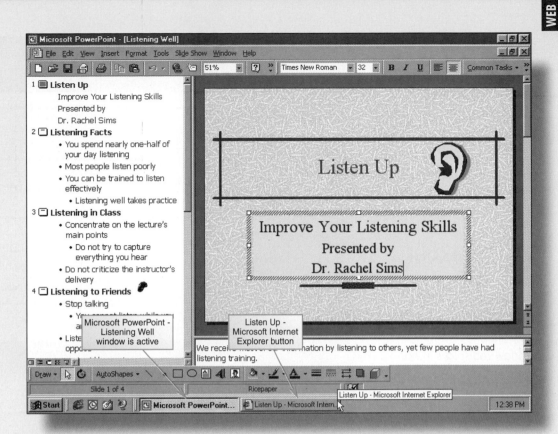

FIGURE 12

5 Click the Listen
Up – Microsoft
Internet Explorer button
and then point to the
Refresh button on the
Standard Buttons toolbar.

*The browser window displays
the title text and clip art on
Slide 1 (Figure 13). Clicking
the Refresh button displays
the most current version of
the Web page.*

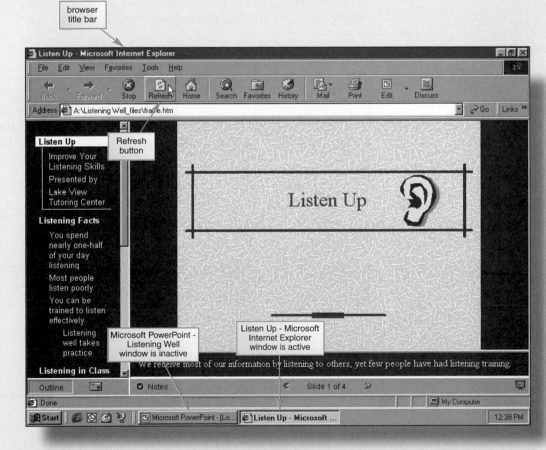

FIGURE 13

Click the Refresh button. Click the slide three times to display all the Object Area placeholder text. Point to the Close button on the browser title bar.

The complete Slide 1 displays (Figure 14). The last line reflects the editing changes.

 Click the Close button.

PowerPoint closes the Listening Well Web presentation, and the PowerPoint window redisplays in normal view.

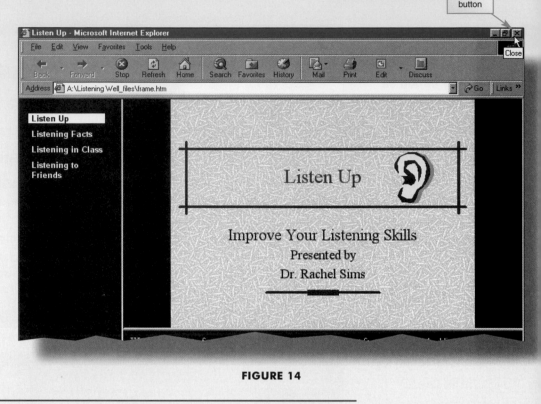

FIGURE 14

The Web page now is complete. The next step is to make your Web presentation available to others on your network, an intranet, or the World Wide Web. Ask your instructor how you can publish your presentation.

CASE PERSPECTIVE SUMMARY

Students attending Dr. Rachel Sims' lecture in the Tutoring Center should learn techniques that will improve their listening skills. Your Listen Up slide show will help to reinforce the key points presented, including facts about listening effectively. The students will be able to apply the theories when they are in class and with their friends. Dr. Sims can publish your presentation to the World Wide Web so that students who cannot attend the lecture also can gain the useful information presented.

Web Feature Smmary

This Web feature introduced you to creating a Web page by saving an existing PowerPoint presentation as an HTML file. You then viewed the presentation as a Web page in your default browser. Next, you modified Slide 1. Finally, you reviewed your Slide 1 change using your default browser. Now that your Listen Up presentation is converted to a Web page, you can post the file to an intranet or to the World Wide Web.

What You Should Know

Having completed this Web feature, you now should be able to perform the following tasks:

▶ Edit a Web Page through a Browser *(PPW 1.9)*

▶ Save a PowerPoint Presentation as a Web Page *(PPW 1.4)*

▶ View a Presentation as a Web Page *(PPW 1.7)*

In the Lab

1 Creating a Web Page from the Studying Presentation

Problem: The advisers at Seaview College want to expand the visibility of the Effective Study Skills presentation created for them in Project 1. They believe the World Wide Web would be an excellent vehicle to help students throughout the campus and at other colleges, and they have asked you to help transfer the presentation to the Internet.

Instructions: Start PowerPoint and then perform the following steps with a computer.

1. Open the Studying presentation shown in Figures 1-2a through 1-2d on page PP 1.9 that you created in Project 1. (If you did not complete Project 1, see your instructor for a copy of the presentation.)
2. Use the Save as Web Page command on the File menu to convert and publish the presentation. Save the Web page using the file name, Effective Studying.
3. View the presentation in a browser.
4. Modify Slide 3 by adding a First level line that states, Arrive a few minutes before class starts, as the last line on the screen.
5. View the modified Web page in a browser.
6. Ask your instructor for instructions on how to post your Web page so others may have access to it.

2 Creating a Web Page from the Scholarship Presentation

Problem: The Searching for Scholarships presentation you developed in Project 2 for the Office of Financial Aid is generating much interest. Students are visiting the office, which has moved to Room 4321, and requesting a date to hear the lecture and to see the slide show. Dr. Mary Halen, the Financial Aid director, has asked you to post the presentation to the school's intranet.

Instructions: Start PowerPoint and then perform the following steps with a computer.

1. Open the Searching for Scholarships presentation shown in Figures 2-1a through 2-1f on page PP 2.5 that you created in Project 2. (If you did not complete Project 2, see your instructor for a copy of the presentation.)
2. Use the Save as Web Page command on the File menu to convert and publish the presentation. Save the Web page using the file name, Scholarship Sources.
3. View the presentation in a browser.
4. Modify Slide 2 by changing the room number to 4321.
5. Modify Slide 4 by changing the word, athletics, to the word, writing, in the Second level paragraph.
6. View the modified Web page in a browser.
7. Ask your instructor for instructions on how to post your Web page so others may have access to it.

In the Lab

3 Creating a Personal Presentation

Problem: You have decided to apply for a job at a company several hundred miles from your campus. You are preparing to send your resume and cover letter to the human resources department, and you want to develop a unique way to publicize your computer expertise. You decide to create a personalized PowerPoint presentation emphasizing your academic strengths and extra-curricular activities. You refer to this presentation in your cover letter and inform the company officials that they can view this presentation because you have saved the presentation as a Web page and posted the page to your school's server.

Instructions: Start PowerPoint and then perform the following steps with a computer.

1. Prepare a presentation highlighting your academic strengths. Create a title slide and at least three additional slides. Use appropriate clip art, animation effects, and slide transition effects.
2. Use the Save as Web Page command to convert and publish the presentation. Save the Web page using the file name, Supplemental Information.
3. View the presentation in a browser.
4. Ask your instructor for instructions on how to post your Web page so others may have access to it.

APPENDIX A
Microsoft Office 2000 Help System

Using the Microsoft Office Help System

This appendix demonstrates how you can use the Microsoft Office 2000 Help system to answer your questions. At any time while you are using one of the Microsoft Office 2000 applications, you can interact with the Help system to display information on any topic associated with the application. To illustrate the use of the Microsoft Office 2000 Help system, the Microsoft Word 2000 application will be used in this appendix. The Help systems in other Microsoft Office applications respond in a similar fashion.

The two primary forms of Help available in each Microsoft Office application are the Office Assistant and the Microsoft Help window. The one you use will depend on your preference. As shown in Figure A-1, you access either form of Help in Microsoft Word by pressing the F1 key, clicking Microsoft Word Help on the Help menu, or clicking the Microsoft Word Help button on the Standard toolbar. Word responds in one of two ways:

1. If the Office Assistant is turned on, then the Office Assistant displays with a balloon (lower-right side of Figure A-1).
2. If the Office Assistant is turned off, then the Microsoft Word Help window displays (lower-left side of Figure A-1)

Table A-1 on the next page summarizes the nine categories of Help available to you. Because of the way the Word Help system works, please review the rightmost column of Table A-1 if you have difficulties activating the desired category of Help.

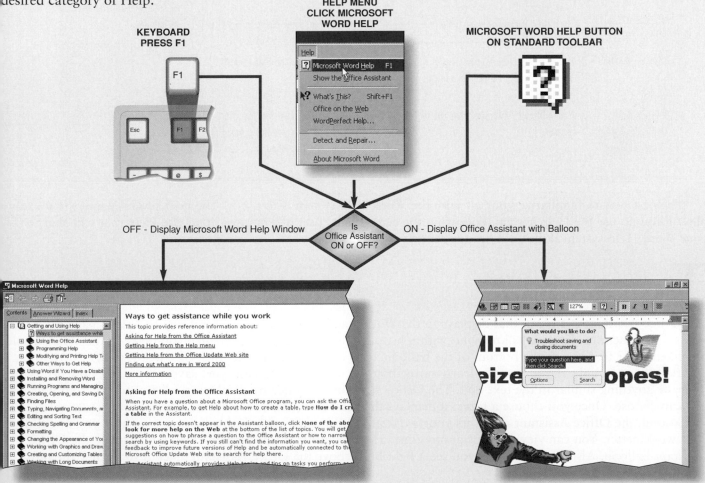

FIGURE A-1

Table A-1 Word Help System

TYPE	DESCRIPTION	HOW TO ACTIVATE	TURNING THE OFFICE ASSISTANT ON AND OFF
Answer Wizard	Similar to the Office Assistant in that it answers questions that you type in your own words.	Click the Microsoft Word Help button on the Standard toolbar. If necessary, maximize the Help window by double-clicking its title bar. Click the Answer Wizard tab.	If the Office Assistant displays, right-click it, click Options on the shortcut menu, click Use the Office Assistant to remove the check mark, click the OK button.
Contents sheet	Groups Help topics by general categories. Use when you know only the general category of the topic in question.	Click the Microsoft Word Help button on the Standard toolbar. If necessary, maximize the Help window by double-clicking its title bar. Click the Contents tab.	If the Office Assistant displays, right-click it, click Options, click Use the Office Assistant to remove the check mark, click the OK button.
Detect and Repair	Automatically finds and fixes errors in the application.	Click Detect and Repair on the Help menu.	
Hardware and Software Information	Shows Product ID and allows access to system information and technical support information.	Click About Microsoft Word on the Help menu and then click the appropriate button.	
Help for WordPerfect Users	Used to assist WordPerfect users who are learning Microsoft Word.	Click WordPerfect Help on the Help menu.	
Index sheet	Similar to an index in a book; use when you know exactly what you want.	Click the Microsoft Word Help button on the Standard toolbar. If necessary, maximize the Help window by double-clicking its title bar. Click the Index tab.	If the Office Assistant displays, right-click it, click Options, click Use the Office Assistant to remove the check mark, click the OK button.
Office Assistant	Answers questions that you type in your own words, offers tips, and provides Help for a variety of Word features.	Click the Microsoft Word Help button on the Standard toolbar or double-click the Office Assistant icon. Some dialog boxes also include the Microsoft Word Help button.	If the Office Assistant does not display, click Show the Office Assistant on the Help menu.
Office on the Web	Used to access technical resources and download free product enhancements on the Web.	Click Office on the Web on the Help menu.	
Question Mark button and What's This? command	Used to identify unfamiliar items on the screen.	In a dialog box, click the Question Mark button and then click an item in the dialog box. Click What's This? on the Help menu, and then click an item on the screen.	

The best way to familiarize yourself with the Word Help system is to use it. The next several pages show examples of how to use the Help system. Following the examples is a set of exercises titled Use Help that will sharpen your Word Help system skills.

The Office Assistant

The **Office Assistant** is an icon that displays in the Word window (lower-right side of Figure A-1 on page MO A.1). It has dual functions. First, it will respond with a list of topics that relate to the entry you make in the What would you like to do? text box at the bottom of the balloon. This entry can be in the form of a word, phrase, or written question. For example, if you want to learn more about saving a file, you can type, save, save a file, how do I save a file, or anything similar in the text box. The Office Assistant responds by displaying a list of topics from which you can choose. Once you choose a topic, it displays the corresponding information.

Second, the Office Assistant monitors your work and accumulates tips during a session on how you might do your work better. You can view the tips at any time. The accumulated tips display when you activate the Office Assistant balloon. Also, if at any time you see a light bulb above the Office Assistant, click it to display the most recent tip.

You may or may not want the Office Assistant to display on the screen at all times. You can hide it, and then show it at a later time. You may prefer not to use the Office Assistant at all. In this case, you use the Microsoft Word Help window (lower-left side of Figure A-1 on page MO A.1). Thus, not only do you need to know how to show and hide the Office Assistant, but you also need to know how to turn the Office Assistant on and off.

Showing and Hiding the Office Assistant

When Word is first installed, the Office Assistant displays in the Word window. You can move it to any location on the screen. You can click it to display the Office Assistant balloon, which allows you to request Help. If the Office Assistant is on the screen and you want to hide it, you click the **Hide the Office Assistant command** on the Help menu. You also can right-click the Office Assistant to display its shortcut menu and then click the **Hide command** to hide it. When the Office Assistant is hidden, then the **Show the Office Assistant command** replaces the Hide the Office Assistant command on the Help menu. Thus, you can show or hide the Office Assistant at any time.

Turning the Office Assistant On and Off

The fact that the Office Assistant is hidden, does not mean it is turned off. To turn the Office Assistant off, it must be displayed in the Word window. You right-click it to display its shortcut menu (right side of Figure A-2). Next, click Options on the shortcut menu. Invoking the **Options command** causes the Office Assistant dialog box to display (left side of Figure A-2).

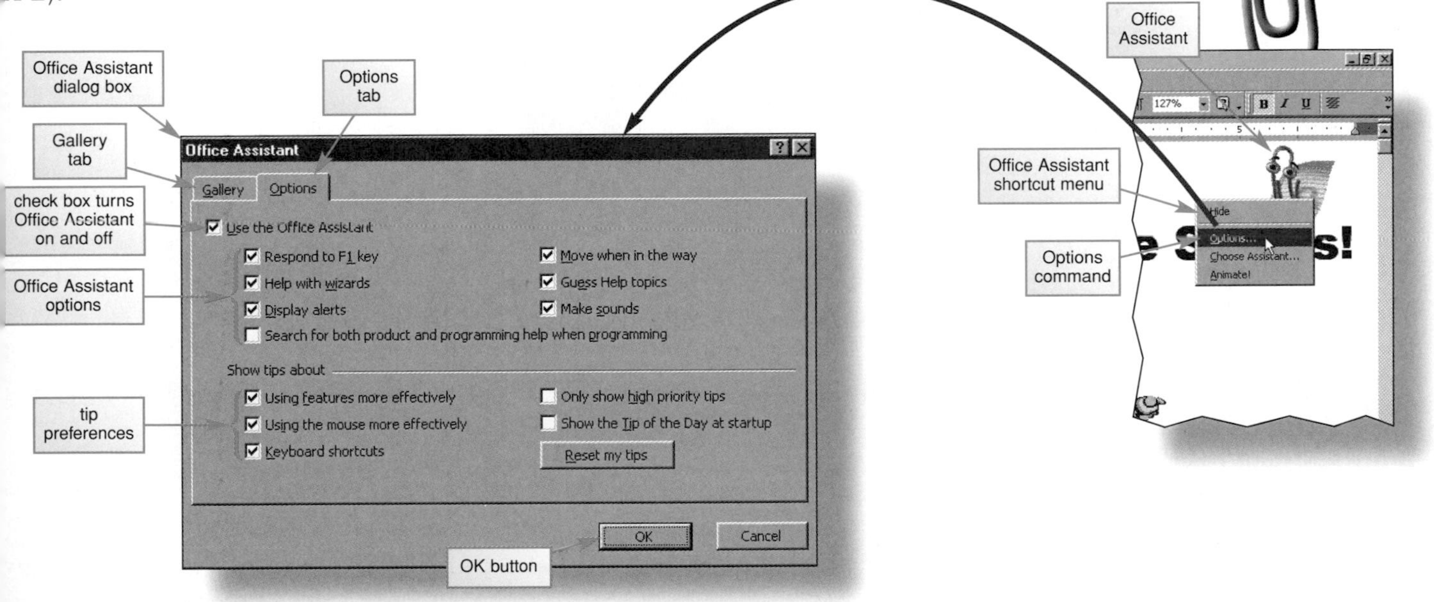

FIGURE A-2

The top check box in the Options sheet determines whether the Office Assistant is on or off. To turn the Office Assistant off, remove the check mark from the **Use the Office Assistant check box** and then click the OK button. As shown in Figure A-1 on page MO A.1, if the Office Assistant is off when you invoke Help, then the Microsoft Word Help window displays instead of the Office Assistant. To turn the Office Assistant on at a later time, click the Show the Office Assistant command on the Help menu.

Through the Options command on the Office Assistant shortcut menu, you can change the look and feel of the Office Assistant. For example, you can hide the Office Assistant, turn the Office Assistant off, change the way it works, choose a different Office Assistant icon, or view an animation of the current one. These options also are available by clicking the Options button that displays in the Office Assistant balloon (Figure A-3 on the next page).

The **Gallery sheet** (Figure A-2) in the Office Assistant dialog box allows you to change the appearance of the Office Assistant. The default is the paper clip (Clippit). You can change it to a bouncing red happy face (The Dot), a robot (F1), a professor (The Genius), the Microsoft Office logo (Office Logo), the earth (Mother Nature), a cat (Links), or a dog (Rocky).

Using the Office Assistant

As indicated earlier, the Office Assistant allows you to enter a word, phrase, or question and then responds by displaying a list of topics from which you can choose to display Help. The following steps show how to use the Office Assistant to obtain Help about online meetings.

Steps To Use the Office Assistant

1 If the Office Assistant is not turned on, click Help on the menu bar and then click Show the Office Assistant. Click the Office Assistant. When the Office Assistant balloon displays, **type** what are online meetings **in the text box. Point to the Search button.**

The Office Assistant balloon displays as shown in Figure A-3.

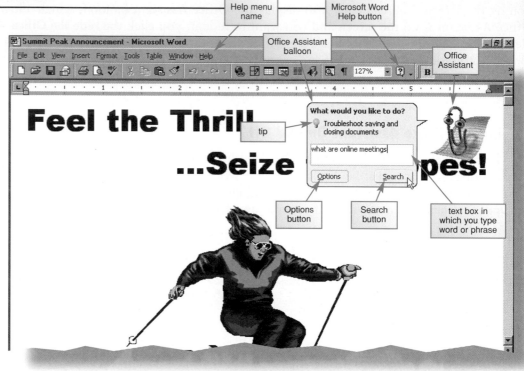

FIGURE A-3

2 Click the Search button. When the Office Assistant balloon redisplays, point to the topic, About online meetings (Figure A-4).

FIGURE A-4

Back and Forward buttons

Print button

Options button

Close button

Show or Hide button

③ Click the topic, About online meetings. Double-click the Microsoft Word Help window title bar to maximize it. If necessary, move or hide the Office Assistant so you can view all of the text in the Microsoft Word Help window.

The Microsoft Word Help window displays the information about online meetings (Figure A-5).

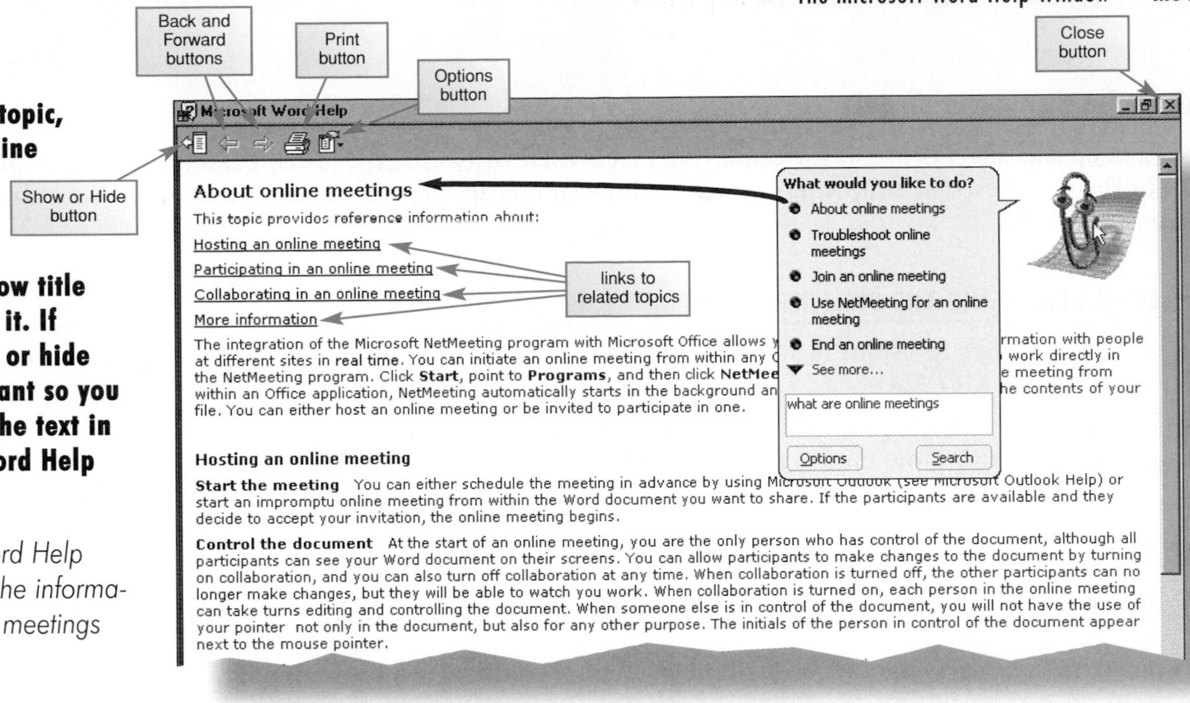

About online meetings

This topic provides reference information about:

Hosting an online meeting
Participating in an online meeting
Collaborating in an online meeting
More information

links to related topics

The integration of the Microsoft NetMeeting program with Microsoft Office allows you to ... work directly in at different sites in real time. You can initiate an online meeting from within any O... the NetMeeting program. Click **Start**, point to **Programs**, and then click **NetMee**... within an Office application, NetMeeting automatically starts in the background an... ... e meeting from file. You can either host an online meeting or be invited to participate in one. ... he contents of your

Hosting an online meeting

Start the meeting   You can either schedule the meeting in advance by using Microsoft Outlook (see Microsoft Outlook Help) or start an impromptu online meeting from within the Word document you want to share. If the participants are available and they decide to accept your invitation, the online meeting begins.

Control the document   At the start of an online meeting, you are the only person who has control of the document, although all participants can see your Word document on their screens. You can allow participants to make changes to the document by turning on collaboration, and you can also turn off collaboration at any time. When collaboration is turned off, the other participants can no longer make changes, but they will be able to watch you work. When collaboration is turned on, each person in the online meeting can take turns editing and controlling the document. When someone else is in control of the document, you will not have the use of your pointer not only in the document, but also for any other purpose. The initials of the person in control of the document appear next to the mouse pointer.

What would you like to do?
- About online meetings
- Troubleshoot online meetings
- Join an online meeting
- Use NetMeeting for an online meeting
- End an online meeting
- See more...

what are online meetings

Options   Search

FIGURE A-5

When the Microsoft Word Help window displays, you can choose to read it or print it. To print the information, click the Print button on the Microsoft Word Help toolbar. Table A-2 lists the function of each button on the toolbar in the Microsoft Word Help window. To close the Microsoft Word Help window shown in Figure A-5, click the Close button on the title bar.

Table A-2 Microsoft Word Help Toolbar Buttons		
BUTTON	**NAME**	**FUNCTION**
or	Show or Hide	Displays or hides the Contents, Answer Wizard, Index tabs
	Back	Displays the previous Help topic
	Forward	Displays the next Help topic
	Print	Prints the current Help topic
	Options	Displays a list of commands

Other Ways

1. If Office Assistant is turned on, on Help menu click Microsoft Word Help, or click Microsoft Word Help button on Standard toolbar to display Office Assistant balloon

The Microsoft Word Help Window

If the Office Assistant is turned off and you click the Microsoft Word Help button on the Standard toolbar, the **Microsoft Word Help window** displays (Figure A-6 on the next page). This window contains three tabs on the left side: Contents, Answer Wizard, and Index. Each tab displays a sheet with powerful look-up capabilities. Use the Contents sheet as you would a table of contents at the front of a book to look up Help. The Answer Wizard sheet answers your queries in the same manner as the Office Assistant. You use the Index sheet in the same manner as an index in a book.

Click the tabs to move from sheet to sheet. The five buttons on the toolbar, Show or Hide, Back, Forward, Print, and Options also are described in Table A-2.

Besides clicking the Microsoft Word Help button on the Standard toolbar, you also can click the Microsoft Word Help command on the Help menu or press the F1 key to display the Microsoft Word Help window to gain access to the three sheets. To close the Microsoft Word Help window, click the Close button in the upper-right corner on the title bar.

Using the Contents Sheet

The **Contents sheet** is useful for displaying Help when you know the general category of the topic in question, but not the specifics. The following steps show how to use the Contents sheet to obtain information about Web folders.

TO OBTAIN HELP USING THE CONTENTS SHEET

1 With the Office Assistant turned off, click the Microsoft Word Help button on the Standard toolbar (Figure A-3 on page MO A.4).

2 When the Microsoft Word Help window displays, double-click the title bar to maximize the window. If necessary, click the Show button to display the tabs.

3 Click the Contents tab.

4 Double-click the Working with Online and Internet Documents book on the left side of the window.

5 Double-click the Creating Web Pages book below the Working with Online and Internet Documents book.

6 Click the About Web Folders subtopic below the Creating Web Pages book.

Word displays Help on the subtopic, About Web Folders (Figure A-6).

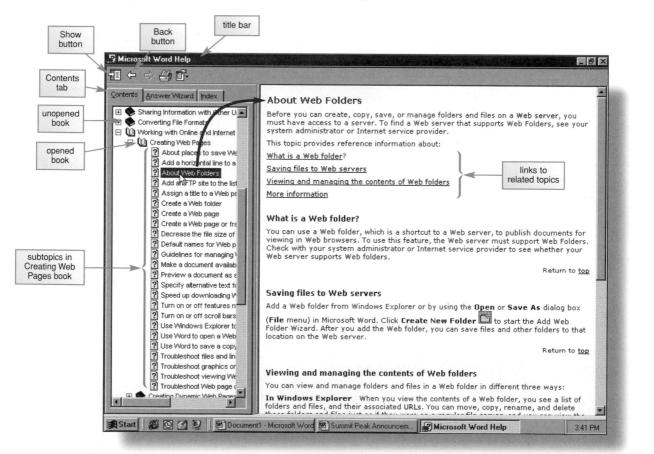

FIGURE A-6

Once the information on the subtopic displays, you can scroll through the window and read it or you can click the Print button to obtain a hard copy. If you decide to click another subtopic on the left or a link on the right, you can get back to the Help page shown in Figure A-6 by clicking the Back button as many times as necessary.

Each topic in the Contents list is preceded by a book icon or question mark icon. A **book icon** indicates subtopics are available. A **question mark icon** means information on the topic will display if you double-click the title. The book icon opens when you double-click the book (or its title) or click the plus sign (+) to the left of the book icon.

Using the Answer Wizard Sheet

The **Answer Wizard sheet** works like the Office Assistant in that you enter a word, phrase, or question and it responds with topics from which you can choose to display Help. The following steps show how to use the Answer Wizard sheet to obtain Help about discussions in a Word document.

TO OBTAIN HELP USING THE ANSWER WIZARD SHEET

1. With the Office Assistant turned off, click the Microsoft Word Help button on the Standard toolbar (Figure A-3 on page MO A.4).

2. When the Microsoft Word Help window displays, double-click the title bar to maximize the window. If necessary, click the Show button to display the tabs.

3. Click the Answer Wizard tab. Type what are discussions in the What would you like to do? text box on the left side of the window. Click the Search button.

4. When a list of topics displays in the Select topic to display list box, click About discussions in Word.

Word displays Help about discussions (Figure A-7).

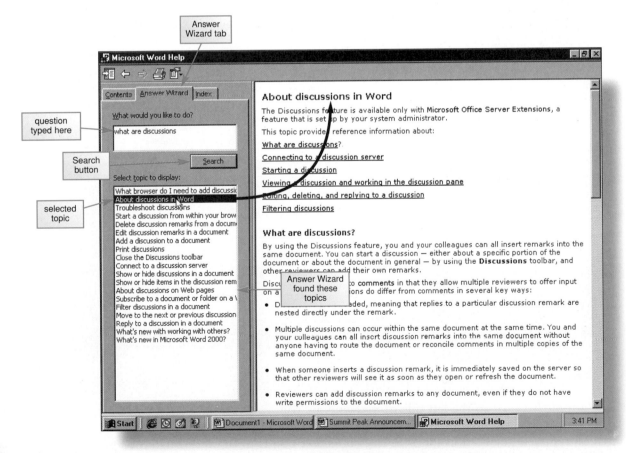

FIGURE A-7

If the topic, About discussions in Word, does not include the information you are searching for, click another topic in the list. Continue to click topics until you find the desired information.

Using the Index Sheet

The third sheet in the Microsoft Word Help window is the Index sheet. Use the **Index sheet** to display Help when you know the keyword or the first few letters of the keyword you want to look up. The following steps show how to use the Index sheet to obtain Help on understanding the readability statistics available to evaluate the reading level of a document.

TO OBTAIN HELP USING THE INDEX SHEET

 With the Office Assistant turned off, click the Microsoft Word Help button on the Standard toolbar (Figure A-3 on page MO A.4).

 When the Microsoft Word Help window displays, double-click the title bar to maximize the window. If necessary, click the Show button to display the tabs.

3 Click the Index tab. Type `readability` in the Type keywords text box on the left side of the window. Click the Search button.

Word highlights the first topic (Readability scores) on the left side of the window and displays information about two readability tests on the right side of the window (Figure A-8).

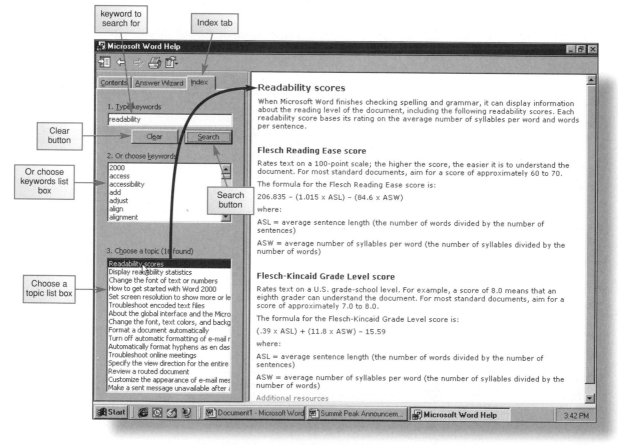

FIGURE A-8

In the Choose a topic list box on the left side of the window, you can click another topic to display additional Help.

An alternative to typing a keyword in the Type keywords text box is to scroll through the Or choose keywords list box (the middle list box on the left side of the window). When you locate the keyword you are searching for, double-click it to display Help on the topic. Also in the Or choose keywords list box, the Word Help system displays other topics that relate to the new keyword. As you begin typing a new keyword in the Type keywords text box, Word jumps to that point in the middle list box. To begin a new search, click the Clear button.

What's This? Command and Question Mark Button • MO A.9

APPENDIX A

What's This? Command and Question Mark Button

Use the What's This command on the Help menu or the Question Mark button in a dialog box when you are not sure what an object on the screen is or what it does.

What's This? Command

You use the **What's This? command** on the Help menu to display a detailed ScreenTip. When you invoke this command, the mouse pointer changes to an arrow with a question mark. You then click any object on the screen, such as a button, to display the ScreenTip. For example, after you click the What's This? command on the Help menu and then click the Zoom box on the Standard toolbar, a description of the Zoom box displays (Figure A-9). You can print the ScreenTip by right-clicking it and clicking Print Topic on the shortcut menu.

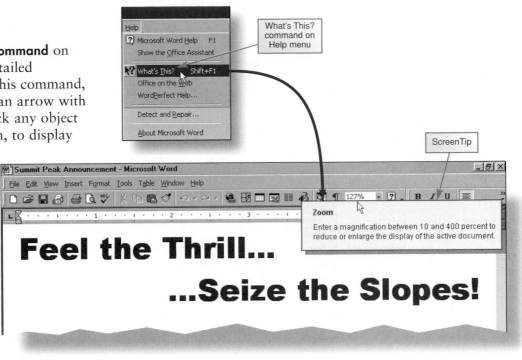

FIGURE A-9

Question Mark Button

In a response similar to the What's This? command, the **Question Mark button** displays a ScreenTip. You use the Question Mark button with dialog boxes. It is located in the upper-right corner on the title bar of dialog boxes, next to the Close button. For example, in Figure A-10, the Print dialog box displays on the screen. If you click the Question Mark button, and then click the Print to file check box, an explanation of the Print to file check box displays in a ScreenTip. You can print the ScreenTip by right-clicking it and clicking Print Topic on the shortcut menu.

If a dialog box does not include a Question Mark button, press the SHIFT+F1 keys. This combination of keys will change the mouse pointer to an arrow with a question mark. You then can click any object in the dialog box to display the ScreenTip.

FIGURE A-10

Office on the Web Command

The **Office on the Web command** on the Help menu displays a Microsoft Web page containing up-to-date information on a variety of Office-related topics. To use this command, you must be connected to the Internet. Once the page displays, you can click the Word link on the left side of the window and then click the Assistance link (Figure A-11). The Word Assistance Web page contains several links such as Knowledge Base Articles about Word and Frequently Asked Questions about Word.

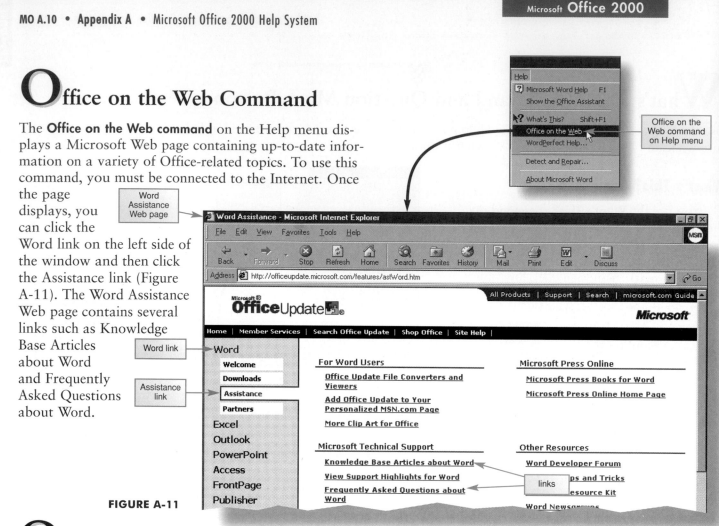

FIGURE A-11

Other Help Commands

Three additional commands available on the Help menu are WordPerfect Help, Detect and Repair, and About Microsoft Word. The WordPerfect Help command is available only if it was included as part of a Custom install of Word 2000. The Help menu of the other Office applications have similar commands that are useful when using each Office application.

WordPerfect Help Command

The **WordPerfect Help command** on the Help menu offers assistance to WordPerfect users switching to Word. When you choose this command, Word displays the Help for WordPerfect Users dialog box. The instructions in the dialog box step the user through the appropriate selections. A similar command is available in each of the other Office applications.

Detect and Repair Command

Use the **Detect and Repair command** on the Help menu if Word is not running properly or if it is generating errors. When you invoke this command, the Detect and Repair dialog box displays. Click the Start button in the dialog box to initiate the detect and repair process.

About Microsoft Word Command

The **About Microsoft Word command** on the Help menu displays the About Microsoft Word dialog box. The dialog box lists the owner of the software and the product identification. You need to know the product identification if you call Microsoft for assistance. The two buttons below the OK button are the System Info button and the Tech Support button. The **System Info button** displays system information, including hardware resources, components, software environment, and applications. The **Tech Support button** displays technical assistance information.

Use Help

1 Using the Office Assistant

Instructions: Perform the following tasks using the Word Help system.

1. If the Office Assistant is turned on, click it to display the Office Assistant balloon. If the Office Assistant is not turned on, click Help on the menu bar, and click Show the Office Assistant.
2. Right-click the Office Assistant and then click Options on the shortcut menu. Click the Gallery tab in the Office Assistant dialog box and then click the Next button to view all the Office Assistants. Click the Options tab in the Office Assistant dialog box and review the different options for the Office Assistant. Click the Question Mark button and then display ScreenTips for the first two check boxes (Use the Office Assistant and Respond to F1 key). Right-click the ScreenTips to print them. Hand them in to your instructor. Close the Office Assistant dialog box.
3. Click the Office Assistant and then type show me the keyboard shortcuts in the What would you like to do? text box at the bottom of the balloon. Click the Search button.
4. Click Keyboard shortcuts in the Office Assistant balloon. If necessary, double-click the title bar to maximize the Microsoft Word Help window. Click the Function keys link and then click the SHIFT+Function key link to view the set of shortcut keys using the SHIFT key and function keys. Click the Print button on the Microsoft Word Help toolbar to print the list of shortcut keys. Hand in the printouts to your instructor.
5. Close all open Help windows.
6. Click the Office Assistant. If it is not turned on, click Show the Office Assistant on the Help menu. Search for the topic, what is a netmeeting. Click the Use NetMeeting for an online meeting link. When the Microsoft Word Help window displays, maximize the window and then click the the Start an impromptu online meeting with Microsoft Word link. Read and print the information. Close the Microsoft Word Help window.

2 Expanding on the Word Help System Basics

Instructions: Use the Word Help system to understand the topics better and answer the questions listed below. Answer the questions on your own paper, or hand in the printed Help information to your instructor.

1. Right-click the Office Assistant. If it is not turned on, click Show the Office Assistant on the Help menu. When the shortcut menu displays, click Options. Click Use the Office Assistant to remove the check mark, and then click the OK button.
2. Click the Microsoft Word Help button on the Standard toolbar. Maximize the Microsoft Word Help window. If the tabs are hidden on the left side, click the Show button. Click the Index tab. Type undo in the Type keywords text box. Click the Search button. Click Reset built-in menus and toolbars. Print the information. Click the Hide button and then the Show button. Click the four links below What do you want to do? Read and print the information for each link. Close the Microsoft Word Help window. Hand in the printouts to your instructor.
3. Press the F1 key. Maximize the Microsoft Word Help window. Click the Answer Wizard tab. Type help in the What would you like to do? text box, and then click the Search button. Click Ways to get assistance while you work. Read through the information that displays. Print the information. Click the first two links. Read and print the information for both.
4. Click the Contents tab. Click the plus sign (+) to the left of the Typing, Navigating Documents, and Selecting Text book. Click the plus sign (+) to the left of the Selecting Text book. One at a time, click the three topics below the Selecting Text book. Read and print each one. Close the Microsoft Word Help window. Hand in the printouts to your instructor.
5. Click Help on the menu bar and then click What's This? Click the E-mail button on the Standard toolbar. Right-click the ScreenTip to print the ScreenTip. Click Format on the menu bar and then click Paragraph. When the Paragraph dialog box displays, click the Question Mark button on the title bar. Click the Special box. Right-click the ScreenTip to print the ScreenTip. Hand in the printouts to your instructor. Close the Paragraph dialog box and the Microsoft Word window.

APPENDIX B
Publishing Office Web Pages to a Web Server

With a Microsoft Office 2000 program, such as Word, Excel, Access, or PowerPoint, you use the **Save as Web Page command** on the File menu to save the Web page to a Web server using one of two techniques: Web folders or File Transfer Protocol. A **Web folder** is an Office 2000 shortcut to a Web server. **File Transfer Protocol (FTP)** is an Internet standard that allows computers to exchange files with other computers on the Internet.

You should contact your network system administrator or technical support staff at your ISP to determine if their Web server supports Web folders, FTP, or both, and to obtain necessary permissions to access the Web server. If you decide to publish Web pages using a Web folder, you must have the Office Server Extensions (OSE) installed on your computer. OSE comes with the Standard, Professional, and Premium editions of Office 2000.

Using Web Folders to Publish Office Web Pages

If you are granted permission to create a Web folder (shortcut) on your computer, you must obtain the URL of the Web server, and a user name and possibly a password that allows you to access the Web server. You also must decide on a name for the Web folder. Table B-1 explains how to create a Web folder.

Office adds the name of the Web folder to the list of current Web folders. You can save to this folder, open files in the folder, rename the folder, or perform any operations you would to a folder on your hard disk. You can use your Office program or Windows Explorer to access this folder. Table B-2 explains how to save to a Web folder.

Using FTP to Publish Office Web Pages

When publishing a Web page using FTP, you first add the FTP location to your computer and then you can save to it. An **FTP location**, also called an **FTP site**, is a collection of files that resides on an FTP server. In this case, the FTP server is the Web server.

To add an FTP location, you must obtain the name of the FTP site, which usually is the address (URL) of the FTP server, and a user name and a password that allows you to access the FTP server. You save and open the Web pages on the Web server using the name of the FTP site. Table B-3 explains how to add an FTP site.

Office adds the name of the FTP site to the FTP locations in the Save As and Open dialog boxes. You can open and save files on this FTP location. Table B-4 explains how to save using an FTP location.

Table B-1   Creating a Web Folder

1. Click File on the menu bar and then click Save As; or click File on the menu bar and then click Open.

2. When the Save As dialog box or the Open dialog box displays, click the Web Folders shortcut on the Places Bar along the left side of the dialog box.

3. Click the Create New Folder button.

4. When the first dialog box of the Add Web Folder wizard displays, type the URL of the Web server and then click the Next button.

5. When the Enter Network Password dialog box displays, type the user name and, if necessary, the password in the respective text boxes and then click the OK button.

6. When the last dialog box of the Add Web Folder wizard displays, type the name you would like to use for the Web folder. Click the Finish button.

7. Close the Save As or the Open dialog box.

Table B-2   Saving to a Web Folder

1. Click File on the menu bar and then click Save As.

2. When the Save As dialog box displays, type the Web page file name in the File name text box. Do not press the ENTER key.

3. Click Web Folders shortcut on the Places Bar along the left side of the dialog box.

4. Double-click the Web folder name in the Save in list.

5. When the Enter Network Password dialog box displays, type the user name and password in the respective text boxes and then click the OK button.

6. Click the Save button in the Save As dialog box.

Table B-3   Adding an FTP Location

1. Click File on the menu bar and then click Save As; or click File on the menu bar and then click Open.

2. In the Save As dialog box, click the Save in box arrow and then click Add/Modify FTP Locations in the Save in list; or in the Open dialog box, click the Look in box arrow and then click Add/Modify FTP Locations in the Look in list.

3. When the Add/Modify FTP Locations dialog box displays, type the name of the FTP site in the Name of FTP site text box. If the site allows anonymous logon, click Anonymous in the Log on as area; if you have a user name for the site, click User in the Log on as area and then type the user name. Type the password in the Password text box. Click the OK button.

4. Close the Save As or the Open dialog box.

Table B-4   Saving to an FTP Location

1. Click File on the menu bar and then click Save As.

2. When the Save As dialog box displays, type the Web page file name in the File name text box. Do not press the ENTER key.

3. Click the Save in box arrow and then click FTP Locations.

4. Double-click the name of the FTP site you want to save to.

5. When the FTP Log On dialog box displays, type your user name and password and then click the OK button.

6. Click the Save button in the Save As dialog box.

Microsoft **Office 2000**

APPENDIX C
Resetting the Menus and Toolbars

When you first install Microsoft Office 2000, the Standard and Formatting toolbars display on one row in some of the applications. As you use the buttons on the toolbars and commands on the menus, Office personalizes the toolbars and the menus based on their usage. Each time you start an application, the toolbars and menus display in the same settings as the last time you used the application. The following steps show how to reset the Word menus and toolbars to their installation settings.

Steps **To Reset My Usage Data and Toolbar Buttons**

1 **Click View on the menu bar and then point to Toolbars. Point to Customize on the Toolbars submenu.**

The View menu and Toolbars submenu display (Figure C-1).

Toolbars command

View menu

Customize command

FIGURE C-1

buttons promoted to Formatting toolbar based on usage

Toolbars submenu

2 **Click Customize. When the Customize dialog box displays, click the Options tab. Make sure the three check boxes in the Personalized Menus and Toolbars area have check marks and then point to the Reset my usage data button.**

The Customize dialog box displays as shown in Figure C-2.

Customize dialog box

Options tab

Reset my usage data button

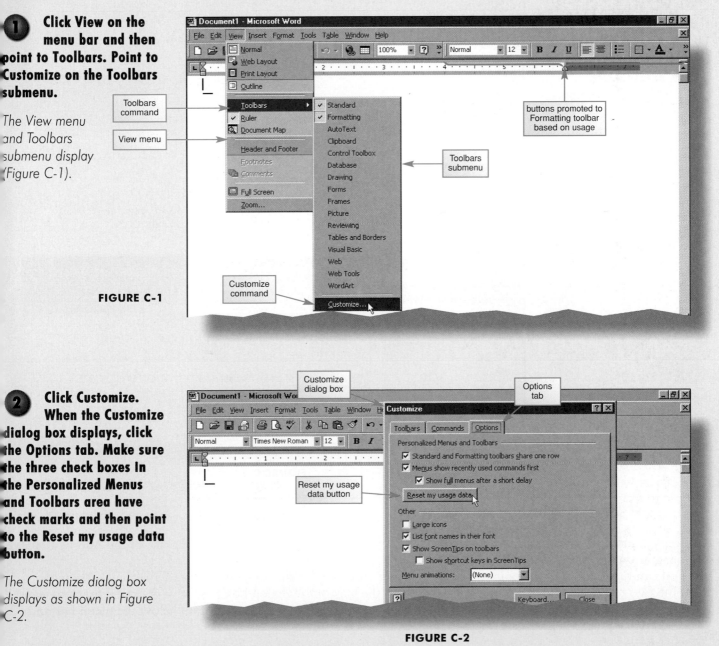

FIGURE C-2

Microsoft **Office 2000**

3 **Click the Reset my usage data button. When the Microsoft Word dialog box displays explaining the function of the Reset my usage data button, click the Yes button. In the Customize dialog box, click the Toolbars tab.**

The Toolbars sheet displays (Figure C-3).

4 **Click Standard in the Toolbars list and then click the Reset button. When the Reset Toolbar dialog box displays, click the OK button. Click Formatting in the Toolbars list and then click the Reset button. When the Reset Toolbar dialog box displays, click the OK button.**

FIGURE C-3

5 **Click the Close button in the Customize dialog box.**

The toolbars display as shown in Figure C-4.

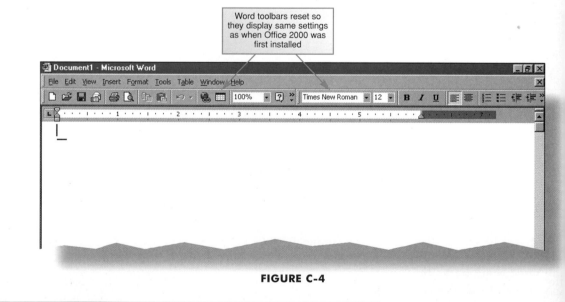

FIGURE C-4

Steps 3 and 4 display or remove any buttons that were added or deleted through the use of the Add or Remove Buttons button on the More Buttons menu.

You can turn off both the toolbars sharing a single row and the short menus by removing the check marks from the two top check boxes in the Options sheet in the Customize dialog box (Figure C-2 on the previous page). If you remove these check marks, Word will display the toolbars on two separate rows below the menu bar and will show only full menus.

APPENDIX D

Microsoft Office User Specialist Certification Program

The Microsoft Office User Specialist (MOUS) Certification Program provides a framework for measuring your proficiency with the Microsoft Office 2000 applications, such as Word 2000, Excel 2000, Access 2000, and PowerPoint 2000. Three levels of certification are available — Master, Expert, and Core. The three levels of certification are described in Table D-1.

Table D-1	Three Levels of MOUS Certification		
LEVEL	DESCRIPTION	REQUIREMENTS	CREDENTIAL AWARDED
Master	Indicates that you have a comprehensive understanding of Microsoft Office 2000	Pass all FIVE of the required exams: Microsoft Word 2000 Expert Microsoft Excel 2000 Expert Microsoft PowerPoint 2000 Core Microsoft Access 2000 Core Microsoft Outlook 2000 Core	Candidates will be awarded one certificate for passing all five of the required Microsoft Office 2000 exams: Microsoft Office User Specialist: Microsoft Office 2000 Master
Expert	Indicates that you have a comprehensive understanding of the advanced features in a specific Microsoft Office 2000 application	Pass any ONE of the Expert exams: Microsoft Word 2000 Expert Microsoft Excel 2000 Expert	Candidates will be awarded one certificate for each of the Expert exams they have passed: Microsoft Office User Specialist: Microsoft Word 2000 Expert Microsoft Office User Specialist: Microsoft Excel 2000 Expert
Core	Indicates that you have a comprehensive understanding of the core features in a specific Microsoft Office 2000 application	Pass any ONE of the Core exams: Microsoft Word 2000 Core Microsoft Excel 2000 Core Microsoft PowerPoint 2000 Core Microsoft Access 2000 Core Microsoft Outlook 2000 Core	Candidates will be awarded one certificate for each of the Core exams they have passed: Microsoft Office User Specialist: Microsoft Word 2000 Microsoft Office User Specialist: Microsoft Excel 2000 Microsoft Office User Specialist: Microsoft PowerPoint 2000 Microsoft Office User Specialist: Microsoft Access 2000 Microsoft Office User Specialist: Microsoft Outlook 2000

Why Should You Get Certified?

Being a Microsoft Office User Specialist provides a valuable industry credential — proof that you have the Office 2000 applications skills required by employers. By passing one or more MOUS certification exams, you demonstrate your proficiency in a given Office application to employers. With nearly 80 million copies of Office in use around the world, Microsoft is targeting Office certification to a wide variety of companies. These companies include temporary employment agencies that want to prove the expertise of their workers, large corporations looking for a way to measure the skill set of employees, and training companies and educational institutions seeking Microsoft Office teachers with appropriate credentials.

The MOUS Exams

You pay $50 to $100 each time you take an exam, whether you pass or fail. The fee varies among testing centers. The Expert exams, which you can take up to 60 minutes to complete, consist of between 40 and 60 tasks that you perform online. The tasks require you to use the application just as you would in doing your job. The Core exams contain fewer tasks, and you will have slightly less time to complete them. The tasks you will perform differ on the two types of exams.

How Can You Prepare for the MOUS Exams?

The Shelly Cashman Series® offers several Microsoft-approved textbooks that cover the required objectives on the MOUS exams. For a listing of the textbooks, visit the Shelly Cashman Series MOUS Web page at www.scsite.com/off2000/cert.htm and click the Shelly Cashman Office Series 2000 Microsoft-Approved MOUS Textbooks link (Figure D-1). After using any of the books listed in an instructor-led course, you will be prepared to take the MOUS exam indicated.

How to Find an Authorized Testing Center

You can locate a testing center by calling 1-800-933-4493 in North America or visiting the Shelly Cashman Series MOUS Web page at www.scsite.com/off2000/cert.htm and then clicking the Locate an Authorized Testing Center Near You link (Figure D-1). At this Web page, you can look for testing centers around the world.

Shelly Cashman Series MOUS Web Page

The Shelly Cashman Series MOUS Web page (Figure D-1) has more than fifteen Web pages you can visit to obtain additional information on the MOUS Certification Program. The Web page (www.scsite.com/off2000/cert.htm) includes links to general information on certification, choosing an application for certification, preparing for the certification exam, and taking and passing the certification exam.

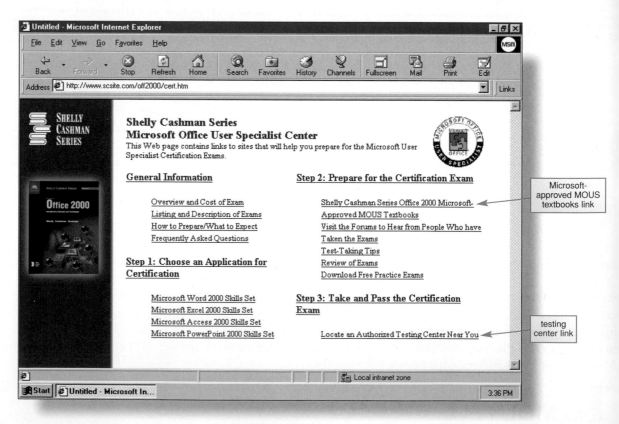

FIGURE D-1

Index

Buttons, INT 1.8, INT 1.11
  adding or deleting, MO C.2
  hiding, E 1.12
  option, A 1.33
  recessed, WD 1.20
  sizing toolbar, E 1.13
  Web toolbar, INT 1.68

Calculate/calculating
  statistics, A 2.38-42
  sum, *see* SUM function
Calculated fields, **A 2.35**-37
Calendar (Outlook), INT 1.73
Camera ready, **INT 1.69**
Cancel box (formula bar), E 1.17, E 1.51
Cancel button (AutoFormat dialog box),
  E 1.33
Cancel command (shortcut menu),
  INT 1.25, **INT 1.26**
Cascading menu, **INT 1.10**
Case sensitive, **E 1.44**
Category axis, **E 1.41**
Cell(s), **E 1.10**
  active, E 1.10, E 1.15, E 1.16
  aligning contents of, E 2.33-34
  bolding, E 1.28-29
  centering data in, E 2.33-34
  clearing, E 1.53
  copying to adjacent cells using fill
    handle, E 1.24-25
  decimal places in, E 2.36
  editing in, E 1.51-52
  formatting, E 1.27-34
  formula in, E 2.9
  range of, *see* Range of cells
  referenced in formula, E 2.24
  selecting for formula, E 2.11
  selecting using mouse, E 1.15
  selecting using Name box, E 1.34-36
  selecting using Point mode, E 2.11
Cell reference, **E 1.10**
  active, E 1.10, E 1.14
  relative, E 1.24
  selecting cell and, E 1.15
Cells command (Excel Format menu)
  alignment, E 1.34, E 2.33
  bold, E 1.29
  border, E 2.32
  currency, E 2.36, E 2.37
  font, E 2.30
  font size, E 1.30
  numbers, **E 2.34**
  patterns, E 2.32
Center button (Formatting toolbar)
  Excel, E 2.33
  Word, WD 1.33, WD 1.46
Centering
  data in cells, E 2.33-34
  graphic, WD 1.46
  moving indent marker before, WD 2.35
  paragraph, WD 1.33, WD 1.40
  worksheet title, E 1.33-34, E 2.30
Cents, E 1.22

Certification, *see* Microsoft Office User
  Specialist
Change All button (Spelling dialog box),
  E 2.50
Change button (Spelling dialog box),
  E 2.50
Change to box (Spelling dialog box),
  E 2.50
Character (Excel), **E 2.43**
Character(s) (Word)
  nonprinting, WD 1.20
  searching for special, WD 2.45
  shortcut keys for formatting,
    WD 2.17-18
  special, WD 2.33
Character formatting, **WD 1.29**-42
Chart (Excel), **E 1.6**
  embedded, E 1.36-41
  legend, E 1.41
  moving, E 1.39-40
  selecting, E 1.38
  sizing, E 1.39-40
  2-D Column, E 1.41
  3-D Column, E 1.36-41
  x-axis, E 1.41
  y-axis, E 1.37
Charting feature (PowerPoint), **PP 1.6**
Chart location, **E 1.37**, E 1.39-40
Chart menu bar, **E 1.12**
Chart types, E 1.38
  default, E 1.41
Chart Wizard button, **E 1.37**-38
Check box (Welcome to Windows 98
  screen), **INT 1.7**
Choose Profile dialog box, E 2.63
Citations, *see* Parenthetical citations
Classic style (desktop), **INT 1.27**
Clear/clearing
  cell or range of cells, E 1.53
  design grid, A 2.16
  embedded chart, E 1.54
  entire worksheet, E 1.54
  formats, E 1.53
  query, A 2.16
Clear command (Excel Edit menu),
  E 1.53, E 1.54
Clear Contents command (shortcut menu),
  E 1.53
Clear Grid command (Access Edit menu),
  A 2.9, A 2.16
Clear the query, **A 2.16**
Click, **INT 1.9**-11
  double-, *see* Double-click
  right-, *see* Right-click/clicking
Click and Type, entering text using,
  WD 2.13
Click and Type pointer, **WD 2.13**
Clip(s), **WD 1.42**
Clip art (PowerPoint), **PP 2.24**
  adding, PP 2.24-31
  animating, PP 2.46-47
  AutoLayout placeholder, PP 2.22
  changing size of, PP 2.32-34

  inserting without clip art region,
    PP 2.30-31
  moving, PP 2.31-32
  placeholders, PP 2.22
  Web sites for, PP 2.29, PP 2.42, PP 2.46
Clip art (Word), **WD 1.42**
  inserting, WD 1.42-48
Clip Art & Text slide layout, PP 2.23,
  PP 2.28
Clip art files, **INT 1.41**
Clip art gallery, Office 2000, INT 1.60
Clipboard, *see* Office Clipboard
Clip Gallery, **WD 1.42**, WD 1.43
Close button, **A 1.12, E 1.33**
Close button (window title bar), **INT 1.19**
Close command (Access File menu),
  A 2.14
Close command (Excel File menu), **E 1.54**
Close command (Windows 98 File menu),
  INT 1.29
Close command (Word File menu),
  WD 1.54
Close Window button, A 1.25
Closing
  application program, INT 1.29
  database, A 1.24-25, A 1.49, A 2.43
  form, A 1.38-39
  note pane, WD 2.29-30
  query, A 2.14
  table, A 1.24-25
  Welcome to Windows 98 screen, INT 1.8
  window, INT 1.19-20, INT 1.24
Closing slide, **PP 2.18**
  creating in outline view, PP 2.18-19
Codes, AutoCorrect entries for, WD 2.22
Collapse All button (Outlining toolbar),
  PP 2.51
Collapsing the folder, **INT 1.33**, INT 1.36
Colors
  number background, E 2.40-41
  font, E 2.30-31
Column(s), **E 1.9**
  centering worksheet title across,
    E 1.33-34
  hidden, E 2.46
  titles, E 1.18-19
Column command (Excel Format menu),
  width, E 2.46
Column heading, **E 1.9**
Column titles, E 2.7
  formatting, E 2.32-33
Column width
  best fit, E 2.43
  changing, E 2.43-46
Column Width command (shortcut menu),
  E 2.46
COMDEX, PP 1.4-5
Commands, **INT 1.10**
  dimmed, E 1.12, INT 1.12, PP 1.14,
    WD 1.12
  hidden, E 1.12, PP 1.14, WD 1.12
  highlighted, WD 1.8
  unavailable, WD 1.12
  undoing, WD 1.33